GO!
with Microsoft®

Excel 2007
Comprehensive First Edition

Shelley Gaskin and Karen Jolly

PEARSON

Prentice
Hall

Upper Saddle River, New Jersey

This book is dedicated to my students, who inspire me every day, and to my husband, Fred Gaskin.
—Shelley Gaskin

This book is dedicated with love to my husband, Paul, for his continued unwavering support, and to my children, Kevin and Trista. Special thanks to Vicky Charlston, who worked side-by-side to complete this project.
—Karen Jolly

Library of Congress Cataloging-in-Publication Data

Gaskin, Shelley.
  Go! with Microsoft Excel comprehensive / Shelley Gaskin and Karen Jolly.
     p. cm.
  ISBN 978-0-13-225559-2
  ISBN 0-13-225559-6
  1. Microsoft Excel (Computer file) 2. Business—Computer programs. 3. Electronic spreadsheets. I. Jolly, Karen. II. Title.
HF5548.4.M523G375 2008
005.54—dc22

2007047460

Vice President and Publisher: Natalie E. Anderson
Associate VP/Executive Acquisitions Editor, Print: Stephanie Wall
Executive Acquisitions Editor, Media: Richard Keaveny
Product Development Manager: Eileen Bien Calabro
Editorial Project Manager: Box Twelve Communications, Inc.
Development Editor: Ginny Munroe
Editorial Assistant: Terenia McHenry
Executive Producer: Lisa Strite
Content Development Manager: Cathi Profitko
Media Project Manager: Alana Coles
Production Media Project Manager: Lorena Cerisano
Director of Marketing: Margaret Waples
Senior Marketing Manager: Tori Olson-Alves

Marketing Assistants: Angela Frey, Kathryn Ferranti
Senior Sales Associate: Rebecca Scott
Senior Managing Editor: Cynthia Zonneveld
Associate Managing Editor: Camille Trentacoste
Production Project Manager: Mike Lackey
Production Editor: GGS Book Services
Photo Researcher: GGS Book Services
Operations Specialist: Natacha Moore
Senior Art Director: Jonathan Boylan
Cover Photo: Courtesy of Getty Images, Inc./Marvin Mattelson
Composition: GGS Book Services
Project Management: GGS Book Services
Cover Printer: Phoenix Color
Printer/Binder: Courier

Microsoft, Windows, Word, PowerPoint, Outlook, FrontPage, Visual Basic, MSN, The Microsoft Network, and/or other Microsoft products referenced herein are either trademarks or registered trademarks of Microsoft Corporation in the U.S.A. and other countries. Screen shots and icons reprinted with permission from the Microsoft Corporation. This book is not sponsored or endorsed by or affiliated with Microsoft Corporation.

Credits and acknowledgments borrowed from other sources and reproduced, with permission, in this textbook are as follows or on the appropriate page within the text.

Pages 2 and 338: PhotoEdit Inc.; page 112: Gunter Marx © Dorling Kindersley; page 236: Greg Nicholas; page 458: Getty Images, Inc.-PhotoDisc; page 540: Helena Smith © Rough Guides; pages 626 and 1064: Getty Images Inc. –Stone Allstock; page 706: The Stock Connection; page 798: M. Eric Honeycutt; page 898: Andrea Gingerich; page 990: Dorling Kindersley Media Library.

10 9 8 7 6 5 4
ISBN 10 0-13-225559-6
ISBN 13 978-0-13-225559-2

Contents in Brief

Table of Contents

Letter from the Editor

Dear Instructors and Students,

The primary goal of the *GO!* Series is two-fold. The first goal is to help instructors teach the course they want in less time. The second goal is to provide students with the skills to solve business problems using the computer as a tool, for both themselves and the organization for which they might be employed.

The *GO!* Series was originally created by Series Editor Shelley Gaskin and published with the release of Microsoft Office 2003. Her ideas came from years of using textbooks that didn't meet all the needs of today's diverse classroom and that were too confusing for students. Shelley continues to enhance the series by ensuring we stay true to our vision of developing quality instruction and useful classroom tools.

But we also need your input and ideas.

Over time, the *GO!* Series has evolved based on direct feedback from instructors and students using the series. *We are the publisher that listens.* To publish a textbook that works for you, it's critical that we continue to listen to this feedback. It's important to me to talk with you and hear your stories about using *GO!* Your voice can make a difference.

My hope is that this letter will inspire you to write me an e-mail and share your thoughts on using the *GO!* Series.

Stephanie Wall
Executive Editor, *GO!* Series
stephanie_wall@prenhall.com

GO! System Contributors

We thank the following people for their hard work and support in making the *GO!* System all that it is!

Additional Author Support

Coyle, Diane	Montgomery County Community College
Fry, Susan	Boise State
Townsend, Kris	Spokane Falls Community College
Stroup, Tracey	Amgen Corporation

Instructor Resource Authors

Amer, Beverly	Northern Arizona University	Paterson, Jim	Paradise Valley Community College
Boito, Nancy	Harrisburg Area Community College	Prince, Lisa	Missouri State
Coyle, Diane	Montgomery County Community College	Rodgers, Gwen	Southern Nazarene University
Dawson, Tamara	Southern Nazarene University	Ruymann, Amy	Burlington Community College
Driskel, Loretta	Niagara County Community College	Ryan, Bob	Montgomery County Community College
Elliott, Melissa	Odessa College		
Fry, Susan	Boise State	Smith, Diane	Henry Ford Community College
Geoghan, Debra	Bucks County Community College	Spangler, Candice	Columbus State Community College
Hearn, Barbara	Community College of Philadelphia	Thompson, Joyce	Lehigh Carbon Community College
Jones, Stephanie	South Plains College	Tiffany, Janine	Reading Area Community College
Madsen, Donna	Kirkwood Community College	Watt, Adrienne	Douglas College
Meck, Kari	Harrisburg Area Community College	Weaver, Paul	Bossier Parish Community College
Miller, Cindy	Ivy Tech	Weber, Sandy	Gateway Technical College
Nowakowski, Tony	Buffalo State	Wood, Dawn	
Pace, Phyllis	Queensborough Community College	Weissman, Jonathan	Finger Lakes Community College

Super Reviewers

Brotherton, Cathy	Riverside Community College	Maurer, Trina	Odessa College
Cates, Wally	Central New Mexico Community College	Meck, Kari	Harrisburg Area Community College
		Miller, Cindy	Ivy Tech Community College
Cone, Bill	Northern Arizona University	Nielson, Phil	Salt Lake Community College
Coverdale, John	Riverside Community College	Rodgers, Gwen	Southern Nazarene University
Foster, Nancy	Baker College	Smolenski, Robert	Delaware Community College
Helfand, Terri	Chaffey College	Spangler, Candice	Columbus State Community College
Hibbert, Marilyn	Salt Lake Community College	Thompson, Joyce	Lehigh Carbon Community College
Holliday, Mardi	Community College of Philadelphia	Weber, Sandy	Gateway Technical College
Jerry, Gina	Santa Monica College	Wells, Lorna	Salt Lake Community College
Martin, Carol	Harrisburg Area Community College	Zaboski, Maureen	University of Scranton

Technical Editors

Janice Snyder
Joyce Nielsen
Colette Eisele
Janet Pickard
Mara Zebest
Lindsey Allen
William Daley
LeeAnn Bates

Student Reviewers

Allen, John	Asheville-Buncombe Tech Community College	Erickson, Mike	Ball State University
		Gadomski, Amanda	Northern Michigan University
Alexander, Steven	St. Johns River Community College	Gyselinck, Craig	Central Washington University
Alexander, Melissa	Tulsa Community College	Harrison, Margo	Central Washington University
Bolz, Stephanie	Northern Michigan University	Heacox, Kate	Central Washington University
Berner, Ashley	Central Washington University	Hill, Cheretta	Northwestern State University
Boomer, Michelle	Northern Michigan University	Innis, Tim	Tulsa Community College
Busse, Brennan	Northern Michigan University	Jarboe, Aaron	Central Washington University
Butkey, Maura	Central Washington University	Klein, Colleen	Northern Michigan University
Christensen, Kaylie	Northern Michigan University	Moeller, Jeffrey	Northern Michigan University
Connally, Brianna	Central Washington University	Nicholson, Regina	Athens Tech College
Davis, Brandon	Northern Michigan University	Niehaus, Kristina	Northern Michigan University
Davis, Christen	Central Washington University	Nisa, Zaibun	Santa Rosa Community College
Den Boer, Lance	Central Washington University	Nunez, Nohelia	Santa Rosa Community College
Dix, Jessica	Central Washington University	Oak, Samantha	Central Washington University
Moeller, Jeffrey	Northern Michigan University	Oertii, Monica	Central Washington University
Downs, Elizabeth	Central Washington University	Palenshus, Juliet	Central Washington University

Pohl, Amanda	Northern Michigan University	Shanahan, Megan	Northern Michigan University
Presnell, Randy	Central Washington University	Teska, Erika	Hawaii Pacific University
Ritner, April	Northern Michigan University	Traub, Amy	Northern Michigan University
Rodriguez, Flavia	Northwestern State University	Underwood, Katie	Central Washington University
Roberts, Corey	Tulsa Community College	Walters, Kim	Central Washington University
Rossi, Jessica Ann	Central Washington University	Wilson, Kelsie	Central Washington University
Shafapay, Natasha	Central Washington University	Wilson, Amanda	Green River Community College

Series Reviewers

Abraham, Reni	Houston Community College	Crawford, Thomasina	Miami-Dade College, Kendall Campus
Agatston, Ann	Agatston Consulting Technical College	Credico, Grace	Lethbridge Community College
Alexander, Melody	Ball Sate University	Crenshaw, Richard	Miami Dade Community College, North
Alejandro, Manuel	Southwest Texas Junior College	Crespo, Beverly	Mt. San Antonio College
Ali, Farha	Lander University	Crossley, Connie	Cincinnati State Technical Community College
Amici, Penny	Harrisburg Area Community College		
Anderson, Patty A.	Lake City Community College	Curik, Mary	Central New Mexico Community College
Andrews, Wilma	Virginia Commonwealth College, Nebraska University	De Arazoza, Ralph	Miami Dade Community College
Anik, Mazhar	Tiffin University	Danno, John	DeVry University/Keller Graduate School
Armstrong, Gary	Shippensburg University		
Atkins, Bonnie	Delaware Technical Community College	Davis, Phillip	Del Mar College
		DeHerrera, Laurie	Pikes Peak Community College
Bachand, LaDonna	Santa Rosa Community College	Delk, Dr. K. Kay	Seminole Community College
Bagui, Sikha	University of West Florida	Doroshow, Mike	Eastfield College
Beecroft, Anita	Kwantlen University College	Douglas, Gretchen	SUNYCortland
Bell, Paula	Lock Haven College	Dove, Carol	Community College of Allegheny
Belton, Linda	Springfield Tech. Community College	Driskel, Loretta	Niagara Community College
		Duckwiler, Carol	Wabaunsee Community College
Bennett, Judith	Sam Houston State University	Duncan, Mimi	University of Missouri-St. Louis
Bhatia, Sai	Riverside Community College	Duthie, Judy	Green River Community College
Bishop, Frances	DeVry Institute—Alpharetta (ATL)	Duvall, Annette	Central New Mexico Community College
Blaszkiewicz, Holly	Ivy Tech Community College/Region 1		
Branigan, Dave	DeVry University	Ecklund, Paula	Duke University
Bray, Patricia	Allegany College of Maryland	Eng, Bernice	Brookdale Community College
Brotherton, Cathy	Riverside Community College	Evans, Billie	Vance-Granville Community College
Buehler, Lesley	Ohlone College	Feuerbach, Lisa	Ivy Tech East Chicago
Buell, C	Central Oregon Community College	Fisher, Fred	Florida State University
Byars, Pat	Brookhaven College	Foster, Penny L.	Anne Arundel Community College
Byrd, Lynn	Delta State University, Cleveland, Mississippi	Foszcz, Russ	McHenry County College
		Fry, Susan	Boise State University
Cacace, Richard N.	Pensacola Junior College	Fustos, Janos	Metro State
Cadenhead, Charles	Brookhaven College	Gallup, Jeanette	Blinn College
Calhoun, Ric	Gordon College	Gelb, Janet	Grossmont College
Cameron, Eric	Passaic Community College	Gentry, Barb	Parkland College
Carriker, Sandra	North Shore Community College	Gerace, Karin	St. Angela Merici School
Cannamore, Madie	Kennedy King	Gerace, Tom	Tulane University
Carreon, Cleda	Indiana University—Purdue University, Indianapolis	Ghajar, Homa	Oklahoma State University
		Gifford, Steve	Northwest Iowa Community College
Chaffin, Catherine	Shawnee State University	Glazer, Ellen	Broward Community College
Chauvin, Marg	Palm Beach Community College, Boca Raton	Gordon, Robert	Hofstra University
		Gramlich, Steven	Pasco-Hernando Community College
Challa, Chandrashekar	Virginia State University	Graviett, Nancy M.	St. Charles Community College, St. Peters, Missouri
Chamlou, Afsaneh	NOVA Alexandria		
Chapman, Pam	Wabaunsee Community College	Greene, Rich	Community College of Allegheny County
Christensen, Dan	Iowa Western Community College		
Clay, Betty	Southeastern Oklahoma State University	Gregoryk, Kerry	Virginia Commonwealth State
		Griggs, Debra	Bellevue Community College
Collins, Linda D.	Mesa Community College	Grimm, Carol	Palm Beach Community College
Conroy-Link, Janet	Holy Family College	Hahn, Norm	Thomas Nelson Community College
Cosgrove, Janet	Northwestern CT Community	Hammerschlag, Dr. Bill	Brookhaven College
Courtney, Kevin	Hillsborough Community College	Hansen, Michelle	Davenport University
Cox, Rollie	Madison Area Technical College	Hayden, Nancy	Indiana University—Purdue University, Indianapolis
Crawford, Hiram	Olive Harvey College		

Hayes, Theresa	Broward Community College	Lord, Alexandria	Asheville Buncombe Tech
Helfand, Terri	Chaffey College	Lowe, Rita	Harold Washington College
Helms, Liz	Columbus State Community College	Low, Willy Hui	Joliet Junior College
Hernandez, Leticia	TCI College of Technology	Lucas, Vickie	Broward Community College
Hibbert, Marilyn	Salt Lake Community College	Lynam, Linda	Central Missouri State University
Hoffman, Joan	Milwaukee Area Technical College	Lyon, Lynne	Durham College
Hogan, Pat	Cape Fear Community College	Lyon, Pat Rajski	Tomball College
Holland, Susan	Southeast Community College	MacKinnon, Ruth	Georgia Southern University
Hopson, Bonnie	Athens Technical College	Macon, Lisa	Valencia Community College, West Campus
Horvath, Carrie	Albertus Magnus College		
Horwitz, Steve	Community College of Philadelphia	Machuca, Wayne	College of the Sequoias
Hotta, Barbara	Leeward Community College	Madison, Dana	Clarion University
Howard, Bunny	St. Johns River Community	Maguire, Trish	Eastern New Mexico University
Howard, Chris	DeVry University	Malkan, Rajiv	Montgomery College
Huckabay, Jamie	Austin Community College	Manning, David	Northern Kentucky University
Hudgins, Susan	East Central University	Marcus, Jacquie	Niagara Community College
Hulett, Michelle J.	Missouri State University	Marghitu, Daniela	Auburn University
Hunt, Darla A.	Morehead State University, Morehead, Kentucky	Marks, Suzanne	Bellevue Community College
		Marquez, Juanita	El Centro College
Hunt, Laura	Tulsa Community College	Marquez, Juan	Mesa Community College
Jacob, Sherry	Jefferson Community College	Martyn, Margie	Baldwin-Wallace College
Jacobs, Duane	Salt Lake Community College	Marucco, Toni	Lincoln Land Community College
Jauken, Barb	Southeastern Community	Mason, Lynn	Lubbock Christian University
Johnson, Kathy	Wright College	Matutis, Audrone	Houston Community College
Johnson, Mary	Kingwood College	Matkin, Marie	University of Lethbridge
Johnson, Mary	Mt. San Antonio College	McCain, Evelynn	Boise State University
Jones, Stacey	Benedict College	McCannon, Melinda	Gordon College
Jones, Warren	University of Alabama, Birmingham	McCarthy, Marguerite	Northwestern Business College
Jordan, Cheryl	San Juan College	McCaskill, Matt L.	Brevard Community College
Kapoor, Bhushan	California State University, Fullerton	McClellan, Carolyn	Tidewater Community College
Kasai, Susumu	Salt Lake Community College	McClure, Darlean	College of Sequoias
Kates, Hazel	Miami Dade Community College, Kendall	McCrory, Sue A.	Missouri State University
		McCue, Stacy	Harrisburg Area Community College
Keen, Debby	University of Kentucky	McEntire-Orbach, Teresa	Middlesex County College
Keeter, Sandy	Seminole Community College	McLeod, Todd	Fresno City College
Kern-Blystone, Dorothy Jean	Bowling Green State	McManus, Illyana	Grossmont College
		McPherson, Dori	Schoolcraft College
Keskin, Ilknur	The University of South Dakota	Meiklejohn, Nancy	Pikes Peak Community College
Kirk, Colleen	Mercy College	Menking, Rick	Hardin-Simmons University
Kleckner, Michelle	Elon University	Meredith, Mary	University of Louisiana at Lafayette
Kliston, Linda	Broward Community College, North Campus	Mermelstein, Lisa	Baruch College
		Metos, Linda	Salt Lake Community College
Kochis, Dennis	Suffolk County Community College	Meurer, Daniel	University of Cincinnati
Kramer, Ed	Northern Virginia Community College	Meyer, Marian	Central New Mexico Community College
Laird, Jeff	Northeast State Community College	Miller, Cindy	Ivy Tech Community College, Lafayette, Indiana
Lamoureaux, Jackie	Central New Mexico Community College	Mitchell, Susan	Davenport University
Lange, David	Grand Valley State	Mohle, Dennis	Fresno Community College
LaPointe, Deb	Central New Mexico Community College	Monk, Ellen	University of Delaware
		Moore, Rodney	Holland College
Larson, Donna	Louisville Technical Institute	Morris, Mike	Southeastern Oklahoma State University
Laspina, Kathy	Vance-Granville Community College		
Le Grand, Dr. Kate	Broward Community College	Morris, Nancy	Hudson Valley Community College
Lenhart, Sheryl	Terra Community College	Moseler, Dan	Harrisburg Area Community College
Letavec, Chris	University of Cincinnati	Nabors, Brent	Reedley College, Clovis Center
Liefert, Jane	Everett Community College	Nadas, Erika	Wright College
Lindaman, Linda	Black Hawk Community College	Nadelman, Cindi	New England College
Lindberg, Martha	Minnesota State University	Nademlynsky, Lisa	Johnson & Wales University
Lightner, Renee	Broward Community College	Ncube, Cathy	University of West Florida
Lindberg, Martha	Minnesota State University	Nagengast, Joseph	Florida Career College
Linge, Richard	Arizona Western College	Newsome, Eloise	Northern Virginia Community College Woodbridge
Logan, Mary G.	Delgado Community College		
Loizeaux, Barbara	Westchester Community College	Nicholls, Doreen	Mohawk Valley Community College
Lopez, Don	Clovis-State Center Community College District	Nunan, Karen	Northeast State Technical Community College

Odegard, Teri	Edmonds Community College	Sterling, Janet	Houston Community College
Ogle, Gregory	North Community College	Stoughton, Catherine	Laramie County Community College
Orr, Dr. Claudia	Northern Michigan University South	Sullivan, Angela	Joliet Junior College
Otieno, Derek	DeVry University	Szurek, Joseph	University of Pittsburgh at Greensburg
Otton, Diana Hill	Chesapeake College		
Oxendale, Lucia	West Virginia Institute of Technology	Tarver, Mary Beth	Northwestern State University
		Taylor, Michael	Seattle Central Community College
Paiano, Frank	Southwestern College	Thangiah, Sam	Slippery Rock University
Patrick, Tanya	Clackamas Community College	Thompson-Sellers, Ingrid	Georgia Perimeter College
Peairs, Deb	Clark State Community College	Tomasi, Erik	Baruch College
Prince, Lisa	Missouri State University-Springfield Campus	Toreson, Karen	Shoreline Community College
		Trifiletti, John J.	Florida Community College at Jacksonville
Proietti, Kathleen	Northern Essex Community College		
Pusins, Delores	HCCC	Trivedi, Charulata	Quinsigamond Community College, Woodbridge
Raghuraman, Ram	Joliet Junior College		
Reasoner, Ted Allen	Indiana University—Purdue	Tucker, William	Austin Community College
Reeves, Karen	High Point University	Turgeon, Cheryl	Asnuntuck Community College
Remillard, Debbie	New Hampshire Technical Institute	Turpen, Linda	Central New Mexico Community College
Rhue, Shelly	DeVry University		
Richards, Karen	Maplewoods Community College	Upshaw, Susan	Del Mar College
Richardson, Mary	Albany Technical College	Unruh, Angela	Central Washington University
Rodgers, Gwen	Southern Nazarene University	Vanderhoof, Dr. Glenna	Missouri State University-Springfield Campus
Roselli, Diane	Harrisburg Area Community College		
Ross, Dianne	University of Louisiana in Lafayette	Vargas, Tony	El Paso Community College
Rousseau, Mary	Broward Community College, South	Vicars, Mitzi	Hampton University
Samson, Dolly	Hawaii Pacific University	Villarreal, Kathleen	Fresno
Sams, Todd	University of Cincinnati	Vitrano, Mary Ellen	Palm Beach Community College
Sandoval, Everett	Reedley College	Volker, Bonita	Tidewater Community College
Sardone, Nancy	Seton Hall University	Wahila, Lori (Mindy)	Tompkins Cortland Community College
Scafide, Jean	Mississippi Gulf Coast Community College		
		Waswick, Kim	Southeast Community College, Nebraska
Scheeren, Judy	Westmoreland County Community College		
		Wavle, Sharon	Tompkins Cortland Community College
Schneider, Sol	Sam Houston State University		
Scroggins, Michael	Southwest Missouri State University	Webb, Nancy	City College of San Francisco
Sever, Suzanne	Northwest Arkansas Community College	Wells, Barbara E.	Central Carolina Technical College
		Wells, Lorna	Salt Lake Community College
Sheridan, Rick	California State University-Chico	Welsh, Jean	Lansing Community College Nebraska
Silvers, Pamela	Asheville Buncombe Tech		
Singer, Steven A.	University of Hawai'i, Kapi'olani Community College	White, Bruce	Quinnipiac University
		Willer, Ann	Solano Community College
Sinha, Atin	Albany State University	Williams, Mark	Lane Community College
Skolnick, Martin	Florida Atlantic University	Wilson, Kit	Red River College
Smith, T. Michael	Austin Community College	Wilson, Roger	Fairmont State University
Smith, Tammy	Tompkins Cortland Community Collge	Wimberly, Leanne	International Academy of Design and Technology
Smolenski, Bob	Delaware County Community College	Worthington, Paula	Northern Virginia Community College
Spangler, Candice	Columbus State		
Stedham, Vicki	St. Petersburg College, Clearwater	Yauney, Annette	Herkimer County Community College
Stefanelli, Greg	Carroll Community College		
Steiner, Ester	New Mexico State University	Yip, Thomas	Passaic Community College
Stenlund, Neal	Northern Virginia Community College, Alexandria	Zavala, Ben	Webster Tech
		Zlotow, Mary Ann	College of DuPage
St. John, Steve	Tulsa Community College	Zudeck, Steve	Broward Community College, North

About the Authors

Shelley Gaskin, Series Editor, is a professor of business and computer technology at Pasadena City College in Pasadena, California. She holds a master's degree in business education from Northern Illinois University and a doctorate in adult and community education from Ball State University. Dr. Gaskin has 15 years of experience in the computer industry with several Fortune 500 companies and has developed and written training materials for custom systems applications in both the public and private sector. She is also the author of books on Microsoft Outlook and word processing.

Karen Jolly, author, is an instructor of computer applications and office systems at Portland Community College in Portland, Oregon. She holds a bachelor's degree in business education from Pacific Lutheran University and a master's degree from Portland State University. Karen has taught in both the high school and the community college for over 25 years. She has authored Excel textbooks for 15 years.

Visual Walk-Through of the *GO!* System

The *GO!* System is designed for ease of implementation on the instructor side and ease of understanding on the student. It has been completely developed based on professor and student feedback.

The *GO!* System is divided into three categories that reflect how you might organize your course—**Prepare**, **Teach**, and **Assess**.

Prepare

GO!

Because the GO! System was designed and written by instructors like yourself, it includes the tools that allow you to Prepare, Teach, and Assess in your course. We have organized the GO! System into these three categories that match how you work through your course and thus, it's even easier for you to implement.

To help you get started, here is an outline of the first activities you may want to do in order to conduct your course.

There are several other tools not listed here that are available in the GO! System so please refer to your GO! Guide for a complete listing of all the tools.

Prepare
1. Prepare the course syllabus
2. Plan the course assignments
3. Organize the student resources

Teach
4. Conduct demonstrations and lectures

Assess
5. Assign and grade assignments, quizzes, tests, and assessments

PREPARE

1. Prepare the course syllabus

A syllabus template is provided on the IRCD in the **go07_syllabus_template** folder of the main directory. It includes a course calendar planner for 8-week, 12-week, and 16-week formats. Depending on your term (summer or regular semester) you can modify one of these according to your course plan, and then add information pertinent to your course and institution.

2. Plan course assignments

For each chapter, an Assignment Sheet listing every in-chapter and end-of-chapter project is located on the IRCD within the **go01_gooffice2007intro_instructor_resources_by_chapter** folder. From there, navigate to the specific chapter folder. These sheets are Word tables, so you can delete rows for the projects that you choose not to assign or add rows for your own assignments—if any. There is a column to add the number of points you want to assign to each project depending on your grading scheme. At the top of the sheet, you can fill in the course information.

Transitioning to GO! Office 2007 — Page 1 of 1

NEW

Transition Guide

New to *GO!*–We've made it quick and easy to plan the format and activities for your class.

GO! with Microsoft Office 2007 Introductory
SAMPLE SYLLABUS (16 weeks)

I. COURSE INFORMATION

Course No.:	Semester:
Course Title:	Credits:
Course Hours:	
Instructor:	Office:
Office Hours:	
Email:	Phone:

II. TEXT AND MATERIALS

Before starting the course, you will need the following:

- GO! with Microsoft Office 2007 Introductory by Shelley Gaskin, Robert L. Ferrett, Alicia Vargas, Suzanne Marks ©2007, published by Pearson Prentice Hall. ISBN 0-13-167990-6
- Storage device for saving files (any of the following: multiple diskettes, CD-RW, flash drive, etc.)

III. WHAT YOU WILL LEARN IN THIS COURSE

This is a hands-on course where you will learn to use a computer to practice the most commonly used Microsoft programs including the Windows operating system, Internet Explorer for navigating the Internet, Outlook for managing your personal information and the four most popular programs within the Microsoft Office Suite (Word, Excel, PowerPoint and Access). You will also practice the basics of using a computer, mouse and keyboard. You will learn to be an intermediate level user of the Microsoft Office Suite.

Within the Microsoft Office Suite, you will use Word, Excel, PowerPoint, and Access. Microsoft Word is a word processing program with which you can create common business and personal documents. Microsoft Excel is a spreadsheet program that organizes and calculates accounting-type information. Microsoft PowerPoint is a presentation graphics program with which you can develop slides to accompany an oral presentation. Finally, Microsoft Access is a database program that organizes large amounts of information in a useful manner.

Syllabus Template

Includes course calendar planner for 8-, 12-, and 16-week formats.

Assignment Sheet

One per chapter. Lists all possible assignments; add to and delete from this simple Word table according to your course plan.

File Guide to the GO! Supplements

Tabular listing of all supplements and their file names.

NEW

Assignment Planning Guide

Description of GO! assignments with recommendations based on class size, delivery mode, and student needs. Includes examples from fellow instructors.

GO! with Microsoft Office 2007 Introductory

Assignment Sheet for GO! with Microsoft Office 2007 Introductory
Chapter 5

Instructor Name: _____
Course Information: _____

Do This (✓ when done)	Then Hand in This — Check each Project for the elements listed on the Assignment Tag. Attach the Tag to your Project.	Submit Printed Formulas	By This Date	Possible Points	Your Points
Study the text and perform the steps for Activities 5.1 – 5.11	Project 5A Application Letter				
Study the text and perform the steps for Activities 5.12 – 5.23	Project 5B Company Overview				
End-of-Chapter Assessments					
Complete the Matching and Fill-in-the-Blank questions	As directed by your instructor				
Complete Project 5C	Project 5C Receipt Letter				
Complete Project 5D	Project 5D Marketing				
Complete Project 5E	Project 5E School Tour				
Complete Project 5F	Project 5F Scouting Trip				
Complete Project 5G	Project 5G Contract				
Complete Project 5H	Project 5H Invitation				
Complete Project 5I	Project 5I Fax Cover				
Complete Project 5J	Project 5J Business Running Case				
Complete Project 5K	Project 5K Services				
Complete Project 5L	Project 5L Survey Form				
Complete Project 5M	Project 5M Press Release				

Copyright © 2008 Pearson Prentice Hall   Page 1 of 1

GO! with Microsoft Office Office 2003
Supplements File Guide - Assess & Grade

GO! with Microsoft Office 2007 Introductory
Assignment Planning Guide

Planning the Course Assignments

For each chapter in GO!, an Assignment Sheet listing every in-chapter and end-of-chapter project is located on the IRCD. These sheets are Word tables, so you can delete rows for the projects that you will not assign, and then add rows for any of your own assignments that you may have developed. There is a column to add the number of points you want to assign to each project—depending on your grading scheme. At the top of the sheet, you can fill in your course information.

Additionally, for each chapter, student Assignment Tags are provided for every project (including Problem Solving projects)—also located on the IRCD. These are small scoring checklists on which you can check off errors made by the student, and with which the student can verify that all project elements are complete. For campus classes, the student can attach the tags to his or her paper submissions. For online classes, many GO! instructors have the student include these with the electronic submission.

Deciding What to Assign

Front Portion of the Chapter—Instructional Projects: The projects in the front portion of the chapter, which are listed on the first page of each chapter, are the instructional projects. Most instructors assign all of these projects, because this is where the student receives the instruction and engages in the active learning.

End-of-Chapter—Practice and Critical Thinking Projects: In the back portion of the chapter (the gray pages), you can assign on a prescriptive basis; that is, for students who were challenged by the instructional projects, you might assign one or more projects from the two *Skills Reviews*, which provide maximum prompting and a thorough review of the entire chapter. For students who have previous software knowledge and who completed the instructional projects easily, you might assign only the *Mastery Projects*.

You can also assign prescriptively by Objective, because each end-of-chapter project indicates the Objectives covered. So you might assign, on a student-by-student basis, only the projects that cover the Objectives with which the student seemed to have difficulty in the instructional projects.

The five Problem Solving projects and the You and GO! project are the authentic assessments that pull together the student's learning. Here the student is presented with a "messy real-life situation" and then uses his or her knowledge and skill to solve a problem, produce a product, give a presentation, or demonstrate a procedure. You might assign one or more of the Problem

GO! Assignment Planning Guide   Page 1 of 1

Student Data Files

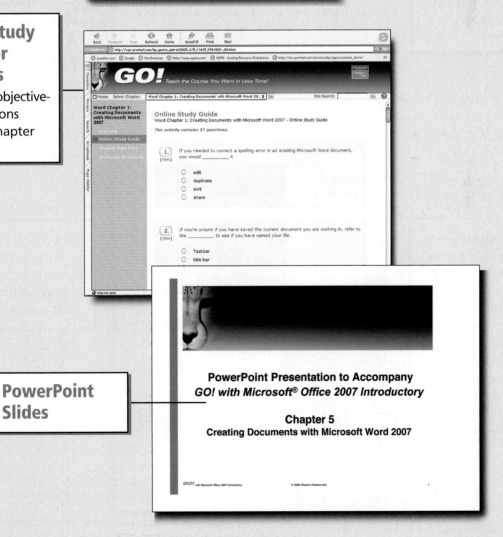

Music School Records discovers, launches, and and develops the careers of young artists in classical, jazz, and contemporary music. Our philosophy is to not only shape, distribute, and sell a music product, but to help artists create a career that can lats a lifetime. too often in the music industry, artists are forced to fit their music to a trend that is short-lived. Music School Records doesn't just follow trends, we take a long-term view of the music industry and help our artists develop a style and repertiore that is fluid and flexible and that will appeal to audiences for years and even decades.

The music industry is constantly changing, but over the last decade the changes have been enormous. New forms of entertainment such as DVDs, video games, and the Internet mean there are more competition for the leisure dollar in the market. New technologies give consomers more options for buying and listening to music, and they are demaning high quality recordings. Young consomers are comfortable with technology and want the music they love when and where they want it, no matter where they are or what they are doing.

Music School Records embraces new technologies and the sophisticated market of young music lovers. We believe that providing high quality recordings of truly talented artists make for more discerning listeners who will cherish the gift of music for the rest of their lives. The expertise of Music School Records includes:

- Insight into our target market and the ability to reach the desired audience
- The ability to access all current sources of music income
- A management team with years of experience in music commerce
- Innovative business strategies and artist development plans
- Investment in technology infrastructure for high quality recordings and business services
- Initiative and proactive management of artist careers

Online Study Guide for Students

Interactive objective-style questions based on chapter content.

PowerPoint Slides

PowerPoint Presentation to Accompany
GO! with Microsoft® Office 2007 Introductory

Chapter 5
Creating Documents with Microsoft Word 2007

Teach

Student Textbook

Learning Objectives and Student Outcomes

Objectives are clustered around projects that result in student outcomes. They help students learn how to solve problems, not just learn software features.

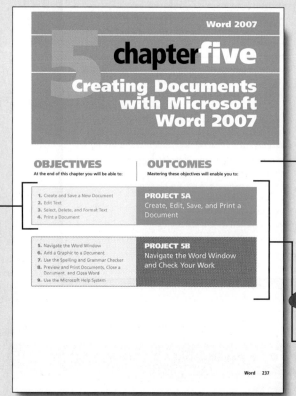

Project-Based Instruction

Students do not practice features of the application; they create real projects that they will need in the real world. Projects are color coded for easy reference and are named to reflect skills the students will be practicing.

A and B Projects

Each chapter contains two instructional projects—A and B.

Each chapter opens with a story that sets the stage for the projects the student will create; the instruction does not force the student to pretend to be someone or make up a scenario.

Each chapter has an introductory paragraph that briefs students on what is important.

Visual Summary

Shows students upfront what their projects will look like when they are done.

Project Summary

Stated clearly and quickly in one paragraph.

NEW

File Guide

Clearly shows students which files are needed for the project and the names they will use to save their documents.

Objective

The skills the student will learn are clearly stated at the beginning of each project and color coded to match projects listed on the chapter opener page.

Teachable Moment

Expository text is woven into the steps—at the moment students need to know it—not chunked together in a block of text that will go unread.

NEW

Screen Shots

Larger screen shots.

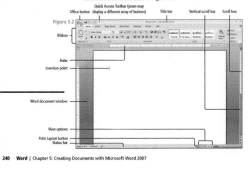

Project 5A Application Letter

In Activities 5.1 through 5.11, you will create and make changes to a letter from John Diamond, Vice President of Creative Development, to William Hawken, an artist interested in becoming a client of Music School Records. Your completed document will look similar to Figure 5.1.

For Project 5A, you will need the following file:

New blank Word document

You will save your document as
5A_Application_Letter_Firstname_Lastname

Figure 5.1
Project 5A—Application Letter

Objective 1
Create and Save a New Document

With a word processing program, you can type, *edit*—make changes to—move, and delete text or change the appearance of text. Because the documents that you create are stored electronically, they can be duplicated, printed, copied, and shared with others. In this project, you will become

Project 5A: Application Letter | **Word** 239

familiar with the parts of the Word window. Then you will create a document, edit and format text, and save your work.

Activity 5.1 Starting Word and Identifying Parts of the Word Window

Note — Comparing Your Screen With the Figures in This Textbook

Your screen will match the figures shown in this textbook if you set your screen resolution to 1024 × 768. At other resolutions, your screen will closely resemble, but not match, the figures shown. To view your screen's resolution, on the Windows desktop, right-click in a blank area, click Properties, and then click the Settings tab.

On the left side of the Windows taskbar, point to, and then click the **Start** button.

From the displayed **Start** menu, locate the **Word** program, and then click **Microsoft Office Word 2007**.
The Word program may be located under All Programs or Microsoft Office or on the main Start menu.
Print Layout view is the ideal view to use when you are learning Microsoft Word 2007 because you can see the document exactly the way it will look when it is printed.

If necessary, on the right side of the status bar, click the **Print Layout** button. If the ruler does not display, click the View tab, and then in the Show/Hide group, click the Ruler check box. Take a moment to study the parts of the Word screen shown in Figure 5.2 and described in the table in Figure 5.3.

240 **Word** | Chapter 5: Creating Documents with Microsoft Word 2007

Steps

Color coded to the current project, easy to read, and not too many to confuse the student or too few to be meaningless.

Sequential Pagination

No more confusing letters and abbreviations.

Microsoft Procedural Syntax

All steps are written in Microsoft Procedural Syntax to put the student in the right place at the right time.

End-of-Project Icon

All projects in the *GO! Series* have clearly identifiable end points, useful in self-paced or online environments.

Press Enter two more times.

In a business letter, insert two blank lines between the date and the inside address, which is the same as the address you would use on an envelope.

Type **Mr. William Hawken** and then press Enter.

The wavy red line under the proper name *Hawken* indicates that the word has been flagged as misspelled because it is a word not contained in the Word dictionary.

On two lines, type the following address, but do not press Enter at the end of the second line:

123 Eighth Street
Harrisville, MI 48740

Note — Typing the Address

Include a comma after the city name in an inside address. However, for mailing addresses on envelopes, eliminate the comma after the city name.

On the **Home tab**, in the **Styles group**, click the **Normal** button.

The Normal style is applied to the text in the rest of the document. Recall that Normal style adds extra space between paragraphs; it also adds slightly more space between lines in a paragraph.

Press Enter. Type **Dear William:** and then press Enter.

This salutation is the line that greets the person receiving the letter.

Type **Subject: Your Application to Music School Records** and press Enter. Notice the light dots between words, which indicate spaces and display when formatting marks are displayed. Also, notice the extra space after each paragraph, and then compare your screen with Figure 5.6.

The subject line is optional, but you should include a subject line in most letters to identify the topic. Depending on your Word settings, a wavy green line may display in the subject line, indicating a potential grammar error.

244 **Word** | Chapter 5: Creating Documents with Microsoft Word 2007

Note — Space Between Lines in Your Printed Document

The Cambria font, and many others, uses a slightly larger space between the lines than more traditional fonts like Times New Roman. As you progress in your study of Word, you will use many different fonts and also adjust the spacing between lines.

From the **Office** menu, click **Close**, saving any changes if prompted to do so. Leave Word open for the next project.

Another Way

To Print a Document

To Print a document:

• From the Office menu, click Print to display the Print dialog box (to be covered later), from which you can choose a variety of different options, such as printing multiple copies, printing on a different printer, and printing some but not all pages.

• Hold down Ctrl and then press P. This is an alternative to the Office menu command, and opens the Print dialog box.

• Hold down Alt, press F, and then press P. This opens the Print dialog box.

End You have completed Project 5A

264 **Word** | Chapter 5: Creating Documents with Microsoft Word 2007

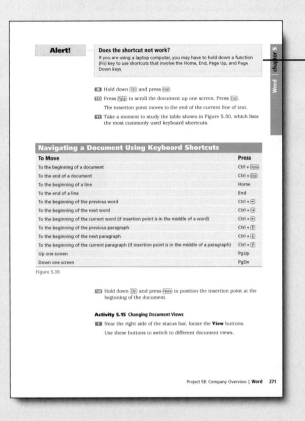

Alert box
Draws students' attention to make sure they aren't getting too far off course.

Another Way box
Shows students other ways of doing tasks.

More Knowledge box
Expands on a topic by going deeper into the material.

Note box
Points out important items to remember.

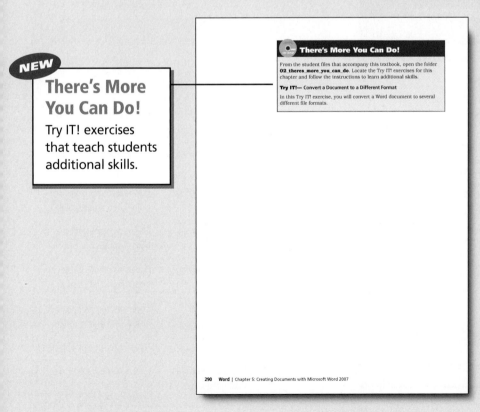

NEW

There's More You Can Do!
Try IT! exercises that teach students additional skills.

End-of-Chapter Material

Take your pick! Content-based or Outcomes-based projects to choose from. Below is a table outlining the various types of projects that fit into these two categories.

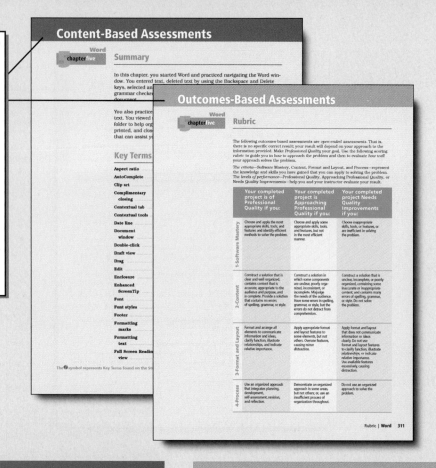

Content-Based Assessments
(Defined solutions with solution files provided for grading)

Project Letter	Name	Objectives Covered
N/A	Summary and Key Terms	
N/A	Multiple Choice	
N/A	Fill-in-the-blank	
C	Skills Review	Covers A Objectives
D	Skills Review	Covers B Objectives
E	Mastering Excel	Covers A Objectives
F	Mastering Excel	Covers B Objectives
G	Mastering Excel	Covers any combination of A and B Objectives
H	Mastering Excel	Covers any combination of A and B Objectives
I	Mastering Excel	Covers all A and B Objectives
J	Business Running Case	Covers all A and B Objectives

Outcomes-Based Assessments
(Open solutions that require a rubric for grading)

Project Letter	Name	Objectives Covered
N/A	Rubric	
K	Problem Solving	Covers as many Objectives from A and B as possible
L	Problem Solving	Covers as many Objectives from A and B as possible.
M	Problem Solving	Covers as many Objectives from A and B as possible.
N	Problem Solving	Covers as many Objectives from A and B as possible.
O	Problem Solving	Covers as many Objectives from A and B as possible.
P	You and GO!	Covers as many Objectives from A and B as possible
Q	GO! Help	Not tied to specific objectives
R	* Group Business Running Case	Covers A and B Objectives

* This project is provided only with the *GO! with Microsoft Office 2007 Introductory* book.

Teach (continued)

Objectives List

Most projects in the end-of-chapter section begin with a list of the objectives covered.

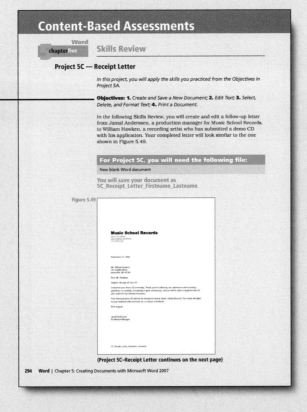

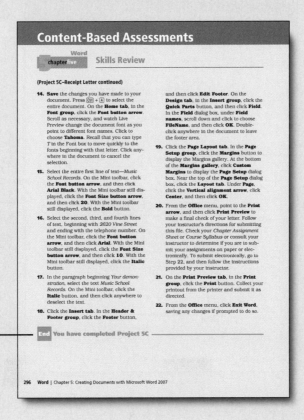

End of Each Project Clearly Marked

Clearly identified end points help separate the end-of-chapter projects.

Teach (continued)

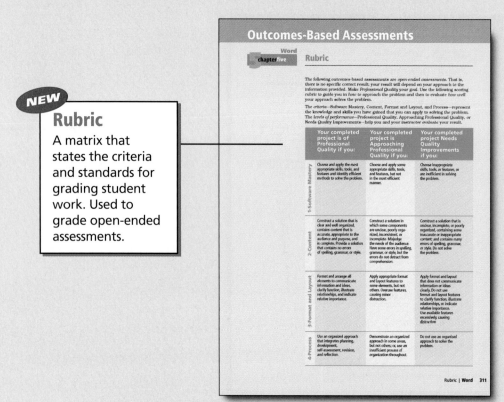

NEW

Rubric
A matrix that states the criteria and standards for grading student work. Used to grade open-ended assessments.

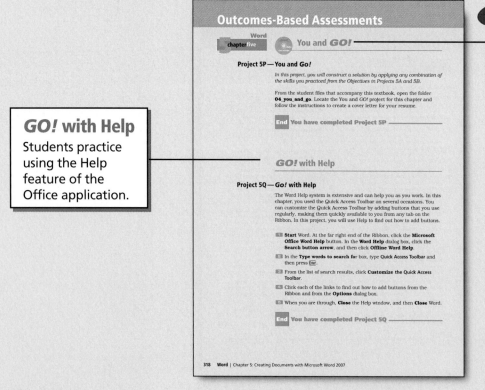

GO! with Help
Students practice using the Help feature of the Office application.

NEW

You and *GO!*
A project in which students use information from their own lives and apply the skills from the chapter to a personal task.

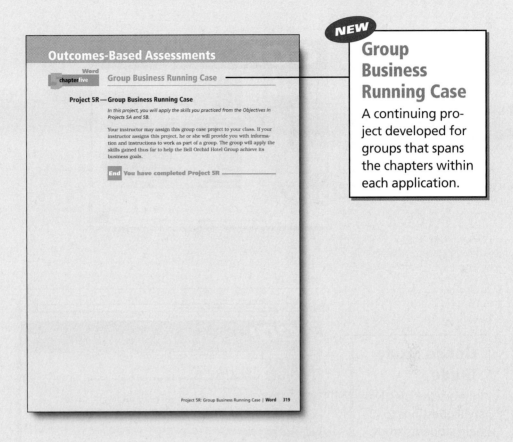

Group Business Running Case

A continuing project developed for groups that spans the chapters within each application.

Student CD includes:

- Student Data Files
- There's More You Can Do!
- Business Running Case
- You and *GO!*

Companion Website

An interactive Website to further student leaning.

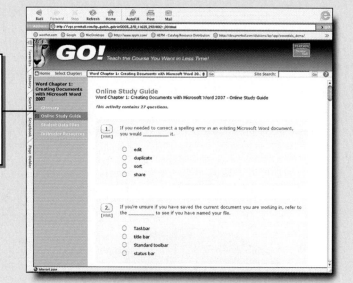

Online Study Guide

Interactive objective-style questions to help students study.

Annotated Instructor Edition

The Annotated Instructor Edition contains a full version of the student textbook that includes tips, supplement references, and pointers on teaching with the *GO!* instructional system.

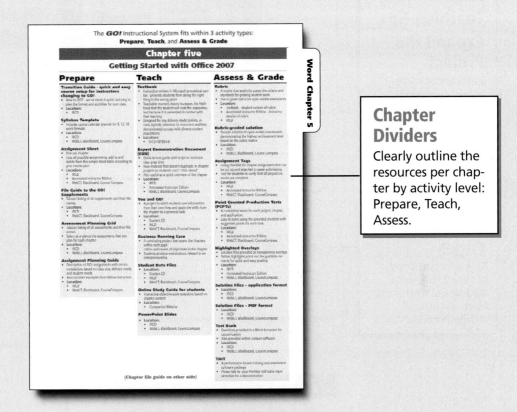

Chapter Dividers

Clearly outline the resources per chapter by activity level: Prepare, Teach, Assess.

Instructor File Guide

Complete list of all Student Data Files and instructor Solution Files needed for the chapter.

Helpful Hints, Teaching Tips, Expand the Project

References correspond to what is being taught in the student textbook.

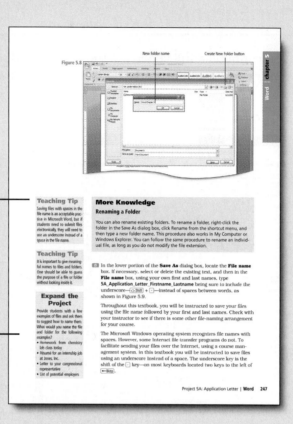

Full-Size Textbook Pages

An instructor copy of the textbook with traditional Instructor Manual content incorporated.

End-of-Chapter Concepts Assessments contain the answers for quick reference.

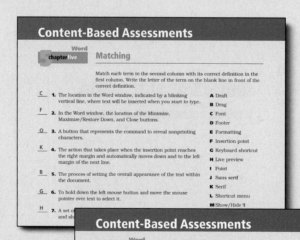

NEW

Rubric

A matrix to guide the student on how they will be assessed is reprinted in the Annotated Instructor Edition with suggested weights for each of the criteria and levels of performance. Instructors can modify the weights to suit their needs.

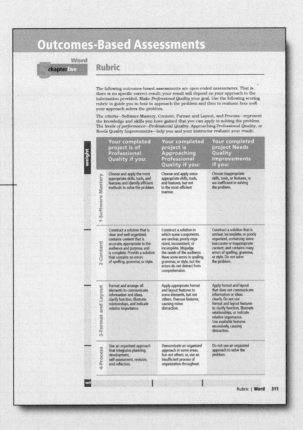

Assess

Assignment Tags

NEW Scoring checklist for assignments. Now also available for Problem-Solving projects.

GO! with Microsoft® Office 2007

Assignment Tags for GO! with Office 2007
Word Chapter 5

Name:	Project:	**5A**
Professor:	Course:	

Task	Points	Your Score
Center text vertically on page	2	
Delete the word "really"	1	
Delete the words "try to"	1	
Replace "last" with "first"	1	
Insert the word "potential"	1	
Replace "John W. Diamond" with "Lucy Burrows"	2	
Change entire document to the Cambria font	2	
Change the first line of text to Arial Black 20 pt. font	2	
Bold the first line of text	2	
Change the 2nd through 4th lines to Arial 10 pt.	2	
Italicize the 2nd through 4th lines of text	2	
Correct/Add footer as instructed	2	
Circled information is incorrect or formatted incorrectly		
Total Points	**20**	**0**

Name:	Project:	**5B**
Professor:	Course:	

Task	Points	Your Score
Insert the file w05B_Music_School_Records	4	
Insert the Music Logo	4	
Remove duplicate "and"	2	
Change spelling and grammar errors (4)	8	
Correct/Add footer as instructed	2	
Circled information is incorrect or formatted incorrectly		
Total Points	**20**	**0**

Name:	Project:	**5C**
Professor:	Course:	

Task	Points	Your Score
Add four line letterhead	2	
Insert today's date	1	
Add address block, subject line, and greeting	2	
Add two-paragraph body of letter	2	
Add closing, name, and title	2	
In subject line, capitalize "receipt"	1	
Change "standards" to "guidelines"	1	
Insert "quite"	1	
Insert "all"	1	
Change the first line of text to Arial Black 20 pt. font	2	
Bold the first line of text	1	
Change the 2nd through 4th lines to Arial 10 pt.	1	
Italicize the 2nd through 4th lines of text	1	
Correct/add footer as instructed	2	
Circled information is incorrect or formatted incorrectly		
Total Points	**20**	**0**

Name:	Project:	**5D**
Professor:	Course:	

Task	Points	Your Score
Insert the file w05D_Marketing	4	
Bold the first two title lines	2	
Correct spelling of "Marketing"	2	
Correct spelling of "geners"	2	
Correct all misspellings of "allready"	2	
Correct grammar error "are" to "is"	2	
Insert the Piano image	4	
Correct/add footer as instructed	2	
Circled information is incorrect or formatted incorrectly		
Total Points	**20**	**0**

Highlighted Overlays

Solution files provided as transparency overlays. Yellow highlights point out the gradable elements for quick and easy grading.

Music School Records

2620 Vine Street
Los Angeles, CA 90028
323-555-0028

— 20 point Arial Black, bold and underline

— 10 point Arial, italic

September 12, 2009

Mr. William Hawken
123 Eighth Street
Harrisville, MI 48740

Dear William:

Subject: Your Application to Music School Records

Thank you for submitting your application to Music School Records. Our talent scout for Northern Michigan, Catherine McDonald, is very enthusiastic about your music, and the demo CD you submitted certainly confirms her opinion.

We discuss our applications from potential clients during the first week of each month. We will have a decision for you by the second week of October.

Yours Truly,

Lucy Burroughs

— Text vertically centered on page

— Body of document changed to Cambria font, 11 point

— Word "really" deleted

— Words "try to" deleted

Point-Counted Production Tests (PCPTs)

A cumulative exam for each **project**, **chapter**, and **application**. Easy to score using the provided checklist with suggested points for each task.

GO! with Microsoft® Office 2007 Introductory

Point-Counted Production Test—Project for GO! with Microsoft® Office 2007 Introductory Project 5A

Instructor Name: _____
Course Information: _____

1. Start Word 2007 to begin a new blank document. Save your document as 5A_Cover_Letter_Firstname_Lastname Remember to save your file frequently as you work.

2. If necessary, display the formatting marks. With the insertion point blinking in the upper left corner of the document to the left of the default first paragraph mark, type the current date (you can use AutoComplete).

3. Press Enter three times and type the inside address:

   Music School Records
   2620 Vine Street
   Los Angeles, CA 90028

4. Press Enter three times, and type Dear Ms. Burroughs:

   Press Enter twice, and type Subject: Application to Music School Records

   Press Enter twice, and type the following text (skipping one line between paragraphs):

   I read about Music School Records in Con Brio magazine and I would like to inquire about the possibility of being represented by your company.

   I am very interested in a career in jazz and am planning to relocate to the Los Angeles area in the very near future. I would be interested in learning more about the company and about available opportunities.

   I was a member of my high school jazz band for three years. In addition, I have been playing in the local coffee shop for the last two years. My demo CD, which is enclosed, contains three of my most requested songs.

   I would appreciate the opportunity to speak with you. Thank you for your time and consideration. I look forward to speaking with you about this exciting opportunity.

5. Press Enter three times, and type the closing Sincerely, Press enter four times, and type your name.

6. Insert a footer that contains the file name.

7. Delete the first instance of the word *very* in the second body paragraph, and insert the word modern in front of *jazz*.

    Page 1 of 1

Test Bank

Available as TestGen Software or as a Word document for customization.

Chapter 5: Creating Documents with Microsoft Word 2007

Multiple Choice:

1. With word processing programs, how are documents stored?

   A. On a network

   B. On the computer

   C. Electronically

   D. On the floppy disk

   Answer: C   **Reference:** Objective 1: Create and Save a New Document   **Difficulty:** Moderate

2. Because you will see the document as it will print, _____ view is the ideal view to use when learning Microsoft Word 2007.

   A. Reading

   B. Normal

   C. Print Layout

   D. Outline

   Answer: C   **Reference:** Objective 1: Create and Save a New Document   **Difficulty:** Moderate

3. The blinking vertical line where text or graphics will be inserted is called the:

   A. cursor.

   B. insertion point.

   C. blinking line.

   D. I-beam.

   Answer: B   **Reference:** Objective 1: Create and Save a New Document   **Difficulty:** Easy

Solution Files–Application and PDF format

Music School Records

Music School Records discovers, launches, and develops the careers of young artists in classical, jazz, and contemporary music. Our philosophy is to not only shape, distribute, and sell a music product, but to help artists create a career that can last a lifetime. Too often in the music industry, artists are forced to fit their music to a trend that is short-lived. Music School Records does not just follow trends, we take a long-term view of the music industry and help our artists develop a style and repertoire that is fluid and flexible and that will appeal to audiences for years and even decades.

The music industry is constantly changing, but over the last decade, the changes have been enormous. New forms of entertainment such as DVDs, video games, and the Internet mean there is more competition for the leisure dollar in the market. New technologies give consumers more options for buying and listening to music, and they are demanding high quality recordings. Young consumers are comfortable with technology and want the music they love when and where they want it, no matter where they are or what they are doing.

Music School Records embraces new technologies and the sophisticated market of young music lovers. We believe that providing high quality recordings of truly talented artists make for more discerning listeners who will cherish the gift of music for the rest of their lives. The expertise of Music School Records includes:

- Insight into our target market and the ability to reach the desired audience
- The ability to access all current sources of music income
- A management team with years of experience in music commerce
- Innovative business strategies and artist development plans
- Investment in technology infrastructure for high quality recordings and business services

pagexxxix_top.docx

Excel 2007

chapterone

Creating a Worksheet and Charting Data

OBJECTIVES

At the end of this chapter you will be able to:

1. Start Excel and Navigate a Worksheet
2. Select Parts of a Worksheet
3. Enter Data, Construct a Formula, and Use the SUM Function
4. Format Data, Cells, and Worksheets
5. Insert a Footer into a Worksheet
6. Delete Unused Worksheets and Preview and Print a Worksheet
7. Print Formulas, Close a Workbook, and Exit Excel

8. Check Spelling and Edit a Worksheet
9. Enter Data by Range
10. Create and Copy Formulas
11. Use Format Painter and Chart Data
12. Use the Microsoft Excel Help

OUTCOMES

Mastering these objectives will enable you to:

Project 1A
Create, Save, and Print a Workbook and Insert a Footer

Project 1B
Create a Workbook with Mathematical Operators and Chart Data

Seattle-Tacoma Job Fair

The Seattle-Tacoma Job Fair is a nonprofit organization that brings together employers and job seekers in the greater Seattle-Tacoma metropolitan area. Each year the organization holds a number of targeted job fairs, and the annual Seattle-Tacoma Job Fair draws 2,000 employers in more than 70 industries and registers more than 5,000 candidates. Candidate registration is free; employers pay a nominal fee to display and present at the fairs. Candidate resumes and employer postings are managed by a state-of-the-art database system, allowing participants quick and accurate access to job data and candidate qualifications.

Creating a Worksheet and Charting Data

Microsoft Office Excel 2007 is used by organizations to analyze, communicate, and manage information for the purpose of making informed decisions. Using Excel, you can create and analyze data that is organized into columns and rows. You can perform calculations, analyze information to make logical decisions, and create visual representations of the data in the form of charts. In addition, Excel can manage and sort your data and it can search for specific pieces of information.

Excel worksheets are used to report financial information such as sales reports, cash flow analyses, business plans and projections, budgets, and what-if analyses. In this chapter, you will create an Excel workbook. You will enter data into the worksheet, and you will edit the data. You will create formulas to make calculations on numbers. You will format a worksheet using text and number styles that will result in a professional-looking worksheet. You will save, preview, and print a worksheet. Finally, you will chart the data in a worksheet.

Project 1A Seattle Payroll

In Activities 1.1 through 1.12, you will assist Michael Dawson, the executive director of the Seattle-Tacoma Job Fair, to prepare a payroll report for the Seattle Job Fair event that was held in May. As a nonprofit organization, the Job Fair prepares this report for each job fair event as part of its financial reporting. The report will list each employee's name, title, taxes withheld, and net pay. Your result will look similar to Figure 1.1.

For Project 1A, you will need the following file:

New blank Excel workbook

You will save your workbook as
1A_Seattle_Payroll_Firstname_Lastname

Seattle-Tacoma Job Fair
Payroll for Seattle Job Fair
Fair Date: May 2, 2009

First	Last	Title	Taxes Withheld	Net Pay
Monica	Eisler	Event Coordinator	$ 248.00	$ 4,000.00
Janice	Strickland	Attendee Registration	18.60	300.00
Janna	Sorokin	Employer Coordinator	150.66	2,430.00
Leslie	Goldhammer	Floor Assistant	24.80	400.75
Chang	Hong	Floor Assistant	24.80	400.75
Julio	Ramirez	Floor Manager	152.70	2,400.00
Timothy	VanHoy	Facilities Coordinator	55.34	892.50
Kevin	London	Advertising Assistant	54.25	875.00
Total			$ 729.15	$ 11,699.00

01A_Seattle_Payroll_Firstname_Lastname

Figure 1.1
Project 1A—Seattle Payroll

Objective 1
Start Excel and Navigate a Worksheet

When you start the Excel program, a new blank **workbook** opens and displays a **worksheet**. By default, three worksheets are available in each workbook. A worksheet—also called a **spreadsheet**—is the primary document that you use in Excel to store and work with data. A worksheet is always stored in a workbook.

Activity 1.1 Starting Excel and Naming and Saving a Workbook

In this activity, you will start Excel and create, name, and save a workbook.

Note — Comparing Your Screen with the Figures in This Textbook

Your screen will match the figures shown in this textbook if you set your screen resolution to 1024 × 768. At other resolutions, your screen will closely resemble, but not match, the figures shown. To view your screen's resolution, on the Windows desktop, right-click in a blank area, click Properties, and then click the Settings tab.

---

1 On the Windows taskbar, click the **Start** button [start], determine where the Excel program is located on your computer—usually in a folder named **Microsoft Office**—point to **Microsoft Office Excel 2007**, and then click once to open the program. Take a moment to compare your screen with Figure 1.2 and study the parts of the Microsoft Excel window described in the table in Figure 1.3.

Figure 1.2

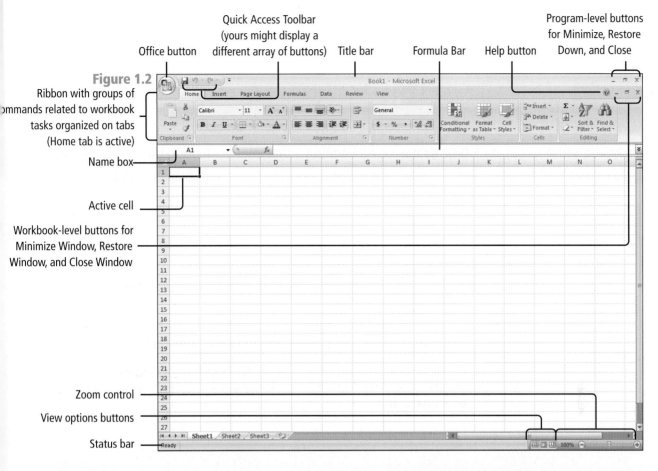

Office button
Quick Access Toolbar (yours might display a different array of buttons)
Title bar
Formula Bar
Help button
Program-level buttons for Minimize, Restore Down, and Close

Ribbon with groups of commands related to workbook tasks organized on tabs (Home tab is active)

Name box

Active cell

Workbook-level buttons for Minimize Window, Restore Window, and Close Window

Zoom control

View options buttons

Status bar

Parts of the Excel Window

Excel Window Element	Description
Active cell	Indicates, with a dark black border, the cell that is ready to receive data or that will be affected by the next Excel command. Its location is also displayed in the Name Box.
Formula Bar	Displays the value or formula contained in the active cell; also permits entry or editing of values or formulas.
Help button	Displays the Excel Help window.
Name Box	Displays the name of the selected cell, table, chart, or object.
Office button	Displays a menu of commands related to things you can do *with* a workbook, such as opening, saving, printing, or sharing.
Program-level buttons	Minimizes, restores, or closes the Excel program.
Quick Access Toolbar	Displays buttons to perform frequently used commands with a single click. Frequently used commands in Excel include Save, Undo, and Redo. For commands that *you* use frequently, you can add additional buttons to the Quick Access Toolbar, such as Print Preview and Print.
Ribbon	Groups the commands used for performing related workbook tasks.
Status bar	Displays, on the left side, the current cell mode, page number, and other information. On the right side, displays buttons to control how the window looks; when numerical data is selected, common calculations such as Sum, Average, and Count display.

(Continued)

(Continued)

Title bar	Indicates the name of the current workbook, the program name, and displays the program-level buttons.
View options	Contains buttons for viewing the workbook in Normal, Page Layout View, or Page Break Preview.
Workbook-level buttons	Minimizes, restores, or closes the Excel workbook.
Worksheet grid	Displays the columns and rows that intersect to form the workbook's cells.
Zoom control	Increases or decreases the number of rows and columns displayed.

Figure 1.3

2 In the upper left corner of your screen, click the **Office** button ⊞, and then from the displayed **Office** menu, point to **Save As**. Compare your screen with Figure 1.4.

The ***Office button*** displays a menu of commands related to things you can do *with* a workbook, such as opening and saving.

A ***ScreenTip*** displays additional information about a command. Here the ScreenTip indicates that pressing F12 will also perform the **Save As** command.

Office button

Figure 1.4

Save As command ———

ScreenTip ———

Office menu of commands ———

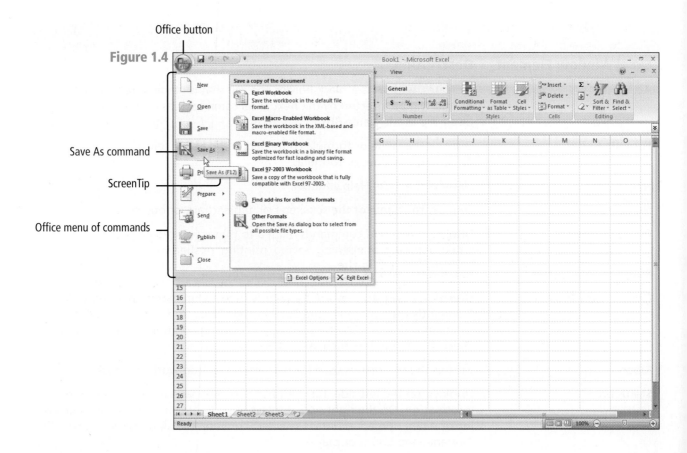

3 Click the **Save As** command. In the displayed **Save As** dialog box, click the **Save in arrow** to view a list of the drives available to you, and then **navigate**—move within—to the drive on which you will be storing your folders and workbooks—for example, a USB flash drive such as the one shown in Figure 1.5.

A **dialog box** requests more information about the command or requires that you make a decision.

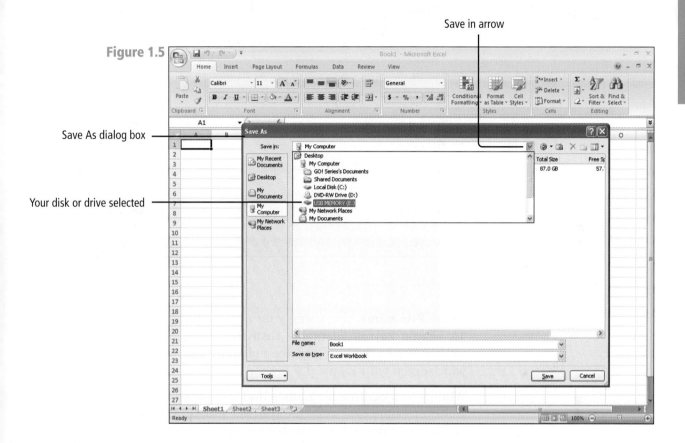

Figure 1.5

Save in arrow

Save As dialog box

Your disk or drive selected

4 Click in the location where your work will be saved. On the **Save As** dialog box toolbar, click the **Create New Folder** button . In the displayed **New Folder** dialog box, in the **Name** box, type **Excel Chapter 1** and compare your screen with Figure 1.6. Then click **OK**.

Windows creates the *Excel Chapter 1* folder and makes it the active folder in the Save in box. At the bottom of the Save As dialog box, in the File name box, *Book1* displays as the default file name.

Figure 1.6

Folder name typed in dialog box   Create New Folder button

Active drive on which
your folder will be created

Save As dialog
box toolbar

New Folder dialog box

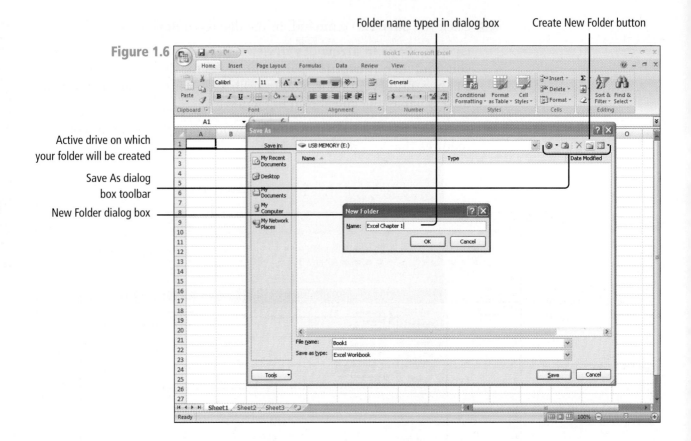

5 In the **File name** box, using your own first and last name, type
1A_Seattle_Payroll_Firstname_Lastname being sure to include the
underscore (⎇ Shift + -) instead of spaces between words. Compare
your screen with Figure 1.7.

Windows recognizes file names that use spaces between words.
However, some electronic file transfer programs do not. In this text,
you will use underscores instead of spaces between words for your
file names.

Figure 1.7

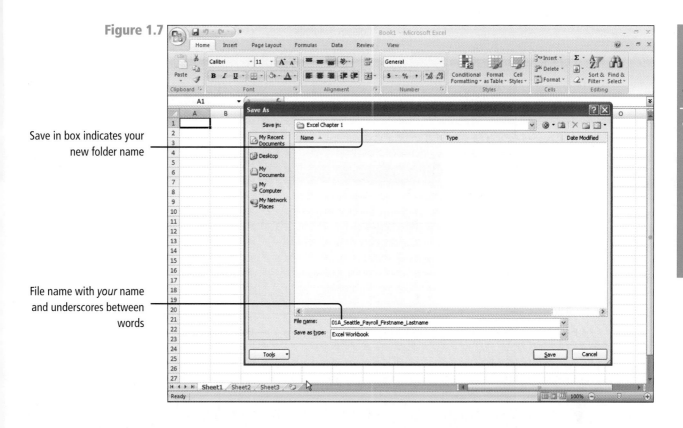

Save in box indicates your new folder name

File name with *your* name and underscores between words

[6] In the lower right corner of the **Save As** dialog box, click **Save** or press Enter.

The file is saved in the new folder with the new name. The worksheet displays, and its new name displays in the ***title bar***—the bar at the top of the workbook window that identifies the program and the name of the workbook.

Activity 1.2 Navigating a Worksheet

In this activity, you will navigate the Excel worksheet window.

[1] Take a moment to study Figure 1.8 and the table in Figure 1.9 to become familiar with the Excel workbook window.

A worksheet is organized in a pattern of uniformly spaced horizontal and vertical lines, called ***gridlines***. The gridlines display on the screen but do not usually display when the worksheet is printed. This grid pattern of the worksheet forms vertical columns and horizontal rows. The intersection of a ***column***—a vertical group of cells in a worksheet—and a ***row***—a horizontal group of cells in a worksheet—forms a small rectangular box referred to as a ***cell***.

Figure 1.8

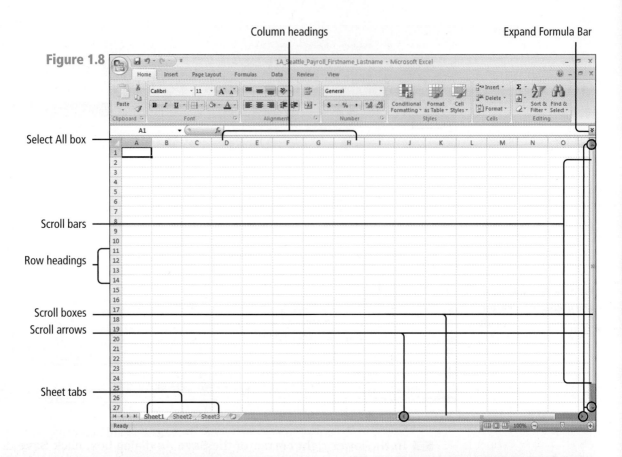

Column headings

Expand Formula Bar

Select All box

Scroll bars

Row headings

Scroll boxes
Scroll arrows

Sheet tabs

Elements of the Excel Workbook Window

Workbook Element	Description
Column headings	Indicate the column letter.
Expand Formula Bar button	Increases the height of the Formula Bar to display lengthy cell content.
Row headings	Indicate the row number.
Scroll arrows	Enable you to scroll one column or row at a time.
Scroll bars	Enable you to scroll the Excel window up and down or left and right.
Scroll boxes	Move the position of a window up and down or left and right.
Select All box	Selects all the cells in a worksheet.
Sheet tabs	Change the active worksheet in a workbook.

Figure 1.9

2 In the horizontal *scroll bar*, click the **right scroll arrow** ▶, and then compare your screen with Figure 1.10.

The workbook window shifts so that column A moves out of view. The number of times you click the arrows on the horizontal scroll bar determines the number of columns by which the window shifts—either to the left or to the right.

Figure 1.10

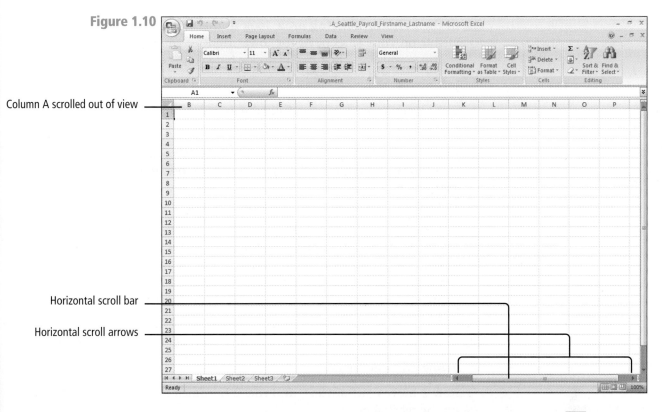

Column A scrolled out of view

Horizontal scroll bar

Horizontal scroll arrows

3 In the horizontal scroll bar, click the **right scroll arrow** ▶ and hold the mouse button down until the columns begin to scroll rapidly to the right; release when you begin to see pairs of letters as the column headings. Compare your screen with Figure 1.11.

The workbook window moves rapidly. *Column headings*—the letters at the top of each column that identify the column—to the right of column Z use two letters starting with AA, AB, AC, and so on. After that, columns begin with three letters beginning with AAA. This pattern is used to provide a total of 16,384 columns. The last column available is column XFD.

Column heading Z

Figure 1.11

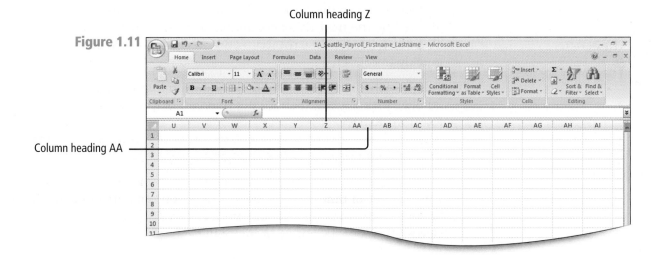

Column heading AA

Excel | chapter 1

4 In the **column heading area**, look at the first column that is visible on your screen. At the lower right of your screen, in the horizontal scroll bar, click in the space between the **scroll box** and the **left arrow** ◀.

The screen moves left one full screen and a different column becomes the first column on your screen.

5 In the horizontal scroll bar, point to the **horizontal scroll box**. Hold down the left mouse button, drag the box to the left to display **column A**, and notice that ScreenTips display the column letters as you drag. Release the mouse button.

To *drag* is to move something from one location on the screen to another; the action of dragging includes releasing the mouse button at the desired time or location. Use the scroll boxes in this manner to bring various parts of the worksheet into view. Scroll boxes change in size to indicate how the visible portion of the worksheet compares to the total amount of the worksheet in use.

6 In the vertical scroll bar, point to and then click the **down scroll arrow** ▼ one time.

Row 1 moves out of view, and row 2 becomes the first available row on the worksheet.

7 Hold down Ctrl and press →.

This is a *keyboard shortcut*, which is an individual keystroke or a combination of keys pressed simultaneously that can either access an Excel command or navigate to another location on your screen.

The last column, XFD, is displayed. Recall that columns are identified by letters beginning with A and ending with XFD.

8 Hold down Ctrl and press ↓.

The last row and column of the worksheet displays. There are 1,048,576 rows available in an Excel worksheet.

9 Hold down Ctrl and press Home.

Cell A1 becomes the *active cell*—the cell ready to accept data or be affected by the next Excel command. The active cell is surrounded by a black border. Use the Ctrl + Home keyboard shortcut to navigate quickly to cell A1.

10 Take a moment to study the table shown in Figure 1.12 to become familiar with keyboard shortcuts that can help you navigate the Excel worksheet.

Keyboard Commands

To Move the Location of the Active Cell:	Press:
Right one cell	Tab
Left one cell	Shift + Tab
Left, right, up, or down one cell	←, →, ↑, ↓
Down one cell	Enter
Up one cell	Shift + Enter
Up one full screen	Page Up
Down one full screen	PgDn
Left one full screen	Alt + Page Up
Right one full screen	Alt + PgDn
To column A of the current row	Home
To cell A1	Ctrl + Home

Figure 1.12

Objective 2
Select Parts of a Worksheet

In Excel, **data** consists of numbers, text, dates, or times of the day. To enter data, you must first select the cell to indicate the location where the data will be entered. You then apply Excel's formatting and functions to any selected cell or cells.

Activity 1.3 Selecting Cells and Ranges and Entering Data

Selecting refers to highlighting cells by clicking or dragging with your mouse. You can edit, format, copy, or move one or more selected cells. Excel treats a selected **range**—group of cells—as a single unit. You can make the same change, or combination of changes, to more than one cell at a time. In the following activity, you will select individual cells and groups of cells in the worksheet.

1 In cell **A1**, type **Seattle-Tacoma Job Fair** and then press Enter.

After you type data into the active cell, you must confirm the entry to store it in the cell. One way to do this is to press the Enter key, which typically moves the selection to the cell *below* to facilitate entry in a column of cells. You can also use other keyboard movements, such as Tab or one of the arrow keys on your keyboard to confirm the entry and make another cell active.

The text extends into columns B and C. If text is too long for a cell and the cells to the right are empty, the text will display. If the cells immediately to the right contain data, only the text that will fit in the cell will display.

2 Point to the cell at the intersection of **column A** and **row 3**, and then click. Compare your screen with Figure 1.13.

Cell A3 is the active cell. A cell is identified by the intersecting column letter and row number, which forms the **cell reference**. The cell reference—also referred to as a **cell address**—displays in the **Name Box**, which displays the name of the selected cell, chart, or object. The column letter and row number of the active cell are highlighted in the column heading area and **row heading** area—the numbers along the left side of the worksheet that indicate the row number.

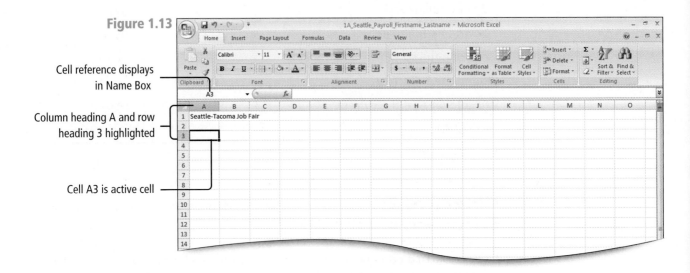

Figure 1.13

Cell reference displays in Name Box

Column heading A and row heading 3 highlighted

Cell A3 is active cell

3 On the keyboard, press → two times and the ↓ three times. Look at the cell address in the **Name Box**.

Cell C6 becomes the active cell. Pressing one of the four direction arrow keys relocates the active cell. The cell reference of the active cell always displays in the Name Box, and the corresponding column and row headings are highlighted.

4 Point to cell **E3**, hold down the left mouse button, drag downward to select cells **E4**, **E5**, and **E6**, and then continue to drag to the right to cell **G6** and release the left mouse button. Alternatively, you can drag diagonally across the range from cell E3 to cell G6. If you are not satisfied with your result, click anywhere, and then begin again. Compare your screen with Figure 1.14.

The 12 cells, E3 through E6, F3 through F6, and G3 through G6 are selected, and cell E3 is the active cell. This range of **adjacent cells** — cells that are next to each other—is identified as *E3:G6*. When you see a colon (:) between two cell references, a range is identified that includes all the cells between the two cell references. The cell references used to indicate the range are the upper left cell and the lower right cell—in this instance, E3 and G6.

When you select a range of cells, the cells are surrounded by a black border, and the cells are shaded except for the first cell in the range, which is the active cell. The cell reference of the active cell displays in the Name Box.

Figure 1.14

Active cell

Column headings (letters)
highlighted

Selected range E3:G6

Name Box indicates reference
of active cell in the range

Row headings (numbers)
highlighted

Black border surrounds
selected range

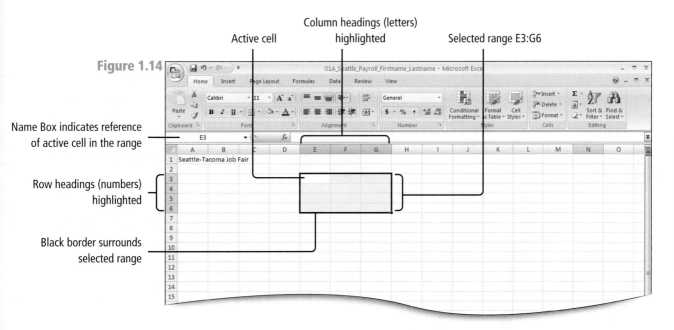

5 At the left edge of the worksheet, point to the number **4** until the ➡️ pointer displays, and then click the **row 4** heading.

Row 4 is selected. A unique number identifies each row. When a row is selected, all the cells in the row are selected, including those that are out of view. The column headings—A, B, C, and so on—are highlighted.

6 In the upper left corner of the worksheet, point to the letter **C** until the ⬇️ pointer displays, and then click the **column C** heading. Compare your screen with Figure 1.15.

Column C is selected. Beginning with the first letter of the alphabet, A, a unique letter identifies each column. When a column is selected, all the cells in the column are selected, including those that are out of view. The row headings—1, 2, 3, etc.—are highlighted.

Select column pointer

Figure 1.15

Active cell reference
displayed in Name Box

Column C heading

Column C selected

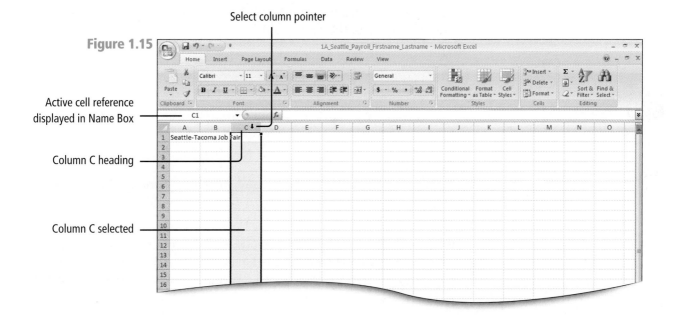

7 Click in the **Name Box** and notice that the cell reference **C1** moves to the left of the box and is highlighted in blue. Text highlighted in blue in this manner will be replaced by your typing. Type **c5:g7** and then compare your screen with Figure 1.16.

Cell references are usually referred to with uppercase letters, but when typing a cell reference, you can use either lowercase or upper-case letters.

Figure 1.16

Range typed in Name Box—can use lowercase or uppercase letters

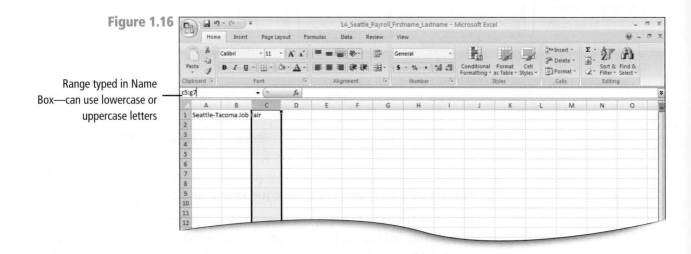

8 Press Enter to select the range you typed into the **Name Box**

Cell C5—the active cell—is identified in the Name Box and is the nonshaded cell within the selected range.

9 Click in the **Name Box**, type **b3:b10,f3:f10** Press Enter, and then compare your screen with Figure 1.17.

Two ***nonadjacent ranges***, which means they are not next to each other, are selected. Nonadjacent ranges of cells can be selected by typing the ranges into the Name Box using a comma to separate them. Cell F3 is the active cell.

Figure 1.17

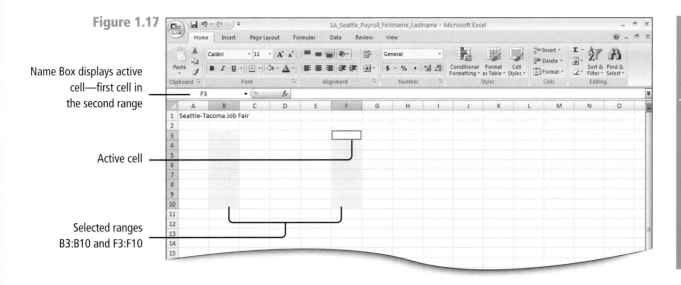

Name Box displays active cell—first cell in the second range

Active cell

Selected ranges B3:B10 and F3:F10

10 Select the range **B3:B5** and notice that the previously selected cells are no longer selected. Then, with the range selected, hold down Ctrl and select the range **E5:E8**.

The selected ranges are B3:B5,E5:E8. The comma separates the range identifications.

11 At the upper left corner of your worksheet, locate and then click the **Select All** button—the small box above **row heading 1** and to the left of **column heading A**—and then compare your screen with Figure 1.18.

The Select All button selects all of the cells in the entire worksheet.

Figure 1.18

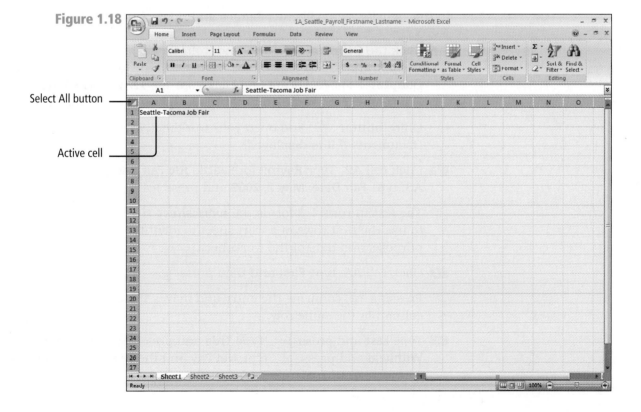

Select All button

Active cell

12 Click cell **A1** to cancel the selection. On the **Quick Access Toolbar**, click the **Save** button 💾 to save the changes.

The **Quick Access Toolbar** displays buttons that perform frequently used commands. Additional buttons can be added to include The commands you use.

As you point to the Save button, the ScreenTip identifies the command name and the keyboard shortcut for the command.

13 Click the **Office** button 🔘, and then click **Close**.

The workbook closes and is no longer visible on the screen, but the Excel program remains open.

Objective 3
Enter Data, Construct a Formula, and Use the SUM Function

Anything typed into a cell is referred to as *cell content*. Cell content is either a *constant value*—referred to as a *value*—or a *formula*. A value is data—numbers, text, dates, or times of day. A formula is an equation that performs mathematical calculations. You can *edit*—change—the values in a cell, or you can clear all values from the cell. *Text* typed into a worksheet provides information about the worksheet's data. For example, a title such as *Fair Date: May 2, 2009* provides the reader with an indication that the data in the worksheet relates to information for a specific date.

Activity 1.4 Opening an Existing Workbook, Entering Text, and Using AutoComplete

In this activity, you will enter names and titles of the Job Fair employees.

1 Click the **Office** button 🔘, and from the displayed menu, click **Open**. In the **Open** dialog box, navigate to the location of your **Excel Chapter 1** folder. Locate and click your file **1A_Seattle_Payroll_Firstname_Lastname** and then click **Open**. Alternatively, click the Office button 🔘, and open your workbook from the list of Recent Documents if it is displayed.

2 Click cell **A2**. Type **Payroll for Seattle Job Fair** and press [Enter]. In cell **A3**, type **Fair Date: May 2, 2009** and press [Enter].

The text in rows 1:3 forms the *worksheet title*. It is good practice to use the first rows of a worksheet to identify the organization, purpose, and date of the worksheet.

3 Click cell **A5**, type **First** and then press [Tab].

Pressing [Tab] confirms the entry and moves the active cell to the next column in the same row.

4 Type **Last** and press [Tab]. Type **Title** and press [Tab], type **Taxes Withheld** and press [Tab], type **Net Pay** and then press [Enter]. Compare your screen with Figure 1.19.

First, Last, Title, Taxes Withheld, and *Net Pay* form the **column titles**—text that identifies the data in the columns. Cell A6 is the active cell. When you enter data in a row, pressing Enter returns the active cell to the first column of the data entered. *Withheld* in cell D5 is **truncated**, which means it does not fully display in the cell—because the cell to the right is not empty.

Column titles   Workbook title

Figure 1.19

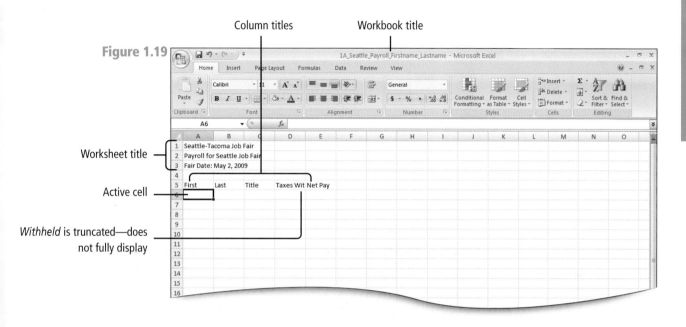

Worksheet title

Active cell

Withheld is truncated—does not fully display

⑤ In cell **A6**, type **Monica** and press Tab, type **Eisler** and press Tab, type **Event Coordinator** and press Enter. Notice that *Event Coordinator* extends into column D.

The active cell returns to column A. Recall that text entries that are longer than the cell will spill over to the cell or cells to the right provided they are empty.

⑥ In cell **A7**, type **Janice** and press Tab, type **Strickland** and press Tab, type **Attendee Registration** and press Enter.

⑦ In cell **A8**, type **J** Notice that the text from the previous cell displays. Compare your screen with Figure 1.20.

If the first few characters you type in a cell match an existing entry in the column, Excel fills in the remaining characters for you. This feature of Excel is called **AutoComplete**. It speeds up the process of typing by helping you type. To accept an AutoComplete suggestion, press Enter. If you don't want to accept a suggestion, continue typing your entry. AutoComplete assists only with alphabetic values; it does not assist with numeric values.

Figure 1.20

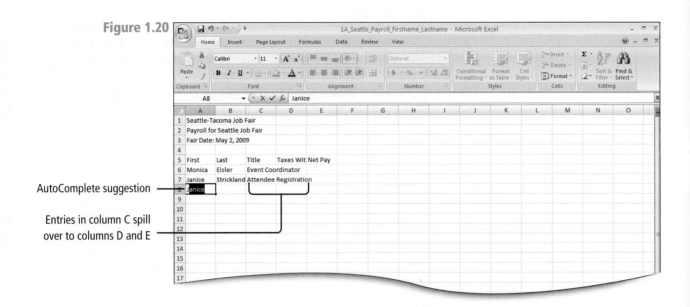

AutoComplete suggestion

Entries in column C spill over to columns D and E

8 Type **an** and notice that the AutoComplete suggestion still displays. Then type **na**

As soon as the text you type differs from the previous text, AutoComplete removes the suggestion.

9 Press [Tab], and type **S** Notice that AutoComplete displays *Strickland*. Continue typing **orokin** and then press [Tab], type **Employer Coordinator** and press [Enter].

10 In cell **A9**, type **Leslie** and press [Tab], type **Goldhammer** and press [Tab], type **Floor Assistant** and press [Enter].

11 In cell **A10**, type **Chang** and press [Tab], type **Hong** and press [Tab], type **F** and notice that AutoComplete displays *Floor Assistant*. Press [Enter] to accept the AutoComplete suggestion.

12 Beginning in cell **A11**, enter the remaining employees listed in the following table. Press [Tab] to confirm your entries and to move across the row. At the end of each row, press [Enter] to move to column A of the next row. Type only the text displayed in bold. When you are finished, compare your screen with Figure 1.21.

First	Last	Title
Julio	**Ramirez**	**Floor Manager**
Timothy	**VanHoy**	**Facilities Coordinator**
Kevin	**London**	**Advertising Assistant**

Figure 1.21

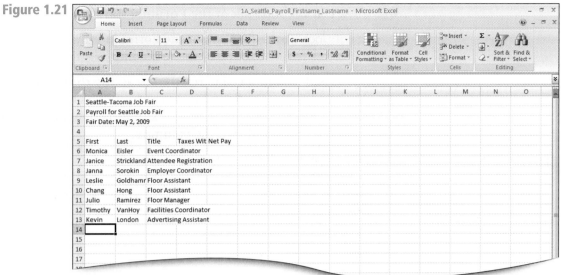

More Knowledge

AutoCorrect Also Assists in Your Typing

AutoCorrect assists in your typing by automatically correcting and formatting some text as you type. Excel compares what you type to a list of commonly mistyped words and when it finds a match, it substitutes the correct word. For example, if you type *abbout*, Excel will automatically correct it to *about*. To view the AutoCorrect options, display the Office menu. At the lower right, click Excel Options; on the left, click Proofing; and then click the AutoCorrect Options button.

Activity 1.5 Entering Numbers and Adjusting Column Width

To type numbers in an Excel worksheet, use either the number keys across the top of your keyboard or the number keys and the Enter key on the numeric keypad. You should practice entering numbers to improve your proficiency in touch control of the numeric keypad. On most keyboards, the number 5 key has a raised bar or dot that helps you identify it by touch. On some desktop computers, the Num Lock light indicates that the numeric keypad is active. In this activity, you will use these techniques to increase your speed while entering the net pay amounts for the workers at the May 2 Job Fair event.

1 Click cell **D6**, and then look at the *Formula Bar*—the area just below the Ribbon that displays cell entries. Notice that although *Coordinator* displays in the cell itself, the cell is empty—no text displays as content in the Formula Bar.

If typed text is too long for a cell and the cell to the right is empty, the display of the text will spill over. *Event Coordinator* is contained in cell C6.

2 In cell **D6,** type **248** and press Tab, type **4000** and then press Enter.

Numbers align at the right edge of the cell. Because cell D6 is no longer empty, the text displayed in cell C6 is truncated.

3 Click cell **C6** and look at the **Formula Bar**.

Event Coordinator displays in the Formula Bar. Only the display in the cell is truncated—all of the text continues to exist as cell content.

Data displayed in a cell is referred to as the ***displayed value***. Data displayed in the Formula Bar is referred to as the ***underlying value***. The number of digits or characters that display in a cell—the value—depends on the width of the columns.

4 Beginning in cell **D7**, enter the following numbers indicating the data in columns D and E. Complete column D first, pressing [Enter] after each entry to move down to the next row. Then, beginning in cell **E7**, enter the amount of the Net Pay. Compare your screen with Figure 1.22.

First	Last	Title	Taxes Withheld	Net Pay
Monica	Eisler	Event Coordinator	248	4000
Janice	Strickland	Attendee Registration	18.60	300
Janna	Sorokin	Employer Coordinator	150.66	2430
Leslie	Goldhammer	Floor Assistant	24.80	400.75
Chang	Hong	Floor Assistant	24.80	400.75
Julio	Ramirez	Floor Manager	148.80	2400
Timothy	VanHoy	Facilities Coordinator	55.34	892.50
Kevin	London	Advertising Assistant	54.25	875

By default, numbers align at the right edge of the cell exactly as you type them. The default ***number format***—a specific way in which Excel displays numbers—is the ***general format***. The general format has no specific characteristics—whatever you type in the cell displays, with the exception that the trailing zeros to the right of a decimal point will not display. For example, when you type *892.50* the cell displays *892.5*.

Figure 1.22

Numbers aligned at right

Cell contents are truncated

Active cell

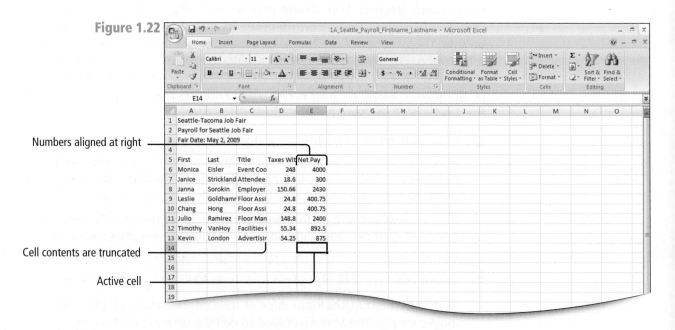

5 Click cell **B9**. On the **Home tab**, in the **Cells group**, click the **Format** button, and then from the displayed menu, click **AutoFit Column Width**.

The column widens to accommodate the contents of the selected cell B9, which happens to be the longest name in the column. The *AutoFit Column Width* command adjusts the column width to fully display the contents of the *selected* cell or cells.

6 From the **column heading area**, select **column C**. In the **Cells group**, click the **Format** button, and then click **AutoFit Column Width**.

Because the entire column is selected, the AutoFit Column Width is applied to the entire column and adjusts the column width to accommodate the longest cell entry in the column.

7 With the ⊹ pointer positioned over the right boundary of **column heading D**, *double-click*—click the left mouse button quickly two times.

The column widens to accommodate the longest entry in the column D—*Taxes Withheld*. Double-clicking the right boundary of a column *heading* applies AutoFit to the entire column—this is a quicker way to apply the AutoFit Column Width command to an entire column.

8 On the **Quick Access Toolbar**, click the **Save** button 🖫 to save the changes.

Activity 1.6 Entering a Formula and Using the Sum Function

A primary reason for using Excel is to perform calculations on numbers. If you make changes to the numbers, Excel automatically *re*calculates the results. You can create tables in other application programs, such as a word processing program, and you can perform simple calculations. Excel, however, performs complex calculations.

A cell contains either a constant value or a formula. A formula is an equation that performs mathematical calculations on values in other cells and then places the result in the cell containing the formula. You can create your own formula, or you can use one of Excel's prewritten formulas. Prewritten formulas are called *functions*. A function is a prewritten formula that takes one or more values, performs an operation, and then returns a value or values.

1 In cell **A14** type **Total** Click cell **D14**, and then type =.

The equal sign ⌐=⌐ displays in the cell with the *insertion point* —the point that indicates where additional text will be entered—blinking and ready to accept data. Formulas begin with the ⌐=⌐ sign. This sign directs Excel to begin a calculation. The Formula Bar displays the ⌐=⌐ sign, and the Formula Bar Cancel and Enter buttons display.

2 At the insertion point, type **d6** and then compare your screen with Figure 1.23.

After you type the letter D, a list of functions that begin with the letter D briefly displays. As you progress in your study of Excel, you will use functions like these. You can use uppercase or lowercase letters in a cell reference while constructing formulas. Cell D6 is surrounded by a blue border with small corner boxes. This indicates that the cell is part of an active formula. The color used in the box matches the color of the cell reference in the formula.

Figure 1.23

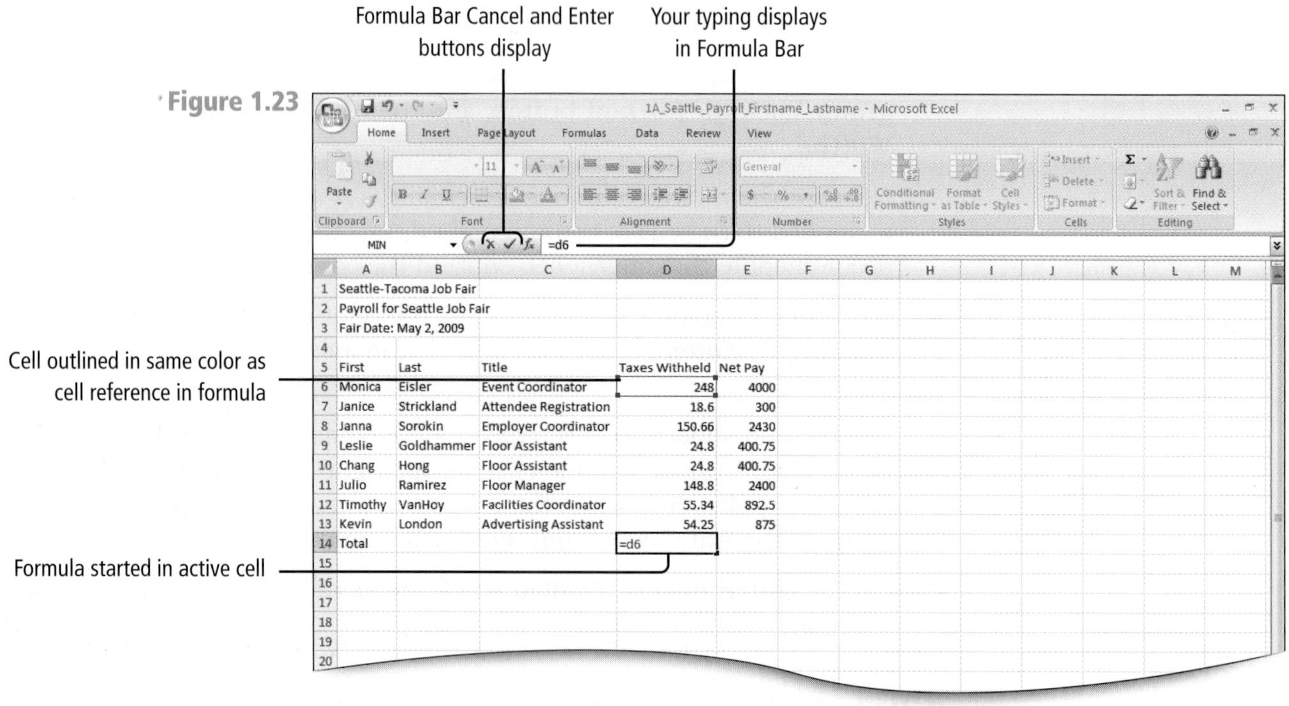
Formula Bar Cancel and Enter buttons display
Your typing displays in Formula Bar
Cell outlined in same color as cell reference in formula
Formula started in active cell
1A_Seattle_Payroll_Firstname_Lastname - Microsoft Excel
=d6
Seattle-Tacoma Job Fair
Payroll for Seattle Job Fair
Fair Date: May 2, 2009
Taxes Withheld
Net Pay
Total

3 At the insertion point, type + and then type **d7** Alternatively, use the + key on your numeric keypad, which does not require the Shift key.

A border of another color surrounds cell d7, and the color matches the color of the cell reference in the active formula.

4 At the insertion point, type **+d8+d9+d10+d11+d12+d13** and then press Enter.

The result of your calculation, *725.25*, displays in the cell. If that is not your result, click cell **D14**, press Delete, and begin again. Also double-check the data you entered in the column to make sure the entries are accurate.

5 Click cell **D14** again to make it the active cell, and then look at the **Formula Bar**. Compare your screen with Figure 1.24.

This formula adds the values in cells D6 through D13. The result of adding the values displays in cell D14. Although cell D14 displays the result of the formula, the formula itself is displayed in the Formula Bar. This is referred to as the ***underlying formula***. View the Formula Bar to be sure of the exact content of a cell—*a displayed number might actually be a formula.*

Underlying formula displays
in the Formula Bar

Figure 1.24

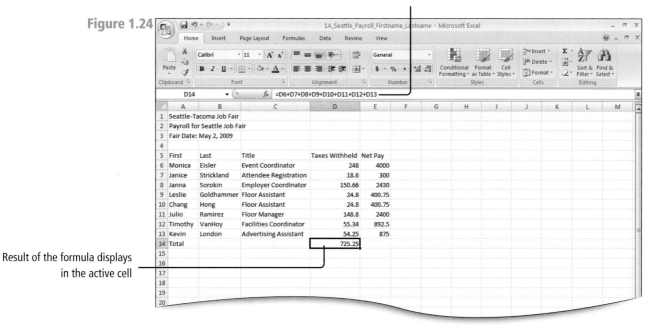

Result of the formula displays
in the active cell

6 Click cell **D11** and change it by typing **152.70** and then watch cell **D14** as you press Enter.

Your result is *729.15*. It not necessary to delete the old value in a cell; selecting the cell and typing a new value replaces the old value with your new typing. Excel *recalculates* formulas if you change the values in a cell that is referenced in a formula.

7 Click cell **E14**. In the **Editing group**, point to the **Sum** button Σ • to display its ScreenTip, click the button to insert the function, and then compare your screen with Figure 1.25.

Cells E6:E13 are surrounded by a moving border and are highlighted in cell E14. The = sign signals the beginning of a formula, *SUM* indicates the type of calculation that will take place (addition), and *(E6:E13)* indicates the range of cells on which the sum operation will be performed. A ScreenTip provides additional information about the action just below the formula.

When the Sum function is activated, Excel first looks above the active cell for a range of cells to add—sum. If no range is above the active cell, Excel looks to the left for a range of cells to add. Excel will propose a range of cells to add, and if the proposed range is not what you had in mind, select a different group of cells.

Figure 1.25

Moving border surrounds range
selected by SUM function

Sum function button on
the Ribbon

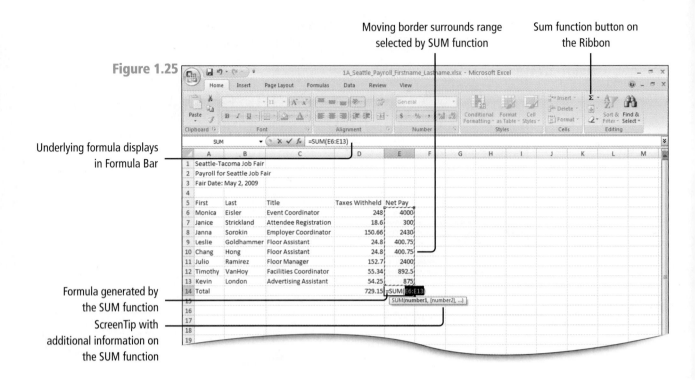

Underlying formula displays
in Formula Bar

Formula generated by
the SUM function

ScreenTip with
additional information on
the SUM function

8 Press Enter, click cell **E14** again, and then look at the **Formula Bar**.

11699—the result of the calculation—displays in the cell. The underlying formula displays in the Formula Bar.

A prewritten formula, such as the SUM function is more efficient than typing the cell reference of every cell in the formula. As you progress in your study of Excel, you will practice additional ways to construct formulas.

9 Select the range **D7:E13**. In the **Number group**, point to the **Comma Style** button to display its ScreenTip, then click the button.

The ***Comma Style*** applies two decimal places and inserts thousand comma separators where appropriate. Comma Style also leaves space at the right to accommodate a parenthesis for negative numbers.

10 Select the range **D6:E6**, hold down Ctrl, and then select the range **D14:E14**. In the **Number group**, click the **Accounting Number Format** button, and then compare your screen with Figure 1.26.

The ***Accounting Number Format*** button formats the number with the default Accounting format using the U.S. dollar sign. It applies a thousand comma separator where appropriate, inserts a fixed U.S. dollar sign aligned at the left edge of the cell, applies two decimal places, and leaves a small amount of space at the right edge of the cell to accommodate a parenthesis for negative numbers.

Applying the Accounting Number Format also widens the column to accommodate the number formatting.

Figure 1.26

Formatted numbers using Comma Style

Accounting Number Format button

Comma Style button

Formatted numbers using Accounting Number Format

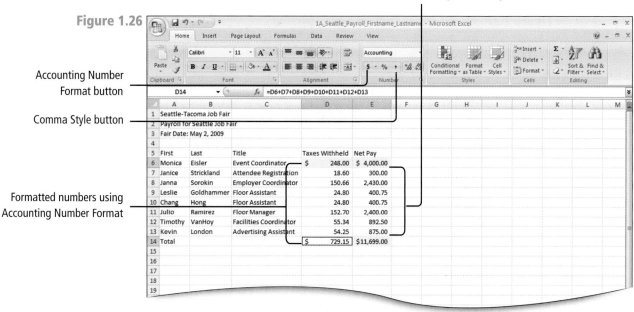

11 Click cell **A1** to cancel the selection and view your results. **Save** the changes you have made to your workbook.

Objective 4
Format Data, Cells, and Worksheets

Formatting is the process of determining the appearance of cells and the overall layout of a worksheet. For example, you can add emphasis to your data by using bold, italic, and underline. You can also align text in the cells.

Activity 1.7 Using Font Styles and Centering Text

A ***font*** is a set of characters with the same design, size, and shape. The default font in Excel is Calibri. In this activity, you will change the font Excel uses in workbooks—the ***default font***—and you will center the text.

1 Select the range **A1:A3**. In the **Font group**, point to the **Bold** button **B** to display its ScreenTip, and then click the button.

The bold ***font style*** is applied to the text in all of the selected cells. A font style is a characteristic such as bold, italic, and underline that is used to emphasize text.

2 Point to the selected range, click the right mouse button—***right-click***—to display a ***shortcut menu*** and the ***Mini toolbar***. The Mini toolbar is a toolbar that contains the most commonly used formatting commands for the selected text. Compare your screen with Figure 1.27.

The Mini toolbar brings common commands closer to the selected text so that your mouse does not have to travel so far to select a commonly used formatting command. A shortcut menu is a list of context-related commands that displays when you right-click selected cells. Because the displayed commands are associated with the selection, the menu is said to be ***context-sensitive***.

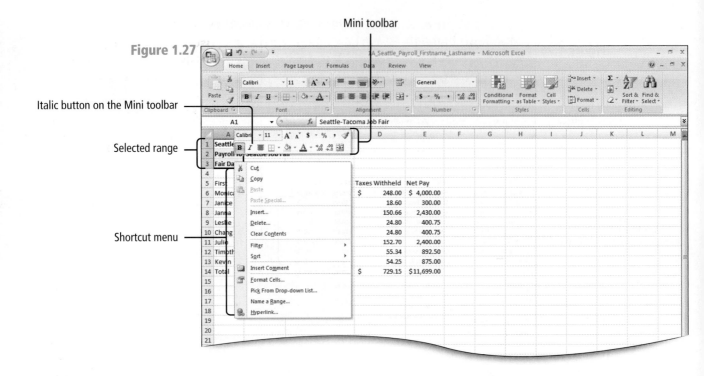

Mini toolbar

Figure 1.27

Italic button on the Mini toolbar

Selected range

Shortcut menu

3 On the Mini toolbar, click the **Italic** button I and notice that the shortcut menu no longer displays. Move the mouse slightly below the Mini toolbar so that the Mini toolbar fades and you can see the result of your formatting. Move the pointer back into the Mini toolbar to display it again. It becomes a functioning toolbar. In the Ribbon, the font style buttons bold and italic are highlighted.

Use commands from either the Ribbon or Mini toolbar to format worksheet cells.

4 In the **Font group**, point to the **Increase Font Size** button A to display its ScreenTip, and then click the button three times.

The ***Increase Font Size button*** increases the font size with each click. The default ***font size***—the size of characters in a font measured in ***points***—is 11. There are 72 points in an inch, with 10 or 11 points being the most commonly used font size in Excel. Point is usually abbreviated as ***pt***.

5 Click in another cell in the worksheet to deselect the range. Point to cell **A3** and right-click to simultaneously select the cell and display the Mini toolbar and shortcut menu. In the Mini toolbar, point to and click the **Decrease Font Size** button A one time.

The worksheet title lines are formatted in bold and italic font styles and increased in size. Worksheet titles are commonly formatted like this to identify the information in the worksheet.

6 Select the range **A5:E5**. In the **Font group**, click the **Bold** button B, the **Italic** button I, and the **Underline** button U. Alternatively, use the keyboard shortcuts for bold—Ctrl + B—, italic—Ctrl + I—and underline—Ctrl + U. Then, click cell **C5** and compare your screen with Figure 1.28.

The formats are applied to all of the selected cells, and the buttons are highlighted in the Ribbon. Frequently used formats have easily accessible buttons on the Ribbon. The most frequently used formats are displayed on the Mini toolbar.

Figure 1.28

Formats applied to selected cell highlighted

Selected column title

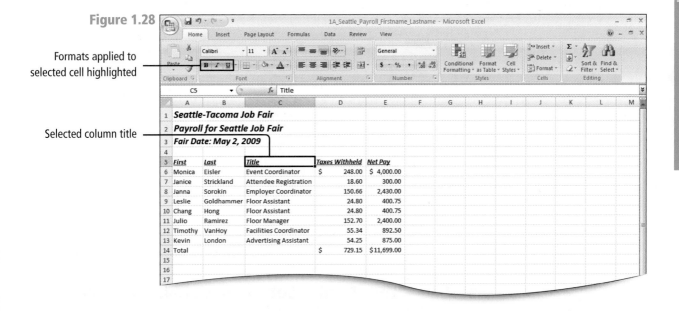

7 Select the range **A5:E5**. In the **Font group**, click the **Underline** button **U ▾** . In the **Alignment group**, click the **Center** button ▤ , and then click in a cell outside the range.

The underlining is removed and the text is centered in each cell. The Bold, Italic, and Underline buttons in the Font group are examples of *toggle buttons*—click the button once to turn the formatting on and click it again to turn it off.

8 Press Ctrl + End to move the active cell to the last cell in the worksheet.

Cell E14 is the active cell. The keyboard shortcut moves the active cell to the last cell of the worksheet that contains data.

9 Select the range **D14:E14**. In the **Font group**, click the **Border button arrow** ⊞ ▾ , and then from the displayed list, click **Top and Double Bottom Border**. Click an empty cell to deselect it, and then compare your screen with Figure 1.29.

It is common to apply the Top and Double Bottom Border style in worksheets that have totals. The single border indicates that calculations were performed on the numbers above, and the double border indicates that the information is complete.

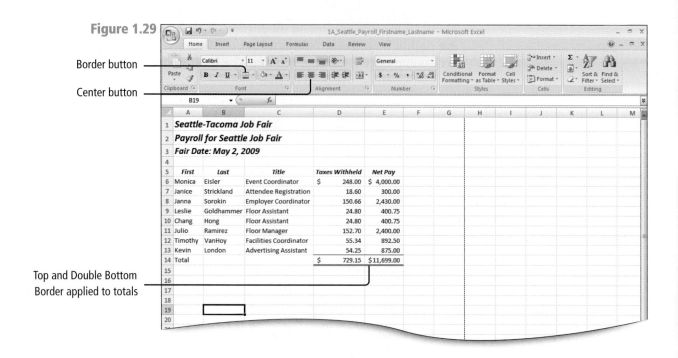

Figure 1.29

Border button

Center button

Top and Double Bottom
Border applied to totals

Note — Your Border Button May Look Different

Many buttons and features display in the manner in which they were last used. For example, after you have applied a top and double bottom border, the Border button displays that usage.

10 Click cell **A14** and apply **Bold** [B]. **Save** [💾] the changes in the workbook.

Activity 1.8 Using Merge and Center

You can merge two or more adjacent cells to become one large cell that is displayed across multiple columns. For example, this is commonly done to make worksheet titles display across columns of data. A ***merged cell*** is a single cell created by combining two or more selected cells. To center the contents with a single command, you use the Merge and Center command. In this activity, you will use the Merge & Center button to enable the Merge and Center command.

1 Select the range **A1:E1**, and then on the **Home tab**, in the **Alignment group**, click the **Merge & Center** button [⊞ ▾].

The Merge and Center command joins the selected cells into one larger cell and centers the contents in the new cell. You can no longer select cells B1:E1 individually because they are merged into cell A1.

2 Select the range **A2:E2**, and then with your mouse pointer positioned over the selected range, right-click to display the Mini toolbar. On the Mini toolbar, click the **Merge & Center** button [⊞]. Select the range **A3:E3** and use either method to merge and center the text across the range. Compare your screen with Figure 1.30.

Figure 1.30

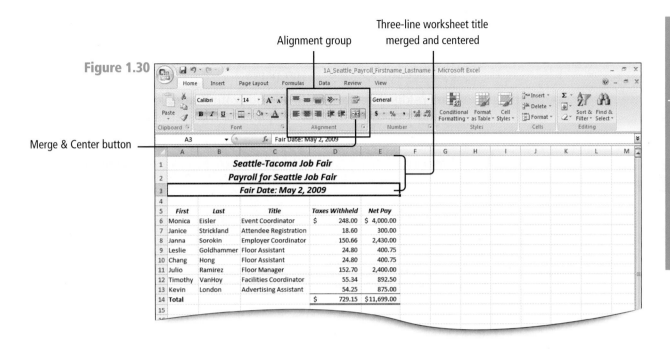

Alignment group

Three-line worksheet title merged and centered

Merge & Center button

Save 💾 your workbook.

Objective 5
Insert a Footer into a Worksheet

Information about a worksheet, such as its file name, the author of the worksheet, and the date, can be placed in a worksheet *header* or *footer*. Headers and footers are text, page numbers, and graphics that display and print at the top (header) or bottom (footer) of every page.

Activity 1.9 Adding a Footer to a Worksheet

For each of your projects in this textbook, you will create a footer containing your name and the project name. This will make it easy to identify your printed documents in a shared printer environment such as a lab or class-room, or if you or your instructor need to view completed work electronically through an online course management system or email.

In this activity, you will add a footer to your worksheet that identifies the document.

1 On the Ribbon, click the **View tab**. In the **Workbook Views group**, click **Page Layout**. Alternatively, on the right side of the status bar, click the **Page Layout** button 🔲. Compare your screen with Figure 1.31.

When you open a workbook, the worksheet displays in *Normal view*, which is the default view. Normal view keeps your rows and columns close to their headings and provides an efficient workspace.

Before you print a worksheet, use **Page Layout view** to get your data ready for printing. Page Layout view displays the worksheet as if it were a sheet of paper. The worksheet margins display. You can also see the space between pages.

Rulers display along both the horizontal and vertical edges. The page number of the worksheet displays in the status bar.

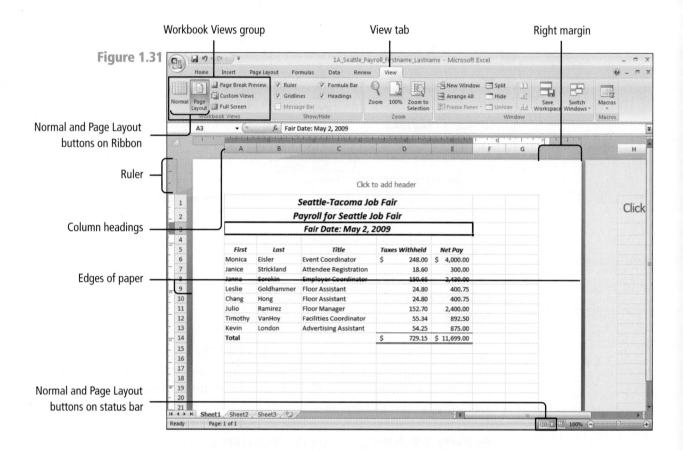

Figure 1.31

In the vertical scroll bar, click the down scroll arrow until the bottom of the page displays and you can see the words *Click to add footer*. Compare your screen with Figure 1.32.

Figure 1.32

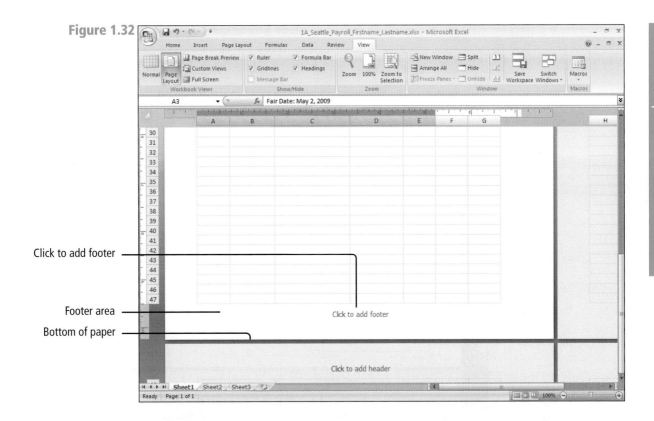

Click to add footer

Footer area

Bottom of paper

3 Point to the text *Click to add footer*.

The highlighted area is the center footer area. Boxes on each side of the center footer area indicate a right and left footer area. There are three footer areas—left, center, right.

4 Point to the **left section** of the **footer area** and click. Compare your screen with Figure 1.33.

The left footer area is active—indicated by the box surrounding it. The blinking insertion point indicates where the text will be added. On the Ribbon, ***contextual tools*** named *Header & Footer Tools* display and add ***contextual tabs*** next to the standard tabs.

Contextual tools enable you to perform specific commands related to the selected area or object. Contextual tools display one or more contextual tabs that contain related groups of commands that you will need when working with the type of area or object that is selected. Contextual tools display only when needed; when you deselect the footer area, the contextual tools no longer display.

Header & Footer Tools contextual tab   Design tab

Figure 1.33

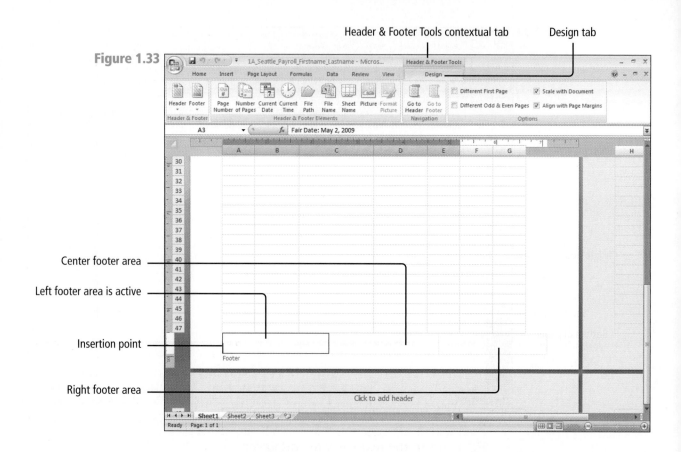

Center footer area

Left footer area is active

Insertion point

Right footer area

5 On the **Design tab**, in the **Header & Footer Elements group**, click the **File Name** button and compare your screen with Figure 1.34.

&[File] displays in the footer, which will cause Excel to enter the file name of your workbook in this location.

Figure 1.34

File Name button

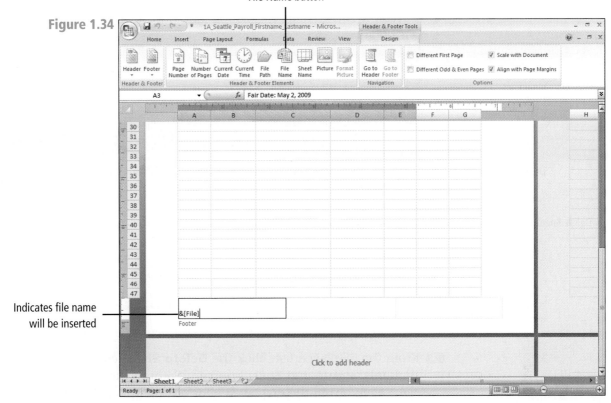

Indicates file name
will be inserted

6 Click any cell in the worksheet to deselect the footer area.

Notice that the name of the file displays in the left footer. The Header & Footer Tools no longer display because you are no longer working in the header or the footer area.

7 **Save** your workbook.

Objective 6
Delete Unused Worksheets and Preview and Print a Worksheet

Before you print your worksheet, display ***Print Preview*** to preview the placement of your worksheet on the page, and then delete unused worksheets.

Activity 1.10 Deleting Unused Worksheets

A new Excel workbook contains three worksheets. Although it is not necessary to delete unused sheets, doing so saves storage space and removes any doubt that additional information is in the workbook.

1 With your worksheet still displayed in **Page Layout** view, press Ctrl + Home to return to cell **A1** and bring the upper portion of your worksheet into view.

2 In the lower left of your screen, click the **Sheet2 tab**.

Sheet2 displays in the Normal view, which is the default view. Changing the view changes only the view of the active sheet.

3 Click the **Home tab**, and then in the **Cells group**, click the **Delete button arrow** to display a list of commands. Compare your screen with Figure 1.35.

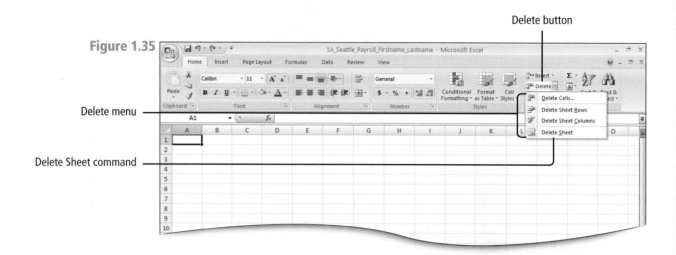

Figure 1.35

Delete button

Delete menu

Delete Sheet command

4 From the displayed list, click the **Delete Sheet** command, and notice that only Sheet1 and Sheet3 remain. Point to the **Sheet3 tab**, and right-click. From the displayed shortcut menu, click **Delete**.

The remaining worksheet, Sheet1, displays in Page Layout view. Recall that deleting unused worksheets removes any doubt that additional information is contained within the workbook.

5 **Save** the workbook.

Activity 1.11 Previewing and Printing a Worksheet

Before you print your worksheet, use Print Preview, which previews its placement on the page. Be sure to use Print Preview before printing documents. If you review your documents before printing them, you can correct mistakes or make adjustments to the presentation of your worksheets.

1 In the upper left corner of your screen, click the **Office** button . From the displayed menu, point to **Print** and compare your screen with Figure 1.36.

A submenu displays to the right of the list providing additional options for printing. A ScreenTip identifies the command and the keyboard shortcut of Ctrl + P.

Figure 1.36

Print Preview command

Print command with ScreenTip

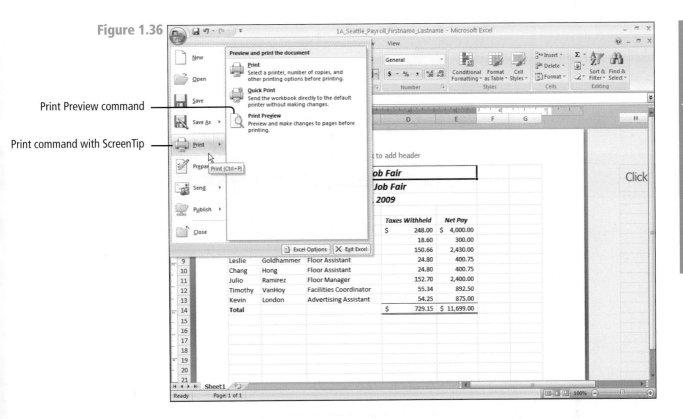

2 In the right side of the displayed menu, click **Print Preview**, and then compare your screen with Figure 1.37. Alternatively, press Ctrl + F2 to display Print Preview.

The Ribbon displays the Print Preview tab, which replaces the standard ribbon when you switch to Print Preview. Your worksheet displays as it will look when printed. Use Print Preview to review the format and placement of your worksheet.

Figure 1.37

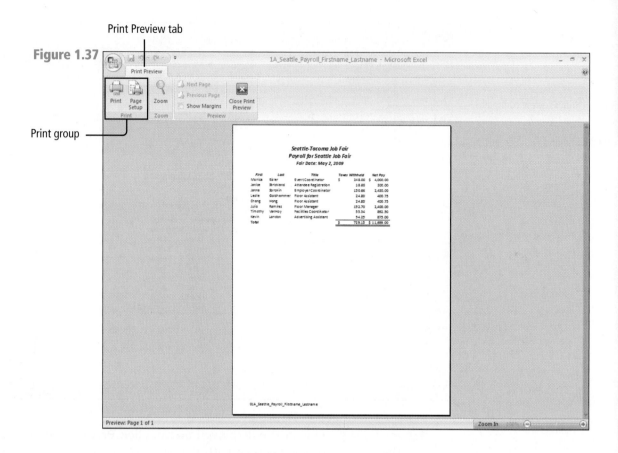

Print group

Preview: Page 1 of 1   Zoom In

3 In the **Print group**, point to the **Page Setup** button to display its ScreenTip, and then click the button. In the displayed **Page Setup** dialog box, click the **Margins tab**, and then compare your screen with Figure 1.38.

The Page Setup dialog box displays. Here you can select commands to change the manner in which the worksheet will print, including placement on the page and margins.

Page Setup button
in Print Preview

Page Setup dialog box

Figure 1.38

Margins tab in Page
Setup dialog box

Center on page area

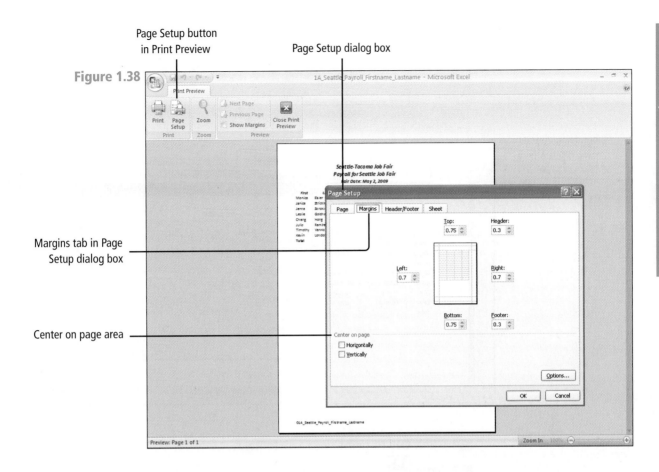

4 In the lower left corner, under **Center on page**, click to select the **Horizontally** check box, and then click **OK**.

Print Preview displays your worksheet with the data centered horizontally on the page.

5 Check your *Chapter Assignment Sheet* or *Course Syllabus*, or consult your instructor, to determine if you are to submit your assignments on paper or electronically using your college's course information management system or email system. To submit electronically, on the Ribbon click Close Print Preview, go to Step 8, and then follow the directions provided by your instructor.

6 To print on paper, on the **Print Preview tab,** in the **Print group**, click **Print**. Compare your screen with Figure 1.39.

The Print dialog box displays. Here you can make additional decisions about how your worksheet is printed, including the number of copies to print.

Figure 1.39

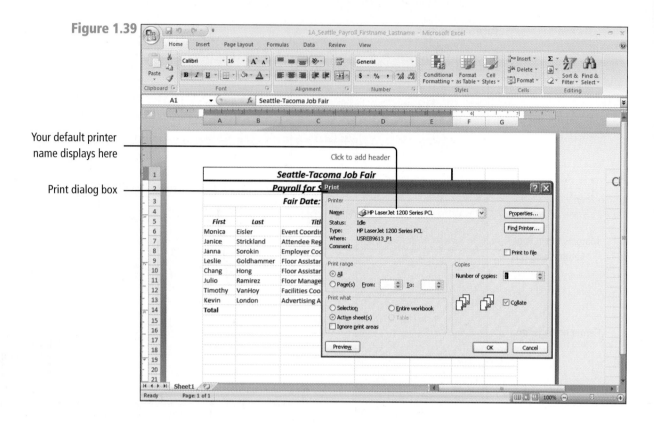

Your default printer name displays here

Print dialog box

7 Click **OK** to print your worksheet.

8 **Save** 💾 your workbook.

Objective 7
Print Formulas, Close a Workbook, and Exit Excel

You can display and print formulas in your worksheet, which is useful when you want to check the accuracy of your worksheet's data and formulas.

Activity 1.12 Displaying and Printing Formulas, Closing a Workbook, and Exiting Excel

For formulas in a cell, the cell displays the results of the formula. You can view and print the underlying formulas in the cells. When you do this, the formula often takes more horizontal space to display than the result of the calculation. Thus, *landscape orientation* is usually a better choice than *portrait orientation* to fit the formulas on one page. In landscape orientation, the paper is wider than it is tall. In portrait orientation, the paper is taller than it is wide.

In this activity, you will print the formulas in Sheet1 in landscape orientation and then close the workbook without saving the changes.

1 **Save** 💾 your workbook, because you are going to make some changes that will be temporary. On the right side of the status bar, click the **Normal** button 🔲 to return to Normal view. Alternatively, on the View tab, in the Workbook Views group, click Normal.

2 Hold down Ctrl and press `'`. Compare your screen with Figure 1.40. Alternatively, on the Formulas tab, in the Formula Auditing group, click the Show Formulas button.

The `'` is usually located below Esc, but the location may vary on laptop computers.

The dotted line indicates where the page would break if printed in the current page layout.

Note — Ctrl + `'` Is a Toggle Function

Displaying formulas using the keyboard shortcut Ctrl + `'` is a toggle function. Use the keyboard shortcut once to display the formulas and use the keyboard shortcut a second time to cancel the display of formulas.

Figure 1.40

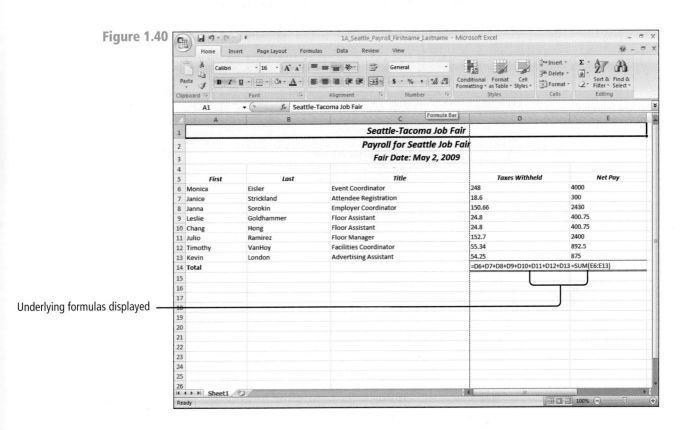

Underlying formulas displayed

3 From the **column heading area**, select columns **A:E**. Point to the right column boundary of any of the selected columns and when the ⊹ displays, double-click to apply the **AutoFit Column Width** command. Alternatively, click the Format button, and from the displayed menu, click AutoFit Column Width.

4 Click any cell to cancel the selection. Click the **Page Layout tab**. In the **Page Setup group**, click the **Orientation** button, and then from the displayed *gallery* —a display of potential results—click **Landscape**. In the **Scale to Fit group**, locate and then point to the **Dialog Box Launcher** button ▣ to show its ScreenTip, as shown in Figure 1.41.

A *Dialog Box Launcher* displays in some groups on the Ribbon and opens a related dialog box. The dialog box provides additional options and commands related to the group.

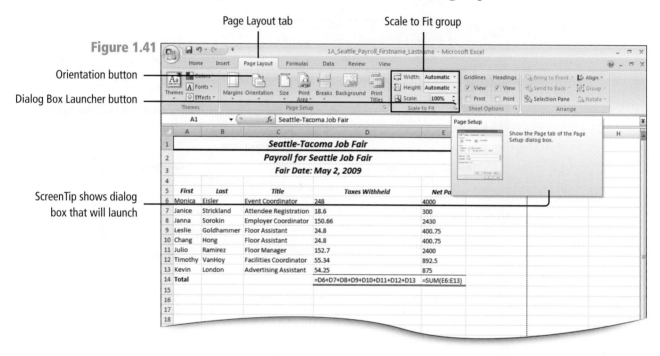

Figure 1.41

Page Layout tab

Scale to Fit group

Orientation button

Dialog Box Launcher button

ScreenTip shows dialog box that will launch

5 Click the **Dialog Box Launcher** button ▣, and under **Scaling**, click the **Fit to** option button. In the lower right corner, click the **Print Preview** button—this is another point from which you can display the Print Preview.

Scaling adjusts the size of the printed worksheet to fit on one page and is convenient for printing formulas. Although it is not always the case, formulas frequently take up more space than the actual data. You will typically want to print them in landscape orientation.

6 Check your *Chapter Assignment Sheet* or *Course Syllabus*, or consult your instructor, to determine if you are to submit your printed formulas on paper or electronically using your college's course information management system. To submit electronically, click **Close Print Preview**, follow the instructions provided by your instructor, and then go to Step 7. To print, click the **Print** button, and then click **OK**.

7 Click the **Office** button and then click **Close**, and when prompted, click **No** so that you do *not* save the changes you made—displaying formulas, changing column widths, orientation, and scaling—to print your formulas.

Your workbook is closed without saving the changes you made to print the formulas. The Excel program remains open.

8 To exit Excel, display the **Office** menu, and in the lower right corner, click **Exit Excel**. Alternatively, at the right end of the title bar, click the program-level **Close** button X .

End **You have completed Project 1A** ——————————

Project 1B Annual Income

In Activities 1.13 through 1.24, you will complete an Excel worksheet for Michael Dawson, director of the Seattle-Tacoma Job Fair. This worksheet will report the revenue from rental fees for the March job fairs—one is in Seattle and one is in Tacoma. In addition, you will chart the total rental fees so Michael can compare the differences between the two fairs. The workbook you complete will look similar to Figure 1.42.

For Project 1B, you will need the following file:

e01B_March_Rentals

You will save your workbook as
1B_March_Rentals_Firstname_Lastname

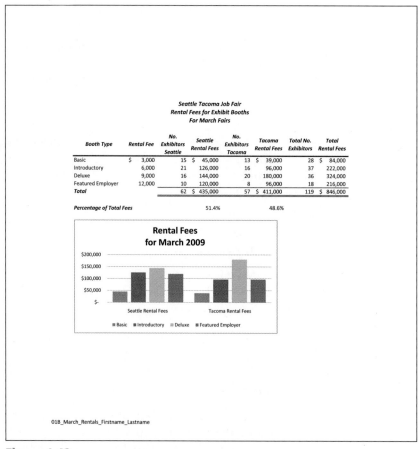

Figure 1.42
Project 1B—March Rentals

Objective 8
Check Spelling and Edit a Worksheet

Excel will check the spelling of your worksheet by comparing the text with words in its built-in dictionary, and then it will suggest changes. After data is entered, you can edit existing text either within the cell or in the Formula Bar.

Activity 1.13 Opening and Saving an Existing Workbook

Michael began a workbook to report the revenue from the March job fairs and has asked you to complete it. In this activity, you will open the workbook and save it in your chapter folder using a different name.

1 **Start** Excel. Click the **Office** button and from the displayed menu, click **Open**. In the displayed **Open** dialog box, click the **Look in** arrow, navigate to the student files that accompany this textbook, click **e01B_March_Rentals**, and then in the lower right corner of the dialog box, click **Open**.

The workbook e01B_March_Rentals displays. Alternatively, you can double-click a file name to open it. The worksheet title and the row and column titles are entered into the worksheet.

2 Click the **Office** button and from the displayed menu, click the **Save As** command. In the displayed **Save As** dialog box, click the **Save in** arrow to view a list of the drives and folders available to you. Navigate to the drive on which you created your **Excel Chapter 1** folder, and then double-click the folder name to display it in the **Save in** box.

3 In the **File name** box, delete any existing text by selecting it and pressing Delete, and then using your own first and last name, type **1B_March_Rentals_Firstname_Lastname** Be sure to include the underscore instead of spaces between words. Alternatively, when you type the file name, the existing text will be replaced.

4 In the lower right corner of the **Save As** dialog box, click **Save**.

The file is saved in your chapter folder with the new name. The workbook remains displayed, and the new name displays in the title bar. In this manner, you can create a new workbook from an existing workbook.

5 On the status bar, click the **Page Layout** button. Scroll to the bottom of the worksheet until the words *Click to add footer* display. Click in the left section of the **footer** area. On the **Design tab**, in the **Header & Footer Elements group**, click the **File Name** button.

6 Click in the worksheet. Press Ctrl + Home to return the active cell to **A1**. On the status bar, click the **Normal** button.

7 On the **Quick Access Toolbar**, click **Save**.

Activity 1.14 Using Wrap Text and the Undo Command

When cell entries are long, use *wrap text* to display them on more than one line within a cell. You can reverse an action or a series of actions by using the *Undo command*. In this activity, you will wrap text, increase the column width, and undo a command.

1 Click cell **C5** and notice that the entry has been truncated but fully displays in the Formula Bar. Note that all of the column titles are truncated. Click cell **I5** and notice that there is no entry displayed in the Formula Bar even though it appears that there is text in cell I5. Recall that text will spill into the adjacent cell if there is no entry in that cell.

2 Select the range **A5:H5**. On the Ribbon, verify that the **Home tab** is selected. In the **Alignment group**, click the **Wrap Text** button and compare your screen with Figure 1.43.

Data in the cells displays on two or three lines. The height of the row adjusted to accommodate the data, but the column widths remained the same. The *s* in *Exhibitors* is separated from the word on a separate line. When formatting the worksheet, the column width will be adjusted.

Wrap Text button

Figure 1.43

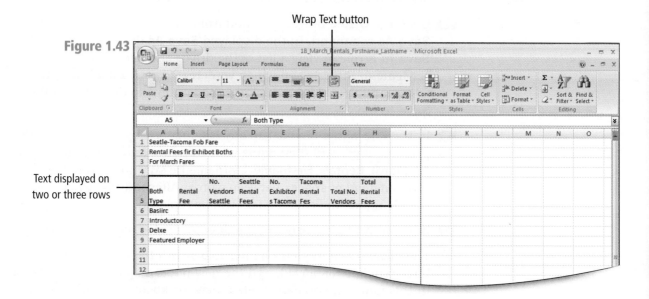

Text displayed on two or three rows

More Knowledge

To Wrap Text in a Cell

To start a new line of text at a specific point in a cell, regardless of column width, double-click the cell, click the location where you want to break the line in the cell, and then press Alt + Enter to insert a line break.

3 In the **Alignment group**, click the **Center** button.

Each line of text is centered horizontally within the cell.

4 In the **Alignment group**, click the **Middle Align** button .

Text is centered vertically within the cell. When text is entered, it aligns at the bottom of the cell. Using the middle align button adjusts the text to display in the middle of the cell.

5 Click cell **A5**. In the **Alignment group**, click the **Top Align** button and compare your screen with Figure 1.44.

The text in cell A5 aligns at the top of the cell.

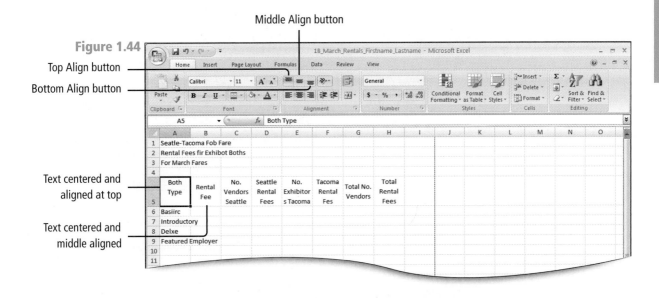

Figure 1.44

Middle Align button

Top Align button

Bottom Align button

Text centered and aligned at top

Text centered and middle aligned

6 On the **Quick Access Toolbar**, point to the **Undo** button and note that the ScreenTip displays *Undo Top Alignment*, and then click **Undo**. Alternatively, you can press Ctrl + Z on the keyboard to reverse (undo) the last action.

The format of the column title is returned to its original centered position—your action was undone. The Undo button identifies the most recent command in its ScreenTip.

7 On the **Quick Access Toolbar**, click the **Undo button arrow** to display the most recent actions.

Undo lists up to the last 16 actions taken and each can be undone by selecting the command from the list.

8 On the **Quick Access Toolbar**, click the **Save** button to save your changes.

Activity 1.15 Checking for Spelling Errors in a Worksheet

The **Spelling Checker** compares the text in the worksheet with a built-in dictionary and identifies words that are possibly misspelled. If a word is not in the dictionary, Excel highlights it and makes suggestions to correct the word. In this activity, you will check the spelling of the text that is entered in the worksheet.

1 Click cell **A1**. On the **Review tab**, in the **Proofing group**, click **Spelling**. Alternatively, press F7, which is the keyboard shortcut for the Spelling command. Compare your screen with Figure 1.45.

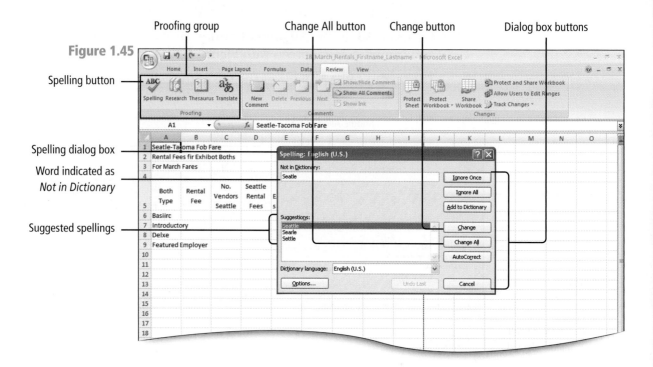

Figure 1.45

2 Take a moment to study the spelling options available in the **Spelling** dialog box, as shown in the table in Figure 1.46.

Spelling Dialog Box

Button	Action
Ignore Once	Ignores the identified word one time, but flags it in other locations in the document.
Ignore All	Discontinues flagging any instance of the word anywhere in the document.
Add to Dictionary	Adds the word to a custom dictionary, which can be edited. This option does not change the built-in Office dictionary.
Change	Changes the identified word to the word highlighted under Suggestions.
Change All	Changes every instance of the word in the document to the word highlighted under Suggestions.
AutoCorrect	Adds the flagged words to the AutoCorrect list, which will subsequently correct the word automatically if misspelled in any documents typed in the future.
Options	Displays the Proofing section of the Excel Options box.

Figure 1.46

Alert ──── **Does a message display asking if you want to continue checking at the beginning of the sheet?**

If a message displays asking if you want to continue checking at the beginning of the sheet, click Yes. The Spelling command begins its checking process with the currently selected cell and moves to the right and down. Thus, if your active cell was a cell after A1, this message will display.

3 In the displayed **Spelling** dialog box, under **Not in Dictionary**, notice the word *Seatle* is displayed.

Several suggestions display in the Suggestions area of the Spelling dialog box. When an error is found, a suggestion is usually provided. You may ignore the suggestion, use the suggestion, or make your own correction. The correct spelling for *Seattle* is highlighted in the Suggestions box of the dialog box, which will be entered when you select the *Change* or *Change All* commands.

4 Click **Change** to accept the suggested spelling.

Seattle is entered in cell A1 and the Spelling Checker displays the next error, *Exhibot*. (If your Spelling dialog box covers the text on your screen, click in the dialog box title bar and drag it out of the way.)

5 The first suggestion, *Exhibit*, is correct. Click **Change**.

The next misspelled word, *Boths*, displays. Because this word is in the same cell, Excel will correct all errors in an individual cell at the same time.

6 The suggestion is *Booths*. Accept that change.

The words *Exhibit* and *Booths* now correctly display in cell A2 and the next misspelled word is highlighted.

7 The word *Basiirc* displays. The correct word, *Basic*, does not display in the list of suggestions. Use the scroll bar to review all suggestions to confirm that *Basic* is not a suggestion. In the **Not in Dictionary** box, double-click the word displayed and type **Basic** then click **Change**.

When the word is not in the dictionary, you can type the correct word in the displayed Spelling dialog box to correct it in the worksheet.

8 Using the procedures just practiced, correct remaining spelling errors in this worksheet. When the message *The spelling check is complete for the entire sheet* displays, click **OK**. Then compare your screen with Figure 1.47.

There are still errors on the worksheet that the Spelling Checker recognizes as correct because these words are in the dictionary. However, they are not the intended words for this worksheet; these will be corrected in the next activity.

Figure 1.47

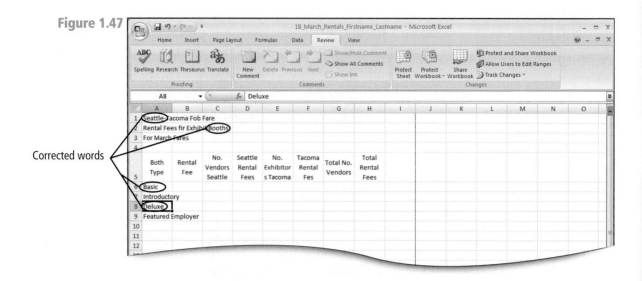

Corrected words

Note — Words Not in the Dictionary Are Not Necessarily Misspelled

Many proper nouns or less commonly used words are not in the dictionary used by Excel. If Excel indicates a correct word as *Not in Dictionary*, you can choose to ignore this word or add it to the dictionary. You may want to add proper names that you expect to use often, such as your own last name, to the dictionary if you are permitted to do so.

9 On the **Quick Access Toolbar**, click the **Save** button [icon] to save your changes.

Activity 1.16 Editing Text in a Worksheet

Data can be edited as it is being entered or after it is confirmed. There are several ways to make corrections as data is entered. In this activity you will edit text in the worksheet.

1 Click cell **A1**. In the **Formula Bar**, double-click the word *Fob*. Type **Job** Use the arrow keys to position the insertion point between the *a* and *r* of *Fare*. Type **i** Use the arrow key to position the insertion point between the *r* and *e* and press [Delete]. Take a few minutes to study Figure 1.48 and familiarize yourself with the editing techniques.

You edited this text in the Formula Bar. Because the Spelling Checker recognized the word *Fob* as spelled correctly, no suggested changes were made. Pressing [Delete] removes the character to the right of the insertion point.

Editing Text

To do this. . .	Use this. . .
Before entry is confirmed	
Delete one character to the left	←Bksp
Delete entire entry	Esc
Delete entire entry	Cancel button [X] on the Formula Bar.
After entry is confirmed, correct entries in the Formula Bar	
Delete characters to the left of insertion point	←Bksp
Delete characters to the right of insertion point	Delete
Delete entire entry	Select cell and type new entry.
Delete entire entry	Select cell and press Del.

Figure 1.48

2 Double-click cell **A2** to display the insertion point in the cell. Use the arrow keys to position the insertion point between the *i* and the *r* of *fir*. Press ←Bksp and type **o** The word is now *for*. Press Enter.

You edited this text in the cell. Pressing ←Bksp deletes the character to the left of the insertion point.

3 In cell **A3**, press F2 to position the insertion point at the end of the cell contents. Use the arrow keys to change *Fares* to *Fairs*.

4 In cell **A5**, use the methods you just practiced to change *Both* to *Booth*. In cells **C5** and **G5**, change *Vendors* to *Exhibitors*. And in cell **F5**, change *Fes* to *Fees*. Press Enter to confirm the entry and then compare your screen with Figure 1.49.

Some of the words in the column titles are split between two lines.

Figure 1.49

Corrected words

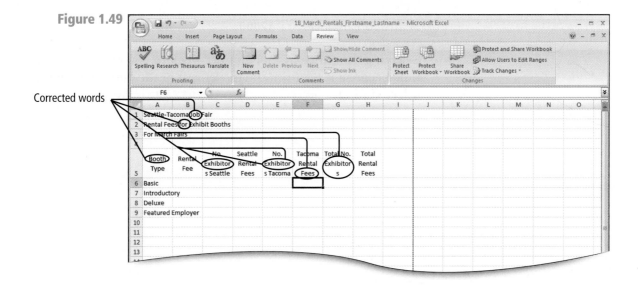

5 On the **Quick Access Toolbar**, click the **Save** button 🖫 to save your changes.

Objective 9
Enter Data by Range

Entering data and numbers in a worksheet can be done more quickly when the movement of the active cell is confined to the range where text and data will be entered. To **enter data by range**, first select the range where the data will be entered so the active cell will move to the next cell where data will be entered.

Activity 1.17 Selecting Cells and Entering Data by Range

Recall that using the 10-key number pad can speed data entry. Selecting a range of cells before entering the data and text speeds data entry.

1 Click cell **A9**. On the **Home tab**, in the **Cells group**, click the **Format** button, and then from the displayed menu, click **AutoFit Column Width**.

2 Select the range **B6:C9**. Beginning in the active cell **B6**, use the 10-key number pad to type the following data and press ⎆Enter on the number pad after each entry. Enter data in the first column, *Rental Fee*. After the last entry is made, the active cell moves to the top of the next column. You will then enter data in the second column. As you enter data by range, use ⎋Bksp to make corrections. Do not use the mouse or arrow keys; they will cancel the selected range. When finished, compare your screen with Figure 1.50.

Booth Type	Rental Fee	No. Exhibitors Seattle
Basic	3000	15
Introductory	6000	21
Deluxe	9000	16
Featured Employer	12000	10

Selecting the range in this manner—before you enter data—saves time because it confines the movement of the active cell to the selected range.

Figure 1.50

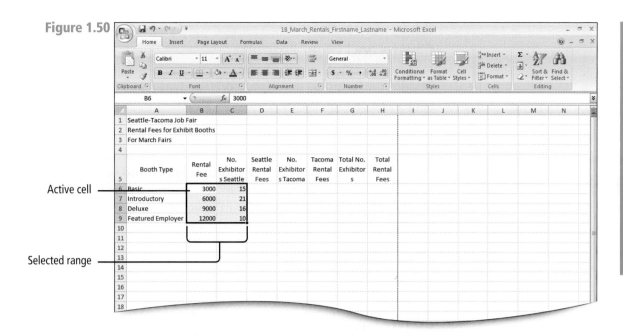

Active cell

Selected range

---

3 Beginning in cell **E6**, enter the number of exhibitors for Tacoma, as shown in the following:

No. Exhibitors Tacoma
13
16
20
8

Only one column of data is entered, so it is not necessary to select the range before you enter the data.

4 Take time to proofread the numbers you have entered.

5 On the **Quick Access Toolbar**, click the **Save** button to save your changes. Then compare your screen with Figure 1.51.

Figure 1.51

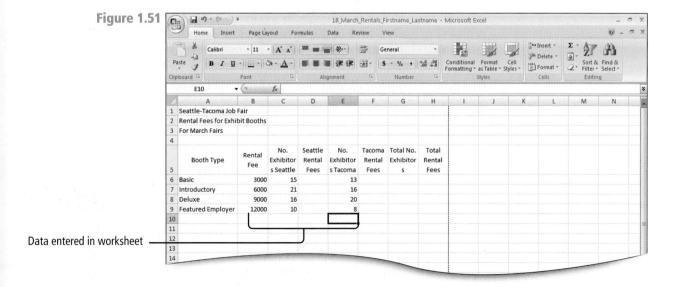

Data entered in worksheet

Objective 10
Create and Copy Formulas

Recall that formulas are equations that perform calculations on values in your worksheet and that a formula starts with an equal sign [=]. **Calculation operators** specify the type of calculation that you want to perform on the elements of a formula. One type of calculation operator is the **arithmetic operator**, which provides basic mathematical operations such as addition, subtraction, multiplication, and division. Arithmetic operators are also used to combine numbers and produce numeric results. There is a default order in which calculations occur, but you can change this order by using parentheses.

In Excel, keyboard characters are used for the mathematical operators. Study the following table to determine the keyboard symbol used in Excel.

Mathematical Symbols Used in Excel	
Operator Symbol	**Operation**
+	Addition
-	Subtraction
*	Multiplication
/	Division
^	Exponentiation

Figure 1.52

Activity 1.18 Using the Point-and-Click Method and Calculation Operators to Create a Formula

Recall that you have entered a formula in a worksheet by typing the entry. You may also enter a cell reference into a formula without typing when you use the **point-and-click method**—clicking in the cell to enter a cell reference in a formula. The Seattle-Tacoma Job Fair provides four types of booth displays: Basic, Introductory, Deluxe, and Featured Employer. The rental fees for exhibit booths vary depending on the size of the display space and the number of services provided, such as advertising and office services available during the fair. In this activity, you will determine the fees generated from exhibit booth rentals for the March job fairs.

1 Click cell **D6**. Type [=] and click cell **B6**. Type [*] click cell **C6**, and notice that the cells used in the formula are color-coded to match the cell references used in the formula. On the **Formula Bar**, click the **Enter** button [✓] to confirm the entry.

Use the Enter button in the Formula Bar to confirm the entry while not moving the active cell. Notice when the entry is completed, the Cancel and Enter buttons no longer display in the Formula Bar.

The total fees for the Basic booths in Seattle—45000—is entered in the cell. You created a multiplication formula without typing the cell references. The formula multiplies the number of exhibitors—15—by the rental fee for the Basic display booth—3000. Recall that the mathematical operator for multiplication is ⊡ and is located on the keyboard in the number row or on the 10-key number pad.

2 In cell **F6**, type ⊡ and click cell **B6**. Type ⊡ click cell **E6**, and then press ⟨Enter⟩.

The total fees for the Basic booths in Tacoma—39000—displays in the cell.

3 In cell **G6**, type ⊡ and click cell **C6**. Type ⊡ and click cell **E6**, and then compare your screen with Figure 1.53.

You may use the point-and-click method to create any formula. However, when creating a formula that uses *nonadjacent cells*—cells that are not next to each other—using the point-and-click method helps to avoid potential typing errors and helps ensure that the correct cell reference is entered in the formula. Alternatively, you may type the formula into the cell. Notice the color coordination of the cells and cell references used in the formula.

Figure 1.53

Active Formula Bar

Cancel button in Formula Bar

Enter button in Formula Bar

Green cell reference and its cell surrounded in green

Blue cell reference and its cell surrounded in blue

Formula not confirmed

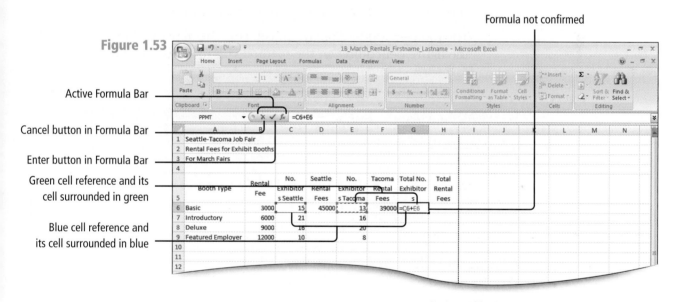

4 On the **Formula Bar,** click the **Enter** button ✔ to confirm the entry, and then compare your screen with Figure 1.54.

The result—28—displays in the active cell and the formula displays in the Formula Bar.

Excel | chapter 1

Figure 1.54

Formula in Formula Bar

Result in active cell

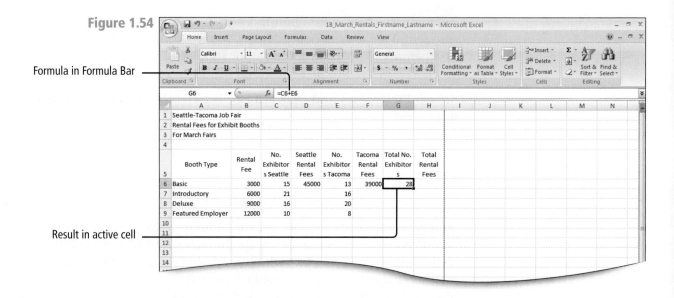

5 Use the techniques you just practiced to complete the formula in cell **H6** to determine the total rental fees received for the rental of the Basic booths. Then compare your screen with Figure 1.55.

The total—84000—displays in cell H6. The active cell may not match the figure depending on the method you used to confirm the entry.

Figure 1.55

Underlying formula

Total rental fees calculated

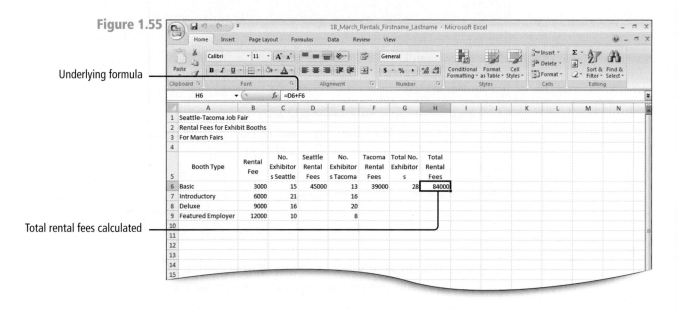

6 On the **Quick Access Toolbar**, click the **Save** button to save your changes.

Activity 1.19 Using the Fill Handle to Copy a Formula

Copying a formula rather than creating a new formula saves time when creating a worksheet. The ***fill handle***—the small black square in the lower right corner of a selected cell—may be used to copy a formula in the worksheet. When a formula is copied from one cell to another, Excel adjusts the cell references to fit the new location of the formula. Cell references that change are called **_relative cell references_**—when the cell reference is copied to a new location, the cell reference changes to reflect the new location. In this activity, you will use the fill handle to copy formulas in the worksheet.

1 Click cell **D6.** Notice the small black square in the lower right corner—the fill handle—as shown in Figure 1.56.

Figure 1.56

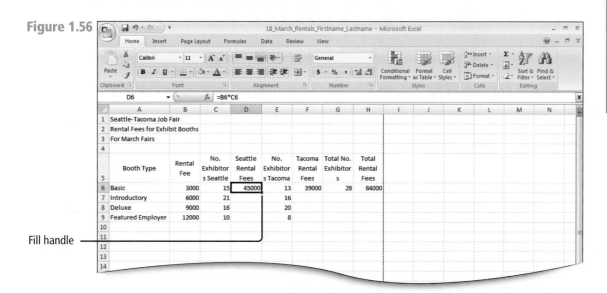

Fill handle

2 Point to the fill handle until the ⊞ pointer displays, hold down the left mouse button, drag down to cell **D9**. Release the left mouse button, point to the **_AutoFill Options button_** 🖳 that displays to view the ScreenTip.

The AutoFill Options button displays after a formula is copied and provides choices on how the selected cells will be filled.

You can drag the fill handle to adjacent cells to copy the formula from one cell to other cells. Excel's AutoFill feature copied the formula in the cell and the AutoFill Options button becomes available. When you point to the AutoFill Options button, the arrow displays, providing access to additional choices.

Alert

Are the formulas in the column incorrect?

In a worksheet, if you enter the Sum functions individually to add a row of numbers, an incorrect formula may result. To make sure your formulas are correct, use the fill handle to copy the formulas that add rows.

3 Click the **AutoFill Options** button 🖳 and compare your screen with Figure 1.57.

The AutoFill Options button displays just below a copied selection after you use the fill handle to copy formulas. When you click the button, a list displays with the options for filling the text or data. The list of options varies depending on the content you are filling, the program you are filling from, and the format of the text or data you are filling.

Copy Cells is selected, indicating the action that was taken. When a cell containing a formula is copied, it is the underlying formula that is copied and not the results of the formula.

Note that you can also *Fill Formatting Only* or *Fill Without Formatting*. Recall that because the options are related to the current task, the button is referred to as being context-sensitive.

Figure 1.57

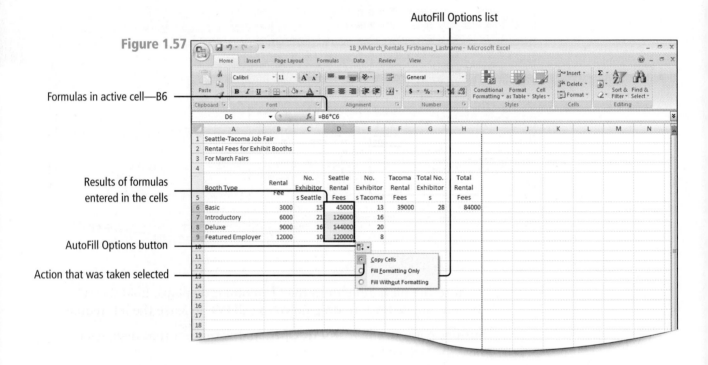

AutoFill Options list

Formulas in active cell—B6

Results of formulas entered in the cells

AutoFill Options button

Action that was taken selected

4 Click cell **D6** to cancel the display of the AutoFill Options list. In the **Formula Bar**, notice the formula that is displayed in cell **D6** —=B6*C6.

The AutoFill Options list no longer displays; however, the AutoFill Options button will display until another screen action takes place.

5 Press Ctrl + ` to display the formulas. Notice that the formula in cell D7 is not identical to the formula in cell D6; it reads =B7*C7. Take a few minutes to study the other formulas that you copied in column D and compare your screen with Figure 1.58.

In each row, Excel copied the formula but adjusted the cell references *relative to* the row number, a reference that is called a relative cell reference. The calculation is the same, but it is performed on the cells in that specific row. Because the cell reference changes when a formula is copied, you can quickly copy similar formulas into the worksheet. The color of the cell references in the formula matches the cells to which they refer.

Figure 1.58

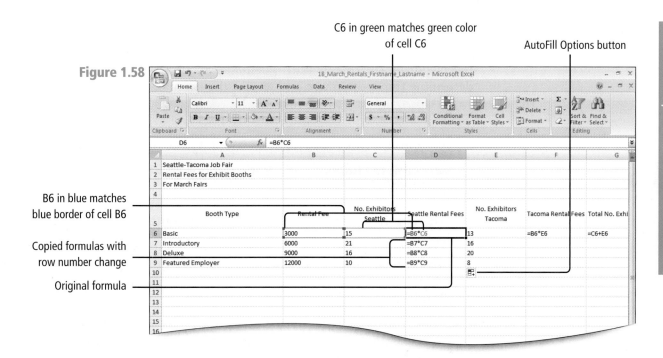

C6 in green matches green color of cell C6

AutoFill Options button

B6 in blue matches blue border of cell B6

Copied formulas with row number change

Original formula

⎡6⎤ Press [Ctrl] + [ˋ] to return to display the worksheet results.

⎡7⎤ Click cell **F6**. Point to the fill handle and when the ⊞ pointer displays, hold down the left mouse button, and drag down to cell **F9**. Release the left mouse button. Then press [Ctrl] + [ˋ] to display the formulas.

The formula in cell F6 has been copied to the range F7:F9. Review how the cell references are changed in the worksheet when they are copied.

⎡8⎤ Press [Ctrl] + [ˋ] to return to display the worksheet results.

⎡9⎤ Select the range **G6:H6**. Point to the fill handle and when the ⊞ pointer displays, hold down the left mouse button, and drag down to row **9**. Release the left mouse button. Then press [Ctrl] + [ˋ] to display the formulas and review how the cell references are changed in the formulas that have been copied.

It is possible to copy more than one formula into adjacent cells at the same time.

⎡10⎤ Press [Ctrl] + [ˋ] to return to display the worksheet results.

⎡11⎤ Click cell **C10**, and in the **Editing group**, click the **Sum** button ∑ ▾ to determine the total number of exhibitors in Seattle. Then in the **Formula Bar**, click the **Enter** button ✓ so cell **C10** remains active.

⎡12⎤ Click the **fill handle** and drag to the right through cell **H10**. Review the formulas that are entered and note how the cell references have changed to reflect their locations in a new column.

The only difference in these formulas is the column identified in each range to reflect the column location of the formula. Recall that a relative cell reference will change the column letter as well as the row number *relative* to the location where it is copied.

⎡13⎤ On the **Quick Access Toolbar**, click the **Save** button 🖫 to save your changes.

Activity 1.20 Determining Percentages

Michael would like to know the percentage of total rental fees that were received from the Seattle and Tacoma fairs. In this activity, you will determine that percentage and format the number as a percentage.

1 In cell **A12**, type **Percentage of Total Fees** and in the **Formula Bar**, click the **Enter** button ✓. Right-click cell **A12** to display the Mini toolbar and click the **Bold** **B** and **Italic** buttons **I**.

2 Click cell **D12**. Type ⊟ Click cell **D10** and type ⊡ and click cell **H10**. Then in the **Formula Bar**, click the **Enter** button ✓.

The decimal number—0.514184—is entered in the cell. The formula determined the rate of rental fees from Seattle by dividing the individual amount by the total amount—Seattle Rental Fees divided by Total Rental Fees.

3 Using the method you just practiced, in cell **F12**, enter the formula to determine the rate of rental fees from Tacoma. The decimal *0.485816* is entered in the cell.

4 Right-click cell **D12** to display the Mini toolbar. Click the **Percent Style** button **%** and then click the **Increase Decimal** button .

once. Alternatively, use the Percent Style and Increase Decimal buttons located on the Home tab in the Number group.

You have changed the percent to display with one decimal place.

5 Use a method you practiced to apply the same format of cell **D12** to cell **F12**. Then compare your screen with Figure 1.59.

Figure 1.59

Percent Style button

Number formatted as a percentage to one decimal place

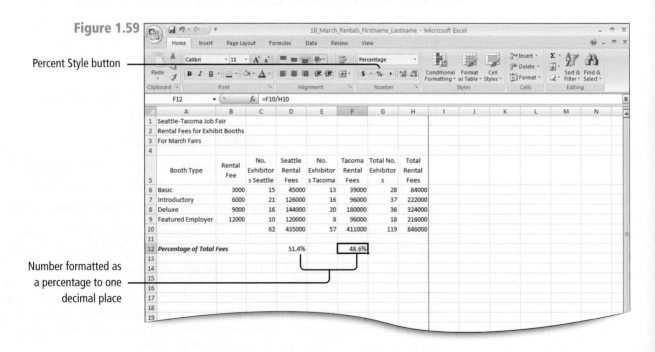

6 On the **Quick Access Toolbar**, click the **Save** button 📄 to save your changes.

Objective 11
Use Format Painter and Chart Data

The **Format Painter** copies a format from one cell and pastes it into another cell or cells. A **chart** is a graphic representation of data in a worksheet. Data presented as a chart is usually easier to understand than a table of numbers. Excel's charting feature assists you in creating an attractive chart.

Activity 1.21 Using Format Painter

In this activity, you will use Format Painter to copy formats in the worksheet.

1 Right-click cell **B6** to display the shortcut menu and Mini toolbar. On the Mini toolbar, click the **Accounting Number Format** button **$ ▾**. Then click the **Decrease Decimal** button 📉 two times.

Because all the numbers on this worksheet will be whole numbers, no decimal places are needed in any of the numbers.

2 In the Mini toolbar, click the **Format Painter** button 🖌, move the mouse onto the worksheet and notice the shape the mouse takes 🔲. Alternatively, in the Clipboard group, click the Format Painter button. Compare your screen with Figure 1.60.

The Format Painter mouse shape displays and the selected cell is surrounded by a moving border, indicating the cell format to be used. The Mini toolbar fades as the mouse is moved on the screen but is still available for further commands.

Figure 1.60

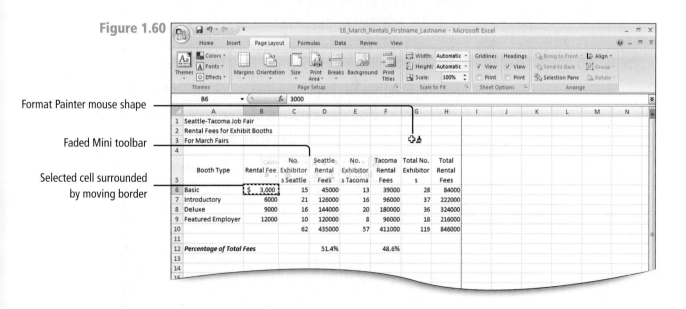

Format Painter mouse shape

Faded Mini toolbar

Selected cell surrounded by moving border

3 With the **Format Painter** button 🖌 , click cell **D6**.

The format from cell B6—Accounting Number style and Decrease Decimal—is applied to cell D6. Use Format Painter to copy the *formatting* of one cell to other cells.

4 Right-click cell **D6** to display the shortcut menu and Mini toolbar.

On the Mini toolbar, double-click the **Format Painter** button 🖌 . Click cells **F6, H6, D10, F10**, and **H10**. In the **Clipboard group**, click the **Format Painter** button 🖌 to turn it off.

When you double-click the Format Painter button, it remains active so the format can be applied to multiple locations. The icon for Format Painter in the Clipboard group is highlighted, providing a visual reminder it is active. Click again in the Format Painter button to turn it off and the icon is no longer highlighted.

When the format is applied to the total row (cells D10, F10, and H10), a series of pound symbols (####) displays in the cell. This happens when a cell width is too narrow to display all of the numbers rather than display only a portion of a whole number, which would be misleading. The underlying values remain unchanged.

5 Select column **B**. Move the mouse to the boundary between columns **B** and **C** to get the ⟷ shape. Click and drag to the right until the ScreenTip indicates a width of **10.00** and then release the mouse button.

To display the words fully within a column that contains wrapped text, drag the column width to the right to display contents.

6 Select columns **C:H**. Point to the right boundary of **column H** to get the ⟷ shape. Click and drag to the right until the ScreenTip indicates a width of **10.00** and then release the mouse button.

When a group of columns is selected, you can change the width for the entire selected group at the same time.

7 Click cell **C6** to clear the selected columns and then right-click cell **C6** to display the shortcut menu and Mini toolbar. On the Mini toolbar, click the **Comma Style** button ⟨,⟩, click the **Decrease Decimal** button ⟨.00⟩ two times, and then double-click the **Format Painter** button 🖌 . Click cells **E6, G6, C10, E10, G10**, and the range **B7:H9**.

In the **Clipboard group**, click the **Format Painter** button 🖌 to turn it off. Click outside the range and then compare your screen with Figure 1.61.

Figure 1.61

Accounting Number Format
with no decimals

Comma Style with no decimals

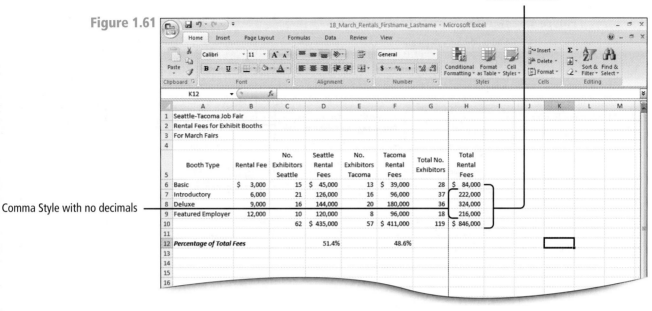

Format Painter can be used to paste a format to a range of cells as well as individual cells.

8 Select cell **A1**. Right-click and from the displayed Mini toolbar, click the **Bold** button **B** and click the **Increase Font Size** button **A** two times.

9 Select the range **A1:H1**. Right-click the selected range to display the shortcut menu and Mini toolbar. On the Mini toolbar, click the **Merge & Center** button and double-click the **Format Painter** button. Click cells **A2** and **A3** and then in the **Clipboard group**, click the **Format Painter** button to turn it off.

The Format Painter copies the entire format of a cell, including the Merge and Center command with the same range of cells.

10 Select the range **C10:H10**. Right-click the selected range to display the shortcut menu and Mini toolbar. Click the **Border button arrow**. In the menu, select the **Top and Double Bottom Border**.

11 Select the range **A5:H5.** Right-click the selected range to display the shortcut menu and Mini toolbar. On the Mini toolbar, click the **Bold B** and **Italic I** buttons, and then display the **Borders** button menu and click **Thick Bottom Border**.

12 In cell **A10**, type **Total** and press Enter. Right-click cell **A10** to display the shortcut menu and Mini toolbar. On the Mini toolbar, click the **Bold** button **B** and the **Italic** button **I**. **Save** your work. Then compare your work with Figure 1.62.

Figure 1.62

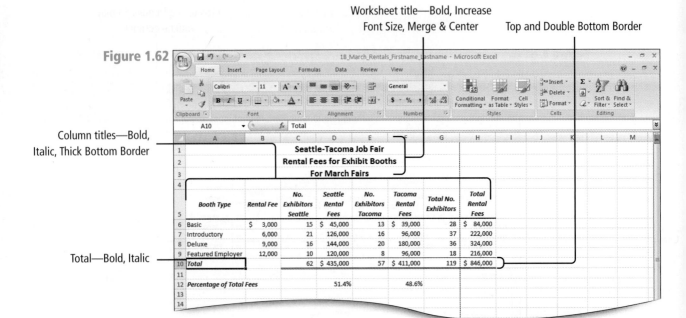

Worksheet title—Bold, Increase Font Size, Merge & Center

Top and Double Bottom Border

Column titles—Bold, Italic, Thick Bottom Border

Total—Bold, Italic

Activity 1.22 Charting Data

In this activity, you will create a column chart showing the rental fees for the Seattle and Tacoma job fairs. This chart will allow Michael Dawson, the director of Seattle-Tacoma Job Fairs, to compare rental income from the different types of display booths.

1 Select the range **A5:A9**. Press Ctrl while you select the ranges **D5:D9** and **F5:F9**. On the Ribbon, click the **Insert tab**, and then in the **Charts group**, click **Column** to display a gallery of column *chart types*.

The data that is selected will be included in the chart. Various chart types are used to chart data in a way that is meaningful to the reader—common examples of chart types are column charts, pie charts, and line charts. A *column chart* is useful for illustrating comparisons among related numbers.

2 From the displayed gallery of column chart types, under **2-D Column**, point to the first chart to display the ScreenTip *Clustered Column*, and then click to select it. Compare your screen with Figure 1.63.

A column chart displays in the worksheet that compares the rental fees for Seattle and Tacoma. Because the chart object is selected—surrounded by a border and displaying sizing handles—the contextual tools named *Chart Tools* displays and adds contextual tabs next to the standard tabs on the Ribbon.

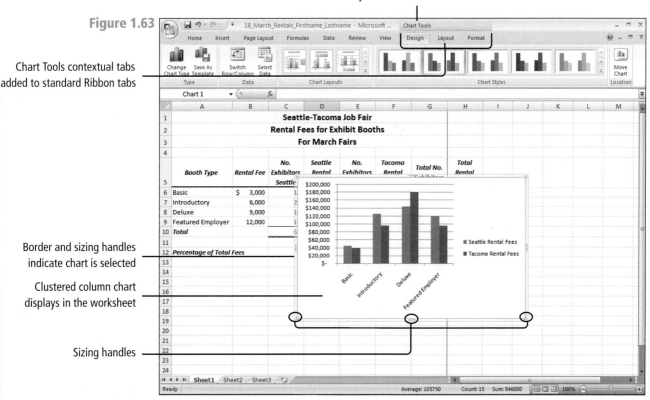

Figure 1.63

Chart Tools indicates tools for selected
object are added to the Ribbon

Chart Tools contextual tabs
added to standard Ribbon tabs

Border and sizing handles
indicate chart is selected

Clustered column chart
displays in the worksheet

Sizing handles

3 Point to the top border of the chart to display the [icon] pointer, hold
down the left mouse button, and then drag the upper left corner of
the chart to the upper left corner of cell **A14**, and as you do, notice
that a border line moves on the screen as you drag the chart to its
new location. This serves as a visual indicator of where the chart will
be placed. Release the mouse button. Use the scroll bar to scroll
down so you can view the entire chart. Compare your screen with
Figure 1.64.

When you release the mouse button, a double border surrounds the
chart, indicating it is an *active chart*—a chart that can be edited.
This border spills into adjacent cells.

Based on the data in your worksheet, Excel constructs a column
chart and adds *category labels*—the labels that display along the
bottom of the chart to identify the category of data. This area is
referred to as the *category axis* or the *x-axis*. Excel uses the row
titles as the category names.

On the left, Excel includes a numerical scale upon which the charted
data is based; this is referred to as the *value axis* or the *y-axis*. On
the right, a *legend* displays, which identifies the patterns or colors
that are assigned to the data in the selected columns in the chart.

Figure 1.64

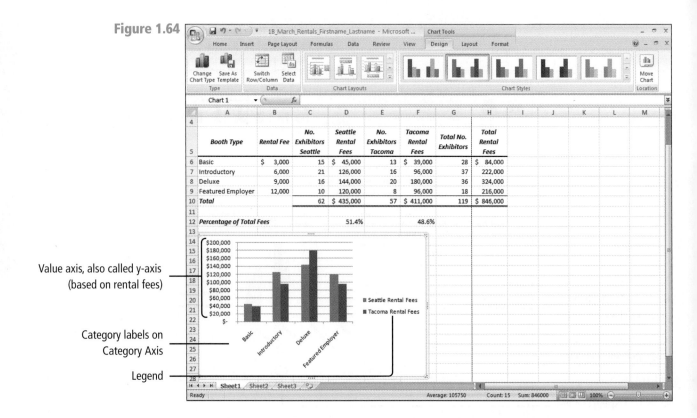

Value axis, also called y-axis (based on rental fees)

Category labels on Category Axis

Legend

4 On the Ribbon, locate the three contextual tabs that are displayed under **Chart Tools—Design**, **Layout**, and **Format**.

When a chart is selected, Chart Tools become available and these three tabs—Design, Layout and Format—provide commands for working with the chart. When the chart is not selected, the Chart Tools do not display.

5 Click the **Design tab**, in the **Data group**, click the **Switch Row/Column** button, and then compare your chart with Figure 1.65.

In this manner, you can easily change the categories of data from the row titles, which is the default, to the column titles. Whether you use row or column titles as your category names depends upon how you want to view your charted data. In this instance, the director wants to compare the Seattle and Tacoma rental fees.

Switch Row/Column button

Figure 1.65

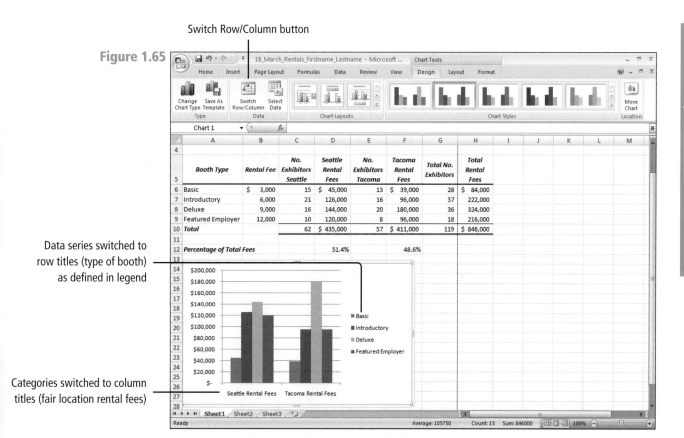

Data series switched to row titles (type of booth) as defined in legend

Categories switched to column titles (fair location rental fees)

6 On the **Design tab**, in the **Chart Layouts group**, point to the **More arrow** ▼, and then compare your screen with Figure 1.66.

Chart Layouts group

Figure 1.66

More arrow

More ScreenTip

7 Click the **More arrow** ![down arrow] to access the gallery. Click several different layouts to see the effect on your chart, and then using the ScreenTips as your guide, locate and click **Layout 3.** Move the mouse into the worksheet and then compare your screen with Figure 1.67.

From the *Chart Layouts gallery*, you can select a predesigned *chart layout*—a combination of chart elements, which can include a title, legend, labels for the columns, and the table of charted cells. This chart now displays a chart title and the legend displays across the bottom of the chart.

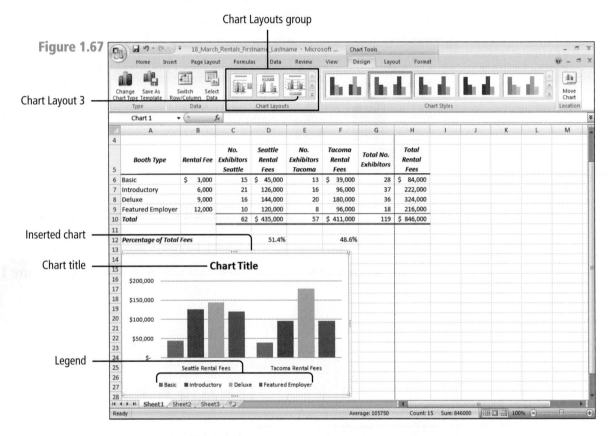

Figure 1.67

Chart Layouts group

Chart Layout 3

Inserted chart

Chart title

Legend

8 In the chart, click on *Chart Title* and drag through it to select it. Type **Rental Fees** Press [Enter] and type **For March 2009** to create a two-line chart title. Click in the worksheet.

Typing over selected text will delete the text while the new text is entered.

9 **Save** ![save icon] your workbook.

Contextual tabs related to contextual tools in Office 2007 applications display when an object is selected, and then are removed from view when the object is deselected.

More Knowledge

A Chart Can Occupy a Separate Sheet in the Workbook

When a chart displays as an object within the worksheet, it is referred to as an *embedded chart*. On the Design tab of the Ribbon, the last button—Move Chart—places the chart on a separate worksheet. An embedded chart is useful when you want to view or print a chart on the same page as its source data.

Activity 1.23 Printing the Worksheet and its Formulas

In this activity, you will print the worksheet and a copy that displays the formulas.

1 Right-click the **Sheet2 sheet tab**. From the shortcut menu, click **Delete**. Use this method to delete **Sheet3**. Then click in the displayed worksheet.

2 On the **Page Layout tab**, in the **Page Setup group**, click the **Margins** button, and then compare your screen with Figure 1.68.

Margins button

Figure 1.68

Margins gallery

Custom Margins selection

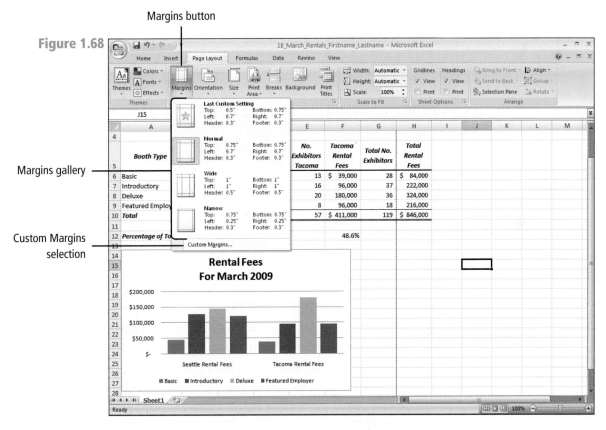

3 In the **Margins** gallery, click **Custom Margins**. In the **Page Setup** dialog box, under the **Center on page** section, click **Horizontally** and **Vertically**. In the lower right corner, click the **Print Preview** button.

The worksheet does not fully display on this page; the last column is missing. In the bottom left corner, the page number indicates that you are viewing page 1 of 2 pages.

4 In the scroll bar at the right, click the **down arrow** to bring page 2 onto the screen.

Page 2 appears with the contents centered both horizontally and vertically.

5 Click **Close Print Preview**. In the **Page Setup group**, click the **Dialog Box Launcher** . In the **Page tab**, under **Scaling**, click the **Fit to** option button. Then click **Print Preview** and compare your screen with Figure 1.69.

The worksheet now displays on one page. The page number indicator displays at the bottom left of the screen. When a worksheet is slightly larger than the page, Excel will fit the entire worksheet on one page using this scaling feature.

Figure 1.69

Page number indicator

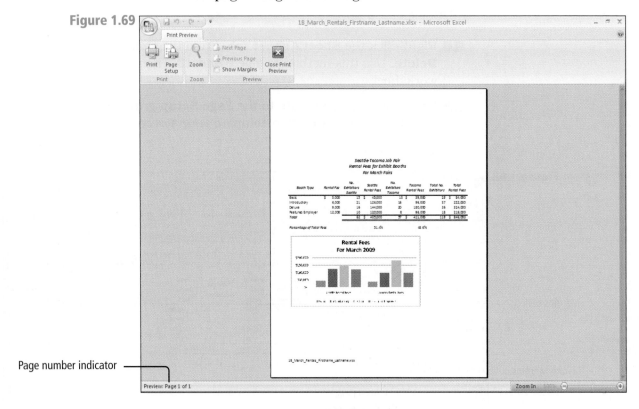

6 In **Print Preview**, click **Print**, and then click **OK**. **Save** your work.

7 Hold down Ctrl and press `. In the **Page Layout tab**, in the **Page Setup group**, click **Orientation**, and then select **Landscape**.

8 Check your *Chapter Assignment Sheet* or *Course Syllabus*, or consult your instructor, to determine if you are to submit your printed formulas on paper or electronically using your college's course information management system. To submit electronically, follow the instructions provided by your instructor, and then go to Step 9. To print, click **OK**.

9 At the upper right side of your screen, point to the Workbook-level **Close Window** button —the ScreenTip displays *Close Window*— and compare your screen with Figure 1.70.

The Close Window button will close only the open workbook and Excel continues running. Recall that the Program-level Close button will close both the workbook and the program.

Workbook-
level buttons

Figure 1.70

Close Window ScreenTip

Close Workbook
Window button

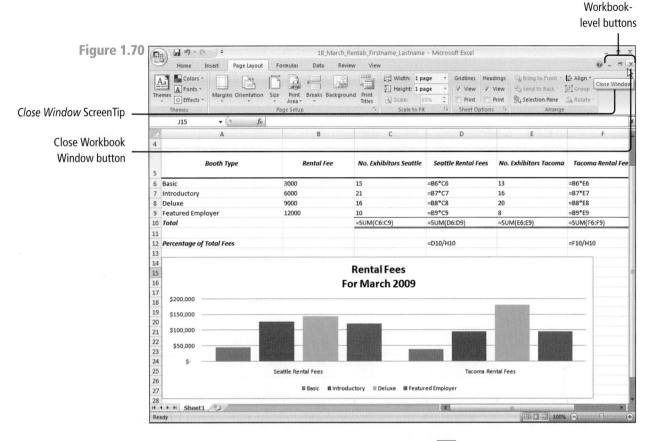

10 Click the Window-level **Close** button ☒ , and when prompted, click
No so that you do *not* save the changes you made—displaying formulas, changing column widths, orientation, and scaling—to print
your formulas.

Your workbook is closed without saving the changes you made to
print the formulas. The Excel program remains open.

Objective 12
Use Microsoft Excel Help

Excel is a complex program and Microsoft recognizes that users sometimes need assistance with some of its many features. Help is available
when using Excel and additional topics are discussed when connected
with the Internet. ***Microsoft Excel Help*** can be used to answer specific
questions and in some cases provide step-by-step instruction.

Activity 1.24 Using Help

In this activity, you will use the Help feature of Excel.

1 Click the **Office** button 🔘 , from the menu click **New,** and compare
your screen with Figure 1.71.

The New Workbook dialog box displays. In the *Blank and recent*
section, Blank Workbook is highlighted.

Figure 1.71

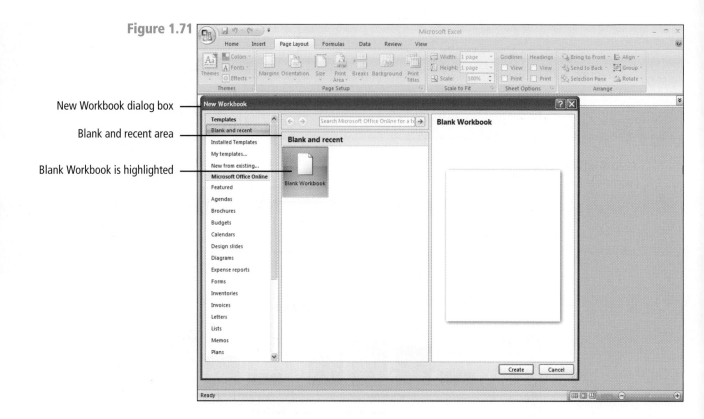

New Workbook dialog box

Blank and recent area

Blank Workbook is highlighted

2 With **Blank Workbook** highlighted, in the lower right corner, click **Create**.

A new, blank workbook displays with its name—*Book2*—displayed in the Title bar. This is the second workbook that has been opened since Excel was last closed. Excel numbers new workbooks used in each session in numerical order, beginning with Book1.

3 In the upper right corner of the screen, click the **Microsoft Office Excel Help** button 🔘 and compare your screen with Figure 1.72.

The Excel Help dialog box displays.

Figure 1.72

Excel Help toolbar

Excel Help dialog box

Type the item to search

List of Help topics

Area that identifies connection to the Internet

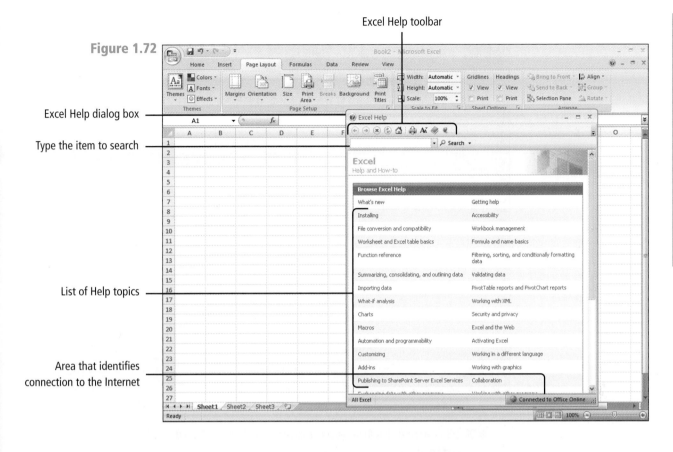

▰▰ In the **Excel Help** window, in the second column, click **Getting help**.

A list of subcategories displays.

▰▰ In the list, click **Find the content you need in the Help window**. Then scroll through the information about the Help. Under the **What do you want to do?** section, click **Restrict a search to a specific feature area** and read the information.

▰▰ In the **Excel Help** window, on the toolbar, at the upper left side of the screen, point to the **Back arrow** button ⬅, confirm the Screen Tip reads *Back*, and then click the **Back arrow** button.

You have returned to the previous screen.

▰▰ In the text box at the top, type **Spelling Checker** and press Enter. Alternatively, you can click the **Search** button to begin the search. Compare your screen with Figure 1.73.

A list of items about spelling displays. Use this text box to search for specific topics.

Figure 1.73

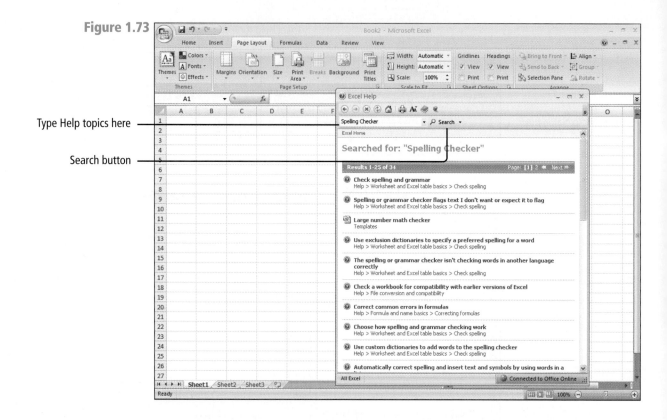

Type Help topics here

Search button

---

8 In the results list, scroll down and click **Find and correct errors in formulas**.

Help provides additional information about this topic. Enter other topics in Help to get assistance in your work with Excel.

9 If you want to do so, click the **Print** button 🖶 to print a copy of this information for your reference. Your name will not print.

10 In the upper right corner of the Excel Help window, click the **Close** button ☒.

11 At the upper right side of your screen, point to the Program-level **Close Window** button ☒—the ScreenTip displays *Close*—compare your screen with Figure 1.74, and then click the **Close** button ☒.

The Program-level button closes both the worksheet and the Excel program. You have exited Excel.

Program-level Close
button with ScreenTip

Figure 1.74

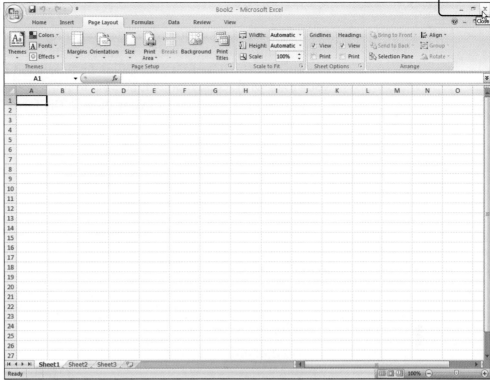

End **You have completed Project 1B**

There's More You Can Do!

From My Computer, navigate to the student files that accompany this textbook. In the folder **02_theres_more_you_can_do**, locate and open the folder for this chapter. Open and print the instructions for this project, which are provided to you in Adobe PDF format.

Try It! 1—Use AutoCalculate

In this Try It! exercise, you will use AutoCalculate to quickly determine the Average and Sum and perform other statistical analysis.

Content-Based Assessments

Summary

Use Microsoft Excel 2007 to create and analyze data organized into columns and rows and to chart and perform calculations on the data and display the data in a professionally formatted manner. By organizing your data with Excel, you will be able to make logical decisions and create visual representations of your data in the form of charts.

Key Terms

Content-Based Assessments

Key Terms

Content-Based Assessments

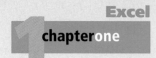

Matching

Match each term in the second column with its correct definition in the first column by writing the letter of the term on the blank line in front of the correct definition.

_____ **1.** A collection of worksheets that are saved in one computer file.

_____ **2.** The primary document used in Excel to store and work with data.

_____ **3.** The uniformly spaced horizontal and vertical lines in a worksheet.

_____ **4.** A small rectangular box formed by the intersection of a column and a row.

_____ **5.** Displays a menu of commands related to things you can do _with_ a workbook, such as opening, saving, printing, or sharing.

_____ **6.** A rectangular box that is used to request more information about a command or where additional decisions are made.

_____ **7.** Displays additional information about a command or descriptive text when you perform various mouse actions such as pointing to screen elements or dragging.

_____ **8.** The area at the top of the worksheet that displays the program icon, the program name, and the workbook name.

_____ **9.** The term used when you move around the worksheet.

_____ **10.** At the right and bottom of the screen, used to move the worksheet window up and down or left and right.

_____ **11.** The letters at the top of each column that identify the column.

_____ **12.** The process used to move something from one location on the screen to another.

_____ **13.** An individual keystroke or a combination of keys pressed simultaneously that can either access an Excel command or navigate to another location on your screen.

_____ **14.** The cell ready to accept data or be affected by the next Excel command.

_____ **15.** Numbers, text, dates, or times of the day that are used in Excel.

A Active cell

B Cell

C Column heading

D Data

E Dialog box

F Drag

G Gridlines

H Keyboard shortcut

I Navigate

J Office button

K ScreenTip

L Scroll bars

M Title bar

N Workbook

O Worksheet

Content-Based Assessments

Fill in the Blank

Write the correct word in the space provided.

1. Highlighting cells by clicking or dragging with your mouse is called _____ cells.

2. A group of cells is referred to as a _____.

3. The intersecting column letter and row number used to identify a cell is called a _____ _____.

4. The area that displays the name of the selected cell, chart, or object is called the _____ _____.

5. The numbers along the left side of the worksheet that indicate the row number are called the _____ _____.

6. Cells that are next to each other are _____.

7. A horizontal group of cells in a worksheet is called a _____.

8. A vertical group of cells in a worksheet is called a _____.

9. Ranges of cells that are not next to each other are _____.

10. The toolbar that displays the buttons that are used most frequently is the _____ _____ _____.

11. Anything typed into a cell is _____ content.

12. Changing values or cell entries is called _____.

13. The first rows of a worksheet that identify the organization, purpose, and date of the worksheet are called the worksheet _____.

14. Text that identifies the data in the columns is called a _____ _____.

15. The feature that will match the first few characters you type and fill in the remaining characters for you is the _____ feature.

Content-Based Assessments

Project 1C — Earnings

In this project, you will apply the skills you practiced from the Objectives in Project 1A.

Objectives: 1. *Start Excel and Navigate a Worksheet;* **2.** *Select Parts of a Worksheet;* **3.** *Enter Data, Construct a Formula, and Use the SUM Function;* **4.** *Format Data, Cells, and Worksheets;* **5.** *Insert a Footer into a Worksheet;* **6.** *Delete Unused Worksheets and Preview and Print a Worksheet;* **7.** *Print Formulas, Close a Workbook, and Exit Excel.*

In the following Skills Review, you will prepare a report of the employee earnings for the year for the Seattle-Tacoma Job Fair. Your completed worksheet will look similar to the one shown in Figure 1.75.

For Project 1C, you will need the following file:

New blank Excel workbook

You will save your workbook as
1C_Earnings_Firstname_Lastname

Figure 1.75

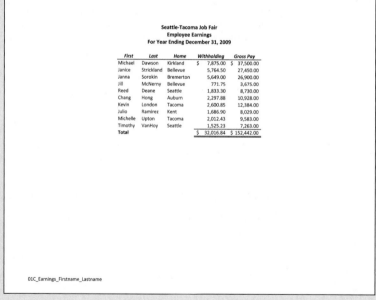

(Project 1C–Earnings continues on the next page)

Content-Based Assessments

(Project 1C–Earnings continued)

1. **Start** Excel. In the new workbook, from the **Office** menu, click the **Save As** command. Navigate to the drive on which you created your **Excel Chapter 1** folder, and then double-click the folder name to display it in the **Save in** box. In the **File name** box, using your own first and last name, type **1C_Earnings_Firstname_Lastname** and then click **Save**.

2. Beginning with cell **A1**, type the following worksheet title:

Seattle-Tacoma Job Fair
Employee Earnings
For Year Ending December 31, 2009

3. Beginning with cell **A5**, type the following column titles:

First	Last	Home	Withholding	Gross Pay

4. Beginning with cell **A6**, type the following data. Most of these employees work part-time for Seattle-Tacoma Job Fair and their earnings reflect that work.

First	Last	Home	Withholding	Gross Pay
Michael	Dawson	Kirkland	7875	37500
Janice	Strickland	Bellevue	5764.5	27450
Janna	Sorokin	Bremerton	5649	26900
Jill	McNerny	Bellevue	771.75	3675
Reed	Deane	Seattle	1833.3	8730
Chang	Hong	Auburn	2297.88	10928
Kevin	London	Tacoma	2600.85	12384
Julio	Ramirez	Kent	1686.90	8029
Michelle	Upton	Tacoma	2012.43	9583
Timothy	VanHoy	Seattle	1525.23	7263

5. In cell **A16**, type **Total** and press Enter. In cell **D16**, type **=d6+d7+d8+d9+d10+d11+d12+d13+d14+d15** and press Enter to calculate the amount of withholding. The result is *32016.84*.

6. Click cell **E16**. On the **Home tab**, in the **Editing group**, click the **Sum** button to calculate the gross pay for all employees. Confirm that the range of cells is correct. Then press Enter. The result is *152442*.

7. Select the range **A1:A3**. Right-click the selected range to display the Mini toolbar, click the **Bold** button and then click the **Increase Font Size** button. Select the range **A5:E5** and right-click the selection. On the Mini toolbar, click the **Bold, Italic, Center**, and **Bottom Border** buttons.

8. Select the range **A1:E1**. Display the Mini toolbar and click the **Merge & Center** button. Repeat this process with the ranges **A2:E2** and **A3:E3**.

(Project 1C–Earnings continues on the next page)

Content-Based Assessments

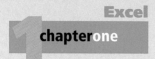
(Project 1C–Earnings continued)

9. Select the range **D6:E6**. Press Ctrl while you select the range **D16:E16**. On the **Home tab**, in the **Number group**, click the **Accounting Number Format** button. Select the range **D16:E16**. Right-click the selected range to display the Mini toolbar, click the **Borders button arrow**, and then click **Top and Double Bottom Border**. Select the range **D7:E15** and right click. In the Mini toolbar, click the **Comma Style** button. Click cell **A16** and from the Mini toolbar, click the **Bold** button.

10. Click cell **B7**. On the **Home tab**, in the **Cells group**, click the **Format** button and click **AutoFit Column Width**. On the column headers, position the mouse on the boundary between **columns C** and **D** and double-click to adjust the column width to fit the text in column C. Adjust the width of **column D** to fit the longest entry.

11. On the **View tab**, in the **Workbook Views group**, click the **Page Layout** button. Scroll to the footer and click in the **Left Footer area**. In the **Header & Footer Tools tab**, in the **Design tab**, in the **Header & Footer Elements group**, click the **File Name** button. Click in the worksheet and press Ctrl + Home to return to cell **A1**. On the **View tab**, in the **Workbook Views group**, click the **Normal** button.

12. Point to the **Sheet2 sheet tab** and right-click. From the displayed shortcut menu, click **Delete**. In **Sheet3**, on the **Home tab**, in the **Cells group**, click the **Delete button arrow**. Then from the menu, click **Delete Sheet**.

13. On the **Page Layout tab**, in the **Page Setup group**, click the **Orientation** button arrow, and then click **Landscape**. In the **Page Setup group**, click the **Dialog Box Launcher** button to display the **Page Setup** dialog box. Click the **Margins tab** and under **Center on page**, select the **Horizontally** check box. Then click **Print Preview**. Save your workbook.

14. Check your *Chapter Assignment Sheet* or your *Course Syllabus* or consult your instructor to determine if you are to submit your assignments on paper or electronically. To submit electronically, click **Close Print Preview** and go to Step 16, and then follow the instructions provided by your instructor.

15. On the **Print Preview tab**, in the **Print group**, click **Print**. In the **Print** dialog box, under **Print what**, verify that **Active sheet(s)** is selected. Under **Copies**, verify that the **Number of copies** is **1**. Click **OK**. **Save** your work. If you are directed to submit printed formulas, refer to **Activity 1.12** to do so.

16. If you printed your formulas, be sure to redisplay the worksheet by pressing Ctrl + `. From the **Office** menu, click **Close**. If the dialog box displays asking if you want to save changes, click **No** so that you do not save the changes to Page Setup that you used for printing formulas. **Exit** Excel.

End You have completed Project 1C ———————————————

Project 1D — Tacoma Revenues

In this project, you will apply the skills you practiced from the Objectives in Project 1B.

Objectives: 8. *Check Spelling and Edit a Worksheet;* **9.** *Enter Data by Range;* **10.** *Create and Copy Formulas;* **11.** *Use Format Painter and Chart Data;* **12.** *Use Microsoft Excel Help.*

In the following Skills Review, you will prepare the income statement for the Tacoma Job Fair that reports the monthly and quarterly income and expenses. You will format the worksheet as a table and also create a chart. Your completed worksheets will look similar to the one shown in Figure 1.76.

For Project 1D, you will need the following file:

e01D_Tacoma_Revenues

You will save your workbook as
1D_Tacoma_Revenues_Firstname_Lastname

Figure 1.76

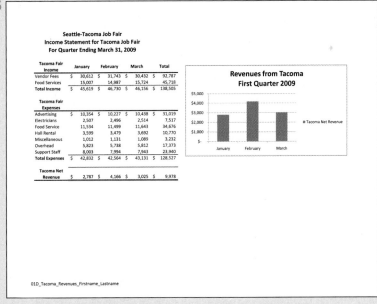

(Project 1D–Tacoma Revenues continues on the next page)

Content-Based Assessments

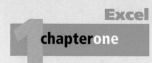

Excel
chapterone   Skills Review

(Project 1D–Tacoma Revenues continued)

1. **Start** Excel. Click the **Office** button and from the displayed menu, click **Open**. Navigate to the student data files that accompany this textbook, and then open the workbook **e01D_Tacoma_Revenues**. From the **Office** menu, click **Save As**. Navigate to the location where you are storing your projects for this chapter. In the **File name** box, type **1D_Tacoma_Revenues_Firstname_Lastname** and then click the **Save** button.

2. In the **Status bar**, click the **Page Layout** button. Scroll to the bottom of the page and click in the **Left Footer area**. In the **Header & Footer Design** tab, locate the **Header & Footer Elements group**, and then click the **File Name** button. Click in the worksheet to exit the footer. In the status bar, click the **Normal** button, and then press Ctrl + Home to return to cell **A1**.

3. Click cell **A5**. On the **Home tab**, in the **Alignment group**, click the **Wrap Text** button. In the **Clipboard group**, double-click the **Format Painter** button. Click cells **A10** and **A20**. Right-click and in the Mini toolbar, click the **Format Painter** button to turn it off.

4. Click cell **A1**. On the **Review tab**, in the **Proofing group**, click **Spelling**. In the Spelling dialog box, in the **Suggestions** area, click **Tacoma**, and then click **Change**. Continue using the Spelling Checker until the dialog box that reads *The spelling check is complete for the entire sheet* displays. Then click **OK**.

5. There are still two spelling errors in the worksheet that Spelling Checker did not find. Use the editing skills you practiced to correct the spelling in the cell or in the Formula Bar. One error is in cell **A17,** which should display *Support Staff*. The other error is in cell **A1**.

6. Double-click cell **A5**. In the cell, position the insertion point between *Tacoma* and *Income*. Type **Fair** and press Space. Click cell **A10**. In the Formula Bar, position the insertion point between *Tacoma* and *Expenses*. Type **Fair** and press Space.

7. Select the range **B6:D7** and enter the following data. Type the data in the January column, then the February column, and then the March column using the **enter data by range** method:

Tacoma Fair Income	January	February	March
Vendor Fees	30612	31743	30432
Food Services	15007	14987	15724

8. Select the range **B11:D17** and type the following expenses using the **enter data by range** method:

Advertising	10354	10227	10438
Electricians	2507	2496	2514
Food Service	11534	11499	11643
Hall Rental	3599	3479	3692
Miscellaneous	1012	1131	1089
Overhead	5823	5738	5812
Support Staff	8003	7994	7943

(Project 1D–Tacoma Revenues continues on the next page)

Content-Based Assessments

(Project 1D–Tacoma Revenues continued)

9. Click cell **A15**. On the **Home tab**, in the **Cells group**, click the **Format** button, and then click **AutoFit Column Width**.

10. Click cell **B8**. From the **Editing group**, click the **Sum** button. On the **Formula Bar**, click the **Enter** button to confirm the entry. The total is *45619*. In cell **B8**, click the **fill handle** and drag through cell **D8**.

11. Click cell **B18**. From the **Editing group**, click the **Sum** button. In the **Formula Bar**, click the **Enter** button to confirm the entry. The total is *42832*. In cell **B18**, click the **fill handle** and drag to the right through cell **D18**.

12. Click cell **E6**. From the **Editing group**, click the **Sum** button. In the **Formula Bar**, click the **Enter** button to confirm the entry. The total is *92787*. In cell **E6**, click the **fill handle** and drag down through cell **E8**. Using the skills you practiced, enter totals for the range **E11:E18**.

13. Click cell **B20**. Type $=$ and click cell **B8**. Type $-$ and click cell **B18**. On the **Formula Bar**, click the **Enter** button to confirm the entry. The net revenue, *2787*, displays. In cell **B20**, click the **fill handle** and drag to the right through cell **E20**.

14. Select the range **A1:E1**. Right-click the selected range to display the Mini toolbar. Click the **Merge & Center** and **Bold** buttons, and then click the **Increase Font Size** button two times. Double-click the **Format Painter** button and click cells **A2** and **A3**. Then in the **Clipboard group**, click the **Format Painter** button to turn it off.

15. Select the range **A5:E5**. Right-click the selected range to display the Mini toolbar. Click the **Bold** and **Center** buttons. From the **Borders** button, select **Thick Bottom Border**. In the **Alignment group**, click the **Middle Align** button.

16. Click cell **A5**. In the **Clipboard group**, double-click the **Format Painter** button and select the range **A10:E10** and cell **A20**. Even though there is no text in the column labels for the range B10:E10, the Format Painter is a quick way to place the bottom border in the cells. Right-click and in the Mini toolbar click the **Format Painter** button to turn it off.

17. Select the range **B6:E6**. Display the Mini toolbar. Click the **Accounting Number Format** button. Click the **Decrease Decimal** button two times. Double-click the **Format Painter** button and drag through the ranges **B8:E8**, **B11:E11**, **B18:E18**, and **B20:E20**. Then in the **Clipboard group**, click the **Format Painter** button to turn it off.

18. Select the range **B7:E7**. Right-click over the selection to display the Mini toolbar. Click the **Comma Style** button. Click the **Decrease Decimal** button two times. Click the **Format Painter** button and select the range **B12:E17**.

19. Select the range **B8:E8**. Press [Ctrl] while you select the range **B18:E18**. Display the Mini toolbar. Click the **Borders** button and then click **Top Border**. Select the range **B20:E20**. Display the Mini toolbar. From the **Borders** list, click **Top and Double Bottom Border**.

20. Click cell **A8** and press [Ctrl] while you click cell **A18**. Right-click one of the selected cells to display the Mini toolbar. Click the **Bold** button. From the **Cells group**, click the **Format** button arrow, and select **AutoFit Column Width**.

(Project 1D–Tacoma Revenues continues on the next page)

Content-Based Assessments

(Project 1D–Tacoma Revenues continued)

21. Select the range **A5:D5**. Press Ctrl and select the range **A20:D20**. On the **Insert tab**, in the **Charts group**, click **Column**. Under **2-D Column**, locate the **Clustered Column** chart and click it.

22. Point to the top border of the chart to display the move pointer and drag the chart to begin in cell **F6**.

23. In the chart, point to the chart title *Tacoma Net Revenue*, right-click, and from the shortcut menu, click **Edit Text**. Delete the text and type **Revenues from Tacoma** Press Enter and then type **First Quarter 2009** Click cell **A1** to deselect the chart.

24. Click the **Excel Help** button. In the **Excel Help** window, in the second column, click **Getting help**. In the list, click **Find the content you need in the Help window**. Scroll down the Excel Help window and under the **What do you want to do?** section, click **Restrict a search to a specific feature area** and read the information. In the Excel Help window click the **Close** button.

25. Point to the **Sheet2 sheet tab** and right-click. From the displayed shortcut menu, click **Delete**. Repeat this process to delete **Sheet3**.

26. On the **Page Layout tab**, in the **Page Setup group**, click the **Dialog Box Launcher** button. In the **Page tab**, under **Orientation**, click **Landscape**, and under **Scaling**, click **Fit to**. Click the **Margins tab**. Under **Center on page**, click **Horizontally** and **Vertically**. Click **Print Preview**. The document fits on one page. Click **Close Print Preview**. On the **Quick Access Toolbar**, click the **Save** button.

27. Check your *Chapter Assignment Sheet* or your *Course Syllabus* or consult your instructor to determine if you are to submit your assignments on paper or electronically. To submit electronically, go to Step 28, and then follow the instructions provided by your instructor. To print your assignment, click the **Office** button, click **Print**. In the **Print** dialog box, click **OK**. If you are directed to submit printed formulas, refer to **Activity 1.12** to do so. If you printed your formulas, be sure to redisplay the worksheet by pressing Ctrl + `.

28. From the **Office** menu, click **Close**. If the dialog box displays asking if you want to save changes, click **No** so that you do not save the changes to Page Setup that you used for printing formulas. **Exit** Excel.

End **You have completed Project 1D** ────────────────────────────

Excel
chapterone

Excel

Mastering Excel

Project 1E — Rentals

In this project, you will apply the skills you practiced from the Objectives in Project 1A.

Objectives: 1. *Start Excel and Navigate a Worksheet;* **2.** *Select Parts of a Worksheet;* **3.** *Enter Data, Construct a Formula, and Use the SUM Function;* **4.** *Format Data, Cells, and Worksheets;* **5.** *Insert a Footer into a Worksheet;* **6.** *Delete Unused Worksheets and Preview and Print a Worksheet; and* **7.** *Print Formulas, Close a Workbook, and Exit Excel.*

In the following Mastering Excel project, you will prepare a report that shows the rental costs for the convention center space used for the June job fairs. Your completed worksheet will look similar to the one shown in Figure 1.77.

For Project 1E, you will need the following file:

New blank Excel workbook

You will save your workbook as
1E_Rentals_Firstname_Lastname

Figure 1.77

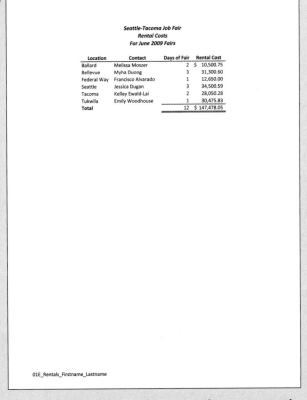

(Project 1E–Rentals continues on the next page)

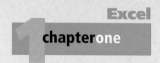
(Project 1E–Rentals continued)

1. **Start** Excel. **Save** the new workbook in your **Excel Chapter 1** folder as **1E_Rentals_Firstname_Lastname**. Add the file name to the left footer and return to **Normal** view.

2. Beginning in cell **A1**, type the following worksheet title:

Seattle-Tacoma Job Fair
Rental Costs
For June 2009 Fairs

3. Beginning in cell **A5**, type the following column titles:

Location	Contact	Days of Fair	Rental Cost

4. Beginning in cell **A6**, type the following data that reports the days and rental costs for each job fair. Adjust the width of the columns so the entries in each column fully display.

Location	Contact	Days of Fair	Rental Cost
Ballard	Melissa Moszer	2	10500.75
Bellevue	Myha Duong	3	31300.60
Federal Way	Francisco Alvarado	1	12650.00
Seattle	Jessica Dugan	3	34500.59
Tacoma	Kelley Ewald-Lai	2	28050.28
Tukwila	Emily Woodhouse	1	30475.83
Total			

5. Click cell **C12**. Type the formula to determine the total number of days of job fairs; use cell references in the formula. Press [Tab]. The total is *12*. Then in cell **D12**, use the **Sum** function to determine the total rental costs. The total is *147478.1*. Depending on the format of your computer, the displayed number of decimal places may vary.

6. Select the column titles—**A5:D5**. Display the Mini toolbar and format the titles with **Bold, Center Alignment**, with a **Bottom Border**. Format cell **D6** and cell **D12** using the **Accounting Number Format**. Format the range **C6:C12** using the **Comma Style** with **no decimals**. Format the range **D7:D11** with **Comma Style**. Format cells **C12** and **D12** with a **Top and Double Bottom Border**. Format cell **A12** with **Bold**.

7. Select the worksheet title—**A1:A3**. Display the Mini toolbar and format the title with **Bold, Italic**, and **Increase Font Size** one size. Select the range **A1:D1**. Display the Mini toolbar and click the **Merge & Center** button. Merge and center the data in cells **A2** and **A3** across to **column D**.

(Project 1E–Rentals continues on the next page)

Content-Based Assessments

Mastering Excel

(Project 1E–Rentals continued)

8. Click the **Page Layout tab** and in the **Page Setup group**, click the **Dialog Box Launcher**. In the **Page Setup** dialog box, click the **Margins tab**. Under the **Center on page section**, click **Horizontally**. Then click **OK**.

9. Right-click the **Sheet2 sheet tab**. In the shortcut menu, click **Delete**. Repeat with **Sheet3**, leaving one worksheet in the workbook. **Save** your work.

10. Check your *Chapter Assignment Sheet* or your *Course Syllabus* or consult your instructor to determine if you are to submit your assignments on paper or electronically. To submit electronically, go to Step 12, and then follow the instructions provided by your instructor.

11. From the **Office** menu, click the **Print** button. In the displayed **Print** dialog box, under **Print range**, verify that the **Active sheet(s)** is selected, and then under **Copies,** verify that the **Number of copies** is **1**. Click **OK.** If you are directed to submit printed formulas, refer to **Activity 1.12** to do so.

12. If you printed your formulas, be sure to redisplay the worksheet by pressing Ctrl + `. From the **Office** menu, click **Close**. If the dialog box displays asking if you want to save changes, click **No** so that you do not save the changes to Page Setup that you used for printing formulas. **Exit** Excel.

End You have completed Project 1E

Content-Based Assessments

Mastering Excel

Project 1F—Expenses

In this project, you will apply the skills you practiced from the Objectives in Project 1B.

Objectives: 8. *Check Spelling and Edit a Worksheet;* **9.** *Enter Data by Range;* **10.** *Create and Copy Formulas;* **11.** *Use Format Painter and Chart Data;* **12.** *Use Microsoft Excel Help.*

In the following Mastering Excel project, Janice Strickland, the employer coordinator for Seattle-Tacoma Job Fair, is reviewing the expenses for the job fairs for the first three months—the first quarter—of the year. You will assist her by preparing a report for the expenses incurred for the job fairs. You will also create a chart that compares the expenses for each job fair. Your completed worksheet will look similar to Figure 1.78.

For Project 1F, you will need the following file:

e01F_Expenses

You will save your workbook as 1F_Expenses_Firstname_Lastname

Figure 1.78

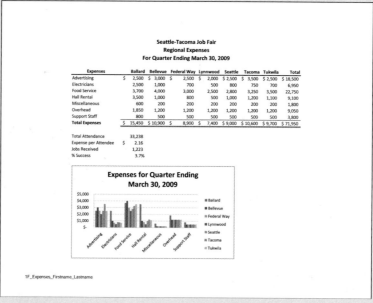

(Project 1F–Expenses continues on the next page)

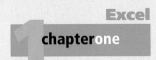

(Project 1F–Expenses continued)

1. **Start** Excel and open the workbook named **e01F_Expenses**. Save it in your **Excel Chapter 1** folder as **01F_Expenses_Firstname_Lastname** Add the file name to the left footer and return to **Normal** view.

2. Spell check the worksheet. Be sure to correct any errors that the Spelling Checker did not find. Cell A17 should display *Jobs Received*.

3. Increase the width of **column A** so the longest data entry, *Expense per Attendee*, fully displays. In the range **F6:H12**, type the following data using the **enter data by range** method:

Seattle	Tacoma	Tukwila
2500	3500	2500
800	750	700
2800	3250	3500
1000	1200	1100
200	200	200
1200	1200	1200
500	500	500

4. In cell **I5,** type **Total** and in cell **A13,** type **Total Expenses**

5. In cell **B13**, enter the formula to determine the total expenses in Ballard. The total is *15450*. Use the fill handle to copy the formula to the right through **column H.**

6. In cell **I6**, enter the formula that provides the total advertising expense for all fairs for the quarter. The total is *18500*. Use the fill handle to copy the formula down through **row 13**.

7. Select **A1:I1** and right-click. In the Mini toolbar, click the **Bold** and **Merge & Center** buttons. Click the **Increase Font Size** button two times. Double-click the **Format Painter** button. Click cells **A2** and **A3**. Then in the **Clipboard group**, click the **Format Painter** button to turn it off.

8. In **row 5**, format the column titles with **Bold** and a **Thick Bottom Border.** Change cell **A5** to **Center** alignment and the range **B5:I5** to **Align Text Right**. Format cell **A13** with **Bold**. Format the ranges **B6:I6** and **B13:I13** with **Accounting Number Format** and **no decimals** and the range **B7:I12** with **Comma Style** and **no decimals**. Place appropriate **borders** around the totals. Increase the width of all columns to fully display all entries.

9. In cell **B16**, enter the expense for each attendee. For planning purposes, Janice wants to know how much the job fairs cost for each person who attends. Divide the total expenses (cell **I13**) by the total number of attendees (cell **B15**). The result is *$2.16*. Be sure cell **B16** is formatted with **Accounting Number Format** with **two decimals**.

10. In cell **B18**, determine the success rate of the job fairs, which is the percentage of attendees who received a job. This rate will be useful in advertising to both attendees and vendors to indicate the successes of the Seattle-Tacoma Job Fair. Divide the jobs received—cell **B17**—by the total attendees—cell **B15**. Format the cell **Percent Style** with **one decimal**.

11. Format cells **B15** and **B17** using **Comma Style** with **no decimals**.

12. Select the range of the worksheet that doesn't include the totals, **A5:H12**, and insert a **2-D Clustered Column** chart. Switch the row and column so the locations display in the legend. Select **Chart Layout 1**. Select the chart title, and type **Expenses for Quarter Ending** press Enter and type **March 30, 2009** The chart title displays on two lines. Click on the chart border and drag until the upper left corner of the

(Project 1F–Expenses continues on the next page)

(Project 1F–Expenses continued)

chart begins in cell **A20**. Click in the worksheet to deselect the chart.

13. Change the worksheet to **Landscape** orientation, **Scaled to fit** on one page and centered **Horizontally** and **Vertically**. Delete unused worksheets and **Save** your work.

14. Check your *Chapter Assignment Sheet* or your *Course Syllabus* or consult your instructor to determine if you are to submit your assignments on paper or electronically. To submit electronically, go to Step 16, and then follow the instructions provided by your instructor.

15. From the **Office** menu, click the **Print** button. In the displayed **Print** dialog box, under **Print range**, verify that the **Active sheet(s)** is selected, and then under **Copies,** verify that the **Number of copies** is **1**. Click **OK.** If you are directed to submit printed formulas, refer to **Activity 1.12** to do so.

16. If you printed your formulas, be sure to redisplay the worksheet by pressing Ctrl + `. From the **Office** menu, click **Close**. If the dialog box displays asking if you want to save changes, click **No** so that you do not save the changes to Page Setup that you used for printing formulas. **Exit** Excel.

End **You have completed Project 1F**

Mastering Excel

Project 1G — Industry Representation

In this project, you will apply the skills you practiced from the Objectives in Projects 1A and 1B.

Objectives: 1. *Start Excel and Navigate a Worksheet;* **2.** *Select Parts of a Worksheet;* **3.** *Enter Data, Construct a Formula, and Use the SUM Function;* **4.** *Format Data, Cells, and Worksheets;* **5.** *Insert a Footer into a Worksheet;* **6.** *Delete Unused Worksheets and Preview and Print a Worksheet;* **7.** *Print Formulas, Close a Workbook, and Exit Excel;* **8.** *Check Spelling and Edit a Worksheet;* **9.** *Enter Data by Range;* **10.** *Create and Copy Formulas;* **11.** *Use Format Painter and Chart Data;* **12.** *Use Microsoft Excel Help.*

In the following Mastering Excel project, you will prepare a worksheet for Janice Strickland, who coordinates the Seattle-Tacoma Job Fair. Janice is responsible for attracting new exhibitors to the fair. She wants to know the pattern of exhibitor participation by industry group that participated in the April job fairs. You will gather that information into a worksheet for Janice. Your completed worksheet will look similar to Figure 1.79.

For Project 1G, you will need the following file:

e01G_Industry_Representation

You will save your workbook as
1G_Industry_Representation_Firstname_Lastname

Figure 1.79

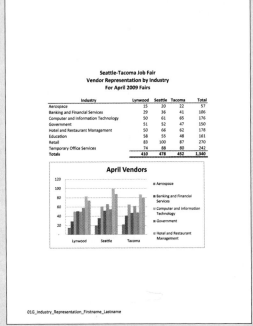

01G_Industry_Representation_Firstname_Lastname

(Project 1G–Industry Representation continues on the next page)

Content-Based Assessments

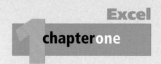
(Project 1G–Industry Representation continued)

1. **Start** Excel and open the workbook named **e01G_Industry_Representation**. Save it in your **Excel Chapter 1** folder as **1G_Industry_Representation_Firstname_Lastname** Add the file name to the footer.

2. Increase the width of **column A** to fully display the types of industries.

3. Run the Spelling Checker to correct misspelled words. Correct any errors that may remain that Spelling Checker could not locate.

4. In the range **B6:D13**, type the following data using the **enter data by range** method:

Industry	Lynnwood	Seattle	Tacoma
Aerospace	15	20	22
Banking and Financial Services	29	36	41
Computer and Information Technology	50	61	65
Government	51	52	47
Hotel and Restaurant Management	50	66	62
Education	58	55	48
Retail	83	100	87
Temporary Office Services	74	88	80

5. In cell **E5**, type **Total** In **row 14**, enter the formulas to determine the total number of exhibitors for each job fair location. In cell **E6**, use the SUM function to determine the total participants for the Aerospace industry. Use the fill-handle to fill the formula down to cell **E14**. In **row 14**, format the totals with **Bold** and appropriate **borders**.

6. Format the three-line worksheet title with **Bold** and **Increase Font Size** two times. **Merge & Center** the three-line worksheet title across **columns A:E**.

7. Format the column titles with **Bold** with a **Bottom Border**. **Center** the column title in cell **A5**, and **Align Text Right** the other column titles. Format cell **A14** with **Bold**. Be sure the column widths are adjusted to fully display the column titles. Format the numbers in the worksheet for **Comma Style** with **zero decimals**.

8. **Center** the worksheet both **Horizontally** and **Vertically** with **Portrait Orientation**. Check the accuracy of your entries.

9. Select the range **A5:D13** and create a **2-D Clustered Column** chart that displays the vendor representation for the April job fairs. Select **Chart Layout 1**. **Switch Rows/Columns**. Move the chart so that it displays below the worksheet data. Enter a chart title that reads **April Vendors**

10. Return to cell **A1**. Delete unused worksheets and **Save** your work.

11. Check your *Chapter Assignment Sheet* or your *Course Syllabus* or consult your instructor to determine if you are to submit your assignments on paper or electronically. To submit electronically, go to Step 13, and then follow the instructions provided by your instructor.

(Project 1G–Industry Representation continues on the next page)

Content-Based Assessments

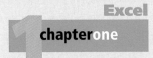
(Project 1G–Industry Representation continued)

12. From the **Office** menu, click the **Print** button. In the displayed **Print** dialog box, under **Print range**, verify that the **Active sheet(s)** is selected, and then under **Copies,** verify that the **Number of copies** is **1**. Click **OK.** If you are directed to submit printed formulas, refer to **Activity 1.12** to do so.

13. If you printed your formulas, be sure to redisplay the worksheet by pressing [Ctrl] + [`]. From the **Office** menu, click **Close**. If the dialog box displays asking if you want to save changes, click **No** so that you do not save the changes to Page Setup that you used for printing formulas. **Exit** Excel.

End **You have completed Project 1G** ————————————————————————

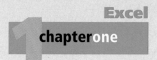

Project 1H — Lynnwood Hours

In this project, you will apply the skills you practiced from the Objectives in Projects 1A and 1B.

Objectives: 1. *Start Excel and Navigate a Worksheet;* **2.** *Select Parts of a Worksheet;* **3.** *Enter Data, Construct a Formula, and Use the SUM Function;* **4.** *Format Data, Cells, and Worksheets;* **5.** *Insert a Footer into a Worksheet;* **6.** *Delete Unused Worksheets and Preview and Print a Worksheet;* **7.** *Print Formulas, Close a Workbook, and Exit Excel;* **8.** *Check Spelling and Edit a Worksheet;* **9.** *Enter Data by Range;* **10.** *Create and Copy Formulas;* **11.** *Use Format Painter and Chart Data;* **12.** *Use Microsoft Excel Help.*

In the following Mastering Excel project, you will assist Janice Strickland by preparing the payroll report to send to the accounting department for the March 7 job fair in Lynnwood. Your saved workbook will look like Figure 1.80.

For Project 1H, you will need the following file:

New blank Excel workbook

You will save your workbook as
1H_Lynnwood_Hours_Firstname_Lastname

Figure 1.80

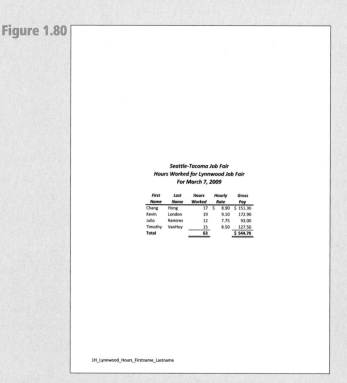

(Project 1H–Lynnwood Hours continues on the next page)

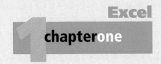

(Project 1H—Lynnwood Hours continued)

1. **Start** Excel and open to a new Excel workbook. Save it in your **Excel Chapter 1** folder as **1H_Lynnwood_Hours_Firstname_Lastname** Add the file name to the footer.

2. In the range **A1:A3**, type the following:

Seattle-Tacoma Job Fair
Hours Worked for Lynnwood Job Fair
For March 7, 2009

3. Select the range **A5:E9** and type the following column and row titles and the data using the **enter data by range** method:

First Name	Last Name	Hours Worked	Hourly Rate	Gross Pay
Chang	Hong	17	8.9	
Kevin	London	19	9.1	
Julio	Ramirez	12	7.75	
Timothy	VanHoy	15	8.5	

4. Format the column titles with **Bold**, **Italic,** and **Wrap Text**. **Center** the data both **Horizontally** and **Vertically** within the cell. Place a **Thick Bottom Border** under the titles.

5. In cell **E6**, create a formula to determine the gross pay for each employee. Gross pay is the number of hours worked times the hourly rate. Use the **fill handle** to copy the formula into the range **E7:E9**.

6. In cell **A10**, type **Total** In cell **C10**, create a formula using the plus key ⊞ to add the hours worked, and in cell **E10**, use the **Sum** function to enter the total gross pay. Format the entries in **row 10** with **Bold**. (Do not total the Hourly Rate column.)

7. Format the two columns that display money amounts using **two decimals**, **Accounting Number Format**, and **Comma Style Format**. Use a **Top and Double Bottom Border** for the totals. Format the hours worked in **column C** using **Comma Style** with **no decimals**. Note: Even though the number in cell **C10** is not a money amount, use the **Top and Double Bottom Border** to show this is a total.

8. Format the three-line title with **Bold** and **Italic**. Increase the **font size** two times and **Merge & Center** the three title rows.

9. Check the spelling of your data entries and delete unused worksheets.

10. **Center** the worksheet both **Horizontally** and **Vertically** on the page. **Save** your work.

11. Check your *Chapter Assignment Sheet* or your *Course Syllabus* or consult your instructor to determine if you are to submit your assignments on paper or electronically. To submit electronically, go to Step 13, and then follow the instructions provided by your instructor.

(Project 1H—Lynnwood Hours continues on the next page)

Content-Based Assessments

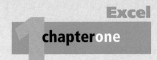

(Project 1H–Lynnwood Hours continued)

12. From the **Office** menu, click the **Print** button. In the displayed **Print** dialog box, under **Print range**, verify that the **Active sheet(s)** is selected, and then under **Copies,** verify that the **Number of copies** is **1.** Click **OK.** If you are directed to submit printed formulas, refer to **Activity 1.12** to do so.

13. If you printed your formulas, be sure to redisplay the worksheet by pressing Ctrl + ⌐. From the **Office** menu, click **Close**. If the dialog box displays asking if you want to save changes, click **No** so that you do not save the changes to Page Setup that you used for printing formulas. **Exit** Excel.

 End **You have completed Project 1H**

Content-Based Assessments

Excel

chapterone

Mastering Excel

Project 1I—Income Statement

In this project, you will apply the skills you practiced from all the Objectives in Projects 1A and 1B.

In the following Mastering Excel project, you will assist Michael Dawson, executive director of Seattle-Tacoma Job Fair, to create a report that shows the income generated for the job fairs for the first quarter of the year. The income statement will report the income and expenses for each fair location and also provide the totals for the quarter. In addition, you will chart the income for the quarter ending March 31, 2009. Your saved worksheet will look similar to Figure 1.81.

For Project 1I, you will need the following file:

e01I_Income_Statement

**You will save your workbook as
1I_Income_Statement_Firstname_Lastname**

Figure 1.81

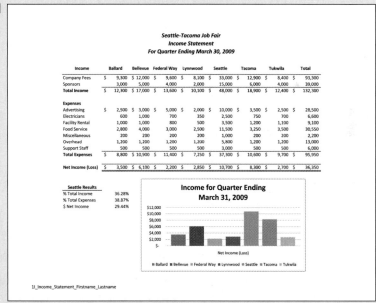

(Project 1I–Income Statement continues on the next page)

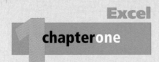

(Project 1I–Income Statement continued)

1. **Start** Excel and open **e01I_Income_Statement**. **Save** the workbook in your **Excel Chapter 1** folder and name it **1I_Income_Statement_Firstname_Lastname** Add the file name to the footer.

2. In the range **A1:A3**, type the following:

Seattle-Tacoma Job Fair
Income Statement
For Quarter Ending March 31, 2009

3. In the range **D5:I5**, type the following column titles. Press ⟨Tab⟩ after each entry to move to the next column:

Federal Way	Lynnwood	Seattle	Tacoma	Tukwila	Total

4. In the range **D6:H7**, type the following using the **enter data by range** method:

Federal Way	Lynwood	Seattle	Tacoma	Tukwila
9600	8100	33000	12900	8400
4000	2000	15000	6000	4000

5. In cell **A8**, type **Total Income** and in the cell **A10**, type **Expenses**

6. In the range **D11:H17**, type the following data using the **enter data by range** method:

5000	2000	10000	3500	2500
700	350	2500	750	700
800	500	3500	1200	1100
3000	2500	11500	3250	3500
200	200	1000	200	200
1200	1200	5800	1200	1200
500	500	3000	500	500

7. In cell **A18**, type **Total Expenses** and in cell **A20**, type **Net Income (Loss)** Adjust **column A** so that the longest entry fits in the cell. Run **Spelling Checker.** Correct cell **A16** to read **Overhead**

8. Format cell **A1** with **Bold**, **Italic**, and **Increase Font Size** two times. **Merge & Center** the row across the worksheet data. Use **Format Painter** to copy the format in cell **A1** to cells **A2** and **A3**.

9. To cells **A8**, **A10**, **A18**, and **A20**, apply **Bold** emphasis. To the range **A5:I5**, apply **Bold** and **Wrap Text**. **Center** and **Middle Align** the text within the cell. If needed, adjust column widths to fully display cell contents. In **row 5**, apply the **Bottom Border** under the **column titles**.

10. In **rows 8** and **18**, calculate the *Total Income* and *Total Expenses*. In **column I**, use the **fill handle** to calculate the total for each row. In cell **B20**, enter a formula that subtracts the *Total Expenses* for *Ballard* from the *Total Income* for *Ballard*. Use the **fill handle** to copy the formula through cell **I20**.

(Project 1I–Income Statement continues on the next page)

Content-Based Assessments

(Project 1I–Income Statement continued)

11. Select the numeric values in **rows 6**, **8**, **11**, **18**, and **20**, and then apply **Accounting Number Format** with no decimals. Use **Comma Style** with **no decimals** for the other numbers in the worksheet. Add a **Bottom Border** to rows **7** and **17** to indicate the amounts above these lines will be included in the total. In the net income cells—**B20:I20**—add a **Top and Double Bottom Border**.

12. Because the Seattle job fair is the largest, Michael requests additional data. In the range **A23:A26**, type the following row titles:

Seattle Results
% Total Income
% Total Expenses
% Net Income

13. Use **Help** to gather information about calculating percentages. In the **Help** text box, type **Percentages** and press ⏎. In the displayed list, click *Calculate percentages*. Under *What do you want to do?* click *Calculate percentage if you know the total and the amount*. Then read the topic so you will be able to calculate the percentage when you know the total and the amount for Steps 14, 15, and 16.

14. In cell **B24**, use cell references to enter the formula to determine the percentage of total income that Seattle fairs generated. Divide the Seattle total income—cell **F8**—by the total income for all fairs—cell **I8**.

15. In cell **B25**, use cell references to enter the formula to determine the percentage of total expenses that Seattle fairs generated. Divide the Seattle total expenses by the total expenses for all fairs.

16. In cell **B26**, use cell references to enter the formula to determine the percentage of net income that Seattle fairs generated. Divide the Seattle net income by the net income for all fairs. Be sure to use cell references in the formula. Format cells **B24:B26** with **Percent Style** and **two decimals**.

17. Use **Format Painter** to copy the format of cell **A5** to cell **A23**.

18. Use Ctrl to select the following nonadjacent ranges: **A5:H5** and **A20:H20**. Insert a **2-D Clustered Column** chart. Position the upper left corner of the chart in cell **C22**, to the right of the percentage calculations and below the worksheet data. Use **Chart Layout 3**. Change the title to **Income for Quarter Ending** on one line and **March 31, 2009** on the next line. **Switch row/column**. Click cell **A1** to deselect the chart.

19. **Center** the worksheet and chart **Horizontally** and **Vertically** on the page in **Landscape** orientation and **Scale to fit** on one page. Delete unused worksheets and **Save** your work. Preview the worksheet to determine that it is accurate and presented professionally.

20. Check your *Chapter Assignment Sheet* or your *Course Syllabus* or consult your instructor to determine if you are to submit your assignments on paper or electronically. To submit electronically, go to Step 22, and then follow the instructions provided by your instructor.

(Project 1I–Income Statement continues on the next page)

Content-Based Assessments

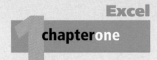
(Project 1I–Income Statement continued)

21. From the **Office** menu, click the **Print** button. In the displayed **Print** dialog box, under **Copies,** verify that the **Number of copies** is **1.** Click **OK.** If you are directed to submit printed formulas, refer to **Activity 1.12** to do so.

22. If you printed your formulas, be sure to redisplay the worksheet by pressing Ctrl + ' . From the **Office** menu, click **Close**. If the dialog box displays asking if you want to save changes, click **No** so that you do not save the changes to Page Setup that you used for printing formulas. **Exit** Excel.

End **You have completed Project 1I**

Content-Based Assessments

Business Running Case

Project 1J — Business Running Case

In this project, you will apply the skills you have practiced from the Objectives in Projects 1A and 1B.

From My Computer, navigate to the student files that accompany this textbook. In the folder **03_business_running_case**, locate and open the folder for this chapter. Open and print the instructions for this project, which are provided to you in Adobe PDF format. Follow the instructions and use the skills you have gained thus far to assist the managers of the Grand Department Store to meet the challenges of keeping records for a large department store.

End **You have completed Project 1J**

Outcomes-Based Assessments

Rubric

The following outcomes-based assessments are *open-ended assessments*. That is, there is no specific correct result; your result will depend on your approach to the information provided. Make *Professional Quality* your goal. Use the following scoring rubric to guide you in *how* to approach the problem and then to evaluate *how well* your approach solves the problem.

The *criteria*—Software Mastery, Content, Format and Layout, and Process—represent the knowledge and skills you have gained that you can apply to solving the problem. The *levels of performance*—Professional Quality, Approaching Professional Quality, or Needs Quality Improvements—help you and your instructor evaluate your result.

	Your completed project is of Professional Quality if you:	Your completed project is Approaching Professional Quality if you:	Your completed project Needs Quality Improvements if you:
1-Software Mastery	Choose and apply the most appropriate skills, tools, and features and identify efficient methods to solve the problem.	Choose and apply some appropriate skills, tools, and features, but not in the most efficient manner.	Choose inappropriate skills, tools, or features, or are inefficient in solving the problem.
2-Content	Construct a solution that is clear and well organized, contains content that is accurate, appropriate to the audience and purpose, and is complete. Provide a solution that contains no errors of spelling, grammar, or style.	Construct a solution in which some components are unclear, poorly organized, inconsistent, or incomplete. Misjudge the needs of the audience. Have some errors in spelling, grammar, or style, but the errors do not detract from comprehension.	Construct a solution that is unclear, incomplete, or poorly organized, containing some inaccurate or inappropriate content; and contains many errors of spelling, grammar, or style. Do not solve the problem.
3-Format and Layout	Format and arrange all elements to communicate information and ideas, clarify function, illustrate relationships, and indicate relative importance.	Apply appropriate format and layout features to some elements, but not others. Overuse features, causing minor distraction.	Apply format and layout that does not communicate information or ideas clearly. Do not use format and layout features to clarify function, illustrate relationships, or indicate relative importance. Use available features excessively, causing distraction.
4-Process	Use an organized approach that integrates planning, development, self-assessment, revision, and reflection.	Demonstrate an organized approach in some areas, but not others; or, use an insufficient process of organization throughout.	Do not use an organized approach to solve the problem.

Problem Solving

Project 1K — Venue Rates

In this project, you will construct a solution by applying any combination of the skills you practiced from the Objectives in Projects 1A and 1B.

For Project 1K, you will need the following file:

e01K_Venue_Rates

**You will save your workbook as
1K_Venue_Rates_Firstname_Lastname**

Michael Dawson, the executive director of Seattle-Tacoma Job Fair, asked you to edit and complete a worksheet that identifies the amount to charge for display booths. The worksheet summarizes information about the size of display space available and the cost per square foot at each location. Seattle-Tacoma rents space from conference centers in each locality. In turn, display space is rented to the exhibitors, who provide attendees with information about their firm. The exhibitors rely on Seattle-Tacoma to advertise the fair and bring job applicants directly to them.

You will edit the worksheet that identifies the locations for the Seattle-Tacoma Job Fair and their rental fees. This worksheet indicates the total space available at each location and the rental cost for that space.

Open the **e01K_Venue_Rates** and save it as **1K_Venue_Rates_Firstname_Lastname**

To determine the Cost per Square Foot, divide the total Rental Cost for the location by the Square Feet Available. Seattle-Tacoma Job Fair then adds 12 percent to that amount to cover its costs, which is the markup. By adding the cost per square foot and the amount of the markup together, you can determine the amount to charge per square foot for each booth rented. Totals are not needed in this worksheet; it is a list of information that will be used to determine charges for exhibiting at the job fairs.

Using skills practiced in this chapter, format the worksheet, including appropriate formats for numbers such as dollar signs and commas, and for text, including changes to fonts, font sizes, and emphasis, as well as placement on the page. All amounts except Square Feet are money amounts, which you will display with two decimals.

Complete a chart that compares the cost per square foot for each location. You will use the location and charge per square foot for the chart. Provide an appropriate chart title and include a legend.

Add the file name to the footer, spell check the worksheet, and delete unused sheets. Save your work and submit it as directed.

End You have completed Project 1K

Outcomes-Based Assessments

Problem Solving

Project 1L—Hires

In this project, you will construct a solution by applying any combination of the skills you practiced from the Objectives in Projects 1A and 1B.

For Project 1L, you will need the following file:

New blank Excel workbook

You will save your workbook as
1L_Hires_Firstname_Lastname

Michael Dawson, executive director of Seattle-Tacoma Job Fair, would like to review the success of the job fairs over the last five years (2005–2009) and has asked you to prepare an Excel worksheet that summarizes the number of hires that resulted from each job fair. You will then chart the data to show the total hires for each year by each location.

Create a worksheet title that includes the name of the organization, what this worksheet reports, and a date line that includes the length of time and the ending date—December 31, 2009.

Location	Year 2005	Year 2006	Year 2007	Year 2008	Year 2009
Ballard	212	260	302	394	350
Bellevue	688	697	832	780	673
Kirkland	276	325	390	323	340
Lynnwood	240	309	196	299	312
Seattle	879	1163	1205	1404	1312
Tacoma	508	546	562	585	603
Tukwila	583	595	607	567	593

Create formulas to determine the total number of hires at each location and for each year. Complete a chart that compares the total hires by year for each location. Select the entire worksheet except for the totals to create the chart. Provide an appropriate chart title. Select a chart layout that includes a legend.

Using the skills you practiced in this chapter, format the worksheet, including appropriate formats for numbers (such as commas) and for text, such as changes to fonts (types, styles, and sizes), as well as placement on the page. Include a footer that identifies the file name. Check the spelling and delete unneeded worksheets. Save your workbook as **1L_Hires_Firstname_Lastname** and submit as directed.

End You have completed Project 1L

Outcomes-Based Assessments

Problem Solving

Project 1M—Cost per Attendee

In this project, you will construct a solution by applying any combination of the skills you practiced from the Objectives in Projects 1A and 1B.

For Project 1M, you will need the following file:

New blank Excel workbook

You will save your workbook as
1M_Cost_Attendee_Firstname_Lastname

Michael Dawson, the executive director of Seattle-Tacoma Job Fair, would like to determine the actual costs for each attendee. This information will help him decide if exhibitors should be charged a higher rental fee. Prepare a worksheet that displays the attendance and expenses for the job fairs over the last five years (2005–2009) using the information in the following table.

Include a three-line title. For the date line, include the length of time and the ending date—December 31, 2009.

Job Fairs	Year 2005	Year 2006	Year 2007	Year 2008	Year 2009
Attendance	7873	6148	9683	10204	10657
Expenses	36250	30550	43335	47890	46060
Cost per Attendee					

Create formulas to determine the cost for each attendee for each year. The cost per attendee is determined by dividing the expenses by the attendance. Totals are not needed in this worksheet.

Using the skills you practiced in this chapter, format the worksheet, including appropriate formats for numbers such as dollar signs and commas, and for text, including changes to fonts, font sizes, and font styles, as well as placement on the page.

Include a chart on the worksheet that compares the cost per attendee for each year of the job fair. You will use the column titles and the cost per attendee information for the chart. Add an appropriate title to the chart.

Add the file name to the footer, check the spelling, and delete unneeded worksheets. Save the workbook as **1M_Cost_Attendee_Firstname_Lastname** and submit it as directed.

End You have completed Project 1M

Outcomes-Based Assessments

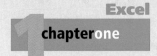
Problem Solving

Project 1N — Phone Costs

In this project, you will construct a solution by applying any combination of the skills you practiced from the Objectives in Projects 1A and 1B.

For Project 1N, you will need the following file:

New blank Excel workbook

You will save your workbook as
1N_Phone_Costs_Firstname_Lastname

Occasionally a location is blocked from receiving a cell phone signal so public phones need to be placed at each exhibit site. Prepare a worksheet that summarizes those phone charges and determines the cost for each minute of use.

Include a three-line title for the worksheet. For the date, use **For Month Ending March 31, 2009** Record the location, amount charged, and number of minutes used for the following locations:

Lynnwood: Charged $93.50 for 850 minutes
Tacoma: Charged $135.35 for 1,035 minutes
Tukwila: Charged $43 for 500 minutes

Create formulas to determine the cost per minute at each location. Provide totals for the phone charges and number of minutes. Also include the total cost per minute for all three locations for the month. You will divide the total amount by the total minutes.

Using the skills you practiced in this chapter, format the worksheet, including appropriate formats for numbers such as dollar signs and commas, and for text, including changes to fonts, font sizes, and font styles, as well as placement on the page. Add the file name to the footer, check the spelling, and delete unneeded worksheets. Save the workbook as **1N_Phone_Costs_Firstname_Lastname** and submit it as directed.

End You have completed Project 1N

Problem Solving

Project 10 — March Income

In this project, you will construct a solution by applying any combination of the skills you practiced from the Objectives in Projects 1A and 1B.

> **For Project 10, you will need the following file:**
>
> New blank Excel workbook

You will save your workbook as
10_March_Income_Firstname_Lastname

Each month, Seattle-Tacoma Job Fair prepares an Income Statement that summarizes the income and expenses for the month and provides the Net Income. The Net Income is the amount of the expenses subtracted from the total income. You will prepare that statement for the month of March.

Be sure to use a three-line title for the worksheet. For the date, indicate the length of time for the worksheet and the ending date, which is the last day of March 2009. The income and expenses for each location are as follows:

Ballard: Income $31,033.33; Expenses $26,908.33
Bellevue: Income $31,575; Expenses $23,741.67
Federal Way: Income $21,975.36; Expenses $18,895.40
Kirkland: Income $11,033.33; Expenses $10,604.17
Lynnwood: Income $32,841.67; Expenses $28,733.33
Seattle: Income $40,350; Expenses $35,108
Tacoma: Income $31,575; Expenses $21,883.40
Tukwila: Income $21,025; Expenses $17,808.33

Create formulas to determine the net income for each location and the totals of the income, expenses, and net income for the month. Net income is the amount that income exceeds expenses. Using the skills you practiced in this chapter, format the worksheet, including appropriate formats for numbers such as dollar signs and commas, and for text, including changes to fonts, font sizes, and font styles, as well as placement on the page. Add the file name to the footer, check the spelling, and delete unneeded worksheets. Save the workbook as **10_March_Income_Firstname_Lastname**

End You have completed Project 10 ——————————

Outcomes-Based Assessments

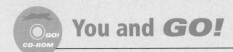
Project 1P — You and *GO!*

In this project, you will construct a solution by applying any combination of the Objectives found in Projects 1A and 1B.

From My Computer, navigate to the student files that accompany this textbook. In the folder **04_you_and_go**, locate and open the folder for this chapter. Open and print the instructions for this project, which are provided to you in Adobe PDF format. Follow the instructions to display your expenses over a three-month period.

 You have completed Project 1P ——————————————

GO! with Help

Project 1Q — *GO!* with Help

The Microsoft Excel Help is extensive and can help you as you work. In this chapter, you used the Quick Access Toolbar on several occasions. You can customize the Quick Access Toolbar by adding buttons that you use regularly, making them quickly available to you from any tab on the Ribbon. In this exercise, you will use Help to find out how to add buttons.

1. **Start** Excel. At the far right end of the Ribbon, click the **Microsoft Office Excel Help** button 🔘.

2. In the **Search** box, type **Quick Access Toolbar** and then press (Enter).

3. From the list of search results, click **Customize the Quick Access Toolbar**.

4. Click each of the links to find out how to add buttons from the Ribbon and from the **Options** dialog box.

5. When you are through, **Close** the Excel Help window, and then **Exit** Excel.

 You have completed Project 1Q ——————————————

chapter two

Using Multiple-Sheet Workbooks

OBJECTIVES

At the end of this chapter you will be able to:

1. Work with a Multiple-Sheet Workbook
2. Enter a Series
3. Copy and Paste Cell Contents
4. Copy and Paste with the Office Clipboard
5. Total the Worksheet Range and Enter a Grand Total
6. Format a Multiple-Sheet Workbook Group
7. Insert Columns and Rows in Multiple Worksheets

8. Copy a Worksheet
9. Create Formulas with Absolute Cell References and Copy Formats
10. Find and Replace Text and Hide and Unhide Columns
11. Conduct a What-If Analysis and Use Statistical Functions
12. Create Accurate Worksheets with Accuracy Tools

OUTCOMES

Mastering these objectives will enable you to:

PROJECT 2A
Work with Multiple-Sheet Workbooks

PROJECT 2B
Create a Worksheet with Absolute Cell References and Correct Errors in a Worksheet

Eastern Cape Inn

Cape Charles is a quiet beach town located in the Eastern Shore area of Virginia, north of Virginia Beach. The Eastern Cape Inn has 20 rooms and is often booked to capacity with returning regular guests who appreciate its comfort, beautiful beachfront location, and the warmth and hospitality of its owners. The dining room, where a full homemade breakfast is served each morning, the expansive porch, and some guest rooms overlook the Chesapeake Bay. Cape Charles is located approximately 200 miles from Washington, DC, Philadelphia, and Baltimore and makes an excellent base for day-trips to Williamsburg, Jamestown, and Assateague Island. Several local restaurants serve outstanding fresh seafood, and the tourist area of Virginia Beach is only a short drive away.

Using Multiple-Sheet Workbooks

When you open Excel, three worksheets are available in the same workbook. When worksheets are grouped, you can enter data or make formatting changes to all the grouped worksheets simultaneously.

In this chapter, you will practice working with multiple worksheets in an Excel workbook. You will insert worksheets, use features to quickly copy and paste data and formulas, insert rows and columns, create formulas using different techniques so they can be accurately copied, use tools that check the accuracy of the worksheet, review the steps needed to plan a worksheet, and conduct a what-if analysis.

Project 2A **Income from Lodging**

In Activities 2.1 through 2.11, you will report the Income from Lodging for the first quarter of the year for Debra Chandler-Walker and Derek Walker, owners of Eastern Cape Inn. You will use multiple worksheets in a workbook; create a series; and cut, copy, and paste data. You will create a formula that displays the grand total of a worksheet. Your completed workbook will look similar to Figure 2.1.

For Project 2A, you will need the following files:

New blank Excel workbook
e02A_Income_External_Data

You will save your workbook as
2A_Income_From_Lodging_Firstname_Lastname

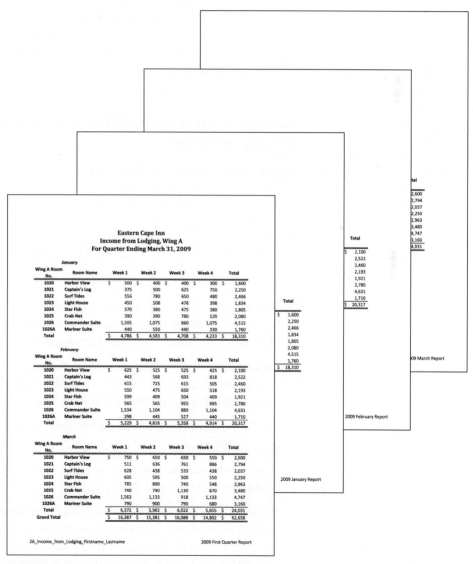

Figure 2.1
Project 2A—Income From Lodging

Objective 1
Use a Multiple-Sheet Workbook

Recall that Excel opens a workbook that contains three worksheets that are saved in one file. Worksheets can be added or deleted from the workbook. The number of worksheets that can be added is limited only by the memory of your computer. Worksheets can be grouped; when grouped, data and formats are entered in all worksheets simultaneously. Worksheet tab names can be changed to identify the worksheet data, and color can be added to a worksheet tab.

Activity 2.1 Inserting a Worksheet and Entering and Formatting Data in a Multiple Sheet Workbook

By default, a workbook contains three worksheets. Recall that you can *navigate* (move) among worksheets by clicking the *sheet tabs*, which identify each worksheet in a workbook. When more than one worksheet of a workbook is selected—*grouped*—data and formatting are entered in all worksheets at the same time. In this activity, you will add a worksheet to a workbook, group the worksheets, and enter and format a title in all worksheets in the workbook.

Note — Comparing Your Screen with the Figures in This Textbook

Your screen will match the figures shown in this textbook if you set your screen resolution to 1024 × 768. At other resolutions, your screen will closely resemble, but not match, the figures shown. To view your screen's resolution, on the Windows desktop, right-click in a blank area, click Properties, and then click the Settings tab.

1 **Start** Excel. Click the **Office button** , and from the displayed menu, click **Save As** and navigate to the drive on which you will be storing your folders and workbooks. Click the **Create New Folder button** . In the displayed **New Folder** dialog box, in the **Name** box, type **Excel Chapter 2** and then click **OK**. In the **File name** area, type **2A_Income_From_Lodging_Firstname_Lastname** and then click **Save**.

2 To the right of the **Sheet3 sheet tab**, click the **Insert Worksheet button** . Alternatively, from the Home tab, in the Cells group, click the **Insert button arrow**, and from the menu click Insert Sheet. Compare your screen with Figure 2.2.

Recall that a workbook opens with three worksheets that are consecutively numbered. You have added a new worksheet that displays the name *Sheet4*. Note also that Sheet4 is the *active worksheet*—the worksheet where text and data will be entered. The sheet tab of the active sheet is highlighted, while the sheet tabs of the inactive sheets are dimmed.

Figure 2.2

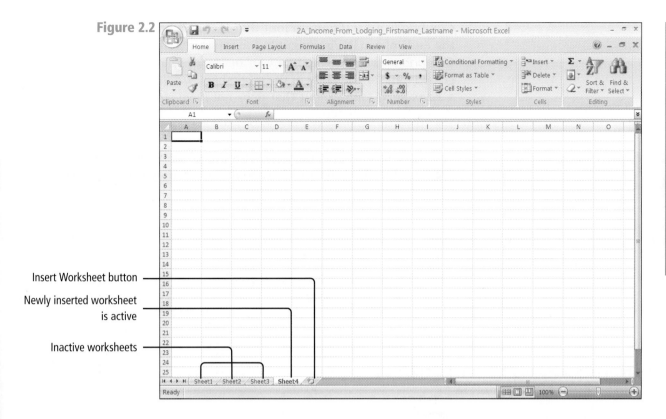

Insert Worksheet button

Newly inserted worksheet is active

Inactive worksheets

3 Hold down the ⬆Shift key while you click the **Sheet1 sheet tab**. Alternatively, on the Sheet4 sheet tab, right-click, and click Select All Sheets. At the top of your screen, look at the title bar and notice that *[Group]* displays.

All the worksheets are selected, as indicated by *[Group]* in the title bar, and the sheet tab names are highlighted. Data that you enter or edit on the active sheet will also be entered or edited in the same manner on all the selected sheets in the same cells.

4 In cell **A1**, type **Eastern Cape Inn** which is the name of the organization. In cell **A2**, type **Income from Lodging, Wing A** the title of the worksheet. In cell **A3**, type the date line **For Quarter Ending March 31, 2009** and then press Enter to confirm the entry.

Because these worksheets are grouped, the entry is made on each of the worksheets, even though it is typed only once.

When the worksheet information covers a period of time, it is generally accepted in a financial report to include that length of time and the ending date in the date line. The worksheets you are creating report the income from lodging that was earned for a quarter—three-month period of time—that ends on March 31, 2009.

5 Select the worksheet title—cells **A1:A3**. On the **Home tab**, in the

Font group, click the **Font button arrow** [Calibri ▾] , use the scroll bar to scroll down the font list and as you do so, point to some of the font choices. Notice *Live Preview* displays the selected font in cells A1:A3, although the menu covers most of the data. Point to **Algerian** and compare your screen with Figure 2.3. Locate and click **Cambria**.

Cambria is a **serif** font—a font that includes small line extensions on the ends of the letters to guide the eye in reading from left to right. *Cambria* is the suggested font for headings, and *Calibri* is the suggested font for the body of the worksheet. *Calibri*, the default font, is a **sans serif** font—a font that does not have small line extensions on the ends of the letters.

Live Preview is a technology that displays the results of applying an editing or formatting change as you move the pointer over the items presented in the gallery or list. Font choices may vary depending on your computer.

List of font styles

Figure 2.3

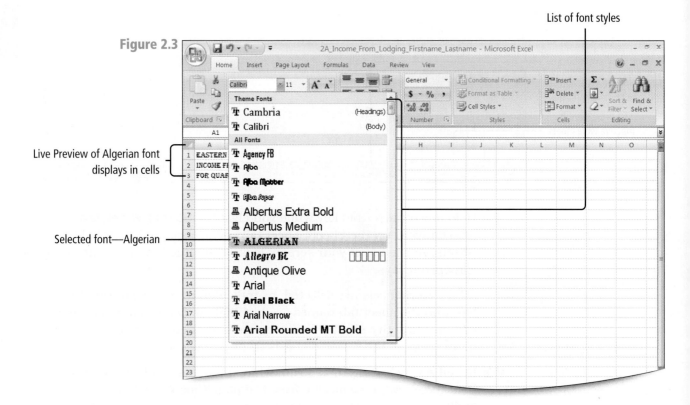

Live Preview of Algerian font displays in cells

Selected font—Algerian

6 In the **Font group**, click the **Bold button** B . Click the **Font Size arrow** 11 ▾ , and then click **14.** Alternatively, from the Mini toolbar, click the **Font Size arrow**, and then click 14.

Specific font sizes are selected in the Font Size list. Recall you can use the Increase and Decrease Font Size buttons to change font sizes in preselected increments.

7 On the status bar, click the **Page Layout button** ▣ and scroll to the end of the worksheet. Click in the **Left Footer area**, and then from the **Header & Footer Elements group**, click the **File Name button**. Click in the **Right Footer area**. From the **Header & Footer Elements group**, click the **Sheet Name button**. Click in any cell in the worksheet and on the status bar, click the **Normal button** ▦ , and then press Ctrl + Home to return to cell **A1**.

Recall that you place the workbook file name in the left footer. Place the worksheet name in the right footer to identify the specific worksheet of the workbook. When a workbook contains more than one worksheet, it is recommended that you include the sheet name in the footer.

8 Click the **Sheet2 sheet tab** and compare your screen with Figure 2.4.

The information was entered simultaneously in all worksheets because they were grouped. When you click a sheet, that sheet becomes active and the worksheets are no longer grouped; the title bar indication—*Group*—no longer displays, but the title remains the same.

Title bar—worksheets not grouped

Figure 2.4

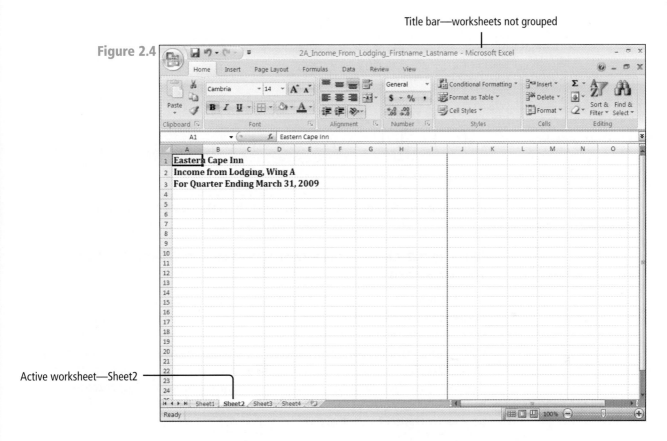

Active worksheet—Sheet2

9 In **Sheet2**, click cell **A3**. In the **Formula Bar**, select the words **Quarter Ending March** and type **Month Ending January** Click **Sheet3** and change the date in cell **A3** to read **For Month Ending February 28, 2009** Click **Sheet4**, and in cell **A3**, change the date to read **For Month Ending March 31, 2009** Compare your screen with Figure 2.5.

Figure 2.5

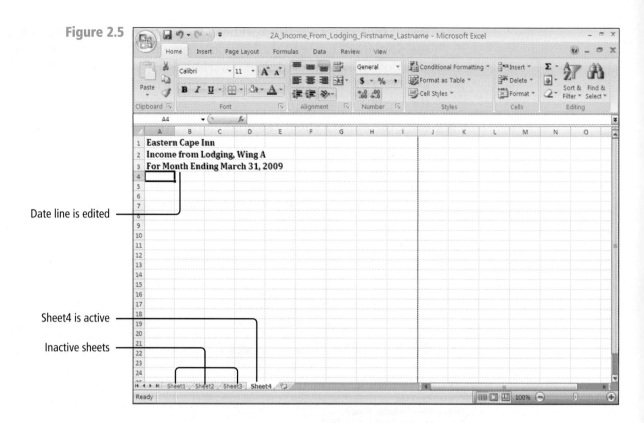

Date line is edited

Sheet4 is active

Inactive sheets

10 Click the **Sheet1 sheet tab**, and then **Save** 💾 your workbook.

Activity 2.2 Changing the Format of Worksheet Tabs and Using the Tab Scrolling Buttons

Excel names the first worksheet in a workbook *Sheet1* and each additional worksheet in order—*Sheet2, Sheet3*, and so on. When you use several worksheets in a workbook, it is helpful to rename the worksheets with names that are more meaningful. Color can also be added to a worksheet tab. When you have more worksheets in the workbook than can be displayed in the sheet tab area, use the four ***tab scrolling buttons***—the buttons containing arrows displayed at the left of the sheet tabs—to access worksheets that are not displayed.

In this activity, you will rename the worksheets, change the color of the worksheet tabs, and use the tab scrolling buttons to navigate among the worksheets.

1 Right-click the **Sheet1 sheet tab** and from the displayed shortcut menu, click **Rename**. Compare your screen with Figure 2.6.

The name of the worksheet—*Sheet1*—is selected.

Figure 2.6

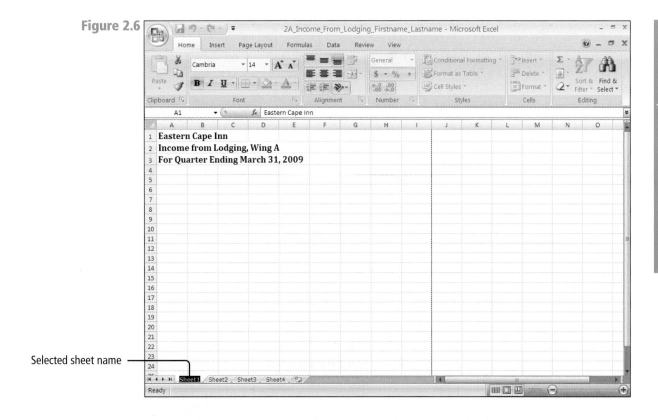

Selected sheet name

Type **2009 First Quarter Report** Click in the worksheet, and then right-click the **Sheet1 sheet tab** again to access the shortcut menu. Point to **Tab Color** to display the **Tab Color gallery**. Compare your screen with Figure 2.7.

The Tab Color gallery displays color choices in several sections—*Theme Colors*, *Standard Colors*, *No Color*, and *More Colors*.

Figure 2.7

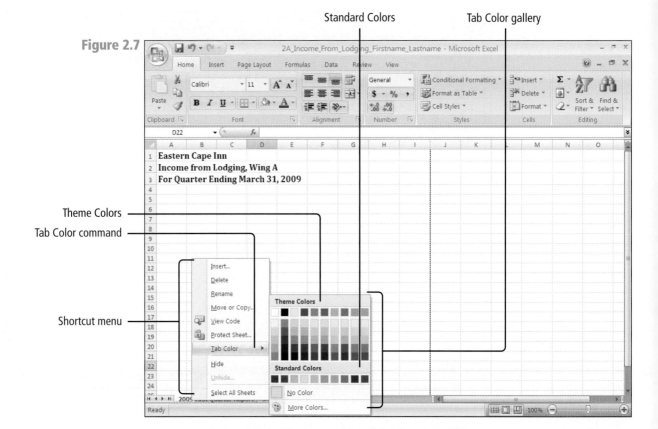

Standard Colors

Tab Color gallery

Theme Colors

Tab Color command

Shortcut menu

▣ In the **Tab Color** gallery, under **Standard Colors** point to the first color—the ScreenTip displays *Dark Red*—and then click **Dark Red**.

When the sheet is active—as is *2009 First Quarter Report*—the tab color displays as an underline.

▣ Click the **Sheet2 sheet tab**. In the **Cells group**, click the **Format button**. In the displayed list, under **Organize Sheets**, click **Rename Sheet**. Type **2009 January Report** and then click anywhere in the **Sheet2** worksheet.

You have used another method to change the worksheet name. The *2009 First Quarter Report*, an inactive worksheet, displays a dark red background with white letters for the sheet name.

▣ In the **Cells group**, click the **Format button**. In the displayed list, under **Organize Sheets**, point to **Tab Color**, and in the **Tab Color gallery**, under **Standard Colors**, click the last color—**Purple**. Compare your screen with Figure 2.8.

The active worksheet, *2009 January Report*, displays with a purple underline, helping you identify it as the active worksheet. The *2009 First Quarter Report* tab is fully displayed in dark red.

Figure 2.8

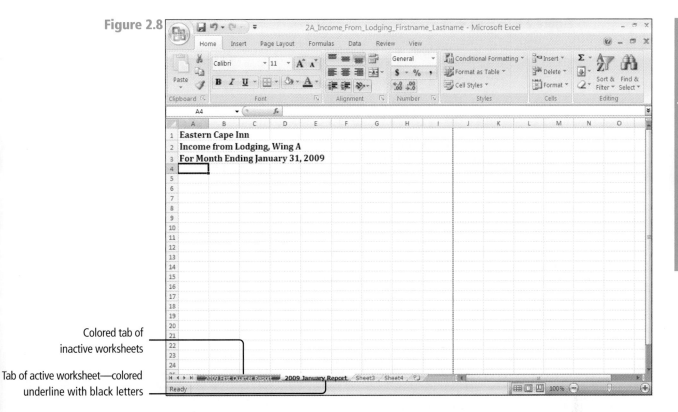

Colored tab of
inactive worksheets

Tab of active worksheet—colored
underline with black letters

6 Double-click the **Sheet3 sheet tab** to select it. Type **2009 February Report** and press Enter to rename the sheet tab. Using the skills you have practiced, from the **Tab Color gallery**, under **Standard Colors** select the seventh color—**Light Blue**.

Double-click directly in the sheet tab to select the worksheet tab so the text can be changed.

7 Using the skills you have practiced, rename the **Sheet4 sheet tab** to **2009 March Report** and under **Standard Colors**, select the sixth color—**Green**. Compare your screen with Figure 2.9.

Because the worksheet names are long, the *2009 First Quarter Report* worksheet no longer displays in the sheet tabs.

Figure 2.9

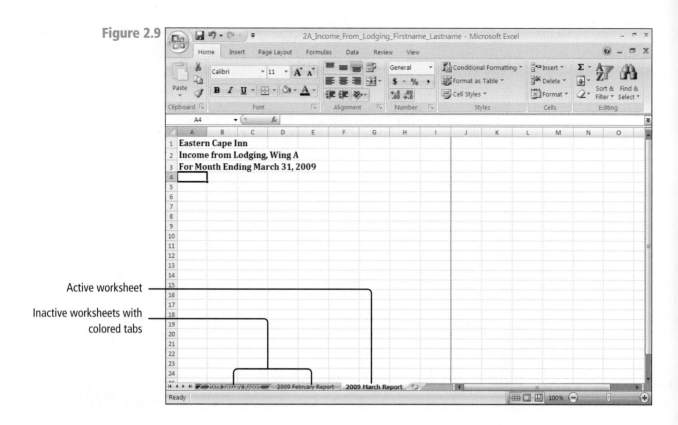

Active worksheet

Inactive worksheets with
colored tabs

8 To the left of the sheet tabs locate the **tab scrolling** buttons. In the

tab scrolling buttons, click the **left-facing arrow** to move the
2009 First Quarter Report worksheet into view, and then compare
your screen with Figure 2.10.

The 2009 First Quarter Report now displays the worksheet tab. The
tab scrolling buttons—located at the left of the sheet tabs—are used
to access worksheets that are not displayed. The number of worksheets available is limited by the computer's memory, and there may
be more worksheets than can be displayed in the space available.

The buttons are used to access the first, last, previous, or next
sheets.

Figure 2.10

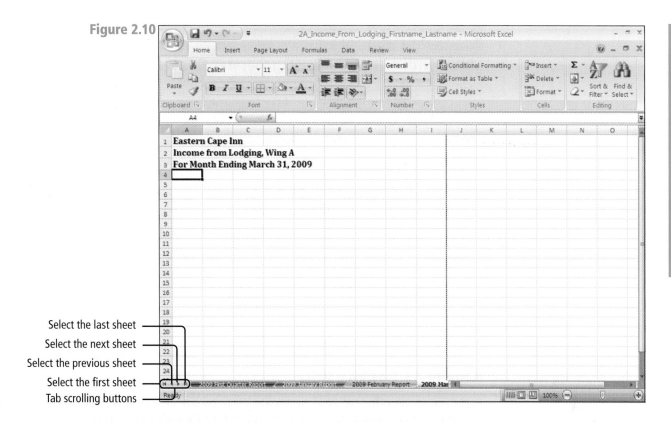

Select the last sheet
Select the next sheet
Select the previous sheet
Select the first sheet
Tab scrolling buttons

◉ Click the **2009 First Quarter Report sheet tab**, and then click **Save** 🔲.

Objective 2
Enter a Series

A **series** is a group of similar or related items that come one after another in succession. For example, January, February, March, April, and so on is a series, as are the days of the week. The numbers 1, 2, 3 and 5, 10, 15 are series. Excel's **Auto Fill** feature completes a series so that you do not have to type every value. Auto Fill enables you to extend a series of values into adjacent cells based on the value of other cells. Examples of Auto Fill series are listed in the table in Figure 2.11.

Auto Fill Series

Start with	Auto Fill generates this series:
Jan	Feb, Mar, Apr . . .
January	February, March, April. . .
Mon	Tue, Wed, Thu . . .
Monday	Tuesday, Wednesday, Thursday. . .
Qtr 1	Qtr 2, Qtr 3, Qtr 4 . . .
Quarter 1	Quarter 2, Quarter 3, Quarter 4 . . .
1st Period	2nd Period, 3rd Period, 4th Period . . .
Product 1	Product 2, Product 3, Product 4 . . .
Text 1	Text 2, Text 3, Text 4 . . .
10:10 AM	11:10 AM, 12:10 PM, 1:10 PM . . .

Figure 2.11

Activity 2.3 Entering a Series

Auto Fill is an efficient and accurate method for entering a related series of data into the worksheet. Recall that when descriptive column and row titles are long, you can display them on two or more lines. In this activity, you will use the fill handle to enter a series as column titles and then to create a series of numbers.

1 In the **2009 First Quarter Report worksheet**, in cell **A6**, type **Wing A Room No.** and in cell **B6**, type **Week 1** and **press** Enter↵.

The entry in cell A6 is truncated when you enter text in the adjoining cell. The format from the title has been applied to cell A6. By default, when you format at least three of the five preceding rows, Excel extends the format to the same number of rows—in this case the next three rows. Because column B was not formatted, the entry in cell B6 displays the default format.

2 Click cell **A6**. In the **Editing group**, click the **Clear button** ⬚. From the list that displays, click **Clear Formats**.

The **Clear command** is used to clear either the format or the contents of the cell—or both. The format in cell A6 is the default format.

3 Click cell **B6** and position the mouse over the **fill handle** until the ➕ pointer displays, and then drag to the right through **column E**. As you drag, notice a ScreenTip displays the series value for each cell. When *Week 4* displays, release the mouse button.

The column titles, *Week 1* through *Week 4*, are entered in row 6. Previously, you used the fill handle to copy a formula into adjacent cells. Excel's Auto Fill feature uses the fill handle to generate a series of values into adjacent cells, based on the value of other cells.

4 In cell **A7**, type **1020** and in the **Formula Bar**, click the **Enter button** ✓. Position the mouse over the **fill handle** to display the ➕

pointer, drag the fill handle down through cell **A13**, and then release the mouse button. Compare your screen with Figure 2.12.

The cell entry, *1020*, is copied in the cells and the ***Auto Fill Options*** button displays just to the right of the filled selection. Recall that the Auto Fill Options button provides choices on how the selected cells will be filled.

Figure 2.12

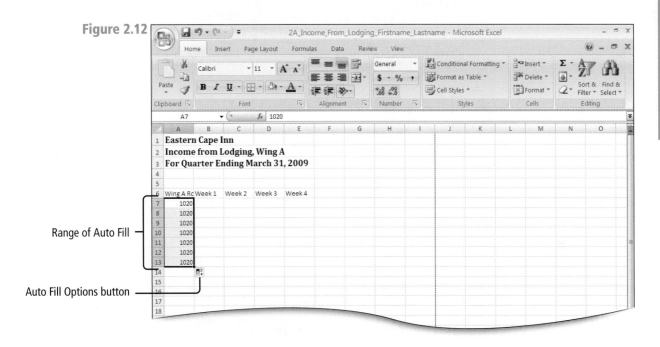

Range of Auto Fill

Auto Fill Options button

5 Click the **Auto Fill Options button** to display the menu. Compare your screen with Figure 2.13.

When you click the Auto Fill Options button, a list displays with options for filling the text or data. The Auto Fill Options is context-sensitive. Recall that a context-sensitive list varies depending on the content you are filling, the program you are filling from, and the format of the text or data you are filling.

Copy Cells is selected, indicating the action that was taken.

Figure 2.13

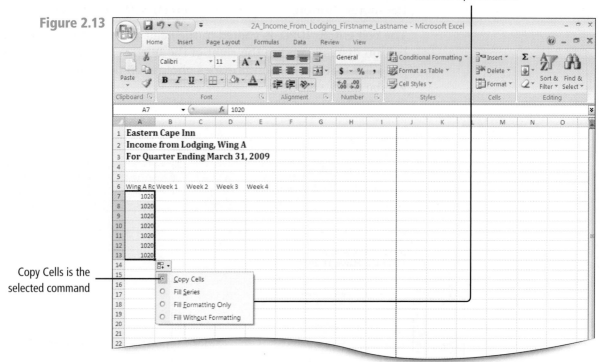

Auto Fill Options menu

Copy Cells is the selected command

⑥ In the **Auto Fill Options** button list [image], click **Fill Series**, and compare your screen with Figure 2.14.

A consecutive series of numbers beginning with *1020* and ending with *1026* has been entered into the range. Using Auto Fill Options, you can select to copy the cells, to enter a series of numbers, to copy only the formatting, or to copy only the cell contents without the format. The options relate to the current task because the command is context-sensitive.

Consecutive numbers entered—result
of Fill Series command

Figure 2.14

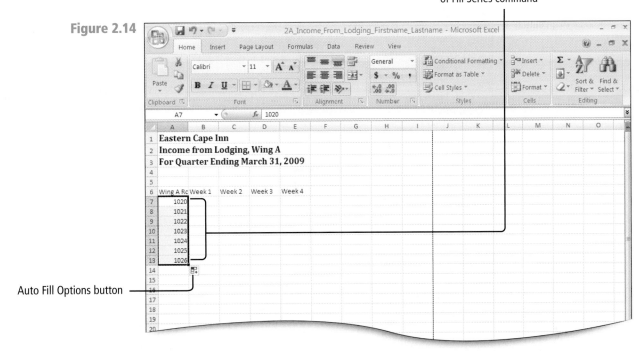

Auto Fill Options button

7 With the range **A7:A13** still selected, right-click and from the Mini toolbar, click the **Bold** **B** and **Center buttons** .

8 Click cell **F6**. Hold down Ctrl and click cell **A14**. Type **Total** and then press Ctrl + Enter.

By first selecting multiple cells, entries typed in a cell are entered in all selected cells when you confirm the entry by pressing Ctrl + Enter.

9 Select the column titles **A6:F6**. Right-click and from the Mini toolbar click the **Bold** **B** and **Center buttons** and add a **Bottom Double Border**. In the **Alignment group**, click the **Wrap Text button** , and then click the **Middle Align button** .

Recall that the *wrap text* feature displays text entries on multiple lines within the cell. As you select wrap text, the height of row 6 increases to fully display the cell entry on three lines.

10 Point to the boundary between columns A and B and when ✛ displays, click and drag so the title in cell **A6** displays on two lines, and then compare your screen with Figure 2.15.

When you adjust the width of column A, the text wraps on two lines. However, the height of row 6 does not decrease.

Figure 2.15

Wrap Text button

Middle Align button

Mouse pointer

Wrapped text

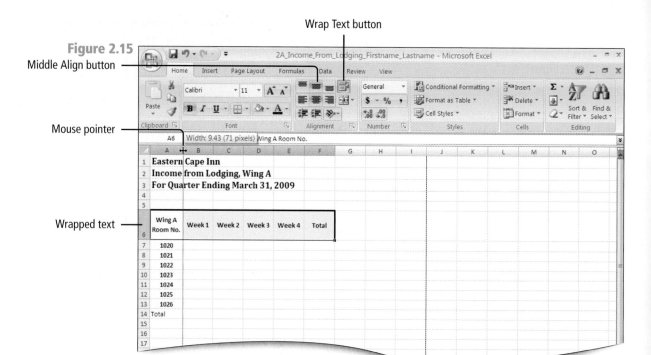

11 Point to the boundary between the **row 6 heading** and the **row 7 heading**. When the ✛ pointer displays, **double-click**.

The height of row 6 has decreased to AutoFit the height of the contents in cell A6. Double-clicking at the bottom row border is another method to AutoFit the height of a row.

12 **Save** 🖫 your workbook.

Objective 3
Copy and Paste Cell Contents

Data from individual cells and groups of cells can be copied to other cells in the same worksheet, to other sheets in the same workbook, or to sheets in another workbook. The action of copying cell contents to another location is called *copy and paste*. The *Copy* command duplicates the selected data—the *source*—and stores it in the *system Clipboard*—or simply *Clipboard*—which is a temporary storage area maintained by the Windows operating system. The *Paste* command inserts the most recent data stored in the Clipboard into a new cell or range of cells—the *destination*.

Activity 2.4 Using Copy and Paste

In this activity, you will copy and paste data and its format to other cells in the worksheet.

1 In the **2009 First Quarter Report** worksheet, select the range **A6:F6**. In the **Clipboard group**, click the **Copy button** 🗎. Alternatively, right-click the selected range and from the displayed shortcut menu, click Copy, or press Ctrl + C, which is the keyboard shortcut for copy. Compare your screen with Figure 2.16.

The range A6:F6 is the ***source range***—the range of cells that will be copied. The source range is surrounded by a moving border, and a message on the left side of the status bar displays *Select destination and press ENTER or choose Paste.* These two results serve as a reminder that this is the active source range.

The data is placed in the Clipboard, where it remains until the Paste command is completed and another action is taken.

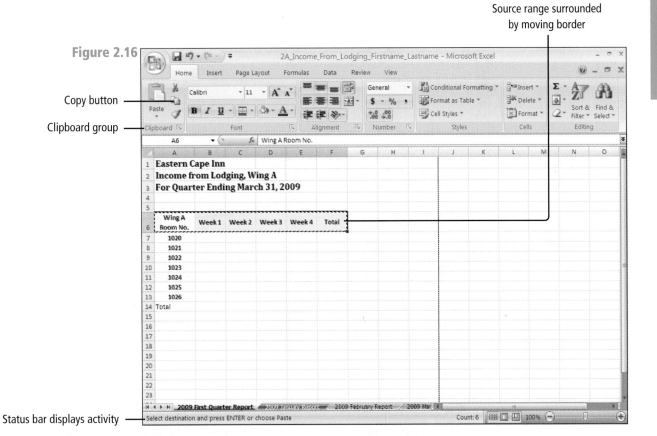

Source range surrounded by moving border

Figure 2.16

Copy button

Clipboard group

Status bar displays activity

2 Right-click cell **A17** and from the shortcut menu, click **Paste**. Alternatively, press Ctrl + V, the keyboard shortcut for paste, or from the Home tab, in the Clipboard group, click the Paste button. Compare your screen with Figure 2.17.

The data stored in the Clipboard is inserted in the ***destination range***—the range of cells into which the copied data is placed. Cell A17 is selected as the upper left cell in the destination range, and the remaining data is placed in adjacent cells in the same order and configuration as in the source range. If there is data in any cell in the destination, it will be overwritten.

The ***Paste Options button*** displays just under and to the right of the destination. The Paste Options button is used to confirm what will be pasted. Choices include data and formatting, formatting only, or values only. When you copy a cell or range of cells, the format is also copied unless you specify a different selection in the Paste Options menu.

Figure 2.17

Source range

Destination range

Paste Options button

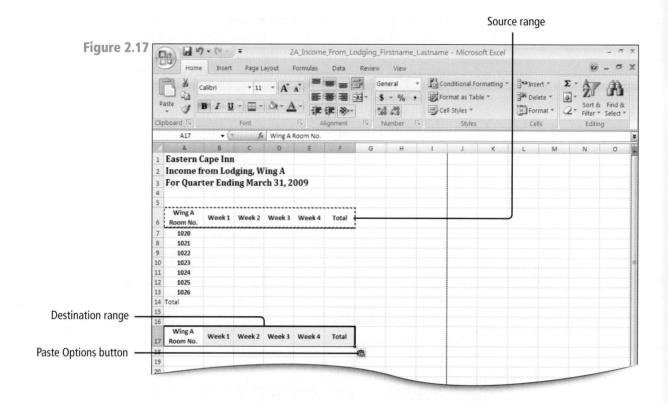

Note — Pressing Enter to Complete a Paste Action

Another technique is to click the destination cell and press [Enter] to paste the copied data to the new location, but doing this removes copied text from the Clipboard. Thus, if you want to paste the same text more than one time, use the Paste button.

3 Click cell **A28**. In the **Clipboard group**, click the **Paste button**.

Because the source range is still active, the contents can be pasted many times. The source range becomes inactive when you type data or select another command.

4 Right-click cell **A13** and from the shortcut menu, click **Copy**. Right-click cell **A14** and from the shortcut menu, click **Paste**.

The room number has been pasted into cell A14, replacing the word *Total*. Cell A13 is the *source cell*—the cell that is copied and stored in the Clipboard—and cell A14 is the *destination cell*—the cell into which the data is placed.

5 Click the **Paste Options button** 📋 to display the menu, and then click **Formatting Only**. Compare your screen with Figure 2.18.

You selected to paste only the format of the source cell—cell A13. The original cell entry—*Total*—displays with the center and bold format used in cell A13. The moving border continues to surround the source cell.

Figure 2.18

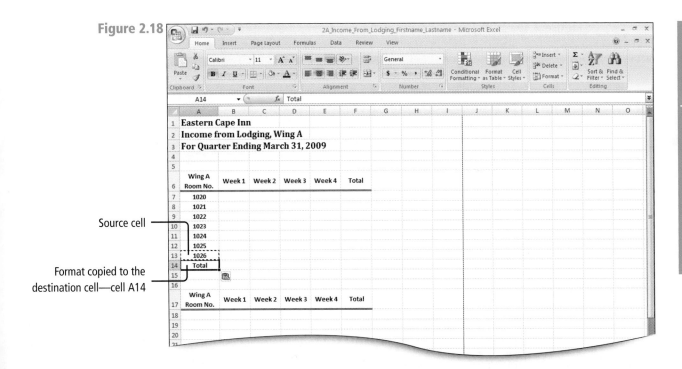

Source cell

Format copied to the
destination cell—cell A14

6 Select the range **A7:A14**. Right-click the selected range and from the
shortcut menu, click **Copy**. Click cell **A18**, and hold down Ctrl
while you click cell **A29**. Release the Ctrl key and then from the
Clipboard group, click the **Paste button**. Compare your screen with
Figure 2.19.

You can paste contents simultaneously to more than one selected
cell or range of cells. The source range is still active and is surrounded by the moving border, indicating it can be pasted again. The
Paste Options button is not available when you paste a group of cells
at the same time.

Figure 2.19

Moving border surrounds source range

Row titles copied to two destination ranges

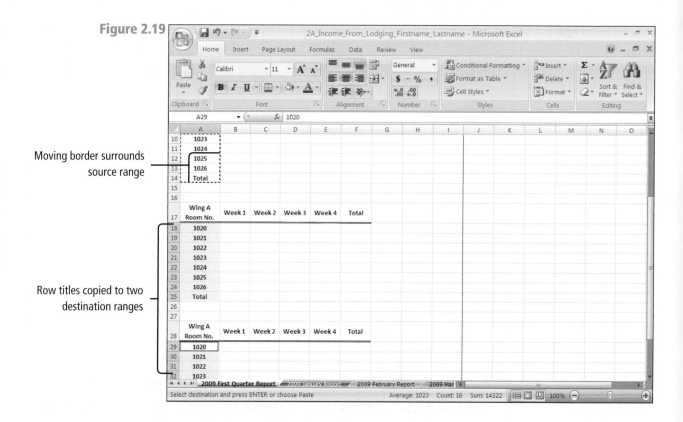

7 Press `Esc` to deselect the source range. **Save** 💾 your workbook.

More Knowledge

Moving Text Using the Cut and Paste Method

The copy and paste method *duplicates* the cell contents. If you prefer to move the cell contents, use the Cut button ✂ instead of the Copy button 📋. The Cut command removes the contents from the source location.

Activity 2.5 Copying Data Between Worksheets

You can use copy and paste to copy data between worksheets. Auto Fill can also be used to copy content, formats, or both to identical cells in other worksheets of the same workbook. In this activity, you will copy the column titles and room numbers to a group of worksheets in the workbook using the Fill command.

1 In the **2009 First Quarter Report** sheet, select the range **A6:F14**. Press `Ctrl` + `C`. Compare your screen with Figure 2.20.

You have used the keyboard shortcut for the Copy command. The source range in the *2009 First Quarter Report* is selected and the moving border surrounds it.

Source range surrounded
by moving border

Figure 2.20

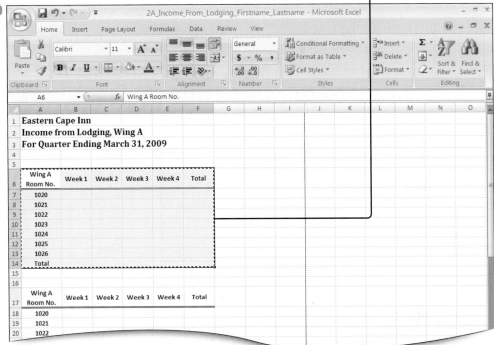

2 Click in the **2009 January Report** worksheet, and then click in cell **A6**. On the **Home tab**, in the **Clipboard group**, click the **Paste button**.

The Paste Options button displays. Because you want to copy both the contents and the format, it is not necessary to use it. Information is copied from one worksheet to another worksheet.

3 Hold down the ⇧ Shift key and click the **2009 March Report tab** to select a group of worksheets.

The monthly worksheets are grouped, but the First Quarter Report is not included in the group. The indication—*[Group]*—displays in the title bar.

4 On the **Home tab**, in the **Editing group**, point to the **Fill button** ⬇▾ to display the ScreenTip, and then click the **Fill button** ⬇▾. Compare your screen with Figure 2.21.

Figure 2.21

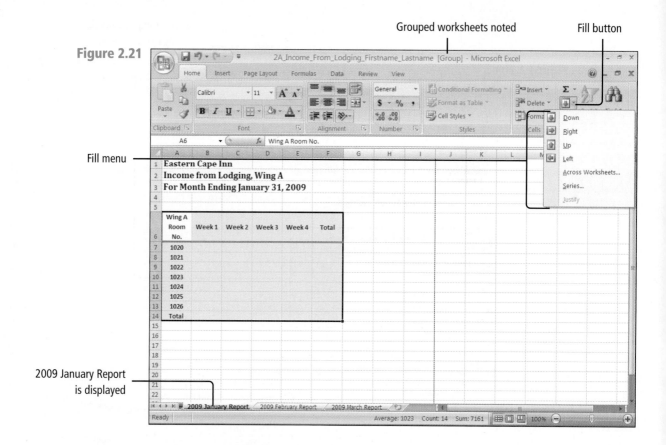

Grouped worksheets noted

Fill button

Fill menu

2009 January Report is displayed

---

5 In the **Fill** menu, click **Across Worksheets**, and compare your screen with Figure 2.22.

In the displayed *Fill Across Worksheets* dialog box, you indicate if you want the contents, the formats, or both (All) to be copied to the selected worksheets. Fill Across Worksheets enables you to copy data and format to the same cells in other worksheets when they are grouped.

Figure 2.22

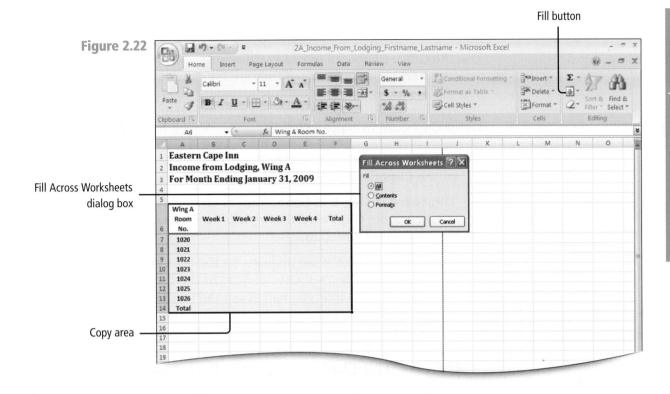

Fill button

Fill Across Worksheets dialog box

Copy area

6. In the **Fill Across Worksheets** dialog box, confirm that the **All** button is selected, and then click **OK**.

7. Click the **2009 February Report sheet tab** to confirm the row and column titles are inserted into the worksheet. Also confirm they are entered in the **2009 March Report** worksheet.

   Using the Fill button enables you to quickly copy cell contents to selected worksheets. The worksheets are still grouped, as noted in the title bar.

8. Use the tab scrolling button to view the **2009 First Quarter Report**. Click the **2009 First Quarter Report tab**, and then click cell **A1**.

   The worksheets are no longer grouped. **Save** your workbook.

Objective 4
Use the Office Clipboard

The **Microsoft Office Clipboard**—also called the **Office Clipboard**—is temporary storage maintained by your Windows operating system. It enables you to copy multiple text and graphical items from different Office applications, such as Word, Excel, or PowerPoint, and paste them into another Office document. When you copy or cut a single item, the data you select is placed on the system Clipboard, which holds only one item. The Office Clipboard, however, holds up to 24 items. These entries are displayed in the **Clipboard task pane**—an area at the left of your screen used to collect copied data. This collected data is available for pasting into other cells, worksheets, workbooks, and even other Office programs.

Activity 2.6 Using the Office Clipboard to Collect and Paste Data Between Workbooks

Use the Office Clipboard to collect data from one source and paste it into another workbook. Dominique Amerline, the inn manager, created a workbook that reports the monthly income. However, it is not in the style that she prefers. In this activity, you will open that workbook and use the Office Clipboard to copy data from one workbook to another.

1 With the **2009 First Quarter Report** sheet active, on the **Home tab**, in the **Clipboard group**, in the lower right corner, point to the **Clipboard Dialog Box Launcher** 🔲 to display the ScreenTip, and then click the **Clipboard Dialog Box Launcher**. Compare your screen with Figure 2.23.

The Clipboard task pane displays on the left side of the window. Items that you copy—or cut—display in the Clipboard task pane and remain visible so that you can select the text or graphic that you want to paste into another location.

Note — The Clipboard Size Is Different

The width of your Clipboard may vary depending on your computer setup. If you wish to alter the size, position the mouse on the right boundary. When the ↔ shape displays, click and drag to the desired size.

Figure 2.23

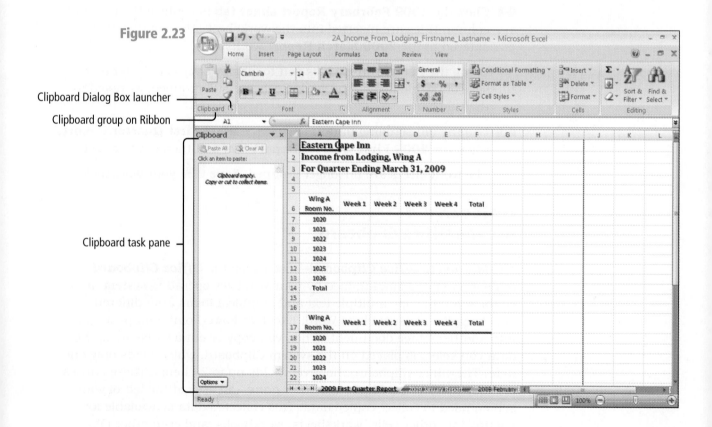

- Clipboard Dialog Box launcher
- Clipboard group on Ribbon
- Clipboard task pane

2 Click the **Office button** , and from the displayed menu, click **Open**. In the **Open** dialog box, navigate to the student files that accompany this textbook, click **e02A_Income_External_Data**, and then click **Open**.

There are two Excel workbooks open on your computer. Several programs and documents may be open at the same time, although only one will be active. Recall the file name of the active document is identified in the title bar.

The newly opened data file contains the income information. You will copy this information into your Income From Lodging workbook.

3 Select the range **B6:E12**. Press Ctrl + C to copy the data to the Office Clipboard. Compare your screen with Figure 2.24.

A moving border surrounds the source range. The copied data displays in the Clipboard task pane on the left.

Moving border

Figure 2.24

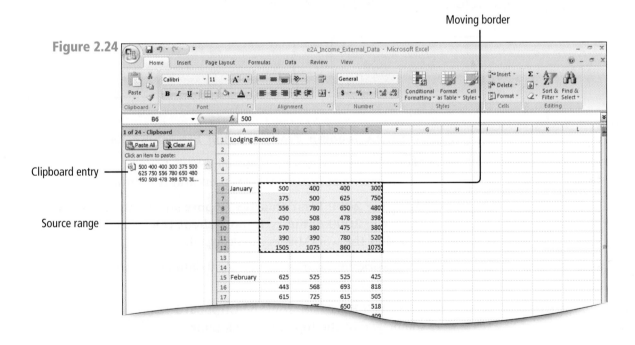

Clipboard entry

Source range

4 Click the **View tab**. In the **Window group**, click the **Switch Windows button** and compare your screen with Figure 2.25.

The View menu displays the names of the open Excel workbooks—*e02A_Income_External_Data* and *2A_Income_From_Lodging_Firstname_Lastname*. The active workbook is indicated by the check mark in front of its name.

Figure 2.25

e02A_Income_External_Data workbook

2A_Income_Firstname_Lastname Excel workbook

Clipboard entry

Inactive worksheet

Active worksheet

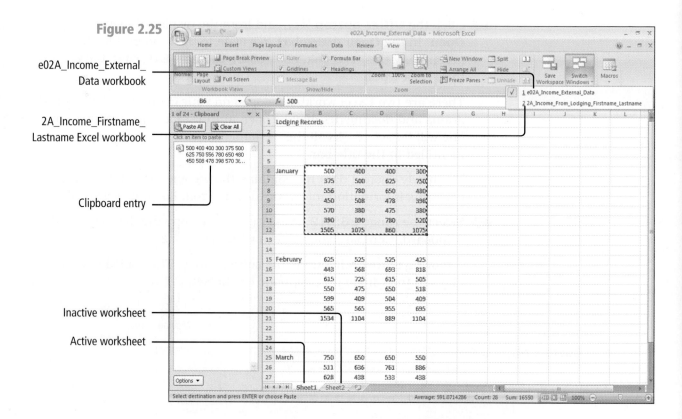

5 Click **2A_Income_From_Lodging_Firstname_Lastname**.

The active workbook, *2A_Income_From_Lodging_Firstname_Lastname*, displays on your screen and is identified in the title bar.

6 With the **2009 First Quarter Report** sheet active, press ⇧Shift and click the **2009 January Report sheet tab** and confirm in the title bar that the worksheets are grouped.

Two worksheets are selected. Any data entries or commands will affect both worksheets.

7 Click cell **B7**. Then from the **Clipboard task pane**, click the entry displayed at the top of the task pane.

The information is pasted from the Income External Data workbook to the Office Clipboard, and then to the Income From Lodging workbook.

8 Click the **2009 January Report sheet tab** to confirm the data is also copied into this worksheet. Right-click the sheet tab and click **Ungroup Sheets**.

The numbers are copied into both the First Quarter and the January worksheets simultaneously because the worksheets are grouped.

9 Hold down Alt and press the Tab key once and do not release the Alt key. Compare your screen with Figure 2.26.

A small box displays icons that represent each open workbook, document, or file. While holding down the Alt key, you can press the Tab key repeatedly to quickly move between open documents. When the name of the document needed displays under the icons, release the Alt key and the document just selected becomes the active document.

The Windows task bar also displays the names of the open workbooks.

Figure 2.26

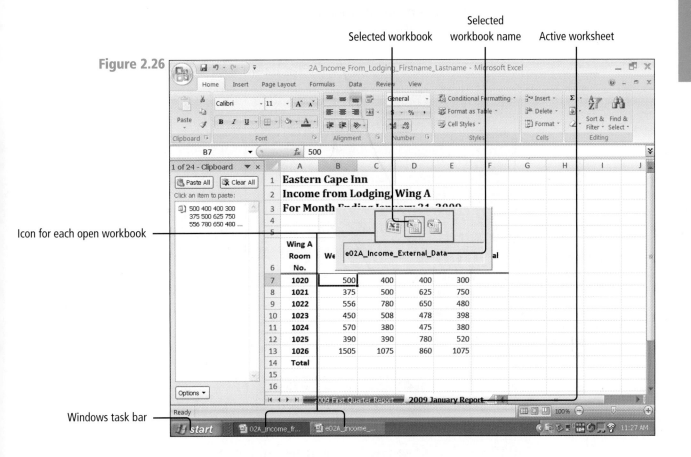

Selected workbook
Selected workbook name
Active worksheet

Icon for each open workbook

Windows task bar

10 Continue holding the Alt key and press Tab to cycle through the open documents. When **e02A_Income_External_Data** displays under the icons, release both keys to make this document the active workbook.

The *e02A_Income_External_Data* workbook displays as the ***active workbook***—the workbook that is visible on the screen where changes can be made.

11 Select the range **A15:E21.** Click on the **Home tab**. In the **Clipboard group**, click the **Copy button** 📋.

The data for February is copied to the Clipboard task pane as the first—top—entry. The previous entry moves down and is now the second entry in the Clipboard task pane. Including the names of the months in the copy area helps identify the group of numbers.

🔢 Using the skills you just practiced, copy the March data, **A25:E31**, from the worksheet to the Office Clipboard, including the name of the month.

🔢 In the **Clipboard task pane**, point to the third set of numbers that begin *500 400 400 300*. These are the numbers for January. Notice a blue box surrounds the numbers and an arrow displays at the right side. Click the **arrow**, and then compare your screen with Figure 2.27. Click **Delete**.

The group is no longer available in the Clipboard task pane. Because there is no identifying month, and the list is simply a set of numbers, deleting them removes confusion over what the numbers represent.

Selected and copied data

Figure 2.27

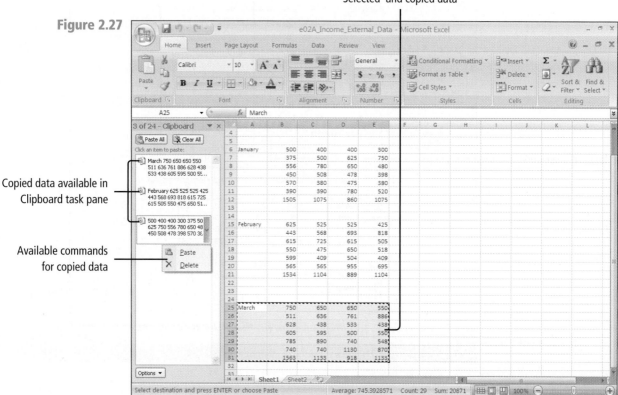

Copied data available in Clipboard task pane

Available commands for copied data

🔢 Using one of the skills you practiced, return to the **2A_Income_ From_Lodging_Firstname_Lastname** workbook and be sure the **2009 First Quarter Report** sheet is active.

🔢 Select the range **A7:A13**. Right-click and from the shortcut menu, click **Copy**.

🔢 Click cell **A18**. In the **Clipboard task pane**, click the entry that begins **February**. Without deselecting the selected destination, click the first entry displayed, which is *room numbers*. Compare your screen with Figure 2.28.

The worksheet now displays the February data and the room numbers. When the February data is copied, it **overwrites**—replaces—any existing cell content, so the room numbers in the range A18:A24 were deleted. The room numbers were pasted into the worksheet as one column beginning in cell A18. The Paste Options button displays at the bottom right of the pasted data.

Figure 2.28

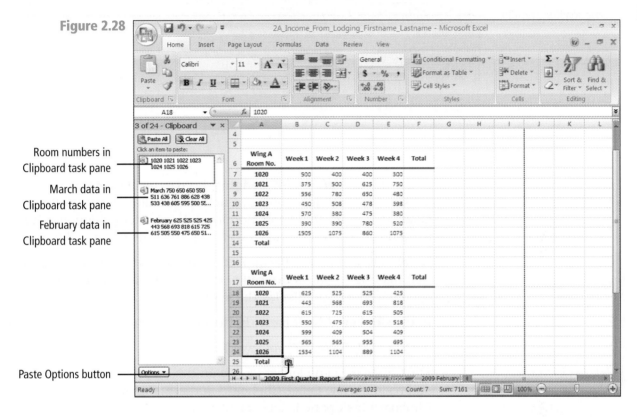

Room numbers in Clipboard task pane

March data in Clipboard task pane

February data in Clipboard task pane

Paste Options button

---

17 Click cell **A29** and in the **Clipboard task pane**, click the **March** data—the second selection in the Clipboard. Then click the first entry displayed in the Clipboard—the *room numbers.*

Data entered in the Clipboard task pane is available and visible to be used in other worksheets.

18 Click the **2009 February Report sheet tab**. Click in cell **A7** and from the **Clipboard task pane**, click the **February** data. Then from the Clipboard, click the *room numbers.*

19 Click the **2009 March Report sheet tab**. Using the method you just practiced, and beginning in cell **A7**, paste the **March** data in this worksheet and then click the *room numbers.*

20 Click the **View tab**. In the **Window group**, click the **Switch Windows button**, and then click the **e02A_Income_External_Data** workbook. In the upper right corner, point to the workbook-level **Close Window button** ☒ and compare your screen with Figure 2.29. Click the **Close Window button** ☒ to close the workbook. If prompted, do not save changes.

One workbook has been closed. Excel remains open and the *2A_Income_From_Lodging_Firstname_Lastname* workbook is active.

Figure 2.29
Workbook-level Close
button—closes workbook

Close Window ScreenTip

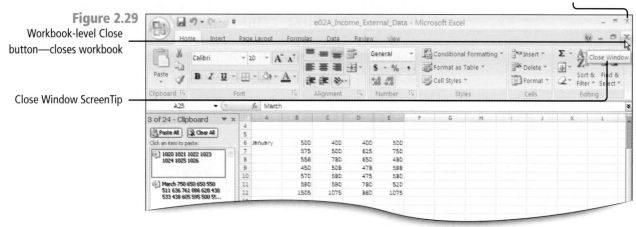

21 In the **2A_Income_From_Lodging_Firstname_Lastname** workbook, click the far left tab scrolling button. Right-click the **2009 First Quarter Report sheet tab**, and from the shortcut menu click **Select All Sheets**. Then press Ctrl + Home to return the active cell to **A1**.

Recall that a command is applied to all worksheets in a group. Recall that making A1 the active cell before saving enables the worksheet to open to cell A1 and display the worksheet title.

22 In the **Clipboard task pane**, in the upper right corner, click the **Close button** ☒. **Save** 🖫 your workbook.

The Clipboard is no longer visible on the screen. However, the entries still reside in the Office Clipboard and are available when the Clipboard task pane is later displayed.

More Knowledge
About Using the Office Clipboard

The Office Clipboard holds up to 24 items. Scroll bars in the task pane are used to access Clipboard entries that are not visible in the display. When the Clipboard is full, the first item entered in it is deleted as each new one is added. The Clipboard is active even when the Clipboard is not displayed on the screen. The data in the Clipboard remains until you quit all Office programs.

Objective 5
Total the Worksheet Range and Enter a Grand Total

Excel is designed to report numeric data and provide totals of that data, so there are many ways to total the worksheet quickly. Selecting the range of data and using the SUM formula will place the row and column totals in the worksheet. When a worksheet contains totals, the grand total feature will add those totals to quickly total the entire worksheet.

Activity 2.7 Totaling the Worksheet in One Step and Correcting Formula Errors

In many worksheets, each column as well as each row needs to have a total. These totals can be entered simultaneously when you group the worksheets prior to entering the SUM formula. Excel also reviews the formula that is entered in a cell. If an error is suspected, a green triangle—an **error indicator**—is placed in the upper left corner of the cell to indicate there is a potential error in the formula. In this activity, you will total the rows and columns and check their accuracy.

1 In the title bar, confirm that the worksheets are grouped—or at a sheet tab, right-click and click Select All Sheets. Select the range **B7:F14**. On the **Home tab**, in the **Editing group**, click the **Sum button** Σ · and compare your screen with Figure 2.30.

Totals are entered in row 14 and column F. In each cell in column F, a green triangle—error indicator—displays in the upper left corner of the cell, indicating a potential formula error.

Totals in column F   Worksheets grouped

Figure 2.30

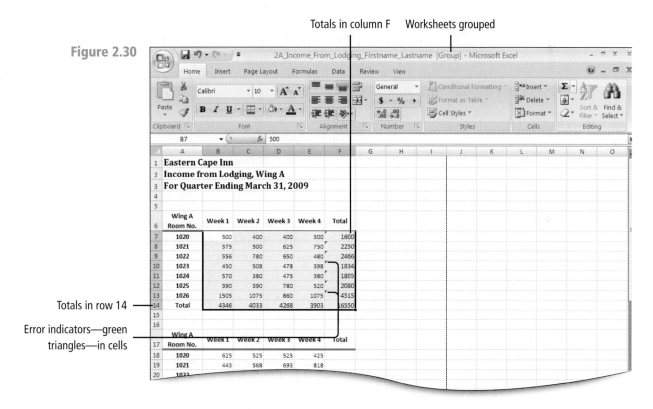

Totals in row 14

Error indicators—green triangles—in cells

2 Click cell **F7** and in the **Formula Bar**, review the formula and confirm that it adds the data in row 7—B7:E7—but not the room numbers in column A. Click in cell **F8** to confirm that the formula also adds the data in row 8 and not the room numbers.

3 Right-click in the **2009 First Quarter Report sheet tab** and select **Ungroup Sheets**. Click cell **F7**. The **Error Checking** button displays.

The **Error Checking button** indicates that Excel has reviewed the formulas that are entered in the worksheet and alerts you to potential errors in a formula. It does not appear when worksheets are grouped.

4 Point to the **Error Checking** button 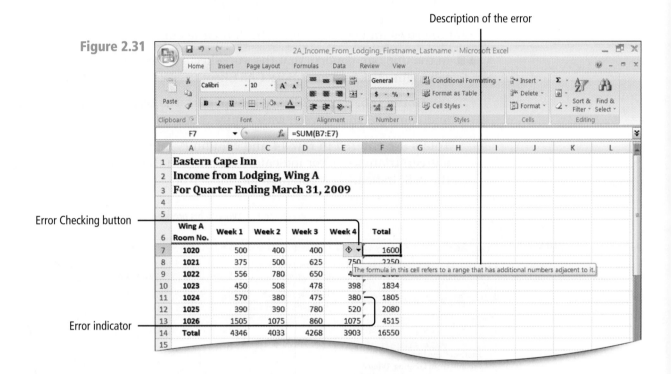 and review the ScreenTip. Compare your screen with Figure 2.31.

The ScreenTip reads *"The formula in this cell refers to a range that has additional numbers adjacent to it."*

Figure 2.31

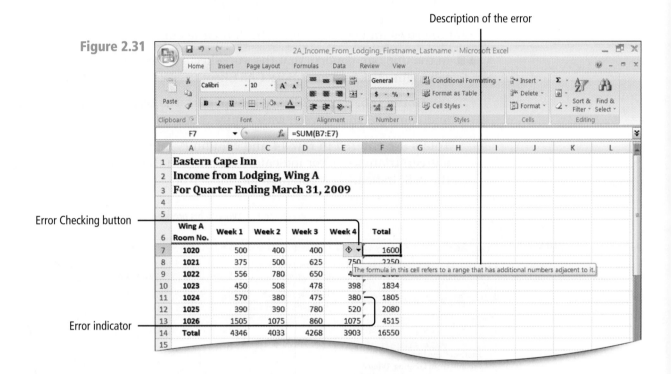

5 Click the **Error Checking button** to view the list of options and compare your screen with Figure 2.32. Because the formula is correct, click **Ignore Error**.

The Error Checking button is context-sensitive and will display different correction options depending on the error. This error indicator displays because numbers are entered in column A. Excel alerts you that these numbers have not been included in the formula.

After you review the error and indicate the formula is correct, the error indicator is removed from the cell.

Figure 2.32

Reason for potential error   Ignore Error command

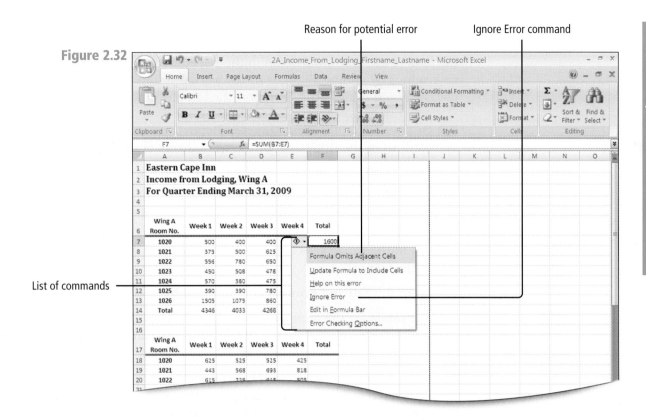

List of commands

6 Select the range **F8:F13**, click the **Error Checking button** , and from the displayed list, click **Ignore Error**.

You can remove multiple error indicators from selected adjacent cells at the same time.

7 In the title bar, confirm that the worksheets are not grouped. Click the **2009 January Report sheet tab**. Using the skills you just practiced, confirm that the correct formulas are entered and remove any error indicators. Repeat this process for the **February** and **March** worksheets.

Although you can group the worksheets to enter a formula, the error indicators must be deleted from individual worksheets.

8 Click the **2009 First Quarter Report sheet tab**. Select the range **B18:F25**. In the **Editing group**, click the **Sum button** . Using the skills practiced, enter the totals for the remaining section— **B29:F36**. In both sections, confirm that the formulas are correct and the error indicators are removed.

9 **Save** your workbook.

Activity 2.8 Creating a Grand Total in One Step

When businesses report information, they often report for shorter periods of time but want to see the total for a longer period of time. For instance, Eastern Cape Inn has been reporting its income on a monthly basis. However, owners Debra Chandler-Walker and Derek Walker would like to know how much income was generated for the entire quarter.

Excel provides a grand total feature that quickly and accurately adds totals within a selected range of a worksheet and provides a *grand total*—the total of the individual sums in the selected range. The grand total is determined by adding all totals in the worksheet. In this activity, you will use the grand total feature to report the total income for the quarter.

1 Be sure the **2009 First Quarter Report** worksheet is active and confirm in the title bar that the worksheets are not grouped.

2 Click cell **B7**. Using the scroll bar, scroll to row **37**. Press ⇧Shift while you click cell **E37**.

The range B7:E37 is selected. When a range is large and not all cells are visible on the screen, pressing ⇧Shift while you click in the last cell in the range selects the entire range, from the first cell selected to the last cell.

3 From the **Editing group**, click the **Sum button** Σ ▾.

The totals for the quarter for each week are placed in row 37. Excel copies the formula in cell F36 to F37. Excel automatically copies formulas that repeat in every row.

4 Click cell **B37** and review the formula. Compare your screen with Figure 2.33. Notice that the cell references used are those that correspond with the total rows—14, 25, and 36. Notice also that the cell references begin with the formula at the end of the worksheet and include each formula in order until the first formula in row 14 is included.

When you select the entire worksheet, a grand total is created when you use the SUM function. Excel recognizes SUM formulas in the range and adds only the cells with the SUM formulas to obtain the grand total.

The grand total formula in cell B37 uses the totals in column B—cells B36, B25, and B14—to determine the total income earned during the first week of the months in the quarter.

Figure 2.33

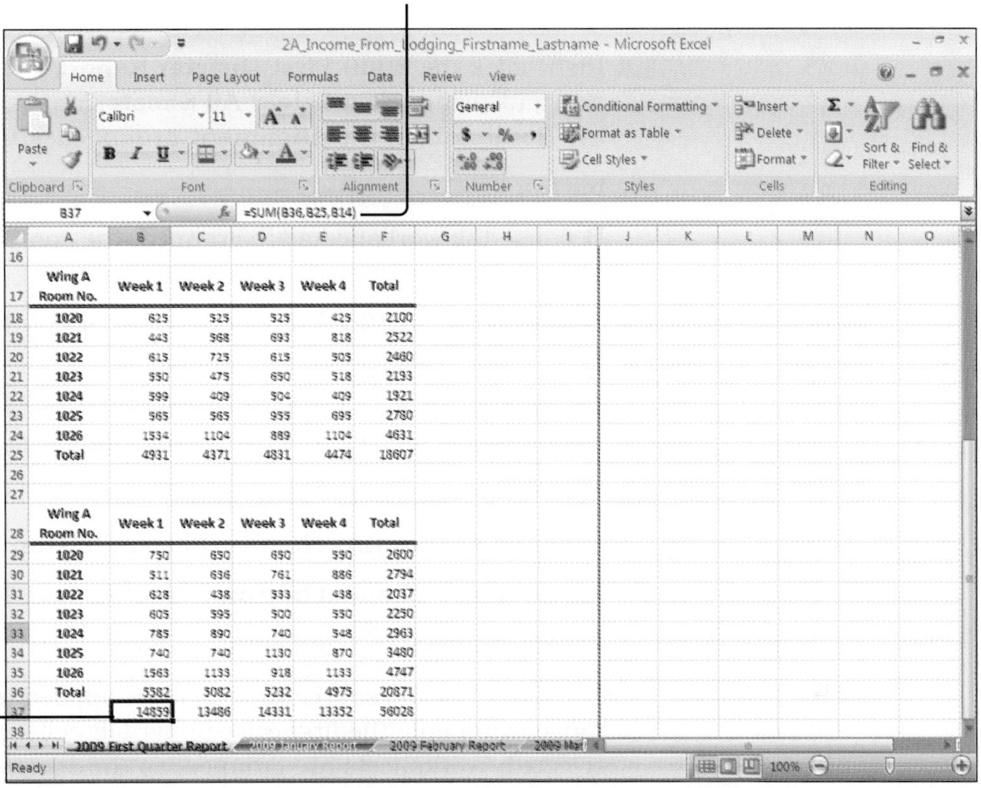

Formula for totals in Week 1

Grand total

5️⃣ Click cell **C37** and review the formula entered. Then click cell **F37** and notice that this formula sums the totals in the grand total row—**row 37**—and not the totals for each month—**rows 14**, **25**, and **36**.

6️⃣ **Save** 💾 your workbook.

Note — The Grand Total Does Not Display or Adds Another Column

Sometimes when you use the grand total feature, a total will not display in the last cell of the grand total row. If that occurs, you will need to enter the formula yourself. Other times, an entire column of numbers will be displayed to the right of the last column. If that occurs, delete those numbers.

Objective 6
Format a Multiple-Sheet Workbook Group

When worksheets are grouped, formats applied in the active worksheet are also applied to all the worksheets that are grouped. Formats can be copied across a group of worksheets in one step or can be copied to exact cells.

Activity 2.9 Formatting a Worksheet Group and Using Print Preview

Grouped worksheets enable you to format the same range of cells in all worksheets of the group simultaneously. Caution is needed to be sure the same formats are needed in identical cells in all worksheets. In this activity, you will format the worksheets as a group.

1 Right-click the **2009 First Quarter Report sheet tab**. From the shortcut menu, click **Select All Sheets**. Select the range **A1:F1**. On the **Home tab**, in the **Alignment group**, click the **Merge & Center button** ⊞ ▾.

Because the worksheets are grouped, the contents in row 1 are centered in the range A1:F1 in all worksheets.

2 Select the range **A2:F2**. Press Ctrl + Y. Select the range **A3:F3** and press Ctrl + Y.

Using the keyboard shortcut command of Ctrl + Y repeats the last command, which was the merge and center command.

3 Select the range **B7:F7** and right-click to display the Mini toolbar. Click the **Accounting Number Format button** $ ▾, and then click the **Decrease Decimal button** .00→.0 two times. Then click the **Format Painter button** 🖌 and click cell **B14**.

The format of the source range can be applied to the destination range when only the first cell—upper left cell—of the range is selected. Worksheets are grouped, so the accounting number format has been applied to the same ranges in all worksheets.

4 With the range **B14:F14** selected, right-click to display the Mini toolbar. Click the **Bottom Border button arrow** ⊞ ▾ and then click **Top and Double Bottom Border**.

5 Select the range **B8:F13** and right-click to display the Mini toolbar. Click the **Comma Style button** ' and the **Decrease Decimal button** .00→.0 two times.

6 On the **Page Layout tab**, in the **Page Setup group**, click the **Dialog Box Launcher** ⬚.

7 In the **Page Setup** dialog box, click the **Margins tab**. In the **Center on page** area, click **Horizontally**, and then click **Vertically**. Click **Print Preview**. At the right edge of the screen, in the vertical scroll bar, click in the space between the scroll box and the down scroll arrow to display page 2, and then compare your screen with Figure 2.34.

At the bottom left of the screen, the page number displays. As you review the worksheets displayed in Print Preview, note that the formatted title is entered on each worksheet and a footer displays on each sheet—the file name displays in the left footer and the sheet name displays in the right footer. The page number displayed in the lower left corner of the screen indicates the page number in the workbook file—this is page 2 of 4 pages.

Figure 2.34

Space between scroll box and down scroll arrow

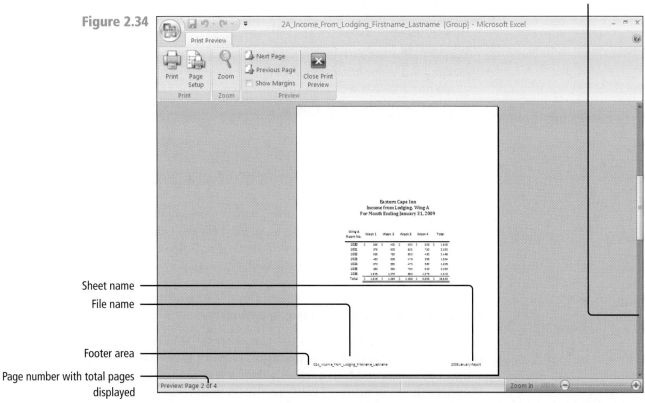

Sheet name

File name

Footer area

Page number with total pages
displayed

8 Use the technique you just practiced to view pages 3 and 4. Then in the Print Preview, click **Close Print Preview**.

9 Right-click the **2009 First Quarter Report sheet tab** and in the shortcut menu, click **Ungroup Sheets**.

10 Click the **Home tab**. In the **2009 First Quarter Report** worksheet, select the range **B7:F14** and right-click to display the Mini toolbar.

Double-click the **Format Painter button** [icon]. Then click cells **B18** and **B29**. In the **Clipboard group**, click the **Format Painter button** [icon] to turn it off.

The Format Painter can be used to format a group of cells as long as it is identical in size—it has the same number of rows and columns—as the group of cells from which the format was copied. When the Format Painter is used to copy the format to a range of cells, click in the first cell—the upper left cell of the range—and the format will be copied to the identical range.

11 Select the range **B37:F37**. On the **Home tab**, in the **Number group**, click the **Accounting Number Format button** [$ icon] and then click the **Decrease Decimal button** [icon] two times. In the **Font group**, click the **Bottom Border button arrow** [icon], and then click **Bottom Double Border**.

12 In cell **A37**, type **Grand Total** Right-click cell **A36** and click the **Format Painter button** [icon]. Then click cell **A37**. **Save** [icon] your workbook.

More Knowledge

Grouping Specific Worksheets

To select adjacent worksheets, click one sheet tab and press ⇧Shift while you click the last sheet tab in the adjacent worksheets you want to group. To group nonadjacent worksheets, hold down Ctrl and click on each sheet tab you want to add to the group.

Objective 7
Insert Columns and Rows in Multiple Worksheets

Columns and rows can be inserted into a worksheet or group of worksheets. Formulas that are created using relative cell references adjust to reflect the new location. If Excel detects a possible error in the formula, an error indicator displays in the cell.

Activity 2.10 Inserting Columns in a Worksheet

When a column is inserted in the worksheet, the existing columns move one column to the right. For instance, column B becomes column C. When a formula is entered into a cell, the cell references in that formula adjust to reflect the new range of cells. In this activity, you will insert a column, enter the room names, and review the formulas to verify that? The relative references changed and that the formulas remain accurate in all worksheets of the workbook.

1 Be sure the worksheets are ungrouped and the **2009 First Quarter Report** sheet is active. Press Ctrl + Home to make cell **A1** active. Point to the **column B** heading and when the mouse takes the ⬇ shape, right-click to select the column. In the shortcut menu, click **Insert**. Alternatively, from the Cells group, click the Insert button arrow, and from the displayed list, click Insert Sheet Columns. Compare your screen with Figure 2.35.

A new column has been entered. Even though you merged the title rows into one cell over columns A through F, when a column is inserted, the erge and center range adjusts to include the inserted column. Just to the right of the inserted column, the *Insert*

Options button 🖌 displays, which, when selected, provides suggestions for formatting the newly inserted column.

Insert Options button

Figure 2.35

Inserted column

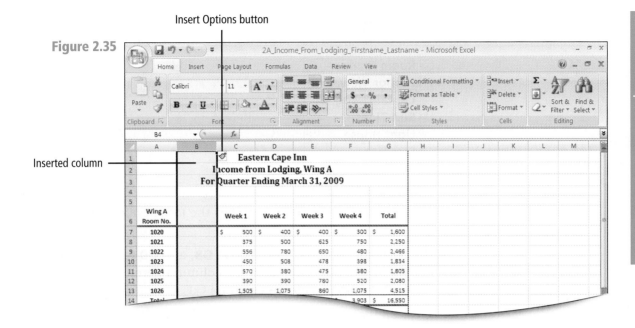

2 Click the **Insert Options button** 🖋 and compare your screen with Figure 2.36. In the displayed menu, click **Clear Formatting**.

A warning box displays indicating you cannot change the format of the merged cells—in rows 1:3. The other choices will format the column as either column A—Format Same as Left—or column B—Format Same as Right.

Insert Options menu

Figure 2.36

Inserted column

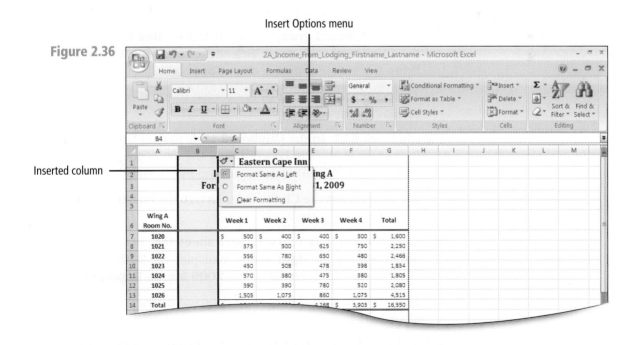

3 In the **Microsoft Office Excel** warning box, click **OK**, and then click cell **B6** and type the following data in **column B**:

| Room Name |
| Harbor View |
| Captain's Log |
| Surf Tides |
| Light House |
| Star Fish |
| Crab Net |
| Commander Suite |

The format of column B matches the format of column A—bold and centered.

4 Review the formulas in cells **G7, G8,** and **G9** to confirm that the Sum function has adjusted the column reference to reflect the new position of the formula—columns C:F.

Recall that a formula that is entered with relative cell references will change to reflect the new position. When the column was inserted, the cell references adjusted and the formulas remained accurate.

5 Select the range **B7:B13**. In the **Alignment group**, click the **Align Text Left button** ☰. Point to the border between the **column B** and **C** headings and when the mouse takes the ✛ shape, double-click to widen **column B** to accommodate the longest entry, *Commander Suite*.

Recall that you can also select the cell, then from the Home tab, in the Cells group, click the Format button arrow, and under Cell Size, click AutoFit Column Width.

6 In the **Clipboard group**, click the **Dialog Box Launcher** to display the **Clipboard task pane**. Select the range **B6:B13** and right-click. From the shortcut menu, click **Copy**.

The contents of the range are copied to the Clipboard task pane and display as the top entry.

7 Click cell **B17**. In the **Clipboard task pane**, click **Room Name**—the first entry in the Clipboard. Using the skills you practiced, paste the room names in the range beginning in cell **B28**.

The entry from the Clipboard task pane is pasted into the worksheet along with the format.

8 Click the **2009 January Report sheet tab**. In the **tab scrolling buttons**, click the **right arrow** to display the **2009 March Report**. Then press ⇧Shift and click the **2009 March Report sheet tab.**

The selected worksheet group does not include the *2009 First Quarter Report* sheet.

9 Right-click the **column B** heading. From the shortcut menu, click **Insert**. Click cell **B6**. In the **Clipboard task pane**, click the first entry, which is the room names.

An additional column has been inserted in all grouped worksheets and the room names have been inserted from the Clipboard task pane. The *Insert Options* button does not display when a column is inserted into a group of worksheets.

10 Adjust the column width to fit the longest entry, *Commander Suite*. In the sheet tab, right-click and select **Ungroup Sheets**.

11 Click the **2009 February Report sheet tab** to confirm the column was inserted and room names are entered in the worksheet. **Save** 💾 your workbook.

Activity 2.11 Inserting Rows That Adjust Relative References and Reviewing Error Messages

When a row is inserted into the worksheet, existing data below the inserted row moves down one row. A row inserted between rows 4 and 5 means that row 5 becomes row 6. Any cells that contain formulas will be located in a new row and the formula containing a reference to that row will adjust to its new location. In this activity, you will insert a row, add data for a missing room, and review the relative references of the formulas in the worksheet.

1 With the **2009 First Quarter Report** active, point to the **row 14** heading until the ➡ pointer displays. Right-click the **row 14** heading and from the shortcut menu click **Insert**. Compare your screen with Figure 2.37.

The Insert Options button displays at the left edge of the screen just below the inserted row.

Inserted row

Figure 2.37

Insert Options button

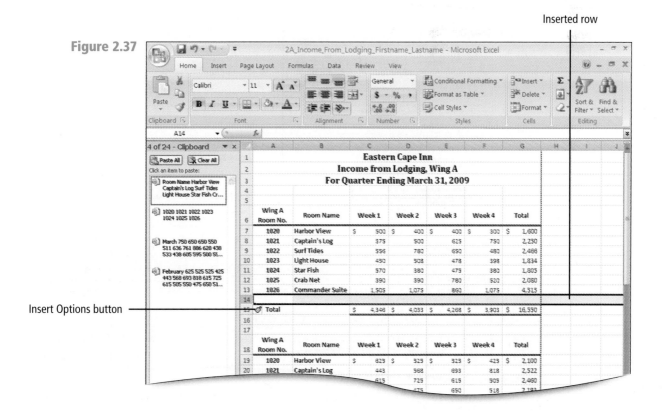

2 Click the **Insert Options button** 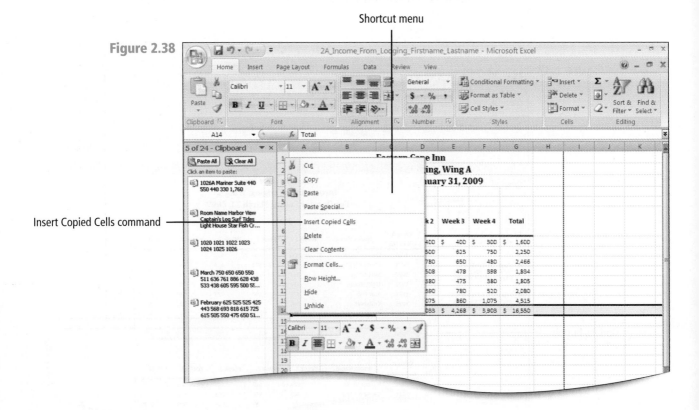. Confirm that the **Format Same As Above** option is selected. Then look at the formulas in cells **C15** and **D15** and note that they have not changed to include the newly inserted row 14.

The Insert Options button provides formatting choices for the inserted row. Additional numbers will be inserted into the row, so it should be formatted like the other data rows of the worksheet.

3 Select the range **A14:F14** and type the following data, pressing [Enter] after each entry.

1026A	Mariner Suite	440	550	440	330

Click cells **C15** and **D15** to review the formulas again.

Note that the formulas in row 15 have changed to include the newly entered data in row 14. Once data is entered, Excel recognizes that data and includes it in the formula. The total for the row is also entered in cell G14. Excel recognizes the pattern of formulas in adjacent cells in column G and entered a new formula for row 14.

4 Select the range **A14:G14** and press [Ctrl] + [C] to copy the data in this row to the Clipboard task pane. Click the **2009 January Report**

sheet tab. Point to the **row 14** heading to display the ➡ pointer and then right-click. Compare your screen with Figure 2.38.

Because the shortcut menu is context-sensitive, the *Insert* command has changed to *Insert Copied Cells*.

Shortcut menu

Figure 2.38

Insert Copied Cells command

5 From the displayed shortcut menu, click **Insert Copied Cells** and compare your screen with Figure 2.39.

The Insert Paste dialog box displays. Here you decide whether existing cells in the worksheet should shift down a row or to the right.

Figure 2.39

Insert Paste dialog box

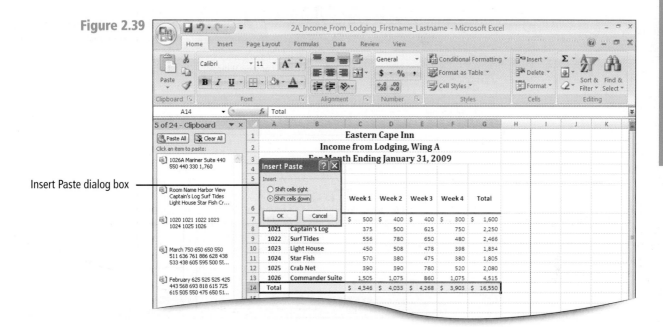

6 Confirm that the **Shift cells down** option is selected, and then click **OK**.

The data is inserted into row 14 and the column totals are now in row 15. Error indicators display in the totals of row 15.

7 Click cell **C15**. The **Error Checking** button ⬧ displays. In the **Formula Bar**, review the formula, then click the **Error Checking button** ⬧ and compare your screen with Figure 2.40.

The formula does not include the data entered in row 14. When the new row was inserted, the formula did not automatically update to include the data in that row.

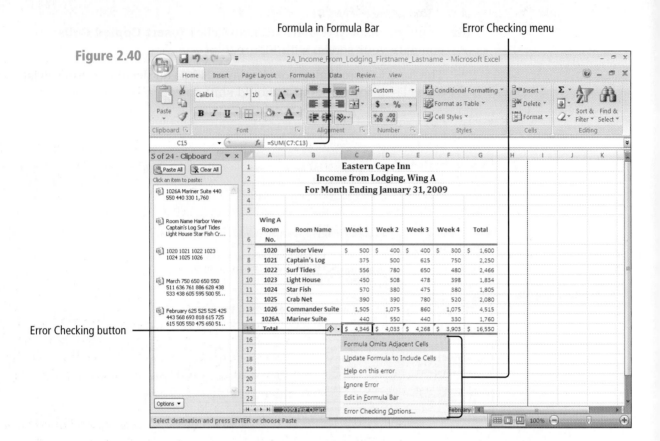

Figure 2.40

Formula in Formula Bar

Error Checking menu

Error Checking button

8 From the **Error Checking** button options, click **Update Formula to Include Cells**.

The formula in cell C15 is updated to include cell C14.

9 Using skills you have practiced, clear the error indicators from the cells in **row 15**. Then click in each cell to confirm that the Sum formula includes the correct range of cells.

When you Update Formula to Include Cells, the formula includes the newly inserted row. This command must be selected in each formula rather than for an entire range of cells.

10 Click the **2009 First Quarter Report sheet tab**. Right-click the **row 26** heading, and then from the shortcut menu, click **Insert**. Click the **Insert Options button** and confirm that **Format Same As Above** is selected.

11 Select the range **A26:F26** and type the following data, pressing Enter after each entry.

1026A	Mariner Suite	298	445	527	440

Then confirm that the formulas in **row 27** and cell **G26** are accurate and include the newly inserted row.

12 Select the range **A26:G26** and right-click. In the shortcut menu, click **Copy**.

The copy range displays as the first entry in the Clipboard task pane.

13 Click the **2009 February Report sheet tab**. Right-click the **row 14** heading. In the shortcut menu, click **Insert Copied Cells**. In the

Insert Paste dialog box, confirm the **Shift cells down** option is selected, and then click **OK**.

14 Click cell **C15** and click the **Error Checking button** and click **Update Formula to Include Cells**. Confirm the formula includes the required range of cells. Using the skills you just practiced, correct the other formulas in row 15.

15 Click the **2009 First Quarter Report sheet tab** and using the skills you practiced, insert a row above **row 38** and format it **Same as Above**. Type the following data beginning in cell **A38**.

| 1026A | Mariner Suite | 790 | 900 | 790 | 680 |

16 Copy the range **A38:G38**. Click the **2009 March Report sheet tab**. Using the skills practiced, right-click the **row 14** heading and insert the copied cells. Shift cells down and update the formulas to remove the error indicators.

17 Click the **2009 First Quarter Report sheet tab**. Press Esc to stop the moving border around the source range and click cell **C40**. Confirm that the formula for the grand total has changed to include the new total rows after they have been inserted and remains accurate. Compare your work with Figure 2.41.

Grand total formula in Formula Bar

Figure 2.41

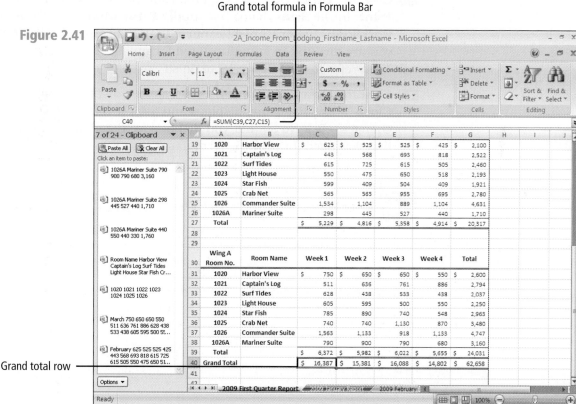

Grand total row

18 Click cell **A5** and type **January** and press Enter. Right-click cell **A5** and from the displayed Mini toolbar, click the **Bold button** B, the **Italic button** I, and the **Bottom Border button** ▦ ▾. Select the range **A5:B5** and in the **Alignment group**, click the **Merge & Center button** ▦ ▾.

19 With cell **A5** selected, right-click and from the shortcut menu, click **Copy**. Click cell **A17**. Press Ctrl while you click cell **A29**. Press Enter. In cell **A17**, type **February** and in cell **A29** type **March Select all sheets** and then Run Spelling Checker to confirm there are no spelling errors. Close the Clipboard task pane and **Save** 💾 your work.

The contents and format have been copied to two cells simultaneously and the cells modified to reference the data displayed for each month. The spelling checker will check the spelling on all selected worksheets.

20 Check your *Chapter Assignment Sheet* or *Course Syllabus*, or consult your instructor, to determine if you are to submit work on paper or electronically. To submit electronically, follow the instructions provided by your instructor, and then go to Step 22.

21 Click the **Office button** 🔘, and from the displayed menu, click **Print**. In the **Print** dialog box, under **Print what**, select **Entire workbook**. Under **Copies**, confirm that **1** is selected. Click **OK**. If you are directed to submit printed formulas, group all worksheets. Then refer to **Activity 1.12** to do so.

22 Click the **Office button** 🔘, and from the displayed menu, click **Close**. If the dialog box displays and asks if you want to save changes, click **No** so that you do not save the changes to Page Setup that you used for printing formulas. **Close** Excel.

End **You have completed Project 2A** ————————————

Project 2B **Hotel Taxes**

In Activities 2.12 through 2.21, you will construct an Excel workbook for Dominique Amerline, the Eastern Cape Inn manager. The workbook contains several worksheets that report the amount of hotel taxes collected for a month, a worksheet that projects taxes with an increase in the tax rate, as well as statistical data such as the average and maximum amounts of lodging income. Your completed workbook will look similar to Figure 2.42.

For Project 2B, you will need the following files:

e02B_Hotel_Taxes
e02B_Income_Analysis

**You will save your workbook as
2B_Hotel_Taxes_Firstname_Lastname**

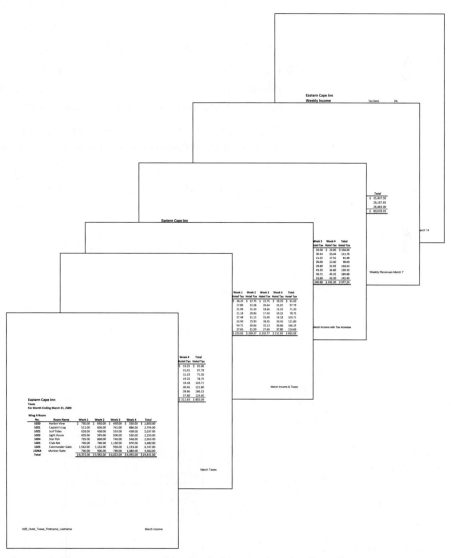

Figure 2.42
Project 2B—Hotel Tax Report

Objective 8
Copy a Worksheet

On occasion, the contents of one worksheet can be used in another worksheet. This can occur when you want to create separate reports using the same data. Rather than create the worksheet again, you can copy it and place the new worksheet within the same workbook or into a different workbook.

Activity 2.12 Copying a Worksheet Within a Workbook

In this activity, you will copy a worksheet and place it in the same workbook.

1 **Start** Excel. Click the **Office button** 🔲, and from the displayed menu, click **Open**. In the **Open** dialog box, navigate to the student files that accompany this textbook. Click **e02B_Hotel_Taxes**, and then click **Open**. **Save** the workbook in the **Excel Chapter 2** folder with the name **2B_Hotel_Taxes_Firstname_Lastname**

This worksheet reports the income for the rooms in Wing A for the month of March.

2 Click cell **A2** and change the title to **Taxes** Right-click the **Sheet1 sheet tab** and from the shortcut menu, click **Rename**. In the sheet tab, type **March Income** and then click in the worksheet or press Enter.

3 Right-click the **March Income sheet tab** and on the shortcut menu, click **Move or Copy**. Compare your screen with Figure 2.43.

The Move or Copy dialog box opens. Using this dialog box, you can copy or move the worksheet. You also specify which workbook the worksheet will be placed into and the location within the workbook.

Name of worksheet that new worksheet will be placed before

Figure 2.43

Name of current workbook—
location for copied worksheet

Active worksheet

Click to create a copy of
current worksheet

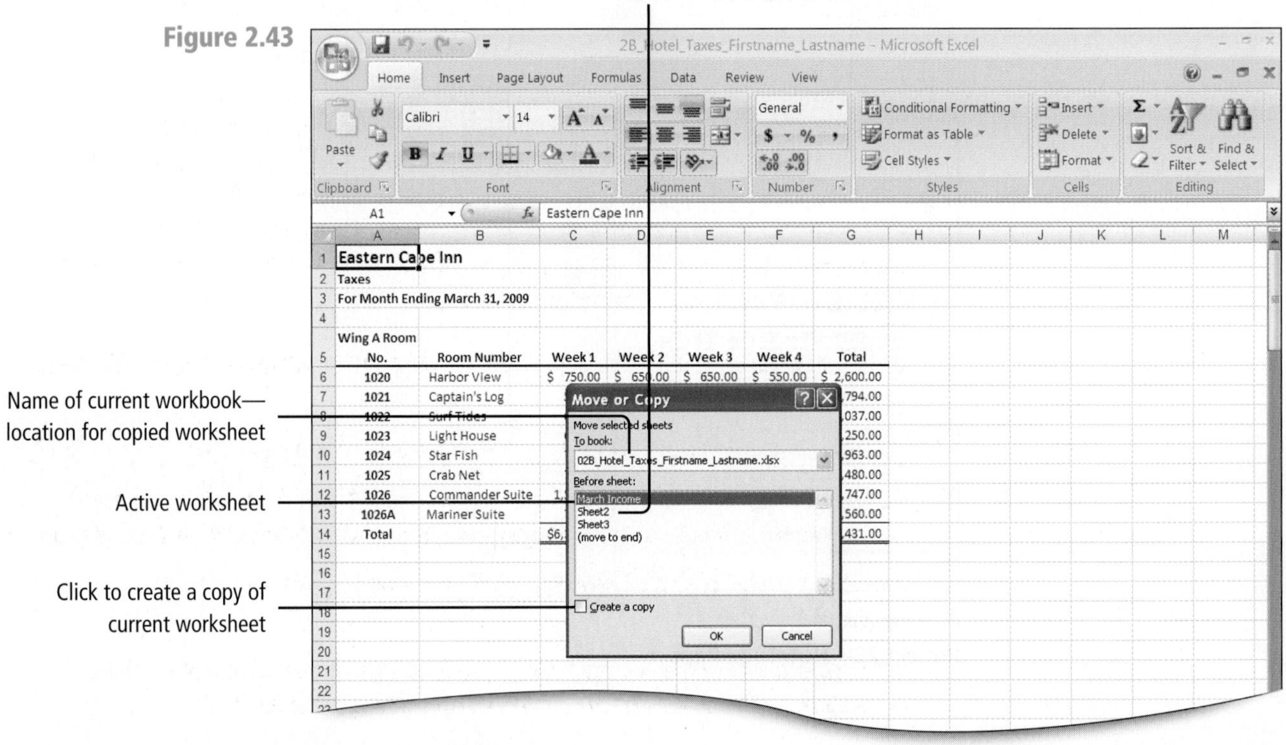

4 In the **To book** section, confirm that 2B_Hotel_Taxes_ Firstname_Lastname displays. In the **Before sheet** section, click **Sheet2**. Click the **Create a copy** check box to select it, and then click **OK**.

A copy of the worksheet, named *March Income (2)*, is placed between the *March Income* and the *Sheet2* worksheets.

Alert

Did you not select Create a copy?

If you have moved the worksheet, then using the skills practiced, copy it back to the original worksheet. If you do not click Create a copy, the worksheet will move to a new location and will be deleted.

5 Using the skills you have practiced, rename *March Income (2)* to **March Taxes**.

6 **Save** 🖫 your workbook.

Objective 9
Create Formulas with Absolute Cell References and Copy Formats

You have seen that a relative cell reference refers to cells by their position in relation to the cell that contains a formula. Relative cell references change when the formula is copied. *Absolute cell references*, on the other hand, refer to cells by their *fixed* position in the worksheet and do not change when the formula is copied.

Activity 2.13 Creating and Copying a Formula That Uses an Absolute Cell Reference

To copy a formula and retain the reference to a specific cell, use an absolute cell reference, which does not change when the formula is copied in the worksheet. To make a cell reference absolute, type a dollar sign ($) to the left of the column letter and row number of the cell reference—$A$1. In this activity, you will create a worksheet that uses an absolute cell reference in a formula that identifies the hotel tax rate and use it to determine the hotel taxes due.

1 In the **March Taxes** worksheet, beginning in cell **H5** enter the following column titles:

Week 1 Tax	Week 2 Tax	Week 3 Tax	Week 4 Tax	Total Tax

2 Click cell **D3** and type **Tax Rate** and in cell **E3** type **3.5%** Press ⏎. Right-click cell **E3**. In the displayed Mini toolbar, click the **Decrease Decimal button** one time to format the number to one decimal place.

By default, when you type the ⍟ key as you enter a number that contains a decimal, two (2) decimal places are entered.

3 Right-click cell **A5** and in the Mini toolbar, click the **Format Painter button** ☑. Drag the Format Painter through the range **H5:L5**.

4 Click cell **H6**. Type = and click in cell **C6**. Type *e3 and then press ⌊F4⌋. On the **Formula Bar**, click the **Enter button** ✔. Alternatively, you can type **$E$3**

The shortcut to change a cell reference to an absolute cell reference is the function key ⌊F4⌋. *Function keys* are located across the top of the keyboard and are labeled F1, F2, F3, and so on,

You have entered a formula in cell H6 that determines the amount of hotel tax that is applied to Room 1020 for the first week of March. This number is determined by multiplying the room charges for Week 1—cell C6—by the tax rate of 3.5%—cell E3. Because you will copy the formula, use an absolute cell reference for the tax rate so that the cell that contains the tax rate will always be referenced in the formula.

5 Right-click cell **H6** and from the displayed shortcut menu, click **Copy**. Click cell **H7**, right-click and from the displayed menu, select **Paste**. Press ⌊Ctrl⌋ + ⌊'⌋ to display the formulas. Using the horizontal scroll bar, scroll to the right to see the formulas and compare your screen with Figure 2.44. In this figure, the column widths have been decreased to display more of the worksheet; your screen will look different.

In the displayed formulas, notice that the relative cell reference in the formula, cell C6, changed to cell C7 when copied to the next row to reflect its new position. The absolute cell reference—$E$3—remained the same when it was copied. Recall that a relative cell reference will change relative to its new position and an absolute cell reference will remain the same when it is copied.

This formula multiplies the income from room 1021 for Week 1 by the tax rate of 3.5%.

Figure 2.44

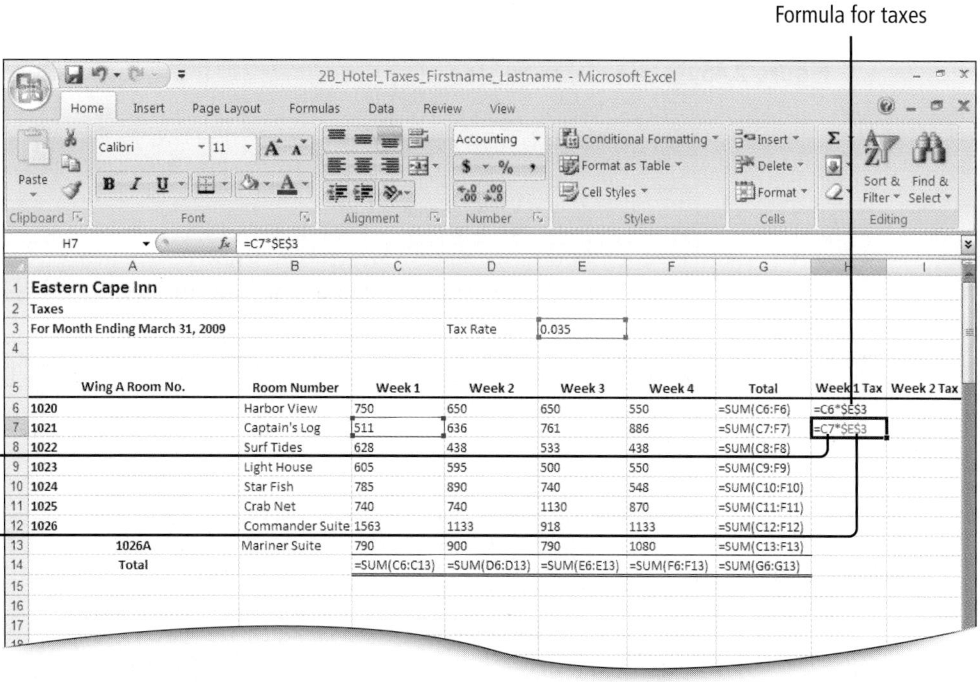

Formula for taxes

Relative cell reference in formula

Absolute cell reference in formula

The screenshot shows a Microsoft Excel window titled "2B_Hotel_Taxes_Firstname_Lastname - Microsoft Excel" with cell H7 selected showing the formula =C7*$E$3.

	A	B	C	D	E	F	G	H	I
1	Eastern Cape Inn								
2	Taxes								
3	For Month Ending March 31, 2009				Tax Rate	0.035			
4									
5	Wing A Room No.	Room Number	Week 1	Week 2	Week 3	Week 4	Total	Week 1 Tax	Week 2 Tax
6	1020	Harbor View	750	650	650	550	=SUM(C6:F6)	=C6*$E$3	
7	1021	Captain's Log	511	636	761	886	=SUM(C7:F7)	=C7*$E$3	
8	1022	Surf Tides	628	438	533	438	=SUM(C8:F8)		
9	1023	Light House	605	595	500	550	=SUM(C9:F9)		
10	1024	Star Fish	785	890	740	548	=SUM(C10:F10)		
11	1025	Crab Net	740	740	1130	870	=SUM(C11:F11)		
12	1026	Commander Suite	1563	1133	918	1133	=SUM(C12:F12)		
13	1026A	Mariner Suite	790	900	790	1080	=SUM(C13:F13)		
14	Total		=SUM(C6:C13)	=SUM(D6:D13)	=SUM(E6:E13)	=SUM(F6:F13)	=SUM(G6:G13)		
15									
16									
17									

6 Press Ctrl + ` to return to the original view that displays the results. With cell **H7** active, point to the **fill handle**. When the ➕ pointer displays, drag through cell **H13**, then release the mouse. Click cells **H8**, **H9**, and **H10** to confirm that the formula used the cell reference for the Week 1 income and the absolute cell reference to cell E3 for the tax rate.

7 Right-click cell **H6** and in the Shortcut menu, click the **Copy button**. Right-click cell **I6** and in the Shortcut menu, click the **Paste button**. Then in the **Formula Bar**, review the formula.

The relative reference changed from C6 to D6 to reflect its new position in the worksheet. The reference to the tax rate in cell E3 remains because it is an absolute cell reference.

8 With cell **I6** active, point to the **fill handle**. When the ➕ pointer displays, drag through cell **I13**, then release the mouse. Click in cells **I7**, **I8**, and **I9** to confirm that the formula used the cell reference for the Week 2 income and the absolute cell reference to cell E3 for the tax rate.

9 Select the range **I6:I13.** In cell **I13**, point to the **fill handle** and drag through cell **K13**, then release the mouse. Press Ctrl + ` to display the formulas. Scroll to the right on the horizontal scroll bar to bring **columns I:K** into view and compare your screen with Figure 2.45. In this figure, the column widths in the displayed worksheet have been changed so more of the worksheet displays.

As a formula is copied, the relative cell reference changes its row or column reference to reflect its new location. The absolute cell reference, on the other hand, always refers to the same cell.

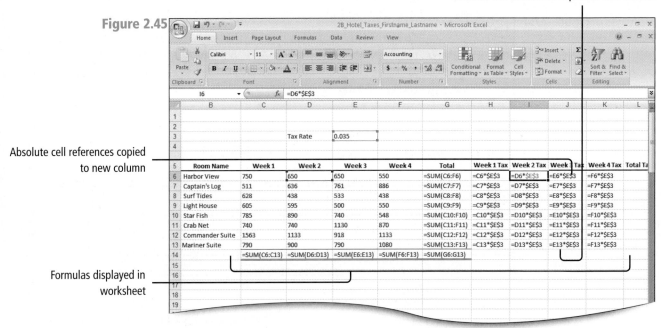

Figure 2.45

Relative cell references copied to new column

Absolute cell references copied to new column

Formulas displayed in worksheet

10 Press [Ctrl]+[`] to return to the results. Select the range **H6:L14**. From the **Editing group**, click the **Sum button** ![Sum](Σ ▾).

Sum formulas have been placed in row 14 and column L to determine totals for the taxes.

11 Select the range **C6:G14** and right-click. On the Mini toolbar, click the **Format Painter button** , and then click cell **H6**.

The format from a group of cells can be selected for the Format Painter. After selecting the range and activating the Format Painter, click with the Format Painter icon in the first cell—the upper left cell—of the range to receive the format. The format from the source range will be copied to the same number of rows and columns.

The worksheet format is completed.

12 Return to cell **A1** and **Save** your workbook.

Objective 10
Find and Replace Text and Hide and Unhide Columns

The Find and Replace dialog box is used to find specific text or values. When a match is found, the text can be replaced with text that you specify. Columns can be hidden in a worksheet so that only the data you need to review is visible. When columns are hidden, the cell contents are not deleted from the worksheet; they are simply hidden from view.

Activity 2.14 Using Find and Replace

The *Find and Replace* feature searches the cells in a worksheet—or in a selected range—for matches and then replaces each match with a replacement of your choice. In this activity you will replace some occurrences of *Tax* with *Hotel Tax*, a title that is more descriptive.

1 In the **March Taxes** worksheet, with cell **A1** active, on the **Home tab**, in the **Editing group**, point to the **Find & Select** button to review the ScreenTip. Click the **Find & Select button**, and then compare your screen with Figure 2.46.

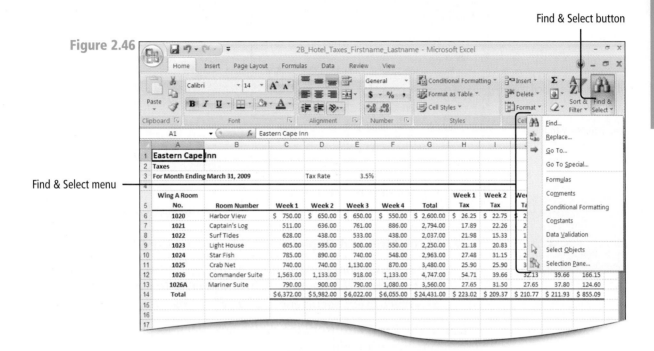

Find & Select button

Figure 2.46

Find & Select menu

2 In the displayed **Find & Select** menu, point to **Replace** and note the ellipses following the command, and then click **Replace**.

The *ellipses*—string of periods—that follow a command indicate that a dialog box will open when that command is selected.

The Find and Replace dialog box displays. There are two tabs in this dialog box—*Find* and *Replace*. The Replace tab is active.

3 Click in the **Find what** box and type **Tax** Press Tab. In the **Replace with** box, type **Hotel Tax** Compare your screen with Figure 2.47.

In a dialog box, pressing Tab will move to the next text box. The instructions in the dialog box tell Excel to search for every occurrence of *Tax*. Unless specified, Excel will match the word, even if the formats are different, the word is not capitalized, or if additional letters are added to the word, such as *Taxes*. When the match is made, you can select to replace that occurrence of *Tax* with *Hotel Tax*.

Figure 2.47

Excel searches for this text

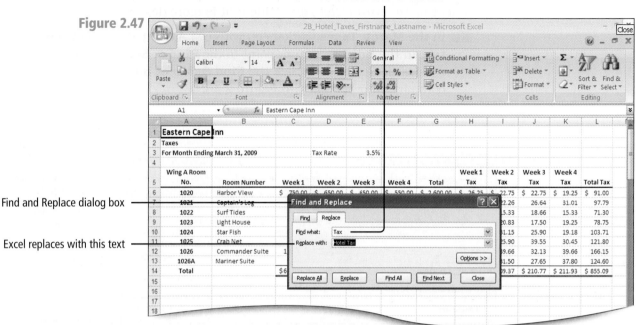

Find and Replace dialog box

Excel replaces with this text

4 In the **Find and Replace** dialog box, click **Find Next**.

The cell that contains the first occurrence of *tax* is highlighted—cell A2. If you wish to replace this occurrence, click *Replace*. If you would like to replace every occurrence of *Tax* with *Hotel Tax*, click *Replace All*.

5 In the **Find and Replace** dialog box, click **Replace**. Compare your screen with Figure 2.48.

Excel replaces the characters *tax* in cell A2 with *Hotel Tax* resulting in *Hotel Taxes* as the worksheet title—the characters *es* from the original word remain in the cell. Excel then finds and highlights cell D3 where the next occurrence of *Tax* displays.

Next occurrence of Tax in cell D3

Figure 2.48

Entry changed in cell A2

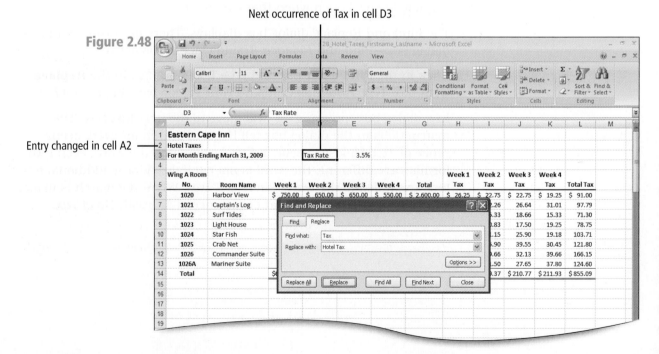

6 In the **Find and Replace** dialog box, click **Find Next**.

The entry in cell D3, *Tax Rate*, is correct, so you move to the next match, which is a column title in cell H5.

7 In the **Find and Replace** dialog box, click **Replace All**. Compare your screen with Figure 2.49. Then click **OK.**

An Information Box opens informing you that the search is complete and there were 7 replacements. Notice that in cells A2, D3, and L5, *tax* has been replaced with *Hotel Tax* in each cell. Cell A2 now reads *Hotel Hotel Taxes* and cell D3 reads *Hotel Tax Rate*. These are not the results that you want. In a worksheet, you need to be cautious about using the Replace All button because it may result in unintentional changes.

Replaced column titles

Figure 2.49

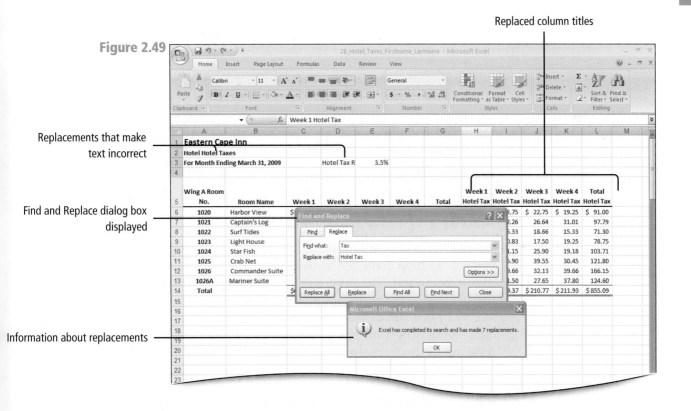

Replacements that make text incorrect

Find and Replace dialog box displayed

Information about replacements

8 In the **Quick Access Toolbar**, click the **Undo button**. Alternatively, press Ctrl + Z.

Recall that Undo deletes the last command, which replaced all instances of *Tax* with *Hotel Tax*. Cell H5 remains active.

9 Using the skills practiced, replace *Tax* with *Hotel Tax* in all cells except for cells **A2** and **D3**. When completed, in the **Find and Replace** dialog box, click **Close**, and then compare your screen with Figure 2.50.

Figure 2.50

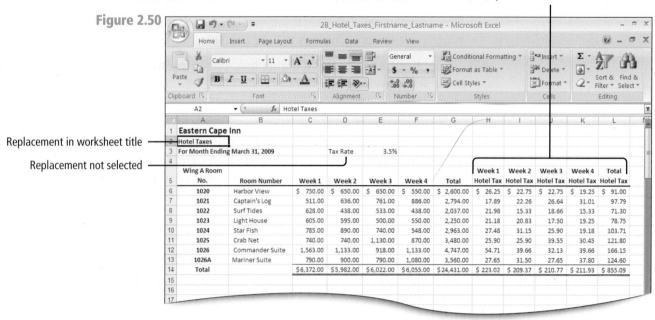

Replacement in worksheet title

Replacement not selected

10 If needed, adjust column widths to fully display contents in the column on one or two lines.

11 **Save** 💾 your workbook.

Activity 2.15 Hiding and Unhiding Columns

A large worksheet contains data that may not be needed for a report. It is possible to hide some of the worksheet rows or columns without losing that information. The process to **hide rows** or **hide columns**—remove the rows or columns from the worksheet view without losing the data—lets you print the worksheet without showing unnecessary or confidential data. Rows and columns that are hidden are not deleted, but are retained in the worksheet. In this activity you will hide columns in the worksheet and print a document that shows only the taxes that are due.

1 In the **March Taxes** worksheet, select **column C**. In the **Cells group**, click the **Format button**. In the displayed menu, under **Visibility**, point to **Hide & Unhide**. In the submenu that displays, click **Hide Columns**. Compare your screen with Figure 2.51.

Column C is no longer visible on the screen. A bold line remains, indicating there is hidden information. Hidden information remains in the worksheet but does not display on the screen.

Figure 2.51

Column C hidden

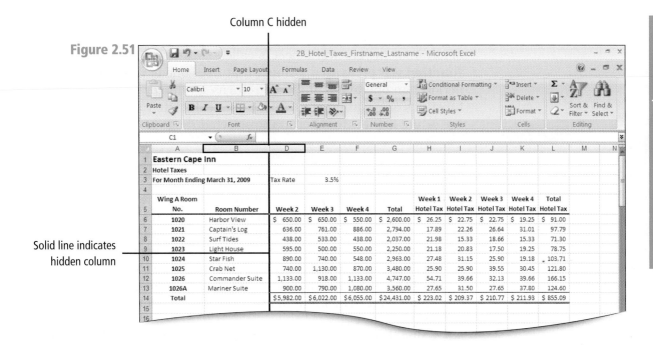

Solid line indicates
hidden column

2 Select **Columns D:G**, and then right-click. In the shortcut menu, click **Hide**.

The columns that report the lodging income are hidden from view and the worksheet displays only the Hotel Taxes.

3 Right-click the **March Taxes sheet tab**, and click **Move or Copy**. In the **Before sheet** section, click **Sheet2**. Click to select the **Create a copy** check box, and then click **OK**.

A copy of this worksheet is inserted just after the *March Taxes* worksheet and is named *March Taxes (2)*.

4 Rename the **March Taxes (2) sheet tab** to **March Income & Taxes**

5 In the **March Income & Taxes** worksheet, select **columns B:H**. In the **Cells group**, click the **Format button**. Under **Visibility**, point to **Hide & Unhide**. From the displayed submenu, click **Unhide Columns**. Alternatively, with the range of columns selected, position the mouse at the boundary between columns B and H and when the ⊞ pointer displays, double-click.

Columns B through H are now displayed in the March Income & Taxes worksheet.

6 Save 🖫 your workbook.

Objective 11
Conduct a What-If Analysis and Use Statistical Functions

Managers use the data in worksheets to analyze financial information and to make decisions. If you change the value of a cell referenced in a formula, Excel recalculates the results. Thus, you can change cell values to see *what* would happen *if* you tried different values. Changing only one number can provide completely different results. The process of changing the values in cells to see how those changes affect the outcome of formulas in your worksheet is called **what-if analysis**. Recall that a **function** is a prewritten formula that uses one or more cell references to perform an operation, and then returns a value or values. Statistical functions are a group of functions that calculate values such as the average or the highest number in the selected range of cells.

Activity 2.16 Performing a What-If Analysis and Using Statistical Functions

Dominique Amerline expects that the hotel tax rate will increase, which would result in an increase in the hotel room rates. Statistical functions are used to calculate various statistics about a group of numbers, such as the average, minimum—lowest number or maximum—highest number. In this activity, you will change the tax rate to evaluate what the taxes will be at a different rate. You will also determine the average, the maximum, and the minimum amount of income for the month.

1 Using the skills you practiced, create a copy of the **March Income & Taxes** worksheet and insert it before **Sheet2** of the workbook. Rename the new worksheet **March Income with Tax Increase**

2 In the **March Income with Tax Increase** worksheet, select cell **E3**. Type **4** and press Enter, and as you do, view the amount of tax in the worksheet columns H:L to see how the results change.

The worksheet is updated to display the result of a 4 percent hotel tax. When you change the value in a cell, the results of the formulas containing that cell also change.

3 Click the **March Income & Taxes sheet tab**. Beginning in cell **A16**, type the following row titles:

Average
Minimum
Maximum

4 Click cell **B16**. Click the **Formulas tab** and in the **Function Library group**, click the **Insert Function button**. Compare your screen with Figure 2.52.

The Insert Function dialog box displays. The top section, *Search for a function*, can be used to enter information you are looking for. You may also select a category in the *Or select a category* list. The *Select a function* area lists the functions that have been most recently used on that particular computer. Below the list of functions is a description of the selected function. Yours may be different from the list shown in Figure 2.52.

Figure 2.52

Formulas tab   Search for a function

Insert Function button ——

Function Library group ——

Insert Function dialog box ——

List of functions ——

Function location—cell B16 ——

Explanation of function ——

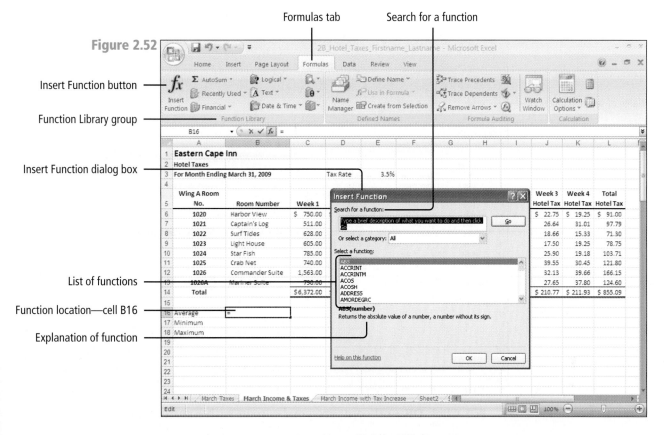

5 To the right of the **Or select a category** box, click the **arrow**, and from the displayed list, click **Statistical**.

A list of statistical functions displays.

6 In the **Select a function** box, click **AVERAGE**. Compare your screen with Figure 2.53.

The AVERAGE function is a statistical function. When used, it will return, or determine, the average of its *arguments*. Arguments are the values that an Excel function uses to perform calculations or operations. The **AVERAGE function** is a formula that adds a group of values and divides the result by the number of values in the group. Information about the selected function displays in the Insert Function dialog box.

Figure 2.53

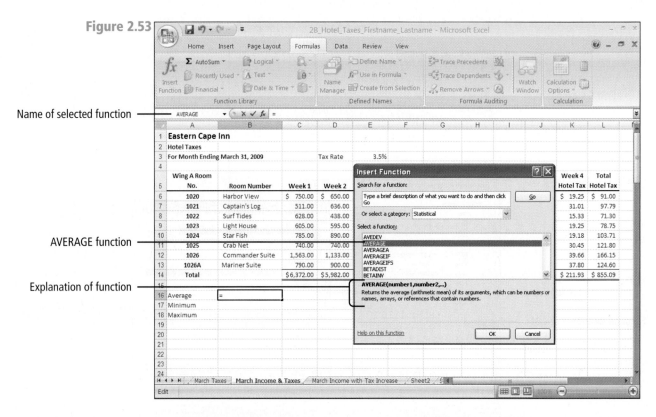

Name of selected function —
AVERAGE function —
Explanation of function —

---

7 Click **OK** and compare your screen with Figure 2.54.

The AVERAGE Function Arguments dialog box displays. This is where you will enter the arguments—values—used for the function. The specific function displays in the upper left corner of the dialog box. Arguments are entered at the *Number1* box and a description of the function displays in the middle area.

Text box used to enter arguments   Collapse Dialog Box button

Figure 2.54

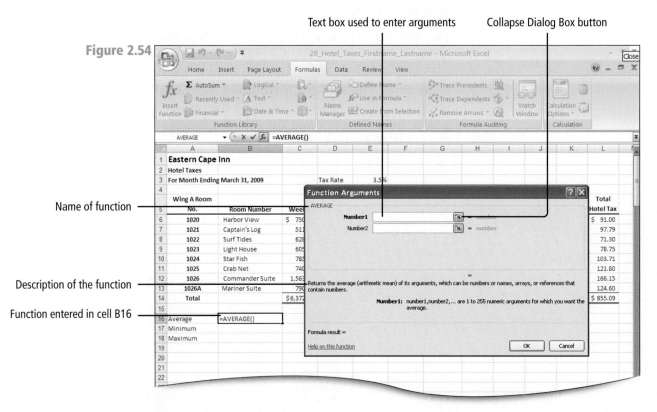

Name of function —
Description of the function —
Function entered in cell B16 —

8 To the right of the **Number1** text box, click the **Collapse Dialog Box button** 📖.

The ***Collapse Dialog Box button*** collapses the Function Arguments dialog box and displays only the entry area for this argument. If the collapsed dialog box covers the worksheet, click the dialog box title bar and drag it to a position that is out of the way.

9 Click cell **C14**, then in the collapsed **Function Arguments** dialog box, click the **Expand Dialog Box button** 📖.

Click the ***Expand Dialog Box button*** to fully display the Function Arguments dialog box. The first argument is entered.

10 Click in the **Number2** text box and notice that another text box — *Number3*—displays. Alternatively, press [Tab] to move to the next argument text box.

11 To the right of the **Number2** text box, click the **Collapse Dialog Box button** 📖. Click cell **D14**, and then in the collapsed **Function Arguments** dialog box, click the **Expand Dialog Box button** 📖.

As the AVERAGE function arguments are entered, the dialog box continues to expand to enable entry areas for the number of entries required.

12 Click the **Number3** text box and type **e14** Press [Tab], and using the skills you practiced, enter the cell **f14** in the *Number4* text box. Compare your screen with Figure 2.55.

Each argument is displayed in the dialog box with each cell value displayed at the right. The results of the function—6107.75—displays in the Function Arguments dialog box.

Figure 2.55

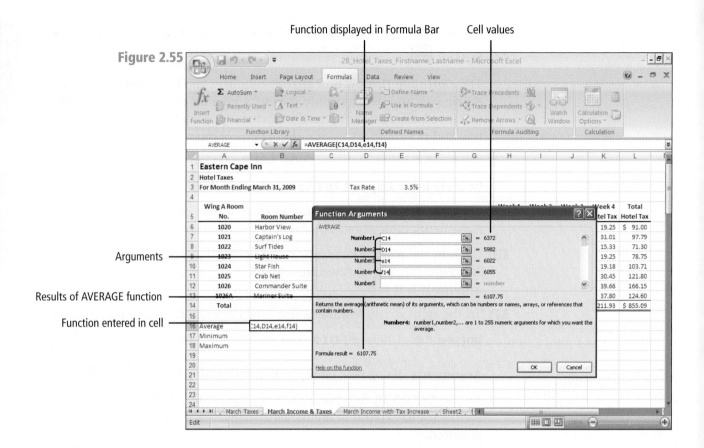

Function displayed in Formula Bar   Cell values

Arguments

Results of AVERAGE function

Function entered in cell

13 Click **OK**. Be sure cell **B16** is active, and then examine the formula in the **Formula Bar** and compare your screen with Figure 2.56.

The Average weekly lodging income—$6,107.75—displays in cell B16. The function displays in the Formula Bar and begins with an equal sign followed by the function name. The function arguments—cell references—are listed within parentheses, with commas separating each argument. The cells used in this function were formatted for Accounting Number Format, so that format is applied to the results of the function.

Figure 2.56

Average function formula

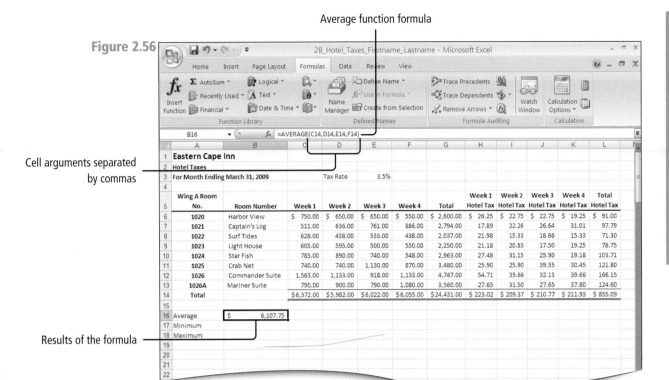

Cell arguments separated by commas

Results of the formula

14 Click cell **B17**. In the **Formula Bar**, point to the **Insert Function** button [fx], display the ScreenTip, compare your screen with Figure 2.57, and then click the **Insert Function button** [fx].

Because functions are used so frequently in Excel, the Insert Function button is always available on the Formula Bar, no matter which tab on the Ribbon is selected. In the *Insert Function* dialog box, *Statistical* is displayed in the *Or select a category* because it was the last used function category.

Figure 2.57

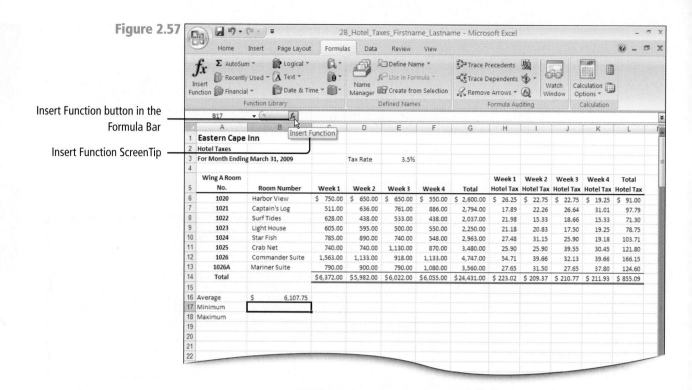

Insert Function button in the Formula Bar

Insert Function ScreenTip

15 Click in the **Select a function** list, type **m** then scroll down and double-click **MIN**.

The lists in the Insert Function dialog box are often long. You can move quickly to the function needed by typing the first letter of the function name. Double-clicking the name of the function is another method to open the Function Arguments dialog box.

The results of the *minimum function (MIN)* will display the smallest number in the selected cell range.

16 Click cell **C14** and drag through cell **F14**.

When you click in the cell, the Function Arguments dialog box collapses so you can see the worksheet. When you release the mouse button, the dialog box is restored.

The arguments—C14:F14—display in the Number1 arguments text box. The individual value of each cell in the range is displayed to the right, and the results of the function display near the center of the Function Arguments dialog box.

17 Press [Enter]. With cell **B17** active, examine the formula in the **Formula Bar**.

The smallest income amount—$5,982.00—is entered in cell B17. In a dialog box, *OK* is the default command and can be executed by pressing [Enter].

Recall that the function arguments—cell references—are listed within parentheses. In the Formula Bar, the function name is included first. The range of cells is displayed in parentheses. When a range of cells is entered in a function dialog box, each cell within the range is considered. Using the range C14:F14 is the same as entering the individual cells C14, D14, E14, and F14.

18 Click cell **B18**. On the **Home tab**, in the **Editing group**, click the **Sum button arrow** and compare your screen with Figure 2.58.

Functions can be accessed from the Sum button. Common ones display in the menu, but they can all be accessed using More Functions at the bottom of the list.

Sum button

Figure 2.58

Max function

Access More Functions

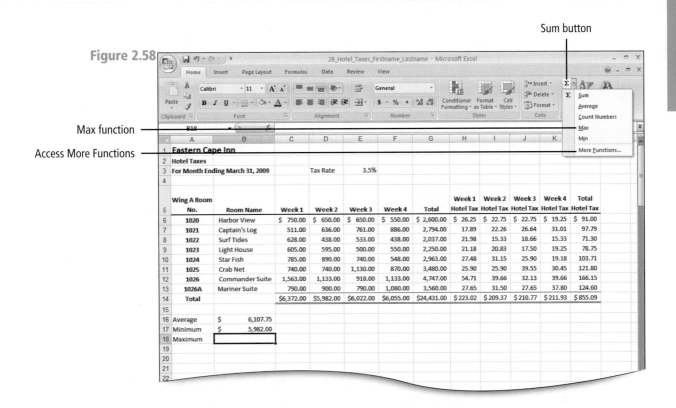

19 From the list, click **Max** to determine the *maximum*—largest—number in the range. In cell **B18**, a selected range is entered. Click and drag through the range **C14:F14** and press Enter. When complete, *$6,372.00* is entered in cell **B18**. With cell **B18** active, compare your screen with Figure 2.59.

The largest income amount—$6,372.00—is entered in cell B18. Examine the formula in the Formula Bar. When entering a function, the name of the function always displays just after the equal sign (=). Excel will suggest a range as it did for this function, but you can override the suggested range by selecting the range you want.

Figure 2.59

Formula for Maximum function

Results of Minimum function—MIN

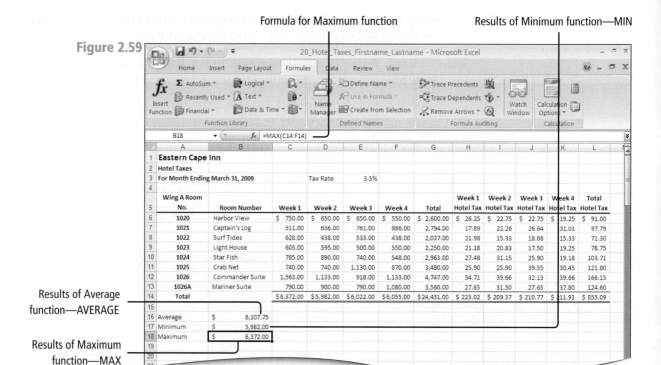

Results of Average function—AVERAGE

Results of Maximum function—MAX

20 **Save** your workbook.

Another Way
To Enter a Function

A function can be typed directly into the Formula Bar, using the specific *syntax*— language—of Excel. The function begins with an equal sign (=) and is followed by the name of the function. The arguments are next entered as a range or individual cells and are enclosed in parentheses.

Planning a Worksheet

When creating the worksheet, the planning stage is perhaps the most critical. You need to decide what data to include and how to organize it in a concise, easy-to-understand manner. The design must present a professional appearance. The following is a guide to planning a worksheet:

- **Determine the information that is critical** and must be included.
- **Determine information that is not critical.** Often there is data that is not relevant. For example, in the current worksheet, it is not necessary to know the total income for each individual room.
- **Determine the worksheet title.** Your title will answer who (name of business), what (identify what the worksheet displays), and when (the date of the worksheet). Although it is generally centered over the worksheet, it may align at the left margin.
- **Express the length of time for the worksheet in the dateline**. If the worksheet covers a period of time, indicate that period of time and the ending date. Use the formal date style of month, day, year—*December 31, 2009*.
- **Provide column and row titles.** All data in the worksheet must be identified or explained. Row and column titles explain the data so the reader can determine the relationship of the data. Totals also need to be identified.
- **Place the time frame along the horizontal (row) of the worksheet**. Use the days of the week, months of the year, quarters of a year, etc., for your column titles.
- **Determine what formulas (totals) are needed.**
- **Determine the format you will use for the numbers, the worksheet title, the row and column titles, and the totals.**
- **Decide what information will be placed in the header or footer.** It's important to know the file name of the document and who prepared it. You may also want to indicate the name of the worksheet, especially if the workbook contains more than one worksheet.
- **Determine where the worksheet will be placed on the page.** Center the worksheet, rather than leaving it in the upper left corner of the page. Be sure the worksheet will look professional when it is printed.

Activity 2.17 Planning and Preparing a Worksheet

In this activity, you will use the guidelines presented in the Planning a Worksheet workshop to prepare a worksheet that summarizes weekly income for room rentals for each day for the Eastern Cape Inn.

1 Double-click the **Sheet2 sheet tab** and type **Weekly Revenues March 7**

2 Beginning in cell **A1** type the worksheet titles—name of the organization, what the worksheet will display, and the date line. Recall that the name of the firm is Eastern Cape Inn. You will report the Weekly Income for the week that ends March 7, 2009. Enter the three title lines, and then compare your screen with Figure 2.60.

Figure 2.60

Purpose of worksheet report

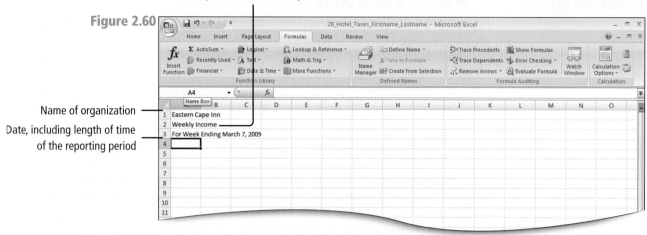

Name of organization

Date, including length of time
of the reporting period

1 Eastern Cape Inn
2 Weekly Income
3 For Week Ending March 7, 2009
4

3 Enter the column titles. The wing will be located in column A and the days of the week entered as column titles. You will want to include the total of each row, so a column title is needed for that total. In cell **A5**, type **Wing** Beginning in cell **B5** type **Sunday** and then use the fill handle to enter the days of the week as column titles extending to **Saturday**. In cell **I5**, type **Total**

Recall that the time frame is placed as row titles, so the days of the week are used as the column titles.

4 Beginning in cell **A6**, type the row titles for the three wings of the inn.

Wing A
Wing B
Wing C
Total

5 Enter the following data in the worksheet. It is not necessary to type the comma in each number as you enter the numbers.

Wing	Sunday	Monday	Tuesday	Wednesday	Thursday	Friday	Saturday
Wing A	3,805.50	2,987.50	3,029.35	3,450.80	2,983.50	4,050.25	5,100.60
Wing B	4,001.55	2,500.60	2,930.25	4,503.85	3,050.50	5,100.75	6,100.35
Wing C	3,800.10	3,000.70	3,100.75	3,500.70	2,900.40	4,800.00	5,380.35

6 Select the range **B6:I9**. With the **Home tab** active, in the **Editing group**, click the **Sum button** to calculate a total of each column and each row. The total sales for the week—*80078.35*—displays in cell **I9**. Verify that each row and column is identified by a title.

As you planned the worksheet, you would want to make sure there are totals for each wing and also totals for each day, so totals are needed in column I and row 9.

7 Select the three-line title range **A1:A3** and in the **Font group**, click the **Bold button**. Select the range **A1:I1**, and in the **Alignment group**, click the **Merge & Center button**. Select the range

A2:I2 and press Ctrl + Y. Use the method you practiced to merge and center the title in **row 3**.

Planning and then formatting the worksheet title is necessary to create a professional worksheet.

8 Select the column titles range **A5:I5**. On the **Home tab**, in the **Font group**, click the **Bold** B and **Italic** I buttons, click the **Border button**, and then click the **Thick Bottom Border button**. In the **Alignment group**, click the **Center button**.

9 Format the numbers in **row 6** with the **Accounting Number Format** $ with **2 decimals**. Format the numbers in **row 7** and **row 8** for **Comma Style** and **2 decimals**. Format the numbers in **row 9** with the **Accounting Number Format** with **2 decimals** and a **Top and Double Bottom Border**.

Planning for the format of the numbers and applying that format is also important for a professional worksheet. Recall that the placement of the worksheet on the page, including headers and footers, should be planned which will be completed for this entire workbook group.

10 **Save** your workbook.

Objective 12
Create Accurate Worksheets with Accuracy Tools

The data and formulas in a workbook must be 100 percent correct. Excel has many tools that help identify potential errors. Some tools are used as you create the worksheet. Others provide a message that a potential error is detected by displaying an error indicator in a cell. You can then check those error indicators and make corrections.

Activity 2.18 Inserting a Worksheet into a Workbook

1 Click the **Office button**, and then click **Open**. In the **Open** dialog box, navigate to the student files that accompany this textbook, click **e02B_Income_Analysis**, and then click **Open**. An **Alert** dialog box displays indicating Excel cannot calculate a formula. Compare your screen with Figure 2.61.

This Alert dialog box displays because there is a *circular reference* error in one of the cells in the worksheet. A circular reference error occurs when the cell that contains the results of the formula is included in the range or arguments used in the formula. You will resolve this error in a subsequent activity.

Figure 2.61

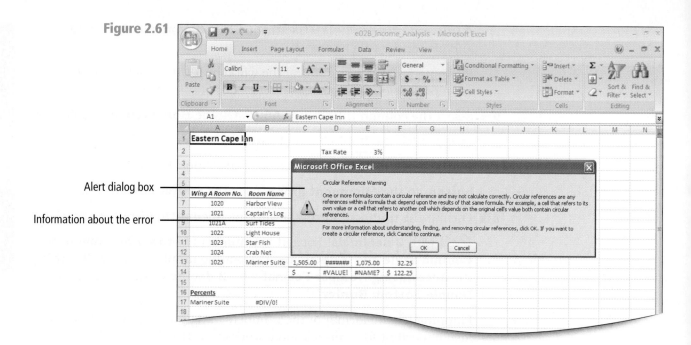

Alert dialog box

Information about the error

2 In the **Alert** dialog box, click **Cancel**. The workbook that opens contains several errors that you will correct, some of which may be indicated by the Error Message indicators—green triangles.

You have two workbooks open; e02B_Income_Analysis is the active workbook. Several cells contain words that begin with a # symbol, which you will correct in a later activity.

3 Right-click the **Sheet1 sheet tab** and click **Move or Copy**.

4 In the displayed **Move or Copy** dialog box, click the **To book arrow** and compare your screen with Figure 2.62.

The status bar displays *Circular Reference: C14* as a reminder of an error in this worksheet.

Arrow used to display available workbooks

Figure 2.62

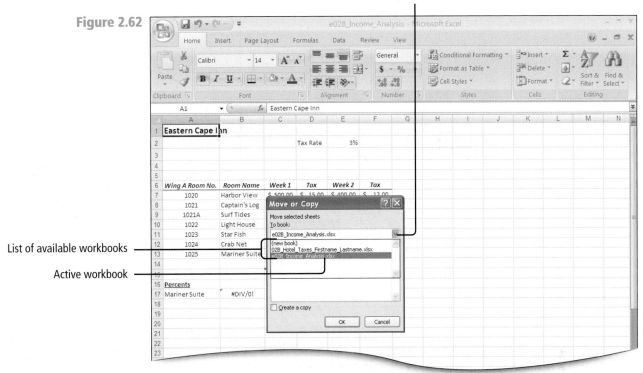

List of available workbooks

Active workbook

5 In the displayed list, click **2B_Hotel_Taxes_Firstname_Lastname**.

In the *Before sheet* area, the list of the worksheets in this workbook are displayed.

6 Click **Sheet3**, click the **Create a copy** check box, and compare your screen with Figure 2.63.

You have selected to place a copy of this worksheet in the *Hotel Taxes* workbook just after the *Weekly Revenues March 11* worksheet.

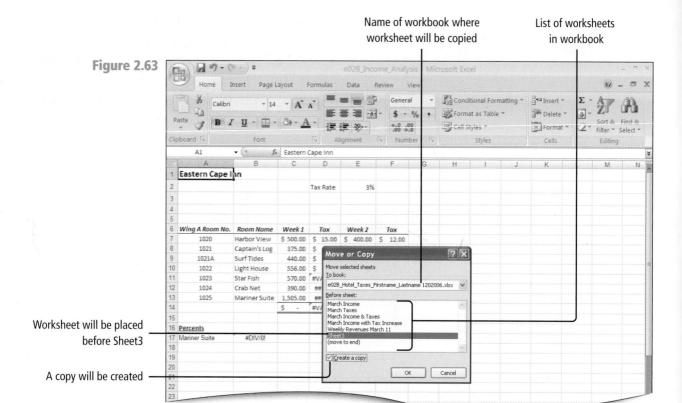

Figure 2.63

Name of workbook where worksheet will be copied

List of worksheets in workbook

Worksheet will be placed before Sheet3

A copy will be created

7 Click **OK**. Double-click the **Sheet1 sheet tab** and rename the worksheet **Two Weeks Ending March 14** and then click cell **A1**.

8 **Save** 💾 your workbook.

9 Click the **View** tab and in the **Window group**, click the **Switch Windows button**. Click **e02B_Income_Analysis**. In the **workbook-level buttons**, click the **Close Window button** ☒—the ScreenTip displays Close Window. When prompted, do not save changes.

Activity 2.19 Using Undo and Redo

Recall that you can reverse an action or a series of actions by using the *Undo* command. If you undo a command by mistake, the *Redo* command will reverse a previous undo action. A list of recent commands is available in the Undo and Redo lists, enabling several commands to be undone or redone at the same time. In this activity, you will use the Undo and Redo commands to correct the worksheet.

1 With the *Two Weeks Ending March 14* worksheet displayed, click in cell **A2** and type **Tax Report** and in cell **A3**, type **For Two Weeks Ending March 14, 2009** and press Enter.

The worksheet title is entered. When the worksheet was first completed, the format for the three-line title was entered. When you enter information into a preformatted range, the format is applied.

2 In the **Quick Access Toolbar**, click the **Undo button** 🔄.

The text is removed from cell A3, the latest data that was entered.

3 Click the **Undo button** 🔄 again.

The Tax Report title is removed. The Undo button reverses the commands or entries in the reverse order they were entered.

4 In the **Quick Access Toolbar**, point to the **Redo** button 🔄, review the ScreenTip, and then compare your screen with Figure 2.64.

The ScreenTip reads *Redo typing 'Tax Report' in A2*.

Redo button

Figure 2.64

Undo button

ScreenTip

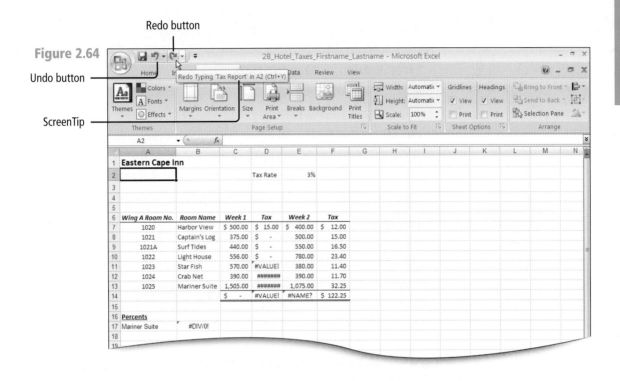

5 Click the **Redo button arrow** 🔄 to display the menu. Scroll to the second entry that reads *Typing 'For Two Weeks Ending March 14. . . ' in A3* and click the entry.

Two entries have been returned to the worksheet. Undo and Redo are quick ways to reverse or repeat one or more of the last entries.

6 Point to the **row 6 heading** until the ➡ pointer displays, and then right-click and from the shortcut menu, click **Delete**.

The row that contains the column titles is deleted from the worksheet.

7 On the **Quick Access Toolbar**, click the **Undo button** 🔄.

Row 6 is inserted again.

8 Using the skills you practiced, delete **row 5**.

When row 6 was deleted by mistake, Undo restored the row and then the correct row—row 5—was deleted.

9 **Save** 💾 your workbook.

Activity 2.20 Identifying and Correcting Errors in Formulas

Excel helps identify potential formula errors. Data entry errors cannot be detected, but other types of errors may be. Excel alerts you to potential errors by displaying an **error value**—an indicator of a type of formula error—in cells when a problem is detected. Error values begin with a number sign (#) followed by the error name. The table in Figure 2.65 identifies the error values that Excel uses and what causes them to occur in the worksheet.

Excel's Error Values

Error Value	Description
#N/A	Occurs when a value is not available to a function or a formula.
#NAME?	Occurs when Excel doesn't recognize text in a formula.
#NULL!	Occurs when an intersection of two areas is included in the formula but the areas do not intersect.
#REF!	Occurs when a cell reference is not valid.
#VALUE!	Occurs when the wrong type of argument or mathematical symbol—an operand—such as + or – is used.
#DIV/0	Occurs when a number is divided by zero (0).
#NUM!	Occurs with invalid numeric values in a formula or function.

Figure 2.65

1 In the **Two Weeks Ending March 14** worksheet, notice that there are a number of cells that contain an error value—*#REF!*, *#VALUE!*, *#NAME?*, and *#DIV/0!*.

When Excel detects a possible formula error, an error value is placed in the cell or cells that contain errors. Notice also there are error indicators displayed in some cells. Recall that an error indicator is a green triangle placed in the upper left corner of the cell to indicate a potential error in the formula.

2 Click cell **D6** and review the formula in the **Formula Bar**.

The formula multiplies the Week 1 income in cell C6 by cell E2 and is accurate.

3 Click cell **D7** and review the formula in the **Formula Bar**.

This formula multiples the Week 1 income in cell C7 by cell E3—an empty cell. The result—which is zero, displayed by $ and a hyphen—is displayed in the cell, but is an incorrect answer. This formula should have used the tax rate in cell E2. The formula in cell D6 was copied in the column. However, because an absolute cell reference was not used for cell E2, an error resulted when the formula was copied.

4 Click cell **D6**. In the **Formula Bar**, position the insertion point at the end of the formula—after cell **E2**. Press [F4] and then press [Enter]. Click cell **D6** and use the fill handle to copy the new formula through cell **D12**.

The formula is now correct. The error values, pound symbols, and empty cells have been removed from column D. Changing the cell reference to an absolute cell corrected the errors.

5 Select the range **D7:D12**, right-click, and from the Mini toolbar, click the **Comma Style button** .

6 Click cell **E13** and review the formula in the **Formula Bar**—=SM (E6:E12). Then click the **Error Checking button** and compare your screen with Figure 2.66.

Invalid Name Error is highlighted and displays the formula error. The error value—#NAME?—in the cell indicates that Excel cannot recognize the text in the formula. The function name, SUM, has been misspelled.

Invalid formula name   Error checking list

Figure 2.66

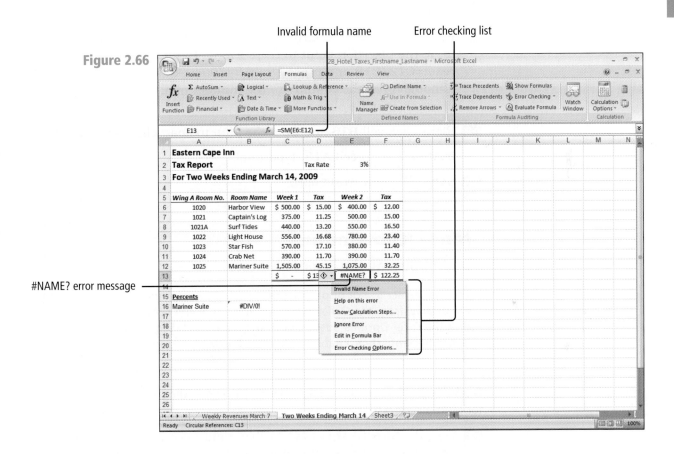

#NAME? error message

7 In the **Error Checking** options listed, click **Edit in Formula Bar** and position the insertion point between the **S** and the **M**. Type **u** and press Enter.

The formula is now correct and the cell displays the correct amount.

8 Click cell **C13** and in the **Formula Bar**, review the formula.

There is no mathematical operator instructing Excel that this range needs to be added. In addition, the range includes cell C13, which is the cell where the formula is located. This is an example of a circular reference, which causes the Alert dialog box to display when this file is opened.

9 In the **Formula Bar**, position the insertion point between the = and the C. Type **sum(** Then position the insertion point at the end of the formula—after the cell reference C13. Press ⌫Bksp and type **2)** The formula reads =*SUM(C6:C12)*. Press Enter.

The formula is correctly entered and the result—$4,336.00—displays in cell C13.

10 Click cell **B16** and click the displayed **Error Checking button** ◈ to display the Error Checking options.

The Error Checking options indicate this is a *Divide by Zero Error*. Recall that when you cannot divide a number by 0, the result is undefined. Cell B13 contains no value, which Excel recognizes as a zero.

This formula should show the percentage of weekly income for the Mariner Suite, the most popular room in this wing. This percentage is found by dividing the income for the room by the total income for the week.

11 From the **Error Checking** options, click **Edit in Formula Bar** to move the insertion point to the Formula Bar. Correct the formula to read **=C12/C13** and press Enter. *0.347094096* is entered in the cell, although on some computers the number may be truncated—fewer decimals may display.

12 Right-click cell **B16** and from the Mini toolbar, click the **Percent button** %. In cell **A13,** type **Total**

13 **Save** 💾 your workbook.

More Knowledge

Do Not Display the Error Indicators

You may select to not display the green triangle error indicators. To turn off the display, from the Office menu, on the bar at the bottom of the menu, click the Excel Options button. Click the Formulas category, and then under Error Checking, clear Enable background error checking.

Activity 2.21 Formatting Page Placement and Adding Footers for Multiple Worksheets

1 With the **Sheet3 sheet tab** visible, right-click the **Sheet3 sheet tab** and click **Delete**. If a Warning Box displays that reminds you there may be data on the sheet, press Delete. At any sheet tab, right-click and click **Select All Sheets**.

2 On the status bar, click the **Page Layout button** ▣ and scroll to the end of the worksheet to display the footer.

3 Click the **Left Footer area** and in the **Header & Footer Elements group**, click **File Name**. Click the **Right Footer area** and in the **Header & Footer Elements group**, click **Sheet Name**. Return to cell **A1**, and then return to **Normal** view.

4 Click the **Page Layout tab** and in the **Page Setup group**, click the **Dialog Box Launcher** ⬚. Click the **Margins tab** and under **Center**

on page, click the **Horizontally** check box and the **Vertically** check box. Then click **OK**.

5 At a worksheet tab, right-click, and then click **Ungroup Sheets**. Click the **March Income & Taxes** worksheet. Click the right tab scrolling button to display the sheet tab of the **Weekly Revenues March 7** worksheet and press ⇧Shift while you click the **Two Weeks Ending March 14 sheet tab**.

To select adjacent worksheets within the workbook, press ⇧Shift while you click in the last worksheet that will be included in the group. Three of the six worksheets in the workbook are grouped and can be formatted differently from the others.

6 On the **Page Layout tab**, in the **Page Setup group**, click the **Orientation button**. From the displayed list, click **Landscape**. In the **Page Setup group**, click the **Dialog Box Launcher** ⬚. In the **Page Setup** dialog box, in the **Page tab**, under **Scaling**, click **Fit to 1 page wide by 1 tall**. Click **OK**.

The page layout was selected for a group of worksheets, but the March Income & Taxes worksheet displays best in Landscape orientation with Fit to Page selected. In situations such as this, it is appropriate to set the Page Layout for individual worksheets. The March Income & Taxes worksheet displays best in Landscape Orientation and Fit to Page. It is recommended to apply a separate page layout style to a single worksheet in a workbook.

7 At a worksheet tab, right-click and click **Select All Sheets**. Press Ctrl + Home to return the active cell to **A1** in all worksheets. Run Spelling Checker to confirm there are no spelling errors. Then right-click a **sheet tab** and click **Ungroup Sheets**. Alternatively, click in each worksheet of the workbook and select cell A1. **Save** 🖫 your workbook.

8 Right-click a sheet tab and click **Select All Sheets**. Click the **Office button** 🗔, point to **Print**, and then click **Print Preview**. Use the scroll bar at the right to access and review each of the six worksheets of the workbook. Click **Close Print Preview**.

9 Check your *Chapter Assignment Sheet* or *Course Syllabus*, or consult your instructor, to determine if you are to submit work on paper or electronically. To submit electronically, follow the instructions provided by your instructor, and then go to Step 11.

10 Click the **Office button** 🗔, and from the displayed menu, click **Print**. In the **Print** dialog box, under **Print what**, select **Entire workbook**. Under **Copies**, confirm that **1** is selected. Click **OK**. If you are directed to submit printed formulas, group all worksheets. Refer to **Activity 1.12** to do so.

11 Click the **Office button** 🗔, and from the displayed menu, click **Close**. If the dialog box displays asking if you want to save changes, click **No** so that you do not save the changes to Page Setup that you may have used for printing formulas. **Exit** Excel.

End **You have completed Project 2B** ——————

There's More You Can Do!

From My Computer, navigate to the student files that accompany this textbook. In the folder **02_theres_more_you_can_do**, locate and open the folder for this chapter. Open and print the instructions for this project, which are provided to you in Adobe PDF format.

Try It! 1—Calculate Common Statistical Functions—Mean, Mode, Median

In this Try It! exercise, you will use Excel's statistical functions to determine the mean (average), median, and mode of the annual sales for the Eastern Cape Inn.

Summary

An Excel workbook contains several worksheets that are saved in the same file. When creating a workbook, the worksheets are related. Worksheets can be grouped and when grouped, entries and formats can be made to all worksheets in the group at the same time. Worksheets can be copied within the workbook or between workbooks. An absolute cell reference is used in a formula when a cell will be referenced no matter where the formula is placed within the worksheet. Error indicators and values help you ensure the accuracy of your worksheet data.

Key Terms

The 🔘 symbol represents Key Terms found on the Student CD in the 02_theres_more_you_can_do folder for this chapter.

Summary | **Excel** 191

Content-Based Assessments

Matching

Match each term in the second column with its correct definition in the first column by writing the letter of the term on the blank line in front of the correct definition.

_____ **1.** The area that identifies each worksheet in a workbook and accesses another worksheet.

_____ **2.** Enables data entries and formats to be entered into several worksheets at the same time.

_____ **3.** The worksheet in which text and data will be entered.

_____ **4.** A font that includes small line extensions on the ends of the letters to guide the eye in reading from left to right.

_____ **5.** A font that does not have small line extensions on the ends of the letters.

_____ **6.** Used to access worksheets that are not displayed.

_____ **7.** A group of similar or related items that come one after another in succession.

_____ **8.** The term for text that is displayed on two or more lines.

_____ **9.** The feature that creates a series using the fill handle and dragging in the worksheet.

_____ **10.** Used to display a list with options for filling the text or data.

_____ **11.** The action of copying cell contents into another location.

_____ **12.** The dialog box where you indicate if you want the contents, formats, or both to be copied to the selected worksheets.

_____ **13.** The data that is copied.

_____ **14.** A temporary storage area maintained by your Windows operating system that contains the latest data in a copy command.

_____ **15.** The cell or range of cells where data will be copied into.

A Active worksheet

B Auto Fill

C Auto Fill Options button

D Copy and paste

E Destination

F Fill Across Worksheets dialog box

G Grouped worksheets

H Sans serif font

I Series

J Serif font

K Source

L System Clipboard

M Tab scrolling buttons

N Worksheet tab

O Wrap Text

Content-Based Assessments

Fill in the Blank

Write the correct word in the space provided.

1. The range of cells that is copied is the _____ range.

2. The range of cells where data will be copied into is the _____ range.

3. Select whether you want to paste the contents, formats, or both (All) to the selected worksheet using the _____ _____ button.

4. The feature that enables you to copy multiple text and graphical items from Office documents and paste them into another Office document is the Microsoft Office _____.

5. The workbook that is visible on the screen where changes can be made is the _____ workbook.

6. When data is pasted into a cell, it _____ existing cell contents.

7. The green triangle placed in a cell where a possible error is detected is the error _____.

8. The total of the individual sums in the selected range is called the _____ _____.

9. When a column or row is inserted in the worksheet, suggestions for formatting the newly inserted row or column is available with the _____ _____ button.

10. The type of cell reference used to refer to cells by their *fixed* position in the worksheet and does not change when the formula is copied is called a(n) _____ cell reference.

11. The keys across the top of the keyboard labeled F1, F2, F3, and so on, which are used for special tasks, are the _____ keys.

12. The feature that searches the cells in a worksheet, identifies matches, and then replaces each match with a replacement of your choice is _____ and _____.

13. Removing the row or column from view on the worksheet without losing the data is called _____ the row or column.

14. A prewritten formula that takes one or more values, performs an operation, and then returns a value or values is called a(n) _____.

15. The values that an Excel function uses to perform calculations or operations are its _____.

Project 2C—Personnel Costs

In this project, you will apply the skills you practiced from the Objectives in Project 2A.

Objectives: 1. *Work with a Multiple-Sheet Workbook;* **2.** *Enter a Series;* **3.** *Copy and Paste Cell Contents;* **4.** *Copy and Paste with the Office Clipboard;* **5.** *Total the Worksheet Range and Enter a Grand Total;* **6.** *Format a Multiple-Sheet Workbook Group;* **7.** *Insert Columns and Rows in Multiple Worksheets.*

In the following Skills Review, you will prepare a report of the personnel costs for Eastern Cape Inn for a year. Individual worksheets will be prepared for each quarter and then combined into one report. Your completed workbook will look similar to the one shown in Figure 2.67.

For Project 2C, you will need the following files:

New blank Excel workbook
e02C_Annual_Personnel_Costs

You will save your workbook as
2C_Personnel_Costs_Firstname_Lastname

Figure 2.67

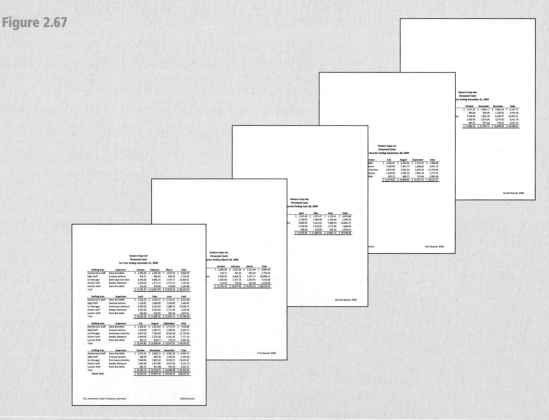

(Project 2C–Personnel Costs continues on the next page)

Content-Based Assessments

(Project 2C–Personnel Costs continued)

1. **Start** Excel. Click the **Office button**, and from the displayed menu, click **Save As** to display the **Save As** dialog box, click the **Save in arrow**, and then navigate to your **Excel Chapter 2** folder. In the **File name** box, type **2C_Personnel_Costs_Firstname_ Lastname** and then click **Save** or press Enter.

2. To the right of the **Sheet3** sheet tab, click the **Insert Worksheet button** to add **Sheet4**. Repeat this process to add **Sheet5**.

3. Right-click any **sheet tab** and click **Select All Sheets**. Confirm that *[Group]* displays in the title bar to indicate that any changes you make will be made to all the worksheets in the group. In cell **A1**, type **Eastern Cape Inn** In cell **A2**, type **Personnel Costs** In cell **A3**, type **For Year Ending December 31, 2009**

4. In the **Status bar**, click the **Page Layout button** and scroll down to display the footer. Click in the **Left Footer area**, and then in the **Header & Footer Elements group**, click the **File Name button**. Click in the **Right Footer area**, and then in the **Header & Footer Elements group** click the **Sheet Name button**. Return to cell **A1** and click the **Normal button** to return to Normal view.

5. Double-click the **Sheet1 sheet tab**, type **2009 Summary** and then press Enter. Repeat this process to select and rename each sheet tab as follows, using the tab scrolling buttons as necessary to navigate between the sheet tabs:

Sheet2	First Quarter 2009
Sheet3	Second Quarter 2009
Sheet4	Third Quarter 2009
Sheet5	Fourth Quarter 2009

6. Click the **tab scrolling button** at the far left. Right-click the **2009 Summary sheet tab**, point to **Tab Color**, and then under **Standard Colors**, click the second color— **Red**. Repeat this process and using the ScreenTips to identify the standard colors, change the tab color for the other sheet tabs as follows:

First Quarter 2009	Light Green
Second Quarter 2009	Light Blue
Third Quarter 2009	Dark Blue
Fourth Quarter 2009	Dark Red

7. Right-click any sheet tab and click **Select All Sheets**. Confirm in the title bar that the worksheets are grouped. In cell **A5**, type **Staffing Area** In cell **B5**, type **January** Click cell **B5**, point to the **fill handle**, and drag to the right to cell **D5** to extend the months to **March**. In cell **E5**, type **Total** Select the range **A5:E5**. Right-click the selected range to display the Mini toolbar and then click the **Bold**, **Center**, and **Bottom Border buttons**.

8. With the sheets still grouped, beginning in cell **A6**, type the following row titles in **column A**:

Maintenance Staff
Night Staff
Inn Manager
Kitchen Staff
Laundry Staff
Total

9. With the worksheets still grouped, click cell **A6**. On the **Home tab**, in the **Cells group**, click **Format**, and then click

(Project 2C–Personnel Costs continues on the next page)

(Project 2C–Personnel Costs continued)

AutoFit Column Width to widen **column A** to fit the longest row title in the column.

10. Right-click any **sheet tab**, click **Ungroup Sheets**, and then confirm in the title bar that *[Group]* no longer displays. If necessary, use the tab scrolling buttons to display the **First Quarter sheet tab**. Click the **First Quarter sheet tab**. In cell **A3**, edit the date to read **For Quarter Ending March 31, 2009** Click the **Second Quarter sheet tab**, and in cell **A3**, edit the date to read **For Quarter Ending June 30, 2009**

11. Click the **Third Quarter sheet tab**, and then in cell **A3**, edit the date to read **For Quarter Ending September 30, 2009** Click the **Fourth Quarter sheet tab** and in cell **A3**, edit the date to read **For Quarter Ending December 31, 2009**

12. On the **Home tab**, in the **Clipboard group**, click the **Dialog Box Launcher** to display the **Clipboard task pane**.

13. Click the **Office button**, and from the displayed menu, click **Open**. Navigate to the student files that accompany this textbook. Locate and **open** the Excel workbook named **e02C_Annual_Personnel_Costs**. Select the range **C4:E9**, right-click the selected range, and from the displayed shortcut menu, click **Copy**. Using the skills you have practiced, copy the data from each quarter displayed in this worksheet to the **Clipboard task pane**. Include the month names and the data in the source range. The ranges to copy are **C12:I17**, **C20:E25**, and **C28:E33**. When you have copied the data from all four quarters to the **Clipboard task pane**, in the **workbook-level** buttons, click the **Close Window button** and if prompted to save changes, click **No**—don't save changes.

14. Click the **2009 Summary sheet tab**. Click cell **B5**. In the **Clipboard task pane**, locate the entry that displays the data that begins **January**, and then click the entry. Click the **Paste Options button** and click **Match Destination Formatting**. Click the **First Quarter 2009 sheet tab**. Click cell **B5**. In the **Clipboard task pane**, locate the entry that displays the data that begins **January**, and then click the entry. Click the **Paste Options button** and click **Match Destination Formatting**.

15. Click the **Second Quarter 2009 sheet tab**. Click cell **B5** and in the **Clipboard task pane**, locate the data that begins **April**, and then click the entry. Click the **Paste Options button**, and from the displayed list, click **Match Destination Formatting**. Click the **Third Quarter 2009 sheet tab**, click cell **B5**, and then click the data that begins with **July** and use the **Paste Options** button to **Match Destination Formatting**. Click the **Fourth Quarter 2009 sheet tab**, click cell **B5**, and using the skills you practiced, enter the data that begins with **October** and maintain the format of the worksheets.

16. Right-click any sheet tab, and from the shortcut menu, click **Select All Sheets**. Select the range **B6:E11**. In the **Editing group**, click the **Sum button**. Select the range **B6:E6**, press Ctrl, and then select the range **B11:E11**. In the **Number group**, click the **Accounting Number Format button**. Select the range **B7:E10** and in the **Number group**, click the **Comma Style button**. Select the range **B11:E11**, and in the **Font group**, click the **Bottom Border button arrow**, and then click **Top and Double Bottom Border**.

17. Click the **Second Quarter 2009 sheet tab** and confirm that the worksheets are no longer grouped. Select the range **A5:D10**.

(Project 2C–Personnel Costs continues on the next page)

Content-Based Assessments

(Project 2C–Personnel Costs continued)

Right-click and from the shortcut menu, click **Copy** to store this data in the **Clipboard task pane**. Click the **Third Quarter sheet tab** and select the range of the worksheet data—**A5:D10**. Right-click, and then click **Copy**. Using the skills you practiced, click the **Fourth Quarter sheet tab** and copy the same data range. The data sections for three worksheets are copied to the **Clipboard task pane**.

18. Click the **2009 Summary sheet tab** and click cell **A13**. In the **Clipboard task pane**, locate the entry that begins *Staffing Area April May* and click it to insert it into the Summary worksheet. Click cell **A21**. In the **Clipboard task pane**, locate the entry that begins *Staffing Area July August* and click it to insert it into the Summary worksheet. Click cell **A29**. Using the skills practiced, insert the fourth quarter data that begins *Staffing Area October November*. Adjust the column widths to fully display the cell entries.

19. Select the range **B14:E19** and in the **Editing group**, click the **Sum button**. Select the range **B22:E27** and in the **Editing group**, click the **Sum button**. Using the skills you practiced, insert totals for the fourth quarter report.

20. Right-click cell **E5**, and then click **Copy**. Click cell **E13**. In the **Clipboard task pane**, click the entry that begins **Total**. Click cell **E21** and from the **Clipboard task pane**, click the entry that says **Total**. Using the skills you practiced, place **Total** in cell **E29**. Click cell **A19**. Hold down (Ctrl) while you click cells **A27** and **A35**. Type **Total** and then press (Ctrl) + (Enter).

21. Select the range **B11:E11** and use the **Format Painter** to copy the format to the ranges beginning in cells **B19**, **B27**, and **B35**.

22. In the **2009 Summary sheet**, select the range **B6:D36**. In the **Editing group**, click the **Sum button**. If necessary, adjust column widths. Select the grand totals—the range **B36:E36**. Apply **Accounting Number Format** to this range where necessary. In the **Font group**, click the **Borders button arrow**, and then click **Thick Bottom Border**. In cell **A36**, type **Grand Total** and confirm the entry. Right-click cell **A36** and on the Mini toolbar, click the **Bold** and **Center buttons**.

23. The supervisor of each staff area should be included in this worksheet, so you will insert a column, and then add that data. Right-click any sheet tab, and click **Select All Sheets**. Right-click the **column B header**, and then click **Insert**. Beginning in cell **B5**, type the following entries in **column B**:

Supervisor
Elena Brondello
Emanuel Jackson
Dominique Amerline
Bradley Matteson
Elena Brondello

24. Click cell **B8**. In the **Cells group**, click **Format**, and then click **AutoFit Column Width**. Right-click the **2009 Summary sheet tab** and from the displayed shortcut menu, click **Ungroup Sheets**. Select the range that includes the supervisors—**B5:B10**. Right-click, and then click **Copy**. Press (Ctrl) while you click in cells **B13**, **B21**, and **B29**. Then right-click and click **Paste**. Recall that you can paste data into several ranges of the worksheet at the same time. In the **Office Clipboard task pane** click the **Close button**.

25. Right-click any **sheet tab** and click **Select All Sheets**. Select the range **A1:F1** and

(Project 2C–Personnel Costs continues on the next page)

Content-Based Assessments

(Project 2C–Personnel Costs continued)

right-click. On the **Mini toolbar**, click the **Bold**, **Italic**, and **Increase Font Size buttons**. On the **Home tab**, in the **Alignment group**, click the **Merge & Center button**. In the **Clipboard group**, double-click the **Format Painter button**. Click cells **A2** and **A3**, and then in the **Clipboard group**, click the **Format Painter button** to turn it off.

26. With all worksheets still grouped, click the **Page Layout tab**, and in the **Page Setup group**, click the **Dialog Box Launcher.** On the **Page** tab, under **Scaling**, click **Fit to 1 page**. Click the **Margins tab**, and under **Center on page**, click **Horizontally** and click **Vertically**. Then click **Print Preview.** Use the vertical scroll bar at the right to preview each of the five pages of the workbook.

27. Click **Close Print Preview**. **Save** your work. Check your *Chapter Assignment Sheet* or your *Course Syllabus* or consult your instructor to determine if you are to submit your assignments on paper or electronically. To submit electronically, go to Step 28, and then follow the instructions provided by your instructor.

28. Click the **Office button** and from the displayed menu, click **Print**. In the **Print** dialog box, under **Print what**, select **Entire workbook**. Under **Copies**, confirm that **1** is selected, and then click **OK**. If you are directed to submit printed formulas, group all worksheets. Then refer to Activity 1.12 to do so.

29. Click the **Office button** and from the displayed menu, click **Close**. If the dialog box displays asking if you want to save changes, click **No** so that you do not save the changes to Page Setup that you used for printing formulas. **Exit** Excel.

End **You have completed Project 2C**

Content-Based Assessments

Project 2D — Salary Projections

In this project, you will apply the skills you have practiced from the Objectives in Project 2B.

Objectives: 8. *Copy a Worksheet;* **9.** *Create Formulas with Absolute Cell References and Copy Formats* **10.** *Find and Replace Text and Hide and Unhide Columns;* **11.** *Conduct a What-If Analysis and Use Statistical Functions;* **12.** *Create Accurate Worksheets with Accuracy Tools.*

In the following Skills Review, you will evaluate the current salaries for the employees of Eastern Cape Inn and determine what the salaries would be with proposed increases. Your completed workbook will look similar to the one shown in Figure 2.68.

For Project 2D, you will need the following files:

e02D_Salary_Projections
e02D_Salary_Increases

You will save your workbook as
2D_Salary_Projections_Firstname_Lastname

Figure 2.68

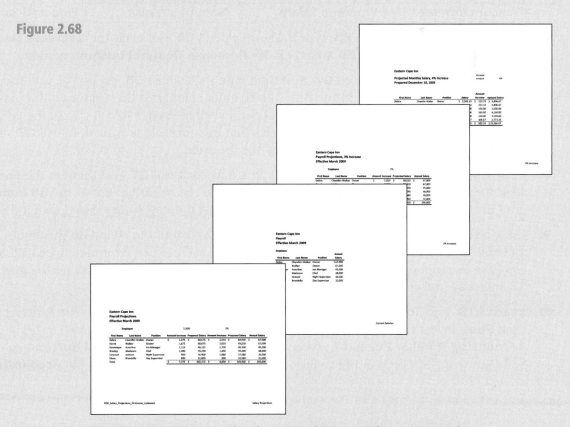

(Project 2D–Salary Projections continues on the next page)

Content-Based Assessments

chapter two   Skills Review

(Project 2D–Salary Projections continued)

1. **Start** Excel. Display the **Open** dialog box, and then from the student files that accompany this text, locate and open **e02D_Salary_Projections**. Click the **Office button**, and from the displayed menu, click **Save As** and navigate to your **Excel Chapter 2** folder. In the **File name** box, type **2D_Salary_Projections_Firstname_Lastname** and then click **Save** or press Enter.

2. Double-click the **Sheet1 sheet tab** and type **Current Salaries** and press Enter to rename the sheet. Right-click the **Current Salaries sheet tab**, point to **Tab Color**, and then under **Standard Colors**, click the fourth color—**Yellow**.

3. To preserve this worksheet, you will make a copy of it to use for the projections. Right-click the **Current Salaries sheet tab** and from the shortcut menu, click **Move or Copy**. In the **Before sheet** area, confirm that **Current Salaries** is selected, click the **Create a copy** check box, then click **OK**. The **Current Salaries (2)** worksheet is the first worksheet of the workbook. Double-click the **Current Salaries (2) sheet tab**, type **Salary Projections** and then press Enter. Right-click the **Salary Projections sheet tab**, point to **Tab Color**, and then under **Standard Colors**, click the sixth color—**Green**.

4. In the **Salaries Projections** sheet, right-click the **column C heading** and from the shortcut menu, click **Insert**. Press Ctrl + Y to insert another column. Insert two more columns so four columns are inserted into the worksheet. The Annual Salary now displays in column G.

5. Beginning in cell **C6**, enter the following column titles:

Amount Increase	Proposed Salary	Amount Increase	Proposed Salary

6. In cell **C5**, type **2.5%** In cell **E5**, type **3.0%**. Click cell **C5** and click the **Decrease Decimal button** one time. Click cell **E5** and click the **Decrease Decimal button** one time.

7. In cell **C7**, type **=** and click cell **G7**, and then type * Click cell **C5**, press F4, and then on the **Formula Bar**, click the **Enter button**. This formula calculates the amount of increase at a rate of 2.5%. In this formula, you created an absolute cell reference to cell C5, so the percentage in cell C5 will be applied to the other salaries when this formula is copied. In cell **C7**, click the **fill handle** and drag through cell **C12** to copy the formula.

8. Click cell **D7**. Type **=** and click cell **C7**. Type **+** and click cell **G7** and then on the **Formula Bar**, click the **Enter button**. $68,675 is entered in cell D7. In cell **D7**, point to the **fill handle** and drag through cell **D12**. In this column you calculated the new salary based on a 2.5% increase.

9. Click cell **E7**. Using the skills you practiced, write a formula to calculate the amount of the increase at 3%. In the formula, be sure to use an absolute cell reference to cell **E5** and then copy the formula to cell **E12**. Click cell **F7** and enter a formula to calculate the new salary at a 3% increase and copy the formula down to cell **F12**.

10. In cell **A13**, type **Total** Select the range **C13:G13**. On the **Home tab**, in the **Editing** group, click **Sum**. Select the range **C7:G7** and right-click to access the Mini toolbar. Click the **Accounting Number Format button** and click the **Decrease Decimal button** two times. Select the range **C13:G13**. Right-click and from the Mini toolbar, click the **Accounting Number**

(Project 2D–Salary Projections continues on the next page)

200   **Excel** | Chapter 2: Using Multiple-Sheet Workbooks

Content-Based Assessments

(Project 2D–Salary Projections continued)

Format button and click the **Decrease Decimal button** two times. In the **Borders** button, click the arrow and click **Top and Double Bottom Border**. Select the range **C8:G12** and right-click. In the Mini toolbar, click the **Comma Style button** and click the **Decrease Decimal button** two times. Even though decimals will result in these formulas, the owners have asked that salaries be stated in whole dollars.

11. Select the range **A5:B5**, right-click, and from the Mini toolbar, click **Merge & Center**. Select the range **C5:D5** and press Ctrl + Y, and then select the range **E5:F5** and press Ctrl + Y to center this data over two columns. In cell **A2**, change the entry so it reads **Payroll Projections** Select **columns C:G** and move the mouse to a boundary between column headings and double-click.

12. Right-click any sheet tab, and from the shortcut menu, click **Select All Sheets**. Click the **column C heading**, right-click, and from the shortcut menu, click **Insert**. In **column C**, beginning in cell **C6**, type the following entries:

Position
Owner
Owner
Inn Manager
Chef
Night Supervisor
Day Supervisor

13. Click in the **Salary Projections sheet tab** and confirm the worksheets are not grouped. Right-click the **Salary Projections sheet tab** and click **Move or Copy**. In the **Before sheet** area, click **(move to end)**. Click the **Create a copy** check box, and then click **OK**. Double-click the **Salary Projections (2) sheet tab**, type **3% Increase** and then press Enter. Right-click the **3% Increase sheet tab**, from the shortcut menu, point to **Tab Color**, and then under **Standard Colors**, click the ninth color—**Dark Blue**.

14. In the **3% Increase** worksheet, select **columns D:E**. Right-click, and from the shortcut menu, click **Hide**. Click the **column H heading** and press Ctrl + Y to repeat the Hide command.

15. In the **3% Increase** worksheet, click cell **A1**. In the **Editing group**, click **Find & Select**. From the displayed menu, click **Replace**. In the **Find and Replace** dialog box, in the **Find what** box, type **Proposed** Press Tab and in the **Replace with** box, type **Projected** Click **Replace All**. A dialog box displays indicating that 2 replacements have been made; one is in the hidden columns. Click **OK**, and then in the **Find and Replace** dialog box, click **Close**. Click cell **A2**; at the end type **, 3% Increase** so the worksheet title displays *Payroll Projections, 3% Increase* and then **Save** your work.

16. Click the **Office button** and from the displayed menu, click **Open**. In the **Open** dialog box, navigate to the student files that accompany this textbook, locate and open **e02D_Salary_Increases**. A warning box opens indicating an error in the document. Click **Cancel** to continue opening the file. Right-click the **Sheet1 sheet tab** and from the shortcut menu, click **Move or Copy**. In the **To book** section, click the **arrow** and from the list, click **2D_Salary_Projections_Firstname_**

(Project 2D–Salary Projections continues on the next page)

(Project 2D–Salary Projections continued)

Lastname. In the **Before sheet** area, click **(move to end)**. Click the **Create a copy** check box, and then click **OK**. The 2D_Salary_Projections_Firstname_Lastname workbook is the active workbook.

17. Click the **View tab**. In the **Window group**, click the **Switch Windows button**. From the displayed menu, click **e02D_Salary_Increases** to make that workbook the active workbook. With the **e02D_Salary_Increases** workbook as the active workbook, click the **Office button**, and from the displayed menu, click **Close**. If you are prompted to save changes, click **No**. The worksheet you copied into the 2D_Salary_Projections workbook displays on the screen.

18. There are several errors in this worksheet that will be corrected. Double-click the **Sheet1 sheet tab** and type **4% Increase** and press [Enter] to rename this sheet. Right-click the **4% Increase sheet tab**, point to **Tab Color**, and under **Standard Colors**, click the third color—**Orange**.

19. Click cell **E7** to review the formula. This formula produces a correct result in this cell, but when it is copied to the next row, the formula still needs to refer to the value in cell F2—the amount of increase. To do this the formula needs to be changed so it uses an absolute cell reference to cell F2. In the **Formula Bar**, click the insertion point after **F2** and press [F4]; and then in the **Formula Bar**, click the **Enter button**. In cell **E7**, point to the fill handle and drag down to cell **E12** to copy this formula to the other cells in this column. The error indicators and error values in column E are removed.

20. Click cell **F7** and review the formula in this cell. Notice that it refers to the row above, which contains column titles. In cell **F7**, type **=d7+e7** and press [Enter]. Click cell **F7** and drag the fill handle to cell **F12**. The salaries are now corrected. Click cell **F6**, type **Proposed Salary** On the **Formula Bar**, click the **Enter button**, and from the **Alignment group**, click the **Wrap Text button**.

21. In cell **A13**, type **Total** The totals in row 13 are not correct. Click cell **F13** and notice that *Sum* is not spelled correctly. In the **Formula Bar**, position the insertion point between **S** and **M**, and type **u** and then in the **Formula Bar**, click the **Enter button**.

22. Click cell **D13** and review the formula. Notice that it contains only a cell range without a function or mathematical operator. Press [Delete] to remove the formula. Select the range **D13:E13** and from the **Editing group**, click the **Sum button**.

23. Select the range **D8:F12** and right-click. In the Mini toolbar, click the **Comma Style button**. Select the range **D13:F13** and right-click. In the Mini toolbar, click the **Border button arrow** and click **Top and Double Bottom Border**. Adjust column widths if needed.

24. Click cell **A2** and change the entry to read **Projected Monthly Salary, 4% Increase** Click cell **A3** and type **Prepared December 10, 2009** Take time to review your work and confirm that cell **A3** is formatted in the same style as cells **A1** and **A2**. Is the format consistent, are correct formulas entered, are all error indicators and error values removed, does text in a column fully display?

25. Right-click any sheet tab and click **Select All Sheets**. Change to **Page Layout** view and scroll to the bottom of the worksheet to display the Footer. Click the **Left Footer area** and in the **Header & Footer Elements group**, click the **File Name** button. Click the **Right Footer area** and in the **Header & Footer Elements group**, click the **Sheet Name** button. Return to cell **A1** and change to **Normal** view.

(Project 2D–Salary Projections continues on the next page)

Content-Based Assessments

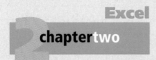
(Project 2D–Salary Projections continued)

26. On the **Page Layout tab**, in the **Page Setup group**, click the **Dialog Box Launcher**. In the **Page tab**, under **Orientation**, click **Landscape** and under **Scaling**, click **Fit to 1 page**. In the **Margins tab**, under **Center on page**, click **Horizontally** and **Vertically**, and then click **Print Preview**. Use the vertical scroll bar at the right to access and review each of the 4 pages of the workbook.

27. Click **Close Print Preview**. **Save** your work. Check your *Chapter Assignment Sheet* or your *Course Syllabus* or consult your instructor to determine if you are to submit your assignments on paper or electronically. To submit electronically, go to Step 29, and then follow the instructions provided by your instructor.

28. Click the **Office button** and from the displayed menu, click **Print**. In the **Print** dialog box, under **Print what**, select **Entire workbook**. Under **Copies**, confirm that **1** is selected. Click **OK**. If you are directed to submit printed formulas, group all worksheets. Then refer to Activity 1.12 to do so.

29. **Close** your file without saving changes, and then **Exit** Excel.

End **You have completed Project 2D**

Mastering Excel

Project 2E — Comparison of Operating Expenses

In this project, you will apply the skills you practiced from the Objectives in Project 2A.

Objectives: 1. *Work with a Multiple-Sheet Workbook;* **2.** *Enter a Series;* **3.** *Copy and Paste Cell Contents;* **4.** *Copy and Paste with the Office Clipboard;* **5.** *Total the Worksheet Range and Enter a Grand Total;* **6.** *Format a Multiple-Sheet Workbook Group;* **7.** *Insert Columns and Rows in Multiple Worksheets.*

The owners of the Eastern Cape Inn are looking for ways to avoid raising room rates and have decided to compare the expenses for the inn over the last three years. In the following Mastering Excel assessment, you will prepare a multiple-sheet report that reports the expenses for the last three years. The worksheets of your workbook will look similar to Figure 2.69.

For Project 2E, you will need the following files:

New blank Excel workbook
e02E_Operating_Expenses

You will save your workbook as
2E_Operating_Expense_Comparison_Firstname_Lastname

Figure 2.69

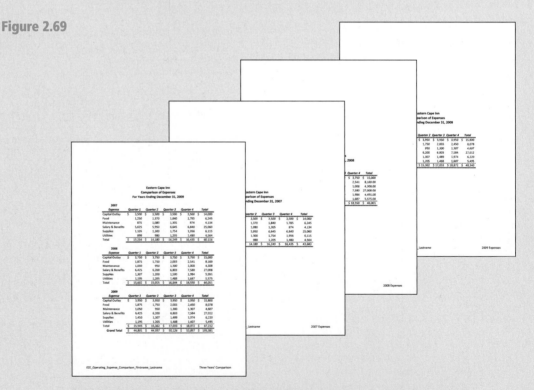

(Project 2E–Comparison of Operating Expenses continues on the next page)

Content-Based Assessments

Excel

chaptertwo

Mastering Excel

(Project 2E–Comparison of Operating Expenses continued)

1. **Start** Excel and display a new blank workbook. **Save** the workbook in your **Excel Chapter 2** folder as **2E_Operating_Expense_Comparison_Firstname_Lastname**

2. Beginning in cell **A1**, type the following worksheet title:

Eastern Cape Inn
Comparison of Expenses
For Three Years Ending December 31, 2009

3. In cell **A6**, type **Expense** and in cell **B6**, type **Quarter 1** Use the from fill handle to extend the column titles to *Quarter 4* in **column E**. In cell **F6**, type **Total**

4. Click cell **A1** and format with **Bold** and change the **Font Size** to **14**. Select the range **A1:F1** and click the **Merge & Center button**. Use the **Format Painter** to paste the format to cells **A2** and **A3** the same as cell **A1**. Select the column titles—the range **A6:F6**. Format the titles with **Bold** and **Italic** emphasis and **Center** alignment. Apply a **Bottom Double Border** to the cells.

5. Click the **Insert Worksheet button** to insert another worksheet. Name the sheet tabs and add tab colors to each sheet tab as follows:

Sheet	Name	Color of Tab
Sheet1	Three Year Comparison	Blue
Sheet2	2007 Expenses	Purple
Sheet3	2008 Expenses	Dark Red
Sheet4	2009 Expenses	Light Green

6. Right-click the **Three Year Comparison sheet tab** and click **Select All Sheets**.

Select the range **A1:F6**. From the **Editing group**, click the **Fill button**, and then click **Across Worksheets**. In the **Fill Across Worksheets** dialog box, confirm that the **All** option is selected, and then click **OK**.

7. Click the **2007 Expenses sheet tab** and confirm that the worksheets are not grouped. Change the date line to read **For Year Ending December 31, 2007** Click cell **A3**, press ⇧Shift, and click the **2009 Expenses sheet tab** to group the three sheets. In the **Editing group**, click the **Fill button** and click **Across Worksheets**. In the **Fill Across Worksheets** dialog box, confirm that the **All** option is selected, then click **OK**. Ungroup the worksheets, and then in the **2008 Expenses** and **2009 Expenses** worksheets, change the date line—in cell **A3**—to match the year in the sheet tab.

8. Click the **Three Year Comparison sheet tab**. In the **Clipboard group**, click the **Dialog Box Launcher** to display the **Clipboard task pane**. **Copy** the range **A6:F6** to the **Clipboard task pane**.

9. Click the **Office button**, and from the displayed menu, click **Open** to display the **Open** dialog box. Locate and open the workbook **e02E_Operating_Expenses**. This worksheet displays the expenses for three quarters of the past three years. Select the expenses for 2007—**A3:D9**—which includes the year and total rows. **Copy** it to the **Clipboard task pane**. Using the skills you have practiced, copy the expenses for the other two years from the following ranges: **A12:D18** and **A21:D27**. When all data is copied to the **Clipboard task pane**, **Close** the e02E_Operating_Expenses workbook.

(Project 2E–Comparison of Operating Expenses continues on the next page)

(Project 2E–Comparison of Operating Expenses continued)

10. Click the **Three Year Comparison sheet tab**. Press ⇧Shift and click the **2007 Expenses sheet tab** to group the two worksheets. Click cell **A6**. On the **Clipboard task pane**, click the entry that begins *2007*, and then click the entry that begins *Expense*. Ungroup the worksheets and click the **Three Year Comparison sheet tab**. Click cell **A15** and on the **Clipboard task pane**, click the entry that begins, *2008* and then click the entry that begins *Expense*. Beginning in cell **A24**, use the data saved in the **Clipboard task pane** to enter the 2009 data and column labels. Click the **2008 Expenses sheet tab** and click cell **A6**. On the **Clipboard task pane**, click the entry that begins, *2008* and then click the entry that begins *Expense*. Enter the data for the 2009 expenses in the **2009 Expenses** worksheet.

11. Right-click the **Three Year Comparison sheet tab**. Click **Select All Sheets**. Adjust column widths so all titles in column A fully display. Select the range of the worksheet data—**B7:F12**—and in the **Editing group**, click the **Sum button** to create a Sum formula. When data is entered in column E, the totals will change to reflect the additional numbers. **Ungroup the worksheets** and create a Sum formula to total the columns and rows for ranges **B16:F21** and **B25:F30**.

12. Select all of the worksheets. Format the numbers in **row 7** using the **Accounting Number Format** with **no decimals**. For **rows 8** through **row 11**, use **Comma Style** with **no decimals**. For **row 12**, use **Accounting Number Format** with **no decimals** and a **Top and Double Bottom Border**. Ungroup the sheets and click the **Three Year Comparison sheet tab**. Select the range **B7:F12**—the 2007 data—right-click, and then double-click **Format**

Painter. Click cells **B16** and **B25**. In the **Clipboard group**, click the **Format Painter** button to turn it off.

13. In cell **A5**, type **2007** and in the **Formula Bar**, click the **Enter button**. Right-click cell **A5** and from the Mini toolbar, click the **Bold** and **Center buttons**, and then double-click the **Format Painter button**. Click cells **A14** and **A23**, and in the **Clipboard group**, click the **Format Painter button** to turn it off. In cell **A14**, type **2008** and in cell **A23**, type **2009**

14. Select all of the worksheets. Right-click the **row 11** heading to select the row and from the shortcut menu, click **Insert**. Ungroup the worksheets and beginning in cell **A11**, type the following in **row 11**:

Supplies	1105	1300	1754

15. Confirm that the formulas are correct after the row has been inserted. Select the range **A11:F11**, right-click, and then click **Copy**. Click the **2007 Expenses sheet tab**, right-click cell **A11**, and then click **Paste**.

16. Click the **Three Year Comparison sheet tab**. Right-click **row 21** and **Insert** a row before the row titled *Utilities*. Type the following:

Supplies	1307	1200	1500

17. Select **row 31** and **Insert** a row. Beginning with cell **A31**, type the following data:

Supplies	1450	1307	1489

18. Confirm the formulas are entered and are correct in both ranges.

19. Select the range **A21:F21** and right-click and click **Copy**. Click the **2008 Expenses sheet tab**, right-click cell **A11**, and click **Paste**. Using the skills you practiced, **Copy** the data for 2009 Supplies to the **2009 Expenses** worksheet.

(Project 2E–Comparison of Operating Expenses continues on the next page)

Excel

chaptertwo   Mastering Excel

(Project 2E–Comparison of Operating Expenses continued)

20. The 2009 data is ready to be entered into the worksheet. **Group** the **Three Year Comparison** and **2007 Expenses** worksheets. Beginning in cell **E7**, type the following data for 2007:

| 3500 |
| 1785 |
| 874 |
| 6840 |
| 1956 |
| 1480 |

21. Enter the formula in cell **E13** and confirm the other formulas in **row 13** and those in **column F** are accurate.

22. **Ungroup** the worksheets. On the **Three Year's Comparison** worksheet, beginning in cell **E17**, type the following data for Quarter 4 of 2008. When finished, enter missing formulas and confirm the accuracy of all formulas.

| 3750 |
| 2541 |
| 1008 |
| 7580 |
| 1984 |
| 1687 |

23. Beginning in cell **E27**, type the following data for 2009. When finished, enter missing formulas and confirm the accuracy of all formulas.

| 3950 |
| 2450 |
| 1307 |
| 7584 |
| 1974 |
| 1607 |

24. From the **Three Year Comparison** worksheet, **Copy** the **Quarter 4** data to the individual worksheets. Confirm the formulas are accurate.

25. In the **Three Year Comparison** sheet, select the range of the worksheet—**B7:E34**—and use the **Sum** button to calculate a grand total in **row 34** and place a **Thick Bottom Border** in that range. In cell **A34**, type **Grand Total** and apply **Bold** and **Center** alignment.

26. Select all sheets. Switch to **Page Layout view**. In the **Left Footer**, insert the **File Name** and in the **Right Footer**, insert the **Sheet Name**. Return to **Normal** view.

27. On the **Page Layout tab**, in the **Page Setup group**, click the **Dialog Box Launcher**. In the **Page** tab, under **Orientation**, click **Portrait**, and under **Scaling**, click **Fit to 1**. In the **Margins** tab, click **Horizontally** and **Vertically**. Then click **OK**.

28. **Save** your workbook. **Print** the **Entire workbook** or submit electronically as directed. If you are directed to submit printed formulas, refer to Activity 1.12 to do so. If you printed your formulas, be sure to redisplay the worksheet by pressing Ctrl + [`]. Click the **Office button** and from the displayed menu, click **Close**. If you are prompted to **Save** changes, click **No**. **Exit** Excel.

End You have completed Project 2E

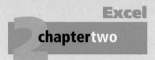
Project 2F — Tax Report

In this project, you will apply the skills you practiced from the Objectives in Project 2B.

Objectives: 8. *Copy a Worksheet;* **9.** *Format Data, Cells, and Worksheets;* **10.** *Find and Replace Text and Hide and Unhide Columns;* **11.** *Conduct a What-If Analysis and Use Statistical Functions;* **12.** *Create Accurate Worksheets with Accuracy Tools.*

In the following Mastering Excel project, you will determine the amount of taxes the Eastern Cape Inn will need to deposit for the year. In addition, you will provide statistical data and prepare a worksheet that reviews the results with a possible increase in the tax rates. The worksheets of your workbook will look similar to Figure 2.70.

For Project 2F, you will need the following files:

e02F_Tax_Report
e02F_Taxes_Q1

You will save your workbook as
2F_Tax_Report_Firstname_Lastname

Figure 2.70

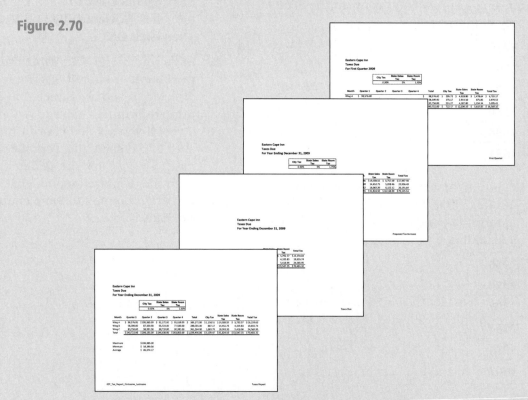

(Project 2F–Tax Report continues on the next page)

(Project 2F–Tax Report continued)

1. **Start** Excel. Locate and open **e02F_Tax_ Report**. **Save** the file in your **Excel Chapter 2** folder as **2F_Tax_Report_ Firstname_Lastname**

2. Select the range **B9:F12** and enter a **Sum** formula. Adjust column widths to display the results. Confirm the format is correct with **Accounting Number Format** used in rows 9 and 12.

3. Click cell **A1**. Use **Find and Replace** to replace **Amount** with **Tax**.

4. In cell **G9**, enter the formula for the City Tax. Multiply the total revenue—**F9**—for Wing A by the city tax rate in cell **C6**. Use an absolute cell reference to the City Tax rate. Copy the formula to **rows 10** and **11**. Adjust the column width.

5. In cell **H9**, enter the formula for the State Sales Tax. Multiply the total for Wing A by the state sales tax rate in cell **D6**. Use an absolute cell reference to the State Sales Tax rate. Copy the formula to **rows 10** and **11**. Adjust the column width.

6. In cell **I9**, enter the formula for the State Room Tax. Multiply the total revenue for Wing A by the state room tax rate in cell **E6**. Use an absolute reference to the State Room Tax rate. Copy the formula to **rows 10** and **11**. Adjust the column width.

7. Select the range of the taxes, **G9:J12**, and enter a **Sum** formula. Select the range **F9:F12**, right-click, and click the **Format Painter**. Then select the range **G9:J12**. Adjust the column widths if needed. There is an **error indicator** in cell **F12**. Click cell **F12** and click the **Error Checking button** to review the type of error. Review the formula in the **Formula Bar**; this formula adds the row—**B12:E12**. Click cell **E12** and review the formula in the **Formula**

Bar; this formula adds the column of numbers—**E9:E11**. Click cell **G12** and confirm that formula also adds the column. Click back in cell **F12**. Click the **Error Checking button** and click **Copy Formula from Left**.

8. The owners would like to see a worksheet that displays only the taxes section. Create a copy of **Sheet1** and place it before **Sheet2** in this workbook. In the new worksheet— **Sheet1 (2)**—hide **columns B:F**.

9. The city and state are considering changing the tax rate for hotel rooms and the owners would like to determine how this change would affect Eastern Cape Inn. Create a copy of the **Sheet1 (2)** sheet and place it before **Sheet2** in this workbook. In the **Sheet1 (3)** sheet, unhide the columns. In cell **C6**, type **.5%** and in cell **E6**, type **1.75%** to change the tax rates.

10. Rename the sheet tabs and change the tab colors as follows:

    Rename **Sheet1** to **Taxes Report** and select the Standard Color **Dark Blue**

    Rename **Sheet1 (2)** to **Taxes Due** and select the Standard Color **Light Green**

    Rename **Sheet1 (3)** to **Proposed Tax Increase** and select the Standard Color **Orange**

11. The owners want to include statistical information about the rentals for the lodge for the year. In the **Taxes Report** beginning in cell **A15**, enter the following row titles:

| Maximum |
| Minimum |
| Average |

(Project 2F–Tax Report continues on the next page)

(Project 2F–Tax Report continued)

12. In cell **C15**, enter the **MAX** function to determine the largest rental income by quarter and Wing using the range **B9:E11**. The highest revenues for the year—$100,385.00—occurred in the second quarter for Wing A.

13. In cell **C16**, use the **MIN** function to determine the lowest rental income for the range **B9:E11**. Then in cell **C17** insert the **AVERAGE** function to determine the average rental for the same range. The smallest revenue—$58,390.00—displays in cell **C16**, and the average revenue—$86,374.17—displays in cell **C17**. **Save** your work.

14. Display the **Open** dialog box. From the student data files, locate and open **e02F_Taxes_Q1**. There are several errors in this worksheet. Copy this worksheet to the **2F_Tax_Report_Firstname_Lastname** workbook and place it before **Sheet2**.

15. This worksheet reviews the first quarter income for the year, although it is designed to include all quarters of the year. As the income is determined for the quarter, each quarter is added to the worksheet. Click cell **F12** and correct the formula by placing parentheses around the range of cells included in the Sum formula.

16. Click cell **G9** and review the formula. This formula multiplies the total revenue in column F times the city tax rate, which should be expressed as an absolute reference. Correct the formula and copy it through cell **G11**. Using the skills practiced, correct the formulas in cells **H9** and **I9** and copy the corrected formulas through **row 11**.

17. Click cell **H12** and review the formula in the **Formula Bar**. Notice that cell **H12** is included in the formula—the cell that will contain the formula. Correct the formula so it reads =SUM(H9:H11) Click cell **I12** and review the formula. Notice that the name of the formula is incorrectly entered. Correct the function name. After corrections, the total tax in cell **J12** is $16,369.10.

18. Copy the formats from the range **F9:F12** to the range **G9:J12**.

19. Click cell **B15** and review the formula. The function for Maximum was not used. Enter the **MAX** function, using the range **B9:B11** for the arguments—which will result in $98,576. Use the correct functions to correct the results in cells **B16** and **B17**.

20. Delete **Sheets 2** and **3**. **Select all worksheets** and in the **Left Footer** area, place the **File Name**. In the **Right Footer** area, place the **Sheet Name**.

21. Format the worksheets for **Landscape** orientation, and **Fit to** page. Center the worksheets **Horizontally** and **Vertically**.

22. **Save** your workbook. **Print** the **Entire workbook** or submit electronically as directed. If you are directed to submit printed formulas, refer to Activity 1.12 to do so. If you printed your formulas, be sure to redisplay the worksheet by pressing Ctrl + `. Click the **Office button** and from the displayed menu, click **Close**. If you are prompted to save changes, click **No**. **Exit** Excel.

End **You have completed Project 2F**

Mastering Excel

Project 2G — Payroll Report

In this project, you will apply the skills you practiced from the Objectives in Projects 2A and 2B.

Objectives: 1. *Work with a Multiple-Sheet Workbook;* **3.** *Copy and Paste Cell Contents;* **5.** *Total the Worksheet Range and Enter a Grand Total;* **6.** *Format a Multiple-Sheet Workbook Group;* **9.** *Create Formulas with Absolute Cell References and Copy Formulas.*

You will prepare a payroll report for the first quarter of the year for the Eastern Cape Inn in one workbook. Employees are paid monthly. You will then prepare a summary report for the payroll for the quarter. The worksheets of your workbook will look similar to Figure 2.71.

For Project 2G, you will need the following file:

New blank Excel workbook

You will save your workbook as
2G_Payroll_Report_Firstname_Lastname

Figure 2.71

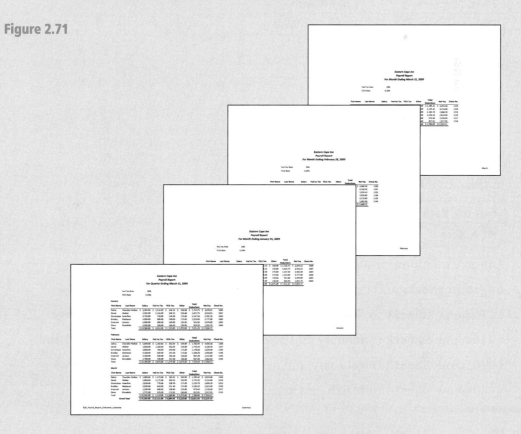

(Project 2G–Payroll Report continues on the next page)

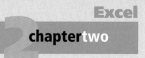
(Project 2G–Payroll Report continued)

1. **Start** Excel and display a new blank workbook. In your **Excel Chapter 2** folder, **Save** the file as **2G_Payroll_Report_Firstname_Lastname**

2. Insert a worksheet and **Select All Sheets**. Enter the worksheet title in rows **A1:A3** as follows:

Eastern Cape Inn
Payroll Report
For Quarter Ending March 31, 2009

3. Beginning in cell **A6**, enter the following column titles:

First Name	Last Name	Salary	Fed Inc Tax	FICA Tax	Other	Total Deductions	Net Pay	Check No.

4. Format the worksheet title with **Bold**, and **Italic**, and increase the **Font Size** to **14 pt**. Format the column titles with **Bold**, **Center**, and **Middle Align**, **Wrap Text** with a **Bottom Border**. Adjust the column widths so the column titles display on two lines and adjust the row height, if necessary.

5. Insert three new rows between the worksheet title and the column titles.

6. Beginning in cell **A10**, type the following data:

First Name	Last Name
Debra	Chandler-Walker
Derek	Walker
Dominique	Amerline
Bradley	Matteson
Emanuel	Jackson
Elena	Brondello
Total	

7. In the range **B5:C6**, type the following:

Fed Tax Rate	20%
FICA Rate	6.2%

8. Adjust the column widths to fully display the employee names.

9. **Ungroup sheets** and rename and add color to the sheet tabs as follows:

   - Rename **Sheet1** to **Summary** and select the Standard Color of **Orange**.

   - Rename **Sheet2** to **January** and select the Standard Color of **Light Blue**.

   - Rename **Sheet3** to **February** and select the Standard Color of **Yellow**.

   - Rename **Sheet4** to **March** and select the Standard Color of **Purple**.

(Project 2G–Payroll Report continues on the next page)

Content-Based Assessments

(Project 2G–Payroll Report continued)

10. Group the **Summary** and **January** worksheets. Beginning in cell **C10**, enter the salary for each employee.

Name	Salary
Chandler-Walker	5583
Walker	5583
Amerline	3750
Matteson	4000
Jackson	3000
Brondello	2650

11. Enter the following salaries in the **February** and **March** worksheets.

Name	February Salary	March Salary
Chandler-Walker	5849	5860
Walker	5849	5860
Amerline	3800	3850
Matteson	4100	4050
Jackson	3100	3200
Brondello	2700	2775

12. Select All Sheets. Enter the following data in the **Other** column. These deductions for the employees remain the same each month. This includes health insurance and pensions.

Name	Other
Chandler-Walker	250
Walker	210
Amerline	175
Matteson	175
Jackson	135
Brondello	130

13. Click cell **D10** and enter the formula, using cell references, to determine the Federal Income tax that will be withheld. The Federal Income Tax rate is 20% for each employee. To determine the amount withheld, multiply the salary by the income tax rate. (*Hint:* Use an absolute reference.)

(Project 2G–Payroll Report continues on the next page)

Excel
chaptertwo

Mastering Excel

(Project 2G–Payroll Report continued)

14. Click cell **E10** and enter the formula to determine the amount of FICA—social security—tax that will be withheld. The FICA Tax rate is 6.2% for each employee. To determine the amount withheld, multiply the salary by the FICA tax rate. (*Hint:* Use an absolute reference.)

15. Click cell **G10** and enter the formula to determine the Total Deductions. This is Chandler-Walker's deductions—Fed Inc Tax, FICA Tax, and Other—**=D10+E10+F10**.

16. Click cell **H10** and enter the formula to determine the Net Pay—Salary minus Total Deductions. Chandler-Walker's net pay is determined by subtracting the total deductions from the Salary.

17. Copy the formulas in **row 10** to **rows 11:15**. In **row 16**, total the columns.

18. Format the first row of numbers—**C10:H10**—using **Accounting Number Format** with **two decimals**. Copy the format in **row 10** to **row 16** and add a **Top and Double Bottom Border**. Format the other rows—**rows 11:15**—for **Comma Style** with **two decimals**. Adjust the column widths if needed.

19. **Merge and Center** the worksheet title over **columns A:I**. In the **Left Footer area**, place the **File Name** and in the **Right Footer area**, place the **Sheet Name**.

20. **Ungroup** the worksheets. Enter the check numbers for each employee for the following months in the respective worksheets. Make certain that the check numbers for January are placed both in the Summary and January sheets.

	January	February	March
Chandler-Walker	1008	1108	1220
Walker	1007	1107	1219
Amerline	1003	1103	1215
Matteson	1006	1106	1218
Jackson	1005	1105	1217
Brondello	1004	1104	1216

21. Click the **Summary sheet tab**, and confirm the total net pay in cell **H16**—$17,054.71. In each of the monthly worksheets, change the date line from *Quarter* to **Month** and the date to the last day in each month. January and March have 31 days and February has 28 days.

22. In the **February** worksheet **copy** the worksheet data, beginning with the column title—**A9**. Click the **Summary sheet tab**, and beginning in cell **A19**, **Paste** the February data. Repeat this process to paste a copy of the March data—beginning with column titles—to the **Summary sheet**, beginning in cell **A29**.

23. In cell **A8**, type **January** In cell **A18**, type **February** and in cell **A28**, type **March** Format these cells with **Bold** emphasis.

(Project 2G–Payroll Report continues on the next page)

Content-Based Assessments

(Project 2G–Payroll Report continued)

24. Select the range **C10:H37** and use the **grand total** feature to create a grand total in **row 37**. In cell **A37**, type Grand Total and format it with **Bold** and **Merge & Center** the title in cells **A37:B37**. Format the grand total row with **Accounting Number Format**, **two decimals**, and **Bold** with a **Thick Bottom Border**. Adjust column width if needed. Confirm that the total salary in cell **C37** is $75,559.00 and the Net Pay in cell **H37** is $52,537.54.

25. Review the worksheets. If necessary, widen the columns to fully display the data, adjust any formats, and correct any error message or error indicator that displays. **Select all worksheets**, change the orientation to **Landscape, Scale to fit** on one page, and center **Horizontally** and **Vertically** on the page. Use **Print Preview** to review the worksheet placement. **Save** your workbook.

26. **Print** the **Entire workbook** or submit electronically as directed. If you are directed to submit printed formulas, refer to Activity 1.12 to do so. If you printed your formulas, be sure to redisplay the worksheet by pressing Ctrl + ˋ. From the **Office** menu, click **Close**. If you are prompted to save changes, click **No**. **Exit** Excel.

End You have completed Project 2G

Content-Based Assessments

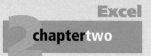

chaptertwo

Excel

Mastering Excel

Project 2H — Souvenir Sales

In this project, you will apply the skills you practiced from the Objectives in Projects 2A and 2B.

Objectives: 2. *Enter a Series;* **3.** *Copy and Paste Cell Contents;* **5.** *Total the Worksheet Range and Enter a Grand Total;* **7.** *Insert Columns and Rows in Multiple Worksheets;* **9.** *Create Formulas with Absolute Cell References and Copy Formats;* **10.** *Find and Replace Text and Hide and Unhide Columns;* **12.** *Create Accurate Worksheets with Accuracy Tools.*

Eastern Cape Inn sells souvenir items to its guests. In the following Mastering Excel assessment, you will create a worksheet for Dominique Amerline, inn manager, which reports the sale of souvenirs for the year. In addition to sales to guests during their stay at the inn, many of the sales come from the inn's Web site. The report will include the sales tax due on the souvenir sales for the year. The worksheet will look similar to Figure 2.72.

You will save your workbook as 2H_Souvenir_Sales_Firstname_Lastname

Figure 2.72

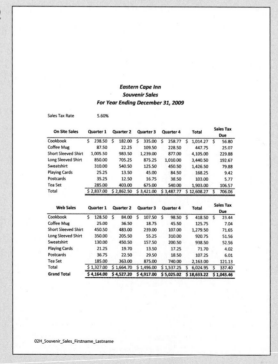

(Project 2H–Souvenir Sales continues on the next page)

Content-Based Assessments

(Project 2H–Souvenir Sales continued)

1. **Start** Excel to a new workbook. **Save** the workbook and name it
   2H_Souvenir_Sales_Firstname_Lastname

2. Create a title in the first three rows of the worksheet. This worksheet is for Eastern Cape Inn
   reports Souvenir Sales and For Year Ending December 31, 2009. Format the title with **Bold**,
   Italic, and **14 pt** font, and **Merge and & Center** the title lines through **column G**. Add the
   File Name in the left footer.

3. In cell **A7**, type **On Site Sales** and in cell **B7**, type **Quarter 1** Use the fill handle to extend the
   quarters to the right as column titles through **Quarter 4**. In cell **F7**, type **Total** and in cell **G7**,
   type **Sales Tax Due** Format the range **A7:G7** with **Bold**, **Wrap Text**, **Center**, and **Middle Align**,
   and with a **Bottom Border**.

4. Beginning in cell **A8**, type the following row titles:

Cookbook
Mug
Short Sleeved Shirt
Long Sleeved Shirt
Sweatshirt
Playing Cards
Postcards
Total

5. In cell **A5**, type **Sales Tax Rate** and in cell **B5**, type **5.6%** Adjust **column A** so the longest entry
   fully displays.

6. Select the worksheet range—**A7:G15**—and select a **Copy** command. Click cell **A17** and select a
   Paste command. Replace the contents of cell **A17** with **Web Sales**

7. Select the range for the On Site Sales data—**B8:E14**. Enter the following sales:

On Site Sales	Quarter 1	Quarter 2	Quarter 3	Quarter 4
Cookbook	238.50	182.00	335.00	258.77
Mug	87.50	22.25	109.50	228.50
Short Sleeved Shirt	1,005.50	983.50	1239.00	877.00
Long Sleeved Shirt	850.00	705.25	875.25	1010.00
Sweatshirt	310.00	540.50	125.50	450.50
Playing Cards	25.25	13.50	45.00	84.50
Postcards	35.25	12.50	16.75	38.50

(Project 2H–Souvenir Sales continues on the next page)

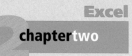
(Project 2H–Souvenir Sales continued)

8. Select the range for the Web Sales data—**B18:B24**. Type the following sales figures for Web Sales.

Web Sales	Quarter 1	Quarter 2	Quarter 3	Quarter 4
Cookbook	128.50	84.00	107.50	98.50
Mug	25.00	36.50	18.75	45.50
Short Sleeved Shirt	450.50	483.00	239.00	107.00
Long Sleeved Shirt	350.00	205.50	55.25	310.00
Sweatshirt	130.00	450.50	157.50	200.50
Playing Cards	21.25	19.70	13.50	17.25
Postcards	36.75	22.50	29.50	18.50

9. In the **On Site Sales** area, in **row 15** and **column F** calculate the totals required. Then in the **Web Sales** area, in **row 25** and **column F** calculate the totals required.

10. In cell **G8**, enter the formula to determine the sales tax due. Multiply the total in cell **F8** by the Sales Tax Rate in cell **B5**. Be sure to use an absolute cell reference to the Sales Tax Rate. Use the fill handle to copy the formula in cell **G8** through cell **G14** and place a total in cell **G15**. Copy the formula in cell **G14** to the range **G18:G24** and place a total in cell **G25**.

11. Format the numbers in **row 8** with **Accounting Number Format** with **two decimals**. Copy that format to **row 15** and add a **Top and Double Bottom Border**. Format the data in **rows 9:14** with **Comma Style** with **two decimals**. Copy the format from the *On Site Sales* area to the *Web Sales* area. Adjust column widths to fully display the totals.

12. In **row 26**, calculate the **grand total**. Confirm the formulas are correct.

13. In cell **A26**, type **Grand Total** and format it with **Bold**. Format the numbers in **row 26** with **Accounting Number Format** with **2 decimals**, **Bold**, and a **Thick Bottom Border**. Adjust column widths if needed.

14. Click cell **A1**. Use **Find & Select** to replace *Mug* with *Coffee Mug*.

15. In the **On-Site Sales** worksheet section, insert a row between **rows 14** and **15**. In the **Insert Options** button, be sure **Format Same As Above** is selected. Type the following data:

Tea Set	285	403	675	540

16. In the **Web Sales** worksheet section, insert a row between **rows 25** and **26** and type the following data:

Tea Set	185	363	875	740

17. Adjust column widths to fully display column entries. Confirm the formulas in both areas are accurate. Remove any **error indicators** and correct any **error values**.

(Project 2H–Souvenir Sales continues on the next page)

Content-Based Assessments

(Project 2H–Souvenir Sales continued)

18. Delete **Sheets 2** and **3**. Rename **Sheet1** as **Souvenir Sales**. Then **Center** the worksheet **Horizontally** and **Vertically** on the page. Use **Print Preview** to review the worksheet placement.

19. **Save** your workbook. **Print** the **Entire workbook** or submit electronically as directed. If you are directed to submit printed formulas, refer to Activity 1.12 to do so. If you printed your formulas, be sure to redisplay the worksheet by pressing Ctrl + `. From the **Office** menu, click **Close**. If you are prompted to save changes, click **No**. **Exit** Excel.

End **You have completed Project 2H**

Excel

chapter two

Project 2I—Lodging Income

In this project, you will apply the skills you practiced from all of the Objectives in Projects 2A and 2B.

Objectives: 1. *Work with a Multiple-Sheet Workbook;* **2.** *Enter a Series;* **3.** *Copy and Paste Cell Contents;* **4.** *Use the Office Clipboard;* **5.** *Total the Worksheet Range and Enter a Grand Total;* **6.** *Format a Multiple-Sheet Workbook Group;* **7.** *Insert Columns and Rows in Multiple Worksheets;* **8.** *Copy a Worksheet;* **9.** *Create Formulas with Absolute Cell References and Copy Formats;* **10.** *Find and Replace Text and Hide and Unhide Columns;* **11.** *Conduct a What-If Analysis and Use Statistical Functions;* **12.** *Create Accurate Worksheets with Accuracy Tools.*

In the following Mastering Excel assessment, you will prepare financial reports for the lodging income for Wings B and C for the third quarter of the year. You will then prepare additional financial information for the same period. The worksheets of your workbook will look similar to Figure 2.73.

For Project 2I, you will need the following files:

New blank Excel workbook
e02I_Rate_Sheets
e02I_Quarterly_Data

You will save your worksheet as
2I_Lodging_Income_Firstname_Lastname

Figure 2.73

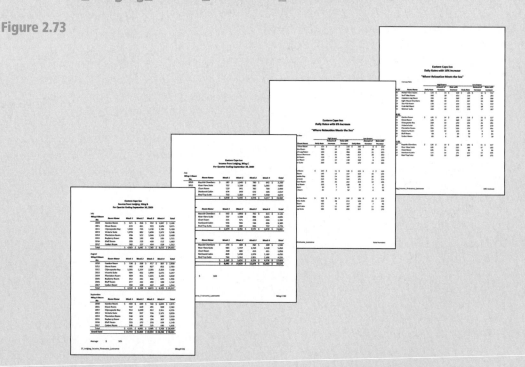

(Project 2I–Lodging Income continues on the next page)

Content-Based Assessments

(Project 2I–Lodging Income continued)

1. **Start** Excel and display a new blank workbook. **Save** it as **2I_Lodging_Income_Firstname_Lastname Group Sheet1** and **Sheet2**. Beginning in cell **A1**, enter a three-line title that includes the name of the inn—**Eastern Cape Inn**—the purpose of the worksheet—**Income from Lodging, Wing B**—and a date line—**For Quarter Ending September 30, 2009**

2. In cell **A6**, type **Wing B Room No.** and in cell **B6**, type **Week 1** Use the **fill handle** to extend the column labels to the right through **Week 4** In cell **F6**, type **Total**

3. Format the worksheet title lines with **Bold**, **12 pt** font. Format the column titles with **Bold**, **Italic**, **Wrap Text**, **Middle Align**, and a **Thick Bottom Border**. In addition, format cell **A6** with **Center** alignment and the titles in **columns B:F** to **Align Text Right**. Adjust the width of **column A** so it displays on two lines, and adjust the row height.

4. Rename **Sheet1** to **Wing B 3Q** and rename **Sheet2** to **Wing C 3Q** Change the tab color of Wing B to **Dark Red** and the tab color of Wing C to **Yellow**.

5. With the worksheets ungrouped, in the **Wing B** worksheet, in cell **A7**, type **2010** Drag the **fill handle** down to cell **A14**. Click the **Auto Fill Options button** and click **Fill Series**. Display the **Clipboard task pane**. Select the column titles—**A6:F6**—and select a **copy** command. Then select the room numbers—the range **A7:A14**—and select a **Copy** command.

6. In the **Wing C 3Q** worksheet, in cell **A7**, type **3010** Drag the **fill handle** to cell **A11**.

Click the **Auto Fill Options button** and click **Fill Series**. Use **Find & Select** to find **Wing B** and replace it with **Wing C**. Adjust the width of **column A** so the column title in cell **A6** fits on two lines. Select the column titles—**A6:F6**—and select a **copy** command. Then select the room numbers—the range **A7:A11**—and select a **copy** command.

7. The data for the income is in another workbook that contains two worksheets. From the student files, locate and open the worksheet **e02I_Quarterly_Data** Confirm that the **Wing B sheet** is selected. Select and copy the range **A2:E11**. In a similar manner, copy the **August** and **September** data to the Clipboard. Then select the **Wing C sheet**. Select and copy the range **A2:E8**. Then copy the **August** and **September** data to the Clipboard. **Close** the **e02I_Quarterly_Data** worksheet.

8. With the **2I_Lodging_Income_Firstname_Lastname** workbook active, in the **Wing B worksheet**, click cell **A5**. From the **Clipboard**, click the entry that begins *July Wing B*. (You may need to use the Clipboard scroll bars to access this entry.) Click cell **A6** and from the **Clipboard**, click the first entry—at the bottom of the Clipboard list—that begins *Wing B Room No.* Click cell **A17**. From the **Clipboard**, click the entry that begins *August Wing B*. Click cell **A18** and from the **Clipboard**, click the first entry that begins *Wing B Room No.* In cell **A29**, paste the Clipboard entry that begins *September Wing B*. In cell **A30**, paste the *Wing B Room No.* column titles.

(Project 2I–Lodging Income continues on the next page)

(Project 2I–Lodging Income continued)

9. Click the **Wing C sheet tab**. Using the skills you practiced on the Wing B worksheet, click cell **A5** and enter the Wing C data into the worksheet beginning with **July**. After the monthly data is copied, you will need to copy the column **titles** that begin **Wing C Room**. Leave **two** blank rows between the monthly data. Row 29 is the last row used in the worksheet.

10. In each worksheet, enter row and column **totals** for each month and place the row title, **Total**, at each row that contains a total. Format the row title *Total* in the same style as the room numbers in each column. Calculate a **grand total** at the end of the data, which provides the quarterly totals for each wing of the inn. On each sheet, enter the row title **Grand Total** in the appropriate cell and format the row with **Bold** emphasis and **Accounting Number Format** with **no decimals**. Place a **Thick Bottom Border** under the grand totals. Format the monthly total rows with **Accounting Number Format** with **no decimals** and add a **Top and Double Bottom Border**.

11. Review the **error alert**. Because numbers display in column A, Excel wants to alert you that these numbers are not included in the formula. Click **Ignore Error**. To quickly remove the **error alert**, select the range of cells that contain the alert and select **Ignore Error**. Remove any error alert in both worksheets.

12. **Group** the **Wing B** and **Wing C** worksheets and insert a column after the **Room Numbers**. In cell **B6**, type **Room Name**. **Ungroup** the sheets, select the **Wing B sheet**, and beginning in cell **B7**, type the room names as follows:

Wing B Room No.	Room Name
2010	**Garden Room**
2011	**Shore Room**
2012	**Chesapeake Bay**
2013	**Victoria Suite**
2014	**Plantation Room**
2015	**Bayberry Room**
2016	**Bluff Room**
2017	**Cedars Room**

13. Select the range **B7:B14** and **clear formats**. Copy the column title and room names—**B6:B14**—to the Clipboard. Click in cell **B18** and paste the room names from the Clipboard. Using the skills you practiced, copy the room names into the **September** data and adjust the column width to display the longest entry in the column.

14. In the **Wing C sheet**, beginning in cell **B7**, type the room names as follows:

Wing C Room No.	Room Name
3010	**Bayside Chambers**
3011	**River View Suite**
3012	**Chart Room**
3013	**Starboard Cabin**
3014	**Roof Top Suite**

15. Select the range **B7:B11** and **clear formats**. Copy the column title and room names—**B6:B11**—into the **August** and **September** areas and adjust the column width to display the longest entry in the column.

(Project 2I–Lodging Income continues on the next page)

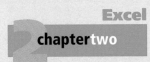
(Project 2I–Lodging Income continued)

16. In the **Wing B sheet**, in cell **A43**, type **Average** In cell **B43**, enter the function that determines the average. In the **Number1 argument** area, click the **Collapse Dialog Box button** and drag through the Week 1 July income—**C7:C14**. Then click the **Expand Dialog Box button**. In the **Number2 argument** area, click the **Collapse Dialog Box button** and drag through the Week 1 August income—**C19:C26**. In the **Number3 argument** area, select the Week 1 data for September. Click **OK**. The value $573 is entered in cell **B43**.

17. In the **Wing C sheet**, in cell **A35**, type **Average** and in cell **B35**, enter the Average function. Using the skills practiced, determine the average of the Week 1 lodging income for Wing C. $594 is entered as the average lodging for Week 1 Wing C.

18. **Save** your work. From the data files, open **e02I_Rate_Sheets**. **Copy** the worksheet and place it in **2I_Lodging_Income_Firstname_Lastname** just before **Sheet3**. Be sure to create a copy. This is a worksheet that displays the rates for the inn. The owners would like to calculate new daily rates with an 8% increase. It is now named *Sheet1*; rename it to **Rate Increases** and change the tab color to **Green**.

19. In cell **A2**, type **Daily Rates with 8% Increase** In cell **E8**, type **Amount of Increase** and in cell **G8**, type **Amount of Increase** Format the column titles for **Wrap Text**.

20. Insert a column to the left of **column F**. In cell **F8**, type **Rate with Increase** In cell **I8**, type **Rate with Increase** Copy the format from **F8** to cell **I8**.

21. In cell **B6**, type **Increase Rate** and in cell **C6**, type **8%** Select the range **E9:E32** and

press Delete. Then delete the numbers in **column H**.

22. In cell **E9**, enter the formula to determine the amount of the increase for *Harbor View Room*. The formula will be the daily rate of the room in cell **D9** times the increase rate in cell **C6**. The formula will read =D9*C6. In cell **F9**, enter the formula to determine the rate with the increase. Select the range **E9:F9**. Click the fill handle and drag through **row 15** to copy two formulas at the same time.

23. Error values are displayed. Review the formulas you entered in cells **E9** and **F9** and make the correction. An absolute cell reference is needed in the formula in cell **E9**. Then make the corrections to the cells that you previously copied.

24. Select the range **E9:F9** and select a **copy** command. Click cell **H9** and select a **paste** command. Click cell **H9** and confirm that the formula is correct. Select the range **H9:I9**. Then use the **fill handle** and drag through **row 15** to copy the two formulas at the same time.

25. In the **Rate Increases** sheet, copy the formulas used for Wing A increases to Wings B and C. For each wing, format the first row for **Accounting Number Format** with **no decimals**. For the other rows, use **Comma Style** with **no decimals**. Even though there is a decimal resulting from the increase, the owners quote room rates in whole dollars. There is no total row in this worksheet, so one dollar sign at the top of each range is correct.

26. Select cell **A1** and click **Merge & Center** to unmerge the name of the inn. Then select the range **A1:I1** and click **Merge & Center** so the title is merged over the columns of

(Project 2I–Lodging Income continues on the next page)

(Project 2I–Lodging Income continued)

the worksheet. Repeat with **row 2** and **row 4**. Select the range **D7:F7** and click **Merge & Center** twice—the first time unmerges the range D7:E7 and the second time merges the cells over the selected range. Use the Format Painter to copy this format to the range **G7:I7**.

27. **Copy** the **Rate Increases** worksheet to a new worksheet, place it before **Sheet3**, and **rename** the sheet **10% Increase** Change the **tab color** to **Purple**. Edit the second line of the worksheet title from *8%* to **10%** In the newly inserted worksheet, change the rate in cell **C6** to **10%** Note that the rates have increased to reflect a 10% increase in rates.

28. In the **Rate Increases** and **10% Increase** worksheets, **hide column C**. In this report, it's not necessary to know the capacity of the room. Even though the rate increase in cell **C6** is hidden, the cell references are

still effective. Notice that the rate, 8%, is in the title of the worksheet.

29. Delete **Sheet3**. **Group** the **Wing B** and **Wing C** worksheets and **Merge and & Center** the title.

30. **Select All Sheets** and in the **Left Footer area**, place the **File Name** and in the **Right Footer area**, place the **Sheet Name**. Return to **Normal view**. Format the worksheets so they are centered both **Horizontally** and **Vertically**. Select **Fit to 1 page**. Use **Print Preview** to review the worksheet placement.

31. **Save** your workbook. **Print** the **Entire workbook**, or submit electronically as directed. If you are directed to submit printed formulas, refer to Activity 1.12 to do so. If you printed your formulas, be sure to redisplay the sheet by pressing Ctrl + `. From the **Office** menu, click **Close**. If you are prompted to save changes, click **No**.

End You have completed Project 2I

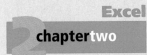

GO!
CD-ROM

Business Running Case

Project 2J—Business_Running_Case

In this project, you will apply the skills you have practiced from the Objectives in Projects 2A and 2B.

From My Computer, navigate to the student files that accompany this textbook. In the folder **03_business_running_case**, locate and open the folder for this chapter. Open and print the instructions for this project, which are provided to you in Adobe PDF format. Follow the instructions and use the skills you have gained thus far to assist the managers of the Grand Department Store to meet the challenges of keeping records for a large department.

End **You have completed Project 2J**

Rubric

The following outcomes-based assessments are *open-ended assessments*. That is, there is no specific correct result; your result will depend on your approach to the information provided. Make *Professional Quality* your goal. Use the following scoring rubric to guide you in *how* to approach the problem, and then to evaluate *how well* your approach solves the problem.

The *criteria*—Software Mastery, Content, Format and Layout, and Process—represent the knowledge and skills you have gained that you can apply to solving the problem. The *levels of performance*—Professional Quality, Approaching Professional Quality, or Needs Quality Improvement—help you and your instructor evaluate your result.

	Your completed project is of Professional Quality if you:	Your completed project is Approaching Professional Quality if you:	Your completed project Needs Quality Improvements if you:
1-Software Mastery	Choose and apply the most appropriate skills, tools, and features and identify efficient methods to solve the problem.	Choose and apply some appropriate skills, tools, and features, but not in the most efficient manner.	Choose inappropriate skills, tools, or features, or are inefficient in solving the problem.
2-Content	Construct a solution that is clear and well organized, contains content that is accurate, appropriate to the audience and purpose, and is complete. Provide a solution that contains no errors of spelling, grammar, or style.	Construct a solution in which some components are unclear, poorly organized, inconsistent, or incomplete. Misjudge the needs of the audience. Have some errors in spelling, grammar, or style, but the errors do not detract from comprehension.	Construct a solution that is unclear, incomplete, or poorly organized, containing some inaccurate or inappropriate content; and contains many errors of spelling, grammar, or style. Do not solve the problem.
3-Format and Layout	Format and arrange all elements to communicate information and ideas, clarify function, illustrate relationships, and indicate relative importance.	Apply appropriate format and layout features to some elements, but not others. Overuse features, causing minor distraction.	Apply format and layout that does not communicate information or ideas clearly. Do not use format and layout features to clarify function, illustrate relationships, or indicate relative importance. Use available features excessively, causing distraction.
4-Process	Use an organized approach that integrates planning, development, self-assessment, revision, and reflection.	Demonstrate an organized approach in some areas, but not others; or, use an insufficient process of organization throughout.	Do not use an organized approach to solve the problem.

Project 2K — Time Card Report

In this project, you will construct a solution by applying any combination of the skills you practiced from the Objectives in Projects 2A and 2B.

For Project 2K, you will need the following file:

New blank Excel workbook

You will save your workbook as
2K_Time_Card_Report_Firstname_Lastname

The owners of Eastern Cape Inn need a Time Card Report to report the hours worked for each employee. The time card will be used each week to summarize the hours worked and will be sent to the accountant to prepare pay checks. The weekly time period runs from Sunday through Saturday. Create a workbook that can be used to record employee work hours each day. Use a three-line title for the worksheet. This report is for the week ending April 11, 2009. The following table provides the hours each employee worked the first week. Provide the total hours worked for each employee and also for each day. These are not money amounts.

Employee	Sun	Mon	Tues	Wed	Thurs	Fri	Sat
Debra Chandler-Walker	6	7	8	9			8
Derek Walker	8	8	7	8	4		6
Dominique Amerline	7			8	8	8	9
Bradley Matteson	6		4	5	8	8	6
Emanuel Jackson	7	5	6			6	8
Elena Brondello	7			6	7	8	7

After reviewing your worksheet, the owners want to use the same format to report each week's payroll. On a separate worksheet, report the hours worked for the week ending April 18, 2009, as shown in the following table.

(Project 2K–Time Card Report continues on the next page)

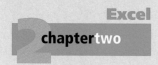
(Project 2K–Time Card Report continued)

Employee	Sun	Mon	Tues	Wed	Thurs	Fri	Sat
Debra Chandler-Walker	7	7	8	9			9
Derek Walker	8	6	7	6	5		8
Dominique Amerline	8			6	8	7	8
Bradley Matteson	8		5	8	7	8	7
Emanuel Jackson	6	7	5			7	6
Elena Brondello	8			7	6	8	8

Create a summary sheet that combines the data from both of these worksheets into one sheet that displays the time card reports for both weeks. Provide a grand total that displays the total hours worked each day of the week and the total hours for the week.

Using the skills you have practiced, format the worksheet attractively and appropriately. Be sure there are no data entry errors, spelling errors, or formula errors. Name each worksheet appropriately and place a different color on each sheet tab. Add a footer to all the worksheets that identifies the file name and sheet name. Center the worksheets on the page and delete unused worksheets. Your final workbook should be professional in every way. Save the workbook as **2K_Time_Card_Report_Firstname_Lastname** and submit it as directed.

 End **You have completed Project 2K**

Problem Solving

Project 2L — Payables

In this project, you will construct a solution by applying any combination of the skills you practiced from the Objectives in Projects 2A and 2B.

For Project 2L, you will need the following file:

e02L_Payables

**You will save your workbook as
2L_Payables_Firstname_Lastname**

Eastern Cape Inn maintains records of the amounts owed to its suppliers. Derek and Debra, the owners, want a workbook that reports the activity that has taken place during the month of May. To create the report, data from several worksheets must be combined and finance charges calculated when payments cannot be made in full.

From your student files, open e02L_Payables. Sheet1 lists the beginning balance for each supplier, Sheet2 lists the total purchases made from each supplier during the month, and Sheet3 lists the payments made during the month. Create a summary worksheet for Eastern Cape Inn that reports the beginning balances, purchases, payments, and balances due at the end of May 2009. When there is a balance due, the suppliers charge a 2 percent finance charge. Include columns as needed to calculate the amount of the finance charges, if any, made by each supplier, and to calculate a new ending balance which includes the finance charge.

Using the skills you have practiced, be sure all worksheets include title lines and are attractively and appropriately formatted. Add suitable sheet names and tab colors. Be sure there are no data entry errors, spelling errors, or formula errors and that all items are identified. Add the file name and sheet name to the footer, delete unused sheets, and format for printing appropriately. Save the workbook as **2L_Payables_Firstname_Lastname** and submit it as directed.

End You have completed Project 2L

Outcomes-Based Assessments

Excel

chapter two

Problem Solving

Project 2M — Maintenance Expenses

In this project, you will construct a solution by applying any combination of the skills you practiced from the Objectives in Projects 2A and 2B.

For Project 2M, you will need the following files:

New blank Excel workbook
e02M_Maintenance_Records

You will save your workbook as
2M_Maintenance_Expenses_Firstname_Lastname

The Maintenance Department at Eastern Cape Inn has created a worksheet that reports the costs of repairs to each room at the inn. You will use this information to prepare a professional-looking report of the maintenance expenses.

Open the document e02M_Maintenance_Records and review the repair information the maintenance staff has gathered. There is a separate worksheet in the workbook for each wing.

Create a new workbook and copy the data for each wing from the e02_Maintenance_Records workbook into your new workbook, using a separate sheet for each wing. Create a summary worksheet that combines the data from each wing and then summarizes the expenses for the year as a total by quarter and by room. On the summary worksheet, also create a grand total for the year.

Using the skills you have practiced, add appropriate title lines to each worksheet, format the worksheet attractively and appropriately, and add descriptive sheet names. Be sure there are no data entry errors, spelling errors, or formula errors and that all items are identified. Add the file name and sheet name to the footer, delete unused sheets, and then arrange for attractive printing. Save the workbook as **2M_Maintenance_Records_Firstname_Lastname** and submit it as directed.

End **You have completed Project 2M**

Problem Solving

Project 2N — Inventory

In this project, you will construct a solution by applying any combination of the skills you practiced from the Objectives in Projects 2A and 2B.

For Project 2N, you will need the following file:

e02N_Inventory

You will save your workbook as 2N_Inventory_Firstname_Lastname

The inventory for the Eastern Cape Inn is used to determine costs of operation and when to reorder supplies and other items. You will prepare an inventory report that identifies the value of the inventory for each wing of the inn and determines the value of items that need to be restocked for the month of July 2009. In addition, owners Derek and Debra have decided that the inventory needs to be increased by 8 percent and would like those amounts included in the workbook report.

Open the document e02N_Inventory and review the information about the inventory that has been reported. There is a separate worksheet in the workbook for each wing. Save this workbook as **2N_Inventory_ Firstname_Lastname** and use it to complete the inventory report. Subtract the ending inventory from the beginning inventory to determine the amount used. The goal is for inventory to increase by 8 percent over the beginning inventory amount. Determine the amount of the increase in inventory—the beginning inventory times 8 percent—and what the goal for the inventory will be after the increase—the beginning inventory plus the amount of the increase. Report the inventory of each wing in a separate worksheet and create a summary worksheet that reports the total inventory. Provide the grand total that reports the entire inventory for the inn.

Using the skills you have practiced, add appropriate title lines to each worksheet, format the worksheets attractively and appropriately, and add descriptive sheet names. Be sure there are no data entry errors, spelling errors, or formula errors and that all items are identified. Add the file name and sheet name to the footer, delete unused sheets, and then arrange for attractive printing. Save the workbook as **2N_Inventory_Firstname_Lastname** and submit it as directed.

End You have completed Project 2N

Outcomes-Based Assessments

Excel
Problem Solving

Project 20 — Fill Rate

In this project, you will construct a solution by applying any combination of the skills you practiced from the Objectives in Projects 2A and 2B.

For Project 20, you will need the following file:

e02O_Fill_Rate

You will save your workbook as
20_Fill_Rate_Firstname_Lastname

The owners of Eastern Cape Inn need a report that determines the fill rate—percentage of rooms that are rented—for a quarter. They want a summary of the quarter on one worksheet that includes a grand total for the quarter.

Open the workbook e02_Fill_Rate and review the data contained on all three worksheets.

There is a separate worksheet for each month in the third quarter. Each worksheet lists the number of rooms for each wing and how many total nights they have been occupied during that month. Complete the worksheet by calculating the total number of rooms that are available for each month for each wing (multiply number of rooms available by number of days in each month). To determine the fill rate, divide the number of filled rooms by the number of rooms available. Use the Sum formula to determine the total number of rooms, rooms available, and rooms filled for each worksheet. Create a summary sheet that shows the data from each month in the quarter and a grand total of the three months.

Using the skills you have practiced, be sure each worksheet includes title lines and is formatted attractively and appropriately. Add identifying sheet names and tab colors to each of the four worksheets. Be sure there are no data entry errors, spelling errors, or formula errors and that all items are identified. Add the file name to the footer, delete unused sheets, and then arrange for attractive printing. Save the workbook as **20_Fill_Rate_Firstname_Lastname** and submit it as directed.

End You have completed Project 20 ———————————

Outcomes-Based Assessments

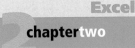
You and *GO!*

Project 2P—You and *GO!*

In this project, you will construct a solution by applying any combination of the Objectives found in Projects 2A and 2B.

From My Computer, navigate to the student files that accompany this textbook. In the folder **04_you_and_go**, locate and open the folder for this chapter. Open and print the instructions for this project, which are provided to you in Adobe PDF format. Follow the instructions to create a worksheet to determine the total cost of your texts the last two semesters you have been in college.

End You have completed Project 2P ——————————

GO! with Help

Project 2Q—*GO!* with Help

In this chapter, you practiced using multiple-sheet workbooks. You copied a worksheet from one workbook to another. You can move the worksheets within the workbook using the mouse.

1 **Start** Excel and confirm that you are connected to the Internet. At the far right end of the Ribbon, click the **Microsoft Office Excel Help button**.

2 In the search box, type **move worksheet** and then press [Enter]. Click the link for **Move or copy a worksheet.**

3 Read the information that displays. There are several ways to move the worksheets within the workbook. Be sure to read the Tips. When you are finished, **Close** the Help window, and then **Close** Excel.

End You have completed Project 2Q ——————————

3 chapterthree

Working with IF Functions and Large Worksheets

OBJECTIVES

At the end of this chapter you will be able to:

1. Construct an IF Function
2. Link Data in Workbooks
3. Create IF Functions That Return Text
4. Emphasize Data Using Conditional Formatting
5. Format with Themes
6. Add Information in the Header and Footer

OUTCOMES

Mastering these objectives will enable you to:

PROJECT 3A
Create a Report That Uses IF Functions, Conditional Formats, and Themes

7. Enter Dates
8. Format Large Worksheets
9. Apply Number Formats
10. Control Print Options

PROJECT 3B
Create a Large Worksheet and Use Freeze Panes and Control Print Options

Laurel County Community College

Laurel County Community College is located in eastern Pennsylvania and serves urban, suburban, and rural populations. The college offers this diverse area a broad range of academic and vocational programs, including associate degrees, certificate programs, and noncredit continuing education and personal development courses. LCCC makes positive contributions to the community through cultural and athletic programs and partnerships with businesses and nonprofit organizations. The college also provides industry-specific training programs for local businesses through its Economic Development Center.

Working with IF Functions and Large Worksheets

Excel enables you to create formulas that compare values. The results that display depend on the outcome of the comparison. For example, if a sales bonus is paid to sales personnel who sell over a specified amount, a formula can be constructed to determine whether or not to pay the bonus. The result will display one amount if the sales goal is met and a different amount if it is not.

Worksheets can be three, five, or even more pages long. When working with large worksheets, you can implement useful techniques to view more of the worksheet on the screen. Techniques include zooming in and freezing column and row titles so they are always visible as you enter data in distant rows and columns. In this chapter, you will create IF functions and work with large worksheets.

Project 3A **Library Payroll**

In Activities 3.1 through 3.11, you will use the IF function to create a Payroll Report for the library at Laurel County Community College. You will display conditional formats for certain data and use themes to format the workbook. Your completed workbook will look similar to Figure 3.1.

For Project 3A, you will need the following file:

e03A_Library_Payroll

You will save your document as
3A_Library_Payroll_Firstname_Lastname

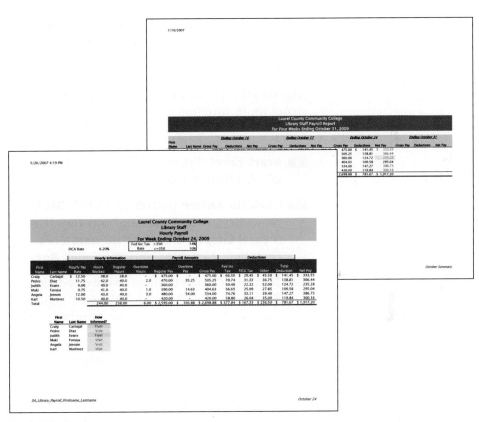

Figure 3.1
Project 3A—Library Payroll

Objective 1
Construct an IF Function

Recall that a function is a prewritten formula that takes one or more values, performs an operation, and then returns a value or values. The **IF function** is a logical function that performs a test to determine whether a condition is true or false. If the condition is true, it returns one value; if it is false, it returns a different value. A **logical test** is any value or expression that can be evaluated as being true or false. For example, a logical test determines if the value in C8 is equal to 100. If cell C8 is 100, the logical test is true. If the value in cell C8 is not 100, the logical test is false.

Activity 3.1 Preparing Regular Hours Worked in a Payroll Report Using an IF Statement

Worksheets are created for payroll records to determine how much each employee has earned. A work week consists of 40 hours and when more than 40 hours are worked, **overtime** is paid. Overtime is all hours worked in excess of 40 hours per week and is paid at a higher rate of pay, usually 1½ times the regular pay rate. In this activity, you will construct an IF function to determine the number of hours worked that will be paid at the regular hourly pay rate for the library employees.

1 **Start** Excel. From your student files, locate and open the file named **e03A_Library_Payroll**.

2 Click the **Office** button [icon], click **Save as**, and navigate to the location where you are saving your files. **Create** a new folder and name it **Excel Chapter 3** In the **File name** box, type **3A_Library_Payroll_Firstname_Lastname** and then click **Save**.

> This workbook contains two worksheets—*October 24* and *October Summary*. The October 24 payroll report is partially completed with the hourly pay rate and the number of hours worked already entered into the worksheet.

3 Review the **October 24** worksheet.

> The payroll worksheet is divided into four areas—Hourly Information, Payroll Amounts, Deductions, and Net Pay—across the width of the worksheet and displayed in rows 8 and 9.

4 Click the **October Summary sheet tab** and review the worksheet.

> This worksheet summarizes the payroll information for four weeks in October. Data from the October 10 and October 17 payrolls has been entered.

5 Click the **October 24 sheet tab**, and click cell **E10**. Click the **Formulas tab**; in the **Function Library group**, click the **Insert Function** button. Click the **Or select a category arrow**, and locate and click **Logical**. Under **Select a function**, click **IF**, and then click **OK**. Compare your screen with Figure 3.2

> The IF Function Arguments dialog box displays. The arguments that are required are Logical_test, Value_if_true, and Value_if_false. Recall that **arguments** are the values that an Excel function uses to

perform calculations or operations. Recall also that the name of the function is displayed just below the dialog box title bar.

Insertion point   Logical_test box

Figure 3.2

IF Function Arguments dialog box

Name of function

Value_if_true box

Value_if_false box

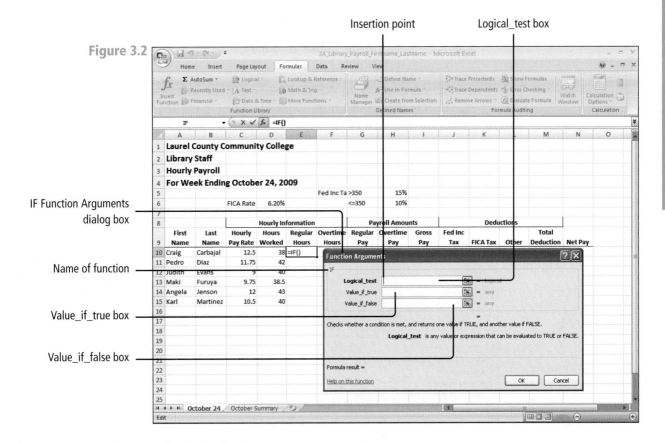

6 At the right side of the **IF Function Arguments** dialog box, at the end of the **Logical_test** box, locate and click the **Collapse Dialog Box** button ![icon].

The dialog box collapses in order to view the worksheet. Recall that you can click the title bar and drag the collapsed dialog box out of the way to display the data in the worksheet.

7 Click cell **D10** and in the collapsed **Function Arguments** dialog box, click the **Expand Dialog Box** button ![icon]. The insertion point blinks just after the cell reference. Type **>=40**

This logical test compares the value in cell D10—*38 hours*—and determines if Craig's hours are greater than or equal to 40. Because overtime is paid for all hours over 40, it is important to know the number of hours that will be paid at the regular rate and the number of hours that will be paid at the overtime rate. The symbol >= is a *comparison operator*—an operator that compares two values—and is entered to compare the value in the cell.

8 Press ⎋Tab. In the **Value_if_true** box, type **40**

In the Value_if_true area, determine what will display in the cell if the logical test is true—the employee works 40 or more hours during the week. Because the first 40 hours worked each week are paid at the regular rate and all hours in excess of 40 are paid at the over-time rate, the maximum number of regular hours is 40.

The result of this function is that if the hours worked are 40 or more, then 40 will display in cell E10.

9 Press Tab. In the **Value_if_false** box, type **d10** and then compare your screen with Figure 3.3.

When fewer than 40 hours are worked, the result of the logical function is false. All hours worked will be paid at the regular rate. Use a cell reference rather than the exact amount in the function so the formula can be copied. The result of this function—38—displays just after the last argument text box and on the lower left side of the Function Arguments dialog box.

Logical test—testing if hours worked are greater than or equal to 40

Result of function—number displayed in the Function Arguments dialog box

Figure 3.3

Value if true—hours worked >=40, display 40

Value if false—hours worked *not* >=40, display the hours worked—cell D10

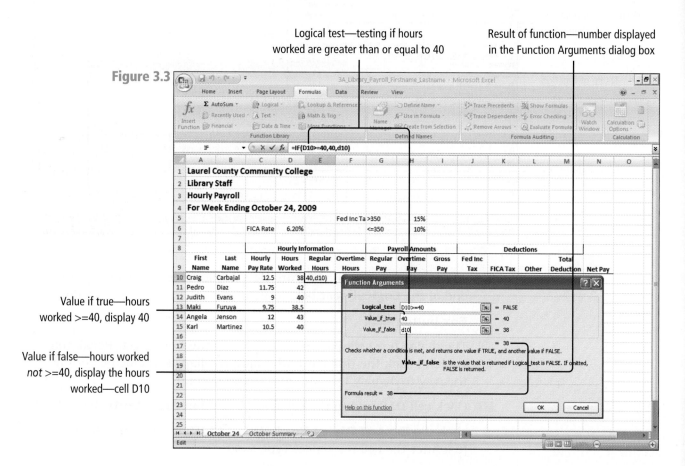

10 Click **OK,** and then compare your screen with Figure 3.4.

The arguments of the function display in the Formula Bar, written as a formula. The name of the function immediately follows the equal sign—=. The arguments of the function are displayed in parentheses with the arguments separated by commas.

The value of cell D10 displays as the result of the function. Because Craig worked fewer than 40 hours during the week, all of his 38 hours worked will be paid at the regular rate.

Figure 3.4

Value if true   Function displays in Formula Bar

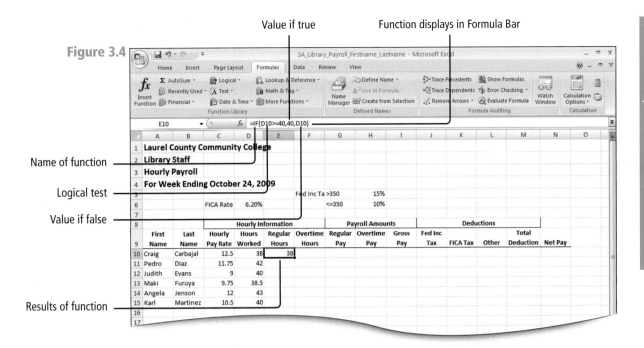

Name of function

Logical test

Value if false

Results of function

11 With cell **E10** as the active cell, drag the fill handle down through cell **E15** to copy the formula from cell **E10**. Review the results of the function in the cells and then compare your screen with Figure 3.5.

For the employees who work 40 hours or fewer—Craig, Judith, Maki, and Karl— the actual hours worked display in column E. Those who work more than 40 hours—Pedro and Angela—display 40 in column E to indicate the number of hours that will be paid at the regular hourly rate.

Function displays in Formula Bar   Results of function

Figure 3.5

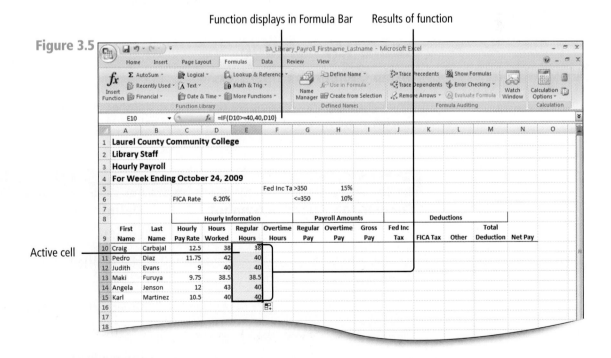

Active cell

12 Press [Ctrl] + [ʼ] to display the formulas and review the results after the function was copied. Compare your screen with Figure 3.6.

Because the function uses relative cell references, they change to reflect their new location in the worksheet.

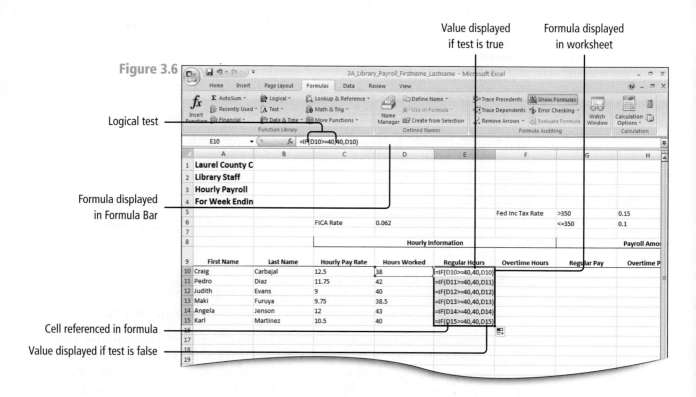

Figure 3.6

13 Press [Ctrl] + [ʼ] to display the results and **Save** 💾 your work.

More Knowledge
Using Comparison Operators

Comparison operators compare one value to another. The table in Figure 3.7 is a list of symbols that are used to compare values.

Comparison Operators

Comparison Operator Symbol	Definition
=	Equal to
>	Greater than
<	Less than
>=	Greater than or equal to
<=	Less than or equal to
<>	Not equal to

Figure 3.7

Payroll Calculations for Hourly Employees

Every organization with employees prepares a payroll. There are several federal and local laws that affect payroll processing such as the minimum wage and mandatory and voluntary deductions. Minimum wage is the minimum hourly pay rate. Mandatory deductions include money deducted from a paycheck to cover federal, state, and social security taxes. Voluntary deductions are chosen by the employee to cover items such as health insurance and retirement contributions.

Determine Gross Pay

The *gross pay* is the total amount of earnings before taxes. Federal law requires that all hours worked in excess of 40 hours per week are overtime and are paid at an overtime rate of at least 1½ times the normal hourly rate. The first 40 hours worked are paid at the regular hourly rate and all hours over 40 are paid at the overtime rate.

To determine the gross pay, determine the amount of pay earned for the regular hours worked—regular hours times hourly rate. Then determine the amount of pay earned for the overtime hours worked—all hours in excess of 40. To determine the overtime hourly rate, multiply the hourly rate by 1.5, and then multiply this result times the hours worked in excess of 40. Then add the earnings from regular hours to the earnings from overtime hours.

Determine Deductions

Net pay—another term for *take-home pay*—is the amount of pay after deductions are withheld. This is determined by subtracting your *deductions*— amount that is withheld from your paycheck—from your gross pay. Mandatory deductions are determined by law and include federal income tax, state income tax (although a few states do not have a state income tax), and FICA— the federal social security tax. In some cities there may also be a local city tax. Other deductions can be taken if the employee requests.

The amount of mandatory deductions varies depending on the employee and his or her choices. The deduction for federal income tax is based on the projected annual earnings and the number of dependents the employee has indicated. FICA tax is required by the federal government. The current rate is 12.4%. Half of that is deducted from the employee's pay and the other half is paid by the employer.

Calculate Net Pay

The formula to determine *net pay* is gross pay minus total deductions.

The calculation of net pay is made in the following sequence:

1. Determine **regular pay**.

   Multiply regular rate of pay by 40 hours or fewer.

2. Determine **overtime pay**.

   Multiply regular rate of pay times overtime hours worked (all hours in excess of 40) times 1.5.

3. Determine the **gross pay**.

   Add the regular pay to the overtime pay:

   Hourly rate × Regular hours + Hourly rate × (1.5 × Overtime hours) = Gross pay

4. Total all **deductions**.

   Deductions include federal income tax, state income tax (if applicable), and FICA tax—social security tax. In addition, some employees may choose to have additional deductions from their wages such as health insurance and savings plans.

5. Subtract the **total of the deductions** from the **gross pay** to determine **net pay**.

Activity 3.2 Reporting Overtime Hours Worked with an IF Formula

Overtime hours are paid at 1½ times the regular hourly rate. In this activity, you will determine the number of overtime hours the library employees worked.

1 Click cell **F10** and on the **Formula Bar**, click the **Insert Function** button ![fx]. In the **Or select a category** section, confirm that **Logical** displays. Alternatively, click the arrow and select Logical.

The Insert Function dialog box displays the category that was most recently used.

2 In the **Select a function** area, click **IF,** and then click **OK** to display the **Function Arguments** dialog box.

3 With the insertion point in the **Logical_test** box, click cell **D10** to place this cell reference in the box, and then type **>40**

The logical test compares the value in cell D10 to determine if it is greater than 40. You can click on a cell to enter its cell reference into the dialog box without collapsing the dialog box.

4 Press ⟨Tab⟩. Type **d10-40** Alternatively, click cell D10 and type **-40**

If the logical test is true—the hours worked are greater than 40—subtract 40 from that number to determine the overtime hours worked. Recall that overtime hours are those in excess of 40.

Values and comparisons can be typed directly into the Function Arguments dialog box.

5 Press ⟨Tab⟩. Type **0** and compare your screen with Figure 3.8, and then click **OK** or press ⟨Enter⟩.

The result—0—displays in the dialog box. The logical test determined that the value in cell D10—38—was less than 40, making the result false. When this test is false, 0 displays in the cell.

Value if true—if hours
worked >40, subtract 40 Result of function—number
from hours worked   to be displayed in the cell

Figure 3.8

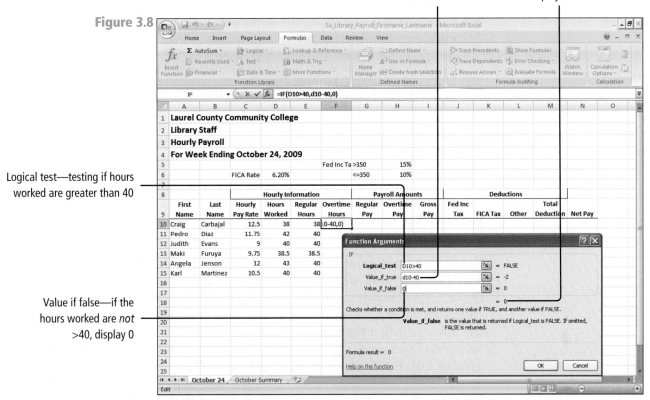

Logical test—testing if hours
worked are greater than 40

Value if false—if the
hours worked are *not*
>40, display 0

6. With cell **F10** active, use the fill handle to copy the formula down through cell **F15**. Select the range **D10:F15** and right-click. In the Mini toolbar, click the **Comma Style** button and the **Decrease Decimal** button one time—the numbers display with one decimal place. Review the results of the formula.

It is standard practice to align decimals within a column. Because some of these numbers require one decimal place, format the entire range for one decimal.

Pedro and Angela both worked more than 40 hours, resulting in overtime hours. Judith and Karl worked exactly 40 hours, which results in no overtime. The others worked fewer than 40 hours and also do not qualify for overtime.

7. Click cell **G10** and type = Click cell **C10**, type * click cell **E10**, and on the **Formula Bar**, click the **Enter** button.

The *regular pay* is calculated by multiplying the hourly wage—cell C10—by the regular hours worked—E10. Craig's regular pay is 475.

8. Click cell **H10** and type = Click cell **C10**, type * click cell **F10** and type ***1.5** and then on the **Formula Bar**, click the **Enter** button.

The amount of pay earned from overtime hours is calculated by multiplying the hourly wage—cell C10—by the number of overtime hours worked—cell F10—by 1.5—the overtime bonus. Even though Craig earns no overtime pay, the formula is entered in every cell in the column.

9 Click cell **I10** and using the skills you have practiced, use cell references to calculate the *gross pay*, which is the regular pay plus the overtime pay. Confirm that Craig earns 475.0.

10 Select the range **G10:I10**. Use the fill handle to copy the formulas down through **row 15**.

Recall that a range of cells can be copied simultaneously when they are adjacent to each other and the copy range is identical.

11 **Save** 💾 your workbook.

Activity 3.3 Determining Payroll Deductions Using Absolute References in Formulas

Recall that an employer is required by law to deduct federal income and social security (FICA) taxes from employee paychecks. The amount of the deductions is based on the amount of earnings. The income tax rate varies depending on the amount of income earned and other factors. For the library staff, a tax rate of 10% is assessed when gross pay is $350 or less each week, and a tax rate of 15% is assessed when the gross pay is greater than $350. The employee's share of FICA tax is 6.2%.

In this activity, you will create an IF function that determines which tax rate applies to each employee, use that tax rate to calculate the deductions for federal income tax, and calculate the amount of FICA tax that will be withheld from the employee's paycheck.

1 Click cell **J10**. On the **Formula Bar**, click the **Insert Function** button 𝑓ₓ. In the **Insert Function** dialog box, select the **Logical** category and double-click **IF**. Click in the dialog box title bar and drag the **Function Arguments** dialog box to the lower part of your screen, below **row 11**.

In the Insert Function dialog box, double-clicking the function name also displays the Function Arguments dialog box.

2 With the insertion point in the **Logical_test** box, click the **Collapse Dialog Box** button 📑. Click cell **I10**. Then click the **Expand Dialog Box** button 📑 and at the insertion point, type **>350**

The logical test compares the gross pay and determines if it is greater than 350.

3 Press Tab and in the **Value_if_true** text box, click the **Collapse Dialog Box** button 📑, click cell **H5,** and then click the **Expand Dialog Box** button 📑. Press F4 to make cell **H5** an absolute cell reference, and then type ***i10**

4 Press Tab and in the **Value_if_false** text box, type **h6** press F4, and type ***i10** and then compare your screen with Figure 3.9. Alternatively, collapse the Function Arguments dialog box, click in cell H6, press F4, and then type ***i10**

If the logical test is true, the tax rate is 15%—located in cell H5. This rate will be multiplied by the gross pay—cell I10—to calculate the amount of federal income tax to be withheld from the paycheck. Use absolute cell references for the tax rate so that the formula can be accurately copied.

If the logical test is false, the tax rate is 10%—located in cell H6. This rate will be multiplied by the gross pay—cell I10—to calculate the amount of federal income tax to be withheld from the paycheck.

Craig's gross pay is greater than 350, so the logical test is true, as stated at the right of the Logical_test box. The result—71.25—displays in the center of the Function Arguments dialog box.

In functions, cell references are used so the resulting formula can be copied in the worksheet. Recall it is faster to copy a formula than to create new formulas in every cell needed.

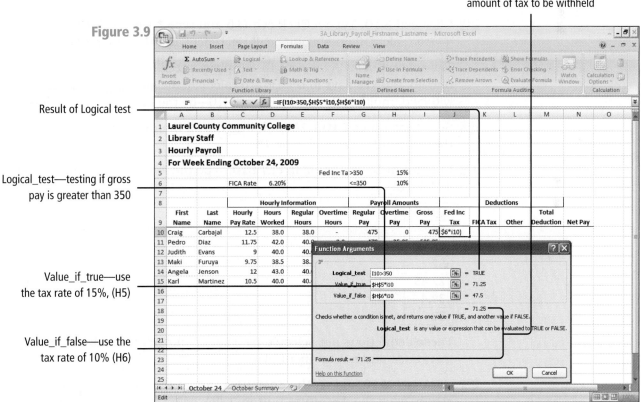

Figure 3.9

Result of function—amount of tax to be withheld

Result of Logical test

Logical_test—testing if gross pay is greater than 350

Value_if_true—use the tax rate of 15%, (H5)

Value_if_false—use the tax rate of 10% (H6)

5 Click **OK**. Review the formula in the Formula Bar and compare your screen with Figure 3.10.

Value_if_true

Figure 3.10

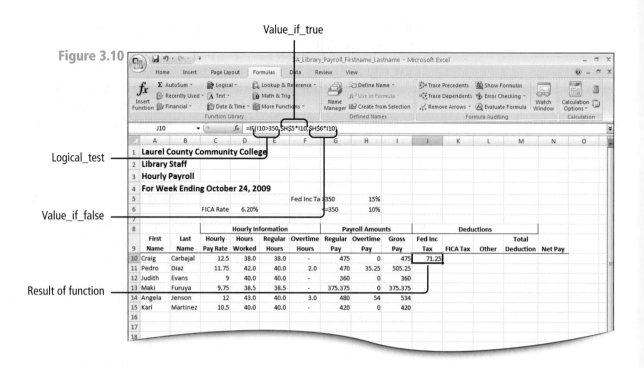

Logical_test

Value_if_false

Result of function

	A	B	C	D	E	F	G	H	I	J	K	L	M	N	O
1	Laurel County Community College														
2	Library Staff														
3	Hourly Payroll														
4	For Week Ending October 24, 2009														
5						Fed Inc Ta >350		15%							
6			FICA Rate	6.20%		<=350		10%							
7															
8				Hourly Information				Payroll Amounts				Deductions			
9	First Name	Last Name	Hourly Pay Rate	Hours Worked	Regular Hours	Overtime Hours	Regular Pay	Overtime Pay	Gross Pay	Fed Inc Tax	FICA Tax	Other	Total Deduction	Net Pay	
10	Craig	Carbajal	12.5	38.0	38.0	-	475	0	475	71.25					
11	Pedro	Diaz	11.75	42.0	40.0	2.0	470	35.25	505.25						
12	Judith	Evans	9	40.0	40.0	-	360	0	360						
13	Maki	Furuya	9.75	38.5	38.5	-	375.375	0	375.375						
14	Angela	Jenson	12	43.0	40.0	3.0	480	54	534						
15	Karl	Martinez	10.5	40.0	40.0	-	420	0	420						
16															
17															
18															

J10 = IF(I10>350,$H$5*I10,$H$6*I10)

6 Click cell **K10**. Type **=** Click cell **I10** and type ***** Click cell **D6**, press F4 to make D6 an absolute cell reference, and then press Enter.

The amount of FICA tax—29.45—displays in cell K10. The FICA tax rate—6.2%—displays in cell D6. To calculate the amount of FICA tax withheld, multiply the total pay—cell I10—by the FICA tax rate—cell D6.

7 Select the range **J10:K10** and drag the fill handle down to copy these formulas through **row 15**.

8 In **column L**, beginning in cell **L10**, type the following amounts to be deducted.

Other
45.5
36.75
52
27.85
39.4
35

These deductions are selected by each employee and include health insurance and a retirement plan.

9 Click cell **M10** and on the **Formulas tab**, in the **Function Library group**, click the **AutoSum** button. Click cell **J10** and drag through cell **L10** and compare your screen with Figure 3.11.

The ScreenTip displays the suggested range, which included the entire row. Because only the total deductions are required, scroll through the range to be included in this function—J10:L10. When Excel selects a range of cells to include in the formula, the range can be changed by dragging through the required cells. The AutoSum button in the Function Library provides the same results as the Sum button ∑ ▾ in the Editing group of the Home tab.

Figure 3.11

AutoSum button in
Function Library group

Sum range surrounded
by moving border

ScreenTip

Sum range

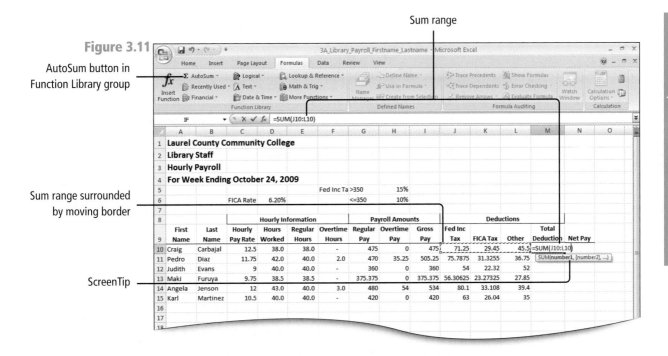

10 Press Enter. Click cell **N10** and type **=i10-m10** to determine the net pay. On the **Formula Bar**, click the **Enter** button ✔. Recall that net pay is the amount of gross pay minus the deductions.

Craig will receive a paycheck for $328.80, his take-home pay.

11 Select the range **M10:N10**. Use the fill handle to copy the formulas down through **row 15**.

12 **Save** 💾 your workbook.

Activity 3.4 Formatting the Worksheet and Merging and Centering a Vertical Range of Cells

1 Click cell **A16** and type **Total** Click cell **D16**. In the **Function Library group,** click the **AutoSum** button. On the **Formula Bar**, click the **Enter** button ✔. In cell **D16**, drag the fill handle to the right through cell **N16** to copy the formula across the worksheet.

2 Select the range **G16:N16**. Right-click, and from the Mini toolbar, click the **Accounting Number Format** button $ ▾. Click the **Borders button arrow** ▦ ▾, and then click **Top and Double Bottom Border**. Select the range **G10:N10**, right-click, and from the Mini toolbar, click **Accounting Number Format** $ ▾. Select the range **G11:N15**, right-click and from the Mini toolbar, click the **Comma Style** button ＇. Select the range **D16:F16**, right-click, and from the Mini toolbar, click the **Borders** button ▦ ▾, and then click **Top and Double Bottom Border**.

3 Right-click cell **C10** and from the Mini toolbar, click the **Accounting Number Format** button ⬛▾. Select the range **C11:C15** and right-click. From the Mini toolbar, click the **Comma Style** button ⬛.

This column displays the hourly wage and a total is not needed. Recall that you place a dollar sign—$—at the top cell and the total cell of the column. Because there is no total in this range, only the first cell requires a dollar sign.

4 Select the range **F5:F6**. Click the **Home tab**, and in the **Alignment group**, click the **Merge & Center** button ⬛▾ and the **Wrap Text** button ⬛.

Recall that Merge & Center combines the selected cells into one cell and centers the text within that cell. In addition to using Merge & Center in a horizontal range of cells, vertical cells can also be merged into one cell with the text centered vertically.

5 Select the range **F5:H6**. In the **Font group**, click the **Borders button arrow** ⬛▾ and from the displayed list, click **Outside Borders**.

6 **Save** ⬛ your workbook.

Objective 2
Link Data in Workbooks

Data used in one worksheet may be used in another worksheet of the workbook. Rather than entering the value of the cell, use a formula that refers to the original cell. By using a formula of this type, the worksheet is automatically updated when a change is made.

Activity 3.5 Constructing Formulas That Refer to Cells in Another Worksheet

In this activity, you will place the results of the payroll into a Summary worksheet using cell references that refer to the original amounts.

1 Click the **October Summary sheet tab**. Select the range **C5:L5**. In the **Font group**, point to the **Underline** button ⬛▾ and read the ScreenTip, and then click the **Underline** ⬛▾, **Bold** ⬛, and **Italic** ⬛ buttons. Alternatively, press Ctrl + U to underline the contents, Ctrl + B for bold, and Ctrl + I for italics.

The **Underline button** is used to place a line under only the text or numbers within a cell or range of cells. Recall that the Border button places a border under the entire width of the selected cell or range of cells.

2 Select the range **C5:E5** and in the **Alignment group**, click the **Merge & Center** button ⬛▾. Select the range **F5:H5** and click the **Merge & Center** button ⬛▾. Using the skills you practiced, merge the remaining ending dates over the ranges **I5:K5** and **L5:N5**.

3 Select the range **C6:E6**. Use the fill handle to copy the content of these cells through cell **N6**. Adjust the column widths to fully display the cell entries; your column titles may display on two lines. Position the mouse between **row 6** and **row 7** and double-click to display the two-line column titles.

The text in each of the selected cells is copied in the same order into adjacent cells. When a range of cells that contain text is selected, using the fill handle will copy the cells and their format and retain the original order. Double-clicking between rows adjusts the row height to accommodate the tallest entry.

4 Click cell **I7**. Type **=** and click the **October 24 sheet tab**. Click cell **I10** and press Enter to redisplay the **October Summary** worksheet.

The value in cell I10—$475.00—is entered into the October Summary worksheet. In a formula of this type, if the value in cell I10 of the October 24 worksheet changes, it will also change in cell I7 of the October Summary worksheet.

5 Click cell **I7** to select it again. In the **Formula Bar,** notice that instead of a value, the cell contains a formula that is equal to the value in a cell in another worksheet. Compare your screen with Figure 3.12.

The value displayed in cell I7 is the same number displayed in cell I10 of the October 24 worksheet. The number—$475.00—is entered in the October Summary worksheet and retains the Accounting Number Format of the source cell.

This formula displays a specific **syntax**—the language rules used by Excel to complete an instruction or command. The name of the worksheet—October 24—is displayed first and enclosed in single quotes followed by an exclamation mark—! After the worksheet name, the cell reference displays. This syntax indicates that the value displayed in cell I7—$475—is found in cell I10 of the October 24 worksheet.

Name of worksheet containing source data

Figure 3.12

Underlying value

Cell reference for the source data

Results

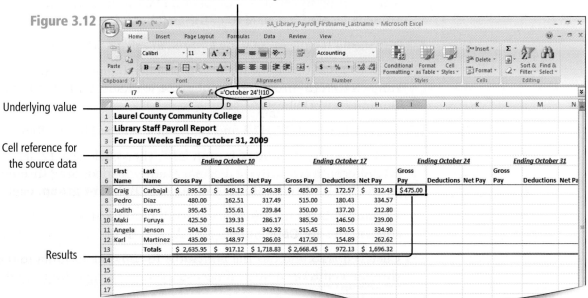

6 With cell **I7** active, use the fill handle to copy the formula down through cell **I12**. Then press Ctrl + ` to display the formulas. Scroll to the right to view **column I** and compare your screen with Figure 3.13.

The amount of gross pay is copied from the October 24 sheet to the October Summary sheet. As you review the formula, note that the reference to the October 24 worksheet remains the same while the cell reference changes to indicate the location of the data in the October 24 worksheet.

Figure 3.13

Worksheet name

Cell Reference

Formulas to reference cells on October 24 worksheet

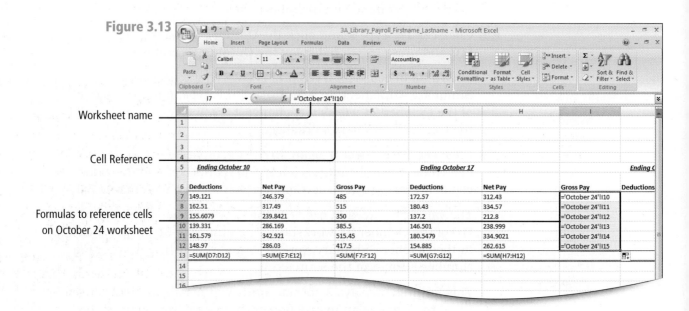

7 Press Ctrl + ` to redisplay the results. In the **October Summary** worksheet, click cell **J7**. Type = and click the **October 24 sheet tab**. Click cell **M10** and press Enter to redisplay the **October Summary** worksheet. Click cell **J7** and in the **Formula Bar**, review the displayed formula.

This formula in cell J7—='October 24'!M10—indicates the source value is located in cell M10 of the October 24 worksheet.

8 Use the fill handle to copy the formula in cell **J7** down through cell **J12**.

9 Click cell **K7**. Using the skills you practiced, place the Net Pay—the range N10:N15—from the **October 24** worksheet into the **October Summary** worksheet, beginning in cell **K7**.

10 Select the range **H7:H12** and right-click. In the Mini toolbar, double-click the **Format Painter** button ✨. Then click cells **I7, J7,** and **K7**. Alternatively, with the Format Painter loaded, drag through the range I7:K12. On the **Home tab**, in the **Clipboard group**, click the **Format Painter** button ✨ to turn it off. Alternatively, press Esc to turn off the Format Painter.

11 Click cell **H13** and use the fill handle to copy the formula to the right through cell **K13**. Adjust. If necessary, adjust the column widths.

12 **Save** 💾 your workbook.

Objective 3
Create IF Functions That Return Text

IF functions are also used to enter text into a cell. What displays in the cell depends on whether the logical test is true or false.

Activity 3.6 Copying Cells and Creating an IF Formula to Enter Text Using Drag-and-Drop

The library has noted that some employees have less money deducted from their paychecks for benefits. The human resources benefits manager has decided to visit employees whose deductions are low. In this activity, you will create an IF function that will determine those employees who will be contacted in person. The others will receive a flyer that describes the benefits.

1 Be sure the **October 24 sheet tab** is the active worksheet, and select the range **A9:B15**. Press Ctrl and position the mouse pointer at any border of the selected range. When the shape displays, drag down and to the right one column until the ScreenTip displays **B19:C25** and as you do, notice the information on the left side of the status bar that displays *Drag to copy cell contents . . . .* Compare your screen with Figure 3.14, release the mouse, and then release Ctrl.

Using the ***drag-and-drop*** method to copy cell content is recommended when both the source and destinations are on the same screen. Drag-and-drop is a technique that uses the mouse to copy selected text from one location to another, when Ctrl is pressed while you drag.

Arrow with plus

Figure 3.14

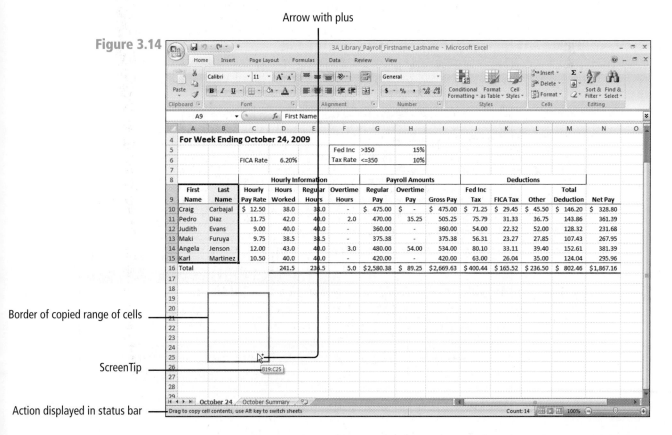

Border of copied range of cells

ScreenTip

Action displayed in status bar

2 In cell **D19**, type **How Informed?** and format it like cell **C19**. If necessary, adjust the column width and row height.

3 Click cell **D20** and from the **Formula Bar**, click the **Insert Function** button ![fx]. In the **Logical** category, double-click **IF** to display the IF Function Arguments dialog box. Drag to the bottom right of your screen so you can see the worksheet data.

4 In the **IF Function Arguments** dialog box, with the insertion point in the **Logical_test** box, click cell **L10** and type **<45** Press `Tab`. At the insertion point that is blinking in the **Value_if_true** box, type **Visit** Press `Tab` and in the **Value_if_false** box, type **Flyer** and then compare your screen with Figure 3.15.

This IF function is designed to determine which employees need additional information about their health care and retirement benefits. Those who have less than $45 deducted each month should be informed personally about the benefits, so *Visit* is entered by the employee's name. The others will receive a flyer explaining these benefits.

The dialog box indicates the arguments. When text is an argument, it is enclosed in quotation marks. *Visit* is enclosed in quotation marks because that entry is confirmed; when the Value_if_false text is confirmed, it will also be enclosed in quotation marks.

Figure 3.15

Logical test

Text enclosed in quotation marks

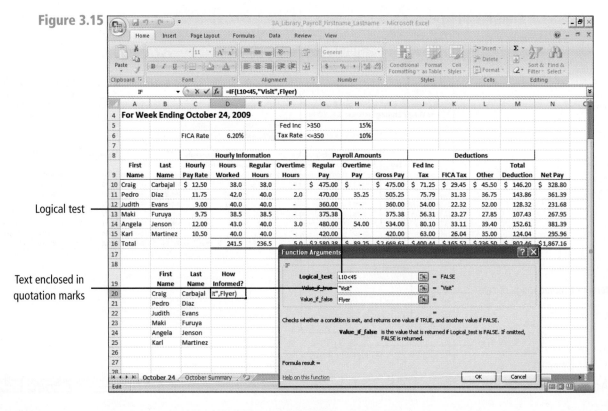

5 Click **OK**. With cell **D20** active, study the formula in the Formula Bar.

Both of the text arguments display in the Formula Bar inside quotation marks. A comma separates the arguments.

6 Drag the fill handle down to extend the formula through cell **D25**. With the range **D20:D25** selected, right-click and from the Mini toolbar, click the **Center** button ▤.

Text is entered and formatted in the cells.

7 **Save** 🖫 your workbook.

More Knowledge

Typing Functions in the Formula Bar

Some Excel users prefer to type the functions directly into the Formula Bar. It's important to understand the syntax when you do that. The function begins with the equal sign and the name of the function is typed. The logical test is entered followed by the value if true and then the value if false. The function is enclosed in parentheses and the arguments are separated with commas. If text is to be entered, it is enclosed in quotation marks. Even one typing error will cause a function error.

Objective 4
Emphasize Data Using Conditional Formatting

A **conditional format** is any format, such as cell shading or font color that is applied to cells that meet certain conditions to emphasize that data. Conditional formatting is used to highlight interesting cells, emphasize unusual values, and visualize data.

Activity 3.7 Highlighting Results with a Conditional Format

It has been determined that several employees are not taking advantage of their benefits package and need additional information. All employees will receive additional information and those with the least number deductions will be visited. In this activity, you will use a conditional format to indicate which employees will receive a visit about the benefits package and which will receive the flyer. You will also use a conditional format to highlight earnings.

1 On the **October 24 sheet** select the range **D20:D25**. On the **Home tab**, in the **Styles group**, click the **Conditional Formatting** button, and then compare your screen with Figure 3.16.

The Conditional Formatting menu displays with arrows indicating submenus will be available.

Figure 3.16

Conditional Formatting button

Conditional Formatting menu

Arrows indicate submenus are available

Selected range to apply conditional formatting

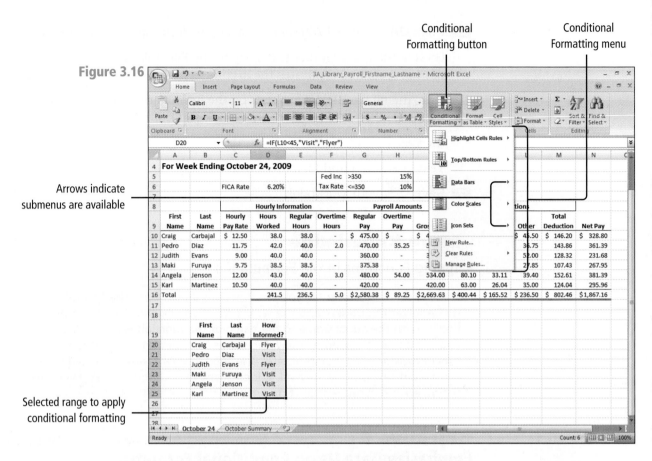

2 Scroll through the **Conditional Formatting** menu to display the submenus of this list. Point to **Highlight Cells Rules** and in the submenu that displays at the right, click **Equal To** and compare your screen with Figure 3.17.

The Equal To dialog box displays. This dialog box is used to set the conditions and the format for the cells. The left side will identify the comparison—what the cell will equal—while the right side will identify the format that will be applied to the cells that meet the condition.

Figure 3.17

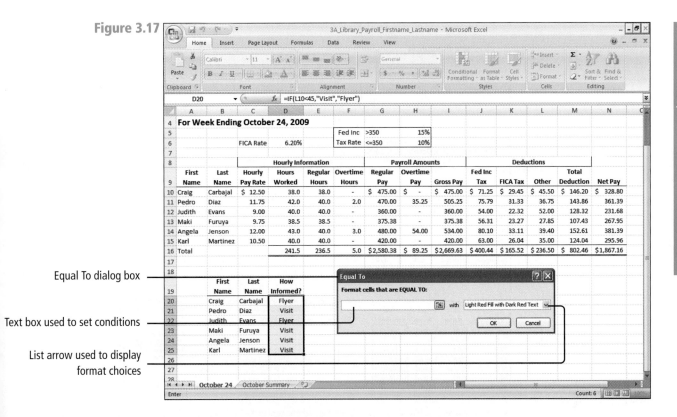

Equal To dialog box

Text box used to set conditions

List arrow used to display format choices

---

3 In the **Equal To** dialog box, the insertion point blinks in the **Format cells that are EQUAL TO** area. Type **Flyer** and notice that the text in the right text box shows that *Light Red Fill with Dark Red Text* is indicated. Click **OK** to accept the selected format.

When the condition is entered in the dialog box, the selected cells display the selected condition and format.

The conditional format is applied to the cells that meet the condition. All cells that contain the word *Flyer* are formatted with Light Red Fill and Dark Red Text.

4 With the range **D20:D25** selected, in the **Styles group**, click the **Conditional Formatting** button. From the displayed list, point to **Highlight Cells Rules** and from the submenu, click **Equal To**. In the **Equal To** dialog box, at the insertion point, type **Visit** On the right side of the **Equal To** dialog box, click the **arrow** and then compare your screen with Figure 3.18.

Figure 3.18

List arrow

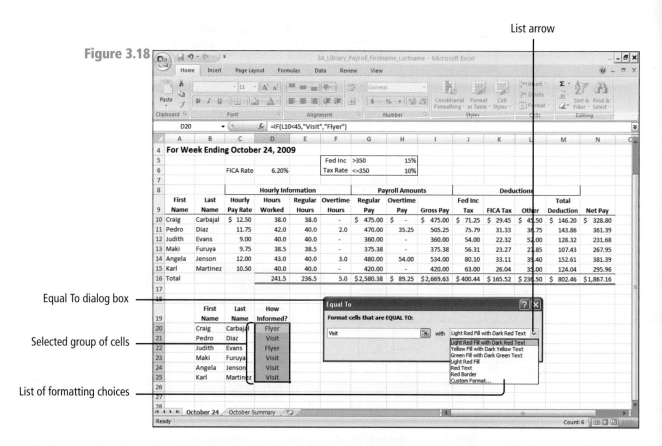

Equal To dialog box

Selected group of cells

List of formatting choices

5 From the displayed list, click **Green Fill with Dark Green Text** and click **OK**. Then click in another cell outside the range and compare your screen with Figure 3.19.

The conditional format highlights in green the employees who will be informed with a personal visit.

Figure 3.19

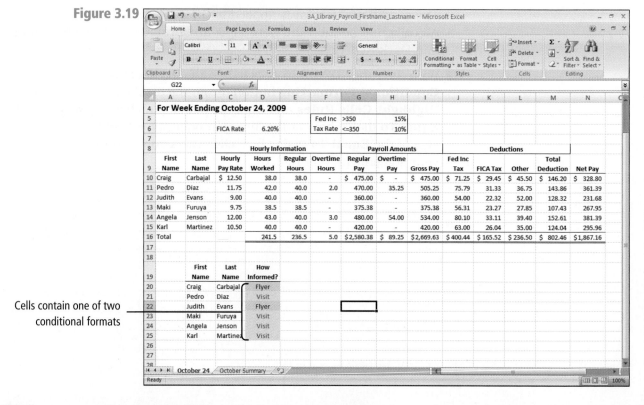

Cells contain one of two conditional formats

6 Click the **October Summary sheet tab**. Select the range **E7:E12** and press Ctrl while you select the ranges **H7:H12** and **K7:K12**.

7 In the **Styles group**, click the **Conditional Formatting** button. In the **Conditional Formatting** menu, point to **Highlight Cells Rules** and from the submenu, click **Greater Than**, and then compare your screen with Figure 3.20.

The Greater Than dialog box displays and a number is suggested.

Selected ranges where format will be applied

Figure 3.20

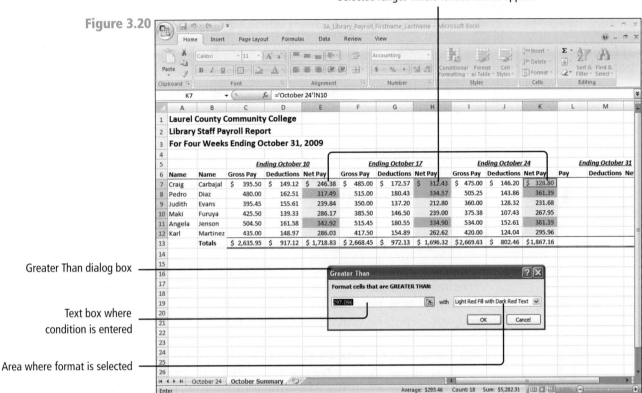

Greater Than dialog box

Text box where condition is entered

Area where format is selected

8 In the **Format cells that are GREATER THAN** area, type **300** and notice in the worksheet that the cells meeting this condition already display in this format. On the right side of the **Greater Than** dialog box, click the **arrow** and from the displayed list, click **Red Text**.

All cells that are greater than $300 will be printed in red text.

9 Click **OK**. With the ranges still selected, in the **Styles group**, click the **Conditional Formatting** button. In the **Conditional Formatting** menu, point to **Highlight Cells Rules** and in the displayed submenu, click **Less Than**.

10 In the **Format cells that are LESS THAN** area, type **250** and on the right side of the **Less Than** dialog box, click the **arrow**. Click **Yellow Fill with Dark Yellow Text**, and then click **OK**. Click in a cell in the worksheet so the cells are no longer highlighted and compare your screen with Figure 3.21.

Figure 3.21

Net pay greater than
$300 displayed in red

Net pay less than $250
displayed with yellow
background

Net pay between $250 and
$300 with no conditional
formatting

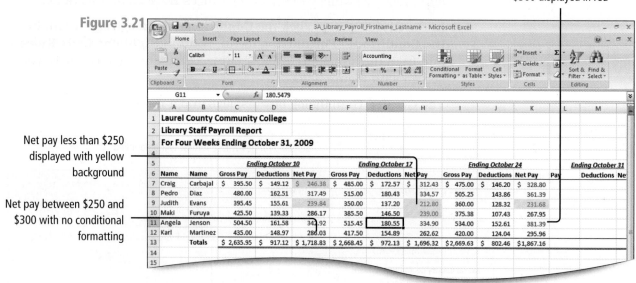

11 **Save** your workbook.

Activity 3.8 Correcting an Error and Reviewing Results

It is good practice to review worksheets to ensure the accuracy of the data. Proofreading data entries is necessary. When an error is corrected, the worksheet is automatically updated and remains accurate. In this activity, you will correct several errors in this worksheet and view the results.

1 Click the **October 24 sheet tab**. Click cell **H5** and type **14** Press Enter and as you do so, observe in the **Fed Inc Tax** column the changes that occur when the percentage rate for taxes is changed and then compare your screen with Figure 3.22.

By using cell references in formulas, rather than the actual amount, all cells that use this cell are automatically updated. The amount of Federal Income Tax—cell J10—changed, which also changed the amount of Total Deductions and Net Pay. The net pay in cell N10 changed from $328.80 to $333.55.

Figure 3.22

Fed Inc Tax Rate changed to 14%

Cell entries change to reflect tax rate

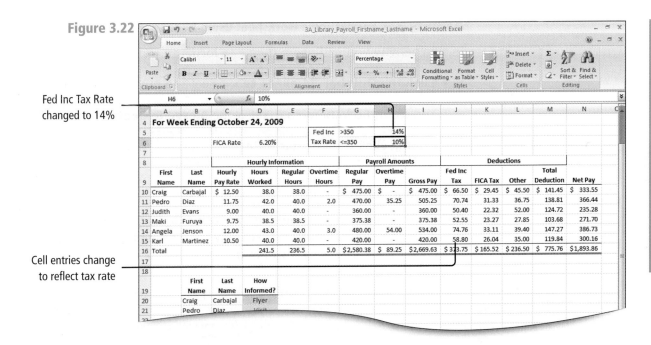

2 Click the **October Summary sheet tab** and review the number entered in cell **K7**.

This number also changed to $333.55. The formula entered in this cell referred to cell N10 in the October 24 worksheet and when that cell was changed, cells that referred to it also changed.

3 Click the **October 24 sheet tab**. Click cell **D13** and type **41** to change the hours worked for Maki Furuya, and as you press Enter, observe the changes in this worksheet and confirm that Maki Furuya's net pay is now $295.04.

4 Click the **October Summary sheet tab** and notice that the net pay in cell **K10** also changed to $295.04.

The number updated to reflect the change in hours and the conditional format was removed from the cell. When creating a worksheet, formulas are created so that when a change is made, the worksheet is automatically updated.

5 **Save** your workbook.

Objective 5
Format with Themes

A **theme** is a combination of complementary colors, fonts, and effects that may be applied to a workbook to give it a professional appearance. A **document theme** is used to format an entire workbook or individual worksheets. The same themes are available in all Microsoft Office applications—Word, Access, PowerPoint—and provide a consistent format throughout a group of documents.

Activity 3.9 Formatting a Worksheet Using a Theme

In this activity you will use a theme to format a worksheet.

1 Click the **October 24 sheet tab,** select the range **A1:N1**, right-click, and from the Mini toolbar, click the **Merge & Center** button ⊞.

Double-click the **Format Painter** button 🖌 and click cells **A2**, **A3**, and **A4**. In the **Clipboard group**, click the

Format Painter button 🖌 to turn it off.

2 On the Ribbon, click the **Page Layout tab**. In the **Themes group**, click the **Themes** button to display the **Themes gallery**, and then compare your screen with Figure 3.23.

Figure 3.23

Themes button

Themes gallery

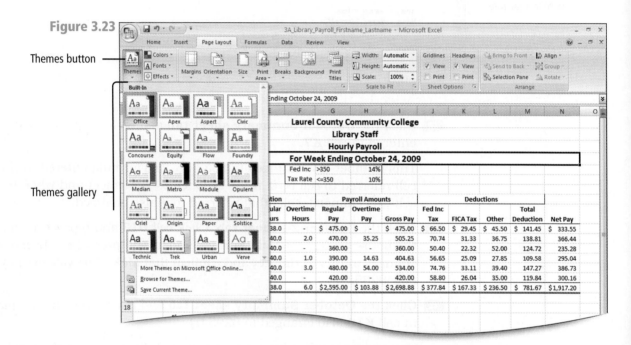

3 Move your mouse pointer over the displayed themes and notice how Live Preview allows the format of the worksheet to change as you scroll over each theme. In the **Themes gallery**, under **Built-In**, click **Flow**—the second row, third column. Click the **Home tab**.

Notice in the Font group that the font of the worksheet changed to Constantia and the font attributes and sizes remained intact.

4 Select the range **A1:A4**. Recall these cells are merged and centered over the range of the worksheet.

5 In the **Font group**, point to the **Fill Color button arrow** ⬦▾ to read the ScreenTip. Click the **Fill Color button arrow** ⬦▾ and then compare your screen with Figure 3.24.

The colors in the gallery change to match the colors of the theme—Flow in this case. Shades of varying intensity are available. Recall that a Color gallery displays both theme and standard colors.

Figure 3.24

Theme Colors   Standard Colors

Fill Color button

Fill Color gallery

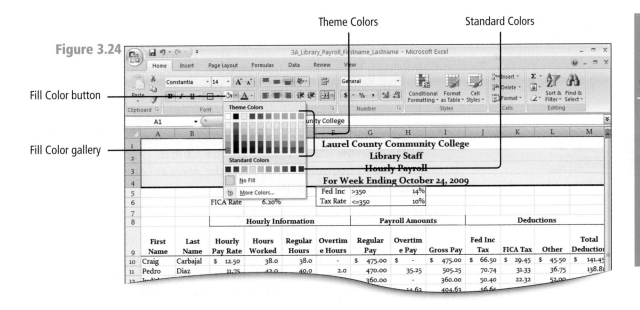

6 Under **Theme Colors**, point to the sixth column—**Turquoise**. Point to the fourth color in the column—the ScreenTip displays *Turquoise, Accent 2, Lighter 40%*. Click to select this color.

7 Select the range **A9:N9**. In the **Font group**, click the **Fill Color button arrow** . Under **Theme Colors**, point to the sixth column—**Turquoise**—and click the last color chip in the column—**Turquoise, Accent 2, Darker 50%**. In the **Font group**, click the **Font Color button arrow** and compare your screen with Figure 3.25.

Font Color button   Font Color gallery

Figure 3.25

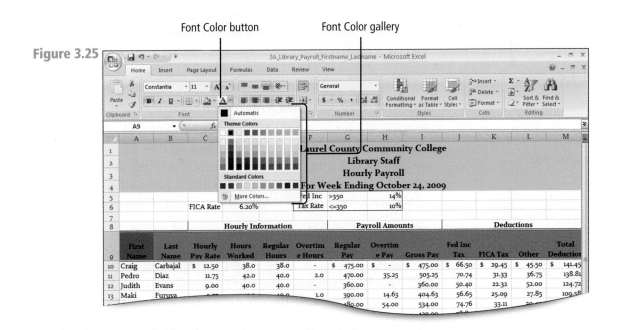

8 Point to the first column and click the first color chip—**White, Background 1**.

Placing a light-colored font over dark background maintains readability. The font color used must be readable both on the screen and when printed and needs to be reviewed when using a color background.

9 Select the range **C8:M8**. In the **Font group**, click the **Fill Color button arrow** ![icon]. Under **Theme Colors**, point to the sixth column—**Turquoise**—and click the second color chip—**Turquoise, Accent 2, Lighter 80%**.

10 If necessary, adjust the column widths to fully display cell contents.

When a theme is changed, the font style also changes. Each font style is a different size. Changing the font may change the size and alter the display in a cell. When changing a theme, it is a good practice to review the text and data in the worksheet.

11 Click the **October Summary sheet tab.** On the **Page Layout tab,** in the **Themes group**, point to **Themes** and notice that the ScreenTip displays *Current: Flow*, indicating the theme applied to this worksheet.

When a theme is changed, it is applied to all worksheets in the workbook.

12 Using the skills you practiced, center the three title lines over the range of the worksheet. Select the range **A1:A3** and on the **Home tab**, in the **Font group**, click the **Fill Color button arrow** ![icon]. Under **Theme Colors**, point to the next-to-last column—**Green**—and click the row 5 chip—**Green, Accent 5, Darker 25%**.

13 Select the range **A5:N6**. Using the skills you practiced, select a fill color of **Green, Accent 5, Lighter 60%**. If necessary, adjust the column widths.

14 **Save** ![icon] your workbook.

Activity 3.10 Changing a Theme and Font

A theme provides a consistency to the worksheets of a workbook. A new theme can be applied quickly, and several themes can be reviewed until the desired look is achieved. Different sections of the theme can be changed, such as the colors or font. In this activity, you will apply a different theme to the worksheet and change the fonts and colors.

1 Click the **October 24 sheet tab.** Click the **Page Layout tab**, and in the **Themes group**, click the **Themes** button. Scroll through the **Theme gallery** and as you do, view the display on the worksheet to see how Live Preview allows the effect of applying that theme to be displayed. Under **Built-In**, in the third column, in the last row, click **Urban**.

2 Click the **October Summary sheet tab.** In the **Themes group**, point to the **Themes** button and review the ScreenTip. Notice that *Current: Urban* displays. Point to the **Colors** button and review the ScreenTip—the current theme is identified as *Urban*—and then in the **Themes group**, point to the **Fonts** button and compare your screen with Figure 3.26.

When the theme was changed in one worksheet, it was changed in the entire workbook. The ScreenTips identify the current theme—Urban. The Theme Fonts ScreenTip also identifies the fonts used in the theme—Trebuchet MS for the Heading and Georgia for the Body.

Figure 3.26

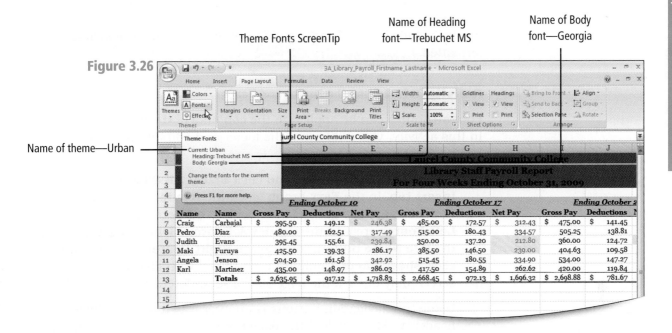

Name of theme—Urban
Theme Fonts ScreenTip
Name of Heading font—Trebuchet MS
Name of Body font—Georgia

3 In the **Themes group**, click the **Colors** button to display the **Color gallery**.

Each theme is listed and displays the array of colors available in the theme. This gallery provides a Live Preview as you move your mouse through the gallery.

4 Click in the worksheet to close the **Color gallery**. In the **Themes group**, click the **Fonts** button to display the **Fonts gallery**. Scroll through the gallery and notice how the font changes in the work-sheet. Locate and click **Concourse Lucida Sans Unicode**.

The Lucida Sans Unicode font has been applied to the workbook.

5 Point to the **Fonts button arrow** and review the ScreenTip. Point to the **Themes** button and review the ScreenTip.

Although the font has changed to the Concourse font, the theme is still Urban. A theme includes a font, but the font can be changed within the theme to personalize the format.

6 Select the range **A1:A3**. Click the **Home tab**, and then click the **Font Color button arrow** . Click the first color—**White, Background 1**.

After the theme was changed, the text in the title of this worksheet was difficult to read. Changing it to a lighter text maintains readability.

7 If necessary, adjust the column widths. **Save** your workbook.

Objective 6
Add Information in the Header and Footer

The ***header*** displays at the top of every page and may be used to print text, page numbers, and graphics—like the footer which displays at the end of every page. There is built-in data, such as file name and sheet name, that can be included in the header and footer, and text may be added and formatted.

Activity 3.11 Editing the Footer and Header

Font attributes can be applied to the contents of the header and footer. In this activity, you will format the footer and add information to the header for the payroll reports.

1 At a sheet tab, right-click and click **Select All Sheets**. Click the **Insert tab**. In the **Text group**, click the **Header & Footer** button. In the **Navigation group**, click the **Go to Footer** button. Click the **Left Footer** area. In the **Header & Footer Elements group**, click the **File Name** button. Click in the **Right Footer** area, and then click **Sheet Name**. Compare your screen with Figure 3.27. (Your screen may differ if the page size is set differently).

Using the Navigation buttons is another way to move between the header and footer. Note the page number indicator in the Status bar that reads *Page: 1 of 2*.

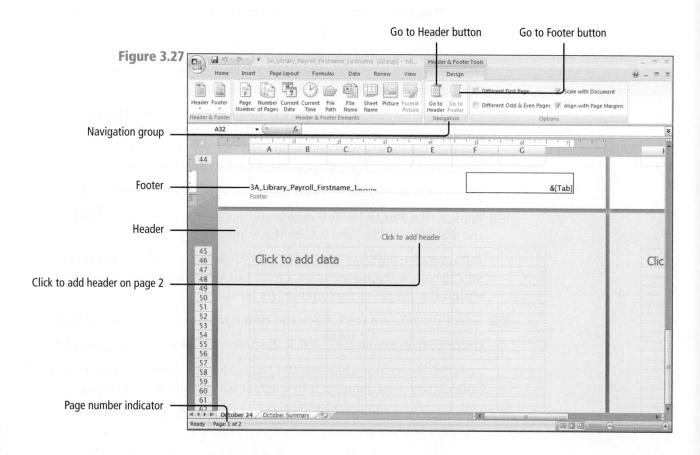

Figure 3.27

Go to Header button

Go to Footer button

Navigation group

Footer

Header

Click to add header on page 2

Page number indicator

2 In the **Right Footer** area, select the code for the sheet name, **&[Tab]**. On the Ribbon, click the **Home tab**. Press Ctrl + B and Ctrl + I to format with bold and italic. Click the **Font Color button arrow** [A ▾] and from the displayed gallery, in the seventh column, click the fifth chip—**Purple, Accent 3, Darker 25%**.

The sheet name in the footer will be formatted in purple, with the other font attributes applied.

3 Click the **Left Footer** area. On the **Home tab**, in the **Font group**, click the **Bold** button [B] and **Italic** button [I]. Click the **Font Color button arrow** [A ▾] to display in purple.

Each area of the footer must be formatted independently. After a font color has been selected, it remains the active color for that button and can be applied to other areas of the worksheet simply by clicking the Font Color button.

4 Click the **Header & Footer Tools Design tab**. In the **Navigation group**, click the **Go to Header** button.

The insertion point moves to the Left Header area. The header prints at the top of each worksheet. Like the footer, three areas display in the header area—left, center, right. The same options are available from the Header & Footer Elements group.

5 In the **Header & Footer Elements group,** click the **Current Date** button.

The code for the current date is entered into the worksheet. The current date will display whenever the worksheet is opened.

6 Press Spacebar and from the **Header & Footer Elements group**, click the **Current Time** button. Click back into the worksheet.

7 Press Ctrl + Home to return to cell **A1**. In the **Status bar**, click the **Normal** button [⊞]. **Save** [💾] your workbook.

8 Click the **Page Layout tab**. In the **Page Setup group**, click the **Dialog Box Launcher** [⌐]. In the **Page Setup** dialog box, in the **Page tab**, under **Orientation**, click **Landscape**. Under **Scaling**, click **Fit to 1**. Click the **Margins tab**. Under **Center on page**, click **Horizontally** and **Vertically**. Then click **Print Preview** and view both worksheets of the completed workbook.

9 Click **Close Print Preview**. Press Ctrl + Home to return the active cell to **A1**. Right-click any sheet tab and click Ungroup Sheets. **Ungroup sheets**. Click the **October 24 sheet tab**. **Save** [💾] your workbook.

10 Check your *Chapter Assignment Sheet* or *Course Syllabus*, or consult your instructor, to determine if you are to submit work on paper or electronically. To submit electronically, follow the instructions provided by your instructor, and then go to Step 11.

11 Click the **Office** button [📄], and then click **Print**. In the **Print** dialog box, under **Print what**, click **Entire workbook**. Under **Copies**, confirm that **1** is selected. Click **OK**. If you are directed to submit printed formulas, group all worksheets and display and print formulas.

12 Click the **Office** button 🔳, and then click **Close**. If the dialog box displays asking if you want to save changes, click **No** so that you do not save the changes to Page Setup that you used for printing formulas. **Exit** Excel.

End You have completed Project 3A ————————————————

Project 3B **Enrollments**

In Activities 3.12 through 3.22, you will report enrollments for Fall semester for the last three years for Michael Schaeffler, vice president of instruction. You will determine where a new page begins, print column and row titles on every page, display column and row headings, and use format tools to assist in the readability of this large worksheet. Your completed worksheet will look similar to Figure 3.28.

For Project 3B, you will need the following file:

e03B_Enrollments

You will save your workbooks as
3B_Enrollments_Firstname_Lastname
3B_Enrollments_Print_Area_Firstname_Lastname

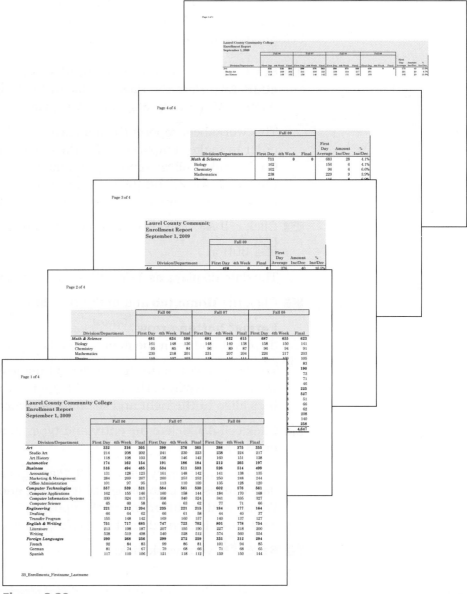

Figure 3.28
Project 3B—Enrollments

Objective 7
Enter Dates

Excel recognizes a date as a number and formats the date in one of many date styles. As a date is entered into the worksheet, the *General Style* is applied. Any one of several date styles may later be applied to the cell, such as 3/14, 14-Mar, or March 14, 2009. You can enter the year as two digits, four digits, or even leave it off. A two-digit year value of 30 through 99 is interpreted by the Windows operating system as the four-digit years of 1930 through 1999. All other two-digit year values are assumed to be in the 2000s, so 03 is interpreted as 2003. Make it a habit to type year values as four digits, even though only two digits may display in the cell.

Activity 3.12 Entering a Date as Text

The preferred date format for business is to write the date in full, such as *July 4, 2009*. Dates are generally recognized as a number. In order for the date to be recognized and formatted as text, type an apostrophe (') before typing the date.

1 **Start** Excel. From your student files locate and open the file named **e03B_Enrollments**. **Save** the file in the **Excel Chapter 3** folder and name it **3B_Enrollments_Firstname_Lastname**

This worksheet reports the fall enrollments for the last three years in order to make comparisons for the current semester. Laurel County Community College reports enrollments for the first day, the end of the fourth week, and the final numbers for each semester. The data for the years evaluated—2006, 2007, and 2008—are already entered.

2 Click cell **A3**. Type **9/1/09** and on the **Formula Bar**, click the **Enter** ✔ button.

The date displays as 1-Sep-09—an abbreviated style.

3 Click the **Home tab** and in the **Number group**, click the **Number Format button arrow** [General ▾] (Custom currently displays) and from the menu, click **Long Date**.

The date is written in the preferred business style, but the day of the week also displays. The date is aligned at the right. Recall that numbers align at the right and the date is recognized as a number.

4 Click cell **A3**, delete the entry and type **'September 1, 2009** and then press [Enter].

The full date displays in the cell. Placing the apostrophe before the date causes Excel to recognize it as text and display it as it is typed. When used in this manner, the apostrophe will not print when the worksheet is printed, and the date cannot be used in a calculation.

5 **Save** 🖫 your workbook.

Objective 8
Format Large Worksheets

It is difficult to create a large worksheet when you cannot see all of it on your screen. Recall that you can view the entire worksheet page in Print Preview, but it cannot be edited. Using the **Zoom control** to quickly decrease or increase the worksheet is one method used to view and work in more areas of the worksheet. When creating a worksheet, it is helpful to have the column and row titles visible to assist in placing data in the correct cell. Any row or column will remain on the screen when you use the **Freeze Panes** command. This allows the rest of the worksheet to be used while the identifying rows and columns remain visible.

Activity 3.13 Indenting Cell Contents and Using Zoom Control

A large worksheet filled with numbers can be formatted to highlight numbers and their relationships. In this activity you will format the worksheet using bold, borders, indent cell contents, zoom, and other techniques.

1 Select the range **A15:A17**. Click the **Home tab**. In the **Alignment group**, click the **Increase Indent** button.

The space increases between the left border and the text in the cell. The departments within the Computer Technologies division are indented to provide a visual separation between divisions and the departments within the divisions.

As you review the worksheet, you can see that these indents have already been completed for the Art and Business divisions and that it is easy to see the departments of each division.

Note — Decreasing Indents

The Decrease Indent button is used to move indented cells to the left until there is no space between the entry and left edge of the cell.

2 Select the range **A19:A20**. Press and hold Ctrl while you select **A22:A23**, **A25:A27**, **A29:A33**, **A35:A37**, and **A40:A44** and from the **Alignment group**, click the **Increase Indent** button. Then adjust the column width so the longest cell entry fully displays in the column width.

Recall that you can apply a format to more than one selected range of cells at the same time.

3 Click the **row 14** heading to select the row. At the right edge of the status bar, locate the **Zoom controls**, and compare your screen with Figure 3.29.

Figure 3.29

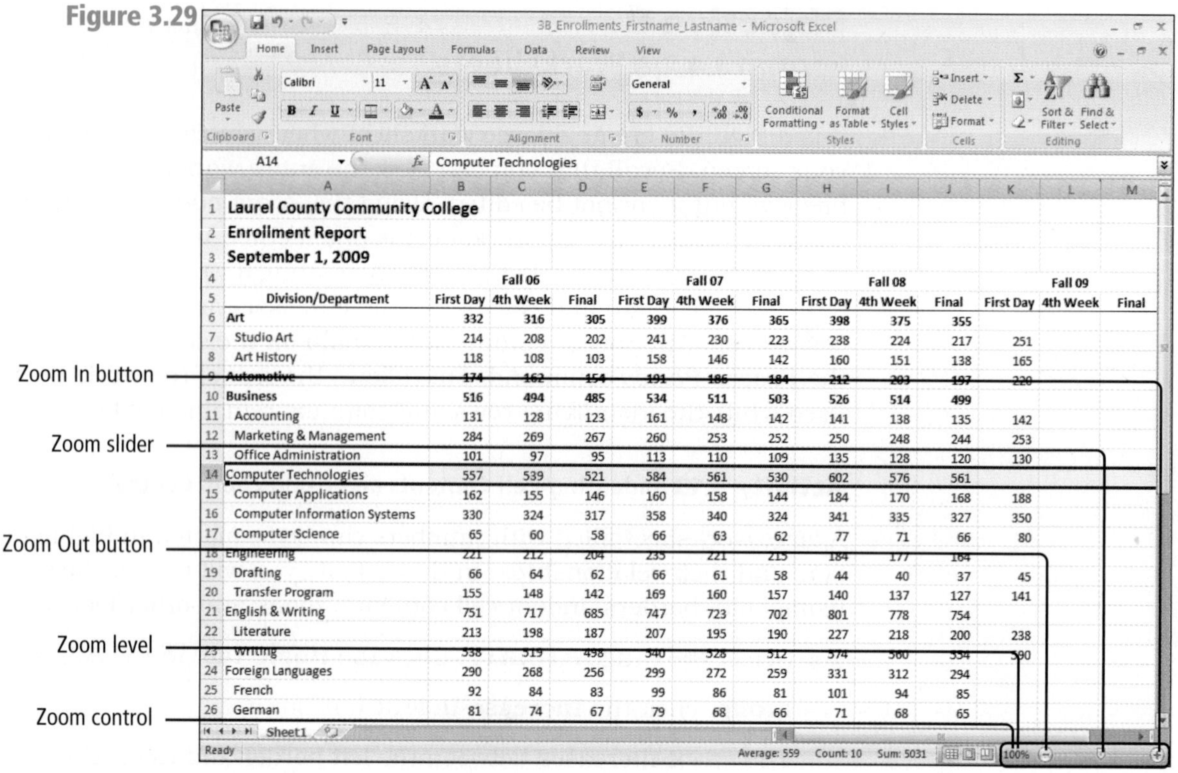

3B_Enrollments_Firstname_Lastname - Microsoft Excel

A14 ▾ (fx Computer Technologies

Division/Department	Fall 06 First Day	4th Week	Final	Fall 07 First Day	4th Week	Final	Fall 08 First Day	4th Week	Final	Fall 09 First Day	4th Week	Final
1 Laurel County Community College												
2 Enrollment Report												
3 September 1, 2009												
6 Art	332	316	305	399	376	365	398	375	355			
7 Studio Art	214	208	202	241	230	223	238	224	217	251		
8 Art History	118	108	103	158	146	142	160	151	138	165		
9 Automotive	174	162	154	191	186	184	212	203	197	220		
10 Business	516	494	485	534	511	503	526	514	499			
11 Accounting	131	128	123	161	148	142	141	138	135	142		
12 Marketing & Management	284	269	267	260	253	252	250	248	244	253		
13 Office Administration	101	97	95	113	110	109	135	128	120	130		
14 Computer Technologies	557	539	521	584	561	530	602	576	561			
15 Computer Applications	162	155	146	160	158	144	184	170	168	188		
16 Computer Information Systems	330	324	317	358	340	324	341	335	327	350		
17 Computer Science	65	60	58	66	63	62	77	71	66	80		
18 Engineering	221	212	204	235	221	215	184	177	164			
19 Drafting	66	64	62	66	61	58	44	40	37	45		
20 Transfer Program	155	148	142	169	160	157	140	137	127	141		
21 English & Writing	751	717	685	747	723	702	801	778	754			
22 Literature	213	198	187	207	195	190	227	218	200	238		
23 Writing	538	519	498	540	528	512	574	560	554	590		
24 Foreign Languages	290	268	256	299	272	259	331	312	294			
25 French	92	84	83	99	86	81	101	94	85			
26 German	81	74	67	79	68	66	71	68	65			

Sheet1

Ready   Average: 559   Count: 10   Sum: 5031   100%

Zoom In button
Zoom slider
Zoom Out button
Zoom level
Zoom control

4 In the **Zoom control** area, click the **Zoom Out** button ⊖. Alternatively, press Ctrl while you use the scroll wheel on your mouse to use the Zoom controls.

The worksheet has decreased in size so more of it can be viewed on the screen.

5 Click the **Zoom Out** button ⊖ until the Zoom level displays 50%.

The worksheet has decreased in size so more of it can be viewed. When formatting a worksheet, it is recommended that you view as much of it as possible.

6 With the **row 14** heading selected, press and hold Ctrl while you click rows **18**, **21**, **24**, **28**, **34**, **38**, **39**, **45**, and **46**. You may need to zoom to a larger display in order to read the row headings. Then, from the

Font group, click the **Bold** button **B**. Click in the worksheet to deselect the rows.

Row 46 is currently blank, but totals will be entered later. The division names and totals were formatted as a group and display at the top of the division data and are highlighted in bold. Using this font attribute to separate divisions highlights the enrollments within each division.

7 Press Ctrl while you select the division names—cells **A6**, **A9**, **A10**, **A14**, **A18**, **A21**, **A24**, **A28**, **A34**, **A38**, **A39**, **A45**, and **A46**—and click the **Italic** button **I**.

8 In the **Zoom control** area, click the **Zoom slider** and drag it back to the center position until the Zoom control monitor displays 100%.

9 Click cell **A5**. Scroll until cell **J46** is visible on the screen. Press ⇧Shift, and then click cell **J46**. Click the **View tab.** In the **Zoom group**, click the **Zoom to Selection** button.

The **Zoom to Selection** feature changes the size of the worksheet so the currently selected range of cells fills the entire window. Another way to select a range of cells—particularly a large range of cells where the first and last cell are not visible at the same time—is to click in the first cell, and then press ⇧Shift while you click in the last cell.

10 Select the range **A18:A20**. In the **Zoom group**, click the **Zoom to Selection** button. Then compare your screen with Figure 3.30.

The selected range of the worksheet displays. You can quickly increase or decrease areas of the worksheet using the Zoom control.

Notice in the Zoom control that the percentage for the worksheet displays. The exact percentage will vary depending on the settings on your computer.

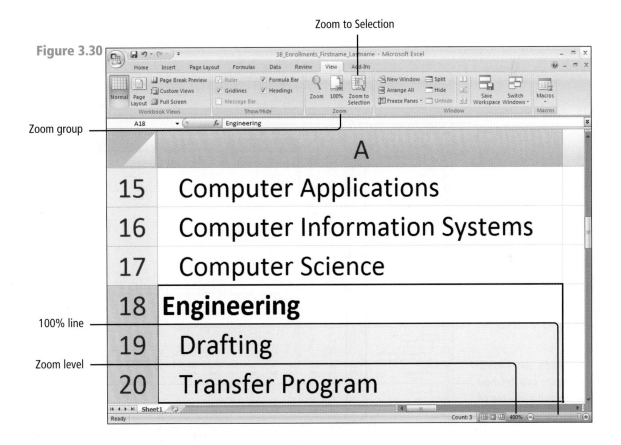

Figure 3.30

11 In the **Zoom group**, click the **100%** button. Alternatively, in the status bar, in the Zoom control buttons, click the 100% line.

To quickly return to view at 100%, use either the Zoom button or the Zoom control buttons.

12 **Save** your workbook.

Activity 3.14 Adding Vertical Borders

Placing vertical borders between sections of data helps define each section. In this activity, you will add vertical borders between the data for each semester.

1 Click cell **A5**. Scroll to the last cell of the worksheet, press ⟨⇧Shift⟩, and click cell **P46**. On the **View tab**, in the **Zoom group**, click the **Zoom to Selection** button.

2 Select the range **B5:B46**. On the **Home tab**, in the **Alignment group**, click the **Dialog Box Launcher** ⬚. In the **Format Cells** dialog box, click the **Border tab** and compare your screen with Figure 3.31.

Recall that you have placed horizontal borders at the top and bottom of rows. The Border tab of the Format Cells dialog box is used to place borders on the cell edges—horizontal, vertical, or at a diagonal—and to select another style and size of line. Colored borders can also be used in the worksheet.

Presets area—use to select a
pre-determined border style

Figure 3.31

Border tab of Format
Cells dialog box

Line area—use to select
the line style and color

Default border style

Buttons used to add borders

Border area—use to
determine exactly where
border will be placed

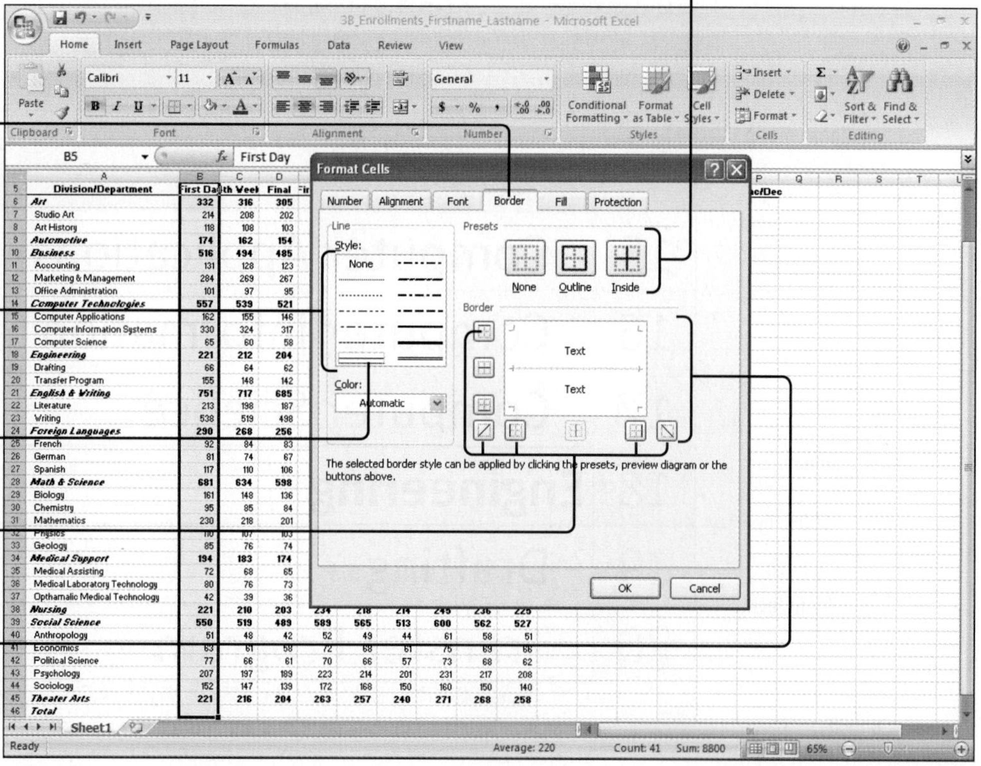

3 In the **Border** area, click the **left vertical** area to display a vertical line at the left edge. Alternatively, click the **Left Vertical Border** button ⬚. Compare your screen with Figure 3.32.

A border will be placed at the left edge of the selected cells.

Border area

Figure 3.32

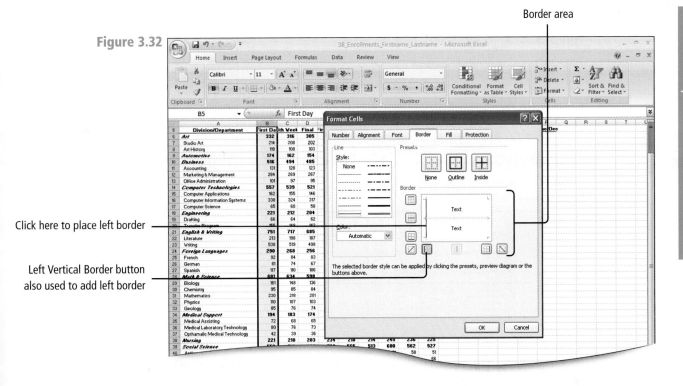

Click here to place left border

Left Vertical Border button also used to add left border

4 Click **OK**. Click outside the selected area and notice the solid line along the gridline between columns A and B.

5 Select the range **E5:E46**. Press Ctrl while you select the ranges **H5:H46**, **K5:K46**, and **N5:N46**. In the **Alignment group**, click the

Dialog Box Launcher and in the displayed **Format Cells** dialog box, click the **Border tab**. In the **Border** area, click at the left edge to place a border on the left side of the Border area, and then click **OK**. Select the range **P5:P46** and using the skills you practiced, access the **Format Cells** dialog box and click in the **Border tab**. In the **Border** area, click at the right edge to place a border on the right side of the cell, and then click **OK**.

Borders have been placed between the enrollment data for each semester. It is now easier to review the data for each semester.

6 Select the range **B4:M4**. In the **Alignment group**, click the **Dialog Box Launcher** and in the **Format Cells** dialog box, click the **Border tab**. In the **Presets** area, click **Outline**. In the **Border** area, click to insert a vertical line in the center of the area. Alternatively, in the **Presets** area, click **Inside**. Compare your screen with Figure 3.33, and then click **OK**.

The *Outline preset* is used to insert a border that outlines the selected range. The *Inside preset* is used to place borders surrounding each cell in the range.

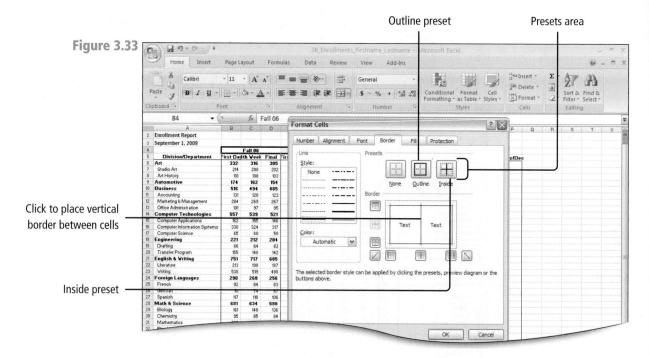

Figure 3.33

Outline preset

Presets area

Click to place vertical border between cells

Inside preset

7 Using the skills you practiced, use **Zoom control** to display the worksheet at 100% and return to cell **A1**.

8 **Save** your workbook.

Activity 3.15 Freezing Panes

To display the row and column titles as you work in distant areas of the worksheet, use the Freeze Panes command. When you freeze panes, the frozen rows and columns remain visible while you scroll through the worksheet. In this activity, you will freeze the column and row titles before you enter data in another part of the worksheet.

1 Scroll the worksheet so that **row 5** is the first row displayed. Click cell **A6**. Click the **View tab**, and in the **Window group**, click the **Freeze Panes** button, and compare your screen with Figure 3.34.

The Freeze Panes menu displays information about each of the choices.

Freeze Panes command

Figure 3.34

Freeze Panes menu

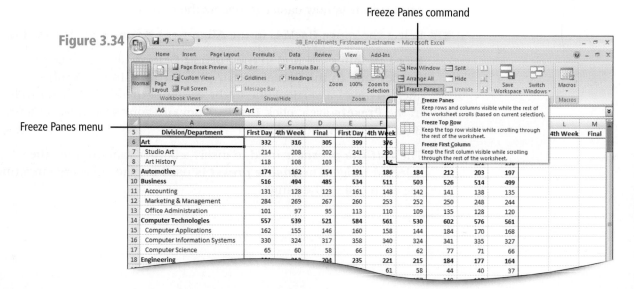

2 In the **Freeze Panes menu**, click **Freeze Top Row**. On the vertical scroll bar, click between the scroll box and the bottom scroll arrow.

The display has moved one full screen. Row 5 remains the first row displayed, but the next row is further down the worksheet; the row number that displays depends on your monitor settings. When Freeze Panes is used, selected rows or columns remain on the screen. When you select Freeze Top Row, the first row that displays on your monitor remains visible as you scroll through the worksheet.

3 Click cell **B46**. Click the **Home tab**. In the **Editing group**, click the **Sum** button Σ . Click cell **B45** to select this cell and delete the suggested range. Type **a comma** and click cell **B39**. Continue entering cell references in this manner—click in a cell that is formatted in bold and type a comma between the cells—until all cells formatted in bold in column B are included in the formula. Press Enter. Click cell **B46** and confirm the formula reads *=SUM(B45,B39,B38,B34,B28, B24,B21,B18,B14,B10,B9,B6)*. Confirm that the total—*4,708*—displays in cell B46.

Because the cells that contained the totals were formatted in bold, it was not difficult to identify the correct cells to enter into the formula.

4 With cell **B46** active, use the fill handle to copy the formula in cell **B46** to the right to cell **M46** and review the column title—*Final*—as confirmation you have selected the correct range.

Recall that when you copy a cell, the format of that cell is also copied. Cell B46 includes the border line at the left of the cell, which has been copied in the range.

5 Select the range **B45:M45** and right-click. From the **Mini toolbar,** click the **Format Painter** button . Click cell **B46** to copy the format. The range **B46:M46** is active. Right-click, and from the Mini toolbar, click the **Border** button and click **Top and Double Bottom Border**. Then click in a cell outside the selected range to view the borders.

Note that when column titles display, it is easier to verify that you have selected the correct range.

6 Confirm that column A is the first column displayed and click cell **B10**. Click the **View tab**, and in the **Window group**, click the **Freeze Panes** button. From the displayed menu, click **Freeze First Column**. On the horizontal scroll bar, click the right arrow one time and compare your screen with Figure 3.35.

Column A remains visible on the screen—it is the frozen column—but column B is no longer visible. The active cell does not display, but there is a bold vertical line in row 10 between columns A and B.

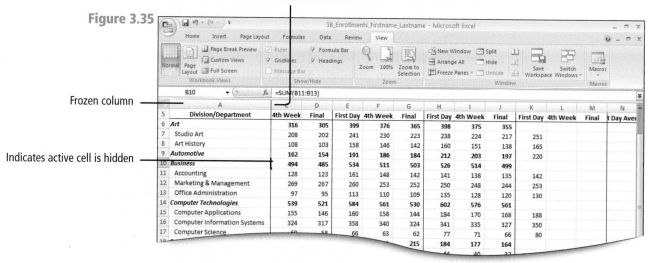

Figure 3.35

Column B hidden from view

Frozen column

Indicates active cell is hidden

7 Scroll through the columns until **column K** displays next to **column A** and compare your screen with Figure 3.36.

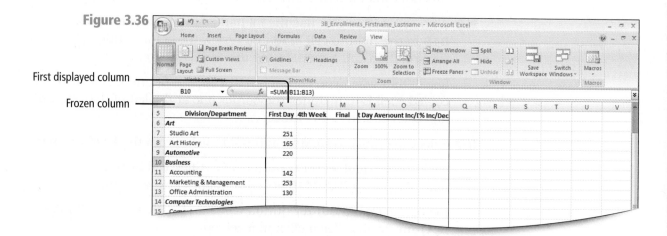

Figure 3.36

First displayed column

Frozen column

8 Beginning in cell **K25**, type the following enrollments for the First Day for 2009 to complete the list. There will be several cells left blank for the division totals, which will be entered later. When all numbers are entered, the total—*756*—displays in cell **K46**.

Foreign Languages	
French	110
German	77
Spanish	162
Math & Science	
Biology	162
Chemistry	102
Mathematics	238
Physics	124
Geology	85

(Continued)

Medical Support	
Medical Assisting	83
Medical Laboratory Technology	79
Opthamalic Medical Technology	55
Nursing	252
Social Science	
Anthropology	62
Economics	77
Political Science	74
Psychology	240
Sociology	167
Theater Arts	284

9 Use the **Horizontal scroll bar** to adjust the columns so **column H** displays next to column **A**. Select the range **H6:J6** and use the fill handle to copy the formulas to the right through **column M**.

Even though there is no data entered into columns L and M, the formula is entered and a hyphen, ⊡, displays in the cells. Recall that when you copy a formula, the format in the cell also copies.

10 Select the range **H10:J10** and use the fill handle to copy the formulas to the right through **column M**. Using the skills you practiced, copy the formulas for the totals in each division from **columns H:J** to **columns K:M** except for rows **9** (Automotive), **38** (Nursing), and **45** (Theater Arts), where the enrollments have already been entered.

11 Confirm that the numbers for Automotive (K9), Nursing (K38), and Theater Arts (K45) are formatted with **Bold** B.

12 Click cell **K39** and notice the green error indicator in the upper left corner of the cell. Click the **Error Checking** button ◇ and click **Ignore Error**. Using the skills you practiced, remove the **Error Indicators** where displayed in **column K**.

Most Excel formulas use numbers that are adjacent to the formula—either from above or from the left. This formula does not use the numbers directly above the formula, therefore Excel indicates a possible error.

13 On the **View tab**, in the **Window Group**, click the **Freeze Panes button arrow**, and then click **Unfreeze Panes**.

14 **Save** 🖫 your workbook.

Objective 9
Apply Number Formats

Numbers can be written as percentages, whole numbers, negative numbers, decimals, fractions, dates, or monetary amounts. Excel refers to the various ways that numbers are displayed as *number formats*—such as General, Accounting Number, Comma Style, and Custom.

Activity 3.16 Formatting Numbers

The General format is the default format for a number that you type in a cell. Unless you apply a different number format to a cell, Excel will use the General format. The General format displays a number exactly as you type it unless the column is too narrow.

1 Click cell **N6** and use the Zoom control so all entries in **row 6** display on the screen. On the **Formula Bar**, click the **Insert Function** button ![fx]. In the **Or select a category** section, click the **arrow** and select **Statistical**. In the **Select a function** area, click **AVERAGE**, and then click **OK**.

2 In the **AVERAGE Function Arguments** dialog box, at the end of the **Number1** text box, click the **Collapse Dialog Box** button ![icon]. Click cell **B6** and click the **Expand Dialog Box** button ![icon]. Type **,e6,h6** and then click **OK**. Alternatively, in the AVERAGE Function Arguments dialog box, click in cells E6 and H6 and type a comma between the cell references.

The average first-day enrollments for the Art Department for the previous three fall semesters—*376*—is entered in the cell.

3 Click cell **O6**. Type **=k6-n6** and on the **Formula Bar**, click the **Enter** button ![check]. Click cell **P6**. Type the formula **=o6/n6** and press [Enter]. Note: use the letter O and not the number 0 in this formula.

These formulas determine the increase or decrease in enrollments and the percentage of increase or decrease. The increase—40—is entered in cell O6 and the decimal indicating the increase or decrease—0.1054—displays in cell P6. The number of decimals that display vary depending on the number format on your computer.

4 Select cells **N6:P6** and use the fill handle to copy the formulas down through **row 46**.

5 Click cell **O11** and in the **Name** box, confirm you have the correct cell reference. In the **Zoom group**, click the **100%** button to increase the size of the screen. The enrollments for Accounting have decreased. This negative number is identified in parentheses. Notice that the negative percentage in cell **P11** is identified with a minus sign. On the **Home tab**, in the **Number group**, in the **Number Format** | General ▾ |, confirm that **Custom** displays. Compare your screen with Figure 3.37.

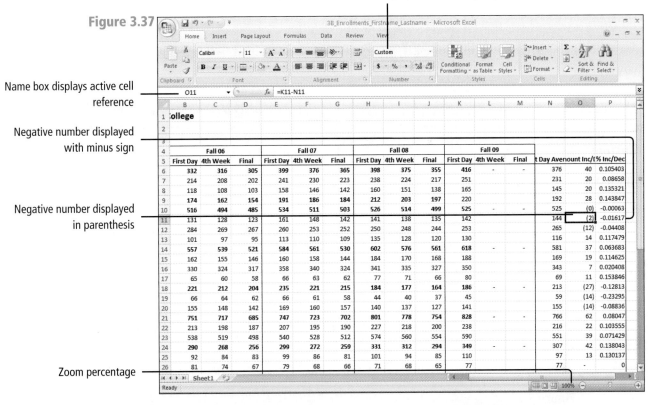

Custom number format displayed in Number group

Figure 3.37

Name box displays active cell reference

Negative number displayed with minus sign

Negative number displayed in parenthesis

Zoom percentage

6 In the **Number group**, click the **Dialog Box Launcher**. Review the different number formats, which are also described in the table in Figure 3.38.

The Format Cells dialog box displays at the Number tab. The category, Custom, is highlighted.

Excel Number Formats

Number Format	Description
General	This is the default format that is applied when you type a number in a cell and usually displays the number exactly as you type it unless the cell is not wide enough to show the entire number. When this occurs, the format rounds the number with decimals or uses scientific notation if the number is larger than 12 digits.
Number	This format is used for the general display of numbers. You can choose the number of decimal places to display, whether or not there is a comma separator for thousands, or how negative numbers will be displayed.
Currency	Currency format is used for general monetary values—the U.S. dollar sign is the default symbol.
Accounting	Also used for monetary values, but aligns currency symbols and decimal places.
Date	Used to displays dates in a worksheet in a variety of styles.
Time	Used to display time in a worksheet in a variety of styles.
Percentage	Percentage format multiplies the cell value by 100 and displays the result with a percent sign.

(Continued)

(Continued)

Fraction	Fraction format displays a number as a fraction.
Scientific	Scientific format displays numbers in scientific (exponential) notation and is useful with large numbers.
Text	Text format treats a number as if it were text and displays exactly as typed.
Special	This format displays numbers as a postal code (ZIP code), phone number, or social security number.
Custom	Custom format is used to modify a number format.

Figure 3.38

7 In the **Category** area, click **Number** and compare your screen with Figure 3.39.

The Number category lists the categories Excel uses for displaying numbers. The Number category is used to identify the way a negative number is displayed in the cell. The Sample area displays how the active cell will look in the selected negative number style.

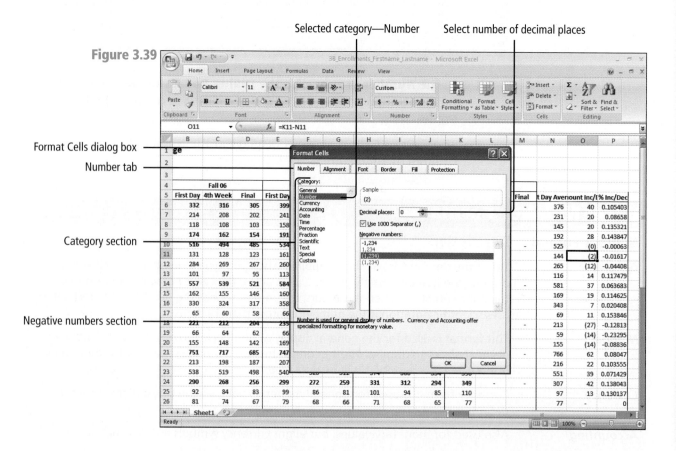

Figure 3.39

8 In the **Negative numbers** area, click the last choice that displays the negative number surrounded by parentheses and displayed in red. Then click **OK**.

Note — Using Negative Numbers in a Worksheet

You can see a small amount of space to the right of each of the formatted number cells. The formats you applied leave this space in the cell in the event that parentheses will be used to indicate negative numbers. If your worksheet contains negative numbers, display the Format Cells dialog box and select from among various formats to accommodate negative numbers.

9 With cell **O11** active, right-click and from the Mini toolbar, click the **Format Painter** button . Drag the **Format Painter** through the range **O6:O46**.

When enrollments have decreased, they are displayed in parentheses with red text.

10 Select the range **P6:P46**. From the **Number group**, click the **Number Format button arrow** that displays **General** and compare your screen with Figure 3.40.

The Number Format list in the Number group displays the most common number styles used and is a quick way to change the style.

Number Format button   List of number formats

Figure 3.40

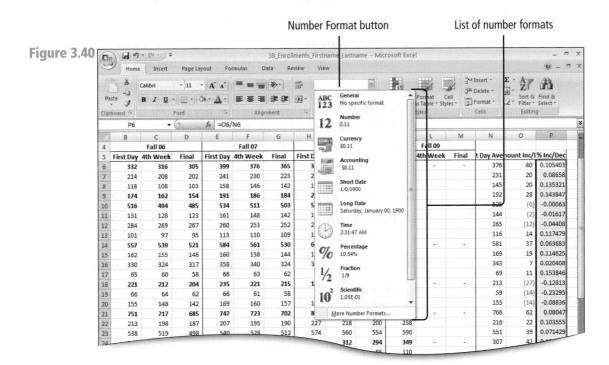

11 From the displayed list, click **Percentage**. Then click the **Decrease Decimal** button to display **one decimal**.

Using the Percentage command in the Number menu displays the percent with two decimals.

12 In the **Styles group**, click the **Conditional Formatting** button. In the **Conditional formatting** menu, point to **Highlight Cells rules** and from the submenu, click **Less Than**. In the **Less Than** dialog box, in the **Format cells that are LESS THAN** area, type **0** Click the **arrow** and from the displayed list, click **Red Text**. Then click **OK**.

When enrollments have decreased, the percentage of that decrease displays in red text. It is common practice to display negative numbers in red text.

13 Select cell **B6** and in the **Number button** `General ▾`, confirm that **Custom** displays—the style that is applied to the cells.

14 Select the range **B6:N46**. In the **Number group**, click the **Dialog Box Launcher**. In the **Category** area, click **Number**, and then click **OK**.

15 Select the range **N46:P46**, right click, and insert a **Top and Double Bottom Border**.

16 Save 💾 your workbook.

Activity 3.17 Using a Theme on Large Worksheets

When working with large worksheets, display the worksheet title at the left margin. Likewise, when applying a theme on the title, select the range of cells to which you will apply the theme.

1 Click the **Page Layout tab**, and in the **Themes group**, click the **Themes** button, and then in the **Themes menu**, click **Oriel**.

2 Select the range **A1:P5**. Click the **Home tab**, and in the **Font group**, click the **Font Color button arrow** 🅰️▾. In the sixth column— Blue—locate and click the color chip that reads *Blue, Accent 2, Darker 50%*.

When applying a color, the range of the cells is first selected.

3 With the range **A1:P5** still selected, in the **Font group**, click the **Fill Color button arrow** 🎨▾. Locate the sixth column, and click the second color chip—**Blue, Accent 2, Lighter 80%**.

4 Select the range **N5:P5**. In the **Alignment group**, click **Wrap Text** button 📳. Adjust the column widths to fully display the text, and then click cell **A1**.

When a format is applied, make it a habit to review the column's widths to confirm that all data within the column is visible. Changing a font style will also change the font size, resulting in text that no longer fully displays within the cell.

5 Save 💾 your workbook.

Objective 10
Control Print Options

When printing a worksheet that displays on more than one page, printing the row and column titles on each page helps track the data across pages. If data is identified only on the first page, the succeeding pages are difficult to review. You can also control where the pages begin and end or specify a portion of the worksheet to print whenever the worksheet is printed.

Activity 3.18 Printing Gridlines and Headings

When creating complex, large worksheets, printing the gridlines and the column and row headings can help with proofreading the worksheet and reviewing the printed data. Recall that gridlines are the horizontal and vertical lines in the worksheet that separate the cells.

1 Click the **Page Layout tab**, and in the **Page Setup group**, click the **Print Titles** button, and then compare your screen with Figure 3.41.

The Page Setup dialog box displays the Sheet tab. This tab area is used for deciding what will be included on the printed page and provides sections for Print area, Print titles, Print, and Page order.

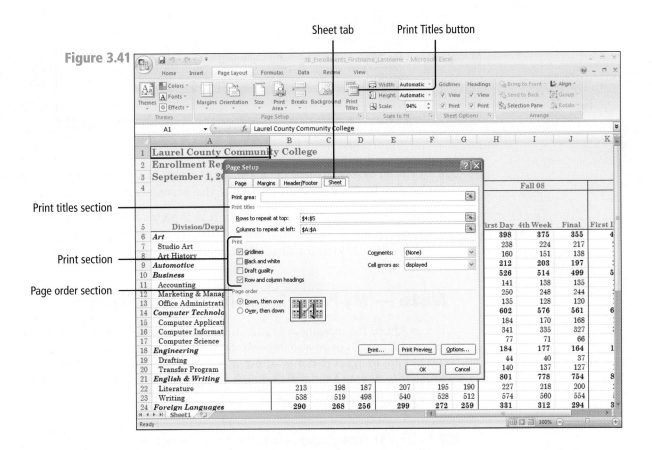

Figure 3.41

2 In the **Print** section, click **Gridlines** and **Row and column headings**, and then click **Print Preview** and compare your screen with Figure 3.42.

Recall that Print Preview displays how the worksheet will look when it is printed. The column headings—A, B, C, and so on—and the row headings—1, 2, 3, and so on—display and will print. The gridlines—which usually do not print—will print as instructed.

Column heading displayed

Figure 3.42

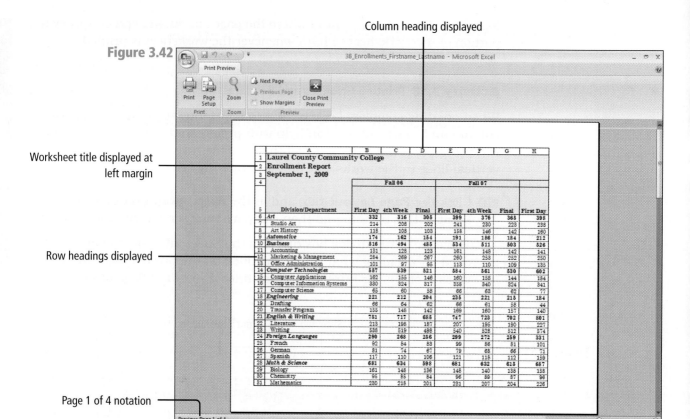

Worksheet title displayed at left margin

Row headings displayed

Page 1 of 4 notation

3 In the **Preview group**, click the **Next Page** button and note the page number in the lower left corner of the screen reads *Page 2 of 4*.

This worksheet prints on 4 pages. It is 2 pages long and 2 pages wide. On this page, notice that column titles do not display on page 2, making it difficult to determine what column E or column H displays.

Note — My Pages Break in Different Places

The widths of the margins are defined in Excel. However, the amount actually displayed on each page also depends on the printer that is used. Each printer sets default margins that may affect what prints on a page. On occasion, your screen may display a different number of pages or items on a page because the printer defaults are different.

4 In the **Preview group**, click the **Next Page** button to display the next page and then click again until you have reviewed all 4 pages. Click the **Previous Page** button until page 1 displays, and then compare your screen with Figure 3.42.

5 Click **Close Print Preview** and **Save** 🔲 your workbook.

Why isn't the title merged and centered?

Generally, worksheet titles have been merged and centered across the width of the worksheet. However, if the worksheet is wide enough to print on more than one page, a title that is centered over the width of the worksheet will not be centered over any of the printed pages. In those circumstances, it is preferable to leave the title lines at the left side of the worksheet.

Activity 3.19 Previewing and Modifying Page Breaks

Page breaks are the locations in a worksheet where the worksheet will split—break—between pages when it is printed. Excel automatically places a page break when the space on a page is filled. Those page breaks can be relocated to make the worksheet more readable. When a group of cells are related, it is easier to read when the entire group is displayed on the same page. In this activity, you will change the page break.

1 In the **Page Layout tab**, in the **Scale to Fit** group, next to **Width**, the button displays *Automatic*. Click the **Width Automatic button arrow** to display the menu and compare your screen with Figure 3.43, and then click **Automatic**.

The Excel default determines the width and height of the worksheet page. Recall that you have used scaling so worksheets display and print on one page.

This worksheet is too large to scale so it fits on one page. If you do so, the text will be too small to be readable.

Width area   Width menu

Figure 3.43

Scale to Fit group

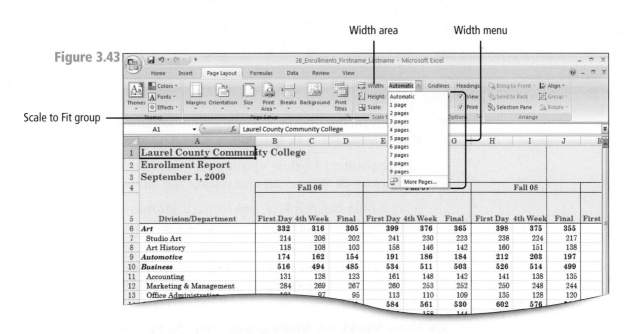

2 Click the **View tab**, and in the **Workbook Views group**, click the **Page Break Preview** button. If the **Welcome to Page Break Preview** dialog box displays, click **OK**. Then compare your screen with Figure 3.44.

The ***Page Break Preview*** displays the suggested page breaks with the ***page break lines***, which are highlighted with a dark blue dotted line.

Page numbers display in the shaded type. The blue dotted line between columns I and J divides the pages horizontally into two pages. The blue line between rows divides the rows vertically into two pages. The page number is displayed in the center of each page but will not print. The positioning of the page breaks may vary depending on your settings.

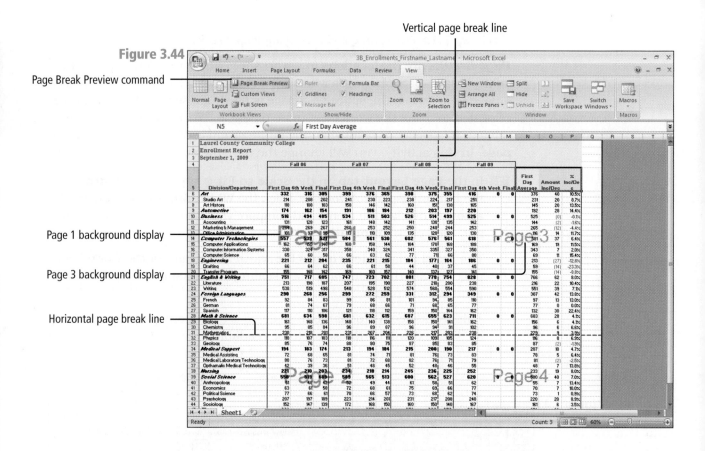

Figure 3.44

Page Break Preview command

Page 1 background display

Page 3 background display

Horizontal page break line

Vertical page break line

3 Position the mouse pointer at the blue *horizontal page break line*—the page break line that is placed between rows. With the mouse pointer, drag up until the page break line displays between **rows 27** and **28** and release the mouse.

A solid blue line displays, indicating a *manual page break line* has been inserted in the worksheet. A manual page break line displays when the page break position is set by the Excel user.

When deciding how to place a worksheet on more than one page, look for natural breaks in the data. In this case, the information for the Math & Science division will be placed on the same page.

4 In the **Workbook Views group**, click the **Full Screen** button and compare your screen with Figure 3.45.

Full Screen hides the Ribbon and Status bar and displays additional rows of the worksheet. When working in this view, all commands will be entered using the Mini toolbar and the shortcut menu. When working with large worksheets, there are several methods available to see more of the worksheet at the same time.

Column headings   Page break line

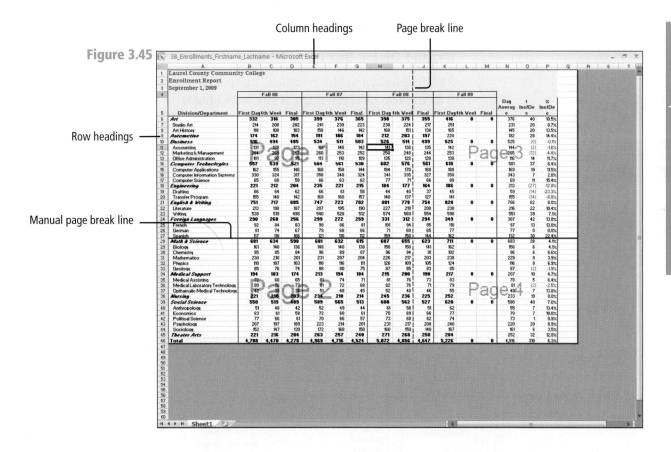

Row headings

Manual page break line

Figure 3.45

5 Position the mouse pointer on the ***vertical page break line***—the page break line that is placed between columns. With the ↔ pointer, drag right until the page break line displays between **columns J and K**.

The vertical page break is moved so all data from one semester is placed on the same page.

6 Right-click and from the shortcut menu, click **Close Full Screen**. On the **View tab**, in the **Workbook Views group**, click the **Normal** button.

7 In the **Workbook Views group**, click the **Full Screen** button.

With a large worksheet, it may be helpful to view more of the worksheet by removing the Ribbon from the screen.

8 In the worksheet, right-click and on the shortcut menu, click **Close Full Screen**.

The Ribbon again displays on the worksheets and the Excel commands are available.

9 Click the **Office** button , point to **Print**, and then click **Print Preview**. Click the **vertical scroll bar** to view page 2 of the worksheet. Then click **Close Print Preview**.

When page 2 displays, there are no column titles, making it difficult to determine what the numbers represent.

10 Click the **Page Layout tab**, and in the **Page Setup group**, click the **Print Titles** button. In the **Page Setup** dialog box, on the **Sheet tab**, under **Print titles**, click in the **Rows to repeat at top** text box, and then click the **Collapse Dialog Box** button .

11 Drag over the row headings for **row 4** and **row 5**, and then click the **Expand Dialog Box** button ⊞.

$4:$5 displays in the text box, instructing Excel to repeat rows 4 and 5 at the top of every page of the worksheet.

12 Press Tab to move to the **Columns to repeat at left** box, and then in the worksheet, click in **column A**. Compare your screen with Figure 3.46.

A moving border surrounds column A, indicating that column will display on every page.

Moving border surrounds column to repeat

Figure 3.46

Rows to repeat at top

Columns to repeat at left

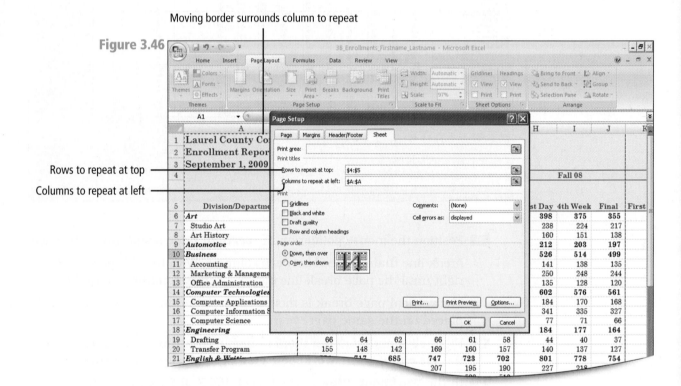

13 Click **Print Preview**. Use the **vertical scroll bar** to display and review the other pages of the worksheet.

The row and column titles display on every page of the worksheet so that all data on the worksheet is identified. The worksheet title on page 3 is truncated—not entirely displayed. When repeating column and row titles, only the text that actually displays in the cell width will be displayed.

14 Click **Close Print Preview** and **Save** ⊞ your workbook.

Activity 3.20 Setting Margins

1 On the **Page Layout tab**, in the **Page Setup group**, click the **Margins** button.

The margins gallery provides suggestions for four types of margins—*Normal*, *Wide*, *Narrow*, and *Custom*. The default margins for Excel are 0.75" top and bottom margins with .7" side margins.

2 Click **Custom Margins** and compare your screen with Figure 3.47.

The Margins tab in the Page Setup dialog box

Use to change Header and Footer margin

Figure 3.47

Use to change Top margin

Use to change Left margin

Use to change Right margin

Use to change Bottom margin

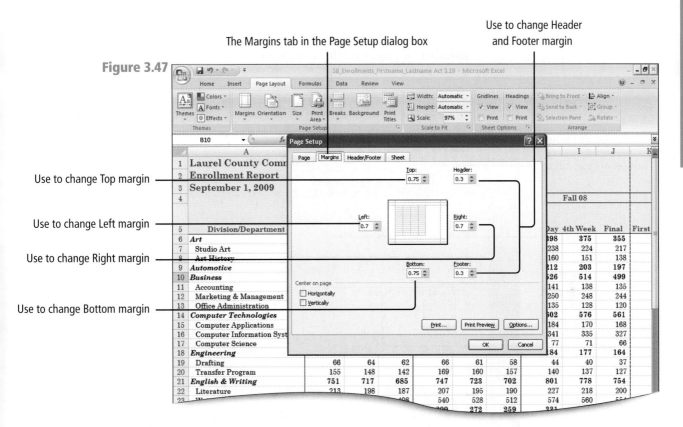

3 In the **Page Setup** dialog box, in the **Top** box, in the Spin Box, click the **up arrow** until **1.5** displays. In the **Header** box, in the Spin Box, click the **up arrow** until **0.55** displays. In the **Center on page** area, click **Horizontally**. Click **Print Preview** and scroll through the worksheet to preview the placement on the page.

You have manually set the top margin and the header margin and centered the worksheet horizontally on the page.

4 Click **Close Print Preview** and **Save** your workbook.

Activity 3.21 Inserting Page Numbers in a Header

In this activity, you will enter the page numbers and the total number of pages in the header.

1 Click cell **A1** and click the **Insert tab**. In the **Text group**, click the **Header & Footer** button. In the **Navigation group**, click the **Go to Footer** button. Click in the **Left Footer** area. In the **Header & Footer Tools Design tab**, in the **Header & Footer Elements group**, click the **File Name** button.

The header area for page 2 displays just below the footer area for page 1.

2 Click the page 2 **Left Header** area, type **Page** and press ⌷Spacebar⌷. In the **Header & Footer Elements group**, click the **Page Number** button and press ⌷Spacebar⌷, then type **of** and press ⌷Spacebar⌷. Click the **Number of Pages** button and compare your screen with Figure 3.48.

When the header/footer area is not displayed, the code & *[Page]* will be replaced by the page number. This is the code that will display the page number. The code *&[Pages]* will be replaced by the total number of pages in the worksheet.

Figure 3.48

Page Number button

Number of Pages button

Footer that prints on every page

Header that prints on every page

Code for page number

Code for number of pages

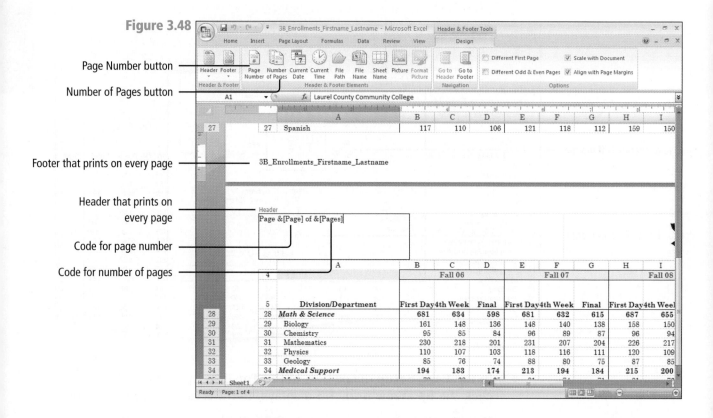

3 Click in the **Footer** at the bottom of Page 1. On the **Navigation group**, click the **Go to Header** button.

4 Click the **Office** button 🔘, point to **Print**, and then on the right, click **Print Preview**.

These worksheets display the column and row headings and gridlines, which are helpful for proofreading but distracting in the final printing. Row and column titles display on every page.

5 Click **Close Print Preview**. On the status bar, click the **Normal** button ▦. On the **Page Layout tab**, under **Page Setup**, click the **Print Titles** button. Under **Print**, click **Gridlines** and **Row and column headings** to clear the check boxes. Click **OK**. **Save** 💾 your workbook.

The row and column headings are helpful when proofreading a document, but they are not usually displayed in the final work.

6 Check your *Chapter Assignment Sheet* or *Course Syllabus*, or consult your instructor, to determine if you are to submit your work on paper or electronically. To submit electronically, follow the instructions provided by your instructor, and then go to Step 8.

7 Click the **Office** button 🔲, and then click **Print**. In the **Print** dialog box, under **Print what**, select **Entire workbook**. Under **Copies**, confirm that **1** is selected. Click **OK**. If you are directed to submit printed formulas, refer to **Activity 1.12**.

8 Click the **Office** button 🔲, and then click **Close**. If the dialog box displays asking if you want to save changes, click **No** so that you do not save the changes to Page Setup that you used for printing formulas.

Activity 3.22 Setting the Print Area

A specific portion of a worksheet can be defined as a ***print area***. Every time you print the worksheet, Excel prints only the data that is specified in the print area.

1 Navigate to your **Excel Chapter 3** folder. Locate and open the worksheet you named **3B_Enrollments_Firstname_Lastname**. Click the **Office** button 🔲, click **Save As**. In the **Save As** dialog box, in the **File name** box, type **3B_Enrollments_Print_Area_Firstname_Lastname** Then click **Save**.

Renaming the document provides a copy of the document with another name.

2 Select the range **A1:P8**. On the **Page Layout tab,** in the **Page Setup group**, click the **Print Area** button, and then compare your screen with Figure 3.49.

A print area is selected by the user. When the worksheet is printed, only the defined area will print.

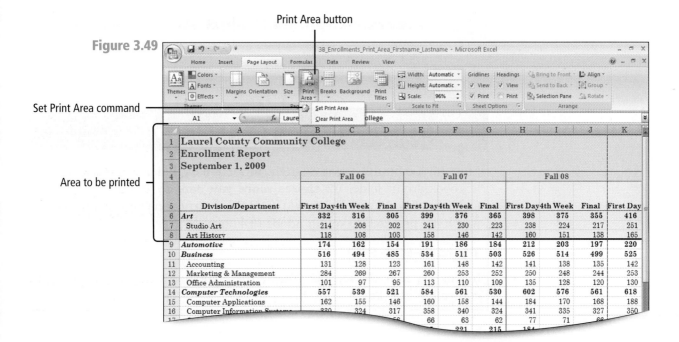

Figure 3.49

3 Click **Set Print Area**. In the **Page Setup group**, click the **Dialog Box Launcher** ⬜. In the **Page Setup** dialog box, under **Scaling**, click **Fit to 1 page**.

4 Click **Print Preview** to view the worksheet. Click **Close Print Preview** and **Save** 💾 your workbook.

Each time this worksheet is printed, only the print area will print.

Note — Clear Print Area

When a print area is set, only that portion of the worksheet will print. To remove the print area and print the entire worksheet, on the **Page Layout tab**, in the **Page Setup group**, click the **Print Area** button and from the list, click **Clear Print Area**.

5 Check your *Chapter Assignment Sheet* or *Course Syllabus*, or consult your instructor, to determine if you are to submit work on paper or electronically. To submit electronically, follow the instructions provided by your instructor and then go to Step 6. If you print your work, click the **Office** button 🔘, point to **Print**, and then click **Quick Print**.

6 Click the **Office** menu, and then click **Close**.

Note — Printing

When a Print Area is set, the entire worksheet can still be printed. In the **Print** dialog box, in the **Print what area**, click **Ignore print areas**.

End **You have completed Project 3B** ————————

🔘 There's More You Can Do!

From My Computer, navigate to the student files that accompany this textbook. In the folder **02_theres_more_you_can_do**, locate and open the folder for this chapter. Open and print the instructions for this project, which are provided to you in Adobe PDF format.

Try It! 1—Scale to Fit

In this Try It! exercise, you will use the Scale to Fit feature as a way of controlling the way a worksheet prints.

Excel
chapterthree

Summary

In this chapter, you used IF functions to compare values and return results that depended on the outcome of the comparison. You created formulas that referenced cells in another worksheet and used conditional formatting to highlight certain values. You practiced techniques for working with information in large worksheets and formatted worksheets using themes, borders, indents, and other techniques to highlight certain data and enhance the readability of the worksheet. Lastly, you used several new print options to control how your worksheet is printed.

Key Terms

Content-Based Assessments

Matching

Match each term in the second column with its correct definition in the first column by writing the letter of the term on the blank line in front of the correct definition.

_____ **1.** A logical function that performs a test to determine whether a condition is true or false.

_____ **2.** Any value or expression that is evaluated as being true or false.

_____ **3.** All hours worked in excess of 40 hours per week and are paid at a higher rate of pay, usually 1½ times the regular pay rate.

_____ **4.** The values that an Excel function uses to perform calculations or operations.

_____ **5.** A mathematical operator that compares two values.

_____ **6.** The amount of earnings before any deduction.

_____ **7.** The amount of pay after deductions are withheld.

_____ **8.** An amount that is withheld from your pay check.

_____ **9.** Places a bottom border under only the text or numbers within a cell or range of cells.

_____ **10.** The language rules Excel uses.

_____ **11.** A technique that uses the mouse to move or copy selected text from one location to another.

_____ **12.** Any format, such as cell shading or font color, that is applied to cells which meet certain conditions and emphasizes that data.

_____ **13.** A combination of complementary colors, fonts, and effects that may be applied to a workbook to give it a professional appearance.

_____ **14.** Provides choices on ways to display the time.

_____ **15.** Displays at the top of every page and may be used to print text, page numbers, and graphics.

A Arguments

B Comparison operator

C Conditional format

D Deduction

E Drag-and-drop

F Gross pay

G Header

H IF function

I Logical test

J Net pay or take-home pay

K Overtime

L Syntax

M Theme

N Time number format

O Underline button

Content-Based Assessments

Fill in the Blank

Write the correct answer in the space provided.

1. To quickly reduce the size of the worksheet so more of it is visible on the screen, use the _____ _____.

2. Specified rows and columns remain visible on the screen even when you scroll to other areas when you use the _____ _____ feature.

3. In order for the currently selected range of cells to completely fill the screen, use the _____ to _____ feature.

4. The default format for displaying a number is the _____ number format.

5. The format that places a dollar sign in the cell and aligns decimal places is the _____ number format.

6. The category of number styles that is used to display the styles for today's date is called the _____ number format.

7. The number format that displays a percentage symbol and two decimals is the _____ number format.

8. The number format used primarily with database functions such as postal codes and telephone numbers is the _____ number format.

9. Suggested locations for page breaks are displayed in the _____ _____ _____.

10. The location in the worksheet that identifies what will be placed on one page and what on another is the _____ _____.

11. The page break line that is placed between rows is the _____ page break line.

12. The page break that is inserted by the Excel user is a(n) _____ page break.

13. The page break line that is placed between columns is the _____ page break line.

14. To display the worksheet without the Ribbon or scroll bars, use the _____ _____ command.

15. When only a portion of a worksheet is to be printed, set the _____ _____.

Project 3C—Bookstore Orders

In this project, you will apply the skills you practiced from the Objectives in Project 3A.

Objectives: 1. Construct an IF Function; **2.** Link Data in Workbooks; **3.** Create IF Functions That Return Text; **4.** Emphasize Data Using Conditional Formatting; **5.** Format with Themes; **6.** Add Information in the Header and Footer.

In the following Skills Review, you will complete the report for computer book orders for the Laurel County Community College bookstore. The bookstore receives a discount for textbook orders and that discount is larger when the order is larger. The results for the winter orders will be combined with the fall semester orders for a report of annual orders. You will complete and format these reports. Your completed worksheets will look similar to Figure 3.50.

For Project 3C, you will need the following file:

e03C_Bookstore_Orders

You will save your workbook as
3C_Bookstore_Orders_Firstname_Lastname

Figure 3.50

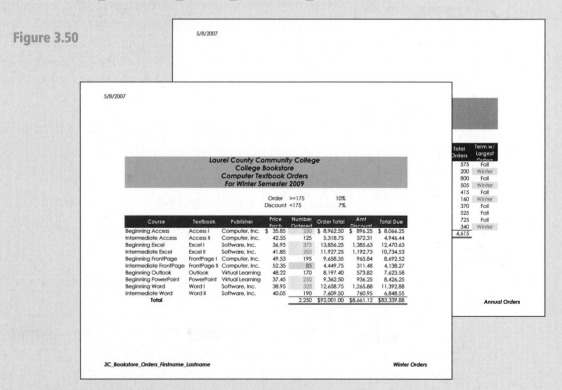

(Project 3C–Bookstore Orders continues on the next page)

Content-Based Assessments

(Project 3C–Bookstore Orders continued)

1. **Start** Excel. From the student files, locate and open the file named **e03C_Bookstore_Orders** and save it in your **Excel Chapter 3** folder as **3C_Bookstore_Orders_Firstname_Lastname**

2. Review the worksheets. The Winter Orders sheet displays the textbooks that have been ordered and their price. The Annual Orders sheet will be used to report the totals from the Winter Orders and add them to the Fall Orders to provide a summary for the year.

3. In the **Winter Orders** sheet, select cells **A1:A4**. Right-click and in the Mini toolbar click the **Bold** and **Italic** buttons and change the **Font Size** to **14**. Select the range **A1:H1** and right-click. From the Mini toolbar, click **Merge & Center** and double-click the **Format Painter** button. Click in cells **A2**, **A3**, and **A4**. Then on the **Home tab,** in the **Clipboard group**, click the **Format Painter** button to turn it off.

4. Select the range **D6:D7**. In the **Alignment group**, click the **Merge & Center** button and **Wrap Text** button. Select the range **A9:H9** and right-click. In the Mini toolbar, click the **Bold**, **Center**, and **Bottom Border** buttons. In the **Alignment group**, click the **Middle Align** button, and then click **Wrap Text**. Adjust columns widths to fully display cell contents.

5. Click cell **F10**. Type **=d10*e10** to multiply the price for each textbook by the number of textbooks ordered. In the **Formula Bar**, click the **Enter** button. The result— *8,962.5*—is the cost of the total order for that book.

6. Click cell **G10**. The publishers provide discounts to college bookstores and the rate of the discount varies depending on the number of texts ordered. A discount of 7% is given to all orders. If the order is for 175

or more texts, the discount rate is 10%. On the **Formula Bar**, click the **Insert Function** button. In the **Or select a category** section, click **Logical**. In the **Select a function** area, click **IF**, and then click **OK**.

7. In the **Logical_test** box at the right end, click the **Collapse Dialog Box** button. Click cell **E10**, and then click the **Expand Dialog Box** button and type **>=175** The logical test compares the number ordered in cell E10 with 175.

8. Press **Tab** and in the **Value_if_true** text box, click the **Collapse Dialog Box** button. Click cell **F10**, type ***** and click cell **F6**, and then press F4. Click the **Expand Dialog Box** button. The value if true indicates that if orders are greater than or equal to 175, then the order is multiplied by the 10% discount.

9. Press **Tab** and in the **Value_if_false** text box, click the **Collapse Dialog Box** button. Click cell **F10**, type ***** and click cell **F7**, and then press F4. Click the **Expand Dialog Box** button. The value if false indicates that orders fewer than 175 will receive the 7% discount.

10. Click **OK.** The amount of the discount, 896.25, is entered into cell G10 and the function formula—*=IF(E10>=175, F10*$F$6,F10*$F$7)*—displays in the Formula Bar.

11. Click cell **H10**. Type **=f10-g10** and press Enter. The total due for the textbooks after the discount was taken is displayed— *8066.25* for Access I texts.

12. Select the range **F10:H10**. Use the fill handle to copy the formulas down through **row 19**.

13. Click cell **A20** and type **Total** and in the **Formula Bar**, click the **Enter** button to

(Project 3C–Bookstore Orders continues on the next page)

(Project 3C–Bookstore Orders continued)

confirm the entry. With cell **A20** active, right-click and in the Mini toolbar, click the **Bold** and **Center** buttons. Select the range **E20:H20** and from the **Editing group**, click the **Sum** button.

14. Select the range **F10:H10** and right-click. From the Mini toolbar, click the **Accounting Number Format** button. Select the range **F11:H19** and right-click. Click the **Comma Style** button. Select the range **F20:H20**, right-click, and then click the **Accounting Number Format** button and apply a **Top and Double Bottom Border**. Adjust column widths to display the full contents, if needed. Right-click cell **D10** and click the **Accounting Number Format** button. Select the range **D11:D19**, right-click, and then click the **Comma Style** button. Select the range **E10:E20**, right-click, and click **Comma Style**, and then click **Decrease Decimal** button **two times**. In cell **E20**, add a **Top and Double Bottom Border**.

15. In the **Annual Orders sheet**, select the range **A1:F1**. Right-click and on the Mini toolbar, click the **Bold** and **Merge & Center** buttons, and change the **Font Size** to **14**. Double-click the **Format Painter**. Click in cells **A2**, **A3**, and **A4**. Then on the **Home tab,** in the **Clipboard group**, click the **Format Painter** button to stop it.

16. Select the range **A7:F7** and right-click. On the Mini toolbar, click the **Bold**, **Center**, and **Bottom Border** buttons. In the **Alignment group**, click the **Wrap Text** button and the **Middle Align** button.

17. This workbook summarizes the orders for the two semesters. The data for fall has been entered and you will now enter the winter data and provide a total. Click cell **D8** and type = Click the **Winter Orders**

sheet tab, click cell **E10**, and then press [Enter]. Use the fill handle to copy the formula down through **row 17**. Review the data in both worksheets to confirm its accuracy.

18. On the **Annual Orders sheet**, click cell **E8** and type = click cell **C8** type + and then click cell **D8** and press [Enter]. You have added the book orders for fall and winter semesters. Click cell **E8** and use the fill handle to copy the formula down through cell **E17**.

19. Click cell **A18** and type **Total** and in the **Formula Bar**, click the **Enter** button. Right-click cell **A18** and in the Mini toolbar, click the **Bold** and **Center** buttons. Select the range **C18:E18** and in the **Editing group** click the **Sum** button. Right-click and in the Mini toolbar, select a **Top and Double Bottom Border**. Select the range **C8:E18** and right click. In the Mini toolbar, click the **Comma Style** button, and then click the **Decrease Decimal** button **two times**.

20. Click cell **F8**. In the **Formula Bar**, click the **Insert Function** button. You will enter an IF function that indicates whether the largest orders were for the fall or winter semester. Select a **Logical** function, locate and click **IF**, and then click **OK**.

21. In the **Logical_test** text box at the right edge, click the **Collapse Dialog Box** button. Click cell **C8**, type > and click cell **D8**—the logical test is the fall orders are larger than the winter orders. Click the **Expand Dialog Box** button. Press **Tab** and in the **Value_if_true** text box, type **Fall**—the text that will be entered if fall orders are the largest. Press **Tab** and in the **Value_if_false** text box, type **Winter**—the text that will be entered if fall orders *are not* the largest. Click **OK**. Because more

(Project 3C–Bookstore Orders continues on the next page)

Content-Based Assessments

(Project 3C–Bookstore Orders continued)

Access I texts were sold in the fall term, *Fall* is entered in the cell. In the **Alignment group**, click the **Center** button.

22. With cell **F8** active, drag the fill handle down to copy the formula through cell **F17**. It is easy to tell at a glance which term had the largest textbook sales.

23. With the range **F8:F17** selected, in the **Styles group**, click the **Conditional Formatting** button. In the list, click **Highlight Cells Rules** and in the **submenu**, click **Equal To**. In the **Equal To** dialog box, in the **Format cells that are EQUAL TO**, type **Fall** and then click **OK**. With the range **F8:F17** still selected, in the **Styles group**, click the **Conditional Formatting** button. In the list, click **Highlight Cells Rules** and in the **submenu**, click **Equal To**. In the **Equal To** dialog box, in the **Format cells that are EQUAL TO**, type **Winter** In the format text box, click the **arrow**, and then click **Green Fill with Dark Green Text**. Click **OK**.

24. Click the **Winter Orders sheet tab** and select the range **E10:E19**. In the **Styles group**, click the **Conditional Formatting** button. In the list, click **Highlight Cells Rules** and from the **submenu**, click **Less Than**. In the **Less Than** text box, type **100** and click **OK**. With the range still selected, click **Conditional Formatting**. In the list, click **Highlight Cells Rules**, and then click **Greater Than**. In the **Greater Than** text box, type **200** In the format text box, click the **arrow**, and then click **Yellow Fill with Dark Yellow Text**. Click **OK**.

25. Right-click the **Winter Orders sheet tab** and click **Select All Sheets**. Click the **Insert tab**. In the **Text group**, click the **Header & Footer** button, and in the

Navigation group, click the **Go to Footer** button. Click the **Left Footer** area. In the **Header & Footer Elements group**, click the **File Name** button. Click the **Right Footer** area and click **Sheet Name**.

26. Select the text in the **Right Footer**. Click the **Home tab** and in the **Font group**, click the **Bold** button and **Italic** button. Using the skills you just practiced, apply the same format to the **File Name** in the **Left Footer** area.

27. Click the **Design tab**, and in the **Navigation group**, click the **Go to Header** button. In the **Left Header** area in the **Header & Footer Elements group**, click the **Current Date** button. Click in the worksheet, and then on the Status bar, click the **Normal** button.

28. Right-click the **Winter Orders sheet tab** and click **Ungroup Sheets**. Select the range **A1:A4**. On the **Home tab**, under **Font group**, click the **Fill Color button arrow** and from the displayed gallery, in the sixth column, click the third color chip in the column—**Red, Accent 2, Lighter 60%**. Select the range **A9:H9** and click the **Fill Color button arrow**. Point to the sixth column and click the last color chip in the column—the ScreenTip displays *Red, Accent 2, Darker 50%*. Click the **Font Color button arrow**, click the first color chip—**White, Background 1**.

29. Click the **Annual Orders sheet tab**. Select the range **A1:A4**. On the **Home tab**, under **Font group**, click the **Fill Color button arrow** and from the displayed gallery, point to the eighth column and the third color chip in the column—**Purple, Accent 4, Lighter 60%**. Select the range **A7:F7** and click the **Fill Color button arrow**. Point to the eighth column and select the last color chip in the column—**Purple, Accent 4,**

(Project 3C–Bookstore Orders continues on the next page)

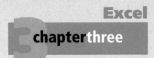

(Project 3C–Bookstore Orders continued)

Darker 50%. Click the **Font Color button arrow**, click the first color chip—**White, Background 1**.

30. Click the **Page Layout tab**, and in the **Themes group**, click the **Themes** button, and then click the **Verve** theme. Review the worksheets and adjust column widths, if needed, to display the contents in each column.

31. Right-click a worksheet tab, and click **Select All Sheets**. On the **Page Layout tab** and in the **Page Setup group**, click the **Dialog Box Launcher**. On the **Page tab**, under **Orientation**, click **Landscape**. Under **Scaling**, click **Fit to 1 page**. Click the **Margins tab** and under **Center on page**, click **Horizontally** and **Vertically**, and then click **OK. Save** your workbook.

32. Check your *Chapter Assignment Sheet* or *Course Syllabus*, or consult your instructor, to determine if you are to submit work on paper or electronically. To submit electronically, follow the instructions provided by your instructor, and then go to Step 31.

33. Click the **Office** button, click **Print**. In the **Print** dialog box, under **Print what**, select **Entire workbook**. Under **Copies**, confirm that **1** is selected. Click **OK**. If you are directed to submit printed formulas, group all worksheets. Then refer to **Activity 1.12** to do so.

34. Click the **Office** button, click **Close**. If the dialog box displays asking if you want to save changes, click **No** so that you do not save the changes to Page Setup that you used for printing formulas. **Exit** Excel.

End You have completed Project 3C

Content-Based Assessments

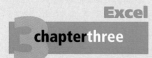

Skills Review

Project 3D — Faculty

In this project, you will apply the skills you practiced from the Objectives in Project 3B.

Objectives: 7. *Enter Dates;* **8.** *Format Large Worksheets;* **9.** *Apply Number Formats;* **10.** *Control Print Options.*

In the following Skills Review, you will prepare a report that identifies the number of sections taught by full-time faculty and the number of sections taught by part-time faculty. You will also report the percentage of sections taught by each faculty category. Your completed worksheets will look similar to Figure 3.51.

For Project 3D, you will need the following file:

e03D_Faculty

You will save your workbook as 3D_Faculty_Firstname_Lastname

Figure 3.51

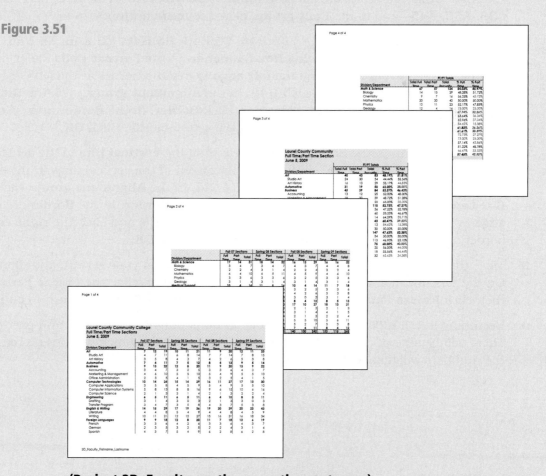

(Project 3D–Faculty continues on the next page)

Content-Based Assessments

chapterthree

Excel

Skills Review

(Project 3D–Faculty continued)

1. **Start** Excel. From the student files locate and open the file named **e03D_Faculty** and then save it in your **Excel Chapter 3** folder as 3D_Faculty_Firstname_Lastname

2. Click cell **A3**. Type 'June 5, 2009 and press **Enter**.

3. Click cell **N4** and type **FT/PT Totals** Select the range **N4:R4** and right-click. In the Mini toolbar, click the **Bold** and **Merge & Center** buttons and add a **Bottom Border**. In cell **N5**, type **Total Full Time** In cell **O5**, type **Total Part Time** In cell **P5**, type **Total Faculty** In cell **Q5**, type **% Full Time** and in **R5**, type **% Part Time** Select the range **N5:R5** and right-click. In the Mini toolbar, click the **Bottom Border** button.

4. Select the range **A7:A8**. On the **Home tab**, in the **Alignment group**, click the **Increase Indent** button. Click on **A11**. Press Ctrl while you select the following ranges: **A11:A13**, **A15:A17**, **A19:A20**, **A22:A23**, **A25:A27**, **A29:A33**, **A35:A37**, **A40:A44**. Then in the **Alignment group**, click the **Increase Indent** button. Click in the worksheet to deselect the ranges.

5. On the status bar, click the **Zoom Out** button until all the data in the worksheet displays. Press Ctrl while you select the following rows: **6, 9, 10, 14, 18, 21, 24, 28, 34, 38, 39, 45, 46**. From the **Font group**, click the **Bold** button. Click in the worksheet to deselect the range. Press Ctrl while you select the Division Names—**A6**, **A9**, **A10**, **A14**, **A18**, **A21**, **A24**, **A28**, **A34**, **A38**, **A39**, **A45**—and in the **Font group**, click the **Italic** button.

6. Press Ctrl as you select the ranges **B5:B46**, **E5:E46**, **H5:H46**, **K5:K46**, **N5:N46**. In the **Alignment group**, click the **Dialog Box Launcher**. In the **Format Cells** dialog box, click **Border**. In the **Border** area, click the **left edge** to insert a border at the left edge of the selected cells. Click **OK**. Select the range **R5:R46**. In the **Alignment group**, click the **Dialog Box Launcher**. In the **Format Cells** dialog box, click **Border**. In the **Border** area, click the **right edge** to insert a border at the right edge of the selected cells. Click **OK**.

7. On the status bar, in the **Zoom control** area, drag the **vertical line** to the center to return to 100%. Review the format and confirm the placement of the vertical lines in the worksheet. Use the Ctrl key to select the cells **B4**, **E4**, **H4**, **K4**, **N4**. In the **Alignment group**, click the **Dialog Box Launcher**. In the **Format Cells** dialog box, click **Border**. In the **Border** area, click the **left edge** to insert a border at the left edge of the selected cells and click the **right edge** to insert a border at the right edge of the selected cells. Then click **OK**.

8. Move the worksheet so **row 4** is the first row displayed on your screen, and then click cell **B6**. On the Ribbon, click the **View tab**. In the **Window group**, click the **Freeze Panes** button, and then click **Freeze Panes**. Move the worksheet so **column K** displays next to **column A**.

9. Beginning in cell **K22**, enter the following sections taught by full-time and part-time faculty. There will be several cells left blank for the division totals, which will be entered later. Some of the numbers will display the format of adjacent cells.

(Project 3D–Faculty continues on the next page)

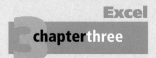

(Project 3D–Faculty continued)

Division/Department	Full Time	Part Time
English & Writing		
Literature	4	5
Writing	16	18
Foreign Languages		
French	4	3
German	3	1
Spanish	6	2
Math & Science		
Biology	4	4
Chemistry	2	2
Mathematics	4	6
Physics	3	3
Geology	3	1
Medical Support		
Medical Assisting	3	3
Medical Laboratory Technology	5	3
Opthamalic Medical Technology	3	1
Nursing	8	5
Social Science		
Anthropology	2	1
Economics	4	1
Political Science	2	2
Psychology	5	6
Sociology	5	3
Theater Arts	8	4

10. Position the screen display so you can view **column J** next to **column A**. The name of the division, along with its totals, displays above the departments within the division. Click cell **J6** and use the fill handle to copy the cell through **column L**. Click the **AutoFill Options** button and click **Fill Without Formatting** so the border is not copied along with the formula. Click cell **J10** and use the fill handle to copy the cell through **column L**. Click the **AutoFill Options** button and click **Fill Without Formatting**. If **Error Indicators** appear, click the **Error Alert** and click **Ignore Error**. Using the skills practiced, copy the formulas for all divisions in the worksheet from **column J** through **column L**.

11. Click cell **M6** and enter a **SUM** formula to add **K6:L6**. Use the fill handle to copy the formula down through **row 45**. Click the **AutoFill Options** button and click **Fill Without Formatting**. With the range **M6:M45** selected, right-click and from the Mini toolbar, click the **Format Painter** button. Click in cell **L6** to copy the formats of **column M** to **column L**.

(Project 3D–Faculty continues on the next page)

(Project 3D–Faculty continued)

12. Click the **View tab**, and in the **Window group**, click the **Freeze Panes** button, and then click **Unfreeze Panes**.

13. Click cell **N6**. Enter a formula to add the total number of full-time faculty. The formula will read =B6+E6+H6+K6. Use the fill handle to copy the formula through cell **P6**. Click the **AutoFill Options** button and click **Fill Without Formatting**.

14. Select the range **N6:P6** and use the fill handle to copy the formulas down through **row 45**. From the **AutoFill Options**, click **Fill Without Formatting**.

15. Click cell **Q6**. Type =n6/p6 and on the **Formula Bar**, click the **Enter** button. Click cell **R6** and type =o6/p6 and on the **Formula Bar**, click the **Enter** button.

16. Select the range **Q6:R6**. Use the fill handle to copy the formulas down through **row 45**. Click the **AutoFill Options** button and click **Fill Without Formatting**. Click the **Home tab**. In the **Number group**, click the **Percent Style** button and click the **Increase Decimal** button two times.

17. Select the range **Q6:Q45**. Use a Conditional Format to display the divisions and departments where the percentage of full-time faculty is greater than 65%. In the **Styles group**, click the **Conditional Formatting** button, point to **Highlight Cells Rules**, and from the submenu, click **Greater Than**. In the **Format cells that are GREATER THAN** text box, type **65%** and in the text box at the right, click the **arrow** and then click **Red Text**. Click **OK**.

18. Select the range **R6:R45**. Use a Conditional Format to display the divisions and departments where the percentage of full-time faculty is less than 45%. In the **Styles group**, click the **Conditional Formatting** button, point to **Highlight Cells Rules**, and from the submenu, click **Less Than**. In the **Format cells that are LESS THAN** text box, type **45%** and in the text box at the right, click the **arrow** and select **Red Text**. Click **OK**.

19. Click cell **B46**. Type = Click cell **B45** and type + Click cell **B39** and type + Continue in this manner, clicking in the cells that are formatted in bold (these are the totals of the divisions) and placing a + between each cell reference. Your formula will read =B45+B39+B38+B34+B28+B24+B21+B18+B14+B10+B9+B6. Use the fill handle to copy the formula through cell **P46**. Click the **AutoFill Options** button and click **Fill Without Formatting**. Right-click and in the Mini toolbar, click the **Border** button, and then click **Top and Double Bottom Border**.

20. On the **Page Layout tab**, in the **Themes group**, click **Themes**, and then click **Verve**. Select the range **A1:R5**. Click the **Home tab**, and in the **Font group**, click the **Fill Color** button and in the fifth column, click the second color—the ScreenTip displays *Pink, Accent1, Lighter 80%*. Select the range **A46:R46** and press Ctrl + Y to repeat the color command.

21. On the Ribbon, click the **View tab**, in the **Workbook Views group**, click the **Page Break Preview** button. If the **Welcome to Page Break Preview** displays, click **OK**. Drag the **Horizontal Page Break line** up until it is between **rows 27** and **28**, and then release the mouse. All of the data for the Math & Science division will display on the same page. Click the **Vertical Page Break line** and drag it to the left until it is between **columns M** and **N**. In the **View tab**, in the **Workbook Views group**, click the **Normal** button to return to Normal view.

(Project 3D–Faculty continues on the next page)

Content-Based Assessments

(Project 3D–Faculty continued)

22. Click the **Page Layout tab**, and in the **Page Setup group**, click the **Print Titles** button. In the **Print titles area**, in the **Rows to repeat at top**, click the **Collapse Dialog Box** button and select **rows 4 and 5**. Click the **Expand Dialog Box** button, and press Tab. In the **Columns to repeat at left** box, click the **Collapse Dialog Box** button and click **Column A**. Click the **Expand Dialog Box** button, and then click **OK**.

23. Click the **Insert tab**. In the **Text group**, click the **Header & Footer** button. In the **Navigation group**, click the **Go to Footer** button. Click the **Left Footer** area and, in the **Header & Footer Elements group**, click the **File Name** button. In the **Navigation group**, click **Go to Header** button. In the **Left Header** area, type **Page** and press Spacebar. In the **Header & Footer Elements group**, click the **Page Number** button, press Spacebar, type **of** and press Spacebar, and then click the **Number of Pages** button.

24. Click in the worksheet. On the status bar, click the **Normal** button. Click the **Page Layout tab** and in the **Page Setup group**, click the **Dialog Box Launcher**. In the **Page Setup** dialog box, in the **Page tab**, under the **Orientation**, verify that **Landscape** is selected. Click the **Margins tab**. In the **Top** box, use the spin arrows to select a top margin of **1.5**. Under **Center on page**, click **Horizontally** and **Vertically**. Click **Print Preview**. Scroll through the worksheet to review how it will display when printed. Then click **Close Print Preview**.

25. **Save** your workbook.

26. Check your *Chapter Assignment Sheet* or *Course Syllabus*, or consult your instructor, to determine if you are to submit work on paper or electronically. To submit electronically, follow the instructions provided by your instructor, and then go to Step 28.

27. Click the **Office** button, click **Print**. In the **Print** dialog box, under **Print what**, select **Entire workbook**. Under **Copies**, confirm that **1** is selected. Click **OK**. If you are directed to submit printed formulas, refer to **Activity 1.12** to do so.

28. Click the **Office** button, click **Close**. If the dialog box displays asking if you want to save changes, click **No** so that you do not save the changes to Page Setup that you used for printing formulas.

End **You have completed Project 3D** —————————————————

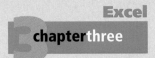

Project 3E — Enrollment Goals

In this project, you will apply the skills you practiced from the Objectives in Project 3A.

Objectives: 1. *Construct an IF Function;* **2.** *Link Data in Workbooks;* **3.** *Create IF Functions That Return Text;* **5.** *Format with Themes;* **6.** *Add Information in the Header and Footer.*

In the following Mastering Excel, you will report the enrollments for Laurel County Community College for Michael Schaeffler, Vice President of Instruction. The college will project its enrollment goal for the next academic year, based on the enrollments for the past three years. You will create a worksheet that displays these numbers. Your completed worksheets will look similar to Figure 3.52.

For Project 3E, you will need the following file:

New blank Excel workbook

You will save your workbook as
3E_Enrollment_Goals_Firstname_Lastname

Figure 3.52

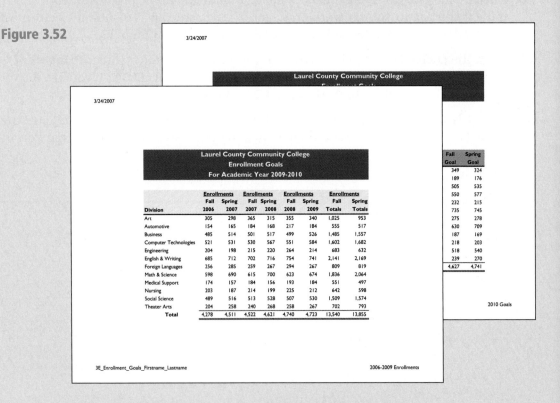

(Project 3E–Enrollment Goals continues on the next page)

Content-Based Assessments

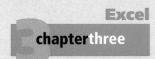
(Project 3E–Enrollment Goals continued)

1. **Start** Excel and display a new blank workbook. **Save** the workbook in your **Excel Chapter 3** folder and name it **3E_Enrollment_Goals_Firstname_Lastname**

2. Delete **Sheet3** and then **Select All Sheets**. In the range **A1:A3**, type the following worksheet title:

| Laurel County Community College |
| Enrollment Goals |
| For Academic Year 2009–2010 |

3. Beginning in cell **A6**, enter the following row titles, ending in cell **A18**:

| Division |
| Art |
| Automotive |
| Business |
| Computer Technologies |
| Engineering |
| English & Writing |
| Foreign Languages |
| Math & Science |
| Medical Support |
| Nursing |
| Social Science |
| Theater Arts |

4. Format the worksheet title with **Bold**, **14 pt font**. Adjust the column widths so the longest row title fully displays within the column. **Ungroup** the sheets. On **Sheet1**, **Merge & Center** each row of the title across columns **A:I**.

5. In the **Sheet1** worksheet, beginning in cell **B6**, type the following column titles:

Fall 2006	Spring 2007	Fall 2007	Spring 2008	Fall 2008	Spring 2009	Fall Totals	Spring Totals

6. In cell **B5**, type **Enrollments** Select the range **B5:C5** and **Underline** the title and **Merge & Center** the heading in these cells. Copy that cell entry into cells **D5**, **F5**, and **H5**.

(Project 3E–Enrollment Goals continues on the next page)

Content-Based Assessments

Mastering Excel

(Project 3E–Enrollment Goals continued)

7. Select the range **B7:G18** and use the enter data by range method—recall that using this method you select the range of cells first and then press ⟨Enter⟩ after each cell entry—to enter the following data:

Fall 2006	Spring 2007	Fall 2007	Spring 2008	Fall 2008	Spring 2009
305	298	365	315	355	340
154	165	184	168	197	184
485	514	501	517	499	526
521	531	530	567	551	584
204	198	215	220	264	214
685	712	702	716	754	741
256	285	259	267	294	267
598	690	615	700	623	674
174	157	184	156	190	184
203	187	214	199	225	212
489	516	513	528	527	530
204	258	240	268	258	267

8. Click cell **H7** and enter a formula that adds the fall enrollments for the last three years. The formula will read =B7+D7+F7. Copy the formula in cell **H7** to cell **I7**. Select the range **H7:I7** and use the fill handle to copy the formula down through **row 18**.

9. Click cell **A19** and type **Total** Format the cell with **Bold** and **Center**. Enter totals in **row 19** and place a **Top and Double Bottom Border** around it. Select the range **B7:I19** and format for **Comma Style** with **no decimals**.

10. Format the column titles in **row 5** and **row 6** with **Bold**. Format cell **A6** with **Align Text Left** and the range **B6:I6** with **Align Text Right** and **Wrap Text**. Place a **Thick Bottom Border** under the titles in **row 6**. Adjust column width so the titles in **row 6** display on two lines.

11. Rename **Sheet1** to **2006–2009 Enrollments** and rename **Sheet2** to **2010 Goals** On the **2010 Goals sheet**, insert three rows between the worksheet title and the row titles so that there is a total of five blank rows. Beginning in cell **B9**, enter the following column titles:

Fall Totals	Fall Average	Spring Totals	Spring Average	Fall Increase Goal	Spring Increase Goal	Fall Goal	Spring Goal

12. In the range **B5:C7**, type the following:

Goals	
>500	3%
<=500	2%

(Project 3E–Enrollment Goals continues on the next page)

Content-Based Assessments

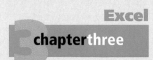
(Project 3E–Enrollment Goals continued)

13. Select the range **B5:C7**, click the **Borders** button, and click the **Outside Borders** button. Merge and center the range **B5:C5**. Click the **Borders** button and click the **Bottom Border**.

14. Click cell **B10** and type = Click the **2006–2009 Enrollments sheet tab**, and click cell **H7** and press ⌷Enter⌷. Click cell **C10**. Enter a formula that divides the fall totals by 3—the number of fall semesters reported. The formula will read =B10/3. The number—341.6667—is entered into the cell and is the average Art enrollments during the last three fall semesters.

15. Select the range **B10:C10**. Use the fill handle to copy the formulas down through **row 21**.

16. Click cell **D10** and type = Click the **2006–2009 Enrollment sheet tab**, click cell **I7**, and then press ⌷Enter⌷. If the **Error Alert** box displays, click **Ignore Error**. (This formula is not consistent with the formula in cell C10.) Click cell **E10**. Enter a formula that divides the spring totals by 3—the number of spring semesters reported. The formula will read =D10/3. The number—317.667—is entered into the cell and is the average Art enrollments during the last three spring semesters.

17. Select the range **D10:E10**. Use the fill handle to copy the formula down through **row 21**. Select the range **D11:D21** and in the **Error Alert** box, click **Ignore Error**.

18. Click cell **F10**. Open the **IF Function Arguments** dialog box. For the Logical test, determine if the fall average enrollments—located in cell C10—are greater than 500. If this test is true, multiply the *Fall Average*—located in cell C10—by 3%—located in cell C6. Because you will copy this formula, use an absolute cell reference for the percentage rate. If this test is false, multiply the *Fall Average*—located in cell C10—by 2%—located in cell C7. Because you will copy this formula, use an absolute cell reference. Click **OK**. The result—6.833333—displays in the cell.

19. Click cell **G10**. Open the **IF Function Arguments** dialog box. Using the skills practiced, determine the Spring Increase Goal. For the Logical test, determine if the spring average enrollments—located in cell E10—are greater than 500. If this test is true, multiply the *Spring Average*—located in cell E10—by 3%. If this test is false, multiply the *Spring Average*—located in cell E10—by 2%. The result—6.353333—displays in the cell.

20. Click cell **H10** and enter the goal for fall. Add the *Fall Average*—located in cell C10—to the *Fall Increase*—located in cell F10. Click cell **I10** and enter the goal for spring. Add the *Spring Average*—located in cell E10—to the *Spring Increase*—located in cell G10. Select the range **F10:I10** and use the fill handle to copy the formulas down through **row 21**.

21. In cell **A22**, type **Total** and format it with **Bold** and **Center**. Select the range **B22:I22** and **SUM** the columns. Add a **Top and Double Bottom Border** to the total row. Format the range **B10:I22** with **Comma Style** and **no decimals**.

22. **Merge & Center** each row of the title across the columns of the worksheet. Format cells **B5:C7** with **Bold**. Format column titles with **Bold**, **Wrap Text**, **Center**, **Middle Align**, with a **Thick Bottom Border**. Adjust the column widths so the titles in **row 6** display on two lines.

23. Format the workbook with the **Equity** theme. Select the **2006–2009 Enrollments sheet tab**. Select the worksheet title and add a **Fill Color** of **Brown, Accent 4, Darker 50%** and a **Font Color** of **White, Background 1**. Format the column titles (rows 5 and 6) with a **Fill Color** of

(Project 3E–Enrollment Goals continues on the next page)

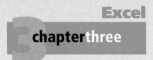
(Project 3E–Enrollment Goals continued)

Brown, Accent 4, Lighter 80%. If necessary, adjust column widths so the column titles still display on two lines.

24. Click the **2010 Goals sheet tab** and select the worksheet title. Select a **Fill Color** of **Brown, Accent 4, Lighter 60%**. Select a **Font Color** of **White, Background 1**. Select the column titles in **row 9**. Select the **Fill Color** of **Gray-50%, Accent 5, Lighter 40%** with a **Font Color** of **Black, Text 1, Lighter 5%**. If necessary, adjust the column widths so that the titles still display on two lines.

25. In the **2006–2009 Enrollments sheet**, correct the **Fall 2008** enrollments as follows:

Automotive	217
Medical Support	193
Social Science	507

26. Change the theme to **Solstice**. In both worksheets, confirm the column widths are wide enough to display the contents when the new theme and its font are selected.

27. Select both worksheets. Place the **File Name** in the **Left Footer** area and the **Sheet Name** in the **Right Footer**. Place the **Current Date** code in the **Left Header**.

28. Place the worksheets in **Landscape Orientation** centered **Horizontally** and **Vertically** and **Fit to 1 page**. Return to **Normal** view. **Save** your work.

29. Check your *Chapter Assignment Sheet* or *Course Syllabus*, or consult your instructor, to determine if you are to submit work on paper or electronically. To submit electronically, follow the instructions provided by your instructor, and then go to Step 31.

30. Click the **Office** menu, click **Print**. In the **Print** dialog box, under **Print what**, select **Entire workbook**. Under **Copies**, confirm that **1** is selected. Click **OK**. If you are directed to submit printed formulas, **Group** all worksheets. Then refer to **Activity 1.12** to do so.

31. Click the **Office** menu, click **Close**. If the dialog box displays asking if you want to save changes, click **No** so that you do not save the changes to Page Setup that you used for printing formulas. **Exit** Excel.

End You have completed Project 3E

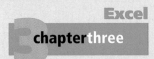

Mastering Excel

Project 3F—Expenses

In this project, you will apply the skills you have practiced from the Objectives in Project 3B.

Objectives: 7. *Enter Dates;* **8.** *Format Large Worksheets;* **9.** *Apply Number Formats;* **10.** *Control Print Options.*

In the following Mastering Excel, you will begin the annual report of expenses for the divisions of Laurel County Community College, which are reported on a monthly basis. Kesia Toomer, Vice President, Administration and Development, prepares one report that includes the expenses for the entire year on a month-by-month basis. The formulas and formats are completed for the entire fiscal year and then each month's expenses are entered. Your completed worksheets will look similar to Figure 3.53.

For Project 3F, you will need the following file:

e03F_Expenses

You will save your workbook as
3F_Expenses_Firstname_Lastname
3F_Expenses_Partial_Firstname_Lastname

Figure 3.53

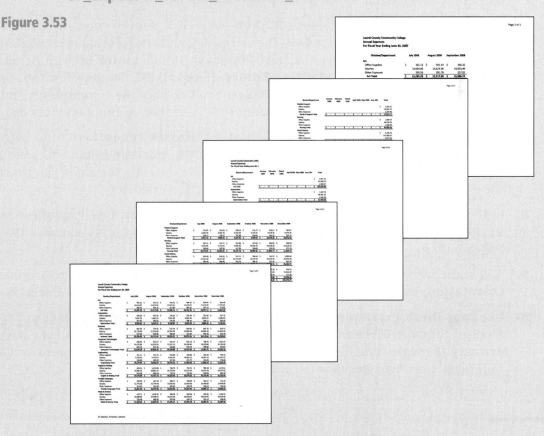

(Project 3F–Expenses continues on the next page)

Content-Based Assessments

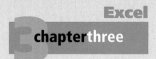

Mastering Excel

(Project 3F–Expenses continued)

1. **Start** Excel. From your student files, locate and open the file named **e03F_Expenses** and **Save** it in your **Excel Chapter 3** folder as **3F_Expenses_Firstname_Lastname**

2. Beginning in cell **H5**, enter the following column titles. The format will match cell **G5** as you enter the data. Recall that a format placed in the three previous cells will be copied into adjacent cells.

'January 2009	'February 2009	'March 2009	'April 2009	'May 2009	'June 2009	Total

3. Select the range **B10:N10** and select a **SUM** formula. To the selected range add **Bold**, **Accounting Number Format**, and a **Top and Double Bottom Border**. Even though some data is not yet entered, the formulas are completed. Then when the data is entered, the worksheet will be formatted and completed.

4. **Copy** the selected range—**B10:N10**—click cell **B15**, and **Paste**. Using the skills practiced, copy the formulas to each of the total rows in the following cells: **B20**, **B25**, **B30**, **B35**, **B40**, **B45**, **B50**, **B55**, **B60**, and **B65**. The formulas and cell formats are copied in the range of the worksheet.

5. Select the range **B7:N7**. Format the range with **Accounting Number Format**. Use **Format Painter** to copy this format to cells **B12**, **B17**, **B22**, **B27**, **B32**, **B37**, **B42**, **B47**, **B52**, **B57**, and **B62**. Format the other numbers on the worksheet with **Comma Style**, including the cells that don't yet contain data.

6. Select the range of the worksheet—**B7:N66**—and click **Sum** to enter the grand total. Recall that a grand total adds the totals of the worksheet and the formula is created from existing totals within the selected range of cells. Format the totals in **row 66** with **Accounting Number Format**, **Bold**, with a **Thick Bottom Border**. Click cell **B6**. On the **View tab**, click the **Freeze Panes** button, and then click **Freeze Panes**. You can view the column titles and the total expenses at the same time. Adjust column widths so that all numbers fully display in the cells.

7. Click the **Freeze Panes** button, and then click **Unfreeze Panes**. Select the range **A7:A10** and on the **Home tab**, in the **Alignment group**, click the **Increase Indent** button. The total column title, *Art Total*, will be increased a second indent. Using the skills you practiced, indent the expenses and totals in the other divisions of the worksheet.

8. In the **Left Footer**, add the **File Name**. In the **Right Header**, type **Page** press Spacebar, and click the **Page Number** button. Press Spacebar, type **of** press Spacebar, and then click the **Number of Pages** button.

9. Adjust the worksheet so there is a **1"** top margin and a **1.5"** left margin, it prints in **Landscape Orientation**; the column titles in **row 5** and the row titles in **column A** print on every page.

10. Use **Page Break Preview** to adjust what will print on each page. Begin Page 2 with the **Medical Support Division**. Place the **July through December** data on one page and the **January through June** data on the next page. Delete **Sheet2** and **Sheet3** and **Save** your workbook. Use **Print Preview** to review the placement.

(Project 3F–Expenses continues on the next page)

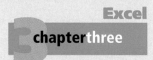

Excel

chapterthree | Mastering Excel

(Project 3F–Expenses continued)

11. Set a **Print Area** to print only the July through September data for the Art, Automotive, and Business divisions. **Save** your workbook and name it **3F_Expenses_Partial_Firstname_Lastname**

12. Check your *Chapter Assignment Sheet* or *Course Syllabus*, or consult your instructor, to determine if you are to submit work on paper or electronically. To submit electronically, follow the instructions provided by your instructor, and then go to Step 15.

13. Click the **Office** menu, click **Print**. Only the Print Area is printed.

14. Locate and open the workbook named **3F_Expenses_Firstname_Lastname** Click the **Office** button and then click **Print**. Under **Copies**, confirm that **1** is selected. Click **OK**. If you are directed to submit printed formulas, refer to **Activity 1.12** to do so.

15. Click the **Office** button, and then click **Close**. If the dialog box displays asking if you want to save changes, click **No** so that you do not save the changes to Page Setup that you used for printing formulas. **Exit** Excel.

End **You have completed Project 3F** ————————————————————————

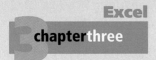

Excel

chapterthree

Mastering Excel

Project 3G—Bookstore Payroll

In this project, you will apply the skills you practiced from the Objectives in Projects 3A and 3B.

Objectives: **1.** Construct an IF Function; **2.** Link Data in Workbooks; **3.** Create IF Functions That Return Text; **4.** Emphasize Data Using Conditional Formatting; **5.** Format with Themes; **6.** Add Information in the Header and Footer; **7.** Enter Dates; **8.** Format Large Worksheets; **9.** Apply Number Formats; **10.** Control Print Options.

In the following Mastering Excel, you will complete the payroll for the Bookstore employees of Laurel County Community College. You will determine the total hours worked, the deductions, and the net pay. Your completed worksheets will look similar to Figure 3.54.

For Project 3G, you will need the following file:

e03G_Bookstore_Payroll

You will save your workbook as
3G_Bookstore_Payroll_Firstname_Lastname

Figure 3.54

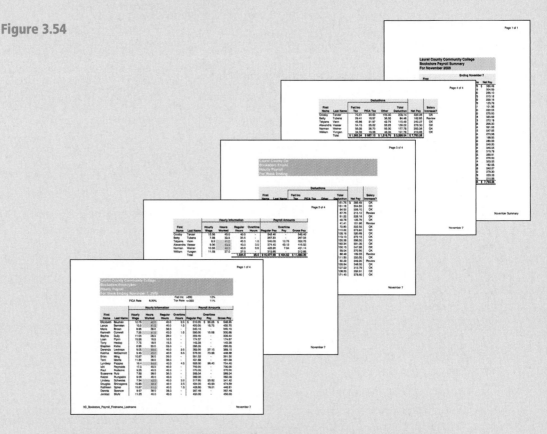

(Project 3G–Bookstore Payroll continues on the next page)

Content-Based Assessments

(Project 3G–Bookstore Payroll continued)

1. **Start** Excel. From the student files, locate and open the file named **e03G_Bookstore_Payroll** and **Save** it in your **Excel Chapter 3** folder as **3G_Bookstore_Payroll_Firstname_Lastname**

2. In the **November 7 sheet**, click cell **E10** and display the **IF Function Arguments** dialog box. Write an IF function to determine the number of hours worked that will be paid at the regular hourly rate. All hours 40 and under are paid at the regular rate. Copy the formula down through **row 37**.

3. Click cell **F10**. In the **IF Function Arguments** dialog box write a function to determine the number of hours worked that will be paid at the overtime rate. All hours over 40 are paid at the overtime rate. Copy the formula down through **row 37**.

4. In cell **G10** enter the formula to determine the total pay at the regular rate. This is the regular hours worked times the hourly wage. The result in cell G10 is 510. In cell **H10**, enter the formula to determine the total pay for overtime. This is the overtime hours worked multiplied by the hourly wage and then by 1.5. In cell **I10**, enter the gross pay, which is the sum of the regular pay plus the overtime pay. Copy the formulas in cells **G10**, **H10**, and **I10** down through **row 37**.

5. In cell **J10**, use the IF function to write the formula to determine the federal income tax. If the gross pay is greater than $350, the tax rate is 13% of the gross pay, and if it is $350 or less, the tax rate is 11%. Create a formula that returns the actual amount of the tax in cell J10. The tax is 71.2725. In cell **K10**, enter the formula to determine the social security tax—*FICA*—shown in cell **D6**. The result displays

33.9915. In both formulas, be sure to use an absolute cell reference where appropriate to facilitate copying the formula. Copy the formulas in cell **J10** and **K10** down through **row 37**.

6. Beginning in cell **L10**, enter the following deductions for each employee. Freezing panes and scrolling column L next to the names in column B is recommended.

Bauman	76.5
Bernsten	47.5
Brown	25.5
Conwell	36
Dully	28
Flynn	18.75
Heslop	16.75
Keller	22
Levinson	38.5
McDermott	42
Ming	44
Morris	52.5
Pappas	18.5
Reynolds	17.75
Rodezno	28
Ruiz	38.95
Rumpakis	42
Schweiss	33.5
Shinagawa	37.5
Sphar	42
Spencer	38
Stuhr	85
Tanzer	105
Tubens	38.5
Vann	42.75
Vassar	58.25
Weiner	95
Yungen	48

(Project 3G–Bookstore Payroll continues on the next page)

Content-Based Assessments

(Project 3G–Bookstore Payroll continued)

7. In cell **M10**, enter a formula to determine the total deductions—the sum of the federal income tax, the FICA tax, and the other deductions. Copy the formula in cell **M10** down through the range of the worksheet, **row 37**. In cell **N10**, enter a formula to determine the net pay—the gross pay minus the total deductions. Copy the formula in cell **N10** down through the range of the worksheet, **row 37**.

8. **Unfreeze Panes** if you used this feature in Step 6. In cell **B38**, type **Total** In cell **D38**, enter a **Sum** formula and copy it through the row to cell **N38**. Format the totals with **Bold, Accounting Number Format**, and add a **Top and Double Bottom Border**. Format cells **D38:F38** for **Comma Style** with **one decimal**.

9. Format the numbers in columns **D:F** for **Comma Style** with **one decimal**. Format the other numbers with **Accounting Number Format** on the top row and **Comma Style** for the rest of the numbers.

10. Use the **Zoom** feature to zoom out to view the worksheet on the screen. Place a **vertical line** from **row 8** through **row 38** between columns **B** and **C**, **F** and **G**, **I** and **J**, **M** and **N**, and **N** and **O**. Select the range **C8:M8** and place a **vertical line** on both the **left** and **right** edges of the cells.

11. In cells **F5:F6**—the title for federal income tax—**Merge & Center** and **Wrap Text**.

12. Click the **November Summary sheet tab**. In cell **A3**, type **For November 2009** Copy the column titles in cells **C6:E6** through cell **N6**. Format the titles in **row 5** with **Bold** and **Merge & Center** each title over the three columns where that week's data will be entered—center cell **C5** over columns **C:E**. Adjust column width if needed.

13. In the **November Summary sheet**, complete the data for the November 7 payroll. Use the formula in each cell that equals the value in the **November 7 worksheet** so that when a value in the November 7 worksheet changes, the November Summary sheet is automatically updated. **Format** the numbers in **row 7** for **Accounting Number Format** and format the other numbers for **Comma Style**.

14. In cell **B35** type **Total** and format it with **Bold, Italic**, and **Center**. In cells **C35:N35**, enter a **Sum** formula. Format the row with **Bold, Accounting Number Format**, and place a **Top and Double Bottom Border**. Adjust column widths if needed.

15. In the **November 7 sheet**, use **Conditional Formatting** to format the hours worked in **column D** over **40** with **Light Red Fill with Dark Red Text**. Click cell **O9** and type **Salary Increase?** and format it to match the other column titles. In cell **O10**, write an **IF formula** that compares the hourly wage to $8. If it is less than $8 an hour, type **Review** and if it is $8 or more, type **OK** Copy the formula down through **row 37**, and then click the **Center** button.

16. Apply the **Technic Theme** to the workbook. Format the **November 7 sheet** as follows. Recall that you first need to select the range that will have fill or font color applied. Format the **Worksheet title rows—A1:O4**—with a **Fill Color** of **Olive Green, Accent 4, Lighter 40%** and a **Font Color** of **White, Background 1, Darker 5%**. Format the **Column titles—rows 8** and **9**—with a **Fill Color** of **Olive Green, Accent 4, Lighter 80%**.

(Project 3G–Bookstore Payroll continues on the next page)

(Project 3G–Bookstore Payroll continued)

17. Format the **November Summary sheet** as follows:
Format the **Worksheet title rows—A1:N3**—with a **Fill Color** of **Gray-50%, Accent 6, Lighter 60%** and **Column titles—rows 5** and **6**—with a **Fill Color** of **Lavender, Accent 3, Lighter 80%**.

18. Review all column titles in both worksheets and adjust column widths if needed so the text and data fully display in the column. **Delete** Sheet3.

19. In both worksheets, in the **Left Footer**, enter the **File Name** and in the **Right Footer**, enter the **Sheet Name**. In the **Right Header**, enter the **Page Number** and the **Number of Pages** and the words so it reads *Page x of xx*.

20. Click the **November 7 sheet tab**. Adjust the worksheet so there is a 1" top margin, it prints in **Landscape Orientation**, and is centered **Horizontally**. Repeat **rows 8** and **9** at the top and **columns A** and **B** at the left. On the **November Summary sheet**, set the **Orientation** to **Portrait** and center the worksheet both **Horizontally** and **Vertically**.

21. Use **Page Break Preview** to adjust what will print on each page. For the **November 7 worksheet**, position the **vertical** page break between the **Gross Pay** and the **Federal Income Tax**. Adjust the bottom page break

so the first row on the second page is for **Crosby Tanzer**. For the **November Summary sheet**, place the **vertical** page break between the **November 7** and the **November 14** data. Use **Print Preview** to review the placement.

22. In the **November Summary sheet**, set a **Print Area** to print only the November 7 data for all employees. **Save** your work.

23. Check your *Chapter Assignment Sheet* or *Course Syllabus*, or consult your instructor, to determine if you are to submit work on paper or electronically. To submit electronically, follow the instructions provided by your instructor, and then go to Step 26.

24. Click the **Office** button, click **Print**. Confirm that under **Print what**, **Active sheet** is selected. Only the selected Print Area prints.

25. Click the **Office** button, click **Print**. In the **Print** dialog box, under **Print what**, select **Entire workbook** and click **Ignore print areas**. Under **Copies**, confirm that **1** is selected. Click **OK**. If you are directed to submit printed formulas, **Group** all worksheets. Then refer to **Activity 1.12** to do so.

26. Click the **Office** button, click **Close**. If the dialog box displays asking if you want to save changes, click **No** so that you do not save the changes to Page Setup that you used for printing formulas. **Exit** Excel.

End **You have completed Project 3G**

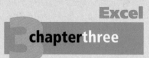

Mastering Excel

Project 3H — Food Service

In this project, you will apply the skills you practiced from the Objectives in Projects 3A and 3B.

Objectives: **1.** *Construct an IF Function;* **2.** *Link Data in Workbooks;* **3.** *Create IF Functions That Return Text;* **4.** *Emphasize Data Using Conditional Formatting;* **5.** *Format with Themes;* **6.** *Add Information in the Header and Footer;* **8.** *Format Large Worksheets;* **9.** *Apply Number Formats.*

In the following Mastering Excel, you will report the income and expenses for the food services of the Laurel County Community College. You will link the detailed report to a summary report. The Laurel County Community College provides most of its services in the cafeteria, but they do have two coffee stands in two classroom buildings. The college's food services also provide catering for many local events. Your completed worksheets will look similar to Figure 3.55.

For Project 3H, you will need the following file:

e03H_Food_Service

**You will save your workbook as
3H_Food_Service_Firstname_Lastname**

Figure 3.55

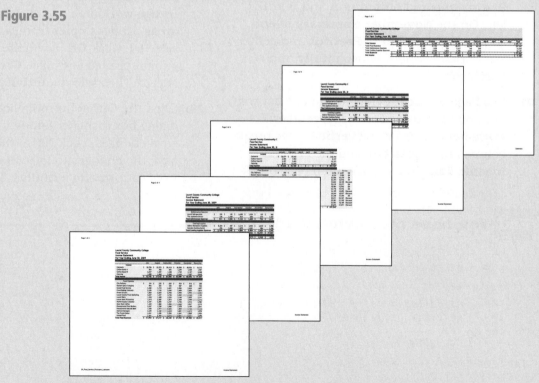

(Project 3H–Food Service continues on the next page)

Content-Based Assessments

(Project 3H–Food Service continued)

1. **Start** Excel. From the student files locate and open the file named **e03H_Food_Service** and **Save** it to your **Excel Chapter 3** folder as 3H_Food_Service_Firstname_Lastname

2. Position the worksheet so **row 6** is the first row displayed. In cell **N6**, enter the column title **Total** and format it to match the other column titles.

3. Click cell **B7** and **Freeze Panes**. Then position **column N** so it is next to **column A**. In cell **N8**, enter a **SUM** formula that adds row 8, including the cells that do not yet contain data—B8:M8. Copy the formula through cell **N11** and to the following ranges: **N15:N29, N33:N34, N38:N39**. Format the data in **column N** to match the entries in **column B**.

4. Format cell **A7** with **Bold** and **Center** alignment. Copy that format to the other section headings, cells **A14, A32, A37**, and **A43**. Format the total headings with **Bold**— cells **A12, A30, A35, A40, A41**. Format the remaining row titles in **column A** with **Increase Indent**.

5. In cell **B12**, enter a formula that sums the total income and copy it through **column N**. Format the row with **Accounting Number Format** with **no decimals**, **Bold**, with a **Top and Double Bottom Border**. Complete formulas and formatting for the worksheet totals in **row 30**—*Total Food Expenses*—**row 35**—*Total Maintenance Expenses*—and **row 40**—*Total Cooking Supplies Expenses*.

6. In **row 41**, enter a formula that totals the expenses. It is suggested that you use the **grand total** method you practiced previously. Recall the grand total method selects the range of the worksheet, including all totals. For this grand total, include column N—totals—in the worksheet range. The number entered in cell **B41** is *$38,599*. In **row 43**, write a formula that

determines the net income—total income minus total expenses. The number entered in cell **B43** is *$(6,243)*.

7. Format the totals in **rows 41** and **43** with **Bold**. Format **row 41** with a **Top Border** and format **row 43** with a **Thick Bottom Border**. If needed, adjust column widths so all entries are fully displayed.

8. With **Freeze Panes** still active, move **column I** next to **column A**. Beginning in cell **I8**, from the following list, type the February data using care not to overwrite the formulas in column I:

Income	February
Cafeteria	35842
Coffee Stand A	1984
Coffee Stand B	2684
Catering	12670
Food Expense	
City Delivery	475
Eastern Spice Service	1250
Grand Food Service	3745
Great Baking Company	3440
Green Grocers	2850
Laurel County Food Marketing	3418
Laurel Dairy	3277
Laurel Meat Processing	3501
Market Supply Company	3363
Moon Dust Coffee	4801
Pennsylvania Food Brokers	3264
Pennsylvania Natural Beef	2457
Seafood Managers	2640
The French Baker	3750
United Food	6514
Maintenance Expense	
Laurel Refrigeration	225
The Appliance Doctor	275
Cooking Supplies	
Adams Restaurant Supplies	1360
Camden Cooking Outlet	750

(Project 3H–Food Service continues on the next page)

Content-Based Assessments

(Project 3H–Food Service continued)

9. Adjust column width if needed to fully display all contents. Select the numbers in the **Food Expense** section of the worksheet—**B15:M29**. Use a **Conditional Format** to highlight all cells with **Light Red Fill with Dark Red Text** that contain an amount greater than $4,000.

10. Click the **Summary sheet tab** and review the values entered into the worksheet. The totals for July through January are entered as values, but they do not link to the Income Statement.

11. Position the worksheet so **row 6** is the first row displayed. Click cell **B7** and **Freeze Panes**. Click cell **N7** and enter a **Sum** formula that adds the numbers in **row 7**. Copy the formula down through cell **N12**. Format **column N** using the same formats as used in **column H**.

12. In the Summary worksheet, you will enter the February data. Click cell **I7** and type = Click the **Income Statement sheet tab**, and click cell **I12** and press Enter to enter the **February Income** on the Summary sheet. Using this same technique, enter the other February totals using a formula that will update automatically when the number in the Income Statement worksheet changes.

13. Notice that the data entered in the Summary worksheet is entered as values and not linked to the data in the Income Statement worksheet. Select the range **I7:I12**. Click the fill handle and drag **to the left** through **column B**. Click in several cells to confirm that the formulas refer to the Income Statement worksheet.

14. In the **Income Statement sheet**, click cell **O14**, type Review. Select the range **O14:P14** and click **Merge & Center**. Click

cell **O15** and enter a **SUM** formula to add the expenses to City Delivery for July through December—the **range B15:G15**. Use the fill handle to copy the formula down through **row 29**. Click the **Error Alert** indicator and click **Ignore Error**. Copy the format from cell **N15** to cell **O15**.

15. Click cell **P15** and display the **IF Function Argument** dialog box. The Food Services director is taking a look at the suppliers to determine the size of the orders. If the total orders for six months are greater than $18,000, she will ask the supplier for a quantity discount. For the **Logical Test**, compare the amount in cell **O15** with 18,000. The Logical Test will read *O15>18000*. For the **Value_if_true**, type **Discount** and for the **Value_if_false**, type **OK** Complete the function and use the fill handle to copy the formula down through **row 29**. **Center** the text.

16. **Unfreeze Panes** in both worksheets. Format the workbook with the **Opulent Theme**. In the **Income Statement sheet**, use the Ctrl key to select the following nonadjacent ranges: **A8:N12**, **A15:P30**, **A33:N35**, **A38:N41**, **A43:N43**. Select a **Fill Color** of **Gold, Accent 4, Lighter 80%**.

17. Select the rows that contain no data—**A5:N5**, **A13:N13**, **A31:N31**, **A36:N36**, and **A42:N42**— and select a **Fill Color** of **Purple, Accent 2, Darker 50%**.

18. Select the remaining rows—**A6:N6**, **A14:P14**, **A32:N32**, and **A37:N37**—and select a **Fill Color** of **Purple, Accent 2, Lighter 80%** and a **Font Color** of **Purple, Accent 2, Darker 50%**. If needed, widen the columns to fully display contents.

19. Click the **Summary sheet tab**. Select the range of the worksheet title through

(Project 3H–Food Service continues on the next page)

Content-Based Assessments

(Project 3H–Food Service continued)

column N. Select a **Fill Color**, **Gold, Accent 4, Lighter 60%**. Select the range of the blank **row 5** through **column N**, and select a **Fill Color** of **Gold, Accent 4, Darker 50%**.

20. Select both sheets. In the **Left Footer** area, add the **File Name** and in the **Right Footer** area, add the **Sheet Name**. In the **Left Header**, enter the **Page Number** and the **Number of pages** and the words so it reads *Page x of xx.*

21. Format the worksheets to **Center Horizontally** in **Landscape Orientation** with a top margin of 1. In the **Income Statement** worksheet, print the worksheet title and column and row titles on all pages and set a vertical page break between the columns for **December** and **January** and a horizontal break just after the **Total Food Expenses**. In the **Summary** worksheet, use **Fit to 1 page**.

22. Adjust columns on both worksheets, if necessary, to fully display data in the worksheet. **Save** your workbook.

23. Check your *Chapter Assignment Sheet* or *Course Syllabus*, or consult your instructor, to determine if you are to submit work on paper or electronically. To submit electronically, follow the instructions provided by your instructor, and then go to Step 25.

24. Click the **Office** button, click **Print**. In the **Print** dialog box, under **Print what**, select **Entire workbook**. Under **Copies**, confirm that **1** is selected. Click **OK**. If you are directed to submit printed formulas, **Group** all worksheets. Then refer to **Activity 1.12** to do so.

25. Click the **Office** button, click **Close**. If the dialog box displays asking if you want to save changes, click **No** so that you do not save the changes to Page Setup that you used for printing formulas. **Exit** Excel.

End **You have completed Project 3H**

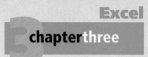

Excel

chapter three Mastering Excel

Project 3I — Faculty Salaries

In this project, you will apply all the skills you practiced from the Objectives in Projects 3A and 3B.

Objectives: **1.** *Construct an IF Function;* **2.** *Link Data in Workbooks;* **3.** *Create IF Functions That Return Text;* **4.** *Emphasize Data Using Conditional Formatting;* **5.** *Format with Themes;* **6.** *Add Information in the Header and Footer;* **7.** *Enter Dates;* **8.** *Format Techniques for Large Worksheets;* **9.** *Apply Number Formats;* **10.** *Control Print Options.*

In the following Mastering Excel, you will complete the January payroll for faculty members. You will then transfer the salary information to a summary sheet and determine the total salaries for each division of Laurel County Community College. Your completed worksheets will look similar to Figure 3.56.

For Project 3I, you will need the following file:

e03I_Faculty_Salaries

You will save your workbook as
3I_Faculty_Salaries_Firstname_Lastname

Figure 3.56

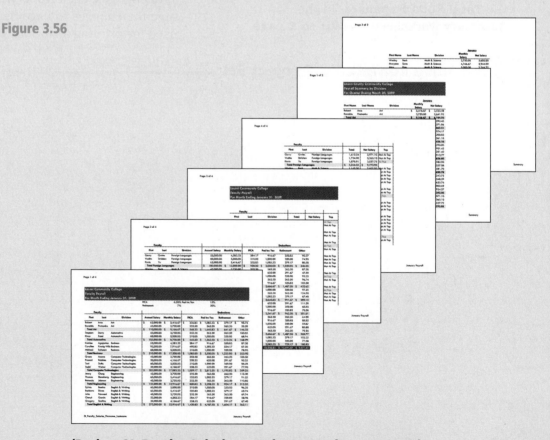

(Project 3I–Faculty Salaries continues on the next page)

Content-Based Assessments

(Project 3I–Faculty Salaries continued)

1. **Start** Excel. From your student files, locate and open the file named **e03I_ Faculty_Salaries** and **Save** it in your **Excel Chapter 3** folder as **3I_Faculty_ Salaries_Firstname_Lastname**

2. Click cell **E9** and write a formula that divides the Annual Salary in cell **D9** by **12** to determine the monthly salary. The amount—*5416.67*—displays in the cell. (Note: depending on your screen, the number of decimals displayed may be different.) Use the fill handle to copy this formula down through **row 59**. It is faster to copy the formula through the range and later remove the formula from the cells where it is not needed.

3. Click cell **F9** and write a formula that uses an absolute cell reference to determine the FICA tax withheld from the monthly salary. The tax rate—6.2%—is in cell **E4**. The amount—*335.833*—displays in the cell. Use the fill handle to copy this formula down through **row 59**.

4. Click cell **G9** and write an IF formula to determine the amount of federal income tax withheld, which is the tax rate times the monthly salary. If the monthly salary is less than $4,500, the tax rate is 15%—displayed in cell **G4**. If it is $4,500 or more, the tax rate is 20%—displayed in cell **G5**. The amount of tax withholding—*1083.33*—displays in cell **G9**. Use the fill handle to copy this formula down through **row 59**.

5. Click cell **H9** and write a formula that determines the amount withheld for retirement. The retirement rate—7%—is in cell **E5** and is multiplied by the monthly salary to determine the amount withheld for retirement benefits. The amount—*379.1667*—displays in the cell. Use the fill handle to copy this formula down through **row 59**.

6. In cell **J9** write a formula to total the deductions (FICA, Fed Inc Tax, Retirement, and Other) and in cell **K9**, create a formula for the Net Income. The Net Income is the Monthly Salary minus the Total Deductions. The amount of net salary for Robert is 3522.58.

7. Select the range **J9:K9** and use the fill handle to copy these formulas down through **row 59**.

8. Select the range of the data, including the total rows—**D9:K61**—and format for **Comma Style** with **two decimals**. Select the range **D9:K9** and format for **Accounting Number Format**.

9. Select the range **D11:K11** and press Delete to remove the formula in the cells. Then enter a **SUM** formula. If an **Error Alert** indicator displays, click it and click **Ignore Error**. This SUM formula is not consistent with the formulas in the surrounding cells.

10. Select the range **D14:K14** and press Delete to remove the formula in the cells. Then enter a **SUM** formula. If an **Error Alert** indicator displays, click it and click **Ignore Error**. Using the skills practiced, enter **SUM** formulas for the totals in all divisions of the college.

11. Select the range of the worksheet— **D9:K61**—and enter a **SUM** formula to enter the grand total. Select the grand total and format with **Accounting Number** format and **Bold**. Click cell **A61** and format with **Bold** and **Increase Indent** two times. The total January Monthly Salary is $184,166.67 and the January Net Salary is $122,964.26.

12. Click cell **A11**. Format with **Bold** and **Increase Indent**. Select the range

(Project 3I–Faculty Salaries continues on the next page)

(Project 3I–Faculty Salaries continued)

D11:K11 and format with **Accounting Format** and **two decimals**. Then select the range **A11:K11**. Use a **Fill Color** of **Blue, Accent 1, Lighter 60%**. Right-click and double-click the **Format Painter**. Click the Format Painter in the division total rows—**A14, A18, A23, A27, A33, A37, A43, A47, A51, A57**, and **A60**. Then stop the **Format Painter**.

13. Select the range **A61:K61**. Use a **Fill Color** of **Dark Blue, Text 2, Darker 25%** and a **Font Color** of **White, Background 1**. Adjust column widths to fully display the contents.

14. Use **Zoom control** to zoom out so you can see the entire worksheet. Starting with **row 7**, place **vertical lines** between data in columns **C:D**, **E:F**, **J:K**, and **K:L**. Place a **right vertical border** in **column L**. Use **Zoom** to return to 100%.

15. Click the **Summary sheet tab**. **Merge & Center** the month names over the two columns that display data for the month—center **January** in columns **D:E**—and format the month names with **Bold** and **Underline**. In cells **J5:K5**, **Merge & Center** Quarterly Total and format to match the other titles in row 5.

16. Position the worksheet so that the column titles in **row 6** and the row titles in **columns A:B** remain visible on the screen and **Freeze Panes**. Position **column D** next to **column B**. Click the **January Payroll sheet tab**. Position the worksheet so **row 8** is the first row displayed on the screen. Click cell **D9** and **Freeze Panes**. Position **column E** next to **column C**.

17. Click the **Summary sheet tab** and click cell **D7** and type = Click the **January Payroll sheet tab** and locate the monthly salary for Robert Arce, cell **E9**. Click cell

E9 and press Enter. Click cell **E7** and type = Click the **January Payroll sheet tab**, and locate the net salary for Robert Arce, cell **K9**. Click cell **K9** and press Enter.

18. Select cells **D7:E7** and use the fill handle to copy the formulas down through **row 59**.

19. In the **Summary worksheet**, **Unfreeze Panes**. Click cell **A9**—the title for the total of salaries for Art faculty—and **Increase Indent**. Select the range **A9:K9**, format with **Bold**, and use a **Fill Color** of **Olive Green, Accent 3, Lighter 60%**. Use **Format Painter** to copy the format to the other total rows—**A12, A16, A21, A25, A31, A35, A41, A45, A49, A55**, and **A58**.

20. Click cell **A59** and format with **Bold**, **Italic**, and **Increase Indent two times**. Select the range **D59:E59** and add a **Top and Double Bottom Border**. Select the range **A59:K59** and use a **Fill Color** of **Olive Green, Accent 3, Darker 50%** and a **Font Color** of **White, Background 1**. Adjust column widths if needed.

21. Select the range **D8:E8** and right-click. Click **Comma Style**, and double-click the **Format Painter**. Beginning with cell **D10**, click in the cells that do not contain a total. Recall that the total rows are formatted with a fill color. Therefore, you will click in cells that are not shaded.

22. The faculty with the top salaries are to be highlighted. In the **January Payroll sheet**, **Unfreeze Panes**. Click cell **L8** and type Top Use **Format Painter** to copy the format from cell **K8** to cell **L8**. Click cell **L9** and enter an IF function that returns the words *At Top* if the **Annual Salary** is $65,000 or greater and the words *Not at Top* if the salary is less than $65,000. *At*

(Project 3I–Faculty Salaries continues on the next page)

Content-Based Assessments

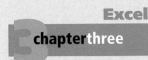
(Project 3I–Faculty Salaries continued)

Top is entered in cell **L9** for Robert. Copy the formula down through **row 59**. Use **Conditional Formatting** to format the words *At Top* in **Green Fill with Dark Green Text**. Delete the entries in the total rows and adjust column widths to fully display contents.

23. Format the workbook using the **Median Theme**. Click the **January Payroll sheet tab**. Select the title range, **A1:L3**, and add a **Fill Color** of **Green, Accent 5, Darker 50%** and **Font Color** of **White, Background 1**. Format the **Summary** worksheet title— **A1:K3**—with a **Fill Color** of **Olive Green, Accent 3, Darker 50%** and a **Font Color** of **White, Background 1**.

24. **Select both sheets**. In the **Left Footer** area, add the **File Name** and in the **Right Footer** area, add the **Sheet Name**. In the **Left Header** area, enter the **Page Number** and the **Number of Pages** and the words so it reads *Page x of xx*.

25. Place the worksheets in **Landscape orientation**, centered both **Vertically** and **Horizontally**. For each worksheet, print the column titles at the top of each page

and print the three-column row titles at the left of each page. In the **January Payroll sheet**, place a horizontal page break line just after the **Total** for **English & Writing**. In the **Summary sheet**, select the range of the data—**A1:E59**—and set a print area. **Save** your workbook.

26. Check your *Chapter Assignment Sheet* or *Course Syllabus*, or consult your instructor, to determine if you are to submit work on paper or electronically. To submit electronically, follow the instructions provided by your instructor, and then go to Step 28.

27. Click the **Office** button, click **Print**. In the **Print** dialog box, under **Print what**, select **Entire workbook**. Under **Copies**, confirm that **1** is selected. Click **OK**. If you are directed to submit printed formulas, **Group** all worksheets. Then refer to **Activity 1.12** to do so.

28. Click the **Office** button, click **Close**. If the dialog box displays asking if you want to save changes, click **No** so that you do not save the changes to Page Setup that you used for printing formulas. **Exit** Excel.

End You have completed Project 3I

Content-Based Assessments

Project 3J — Business Running Case

In this project, you will apply the skills you have practiced from the Objectives in Projects 3A and 3B.

From My Computer, navigate to the student files that accompany this textbook. In the folder **03_business_running_case**, locate and open the folder for this chapter. Open and print the instructions for this project, which are provided to you in Adobe PDF format. Follow the instructions and use the skills you have gained thus far to assist the managers of the Grand Department Store to meet the challenges of keeping records for a large department.

End You have completed Project 3J

Outcomes-Based Assessments

Rubric

The following outcomes-based assessments are *open-ended assessments*. That is, there is no specific correct result; your result will depend on your approach to the information provided. Make *Professional Quality* your goal. Use the following scoring rubric to guide you in *how* to approach the problem and then to evaluate *how well* your approach solves the problem.

The *criteria*—Software Mastery, Content, Format and Layout, and Process—represent the knowledge and skills you have gained that you can apply to solving the problem. The *levels of performance*—Professional Quality, Approaching Professional Quality, or Needs Quality Improvement—help you and your instructor evaluate your result.

	Your completed project is of Professional Quality if you:	Your completed project is Approaching Professional Quality if you:	Your completed project Needs Quality Improvements if you:
1-Software Mastery	Choose and apply the most appropriate skills, tools, and features and identify efficient methods to solve the problem.	Choose and apply some appropriate skills, tools, and features, but not in the most efficient manner.	Choose inappropriate skills, tools, or features, or are inefficient in solving the problem.
2-Content	Construct a solution that is clear and well organized, contains content that is accurate, appropriate to the audience and purpose, and is complete. Provide a solution that contains no errors of spelling, grammar, or style.	Construct a solution in which some components are unclear, poorly organized, inconsistent, or incomplete. Misjudge the needs of the audience. Have some errors in spelling, grammar, or style, but the errors do not detract from comprehension.	Construct a solution that is unclear, incomplete, or poorly organized, containing some inaccurate or inappropriate content; and contains many errors of spelling, grammar, or style. Do not solve the problem.
3-Format and Layout	Format and arrange all elements to communicate information and ideas, clarify function, illustrate relationships, and indicate relative importance.	Apply appropriate format and layout features to some elements, but not others. Overuse features, causing minor distraction.	Apply format and layout that does not communicate information or ideas clearly. Do not use format and layout features to clarify function, illustrate relationships, or indicate relative importance. Use available features excessively, causing distraction.
4-Process	Use an organized approach that integrates planning, development, self-assessment, revision, and reflection.	Demonstrate an organized approach in some areas, but not others; or, use an insufficient process of organization throughout.	Do not use an organized approach to solve the problem.

Outcomes-Based Assessments

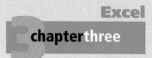
Problem Solving

Project 3K—Purchases

In this project, you will construct a solution by applying any combination of the skills you practiced from the Objectives in Projects 3A and 3B.

For Project 3K, you will need the following file:

e03K_Payments

You will save your workbook as
3K_Payments_Firstname_Lastname

The Accounting Department of Laurel County Community College uses an Excel worksheet to record the purchases that are made and the payments for those purchases. You will complete the worksheet recording the payments that were made and any amounts still unpaid.

From your student files, open e03K_Payments. This file reports the payments made during a week in February. The college has an agreement with its vendors—the agencies the college purchases from—to receive a discount for purchases. The rate of the discount varies depending on the quantity of the purchase. You will determine the discount rate, the amount of the discount, and any balance that is still due if the invoice was not paid in full.

Use an IF function to determine the discount rate. All invoices will receive a 1% discount. If the invoice is larger than $3,000, then a 2% discount will be given. To determine the amount of the discount, multiply the discount rate times the amount of the invoice. To determine the amount still due, from the Amount of the Invoice, subtract the Amount of the Payment and the Amount of the Discount. Provide totals for the columns that contain money amounts. Use Conditional Formatting to highlight the Amounts Due that are greater than $1,000.

Use borders, themes, and font attributes to prepare a professional worksheet. If the worksheet prints on more than one page, repeat appropriate row and column titles on each page. For the row titles on the additional pages, use only the invoice numbers. Insert a left footer that includes the file name and a right footer that displays the page number. Save the workbook as **3K_Payments_Firstname_Lastname**

End **You have completed Project 3K** ⎯⎯⎯⎯⎯⎯⎯⎯⎯

Outcomes-Based Assessments

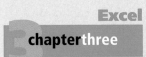
Problem Solving

Project 3L — Bookstore Income

In this project, you will construct a solution by applying any combination of the skills you practiced from the Objectives in Projects 3A and 3B.

For Project 3L, you will need the following file:

e03L_Bookstore_Income

You will save your workbook as
3L_Bookstore_Income_Firstname_Lastname

In this project, you will complete a workbook that displays the income for the bookstore for the first quarter of 2009. The Bookstore of Laurel County Community College sells all textbooks for the college, in addition to supplies, cards, snacks, college logo items, and clothing. The data for the quarter has been entered for you. You will complete and format the worksheet.

From the student files, locate and open e03L_Bookstore_Income. Books are sold at the beginning of the semester and returned throughout the semester. That pattern is reflected in the income of this report. Calculate the total of General sales, and Textbook sales, and a total of all sales for the bookstore for each week. In column N, calculate the total sales for each category listed for the quarter.

The bookstore is required to share its profits with the college. Below the total sales, enter the information for the amount that will be shared. If the total income is greater than $10,000 in any week, 30% of those profits will be returned. If the income is $10,000 or less, then 20% of those profits will be returned. This information should be entered on the worksheet as a reference for the user. Under the total row, write an IF formula to determine the percent shared each week. Then add a row that reports the amount of income that will be shared with the college.

Use borders, themes, and font attributes to prepare a professional worksheet. Add a footer that includes the file name in the left footer and page number information in the right footer. Save the workbook as **3L_Bookstore_Income_Firstname_Lastname** and submit it as directed.

End **You have completed Project 3L**

Outcomes-Based Assessments

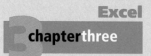
Problem Solving

Project 3M — Budget

In this project, you will construct a solution by applying any combination of the skills you practiced from the Objectives in Projects 3A and 3B.

> **For Project 3M, you will need the following file:**
>
> e03M_Budget

**You will save your workbook as
3M_Budget_Firstname_Lastname**

In this project, you will complete a workbook that displays the budget for the academic year for the Vice President of Instruction, Michael Schaeffler. The workbook has been started and displays the budget and actual expenses for the last two years. You will complete that worksheet and determine the budget amount for the next year.

To determine the average of the actual expenses, add the actual expenses for the last two years together and then divide by 2. The formula in cell G7 will read =(D7+F7)/2. In the column titled *Increase Budget?*, enter an IF statement to determine whether or not an increase in the budgeted amount is needed. If the Average Actual expenses—column G—exceed the 2008–2009 YTD Actual expenses—column F—enter *Increase*. If not, enter *No Increase*. In column I write an IF formula to determine the budget amount. If the budget should be increased, then add $200 to the 2008–2009 Budget amount—the amount in column E, otherwise the budget will be the same as the 2008–2009 Budget. In the *Increase Budget?* column, use Conditional Formatting to indicate the areas where the budget has increased. Calculate totals for each division. In row 108, calculate a Total College Budget for all amounts.

In another worksheet, prepare a report that displays only the 2009–2010 proposed budget for each division—the totals for each division that display in the 2009–2010 Proposed Budget column. Make sure that the worksheet amounts are linked to the division totals in the original budget. Sum the Total Budget on this sheet. Name each sheet to reflect its content.

Use borders, themes, and font attributes to prepare a professional workbook. Add a footer that includes the file name at the left and sheet name at the right. Repeat the column headings in row 5 on subsequent pages, and adjust the page breaks to prevent divisions from breaking across pages. Save the workbook as **3M_Budget_Firstname_Lastname** and submit it as directed.

End You have completed Project 3M ————————

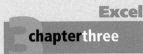

Problem Solving

Project 3N — Financial Aid

In this project, you will construct a solution by applying any combination of the skills you practiced from the Objectives in Projects 3A and 3B.

For Project 3N, you will need the following file:

e03N_Financial_Aid

You will save your workbook as
3N_Financial_Aid_Firstname_Lastname

In this project, you will complete a workbook that displays the financial aid awards for the year. A workbook has been started and the financial aid awards have been entered into the worksheet. You will complete and format the worksheet.

Complete the worksheet as follows: In column C, enter the total amount of the aid from all sources for each student. In row 47, provide totals for each type of aid granted and for the Amount of Award column.

Students who have been awarded a PELL grant will be invited to a reception in their honor hosted by the college president, Diane Gilmore. Enter an IF statement that identifies which students will receive this invitation. Use Conditional Formatting to identify all students who have total awards of $2,500 or greater.

Use borders, themes, and font attributes to prepare a professional workbook. Add a footer that includes the file name at the left and page numbers at the right. Repeat the column headings in row 6 on subsequent pages. Save the workbook as **3N_Financial_Aid_Firstname_Lastname** and submit it as directed.

 End You have completed Project 3N _____

Outcomes-Based Assessments

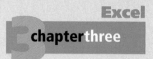
Problem Solving

Project 30 — Bookstore Inventory

In this project, you will construct a solution by applying any combination of the skills you practiced from the Objectives in Projects 3A and 3B.

For Project 30, you will need the following file:

e03O_Bookstore_Inventory

You will save your workbook as
30_Bookstore_Inventory_Firstname_Lastname

In this project, you will complete a workbook that identifies the bookstore inventory. The beginning inventory, number of purchases, and number remaining in the ending inventory are entered into the worksheet. You will complete the number sold, determine if an increase in inventory is needed, what the desired beginning inventory will be, and then determine the number to order.

Open the workbook and on row 1 enter the college name and on row 3 add the date of September 30, 2009. Complete the information in the workbook, calculating a total for each inventory type. Determine the number sold by adding the purchases to the beginning inventory, then subtracting the ending inventory. If the number sold is 75% or more of the beginning inventory, an increase in inventory is needed. In column F, write a formula to determine 75% of the beginning inventory. In column G, use an IF function to determine whether the inventory should increase. It should increase if the number sold in column E is greater than or equal to column F—75% of the beginning inventory. If an increase in inventory is needed, in column H calculate an increase of 15% of the beginning inventory. Next, write a formula to determine the new beginning inventory, which is the beginning inventory plus the amount of increase. Then determine the number to order to bring the inventory to the desired level, which is the amount of the desired beginning inventory minus the ending inventory. For each total row, sum the new amounts you calculated in columns H:J.

Use borders, themes, and font attributes to prepare a professional workbook. These numbers are not money amounts; round to 0 decimal places. Add a footer that includes the file name and delete the unused sheets. Adjust column widths so the worksheet prints on one page. Save the workbook as **30_Bookstore_Inventory_Firstname_Lastname** and submit it as directed.

End **You have completed Project 30** ——————————

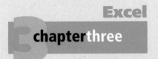

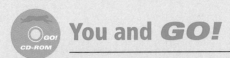 You and *GO!*

Project 3P — You and *GO!*

In this project, you will construct a solution by applying any combination of the Objectives found in Projects 3A and 3B.

From My Computer, navigate to the student files that accompany this textbook. In the folder **04_you_and_go**, locate and open the folder for this chapter. Open and print the instructions for this project, which are provided to you in Adobe PDF format. Follow the instructions to create a worksheet that displays something that you collect. You will use a Conditional Format to highlight a portion of your collection.

End You have completed Project 3P ——————————

GO! with Help

Project 3Q — *GO!* with Help

In this chapter, you used a Theme to format the workbook. You then changed from one Theme to another. You can create a custom theme of your choice and save that theme so you can use it multiple times.

   1 **Start** Excel and confirm that you are connected to the Internet. At the far right end of the Ribbon, click the **Microsoft Office Excel Help** button.

   2 In the search box, type **custom theme** and then press `Enter`. Locate and click **Apply or customize a document theme**.

   3 In the **What do you want to do?** section, click **Customize a document theme**.

   4 Read the information that displays, including the sections **Customize the theme colors**, **Customize the theme fonts**, **Select a set of theme effects**, and **Save a document theme**. When you are finished, close the Help window and then **Exit** Excel.

End You have completed Project 3Q ——————————

chapterfour

Creating Charts and Tables; Sorting and Filtering Data

OBJECTIVES

At the end of this chapter you will be able to:

1. Use Text Orientation
2. Create a Column Chart
3. Create a Chart Sheet and Edit the Chart
4. Create and Modify a Pie Chart
5. Apply a Theme to a Chart
6. Print Charts

7. Sort Data
8. Convert Text into Columns
9. Apply Conditional Formatting Using Data Bars and Color Scales
10. Insert a Table and Filter Data

OUTCOMES

Mastering these objectives will enable you to:

PROJECT 4A
Create and Modify Charts

PROJECT 4B
Filter and Sort a Table

Providence and Warwick Hospital

Providence and Warwick Hospital serves the metropolitan area of Providence, Rhode Island, and the surrounding cities of Warwick, Rhode Island, and Fall River, Massachusetts. It is a world-class medical facility providing care to adults and children through the hospital and a number of social service and multidisciplinary facilities, such as the Asthma Center and Adult Metabolism Clinic. Scientists at the hospital conduct research and clinical trials of new drugs. The hospital's medical staff focuses on innovation and new technologies to provide quality care to patients at every stage of life.

Creating Charts and Tables

Data displayed in a worksheet is prepared to report information and is often used to make business decisions. Placing the data in a chart provides visual comparisons and displays patterns with which to make decisions. Sorting the data in different ways and displaying only a portion of it are other ways to rearrange data for review.

In this chapter, you will create charts and sort and filter data displayed as a table. You will practice the basics of chart design, create a separate chart sheet, modify a chart, use themes in a chart, and print the chart. You will sort data within a worksheet, filter the data, convert text entered into one cell into several columns, and insert a table. You will use a workbook that has several worksheets and charts.

Project 4A Census

In Activities 4.1 through 4.14, you will construct a portfolio of Excel worksheets and charts for Maria Benitez, vice president of operations at Providence and Warwick Hospital, that displays the number of patients—called *census*—for a day at the hospital. Records of all patient contact are tracked on a daily basis and used to analyze trends in patient care needs and assist with staffing. Your report will include the number of beds available in each unit—department in the hospital—the number of patients admitted and discharged, and the number of beds filled at the end of the day. Your completed workbook will look similar to Figure 4.1.

For Project 4A, you will need the following file:

New blank Excel workbook

**You will save your workbook as
4A_Census_Firstname_Lastname**

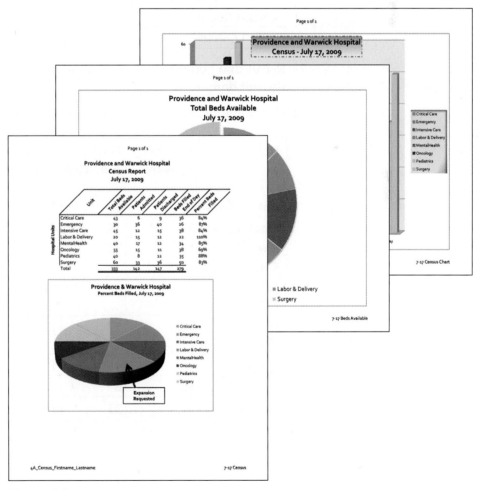

Figure 4.1
Project 4A—Census

Objective 1
Use Text Orientation

Information in cells can be displayed at an angle or vertically. Not only do these formats save space but they also add interest and a professional look to the worksheet.

Activity 4.1 Rotating Text in Cells

Long column titles are sometimes disproportionate to the data in the column. Placing the titles at an angle is a method used to maintain the worksheet data in close proximity and to balance the data with the column and row titles. Other text can also be placed vertically in a cell.

In this activity, you will create a report that displays the July 17 census—number of patients—for the hospital. You will format a worksheet, place column titles at an angle, and insert a vertical worksheet heading.

1 **Start** Excel and open to a new, blank workbook. Beginning in cell **A1**, type the following worksheet title:

Providence and Warwick Hospital
Census Report
'July 17, 2009

Recall that you type an apostrophe in front of a date so it displays the full date.

2 Beginning in cell **A5**, type the following data:

Unit	Total Beds Available	Patients Admitted	Patients Discharged	Beds Filled End of Day	Percent Beds Filled
Critical Care	43	6	9	36	
Emergency	32	36	40	26	
Intensive Care	45	12	15	38	
Labor & Delivery	20	15	12	22	
Mental Health	40	17	12	34	
Oncology	60	15	11	38	
Pediatrics	40	8	12	35	
Surgery	60	33	36	50	

3 Click the **Office** button 🖼, click **Save As**, and navigate to the location where you are saving your files for this chapter. Click the **Create New Folder** button 🖼. In the displayed **New Folder** dialog box, in the **Name** box, type **Excel Chapter 4** and click **OK**. In the **File name** area, type **4A_Census_Firstname_Lastname** and then click **Save**.

4 In cell **A14**, type **Total** Right-click the **column A** heading. From the shortcut menu, click **Insert**. In cell **A6**, type **Hospital Units** and press Enter.

5 Click cell **G6**. Enter the formula to determine the percentage of beds filled. This is determined by dividing the beds filled at the end of the day by the number of beds available—**=F6/C6** Copy the formula down through cell **G13**. With the range **G6:G13** selected, right-click and click the **Percent Style** button ⍣.

The Labor & Delivery unit needed to bring in temporary beds to cover the number of patients. Therefore, the percentage of beds filled exceeds 100%.

6 Select the worksheet title—**B1:B3**. Point to the border of the range and when the ⍣ pointer displays, drag the cells to the range **A1:A3**.

Recall that you copied cells using the drag-and-drop method. This same method can be used to move cells and ranges.

7 In the range **A1:A3**, apply **Bold** **B** emphasis and change the **Font Size** ⍣ to **14**. Select the range **A1:G1** and **Merge & Center** ⍣ the title. Using the skills you practiced, **Merge & Center** the title in **rows 2** and **3**.

8 Select the range **B5:G5**. Apply **Bold** **B** emphasis. Click the **Borders button arrow** ⍣ and click **All Borders**. In the **Alignment group**, click the **Wrap Text** ⍣, **Center** ⍣ and **Middle Align** ⍣ buttons.

9 With **B5:G5** still selected, in the **Alignment group**, point to the **Orientation** button ⍣ and review the ScreenTip. Then click the **Orientation button arrow** ⍣ to view the list and compare your screen with Figure 4.2.

The icon at the left of the menu displays the angle of the text for that specific selection.

Figure 4.2

Orientation button

Orientation menu

Icons display orientation of
text with each choice

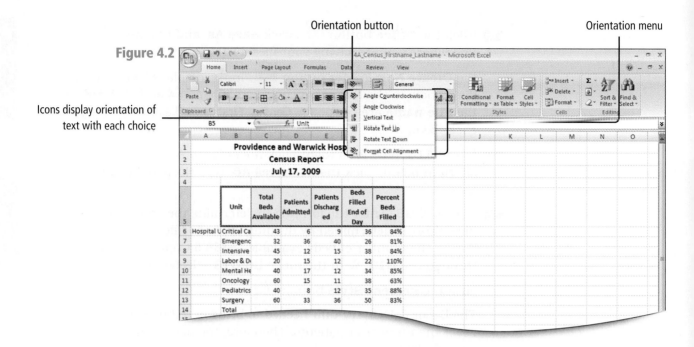

10 From the **Orientation list**, click **Angle Counterclockwise**. If necessary, adjust the height of **row 5** so that the column titles display on two lines, and then compare your screen with Figure 4.3.

Orientation in this context refers to a diagonal angle or vertical position of data within a cell. The default orientation is horizontal.

Figure 4.3

Column titles displayed at
angle on two lines

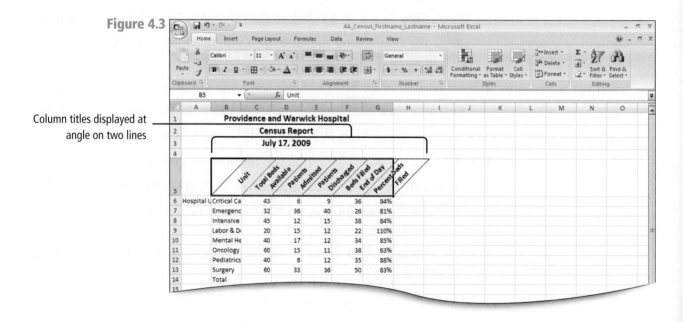

11 Click cell **B9**—the longest cell entry in column B—and in the **Cells group**, click the **Format button arrow**. Under **Cell Size**, click **AutoFit Column Width**.

12 Select the total row—**C14:F14**—and in the **Editing group**, click the **Sum** button ▢. Click the **Borders button arrow** ▢ and click **Top and Double Bottom Border**. Select the range of the worksheet—**C6:F14**—and in the **Number group**, click the **Comma Style** button ▢ and then click the **Decrease Decimal** button ▢ two times.

13 Select the range **A6:A13**. In the **Alignment group**, click the **Merge & Center** button ▢ and then click the **Middle Align** button ▢ Click the **Orientation button arrow** ▢ and from the displayed list, click **Rotate Text Up**. In the **Font group**, click the **Bold** button ▢. Click the **Borders button arrow** ▢ and from the list, click **Right Border**. Point to the boundary between **columns A** and **B** until the ▢ pointer displays, and drag to the left to reduce the column width until the ScreenTip displays **5.00 (40 pixels)**.

14 **Save** ▢ your workbook.

Objective 2
Create a Column Chart

A **chart** is a visual representation of numeric data found in a worksheet. In the hospital, charts graphically display comparisons in the number of beds filled, the relationship in number of patients between hospital departments, or salaries between employees. There are several chart types available with Excel, and deciding which style to use depends on the type of data to be charted. A **column chart** is used to display changes over a period of time or for illustrating comparisons among categories.

Activity 4.2 Creating a 3-D Column Chart

A column chart uses vertical columns to display the data. Each column represents the value in a cell in the worksheet and is called a **data marker**. Columns may be two-dimensional—height and width—or display with a 3-D effect, which adds depth to the column. In this activity, you will create a 3-D column chart in order to have a visual comparison of the hospital census for one day.

1 Select the range **B5:F13**.

When creating a chart, first select the data that will be charted. Include the column and row titles and the range of data. Do not include totals unless the chart will compare only the totals. In this chart, you will compare the actual number of beds filled for the different units in the hospital.

2 Click the **Insert tab**, and in the **Charts group**, click the **Column** button. From the displayed gallery, under **3-D Column**, point to the first chart and review the ScreenTip that reads *3-D Clustered Column*. Then click **3-D Clustered Column**, and compare your screen with Figure 4.4.

A 3-D column chart is inserted in the worksheet and covers part of the data. This chart is an ***embedded chart***—a chart that displays as an object within the worksheet. It is also an ***active chart***—a chart that is surrounded by a double border indicating that it may be edited, formatted, and moved.

The contextual tab—Chart Tools—displays on the Ribbon with three additional contextual tabs—Design, Layout, and Format—added.

The clustered chart displays all data markers for each unit together, beginning with the four data markers for the Critical Care unit. Each column in the chart is a data marker and represents one number in the worksheet. The ***legend*** at the right identifies the patterns or colors that are assigned to the data series or categories in a chart. For instance, the blue data markers represent the total beds available in each unit.

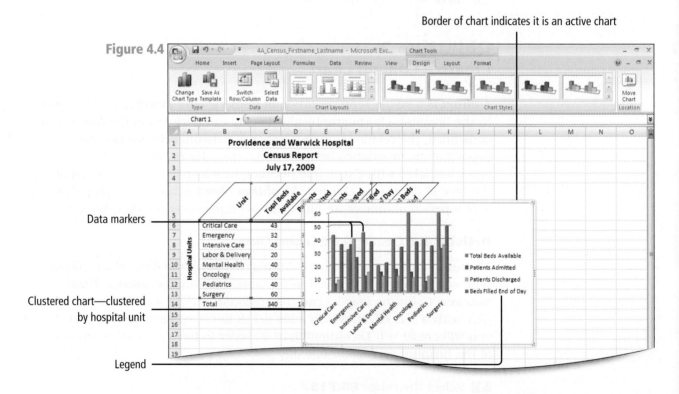

Figure 4.4

Border of chart indicates it is an active chart

Data markers

Clustered chart—clustered by hospital unit

Legend

3 Point to the top border of the chart to display the ⬚ pointer. Drag the upper left corner of the chart to the upper left corner of cell **A17**. In the worksheet, notice the solid borders that outline the ***chart range***—the range of cells that are included in the chart—and compare your screen with Figure 4.5.

Recall that a jagged border line moves on the screen as you drag the chart to its new location, serving as a visual indicator where the chart will be placed.

The range of the data values—C6:F13—is surrounded by blue lines and is represented by the columns of the worksheet. The information included in the legend—C5:F5—is surrounded by green borders and the labels at the bottom—the *Horizontal axis*—also called the *Category axis*—are outlined with purple lines.

Figure 4.5

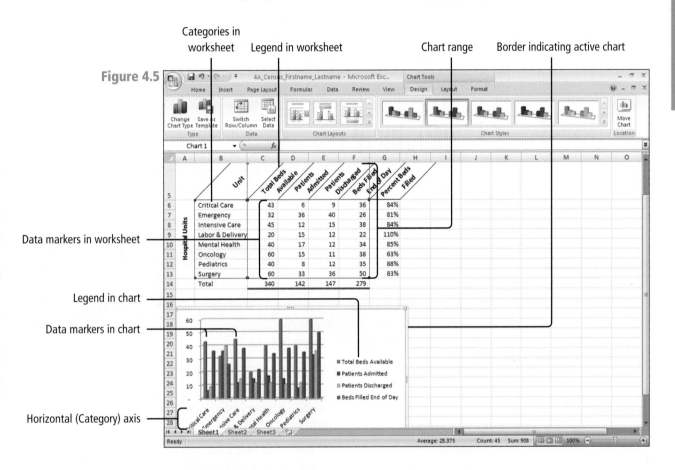

Categories in worksheet
Legend in worksheet
Chart range
Border indicating active chart

Data markers in worksheet

Legend in chart

Data markers in chart

Horizontal (Category) axis

4 Scroll to display the entire chart. On the **Design tab**, in the **Chart Layouts group**, click the **More** button ▾. In the displayed gallery, locate and click the chart style in the third row, the third chart— **Layout 9**. Compare your screen with Figure 4.6 and review the description of the elements of charts in the table in Figure 4.7.

The *chart layout* is the look of the chart, including the elements of the chart—for example, the legend, title, and gridlines.

Figure 4.6

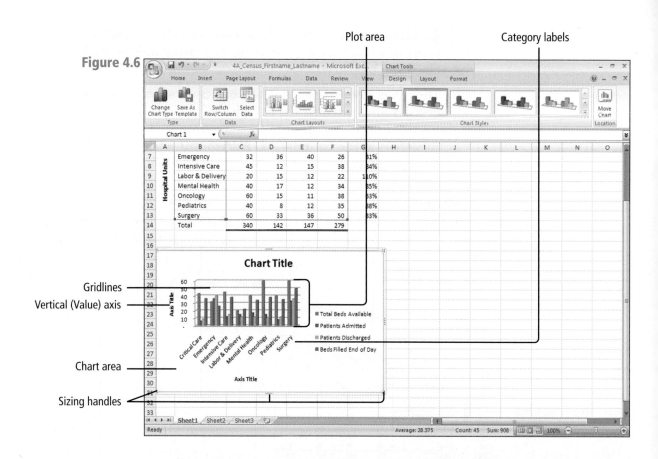

Plot area

Category labels

Gridlines

Vertical (Value) axis

Chart area

Sizing handles

	A	B	C	D	E	F	G
7		Emergency	32	36	40	26	81%
8		Intensive Care	45	12	15	38	84%
9		Labor & Delivery	20	15	12	22	110%
10		Mental Health	40	17	12	34	85%
11		Oncology	60	15	11	38	63%
12		Pediatrics	40	8	12	35	88%
13		Surgery	60	33	36	50	83%
14		Total	340	142	147	279	

Description of Chart Elements

Excel Chart Element	Description
Chart area	The entire chart and all of its elements.
Plot area	The area bordered by the axes, including all data series, category names, tick-mark labels, and gridlines.
Legend	The list that identifies the patterns or colors that are assigned to the data series or categories in a chart.
Data marker	Represents a single data point or value that originates from a worksheet cell.
Vertical (Value) axis	The axis on the left edge of the chart, which usually contains numeric values. A second vertical axis may also display on the right edge of the chart.
Horizontal (Category) axis	The axis along the lower edge of the chart data that contains categories on the horizontal plane.
Gridlines	Horizontal and vertical chart lines that extend from any horizontal and vertical axes across the plot area of the chart.

(Continued)

(Continued)

Data series	Related values in a single row or column that are plotted in a chart.
Chart titles	Descriptive text that is aligned to an axis or centered at the top of a chart.
Data labels	A label that provides additional information about a data marker, which represents a single data point or value that originates from a worksheet cell.
Category labels	The labels that identify specific categories of a chart.
Axis titles	Titles that display at the far left and bottom of the chart that identify the type of data in that area.

Figure 4.7

[5] Click in the worksheet and outside the chart. Compare your screen with Figure 4.8. **Save** 💾 your workbook.

The border of the chart becomes a single line, which indicates this is an *inactive chart*. An inactive chart cannot be edited.

Solid border indicating inactive chart

Figure 4.8

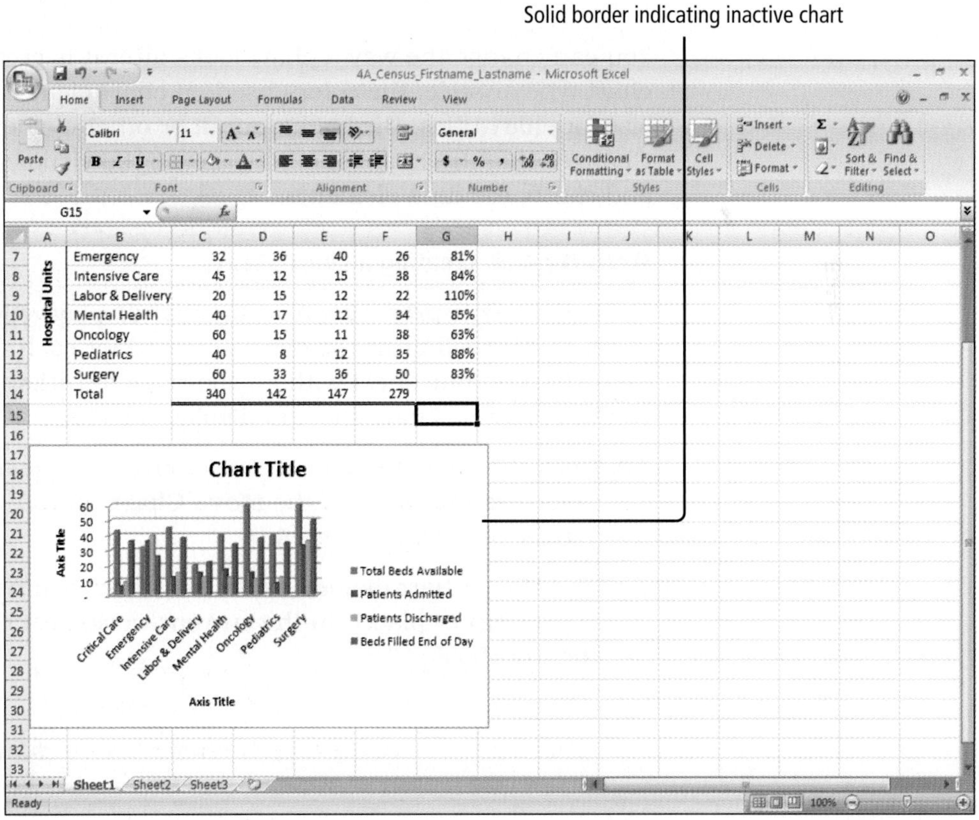

More Knowledge

Changing the Size of an Embedded Chart

The size of an embedded chart can be changed using the *sizing handles* at each corner and in the center of each border of the *active chart*, identified by small dots. As you position the pointer over the sizing handles, a double-headed arrow displays, indicating the directions that the chart can be moved. The ↕ pointer is used to increase or decrease the height of the chart. The ↔ pointer is used to increase or decrease the width of the chart. The ⬉ and the ⬈ pointer shapes increase or decrease both the height and width at the same time.

Objective 3
Create a Chart Sheet and Edit the Chart

When a chart is created, the chart elements use default settings that affect how the data displays. By default, charts are embedded in a worksheet that displays both the chart and the worksheet. A chart may display on a separate sheet in a workbook, called a *chart sheet*.

You can change the way a chart looks after it is created by changing the chart type or style, the colors used on chart elements, the font and font size for chart titles, the background, or other elements in the chart. Changes that are made should increase the visual appeal of the chart and clarify the data elements.

Activity 4.3 Creating a Chart Sheet

Maria Benitez is preparing a report that displays the daily census for the hospital. She will print the charts created for each day and will display each chart on one sheet without the related worksheet. In this activity, you will create a chart sheet to display the chart.

1. Click the chart to make it active. From the **Design tab**, and in the **Location group**, click the **Move Chart** button, and then compare your screen with Figure 4.9.

   The Move Chart dialog box is used to determine the placement of the chart—either placed in the current worksheet or in a new sheet of the workbook.

Figure 4.9

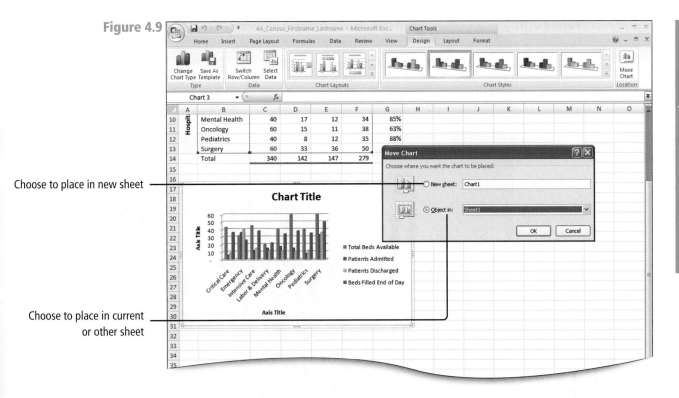

Choose to place in new sheet

Choose to place in current or other sheet

In the **Move Chart** dialog box, click **New sheet**. At the right, in the text box, type **7-17 Census Chart** and then click **OK**. Compare your screen with Figure 4.10.

A new active worksheet named *7-17 Census Chart* is inserted to the left of Sheet1, which contains the data range. You have created and named the new chart sheet at the same time.

Figure 4.10

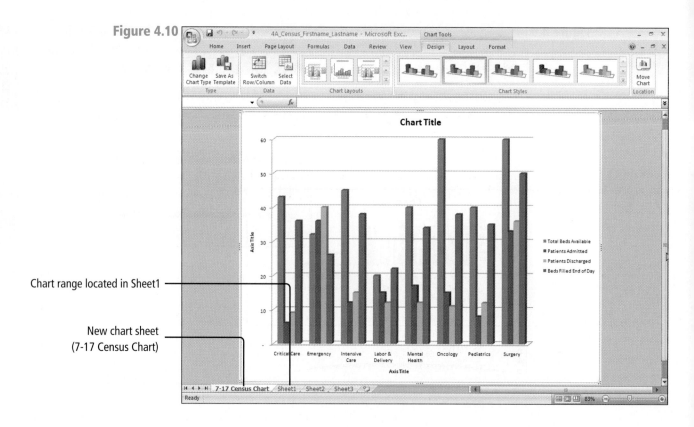

Chart range located in Sheet1

New chart sheet
(7-17 Census Chart)

3 Click the **Chart Title** to make it active—surrounded by solid lines with sizing handles at each corner. Type **Providence & Warwick Hospital** and as you do, notice it is inserted in the Formula Bar. Press Enter. Right-click in the chart title and change the **Font Size** ⌷11 ▾⌷ to **20**.

In a chart sheet, the double border surrounds the chart. The only visual cues that indicate it is active are the dots at each corner and in the center of each border.

Alert

Are you typing in the chart title and not the Formula Bar?

If the new title is inserted into the *Chart Title* text, click the Undo button ⌷↩⌷ and click outside the chart title to deselect it. Click again in the chart title—which will be surrounded by a solid border—and immediately begin typing.

4 Click in the **Chart Title** box, position the insertion point at the end of the word *Hospital*, press Enter, and type **Census – July 17, 2009** and then click in the chart to deselect the title. **Save** ⌷💾⌷ your workbook.

Activity 4.4 Changing Chart Type and Style

The ***chart type*** determines the way the data is presented—as a column, line, bar, pie, or some other graphical element that displays the relationship among the data—whereas ***chart styles*** determine the colors used in the chart. There are several chart types and chart styles available. In this activity, you will change the type and style of the chart. The chart that was created for Maria Benitez will be enhanced to better display the relationships in a professional manner.

1 Click the **7-17 Census Chart sheet** to make it active. On the **Design tab**, in the **Type group**, click the **Change Chart Type** button. Compare your screen with Figure 4.11.

The Change Chart Type dialog box displays the types of charts available in the left section, which includes Column, Line, Pie, Bar, and other charts. The right area of this dialog box displays the way each specific chart subtype will display when it is selected. The displayed chart is highlighted by a yellow-orange border.

Alert

Does your Change Chart Type dialog box display a different number of icons on each row?

The Change Chart Type dialog box can be adjusted in size using the sizing handles in the lower right corner of the dialog box. The number of chart icons that display on each line depends on the size of your Change Chart Type dialog box.

Figure 4.11

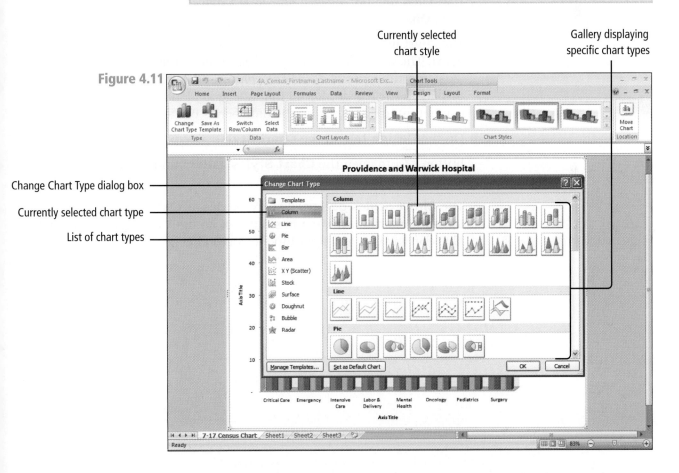

Currently selected chart style

Gallery displaying specific chart types

Change Chart Type dialog box

Currently selected chart type

List of chart types

2 In the **Change Chart Type** dialog box, on the left side, click **Bar**. At the right, click the dialog box **scroll bar** to display the rows of bar charts.

3 In the right section of the **Change Chart Type** dialog box, under **Bar**, using the ScreenTips as your guide locate and click the **Clustered Horizontal Cone**, and then click **OK**.

The chart in your worksheet has been changed to the Clustered Horizontal Cone style. As you review the chart, notice that it is difficult to compare the data in the worksheet. The values of the data in this chart cause the cones to display as paper-thin cones, making the data markers difficult to compare.

4 In the **Type group**, click the **Change Chart Type** button to display the **Change Chart Type** dialog box. On the left side of the **Change Chart Type** dialog box, click **Line**. Click the highlighted suggestion—*Line with Markers*—and then click **OK**.

A line chart displays, showing the comparison for each unit. Although it is easy to see the relationships among the data, a line chart is typically used to show a trend over time and is not a good choice for this data.

5 In the **Type group**, click the **Change Chart Type** button, and then in the **Change Chart Type** dialog box, click **Column**. On the first row, click the fourth selection—**3-D Clustered Column**—and then click **OK**.

The chart in the worksheet has changed to the 3-D Clustered Column chart. The hospital units display along the lower edge in the category axis, and the types of data—the column titles in the worksheet—display in the legend. Recall that a legend identifies the patterns or colors that are assigned to the data series or categories in a chart.

6 On the **Design tab**, in the **Chart Styles group**, click the **More** button ⬇ to open the **Chart Styles gallery** and compare your screen with Figure 4.12.

The *Chart Styles gallery* displays styles available for the chart and includes charts formatted in shades of an individual color, shades of black and white, and a multiple-colored chart.

Currently active
chart style

Chart Tools
Design tab

Figure 4.12

Chart Styles gallery

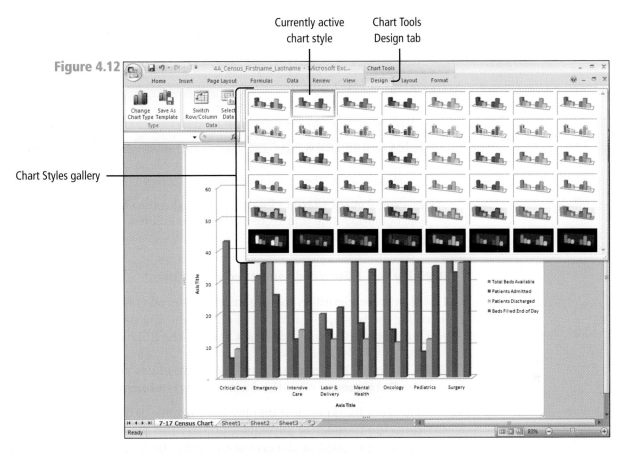

7 On the **Chart Styles gallery**, in the second column, locate and click the fifth choice—**Style 34**. **Save** your workbook.

The Chart Styles gallery closes and the style of the chart is changed to reflect the selected style, which includes a 3-D effect on the data markers, and the background of the chart displays in gray color.

More Knowledge

Determining Which Chart Type to Use

Column chart	Shows data changes over a period of time or for illustrating comparisons among items.
Line chart	Displays continuous data over time. Use for showing trends in data at equal intervals.
Pie chart	Shows the proportion of each data item to the sum of the whole. All data points must be positive values and only one data range—row or column—may be charted.
Bar chart	Used to illustrate comparisons among individual items.

Planning the Chart

Like worksheets, charts require a professional appearance and accuracy. In addition to selecting the correct chart to illustrate the data, it needs to be easy to read. Below are guidelines for creating a chart.

- **Determine the purpose of the chart**. Match the chart type to the purpose of the chart and select an appropriate style.

- **Include a title**. Like worksheets, charts need identifying information that includes the organization name, the purpose of the chart, and the date of the charted data. This information may be included in the header or footer.

- **Be careful about charting totals**. Charts that compare data within the chart will not include the totals. Charts that include totals chart only the totals.

Activity 4.5 Editing and Formatting a Chart Title

The chart title identifies the organization—even if it is an internal document for the hospital—purpose of chart, and the date. In this activity, you will edit and format the chart title for the July 17 census.

1. With the **7-17 Census Chart** the active sheet, on the **Design tab**, in the **Data group**, click the **Switch Row/Column** button.

   The data markers now display the number of beds available in each unit, the number of patients admitted and discharged, and the number of beds filled at the end of the day. The legend displays the units in the hospital.

2. Click the **chart title** to make it active—a border surrounds the perimeter of the selected element. Sizing handles display at each corner. Compare your screen with Figure 4.13.

Figure 4.13

Chart title · Border indicating title is active

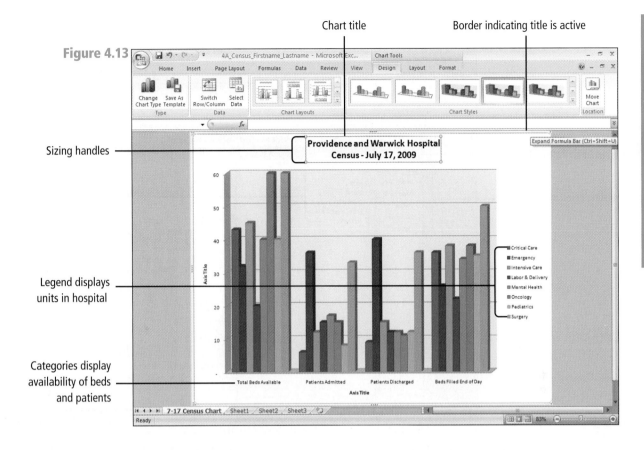

Sizing handles

Legend displays
units in hospital

Categories display
availability of beds
and patients

3 Click the **Layout tab**, and in the **Labels group**, click the **Chart Title** button. In the displayed list, click **Centered Overlay Title**.

When you select to overlay the title, the space reserved for the title decreases. The **plot area**—the area bordered by the axes—increases in size.

4 With the chart title active, click the **Format tab**. In the **Current Selection** group, click the **Format Selection** button, and then compare your screen with Figure 4.14.

The Format Chart Title dialog box opens. This dialog box is divided into two sections. The left section lists the types of formatting available for a chart title. The section at the right displays format choices for the type of formatting that has been selected.

When options are changed in this dialog box, the changes are immediately applied to the selected chart element, making it easy to see the effects of the change without closing the dialog box.

Fill is selected at the left and the Fill options—*No fill, Solid fill, Gradient fill,* etc.—display at the right. **Fill** refers to the color or pattern in the interior of a shape, line, or character.

Figure 4.14

Specific formatting choices for Fill

Format Chart Title dialog box

Formatting selections available

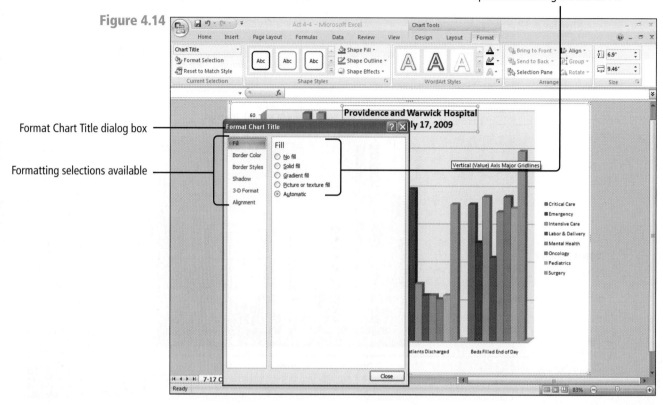

5 In the **Format Chart Title** dialog box, with **Fill** selected, click **Gradient fill**. Point to the title bar of the **Format Chart Title** dialog box and drag it to the left side of your screen until you can see most of the Chart Title area.

With this selection, additional information is requested. A *gradient fill* is a gradual progression of colors and shades, usually from one color to another color, or from one shade to another shade of the same color.

Specific instructions about the gradient fill can be selected in this dialog box.

6 Click the **Preset colors button arrow** to display the gallery. Then compare your screen with Figure 4.15.

The Preset colors display a gallery of colors that can be used for the fill of the selected chart element.

Preset colors buton

Figure 4.15

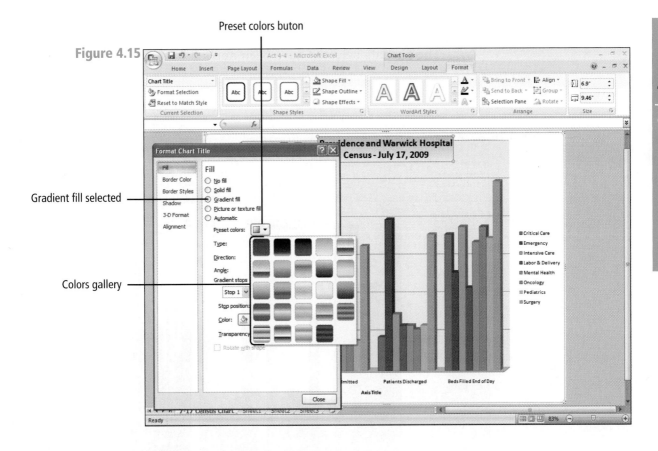

Gradient fill selected

Colors gallery

7 On the top row, locate and click the fourth color—**Daybreak**.

The gradient color in the title box begins with a darker blue color and gradually progresses to a very light blue color with a tinge of pink. The gradient color is immediately applied to the chart title.

8 In the **Format Chart Title** dialog box, in the list at the left, click **Border Color**. At the right side of the dialog box, click **Solid line**. Click the **Color** button to display the **Color gallery**, and then in the eighth column, click the last color—**Purple, Accent 4, Darker 50%**.

When Solid line is selected, choices about its color display. The Color gallery displays both the theme and standard colors.

9 In the **Format Chart Title** dialog box, on the left side, click the **Border Styles**. On the right side, click the **Dash type** button and then click the fifth selection—**Dash Dot**. In the **Width** box, click the **up spin arrow** until **1.5 pt** displays.

The *border style* is the style of the *border line*—the line that surrounds the title or other chart element. The width of the border can be adjusted.

10 In the **Format Chart Title** dialog box, on the left side, click **Shadow**. On the right side, click the **Presets** button. Under **Outer**, in the third row, click the first option—**Offset Diagonal Top Right**.

A small shadow is added to the title at the top and right of the chart title. In this section, the color of the shadow can also be specified.

11 Click **Close** and compare your screen with Figure 4.16.

The formats selected have been applied to the worksheet title.

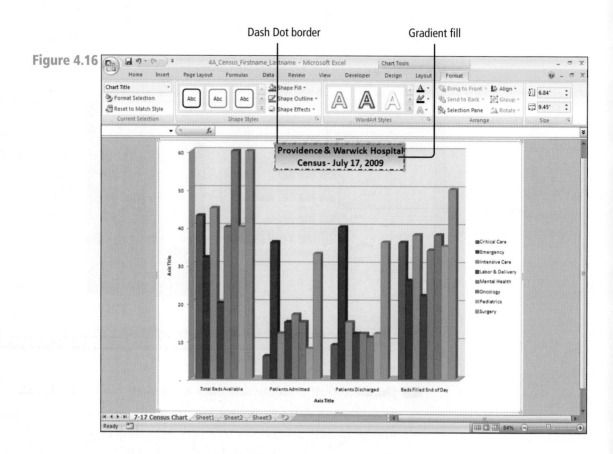

Figure 4.16

Dash Dot border

Gradient fill

12 On the **Quick Access Toolbar**, click the **Undo button arrow** and display the list of recently applied commands. Compare your screen with Figure 4.17.

Figure 4.17

Shadow command

List of commands in order of completion

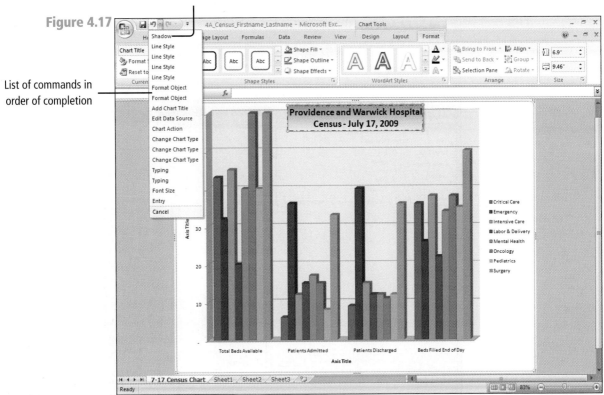

13 Click the first choice—**Shadow**—to remove the shadow from the title. **Save** your workbook.

Recall that the Undo button is used to undo commands made in the worksheet. Recall also that once a command is selected in the Format Chart Title dialog box, it is immediately applied to the cell and Undo is used to remove it.

Activity 4.6 Editing and Formatting a Chart Legend

The legend is used to identify the data markers in the chart, so it should be easy to review. In this activity, you will edit the chart legend.

1 In the chart, click anywhere on the **legend** to make it active.

Recall that a chart element is active when a solid line surrounds it and the sizing handles display. Because the legend is large, sizing handles also display in the center of each side.

2 Click the **Layout tab** and in the **Current Selection group**, click **Format Selection** and compare your screen with Figure 4.18.

The Current Selection group is available on both the Layout and the Format Chart Tools tabs. The Format Legend dialog box displays and is similar to the Format Chart Titles dialog box. When working with charts, each element can be independently formatted using a dialog box similar to this.

Figure 4.18

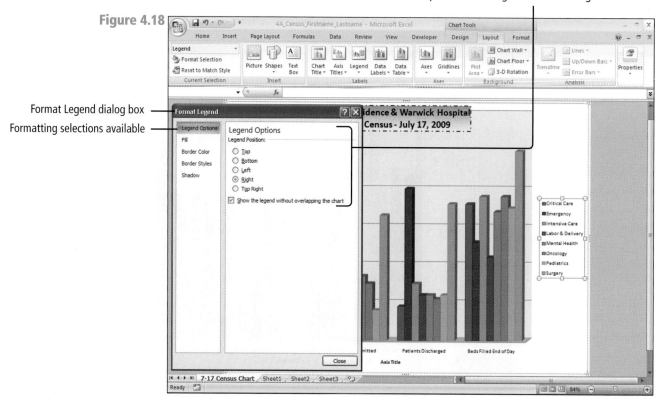

Format Legend dialog box

Formatting selections available

3 On the **Format Legend** dialog box, at the left side, click **Fill**. On the right, click **Gradient fill**. Click the **Preset colors** button to display the **Color gallery**, and then in the second row, click the last option—**Fog**—and as you do, watch the color of the legend change. Click the **Direction** button to display the gallery and then click the first choice—**Linear Diagonal**—and as you do, watch the color of the legend change. Click the **Color** button to display the **Color gallery**. In the eighth column, click the third color—**Purple, Accent 4, Lighter 60%**. Click **Close** and compare your screen with Figure 4.19.

Figure 4.19

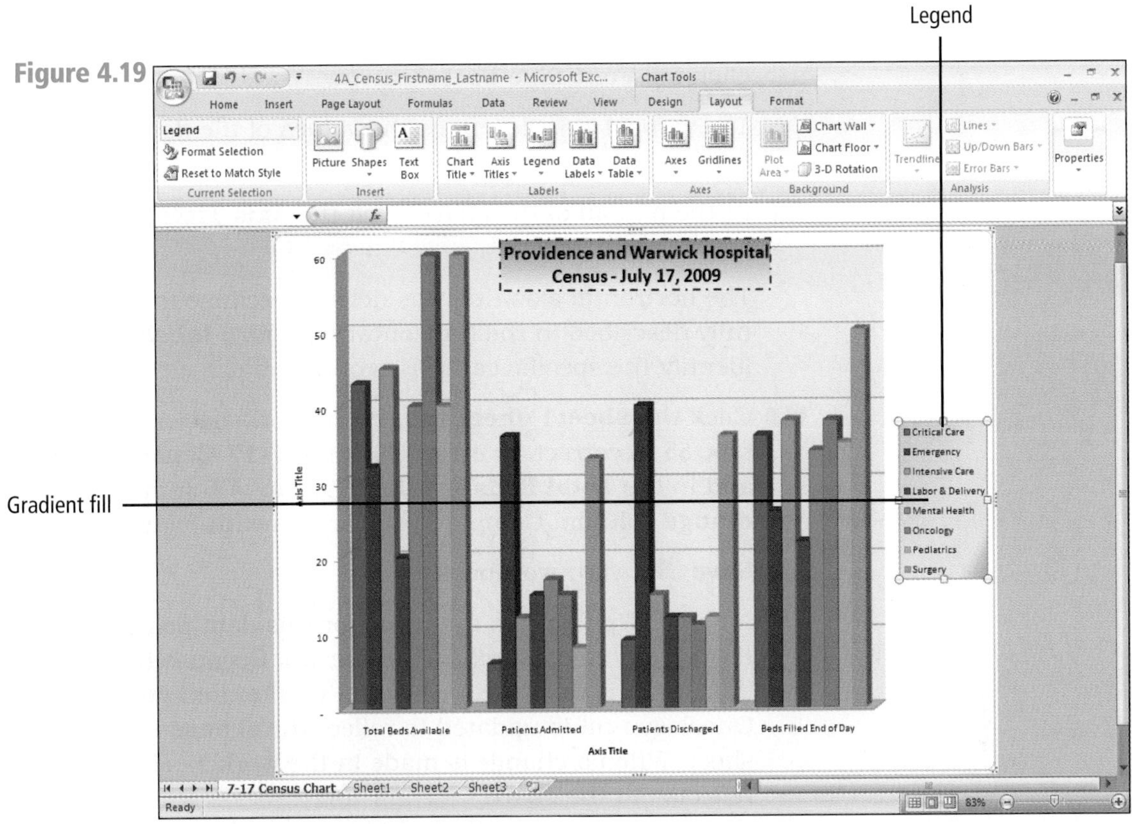

Legend

Gradient fill

4 In the active **Legend** right-click and from the shortcut menu, click **Format Legend**. In the **Format Legend** dialog box, on the left, click **Shadow**. Under **Shadow** on the right, click the **Presets** button, and then under **Inner**, in the first row, click the third style—**Inside Diagonal Top Right**. Click **Close**. **Save** your workbook.

To format a chart element, you can access the Format dialog box using the Current Selection button in the Ribbon, or you can select the command from the shortcut menu.

Activity 4.7 Adding Axis Titles and Editing Worksheet Data

The chart style provides a place for *axis titles*, which further describe the data displayed in the chart. When the worksheet data is edited, the changes are reflected in the chart because the worksheet is *linked*—connected—to the chart. In this activity, you will add **axis titles** and edit the data in the worksheet so the chart provides better explanation to the hospital staff.

1 In the **7-17 Census Chart sheet**, at the left edge of the chart, click the **Axis Title** to select it. Type **Census** which displays in the Formula Bar. Watch the title at the left edge as you press Enter.

As you type data into the active chart element, it is entered into the Formula Bar. When you press Enter, the typed text replaces the text in the selected element—Axis Title.

2 Right-click the **Census** axis title and on the displayed Mini toolbar, click the **Font Size button arrow** `11 ▾`, and then click **16**.

The vertical axis describes the values of the data markers—the census.

3 At the bottom of the chart, click the **Axis Title** to select it, and then press Delete.

The horizontal axis title was deleted because the data markers are fully described in the horizontal *category labels*—the labels that identify the specific categories of the chart.

4 Click the **Sheet1 sheet tab**. In the worksheet, click cell **C11** and type **55** to correct an error. Click the **7-17-Census Chart sheet tab** and in the **Total Beds Available** group of columns, point to the **orange** column. Compare your screen with Figure 4.20, and then **Save** 💾 your workbook.

A ScreenTip displays the value for this data point—*Series "Oncology" Point "Total Beds Available" Value: 55*. Because the chart data is linked to the worksheet, the data marker for beds available in the Oncology unit is updated to reflect the change made in the worksheet. When a change is made in the worksheet, the change is also reflected in the chart.

ScreenTip reflects value for this data point

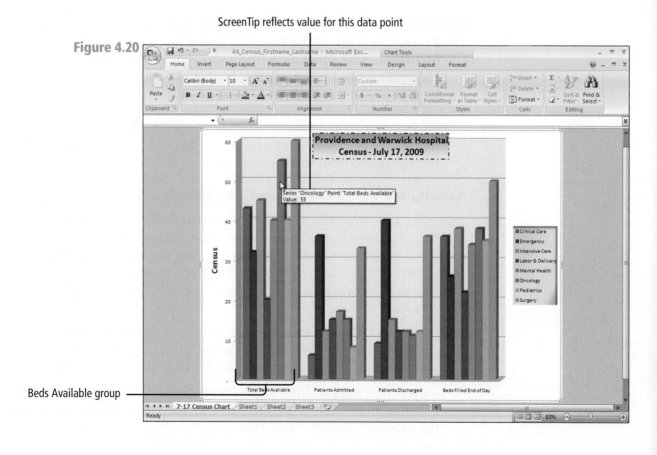

Figure 4.20

Beds Available group

Objective 4
Create and Modify a Pie Chart

A ***pie chart*** is a round chart that shows the relationship of parts to the whole. In a pie chart, each data marker—value from a worksheet cell—is a portion of the pie. Pie charts display only one data series and negative numbers cannot be displayed. When creating a pie chart, using fewer than seven categories is recommended.

Activity 4.8 Creating a Pie Chart

The hospital is considering an expansion and Paul Scheinman, the CEO, has requested that reports and charts be provided for the daily census. Because the Surgery area has the most beds, it will be highlighted in the chart. In this activity, you will create a pie chart that will compare the beds available.

1 Click the **Sheet1 sheet tab**. Select the range **B5:C13**. Click the **Insert tab**, and in the **Charts group**, click **Pie** to display the **Pie chart gallery**. Under **2-D Pie**, point to and click the first chart—**Pie**. Compare your screen with Figure 4.21.

The 2-D pie chart displays in the worksheet. The title of the chart matches the column title in the worksheet. Each department is displayed in a different color. By reviewing the size of the pieces of the pie, a comparison of the available beds in each unit can be made.

Pie chart title matches worksheet column title

Figure 4.21

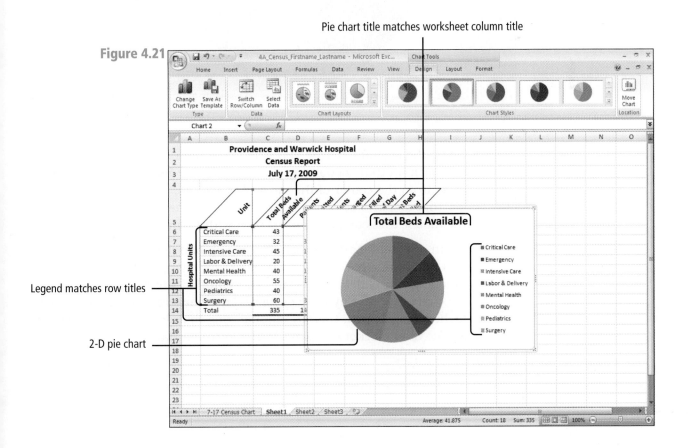

Legend matches row titles

2-D pie chart

2 With the chart active, in the **Location group**, click **Move Chart**. In the **Move Chart** dialog box, click **New sheet**. In the text box, type **7-17 Beds Available** and then click **OK**.

3 Click in the center of the pie chart and compare your screen with Figure 4.22.

Sizing handles display at the edge of each data marker—piece of pie—in the chart and in the center.

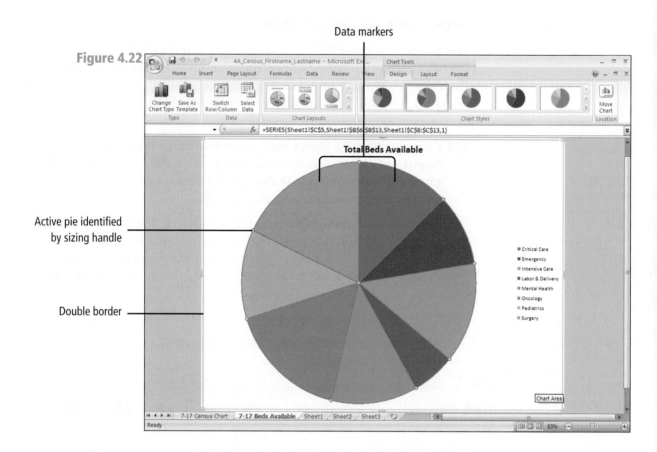

Figure 4.22

Active pie identified by sizing handle

Double border

4 Using the legend to assist you, locate the data marker for **Surgery** and click on that section to select it. Drag the **Surgery** piece slightly away from the center of the pie and as you do, notice the dash border that displays as a visual indicator of the new location. Release the mouse and compare your screen with Figure 4.23.

When one data marker is selected, sizing handles are active only on that data marker. When the data markers on a pie chart are not touching, the chart has become an **exploded pie chart**—a style of pie chart that displays one or more data markers "outside" or unattached to the chart, thereby emphasizing that data. The source data for the data markers displays in the Formula Bar.

Sizing handles on data marker   Pie chart

Figure 4.23

Data marker source displays on the Formula Bar

Exploded data marker

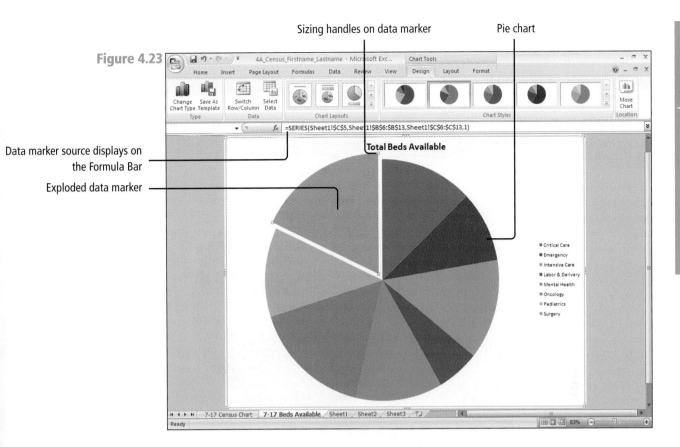

5 Click the **chart title** to make it active. Position the insertion point to the left of the word *Total*. Press Enter, and then press the ↑ and type **Providence & Warwick Hospital**

6 Position the insertion point at the end of the second line—after *Available*—press Enter, and type **July 17, 2009**

The chart title fully describes the chart—the name of organization, what the chart displays, and the date.

7 Click the pie chart to make the entire chart active. On the **Design tab**, in the **Chart Styles group**, click the **More** button [▼].

The Chart Styles gallery displays the styles available for the pie chart.

8 On the **Chart Styles gallery**, in the second column, point to and click the last chart—**Style 42**.

The chart style with black background is applied to the chart. The text displays in white so it contrasts with the background. With the black background, the chart is effective in Excel or in a PowerPoint presentation. However, it is inappropriate to use if the chart will be printed.

9 Display the **Chart Styles gallery**, and in the second column, point to and click the second chart—**Style 10**.

10 Click the **Layout tab**, and in the **Labels group**, click the **Legend** button. Compare your screen with Figure 4.24.

At the left side of the Legend gallery, the figure displays the legend in yellow and provides visualization of where the legend will be placed in the chart.

Figure 4.24

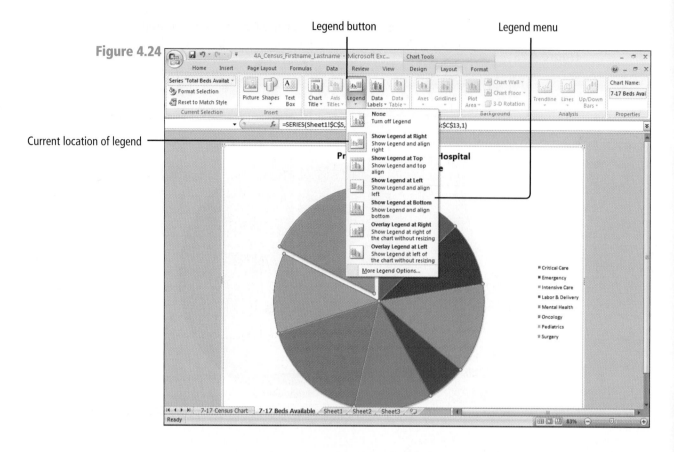

Legend button

Legend menu

Current location of legend

11 From the displayed **Legend gallery**, click **Show Legend at Bottom**.

The legend displays at the bottom of the chart.

12 Right-click the **Legend** and on the Mini toolbar, click the **Font Size button arrow** `11 ▾`, and then click **14**. **Save** 🖫 your workbook.

The legend text has been increased in size. It is recommended that text in a worksheet or chart be large enough to be easily read.

Activity 4.9 Creating a 3-D Pie Chart Using Nonadjacent Cells

Recall that a pie chart uses only one *data series*—a single row or column of data. The row or column titles are selected to identify the values, but sometimes the data series are not adjacent to the titles. Because the hospital is considering an expansion, Paul Scheinman, the CEO, has requested that daily reports and charts be provided for the daily census. In this activity you will create a pie chart that will compare the percentages of beds that are filled July 17.

1 Click the **Sheet1 sheet tab**. In the **Name Box**—recall the Name Box is at the far left edge of Formula Bar—type **b5:b13,g5:g13** and press Enter to select these two nonadjacent ranges. Alternatively, select the range B5:B13, press Ctrl, and select the range G5:G13.

This pie chart will compare the percent of beds filled in each unit, which is one data series. Recall that you use the Ctrl key to select nonadjacent ranges.

2 Click the **Insert tab**, and in the **Charts group**, click the **Pie** button. Under **3-D** click the first choice—**Pie in 3-D**.

A 3-D pie chart titled *Percent Beds Filled* displays on the worksheet.

3 Point to the edge of the chart and when the 🔀 pointer displays, drag the chart to position the upper left corner of the chart in cell **A16**.

4 Click the **chart title** to make it active; a solid border surrounds the chart title. Position the insertion point to the left of the title, *Percent Beds Filled*. Press Enter, and then press ↑ and type **Providence & Warwick Hospital** Select the hospital name, and from the faded Mini toolbar that displays, click the **Font Size button arrow** `11 ▾` and click **14**.

5 Select **Percent Beds Filled** and from the Mini toolbar, click the **Font Size button arrow** `11 ▾` and click **11**. To the right of *Percent Beds Filled* type **July 17, 2009 Save** 💾 your workbook.

The chart title identifies the chart and is placed on two lines.

Activity 4.10 Rotating a Pie Chart

When creating a pie chart, it is recommended that the largest data marker be displayed immediately to the right of the 12 o'clock position. In this activity, you will rotate the pie chart.

1 On **Sheet1**, in the chart, click on the pie to select it. Click the **Layout tab**, and in the **Current Selection group**, click the **Format Selection** button. If the **Format Data Series** dialog box covers the pie chart, click in the title bar and drag it to the right to fully view the chart.

The Format Data Series dialog box is similar to the Chart Title and Legend dialog boxes you have previously used. Recall that each chart element can be formatted independently using a similar dialog box.

2 In the **Format Data Series** dialog box, confirm that the left side indicates **Series Options**. On the **right side**, in the **Series Options** area, under **Angle of first slice**, drag the **slide** until a number between **228–232** displays in the box below the slide—it is difficult to move the slide to the exact number. Alternatively, type **228** in the rotation display box. Compare your screen with Figure 4.25, and then click **Close. Save** 💾 your workbook.

Rotation changes the orientation and perspective of the selected chart element. The slide can be used to change the angle of the first slice in the pie; and when you release the slide, the live preview displays the change to the chart.

The orientation of the chart has changed. The largest piece—Labor & Delivery—has moved to the top right data marker, a recommended location for the largest data marker.

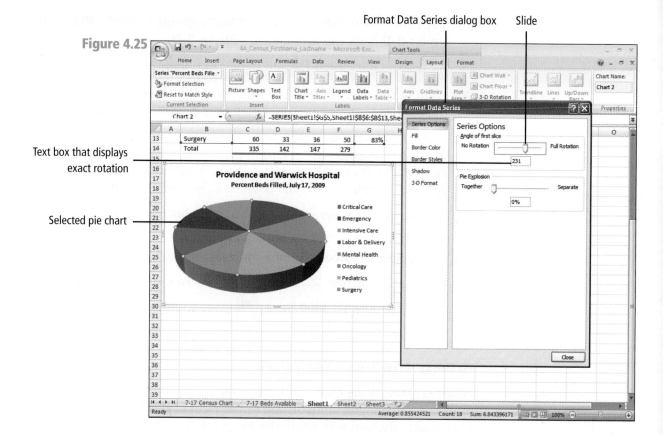

Figure 4.25

Format Data Series dialog box   **Slide**

Text box that displays exact rotation

Selected pie chart

Activity 4.11 Inserting a Text Box in a Chart

A *text box* is used to add additional information to a chart or worksheet and can be formatted and moved independently from cells on the worksheet or elements of the chart. An arrow from the text box to the data marker is used to indicate the specific data marker referenced. In this activity, you will add a text box and place an arrow from the text box to the data marker.

1 Double-click the **Sheet1 sheet tab**, type **7-17 Census** and then press [Enter].

2 Click the chart to make it active and on the lower border of the chart, point to the center sizing handle. When ↕ displays, drag down until the lower edge of the chart covers **row 36**.

The size of the chart is expanded. Similarly, you can increase the width of the chart by clicking a sizing handle on the side of the chart and dragging to the right.

3 Confirm the chart is active. Click the **Layout tab** and in the **Insert group**, click the **Text Box** button.

When you click the text box nothing appears to change. However, when you move the mouse pointer onto the worksheet, it will take a new shape, which will enable you to "draw" a text box by dragging the mouse.

4 Position the ↓ pointer in the upper right corner of the chart, at approximately the **row 19** header and under the **column D** header. Drag down to about **row 21** and to the right to cover approximately

columns D and **E** to insert a text box. Compare your screen with Figure 4.26.

A box is formed. A text box is used to enter text in a chart—or worksheet—and can overlay the existing data. The insertion point blinks in the text box.

When the text box is inserted, the Ribbon displays the Drawing Tools Format tab, and when the text box is active, the Home tab is active.

Note

If you are not satisfied with the size and shape of the text box, press Delete and try again.

Home tab (displays when text box is active)

Drawing Tools Format tab (inactive)

Figure 4.26

Text box (active)

Chart expanded to row 36

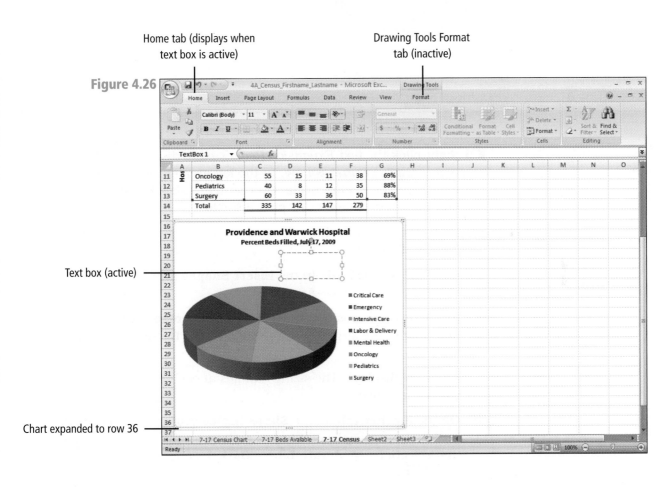

At the insertion point, type **Expansion Requested** Select the text you typed and on the **Home tab**, in the **Font group**, click the **Bold** button **B**. In the **Alignment group**, click the **Center** button and **Middle Align** button and compare your screen with Figure 4.27.

Figure 4.27

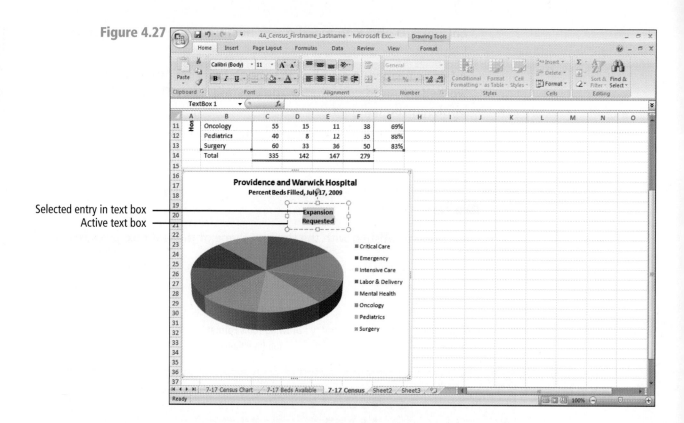

Selected entry in text box —

Active text box —

6 Right-click the text *Expansion Requested* to display the shortcut menu. Click **Format Shape**. In the left area of the **Format Shape** dialog box, click **Line Style**. On the right side, click the **Width spin box up arrow** to select **.75 pt**. Click **Close**.

Right-clicking on a chart element is another method of accessing its Format dialog box.

7 Click the **Format tab**. In the **Insert Shapes group**, in the first row, click the third shape—**Arrow**.

8 At the text box, position the pointer at the **bottom border**, and click and drag to the largest piece of the pie—the **Labor & Delivery** data marker.

An arrow displays. The sizing handles at each edge of the arrow indicates it is active.

9 On the **Format tab**, in the **Shape Styles group**, click the **More** button. In the displayed **Shapes gallery**, in the second row, click the first selection—**Moderate Line – Dark 1**—and compare your screen with Figure 4.28.

Figure 4.28

Arrow in Insert Shapes group

Selected arrow style

Shape Styles group

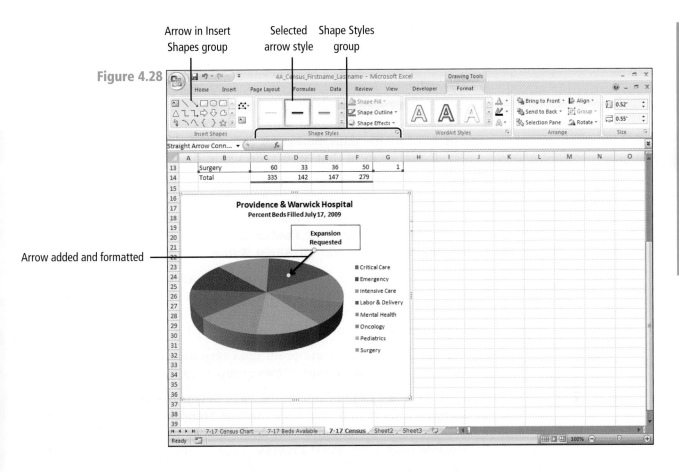

Arrow added and formatted

10 Click in the chart to deselect the arrow and **Save** your workbook.

Objective 5
Apply a Theme to a Chart

Recall that worksheets are formatted according to a **_theme_**—a combination of complementary colors, fonts, and effects. When a chart is created in the workbook, it uses the same theme as the rest of the workbook.

Activity 4.12 Changing the Theme in a Chart

When a theme is applied, it is applied to all sheets in the workbook, including those containing a chart. In this activity you will change the theme in the workbook, which will affect the charts.

1 With the **7-17 Census sheet** active, click the **Page Layout tab**, and in the **Themes group**, click the **Themes** button. In the displayed **Themes gallery**, under Built-In, in the last row, click the second choice—**Trek**.

This theme displays the Franklin Gothic and Franklin Gothic Book fonts. The chart has enlarged and the text box spills onto the pie chart.

2 Display the **Themes gallery** again; in the third row, click the third choice—**Module**.

This theme provides more color in the chart.

3 Click each of the sheets in the workbook and review the colors that the Module theme uses for the worksheet and charts.

Recall that when you change a theme, the font also changes and formats may be altered. If your text box spills into the chart, use the handles to adjust the size of the text box or move it out away from the chart.

4 On the **7-17 Census** sheet, click cell **C7** and type **30** to change the number of beds available in the Emergency Room. Then review each chart, locate the data marker for *Beds Available in the Emergency Room*, and confirm that **30** is reflected in the charts.

5 **Delete Sheet2** and **Sheet3**. Click the **7-17 Census sheet tab** and confirm the chart is not selected. Click the **Insert tab**, and in the **Text group**, click **Header & Footer**. In the **Navigation group**, click **Go to Footer**. In the **Left Footer** area, add the **File Name** and in the **Right Footer** area add the **Sheet Name**.

6 Just below the footer, click **Click to add header**. Type **Page** press Spacebar, and in the **Header & Footer Elements group**, click the **Page Number** button. Then press Spacebar and type **of** press Spacebar, and then in the **Header & Footer Elements group**, click **Number of Pages**.

7 Click in the worksheet and press Ctrl + Home to return to cell **A1**. On the **View tab**, in the **Workbook Views group**, click the **Normal** button.

8 Click the **Page Layout tab**. In the **Page Setup group**, click the **Margins** button, and then click **Custom Margins**. In the **Page Setup** dialog box, on the **Margins tab**, under **Center on page**, click **Horizontally**. Click **Print Preview**. Confirm the worksheet is centered.

9 **Close Print Preview** and **Save** 🖫 your workbook.

Objective 6
Print Charts

Like worksheets, a chart sheet may include a header and footer, be centered on the page, and print in either portrait or landscape orientation. A chart that is embedded on the same sheet as a worksheet can be printed with the worksheet or as a separate document.

Activity 4.13 Inserting Headers and Footers for Chart Sheets

Excel recognizes two types of sheets in a workbook—worksheets and chart sheets—and will add a header or footer to only one type of worksheet, even if they are grouped. Therefore, when you enter a header or footer, you need to group the two types of sheets separately. In this activity, you will group the chart sheets and enter headers and footers.

1 Click the **7-17 Census Chart sheet**, press Shift, and click the **7-17 Beds Available sheet**. Click the **Insert tab**, and in the **Text group**, click **Header & Footer**. Compare your screen with Figure 4.29.

The chart sheets have been grouped so that headers and footers can be inserted into the group of chart sheets at the same time.

The Header/Footer tab of the Page Setup dialog box displays. The Custom Header and Custom Footer buttons can be used to create the header or footer that you want, or you can select options from the Header or Footer list boxes.

Figure 4.29

Page Setup dialog box

Header/Footer tab

Custom Footer button

Arrow to display header or footer options

Custom Header button

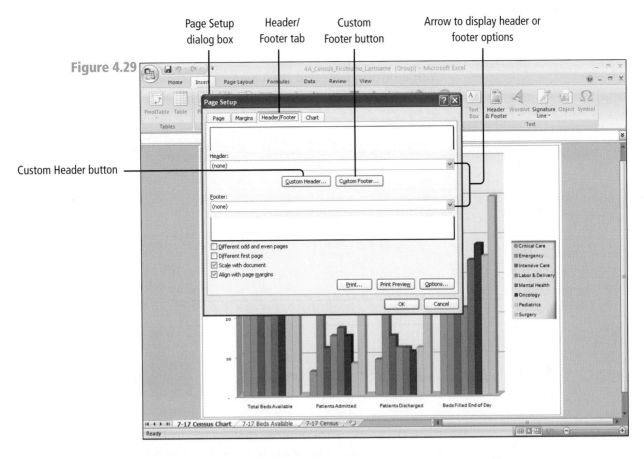

2 Click the **Custom Footer** button and compare your screen with Figure 4.30.

The Footer dialog box displays with the three sections in the footer and a group of buttons similar to those found in the Header and Footer Elements group.

Figure 4.30

Footer dialog box

Insert File Name button

Insert Sheet Name button

Three sections of the footer area

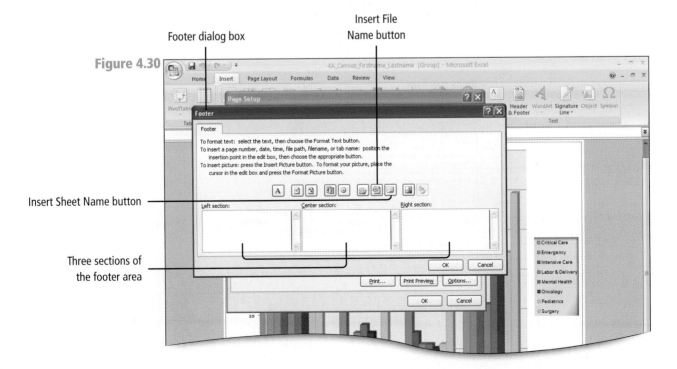

3 With the insertion point in the **Left section** click the **Insert File Name** button 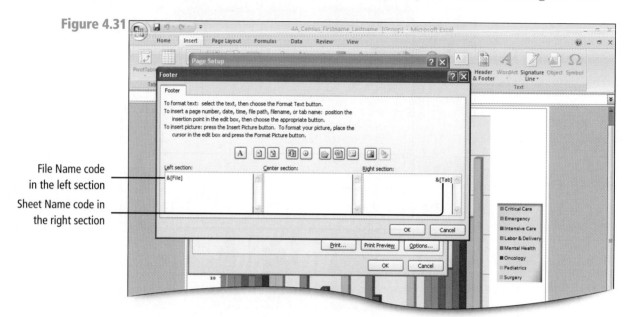. Click the **Right section** and click the **Insert Sheet Name** button, and then compare your screen with Figure 4.31.

Figure 4.31

File Name code in the left section

Sheet Name code in the right section

4 Click **OK** to close the **Footer** dialog box. In the **Page Setup** dialog box, click **Custom Header**. In the displayed **Header** dialog box, click in the **Center section**. Type **Page** and press Spacebar. Click the **Insert Page Number** button, press Spacebar, type **of** and press Spacebar, and then click the **Insert Number of Pages** button. Compare your screen with Figure 4.32.

The codes used display the page number and the total number of pages in the center section of the Header dialog box. When the Header dialog box is closed, the headers and footers are complete.

Figure 4.32

Insert Page Number button

Insert Number of Pages button

Page Number code
Number of Pages code

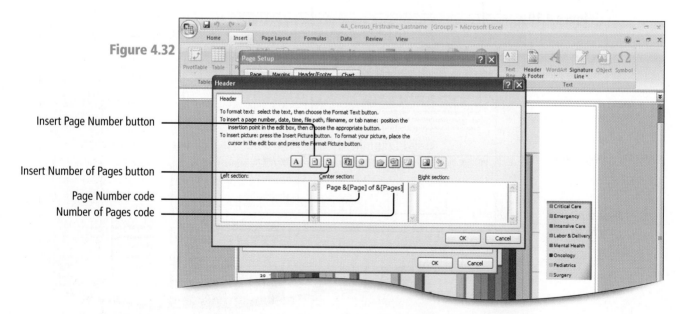

5 Click **OK** to close the **Header** dialog box.

A preview of the header and footer displays in the Page Setup dialog box.

6 Click **OK** to close the **Page Setup** dialog box. At the **7-17 Census Chart tab**, right-click and **Select All Sheets**. Click the **Office** button [image], point to **Print**, and at the right side, click **Print Preview.** Scroll through the worksheets and confirm the placement of the footer and page number.

7 Click **Close Print Preview.** Click the **7-17 Census Chart sheet tab** to ungroup the sheets, click and hold down the mouse button, and compare your screen with Figure 4.33.

The mouse pointer includes an icon that resembles a sheet of paper. This icon represents this worksheet and will move with the mouse arrow as you drag the mouse. With the mouse pointer active, you can move the sheet to another location within the workbook.

Figure 4.33

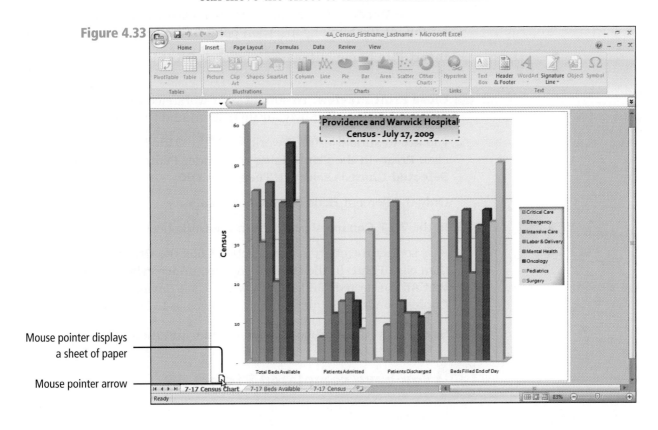

Mouse pointer displays a sheet of paper

Mouse pointer arrow

8 Drag the pointer to the right of the **7-17 Census sheet** and when a small downward pointer arrowhead displays to the right of the 7-17 Census sheet, release the mouse. Using the skills you have practiced, move the **7-17 Beds Available sheet** to the the right of the 7-17 Census sheet. Confirm that the order of the worksheets is *7-17 Census, 7-17 Beds Available, 7-17 Census Chart.* **Save** [image] your workbook.

The 7-17 Census sheet is now the first worksheet of the workbook. Use the drag-and-drop method to rearrange worksheets in a workbook. With both of the chart sheets selected, it is possible to move both sheets in one step. Alternatively, you can drag individual sheets to reorder them as needed. In a workbook, it is recommended that the worksheet containing the data be the first worksheet of the workbook so the data displays when the workbook is opened.

Activity 4.14 Printing a Chart

The chart that is embedded into the worksheet will be added to the portfolio of data that will be presented to management. In this activity, you will print this chart as a separate sheet apart from the worksheet data.

1 Click the **7-17 Census sheet tab** and click in the **Chart** to make it active. Click the **Office** button, point to **Print**, and then click **Print Preview**.

Only the chart displays in Print Preview. There are no headers or footers on this sheet.

2 In the **Print group**, click **Page Setup**. In the **Page Setup** dialog box, click the **Header/Footer tab**, and then click the **Custom Footer** button. At the blinking insertion point in the **Left section**, click the **Insert File Name** button and click **OK** twice to close the two dialog boxes.

3 **Close Print Preview**. To submit your work electronically, follow the instructions provided by your instructor, and then go to Step 5. If you are to submit printed work, click the **Office** button and click **Print**. In the **Print** dialog box, under **Print what**, confirm that **Selected Chart** is selected. Then click **OK**.

Only the Percent Beds Filled chart prints.

4 In the **7-17 Census** sheet, click in the worksheet and then press Ctrl + Home so that the chart is not selected. Click the **Office** button, and then click **Print**. In the **Print** dialog box, under **Print range**, confirm that **All** is selected. Under **Print what**, click **Entire workbook**. Under **Copies**, confirm that the number of copies is **1**. Click **OK**.

5 **Save** your workbook, **Close** the file, and then **Exit** Excel.

End **You have completed Project 4A** ———————————

Project 4B **Employees**

In Activities 4.15 through 4.27, you will prepare a portfolio—a group of worksheets—that will assist the Human Resource Department of Providence and Warwick Hospital to evaluate the salary ranges of its employees in order to make recommendations about the potential salary increases. The HR director, Georgia Burns, will use this data as she prepares her report to Maria Benitez, vice president of operations, who will make salary recommendations.

Your completed worksheet will look similar to Figure 4.34.

For Project 4B, you will need the following files:

e04B_Employees
e04B_New_Hires

You will save your workbook as
4B_Employees_Firstname_Lastname

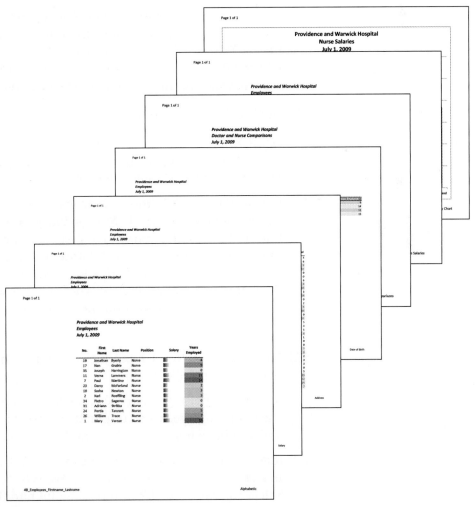

Figure 4.34
Project 4B—Employees

Objective 7
Sort Data

A *table*—also called a *list* or a *database*—is a collection of data. For example, a list of doctors, a list of patients, or a list of supplies used in surgery can be organized into a list or table. In Excel, the table is organized in rows and columns that contain related data. Each row of data constitutes a *record*—all of the related data for that person, place, thing, or event.

Each column title describes a *field*—an individual category of data. Each entry in a row is a value under the field or category that is identified in the column title.

Arranging data according to its value or alphabetically is *sorting* data. Data can be sorted in alphabetical order from A to Z or in reverse alphabetical order from Z to A. Numeric values can be arranged in *ascending order*—from the smallest number to the largest number—or in *descending order*—from the largest to the smallest number.

Activity 4.15 Sorting Alphabetical Data

It is customary to sort a table of names in alphabetical order by last names. When the last names are the same, then the first name is used to determine the order of the records. Georgia Burns, HR director, is updating the records of the hospital and you will assist her with this project. In this activity, you will use Excel to sort names of employees in alphabetical order.

1 **Start** Excel. From your student files, locate and open the file named

e04B_Employees. Click the **Office** button, click **Save As,** and navigate to the **Excel Chapter 4** folder. In the **File name** box, type **4B_Employees_Firstname_Lastname** and then click **Save**.

2 Click the **Insert tab**. In the **Text group**, click **Header & Footer**. On the **Design tab**, in the **Navigation group**, click the **Go to Footer** button. In the **Left Footer** area insert the **File Name**. In the **Right Footer** area, insert the **Sheet Name**. In the **Navigation group**, click **Go to Header**. In the **Left Header** area, enter the **Page Number** and the **Number of Pages** and the words so it reads *Page x of xx.* In the worksheet, click cell **A1**, and then in the status bar, click the **Normal** button.

3 Right-click the **row 1 heading** and on the shortcut menu, click **Insert**. Press Ctrl + Y three times so that four rows are inserted.

Recall that Ctrl + Y will repeat the last command. When the worksheet for employees was originally saved, the title was not included and you have inserted rows to make room for the identifying title.

4 Right-click the **column A heading** and on the shortcut menu, click **Insert**. In cell **A5**, type **No.** In cell **A6**, type **1** and in cell **A7**, type **2** Select the range **A6:A7** and use the fill handle to extend the numbers through **row 33** until the ScreenTip displays **28**. Click the **Home tab**, and in the **Alignment group**, click **Center**.

Recall that the fill handle is used to extend a consecutive list of numbers. When working with a table, it is helpful to sequentially number the items on the original worksheet. In this way, it is easy to return the table to the original order if needed.

5 Beginning in cell **A1**, type the following worksheet title:

| Providence and Warwick Hospital |
| Employees |
| 'July 1, 2009 |

6 Select the worksheet title—**A1:A3**—and apply **Bold** **B** and **Italic** **I** emphasis, and change the **Font Size** **11 ▾** to **14**.

7 Select the column titles—**A5:K5**—and apply **Bold** **B**, with a **Bottom Border** **⊞ ▾**. In the **Alignment group**, click the **Wrap Text** **≣**, **Center** **≣**, and **Middle Align** buttons **≡**. Adjust column widths to fully display column contents. Adjust the height of **row 5** without extra space above or below the column titles.

First Name, *Postal Code*, and *Years Employed* display on two lines.

8 Click cell **C6**. On the **Home tab**, in the **Editing group**, click the **Sort & Filter** button to display the list. Compare your screen with Figure 4.35.

Because this table will be sorted by last name, you can click in any cell in the **Last Name** column. When sorting in this manner, Excel sorts the table based on the field where the active cell resides.

Active cell

Column titles identify field categories

Sort & Filter button

Sort & Filter list

Figure 4.35

Column on which to sort

A row—record— contains all of the data about one employee

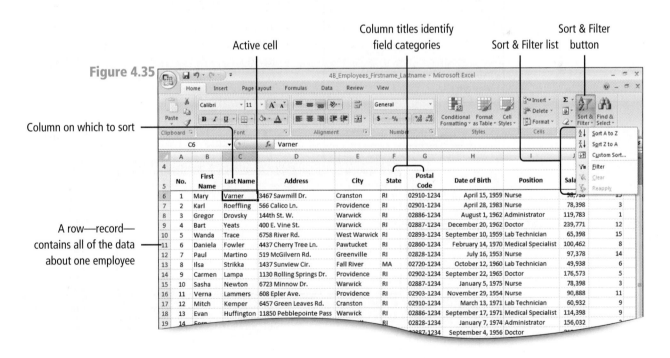

9 From the displayed list, click **Sort A to Z** and as you do, notice that the order of the lists changes.

The table is sorted in alphabetical order by last name. Sorting a worksheet in this manner is quick when one field is sorted.

10 Scroll down the table and notice that two employees have the last name *Lammers* and three employees have the last name *Trace*.

It is standard practice to sort by first name when the last names are identical.

11 With cell **C6** active, click the **Data tab**, and in the **Sort & Filter group**, click the **Sort** button. If necessary, move the Sort dialog box in the worksheet so the column titles display. Compare your screen with Figure 4.36.

The Sort dialog box displays. The first sort instruction is displayed in the dialog box. Excel sorted by Last Name from A to Z.

When records match, this dialog box is used to instruct Excel on the order that the other fields will be sorted. When the first sort—the *primary sort*—results in identical entries, additional fields will be sorted next. Each sort after the first is a *secondary sort* and those fields will be added to this dialog box.

Sort dialog box

Figure 4.36

Instructions for primary sort

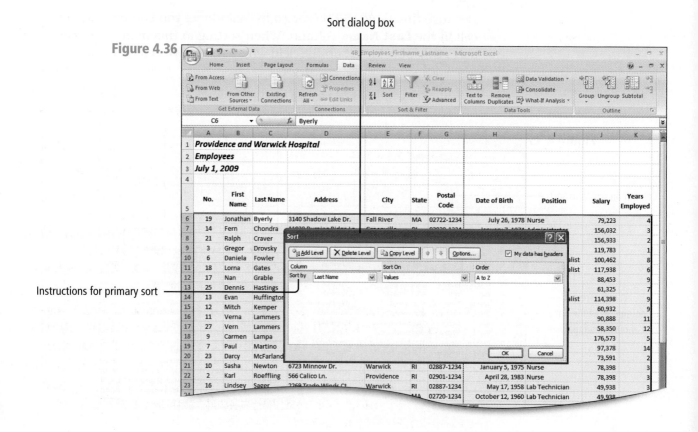

12 In the **Sort** dialog box, click the **Add Level** button, and then compare your screen with Figure 4.37.

The next level is the secondary sort field. When the primary sort results match, the secondary sort field is used. At the right edge of the Sort dialog box, *My data has headers* is checked. These headers are the column titles. When this box is checked, Excel recognizes that the first row contains column titles and will not include those cells when the table is sorted.

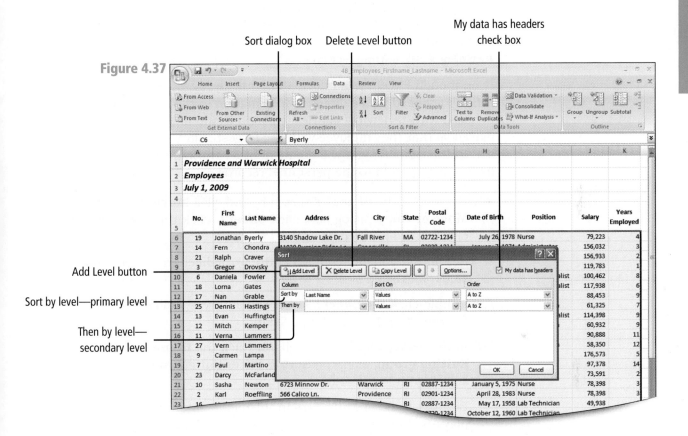

Figure 4.37

Sort dialog box   Delete Level button

My data has headers check box

Add Level button

Sort by level—primary level

Then by level—secondary level

13 In the **Then by** section, click the **arrow** and from the displayed list, click **First Name**. In the middle section, confirm that **Values** is selected. In the last box—the **Order** area—click the **arrow** to view the displayed choices, and then click to confirm **A to Z**.

The list in the Then by section of the table displays the column titles used in this worksheet. Any column title—field—may be sorted. The choice is to sort from A to Z—alphabetical order—or Z to A—reverse alphabetical order—or Custom List—a list you can create.

14 Click the **Add Level** button. In the displayed **Then by** section, click the **arrow**, and then click **Position**. Confirm that **Values** is selected and the **Order** is **A to Z**.

Another sort level is added. Every column title can be included in the sort levels. In large tables, additional sort orders may be needed to accurately sort the records in the table. This table will be sorted by last name. When the last name is the same, those names will be sorted by first name. If both the first and last names are the same, then the table will be sorted by position.

15 Click **OK**. Then review the data in the worksheet and confirm that the two records with the last name *Lammers* have been sorted correctly and that the three records with the last name *Trace* have also been sorted correctly. **Save** 🖫 your workbook.

Wanda Trace the Doctor is placed before Wanda Trace the Lab Technician because the third sort—*Position*—differentiated the identical names by using the Position field to determine which of the two records should be listed first.

Activity 4.16 Sorting by Numbers

Even though Excel sorts information quickly, personnel within an organization may need to see different information in the same table. In order to assist with reviewing salaries, Georgia would like to see the table displayed so that the employee with the largest salary is at the top of the list. In this activity, you will create another worksheet and sort the table by numbers to add to the personnel records.

1 Right-click the **Sheet1 sheet tab**, and click **Move or Copy**. In the **Move or Copy** dialog box, click **Sheet2**, click the **Create a copy** check box, and then click **OK**.

Recall that you can copy an entire worksheet and place it in the same workbook.

2 Double-click the **Sheet1 sheet tab** and type **Alphabetic** Double-click the **Sheet1 (2) tab** and type **Salary**

3 In the **Salary sheet**, click cell **J6**. Click the **Home tab**. In the **Editing group**, click the **Sort & Filter** button and compare your screen with Figure 4.38.

Because there are numbers in this field—column—the sort list displays *Sort by Smallest to Largest*, which is how numbers are sorted. Recall that when the list contained text, the sort instructions were Sort A to Z.

Figure 4.38

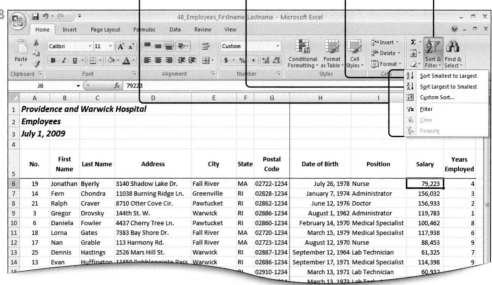

Sort & Filter List · Sort Largest to Smallest command · Sort Smallest to Largest command · Sort & Filter button

4 In the **Sort & Filter** list, click **Sort Largest to Smallest**. Scroll down the salary column and notice that *Karl Roeffling* and *Sasha Newton* both have the same salary, as do *Ilsa Strikka* and *Lindsey Sager*.

The table is sorted and displays the employee with the highest salary at the top of the list. You can further refine the sort by adding another sort level.

5 Click the **Data tab**, and in the **Sort & Filter group**, click the **Sort** button. In the **Sort** dialog box, review the data for the first sort by *Salary* from *Largest to Smallest*. Click the **Add Level** button, and in the **Then by** section, click the **arrow** and then click **Position**. Confirm that the **Order** is **A to Z**.

The first sort—salary—displays that it was sorted from largest to smallest. Excel is now instructed that when the salaries are the same, use the position to determine the sort order.

6 Click the **Add Level** button again, click the **Then by arrow**, and then click **Last Name**. Confirm that the **Order** is **A to Z**, and compare your screen with Figure 4.39.

Excel is instructed to sort the table by salary with the highest salary listed first. If the salaries match, then use the position to determine the order of the list. If both the salary and the position match, then sort by last name.

Figure 4.39

Numeric sort order   Text sort order

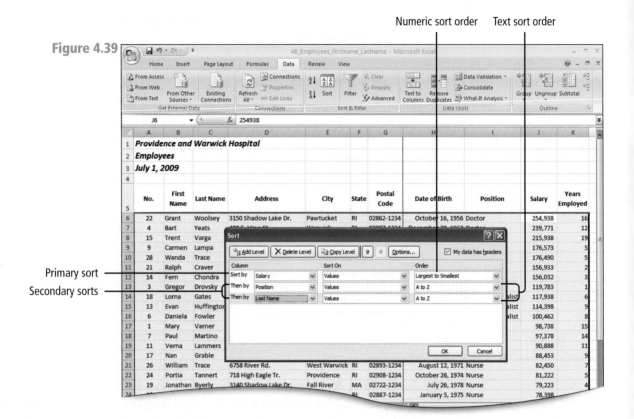

Primary sort

Secondary sorts

7 Click **OK** and review the order of the list. Confirm that the employees with the same salaries have been sorted according to your instructions.

Newton is sorted alphabetically before Roeffling, and Sager is before Strikka. In both cases, the salaries and position are the same, so the third sort by last name determines which employee record is listed first.

8 Right-click the **Salary sheet tab**, and click **Move or Copy**. In the **Move or Copy** dialog box, click **Sheet2**, click the **Create a copy** check box, and then click **OK**. Double-click the **Salary (2) sheet tab** and type **Address** and then click in the worksheet.

9 On the **Data tab**, in the **Sort & Filter group**, click the **Sort** button. In the **Sort** dialog box, in the **Sort by** box, click the **arrow** and from the list, select **State**. Confirm that the **Order** is **A to Z**. Click the **Add Level** button. Click the **Then by arrow** and click **City**, and confirm that the **Order** is **A to Z**. Using the skills you have practiced, add another level to sort alphabetically by **Last Name** and a fourth level to sort alphabetically by **First Name**. Compare your screen with Figure 4.40.

Figure 4.40

Sort order

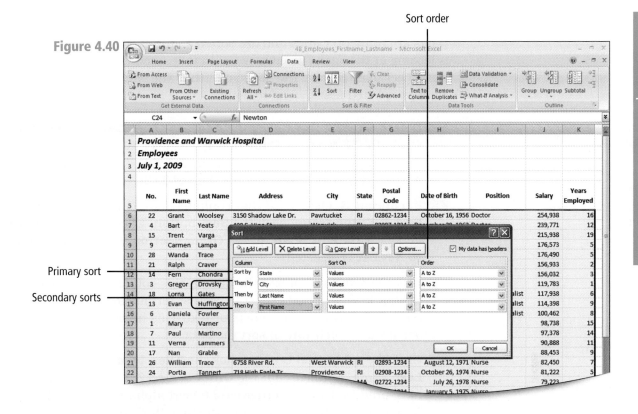

Primary sort

Secondary sorts

10 Click **OK**. Review the order of the table to confirm the accuracy of the sort. **Save** 💾 your workbook.

Both Wanda and William Trace live in West Warwick, Rhode Island. Because the sort order included first and last name, they are listed correctly in alphabetical order.

This table is sorted first by state. When the state is the same, then it is sorted by city. When both the city and state are identical, the table is sorted by last name and then by first name.

More Knowledge

To Remove a Sort Field

If you discover that a sort field should be removed from the list, click in the sort field and in the Sort dialog box, click Delete Level. You can also insert a sort field between existing fields. To do so, click in the field that will be first sorted and then click Add Level.

Activity 4.17 Sorting by Date

Dates are numeric values and are sorted as numbers. The HR Department is looking at the age of its employees. In this activity, you will create a worksheet that displays the dates of birth of the employees with the oldest employees listed first.

1 **Delete Sheet3**. Right-click the **Address sheet tab** and click **Move or Copy**. In the **Move or Copy** dialog box, click **Sheet2**, click the **Create a copy** check box, and then click **OK**. Double-click the **Address (2) sheet tab** and type **Date of Birth**

2 In **column H**, click a cell that contains data. On the **Data tab**, in the **Sort & Filter group**, click the **Sort** button. Click the **Sort by arrow** and click **Date of Birth**. In the **Order section**, confirm that **Oldest to Newest** is selected.

Because Excel recognizes the data in this column as dates, it uses Newest to Oldest and Oldest to Newest terminology rather than the terminology used for numbers or text. This helps you determine accurately which way to sort the data.

3 Click the **Add Level** button, click the **Then by arrow**, and then click **Last Name**. Confirm that the **Order** is **A to Z**. Using the skills you have practiced, add another level to sort alphabetically by **First Name**, and then compare your screen with Figure 4.41.

This table will be sorted by date of birth. If they are the same, then it will be sorted by last name and then by first name.

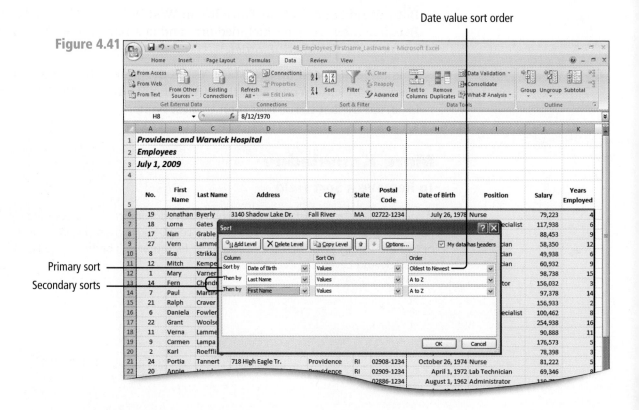

Figure 4.41

Date value sort order

Primary sort

Secondary sorts

4 Click **OK** and **Save** 🖫 your workbook.

The table is sorted by birthday with the oldest employee listed at the top.

Objective 8
Convert Text into Columns

Worksheet data, such as first and last name, that is entered into one cell can be split into two or more cells. Using the **_Text to Columns_** feature converts data in one cell into several fields and places the data in the number of cells required to display the fields separately.

Activity 4.18 Splitting Cell Contents into Multiple Cells and Copy and Paste

The table of newly hired employees was created with all information placed into one cell. To use the data, the worksheet needs to be converted into a table. In this activity, you will use the Text to Columns feature to add the new employees to the existing table of employees.

1 From your student files, locate and open the file named **e04B_New_Hires**. Select the range **A3:A9**, right-click, and click **Copy**.

A table of employees hired in June was prepared in an Excel spreadsheet. However, the data for each employee is entered into one cell and spills across several columns. Two workbooks are now open.

2 Click the **View tab**. In the **Window group**, click the **Switch Windows** button. Compare your screen with Figure 4.42.

The list of the open Excel workbooks displays. A check mark displays to the left of the active workbook, which is the New Hires workbook.

Active workbook   Switch Windows button

Figure 4.42

List of open workbooks

Selected range of cells

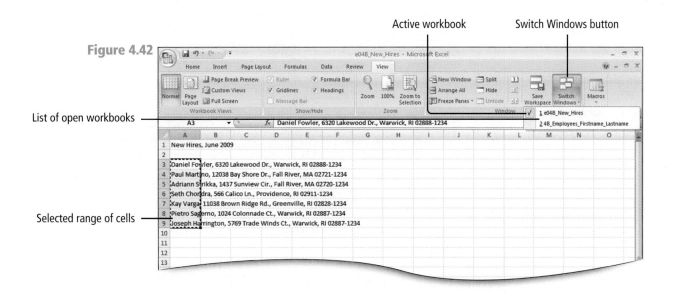

3 From the displayed list, click **4B_Employees_Firstname_Lastname**. On the **Date of Birth sheet**, right-click cell **B37**, and then click **Paste**.

The 4B_Employees_Firstname_Lastname worksheet displays on the screen. The data has been pasted in column B and spills into the cells to the right. Leaving space between the worksheet and the newly inserted data provides a visual separation of the data.

4 On the **View tab**, in the **Window group**, click the **Switch Windows** button. From the list, click **e04B_New_Hires** and in the workbook-level buttons, click **Close Window** ☒; if you are asked to save changes, click **No**.

5 Confirm the newly inserted data—**B37:B43**—is selected. Click the **Data tab**, in the **Data Tools group**, click the **Text to Columns** button, and then compare your screen with Figure 4.43.

The Convert Text to Columns Wizard – Step 1 of 3 dialog box displays. The top portion is used to set the type of data that will result. The area near the bottom of the dialog box displays the data.

Two choices for the file type are available—delimited and fixed width. A **delimited** column width sets the fields by a symbol, such as a space, comma, tab, or semicolon, which are called **delimiters**. Using the **fixed width** aligns the fields by specified width for the column break.

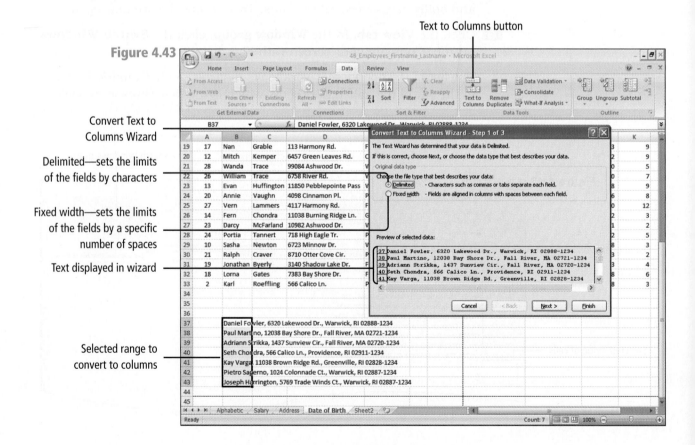

Figure 4.43

6 Click **Next** to display the **Convert Text to Columns Wizard – Step 2 of 3**.

The specific delimiters are displayed on the left side of the dialog box. *Tab* is selected.

Alert!

Do you have different delimiters checked?

Because Excel is intuitive, the delimiters that display in this dialog box maintain the choices of the previous use. The delimiters on your screen will reflect the delimiters last used.

7 Under **Delimiters**, click **Comma** to select it, and then click any others that may be selected to remove all other check marks. Review the display in the **Data preview** section, and compare your screen with Figure 4.44.

There are four fields in the worksheet. In the Data review section of the wizard, a vertical line is placed between each suggested field. A new field is created whenever there is a comma, tab, or space in the original list, as instructed by the delimiters.

State and postal code displayed in one field

Figure 4.44

City displayed in one field

Data preview section

First and Last Name in one field

Address in one field

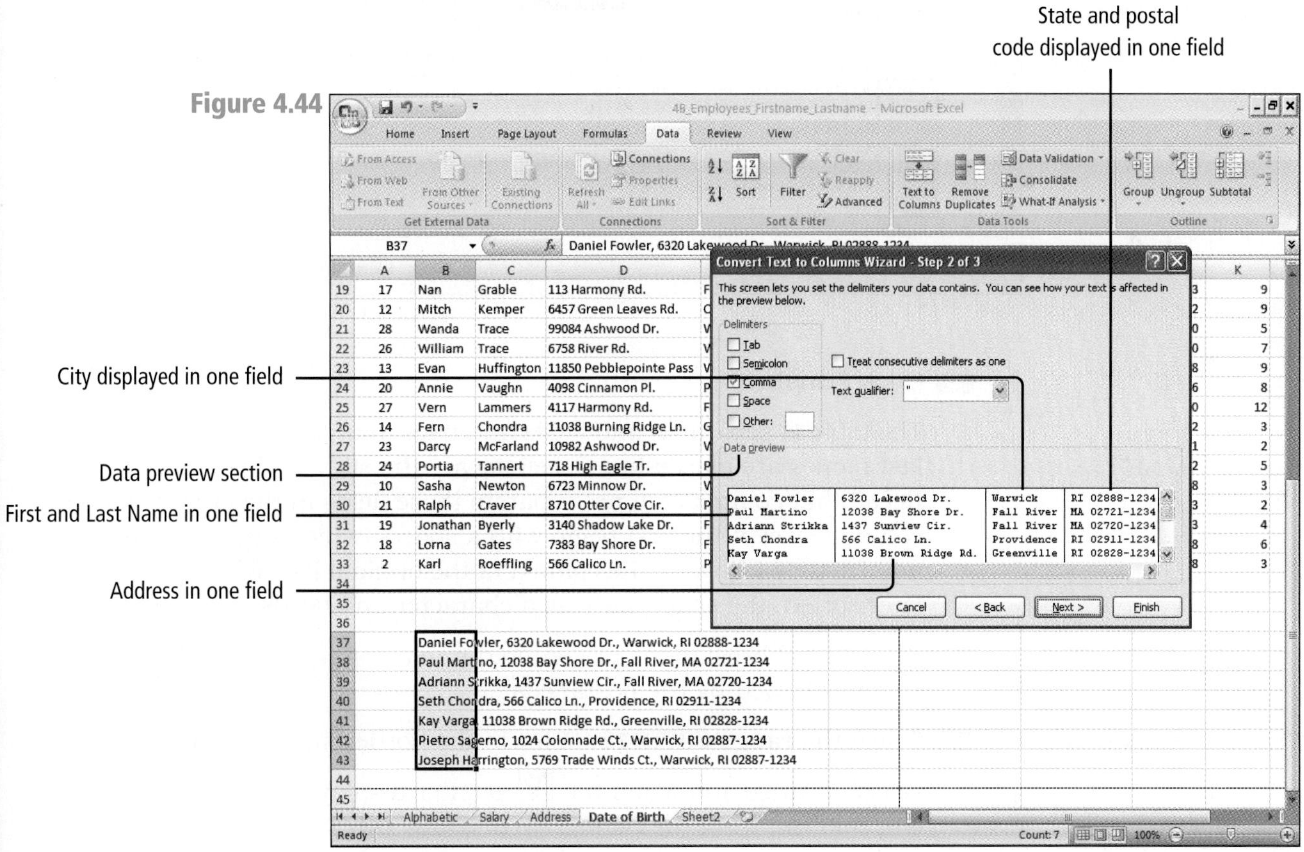

8 Click **Next** and compare your screen with Figure 4.45.

At the top of this screen are instructions for displaying the data. *General* is selected and information about this format is displayed at the right. In the center of the dialog box, the *Destination* box indicates the position of the first cell—where the new table will be entered in the worksheet.

Information about data format

Figure 4.45

Column data format

Destination—where the data will be placed in the worksheet

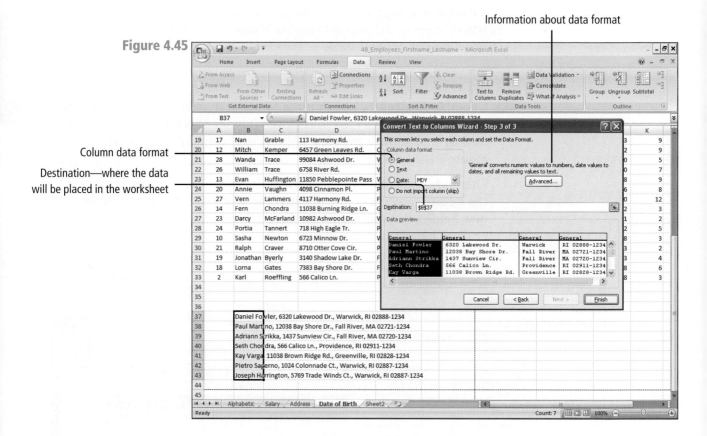

9 Click **Finish**.

The table is separated into fields and uses four columns. The first and last names are placed in one cell, as are the state and postal code. Recall that commas did not separate these fields in the original list. All columns except the first begin with a space—which was the character immediately following the comma in the original list. When the list is later sorted, the space sorts as a character and needs to be omitted.

The state abbreviations are entered into a column and begin with a space, followed by the postal code.

10 Select the range **C37:E43**. Point to the border surrounding the selected range and when the ⬚ pointer displays, drag to the right one column, until the ScreenTip displays *D37:G43*.

Recall that you can move data using the drag-and-drop method.

11 Select the range **B37:B43**. In the **Data Tools group**, click the **Text to Columns** button. In the **Step 1** box, confirm that **Delimited** is selected, and click **Next**. In the **Step 2** box, click **Space** and click to deselect the other boxes. Click **Next**. In the **Step 3** box, click **Finish**.

12 Select the range **F37:F43** On the **Data tab**, in the **Data Tools group**, click the **Text to Columns** button. In the **Step 1** box, confirm that **Delimited** is selected, and click **Next**. In the **Step 2** box, click to select **Space** and delete the others that are selected. Click **Next**. In the **Step 3** box, notice that the first column will be blank. Then click **Finish**.

In the selected list, when a space occurs, a new column is created. Because the state abbreviations began with a space, a column was inserted. Now there are no spaces in front of the state abbreviations listed in column E. The cells F37:F43 remain selected.

13 With the range **F37:F43** selected, on the **Home tab**, in the **Cells group**, click the **Delete button arrow** and compare your screen with Figure 4.46. Then click **Delete Cells**. In the **Delete** dialog box, confirm that **Shift cells left** is selected and click **OK**. **Save** 💾 your workbook.

The Delete menu displays the choices for deleting cells, rows, columns, or the entire sheet. *Deleting cells* is like cutting them from the worksheet and sliding the adjoining cells to the left.

Figure 4.46

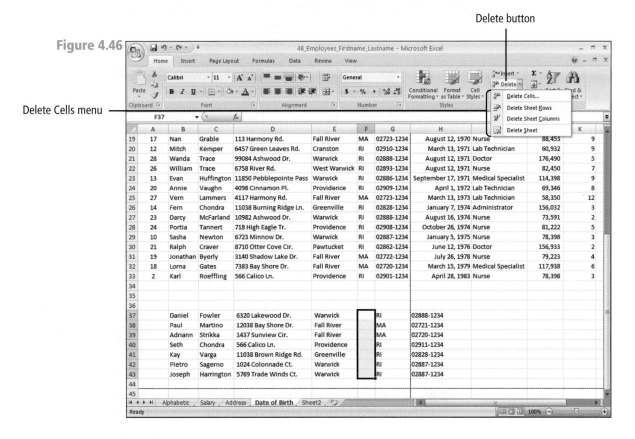

Delete button

Delete Cells menu

Activity 4.19 Using the TRIM Function

When using Convert to Text, a space—called a leading space—remains as the first character in some of the cells. When sorting a list, that space is identified as a character and alters the sort order. In this activity, you will use the TRIM function to remove spaces in a list.

1 Click cell **D45**. Click the **Formulas tab** and in the **Function Library group**, click the **Text** button and from the list click **Trim**.

The Trim dialog box displays. The ***TRIM function*** is a Text function that removes all spaces from text except for spaces between words.

2 In the **TRIM Function Arguments** dialog box, in the **Text** section, click cell **D37,** compare your screen with Figure 4.47, and then click **OK**.

The space at the beginning of the text has been deleted while the spaces within the text remain.

Function in Formula Bar   Results of function

Figure 4.47

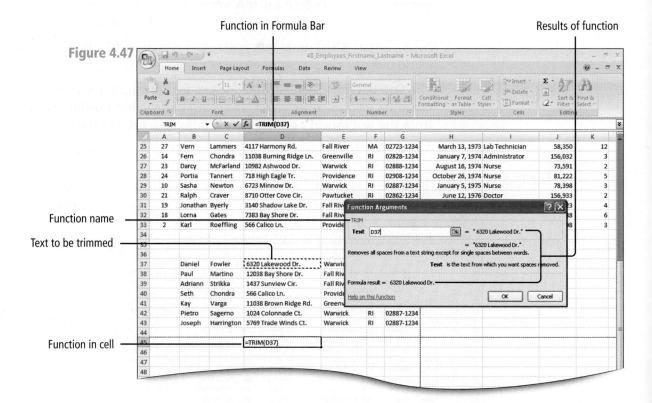

Function name

Text to be trimmed

Function in cell

3 With cell **D45** active, click the fill handle, and drag down through cell **D51**, and then drag to the right to cell **G51** to copy the function.

The function has been copied through the range of the worksheet. Any space at the beginning of the cells is eliminated.

4 Click in each of the four worksheets in this workbook and confirm that **row 34** does not contain data.

5 In the **Date of Birth sheet**, with the range **D45:G51** selected, right-click and select **Copy**. Click cell **D37**, right-click and select **Paste Special**. Under **Paste** click **Values**, and then click **OK**.

Recall that copying a cell containing a formula also copies that formula. The formula contained in the copy range is not needed in this table, so you will copy only the values of the cell—the dates without the leading space within each cell.

6 Select the range **D45:G51** and press Delete.

7 Select the range **B37:G43**. Point to the border of the selected range and when the [pointer icon] pointer displays drag up and left to the range **B34:G40**.

8 Press ⇧Shift and click the **Alphabetic sheet tab**. On the **Home tab**, in the **Editing group**, click the **Fill** button [icon] and from the list, click **Across Worksheets**. In the **Fill Across Worksheets** dialog box, confirm that **All** is selected, and then click **OK**.

9 Scroll the worksheet so that **row 5** is the top row visible on the screen and **column B** is the first column on the screen. Click cell **D6**. On the **View tab**, in the **Window group**, click the **Freeze Panes** button, and from the displayed list, click **Freeze Panes**. Scroll the worksheet so that **column H** displays next to **column C** and **row 24** displays next to **row 5**. Compare your screen with Figure 4.48.

Columns C and H next to each other

Figure 4.48

Rows 5 and 24 next to each other

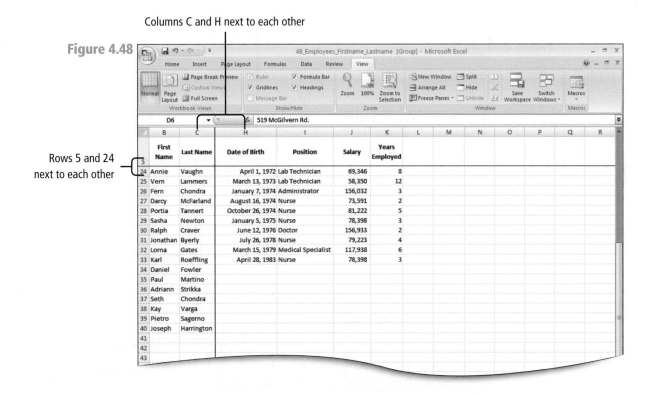

10 With the worksheets still grouped, beginning in cell **H34**, type the following data:

Last Name	Date of Birth	Position	Salary	Years Employed
Fowler	9/27/73	Doctor	157,000	0
Martino	7/4/81	Medical Specialist	85,500	0
Strikka	7/12/75	Nurse	75,500	0
Chondra	8/29/80	Lab Technician	45,000	0
Varga	2/14/76	Lab Technician	45,000	0
Sagerno	10/28/68	Nurse	76,000	0
Harrington	12/14/76	Nurse	77,000	0

11 Select the dates of birth just inserted in the worksheet—**H34:H40**. Click the **Home tab**, and in the **Number group**, click the **Dialog Box Launcher** . In the **Format Cells** dialog box, on the **Number tab**, under the **Category**, click **Date**. At the right, in the **Type** section, scroll to and click the style displayed as *March 14, 2001*. Compare your screen with Figure 4.49, and then click **OK**.

Number tab of Format Cells dialog box

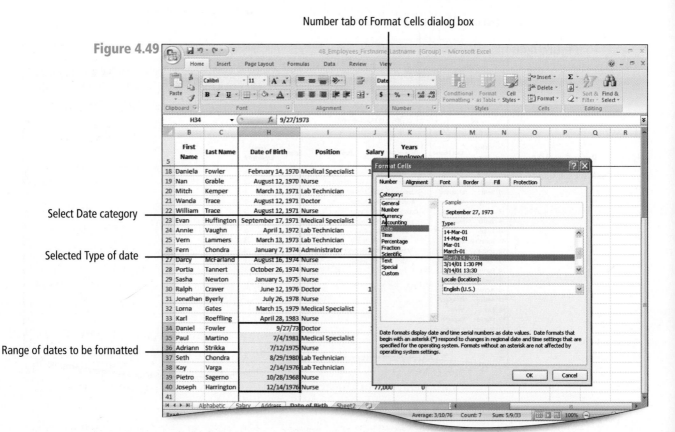

Figure 4.49

Select Date category

Selected Type of date

Range of dates to be formatted

12 Right-click cell **J33** and on the Mini toolbar, click the **Format Painter** button ![icon] and drag the range **J34:J40** to copy the format.

13 On the **View tab**, in the **Window group**, click the **Freeze Panes** button, and from the displayed list, click **Unfreeze Panes**. In cell **A34**, type **29** and in cell **A35**, type **30** Select the range **A34:A35** and use the Fill handle to extend the numbers to **row 40** and number **35**.

Right-click and from the Mini toolbar, click the **Center** button ![icon].

14 Right-click a **sheet tab** and then click **Ungroup Sheets**. Click in the four worksheets to confirm the entries have been made and formatted.

15 Click the **Alphabetic sheet tab**. Click in a cell in the data of the worksheet—below row 5 and above row 41. Click the **Data tab**, in the **Sort & Filter group**, click the **Sort** button.

The Sort dialog box displays. The sort instructions have been retained by Excel, making it easy to complete the same sort after additional entries are made.

16 Click **OK** to complete the sort. Click the **Salary sheet tab**. Click in a cell in the data of the worksheet. Display the **Sort** dialog box. Confirm the sort levels are correct and click **OK**. Using the skills you have practiced, sort the **Address** and **Date of Birth** sheets to include the new hires. **Save** ![icon] your workbook.

Objective 9
Apply Conditional Formatting Using Data Bars and Color Scales

Conditional formatting not only applies a format to specific cells, it can show the relationship of the data within the cells without modifying the worksheet. Conditional formatting highlights data and highlights comparisons. For instance, you can easily display the top 10 items in a table or use conditional formatting to apply different colors to different data.

Activity 4.20 Highlighting Cell Rules

Cells that meet a specific condition, such as greater than, less than, or equal to, can be highlighted using conditional formatting. The HR Department is analyzing salary ranges and will use the worksheet with the hospital board, so specific salaries will not be included in this worksheet. In this activity, you will highlight salaries between a certain range and the number of years an employee has worked for the hospital.

1 Click the **Salary sheet tab**. Select the salary range—**J6:J40**. Click the **Home tab**, and in the **Styles group**, click the **Conditional Formatting** button. From the displayed list, point to **Highlight Cells Rules** and from the submenu, click **Between**. Compare your screen with Figure 4.50.

Using Conditional Formatting, data that falls within a specific range will be highlighted.

Type largest number of range   Format to apply

Figure 4.50

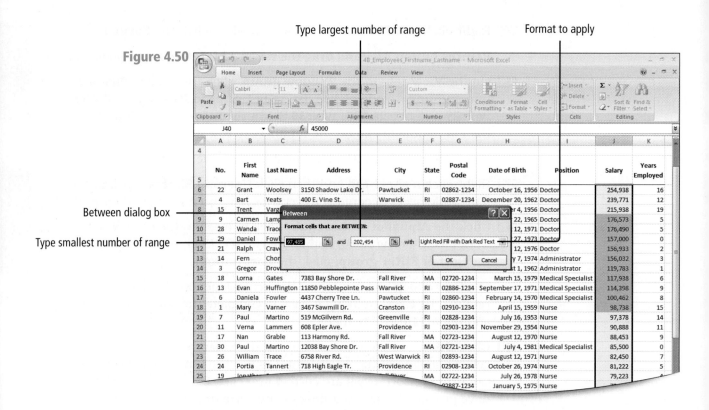

Between dialog box

Type smallest number of range

In the dialog box, in the first text box, type **75000** and in the second text box, type **125000** and then click **OK**.

The salaries between $75,000 and $125,000 are highlighted in Light Red Fill with Dark Red Text in the worksheet.

Select the range of years employed—**K6:K40**. In the **Styles group**, click the **Conditional Formatting** button. From the displayed list, point to **Highlight Cells Rules** and from the submenu, click **Greater Than**. In the **Greater Than** dialog box, in the left box, enter **10** In the box that displays the format style, click the arrow, and then click **Red Border**. Click **OK** and click outside the selected range, and then compare your screen with Figure 4.51

All employees who have been employed with the hospital for more than 10 years are identified.

Displays more than 10 years worked

Figure 4.51

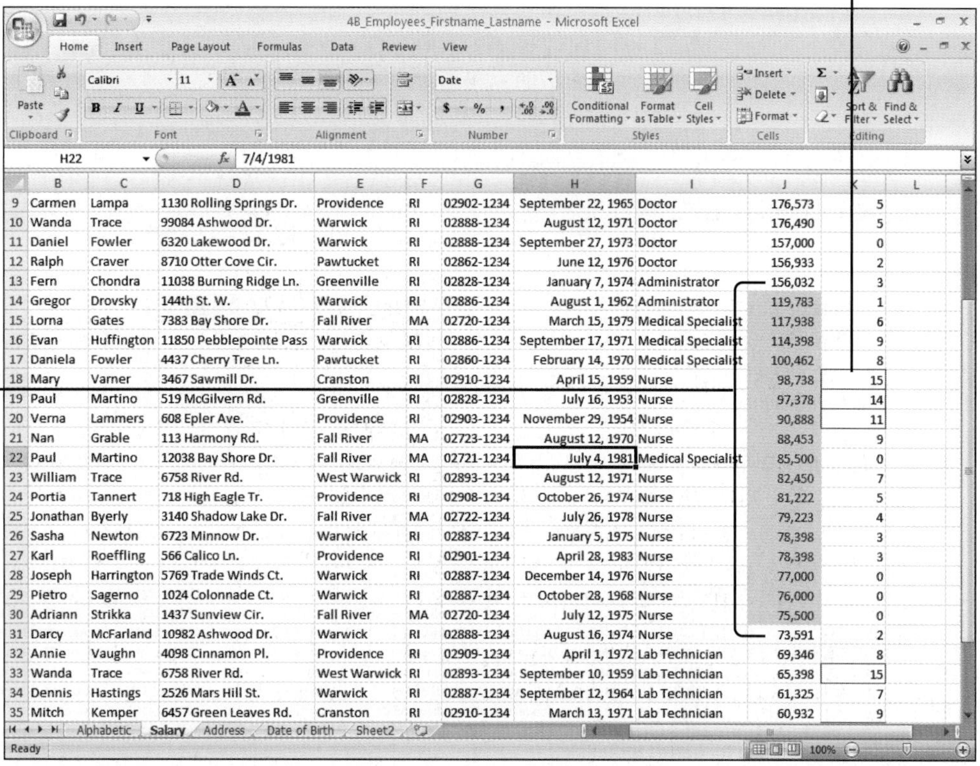

Displays salary between
$75,000 and $125,000

4 Click the **Insert tab**. In the **Text group**, click the **Header & Footer** button. On the **Header & Footer Tools Design tab**, in the **Navigation group**, click the **Go to Footer** button. In the **Center Footer** area type **Displays Salaries Between $75,000 and $125,000** Then press Enter and on the next line, type **Displays Years Employed Over 10**

When conditional formats are applied to the worksheet, it is recommended that the formats are explained, which can be included in the footer. Use the Enter key to display information in the footer on two lines.

5 In the **Navigation group**, click the **Go to Header** button to return to the top of the worksheet, click any cell in the worksheet and on the status bar, click the **Normal** button⊞. **Save** 🖫 your workbook.

Activity 4.21 Using Top/Bottom Rules

In this activity you will highlight the employees with the top eight and bottom eight salaries. In addition, you will highlight the employees who have been with the hospital above the average years of employment.

1 Click the **Address sheet tab**. Select the **Salary** range of cells— **J6:J40**. Click the **Home tab**. In the **Styles group**, click the **Conditional Formatting** button. Point to **Top/Bottom Rules** and in the displayed submenu, click **Top 10 Items** and compare your screen with Figure 4.52.

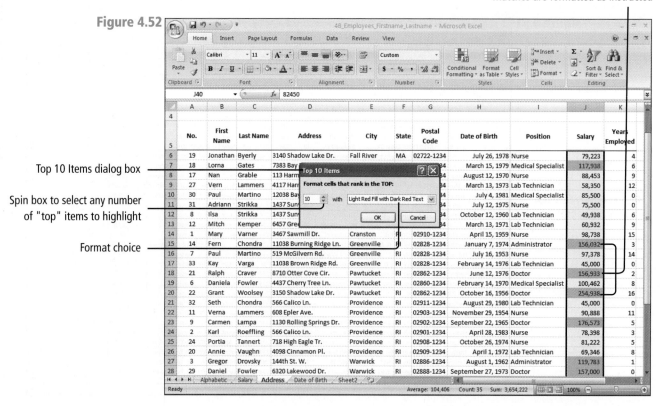

Figure 4.52

Matches are formatted as instructed

Top 10 Items dialog box

Spin box to select any number of "top" items to highlight

Format choice

2 In the **Top 10 Items** dialog box, in the left box, click the **down spin arrow** two times until **8** displays and as you do, notice changes that take place in the selected column. In the box on the right, click the arrow, select **Light Red Fill**, and then click **OK**.

In the worksheet, the highest—top—eight salaries are displayed with a light red fill.

3 With the **Salary** range still selected, in the **Styles group**, click the **Conditional Formatting** button. Point to **Top/Bottom Rules** and in the displayed submenu, click **Bottom 10 Items**. In the **Bottom 10 Items** dialog box, in the left box, click the **down spin arrow** two times until **8** displays and as you do, notice changes that take place in the selected column. In the box on the right, click the arrow, select **Yellow Fill with Dark Yellow Text**. Click **OK** and compare your screen with Figure 4.53.

As the salaries are reviewed, the highest salaries are indicated with a red background and the lowest salaries are highlighted with a yellow background. Highlighting salaries in this manner allows comparisons of salaries to be easily made.

Figure 4.53

Highest salaries

Lowest salaries

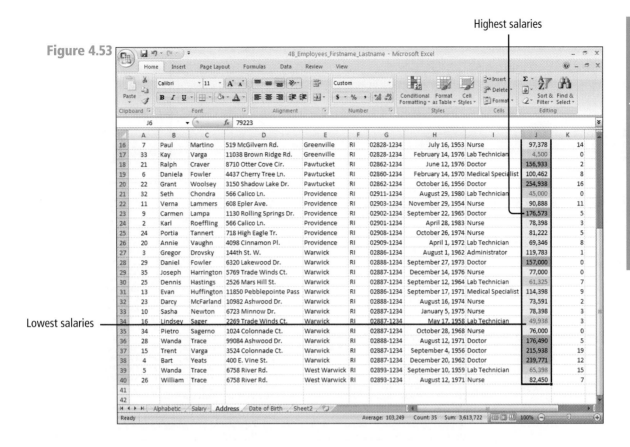

4 Select the Years Employed range—**K6:K40**. In the **Styles group**, click the **Conditional Formatting** button, point to the **Top/Bottom Rules**, and from the displayed submenu, click **Above Average**.

The Above Average dialog displays so that you can choose the conditional format. When the list is selected, Excel calculates the average and then highlights all data that is above average, thereby highlighting the employees who have had the longest service at the hospital.

5 In the **Above Average** dialog box, select a format of **Green Fill with Dark Green Text**, and then click **OK**. Click outside the selected range and compare your screen with Figure 4.54.

The years of service that are above the average are highlighted in the worksheet.

Figure 4.54

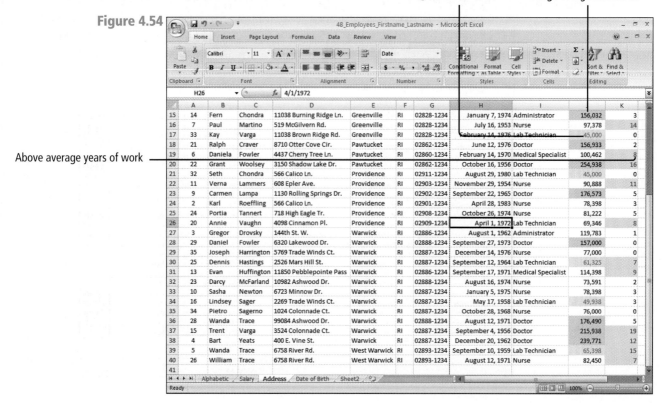

Within the range of lowest salaries

Within the range of highest salaries

Above average years of work

	A	B	C	D	E	F	G	H	I		K
15	14	Fern	Chondra	11038 Burning Ridge Ln.	Greenville	RI	02828-1234	January 7, 1974	Administrator	156,032	3
16	7	Paul	Martino	519 McGilvern Rd.	Greenville	RI	02828-1234	July 16, 1953	Nurse	97,378	14
17	33	Kay	Varga	11038 Brown Ridge Rd.	Greenville	RI	02828-1234	February 14, 1976	Lab Technician	45,000	0
18	21	Ralph	Craver	8710 Otter Cove Cir.	Pawtucket	RI	02862-1234	June 12, 1976	Doctor	156,933	2
19	6	Daniela	Fowler	4437 Cherry Tree Ln.	Pawtucket	RI	02860-1234	February 14, 1970	Medical Specialist	100,462	8
20	22	Grant	Woolsey	3150 Shadow Lake Dr.	Pawtucket	RI	02862-1234	October 16, 1956	Doctor	254,938	16
21	32	Seth	Chondra	566 Calico Ln.	Providence	RI	02911-1234	August 29, 1980	Lab Technician	45,000	0
22	11	Verna	Lammers	608 Epler Ave.	Providence	RI	02903-1234	November 29, 1954	Nurse	90,888	11
23	9	Carmen	Lampa	1130 Rolling Springs Dr.	Providence	RI	02902-1234	September 22, 1965	Doctor	176,573	5
24	2	Karl	Roeffling	566 Calico Ln.	Providence	RI	02901-1234	April 28, 1983	Nurse	78,398	3
25	24	Portia	Tannert	718 High Eagle Tr.	Providence	RI	02908-1234	October 26, 1974	Nurse	81,222	5
26	20	Annie	Vaughn	4098 Cinnamon Pl.	Providence	RI	02909-1234	April 1, 1972	Lab Technician	69,346	8
27	3	Gregor	Drovsky	144th St. W.	Warwick	RI	02886-1234	August 1, 1962	Administrator	119,783	1
28	29	Daniel	Fowler	6320 Lakewood Dr.	Warwick	RI	02888-1234	September 27, 1973	Doctor	157,000	0
29	35	Joseph	Harrington	5769 Trade Winds Ct.	Warwick	RI	02887-1234	December 14, 1976	Nurse	77,000	0
30	25	Dennis	Hastings	2526 Mars Hill St.	Warwick	RI	02887-1234	September 12, 1964	Lab Technician	61,325	7
31	13	Evan	Huffington	11850 Pebblepointe Pass	Warwick	RI	02886-1234	September 17, 1971	Medical Specialist	114,398	9
32	23	Darcy	McFarland	10982 Ashwood Dr.	Warwick	RI	02888-1234	August 16, 1974	Nurse	73,591	2
33	10	Sasha	Newton	6723 Minnow Dr.	Warwick	RI	02887-1234	January 5, 1975	Nurse	78,398	3
34	16	Lindsey	Sager	2269 Trade Winds Ct.	Warwick	RI	02887-1234	May 17, 1958	Lab Technician	49,938	3
35	34	Pietro	Sagerno	1024 Colonnade Ct.	Warwick	RI	02887-1234	October 28, 1968	Nurse	76,000	0
36	28	Wanda	Trace	99084 Ashwood Dr.	Warwick	RI	02888-1234	August 12, 1971	Doctor	176,490	5
37	15	Trent	Varga	3524 Colonnade Ct.	Warwick	RI	02887-1234	September 4, 1956	Doctor	215,938	19
38	4	Bart	Yeats	400 E. Vine St.	Warwick	RI	02887-1234	December 20, 1962	Doctor	239,771	12
39	5	Wanda	Trace	6758 River Rd.	West Warwick	RI	02893-1234	September 10, 1959	Lab Technician	65,398	15
40	26	William	Trace	6758 River Rd.	West Warwick	RI	02893-1234	August 12, 1971	Nurse	82,450	7
41											

6 Using the skills you have practiced, display the **Footer area**. In the **Center Footer area**, type **Salaries: Top 8 light red fill and bottom 8 yellow** Press Enter and type **Years Employed: Those working more than average years display in green**

Recall that providing an explanation of the conditional formats helps the reader review the data. The footers will overlap as you type them but will not overlap when they are displayed or printed.

7 Click in the worksheet and switch to Normal view. Switch to **Normal** view. **Save** 💾 your workbook.

More Knowledge

Top/Bottom Rules

The Top/Bottom Rules apply for the highest or lowest actual number. You may also determine the highest or lowest percentages or averages in the table. The number of items to include in the top or bottom list can also be changed.

Activity 4.22 Formatting and Editing Data Bars

A ***data bar*** is a colored bar that displays in a worksheet cell where the length of the data bar represents the value in the cell. A longer bar represents a higher value, a shorter bar represents a lower value. Data bars illustrate the relationship between the values in selected data range and will be used to display the salary ranges. In this activity, you will add data bars to a worksheet and edit the rules.

1 Click the **Alphabetic sheet tab**. Select the **Salary** range—**J6:J40**. Click the **Home tab**, and in the **Styles group**, click the **Conditional Formatting** button. Point to **Data Bars** and in the submenu, move the pointer over the displayed choices. As you do, observe the live preview changes the way the salaries are displayed on the screen. On the **Data Bar gallery**, point to the second row, third item—the ScreenTip displays *Purple Data Bar*. Compare your screen with Figure 4.55.

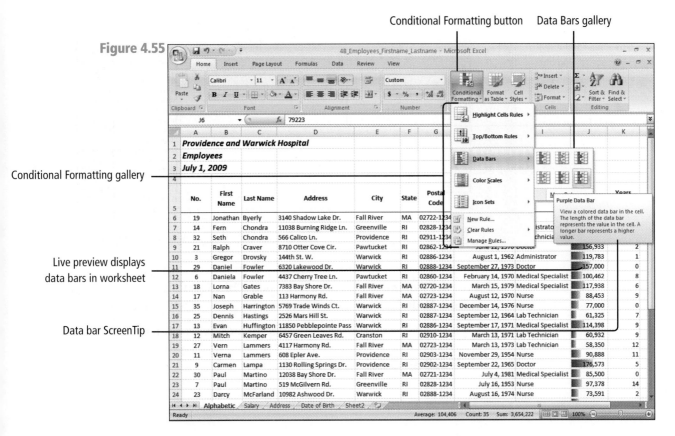

Figure 4.55

2 In the **Data Bar gallery**, click the **Purple Data Bar**.

Data bars have been placed in the cells in the salary column. The longer the data bar, the higher the salary. In this manner, the salaries can be compared without further sorting or altering the worksheet.

3 Click the **Conditional Formatting** button, and from the list, click **Manage Rules**.

The ***Conditional Formatting Rules Manager*** displays. The Conditional Formatting Rules Manager uses predetermined rules for applying a conditional format. New rules can be added or rules can be edited or removed. The Rules Manager provides a space for rules to be added, deleted, or edited. In addition, changes in the color format may be suggested.

4 At the top of the **Conditional Formatting Rules Manager**, in the **Show formatting rules for** box, click the arrow to display the list of choices and compare your screen with Figure 4.56.

Figure 4.56

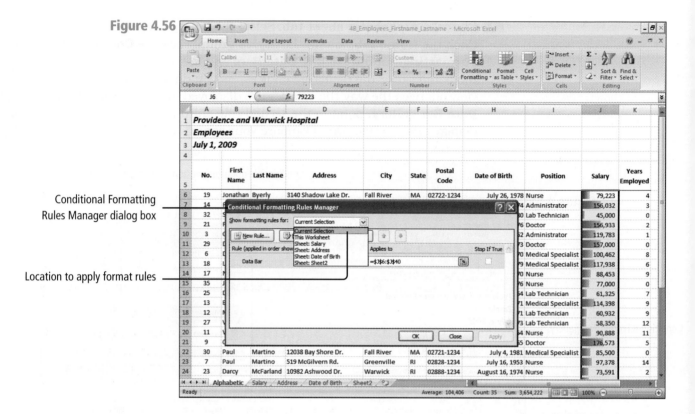

Conditional Formatting Rules Manager dialog box

Location to apply format rules

5 In the **Formatting rules** list, click **This Worksheet**. Then click the **Edit Rule** button and compare your screen with Figure 4.57.

The Edit Formatting Rule dialog box displays. A list of the rule types display, which can be edited. The rule description can also be edited as well as the color of the data bar.

Rules

Figure 4.57

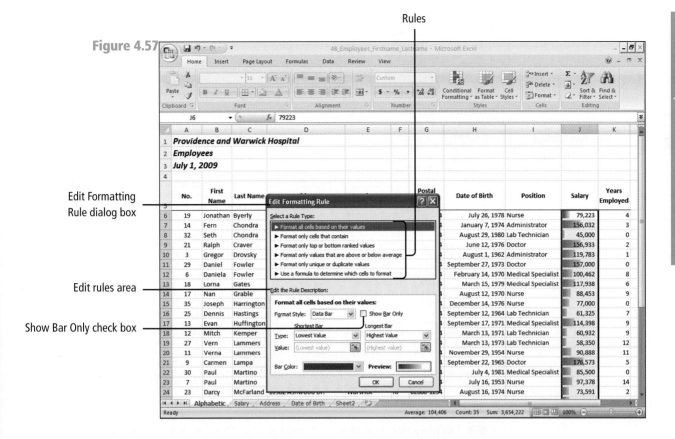

Edit Formatting
Rule dialog box

Edit rules area

Show Bar Only check box

6. In the lower part of the dialog box, under the **Format all cells based on their values** section, click **Show Bar Only**, and then click **OK**. In the **Conditional Formatting Rules Manager** dialog box, click **OK**. Compare your screen with Figure 4.58.

The actual salary numbers have been removed from the worksheet but the data bars remain. Confidential information is not available, although it is easy to compare the salaries among the employees.

Figure 4.58

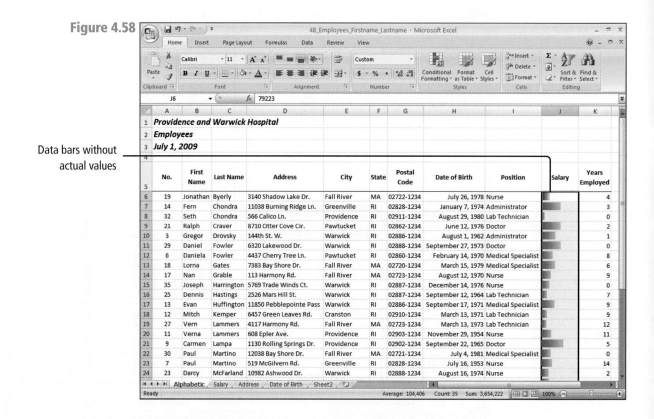

Data bars without actual values

7 Display the **Footer** area and in the **Center Footer** area, type **Salary data bars indicate salary level**

8 In the **Navigation group**, click the **Go to Header** button. Click in the worksheet, and then in the status bar, click the **Normal** button. **Save** your workbook.

Activity 4.23 Formatting and Editing Color Scales

Color scales uses gradients of the color to visually compare values. A two-color template assigns one color to the lowest value and a different color to the highest value and uses gradients of color for the values in between. Three-color templates are also available. In this activity, you will add color scales to a worksheet and edit the rules in order to visually review the relationships of the data.

1 In the **Alphabetic sheet**, select the **Years Employed** range—**K6:K40**. On the **Home tab**, in the **Styles group**, click the **Conditional Formatting** button and point to **Color Scales**. In the submenu, move the pointer over the options to view the live preview.

2 In the **Color Scales gallery**, point to the first choice in the first row—the ScreenTip displays *Green-Yellow-Red Color Scale*—and compare your screen with Figure 4.59. Then click the first choice.

The Years Employed are compared using color scales. The darker the color, the longer the years of employment for each employee.

Conditional Formatting button   Color Scales gallery

Figure 4.59

Color Scales command

ScreenTip

Color Scales applied using
Live Preview

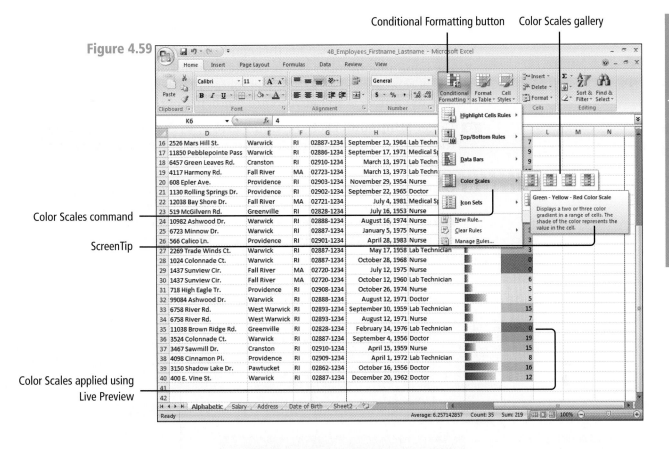

3 Display the **Conditional Formatting** list, and then click **Manage Rules**. In the **Show formatting rules for** box, click the **arrow**, and then click **This Worksheet** and compare your screen with Figure 4.60.

The Data Bar rule is displayed, along with the Graded Color Scale rule. When more than one rule is created in a worksheet, they are included in the Rules Manager.

Figure 4.60

Conditional Formatting
Rules Manager

Graded Color Scale

Data Bar

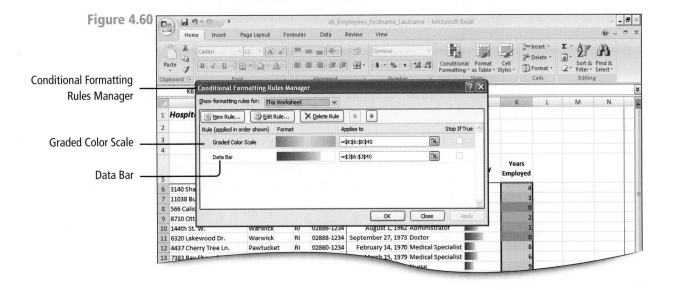

4 In the **Conditional Formatting Rules Manager**, click **Edit Rule**.

A 3-Color Scale is used for this conditional format. In the dialog box, the minimum number is represented by pink and the highest number is represented by green. The midpoint is represented by yellow, and the numbers in between are gradients of these colors.

5 Under **Minimum**, click the **Color arrow**. In the **Color gallery**, locate the eighth column and click the second color—**Purple, Accent 4, Lighter 80%**.

6 Under **Maximum**, click the **Color arrow**. In the **Color gallery**, in the eighth column, click the second-to-last color—**Purple, Accent 4, Darker 25%**. Under **Midpoint**, use the skills you have practiced to change the color to **Purple, Accent 4, Lighter 40%**. Compare your screen with Figure 4.61.

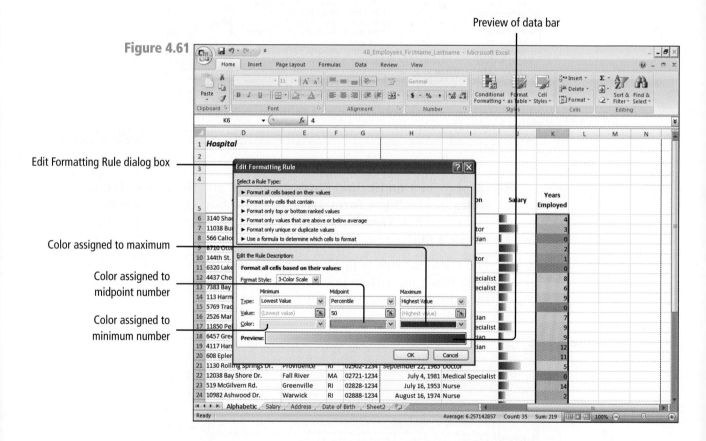

Figure 4.61

Preview of data bar

Edit Formatting Rule dialog box

Color assigned to maximum

Color assigned to midpoint number

Color assigned to minimum number

7 Click **OK**. In the **Conditional Formatting Rules Manager**, click **OK**.

The color bar has been edited to a purple color.

8 Display the **Footer** area and in the **Center Footer** area, position the insertion point at the end of the text and press Enter, and then type **Years Employed: darker displays those employed longer**

9 Click in the worksheet. Return to the **Normal** view ⊞ and **Save** 💾 your workbook.

Objective 10
Insert a Table and Filter Data

Recall that a table is a series of rows and columns that contain related data that can be manipulated separately from other data on the same worksheet. Using an existing worksheet, you can create a table that is already formatted and ready to use for sorting and filtering data. In a table, data that meets *criteria*—conditions you specify—can be *filtered* so only the rows that meet the criteria are displayed in the worksheet. Filtering data enables you to display a specific set of data.

Activity 4.24 Filtering a Table

When a filter is applied to a list, only the records that match the criteria—conditions—will display in the worksheet. Data is not lost, even though it does not display. In this activity, you will create a table that displays the doctors who live in Warwick.

1 Click the **Alphabetic sheet tab**, and click in a cell within the worksheet data. Click the **Data tab** and in the **Sort & Filter group**, click the **Filter** button, and then compare your screen with Figure 4.62.

Sorting and filtering arrows display with each column title indicating that this worksheet is ready to be sorted or filtered.

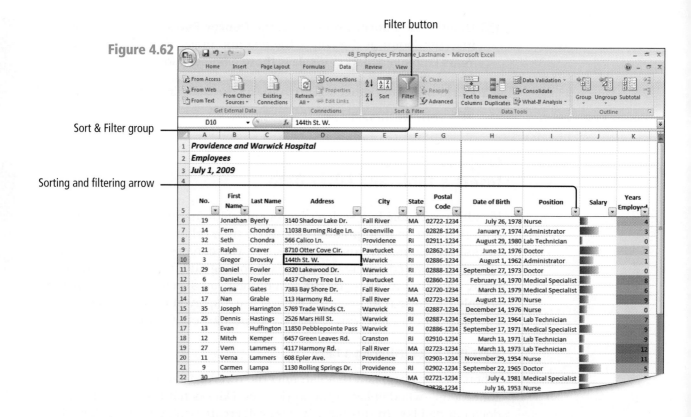

Filter button

Figure 4.62

Sort & Filter group

Sorting and filtering arrow

2 Point to the **column D header** and when the ⬇ pointer displays, click and drag through **column H** to select the columns. Click the **Home tab**, and in the **Cells group**, click the **Format** button. On the displayed list, under **Visibility**, point to **Hide & Unhide**. Then in the submenu that displays, click **Hide Columns**.

The selected columns no longer display. A solid vertical border indicates the hidden columns.

3 In the **Position** column title, click the **Sorting and Filtering arrow** ▼ to display the menu, and compare your screen with Figure 4.63.

When you click the arrow, a list of sorting and filtering options displays. The top portion of the list is used to sort the data, the center section is used for additional instructions, and the bottom section displays all the entries in the column. All filter choices are selected. This means that all of the data in this column is shown in the table. Although the sorting and filtering arrows display in the worksheet, they will not print.

Sorting instructions

Figure 4.63

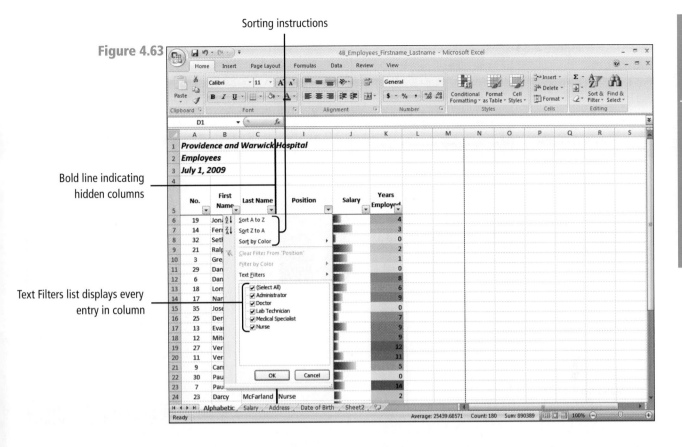

Bold line indicating hidden columns

Text Filters list displays every entry in column

4 In the filter area, click **Select All** to deselect all of the positions, click **Doctor**, and then click **OK**. Compare your screen with Figure 4.64.

Excel now displays only the name, position, salary, and

years employed of the doctors. A *filter button* displays in the Position column—cell I5. A filter button displays when the column is filtered. This worksheet has been filtered on one criterion—*Doctor*—the condition you specified to limit the records included in the results.

The row numbers display in blue text, indicating there are hidden rows. The status bar displays the status of the filter—7 of the 35 records display.

Figure 4.64

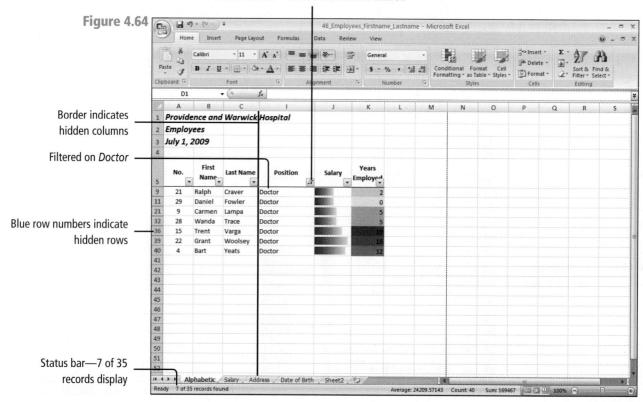

Border indicates hidden columns

Filtered on *Doctor*

Blue row numbers indicate hidden rows

Status bar—7 of 35 records display

5 Point to the **Position Filter** button [filter icon] and review the ScreenTip. Then compare your screen with Figure 4.65.

The ScreenTip displays *Position: Equals "Doctor"*. The filter button indicates that this field has been filtered—limited so that not all of the data displays.

Filter button

Figure 4.65

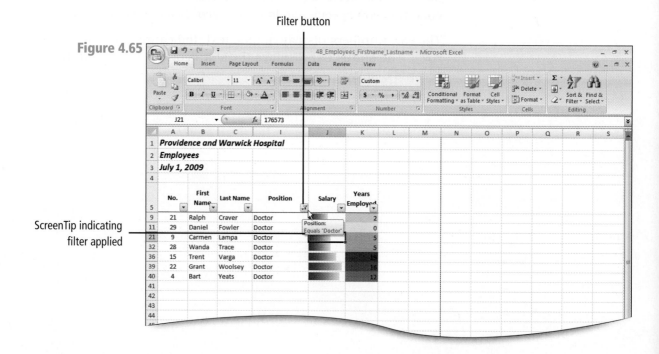

ScreenTip indicating filter applied

6 Select the range of the worksheet—**A1:K40**—and right-click. Click **Copy**, and then click the **Sheet2 tab**. Right-click cell **A1** and click **Paste**. Adjust column widths, if necessary.

The filtered list has been copied to the worksheet exactly as displayed. The hidden columns and rows are no longer available.

7 Click the **Alphabetic sheet tab**. Click the **Position Filter** button ▼ and from the list, click **(Select All)**, and then click **OK**.

All rows of the table display. The sorting and filtering arrow returns at the Position column title. The moving border remains active around the previous copy range. Recall that the copy range remains selected until another command is selected.

8 Click the **Position Sorting and Filtering** button ▼ , click **Select All** to deselect it, and click **Nurse**, and then click **OK**.

Only the nurses are now displayed in the range. The row headings display in blue with many row numbers hidden.

9 Select the range of the worksheet—omitting the worksheet title but including the column title—**A5:K37**. Right-click and click **Copy**. Click the **Sheet2 sheet tab**, right-click cell **A16**, and then click **Paste**. Double-click the **Sheet2 sheet tab** tab and type **Doctor Nurse Comparisons**

10 Select the salary range for the doctors—**E6:E12**. Press Ctrl and select the salary range for the nurses—**E17:E29**. On the **Home tab**, in the **Styles group**, click the **Conditional Formatting** button, and then click **Manage Rules**. Compare your screen with Figure 4.66.

There are two rules in the dialog box, both titled *Data Bar*. You can tell them apart by the ranges they refer to. The first data bar—E17:E29—is shaded, indicating it is the active data bar.

Figure 4.66

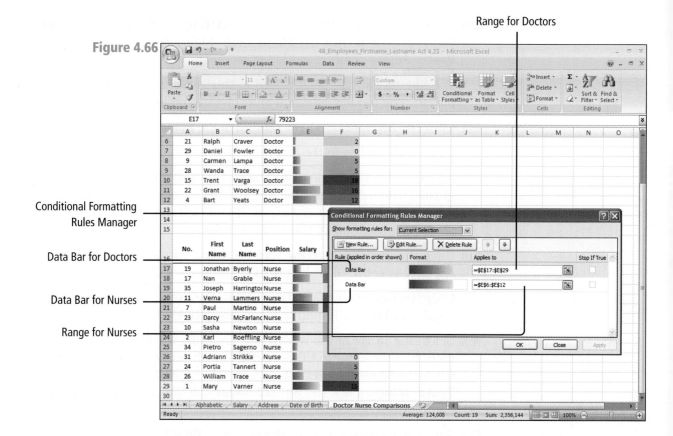

Range for Doctors

Conditional Formatting Rules Manager

Data Bar for Doctors

Data Bar for Nurses

Range for Nurses

11 With the first Data Bar selected, click **Edit Rule**. Under **Format all cells based on their values**, click **Show Bar Only** to deselect it. Then click **OK**.

12 Click the second Data Bar with the corresponding range **E6:E12**. Click **Edit Rule**. Under **Format all cells based on their values**, click **Show Bar Only** to deselect it. Then click **OK**. In the **Conditional Formatting Rules Manager**, click **OK**.

The data is again displayed for the doctors and the nurses. You can edit more than one range without exiting the Conditional Formatting Rules Manager dialog box.

13 Select the range **A5:F12**. On the **Insert tab**, in the **Tables group**, click the **Table** button. In the **Create Table** dialog box, the range of the table is identified. Confirm that **My table has headers** is checked, click **OK**, and then compare your screen with Figure 4.67.

The Table Tools Design tab now displays on the Ribbon. The selected cells display as a table with each row displaying alternating colors—referred to as banded colors. The sorting and filtering buttons remain and the conditional formatting displays.

A table is used to quickly format the data and helps organize your work. The Sorting and Filtering arrows display and there are several styles that add designer-quality formatting to the table.

Table Tools Design tab   Table format applied to selection

Figure 4.67

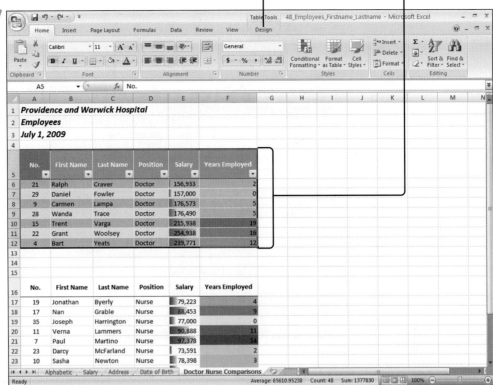

14 Select the range **A16:F29**. On the **Insert tab**, in the **Tables group**, click the **Table** button. In the **Create Table** dialog box, the range of the table is identified. Confirm that **My table has headers** is checked, and then click **OK**.

15 On the **Table Tools Design tab**, in the **Table Styles group**, click the **More** button ⬇ to display the **Table Styles gallery.** Compare your screen with Figure 4.68.

The *Table Styles gallery* displays the styles that can be applied to a table. The scroll bar at the right side of the gallery indicates there are additional choices.

Figure 4.68

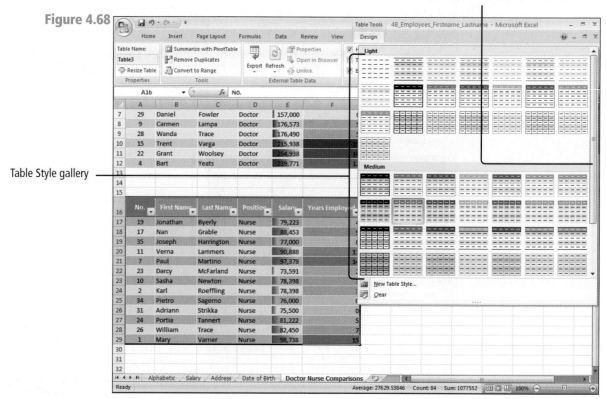

Table Style gallery

16 Under **Medium**, in the fifth column, click the first choice—**Table Style Medium 5**. Then click outside the selected range of cells.

The table that displays the nurse's information is displayed in a banded purple color.

17 In the **Left Footer** area, place the **File Name** and in the **Right Footer** area, place the **Sheet Name**. Return to cell **A1** and switch to **Normal** view . **Save** your workbook.

More Knowledge

Insert and Delete Rows in a Table and Apply Themes to the Design

When a row is inserted or deleted from a table, the row format of alternating styles is maintained.

When a workbook theme is changed, the display in the table changes to match the selected theme. Color and font choices match those in the rest of the workbook.

Activity 4.25 Filtering and Sorting on Two Tables

The data in the tables will be sorted and filtered so that comparisons about the salaries can be made. In this activity, you will filter the tables.

1 Click the **Doctor Nurse Comparisons sheet tab**. In the **Doctor** table, click the **Salary Sorting and Filtering arrow**, and click **Sort Smallest to Largest**. In the Nurse table, click the **Salary Sorting and Filtering arrow**, and click **Sort Largest to Smallest**.

Maria Benitez notices that the least-paid doctor is paid more than the highest-paid nurse.

2 In the **Doctor** table, click the **Years Employed Sorting and Filtering arrow**, point to **Number Filters**, and compare your screen with Figure 4.69.

The submenu displays the filtering choices for numbers, which include the comparison operators you have used previously, along with Top 10, Above Average, Below Average, and Custom Filter.

Number Filters command   Number filter submenu

Figure 4.69

Sort and Filter list

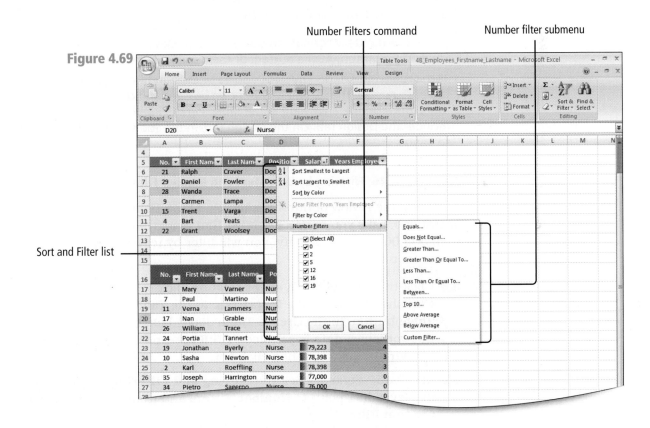

3 In the submenu, click **Less Than**. At the right side of the dialog box, in the box with the blinking insertion point, type **10** and then click **OK**.

Four records display. Those that are not displayed are still included in the table. The row headings at the left display in blue, indicating there are hidden rows.

4 In the **Nurse** table, click the **Years Employed** column **Sorting and Filtering arrow**, point to **Number Filters**, and in the submenu, click **Greater Than**. In the box with the blinking insertion point, type **10** and then click **OK**.

The nurses who have been employed more than 10 years display. Maria can now compare the salaries and years of service of the nurses and doctors at the hospital.

5 Click cell **A2** and type **Doctor and Nurse Comparisons**

This document will be used by the HR Department for comparison purposes. When a worksheet is prepared only for the user, it is not necessary to provide a formatted title. It is critical, however, to identify the document and the date.

6 Save 🖫 your workbook.

More Knowledge

To Convert a Table into a Range of Data and Remove the Table Format

To remove the table format, on the Table Tools Design tab, click the Table Styles More button. At the bottom of the display, click Clear.

The sorting and filtering buttons display to assist in filtering and sorting the table. To remove the sorting and filtering buttons and convert a table to a range of cells, click anywhere in the table. On the Ribbon, the Table Tools includes the Design tab. On the Design tab, in the Tools group, click Convert to Range.

Activity 4.26 Filtering by Using Text and Number Filters

As part of the review of nursing salaries, Maria Benitez, vice president of operations, asks you to prepare a list that displays nurses earning more than $85,000. In this activity, you will filter by text and by numbers to create that list.

1 Click the **Date of Birth sheet tab** and click on a cell within the worksheet data. On the **Insert tab**, in the **Tables group**, click the **Table** button. In the **Create Table** dialog box, confirm the range of the worksheet data is selected—**A5:K40**—and that **My table has headers** is checked. Then click **OK**.

2 In cell **J5**—Salary—click the **Sorting and Filtering arrow**. From the displayed list, point to **Number Filters** and from the submenu, click **Custom Filter**.

3 In the displayed **Custom AutoFilter** dialog box, under **Salary**, click the arrow and click **is greater than or equal to**. Press Tab and in the top right text box, type **85000** Compare your screen with Figure 4.70, and then click **OK**.

The Custom AutoFilter dialog box is used to enter the specific instructions for filtering numbers. Here you can also apply more than one criterion for your filter.

In the table, only the salaries that are $85,000 or greater display. The Filter button displays in the column title.

Figure 4.70

Custom AutoFilter dialog box —

Enter filter specifications —

Display filter instructions —

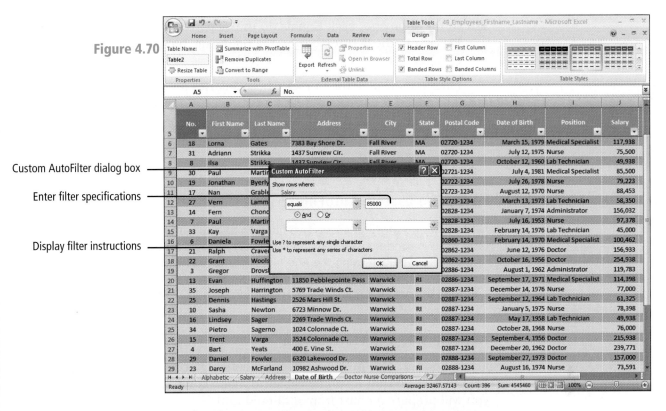

4 Click the **Position Sorting and Filtering arrow**. From the displayed list, point to **Text Filters** to display the submenu and compare your screen with Figure 4.71.

The submenu displays the filtering choices for text. The status bar indicates that 17 of 35 records were found.

Text Filters command   Sort and Filter list

Figure 4.71

Text filter submenu —

Status bar displays
17 of 35 records found —

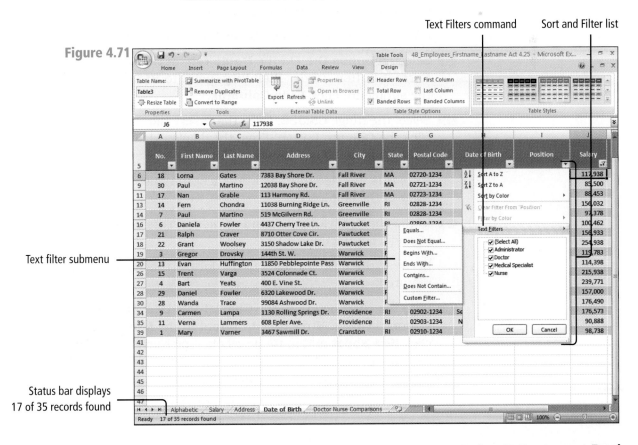

5 In the submenu, click **Equals**. In the displayed **Custom AutoFilter** dialog box, in the first textbox on the right side, type **Nurse** and click **OK**.

The Filter button now displays in the Position column title. The table is filtered to display the nurses whose salaries are greater than $85,000.

6 **Save** 💾 your workbook.

More Knowledge

Why Use Custom AutoFilter?

The Custom AutoFilter allows two filters to be applied to the table. You can filter for two conditions—nurses and years of employment over 5, for example—or for either field. If using the And filter, your list will display only the nurses who have been employed more than 5 years. If using the Or filter, your list will include the field if it matches either criterion—a nurse or employed over 5 years.

Activity 4.27 Chart Filtered Data

Maria Benitez, vice president of operations, charts the data of the higher-paid nurses so that it will be easier to make comparisons. In this activity, you will prepare a chart from a filtered table.

1 Right-click the **Date of Birth sheet tab** and click **Move or Copy**. In the **Move or Copy** dialog box, under **Before sheet**, click **(move to end)**. Click **Create a copy**, and then click **OK**.

2 Double-click the **Date of Birth (2) sheet tab** and type **Nurses' Salaries** and then click in the worksheet. Click the **Salary AutoFilter** button ▼ and from the list, click **Clear Filter From "Salary"**.

3 Select **columns D:I**. On the **Home tab**, in the **Cells group**, click the **Format** button. Under **Visibility**, point to **Hide & Unhide** and from the submenu, click **Hide Columns**.

4 Select the range **C5:J39**. Click the **Insert tab**. In the **Charts group**, click the **Column** button. From the displayed list, under **2-D Column**, click the first choice—**Clustered Column**.

A chart is inserted into the worksheet that displays the salaries of some of the employees.

5 In the chart, click the **Legend**—*Salary*. Press ⌈Delete⌋ to delete the legend from the chart.

Because there is only one type of data in this chart, a legend is not required.

6 With the chart active, in the **Chart Tools Design tab**, in the **Location group**, click the **Move Chart** button. In the **Move Chart** dialog box, click **New sheet** and in the text box, type **Nurse Salary Chart** Click **OK**.

7 Click the **Nurses' Salaries sheet tab**. Click the **Salary** column **Sorting and Filtering arrow** and from the list, click **Sort Largest to Smallest**. Click the **Nurse Salary Chart sheet tab** and as you do, notice the data markers on the chart are altered to match the newly sorted data.

Because the worksheet is linked to the chart, changes made in the worksheet are reflected in the chart, including the order of the display for the data markers.

8 Click the **Chart Title**. Select the title and then type **Nurse Salaries** and press Enter. Type **July 1, 2009** Position the insertion point before *Nurse Salaries*, press Enter, press the ↑, and type **Providence and Warwick Hospital**. Compare your screen with Figure 4.72.

Figure 4.72

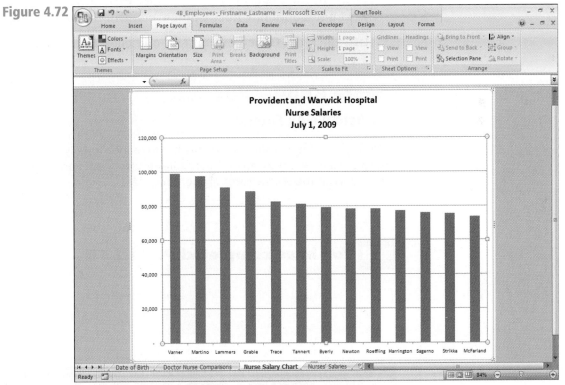

9 Click the **Nurses Salary Chart sheet tab** and drag to the right to move the chart sheet to the last sheet of the workbook.

10 Click the **Insert tab**. In the **Text group**, click the **Header & Footer** button. Click **Custom Footer**. In the **Left section** click the **Insert File Name** button . Click the **Right section** and click the **Insert Sheet Name** button . Click **OK**. Click **Custom Header**. In the **Left section**, enter the page number using the *Page x of xx* style. Click **OK** two times to close both dialog boxes.

11 Click the **Nurses' Salaries sheet tab**, and use the **tab scrolling bars** to display the **Alphabetic sheet**. Press ⟨⇧ Shift⟩ as you click the **Alphabetic sheet tab**. Click the **Page Layout tab**. In the **Page Setup group**, click the **Dialog Box Launcher** 🔲. In the **Page Setup** dialog box, under **Orientation**, click **Landscape**. Under **Scaling**, click **Fit to**. Click the **Margins tab**. At the **Top** spin box, click the **up arrow** to change the **Top** margin to **1.25"**. Under **Center on page**, click **Horizontally** and click **OK**. Click cell **A1**, **Ungroup the sheets**, and click the **Alphabetic sheet tab**.

12 **Save** 💾 your workbook.

13 To submit your work electronically, follow the instructions provided by your instructor. To print, click the **Office** button 🔲 and click **Print**. In the **Print** dialog box, under **Print what**, click the **Entire workbook** option. Under **Copies**, confirm that **1** is selected. Click **OK**. Click the **Office** button 🔲 and click **Exit Excel**.

More Knowledge

To Remove All Filters

Removing a filter from a table may be done individually by field. When all filters are to be removed and the table restored to its original form, on the Data tab, in the Sort & Filter group, click Clear.

End **You have completed Project 4B** ———————————

There's More You Can Do!

From My Computer, navigate to the student files that accompany this textbook. In the folder **02_theres_more_you_can_do**, locate and open the folder for this chapter. Open and print the instructions for this project, which are provided to you in Adobe PDF format.

Try It! 1—Use Table Tools Design

In this Try It! exercise, you will use the Table Tools Design tab to format a Table.

Content-Based Assessments

Summary

Charts create a visual representation of numbers to help you analyze and communicate information about the data in your worksheet. Excel tables contain related data that is organized into columns and rows which can be manipulated separately from other data in the worksheet. Sort and filter tables to organize and limit the data displayed to create information that can be used to make decisions. By organizing your data with Excel charts and tables, you will be able to make logical decisions and create visual representations of your data.

Key Terms

The ❷ symbol represents Key Terms found on the Student CD in the 02_theres_more_you_can_do folder for this chapter.

Content-Based Assessments

Matching

Match each term in the second column with its correct definition in the first column. Write the letter of the term on the blank line in front of the correct definition.

_____ **1.** The angle of text within a cell.

_____ **2.** A visual representation of numeric data found in a worksheet.

_____ **3.** A chart that displays changes over a period of time or illustrates comparisons.

_____ **4.** In a chart, the representation of the value in the worksheet cell.

_____ **5.** A chart that displays as an object within a worksheet.

_____ **6.** A chart identified by a double border that may be edited.

_____ **7.** The range of cells that are charted.

_____ **8.** The area of a chart that identifies the colors of the data markers.

_____ **9.** Located at the edge of a chart and used to change the size of the chart.

_____ **10.** The look of the chart including the chart elements.

_____ **11.** The entire chart and all of its elements.

_____ **12.** In a chart, the area bordered by the axes, including all data series, category names, tick-mark labels, and gridlines.

_____ **13.** Horizontal and vertical chart lines that extend from any horizontal and vertical axes across the plot area of the chart.

_____ **14.** Related data points that are plotted in a chart.

_____ **15.** A chart that cannot be edited.

A Active chart

B Chart

C Chart area

D Chart layout

E Chart range

F Column chart

G Data marker

H Data series

I Embedded chart

J Gridlines

K Inactive chart

L Legend

M Orientation

N Plot area

O Sizing handles

Content-Based Assessments

Fill in the Blank

Write the correct word in the space provided.

1. A chart that is placed within a worksheet is a(n) _____ chart.

2. Selecting a column chart, a line chart, a bar chart, or a pie chart is selecting a chart _____.

3. Determining the colors used in a chart is selecting the chart _____.

4. A gradual progression of colors and shades that may move from one color to another that is often used as background is _____ fill.

5. The look of the border line is the border _____.

6. The line that surrounds the title or legend of a chart is the border _____.

7. The worksheet is connected to the chart because the chart and worksheet are _____.

8. The labels that identify the markers of the chart are the _____ labels.

9. Charts that are round are _____ charts.

10. When a data marker in a pie chart is displayed detached from the chart, you have a(n) _____ pie chart.

11. Change the orientation or angle of the chart element by _____ the chart element a specified number of degrees.

12. Additional information can be included in a chart or worksheet in a _____ _____ that is independent from the worksheet cells.

13. A series of rows and columns that contains related data is a _____.

14. Each row of information consists of a(n) _____.

15. Each column of information consists of a(n) _____.

Content-Based Assessments

Project 4C — ICU

In this project, you will apply the skills you practiced from the Objectives in Project 4A.

Objectives: **1.** *Use Text Orientation;* **2.** *Create a Column Chart;* **3.** *Create a Chart Sheet and Edit the Chart;* **4.** *Create and Modify a Pie Chart;* **5.** *Apply a Theme to a Chart;* **6.** *Print Charts.*

In the following Skills Review project, you will create a workbook for Maria Benitez, vice president of operations, which displays the types of cases in the Intensive Care Unit for four days. Charts will be completed to compare the days. Your completed workbook will look similar to the one shown in Figure 4.73.

For Project 4C, you will need the following file:

New blank Excel workbook

**You will save your workbook as
4C_ICU_Firstname_Lastname**

Figure 4.73

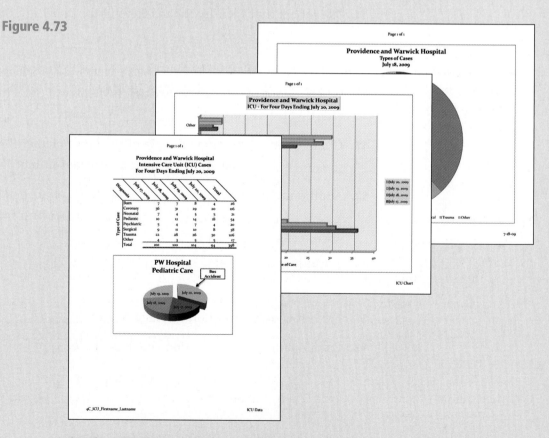

(Project 4C–ICU continues on the next page)

Content-Based Assessments

(Project 4C–ICU continued)

1. **Start** Excel and display a new blank workbook. Save the file in your **Excel Chapter 4** folder as 4C_ICU_Firstname_Lastname

2. Beginning in cell **A1**, type the following worksheet title:

Providence and Warwick Hospital
Intensive Care Unit (ICU) Cases
For Four Days Ending July 20, 2009

3. Beginning in cell **A5**, type the following data. Recall that to enter a date in this style, place an apostrophe before the month. Recall that entering data by range is recommended.

Diagnosis	July 17, 2009	July 18, 2009	July 19, 2009	July 20, 2009
Burn	7	7	8	4
Coronary	36	31	29	20
Neonatal	7	4	5	5
Pediatric	10	12	14	15
Psychiatric	5	4	7	4
Surgical	9	11	10	8
Trauma	22	28	26	30
Other	4	3	5	5

4. Right-click the **column A heading**, and then click **Insert**. In cell **A6**, type Type of Case Select the range **A6:A14** and in the **Font group**, click the **Bold** button. In the **Alignment group**, click the **Merge & Center** button and **Middle Align** button. Click the **Orientation** button and from the displayed list, click **Rotate Text Up**. In the **Font group**, click the **Borders button arrow** and from the displayed list, click **Right Border**. Adjust the width of **column A** to **4.00**.

5. Click cell **B10**. On the **Home tab**, in the **Cell group**, click the **Format** button. Under **Cell Size**, click **AutoFit Column Width**. Select the worksheet title—cells **B1:B3.** Apply **Bold** emphasis and change the **Font Size** to **14**. Select the range **A1:G1** and **Merge & Center** the title. Using the skills you just practiced, **Merge & Center** each line of the worksheet title.

6. In cell **G5**, type Total In cell **B14**, type Total Select the range of the worksheet—**C6:G14**—and in the **Editing group**, click the **Sum** button. With the range selected, apply the **Comma Style** with **no decimals**. Select the range **C14:G14** and apply a **Top and Double Bottom Border**.

7. Select the range **B5:G5**. In the **Font group**, click the **Bold** button. In the **Alignment group**, click the **Center** button and **Middle Align** button. Click the **Orientation** button and from the displayed list, click **Angle Clockwise**. In the **Font group**, click the **Borders button arrow** and from the displayed list, click **All Borders**.

8. Select the range of the worksheet that will be charted—**B5:F13**. Click the **Insert tab**, and in the **Charts group**, click the **Column** button. In the displayed list, under **Cylinder**, click the first choice—**Clustered Cylinder**.

(Project 4C–ICU continues on the next page)

(Project 4C–ICU continued)

9. In the **Type group**, click the **Change Chart Type** button. In the area at the left, click **Bar**. In the area at the right, under **Bar** in the first row, click the fourth choice—**Clustered Bar in 3-D**, and then click **OK**.

10. Rename **Sheet1** to **ICU Data** Click in the chart to make it active. On the **Design tab**, in the **Location group**, click the **Move Chart** button. In the **Move Chart** dialog box, click **New Sheet** and in the text box, type **ICU Chart**, and then click **OK**.

11. On the **Design tab**, click the **Chart Styles More** button. In the displayed **Chart Styles gallery**, in the sixth column, click the fifth choice—**Style 38**. As you review the chart, notice that there is not much difference in the colors for the number of data markers. Again click the **Chart Styles More** button. From the displayed **Chart Styles gallery**, in the second column, click the fifth choice—**Style 34**.

12. Click the **Layout tab,** and in the **Labels group**, click **Chart Title**, and then click **Above Chart**. Select the text, *Chart Title*, and type **Providence and Warwick Hospital** Press ⏎ and type **ICU – For Four Days Ending July 20, 2009**

13. With the chart title active, click the **Layout tab**, and in the **Current Selection group**, click **Format Selection**. In the **Format Chart Title** dialog box, confirm that **Fill** is selected. On the right side, click **Solid fill**. Click the **Color** button and in the fourth column, click the third color—**Dark Blue, Text 2, Lighter 60%**. Under **Transparency**, move the slider until **50%** displays in the slider display box. Alternatively, in the slider box type **50%**

14. In the **Format Chart Title** dialog box, on the left side, click **3-D Format**. On the right side— 3-D Format—under **Bevel**, click the **Top** button. In the displayed gallery, under **Bevel**, in the second row, click the second choice—**Soft Round**. Click the **Bottom** button and under **Bevel**, in the second row, click the second icon—**Soft Round**. Click **Close**.

15. In the chart title, select the hospital name and right-click. From the Mini toolbar, click the **Font Size button arrow**, and click **16**. Select the name of the unit and the date, right-click and from the Mini toolbar, change the **Font Size** to **14**.

16. In the active chart, click the **legend**. On the **Layout tab**, in the **Current Selection group**, click **Format Selection**. In the **Format Legend** dialog box, on the left side, click **Fill**. On the right side, click **Solid fill**. Click the **Color** button and from the displayed color gallery, in the fourth column, click the third color chip—**Dark Blue, Text 2, Lighter 60%**. Under **Transparency**, move the slider until **50%** displays in the slider box.

17. In the **Format Legend** dialog box, on the left side, click **Border Color**. On the right side, click **No line**. In the **Format Legend** dialog box, on the left side, click **Shadow**. On the right side, click the **Presets** button. Under **Outer**, in the first row, click the last icon—**Offset Diagonal Bottom Left**. Click the **Color** button. In the color gallery, in the fourth column, click the third color—**Dark Blue, Text 2, Lighter 60%**. Click **Close**.

18. On the **Layout tab**, in the **Labels group**, click the **Axis Titles** button. In the displayed list, point to **Primary Horizontal Axis Title** and from the submenu, click **Title Below Axis**. Select the text, *Axis Title*, and type **Number of Patients**

(Project 4C–ICU continues on the next page)

Content-Based Assessments

(Project 4C–ICU continued)

19. **Save** your workbook. Click the **ICU Data sheet tab**. Click cell **A1**. In the **Name Box**, type **b5:b13,d5:d13** and press Enter to select the ranges to be charted. Alternatively, in the worksheet, select the range **B5:B13**. Press Ctrl and select the range **D5:D13**. Click the **Insert tab**, and in the **Charts group**, click the **Pie** button. In the displayed gallery, under **2-D Pie**, in the first row, click the second chart type—**Exploded Pie**. On the **Design tab**, in the **Chart Layouts group**, click the last icon—**Layout 3**. This removes the chart title and places the legend under the pie.

20. In the **Type group**, click the **Change Chart Type** button. On the right side, under **Pie**, click the first choice—**Pie**—and then click **OK**.

21. With the chart active, on the **Design tab**, in the **Location group**, click **Move Chart**. In the **Move Chart** dialog box, click **New Sheet** and in the text box, type **7-18-09** and then click **OK**.

22. Click the **Layout tab**. In the **Labels group**, click the **Chart Title** button, and then click **Above Chart**. In the chart title, click to position the insertion point to the left of the date. Type **Providence and Warwick Hospital** press Enter, and type **Types of Cases,** and press Enter. Select the second and third lines of the chart title, right-click, and change the **Font Size** to **14**.

23. Click the **Design tab**, and in the **Chart Styles** group, click the **More** arrow to display the gallery. From the second column, click the next-to-last icon—**Style 34**—to show greater definition between the data markers.

24. Click the **ICU Data sheet tab**. Select the range **B5:F5**. Press Ctrl and select **B9:F9**. Click the **Insert tab**, and in the **Charts group**, click the **Pie** button. Under **3-D Pie**, click the first choice—**Pie in 3-D**. Point to the edge of the chart and when the ⬉ pointer displays, drag the chart and position the upper left corner of the chart in cell **A16**.

25. On the **Design tab**, in the **Chart Layouts group**, click the **More** button. In the displayed gallery, in the second row, click the second choice—**Layout 5**. Select the text in the title and type **PW Hospital** press Enter, and type **Pediatric Care**

26. In the chart, click the pie to select it. Click the **Layout tab**, and in the **Current Selection group**, click **Format Selection**. In the **Format Data Series** dialog box, confirm that **Series Options** is selected. In the right side, under **No Rotation**, use the slider to move the rotation until **106** displays in the box. Then click **Close**.

27. Click the pie, then click the **July 20** data marker to select it. Drag the marker slightly away from the center of the pie to "explode" it. On the **Layout tab**, in the **Insert group**, click the **Text Box** button. Move the pointer to the upper right side of the **July 20** data marker approximately aligned with the upper edge of cell F19, and drag down and to the right to create a text box that ends approximately in the middle of column G and through row 20. Type **Bus Accident** Select the text in the text box, right-click, and from the Mini toolbar, click the **Bold** button and **Center** button. In the **Alignment group**, click **Middle Align**. If necessary, drag one of the corner sizing handles to adjust the size of the text box so that the text displays on two lines.

28. With the text box active, click the **Format tab**. Under **Shape Styles**, click the **Shape Outline** button. In the **Color gallery**, click **Automatic**. In the **Insert Shapes group**, on the top row, click the third choice—**Arrow**. Position the pointer at the edge of the text box and drag to the July 20

(Project 4C–ICU continues on the next page)

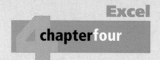
(Project 4C–ICU continued)

data marker. With the arrow selected, click the **Shape Styles More** button. From the displayed gallery, in the first column, click the second choice—**Moderate Line – Dark 1.** Click cell **A1.**

29. Click the **Page Layout tab**, and in the **Themes group**, click the **Themes** button, and then click **Flow**. In each sheet, review that text and data still fully display and are readable.

30. There is a correction for the July 20 pediatric cases. In the **ICU Data sheet**, in cell **F9**, type **18** and then press [Enter]. Confirm this change was made in all worksheets. Click the **ICU Data sheet tab**. In the chart, click the pie to make it active. Click the **Layout tab**, and in the **Current Selection group**, click **Format Selection**. Adjust the **rotation** to **120**.

31. **Delete Sheet2** and **Sheet3**. Click the **ICU Data sheet tab** and drag the displayed icon to the left of the **ICU Chart sheet tab**. Spell check all worksheets in the workbook.

32. Click the **ICU Chart sheet tab**, press [⇧ Shift], and click the **7-18-09 sheet tab** to select both chart sheets. Click the **Insert tab**, and in the **Text group**, click the **Header & Footer** button. In the **Page Setup** dialog box, click **Custom Footer**. In the **Left section**, click the **Insert File Name** button—the code *&[File]* displays. Click in the **Right section** and click the **Insert Sheet Name** button—the code *&[Tab]* displays. Click **OK**. Click **Custom Header**. Click in the **Center section**, type **Page** and press [Spacebar]. Click the **Insert Page Number** button, press [Spacebar], type **of** press [Spacebar], and then click the **Insert Number of Pages** button. The code in the center section displays *Page &[Page] of &[Pages]*. Click **OK**, and then in the **Page Setup** dialog box, click **OK**.

33. Click the **ICU Data sheet tab**. Click in the worksheet to confirm the chart is not active. In the **Text group**, click the **Header & Footer** button. In the **Navigation group**, click the **Go to Footer** button. Click in the **Left Footer** area, and then click the **File Name** button. Click in the **Right Footer** area, and then click the **Sheet Name**. In the header displayed on the top of the next page, click in the **Center Header** area and type **Page** and press [Spacebar]. Click the **Insert Page Number** button, press [Spacebar], type **of** press [Spacebar], and then click the **Insert Number of Pages** button. Click in the worksheet and press [Ctrl] + [Home] to return to cell **A1**. Switch to **Normal** view.

34. Click the **Page Layout tab**. In the **Page Setup group**, click the **Dialog Box Launcher**. In the **Page Setup** dialog box, click the **Margins tab**. Under **Center on Page**, click **Horizontally** and **Vertically**. Click **OK**.

35. **Save** your workbook. Right-click any sheet tab and click **Select All Sheets**. Click the **Office** button, point to **Print**, and then click **Print Preview** and review the worksheets. Click **Close Print Preview**.

36. Click the **ICU Data sheet tab**. To submit your files electronically, follow the instructions provided by your instructor. To print, click the **Office** button, and then click **Print**. In the **Print** dialog box, under **Print range**, confirm that **All** is selected. Under **Print what**, click **Entire workbook**, and then click **OK**.

37. To exit Excel, click the **Office** button, and in the lower right corner, click **Exit Excel**. Alternatively, at the right end of the title bar, click the program **Close** button.

End **You have completed Project 4C**

Content-Based Assessments

Project 4D — Doctors

In this project, you will apply the skills you practiced from the Objectives in Project 4B.

Objectives: 7. *Sort Data;* **8.** *Convert Text into Columns;* **9.** *Apply Conditional Formatting Using Data Bars and Color Scales;* **10.** *Insert a Table and Filter Data.*

In the following Skills Review project, you will create a workbook for the Human Resources Department that identifies the doctors on staff, their specialty, and both the pager and phone number. You will sort and filter the list to prepare a collection of different tables that display the data in several ways. Your completed workbook will look similar to the one shown in Figure 4.74.

> ### For Project 4D, you will need the following files:
>
> e04D_Doctors
> e04D_New_Doctors
>
> You will save your workbook as
> 4D_Doctors_Firstname_Lastname

Figure 4.74

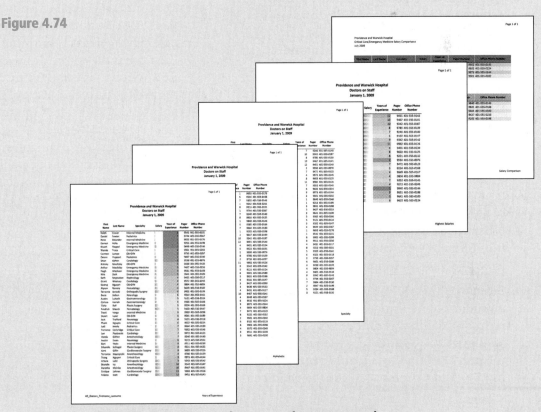

(Project 4D–Doctors continues on the next page)

Content-Based Assessments

(Project 4D–Doctors continued)

1. **Start** Excel. From the student files locate and open the file named **e04D_Doctors** and then save it in your Excel Chapter 4 folder as **4D_Doctors_Firstname_Lastname**

2. Right-click the **row 3 heading** and then click **Insert**. In cell **A3**, type **'January 1, 2009** Select the range **A1:A3**, right-click, and format with **Bold**, and **14 point** font. **Merge & Center** each row across the range of the worksheet—**columns A:G**.

3. Select the column titles—**A5:G5**. Format with **Bold**, **Center**, **Middle Align**, **Wrap Text**, and a **Bottom Border**. Confirm that all items fully display in each column and the titles display on two lines with no extra space above and below the text.

4. From your student files locate and open the file named **e04D_New_Doctors**. Select the range **A4:A7**, right-click and click **Copy**. On the **View tab**, in the **Window group**, click the **Switch Windows** button, and from the displayed list, click **4D_Doctors_Firstname_Lastname**. Right-click cell **A44** and select **Paste**.

5. With the range **A44:A47** selected, click the **Data tab** and in the **Data Tools group**, click the **Text to Columns** button. In the **Convert Text to Columns Wizard - Step 1 of 3** dialog box, be sure **Delimited** is selected, and then click **Next**. In the **Step 2 of 3** dialog box, under **Delimiters**, click to select **Semicolon** and click to clear any other check marks. Click **Next**. In the **Step 3 of 3** dialog box, confirm the destination is cell $A$44, and then click **Finish**.

6. Select the range **B44:F47**. Point to the boundary of the range, and drag to the right one column until the ScreenTip displays **C44:G47**. Select the range **A44:A47**. In the **Data Tools group**, click the **Text to Columns** button. In the **Step**

1 of 3 dialog box, click **Next**. In the **Step 2 of 3** dialog box, under **Delimiters**, click **Space** to select it and click to clear any other check marks. Click **Next**. In the **Step 3 of 3** dialog box, confirm the destination is cell $A$44, and then click **Finish**. In the worksheet, adjust the column widths so that the data fully displays.

7. On the **View tab**, in the **Window group**, click the **Switch Windows** button. From the list, click **e04D_New_Doctors**. In the workbook-level buttons, click **Close Window**. If asked to save changes, click **No**.

8. The **4D_Doctors_Firstname_Lastname** sheet displays. In the newly added data, there are added spaces in columns C and G. Select cell **C49**. On the **Formulas tab**, in the **Function Library group**, click the **Text** button. Scroll to and click **TRIM**. In the **TRIM Function Arguments** dialog box, click cell **C44**, and then click **OK**. Use the fill handle to drag down through cell **C52**. With the range **C49:C52** selected, right-click and click **Copy**. Click cell **G49**, right-click, and select **Paste**. With the copy range **C49:C52** selected—the moving border surrounds the range—right-click cell **C44**, and select **Paste Special**. In the **Paste Special** dialog box, click **Values**, and then click **OK**. Select and copy the range **G49:G52** and beginning in cell **G44**, paste the values. Delete the contents in the ranges **C49:C52** and **G49:G52**.

9. Click cell **E6**. Click the **Home tab**, and in the **Editing group**, click the **Sort & Filter** button. From the displayed list, click **Sort Smallest to Largest**. Double-click the **Sheet1 sheet tab** and type Years of Experience and press Enter.

(Project 4D–Doctors continues on the next page)

Content-Based Assessments

(Project 4D– Doctors continued)

10. Right-click the **Years of Experience sheet tab**, and, click **Move or Copy**. In the **Move or Copy** dialog box, click **Sheet2**, click the **Create a copy** check box, and then click **OK**.

11. Rename the **Years of Experience (2) sheet tab** as **Alphabetic** Click cell **A6**, then click the **Data tab**. In the **Sort & Filter group**, click the **Sort** button. In the **Sort** dialog box, confirm that **My data has headers** is checked. In the **Column area**, click the **Sort by arrow**, and then click **Last Name**. At the top of the **Sort** dialog box, click the **Add Level** button. In the newly added **Then by** section, click the **arrow**, and then click **First Name**. Click the **Add Level** button again, click the new **Then by arrow**, and click **Specialty**. Click **OK**. The data is sorted first by last name, then by first name, and then by specialty.

12. Right-click the **Alphabetic sheet tab**. In the list, click **Move or Copy**. In the **Move or Copy** dialog box, click **Sheet2**, click the **Create a copy** check box, and then click **OK**. Rename the **Alphabetic (2) sheet tab** as **Specialty**

13. Click cell **C6**. In the **Sort & Filter group**, click the **Sort** button. In the **Sort** dialog box, confirm that **My data has headers** is checked. In the **Column area**, click the **Sort by arrow** and click **Specialty**. At the top of the **Sort** dialog box, click **Add Level**. Click the **Then by arrow** and click **Last Name**. Click the **Add Level** button, click the new **Then by arrow**, and then click **First Name**. Add another level, click the **Then by arrow**, and click **Salary**. Confirm Salary is sorted from **Smallest to Largest** and click **OK**.

14. Click the **Alphabetic sheet tab** and click in a cell in the worksheet. On the **Data tab**, in the **Sort & Filter group**, click **Filter**. Click the **Specialty Sorting and Filtering arrow** and click **(Select All)**, and then click **Critical Care**. Click **OK**. Copy the data—**A5:G42**—and click the **Sheet2 sheet tab**. Click cell **A6** and paste the data. Click the **Insert tab** and in the **Tables group**, click the **Table** button. Confirm the correct range is selected and that **My table has headers** is selected. Click **OK**.

15. Click the **Alphabetic sheet tab** and click in a cell in the worksheet. In the **Specialty** cell, click the **Filter** button. In the list, click **Critical Care** to deselect it, and then click **Emergency Medicine**. Click **OK**. Copy the data—**A5:G47**—and click the **Sheet2 sheet tab**. Click cell **A15** and **paste** the data. On the **Insert tab**, in the **Tables group**, click the **Table** button. Confirm the correct range is selected and that **My table has headers** is selected. Click **OK**.

16. Adjust column widths and row height. In cell **A1**, type **Providence and Warwick Hospital** and in cell **A2**, type **Critical Care/Emergency Medicine Salary Comparisons** In cell **A3** type **'January 2009** Click cell **D7** and click the **Table Tools Design tab** and in the **Table Styles group**, click the **More** button. Under **Medium**, in the third column, click the second choice—**Table Style Medium 10**. Click cell **D16** and click the **Table Tools Design tab** and in the **Table Styles group**, click the **More** button. Under **Medium**, in the last column, click the second choice— **Table Style Medium 14**.

(Project 4D–Doctors continues on the next page)

Content-Based Assessments

(Project 4D– Doctors continued)

17. With the active cell in the **Emergency Medicine** table, click the **Salary Sorting and Filtering arrow**. Click **Sort Largest to Smallest**. Click in the **Critical Care** table, and click the **Salary Sorting and Filtering arrow**. Click **Sort Largest to Smallest**. Double-click the **Sheet2 tab** and type Salary Comparison

18. Click the **Alphabetic sheet tab**. Click the **Specialty Filter button** and click **Clear Filter From "Specialty"** Click the **Data tab** and in the **Sort & Filter group**, click the **Filter** button.

19. **Save** your work. Click the **Years of Experience sheet tab** and click in the worksheet. In the **Sort & Filter group**, click the **Sort** button. In the **Sort by area**, confirm the list is sorted by **Years of Experience** with the **Order** from **Smallest to Largest**. Click the **Add Level** button, click the **Then by arrow**, and then click **Salary**. Add another level and sort by **Specialty**, then add a fourth level and sort by **Last Name**. Click **OK**.

20. Select the range that contains the years of experience—**E6:E47**. Click the **Home tab**, and in the **Styles group**, click the **Conditional Formatting** button. In the list, point to **Data Bars** and from the sub-menu, in the second row, click the middle data bar—**Light Blue Data Bar**.

21. In the **Styles group**, click the **Conditional Formatting** button, and then click **Manage Rules**. In the **Conditional Formatting Rules Manager** dialog box, click **Edit Rule**. In the **Edit Formatting Rule** dialog box, under **Format all cells based on their values**, click the **Format Style arrow**, and then click **3-Color Scale**. Then click **OK**. In the **Conditional Formatting Rules Manager**, click **OK**. The lower number of years worked are in

shades of pink, the middle range in shades of yellow, and the higher number of years employed are in shades of green.

22. Select the range that contains the salaries—**D6:D47**. In the **Styles group**, click the **Conditional Formatting** button. In the list, point to **Data Bars** and click the first data bar—**Blue Data Bar**. In the **Styles group**, click the **Conditional Formatting** button, and then click **Manage Rules**. In the **Conditional Formatting Rules Manager** dialog box, click **Edit Rule**. In the **Edit Formatting Rule** dialog box, under **Format all cells based on their values**, click **Show Bar Only**. Click **OK** and in the **Conditional Formatting Rules Manager**, click **OK**.

23. Right-click the **Years of Experience sheet tab** and click **Move or Copy**. In the displayed dialog box, click **Sheet3**; click **Create a copy**, and then click **OK**. Rename the **Years of Experience (2) sheet tab** as Highest Salaries

24. Select the range that contains the years of experience—**E6:E47**. Select a **Conditional Format** of **Data Bars** with the **Blue Data Bar**.

25. Select the range that contains the **Salary**— **D6:D47**. In the **Styles group**, click the **Conditional Formatting** button and from the list, click **Manage Rules**. In the **Conditional Formatting Rules Manager**, click **New Rule**. In the **Edit the Rule Description** area, under **Format Style**, click the arrow and select **3-Color Scale** and then click **OK**.

26. Click any cell in **row 6**. Click the **Data tab**, and in the **Sort & Filter group**, click the **Filter** button. In **column D**, click the **Salary filter arrow**. In the displayed list,

Project 4D–Doctors continues on the next page)

Content-Based Assessments

(Project 4D– Doctors continued)

point to **Number Filters** and from the sub-menu, click **Greater Than Or Equal To**. In the **Custom AutoFilter** dialog box, in the right text area, type **250,000** and then click **OK**. Click the **Salary filter arrow** and from the list, click **Sort Largest to Smallest**.

27. **Delete Sheet3**. Right-click a **sheet tab** and click **Select All Sheets**. Use **AutoFit Column Width** to adjust column widths on all worksheets. Click the **Office** button, point to **Print**, and then click **Print Preview**. Scroll through the worksheets to review how they display. Then click **Close Print Preview**.

28. Click the **Insert tab**. In the **Text group**, click the **Header & Footer** button. In the **Right Header** area, enter the **Page Number** and the **Number of Pages** and the words so it reads *Page x of xx*.

29. In the **Navigation group**, click **Go to Footer**. In the **Left Footer** area, insert the **File Name**. In the **Right Header** area, insert the **Sheet Name**. The sheet name identifies the data in the worksheet, so the title does not need to be changed. In the **Navigation group**, click the **Go to Header** button. Then click in cell **A1** and return to **Normal** view.

30. Click the **Page Layout tab**. In the **Page Setup group**, click the **Dialog Box**

Launcher. In the **Page Setup** dialog box, in the **Page tab**, click **Landscape**. Click the **Margins tab** and select a **Top** margin of **1** inch. Under **Center on page**, click **Horizontally**. Click **Print Preview**. Notice that the first three worksheets display on two pages. Click **Close Print Preview**.

31. Right-click a **sheet tab** and click **Ungroup Sheets**. Click the **Salary Comparison sheet tab** and adjust **column A** to display the first name and allow the worksheet title to spill into adjacent cells. Click the **Years of Experience sheet tab**. Press ⇧Shift and click the **Specialty sheet tab**. (Three work-sheets are grouped: *Years of Experience, Alphabetic,* and *Specialty.*) In the **Page Setup group**, click **Orientation** and from the list, click **Portrait**. In the **Page Setup group**, click the **Dialog Box Launcher**. Click the **Page tab**, and then under **Scaling**, click **Fit to**. Click **OK**. Now these three pages will each fit on a single page.

32. **Save** your work. To submit electronically, follow the instructions provided by your instructor, and then go to Step 30. To print, click the **Office** button, click **Print**. In the **Print** dialog box, under **Print what**, select **Entire workbook**. Under **Copies**, confirm that **1** is selected. Click **OK**.

33. **Close** your file and **Exit** Excel.

End **You have completed Project 4D**

Project 4E — Cardiac Care

In this project, you will apply the skills you practiced from the Objectives in Project 4A.

Objectives: **1**. *Use Text Orientation;* **2.** *Create a Column Chart;* **3.** *Create a Chart Sheet and Edit the Chart;* **4.** *Create and Modify a Pie Chart;* **5.** *Apply a Theme to a Chart;* **7.** *Print Charts.*

In the following Mastering Excel project, you will create a workbook for Maria Benitez, vice president of operations, which displays the types of cases in the Cardiac Care Unit for four days. Charts will be completed for Maria to use in order to make decisions. Your completed workbook will look similar to the one shown in Figure 4.75.

For Project 4E, you will need the following file:

New blank Excel workbook

You will save your workbook as
4E_Cardiac_Care_Firstname_Lastname

Figure 4.75

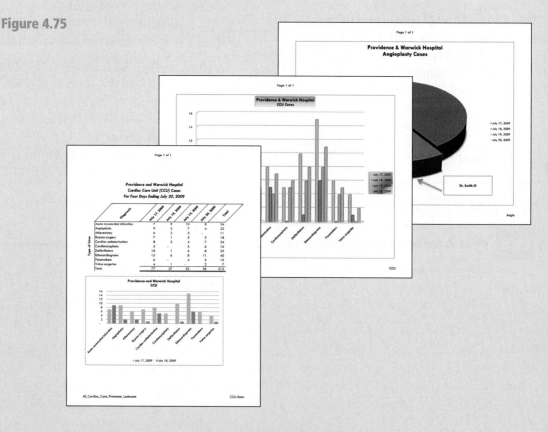

(Project 4E–Cardiac Care continues on the next page)

Content-Based Assessments

(Project 4E–Cardiac Care continued)

1. **Start** Excel and display a new blank workbook. Save the file in your **Excel Chapter 4** folder as 4E_Cardiac_Care_Firstname_Lastname

2. Beginning in cell **A1**, type the following worksheet title:

| Providence and Warwick Hospital |
| Cardiac Care Unit (CCU) Cases |
| For Four Days Ending July 20, 2009 |

3. Beginning in cell **A5**, type the following data. Recall when entering a date in this style, you place an apostrophe before the month.

Diagnosis	July 17, 2009	July 18, 2009	July 19, 2009	July 20, 2009
Acute myocardial infarction	7	9	10	8
Angioplasty	9	2	7	4
Atherectomy	6	2	3	0
Bypass surgery	7	1	5	5
Cardiac catheterization	8	5	4	7
Cardiomyoplasty	5	0	5	6
Defibrillators	10	1	6	8
Echocardiograms	15	6	8	11
Pacemakers	6	0	4	5
Valve surgeries	4	1	0	2

4. Adjust column widths to fully display cell contents and insert a column to the left of **column A**. Click cell **A6** and type **Type of Case** Select the range **A6:A16**. Format with **Bold**, **Center**, **Middle Align**, **Merge and Center**, and select an **orientation** of **Rotate Text Up**. Add a **Right Border**, and change the width of **column A** to **5.0**. In cell **B16**, type Total and in cell **G5**, type Total

5. Select the worksheet title, cells **B1:B3** and format with **Bold**, **Italic**, and a **Font Size** of **14**. Select the range **A1:G1** and **Merge & Center**. Using the skills you practiced, merge and center the other two lines of the worksheet title.

6. Format the column titles—**B5:G5**—with **Bold** and an **orientation** of **Angle Counterclockwise**. Use the alignment of **Center** and **Middle Align**, and add the border of **All Borders**.

7. Place totals in **row 16** and **column G**. Format the numbers for **Comma Style** with **no decimals**. In the total row, add a **Top and Double Bottom Border**.

8. Create a chart that compares the types of cases for each day. Select the range of the worksheet that does not include totals—**B5:F15.** Insert a **Column Chart** and select the **Clustered Cylinder**. Use **Chart Layouts** to select a style that places a title at the top and a legend at the right—*Layout 1*. Move the chart to a chart sheet and name the sheet **CCU**

(Project 4E–Cardiac Care continues on the next page)

Content-Based Assessments

(Project 4E–Cardiac Care continued)

9. Change that chart title to read **Providence & Warwick Hospital** on the first line and **CCU Cases** on the second line. Format the hospital name in **14 point** font and the second line with **12 point** font. Format the title, with a **Gradient fill** of **Daybreak**, **Border Color** set to **No line**, and a **Shadow** of **Outer–Offset Diagonal Top Left**.

10. Select the chart legend and format it with a **Gradient fill** of **Calm Water**, **Type** of **Radial**, and a **Shadow** of **Outer–Offset Left**.

11. Create a pie chart that compares the Angioplasty cases for the four days. On Sheet1, select the nonadjacent ranges of **B5:F5** and **B7:F7**. Create a *Pie in 3-D* with a *Chart Style 12* and place it on a separate sheet named **Angio**

12. Change the chart title to read **Providence & Warwick Hospital** with **Angioplasty Cases** on the second line. Explode the section that represents July 18. Add a text box that reads **Dr. Smith ill** and format the text with **Bold**, **Center**, and **Middle** alignment. Format the text box with a **Shape Outline** of **Orange, Accent 2, Darker 25%** around the text box. Position an arrow from the text box to the July 18 data marker. Format the **arrow** for **Intense Line – Accent 2**.

13. On **Sheet1**, create an embedded chart that compares the types of cases for July 17 and 18. Select the range of **B5:D15**. Insert a **2-D Clustered Column Chart**. Select **Chart Layout 3**. Change the title to read **Providence & Warwick Hospital** on the first line and **CCU** on the second line, and change the title **Font Size** to **12**. Move the chart so it displays beginning in cell **A18**. Use the sizing handles to increase the height of the chart so it displays through **row 37**—the entire label *Acute myocardial infarction* displays in the chart. Increase the width of the chart so it covers **column G** and is the same width as the worksheet data.

14. Apply the **Median theme**. Rename **Sheet1** to **CCU Data** and delete unused sheets. On all sheets, enter a **header** that places the page number and total number of pages in the center header. Enter a **footer** that places the file name in the left footer and the sheet name in the right footer. Format the **CCU Data sheet** so it is centered **Horizontally** and **Vertically** on one page.

15. Move the **CCU Data** sheet so it is the first worksheet in the workbook. In **Print Preview**, verify that the CCU Data sheet will print in portrait on one page and the Chart sheets will print in landscape orientation. **Save** your workbook.

16. Click the **CCU Data sheet tab** and click cell **A1**. **Print** all the sheets in the workbook or submit electronically as directed. **Close** the file and **Exit** Excel.

End You have completed Project 4E

Project 4F — Vendors

In this project, you will apply the skills you have practiced from the Objectives in Project 4B.

Objectives: 7. *Sort Data;* **8.** *Convert Text into Columns;* **9.** *Apply Conditional Formatting Using Data Bars and Color Scales;* **10.** *Insert a Table and Filter Data.*

In the following Mastering Excel project, you will list the food service vendors to prepare various reports for Henrietta Faulkner, the hospital nutritionist. You will display the vendors in various ways that will assist her in making determinations about the purchasing patterns for the department. Your completed workbook will look similar to the one shown in Figure 4.76.

For Project 4F, you will need the following files:

e04F_Vendors
e04F_New_Vendors

You will save your workbooks as
4F_Vendors_Firstname_Lastname

Figure 4.76

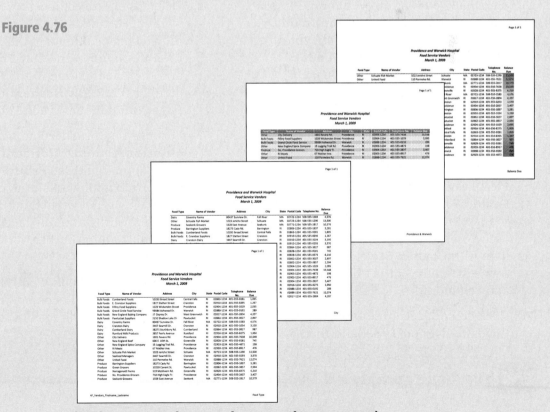

(Project 4F–Vendors continues on the next page)

Content-Based Assessments

Excel
chapterfour Mastering Excel

(Project 4F—Vendors continued)

1. **Start** Excel. From the student files locate and open the file named **e04F_Vendors** and then save it in your **Excel Chapter 4** folder as **4F_Vendors_Firstname_Lastname**

2. Select the worksheet title—**A1:A3**. Format with **Bold**, **Italic**, a **Font Size** of **14 points**, and **Merge & Center** each row across the worksheet—through **column H**.

3. Click cell **A3**. In the **Number group**, click the **Dialog Box Launcher**. In the **Format Cells** dialog box, in the **Number tab**, under **Category**, click **Date**. In the **Type** section, click **March 14, 2001**, and then click **OK**.

4. Select the column titles—**A5:H5**—and format with **Bold**, **Center**, **Wrap Text**, **Middle Align**, with a **Bottom Border**. **Save** your work.

5. From the student files locate and open the file named **e04F_New_Vendors**. Copy the data into the **4F_Vendors_Firstname_Lastname** worksheet beginning in cell **A24**. Close the **e04F_New_Vendors** workbook without saving changes.

6. Use the **Text to Columns** command to convert the data in the worksheet to match the fields of the Vendors worksheet. The fields used in the worksheet are Food Type, Name of Vendor, Address, City, State, Postal Code, Telephone Number, and Balance Due. Use the TRIM function to remove unneeded spaces in the beginning of the cells, and format the **Balance Due** data with **Comma Style** and **no decimals**. Adjust column widths to fully display data and column titles.

7. Click cell **A6**. Click the **Data tab**. **Sort** the data by **Food Type**, and then by the

following levels in this order: **Name of Vendor**, **State**, **City**. Then click **OK**.

8. Rename **Sheet1** to **Food Type** Copy the *Food Type* worksheet into a new sheet and rename it **City** Sort the worksheet in the following levels: **State**, **City**, **Food Type**, **Name of Vendor**.

9. Copy the *City* worksheet into a new sheet and name the sheet **Providence & Warwick** Insert a **Table** into this worksheet. **Filter** the list by the cities **Providence** and **Warwick**. **Sort** the list by **Name of Vendor**.

10. Copy the *Food Type* worksheet into a new sheet and name the sheet **Balance Due** Use a **Conditional Format** to apply the **Blue-Yellow-Red Color Scale** to the **Balance Due** column. Sort the list by **Balance Due** from the **Largest to the Smallest**.

11. Delete the unused sheets. Select all the worksheets and adjust column widths to fully display contents of the column. Place the **File Name** in the **Left Footer** area, and the **Sheet Name** in the **Right Footer** area. In the **Right Header** area, place the **Page Number** so it reads *Page x of xx*.

12. Format the worksheets in **Landscape orientation**, centered **Horizontally**, with a **1.5"** top margin. Use **Print Preview** to confirm that all worksheets display on one page. If they do not, adjust the column widths and row heights in order to display and print the worksheet on one page.

13. **Save** your workbook. **Print** all the sheets in the workbook or submit electronically as directed. **Close** the file and **Exit** Excel.

End You have completed Project 4F

Content-Based Assessments

Excel

chapter four

Mastering Excel

Project 4G — Quarterly Census

In this project, you will apply the skills you practiced from the objectives in Projects 4A and 4B.

Objectives: 1. *Use Text Orientation;* **2.** *Create a Column Chart;* **3.** *Create a Chart Sheet and Edit the Chart;* **4.** *Create and Modify a Pie Chart;* **6.** *Print Charts;* **7.** *Sort Data.*

In the following Mastering Excel project, you will create a workbook for Maria Benitez, vice president of operations. The quarterly census numbers are completed and Maria would like a report of the census. You will create a worksheet that reports the census and charts that display the census. You will prepare a pie chart that compares the critical care census for the quarter. Your completed workbook will look similar to the one shown in Figure 4.77.

> **For Project 4G, you will need the following file:**
>
> New blank Excel worksheet

You will save your workbook as
4G_Quarterly_Census_Firstname_Lastname

Figure 4.77

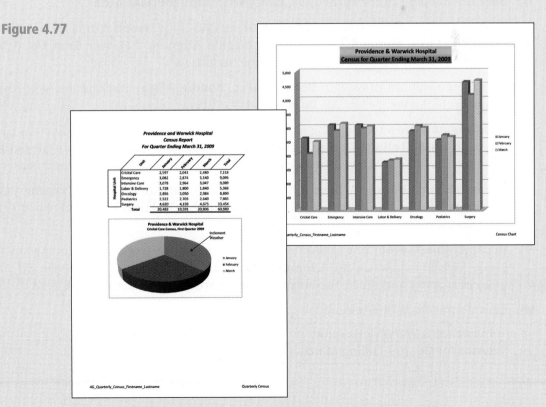

(Project 4G–Quarterly Census continues on the next page)

Content-Based Assessments

(Project 4G–Quarterly Census continued)

1. **Start** Excel, and open a new Excel worksheet. Navigate to the **Excel Chapter 4** folder and save the file as **4G_Quarterly_Census_Firstname_Lastname**

2. Beginning in cell **A1**, enter the worksheet title as follows:

Providence and Warwick Hospital
Census Report
For Quarter Ending March 31, 2009

3. Beginning in cell **A5**, enter the following row and column titles and the data for the worksheet:

Unit	January	February	March	Quarterly Total
Emergency	3082	2874	3140	
Oncology	2856	3050	2984	
Surgery	4620	4159	4675	
Intensive Care	3078	2964	3047	
Critical Care	2397	2041	2480	
Pediatrics	2522	2703	2640	
Labor & Delivery	1728	1800	1840	
Total				

4. **Sort** the hospital units so they are arranged in **alphabetical order**.

5. Insert a column to the left of **column A**. In cell **A6**, type **Hospital Unit**. Select the range **A6:A12** and format with **Merge & Center, Bold, Middle Align**, and **Rotate Text Up**. Adjust **column A** width to **6**. Place **Outside Borders** around the range.

6. Format the column titles with **Bold, Center, Middle Align**, and alignment of **Angle Counterclockwise**. Select **All Borders** for the titles.

7. Use **drag-and-drop** to move the worksheet title to begin in **column A**. Format the worksheet title with **Bold, Italic, 14 point Font Size**, and **Merge & Center** across the worksheet. Because the column titles are angled, include column G in the merge and center range.

8. In **row 13** and **column F**, **Sum** the totals. Format the numbers with **Comma Style** and **no decimals**. On the total row, place a **Top and Double Bottom Border**. Format cell **B13** with **Bold** and **Center**.

9. Rename **Sheet1 Quarterly Census** Select the range of the worksheet that does not include the totals—**B5:E12**. Insert a **3-D Clustered Column** chart. Select **Chart Style 39. Move** the chart to a chart sheet and name the sheet **Census Chart** Select **Chart Layout 1**.

10. Change the chart title to read

Providence & Warwick Hospital
Census for Quarter Ending March 31, 2009

(Project 4G–Quarterly Census continues on the next page)

Content-Based Assessments

Excel

Mastering Excel

(Project 4G–Quarterly Census continued)

11. Format the title with **18 point** for the first line and **16 point** for the second line of the title.

12. **Format** the chart title with a **Gradient fill** with a **Preset color** of **Ocean**. Select a **Shadow** of **Outer Offset Top** with a color of **Blue, Accent 1, Lighter 80%**. Select a **3-D Format** of **Top No Bevel** and **Bottom Bevel Soft Round**.

13. Create a pie chart that displays the Critical Care census for each month of the quarter. Select the data range—**B5:E6**—and insert a **Pie in 3-D** chart. Move the chart so it is placed at the left margin under the worksheet data. Change the title to read **Critical Care Census, First Quarter 2009** and format it with **10 point font size**. Insert a line above this title and type **Providence & Warwick Hospital** and format it with **12 point font size**.

14. Insert a **text box** and an **arrow** that points to the January data marker. In the text box, type **Inclement Weather** Format the arrow with a **Shape Style** of **Subtle Line – Dark 1**. Change the value of the January critical care patients in cell **C6** to **2,597**

15. Delete any unused sheets. Move the **Quarterly Census sheet** so that it is to the left of the **Census Chart**. In both sheets, place the **File Name** in the **Left Footer** and the **Sheet Name** in the **Right Footer**. Use **Print Preview** to confirm the footer displays in both worksheets and the placement on each page is appropriate.

16. Format the **Quarterly Census sheet** in **Portrait Style** centered **Horizontally**.

17. **Save** your work. **Print** all the sheets in the workbook or submit electronically as directed. **Close** the file and **Exit** Excel.

End **You have completed Project 4G** ——————————————————————————

Content-Based Assessments

Project 4H — Accounts Receivable

In this project, you will apply the following Objectives found in Projects 4A and 4B.

Objectives: 2. *Create a Column Chart;* **3**. *Create a Chart Sheet and Edit the Chart;* **6**. *Print Charts;* **7**. *Sort Data;* **9**. *Apply Conditional Formatting Using Data Bars and Color Scales;* **10**. *Insert a Table and Filter Data.*

In the following Mastering Excel project, you will create a workbook for Maria Benitez, vice president of operations. The hospital maintains a list of patients and other businesses that owe it money—its accounts receivable— which are uninsured patients and other companies. Each month the list is reviewed in order to assist in collections. You will prepare a portfolio of worksheets that report the accounts receivable. You will arrange the accounts in different orders and chart the results. Your completed workbook will look similar to the one shown in Figure 4.78.

For Project 4H, you will need the following file:

e04H_Accounts_Receivable

You will save your workbook as
4H_Accounts_Receivable_Firstname_Lastname

Figure 4.78

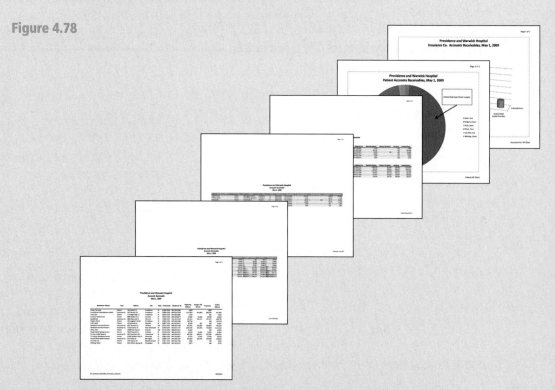

(Project 4H–Accounts Receivable continues on the next page)

Content-Based Assessments

(Project 4H–Accounts Receivable continued)

1. **Start** Excel. Locate and open the file **e04H_Accounts_Receivable** and save it in your **Excel Chapter 4** folder as **4H_ Accounts_Receivable_Firstname_Lastname**

2. Click cell **A3** and type **'May 1, 2009** Select the worksheet titles—**A1:A3**. Format for **Bold** and **Italic**. **Merge & Center** the title over the range of the worksheet. Format **row 1** with **16 point** and **rows 2** and **3** with **14 point**.

3. Select the column titles—**A5:K5**—and format with **Bold**, **Center**, **Middle Align**, and **Wrap Text**, with a **Bottom Double Border**. Adjust the column widths so the column titles display on two rows and the data fully displays in the columns.

4. Format the columns that will display money—**columns H, I, J,** and **K**—with **Comma Style** with **no decimals**. In **column K**, determine the **Ending Balance** for each business. The **Ending Balance** is the **Beginning Balance** plus the **Charges This Month** minus the **Payments**.

5. **Sort** the table by Business or Patient. For the secondary sorts, sort by state and then by city. **Rename** this sheet **Alphabetic**

6. Copy the **Alphabetic sheet** into a new sheet, and name the new sheet **Current Charges** Insert a **Table** in this worksheet. **Filter** the table to remove the **Blanks** in the **Charges This Month** column, so that it displays only the businesses and patients who made charges this month. Sort the table from the smallest charge to the largest charge. Add **Red Data Bars** to the **Charges This Month** column, and add **Purple Data Bars** to the **Ending Balance** column.

7. Copy the **Current Charges sheet** into a new sheet and name the sheet **Payments < $1,000**. Remove the filter. Arrange the list

in **alphabetical order** by name of business or patient. **Filter** the table to display all clients who paid $1,000 or less. **Sort** by payment amount from **Largest to Smallest**.

8. Click the **Alphabetic sheet tab**. Filter the table so the **Type** column displays only **Patient**. Copy this filtered data, including the worksheet title, to **Sheet2**, cell **A1**. Sort the table from the largest ending balance to the smallest ending balance. **Filter** ending balance so the data displayed is **Greater Than 0**. Rename **Sheet2** to **Outstanding Balance**

9. Click the **Alphabetic sheet tab**. Filter the table so the **Type** column displays only **Insurance Co**. Copy this filtered data including the column title to the **Outstanding Balance** worksheet, leaving three blank rows between the two tables. Sort the table from the largest ending balance to the smallest ending balance. Adjust column widths.

10. Insert a table into each of these ranges. For the Patients table, use **Table Style Medium 25** and for the Insurance Co., use a **Table Style Medium 27**. Adjust row height and column width if needed.

11. Based on the filtered patient table, create a **2-D pie chart** that displays the patient name and their ending balances. Position the chart in a separate sheet and name the sheet **Patient AR Chart** Place a text box in the upper right corner of the chart between the title and the legend. In the text box, type **Patient had open heart surgery** Right-click the text box and select **Format Shape**. In the **Format Shape** dialog box, click **Line Color** and in the right side, confirm that **Solid line** displays. Click **Close**. With the text box active, place an arrow from the text box to the data marker for Brian Holguin and use a **Shape**

(Project 4H–Accounts Receivable continues on the next page)

Content-Based Assessments

(Project 4H–Accounts Receivable continued)

Style of **Intense Line – Dark 1**. Insert a chart title above the chart that reads

| Providence and Warwick Hospital |
| Patient Accounts Receivables, May 1, 2009 |

12. Based on the filtered insurance table, create a **3-D Cylinder Chart** that displays the name of the insurance company and their ending balances. Position the chart in a separate sheet and name the sheet **Insurance Co. AR Chart** Insert a chart title above the chart that reads

| Providence & Warwick Hospital |
| Insurance Co. Accounts Receivables May 1, 2009 |

13. Click the **Alphabetic sheet tab**. Click the **Type filter** button and click **Clear Filter from "Type"**. In the **Sort & Filter group**, click **Filter**.

14. Arrange the sheets in the following order: **Alphabetic**, **Current Charges**, **Payments < $1000**, **Outstanding Balance**, **Patient**

AR Chart, and **Insurance Co. AR Chart**. Delete **Sheet3**.

15. **Group** the **Alphabetic**, **Current Charges**, **Payments < $1,000**, and **Outstanding Balance** worksheets. **Format** for **Landscape Orientation**, centered both **Horizontally** and **Vertically** and **Fit to Page**. In the **Left Footer** area, place the **File Name**. In the **Right Footer** area, place the **Sheet Name**. In the **Right Header** area, enter the **Page Number** and the **Total Number of Pages** and the words so it reads *Page x of xx*.

16. **Group** the **Charts**. In the **Left Footer** area, place the **File Name**. In the **Right Footer** area, place the **Sheet Name**. In the **Right Header** area, enter the **Page Number** and the **Total Number of Pages** and the words so it reads *Page x of xx*.

17. **Save** your workbook. **Print** all the sheets in the workbook or submit electronically as directed. **Close** the file and **Exit** Excel.

End **You have completed Project 4H**

Content-Based Assessments

Project 4I — ER Patients

In this project, you will apply all the skills you practiced from the objectives in Projects 4A and 4B. 1. Use Text Orientation; 2. Create a Column Chart; 3. Create a Chart Sheet and Edit the Chart; 4. Create and Modify a Pie Chart; 5. Apply a Theme to a Chart; 6. Print Charts; 7. Sort Data; 8. Convert Text into Columns; 9. Apply Conditional Formatting Using Data Bars and Color Scales; 10. Insert a Table and Filter Data.

In the following Mastering Excel Project, you will edit a workbook for Maria Benitez, vice president of operations, that displays the patients seen in the ER on July 8. You will create a portfolio of worksheets for Maria that evaluates the activity in the ER. You will display the patients for a doctor for the day and chart the amounts billed. Maria can use the information to evaluate the effectiveness of the ER. Your completed workbook will look similar to the one shown in Figure 4.79.

For Project 4I, you will need the following files:

e04I_ER_Patients
e04I_11PM_ER_Patients

You will save your workbook as
4I_ER_Patients_Firstname_Lastname

Figure 4.79

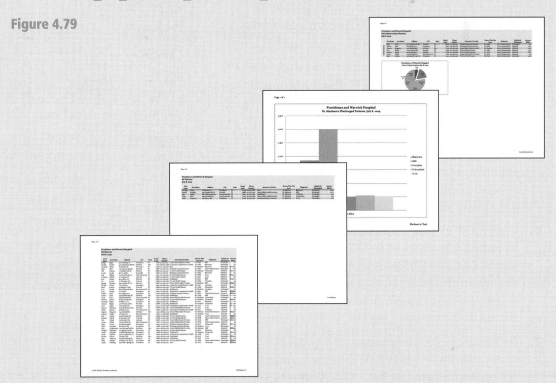

(Project 4I–ER Patients continues on the next page)

Content-Based Assessments

(Project 4I–ER Patients continued)

1. **Start** Excel. From the student files locate and open the file named **e04I_ER_Patients** and then save it in your **Excel Chapter 4** folder as 4I_ER_Patients_Firstname_Lastname

2. Insert four rows at the top of the worksheet. Enter the worksheet title and format it with **Bold**, **Italic**, **14 point** font.

Providence and Warwick Hospital
ER Patients
'July 8, 2009

3. Apply the **Flow Theme**.

4. In cell **L5**, type **Amount Billed** Click cell **K5** and place a space after the **/** so the column title will display on two lines. Format the column titles with **Bold**, **Center**, **Wrap Text**, **Middle Align**, with a **Bottom Border**. Adjust column widths so the data fully displays. Place the column titles *First Name*, *Postal Code*, *Phone Number*, *Doctor Who Was Seen*, *Admitted/Discharged*, and *Amount Billed* on two lines.

5. From the student files, locate and open the file named **e04I_11PM_ER_Patients** and copy the data into the **4I_ER_Patients_Firstname_Lastname** worksheet, leaving blank rows under the original data. The patients that are seen late at night are usually entered after the main spreadsheet has been completed. Then close the e4I_11PM_ER_Patients file.

6. Convert the data from the 11PM worksheet to match the fields of the ER Patients worksheet. Use the **TRIM** function to remove spaces from the beginning of the cells. When the fields align, delete the blank rows so the data becomes part of the worksheet.

7. Select the cells that contain the postal code—**F6:F45**—and click the error indicator button. From the list, click **Convert to**

Number. Use a **Number format** of the **Category** of **Special** and a **Type** of **Zip Code**.

8. Click cell **C6** and **Freeze Panes**. Adjust the worksheet so the following data can be correctly entered. Beginning in cell **L6**, type the following:

First Name	Last Name	Amount Billed
Camilla	Cardow	450
Christian	Deibert	800
Clayton	Mcgarrah	2,500
Colin	Gertracht	500
Dany	Chhy	800
Delores	Jones	2,750
Dennis	Sutton	2,400
Edwina	Maiorano	750
Emilia	Bigby	400
Erik	Deford	2,000
Fernando	Magar	1,100
Fraser	Mayers	650
Jared	Greene	2,500
Javier	Perrett	1,950
Jennifer	Orbell	2,500
Julianne	Noblin	750
Katy	Prudhomme	3,100
Kelly	Welden	3,050
Kurt	Forbus	2,050
Kurt	Hoskie	500
Kurt	Villanova	1,100
Letitia	Schaeffer	2,350
Lyndi	Stafford	875
Michele	Gibson	835
Morgan	Robertson	285

(Project 4I–ER Patients continues on the next page)

(Project 4I–ER Patients continued)

First Name	Last Name	Amount Billed
Neil	Clapton	1,950
Neil	Orbell	2,350
Noemi	Cordle	950
Russell	Pershing	3,005
Skylar	Whitling	2,875
Theresa	Leston	2,500
Tony	Hoskie	2,850
Tyrese	Orbell	435
Vic	Fowler	525
Yoo Jung	Chang	1,850
Fred	Magar	1,500
Julie	Noblin	3,750
Donna	Jones	1,050
Frances	Magar	1,580
Doug	Jones	550

9. **Unfreeze Panes**. Format the numbers in **column L** with **Comma Style** and **no decimals**.

10. Click cell **A6** and **Sort** the worksheet by the following fields: **Last Name**, **First Name**, **State**, **City**. Change the sheet name to read **ER Patients 7-8**

11. Copy the worksheet into a new sheet and rename it **Dr. Mackson** Change the title in cell **A2** to **Dr. Mackson's Discharged ER Patients** Insert a **Table** and **Filter** the list to include the patients that Dr. Mackson saw in the ER and the patients who have been discharged. **Sort** the list by diagnosis.

12. Create a chart that displays the diagnosis and amount billed for Dr. Mackson. Use the Ctrl key to select the nonadjacent ranges of **J5:J37** and **L5:L37**. Insert a **3-D Clustered Column Chart** and **Switch Row/Column** so the diagnoses are listed

in the legend. Select **Chart Layout 1**. Enter a title that reads **Providence and Warwick Hospital** on the first line. Place **Dr. Mackson's Discharged Patients, July 8, 2009** on the second line. Use a **14 point** font size for the hospital name and a **12 point** font size for the second line.

13. Place the chart in a separate chart sheet and name the sheet **Mackson's Chart**. Move the chart sheet to the right of the **Dr. Mackson sheet**.

14. Copy the **Dr. Mackson** worksheet into a new sheet and rename it **Heart Catheterization** Clear existing filters. Change cell **A2** to read **ER Catheterization Patients** Insert a column to the left of **column A**. Move the worksheet title so it begins in **column A**. In cell **A6**, type **Catheterizations** and format with **Bold**. Select the range—**A6:A45**. **Merge & Center** the cells and apply the text orientation **Rotate Text Up**. Confirm the format is **Center** and **Middle Align**. Change the column width to **6.0**.

15. Filter the list for the **Heart catheterization** diagnosis. From this data, create a **2-D Pie Chart** that displays the Patients' last name and the **Amount Billed**. Change the **Chart Layout** to *Layout 1*. Explode the section for **Delores Jones**. Change the title to the following and format the first line with **14 point** font and the second line with **12 point** font:

Providence & Warwick Hospital
Heart Catheterizations, July 8, 2009

16. Move the chart so it is at the left edge of the worksheet below the table.

17. Click the **ER Patients 7-8 sheet tab**. Select the data for the Amount Billed— **L6:L45**. Insert the **Red Data Bars**.

(Project 4I–ER Patients continues on the next page)

Content-Based Assessments

(Project 4I–ER Patients continued)

18. Delete the unused sheets. Arrange the worksheets in the following order: **ER Patients 7-8**, **Dr Mackson**, **Mackson's Chart**, **Heart Catheterization**. For all worksheets and chart sheets, in the **Left Footer** area, place the **File Name**. In the **Right Footer** area, place the **Sheet Name**. In the **Left Header** area, enter the **Page Number** and the **Total Number of Pages** and the words so it reads *Page x of xx*. Use **Print Preview** to confirm the header and footer placement in all worksheets and enter the footer in the chart sheet if necessary.

19. Each worksheet should display in **Landscape Orientation**. **Center** the worksheet **Horizontally** and **Fit to page**. For the **Dr Mackson** and **Hearth Catheterization sheets**, adjust the column widths to display column titles on two lines and to a smaller width. It may be necessary to adjust row heights.

20. Save your workbook. **Print** all the sheets in the workbook or submit electronically as directed. **Close** the file and **Exit** Excel.

End You have completed Project 4I

Content-Based Assessments

Project 4J—Business Running Case

In this project, you will apply the skills you have practiced from the Objectives in Projects 4A and 4B.

From My Computer, navigate to the student files that accompany this textbook. In the folder **03_business_running_case**, locate and open the folder for this chapter. Open and print the instructions for this project, which are provided to you in Adobe PDF format. Follow the instructions and use the skills you have gained thus far to assist the managers of the Grand Department Store to meet the challenges of keeping records for a large department.

End **You have completed Project 4J**

Outcomes-Based Assessments

Rubric

The following outcomes-based assessments are *open-ended assessments*. That is, there is no specific correct result; your result will depend on your approach to the information provided. Make *Professional Quality* your goal. Use the following scoring rubric to guide you in *how* to approach the problem, and then to evaluate *how well* your approach solves the problem.

The *criteria*—Software Mastery, Content, Format and Layout, and Process—represent the knowledge and skills you have gained that you can apply to solving the problem. The *levels of performance*—Professional Quality, Approaching Professional Quality, or Needs Quality Improvements—help you and your instructor evaluate your result.

	Your completed project is of Professional Quality if you:	Your completed project is Approaching Professional Quality if you:	Your completed project Needs Quality Improvements if you:
1-Software Mastery	Choose and apply the most appropriate skills, tools, and features and identify efficient methods to solve the problem.	Choose and apply some appropriate skills, tools, and features, but not in the most efficient manner.	Choose inappropriate skills, tools, or features, or are inefficient in solving the problem.
2-Content	Construct a solution that is clear and well organized, contains content that is accurate, appropriate to the audience and purpose, and is complete. Provide a solution that contains no errors of spelling, grammar, or style.	Construct a solution in which some components are unclear, poorly organized, inconsistent, or incomplete. Misjudge the needs of the audience. Have some errors in spelling, grammar, or style, but the errors do not detract from comprehension.	Construct a solution that is unclear, incomplete, or poorly organized, containing some inaccurate or inappropriate content; and contains many errors of spelling, grammar, or style. Do not solve the problem.
3-Format and Layout	Format and arrange all elements to communicate information and ideas, clarify function, illustrate relationships, and indicate relative importance.	Apply appropriate format and layout features to some elements, but not others. Overuse features, causing minor distraction.	Apply format and layout that does not communicate information or ideas clearly. Do not use format and layout features to clarify function, illustrate relationships, or indicate relative importance. Use available features excessively, causing distraction.
4-Process	Use an organized approach that integrates planning, development, self-assessment, revision, and reflection.	Demonstrate an organized approach in some areas, but not others; or, use an insufficient process of organization throughout.	Do not use an organized approach to solve the problem.

Problem Solving

Project 4K—Census Comparison

In this project, you will construct a solution by applying any combination of the skills you practiced from the Objectives in Projects 4A and 4B.

> **For Project 4K, you will need the following file:**
>
> New blank Excel workbook
>
> You will save your workbook as
> 4K_Census_Comparsion_Firstname_Lastname

You will construct a portfolio of worksheets that report the hospital census for three years. You will then create charts that will compare the years. In a new workbook, enter the appropriate title lines. Use the following data for the original worksheet. *Hint:* Enter the years as column titles so they will be displayed as text.

Unit	2006	2007	2008
Oncology	4056	3874	3674
Emergency	4520	4183	5087
Critical Care	3145	2875	2985
Surgery	4985	4758	4863
Intensive Care	4005	4168	3994
Mental Health	3587	3984	3745
Pediatrics	4087	3874	4120
Labor & Delivery	2845	3158	3258

In the worksheet, display the units in alphabetical order and determine the total census for each year and each unit. Prepare a 3-D clustered column chart that displays the census for each unit for each of the three years and displays the years in the legend. Prepare a pie chart that compares the Surgery cases over the three years.

Use borders, themes, and font attributes to prepare a professional worksheet. Use chart styles, chart layouts, titles, and chart formatting techniques to prepare professional charts. Add footers that include the file name and sheet name. Save the workbook as **4K_Census_Comparison_Firstname_Lastname** and submit it as directed.

End You have completed Project 4K ————————————

Outcomes-Based Assessments

Problem Solving

Project 4L — Accounts Payable

In this project, you will construct a solution by applying any combination of the skills you practiced from the Objectives in Projects 4A and 4B.

For Project 4L, you will need the following file:

e04L_Accounts_Payable

**You will save your workbook as
4L_Accounts_Payable_Firstname_Lastname**

The accounts payable report for the hospital for the month of July, 2009, is in the worksheet that is supplied. You will complete the worksheet to determine the amounts the hospital owes to each of its creditors. From this data, you will create reports for Patricia Jones, the accounts payable manager.

From your student files, open e04L_Accounts_Payable. Write a formula that determines the Ending Balance, which is the Beginning Balance plus Purchases minus Payments.

Display the list in alphabetical order by name of business. In another worksheet, display a table that shows all accounts with Ending Balances sorted from smallest to largest. On another sheet, insert a table and filter it to display the Ending Balances greater than $5,000 from businesses in the state of Rhode Island. Based on this data, prepare a chart that displays the vendor and the ending balance and place it in a separate chart sheet. Name each worksheet appropriately to identify its contents.

Use borders, themes, and font attributes to prepare professional worksheets. Use chart styles, chart layouts, titles, and chart formatting techniques to prepare a professional chart. Add footers that include the file name and sheet name. Format each worksheet and chart so it prints on only one page. Save the workbook as **4L_Accounts_Payable_Firstname_ Lastname** and submit it as directed.

End You have completed Project 4L _____

Problem Solving

Project 4M — ICU Patients

In this project, you will construct a solution by applying any combination of the skills you practiced from the Objectives in Projects 4A and 4B.

For Project 4M, you will need the following file:

e04M_ICU_Patients

You will save your workbook as
4M_ICU_Patients_Firstname_Lastname

You will complete the report for the ICU patients for the week ending March 21, 2009. Patients are billed at $1,215 each day in the ICU. Complete the amount billed. Display the list in alphabetical order by patient's last name. If the patients have the same name, then use the state, city, and then doctor to determine the sort order.

On a separate sheet, prepare a table that displays all patients that live in Providence and chart the Total Billed amount for each patient. In the chart, include each patient's last name and their bill. Place the chart in a separate sheet.

On another sheet, prepare a table that displays all patients of Dr. Trace and chart their total amounts billed. In the chart, include each patient's last name and the amount of their bill. Place the chart in a separate sheet. Name each sheet to indicate its contents.

Use borders, themes, and font attributes to prepare a professional worksheet. Use chart styles, chart layouts, titles, and chart formatting techniques to prepare a professional chart. Add footers that include the file name and sheet name. Format the worksheets so each prints on one page. Save the workbook as **4M_ICU_Patients_Firstname_Lastname** and submit it as directed.

End **You have completed Project 4M** ————————

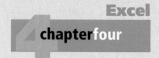
Problem Solving

Project 4N — Pediatrics

In this project, you will construct a solution by applying any combination of the skills you practiced from the Objectives in Projects 4A and 4B.

For Project 4N, you will need the following file:

e04N_Pediatrics

You will save your workbook as
4N_Pediatrics_Firstname_Lastname

The admittance clerk of the pediatrics unit has prepared the list of patients for the week ending April 18, 2009. You will complete that worksheet and determine the amount to be billed for each patient. The Pediatrics daily rate is $895.

The data in the worksheet is entered into column A. Use the Text to Columns feature to display the worksheet and remove unnecessary spaces. You will have the following column titles: First Name, Last Name, Address, City, State, Postal Code, Telephone Number, Doctor, Days Admitted, Daily Rate, Amount Billed. Display the worksheet in alphabetical order by last name. If the last name is the same, then use first name, then doctor, then state, and then city to determine the final list.

Prepare a table that displays the patients for Dr. Fowler and chart the amount billed. In the chart, include the patient's last name and the amount billed and place the chart in a separate sheet.

Prepare another table that displays the patients for Dr. Herda and chart the amount billed. Display the chart at the bottom of the worksheet. Prepare the chart so the data markers display with the largest marker at the left and the smallest marker at the right. *Hint*: sort the data before creating the chart.

Use borders, themes, and font attributes to prepare a professional worksheet. Use chart styles, chart layouts, titles, and chart formatting techniques to prepare a professional chart. Add footers that include the file name and sheet name. Format the worksheets so each prints on one page. Save the workbook as **4N_Pediatrics_Firstname_Lastname** and submit it as directed.

 End You have completed Project 4N _____

Problem Solving

Project 4O — Nurse Shifts

In this project, you will construct a solution by applying any combination of the skills you practiced from the Objectives in Projects 4A and 4B.

For Project 4O, you will need the following file:

e04O_Nurse_Shifts

**You will save your workbook as
4O_Nurse_Shifts_Firstname_Lastname**

Kathy Ring is the nursing manager for the hospital and each unit reports to her. You will complete the required reports for the Pediatric Department, reporting the data for June 12, 2009, which includes charts that display work patterns. There are three shifts for the nurses—day, swing, and night. There is a shift bonus of an additional 10% of pay for the night shift and 5% for the swing shift.

Open e04O_Nurse_Shifts and complete the worksheet by entering the wages earned—hours worked times the hourly wage. Determine any bonus earned for swing or night shifts by multiplying the shift bonus times the wages earned. Then determine the total wage by adding the wages earned to the bonus earned.

Sort the worksheet by shift, then by last name, and then by first name. Create a column chart that displays night shift nurses and their total wage and place it in a chart sheet.

On a new sheet, sort the data by profession and filter for LPNs. Create a 3-D Clustered Column chart that displays the shift and the total wage and place it in a separate chart sheet. Create another worksheet that displays all nurses and sort in alphabetical order by last name, first name, profession, and shift.

Name each worksheet to indicate its contents. Use borders, themes, and font attributes to prepare a professional worksheet. Use chart styles, chart layouts, titles, and chart formatting techniques to prepare a professional chart. Add footers that include the file name and sheet name. Save the workbook as **4O_Nurse_Shifts_Firstname_Lastname** and submit it as directed.

End You have completed Project 4O ————————

Outcomes-Based Assessments

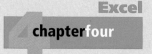
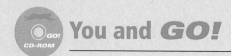 You and *GO!*

Project 4P—You and *GO!*

In this project, you will construct a solution by applying any combination of the Objectives found in Projects 4A and 4B.

From My Computer, navigate to the student files that accompany this textbook. In the folder **04_you_and_go**, locate and open the folder for this chapter. Open and print the instructions for this project, which are provided to you in Adobe PDF format. Follow the instructions to create a worksheet that displays your expenses for one week and then create a chart for those expenses.

 End You have completed Project 4P —————————

GO! with Help

Project 4Q—*GO!* with Help

In this chapter, you used data bars and color scales to highlight numeric values. You can also use Icon Sets to highlight the numeric values.

1. **Start** Excel and confirm that you are connected to the Internet. From the Student files, locate and open the file named **e04_go_with_help** and then save it in your **Excel Chapter 4** folder as **4_go_with_help_Firstname_Lastname**

2. At the far right end of the Ribbon, click the **Microsoft Office Excel Help** button.

3. In the search box, type **conditional formatting** From the displayed list, locate and click **Add, change, or clear conditional formats** Under **What do you want to do?** click **Format all cells by using an icon set**.

4. In the **Excel Help** menu, click **Print**. Use these instructions to add an icon set of your choice to the salary column.

5. **Save** your work and submit as directed. **Close** the file, and then **Exit** Excel.

 End You have completed Project 4Q —————————

chapterfive

Making Decisions with Functions

OBJECTIVES

At the end of this chapter you will be able to:

1. Create Text Functions
2. Create Statistical Functions
3. Insert Date and Time Functions
4. Create Logical Functions and Insert a Comment

OUTCOMES

Mastering these objectives will enable you to:

PROJECT 5A
Create a Workbook that Uses Text, Statistical, Date, Time, and Logical Functions, and Insert and Format Comments

5. Insert Financial Functions
6. Create What-If Analysis with Goal Seek
7. Determine Future Value and Present Value

PROJECT 5B
Create a Workbook that Uses Financial Functions and Goal Seek

Westland Plains City Government

Westland Plains, Texas, is a city of approximately 800,000 people in the western portion of the second most populous state in the United States. The city's economy is built around the oil industry, a regional airport serving western Texas and eastern New Mexico, a multi-location medical center, and a growing high-tech manufacturing industry. Westland Plains has a rich cultural history that is kept alive by a number of civic organizations and museums; new culture and traditions are encouraged through the city's Arts Council. City residents of all ages enjoy some of the finest parks, recreation areas, and sports leagues in the state.

Making Decisions with Functions

Functions are built-in formulas that complete tasks quickly. While functions are usually used for complex mathematical calculations, they are also used for formatting purposes. Text functions are used to work with the words—text—in a spreadsheet. Logical functions compare data in the cells, analyze that data, and place the results in a cell. Statistical functions quickly provide analysis of the data, such as determining the average. Financial functions use the data in the worksheet, perform calculations, and determine financial results, such as the interest paid on a loan.

In this chapter, you will use Excel functions to format text and provide statistical analysis. You will determine information about loans, including the amount of interest and principal paid. You will analyze the data and make recommendations for using that data. In addition, you will complete a What-if analysis to review financial information and change the data to see the results in order to make decisions.

Project 5A Building Permits

In Activities 5.1 through 5.9, you will construct an Excel worksheet for Joaquin Alonzo, city manager of Westland Plains, Texas. The worksheet will display the building permits issued for the month of March. Statistical information about the permits will be completed and a schedule for inspections will be created. A copy of the original worksheet will be used to increase information that assists in establishing department statistics. Your completed worksheet will look similar to Figure 5.1.

For Project 5A, you will need the following file:

e05A_Building_Permits

You will save your workbook as
5A_Building_Permits_Firstname_Lastname

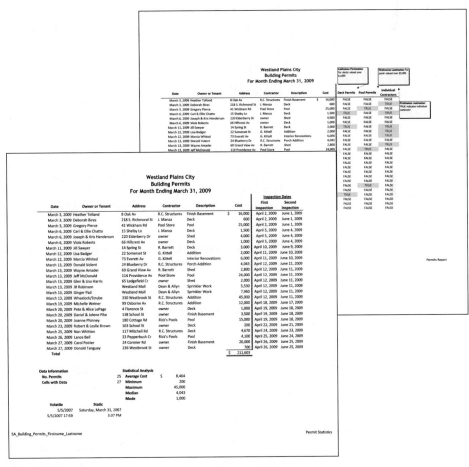

Figure 5.1
Project 5A—Building Permits

Objective 1
Create Text Functions

Recall that a function is a formula that has already been written. Recall also that Excel has many categories of functions. You have used the SUM function to add a series of numeric cell values. It is used so often that a button for this function is placed on the Home tab.

Text functions, such as the TRIM or PROPER function, are used to format text or to add text to a cell.

Activity 5.1 Using the PROPER Function

The *PROPER function* is a text function that capitalizes the first letter of each word in a cell entry that contains text. Joaquin Alonzo, city manager, reviewed the building permits issued in March and found that some of the data needs to be formatted. In this activity, you will use the PROPER text function to format the worksheet to add capital letters in the cells.

1 **Start** Excel. From your student files, locate and open the file named **e05A_Building_Permits**. Navigate to the location where you are saving your files, create a new folder named **Excel Chapter 5**, and then save the file in that folder as **5A_Building_Permits_Firstname_Lastname**

The worksheet reports the building permits that were issued in Westland Plains for the month of March. The list displays the date the permit was issued, who it was issued to, the name of the contractor, what the work is, and the estimated cost of the project.

2 Point to the **column F heading** and when the ⬇ pointer displays, right-click, and then click **Insert**.

A column is inserted between columns E and F. In this worksheet, the text for the description is not capitalized. Rather than change each cell manually, you will use the PROPER text function to make the change.

3 Click cell **F6**. Click the **Formulas tab**. In the **Function Library group**, click the **Text button** and from the list, click **PROPER**.

Recall that a dialog box displays so the arguments—variables—can be entered. In the dialog box is a description of the function. The description for the PROPER function states that it will convert a text string to proper case—the first letter in each word displays in uppercase.

4 Click in the **Function Arguments** title bar and drag the dialog box down so you can view cells **E6:F6**. With the insertion point in the **Text** box, click cell **E6** and compare your screen with Figure 5.2. Click **OK**.

"Finish Basement" is displayed in the cell with a capital letter beginning each word.

Figure 5.2

Location of original text   Description of function

PROPER Function Arguments dialog box

Text currently displayed in cell

Result that will display

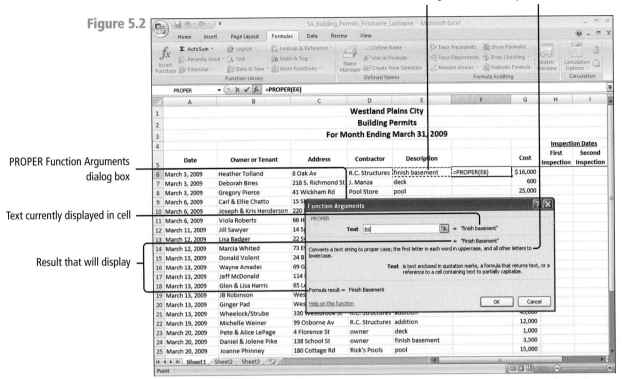

5 Use the fill handle to copy the formula down through **row 30**.

All words in the range begin with a capital letter. Recall that when you copy a formula containing a relative reference, that reference changes to reflect its new location.

6 Confirm the range **F6:F30** is selected. Right-click and from the list, click **Copy**. Click cell **E6**, click the **Home tab**, and in the **Clipboard group**, click the **Paste button arrow**. Compare your screen with Figure 5.3, and then click **Paste Values**.

The Paste button displays a list of choices about pasting the data. The **Paste Values** command pastes only the results of the cell and clears any underlying formula. The PROPER function was entered in column F. When the values are pasted in column E, only the results display in the cells.

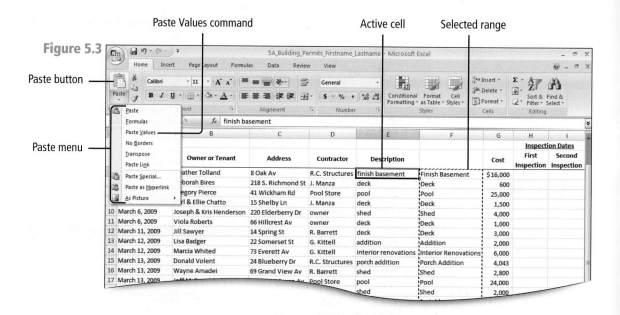

Figure 5.3

Paste button

Paste menu

Paste Values command   Active cell   Selected range

Point to the **column F heading** and when the ⬇ pointer displays, right-click, and then click **Delete** to remove column F.

Select the range **A1:A3**. In the **Font group**, display the **Font** list, scroll to and then click **Trebuchet MS**.

Save 💾 your workbook.

Objective 2
Create Statistical Functions

Statistical functions are a group of functions that provide statistical analysis of the worksheet and are used in evaluating data. Recall that you have used the AVERAGE, MIN (Minimum), and MAX (Maximum) functions There are other statistical functions that determine the median and mode of a group of cells. Statistical functions are also used to count the number of cells that are in the group, the number that have data, and the number that are empty.

Activity 5.2 Using the MEDIAN and MODE Functions and Formula AutoComplete

Excel's functions are designed for statistical analysis. The **median** is the value at the midpoint of a series of numbers, and the **mode** is the value that occurs the most often in a list of numbers. After you type an = (equal sign) and the beginning letters of the function, Excel displays a dynamic list of valid functions, arguments, and names that match the letters—a feature called **Formula AutoComplete**. You can insert an item from the list into the formula. This minimizes typing and syntax errors. In this activity, you will determine the median—middle value—of the estimated cost of the remodels for Joaquin Alonzo.

1 Beginning in cell **A34**, type the following row titles:

| Statistical Analysis |
| Average Cost |
| Minimum |
| Maximum |
| Median |
| Mode |

2 Select the range **A34:A39** and format with **Bold** [B]. Select the range **A35:A39**. In the **Alignment group**, click the **Increase Indent** button [≡].

3 Click cell **A31** and type **Total** Format it with **Bold** [B] and **Center** [≡]. In cell **F31**, use the SUM formula to enter the total. Place a **Top and Double Bottom Border** around the cell and confirm it is formatted with **Accounting Number Format** [$ ▾] with **zero decimals**. If necessary, increase the column widths.

4 Click cell **B35**. Click the **Formulas tab** and in the **Function Library group**, click the **Insert Function** button. In the **Insert Function** dialog box, click the **Or select a category arrow**, click **Statistical**, and from the **Select a function** list, click **AVERAGE**, and then click **OK**.

5 In the **Function Arguments** dialog box, with the insertion point in the **Number1** text box, click the **Collapse Dialog Box** button [▦] and select the range of Costs—**F6:F30**. Click the **Expand Dialog Box** button [▦] and immediately press [F4] to make this range an absolute reference. Displayed in the Number1 text box is *$F$6:$F$30*. Alternatively, press [F4] and then position your cursor after F6 and press [F4]. Click **OK**.

The average—*$8,464*—displays in cell B35.

6 Click cell **B35** and use the fill handle to copy the AVERAGE function formula down through cell **B37**.

7 Click cell **B36**. In the **Formula Bar**, double-click the function name *AVERAGE* and compare your screen with Figure 5.4.

Formula in Formula Bar with function name selected

Figure 5.4

ScreenTip displays formula syntax

Copied formulas

Formula in cell

Average of costs

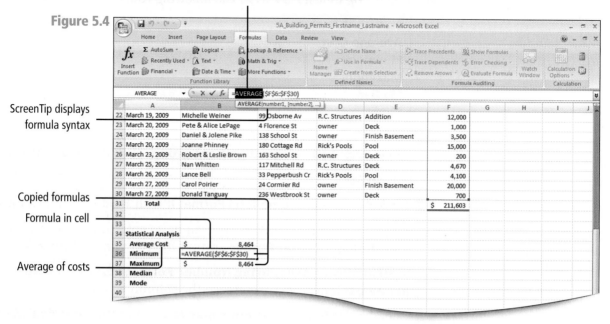

8 Type **M** to display the function list and compare your screen with Figure 5.5.

The Formula AutoComplete list displays an alphabetical list of functions that begin with M. Icons at the left represent the type of entry, such as a function or table reference.

ScreenTip explanation of the first function that begins with M

Figure 5.5

List of function choices beginning with M
Icon indicating a function

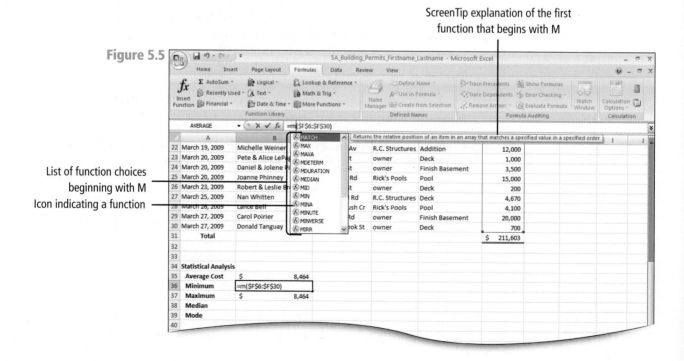

9 In the displayed list, click **MIN**.

The MIN function is the term Excel uses to describe the ***MINIMUM function***. The ScreenTip displays that this function "Returns the smallest number in a set of values."

10 From the list, double-click **MIN**. In the Formula Bar and in cell **B36**, MIN is entered into the function, replacing AVERAGE. Then press Enter.

The syntax for both the MINIMUM and AVERAGE functions uses the same range of cells. Copying the formula and changing the name of the function is an efficient way to enter another function for the same range of data. Recall that you can type the syntax of the entire function into a cell without using the Insert Function dialog box.

Recall that the MINIMUM function displays the smallest number in the selected range of cells. The green error indicator displays in the upper left corner of the cell because this formula does not match the previous formula.

11 With cell **B37** active, on the **Formula Bar**, double-click the function name **AVERAGE** and type M In the **Formula AutoComplete** list, double-click **MAX**, and then press Enter.

12 In cell **B38**, type **=m** and in the **Formula AutoComplete** list, click **MEDIAN**. Compare your screen with Figure 5.6.

Formula AutoComplete displays a list of functions that begin with M.

List of functions used in Formula AutoComplete

Figure 5.6

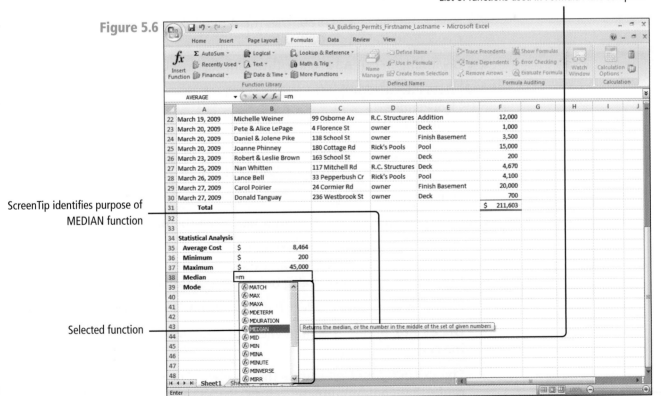

ScreenTip identifies purpose of MEDIAN function

Selected function

13 In the displayed **Formula AutoComplete** list, double-click **MEDIAN**. Select the range **F6:F30**. Press `F4`, type **)** and then press `Enter`.

The median—*$4,043*—displays. Recall that typing the first letter of the function scrolls immediately to functions beginning with that letter.

14 Click cell **B39** and on the **Formula Bar**, click the **Insert Function** button `fx`. Confirm the category is **Statistical**. Click in the **Select a function** area, type **M,** and then scroll to and click **MODE**. Click **OK**.

The range just above the active cell is suggested in the dialog box. Recall that when a range of cells is selected, the next character you type or enter automatically replaces the highlighted numbers.

15 In the **Function Arguments** dialog box, in the **Number1** box click the **Collapse Dialog Box** button. Select the range of the costs—**F6:F30**. Click the **Expand Dialog Box** button, and then click **OK**. Format the range **B36:B39** with **Comma Style** `,` with **no decimals**. **Save** your workbook.

Using the MODE function determines that projects costing $1,000 are the most common ones for March.

Activity 5.3 Counting Cells

When you need to count the number of cells or values in a group of data, use one of the Count functions. In this activity you will count the number of cells that contain values to determine the number of permits issued and count all cells in the list that contain data.

1 Select the range **A34:B39**. Use the drag-and-drop method to move the cells to the range **C34:D39**.

2 Beginning in cell **A34**, enter the following row titles:

Data Information
No. Permits
Cells with Data

3 Select the range **A34:A36**. Format it with **Bold** `B`. Select the range **A35:A36** and in the **Alignment group**, click the **Increase Indent** button.

4 Click cell **B35**. On the **Formula Bar**, click the **Insert Function** button `fx`. Click the **Statistical** category, and in the **Select a function** column, click **COUNT**, and then click **OK**. In the **COUNT Function Arguments** dialog box, click the **Collapse Dialog Box** button, and then select the range **A5:A31**. Click the **Expand Dialog Box** button, and click **OK**. The number *25* displays in the cell.

The *COUNT function* counts the number of cells in the selected range that contain numeric values. Recall that dates are numeric values. Use the COUNT function to determine the number of cells that actually contain data, especially when a worksheet is longer than one page. The cells that contain text (A5 and A31) were not counted with this function even though they were included in the selected range.

5 Click cell **B36**. On the **Formula Bar**, type **=co** and in the displayed **Formula AutoComplete** list, scroll to and click **COUNTA**, and then compare your screen with Figure 5.7.

An explanation of the function displays. The *COUNTA function* counts the number of cells in the range that are not empty. This count includes column and row titles and any other cell that contains data.

List of functions beginning with *co*   ScreenTip that explains function

Figure 5.7

Entry in cell and in Formula Bar

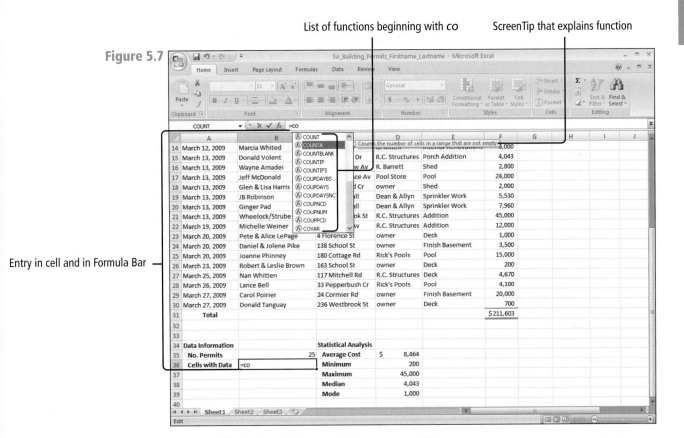

Note — The List Displays Below the Cell

The list that displays in the Formula AutoComplete will display above or below the selected cell, depending on the amount of screen space available. If the cell is at the bottom of the screen, the list will display above the selected cell. If the cell is at the top of the screen, the list will display below the selected cell.

6 Double-click **COUNTA**, select the range **A5:A31**, and then press Enter.
The number *27* displays in the cell. **Save** 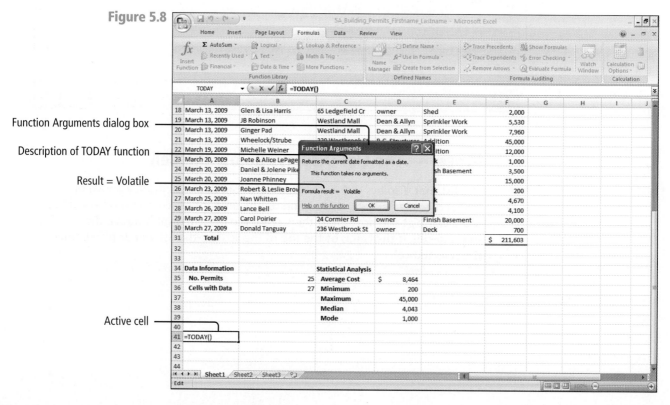 your workbook.

Objective 3
Insert Date and Time Functions

Entering the date and time of completion in a worksheet is useful. Date
and time functions can be static or volatile. A **static** date or time
remains the same and does not change. A **volatile** date or time is
updated each time the worksheet is used.

Activity 5.4 Using Date and Time Functions

The worksheet you are using will be reviewed and edited frequently. To
note when the worksheet is updated, you will enter a date that changes
each time the worksheet is used. In addition, you will enter the date for
the worksheet information that does not change. In this activity, you will
enter a static date and time and a volatile date and time that will change
when the worksheet is updated.

1 Click cell **A41**. Click the **Formulas tab**, and in the **Function Library
group**, click the **Date and Time** button. From the displayed list,
click **TODAY**. Compare your screen with Figure 5.8.

The **TODAY function** returns the current date. Each time the worksheet is opened, the TODAY function recalculates so the current date
always displays. The Function Arguments dialog box explains that
the function does not use any arguments. Notice that it states that
the formula is **Volatile**—the data in the cell will update to remain
current. A **volatile date** will update to display the current date and
a **volatile time** will update to display the current time.

Figure 5.8

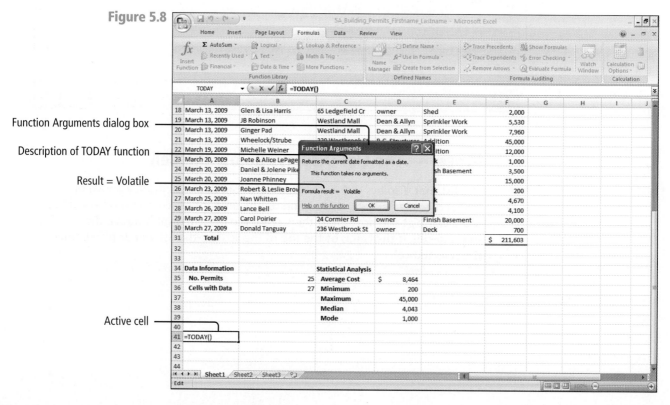

Function Arguments dialog box

Description of TODAY function

Result = Volatile

Active cell

2 Click **OK** to enter today's date in cell A41.

3 Click cell **A42**. In the **Function Library group,** click the **Date & Time** button, and from the displayed list, click **NOW**. Click **OK** to insert the current date and time in cell A42.

Like the TODAY function, no arguments are needed for the NOW function. The **NOW function** returns the current date and time in the cell. It recalculates the date and time when the worksheet is calculated or opened. The current date and time display in the cell and the time displays using the 24-hour clock.

4 Click cell **B41** and press Ctrl + ; and then press Enter.

The current date is quickly entered into the worksheet. This is a **static date**—a date that will not update and will always remain this date.

5 In cell **B42**, press Ctrl + ⇧ Shift + ; and then press Enter.

The current time is entered into the worksheet. This is a **static time**—a time that will not update. The time displays using the AM/PM label.

6 Click cell **B41**. Click the **Home tab**, and in the **Number group**, click the **Number Format button arrow** | General ▾ |—the number format now displays *Date*—to display the list. Compare your screen with Figure 5.9, and then click **Long Date**. Adjust the column width if necessary.

The number format menu displays an icon to the left of each format type and an example of the format displays just below the name of the format type. The **Long Date** displays the day of the week and the date written in full.

Sample format results   Number menu

Figure 5.9

Icon visually indicates the type of format

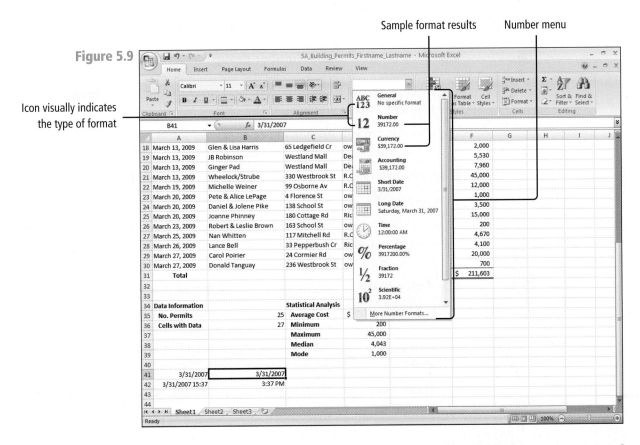

7 Click cell **D42**. Compare the time that displays in cells **A42**, **B42**, and the time that displays on your computer monitor.

Notice that the time that displays is different from the current time.

8 In the **Editing group**, click the **Sum** button and as you do, notice that the time displayed in cell **A42** updated to the current time while the time in cell **B42** did not change. Press Esc.

The static time in cell B42 remained the same while the volatile time in cell A42 updated. The time and date are updated each time Excel completes a calculation, such as using the SUM function.

Recall that Esc is used when you change your mind and don't want to complete the task.

9 Click cell **A40** and type **Volatile** and click cell **B40** and type **Static**

Format cells **A40:B40** with **Bold** **B** and **Center** ☰. **Save** 💾 your workbook.

Activity 5.5 Using Dates in a Formula

Recall that Excel stores dates as sequential serial numbers so they can be used in calculations. By default, January 1, 1900, is serial number 1 and January 1, 2008, is serial number 39448 because it is 39,448 days after January 1, 1900.

Because dates are stored as a serial number, numbers can be added to dates to determine a future date. The city building department completes two inspections on the progress of the work, once 30 days after the date of the permit and a second inspection 60 days after that. In this activity, you will determine future dates by adding numbers to a date.

1 Click cell **A6**. In the **Number group**, click the **Number Format button arrow** | General ▾ |, and then click **General**. The number *39875* displays in the cell.

The date in cell A6 has changed to the serial number for March 3, 2009, which is 39,875 days after January 1, 1900.

2 Click cell **G6**. Type **=a6+30** and on the **Formula Bar**, click the **Enter** button ✔.

The serial number—*39905*—displays in the cell because the number format is **General**. The formula in cell G6 adds 30 to the serial number in cell A6 with the result—*39905*—displayed in cell G6.

3 With cell **G6** active, in the **Number group**, click the **Number Format button arrow** | General ▾ |, and then click **More Number Formats**. In the **Format Cells** dialog box, on the **Number tab**, under **Category**, click **Date**. Under **Type**, scroll to and click **March 14, 2001**, and compare your screen with Figure 5.10.

There are several date styles available. The selected style displays in the *Sample* area.

Figure 5.10

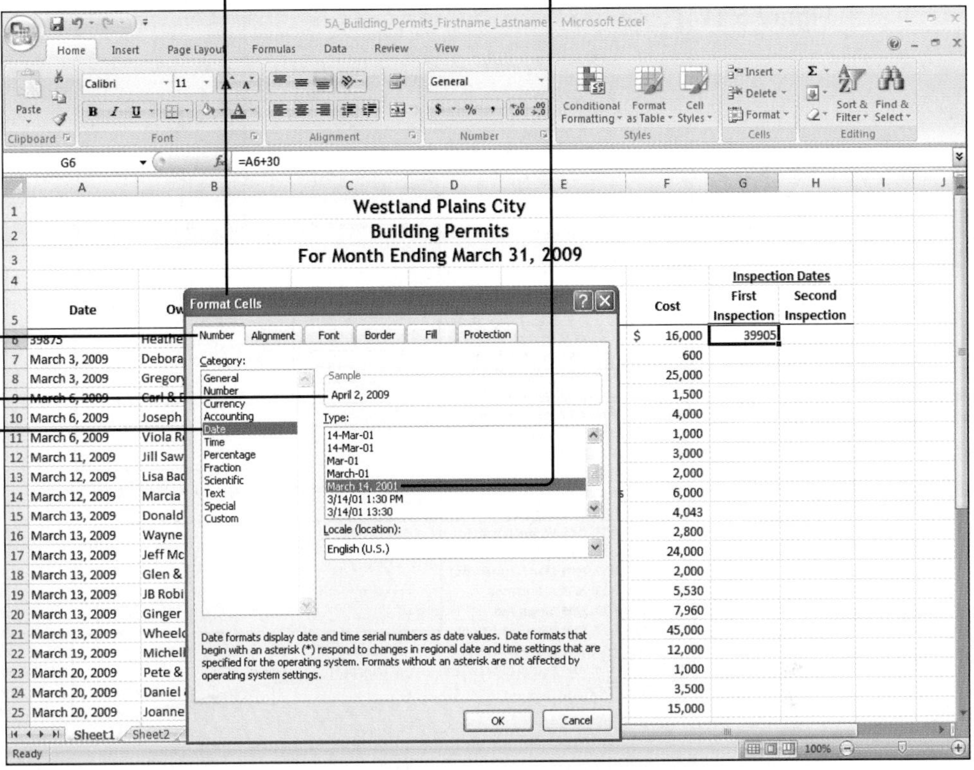

Format Cells dialog box   Type of date is highlighted

Number tab of dialog box

Sample of date
Selected category—Date

4 Click **OK**. Increase the column width of **column G**. Use the **Format Painter** to copy the format from cell **G6** to cell **A6** and in the **Number group**, confirm the format *Date* is displayed.

The date entered in cell G6 is the date the first inspection is due. The date format was copied from cell G6 to cell A6.

5 Click cell **H6** and type **=g6+60** and press Enter to add 60 days to the date in cell **G6**.

6 Select the range **G6:H6** and copy the formulas through **row 30**, and then adjust the widths of **columns G** and **H**.

7 Right-click cell **A6**, and then click the **Format Painter** button. Select the range **A7:A30** to copy the date format in column A.

8 Select the range **F4:F30**. In the **Number group**, click the **Dialog Box Launcher**. In the **Format Cells** dialog box, click the **Border tab**. On the left side, under **Style**, click the border style that is the last one in the second column—a double border. At the right side, under **Border**, click the **Vertical Right Border** button, and then compare your screen with Figure 5.11.

Figure 5.11

Border tab   Border area

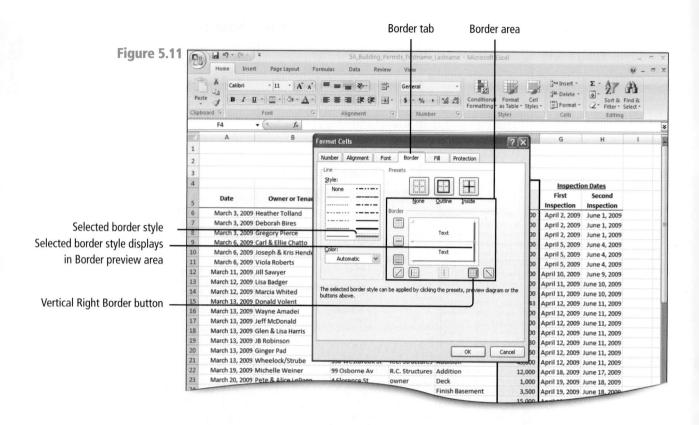

Selected border style
Selected border style displays
in Border preview area

Vertical Right Border button

9 Click **OK** and **Save** 💾 your workbook. Click in another cell to deselect the range and notice the double vertical border.

Objective 4
Create Logical Functions and Insert a Comment

Logical functions test a logical comparison between expressions and
determine if the conditions are true or false. Recall that the IF function is
a logical function that tests data against a set of criteria and, depending
on the results of the test, returns one value if the comparison is true and
another value if the comparison is false. Other logical functions work in a
similar fashion.

Activity 5.6 Using the AND Function

The *AND function* tests two or more arguments to see if they are true or
false and returns TRUE if all arguments are true and FALSE if any argument is not true. The city tracks the types of permits issued and maintains statistical analysis of the permits. This year, city officials want to
review the building of decks and pools more carefully. In this activity,
you will compare the permits for decks and pools and their costs.

1 **Rename Sheet1** to **Permits Statistics Copy** the worksheet into a new
sheet before **Sheet2** and name the new sheet **Permits Report**

2 In the **Permits Report sheet**, select **row headings 34:42**. In the
Editing group, click the **Clear** button 🔲 and from the list, click
Clear All to clear all data and formats from the selected rows.

Recall that you can remove the data and format of a cell or range of cells using the Clear All button.

3 Select **columns G:H**. In the **Editing group**, click the **Clear** button and from the list, click **Clear All**.

The entire worksheet is selected and a warning box displays that indicates you cannot change part of a merged cell. The worksheet title in rows 1 through 3 are merged cells, as are cells G4:H4, so the data in the column cannot be deleted in this manner.

4 Click **OK**. Select the range **G4:H30** and press Delete.

The format of the cells remains, but the formulas and entries are deleted.

5 In cell **G5**, type **Deck Permits** and in cell **H5**, type **Pool Permits** Click cell **G6**, click the **Formulas tab**, and in the **Function Library group**, click the **Logical** button, and from the list, click **AND**.

The AND Function Arguments dialog box displays. A comparison argument is entered and if it is true, then TRUE is entered in the cell. If it is not true, then FALSE is entered.

6 Move the **Function Arguments** dialog box so rows 6 and 7 display. With the insertion point in the **Logical1** box, click cell **F6**, and type **>1000** In the **Logical2** box, click cell **E6** and type **="Deck"** Then click **OK** and compare your screen with Figure 5.12. Alternatively, in the Logical1 text box, type **f6>1000** and in the Logical2 text box, type **e6="Deck"** and then compare your screen with Figure 5.12.

In this logical test, the city wants to identify all deck permits that are valued at more than $1,000. One logical test is for the cost of the permit greater than 1000 and the other logical test is that the permit is issued for a deck. Because the permit in row 6 is not for a deck, FALSE is entered. Even though the cost was greater than $1,000, all arguments needed to be true in order to result in TRUE. Text arguments are entered with quotation marks ["] surrounding the text.

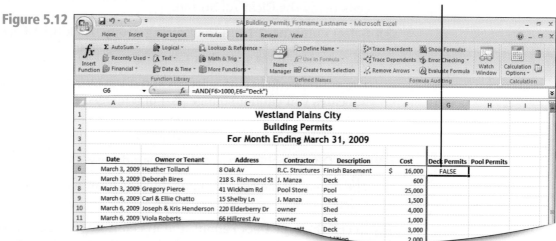

Function displayed in Formula Bar

Result of AND function

Figure 5.12

G6 = AND(F6>1000,E6="Deck")

	A	B	C	D	E	F	G	H	I
1				Westland Plains City					
2				Building Permits					
3				For Month Ending March 31, 2009					
4									
5	Date	Owner or Tenant	Address	Contractor	Description	Cost	Deck Permits	Pool Permits	
6	March 3, 2009	Heather Tolland	8 Oak Av	R.C. Structures	Finish Basement	$ 16,000	FALSE		
7	March 3, 2009	Deborah Bires	218 S. Richmond St	J. Manza	Deck	600			
8	March 3, 2009	Gregory Pierce	41 Wickham Rd	Pool Store	Pool	25,000			
9	March 6, 2009	Carl & Ellie Chatto	15 Shelby Ln	J. Manza	Deck	1,500			
10	March 6, 2009	Joseph & Kris Henderson	220 Elderberry Dr	owner	Shed	4,000			
11	March 6, 2009	Viola Roberts	66 Hillcrest Av	owner	Deck	1,000			
12					Deck	3,000			
						2,000			

7 With cell **G6** active, use the fill handle to copy the formula down through **row 30**.

As a result of the function, you can determine that there are three deck projects that cost more than $1,000—indicated by TRUE in the results. In Westland Plains, more expensive deck projects require additional review—the results in column G identify which deck projects need additional review.

8 Click cell **H6**. In the **Function Library group**, click the **Recently Used** button, and then click **AND**.

The *Recently Used* menu displays a list of functions that have most recently been used.

9 In the **Logical1** box, type **f6>5000** In the **Logical2** box, type **e6="pool"** and then click **OK**. Alternatively, use the collapse and expand dialog box buttons and click in the cells to enter the logical comparisons.

FALSE is entered in cell H6. In this column, you are determining the permits for a pool that costs more than $5,000. Although the permit in row 6 was issued for more than $5,000, it was not for a pool, so FALSE is the result.

10 Copy the formula in cell **H6** down through **row 30**. **Save** 🖫 your workbook.

There are three pool projects that cost more than $5,000 that will require additional review.

Activity 5.7 Using the OR Function

The *OR function* tests two or more arguments to see if they meet the condition. When any of the arguments is true, TRUE is entered into the cell. Periodically, the city reviews its contractors and this year it is reviewing J. Manza, R. Barrett, and G. Kittell. In this activity, you will identify the building permits these contractors have received.

1 Click cell **I5** and type **Individual Contractors** Use the **Format Painter**
to copy the format from cell **H5** to cell **I5**. Adjust column widths
and row heights if needed—the row height should be adjusted so the
borders are close to the top and bottom of the two-line titles.

2 Click cell **I6**. On the **Formulas tab**, in the **Function Library group**,
click the **Logical** button, and then click **OR**.

3 In the **Function Arguments** dialog box, in the **Logical1** box, click
cell **D6** and type **="J. Manza"** Press Tab and in the **Logical2** box, click
cell **D6** and type **="R. Barrett"** Press Tab, and in the **Logical3** box,
type **d6="G. Kittell"** Compare your screen with Figure 5.13 and then
click **OK**.

Because the contractor for this project is not one of the three
selected contractors, FALSE is entered into the cell. Recall that text
in the Function Arguments dialog boxes is surrounded by quotation
marks.

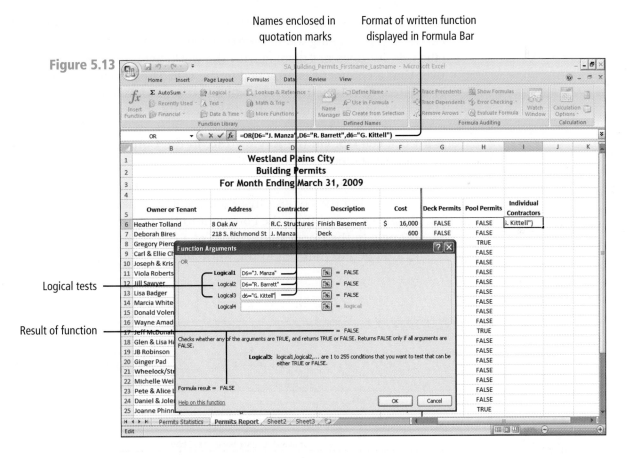

Figure 5.13

4 Copy the formula in cell **I6** through **row 30**.

The six jobs that will be worked by one of these contractors
display TRUE, which identifies these projects for the building codes
department.

5 Select the range **G6:I30**. On the **Home tab**, in the **Styles group**, click the **Conditional Formatting** button. In the displayed list, point to **Highlight Cells Rules**, and in the submenu, click **Equal To**. In the **Format cells that are EQUAL TO** text box, type **true** and then click **OK**.

The cells that display TRUE are formatted in red. This highlights the areas to which the building department will pay special attention. In this dialog box, text is not case sensitive—TRUE is the same as true.

6 Select the range **H5:H30**. In the **Font group**, click the **Borders button arrow** , and click the **Right Border** button. Access the list again and click the **Left Border** button to place borders on both sides of the column. Select the range **I5:I30** and using the skills you practiced, place the **Right Border** on the column. **Save** your workbook.

Activity 5.8 Inserting a Comment

Additional information that further explains the data of the worksheet can be inserted using a ***comment***—a remark that is attached to a specific cell but does not display with the worksheet. An indicator alerts the user that a comment is attached in the cell. The comment can be edited or deleted. In this activity, you will insert and format comments that provide additional information about the results of functions.

1 Click cell **G5**. On the **Review tab**, in the **Comments group**, click the **New Comment** button, and then compare your screen with Figure 5.14.

A comment box displays with the registered computer user's name displayed in the box. An insertion point is blinking in the second line. An arrow points from the comment to the ***comment indicator***—a red triangle in the upper right corner of a cell that indicates a comment is attached to that cell in the worksheet.

Figure 5.14

Comment

Comment indicator in cell

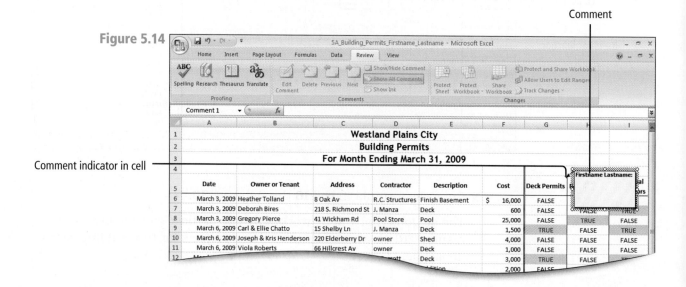

2 In the **Comment** text box, at the insertion point, type **Valued over $1,000** and then compare your screen with Figure 5.15.

Comments group   Comment

Figure 5.15

Red triangle indicates
comment is in cell

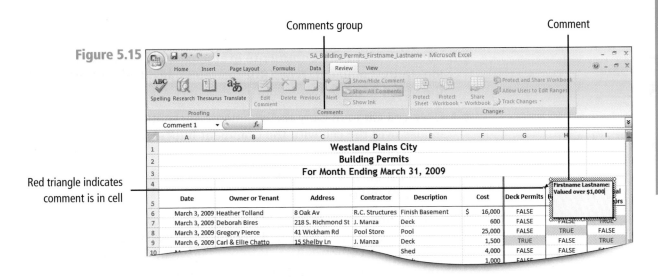

3 Click in cell **A1**. In the **Comments group**, click **Show All Comments** until comments do not display, and compare your screen with Figure 5.16.

The comment no longer displays but the comment indicator remains in the cell.

Alert!

Do your comments display?

The Show All Comments command is a toggle command. It is turned on—comments show—or turned off—comments do not show. When the button is turned on, it displays with a yellow background. The toggle does not change until a computer user clicks on the Show All Comments button. If your comments show, at an earlier time they were requested to show.

Show All Comments command   Comment indicator

Figure 5.16

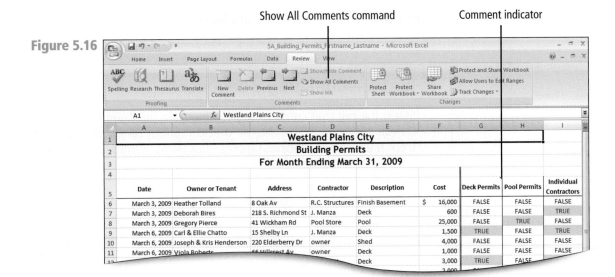

4 Confirm that comments do not show and click cell **H5**. In the **Comments group**, click the **New Comment** button. In the comment, type **Valued over $5,000** and then click outside the comment.

When the active cell does not include a comment, the comments do not display because you have instructed Excel to hide comments.

5 Click cell **I5**. In the **Comments group**, click the **New Comment** button. In the comment, type **TRUE indicates individual contractor** and then click in cell **A1**.

6 Click cell **G5** to display the comment. Alternatively, position the mouse over the cell with the Comment Indicator to display the comment.

When comments do not display, point to or click in the cell with the comment indicator.

7 In the **Comments group**, click the **Next** button to move to the next cell that contains a comment and display the comment. In the same manner, click the **Previous** button to move to the previous cell that contains a comment and display the comment.

8 In the **Comments group**, click the **Show All Comments** button.

All comments display in the worksheet.

9 Click cell **G5** and in the **Comments group**, click the **Edit Comment** button.

The insertion point blinks in the comment.

10 Edit the comment to read **For decks valued over $1,000** Select **decks**, click the **Home tab**, and in the **Font group**, click the **Italic** button _I_ .

Text within a comment may be edited or formatted.

11 Click cell **H5**. Click the **Review tab**, and in the **Comments group**, click **Edit Comment**. Edit the comment to read **For pools valued over $5,000** Double-click **pools** to select it. Click the **Home tab**, and in the **Font group**, click the **Italic** _I_ button.

12 Click in the worksheet and **Save** your workbook.

Note — Deleting a Comment

Select the cell that contains the comment. In the Comments group, click Delete. Alternatively, in the cell that contains a comment, right-click and from the displayed shortcut menu, click Delete Comment.

Activity 5.9 Printing Comments

Comments can be printed as they are displayed or as text at the end of the worksheet. In this activity you will print the worksheet and the comments.

1 Delete **Sheet2** and **Sheet3**. Right-click and click **Select All Sheets**. In the **Left Footer** area enter the **File Name** and in the **Right Footer** area, enter the **Sheet Name** and return to **Normal** view ▦ .

2 Click the **Page Layout** tab and format the worksheets in **Landscape orientation** and centered both **Horizontally** and **Vertically**. On the **Page Layout tab**, in the **Scale to Fit group**, click the **Width button arrow** and from the list, click **1 page**. In the **Scale to Fit group**, click the **Height button arrow** and from the list, click **1 page** and confirm that the Scale is between 70% and 90%. Confirm that **Permits Statistics** is the active sheet, and then compare your screen with Figure 5.17.

The Scale to Fit command may be entered on the Page Layout tab in the Scale to Fit group. The differences in the scaling percentage depend on the default printer you are using.

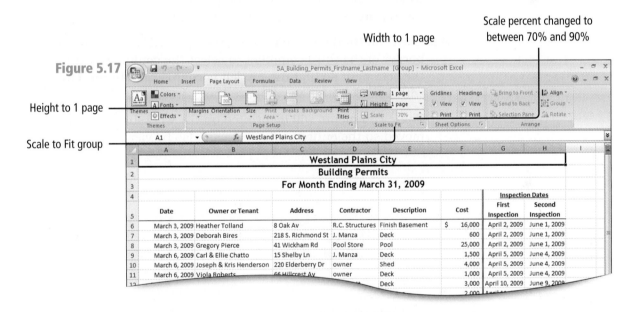

Figure 5.17

3 With all sheets selected, use **Print Preview** to review how the worksheets will display when printed. Notice that the **Permits Report** worksheet title is not centered over the width of the worksheet. **Close Print Preview**.

Columns were added to the Permits Report worksheet causing the title to no longer be centered.

4 **Ungroup** the sheets. Click the **Permits Report sheet tab**. Select the range **A1:I1**. On the **Home tab**, in the **Alignment group**, click the **Merge & Center button arrow** 🖼 ▾ and compare your screen with Figure 5.18.

The menu of choices about Merge & Center displays.

Figure 5.18

Merge & Center button   Merge & Center menu

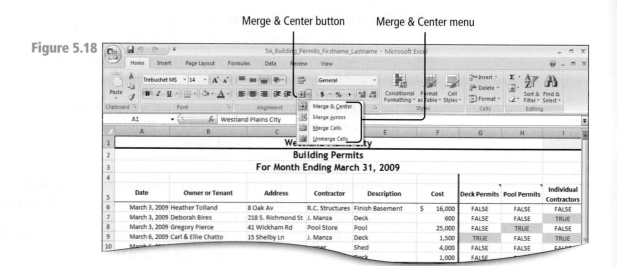

⑤ Click **Merge Across**. Select the range **A2:I2** and click the **Merge & Center button arrow** 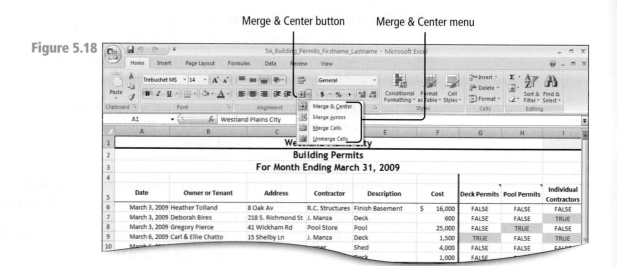 and click **Merge Across**. Using the skills you practiced, merge and center **row 3** to include **column I**. On the **Review tab**, in the **Comments group**, if necessary, click **Show All Comments** to display all comments in the worksheet.

⑥ Click the third comment—it starts with *TRUE*—and then click in the border of the third comment to select the comment text box. Drag the comment so that the top left corner is in **column J** and aligns with **row 7**, and then compare your screen with Figure 5.19.

These comments will be printed on the worksheet and should be moved so the entire worksheet can also be viewed.

Moved comment—border
indicates it is active comment

Show All Comments button

Figure 5.19

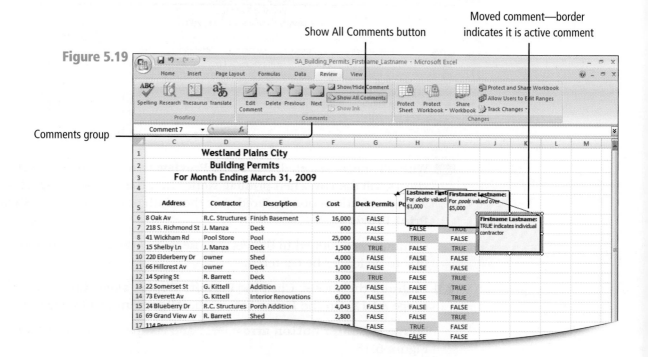

Comments group

7 Using the skill practiced, move the **comment for Pool Permits** to **row 1**, beginning in the center of **column I**, and position the **comment for Deck Permits** in **row 1**, beginning in **column G**.

8 Click the **Page Layout tab**, in the **Page Setup group**, click the **Dialog Box Launcher** [⧉]. In the **Page Setup** dialog box, click the **Sheet tab**. Under **Print**, at the right side, click the **Comments arrow** From the list, click **At end of sheet**, and then click **Print Preview**. On the **Print Preview tab**, in the **Preview group**, click the **Next Page** button to display page 2. If your instructor suggests, print this document.

The comments display at the end of the worksheet in a text format. The cell number is identified for each comment but does not display on the worksheet.

9 Click **Close Print Preview**. Display the **Page Setup** dialog box again, and then click the **Sheet tab**. Under **Print**, at the right side, click the **Comments arrow** and select **As displayed on sheet**. Then click **Print Preview** and review the placement of the worksheet.

The comments are added to the worksheet with arrows pointing to the appropriate cell title.

10 Click **Close Print Preview**. **Save** [💾] your work.

11 To submit electronically, follow the instructions provided by your instructor. To print, from the **Office** menu, click **Print**. In the **Print** dialog box, under **Print what**, select **Entire workbook**, and then click **OK**. From the **Office** menu, click **Close**. **Close** Excel.

More Knowledge
Changing the Comment Identification

By default, the comment displays the registered computer name. You can delete the computer name and insert your name in its place.

End **You have completed Project 5A** ————————

Project 5B City Financial

In Activities 5.10 through 5.17, you will create a workbook for Joaquin Alonzo, city manager, which displays the financial results of a loan. The workbook will include an amortization table that displays the amount of the loan, the payments, and the interest paid. You will use Goal Seek to evaluate the financial impact of the development of a new park. You will change the data to see different results that will assist in making a decision about the size of the park and the total costs. You will also use Excel to make financial decisions regarding an investment for a project and retirement information for a new employee. Your completed worksheet will look similar to Figure 5.20.

For Project 5B, you will need the following file:

New blank workbook

You will save your workbook as
5B_City_Financial_Firstname_Lastname

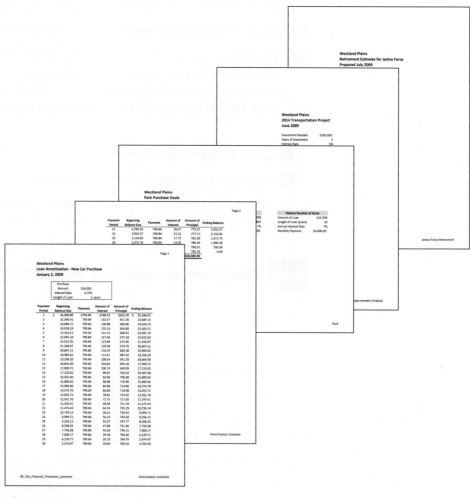

Figure 5.20
Project 5B—City Financial

Objective 5
Insert Financial Functions

In the business world, financial information is used on a daily basis. Excel's built-in *financial functions* assist businesses in making financial decisions, such as calculating a loan payment or reviewing the depreciation allowed on an asset. Currently, the city is negotiating for the purchase of a fleet of new cars. City Manager Joaquin Alonzo will prepare a report to present to the mayor. You will review the financial impact of each car purchase, which will help determine the amount to be budgeted each year for their purchase. Financial functions are used to provide a clear picture to the mayor so that he knows the price of the car and how much interest will be paid.

Activity 5.10 Creating an Amortization Table

When you borrow money, you will usually make equal monthly payments to pay off the loan over time. A portion of that payment will be *interest*, the amount of money that is charged by the lending institution. To review the amount that is paid to interest and the amount still owed, an *amortization table*—also called a *loan payment schedule*—is used to report each monthly payment, the amount paid for interest, and the amount the loan is decreased with each payment. In this activity, you will create a worksheet that will be used for an amortization table for each new vehicle.

1 **Start** Excel and display a new blank workbook. **Save** the workbook in the **Excel Chapter 5** folder as **5B_City_Financial_Firstname_Lastname** Beginning in cell **A1**, type the following worksheet title lines:

Westland Plains
Loan Amortization – New Car Purchase
'January 2, 2009

2 Format the three-line worksheet title with **Bold** B, and **14-point font**.

3 Beginning in cell **B5**, type the following information:

Purchase Amount	$26,000	
Interest Rate	6.25%	
Length of Loan	3	Years

4 Select the range **B5:B7** and format it with **Center** ≡ alignment and **Wrap Text** ≣, and then select the range **B5:D7** and add an **Outside Border**. If necessary, adjust row heights to fit the cell contents.

5 Select the range **A9:F9** and format with **Bold** B, **Center** ≡, **Middle Align** ≡, **Wrap Text** ≣, and a **Bottom Border** . Beginning in cell **A9**, enter the following column titles across the row and adjust column widths so the column titles display on two lines and the row height is adjusted without extra space in the row.

Compare your screen with Figure 5.21 and **Save** 🖫 your workbook.

Payment Period	Beginning Balance Due	Payment	Amount of Interest	Amount of Principal	Ending Balance

To fully report the effects of loan payments, the amortization table will display the beginning balance for each payment, the amount of the payment, how much of the payment is the interest charge and how much is applied to the principal, as well as the ending balance. You will also number the payments of the loan.

Titles entered in row 9

Figure 5.21

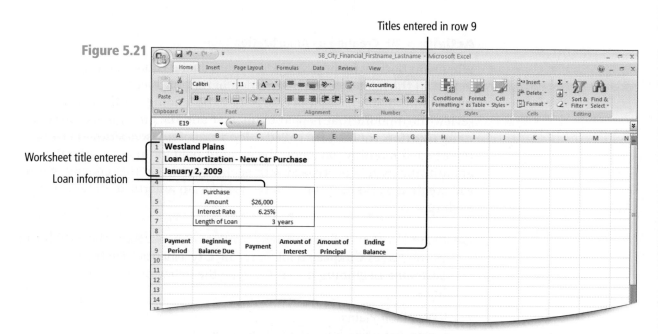

Worksheet title entered

Loan information

Payments Workshop

Borrowing Money

When you borrow money from a bank or similar financial institution, you are charged for using the money, which is interest. Loans are typically made for a period of years, and the interest that is charged is calculated as a percentage of the amount that is borrowed, times the length of time for which the loan is made. This interest percentage is referred to as the *interest rate* or, in Excel, simply *rate*.

When you borrow money, you usually make equal payments over the length of the loan until the loan is completely paid. These payments include an amount for interest and an amount that decreases the *principal*—amount still owed—of the loan. The *time* is the length of time it takes to pay off the loan.

Suppose that you need to borrow $1,000 for a year at a 5% interest rate in order to pay your college expenses. How much will you need in order to pay back the loan?

First you need to identify the principal, rate, and time. **Principal (P)** is $1,000—the amount of the loan. The **interest rate (R)** is 5%, which is expressed as an annual interest rate. The **time (T)** of the loan is 1 year. Using the formula I = PRT, the amount of interest is $50, so you will pay $1,050 to completely pay off this loan at the end of the year.

Usually, loans are paid back in equal monthly payments. When this occurs, the amount of principal is decreased each month, which decreases the amount of interest that is paid. Manually computing the amount of interest due with each payment requires using a complex formula each time a payment is made. Excel's PMT (payment) function is designed to quickly determine the amount of the monthly payment when equal payments are made. Other financial functions include those that will compute the amount of interest and the amount that is applied to the principal of the loan.

Activity 5.11 Using the PMT (Payment) Function

The **PMT (Payment) function** calculates the payments for a loan based on constant payments and a constant interest rate. To determine the amount of the monthly payment, the amount of the loan, the interest rate, and the length of the loan—the number of years or months that will be required to pay off the loan—must be known. In this activity, you will determine the amount of the monthly payment for the car loan.

1 Click cell **A10** and type **1** and in cell **A11**, type **2** Select the range **A10:A11** and use the fill handle to fill the pattern of numbers down through **row 45**—the ScreenTip displays **36**. Format the column with **Center** ☰ alignment.

With three years of monthly payments, this loan will require 36 payments to pay it in full. In this amortization table, each row represents one payment.

2 Click cell **B10**, type **=c5** press Enter, and then format cell **B10** with **Accounting Number Format** $ ▾ .

The first payment is displayed on row 10. The value displayed in column B is the amount of the loan that is still due. For this first payment, the purchase price of the car—$26,000—is the balance due.

3 Click cell **C10**. Click the **Formulas tab**, and in the **Function Library group**, click the **Financial** button. Scroll down the list and click **PMT**.

As displayed in the PMT Function Arguments dialog box, the PMT—Payment—function determines the payment for the loan, which is based on making constant payments with a constant interest rate.

4 Click the **Function Arguments** dialog box title bar, and drag the dialog box to the right of the screen so that **columns A:D** are visible. Compare your screen with Figure 5.22.

The PMT Function Arguments dialog box displays and includes several arguments. The required arguments are indicated in bold and are *Rate*, *Nper*, and *Pv*.

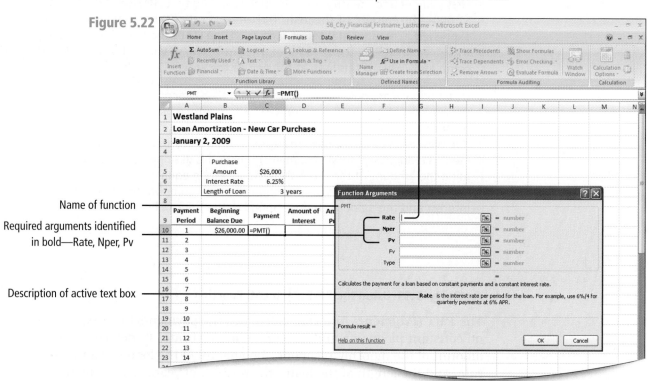

Figure 5.22

Insertion point in active text box—Rate

Name of function

Required arguments identified in bold—Rate, Nper, Pv

Description of active text box

5 With the insertion point blinking in the **Rate** box, click cell **C6**, press [F4], and type **/12**. Alternatively, in the Rate area, type **c6/12**

The interest rate is expressed as an annual percentage rate. Because this loan will require monthly payments, the amount of interest will be expressed on a per-month basis, which is done by dividing the annual interest—6.25%—by the number of months in the year—12. Because the formula will be copied, express the reference to cell C6 as an absolute reference.

6 Press [Tab] to move the insertion point to the **Nper** box and in the dialog box, review the explanation for the *Nper argument*— the total number of payments for the loan. Click cell **C7**, press [F4], and type ***12** Alternatively, in the Nper box, type **c7*12**

This three-year loan will be paid back in monthly payments. To determine the total number of payments, multiply the length of the loan—3 years—by 12—the number of months in a year.

7 Press [Tab] to move to the **Pv** box and review the *Pv argument*—the *present value*—which is defined in the dialog box as the total amount that a series of future payments is worth now, which is the amount of the loan. The present value can also be the lump sum payment needed today to have a specific amount at a future time. Click cell **C5,** press [F4], and compare your screen with Figure 5.23.

As each payment is made, the balance due—the beginning balance—will decrease. The amount due is entered in column B and is expressed as a relative reference.

Figure 5.23

Rate argument Nper argument Pv argument

PMT Function Arguments dialog box

Name of function

Result

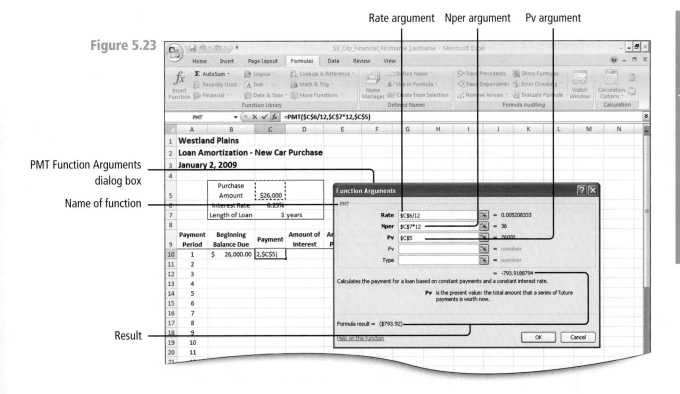

Note — Optional Arguments

The PMT function contains two arguments not indicated in bold that are optional. The Future value (Fv) argument assumes that the unpaid portion of the loan should be zero at the end of the last period. The Type argument assumes that the payment will be made at the end of each period. These default values are typical of most loans and may be left blank.

8 In the displayed dialog box, click **OK**, and then compare your screen with Figure 5.24.

The result displays in the cell and the formula displays in the Formula Bar. Because the payment reduces the amount of the loan, it is entered as a negative number in the cell and is identified by red text and parentheses.

Figure 5.24

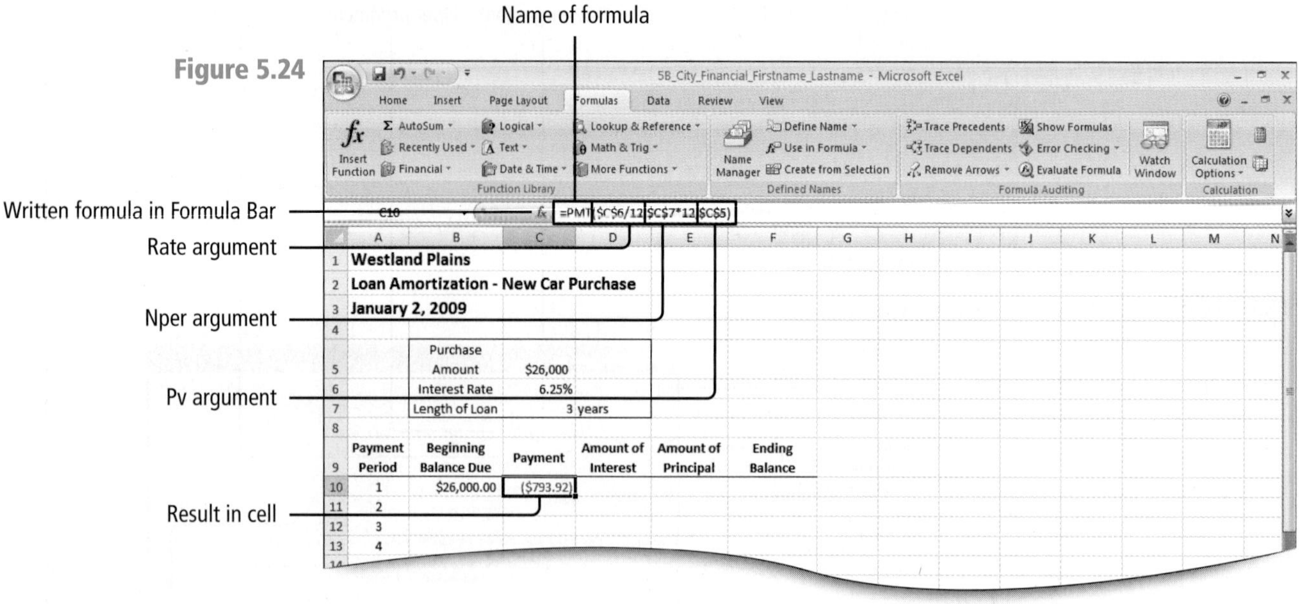

Name of formula

Written formula in Formula Bar

Rate argument

Nper argument

Pv argument

Result in cell

9 Click in the **Formula Bar** between the equal sign (=) and the *P* of *PMT* and type – so that the result will display as a positive number.

In the **Formula Bar**, click the **Enter** button ✔. **Save** 💾 your workbook.

The amount of the monthly payment—*$793.92*—displays as a positive number in cell C10.

Another Way — **To Get a Positive Result**

As you complete the Function Arguments, you are entering positive numbers. Place a minus sign in the principal value (Pv) argument and the result will display as a positive number.

Activity 5.12 Using the IPMT (Interest Payment) Function

The *IPMT—Interest Payment function*—calculates the amount of interest that will be charged for a given period. The amount of interest is determined by the amount of the loan that is remaining and assumes the payments are periodic—monthly, for example—and constant—each payment is the same, the length of time from the last payment is the same, and the interest rate is the same. In this activity, you will determine the amount of the loan payment that is used to pay the interest charge.

1 Click cell **D10**. In the **Function Library group**, click the **Financial** button, and then click **IPMT.** If necessary, click in the **Function Arguments** dialog box title bar and drag it to the right of the screen so the **columns A:D** are visible, and then compare your screen with Figure 5.25.

The IPMT—Interest Payment—Function Arguments dialog box displays with the required arguments—*Rate, Per, Nper,* and *Pv*—displayed in bold. The explanation of the IPMT function states that the interest payment function calculates the interest payment for a given period based on periodic constant payments and a constant interest rate. The insertion point is in the Rate box where the interest rate for the period is entered, making it the active argument box. An explanation of the argument displays in the dialog box.

Figure 5.25

Required arguments

IPMT Function Arguments dialog box

Explanation of function

Explanation of Rate argument

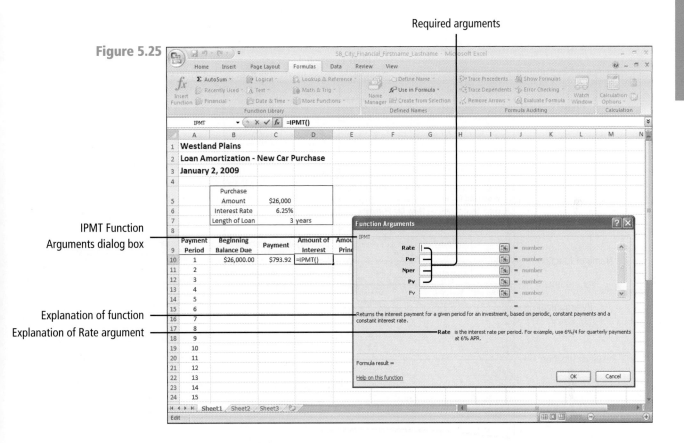

2 With the insertion point in the **Rate** box, click cell **C6**, press F4, and type **/12** Alternatively, in the Rate box, type **c6/12**

Again, divide the interest rate by 12 to calculate the rate used for a monthly payment.

3 Press Tab and review the **Per argument** explanation—the period for which you want to find the interest. Click cell **A10**. This is the first period, as displayed in cell **A10**.

Because this is the first payment, the *per* will be 1. If it were the second payment—period—the *per* would be 2, and so on.

4 Press Tab and with the insertion point in the **Nper** box, click cell **C7**, press F4, and type ***12** Alternatively, in the Nper box, type **c7*12**

Recall that this calculates the total number of payments for the loan. Because the loan is expressed in years, multiply the number of years by 12 months in a year to get the total number of payments.

5 Press Tab and in the **Pv** box, click cell **C5**, press F4, and then compare your screen with Figure 5.26.

The **Pv** is the present value of the loan—the amount that it would take today to completely pay off the loan or the amount still owed. The results displayed in the dialog box indicate that the amount of interest for the first payment is *–135.4166667.*

IPMT Function
Arguments dialog box   Rate argument   Nper argument

Figure 5.26

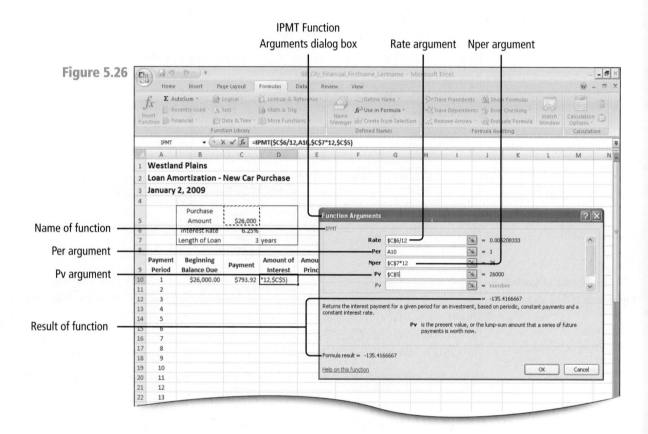

Name of function

Per argument

Pv argument

Result of function

6 Click **OK** and compare your screen with Figure 5.27.

The result—the amount of interest that will be paid this month—displays as a negative number in the cell and the formula displays in the Formula Bar.

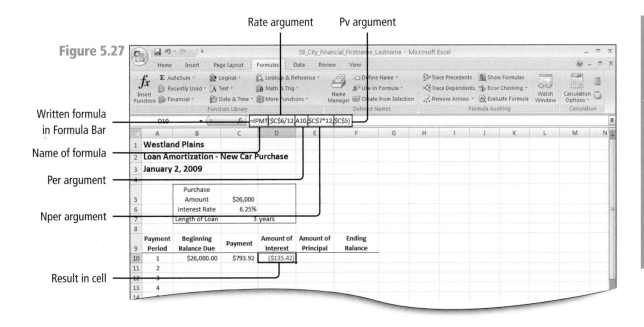

Figure 5.27

Rate argument   Pv argument

Written formula in Formula Bar

Name of formula

Per argument

Nper argument

Result in cell

7 In the **Formula Bar**, click between the equal sign (=) and the *I* of *IPMT* and type – so that the result will display as a positive number, and then click the **Enter** button ✓. **Save** 💾 your workbook.

The amount of the payment that is applied to interest—*$135.42*—displays in the cell.

Activity 5.13 Using the PPMT (Principal Payment) Function and Determining the Ending Balance

The **PPMT—Principal Payment function**—calculates the amount of the payment that will be applied to the principal—the amount of money borrowed. The amount of the loan—the principal—decreases with each payment. The amount of the payment that is applied to the principal is based on equal periodic payments with a constant interest rate. In this activity, you will determine the amount of the loan payment that is used to reduce the principal of the loan.

1 Click cell **E10**. In the **Function Library group**, click the **Financial** button, and then click **PPMT**. If necessary, drag the **Function Arguments** dialog box to the right of the screen so that **columns A:E** are visible, and then compare your screen with Figure 5.28.

The Function Arguments dialog box displays. The required arguments are *Rate*, *Per*, *Nper*, and *Pv*. The insertion point is blinking in the Rate argument box, making it active.

Figure 5.28

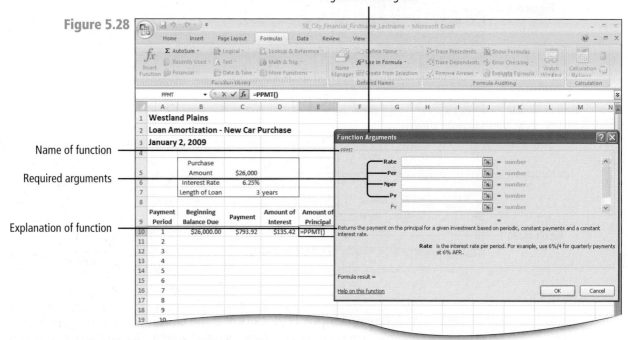

Name of function

Required arguments

Explanation of function

2 With the insertion point in the **Rate** box, click cell **C6**, press F4, and type **/12** to divide the interest rate by 12 to determine the rate used when the payments are made monthly.

3 Press Tab and review the **Per** argument—the period for which you want to find the interest. The payment periods are displayed in **column A**, so click cell **A10**.

Because this is the first payment, the *per* will be 1, which is the value of cell A10. If it were the second payment, the *per* would be 2—displayed in cell A11—and so on.

4 Press Tab and in the **Nper** box, click cell **C7**, press F4, and type ***12** to calculate the total number of payments for the loan.

5 Press Tab and in the **Pv** box, click cell **C5**, press F4, and compare your screen with Figure 5.29.

Recall that Pv is the amount of the loan that is still owed, which is the beginning balance due. As the loan is paid, the beginning balance will be different for each payment.

Figure 5.29

PPMT Function
Arguments dialog box   Per argument   Result

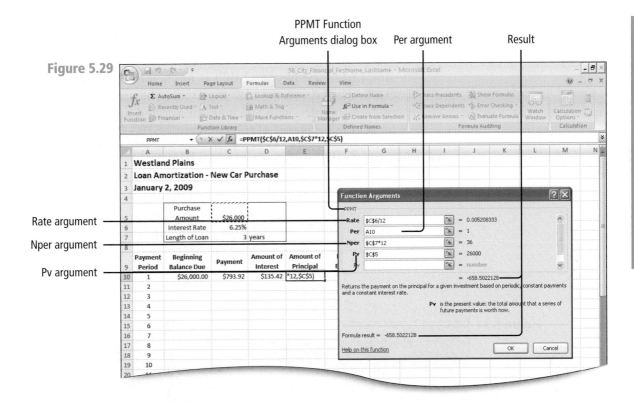

Rate argument

Nper argument

Pv argument

6 Click **OK** and compare your screen with Figure 5.30.

The result—the amount of the payment that reduces the principal—displays in the cell while the formula displays in the Formula Bar.

Rate argument   Pv argument

Figure 5.30

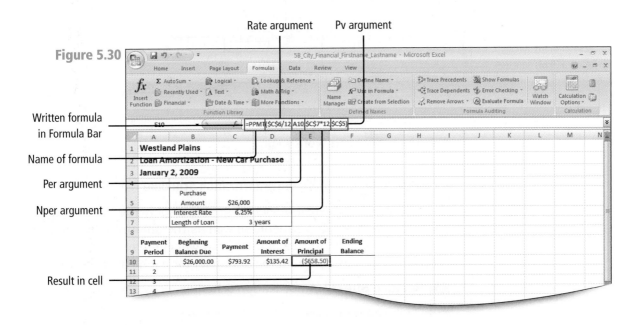

Written formula
in Formula Bar

Name of formula

Per argument

Nper argument

Result in cell

7 In the **Formula Bar**, click between the equal sign (=) and the *P* of *PPMT* and type – and then click the **Enter** button 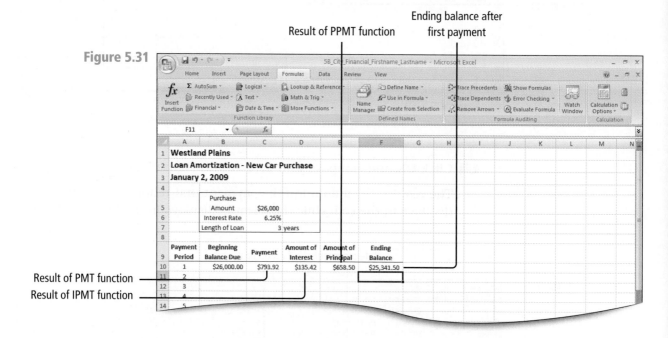.

The amount of the payment that is applied to the principal—$658.50—displays in the cell. If you add the amount applied to interest—$135.42—with the amount applied to principal—$658.50—the total is the amount of the payment—$793.92.

8 Click cell **F10** and type = Click cell **B10** and type – Click cell **E10** and press Enter. Alternatively, you can type the formula in cell F10— =b10-e10. Compare your screen with Figure 5.31.

The ending balance—$25,341.50—displays in cell F10 and is the balance of the loan after the first payment. The amount of the payment that was applied against the principal displays in cell E10.

Result of PPMT function

Ending balance after first payment

Figure 5.31

Result of PMT function

Result of IPMT function

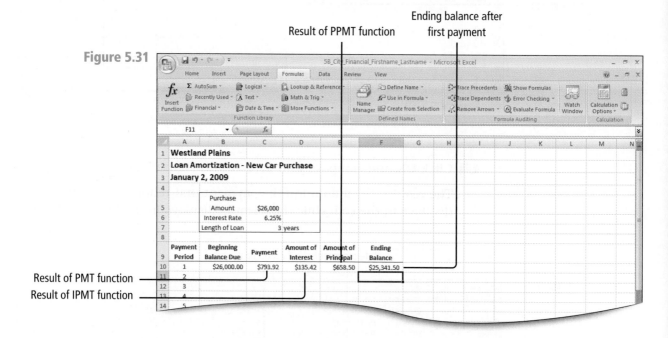

9 **Save** your workbook.

Activity 5.14 Complete the Amortization Schedule

The completed amortization schedule will display the interest and principal amounts for each payment, as well as the amount of the payment and the ending balance. In this activity, you will complete the amortization schedule that shows the financial impact for each car until it is paid for.

1 Rename **Sheet1 Amortization Schedule**

2 Click cell **B11**, type =f10 and press Enter.

The balance after the first payment—ending balance—is the amount of the beginning balance for the next payment period.

3 Select the range **C10:F10** and use the fill handle to copy the range to the next row—**row 11**. Select the range **B11:F11** and use the fill handle to copy the formulas down to **row 45**.

The ending balance after the second payment—$24,679.57—displays in cell F11. The formulas contained absolute references to the loan information and are copied correctly. Notice that the amount of interest decreases with each payment and the amount that is applied to the principal increases. The ending balance is 0.00.

4 Format the numeric values in **row 10** with **Accounting Number Format** $\boxed{\$\ \cdot}$. Format the other cells—**B11:F45**—with **Comma Style** $\boxed{'}$.

5 Select the range **C46:E46** and in the **Function Library group**, click the **AutoSum** button. Format these totals with **Bold** and place a **Top and Double Bottom Border** around them. Adjust column widths if necessary. Compare your screen with Figure 5.32.

Principal total
equals loan amount   Ending balance

Figure 5.32

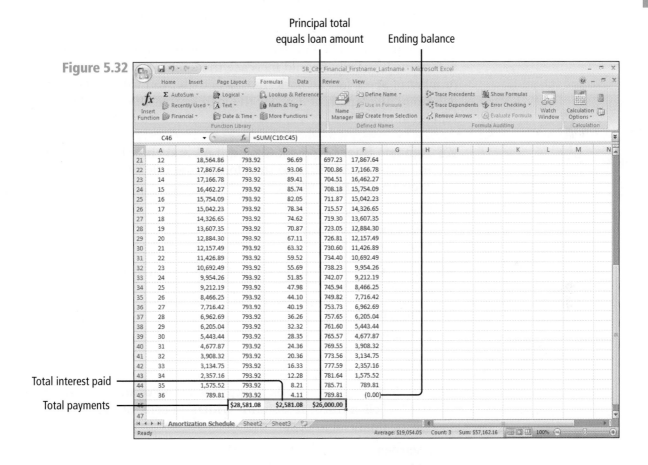

Total interest paid

Total payments

6 In cell **A46**, type **Total** and format it with **Bold** $\boxed{B}$. As the city manager reviewed the worksheet, he noticed that the interest rate is incorrect and should be **6.75%**. In cell **C6**, change the value to **6.75%** and as you press Enter, review the changes made in this worksheet.

Save $\boxed{\blacksquare}$ your workbook.

Objective 6
Create What-If Analysis with Goal Seek

Goal Seek is one of Excel's "what-if" analysis tools that is used to find a specific value for a cell by adjusting the value in another cell. You can use Goal Seek to determine a desired outcome by changing one of the variables in the formula, such as the interest rate, the length of time, or the amount borrowed.

Activity 5.15 Using Goal Seek to Determine Length of Loan

The city is considering the purchase of a new 20-acre park site. The purchase price of the land is $600,000. The city manager, Joaquin Alonzo, is considering how he should recommend the purchase terms for the land. The property owner has agreed to finance the transaction over 20 years at an interest rate of 7%. However, the city accountant requires that the monthly payments be limited to $4,000 each month. Joaquin wants to determine if the city should increase the length of the loan or reduce the number of acres for the park. In this activity, you will use Goal Seek to determine the length of time for the loan so that the monthly payments remain at $4,000.

1 **Rename Sheet2** to **Park** Click cell **A1** and enter the worksheet title in the range **A1:A3**, and then format the title lines with **Bold** and increase the **Font Size** to **14**.

Westland Plains
Park Purchase Goals
'January 12, 2009

2 In cell **A5**, type **20-Acre Park** and beginning in cell **A6**, type the following row titles:

Amount of Loan
Length of Loan (years)
Annual Interest Rate
Monthly Payment

3 Click cell **A7**. In the **Cells group**, click the **Format** button, and from the list, click **AutoFit Column Width**. In cells **B6:B8**, enter the following financial information:

600,000
20
7%

4 Click cell **B9**. Click the **Formulas tab**, and in the **Function Library group**, click the **Financial** button, and then click **PMT**. In the **Rate** box, click cell **B8** and type **/12** to calculate the monthly interest rate—divide the interest rate in cell B8 by the number of months in the year. Alternatively, in the Rate box, type **=b8/12**

5 Press [Tab] and in the **Nper** box, click cell **B7** and type ***12** to calculate the number of payments, which is the total years for the loan times 12 months in a year. Alternatively, type **=b7*12**

6 Press (Tab) and in the **Pv** box, type **-b6** to enter the amount of the loan as a negative amount. Click **OK** and compare your screen with Figure 5.33.

By entering the amount of the loan as a negative number, the amount of the monthly payment—$4,651.79—displays as a positive number. The result is larger than the $4,000 payment that the city can afford.

Formula in Formula Bar

Figure 5.33

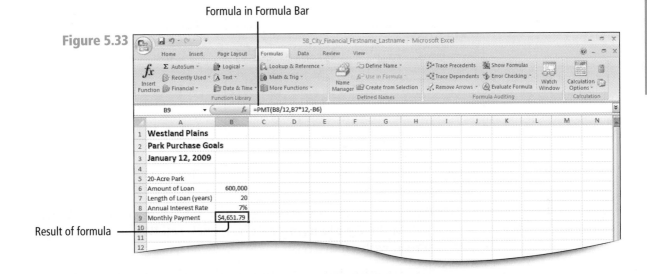

Result of formula

7 Select the range **A6:B9**. Right-click and click **Copy**. Click cell **D6**, right-click and click **Paste**, and then click cell **G6**, right-click, and click **Paste.** Adjust column widths to fully display the cell contents.

8 In cell **D5**, type **Increase Length** and in cell **G5**, type **Reduce Number of Acres** Select the range **A5:B5**. Press (Ctrl) while you select the ranges **D5:E5** and **G5:H5**. On the **Home tab**, in the **Font group**, click the **Bold** button **B** and click the **Fill button arrow** and from the last column, click the third color—**Orange, Accent 6, Lighter 60%**. In the **Alignment group**, click the **Merge & Center** button .

9 Click cell **E9**. Click the **Data tab**, and in the **Data Tools group**, click the **What-If Analysis** button, and in the displayed list, click **Goal Seek** and notice that E9 is entered as the Set cell. Move the dialog box below the worksheet data, and then compare your screen with Figure 5.34.

The Goal Seek dialog box displays. The Set cell reference in the Goal Seek dialog box displays cell E9, the result of the PMT formula. The **Set cell** is the cell that contains the result of the formula that will be set to a specific value by changing the value in another cell used in the formula.

Figure 5.34

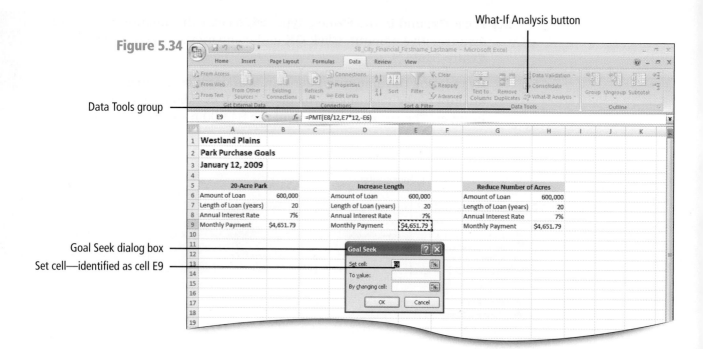

Figure 5.34

What-If Analysis button

Data Tools group

Goal Seek dialog box

Set cell—identified as cell E9

10 Press Tab. In the **To value** box, type the payment goal of **4000**. Press Tab. In the **By changing cell** box, click cell **E7** and compare your screen with Figure 5.35.

The **To value box** is the amount that you want the Set cell to display. The **By changing cell** is the cell that will change to achieve a payment that is set to $4,000. This method to limit the monthly payment will increase the length of the loan.

Set cell—cell containing the result of the formula

To value—the maximum amount for the set cell

Figure 5.35

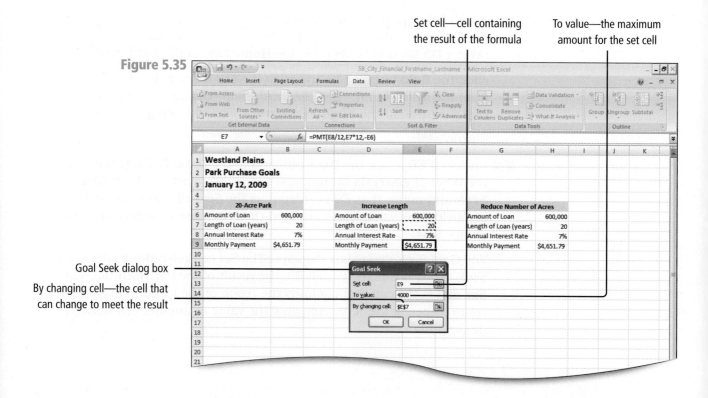

Goal Seek dialog box

By changing cell—the cell that can change to meet the result

11 Click **OK** to close the **Goal Seek** dialog box, and compare your screen with Figure 5.36. Then click **OK** again to close the **Goal Seek Status** dialog box.

When the monthly payment is $4,000, the length of the loan must be increased to almost 30 years. The Goal Seek Status dialog box indicates a solution was found.

Length of Loan with monthly payments of $4,000

Figure 5.36

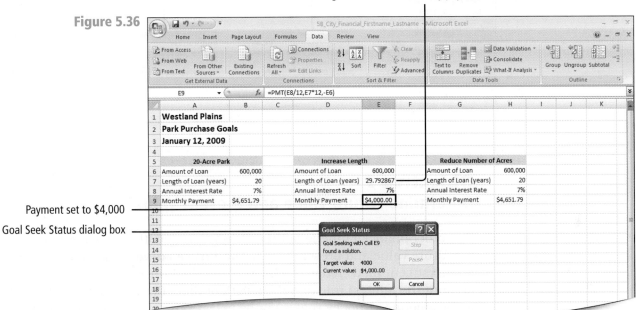

Payment set to $4,000

Goal Seek Status dialog box

12 Click cell **H9**. On the **Data tab**, in the **Data Tools group**, click the **What-If Analysis** button, and then from the list, click **Goal Seek**.

13 In the **Goal Seek** dialog box, confirm that cell **H9** is the Set cell. In the **To value** box, type **4000** In the **By changing cell** box, click **H6**, and then click **OK**.

14 In the **Goal Seek Status** dialog box, click **OK.**

The amount of the loan is reduced to $515,930. To meet the goal of a $4,000 monthly payment, the number of acres purchased must be reduced.

15 **Save** your workbook and compare your screen with Figure 5.37.

Figure 5.37

Results if you increase Length to nearly 30 years   Results if you reduce number of acres purchased

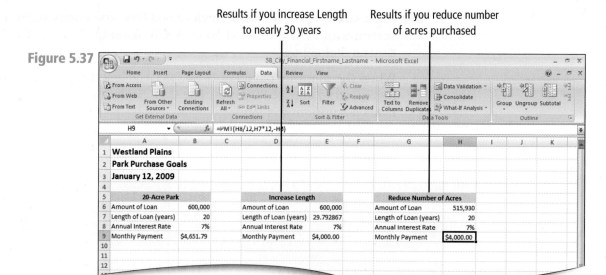

Objective 7
Determine Future Value and Present Value

Two other financial functions that are used frequently in business are the future value and present value. The **future value** is the amount that an investment made today will be worth in the future. This takes into account the interest rate and the length of time. Recall that present value is the amount of money that must be invested today in order to have a specific amount of money at a future time at a specified interest rate, whether the investment is a lump sum or a series of payments. Knowing the present value may be used to determine the amount of money needed to start a business, to purchase a large item, to save for a college education, or to save for a vacation. The present value is always less than the future value and may be a lump sum or a series of payments that will be made.

Activity 5.16 Determining Present Value

The city routinely sets aside money for contingency funds and future payments. Joaquin Alonzo has planned to enhance the transportation system beginning in five years and knows the city will need $500,000 in order to begin the project. The current interest rate is 5%. In this activity, you use the present value function to determine the amount to set aside today in order to have the available funding.

1 Click the **Park sheet tab** and press ⇧Shift and click the **Sheet3 sheet tab**. Select the range **A1:A3**. Click the **Home tab**, and in the Editing group, click the **Fill** button ⬇️▾, and then click **Across Worksheets**. In the **Fill Across Worksheets** dialog box, confirm **All** is selected, and then click **OK**.

2 Right-click the **Sheet3 sheet tab** and click **Ungroup Sheets**. Click the **Sheet 3 sheet tab** and change cell **A2** to read **2014 Transportation Project** and change cell **A3** to read **'June 2009**.

3 **Rename** the **Sheet3 sheet tab** to **Improvement Analysis** Beginning in cell **A5**, enter the following row titles:

| Investment Needed |
| Years of Investment |
| Interest Rate |
| Amount to Invest |

4 Click cell **A5**, and in the **Cells group**, click the **Format** button. Under **Cell Size**, click **AutoFit Column Width**.

5 In cell **B5**, type **$500,000** In cell **B6**, type **5** and in cell **B7**, type **5%**

6 With cell **B8** active, click the **Formulas tab**, and in the **Function Library group**, display the **Financial** list, and then click **PV**.

The Present Value dialog box displays with three required arguments—*Rate*, *Nper*, and *Pmt*.

7 Move the dialog box so the worksheet data can be seen. In the **Rate** box, click cell **B7**. In the **Nper** box, click cell **B6**. In the **Fv** box, click cell **B5** and compare your screen with Figure 5.38.

The Pmt argument is bold, indicating it is a required field. This field is used when monthly payments will be made. Because this is a lump-sum investment without monthly payments, the Pmt field will be left empty. The Fv argument is used to enter the amount desired at the end of 5 years. That is why the interest rate and number of periods are not expressed as monthly rates.

Arguments—Rate, Nper, Fv   Result of function

Figure 5.38

PV Function Arguments dialog box

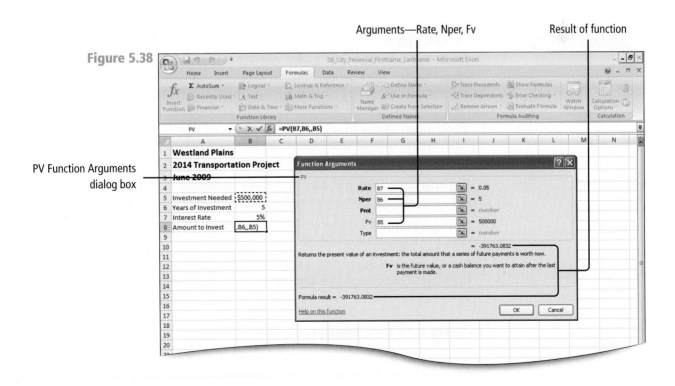

8 Click **OK**. On the **Formula Bar**, position the insertion point between the = and the *P* of *PV* and type ⊡ and then click the **Enter** button ✔. Compare your screen with Figure 5.39.

If the city invests $391,763.08 today, it will have the needed $500,000 ready for the improvement project in 5 years.

Function displayed in Formula Bar

Figure 5.39

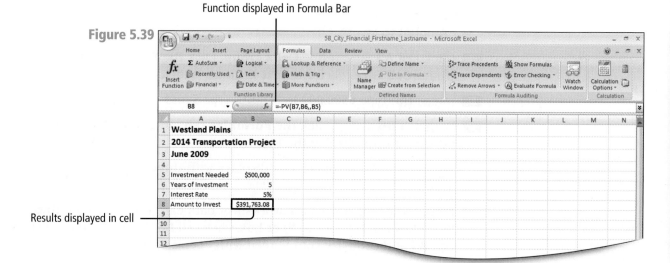

Results displayed in cell

9 In cell **B8**, place a **Bottom Double Border** indicating this total is the result of the calculation. **Save** 🖫 your workbook.

Workshop

Future Value

When you save money, you earn interest on that money and that interest is added to your savings. Next month when you earn interest, you also earn interest on the previous interest you earned. This is called *compound interest*—the interest paid on previously accumulated interest.

If you invest $1,000 today, how much will it be worth in 3 years with an interest rate of 5%? The interest the first year is $50 ($1,000*5%). At the end of the first year, the amount of money you have is $1,050 ($1,000+$50).

The interest the second year is $52.50 ($1,050*5%). At the end of the second year, the amount of money you have is $1,102.50 ($1,050+$52.50).

The interest the third year is $55.12 ($1,102.50*5%). At the end of the third year, the amount of money you have is $1,157.62 ($1,102.50+$55.12).

The future value for your $1,000 is $1,157.62. Excel provides a Future Value function to determine this amount.

Activity 5.17 Determining Future Value

The city's HR department contributes to the employee retirement fund. Each year they invest $2,000 until retirement. The interest rate is 6% for each year. New employees are provided with this information and a table that estimates the value of this fund upon their retirement. In this activity, you will use the Future Value function to estimate the retirement fund for Janice Force, a 30-year-old employee who was just hired.

1 Click the **Insert Worksheet** button. Beginning in cell **A1**, enter the worksheet title. Format the title with **Bold** **B** and increase the **Font Size** to **14**.

| Westland Plains |
| Retirement Estimate for Janice Force |
| Prepared July 2009 |

2 Beginning in cell **A6**, enter the following data:

Yearly Investment	$2,000
Interest Rate	6%
Time (in years)	32

3 Click cell **A10** and type **Estimated Value at Retirement** and format cell **A10** with **Wrap Text**. Select the range **A6:A10** and format with **11-point** font size and **Bold** **B**. Click cell **A6** and in the **Cells group**, click the **Format** button, and under **Cell Size**, click **AutoFit Column Width**. Double-click the **Sheet4 sheet tab** and type **Janice Force Retirement**

4 Click cell **B10**. Click the **Formulas tab** and in the **Function Library group**, click the **Financial** button, and then click **FV**.

5 In the **Rate** box, click cell **B7**. Press Tab and in the **Nper** box, click cell **B8**. Press Tab, and in the **Pmt** box, type **-b6**. Compare your screen with Figure 5.40, and then click **OK**. Adjust column widths and row heights.

Even though you have the exact amounts in the worksheet, enter the variables using cell references. The results of this calculation show that if $2,000 is invested annually, when Joyce retires in 32 years, at age 62, her investment will be $181,779.56.

Figure 5.40

Nper argument—cell B8   Result

Rate argument—cell B7

Pmt argument—cell B6

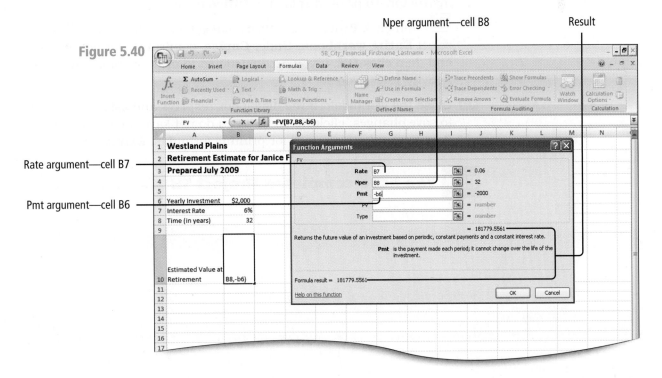

6 **Select all sheets** and click the **Page Layout tab**, and in the **Page Setup group**, click the **Dialog Box Launcher** ⧉. Click the **Margins tab** and under **Center on page**, click **Horizontally**. Click **OK** and then right-click a sheet tab and click **Ungroup sheets**.

7 Click the **Park sheet tab**. In the **Page Setup group**, click the **Orientation** button and click **Landscape**. Click the **Amortization Schedule sheet tab**, and in the **Page Setup group**, click **Print Titles**. Under **Print Titles**, click in the **Rows to repeat at top** box. Then click the **row 9 heading** so that **$9:$9** displays, and then click **OK**.

Recall that on large worksheets, titles printed on each page help in reading the data.

8 In the **Status bar**, click the **Page Break Preview** button 🔲 and at the **Welcome to Page Break Preview** dialog box, click **OK**. Point to the page break line at **row 42**, and drag the line so it is placed between **rows 39** and **40**—between payments 30 and 31. In the **Status Bar**, click the **Normal** button ▦.

9 Click the **Park sheet tab**. Press ⇧ Shift while you click the **Janice Force Retirement sheet tab**. In the **Page Layout tab**, in the **Page Setup** group, click the **Dialog Box Launcher** ⧉. In the **Page Setup** dialog box, click the **Margins tab**. In the **Top** margin area, click the **spin box up arrow** until the number **2** displays. Click **OK**.

10 On all sheets, in the **Left Footer**, place the **File Name** and in the **Right Footer**, place the **Sheet Name**. In the **Amortization Schedule**, in the **Right Header**, type **Page** insert a space, and then click the **Page Number** button. Return to **Normal** view. **Save** 💾 your workbook.

11 To submit electronically, follow the instructions provided by your instructor. To print, display the **Office** menu 🔲 , and click **Print**. In the **Print** dialog box, under **Print what**, select **Entire workbook**. Under **Copies**, confirm that **1** is selected, and then click **OK**. If you are instructed to print formulas, refer to Activity 1.12 to do so.

12 **Close** the workbook. If the dialog box displays and asks if you want to save changes, click **No** so that you do not save the changes to Page Setup that you used for printing formulas. **Exit** Excel.

End **You have completed Project 5B** ——————————

There's More You Can Do!

From My Computer, navigate to the student files that accompany this textbook. In the folder 02_theres_more_you_can_do, locate and open the folder for this chapter. Open and print the instructions for this project, which are provided to you in Adobe PDF format.

Try It! 1—Customize the Quick Access Toolbar

In this Try It! exercise, you will customize the Quick Access Toolbar.

Try It! 2—Use Access Keys and Other Methods to Work with the Ribbon

Using the combination keyboard shortcuts is another method to access commands, and these shortcuts have been introduced within the text. In this Try It! exercise, you will use the access keys and KeyTips to work with the Excel Ribbon.

Content-Based Assessments

Summary

Functions are used to format a worksheet and provide a fast way of inserting complex formulas. Text functions apply formats to the words in the worksheets. Statistical functions analyze data, and date and time functions insert dates and time in various formats. Logical functions compare data in a worksheet. Financial functions are useful to create complex calculations quickly by entering only a few numbers. They are useful in reporting data and making business decisions. Goal Seek provides additional assistance in making decisions by altering data to view the results. Comments can be inserted to add additional information in the worksheet.

Key Terms

The ⊙ symbol represents Key Terms found on the Student CD in the 02_theres_more_you_can_do folder for this chapter.

Content-Based Assessments

Matching

Match each term in the second column with its correct definition in the first column. Write the letter of the term on the blank line in front of the correct definition.

____ **1.** The text function that capitalizes the first letter of each word in a cell entry.

____ **2.** A command that is used to paste only the results of a formula into a cell.

____ **3.** The midpoint of a series of numbers.

____ **4.** The list of functions that displays after you begin typing a formula.

____ **5.** The function that displays the smallest number in the selected range of cells.

____ **6.** In a range of cells, the number that displays the most often.

____ **7.** The function that counts the number of cells that contain numeric values in a range of cells.

____ **8.** The function that counts the number of cells in a range that are not empty.

____ **9.** A date that remains the same and does not change.

____ **10.** The function used to return the current date.

____ **11.** The function that returns the current date and time.

____ **12.** The command used so the date displays the day of the week and the full date.

____ **13.** A function that compares data and returns information about that data.

____ **14.** A function that compares data and returns TRUE if all arguments are true and FALSE if any argument is not true.

____ **15.** A function that compares data and returns TRUE if any of the arguments agree.

A AND function

B COUNT function

C COUNTA function

D Formula AutoComplete

E Logical functions

F Long Date

G Median

H MINIMUM function

I Mode

J NOW function

K OR function

L Paste Values

M PROPER function

N Static

O TODAY function

Content-Based Assessments

Fill in the Blank

Write the correct word in the space provided.

1. The feature that is used to insert a remark attached to a cell in a worksheet is a(n) _____.

2. A red triangle in the upper right corner of a cell is a(n) _____ _____.

3. Functions used to help make financial decisions such as Interest Payment are _____ functions.

4. The cost of borrowing money or the amount earned from a savings account is _____.

5. The amount of money borrowed for a loan is the _____.

6. In a function, the argument that is used to enter the interest rate is the _____ argument.

7. The function that calculates the payments for a loan based on constant payments and a constant interest rate is the _____ function.

8. In a function, the total number of payments needed to pay off a loan is the _____ argument.

9. In a function, the argument that displays the original amount of the loan is the _____ argument.

10. The function that calculates the amount of interest that will be charged each month is the _____ function.

11. The argument that identifies the period for which you will find the interest is the _____ argument.

12. The amount of money it would take today to completely pay off a loan is _____ _____.

13. The function that calculates the amount of a payment that is applied to the principal is the _____ function.

14. An analysis tool that is used to find a specific value for a cell by adjusting another cell is _____.

15. When using Goal Seek, the cell that contains the formula that will be set to a specific value by changing the value in another cell is called the _____ cell.

Content-Based Assessments

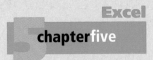

Skills Review

Project 5C—Tax Roll

In this project, you will apply the skills you practiced from the Objectives in Project 5A.

Objectives: 1. *Create Text Functions;* **2.** *Create Statistical Functions;* **3.** *Insert Date and Time Functions;* **4.** *Create Logical Functions and Insert a Comment.*

In the following Skills Review project, you will create a workbook for Westland Plains City that reports a portion of the real estate tax rolls. You will determine the amount of taxes due for each property owner. At the same time, you will determine the date that a late fee will be applied. In addition, you will complete a statistical analysis of the report for the city auditor to use in her reviews. Your completed workbook will look similar to the one shown in Figure 5.41.

For Project 5C, you will need the following file:

e05C_Tax_Roll

You will save your workbook as
5C_Tax_Roll_Firstname_Lastname

Figure 5.41

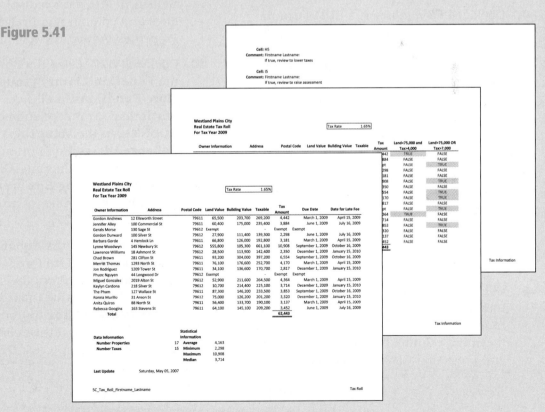

(Project 5C–Tax Roll continues on the next page)

(Project 5C–Tax Roll continued)

1. **Start** Excel. Open the file named **e05C_Tax_Roll** and then save it in your **Excel Chapter 5** folder as **5C_Tax_Roll_ Firstname_Lastname**

2. Select **column B** and **Insert** a column. Click cell **B6**. In the **Formula Bar**, click the **Insert Function** button. In the **Insert Function** dialog box, select the **Text** category. In the list, click **PROPER**, and then click **OK**. In the **Function Arguments** dialog box, in the **Text** area, click cell **A6** and then click **OK**.

3. With cell **B6** active, use the fill handle to copy the formula through cell **B22**. With the range **B6:B22** selected, right-click, and from the menu, click **Copy**. Click cell **A6**, and in the **Clipboard group**, click the **Paste button arrow**, and then click **Paste Values**. Right-click the **column B heading**, and then click **Delete**.

4. Click cell **F6** and insert a **SUM** formula to add the range **D6:E6**. Press [Enter] and click cell **F6**. Use the fill handle to copy the formula through cell **F22**—including the cells for the two exempt properties. At the top of the selected range, click the **Error Alert Indicator** and click **Ignore Error**.

5. Click cell **G6**. Type =f6*f2 and then press [F4]. Press [Enter] to confirm the entry. Click cell **G6** and use the fill handle to copy the formula through cell **G22**. In the cells in column G that are empty because the *Land Value* is marked *Exempt*—cells **G8** and **G16**—type **Exempt**

6. Click cell **G23** and enter a **SUM** formula that adds the tax amount. The suggested range of the SUM formula does not include the entire column. Select the range **G6:G22** and press [Enter]. Click cell **G23** and format

this cell with **Bold** and a **Top and Double Bottom Border**. In cell **A23**, type **Total** and format with **Bold** and **Center**.

7. Beginning in cell **A26,** enter the following row titles:

| Data Information |
| Number Properties |
| Number Taxes |

8. Beginning in cell **C26** and continuing down the column, enter the following titles:

| Statistical Information |
| Average |
| Minimum |
| Maximum |
| Median |

9. Format cells **A26** and **C26** with **Bold** and **Wrap Text**. Format the ranges **A27:A28** and **C27:C30** with **Bold** and **Increase Indent** once. Adjust column widths so *Statistical Information* displays on two lines and column A entirely fits *Number Properties*. Adjust the row height.

10. Click cell **B27**. Click the **Formulas tab**, in the **Function Library group**, point to **More Functions**, and then click **Statistical**. From the submenu, click **COUNTA**. In the **Value1** text area, click the **Collapse Dialog Box** button. Select the range of the tax amount—**G6:G22**—click the **Expand Dialog Box** button, and then click **OK**. The number of properties—*17*—displays in cell B27.

11. Click cell **B28**. In the **Function Library group**, point to **More Functions**, and then click **Statistical**. From the submenu, click **COUNT**. In the **Value1** text area, click the **Collapse Dialog Box** button. Select the range **G6:G22**, and then click the **Expand Dialog Box** button. Click **OK**. The number

(Project 5C–Tax Roll continues on the next page)

Content-Based Assessments

(Project 5C– Tax Roll continued)

of properties that pay taxes—*15*—displays in cell B28.

12. Click cell **D27**. In the **Function Library group**, click **More Functions**, point to **Statistical**, and then click **Average**. In the **Number1** text box, click the **Collapse Dialog Box** button. Select the range **G6:G22**, click the **Expand Dialog Box** button, press [F4] and then click **OK**. The average tax—*4,163*—displays in cell D27.

13. Click cell **D27** and use the fill handle to copy the function to cell **D30**. Click cell **D28** and in the **Formula Bar**, select the name of the function—**AVERAGE**—type **min** and then press [Enter]. The smallest number displays—*2,298*—which is the least amount of property taxes. Cell **D29** is active. In the **Formula Bar**, select **AVERAGE**, type **max** and then press [Enter]. The largest number displays—*10,908*—which is the largest amount of property taxes. Using these skills you just practiced, in cell **D30** replace **AVERAGE** with **MEDIAN**.

14. Click cell **A32** and type **Last Update** and format with **Bold**. Click cell **B32** and in the **Formula Bar**, click the **Insert Function** button. In the **Insert Function** dialog box, in the **Category** section, click **Date & Time**. In the list, type **T** and scroll to and double-click **Today**. Click **OK**. Click the **Home tab** and in the **Number group**, click the **Number Format button arrow** and from the displayed list, click **Long Date**. Adjust the column widths as needed to display the date.

15. Click cell **H5** and type **Due Date** and in cell **I5**, type **Date for Late Fee** Select the range **H5:I5** and in the **Font group**, click the **Border button arrow** and from the list, click **Bottom Border**.

16. Select **column H**. In the **Number group**, click the **Number Format button arrow** and from the list, click **More Number Formats**. In the **Format Cells** dialog box, in the **Category** area, click **Date**. In the **Type** list, click **March 14, 2001**, and then click **OK**.

17. Beginning in cell **H6** type the following. Alternatively, type the dates using numbers. Because the range is formatted in date style, they will be correctly displayed.

Tax Amount	Due Date
4,442	March 1, 2009
3,884	June 1, 2009
Exempt	Exempt
2,298	June 1, 2009
3,181	March 1, 2009
10,908	September 1, 2009
2,350	December 1, 2009
6,554	September 1, 2009
4,170	March 1, 2009
2,817	December 1, 2009
Exempt	Exempt
4,364	March 1, 2009
3,714	December 1, 2009
3,853	September 1, 2009
3,320	December 1, 2009
3,137	March 1, 2009
3,452	June 1, 2009

18. Click cell **I6**. Type **=h6+45** to enter the date late fees will be assessed, which is 45 days after the Due Date. Click cell **I6** and use the fill handle to copy the formula down through cell **I22**. Click cell **I8** and press [Delete]. Click cell **I16** and delete the cell contents. Adjust the column widths if necessary.

(Project 5C–Tax Roll continues on the next page)

Content-Based Assessments

(Project 5C–Tax Roll continued)

19. **Rename Sheet1** to Tax Roll **Copy** the sheet and place it before **Sheet2**.

20. Rename the **Tax Roll(2) sheet** to Tax Information If error indicators display in column F, select cells F6:F22, click the **Error Alert Indicator**, and then click **Ignore Error**.

21. In the **Tax Information sheet**, select **columns H** and **I** and press Delete. Click cell **H5** and type Land<75,000 and Tax>4,000 In cell **I5**, type Land>75,000 OR Tax>7,000

22. Click cell **H6**. Click the **Formulas tab** and in the **Function Library group**, click the **Logical** button, and then click **AND**. Position the dialog box out of the way so that rows 6 and 7 are visible. With the insertion point in the **Logical1** box, click cell **D6** and type <75000 Press Tab and in the **Logical2** box, click cell **G6** and type >4000 and then click **OK**. Use the fill handle to copy the formula down through cell **H22**. Two properties, owned by Gordon Andrews and Miguel Gonzalez, will be reviewed to lower property taxes.

23. Click cell **I6**. On the **Formulas tab**, in the **Function Library group**, click the **Logical** button and then click **OR**. If necessary, position the dialog box so that rows 6 and 7 are visible. In the **Logical1** box, click cell **D6** and type >75000 Press Tab and in the **Logical2** box, click cell **G6** and type >7000 and then click **OK**. Use the fill handle to copy the formula down through cell **I22**.

24. Select the range **H6:I22**. On the **Home tab**, in the **Styles group**, click the **Conditional Formatting** button.

Point to **Highlight Cells Rules** and from the submenu, click **Equal To**. In the **Equal To** dialog box, in the left text box, type **true** and then click **OK**.

25. Click cell **H5**. Click the **Review tab**, and in the **Comments group**, click the **New Comment** button. In the comment text box, type **If true, review to lower taxes** Click the border and move the comment above the column. Click cell **I5**. In the **Comments group**, click the **New Comment** button. In the comment text box, type **If true, review to raise assessment** Click in the border of the comment box and move it above the column.

26. **Delete Sheet2** and **Sheet3**. Right-click a sheet tab, and then click **Select All Sheets**. Format the sheets for **Landscape**, **Fit to one page**, and center **Horizontally** and **Vertically**. Place the **File Name** in the **Left Footer** and the **Sheet Name** in the **Right Footer**.

27. Display the **Page Setup** dialog box, click the **Sheet tab**. Under **Print**, on the right side, click the **Comments arrow**. From the list, click **At end of sheet**, and then click **Print Preview**. In **Print Preview**, click the **Next Page** button to display page 3. **Close** Print Preview. **Save** your workbook.

28. To submit electronically, follow the instructions provided by your instructor. To print, from the **Office** menu, click **Print**. In the **Print** dialog box, under **Print what**, select **Entire workbook**. Under **Copies**, confirm that **1** is selected. Print formulas if you are instructed to do so. Click **OK**. From the **Office** menu, click **Close**.

End **You have completed Project 5C**

Content-Based Assessments

Project 5D—Fire Department

In this project, you will apply the skills you practiced from the Objectives in Project 5B.

Objectives: 5. *Insert Financial Functions;* **6.** *Create What-If Analysis with Goal Seek;* **7.** *Determine Future Value and Present Value.*

The Fire Chief, Kevin Charleston, is researching the purchase of a new fire truck and has several choices. Although he would prefer to purchase a new truck with many features that would benefit the fire department, it is the most expensive. There are two other trucks that would include the minimum requirements, but aren't as desirable. You will use Goal Seek to assist Kevin in his decision to purchase a truck that will keep the monthly payments close to $5,000.

In the following Skills Review project, you will create a workbook for Kevin that uses Goal Seek for making a decision. You will then prepare an amortization table for the selected truck and prepare a worksheet that displays the amount to set aside today for the purchase of another truck in three years. Your completed workbook will look similar to the one shown in Figure 5.42.

For Project 5D, you will need the following file:

e05D_Fire_Department

You will save your workbook as
5D_Fire_Department_Firstname_Lastname

Figure 5.42

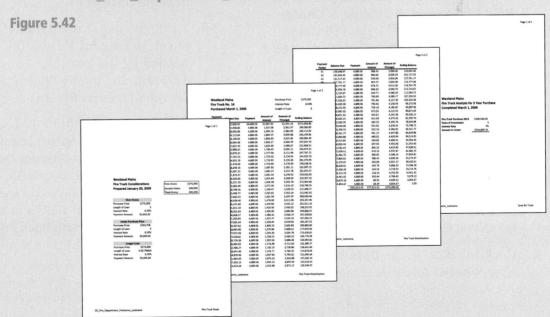

(Project 5D– Fire Department continues on the next page)

(Project 5D–Fire Department continued)

1. **Start** Excel. Open the file named **e05D_Fire_Department** and then save it in your **Excel Chapter 5** folder as 5D_Fire_Department_Firstname_Lastname

2. Click cell **B10**. Click the **Formulas tab**, and in the **Function Library group**, click the **Financial** button, and then click **PMT**. Move the dialog box aside so you can see the data in the worksheet. In the **Rate** box, click cell **B9**, and type **/12** Press Tab, and in the **Nper** box, click cell **B8** and type ***12** Press Tab, and in the **Pv** box, click cell **B7**, and then click **OK**. In the **Formula Bar**, position the mouse between the equal sign = and the *P* of *PMT* and type – and then press Enter.

3. **Copy** the range **A7:B10** and **Paste** the cells beginning in cell **A13** and again in cell **A19**. Press Esc to stop the moving border.

4. In cell **A12**, type **Lower Purchase Price** and in cell **A18**, type **Longer Loan** Select the range **A6:B6**, press Ctrl, and select the ranges **A12:B12** and **A18:B18**. On the **Home tab**, in the **Font group**, click the **Bold** button and the **Merge & Center** button, and then click the **Fill Color** button and click **Olive Green, Accent 3, Lighter 40%**.

5. Click cell **B16**. Click the **Data tab**, and in the **Data Tools group**, click **What-If Analysis**. From the menu, click **Goal Seek**. Confirm the **Set cell** is **B16**. In the **To value** box, type **5000** and in the **By changing cell** box, click cell **B13**. Click **OK** two times. To keep the payment at $5,000, the loan amount would need to be $243,706 for a 5-year loan at 8.50%.

6. Click cell **B22**. In the **Data Tools group**, click **What-If Analysis**. From the menu,

click **Goal Seek**. Confirm the **Set cell** is **B22**. In the **To value** box, type **5000** and in the **By changing cell** box, click cell **B20**, the length of the loan. Click **OK** two times. This option changes the length of the loan to almost 6 years. After reviewing the results, the fire chief has decided to purchase the first-choice truck and increase the loan length to 6 years.

7. Group **Sheet1** and **Sheet2** and select the title—the range **A1:A3**. Click the **Home tab**. In the **Editing group**, click the **Fill** button and from the menu, click **Across Worksheets** and confirm that you will fill **All**. **Rename Sheet1** Fire Truck Goals and **Sheet2** Fire Truck Amortization

8. **Ungroup** the sheets. In the **Fire Truck Amortization sheet**, click cell **A2** and edit the cell to read **Fire Truck No. 14** and edit cell **A3** to read **Purchased March 1, 2009**

9. Select the range **E1:E3** and enter the following row titles:

Purchase Price
Interest Rate
Length of Loan

10. Using the data from the **Fire Truck Goals** sheet, in **column F** enter the information needed for the loan. The *Purchase Price* is **$275,000**, the *Interest Rate* is **8.5%**, and the *Length of Loan* is **6** years.

11. Select the range **A5:F5** and format the cells with **Bold**, **Center**, **Middle Align**, **Wrap Text**, with a **Bottom Double Border**. Beginning in cell **A5**, enter the column titles displayed on the next page. Adjust the column widths so that all titles display on one or two lines and adjust the row height to fit the data entries.

(Project 5D–Fire Department continues on the next page)

(Project 5D–Fire Department continued)

Payment Period	Balance Due	Payment	Amount of Interest	Amount of Principal	Ending Balance

12. In cell **A6**, type **1** and in cell **A7**, type **2** Select the range **A6:A7** and use the fill handle to copy the pattern down until **72** displays in the ScreenTip—**row 77**. Format the range with **Center** alignment.

13. Click cell **B6**, and type **=f1** Click cell **C6**. Click the **Formulas tab** and in the **Function Library group**, click the **Financial** button. From the list, click **PMT**. In the **Rate** box, click cell **F2**, press F4, and type **/12** Press Tab and in the **Nper** box, click cell **F3** and press F4 and type ***12** Press Tab and in the **Pv** box, click cell **F1** and press F4. Click **OK**. On the **Formula Bar**, position the insertion point between the = and the *P* of *PMT* and type – and then press Enter. Recall that the absolute cell reference is required in order to copy the formulas in the amortization table.

14. Click cell **D6**, and on the **Formulas tab**, in the **Function Library group**, click the **Financial** button, and then click **IPMT**. For the **Rate**, click cell **F2**, press F4, and type **/12** Press Tab and in the **Per** box, click cell **A6**. Press Tab and in the **Nper** box, click cell **F3**, press F4, and type ***12** Press Tab, and in the **Pv** box, click cell **F1** and press F4. Then click **OK**. In the **Formula Bar**, position the insertion point between the = and the *I* of *IPMT* and type – and then press Enter.

15. Click cell **E6**. In the **Formulas tab**, in the **Function Library group**, click the **Financial** button, and then click **PPMT**. For the **Rate**, click cell **F2**, press F4, and type **/12** Press Tab and in the **Per** box, click cell **A6**. Press Tab and in the **Nper** box, click **F3**, press F4, and type ***12** Press Tab. In the **Pv** box, click cell **F1** and press F4. Click **OK** and then in the **Formula Bar**, position the insertion point between

the = and the *P* of *PPMT* and type – and then press Enter.

16. In cell **F6**, type the formula **=b6-e6** and press Enter. Click cell **B7** and type **=f6** Copy the range **C6:F6** to **row 7**, and then copy the range **B7:F7** through the rest of the worksheet—**row 77**.

17. With the range selected, on the **Home tab**, in the **Number group**, click the **Comma Style** button. Select the range **C78:E78** and click the **Sum** button. Place a **Top and Double Bottom border** in the range and confirm that the **Accounting Number Format** is selected. In cell **A78**, type **Total** and format it with **Bold**. Adjust column widths if needed, and then format cell **B6** with **Accounting Number Format** with **2 decimals**.

18. The Fire Department is planning to purchase another truck in three years and would like to start setting aside funds now for that truck. Place this analysis in a new sheet. Click the **Sheet3 sheet tab** and beginning in cell **A1**, type

Westland Plains
Fire Truck Analysis for 3 Year Purchase
Completed March 1, 2009

19. Format the title with **14 point** and **Bold**. **Rename Sheet3** to **Save for Truck**

20. Beginning in cell **A6**, type the following entries, and then format the row titles in **column A** with **11 point font** with **Bold**.

Fire Truck Purchase 2012	300,000.00
Years of Investment	3
Interest Rate	7%
Amount to Invest	

21. Click cell **A6** and in the **Cells group**, click the **Format** button and click **AutoFit Column Width**.

22. Click cell **B9**. On the **Formulas tab**, in the **Function Library group**, click the

(Project 5D– Fire Department continues on the next page)

(Project 5D–Fire Department continued)

Financial button, and then click **PV**. In the **Rate** box, click **B8**. In the **Nper** box, click **B7**. Because this is a lump sum, the **Pmt** box will remain empty. In the **FV** box, click **B6**. Click **OK**. In the **Formula Bar**, place the insertion point between the = and the *P* of *PV* and type – and then press [Enter]. In cell **B6**, place a **Thick Bottom Border**.

23. **Select All Sheets**. In the **Left Footer** enter the **File Name,** and in the **Right Footer** enter the **Sheet Name**. In the **Right Header**, enter the **Page Number** using the style that reads *Page x of xx pages*. Return to cell **A1** and **Normal** view.

24. Display all worksheets in **Portrait orientation**. **Center** the *Fire Truck Goals* and *Save for Truck* sheets **Horizontally** and **Vertically**. **Center** the *Fire Truck Amortization* sheet **Horizontally** and place the column titles on all pages. **Save** your workbook.

25. To submit electronically, follow the instructions provided by your instructor. To print, from the **Office** menu, click **Print** In the **Print** dialog box, under **Print what**, select **Entire workbook**. Under **Copies**, confirm that **1** is selected and click **OK**. Print formulas if you are instructed to do so. From the **Office** menu, click **Close** and do not resave your work. **Close** Excel.

End **You have completed Project 5D**

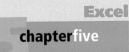

Excel

chapterfive

Mastering Excel

Project 5E — Park Rentals

In this project, you will apply the skills you practiced from the Objectives in Project 5A.

Objectives: 1. *Create Text Functions;* **2.** *Create Statistical Functions;* **3.** *Insert Date and Time Functions;* **4.** *Create Logical Functions and Insert a Comment.*

In the following Mastering Excel project, you will complete a workbook for Yvonne Guillen, chair of the Parks & Recreation Commission, which details the fees for the Westland Plains Lake Park for four weeks in July. This large city park generates income to the city from rental of boats, two-wheeled transportation—bikes and scooters—a large, natural-springs swimming hole, 12 lighted tennis courts, and a golf course. You will prepare the worksheet that reports the weekly totals for the month of July and provide statistical analysis. Your completed workbook will look similar to the one shown in Figure 5.43.

For Project 5E, you will need the following file:

e05E_Park_Rentals

You will save your workbook as
5E_Park_Rentals_Firstname_Lastname

Figure 5.43

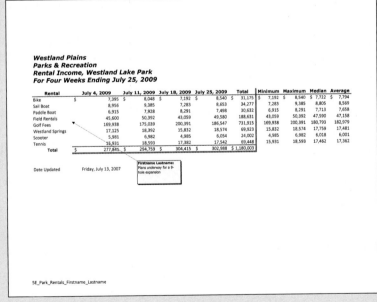

(Project 5E–Park Rentals continues on the next page)

(Project 5E–Park Rentals continued)

1. **Start** Excel. Open the file named **e05E_ Park_Rentals**, and then save it in your **Excel Chapter 5** folder as **5E_Park_Rentals_ Firstname_Lastname**

2. Insert a column between **columns A** and **B**. In cell **B1**, insert the **PROPER** function to convert cell **A1** to proper text format. Copy the function through the range of the worksheet—cell **B18**.

3. Copy the data in **column B** and use **Paste Values** to paste only the values to **column A**. Then delete **column B**.

4. Format the four worksheet title lines with **Bold**, **Italic** and change the font to **Verdana**, **14-point font**. Select the range **B6:E6**. Change the date format to the **March 14, 2001** style. In **row 6**, format the column titles with **Bold**, **Center**, **Verdana font**, **10 point**, with a **Bottom Border**. If necessary, adjust column widths to fully display the column titles.

5. Use the **SUM** formula to place a total in **column F** and a total in **row 15**. Format the range **B7:F7** with **Accounting Number Format** with **no decimals**. Format the range **B8:F14** with **Comma Style** and **no decimals**. Format the totals, **B15:F15**, with **Accounting Number Format** with **no decimals** and a **Top and Double Bottom border**. If the **Error Alert** button displays, choose to **Ignore Error**. Format cell **A15** with **Bold** and **Center**.

6. Click cell **G7**. Access the **MIN** function and determine the smallest profit from bike sales from the range of weekly rentals— **B7:E7**. Use the fill handle to fill the formula down to cell **G14**.

7. Click cell **H7**. In the **Formula Bar**, type **=m** and double-click **MAX**. Drag through the range **B7:E7**, type **)** and then press Enter. Use the fill handle to fill the formula down the range of the worksheet—**H7:H14**.

8. Using the skills you practiced, determine the **Median**—**column I**—and **Average**— **column J**—of the weekly rentals in **columns B:E**. Then select the range **I7:J7** and use the fill handle to copy the formulas through the range of the worksheet— **row 14**.

9. Format the data in the range **G7:J14** using the same formats used in **column F**. If necessary, adjust column widths.

10. Place a **Double Border** between the data in **columns F** and **G**—cells **F6:F15**.

11. Click cell **B18** and enter the **TODAY** function. Format it with the **Long Date** format, and adjust column width if needed.

12. In cell **A11**, enter the following comment: **Plans underway for a 9-hole expansion** Move the comment out of the way so that it is not on top of the data. Delete unused worksheets.

13. **Print** the comments as displayed on the worksheet. Format the worksheet in **Landscape** orientation, **fit to one page**, and centered both **Horizontally** and **Vertically**. In the **Left Footer**, place the **File Name**. **Save** your workbook.

14. To submit electronically, follow the instructions provided by your instructor. To print, from the **Office** menu, click **Print**. In the **Print** dialog box, under **Print what**, select **Entire workbook**. Under **Copies**, confirm that **1** is selected. Print formulas if you are instructed to do so. From the **Office** menu, click **Close**. If you are prompted to save changes, click **No**. **Exit** Excel.

End You have completed Project 5E

Project 5F—Transportation

In this project, you will apply the skills you practiced from the Objectives in Project 5B.

Objectives: 5. *Insert Financial Functions;* **6.** *Create What-If Analysis with Goal Seek;* **7.** *Determine Future Value and Present Value.*

In the following Mastering Excel project, you will complete a workbook for Joaquin Alonzo, the city manager, that evaluates data about the Transportation Department's vehicles. You will create a report that evaluates recent bus and car purchases for the city by determining the amount of monthly payments and the accompanying payment for interest. You will use Goal Seek to begin planning for the light rail project. Your completed workbook will look similar to the one shown in Figure 5.44.

For Project 5F, you will need the following file:

e05F_Transportation

You will save your workbook as
5F_Transportation_Firstname_Lastname

Figure 5.44

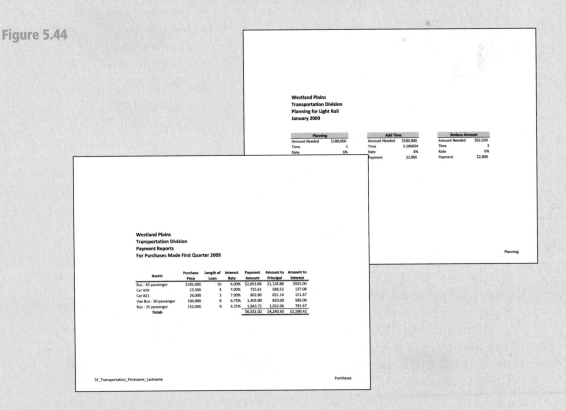

Planning

Westland Plains
Transportation Division
Planning for Light Rail
January 2009

Planning		Add Time			Reduce Amount	
Amount Needed	$100,000	Amount Needed	$100,000		Amount Needed	$92,039
Time	3	Time	3.286694		Time	3
Rate	6%	Rate	6%		Rate	6%
		Payment	$2,800		Payment	$2,800

Westland Plains
Transportation Division
Payment Reports
For Purchases Made First Quarter 2009

Assets	Purchase Price	Length of Loan	Interest Rate	Payment Amount	Amount to Principal	Amount to Interest
Bus - 45 passenger	$185,000	10	6.00%	$2,053.88	$1,128.88	$925.00
Car #20	23,500	3	7.00%	725.61	588.53	137.08
Car #21	26,000	3	7.00%	802.80	651.14	151.67
Van Bus - 20 passenger	104,000	8	6.75%	1,405.00	820.00	585.00
Bus - 35 passenger	152,000	9	6.25%	1,843.72	1,052.06	791.67
Totals				$6,831.02	$4,240.60	$2,590.42

5F_Transportation_Firstname_Lastname

Purchases

(Project 5F—Transportation continues on the next page)

(Project 5F–Transportation continued)

1. **Start** Excel. Open the file named **e05F_Transportation**, and then save it in your **Excel Chapter 5** folder as 5F_Transportation_Firstname_Lastname

2. **Rename Sheet1** to **Purchases**. Click cell **E8** and access the **PMT** function in order to determine the amount of the payment for the bus. In the **Rate** box, type cell **d8/12**. For the **Nper** box, type **c8*12**. For the **Pv**, type **b8**. Click **OK**. In the **Formula Bar**, place a – between the = and the *P* of *PMT*. Use the fill handle to copy the formula in cell **E8** through the range of the worksheet to cell **E12**.

3. Click cell **F8** and access the **PPMT** function in order to determine the amount of the payment that is applied to the principal. For the **Rate** box, type cell **d8/12** For the **Per**, type **1** For the **Nper** box, type **c8*12** For the **Pv**, type **b8** Click **OK**. In the **Formula Bar**, place a – between the = and the *P* of *PPMT*. Use the fill handle to copy the formula in cell **F8** through the range of the worksheet to cell **F12**.

4. Click cell **G8** and access the **IPMT** function in order to determine the amount of the payment that is applied to interest. Using the skills you practiced, enter the information in the Function Arguments dialog box. Adjust the formula to display the result as a positive number. Copy the formula in cell **G8** through the range of the worksheet to cell **G12**.

5. Click cell **A13** and type **Totals** and format the cell with **Bold**, **Italic**, and **Center**. Select the range **E13:G13** and enter a **Sum** function. Format the selected range with **Accounting Number Format** and a **Top and Double Bottom Border**. Select the range **E9:G12** and format with the **Comma Style**.

6. **Rename Sheet2** to **Planning** Joaquin is leading the study to bring light rail to Westland Plains in about three years. The group expects to need $100,000 in start-up funds but can afford to invest only about $3,000 monthly.

7. Data is entered into the worksheet but has not been completed. Click cell **B11** and display the **PMT** function. Complete the function: For the **Rate**, use **B10/12** For the **Nper**, use **B9*12** For the **Pv**, use **B8** Format the results for a positive number.

8. Copy the formula in cell **B11** to cells **E11** and **H11**. Click cell **E11**. Display the **Goal Seek** dialog box. For the **Set cell**, use cell **E11**. For the **To value**, use $2,800 and for the **By changing cell**, use the time in cell **E9**. Click **OK** two times.

9. Click cell **H11** and access **Goal Seek**. For the **Set cell**, use cell **H11**. For the **To value**, use $2,800 and for the **By changing cell**, use the amount in cell **H8**. Click **OK** two times.

10. It has been determined that the plan used will be to reduce the amount to $92,039. The city realized an unexpected increase in reserves and there is $25,000 that could be set aside today for this project. Use the **FV** function to determine the future value of this amount. Click cell **A14** and type **Invest Today** and copy the format from cell **A7** to **A14**.

11. Beginning in cell **A15**, enter the following row titles:

| Amount |
| Interest Rate |
| Length of Time |
| Ending Value |

(Project 5F– Transportation continues on the next page)

(Project 5F–Transportation continued)

12. In **column B**, for the amount, enter **$25,000** with an interest rate of **7%** for **3** years. In cell **B18**, access the **FV** function. For the **Rate**, enter **B16/12** and for the **Nper**, enter **B17*12** Because this is a lump-sum payment, nothing is entered in **Pmt**. For the **Pv**, enter **B15** Click **OK** and format the cell for a positive number. Format cell **B18** with **Bold** and a **Bottom Double Border**. Format cell **B15** with **Accounting Number Format** with **no decimals**.

13. Delete **Sheet3**. **Select All Sheets** and enter a footer that displays the **File Name** in the **Left Footer** area and the **Sheet Name** in the **Right Footer** area. Place the documents centered both **Horizontally** and **Vertically** in **Landscape** orientation. **Save** your workbook.

14. To submit electronically, follow the instructions provided by your instructor. To print, from the **Office** menu, click **Print**. In the **Print** dialog box, under **Print what**, select **Entire workbook**. Under **Copies**, confirm that **1** is selected. Print formulas if you are instructed to do so. From the **Office** menu, click **Close**. If you are prompted to save changes, click **No**. **Exit** Excel.

End You have completed Project 5F

Content-Based Assessments

Project 5G — Paving Equipment

In this project, you will apply the skills you practiced from the Objectives in Projects 5A and 5B.

Objectives: 2. *Create Statistical Functions;* **3.** *Insert Date and Time Functions;* **4.** *Create Logical Functions and Insert a Comment;* **5.** *Insert Financial Functions.*

In the following Mastering Excel project, you will create amortization tables. The Transportation Department has recently purchased equipment—a roller and a paver. The Accounting Department has asked for an amortization table for its records. You will assist the transportation manager by completing this report. Your completed workbook will look similar to the one shown in Figure 5.45.

For Project 5G, you will need the following file:

e05G_Paving_Equipment

You will save your workbook as
5G_Paving_Equipment_Firstname_Lastname

Figure 5.45

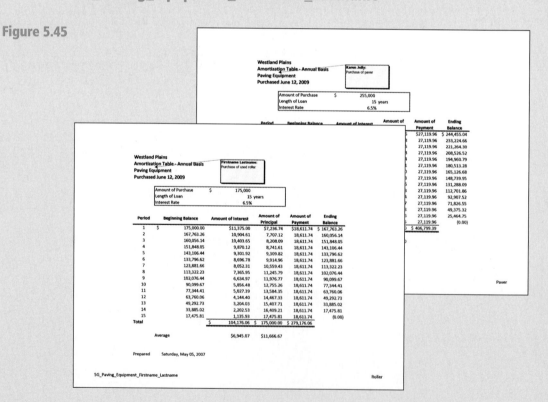

(Project 5G–Paving Equipment continues on the next page)

Content-Based Assessments

(Project 5G–Paving Equipment continued)

1. **Start** Excel and open the file named **e05G_ Paving_Equipment**, and then save it in your **Excel Chapter 5** folder as **5G_Paving_Equipment_Firstname_Lastname**

2. Click cell **A11** and type **1** and in cell **A12**, type **2** Select the range **A11:A12** and use the fill handle to increase the numbers until the ScreenTip displays **15**. **Center** the numbers.

3. Click cell **B11** and enter the beginning balance **=C6** and format cell **B11** with **2 decimals**. Click cell **C11** and access the **IPMT** function. Complete the **Function Arguments** dialog box. This is an annual payment, so express the interest rate as an annual rate. These formulas will be copied, so express the variables—except the *Per* variable—as absolute references. Express the result as a positive number. The amount—$11,375.00—is entered in the cell.

4. Click cell **D11** and access the **PPMT** function. Complete the **Function Arguments** dialog box. This is an annual payment, so express the interest rate as an annual rate. These formulas will be copied, so express the appropriate variables as absolute references. Express the number as a positive number. The amount— $7,236.74—is entered in the cell.

5. Click cell **E11** and access the **PMT** function. Complete the **Function Arguments** dialog box. This is an annual payment, so express the interest rate as an annual rate. These formulas will be copied, so express the appropriate variables as absolute references. Express the number as a positive number. The amount — $18,611.74—is entered in the cell.

6. Click cell **F11** and enter the ending balance—**=B11-D11**. In cell **B12**, enter the beginning balance, which is the ending balance from the first year. Copy the range **C11:F11** to **C12:F12**. Then copy the data—**B12:F12**—through the end of the worksheet—**row 25**.

7. Confirm that **row 11** is formatted with **Accounting Number Format** with **2 decimals**. Format the other numbers with **Comma Style** with **2 decimals**. In cell **A26**, type **Total** and format with **Bold**. Place totals in columns **C:E**. Format the totals with **Accounting Number Format**, **2 decimals**, and a **Top and Double Bottom Border**.

8. Click cell **A3**, and insert a comment that reads **Purchase of used roller** Move the comment to a place where it doesn't block existing text. **Rename Sheet1** to **Roller Print** the **Comments As displayed on sheet**.

9. **Copy** the **Roller sheet** to a new sheet and rename the new sheet **Paver** The city has also purchased a paver using the same loan information—15 years at 6.5%. Change the amount of purchase to **$255,000** and change the comment to read **Purchase of paver**

10. **Delete Sheet2** and **Sheet3**. **Group** the two worksheets and in cell **B28**, type **Average** and in cell **A31**, type **Prepared** Click cell **C28** and insert the **AVERAGE** function and determine the average amount of interest from the data in **column C** and in cell **D28**, insert the **AVERAGE** function, to determine the average amount of principal from the data in **column D**. Click cell **B31**, insert the **TODAY** function, to enter the current date. Format it with the **Long Date** format.

(Project 5G–Paving Equipment continues on the next page)

(Project 5G–Paving Equipment continued)

11. In the **Left Footer**, display the **File Name**; in the **Right Footer** display the **Sheet Name**. **Center** both worksheets **Horizontally** and **Vertically** in **Landscape orientation**. **Save** your workbook.

12. To submit electronically, follow the instructions provided by your instructor. To print, from the **Office** menu, click **Print**. In the **Print** dialog box, under **Print what**, select **Entire workbook**. Under **Copies**, confirm that **1** is selected. Print formulas if you are instructed to do so. From the **Office** menu, click **Close**. If you are prompted to save changes, click **No**. **Exit** Excel.

End You have completed Project 5G

Excel

chapterfive

Mastering Excel

Project 5H — Retirement Funds

In this project, you will apply the skills you practiced from the Objectives in Projects 5A and 5B.

Objectives: 3. *Create Date and Time Functions;* **4.** *Create Logical Functions and Insert a Comment;* **7.** *Determine Future Value and Present Value.*

In the following Mastering Excel project, you will complete a worksheet for the Transportation Department that reports the annual $2,000 retirement contribution for each employee. You will create a worksheet that adds the contribution for 2009 to each employee's existing retirement funds and determine the value of the funds for each employee at his or her retirement age. Your completed workbook will look similar to the one shown in Figure 5.46.

For Project 5H, you will need the following file:

e05H_Retirement

You will save your workbook as
5H_Retirement_Firstname_Lastname

Figure 5.46

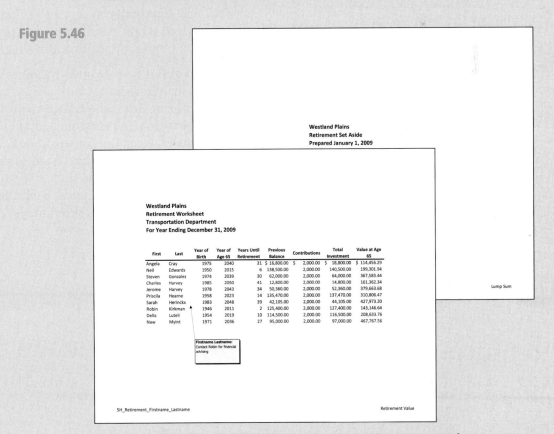

(Project 5H–Retirement Funds continues on the next page)

Content-Based Assessments

(Project 5H–Retirement Funds continued)

1. **Start** Excel and open the file **e05H_ Retirement**, and then save it in your **Excel Chapter 5 folder** as 5H_Retirement_Firstname_Lastname

2. In cell **D8**, enter the formula that determines the year the employee will turn 65 by adding 65 to the year of birth. Copy the formula through the range of the worksheet—cell **D17**.

3. In cell **E8**, enter the formula to determine the years to retirement. Determine that amount by subtracting the current year— use the year 2009 for this activity—from the year of retirement. Angela has 31 years until she can retire. Copy the formula in cell **E8** through the range of the worksheet—cell **E17**.

4. In cell **H8**, enter the total investment—the previous balance plus the contributions— and copy the formula through the range of the worksheet—cell **H17**.

5. Click cell **I8** and insert the **Future Value (FV)** function. For the interest rate, use **6%** The **Nper**—number of periods—are the years until retirement in column E. Because this is a lump-sum contribution, the **Pmt** argument is left empty. The **Pv** is the total investment. Express the result as a positive number. Copy the formula through the range of the worksheet—cell **I17**.

6. Format the numbers in the range **F8:I8** with the **Accounting Number Format**

with **2 decimals**. Format the other money amounts with **Comma Style**. Click cell **B15**, and insert a comment that says **Contact Robin for financial advising** and position the comment so it doesn't cover the worksheet data.

7. **Rename Sheet1** to **Retirement Value** and **Sheet2** to **Lump Sum** In the **Lump Sum sheet**, click cell **B9**. Access the **PV** function. Enter the variables using cell references and express the result as a positive number. Place a **Thick Bottom Border** under the cell. Click cell **A12**, insert the **TODAY** function, and format in the preferred business style—March 14, 2001.

8. **Delete Sheet3** and then **Select All Sheets**. In the **Left Footer**, place the **File Name** and in the **Right Footer,** place the **Sheet Name. Center** the worksheets **Horizontally** and **Vertically** and print in **Landscape orientation**. Format the worksheet so the comment will print on the sheet.

9. To submit electronically, follow the instructions provided by your instructor. To print, from the **Office** menu, click **Print**. In the **Print** dialog box, under **Print what**, select **Entire workbook**. Under **Copies**, confirm that **1** is selected. Print formulas if you are instructed to do so. From the **Office** menu, click **Close**. If you are prompted to save changes, click **No. Exit** Excel.

End **You have completed Project 5H**

Project 5I — Golf Course

In this project, you will apply all the skills you practiced from the Objectives in Projects 5A and 5B.

In the following Mastering Excel Project, you will create a portfolio of worksheets for the Revenue Department. A golf course will be built in the Western Ridge subdivision and the property owners have agreed to an increase in their taxes to partially pay for this golf course. You will create a worksheet that displays the taxes for each property owner. You will then use Goal Seek to determine the amount for the golf course, and then add that increase to the taxes. Finally, you will prepare a statement for one family who wishes to pay its property taxes in advance. Your completed portfolio of worksheets will look similar to the ones shown in Figure 5.47.

For Project 5I, you will need the following file:

e05I_Golf_Course

You will save your workbook as
5I_Golf_Course_Firstname_Lastname

Figure 5.47

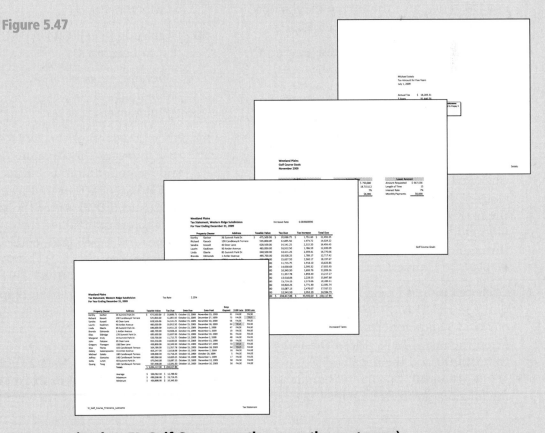

(Project 5I–Golf Course continues on the next page)

Content-Based Assessments

(Project 5I–Golf Course continued)

1. **Start** Excel and open the file named **e05I_Golf_Course**, and then save it in your **Excel Chapter 5** folder as **5I_Golf_Course_Firstname_Lastname**

2. Click cell **A25**. Insert the **Text** function named **PROPER**. In the **Text** box, type **A6**, and click **OK**. Use the fill handle to copy the results through cell **A40**. Select the range **A25:A40** and use the fill handle to copy the cells into **columns B** and **C**. Select and **Copy** the range **A25:C40**. Click cell **A6** and use **Paste Values** to replace the data. Delete the range **A25:C40**.

3. Click cell **E6** and enter a formula that determines the tax due. The tax rate in the Western Ridge subdivision is 2.25%—identified in cell **F2**—of the taxable value—found in **column D**. In this formula, use an absolute reference to the tax rate. With cell **E6** active, use the fill handle to copy the formula down through cell **E21**.

4. Click cell **F6** and enter the due date in the column. All taxes are due on October 15, 2009. Format the date for the style preferred in business—*October 15, 2009*. Use the fill handle to copy the dates through cell **F21**. Use the **Auto Fill Options** to copy the cells.

5. Click cell **H6** and determine the days elapsed. Enter the formula that subtracts the *Date Due* from the *Date Paid*. Use the fill handle to copy the formula down through cell **H21**. Confirm that **column H** displays in **General number format.**

6. Click cell **I6** and insert the **AND** function that returns TRUE if the homeowner will pay a $100 late fee. This fee is assessed when the taxes due are **less than or equal to $12,000** and the days elapsed are greater than **60**. Use the fill handle to copy the formula down through cell **I21**.

7. Click cell **J6** and enter an **AND** function that returns TRUE if the homeowner will pay a $200 late fee. This fee is assessed when the taxes due are **more than $12,000** and the days elapsed are greater than **60**. Use the fill handle to copy the formula down through cell **J21**.

8. Select the range **I6:J21** and select **Conditional Formatting**. For all cells that read *TRUE*, format for **Light Red Fill with Dark Red Text**. Confirm that cell **E6** is formatted with **Accounting Number Format** and **2 decimals** and format the rest of the column with **Comma Style** and **2 decimals**.

9. Click cell **C22** and type **Totals** and format with **Bold**. Enter **Sum** totals in cells **D22** and **E22** and format with a **Top and Double Bottom Border**. Adjust column widths if necessary.

10. Beginning in cell **C24** type the following text in **column C**:

Average
Maximum
Minimum

11. In cell **D24**, enter the **AVERAGE** function that averages the **Taxable Value** for the subdivision, and in cell **E24**, enter the **AVERAGE** function that averages the **Tax Due**. In cell **D25**, enter the **MAXIMUM** function that displays the largest **Taxable Value**, and in cell **E25**, enter the **MAXIMUM** function that displays the largest amount of **Tax Due**. In cell **D26**, enter the **MINIMUM** function that displays the lowest **Taxable Value**, and in cell **E26**, enter the **MINIMUM** function that displays the lowest **Tax Due**. Adjust column widths if needed. Display cells **D24:E24** with **Accounting Number Format** and **two decimals**.

(Project 5I–Golf Course continues on the next page)

(Project 5I–Golf Course continued)

12. Press ⬆Shift and click the **Sheet2 sheet tab** to group the sheets. Select **A1:A3** and use **Fill Across Worksheets** to copy the worksheet title. **Ungroup sheets** and in **Sheet2**, change cell **A2** to read **Golf Course Goals** and change cell **A3** to read ˙November 2009

13. Beginning in cell **A6**, type the following row titles and data into the range **A6:B10**:

Golf Course	
Amount Requested	750,000
Length of Time	15
Interest Rate	7%
Monthly Payments	

14. Widen columns so the longest entries fully display. Click cell **B10** and enter a **PMT** function to determine the monthly payments for the golf course and express the result—$6,741.21—as a positive number.

15. Format the title of this section—*Golf Course*—with **Bold** and **Merge & Center** over **columns A and B** and use a **Fill Color** of **Purple, Accent 4, Lighter 60%**. Format cell **B7** for **Accounting Number Format** with **no decimals** and format the payment in cell **B10** for **Accounting Number Format** with **no decimals** and a **Bottom Double Border**.

16. **Copy** the range **A6:B10** and **Paste** it to begin in cell **D6** and in cell **G6**, and then adjust column widths. Click cell **E10** and access **Goal Seek**. The goal is a monthly payment of $6,000. Determine the *Length of Time* for the loan to maintain a $6,000 monthly payment. Change the title for this Goal Seek to read **Longer Time** Click cell **H10** and use **Goal Seek** to determine the maximum *Amount Requested* with monthly payments of $6,000. Change the title for this Goal Seek to read **Lower Amount** In

reviewing the results, Joaquin Alonzo, the city manager, has decided to trim the golf course budget to $670,000 to keep the payments at $6,000.

17. **Rename Sheet1** to Tax Statement **Sheet2** to **Golf Course Goals** and **Sheet3** to **Increased Taxes** The fourth sheet is already named *Sotelo*. Move the **Tax Statement sheet** so it is between the **Golf Course Goals** and the **Increased Taxes sheets**. Select the **Tax Statement** and **Increased Taxes sheets**. In the **Tax Statement sheet**, select the range **A1:D21** and **Fill Across Worksheets**.

18. **Ungroup** the sheets and in the **Tax Statement sheet**, select and copy the range **E5:E21**. Click the **Increased Taxes sheet tab**, and click cell **E5** and **Paste Values**. Adjust column widths to fully display contents.

19. In cell **F5**, type **Tax Increase** and in cell **G5**, type **Total Due** and copy the format from cell **D5** to cells **E5:G5** In cells **D22** and **E22**, enter the total property values and taxes. In cell **E2**, type **Increase Rate** and in cell **F2**, type **.003683696** Click cell **F6** and enter the formula that multiplies the **Taxable Value** by the **Increase Rate**—cell **F2**—using an absolute cell reference for the increase rate. Copy the formula down through cell **F21**.

20. In cell **G6**, enter the formula that adds the **Tax Due** to the **Tax Increase** and copy the formula down through cell **G21**. Format the numbers in cells **E6:G6** for **Accounting Number Format** with **two decimals**. Format the numbers in cell **E7:G21** with **Comma Style** with **two decimals**. Place totals in cells **F22:G22** and format the total cells—**D22:G22**—with **Accounting Number Format** with a **Top and Double**

(Project 5I–Golf Course continues on the next page)

Content-Based Assessments

(Project 5I–Golf Course continued)

Bottom Border. In cell **A22**, type **Total** and format with **Bold** and adjust column widths if needed.

21. In the **Increased Taxes sheet tab**, **Copy** cell **G18**—the amount of the Sotelo taxes for one year. Click the **Sotelo sheet tab.** In this worksheet, you will determine how much Sotelo can invest now so property taxes will be paid for the next 5 years. Click cell **B6** and **Paste** the **Values**. In cell **B7**, enter the formula for the tax amount for 5 years—=B6*5. In cell **B9**, access the **PV Financial** function. Complete this for an annual basis. For the **Rate**, use **B8**. For the **Nper**, type **5** Because this is a lump-sum payment, skip the **Pmt** argument. For the **Fv**, use **B7**. Click **OK** and express the value as a positive number. Format cell **B6** with **Accounting Number Format** with **two decimals** and cell **B7** with **Comma Style** with **two decimals**. Increase the width of the columns as needed.

22. Click cell **B9** and insert a comment that reads **Funds Needed to Prepay 5 Years'**

Taxes Confirm that **Show All Comments** is selected.

23. Place the worksheets in this order: Tax Statement, Increased Taxes, Golf Course Goals, and Sotelo. **Select All Sheets** and insert the **File Name** in the **Left Footer** area, and the **Sheet Name** and in the **Right Footer** area. Place the worksheets in **Landscape orientation**, **Fit to one page**, centered both **Horizontally** and **Vertically**.

24. Click the **Sotelo sheet tab** and set it to display the comment **As displayed on sheet. Save** your workbook.

25. To submit electronically, follow the instructions provided by your instructor. To print, from the **Office** menu, click **Print**. In the **Print** dialog box, under **Print what**, select **Entire workbook**. Under **Copies**, confirm that **1** is selected. Print formulas if you are instructed to do so. From the **Office** menu, click **Close**. If you are prompted to save changes, click **No**. **Exit** Excel.

End You have completed Project 5I

Content-Based Assessments

Business Running Case

Project 5J—Business Running Case

In this project, you will apply the skills you have practiced from the Objectives in Projects 5A and 5B.

From My Computer, navigate to the student files that accompany this textbook. In the folder **03_business_running_case**, locate and open the folder for this chapter. Open and print the instructions for this project, which are provided to you in Adobe PDF format. Follow the instructions and use the skills you have gained thus far to assist the managers of the Grand Department Store to meet the challenges of keeping records for a large department.

End **You have completed Project 5J** ————————————————

Outcomes-Based Assessments

Rubric

The following outcomes-based assessments are *open-ended assessments*. That is, there is no specific correct result; your result will depend on your approach to the information provided. Make *professional quality* your goal. Use the following scoring rubric to guide you in *how* to approach the problem, and then to evaluate *how well* your approach solves the problem.

The *criteria*—Software Mastery, Content, Format and Layout, and Process—represent the knowledge and skills you have gained that you can apply to solving the problem. The *levels of performance*—Professional Quality, Approaching Professional Quality, or Needs Quality Improvement—help you and your instructor evaluate your result.

	Your completed project is of Professional Quality if you:	Your completed project is Approaching Professional Quality if you:	Your completed project Needs Quality Improvements if you:
Software Mastery	Choose and apply the most appropriate skills, tools, and features and identify efficient methods to solve the problem.	Choose and apply some appropriate skills, tools, and features, but not in the most efficient manner.	Choose inappropriate skills, tools, or features, or are inefficient in solving the problem.
Content	Construct a solution that is clear and well organized, contains content that is accurate, appropriate to the audience and purpose, and is complete. Provide a solution that contains no errors of spelling, grammar, or style.	Construct a solution in which some components are unclear, poorly organized, inconsistent, or incomplete. Misjudge the needs of the audience. Have some errors in spelling, grammar, or style, but the errors do not detract from comprehension.	Construct a solution that is unclear, incomplete, or poorly organized, containing some inaccurate or inappropriate content; and contains many errors of spelling, grammar, or style. Do not solve the problem.
Format and Layout	Format and arrange all elements to communicate information and ideas, clarify function, illustrate relationships, and indicate relative importance.	Apply appropriate format and layout features to some elements, but not others. Overuse features, causing minor distraction.	Apply format and layout that does not communicate information or ideas clearly. Do not use format and layout features to clarify function, illustrate relationships, or indicate relative importance. Use available features excessively, causing distraction.
Process	Use an organized approach that integrates planning, development, self-assessment, revision, and reflection.	Demonstrate an organized approach in some areas, but not others; or, use an insufficient process of organization throughout.	Do not use an organized approach to solve the problem.

Outcomes-Based Assessments

Project 5K — Library

In this project, you will construct a solution by applying any combination of the skills you practiced from the Objectives in Projects 5A and 5B.

For Project 5K, you will need the following file:

e05K_Library

You will save your workbook as
5K_Library_Firstname_Lastname

The Westland Plains Library will be renovated to add additional shelf space and reading areas. The renovation will cost over $250,000 and the library would like to have about $150,000 available when the project begins in three years. On the Library Renovation sheet, you will determine the amount of money that needs to be set aside today so that the necessary funds are available in three years.

The City Records Library is currently being renovated. Several sets of plans—blueprints—are available for the city engineers and other employees to use. The Blueprint Use worksheet lists which employees have checked out the blueprints and when they were returned. Make the changes necessary in this worksheet to present a professional report. Determine the due date—14 days from checkout—and the time elapsed since the blueprints were out. In the Prompt Return? column, enter a formula to determine if the blueprints were returned within 14 days or were renewed. Display TRUE if these conditions are met.

Use Conditional Formatting to highlight those who returned the blueprints within 14 days or renewed the checkout. If there is an employee who has blueprints that are not yet due, insert a comment indicating that information. Because this report is completed on April 15, there are blueprints that are not yet due. If the blueprints were properly handled—returned on time or renewed—insert a comment reminder that a note of appreciation is needed.

Using the skills you have practiced in this chapter, complete and format the workbook attractively and appropriately and confirm its accuracy. Save your workbook as **5K_Library_Firstname_Lastname** Include the file name and sheet name in the footer. Save your work and submit it as directed.

End You have completed Project 5K

Outcomes-Based Assessments

Excel

chapterfive

Problem Solving

Project 5L — Parking

In this project, you will construct a solution by applying any combination of the skills you practiced from the Objectives in Projects 5A and 5B.

For Project 5L, you will need the following file:

e05L_Parking

You will save your workbook as
5L_Parking_Firstname_Lastname

In this project, you will assist the Westland Plains City Manager, Joaquin Alonzo, with several projects that he needs completed. Worksheets have been named and two of them contain data.

A new water treatment plant is needed in 2015—six years from now. Determine the amount of funds needed to be set aside so that the plant can be fully funded before it is constructed. The required data is available on the Investment Analysis worksheet. Complete the proper formula to provide Joaquin with the amount of investment needed.

The city is in the process of planning for a 1,000-space parking structure and is negotiating for the land, which will cost $50,500. Before a final decision can be made, Joaquin would like to see a payment amortization schedule. Prepare the schedule for this 2-year, 7.5% loan, with the city making monthly payments.

In planning for the structure, the Budget Office has requested that monthly payments for the structure not greater than $6,100. The initial plans indicate that the cost of the structure will be $750,000 with an interest rate of 7% for 15 years. The budget office has indicated these terms will result in a higher monthly payment. On the Parking Structure sheet, create What-If Analysis with Goal Seek to determine the length of the loan needed to maintain payments of $6,100 and also the total amount if the number of parking spaces is reduced.

Using the skills you have practiced in this chapter, complete and format the workbook attractively and appropriately and confirm its accuracy. Construct appropriate formulas as needed. Save your workbook as **5L_Parking_Firstname_Lastname** Include the file name and sheet name in the footer. Save your work and submit it as directed.

End You have completed Project 5L

Problem Solving

Project 5M—Bus Drivers

In this project, you will construct a solution by applying any combination of the skills you practiced from the Objectives in Projects 5A and 5B.

For Project 5M, you will need the following file:

e05M_Bus_Drivers

**You will save your workbook as
5M_Bus_Drivers_Firstname_Lastname**

The bus drivers have just settled a strike and a small portion of the agreement is a $2,000 IRA for each driver. Bill Aycock, the mayor, would like to see a worksheet that displays the amount of each IRA and its predicted value upon retirement of each employee. Using the skills you have practiced in this chapter, complete and format the workbook attractively and appropriately and confirm its accuracy. The retirement age is 65, and you will need to determine the years until the driver reaches the retirement age and then the number of years left to work from 2009. The current interest rate is 6.5%. Save your workbook as **5M_Bus_Drivers_Firstname_Lastname** Include the file name in the footer. Save your work and submit it as directed.

End **You have completed Project 5M** _____

Outcomes-Based Assessments

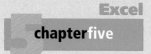

Problem Solving

Project 5N — Health Inspections

In this project, you will construct a solution by applying any combination of the skills you practiced from the Objectives in Projects 5A and 5B.

For Project 5N, you will need the following file:

e05N_Health_Inspections

You will save your workbook as
5N_Health_Inspections_Firstname_Lastname

Amanda Lauritzen oversees the Health Department and has requested a worksheet that summarizes the inspections for May. You will complete that worksheet for Amanda. Each restaurant in the city has periodic inspections by the Health Department and receives a score based on cleanliness of kitchen, rest rooms, and dining facilities, health concerns of the staff, and other factors. The restaurant is then rated on a score of 1–100. An establishment is visited at least twice a year, with the second inspection 30 days after the first. If each score from both inspections is less than 75, the restaurant will be fined $100, unless it is a Fine Dining restaurant, which will be fined $500 and closed until improvements are made. Provide comments that explain the results.

Create a formula to determine the date of the second inspection. Then use logical functions (AND, OR) and Conditional Formatting to identify the restaurants that will be fined. Using the skills you practiced in this chapter, complete the worksheet, format it appropriately, and confirm its accuracy. Save your workbook as **5N_Health_Inspections_Firstname_ Lastname** Include a footer that displays the file name. Save your work and submit it as directed.

End You have completed Project 5N

Outcomes-Based Assessments

Problem Solving

Project 5O—Pool

In this project, you will construct a solution by applying any combination of the skills you practiced from the Objectives in Projects 5A and 5B.

For Project 5O, you will need the following file:

New blank Excel Workbook

You will save your workbook as
5O_Pool_Firstname_Lastname

The Chair of the Parks & Recreation Commission, Yvonne Guillen, recognizes that a replacement swimming pool will be needed in the city park in several years. Her preliminary studies indicate the pool, pool house, and landscaping will cost $970,000 and she would like to set that money aside in monthly investments. In her analysis, she is considering several options.

Create a workbook to determine the monthly investment of the pool using an interest rate of 5.5% for 20 years. Create What-If Analysis with Goal Seek to create the financial picture for Yvonne using these variables. Determine the length of time if the monthly investment is $1,500 and determine the cost of the pool if the monthly investment is $2,100.

Use the skills you have practiced in this chapter to format these financial forecasts attractively and appropriately and confirm their accuracy. Complete this estimate for Yvonne on May 31, 2009, and include that in the date line. Save the workbook as **5O_Pool_Firstname_Lastname** Include the file name in the footer. Save your work and submit it as directed.

End **You have completed Project 5O** _____

Outcomes-Based Assessments

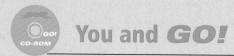

You and *GO!*

Project 5P—You and *GO!*

In this project, you will construct a solution by applying any combination of the Objectives found in Projects 5A and 5B.

From the student files that accompany this textbook, open the folder **04_you_and_go**. Locate **5P_You_and_GO** and follow the instructions to create a worksheet that displays an amortization table for a car purchase.

End You have completed Project 5P

GO! with Help

Project 5Q — *GO!* with Help

In this chapter, you used date and time functions to enter the current date and time in a worksheet. You will use Help to assist you in entering the day of week that you were born into a worksheet.

 If necessary, **Start** Excel to open a new workbook. At the right edge of the menu bar, click the **Microsoft Office Excel Help** button . Alternatively, press F1.

2 Use Help to determine the date style to apply so the day of the week displays in the cell.

3 In the worksheet, type your name in one cell and your birth date in another. Format the date of birth so it displays both the day of the week along with the date.

4 In the **Left Footer**, place the **File Name** and display the work in the center of the printed page. **Print** a copy of the worksheet and one that displays formulas.

5 **Save** your worksheet, **Close** the Help window, and **Close** the task pane.

End You have completed Project 5Q

chaptersix

Using Named Ranges, Templates, Lookup Values, and 3-D References

OBJECTIVES

At the end of this chapter you will be able to:

1. Create Formulas Using Named Ranges
2. Utilize Lookup Lists
3. Customize and Use Microsoft-Created Templates

4. Transpose Data in a Worksheet and Apply Cell Styles
5. Use 3-D References to Link Data in Worksheets and Workbooks and Create a Workspace
6. Create Hyperlinks

OUTCOMES

Mastering these objectives will enable you to:

PROJECT 6A
Create Worksheets with Named Ranges, Use Lookup Lists, and Customize Microsoft-Created Templates

PROJECT 6B
Transpose a Worksheet, Apply Cell Styles, Use 3-D References in Worksheets and Workbooks, and Use Hyperlinks to Navigate Between Workbooks, Including Those in a Workspace

Board Anywhere Surf and Snowboard Shop

College classmates Dana Connolly and J. R. Kass grew up in the sun of Orange County, California, but they also spent time in the mountain snow. After graduating with business degrees, they combined their business expertise and their favorite sports to open Board Anywhere, a snowboard and surf shop. The store carries top brands of men's and women's apparel, goggles and sunglasses, and boards and gear. The surfboard selection includes both classic and the latest high-tech boards, and snowboarding gear can be purchased in packages or customized for the most experienced boarders. In response to growing customer needs, Connolly and Kass have expanded into Malibu and Big Bear rather than relocate into larger space in the home location at Redondo Beach. Connolly and Kass are proud to count many of Southern California's extreme sports games participants among their customers.

Using Named Ranges, Templates, Lookup Values, and 3-D References

The power of Excel is in its capability to complete complex tasks. Using a lookup list, Excel can match an item in one row or column and retrieve data from a related row or column and insert the data into a worksheet.

Workbooks can be customized and used over and over when saved as a template. Using a formula that contains cell references from other worksheets or workbooks helps maintain accuracy in the worksheet so that when a change is made, the related formulas in other worksheets are updated.

In this chapter, you will create an Excel workspace that contains linked workbooks. You will use a lookup list to enter variable information into the worksheet. In addition, you will customize and use a built-in template.

Project 6A Third Quarter

In Activities 6.1 through 6.12, J. R. Kass and Dana Connolly prepare several monthly and quarterly reports to keep track of their sales and sales taxes collected from customers. In addition, they report the lessons that were sold. You will create a workbook that reports the September sales tax that is due, and you will create a quarterly sales report using named cells and named ranges in the formula. In addition, you will complete the worksheet that reports the lessons sold in September. Your completed worksheet will look similar to Figure 6.1.

For Project 6A, you will need the following files:

e06A_Third_Quarter

Services_invoice_with_tax_calculation (Excel template)

You will save your workbooks as
6A_Third_Quarter_Firstname_Lastname
6A_McKinley_Firstname_Lastname
6A_Invoice_Template_Firstname_Lastname

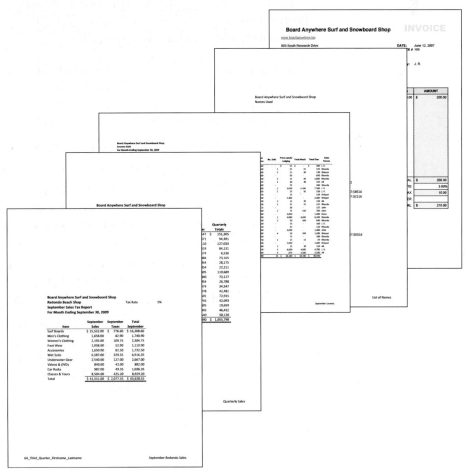

Figure 6.1
Project 6A—Third Quarter

Objective 1
Create Formulas Using Named Ranges

By using named cells or named ranges rather than cell references to create formulas, the formulas are easier to understand and proofread. A **named cell** is identified by a name, which is used in a formula, rather than the cell reference. Likewise, a **named range** identifies a group of cells that can be used in a formula—rather than the cell references.

Using a name in a formula makes it easier to understand the purpose of a cell reference in the formula. It may be difficult to understand the relationship or purpose of cell references used in a formula, but reviewing a formula like =SUM(FirstQuarterSales) rather than =SUM(C20:C30) is easy to understand.

Activity 6.1 Defining and Using a Named Cell

You can define a name for a cell range, function, constant, or table. After names are defined—created—they can easily be updated, audited, and managed. The Redondo Beach shop has created a sales record for its September sales, but Dana, the owner, realizes that the sales tax has not been recorded. In this activity, you will enter the sales tax for the September sales using a named cell.

1 **Start** Excel. Open the file named **e06A_Third_Quarter**. Navigate to the location where you are saving your files, create a new folder named **Excel Chapter 6** and then save the file in that folder as **6A_ Third_Quarter_Firstname_Lastname** and confirm that **Sheet1** is active.

2 Click cell **E2**. On the left side of the **Formula Bar**, click in the **Name Box**, type **Sales_Tax_Rate** and then press Enter. Compare your screen with Figure 6.2.

When you click in the Name Box, the cell reference—E2—moves to the left of the box and is selected—highlighted in blue. After you type the name and press Enter, cell E2 is named *Sales_Tax_Rate*. Pressing Enter sets the name. Range names cannot include spaces; therefore, an underscore is used in place of a space. This is a **defined name**— a name that represents a cell, range of cells, formula, or constant value. When creating a formula, the defined name may be used instead of the cell reference.

This defined name was created by clicking in the cell to make it active, and then typing the name in the Name Box. By default, names are absolute cell references.

Figure 6.2

Name Box with cell
defined—named

Named cell is active

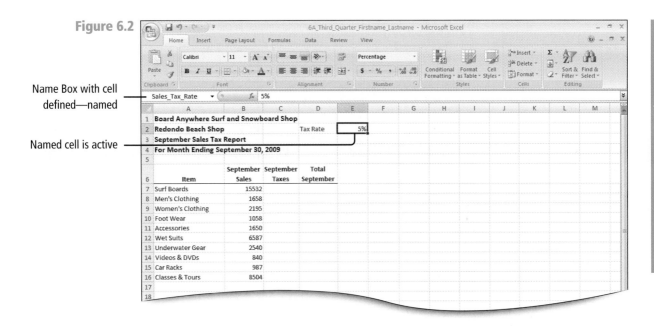

3 Click cell **C7** and type **=** Click cell **B7** and type ***** Click the **Formulas tab**, and in the **Defined Names group**, click the **Use in Formula** button, and then click **Sales_Tax_Rate**. Alternatively, click cell E2 and notice that the name of the cell displays, rather than the cell reference. Compare your screen with Figure 6.3 and then on the

Formula Bar, click the **Enter** button ✓.

Rather than use the cell reference—E2—the cell name *Sales_Tax_Rate* is used. The formula is color-coded, with cell B7 and its cell reference bordered in blue and the Sales Tax Rate and its cell reference bordered in green. The ***Use in Formula list*** displays the names of defined cells and ranges available. By using named cells, when the formula is reviewed, it is easy to understand that this formula multiplies the contents of cell B7 by the sales tax rate.

Figure 6.3

Formula entered in cell and
Formula Bar using named cell

Green border surrounds
cell containing tax rate

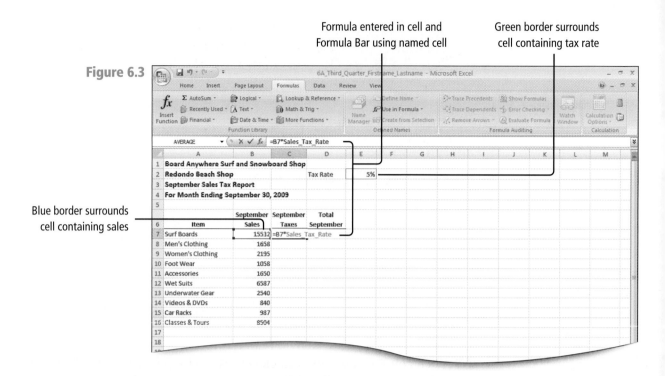

Blue border surrounds
cell containing sales

4 Take a few moments to study the table in Figure 6.4, which identifies the rules for naming cell ranges.

Rules for Naming a Range of Cells in Excel

Characteristic	Rule
Characters	The first character of the name must be a letter or an underscore (_). Using short, meaningful names is recommended. Numbers can be part of a name, but symbols other than the underscore (_) or period (.) cannot be used.
Words	Names can be more than one word, but there cannot be spaces between the words. Use an underscore or a period to separate the range names that contain multiple words.
Cell references	Names cannot be the same as cell references, for example, A1.
Case	Names can contain uppercase and lowercase letters. Excel does not distinguish between uppercase and lowercase characters in range names. For example if you have created the name Total and then create another name called TOTAL in the same workbook, the second name will replace the first.

Figure 6.4

5 Use the fill handle to copy the formula through the range of the worksheet—cell **C16**. On the **Formulas tab**, in the **Formula Auditing group**, click the **Show Formulas** button, and then compare your screen with Figure 6.5.

The formula in each of the cells uses the name of the cell—Sales_Tax_Rate—rather than the cell reference. A defined cell reference in a formula becomes an absolute cell reference.

Show Formulas button

Figure 6.5

Formulas that use named cell

Named cell in green refers to the cell reference—bordered in green

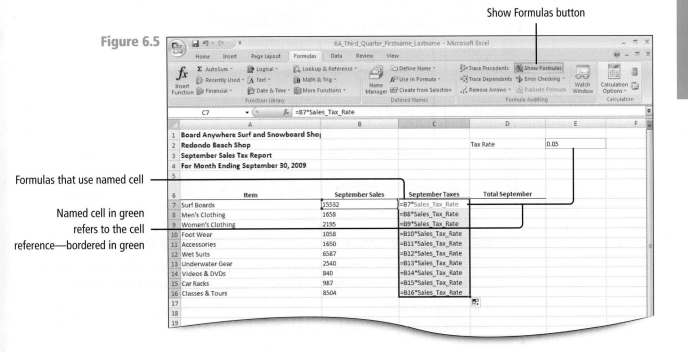

6 In the **Formula Auditing group**, click the **Show Formulas** button to redisplay the results in the cells.

7 Click cell **D7**, and enter the formula for the total sales and taxes for September by adding cell **B7** to cell **C7**, and then fill the formula down through cell **D16**. **Save** your workbook.

Activity 6.2 Creating Names from Row and Column Titles

A cell or a range of cells can be named using several different methods. In this activity, you will create names from column titles and use those names to create the formulas in the worksheet.

1 In cell **A17**, type **Total** Select the range **B6:D16**, and on the **Formulas tab**, in the **Defined Names group**, click the **Create from Selection** button. Compare your screen with Figure 6.6.

The *Create from Selection* feature creates range names from the titles in adjacent rows or columns and applies those titles to the selected cells. The cell names are confirmed in the Create Names from Selection dialog box.

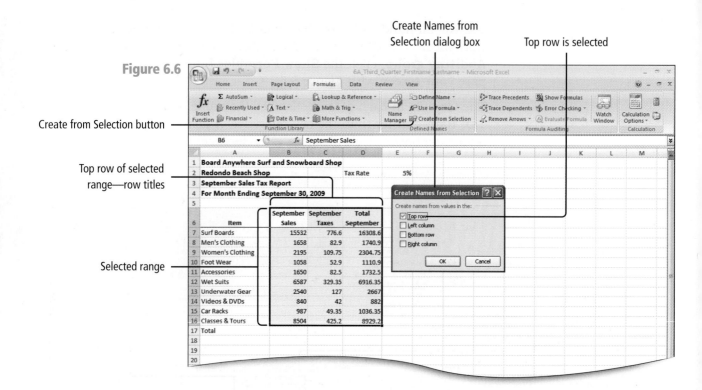

Figure 6.6

Create Names from Selection dialog box

Top row is selected

Create from Selection button

Top row of selected range—row titles

Selected range

2 Confirm that **Top row** is selected, and then click **OK**.

When naming ranges of cells, it is convenient to use the titles already used in the worksheet to name the cells in that row or column.

3 Click cell **B17** and type **=sum(** In the **Defined Names group**, click the **Use in Formula** button, and then compare your screen with Figure 6.7.

A list displays that includes all of the defined names for this workbook. The column titles match the named cells and an underscore replaces the space.

List of defined names

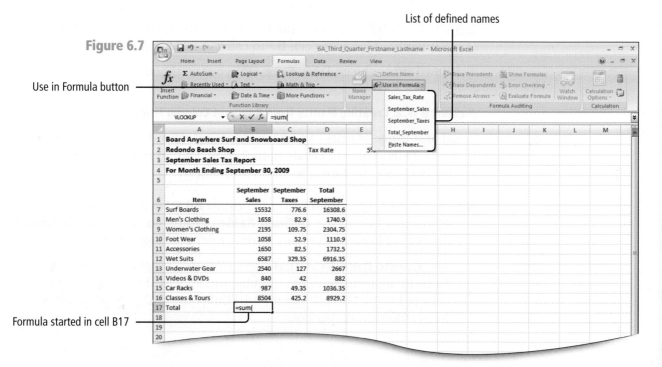

Figure 6.7

Use in Formula button

Formula started in cell B17

4 From the list, click **September_Sales**.

The range name—*September_Sales*—is displayed in the formula and the associated range is outlined with a blue border.

5 Type **)** and on the **Formula Bar**, click the **Enter** button ✓.

The total September Sales—41551—displays in cell B17. The formula— =SUM(September_Sales)—more accurately identifies the purpose of the formula than =SUM(B7:B16).

6 Click cell **C17** and type **=sum(s** and compare your screen with Figure 6.8.

The *Formula AutoComplete* list displays the functions that begin with an S along with the named cells and ranges that begin with S. The icon before the listed name indicates the function name or the range name.

Formula AutoComplete list

Figure 6.8

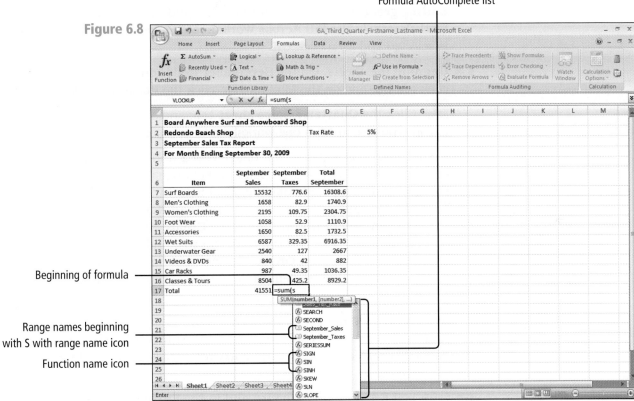

Beginning of formula

Range names beginning with S with range name icon

Function name icon

7 In the **Formula AutoComplete** list, double-click **September_Taxes**, type **)** and then on the **Formula Bar**, click the **Enter** button ✓. With cell **C17** active, fill the formula across to cell **D17** and notice that the formula result is the same because the named range is an absolute cell reference.

8 Click cell **D17**, and on the **Formula Bar**, select *September_Taxes*. In the **Defined Names group**, click the **Use in Formula** button and from the list, click **Total_September** and then press Enter.

The named range is replaced with the one for column D and the formula is corrected. The result—43628.55—displays in cell D17.

9 Format the cells **B17:D17** with **Accounting Number Format** $ ▾ and apply a **Top and Double Bottom Border** to the range. Format the range **B8:D16** with **Comma Style** ' . Format the range **B7:D7** with **Accounting Number Format** $ ▾ .

10 Rename **Sheet1** to **September Redondo Sales** and **Save** 🖫 your workbook.

Activity 6.3 Creating Formulas Using Named Ranges

In this activity, you will create and edit names for ranges in the worksheet and create formulas in the worksheet that use named ranges.

1 Rename **Sheet2** to **Quarterly Sales** and then **Group** the **September Redondo Sales** and the **Quarterly Sales** worksheets. In the **September Redondo Sales** sheet, select the range **A1:A4**. On the **Home tab**, in the **Editing group**, click the **Fill** button ⬇▾ , and then click **Across Worksheets**. In the **Fill Across Worksheets** dialog box, confirm that **All** is selected and then click **OK**.

2 **Ungroup** the sheets. On the **September Redondo Sales** sheet, right-click cell **B6**, and on the Mini toolbar, click the **Format Painter** button ⬗ . Click the **Quarterly Sales sheet tab**, and select the range **A6:E6** to copy the format from one worksheet to another.

3 In the **Quarterly Sales** sheet, delete **row 2** and change the title in cell **A2** to read **Third Quarter Sales** and change the date line to read **For Quarter Ending September 30, 2009** Select the range **A5:D21**. Click the **Formulas tab**, and in the **Defined Names group**, click the **Create from Selection** button. In the **Create Names from Selection** dialog box, confirm that **Top row** and **Left column** are checked, and then click **OK**. An information box displays asking if you want to replace the definition of Accessories. Click **No**.

In the list of items in column A, Accessories is listed in both cells A10 and A15. A name can be used to refer to only one cell or range of cells. The first entry of Accessories in the list—cell A10—is defined. This leaves the second entry for Accessories undefined—unnamed.

4 Click cell **E6**, and type **=sum(su** and in the **Formula AutoComplete** list, double-click **Surf_Boards**—the row title—type **)** and then press Enter .

5 In cell **E7**, type **=sum(** In the **Defined Names group**, click the **Use in Formula** button, and from the displayed list, click **Men_s_Clothing**, type **)** and press Enter .

Formulas that contain named ranges cannot be easily copied. If they are copied, the name of the range must be changed to reflect the current range. Although the cell contains the word *Men's* with the apostrophe, this symbol is not recognized in named ranges and is changed to the underscore. All of the names that are used in this workbook display in the Use in Formula list.

6 In cell **E8**, in the **Function Library group**, click the **AutoSum** button. With the range **E6:E7** selected, click the **Use in Formula button arrow**, scroll to and click **Women_s_Clothing**, and then press Enter.

As is usual with Excel, there are several ways to insert a defined name. When creating a worksheet, you may select any of these methods.

7 Copy cell **E8** to cell **E9**. Click cell **E9**, and on the **Formula Bar**, double-click the name *Women_s_Clothing* to select it. In the **Defined Names group**, click the **Use in Formula** button, and then click **Foot_Wear**—the row title—and press Enter.

8 In cell **E10**, in the **Function Library group**, click the **AutoSum** button. Select the range **B10:D10** and press Enter.

The name of the range, Accessories, is entered into the formula with no additional typing.

9 Using the skills you have practiced, enter the formulas in **column E** that contain named ranges through **Boots, row 14**. Click cell **E15**, and in the **Function Library group**, click the **AutoSum** button. Click the **Use in Formula button arrow**, and then click **Accessories**.

The range that Accessories is related to is B10:D10, which is outlined with a blue line. This is an incorrect range. Because there are two row titles with the same name, Excel assigned the first range to the name Accessories.

10 Press Esc. Click cell **A10** and type **Surf** before *Accessories*. In cell **A15**, change the row title to **Snow Accessories** and in the **Formula Bar**, click the **Enter** ✔ button. In the **Defined Names group**, click the **Name Manager** button, and then click **Accessories**—the first name in the list. At the bottom of the **Name Manager** dialog box, under **Refers to**, the range **B10:D10** displays as absolute references. Compare your screen with Figure 6.9.

Use the *Name Manager* to access the dialog box that displays all of the names defined in the workbook, their cell references, and the sheet name in which you can create, edit, or delete names. There are several worksheets in this workbook, so the defined name refers to a range in a specified worksheet. The sheet name displays with apostrophes around the title and an exclamation mark is placed between the sheet name and the selected range.

Name Manager button

Figure 6.9

Name Manager dialog box

Data for Accessories range

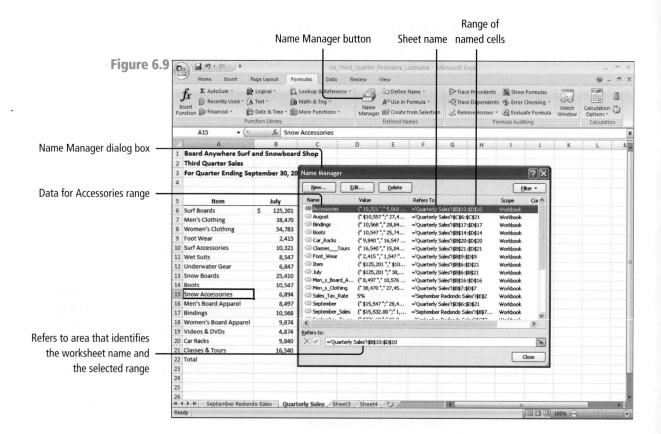

Refers to area that identifies
the worksheet name and
the selected range

Alert!

Can you see the name of the range?

If you cannot see the name of the range, in the Name Manager dialog box,
position your mouse at the right border of the Refers to column heading
and drag to the right.

11 At the top of the **Name Manager** dialog box, click the **Edit** button to
display the **Edit Name** dialog box, change **Accessories** to
Surf_Accessories and then click **OK**. The **Name Manager** dialog box
displays again. Click the **New** button.

12 In the **New Name** dialog box, confirm **Snow_Accessories** is entered,
and in the **Refers to** box, click the **Collapse Dialog Box** button
and select the range **B15:D15**. Click the **Expand Dialog Box**
button, confirm the range is correct, and compare your screen
with Figure 6.10.

The New Name dialog box displays and enables you to enter a new
name for a defined range of cells. The name can be up to 255 characters and cannot contain a space. The named range can be applied
to the entire workbook or an individual worksheet.

Figure 6.10

Range of defined cell

New Name dialog box

Name of worksheet
location of defined range

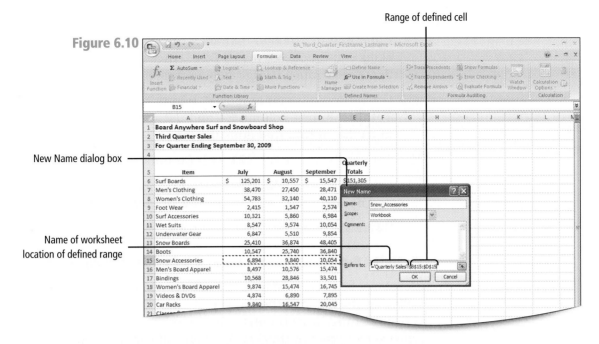

13 Click **OK**. In the **Name Manager** dialog box, confirm the accuracy of the **Snow Accessories** range, and then click **Close**. Click cell **E10** and confirm that the name in the formula has changed to *Surf_Accessories*.

14 Beginning in cell **E15**, continue entering the formulas required in the rest of **column E** for the quarterly totals using named ranges.

15 Click cell **B22**, and in the **Function Library group**, click the **AutoSum** button, and then compare your screen with Figure 6.11.

The range named *July* is selected and is the desired range.

AutoSum button in
Function Library group

Formulas entered in column E

Figure 6.11

Suggested cells for
the Sum function

Range name suggested for total

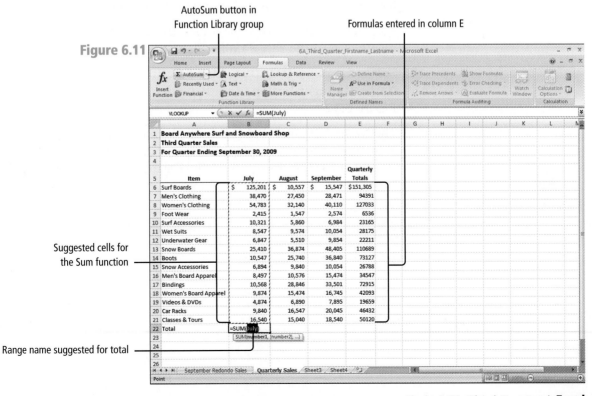

16 Press `Tab` to accept the recommended range and activate cell **C22**. Enter a Sum function that adds the August range of cells. Using the skills you practiced, in cell **D22**, enter a formula that sums the September range using range names.

17 Using the skills you practiced, **name** the cells in the **Quarterly Totals** column—column E—and use named ranges to enter a formula in cell **E22** that adds the totals.

18 Format the range **B7:E21** with **Comma style** [,] and **no decimals**. Format the range **B22:E22** with **Accounting Number Format** [$ ▾] and **no decimals**. Add a **Top and Double Bottom Border** to range **B22:E22**. **Save** [💾] your workbook.

Activity 6.4 Inserting Rows Within a Range and Editing the Worksheet

Cells may be used in more than one defined name. The defined range of cells and the name of the range may be edited. Cells that are inserted in a defined range are automatically included in that range. Dana has identified some errors in this list that you will correct. In this activity, you will insert rows, define new ranges, and edit existing named ranges.

1 In the **Quarterly Sales** sheet, select the range **B6:D12**. Click in the **Name Box** and type **Surf_Sales** and then press `Enter`.

This portion of the worksheet lists the surfing items that were sold. The selected range that includes the surfing items has been named *Surf_Sales*. These cells have been previously used in other range names.

2 Select the range **B13:D18**. Click the **Formulas tab**, and in the **Defined Names group**, click the **Define Name button arrow** and from the list, click **Define Name**. In the **New Name** dialog box, in the **Name** box, type **Snow_Sales** and then click **OK**.

This portion of the worksheet lists the snow items and is grouped together with the range name *Snow Sales*.

3 Select the range **B19:D21**. In the **Defined Names group**, click the **Name Manager** button, and then compare your screen with Figure 6.12.

The Name Manager dialog box displays the *Name*, *Value*, and *Refers To* columns, which display the ranges of the named cells in this workbook. The scope of the defined ranges are the entire workbook. New ranges can be defined and added in this dialog box.

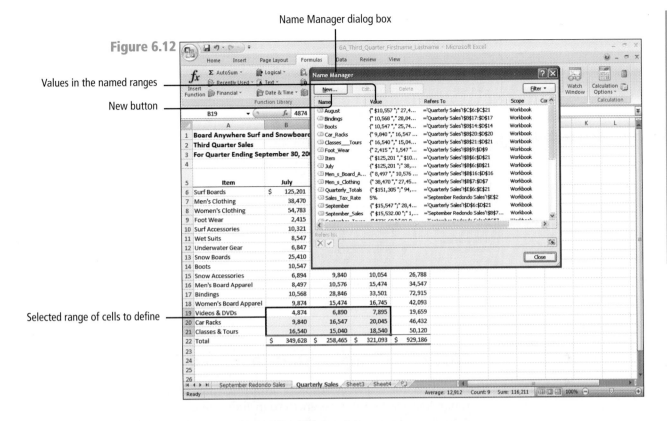

Name Manager dialog box

Figure 6.12

Values in the named ranges

New button

Selected range of cells to define

4. In the **Name Manager** dialog box, click **New**. In the **New Name** dialog box, in the **Name** text box, type **Accessories** and then click **OK**.

The Name Manager dialog box displays again and the newly defined range is included in the list. The choices *Edit* and *Delete* are active, as is the *Filter* button.

5. Click **Close**. Insert a row after **row 8**—*Women's Clothing*—and beginning in cell **A9**, type the following data. You do not need to type the comma in the cells; the cells are already formatted for the numbers.

Children's Clothing	39,283	21,029	23,819

6. In the **Name Box**, click the **arrow** and click **Surf_Sales** to select the range, and then compare your screen with Figure 6.13.

The data for children's clothing is inserted in the area of the worksheet that contains the surfing equipment. The newly inserted row is included in the defined range for surf sales; the range for the surf sales is adjusted to include row 13.

Figure 6.13

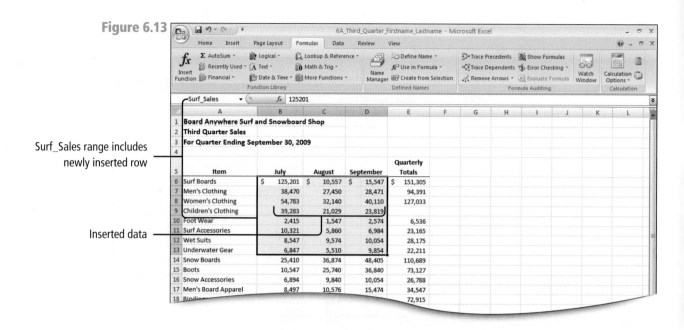

Surf_Sales range includes newly inserted row

Inserted data

Note — Changing Data in Named Ranges

A range name is always absolute. Inserting rows or columns within a named range adjusts the cell references to include the inserted cells. If the range is moved, the range name is also moved to the new location. If a cell or range of cells is entered at the end of the range, though, the range needs to be redefined to include the additional cells.

7 Insert a row after **row 17**—*Men's Board Apparel*—and beginning with cell **A18**, type the following data:

Children's Board Apparel	8,456	12,547	21,478

8 Click the **Name Box arrow** and click **Snow_Sales** to identify the range of cells included in the named range.

Recall that when a row is inserted within a range, the range adjusts to include the newly inserted row.

9 Select the range **A9:D9**, On the **Formulas tab**, in the **Defined Names group**, click the **Create from Selection** button. Confirm that **Left column** is checked, and then click **OK**. In cell **E9**, using the skills you have practiced, enter the total sales using the named range in the formula. In **row 18**, using the skills you practiced, define a name for Children's Board Apparel. In cell **E18**, enter a formula that totals the sales using a formula that contains the named range.

10 In the **Defined Names group**, click the **Name Manager** button. In the list in the dialog box, click **Accessories**, and then click **Edit**.

The Edit Name dialog box displays. This dialog box is similar to the New Name dialog box. Use this dialog box to edit the name or range of the cells or to add comments about the range.

11 Replace *Accessories* with **Miscellaneous** and then click **OK**. Compare your screen with Figure 6.14, and then click **Close**.

The range name for Accessories has been deleted and that same range—B21:D23— has been renamed Miscellaneous. All named ranges are displayed with their values and ranges displayed.

Figure 6.14

Changed name

Range of Miscellaneous

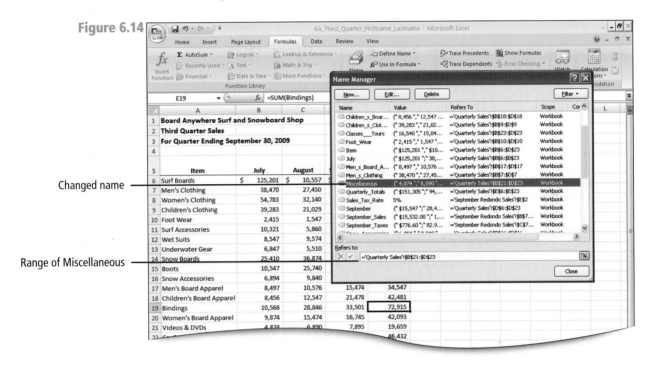

12 **Save** your workbook.

Activity 6.5 Using Named Cells to Create Quarterly Totals

Dana has asked to review the totals of each department in the Redondo Beach shop. In this activity, you will enter totals for the three departments of the Redondo Beach shop—Surfing, Snow Boarding, and Miscellaneous—using named ranges rather than cell references.

1 Beginning in cell **A27**, enter the following row titles:

Totals by Merchandise Departments
Surfing Totals
Snow Boarding Totals
Miscellaneous Totals
Totals

2 Format cell **A27** with **Bold** , **Wrap Text** , and **Center** .
Format cell **A31** with **Bold** . In cell **B27**, type **Quarterly Totals** and format it to match cell **A27**.

3 Click cell **B28**. Click the **Formulas tab**, and in the **Function Library group**, click the **AutoSum** button. In the **Defined Names group**, click the **Use in Formula** button, and from the list, click **Surf_Sales**. Compare your screen with Figure 6.15, and then press Enter.

When the SUM function was selected, a cell or range of cells may be surrounded by a moving border. The Surf Sales range of cells is also bordered in blue, providing a visual indicator of the range that is included in the Sum function. When the function is confirmed, the total for surfing equipment—536947—is entered in the cell.

Formula entered in cell and Formula Bar

Figure 6.15

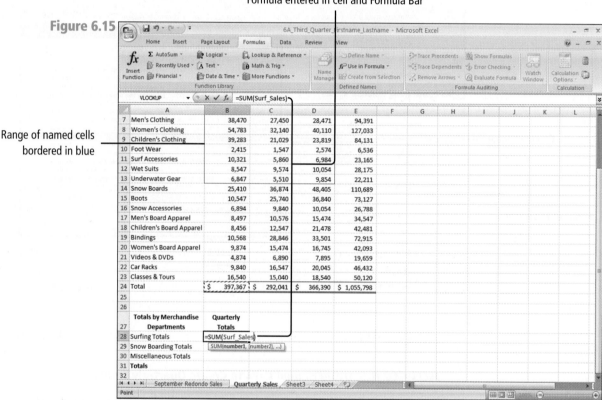

Range of named cells bordered in blue

4 In cell **B29**, type **=sum(** In the **Defined Names group**, click the **Use in Formula** button and at the bottom of the list, click **Paste Names**.

The Paste Name dialog box displays all of the names available in this worksheet.

5 Scroll to and click **Snow_Sales**, click **OK**, type **)** and then press Enter.

When named, the range of the snow sales is enclosed in blue border to visualize the cells included in the range. The total snow equipment sales—402640—displays in cell B29.

6 Click cell **B30** and type **=sum(mi** and then from the **Formula AutoComplete** list, double-click **Miscellaneous**, type **)** and press Enter.

7 Select the range **B27:B30** and in the **Defined Names group**, click the **Create from Selection** button. In the **Create Names from Selection** dialog box, confirm that **Top row** is selected, and then click **OK**.

An Information box displays warning that another range has been named Quarterly Totals and you will replace this range.

8 Click **No**. In the **Defined Names group**, click the **Define Name button arrow** and from the displayed list, click **Define Name**. In the **New Name** text box, type **Summary_Q_Totals** and then click **OK**.

9 Click cell **B31**, and create a formula that uses named ranges to display the quarterly totals from the summary and confirm the total in cell **B31** matches the total in cell **E24**. Format cells **B28** and **B31** with **Accounting Number Format** $ with **no decimals**, and format the range **B29:B30** with **Comma Style** and **no decimals**. In cell **B31**, apply a **Top and Double Bottom Border**. **Save** your workbook.

Activity 6.6 Pasting a List of Named Ranges

It is helpful to have a list of names used in a workbook that includes the corresponding cell or range of cells. Dana has asked for this list to assist her in evaluating the sales. In this activity, you will create a list of names and the ranges used.

1 Press Shift + F11 to insert a new worksheet.

A new Sheet1 is inserted into the workbook to the left of the active worksheet.

2 Rename **Sheet1** to **List of Names**. Click in the worksheet, and then point to the **List of Names sheet tab**, and drag the sheet tab to the right and when the small arrow is between the **Sheet4** and the **Insert Worksheet** button, release the mouse button.

Recall that as you move a worksheet, an icon displays that resembles a piece of paper and a small arrow and indicates the location of the moved sheet.

3 Beginning in cell **A1**, type the following title:

| Board Anywhere Surf and Snowboard Shop |
| Names Used |

4 Click cell **A5**. Click the **Formulas tab**, and in the **Defined Names group**, click the **Use in Formula** button and from the displayed list, click **Paste Names** and compare your screen with Figure 6.16.

The Paste Name dialog box displays with an alphabetic list of the names used in the workbook.

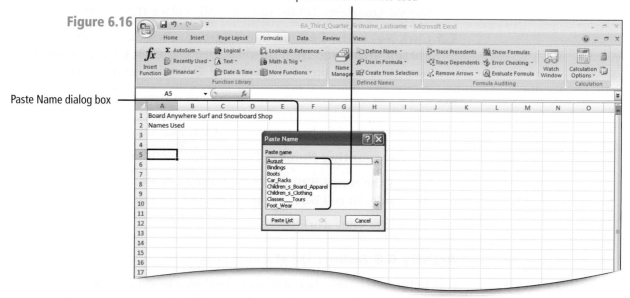

Figure 6.16

Alphabetic list of names used

Paste Name dialog box

5 At the lower left corner of the **Paste Name** dialog box, click **Paste List**.

A list of the names and their ranges displays in the workbook. The list includes the name of the worksheet and the range of cells included in the named range.

6 Adjust the column widths so the contents fully display, and then **Save** your workbook.

Objective 2
Utilize Lookup Lists

Data can be retrieved quickly from another worksheet or workbook using a lookup function. The first step in a lookup function is to create a *table array*—also called a *lookup list*—a table of text, numbers, or logical values in which data can be easily retrieved. When Excel finds a match, it retrieves the data specified by the lookup function and places the value in the cell of the original worksheet. A table array can be used to look up a variety of data—telephone numbers, number of payroll exemptions, bonus amounts, to name a few. The value that is looked up can be used in calculations. The lookup data that is retrieved can then be inserted in the same worksheet, another worksheet, or even another workbook.

Activity 6.7 Creating a Lookup List

Board Anywhere has established a Surf/Snow School that provides several types of lessons, including lessons in other locations such as Hawaii. In addition to the classes, Board Anywhere provides a package deal that includes meals and lodging. Dana and J. R. would like the price of the lesson and any additional costs to be automatically inserted in a worksheet. In this activity, you will create a table array—a lookup list—that displays the lessons available.

1 Click **Sheet3** and rename it **Lesson Prices** Review the lesson rates and cost for add-ins—meals and lodging—for Board Anywhere lessons and trips. This list will be used when completing the report on lessons sold for September.

A lookup list can be large and is often several columns wide. Although these numbers are money amounts, it is not necessary to include dollar signs in the list.

2 Select the range—**A6:C16**. In the **Defined Names group**, click the **Define Name** button. In the **New Name** dialog box, in the **Name** box, type **Lesson_Rates** Confirm that the range is correct—*A6:C16*—and then click **OK**.

3 Click cell **A17** and add the entries displayed below.

| Snowboard Camp | 370 | 50 |
| Skiing Camp | 350 | 15 |

4 On the **Formula Bar**, click the **Name Box arrow**, and from the displayed list, click **Lesson_Rates**. Notice that the range does not include the newly inserted rows.

When a range is named, it will adjust the references to include inserted or deleted rows within the range, but it does not include cells that are entered at the end of the range.

5 In the **Defined Names group**, click the **Name Manager** button. In the **Name Manager** dialog box, click **Lesson_Rates**. In the **Refers to** section, change the reference to read =**'Lesson Prices'!$A$5:$C$18** and then click **Close**. When asked if you want to save changes, click **Yes**.

6 On the **Formula Bar**, click the **Name Box arrow** and from the displayed list, click **Lesson_Rates** to confirm that the named range now includes all rows.

7 Click cell **A6**. Click the **Data tab**, and in the **Sort & Filter group**, click the **Sort** button. Confirm that the range is selected. In the **Sort** dialog box, confirm that **My data has headers** is checked. Click the **Sort by arrow**, and then click **Lesson**. Confirm that you will sort on values from *A to Z* and then click **OK**. Alternatively, click anywhere in the range A5:A18 and from the Home tab, in the Editing group, click Sort & Filter and click Sort A to Z.

When creating a lookup list—table array—the text in the first column must be in alphabetical order. Likewise, if the first column contains numbers, the list must be sorted from smallest to largest. This list is now displayed in alphabetical order with Skiing Camp as the first entry.

8 **Save** your workbook.

Activity 6.8 Looking Up Text in a Worksheet Using VLOOKUP

To retrieve values in a vertically arranged table, use the ***VLOOKUP function***. The VLOOKUP function looks for a value in the left column of a table, and then returns a value in the same row from another column in the table array that you specify. When querying a table array, Excel searches the data in the first column of the table. When a match is found in the list, a corresponding value—text or number—from the specified row or column in the table is placed in the cell that contains the lookup formula. In this activity, you will use the VLOOKUP function to enter prices for the lessons from the Lesson_Rates table array.

1 Rename the **Sheet4 sheet tab** to **September Lessons** Click cell **G6**. Click the **Formulas tab** and in the **Function Library group**, click the **Lookup & Reference** button, and then click **VLOOKUP**. Compare your screen with Figure 6.17.

The VLOOKUP Function dialog box displays with three required arguments—Lookup_Value, Table_array, Col_index_num. Recall that a required argument displays in bold in the dialog box and the definition of the argument—Lookup Value—is displayed in the dialog box. VLOOKUP is an abbreviation for **Vertical Lookup**.

Figure 6.17

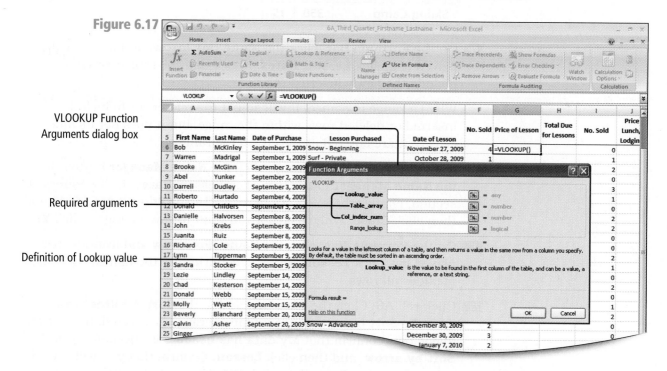

VLOOKUP Function Arguments dialog box

Required arguments

Definition of Lookup value

2 With the insertion point in the **Lookup_value** box, click cell **D6**—the cell that contains the lesson that was purchased. Alternatively, in the Lookup value box, type **d6**

This function will compare the lesson purchased—Snow – Beginning—with the lookup list to determine the cost for that lesson. The **lookup value** is the entry in the worksheet that will be compared in the lookup list. The lookup value can be numbers or text. The entry in the selection—snow—displays to the right of the text box.

3 Press [Tab] and in the dialog box, review the definition of Table_array, type **Lesson_Rates** and then compare your screen with Figure 6.18.

The name of the lookup list—Lesson_Rates—displays in the Table_array box. Recall the table array is a table of text, numbers, or logical values used to look up data. The data in the table array displays to the right of the name box.

Figure 6.18

Data displayed in Table array

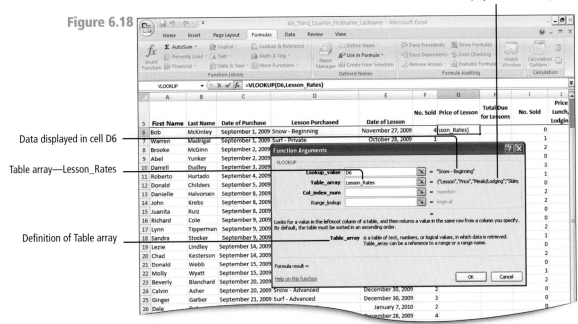

Data displayed in cell D6

Table array—Lesson_Rates

Definition of Table array

4 Press Tab and in the **Col_index_num** box—which is the Column Index Number—type **2** and then compare your screen with Figure 6.19.

The amount for the lesson is in column 2 of the Lesson_Rates lookup list. Excel will compare the value in cell D6—the name of the lesson—and when it finds a match in the Lesson_Rates list, it will return the value that is in the second column of the list for the row that matches the value that is looked up. The **Column Index Number** is the column number in a table from which the matching value will be returned. In the table the first column is column 1, the second column 2, and so forth.

Row index number—column 2 of the
Lesson _Rates table array on the Lesson Prices sheet

Figure 6.19

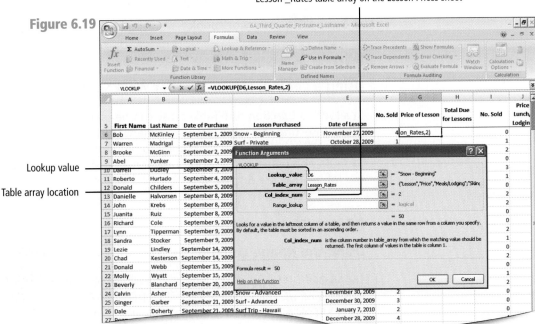

Lookup value

Table array location

5 Click **OK**. The price of the beginning snow lesson is 50 and is now displayed in cell G6. Use the fill handle to copy the formula through cell **G33**.

6 Click cell **H6** and enter a formula for the total due, which is the price of the lesson—found in column G—times the number sold—found in column F. The total due—200—is entered. Use the fill handle to copy the formula through cell **H33**.

7 Click cell **J6**, and in the **Function Library group**, click the **Lookup & Reference** button, and from the list, click **VLOOKUP**. In the **Lookup_Value** box, click cell **D6**. Alternatively, type **d6** In the **Table_array** box, type **Lesson_Rates** In the **Col_index_num**, type **3** and then click **OK**. The result—15—is entered in cell **J6**. Use the fill handle to copy the formula through cell **J33**.

In the table array, the prices for lunch and lodging are in the third column of the table. When a match is made, Excel selects the data in the corresponding cell in the third column and places it in the worksheet.

8 Click cell **K6** and enter a formula to determine the total income from meals/lodging—**=i6*j6**—and copy the formula through **K33**. Click cell **L6** and enter the formula for the total due—Total Meals plus Total Due for Lessons—**=h6+k6**—The value 0 is entered in cell **K6**. Copy the formula through cell **L33**.

9 Select the range **F34:L34**. In the **Function Library group**, click the **AutoSum** button. Place a **Top and Double Bottom Border** around the cell range. Format the ranges **G34:H34** and **J34:L34** with **Accounting Number Format** $ ▾ with **no decimals**. Format the ranges **G6:H6** and **J6:L6** with **Accounting Number Format** $ ▾ with **no decimals**. Format the range **F7:L33** with **Comma Style** ' with **no decimals** and format cells **F6**, **I6**, **F34**, and **I34** with **Comma Style** ' with **no decimals**. In cell **D34**, type **Total** and format it with **Bold** B and **Center** ≡ alignment.

10 **Save** 💾 your workbook.

More Knowledge

Using a Lookup List in Another Workbook

In a lookup function, the table array can be placed in another workbook. When inserting the Table_array argument, click the Collapse Dialog Box button and click in the other workbook to highlight the range. In the resulting formula, the name of the workbook and worksheet along with the range of the table array are displayed.

More Knowledge

Using the Range Lookup

The VLOOKUP function arguments dialog box displays an optional argument *Range_lookup*. This argument is used when an exact match must be made. Enter FALSE in the Range Lookup argument so only an exact match is returned.

Activity 6.9 Editing the Lookup List

Data in a lookup list may need to be changed or updated. Editing the data or inserting or deleting rows or columns keeps the list current. Dana and J. R. added a lesson in the fall that was not included in this list. One of the lessons was incorrectly billed because the new lesson was not listed. In this activity, you will correct the September Lessons worksheet and add the lesson to the price list.

1 Click the **Lesson Prices sheet tab** and insert a row above **row 10**. In cell **A10**, type **Snow Trip - Colorado** Be sure to leave a space before and after the hyphen. In cell **B10**, type **600** and in **C10**, type **2400**.

2 Click the **Name Box arrow**, click **Lesson_Rates**, and confirm that the range—*A5:C19*—displays. Compare your screen with Figure 6.20, and then click **Close**.

Recall that when a row is inserted into the list, the named range changes to include the newly inserted range.

Cells included in the Lesson_Rates range

Figure 6.20

Name of range—Lesson_Rates

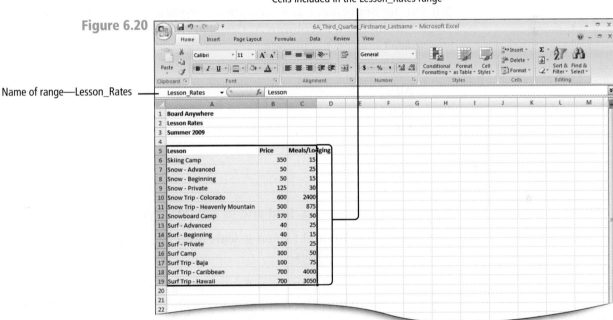

3 Display the **September Lessons sheet** and locate the lessons purchased by Richard Cole—**row 16**. In cell **D16**, select *Heavenly Mountain* and type **Colorado** and as you press Enter, watch the price of the lesson in cell **H16** change to 2,400.

4 **Save** your workbook.

More Knowledge

Using the HLOOKUP Function

The **HLOOKP Function—Horizontal Lookup**—is similar to the VLOOKUP function except Excel searches the value in the top row of a table and returns a value in the same column from a row you specify.

Use the HLOOKUP Function when your comparison values are located in a row across the top of a table of data and you want to look down a specified number of rows. Use VLOOKUP when your comparison values are located in a column to the left of the data you want to find.

Activity 6.10 Determining Sales Amounts Using the COUNTIF Function

Recall that you have used the statistical functions COUNT and COUNTA. Another statistical function—COUNTIF—will count the cells that match a criteria. For Board Anywhere, each employee sells lessons, meals, and lodging, and each month a bonus is provided depending on the number of lessons sold. In this activity, you will use the COUNTIF function to determine the number of lessons each employee sold during September.

1 On the **September Lessons** sheet, beginning in cell **A36**, type the following titles in column A. Confirm that the name J. R. includes a space between his initials.

Sales
Ali
Dana
J. R.
John
Rhonda
Shinpei

2 In cell **B36**, type **No. Sold** and in cell **C36**, type **Bonus** Select the range **A36:C36** and format it with **Bold** [B], **Center** [≡], and with a **Bottom Border** [⊞ ▾].

3 Beginning in cell **F37**, type the following data. The numbers in the first column must be displayed in ascending order—from smallest to largest—as they have been entered.

0	None
2	$5 certificate
3	$15 certificate
9	$20 dinner
12	$30 dinner

4 Click cell **B37**. Click the **Formulas tab**, and in the **Function Library group**, click the **More Functions** button. Point to **Statistical** and from the submenu, click **COUNTIF**, and compare your screen with Figure 6.21.

The COUNTIF Function Arguments dialog box displays with two required arguments—Range and Criteria. The **COUNTIF function** counts the number of cells within a range that meet the given condition.

Figure 6.21

COUNTIF Function
Arguments dialog box

Describes the function

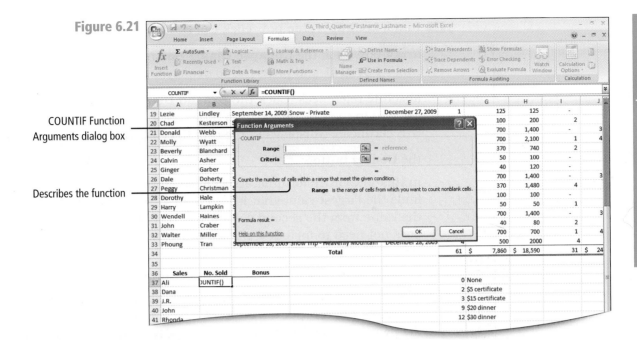

5 In the **Range** box, click the **Collapse Dialog Box** button and select the range **M6:M33**, press F4 to display the range as an absolute reference, and then click the **Expand Dialog Box** button

. In the **Criteria** box, click cell **A37**. Alternatively, in the Criteria box, type **a37** Compare your screen with Figure 6.22, and then click **OK**.

The Function Arguments dialog box displays the completed criteria and the result—4. Ali has sold 4 lessons or trips this month.

The result

Figure 6.22

Range of list

Criteria—the cell that
contains the name *Ali*

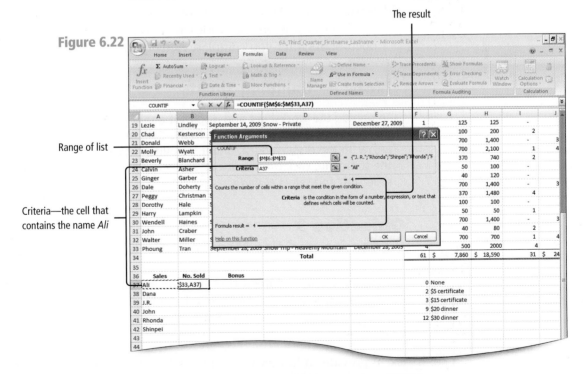

6 Copy the formula in cell **B37** through cell **B42**.

7 Click cell **C37**. You will use the table in columns F and G to insert the bonus each sales person will receive. In the **Function Library group**, click the **Lookup & Reference** button, and then click **VLOOKUP**.

8 In the **Lookup_value** box, click cell **B37** and press ⟨Tab⟩. In the **Table_array** box, click the **Collapse Dialog Box** button 🔳 and select the range **F37:G41** and press ⟨F4⟩ to display both cell references with absolute references. Click the **Expand Dialog Box** button 🔳. Press ⟨Tab⟩ and in the **Col_index_num** box, type **2** Click **OK**. The result—$15 certificate—displays in the cell. In cell **C37**, right-click and click the **Center** button 🔳.

In this VLOOKUP formula, Excel looks in the first column for 4. It finds the largest value that is less than 4, which is 3. It then returns the value from the second column—$15 certificate. A lookup list does not need to include a named range; instead use absolute cell references to identify the lookup range.

9 Use the fill handle to copy the formula through cell **C42**.

10 Select all sheets and in the **Left Footer**, place the **File Name** and in the **Right Footer**, place the **Sheet Name**. Center the worksheets on the page both **Horizontally** and **Vertically**. Display the **September Lessons** sheet in **Landscape Orientation** and **Fit to 1 page**.

11 Click the **Lesson Prices** worksheet, and on the **Home tab**, in the **Cells group**, click the **Format** button. In the displayed list, under **Visibility**, point to **Hide & Unhide**, and from the submenu, click **Hide Sheet**. Alternatively, right-click the Lesson Prices sheet tab and click Hide.

The worksheet is now hidden from view. When you use the **Hide Sheet** command, it does not display in Print Preview and it does not print with the workbook group but it remains a part of the workbook.

12 **Save** 💾 your workbook. If your instructor asks you to submit printed work, **print** the workbook and formulas. You will submit these documents after you complete Activity 6.12. **Close** the workbook.

Note — Unhiding Sheets

To unhide the worksheet and display it again in the workbook, use one of two methods. On the Home tab, in the Cells group, click the Format button arrow. In the displayed list, under Visibility, click Hide & Unhide, and from the submenu, click Unhide Sheet. The second method is to right-click any sheet tab and select *Unhide*.

Objective 3
Customize and Use Microsoft-Created Templates

A **template** is a workbook that has the structure already determined—the format and formulas are completed. A template is useful for workbooks that will be used over and over again, saving much time in creating the worksheet.

Excel provides a library of templates that have been created by Microsoft. You can download a prebuilt template, personalize it for your firm, and save it for future use. Then you can enter the variable information and save the workbook as a regular Excel workbook.

Excel saves templates in a special directory on the hard drive of the computer. The template can also be saved on your removable storage device.

Activity 6.11 Downloading and Personalizing a Template

J. R. and Dana have asked that you prepare an invoice that can be used over and over again, which saves time in creating worksheets. In this activity, you will download, personalize, and save an invoice for Board Anywhere. (It is advisable that you complete Activity 6.11 and 6.12 in the same work session at the same computer.)

1 Click the **Office** menu ⬚ , and click **New**. In the left section, of the **New Workbook** dialog box, under **Microsoft Office Online**, click **Invoices** and compare your screen with Figure 6.23.

The list at the left displays the various types of templates available. *Invoices* is the selected type and several styles display in the center section. The selected invoice displays in the center with a yellow/orange background and is fully displayed at the right, along with a 4-star rating.

Figure 6.23

New Workbook dialog box

List of available templates

The selected invoice

Invoices available

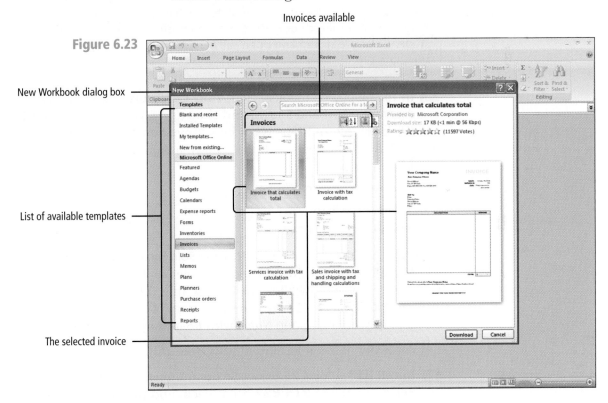

2 In the **Invoices section**, locate and click the invoice named *Services invoice with tax calculation*. Review the display at the right, and then click **Download**.

Alert!

Does your template window match the window in the figure?

When you select a template, it may not always be positioned in the same location in the New Workbook window. Microsoft is intuitive and moves the position of selected templates so the most frequently used ones display at the top of the window.

3 The **Microsoft Office Genuine Advantage** box displays. Click **Continue**.

The first time you download a template, you see a dialog box explaining that this feature is available only to people with genuine Microsoft Office. After Microsoft verifies that your software is legitimate, the messages will no longer appear if you click **Do not show this message again**. If you do not have genuine Microsoft Office software, another dialog box tells you which Microsoft Office programs are installed that are not genuine.

Alert!

Is the template not available?

The Services invoice with tax calculation template may not be available, depending on the installation and version of Office 2007 on your computer. If it is not available, you have two choices—you can search for the template on the Microsoft Web site or you can use the *Services_invoice_with_ tax_calculation.xltx* template included with your student files. To search the Microsoft Web site, under Microsoft Office Online, scroll down and click the Letters option and locate the template—it may be faster to type *Invoice template* in the Search box. Otherwise, navigate to the location where your student files are stored and open the Services_invoice_with_tax_calculation template file.

4 In the displayed invoice, click **Your Company Name** and type **Board Anywhere Surf and Snowboard Shop** and format with **16-point font**. Click cell **A2** and type **www.boardanywhere.biz** Beginning in cell A4, replace the address with the following data and delete the FAX information:

903 South Research Drive
Irvine, CA 92618
Phone (949) 555-0049

5 Click cell **C8** that reads *FOR*. Type **Sold by:** Click cell **D8** and type **Name** Delete **row 10**—*Company Name*—as Board Anywhere does business primarily with individuals. In cell **B14**, type **NUMBER** and in cell **C14** type **PRICE** Scroll to the bottom of the template. In cell **A35**, replace *Your Company Name* with **Board Anywhere** and confirm the company name is formatted with **Bold** **B** .

6 In cell **B15**, type **4.25** to review the number of decimals displayed. Select the range **B15:B27**, right-click, and then click the **Decrease Decimal** button ▪ two times and then delete the contents of cell **B15**. Click cell **C15** and click the **Accounting Number Format** button **$ ▾** . Click cell **D29**—Tax Rate—and type **5%** Click the **Enter** button ✔ on the **Formula Bar**, and then click the **Decrease Decimal** button ▪ two times.

A template is preformatted. In order to display the data in the style for your company, you can alter the format to personalize the template.

7 Click the **Insert tab**, in the **Text group**, click the **Header & Footer button**. In the **Page Setup** dialog box, in the **Header/Footer tab**, click **Custom Footer**. In the **Left** section, click the **Insert File Name** button 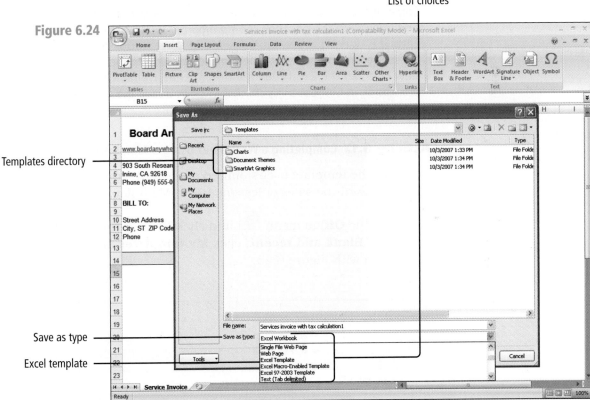 and click **OK** two times.

When using a template, the header and footer is entered using the Header/Footer dialog box. Recall that the insertion point blinks first in the left footer area. The standard entries—file name, sheet name, etc.—can be inserted using the buttons in the dialog box.

8 Click the **Office** menu and click **Save As**. In the **Save As** dialog box, at the bottom under **Save as type**, click the **arrow**, scroll until *Excel Template* displays in the list. Point to **Excel Template** and compare your screen with Figure 6.24.

Excel workbooks are generally saved as Excel files, but they can be saved in other formats. The drop-down list displays those format styles. The default directory for saving a template is the *Templates* directory, which Excel displays.

List of choices

Figure 6.24

Templates directory

Save as type

Excel template

9 Click **Excel Template**.

The Save As dialog box again displays, with **Templates** displayed in the *Save in* area. Excel saves all templates in one location on the computer.

10 In the **File name** box, type **6A_Invoice_Template_Firstname_Lastname** Notice that the **Save in** area is *Templates*, and then click **Save**.

11 From the **Office** menu, , click **Save as**. Navigate to the **Excel Chapter 6** folder, confirm the file name is **6A_Invoice_Template_Firstname_Lastname** and that the **Save as type** is **Excel Template**. Then click **Save**.

12 Click the **Close Window** button .

More Knowledge

Saving and Using Templates

When a template is saved on a shared computer, such as one in a classroom, it can be used or deleted by any student. Because you will use your template later and want to safeguard it, you will save your template on your removable disk. To open a template that has been saved in the template directory, from the Office menu, click New. In the New Workbook dialog box, under Templates, click My Templates. Locate the template and click OK.

When a template is used and saved, it saves as an Excel workbook and not as a template.

More Knowledge

My Template Displays Compatibility Mode in the Title Bar

Some of the templates are created in an earlier version of Microsoft Excel and open with the notation *[Compatibility Mode]* in the Title bar. This indicates it is opened in **Compatibility Mode.** A workbook that was created in an earlier version of Excel will open in Excel 2007 in Compatibility Mode. The new or enhanced Excel 2007 features are not available when working in a workbook in Compatibility Mode. When you save the workbook, it is saved in an earlier version unless you convert it to Excel 2007.

Activity 6.12 Completing a Worksheet Using a Template

Now that the template is customized and saved, you will use this template to record the sales of lessons to Mr. McKinley.

1 Click the **Office** menu and click **New**. In the **Templates** section, under **Blank and recent**, click **My templates** and compare your screen with Figure 6.25.

Figure 6.25

New dialog box

My Templates tab

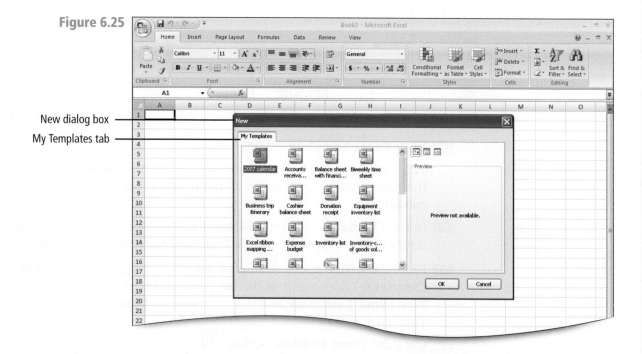

A list of templates that have been created displays in the My Templates tab of the New dialog box. The templates are arranged in alphabetical order and include those built into Excel and those that you create. The list of templates displayed on your screen may differ from the ones shown in the figure.

2 Locate the **6A_Invoice_Template_Firstname_Lastname** icon, click it to select it, and then click **OK**.

The template that you personalized and saved as a template opens as a workbook. Notice that the name in the title bar displays a 1 after the name of the template. In this manner, the original template is preserved so that you can use it over and over again. You will use this invoice to record data about a sale that was made.

3 Click cell **D4** and notice that the **Today** function was entered so that the current date displays.

4 Beginning in cell **A9**, enter the following data about the customer:

Bob McKinley
1340 No. Pine Lane
Cedarville, CA 96104
(500) 555-1234

5 Click cell **D8**, and type **J. R.** to record the person who made this sale. Click cell **A15**, and type **Beginning Snowboard Lessons** Press Tab and under **Hours**, type **4** Press Tab and for **Price** type **50** and then press Enter.

The amount due for the lessons—$200—displays in cell D15 under Amount. Part of the format of this built-in invoice is a formula to calculate sales for each row of data entered.

6 Scroll to the bottom of the invoice and notice that the total due— $210.00—is completed.

When you complete a template, only the variable information needs to be entered. All the formatting and formulas are entered and the invoice is complete. The sales tax has been calculated and the total is determined.

7 From the **Office** menu , click **Save As**. In the **Save As** dialog box, navigate to your **Excel Chapter 6** folder. Name the workbook **6A_McKinley_Firstname_Lastname** and then click **Save**.

8 To submit electronically, follow the instructions provided by your instructor. You will submit these workbooks: **6A_Third_Quarter_Firstname_Lastname**, the template **6A_Invoice_Template_Firstname_Lastname**, and **6A_McKinley_Firstname_Lastname**.

To print, from the **Office** menu , click **Print**. In the Print dialog box, under **Print what**, select **Entire workbook** and click **OK**. From the **Office** menu , click **Close**. **Exit** Excel.

End You have completed Project 6A

Project 6B Quarter 2 Sales

In Activities 6.13 through 6.19, you will prepare sales reports for Board Anywhere. John Smith, the accountant, prepares monthly, quarterly, and annual sales reports, which you will complete. You will link the data in the worksheets in order to ensure accuracy. Your completed work-sheets will look similar to those in Figure 6.26.

For Project 6B, you will need the following files:

e06B_Quarter_1_Sales
e06B_Quarter_2_Sales

You will save your workbooks as
6B_Quarter_2_Sales_Firstname_Lastname
6B_Quarter_1_Sales_Firstname_Lastname
6B_Annual_Sales_Firstname_Lastname
6B_Sales_09_Workspace_Firstname_Lastname

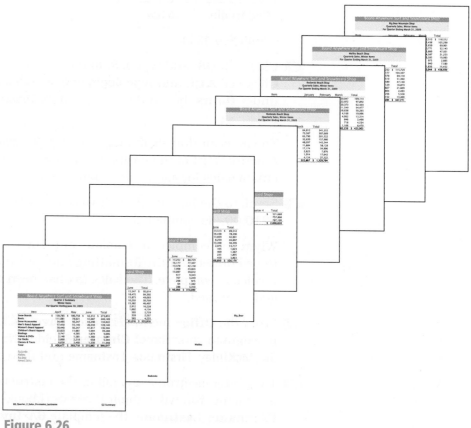

Figure 6.26
Project 6B—Quarter 2 Sales

Objective 4
Transpose Data in a Worksheet and Apply Cell Styles

Data in columns and rows on a worksheet can be rearranged without retyping them. When you *transpose* a block of data, you shift the vertical and horizontal orientation of the data. Styles can be applied to individual cells quickly using the Cell Styles gallery.

Activity 6.13 Transposing Data in a Worksheet

At Board Anywhere, each store location completes quarterly sales reports—one for the winter equipment and one for the summer equipment. The sales reports are then sent to the accounting department. John Smith, the accountant, then combines the totals into a summary worksheet. The report from the Redondo Beach Shop is arranged incorrectly and John has asked you to transpose the data.

1 **Start** Excel. Open the file named **e06B_Quarter_2_Sales** and then **Save** it in your **Excel Chapter 6** folder as **6B_Quarter_2_Sales_ Firstname_Lastname**

This workbook displays the quarterly sales report from each of the three branches—Redondo, Malibu, and Big Bear.

2 In the **Redondo sheet**, notice that the months are entered as row titles and the items are column titles. Recall that it is preferable to place references to time—such as months—as column titles. Click in the **Malibu sheet tab** and notice that the months are displayed as column titles while the items are displayed as row titles. Then click in the **Big_Bear sheet tab** and notice that, like the Malibu sheet, the months are displayed as column titles while the items are displayed as row titles.

In order for the data to be displayed in a similar pattern, the data in the Redondo sheet will be transposed so the row and column titles match those of the other worksheets.

3 Click in the **Redondo sheet tab** and select the range of the worksheet—**A6:K9**. Right-click and click **Copy**.

4 Click cell **A11**. On the **Home tab**, in the **Clipboard group**, click the **Paste button arrow**, click **Paste Special**, and then compare your screen with Figure 6.27.

Figure 6.27

Selected copy range of worksheet

Paste Special dialog box

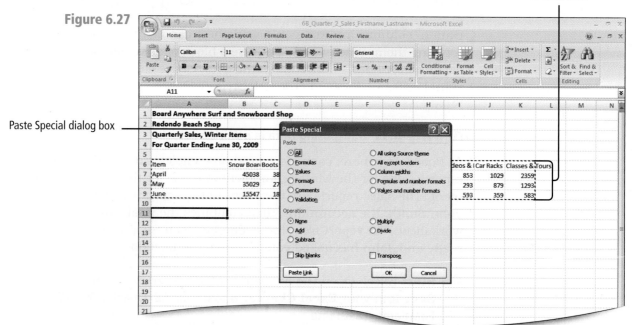

5 In the second column in the last row, click **Transpose**, click **OK**, and then compare your screen with Figure 6.28. Alternatively, on the Paste list, click Transpose.

The data now displays the months as column titles and the items as row titles. Because the copy and paste areas cannot overlap unless they are the same size and shape, the data is pasted into another area of the worksheet. The row titles are now the column titles and the column titles are now the row titles.

Original data range

Figure 6.28

Transposed data

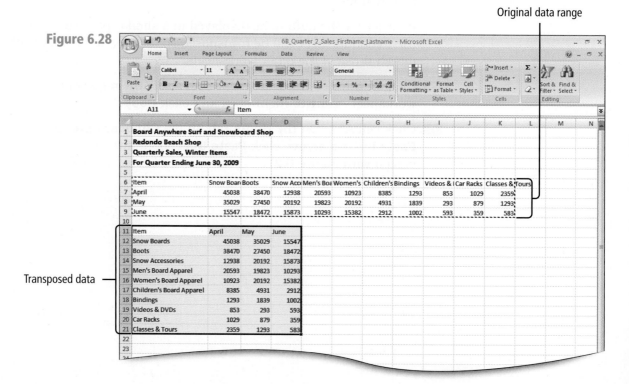

6 Select rows **6:10**, right-click and click **Delete**. Confirm that the column titles display in **row 6**. **Save** your workbook.

Activity 6.14 Applying Cell Styles to a Worksheet

There are various ways to format a worksheet, including the use of *cell styles*—a defined set of formatting characteristics, such as fonts and font sizes, number formats, cell borders, and cell shading. In this activity, you will apply cell styles to a worksheet.

1 In the **Redondo sheet**, click cell **E6**, and type **Total** In cell **A17** type **Total**

2 **Select all sheets**, and then select the range **B7:E17**. In the **Editing group**, click the **Sum** button **Σ ▾** .

Recall that rows and columns can be added simultaneously when the range is selected. Also recall that the Sum function is applied to all worksheets when they are grouped. In this manner, all of the data in this range of cells is summed on all sheets at the same time. For this to work properly, the data must be arranged in the same location on each worksheet.

3 Select the column titles—the range **A6:E6**. In the **Styles group**, click the **Cell Styles** button, and then compare your screen with Figure 6.29.

The *Cell Styles gallery* displays a palette of styles that can be applied to selected cells or ranges. Number formats can also be applied in this gallery.

Figure 6.29

Worksheets grouped

Cell Styles button

Cell Styles gallery

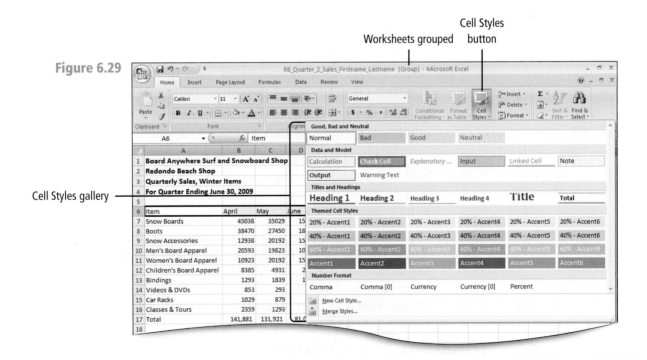

4 In the **Cell Style gallery**, under the **Titles and Headings section**, point to *Heading 1* and as you do, notice that Live Preview is used to display the style on the worksheet. Point to *Heading 2* and view this style, and then point to *Heading 3*. Click **Heading 2**, and then click the **Center** button ▤.

5 Select the total row—**B17:E17**. In the **Styles group**, click the **Cell Styles** button and under **Titles and Headings**, click the last style—**Total**.

The Cell Styles gallery applies one format at a time. In order to apply several selections to the range, the gallery must be accessed again.

6 In the **Styles group**, click the **Cell Styles** button and from the displayed gallery, under **Number Format**, click **Currency [0]**. Select the range **B7:E7** and using the skills practiced, in the **Cell Styles gallery** click **Currency [0]** to apply this style to the range.

This style applies the Accounting Number Format without decimals. If you want to display decimals, use the Currency Style.

7 Select the range **B8:E16** and in the **Styles group**, click the **Cell Styles** button and under **Number Format**, click **Comma [0]**.

8 Click cell **A1**. In the **Styles group**, click the **Cell Styles** button and from the gallery, under **Themed Cell Styles**, click the first column, fourth choice—**Accent1**. Select the range **A2:A4**. In the **Styles group**, click the **Cell Styles** button and from the gallery, under **Themed Cell Styles**, click the first column, first choice—**20% - Accent1**.

When a theme is changed, this color scheme will also change to match the new theme. When colors are selected from the themed colors, they will change when the theme is changed. A standard color does not change when a different theme is selected.

9 Select cell **A1**. In the **Font group**, click the **Font size button** ⌸11 ▾⌸, and then click **18**. Select the range **A1:E1** and in the **Alignment group**, click the **Merge & Center** button ▣▾. Using the skills you practiced, **Merge and Center rows 2**, **3**, and **4** of the title.

10 On the **Page Layout tab**, in the **Themes group**, click the **Themes** button and from the displayed gallery, under Built-In in the first column of the second row, click **Concourse**. Adjust the column widths to fully display the data.

11 On all worksheets, insert a **Left Footer** that displays the **File Name** and in the **Right Footer** display the **Sheet Name**. Format the worksheets so they are centered both **Vertically** and **Horizontally**. **Ungroup** the worksheets and click in the **Malibu sheet tab** and change **row 2** to read **Malibu Shop** In the **Big_Bear sheet tab**, change **row 2** to read **Big Bear Shop**

12 Save 🖫 your workbook.

Objective 5
Use 3-D References to Link Data in Worksheets and Workbooks and Create a Workspace

Data in a worksheet can be linked to help ensure the accuracy of the resulting data. When changes are made in one workbook, they are also made in all linked workbooks. When worksheets are created using the same pattern, linking the workbooks is a useful and convenient way to reference several worksheets that follow the same pattern and the cells on each worksheet in order to summarize the data. Several related Excel workbooks can be saved as one file and opened at the same time when saved as a workspace.

Activity 6.15 Linking Worksheet Data Using a 3-D Reference

Information from several worksheets of a workbook may be linked or summarized into one worksheet using a **3-D Reference**—a reference that refers to the same cell or range of cells on multiple sheets. In this activity, you will report the quarterly sales by using 3-D References to link the amounts in the reports from each branch.

1 Right-click the **Redondo sheet tab** and click **Move or Copy**. In the **Move or Copy** dialog box, confirm that **Redondo** is selected, click **Create a copy**, and click **OK**.

You have inserted a copy of the Redondo sheet as the first worksheet of the workbook. This worksheet has a format, which you will choose to retain. Removing the data and editing the title is all that is needed for the Summary sheet to be ready for new data.

2 Rename **Redondo (2)** to **Q2 Summary** In the **Q2 Summary** sheet, in cell **A2**, type **Quarter 2 Summary** and in cell **A3**, delete **Quarterly Sales** so the cell reads *Winter Items*. Select the range **B7:D16** and press Delete.

3 Click cell **B7** and type **=sum(** Click the **Redondo sheet tab** and click cell **B7**. Press Shift and click the **Big_Bear sheet tab**. Release Shift and in the **Formula Bar**, click the **Enter** button ✔, and then compare your screen with Figure 6.30.

The total snow board sales for April—$130,785—is entered in cell B7 on the Q2 Summary sheet. The formula that displays in the Formula Bar indicates the name of the function—SUM—and the range of the worksheets included in the function. This formula begins with the sheet named Redondo and includes all worksheets through Big Bear. The exclamation mark separates the worksheet names from the cell referenced in each worksheet—cell B7. The 3-D Reference can be used only when the data is in the same cell in all worksheets.

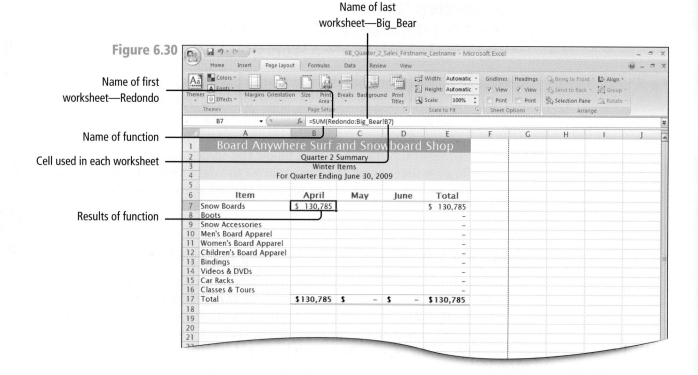

Figure 6.30

Name of last worksheet—Big_Bear

Name of first worksheet—Redondo

Name of function

Cell used in each worksheet

Results of function

=SUM(Redondo:Big_Bear!B7)

4 Click cell **C7** and type **=sum(** Click the **Redondo sheet tab** and click cell **C7**. Press ⇧Shift and click the **Big_Bear sheet tab** and in the **Formula Bar**, click the **Enter button** ✓. The May snow board sales—$100,758—displays in the cell.

5 Using the skills you practiced, enter a 3-D Reference in cell **D7** that adds the June sales for the three branches.

6 In the **Q2 Summary sheet**, select the range **B7:D7**. Use the fill handle to copy the formulas in **row 7** through **row 16**. Click in the cells to confirm the accuracy of the formulas.

7 Format the range **B8:D16** with **Comma Style** ٬ and **no decimals**. Adjust the column widths if needed. **Save** 🖫 your workbook.

Activity 6.16 Linking Workbook Data with a 3-D Reference

Data can be linked between workbooks. In this activity, you will create a workbook that summarizes the sales for each store for the year. In this activity, you will link the quarterly sales for each store into a workbook that reports the total sales by quarter for the year.

1 Open a new, blank workbook and **Save** it in your **Excel Chapter 6** folder as **6B_Annual_Sales_Firstname_Lastname** Click the **View tab**. In the **Window group**, click the **Switch Windows** button and from the list, click **6B_Quarter_2_Sales_Firstname_Lastname**.

2 Select the range **A1:E6** and right-click. Click **Copy** and in the **Window group**, click **Switch Windows** and from the list click **6B_Annual_Sales_Firstname_Lastname**. Right-click cell **A1** and click **Paste**. Change cell **A2** to **Annual Sales** and change cell **A4** to read **For Year Ending December 31, 2009** On the **Page Layout tab**, in the **Themes group**, click the **Themes** button and click **Concourse**.

3 Point to the **column E** heading and when the ⬇ pointer displays, right-click and click **Insert**. Delete the column titles in the range **A6:D6**. In cell **A6**, type **Store** In cell **B6**, type **Quarter 1** and press Enter. Click cell **B6**, and drag the fill handle to the right through **Quarter 4** in cell **E6**. Adjust column widths to accommodate the longest entries.

4 Beginning in cell **A7**, type the following row titles and adjust column widths:

| Redondo |
| Malibu |
| Big Bear |

5 From your data files, open the file named **e06B_Quarter_1_Sales** and save it to your **Excel Chapter 6** folder as **6B_Quarter_1_Sales_Firstname_Lastname**.

Notice that this workbook contains the same format as the Quarter 2 workbook you have completed. It is helpful to follow the same arrangement of data in workbooks with similar reports that are created periodically.

6 On the **View tab**, the **Window group**, use the **Switch Windows** button to return to the **6B_Annual_Sales_Firstname_Lastname** workbook.

The annual sales workbook will be used to collect the income data from each of the shops on a quarterly basis.

7 Click cell **B7**, and type = In the **Window group**, click **Switch Windows** and click **6B_Quarter_1_Sales_Firstname_Lastname**. Click the **Redondo sheet tab**, click cell **E17**, and then press Enter. Click cell **B7**, and then compare your screen with Figure 6.31.

The total sales, for the first quarter, for Redondo, is entered into the cell, using a linked cell reference to a different workbook. When you press Enter, you are returned to the workbook that contains the formula.

Figure 6.31

File name of workbook   Name of worksheet

Formula displayed in Formula Bar

Cell identified

Result in cell is total Quarter 1 sales of Redondo

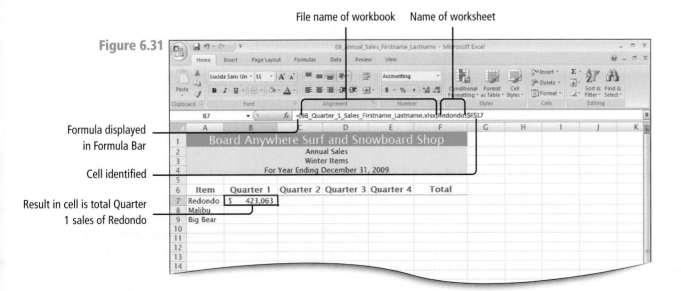

8 In the **6B_Quarter_1_Sales_Firstname_Lastname** workbook, click the **Malibu sheet** and click cell **E17**, right-click, and click **Copy**. Use **Switch Windows** to return to the **6B_Annual_Sales_Firstname_Lastname** workbook. Click cell **B8**. On the **Home tab**, in the **Clipboard group**, click the **Paste** button and from the list, click **Paste Link**.

An alternative method to link a cell from one workbook to another is to use the Paste Link command.

9 Press Ctrl + ' to display formulas and notice that the formula contains the same context using either method of linking the cell. Then press Ctrl + ' to redisplay the results.

10 Use the fill handle to copy the formula in cell **B8** to cell **B9**. Click cell **B9** and in the **Formula Bar**, select **Malibu**, type **Big_Bear** and then press Enter.

The total quarterly sales for the stores are entered into the annual sales report. When you link data in this manner, the worksheet names cannot have a space, which is the reason the Big_Bear sheet is named in this manner.

11 Click cell **C7** and type **=sum(** On the **View tab**, in the **Window group**, click **Switch Windows**, and then click **6B_Quarter_2_Sales_Firstname_Lastname**. Click the **Redondo sheet tab**, click cell **E17**, and press Enter.

12 Use the fill handle to copy the formula in cell **C7** through cell **C9**. Click cell **C8**, and in the **Formula Bar**, select **Redondo**, and type **Malibu**, and then press Enter. Click cell **C9**, and in the **Formula Bar**, select **Redondo**, and then type **Big_Bear** and press Enter.

Because each workbook uses the same naming conventions and organization for the data, it is easy to edit the 3-D formulas to achieve the results you desire.

13 Click cell **A10** and type **Total** Select the range **B7:F10** and on the **Home tab**, in the **Editing group**, click the **Sum** button Σ ▾ .

Format the range **B8:F9** with **Comma Style** ' with **no decimals**. Select the range **B10:F10**. In the **Styles group**, click the **Cell Styles** button. In the **Cell Styles gallery**, under **Titles and Headings**, click **Total**. Adjust column widths if needed.

14 **Delete Sheet2** and **Sheet3**. In the **Left Footer** insert the **File Name**. Center the worksheet both **Horizontally** and **Vertically**.

15 **Save** 💾 your workbook.

Activity 6.17 Saving a Workspace and Editing Linked Data

When the accountant, John Smith, works on one of the quarterly reports, he often works in all of them in the group. A **workspace** is a group of worksheets that are saved together with a file name that can open all of the files simultaneously. When you save a workspace, information about the workbook is saved, including window sizes and screen positions. However, the workspace does not contain the workbooks; it contains only links to the original workbooks. In this activity, you will save in a workspace the workbooks that report the quarterly and annual sales.

1 On the **View tab**, in the **Window group**, click the **Switch Windows** button and confirm that you have three worksheets open: **6B_Quarter_1_Sales_Firstname_Lastname**, **6B_Annual_Sales_Firstname_Lastname**, and **6B_Quarter_2_Sales_Firstname_Lastname**. If you have other worksheets open, close them.

2 In the **Window group**, click the **Save Workspace** button. Navigate to your **Excel Chapter 6** folder. In the **File name** box, type **6B_Sales_09_Workspace_Firstname_Lastname** and then compare your screen with Figure 6.32. Then click **Save**. If a warning box displays asking if you want to save changes to other workbooks, click **Yes**. **Close** all workbooks.

The Save Workspace dialog box opens and only saved workspaces are displayed in the workbook list. The Save as type box indicates Workspaces.

A workspace contains no data but only the information to locate the worksheets contained in the workspace. In order for the workspace to work, all related documents must be located on the computer. If you later rename any of the worksheets, the workspace becomes invalid.

Save Workspace button

Figure 6.32

Save Workspace dialog box

File name

Save as type: Workspaces

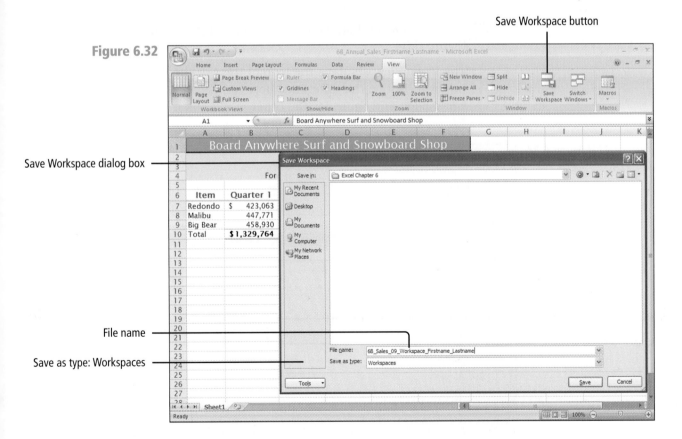

3 Click the **Office button** and click **Open**. Navigate to your **Excel Chapter 6** folder. In the **Open** dialog box, at the right side, locate and click the **Views button arrow**, and compare your screen with Figure 6.33.

Figure 6.33

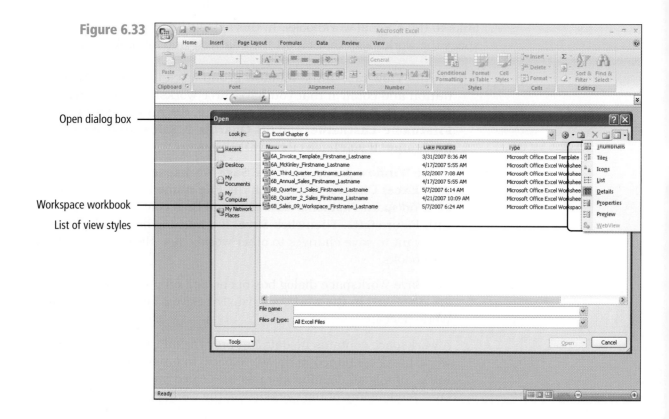

Open dialog box

Workspace workbook

List of view styles

4 In the displayed list, click **Icons** and compare your screen with Figure 6.34.

The Icons view displays the icon of the workbook with the name under it. Notice the difference between the icon displayed for the workspace and those for the other workbooks.

Figure 6.34

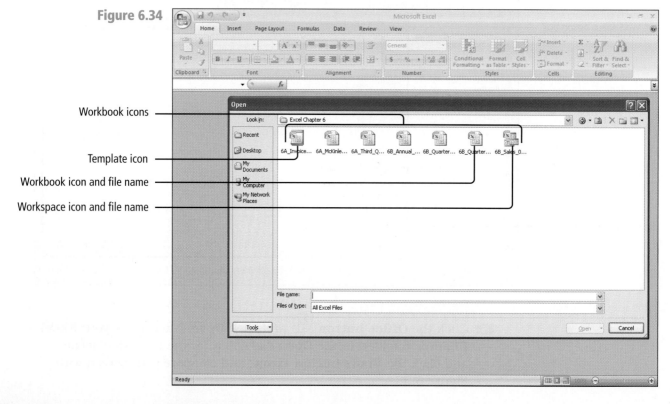

Workbook icons

Template icon

Workbook icon and file name

Workspace icon and file name

5 Click the **View button arrow**, and then click **Details**. Locate the workspace saved as **6B_Sales_09_Workspace_Firstname_Lastname**.

In this view, notice the icon displays at the left. In the dialog box, under the Type heading, the workspace is indicated by *Microsoft Office Excel Workspace.* A workspace is saved with the extension .xlw.

Alert! — **Why doesn't my computer display file extensions?**

The extension of the workbook name may not display, depending on the default of your computer system. To change to display the extension—or to remove the extension from the display—click the **Start** button. In **My Computer**, open the folder that contains the files you want to view. On the **Tools** menu, click **Folder Options**, and then click the **View tab**. To see the file name extensions, clear the **Hide file extensions for known file types** check box, and then click **Apply** and then **OK**.

The default for the files in this chapter is not to display the extension in the Title bar of the workbook.

6 Click the **6B_Sales_09_Workspace_Firstname_Lastname** workspace and click **Open**.

The three workbooks of the workspace all open at the same time. Recall that the workspace saves only links to the workbooks.

Alert! — **Why isn't the file name displayed in the title bar?**

When the workbooks in the workspace open, they may display in minimized view. The title of the worksheet displays just under the Formula Bar and the sheet tabs may not display. To display in full view, click the **Maximize** button on the title bar of the worksheets.

7 In the Title bar, click the **Maximize** button. Click the **View tab**, and in the **Window group**, click the **Switch Windows** button. Click the **6B_Quarter_2_Sales_Firstname_Lastname**. Click the **Redondo sheet tab** and click cell **C14** and change the number of Video sales for May to **1,293**. Then click the **Big_Bear sheet tab** and click cell **B11** and change the number of Women's Apparel to **18,889** Click in the **Q2 Summary sheet tab** and notice that the total in cell **E17** is now changed from $983,077 to $994,077 to reflect the changes.

When you choose to maximize one open worksheet of the workgroup, all worksheets are maximized. Because the totals refer to the information that was corrected and the data is linked with 3-D references, all workbooks are updated when edited.

8 In the **Window group**, click the **Switch Windows** button, and then click the **6B_Annual_Sales_Firstname_Lastname** workbook. Notice that the total sales for Quarter 2 in cell **C10** has been updated to *$994,077* to reflect the changes. Compare your screen with Figure 6.35 and then **Save** your workbooks.

Figure 6.35

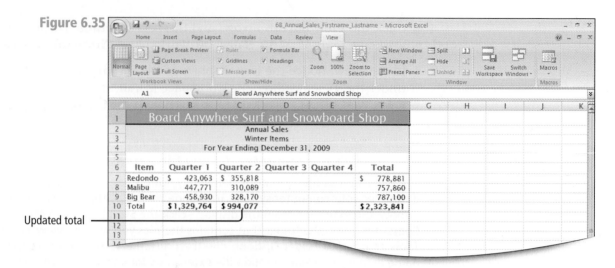

Updated total

Objective 6
Create Hyperlinks

Moving between worksheets is usually accomplished by clicking the worksheet tab, but moving between workbooks is completed in several different ways. A **hyperlink** is text in a cell that you click to go to another location in a worksheet or workbook. Inserting hyperlinks in a worksheet is a useful and convenient way to move between worksheets of a workbook or between different workbooks.

Activity 6.18 Inserting a Hyperlink in a Worksheet

When the accountant, John Smith, works on one of the quarterly reports, he would like to use links to provide a faster way to move between the worksheets and workbooks. In this activity, you will insert hyperlinks in a workbook so that John can move quickly between the worksheets.

1 With the workbooks of the workspace open, on the **View tab**, in the **Window group** click **Switch Windows** and display the **6B_Quarter_ 2_Sales_Firstname_Lastname** workbook. Click the **Q2_Summary sheet tab**.

2 Beginning in cell **A19** and continuing through cell **A21**, type the following worksheet names:

Redondo
Malibu
Big Bear

3 Click cell **A19**—*Redondo*. Click the **Insert tab** and in the **Links group**, click the **Hyperlink** button, and then compare your screen with Figure 6.36. Alternatively, right-click and on the shortcut menu, click Hyperlink.

The Insert Hyperlink dialog box displays the workbooks available in the folder. The *Link to* area displays the type of locations where the link can be entered, and the *Look in* box indicates the exact location for the link. Redondo is entered in the *Link to* box because that is what displays in the selected cell. This text can be entered when the cell is empty, but if the cell contains data, it cannot be altered.

Look in area

Figure 6.36

Insert Hyperlink dialog box

Link to area

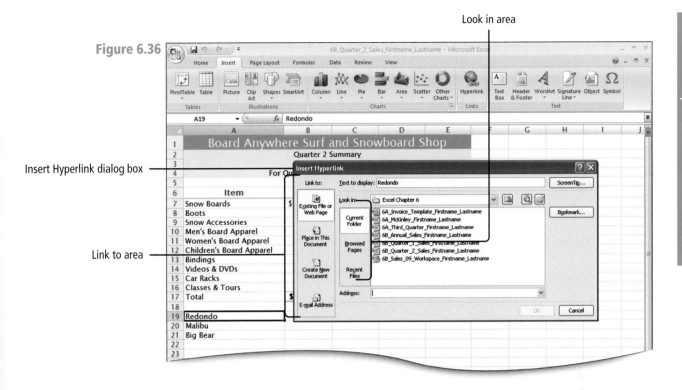

4 In the **Link to** area, click **Place in This Document** and compare your screen with Figure 6.37.

The Insert Hyperlink dialog box now displays the worksheets of the workbook. At the upper right corner is a button where you can add a ScreenTip to the hyperlink.

Place hyperlink in
this worksheet

Text for the
hyperlink

ScreenTip button

Figure 6.37

Cell that will become active

Place hyperlink in
this document command

Worksheets of this document

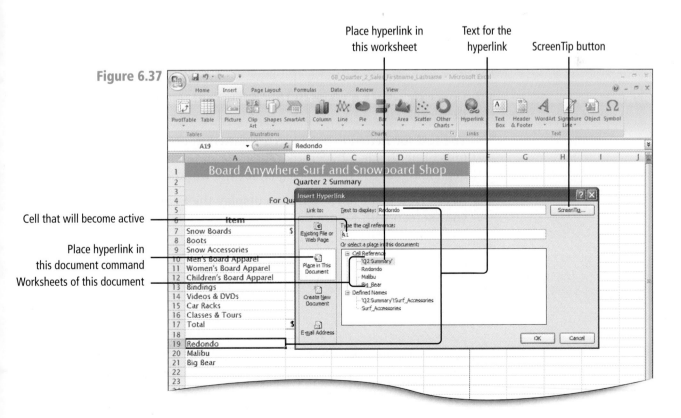

5 In the **Text to display** section, confirm that *Redondo* is displayed. At the right, click **ScreenTip**, compare your screen with Figure 6.38, and then in the **ScreenTip** text box, type **Click to move to the Redondo sheet** Click **OK**.

The Set Hyperlink ScreenTip dialog box displays. The text that displays in the worksheet displays the Text to display area, which can be changed in the dialog box.

You can enter a ScreenTip that will display in the worksheet when you point to the cell that contains the hyperlink. Recall you have used ScreenTips to identify the buttons that display on the Ribbon.

Figure 6.38

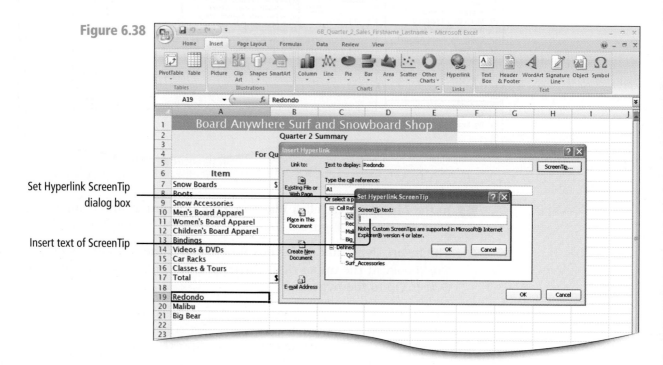

Set Hyperlink ScreenTip dialog box

Insert text of ScreenTip

6 Under **Or select a place in this document**, click **Redondo**, and then click **OK**.

The text for *Redondo* has been formatted in orange and underlined, indicating this is a hyperlink. The color of the hyperlink differs depending on the theme selected for the workbook.

7 In cell **A19** point to **Redondo** to display the ScreenTip and compare your screen with Figure 6.39.

Figure 6.39

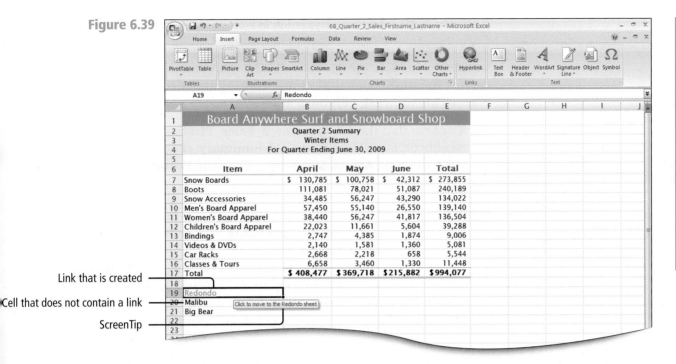

Link that is created

Cell that does not contain a link

ScreenTip

8 Click cell **A19**—**Redondo**—to display the Redondo worksheet. Click cell **A19** and type **Quarter 2 Summary** and in the **Formula Bar**, click the **Enter** button ✔. In the **Links group**, click the **Hyperlink** button. Confirm that under **Link to**, **Place in This Document** is selected. In the **Text to display** text box, confirm that **Quarter 2 Summary** sheet is displayed. Click the **ScreenTip** button and in the **Set Hyperlink ScreenTip**, type **To access the Quarter 2 Summary** and then click **OK**. In the **Or select a place in this document**, click **Q2 Summary**, and then click **OK**.

9 Click cell **A19** to use the hyperlink to display the **Q2 Summary** worksheet. Notice the color of the hyperlink to Redondo has changed to turquoise.

After a hyperlink has been used, the color of the link changes color. The hyperlink will access the other worksheet, no matter the color of the link.

10 Using the skills you practiced, click cell **A20** and insert a hyperlink to the **Malibu** worksheet. Insert a ScreenTip that reads **Click to move to the Malibu sheet** Use the hyperlink to display the **Malibu** worksheet and click cell **A19**. Type **Quarter 2 Summary** and insert a hyperlink to the **Q2 Summary** worksheet. For the hyperlink, display a ScreenTip that displays **To access Quarter 2 Summary** Then use the hyperlink to return to the Q2 Summary.

11 Using the skills you practiced, insert a hyperlink from cell **A21** of the **Q2 Summary** sheet to the **Big_Bear** worksheet. Include a ScreenTip that displays **Click to move to the Big Bear sheet** In the **Big_Bear** worksheet, in cell **A19**, type **Quarter 2 Summary** Include a ScreenTip that displays **To access Quarter 2 Summary** and insert a hyperlink back to the **Q2 Summary** sheet.

12 **Save** 🖫 your workbook.

Activity 6.19 Inserting a Hyperlink in Workbooks

John Smith would like to be able to quickly access the annual summary workbook. In this activity, you will link the annual summary workbook to each of the workbooks that contain the quarterly reports and provide ScreenTips to assist with navigation.

1 Confirm that the **6B Quarter_2_Sales_Firstname_Lastname** workbook is active with the **Q2 Summary sheet** displayed. Click cell **A22** and type **Annual Summary** and on the **Formula Bar**, click the **Enter** button ☑.

2 On the **Insert tab**, in the **Links group**, click the **Hyperlink** button. In the **Link to** section, click **Existing File or Web Page**. From the list in the **Current Folder**, locate and click the **6B_Annual_Sales_Firstname_Lastname** workbook. In the **Text to display** text box, confirm **Annual Summary** displays. Click the **ScreenTip** button and in the **Set Hyperlink ScreenTip** dialog box, type **Click to access the Annual Summary** and then click **OK two times**.

Alert! | **Why do I have two documents with the same name?**

While you are working on a file, a temporary file is created. In the directory, the temporary file is recognized by the tilde ~ in front of the file name. When you save and close the file, this temporary file disappears. A file name that includes the tilde cannot be opened.

3 Click cell **A22**—the link to the **Annual Summary** workbook.

Clicking this link quickly displays the Annual Sales workbook.

4 Click cell **C6**—the column title for Quarter 2. In the **Links group**, click **Hyperlink**. In the **Insert Hyperlink** dialog box, confirm that the **Link to** is **Existing File or Web Page**. In the **Look in** box, click the **6B_Quarter_2_Sales_Firstname_Lastname** file. At the top right corner of the dialog box, click the **ScreenTip** button.

5 In the **Set Hyperlink ScreenTip** dialog box, in the **ScreenTip** text box, type **Click to access Quarter 2 Sales report** and then click **OK**. In the **Insert Hyperlink** dialog box, click **OK**.

6 Right-click cell **B6** and click the **Format Painter** button ☑ and then click cell **C6** to format the column title to match the other column titles. Click in another cell in the worksheet and then point to cell **C6** to display the ScreenTip, indicating this is a link even though it is no longer formatted as a link, and compare your screen with Figure 6.40.

Figure 6.40

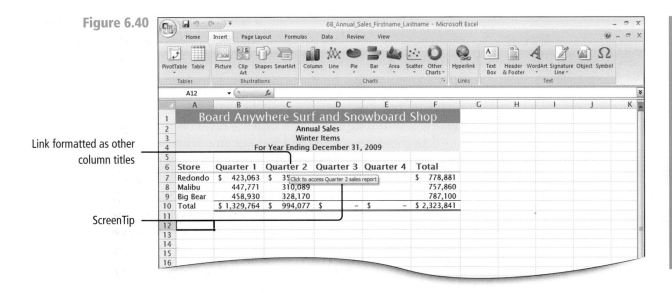

Link formatted as other column titles

ScreenTip

7 **Save** 💾 your workbooks.

8 To submit electronically, follow the instructions provided by your instructor to submit the four files associated with this workspace, **6B_Quarter_1_Sales_Firstname_Lastname**, **6B_Annual_Sales_Firstname_Lastname**, **6B_Quarter_2_Sales_Firstname_Lastname**, and **6B_Sales_09_Workspace_Firstname_Lastname**. To print, from the **Office** menu, click **Print**. In the **Print** dialog box, under **Print what**, select **Entire workbook** and click **OK**. From the **Office** menu, click **Close**. **Exit** Excel.

End **You have completed Project 6B** ——————

🔘 There's More You Can Do!

From My Computer, navigate to the student files that accompany this textbook. In the folder **02_theres_more_you_can_do**, locate and open the folder for this chapter. Open and print the instructions for this project, which are provided to you in Adobe PDF format.

Try It!—Saving Excel Workbooks in PDF and Other Formats

In this Try It! exercise, you will save a workbook in a previous version of Excel and in Binary format. You will also create a PDF file of the worksheet.

Content-Based Assessments

Summary

Worksheets that use named ranges in formulas provide a description of the result of the formula. Worksheets have been transposed so the columns become rows and the rows become columns. The cell styles and themes have been used to provide a professional worksheet. Customizing a built-in template that can be used again and again saves time and provides a consistent format for the workbook. Linking data in worksheets of a workbook and between different workbooks maintains accuracy because a change in one place will be updated in all places that use that data. Hyperlinks are inserted to move quickly between worksheets and workbooks.

Key Terms

Content-Based Assessments

Matching

Match each term in the second column with its correct definition in the first column. Write the letter of the term on the blank line in front of the correct definition.

_____ **1.** A cell that is identified by a name, which is used in a formula rather than the cell reference.

_____ **2.** A range that is identified by a name, which is used in a formula rather than the cell references.

_____ **3.** A name that represents a cell, range of cells, formula, or constant value.

_____ **4.** A list that displays all names of defined cells and ranges available to use in the active workbook where the name can be selected to use in the formula.

_____ **5.** The dialog box that displays all of the names available in the workbook, their cell references, and sheet names.

_____ **6.** Used to create cell and range names from existing row and column titles by using a selection of cells in the worksheet.

_____ **7.** The list that displays the functions and named cells and ranges as the formula is typed into the cell and is used to complete the formula.

_____ **8.** In a lookup function, the argument that is used when an exact match is required.

_____ **9.** Without using Defined Names, the area where you define a cell or range name.

_____ **10.** A function that compares the values in a cell with a defined vertical list and when a match is found, places a corresponding value in the original worksheet

_____ **11.** The full name of the VLOOKUP function.

_____ **12.** The entry in the worksheet that will be compared to a value in the lookup list.

_____ **13.** A table of text, numbers, or logical values in which data is looked up.

_____ **14.** In a lookup list, the column number in a table from which the matching value will be returned.

_____ **15.** A function that compares the values in a cell with a defined horizontal list and when a match is found, places a corresponding value in the original worksheet

A Column Index Number

B Create from Selection

C Defined Name

D HLOOKUP function

E Formula AutoComplete

F Lookup value

G Name Box

H Name Manager

I Named cell

J Named range

K Range lookup

L Table array

M Use in Formula

N Vertical Lookup

O VLOOKUP function

Content-Based Assessments

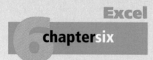
Fill in the Blank

Write the correct word in the space provided.

1. In a four-column lookup table, if the value that will be entered into the worksheet displays in the third column, then the column index number is _____.

2. The full name of the HLOOKUP function is _____ _____.

3. The function that counts the number of cells within a range that meet the given condition is the _____ function.

4. The command that conceals the worksheet so it does not display in Print Preview and does not print with the workbook group is the _____ _____ command.

5. When a worksheet is hidden and you wish to display it again, select the _____ _____ command.

6. A workbook that has a predetermined structure and is saved so it can be used over and over again is a(n) _____.

7. To shift the vertical and horizontal orientation of the worksheet, use the _____ feature.

8. When naming a cell or range of cells, use an underscore to replace a(n) _____.

9. A defined set of formatting characteristics, such as fonts and font sizes, number formats, borders, and shading that is available from a gallery is accessed from the _____ group.

10. A cell reference that refers to the same cell or range of cells on multiple sheets is a(n) _____ reference.

11. A group of workbooks saved together so they can be opened simultaneously is a(n) _____.

12. A link that is used to move between worksheets or workbooks is a(n) _____.

13. When a worksheet or template is created in an earlier version of Excel, _____ Mode displays in the worksheet title.

14. In a 3-D Reference, the _____ is used to separate the sheet name from the cell reference.

15. All open workbooks are saved as one file when you save as a(n) _____.

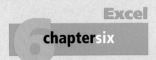
Skills Review

Project 6C — Payroll

In this project, you will apply all the Objectives found in Project 6A.

Objectives: 1. *Create Formulas Using Named Ranges;* **2.** *Utilize Lookup Lists;* **3.** *Customize and Use Microsoft-Created Templates.*

In the following Skills Review project, you will create a workbook for Board Anywhere that reports the payroll for one week. Your completed workbook will look similar to the one shown in Figure 6.41.

For Project 6C, you will need the following files:

e06C_Payroll
Weekly_time_sheet_with _breaks (Excel template)

You will save your workbooks as
6C_Payroll_Firstname_Lastname
6C_McKinley_Time_Card_Firstname_Lastname
6C_Time_Card_Firstname_Lastname (Excel template)

Figure 6.41

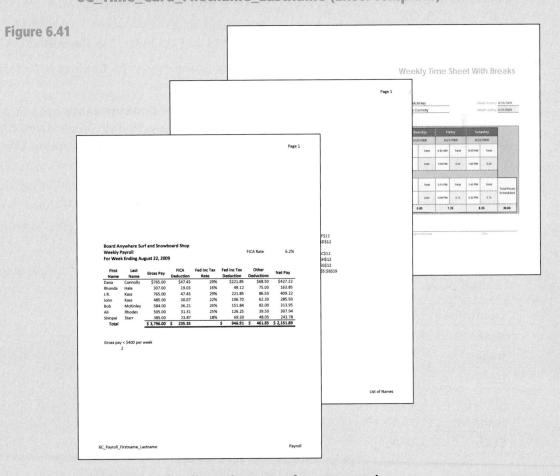

(Project 6C–Payroll continues on the next page)

(Project 6C–Payroll continued)

1. **Start** Excel. Open the file named **e06C_Payroll**, and then save it in your **Excel Chapter 6** folder as **6C_Payroll_Firstname_Lastname**

2. On **Sheet1**, click cell **B6** and on the **Home tab**, in the **Editing group**, click the **Sort & Filter** button, and from the displayed list, click **Sort A to Z**.

3. Click cell **H2**. On the **Formulas tab**, in the **Defined Names group**, click **Define Name**. In the displayed **New Name** dialog box, confirm the name *FICA_Rate* and click **OK**.

4. Click cell **D6** and type =c6* In the **Defined Names group**, click **Use in Formula** and click **FICA_Rate**. In the **Formula Bar**, click the **Enter** button. The FICA deduction—*$47.43*—displays in the cell.

5. Use the fill handle to copy the formula in cell **D6** through cell **D12**.

6. Click the **Sheet2 sheet tab**. This sheet contains the lookup table for the federal income tax rate. Click cell **A4**. On the **Data tab**, in the **Sort & Filter group**, click the **Sort Smallest to Largest** button to sort this lookup table correctly in ascending numeric order.

7. Select the range **A4:B19**. On the **Formulas tab**, in the **Defined Names group**, click the **Define Name** button. In the **New Name** dialog box, in the **Name** box, type **Tax_Withholding** and then click **OK**.

8. Rename **Sheet2** to **Tax Rates** and rename **Sheet1** to **Payroll** On the **Payroll sheet**, click cell **E6**.

9. On the **Formulas tab**, in the **Function Library group**, click the **Lookup & Reference** button, and from the displayed list, click **VLOOKUP**.

10. In the VLOOKUP Function Arguments dialog box, in the **Lookup_value** box, click cell **C6** and press Tab. In the **Table_array** text area, click the **Collapse Dialog Box** button. Click the **Tax Rates sheet tab**, and select the range **A4:B19** and click the **Expand Dialog Box** button. Alternatively, in the **Table_array** text area, type **Tax_Withholding**

11. Click in the **Col_index_num** box, type **2** and then click **OK**. Right-click cell **E6** and click the **Percent Style** button. Use the fill handle to copy the formula in cell **E6** through cell **E12**.

12. Click cell **F6** and type a formula to determine the federal tax deductions— =c6*e6 Copy the formula in cell **F6** through cell **F12**.

13. Click cell **G6** and enter the following data for each employee. Type the numbers as displayed; they will be formatted later.

Connolly	68.5
Hale	75
Kass	86.5
Kass	62.3
McKinley	82
Rhodes	39.5
Starr	48.05

(Project 6C–Payroll continues on the next page)

Content-Based Assessments

(Project 6C–Payroll continued)

14. Click cell **H6** and enter the formula to determine net pay—**=c6-d6-f6-g6** Copy the formula through cell **H12**.

15. Select the range **C6:C12**. On the **Formulas tab**, in the **Defined Names group**, click the **Define Name** button. In the **New Name** dialog box, confirm the name is Gross_Pay and the range is C6:C12. Click **OK**.

16. Select the range **D5:D12**. On the **Formulas tab**, in the **Defined Names group**, click the **Create from Selection** button. In the **Create Names from Selection** dialog box, confirm that **Top Row** is selected. Click **OK**.

17. Using this skills you practiced, name the range **F6:F12** to **Fed_Inc_Tax_Deduction**. Name the range **G6:G12** to **Other_Deductions** and the range **H6:H12** to **Net_Pay**

18. Click cell **A13** and type **Total** and format with **Bold** and **Center**. Click cell **C13** and type **=sum(** In the **Defined Names group**, click **Use in Formula** and click **Gross_Pay**. Type **)** and press [Tab] to move to the next cell. Using the skills practiced, enter formulas using named ranges to sum the columns in cells **D13**, **F13**, **G13**, and **H13**.

19. Select the range **C6:C12**, right-click, and double-click the **Format Painter**. Click in cells **D6**, **F6**, **G6**, and **H6**. Press [Esc] to stop the **Format Painter**. Select the totals—**C13:D13** and **F13:H13**—and format with **Bold**, **Accounting Number format**, and place a **Top and Double Bottom Border**.

20. Click cell **A16** and type **Gross pay <$400 per week** Click cell **A17** and on the **Formulas tab**, in the **Function Library group**, click the **More Functions button arrow**. Point to **Statistical** and from the submenu, click **COUNTIF**. In the **Range** box, type **Gross_Pay** and for the **Criteria**, type **<400** Click **OK**.

21. Click the **Sheet3 sheet tab** and rename it **List of Names**. In cell **A1**, type **Boards Anywhere** and in cell **A2**, type **List of Names** Click cell **A5**. On the **Formulas tab**, in the **Defined Names group**, click the **Use in Formula** button, and then click **Paste Names**. In the **Paste Names** dialog box, click **Paste List**. Adjust the width of **columns A** and **B** to display the entries in the columns.

22. On all sheets, in the **Left Footer**, place the **File Name** and in the **Right Footer**, place the **Sheet Name**. In the **Right Header**, type **Page** followed by the **Page Number**. Center all sheets **Horizontally** and **Vertically**. **Ungroup** the worksheets, right-click the **Tax Rates sheet tab**, and click **Hide**.

23. **Save** your workbook. To submit electronically, follow the instructions provided by your instructor, and then go to Step 24. To print, display the **Office** menu, and click **Print**. In the **Print** dialog box, under **Print what**, select **Entire workbook**. Under **Copies**, confirm that **1** is selected, and then click **OK**. If you are instructed to print formulas, refer to Activity 1.12 to do so, and then **close** the workbook without saving changes made for printing the formulas.

24. From the **Office** menu, click **New**. In the **New Workbook** dialog box, at the left under **Microsoft Office Online**, scroll to and click **Time sheets**. From the **Time sheets** displayed in the center, from the first column, click the first choice—the name reads *Weekly time sheet with breaks*—and then click **Download**. At the **Microsoft Office Genuine Advantage** box, click **Continue** and notice that the document displays in Compatibility Mode.

(Project 6C–Payroll continues on the next page)

Content-Based Assessments

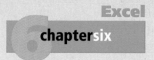
(Project 6C–Payroll continued)

> Note: If you do not have access to the network, this template can be found in your student files named as *Weekly_time_sheet_with_breaks*.

25. In the template, click **Company Name** and type **Board Anywhere Surf and Snowboard Shop** and press Enter. Select the range **D2:M2**—notice that columns A:C are narrow in this template—and click the **Merge & Center** button. Click cell **D4** and type **903 South Research Drive** In cell **D5**, type **Irvine, CA 92618** and in cell **D6** type **Phone (949) 555-0049** and press Enter.

26. On the **Insert tab**, in the **Text group**, click **Header & Footer**. In the **Page Setup** dialog box, click **Custom Footer**. In the **Left section**, click the **Insert File Name** button. Click **OK** two times.

27. From the **Office** menu, click **Save As**. At the bottom of the **Save As** dialog box, under **Save as type**, click the **arrow** and then click **Excel Template**. In the **File Name** text box, type **6C_Time_Card_Template_Firstname_Lastname** At the top of the dialog box, in the **Save in** area, navigate to your **Excel Chapter 6** folder. Under **Save as type**, confirm that **Excel Template** is selected, and then click **Save**. Click the **Close Window** button to close the workbook. The template is saved on you data disk and will be available for you to use.

28. From the **Office** menu, click **New**. At the left, under **Templates**, click **New from existing**. In your **Excel Chapter 6** folder, click **6C_Time_Card_Template_Firstname_Lastname** and then click **Create New**. This creates a new copy of your template.

29. Click cell **M4**—next to *Employee name*—and type **Bob McKinley** Click cell **M5** and type **Dana Connolly** Click cell **S4** and type **8/16/2009** and as you press Enter notice the ending date and all days on the time card change.

30. Click cell **G11** for the Time In on Monday. Type **10 am** and in cell **G12** type **1 pm** Click cell **G14** and type **1:30 pm** and in cell **G15** type **6:30 pm** As you enter the starting and ending times, the total hours worked are calculated and display in cell G16.

31. Enter the following start and end times for the rest of the week.

	Tuesday	Wednesday	Friday	Saturday
Time In	9:30 am	9:45 am	9:30 am	9:30 am
Time Out	1:15 pm	12:45 pm	1 pm	1 pm
Time In	2:00 pm	1:15 pm	2:15 pm	1:45 pm
Time Out	6:30 pm	5:30 pm	6 pm	6:30 pm

32. **Save** the workbook to your **Excel Chapter 6** folder as **6C_McKinley_Time_Card_Firstname_Lastname** In the **Save as type** box, confirm that it is an Excel workbook, and then click **Save**.

33. To submit electronically, follow the instructions provided by your instructor. To print, from the **Office** menu, click **Print**. In the **Print** dialog box, under **Print what**, select **Entire workbook**. Under **Copies**, confirm that **1** is selected. From the **Office** menu, click **Close**. If you are prompted to save changes, click **No**. **Exit** Excel.

 You have completed Project 6C

Project 6D — Inventory

In this project, you will apply all the Objectives found in Project 6B.

Objectives: 4. *Transpose Data in a Worksheet and Apply Cell Styles;* **5.** *Use 3-D References to Link Data in Worksheets and Workbooks and Create a Workspace;* **6.** *Create Hyperlinks.*

In the following Skills Review project, you will create a workbook for J. R. Kass, co-owner of Board Anywhere, which records the inventory for each shop at the end of January and a summary sheet. You will also start a report used for the annual inventory report. Your completed worksheets will look similar to those shown in Figure 6.42.

> **For Project 6D, you will need the following file:**
>
> e06D_Inventory
>
> You will save your workbook as
> 6D_Inventory_Firstname_Lastname

Figure 6.42

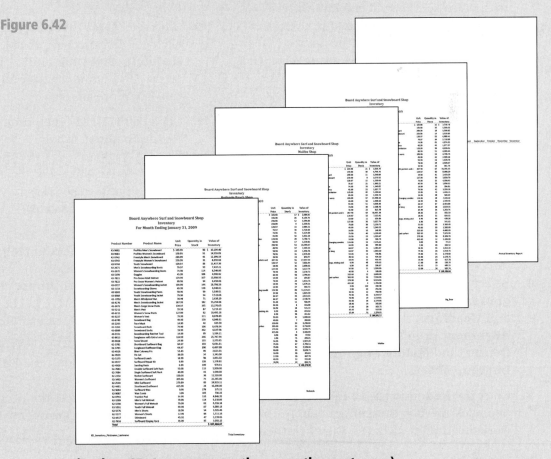

(Project 6D–Inventory continues on the next page)

Content-Based Assessments

(Project 6D–Inventory continued)

1. **Start** Excel. Open the file named **e06D_Inventory**, and then save it in your **Excel Chapter 6** folder as **6D_Inventory_Firstname_Lastname** This workbook displays the inventory report for each of the branches.

2. In the **Total Inventory sheet**, click cell **E6** and type **Value of Inventory**

3. Click in the **Redondo sheet tab**. Press ⇧ Shift and click the **Big_Bear sheet tab** to select three worksheets. Click cell **F6** and type **Value of Inventory** In cell **F7** enter a formula to multiply the unit price by the quantity in stock—**=d7*e7** Use the fill handle to copy the formula through **row 56**.

4. Click cell **F57**, and on the **Home tab**, in the **Editing group**, click the **Sum** button, then press Enter. Format cell **F57** with **Accounting Number Format**. Click cell **A57** and type **Total** Select the range **A57:F57** and in the **Styles group**, click **Cell Styles**. In the **Cell Styles gallery**, under **Titles and Headings**, click the last choice—**Total**. Adjust column widths if needed.

5. Click the **Big_Bear sheet tab**. Press ⇧ Shift and click the **Total Inventory sheet tab**. Select the worksheet title—**A1:A4**. In the **Styles group**, click **Cell Styles**. From the **Cell Styles gallery**, under **Titles and Headings**, click the fifth selection—**Title**. In the **Font group**, click the **Font Size button arrow** and click **16**.

6. Select the range **A6:E6** and in the **Styles group**, click **Cell Styles**. Under **Titles and Headings**, click **Heading 2**. In the **Alignment group**, click the **Wrap Text**, **Center**, and **Middle Align** buttons, **Ungroup sheets**.

7. Click the **Redondo sheet tab**. Press ⇧ Shift and click the **Big_Bear sheet tab**. In the worksheet, right-click cell **E6**, click the

8. Select the range **A1:F1** and in the **Alignment group**, click the **Merge & Center** button. In the **Clipboard group**, double-click the **Format Painter** button and click in cells **A2**, **A3**, and **A4**. Then in the **Clipboard group**, click the **Format Painter** button to stop it.

9. Click cell **D7** and press Ctrl while you click cell **F7** to select both cells. In the **Number group**, click the **Accounting Number Format** button. Select the range **D8:D56** and in the **Number group**, click the **Comma Style** button. In the **Clipboard group**, click the **Format Painter** button, and then click cell **F8**.

10. Click the **Total Inventory sheet tab** and click cell **D7** and type **=sum(** Click the **Redondo sheet tab** and click cell **E7**. Press ⇧ Shift and click the **Big_Bear sheet tab**. Then press Enter.

11. Click cell **E7** and type **=sum(** Click the **Redondo sheet tab** and click cell **F7**. Press ⇧ Shift and click the **Big_Bear sheet tab**, and then press Enter. Select the range **D7:E7** and use the fill handle to copy the formulas through **row 56**.

12. Select cells **C7** and **E7** and in the **Number group**, click the **Accounting Number Format** button. Select the range **C8:C56** and in the **Number group**, click the **Comma Style** button. In the **Clipboard group**, click the **Format Painter** button, and then click cell **E8**.

13. Click cell **E57**, and in the **Editing group**, click **Sum** and press Enter. Click cell **A57** and type **Total** Select the range **A57:E57** and in the **Styles group**, click the **Cell**

Format Painter button, and click cell **F6**. Adjust column widths so the data fully displays in the columns.

(Project 6D–Inventory continues on the next page)

Content-Based Assessments

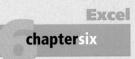

(Project 6D–Inventory continued)

Styles button and in the gallery, under
Titles and Headings, click the last
choice—**Total**. Select the range **A1:E1** and
in the **Alignment group**, click the **Merge
& Center** button. **Merge & Center rows 2
and 3**. Adjust column widths if necessary.

14. Click the **Annual Inventory Report sheet
tab**. Select the range **A5:E17**, right-click
and click **Copy**. Click cell **A19**. On the
Home tab, in the **Clipboard group**, click
the **Paste button arrow**, and then click
Transpose. Select **rows 5:18**, right-click,
and click **Delete**.

15. Select the range **A1:A3** and in the **Styles
group**, click **Cell Styles**. In the **Cell Styles
gallery**, under **Titles and Headings**, click
Title. Change the **Font Size** to **16 pt**.
Select the column titles—**A5:M5**. In the
Styles group, click the **Cell Styles button
arrow** and under **Titles and Headings**,
click **Heading 3**. In the **Alignment group**,
click the **Center** button. Adjust column
widths if needed.

16. Click cell **B6**. Type = and click the
Redondo sheet tab, click cell **F57**, and
then press [Enter]. Click cell **B7**. Type = and
click the **Malibu sheet tab**, click cell **F57**,
and then press [Enter]. Using the skill you
practiced, enter the total January inventory for the Big Bear store. Adjust column
widths if needed.

17. Click cell **B9** and enter a Sum function.
Format cell **B6** with **Accounting Number
Format**, and the range **B7:B8** with
Comma Style. Click cell **B9**. In the **Styles
group**, click the **Cell Styles** button and
under **Titles and Headings**, click **Total**.
The total January sales—$437,075.82—
displays in the cell.

18. There were errors in the inventory. Make
the following corrections:

Sheet	Cell Number	Correction
Redondo	E30	74
Big Bear	E33	54
Redondo	D37	39.50
Malibu	D37	39.50
Big_Bear	D37	39.50

19. Click the **Annual Inventory Report** and
review the total now entered after the
changes. Notice that it has been changed
to reflect the changes in the worksheets.

20. **Select all sheets**. Insert a **Left Footer**
that displays the **File Name**. In the **Right
Footer**, display the **Sheet Name**. On the
Page Layout tab, in the **Scale to Fit
group**, click the **Height arrow** and click **1
page**, and click the **Width** arrow and click
1 page. In the **Page Setup group**, click the
Dialog Box Launcher. Click the **Margins
tab**, and under **Center on page**, click
Horizontally and **Vertically**, and then
click **OK**. **Ungroup** worksheets.

21. Click the **Annual Inventory Report
sheet tab**. Click cell **A6**. On the **Insert
tab**, in the **Links group**, click the
Hyperlink button. At the left edge, click
Place in This Document. In **Or select a
place in this document**, click **Redondo**.
At the top right, click **ScreenTip** and in
the **Set Hyperlink ScreenTip** dialog box,
type **Click to access Redondo sheet** Click
OK two times. Using the skills you just
practiced, insert a hyperlink to the
Malibu sheet in cell **A7** and insert a
ScreenTip that reads **Click to access
Malibu sheet** Then insert a hyperlink to
the Big_Bear sheet in cell **A8** and insert a
ScreenTip that reads **Click to access Big
Bear sheet Save** the workbook.

(Project 6D–Inventory continues on the next page)

(Project 6D–Inventory continued)

22. To submit electronically, follow the instructions provided by your instructor. To print, from the **Office** menu, click **Print**. In the **Print** dialog box, under **Print what**, select **Entire workbook**. Under **Copies**, confirm that **1** is selected. Print formulas if you are instructed to do so. From the **Office** menu, click **Close**. If you are prompted to save changes, click **No**. **Exit** Excel.

 End **You have completed Project 6D** ———————————

Content-Based Assessments

Project 6E — Sales Awards

In this project, you will apply the skills you practiced from the Objectives in Project 6A.

Objectives: 1. *Create Formulas Using Named Ranges;* **2.** *Utilize Lookup Lists;* **3.** *Customize and Use Microsoft-Created Templates.*

In the following Mastering Excel project, you will create a workbook for Board Anywhere that shows prizes won by the sales staff for the amount of sales made within one month. Your completed workbooks will look similar to the ones shown in Figure 6.43.

For Project 6E, you will need the following files:

e06E_Sales_Awards

Travel_expense_report (an Excel Template)

You will save your workbooks as
6E_Sales_Awards_Firstname_Lastname
6E_Expense_Template_Firstname_Lastname (an Excel template)

Figure 6.43

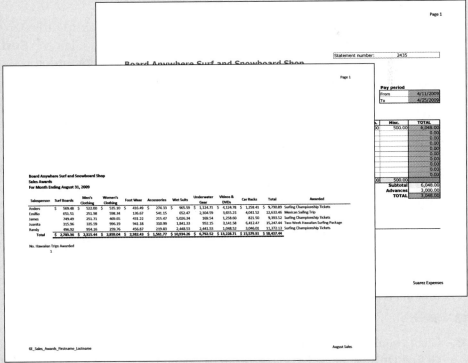

(Project 6E–Sales Awards continues on the next page)

Excel

chaptersix   Mastering Excel

(Project 6E–Sales Awards continued)

1. **Start** Excel. Open the file named **e06E_Sales_Awards**, and then save it in your **Excel Chapter 6** folder as **6E_Sales Awards_Firstname_Lastname**

2. Name **Sheet1 August Sales** and **Sheet2 Awards** On the **August Sales** sheet, select the range **A5:J10** and on the **Formulas tab** in the **Defined Names group**, click the **Create from Selection** button. In the **Create Names from Selection** dialog box, confirm that **Top row** and **Left column** are selected, and then click **OK**.

3. Click cell **A11** and type **Total** and format with **Bold** and **Center**. Click cell **B11** to enter the total sales of Surf Boards. Type **=sum(** In the **Defined Names group**, click **Use in Formula** and click **Surf_Boards**. Type **)** and press Tab to move to the next cell. Using the skills you have practiced, enter formulas that use named ranges in cells **C11** through **J11**.

4. Click in cell **K6** and type **=sum(anders)** and press Enter to move to the next cell. Using the skills you have practiced, enter formulas that use named ranges for each employee in cells **K7** through **K10**.

5. Select the range **K5:K10**. In the **Defined Names group**, click the **Create from Selection** button. In the **Create Names from Selection** dialog box, confirm that **Top row** is selected, and then click **OK**. Click cell **K11** and type **=sum(to** In the **Formula AutoComplete** list, double-click the word **Total** Type **)** and then press Enter.

6. Select the total row—**B11:K11**—and format with **Bold**, **Accounting Number Format**, and place a **Top and Double Bottom Border**. Select **J6:J10** and right-click. Click the **Format Painter** button and then click cell **K6**.

7. Click the **Awards sheet tab**. This sheet contains the lookup table for sales awards. Click cell **A4**. Click the **Data tab**, and in the **Sort & Filter group**, click the **Sort Smallest to Largest** sort button to sort this lookup table in ascending numeric order.

8. Select the range **A4:B7**. On the **Formulas tab**, in the **Defined Names group**, click the **Define Name** button. Name this range **Rewards** and then click **OK**.

9. Click the **August Sales sheet tab** and click cell **L6**. On the **Formulas tab**, in the **Function Library group**, click the **Lookup & Reference** button, and then click **VLOOKUP**.

10. In the **VLOOKUP Function Arguments** dialog box, in the **Lookup_value** box, click cell **K6**, and then press Tab. In the **Table_array** box, type **Rewards** In the **Col_index_num** box, type **2** and then click **OK**. Copy the formula in cell **L6** through cell **L10**. Adjust column widths if needed.

11. Click cell **A13** and type **No. Hawaiian Trips Awarded** Click cell **A14**. In the **Function Library group**, click the **More Functions** button, point to **Statistical**, and from the submenu click **COUNTIF**. In the **Range** box, select the range **L6:L10** and in the **Criteria** box, type **Two-Week Hawaiian Surfing Package** Click **OK**.

12. **Save** your workbook and leave it open.

13. Click the **Office** button and click **New**. In the **New Workbook** dialog box, under **Microsoft Office Online**, click **Expense reports**. From the expense reports displayed, click the **Travel expense report**, and then click **Download**. In the **Microsoft Office Genuine Advantage** box, click **Continue**.

(Project 6E–Sales Awards continues on the next page)

Excel
chaptersix **Mastering Excel**

(Project 6E–Sales Awards continued)

Note: If you do not have access to the network, in your student files use the file named **Travel_expense_report**

14. Right-click cell **A3**, click the **Format Painter** button, and then click cell **A2**. Type **Board Anywhere Surf and Snowboard Shop** Select the range **A2:A3** and change the **Font Size** to **18** In the **Left Footer**, place the **File Name** and in the **Right Footer**, place the **Sheet Name**.

15. Click the **Office** menu and click **Save As**. In the **Save As** dialog box, change the **Save as type** to **Excel Template**. In the **File name** box, type **6E_Expense_Template_Firstname_Lastname** Navigate to your **Excel Chapter 6** folder, and then click **Save**. Click the **Close Window** button The template is saved to your data storage device.

16. Click the **Office** button, and then click **New**. Click **New from existing**, and in the **New** dialog box, click the template titled **6E_Expense_Template_Firstname_Lastname**, and then click **Create New**.

17. Type the following data in the template:

Statement number	2435	Department	Sales
Name	Juanita Suarez	Manager	Johnson
Employee ID	555-44-3333	Pay Period (From)	4/11/09
Position	Sales	Pay Period (To)	4/25/09

18. In **row 12**, type the following data entries:

Date	Account	Description	Hotel	Transport	Meals	Entertain.	Misc
4/25/2009	1452	2-Wk Hawaiian Trip	2500	673	1400	975	500

19. In cell **K24**, enter 3000 for the advances.

20. Right-click the **Expense statement sheet tab**. Click **Move or Copy**. In the **To book** section, click **6E_Sales_Awards_Firstname_Lastname**. Under **Before sheet**, click **(move to end)**, and then click **OK**. The colors of the document change. In the **6E_Sales_Awards_Firstname_Lastname** workbook, rename the **Expense statement** sheet to **Suarez Expenses**

21. On all sheets, in the **Left Footer**, place the **File Name** and in the **Right Footer**, place the **Sheet Name**. In the **Right Header**, type **Page** and then click the **Page Number** button. Change the orientation to **Landscape** and **Fit to 1 Page**. **Hide** the **Awards** sheet. Center the remaining worksheets **Horizontally** and **Vertically**. Hide the **Awards** worksheet.

22. Save your workbook and submit your files as directed. **Close** the workbook. **Exit** Excel.

End You have completed Project 6E

Mastering Excel

Project 6F — Surf Lessons

In this project, you will apply the skills you have practiced from the Objectives in Project 6B.

Objectives: 4. *Transpose Data in a Worksheet and Apply Cell Styles;* **5.** *Use 3-D References to Link Data in Worksheets and Workbooks and Create a Workspace;* **6.** *Create Hyperlinks.*

In the following Mastering Excel project, you will create a workbook for J. R. Kass, co-owner of Board Anywhere, which records the surf lessons sold for each shop for the month of July and a summary sheet for the third quarter. Your completed workbook will look similar to the one shown in Figure 6.44.

For Project 6F, you will need the following files:

e06F_Malibu_Surf_Lessons
e06F_Redondo_Beach_Surf_Lessons
e06F_Big_Bear_Surf_Lessons
New blank Excel worksheet

You will save your workbooks as
6F_Big_Bear_Surf_Lessons_Firstname_Lastname
6F_Malibu_Surf_Lessons_Firstname_Lastname
6F_Redondo_Beach_Surf_Lessons_Firstname_Lastname
6F_Surf_Lessons_Firstname_Lastname
6F_Q3_2009_Surf_Lessons_Firstname_Lastname (Workspace)

Figure 6.44

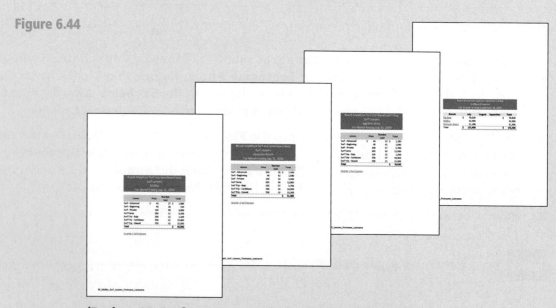

(Project 6F–Surf Lessons continues on the next page)

Content-Based Assessments

(Project 6F–Surf Lessons continued)

1. **Start** Excel. Display your student files for this chapter. Press Ctrl and click the files named **e06F_Big_Bear_Surf_Lessons**, **e06F_Malibu_Surf_Lessons**, and **e06F_Redondo_Beach_Surf_Lessons**, and then click **Open** to open all of these files at once.

2. In your **Excel Chapter 6** folder, save **e06F_Malibu_Surf_Lessons** as 6F_Malibu_Surf_Lessons_Firstname_Lastname and **e06F_Redondo_Beach_Surf_Lessons** as 6F_Redondo_Beach_Surf_Lessons_Firstname_Lastname and **e06F_Big_Bear_Surf_Lessons** as 6F_Big_Bear_Surf_Lessons_Firstname_Lastname

3. Open a new blank workbook. Save it the **Excel Chapter 6** folder and name the workbook 6F_Surf_Lessons_Firstname_Lastname This workbook will display a summary of income from surfboard lessons at each of the branches.

4. In cells **A1:A3** type the following:

Board Anywhere Surf and Snowboard Shop
Surfboard Lessons
For Quarter Ending September 30, 2009

5. Beginning with **A5**, type the following column titles:

Branch	Big Bear	Malibu	Redondo Beach	Total

   Beginning with cell **A6**, type the following row titles: **July**, **August**, **September**, **Total**

6. Merge and center the title—**A1:A3**— over the columns of the worksheet. Format **A1:A3** using **Cell Styles**. Select **Accent4** and change **Font Size** to **12**.

7. **Transpose** the columns and rows of the worksheet so that *Branch, July, August, September,* and *Total* are column titles and *Big Bear, Malibu, Redondo Beach,* and *Total* are row titles. Adjust column widths

so the data fully displays and **delete rows** so the column titles display on **row 5**.

8. In cell **B6**, use a 3-D cell reference to display the July total of surf lessons from the **6F_Big_Bear_Surf_Lessons** workbook. In cell **B7**, use a 3-D cell reference to display the Malibu sales, and in cell **B8** the Redondo Beach sales.

9. In cells **B9** and **E9**, **sum** the column, and in **column E**, **sum** the rows, even though there is only one entry in the row. Format amounts in **rows 6** and **9** with **Accounting Number Format** with **no decimals**. Format amounts in **rows 7** and **8** with **Comma Style** with **no decimals**. Format the total row with **Cell Styles** using the **Total** format. **Delete Sheet2** and **Sheet3**.

10. Format column titles using **Cell Styles** with **20%-Accent4**, **bold**, and **center**. Adjust column widths if needed.

11. In the **Left Footer** enter the **File Name**. Center the worksheet on the page **Vertically** and **Horizontally**. **Save** your workbook.

12. Confirm that only the following workbooks are open:
    6F_Malibu_Surf_Lessons_Firstname_Lastname
    6F_Redondo_Beach_Surf_Lessons_Firstname_Lastname
    6F_Big_Bear_Surf_Lessons_Firstname_Lastname and
    6F_Surf_Lessons_Firstname_Lastname

13. On the **View tab**, in the **Window group**, click the **Save Workspace** button, navigate to your **Excel Chapter 6** folder, and save the open files as a workspace named 6F_Q3_2009_Surf_Lessons_Firstname_Lastname **Close** all open workbooks.

14. From the **Office** menu, click **Open**. Navigate to the **Excel Chapter 6** folder and click

(Project 6F–Surf Lessons continues on the next page)

Content-Based Assessments

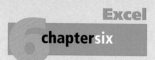
(Project 6F–Surf Lessons continued)

6F_Q3_2009_Surf_Lessons_Firstname_Lastname.xlsw—the workspace. Maximize the worksheets and make the **6F_Malibu_Surf_Lessons_Firstname_Lastname** workbook active and change the number of private surf lessons in cell **C9** to **48** Select the **6F_Surf_Lessons_Firstname_Lastname** worksheet and confirm that the Malibu total has updated to 43,000.

15. In the **6F_Surf_Lessons_Firstname_Lastname** workbook, insert a **hyperlink** from the row headings of *Big Bear*, *Malibu*, and *Redondo Beach* to their respective workbooks. Click the **Big Bear** hyperlink. Recall that your directory may display a temporary file—identified by the tilde ~ —at the beginning of the list of files.

16. Use the hyperlink to display the **6F_Big_Bear_Surf_Lessons** workbook, and then click in cell **A16**. Type **Quarter 3 Surf Lessons** In cell **A16**, insert a hyperlink to the workbook named **6F_Surf_Lessons_Firstname_Lastname** and add a ScreenTip that reads **Total surf lessons from all branches**

17. Click the hyperlink to go back to the **6F_Surf_Lessons_Firstname_Lastname** workbook. Click the **Malibu** link. Using the skills you practiced, place a link and a ScreenTip in the Malibu and Redondo Beach worksheets the same as you did in **6F_Big_Bear_Surf_Lessons**.

18. **Save** your workbooks and submit your files as directed. **Close** the workbooks and **Exit** Excel.

End You have completed Project 6F

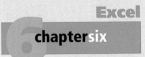

Excel

chaptersix

Mastering Excel

Project 6G — Tax Deposits

In this project, you will apply the following Objectives found in Projects A and B.

Objectives: 1. *Create Formulas Using Named Ranges;* **2.** *Utilize Lookup Lists;* **4.** *Transpose Data in a Worksheet and Apply Cell Styles;* **5.** *Use 3-D References to Link Data in Worksheets and Workbooks and Create a Workspace;* **6.** *Create Hyperlinks.*

In the following Mastering Excel project, you will create and complete a group of worksheets that report the payroll for two weeks. You will determine the payroll for employees and the payroll report for each shop. You will then determine the amount of taxes that will be deposited. You will use a lookup table to determine the amount of tax deductions and create hyperlinks for navigation between the worksheets and workbooks. Your completed workbooks will look similar to the ones shown in Figure 6.45.

For Project 6G, you will need the following files:

e06G_Payroll
e06G_Malibu_Employees

You will save your workbooks as
6G_Payroll_Firstname_Lastname
6G_Malibu_Employees_Firstname_Lastname
6G_Tax_Deposits_Firstname_Lastname
6G_Payroll_Docs_Workspace_Firstname_Lastname (Workspace)

Figure 6.45

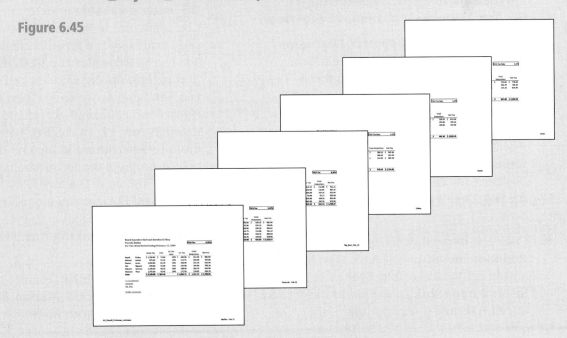

(Project 6G–Tax Deposits continues on the next page)

Content-Based Assessments

(Project 6G–Tax Deposits continued)

1. **Start** Excel, and from the student files, click **e06G_Tax_Deposits**, press `⇧ Shift` and click **e06G_Payroll** and **e06G_Malibu _Employees**. Then click **Open**. Save the workbooks to your **Excel Chapter 6 folder**. Save **e06G_Tax_Deposits** as 6G_Tax_Deposits_Firstname_Lastname. Save **e06G_Malibu_Employees** as 6G_Malibu_Employees_Firstname_Lastname, and save **e06G_ Payroll** as 6G_Payroll_Firstname_Lastname.

2. With the three workbooks open, save a **Workspace** and name the workspace **6G_Payroll_Docs_Workspace_Firstname_Lastname**

3. In the **6G_Tax_Deposits_Firstname_Lastname** workbook, delete **Sheet2** and **Sheet3**. Click cell **E1** and type **To Weekly Payroll** and then from cell E1 insert a **Hyperlink** to the workbook named **6G_Payroll_Firstname_Lastname**.

4. Click the new **hyperlink** and in the **6G_Payroll_Firstname_Lastname**, click cell **A14**, type **To Tax Deposits** and then insert a **hyperlink** to the worksheet named **6G_Tax_Deposits_Firstname_Lastname**.

5. Access the **6G_Tax_Deposits_Firstname_Lastname** and then in cell **E1**, click the **hyperlink** *To Weekly Payroll*. In the **6G_Payroll_Firstname_Lastname** workbook, on the **Malibu** sheet, click cell **A15** and type **Redondo** In cell **A16**, type **Big_Bear** Insert a **hyperlink** in cell **A15** to the **Redondo-Feb 15** worksheet in this workbook and in cell **A16** insert a **hyperlink** to the **Big_Bear_Feb_15** sheet in this workbook.

6. Click the **hyperlink** to *Redondo*. In the **Redondo sheet**, in cell **A15**, type **Malibu** and in cell **A16** type **Big_Bear** In cell **A15** insert a **hyperlink** to the Malibu sheet and in cell **A16** insert a hyperlink to the Big_Bear sheet. Using the skills you practiced, in the **Big_Bear sheet**, insert hyperlinks to the Malibu and Redondo sheets.

7. Click the hyperlink to the **Malibu sheet**. Click cell **A18**, and type **Malibu Employees** Insert a hyperlink to the **6G_Malibu_Employees_Firstname_Lastname** workbook, and click the **hyperlink**.

8. In the **6G_Malibu_Employees_Firstname_Lastname** workbook, in the **Dulley** sheet, click cell **A16** and type **Payroll workbook** Insert a **hyperlink** to 6G_Payroll_Firstname_Lastname, and type a ScreenTip that says **Click to access Tax Deposits workbook**

9. In the **6G_Payroll_Firstname_Lastname** workbook, click cell **H2** and define a name for the cell based on the text in cell **G2**. Click the **Tax Rate sheet tab**, and define the range **A4:B18**, naming it *Fed_Tax*. Confirm the range is sorted from smallest to largest.

10. Click in the **Malibu sheet tab** and in cell **D6**, enter a formula to determine the FICA tax, using the named cell for the FICA rate, and copy the formula through **row 11**. In cell **E6**, enter the **VLOOKUP** function to look up the value in cell **C6** from Fed_Tax table array and return the value in the second column. Copy the formula through **row 11**. In cell **F6**, enter the formula to determine the income tax to withhold. Complete the formulas in cells **G6** and **H6** and copy the formulas through the worksheet. Format the monetary amounts in the same format style that is used in **column C**. Confirm that the Net Pay in cell H6 is $885.60.

11. Select the range **C6:H6**. Right-click and select **Copy**. In the **6G_Malibu_Employees_Firstname_Lastname** workbook, click

(Project 6G–Tax Deposits continues on the next page)

Content-Based Assessments

Mastering Excel

(Project 6G–Tax Deposits continued)

cell **B9** and on the **Home tab**, in the **Clipboard group**, click the **Paste button arrow** and select **Paste Link**. Using the skills practiced and the hyperlinks you have inserted, copy the payroll data from **6G_Payroll_Firstname_Lastname** for the other employees—*Hanke, Jones, Nguyen, Sanchez, Thue*—into their individual payroll sheets in the **6G_Malibu_Employees_Firstname_Lastname** workbook. Be sure to use the **Paste Link** command for each record that is copied. Confirm that the format in row 6 is accurate.

12. In the **6G_Malibu_Employees_Firstname_Lastname** workbook, confirm that the copied data is formatted to match the entries for January 31.

13. Display the **6G_Tax_Deposits_Firstname_Lastname** workbook. Select the range **A1:A3** and in the **Styles group**, click **Cell Styles**, select the **Title** style, and reduce the **Font Size** to 14. In cell **H5**, type **Total** Format the column titles using **Cell Styles** with **Heading 3** and format with **Center** alignment. Adjust column widths.

14. Click cell **D6** and create a 3-D formula that **sums** the **FICA** due from the **6G_Payroll_Firstname_Lastname** workbook, on the **Malibu**, **Redondo**, and **Big Bear_Feb_15 sheets** in cell **D12**. The value

1102.05 is entered in the cell. In the **6G_Tax_Deposits_Firstname_Lastname** workbook, click cell **D7** and enter a similar formula that sums the Federal Income Tax due for all three stores for the February 15 payroll, which is found in cell **F12**.

15. In **row 8**, enter a **sum** function through **column H** and format with **Accounting Number Format** with **two decimals** and include a **Top and Double Bottom Border**. In the range **H6:H8**, enter a formula that sums the rows, including those cells not yet completed.

16. Format the numbers in cells **B6:H6** with **Accounting Number Format** with **two decimals**. Format the numbers in **row 7** with **Comma Style** with **two decimals**. Increase column widths if needed.

17. In all workbooks, format all worksheets with the **File Name** in the **Left Footer** and the **Sheet Name** in the **Right Footer** (if there is more than one worksheet in the workbook), centered both **Horizontally** and **Vertically** and in **Landscape Orientation**. In the **6G_Payroll_Firstname_Lastname** workbook, hide the **Tax Chart** sheet.

18. **Save** your workbooks and submit your files as directed. **Close** your workbooks and **Exit** Excel.

End You have completed Project 6G

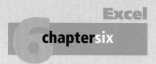
Project 6H — Purchase Order

In this project, you will apply the following Objectives found in Projects A and B.

Objectives: 2. *Utilize Lookup Lists;* **3.** *Customize and Use Microsoft-Created Templates.*

In the following Mastering Excel project, you will create a template for a purchase order that includes a lookup table. You will then use that template to prepare a purchase order. Your completed worksheets will look similar to the ones shown in Figure 6.46.

For Project 6H, you will need the following files:

e06H_Vendors

Purchase_order_(Garamond_Gray_design) (a template)

You will save your workbooks as
6H_Vendors_Firstname_Lastname
6H_Purchase_Order_Template_Firstname_Lastname
(an Excel template)
6H_PO1001_Firstname_Lastname

Figure 6.46

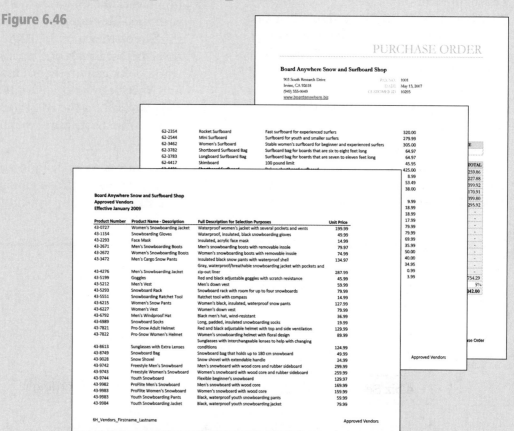

(Project 6H–Purchase Order continues on the next page)

Content-Based Assessments

(Project 6H–Purchase Order continued)

1. **Start** Excel. Display the **New Workbook** dialog box, and under **Microsoft Office Online** click **Purchase orders**, and then download the template named **Purchase order (Garamond Gray design)**. (Note: If you do not have online access, use the file from your student data named **Purchase_order_(Garamond_Gray_design)**.) You will customize this template and then move it into another workbook, so you do not need to save it at this time.

2. Click in the words *YOUR LOGO HERE* and when they are surrounded by a box, press Delete. Click in cell **B1** and delete the contents. In **row 3**, replace *[Your Company Name]* with **Board Anywhere Snow and Surfboard Shop** Use merge tools so the title fully displays. Format the company name with **bold**, **14-point font**, and, if needed, increase the height of **row 3**.

3. Select the range **A5:G19**. Increase the **Font Size** to **10 points**. Select the range **A20:G41** and increase the **Font Size** to **12 points. Delete** the column title in cell **E19** and remove the border between **columns D** and **E** from **row 20:35**. Change the formula in cell **G20** to read **=a20*f20** and **copy** the formula to **row 35**. Format the range **F20:G36** with **Comma Style**. Select the range **A20:A35** and click the **Decrease Decimal** button two times, and then click the **Center** button.

4. Click in cell **A36**; a dashed border surrounds the text. Click on the border line and when it becomes a solid line, press Delete. In cell **A5**, replace the text with **903 South Research Drive** In cell **A6**, replace the text with **Irvine, CA 92618** In cell **A7**, replace the text with **(949) 555-0049** and in cell **A8**, replace the text with **www.boardanywhere.biz** Select the range

E40:G41 and **Clear All**. In cell **G37**, type **5%**

5. Replace the **SHIP TO** information. Click cell **E11** and replace *Company Name* with **Board Anywhere** In the next cell, replace *Street Address* with **903 South Research Drive** Replace *City, ST ZIP Code* with **Irvine, CA 92618** and replace *Phone* with **(949) 555-0049**

6. Display the **Open** dialog box, navigate to the student data, and open the file **e06H_Vendors. Save** the file in your **Excel Chapter 6** folder as **6H_Vendors_Firstname_Lastname** Display the worksheet in **Landscape Orientation**. This is a list of approved vendors—businesses that the Board Anywhere purchases goods from. Rename **Sheet1** as **Approved Vendors**

7. **Sort** the vendor list in ascending order by **product number**. Select the range of the worksheet—**A6:D55**—and name the range as **Vendors**

8. Display the **Purchase Order** workbook. Click cell **C20**, which has been merged with column D. Insert the **VLOOKUP** function and for the lookup value, use the item number—cell **B20**. For the table array, click the **Collapse Dialog Box** button and access the **6H_Vendors_Firstname_Lastname** workbook. Click in the worksheet and when the information is entered in the Function Arguments, select the cell reference and replace it with **Vendors** Click the **Expand Dialog Box** button and for the column index number, use the column number that returns the Product Name - Description—**2**

9. To confirm that this lookup works, in cell **B20**, type **43-0727** and confirm that *Women's Snowboarding* is the description.

(Project 6H–Purchase Order continues on the next page)

(Project 6H–Purchase Order continued)

10. In **column F**, insert a **VLOOKUP** function that returns the unit price for the item in cell **B20** from the Vendor table array—**column 4**. Confirm that *$199.99* is entered in the cell. Delete cell **B20** to allow the worksheet to be saved as a template. #N/A displays in some of the cells.

11. In the **Left Footer**, place the **File Name**, and save the worksheet named **6H_Purchase_Order_Template_Firstname_Lastname** as an **Excel Template** in your **Excel Chapter 6** folder. **Close** the template.

12. Open the **6H_Purchase_Order_Template_Firstname_Lastname** as a worksheet. In the Security Warning message bar that appears under the ribbon, click the **Options** button. Click **Enable this content**, and then click **OK**. In the warning box, click **Continue**. Save it as an Excel workbook named **6H_PO1001_Firstname_ Lastname** Confirm that *6H_Vendors_Firstname_Lastname* is also open. Enter the information for the following purchase order, number **1001** with a customer ID of **10293**. The vendor is

Robert Hurtado, **Winter Sports Supplies, 2784 Kingsley Dr., St. Cloud, MN, 56395, (111) 555-1115**. Ship the order to **J. J. Kass**. The order follows:

Number Ordered	Item #
14	43-7822
12	62-5173
8	43-8749
9	62-5173
20	43-9982
8	43-6792

13. Copy the formula in cell **D20** through **D25** and copy the formula in cell **F20** through **F25**.

14. In the **6H_Vendors_Firstname_Lastname** worksheet, in the **Left Footer**, place the **File Name**, and place the **Sheet Name** in the **Right Footer**. **Save** your completed template.

15. **Save** your workbooks and submit your files as directed. **Close** the workbooks. **Exit** Excel.

 You have completed Project 6H

Project 6I — Weekly Sales

In this project, you will apply all the Objectives found in Projects A and B.

Objectives: 1. *Create Formulas Using Named Ranges;* **2.** *Utilize Lookup Lists;* **3.** *Customize and Use Microsoft-Created Templates;* **4.** *Transpose a Worksheet and Apply Cell Styles;* **5.** *Use 3-D References to Link Data in Worksheets and Workbooks and Create a Workspace;* **6.** *Create Hyperlinks.*

In the following Mastering Excel project, you will create and complete a group of worksheets that report the weekly sales in each store and then combine the sales from all stores into one worksheet. You will use a lookup table to determine the price of the items and use a 3-D Reference to link the data in the workbook. You will also create hyperlinks for navigation between the worksheets. You will also create, save, and use a template for tour sales.

Your completed workbooks will look similar to the ones shown in Figure 6.47.

For Project 6I, you will need the following files:

e06I_Weekly_Sales
e06I_Weekly_Summary_Sales
Donation_receipt (Excel template)

You will save your workbooks as
6I_Weekly_Sales_Firstname_Lastname
6I_Weekly_Sales_Summary_Firstname_Lastname
6I_Tour_Receipt_Template_Firstname_Lastname (Excel template)
6I_Santez_Firstname_Lastname

Figure 6.47

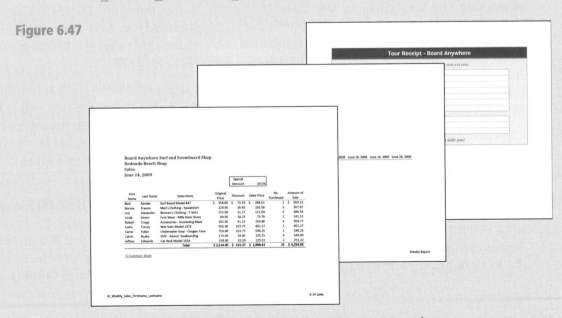

(Project 6I–Weekly Sales continues on the next page)

Content-Based Assessments

(Project 6I–Weekly Sales continued)

1. **Start** Excel. Locate and open the file **e06I_ Weekly_Sales**, and then **Save** it to the **Excel Chapter 6 folder** as **6I_Weekly_ Sales_Firstname_Lastname** There are two worksheets in this workbook—*6–14 Sales* and *Price Sheet*.

2. In the **6-14 Sales** worksheet, select the range **A1:A4**. In the **Styles group**, click the **Cell Styles button arrow**, and then click **Title**. Change the **Font Size** to **14 pt**.

3. Select the range **A7:H7** and in the **Style group**, click Cell Styles, apply **Heading 3**. In the **Alignment group**, click **Center**, **Middle Align**, and **Wrap Text**.

4. Format cell **E5** with **Bold** and **Wrap Text** and define the name of cell **F5** to **Special_ Discount** Select the range **E5:F5** and format with **Outside Borders**.

5. Click the **Price Sheet sheet tab** and select the range **A5:B13**. **Sort** the list in alphabetical order. Name the range **Price_List**. Select the range **A1:A3** and format with **Bold**.

6. You will use a lookup to determine the price of the item. Click the **6–14 Sales sheet tab**, and then click cell **D8**. Insert a **VLOOKUP** function to look up the price of the Sales Items in the Price Sheet in the range you named Price_List. The price of the surf board—358—is entered in the cell. Fill the formula in cell **D8** down through **row 16**.

7. Click cell **E8**, and type **=d8*** and in the **Defined Names group**, click the **Use in Formula** button, and then click **Special_Discount**. Press Enter. Click cell **E8** and fill the formula through **row 16**.

8. Click cell **F8** and type the formula to determine the sales price—**=d8–e8 Copy** the formula through **row 16**. Beginning

in cell **G8**, enter the number of items purchased displayed below:

2
3
4
2
6
1
1
4
2

9. Click cell **H8** and enter a formula that multiplies the *Sales Price* times the *No. Purchased* —**=f8*g8**—and copy the formula through **row 16**.

10. Click cell **D8** and format with **Accounting Number Format**. Copy the format to **E8**, **F8**, and **H8**. Select the range **D9:D16** and format with the **Comma Style**. Copy the format in the range **D9:D16** to the ranges **E9:E16**, **F9:F16**, and **H9:H16**. Use **Comma Style** with **no decimals** to format **column G**.

11. Select the range **D7:H16**. Use the **Create Names from Selection** dialog box to name this range for the **Top row**, and then click **OK**.

12. Click cell **C17**, type **Total** and format with **Bold** and **Center**. Click cell **D17** and type **=sum(** and complete the formula using the name *Original_Price* in the formula. In the range **E17:H17**, use Names to enter the formulas.

13. Format the range **D17:H17** using the **Cell Style** of **Total**. Format the totals in columns **D**, **E**, **F**, and **H** with the **Cell Style** of **Currency** and the total in column **G** with a **Cell Style** of **Comma [0]**. **Save** your workbook.

(Project 6I–Weekly Sales continues on the next page)

Content-Based Assessments

(Project 6I–Weekly Sales continued)

14. In the student files, locate and open **e06I_Weekly_Sales_Summary**, and save it in your **Excel Chapter 6** folder as **6I_Weekly_Sales_Summary_Firstname_Lastname**. Transpose the worksheet—the range **A5:D12**—leaving one blank cell between the worksheet title and the column titles. Format the column titles with **Cell Styles Heading 3**.

15. Click cell **B6** and type = and access the **6I_Weekly_Sales_Firstname_Lastname** workbook. In the **6–14 Sales** sheet, click cell **H17**, and then press Enter. Confirm that it is formatted with **Accounting Number Format**.

16. Click cell **A12** and insert a **Hyperlink** to the **6I_Weekly_Sales_Firstname_Lastname**. In the **Text to display** box, type **To Weekly Sales** Click cell **A12** to test the hyperlink and move to the weekly sales workbook.

17. In the **6I_Weekly_Sales_Firstname_Lastname** workbook, from cell **A19**, insert a **Hyperlink** back to the **6I_Weekly_Sales_Summary_Firstname_Lastname**. In the cell, type the text **To Summary Sheet** Use the link to return to the **Summary** sheet.

18. In the **8I_Weekly_Sales_Firstname_Lastname** workbook, **Hide** the **Price List** sheet. In all workbooks, in the **Left Footer**, enter the **File Name** and in the **Right Footer**, enter the **Sheet Name**. Center all worksheets both **Horizontally** and **Vertically** in **Landscape Orientation**. **Save** your workbooks.

19. Download the template for **Donation receipt**. (Note: If you do not have access to the network, this template can to found in your student files as **Donation_report**.) Customize the template as follows: Replace the title text in **row 2** with **Tour Receipt – Board Anywhere** Edit cell **B4** as follows: Delete *the* and replace *[name of organization]* with **Board Anywhere** and then replace *[phone number]* with **(949) 555-0049**

20. Replace *Donor name* with **Name** Delete *Total pledge amount* Replace *Type of donation* with **Tour Selected** Replace *Description* with **Dates** and replace *Value* with **Deposit** Delete the text in cells **D14:D16**. Replace *Thank you for your generous support!* with **We look forward to touring with you!** Rename the **sheet tab** to **Tour Receipt**

21. In the **Left Footer**, place the **File Name**, and in the **Right Footer**, place the **Sheet Name**. **Save** the workbook as an **Excel Template** named 6I_Tour_Receipt_Template_Firstname_Lastname in your **Excel Chapter 6** folder. **Close** the template.

22. Locate and open **6I_Tour_Receipt_Template_Firstname_Lastname** as a new file. Enter the following information about the tour: **Joseph Santez, 365 La Paz Lane, Malibu, CA, 97100, (100) 555-1234,** purchased the **April 18** trip to **Surf in the Caribbean** and deposited **$700**. **Save** the worksheet and name it 6I_Santez_Firstname_Lastname

23. **Save** your workbooks and submit your files as directed. **Close** the workbooks. **Exit** Excel.

End You have completed Project 6I

Project 6J — Business Running Case

In this project, you will apply the skills you practiced from the Objectives found in Projects 6A and 6B.

From the student files that accompany this textbook, open the folder **03_business_running_case**. Locate and open the folder for this chapter. Open and print the instructions for this project, which are provided to you in Adobe PDF format. Follow the instructions and use the skills you have gained thus far to assist the managers of the Grand Department Store to meet the challenges of keeping records for a large department store.

 End You have completed Project 6J _____

Outcomes-Based Assessments

Rubric

The following outcomes-based assessments are *open-ended assessments*. That is, there is no specific correct result; your result will depend on your approach to the information provided. Make *professional Quality* your goal. Use the following scoring rubric to guide you in *how* to approach the problem and then to evaluate *how well* your approach solves the problem.

The *criteria*—Software Mastery, Content, Format and Layout, and Process—represent the knowledge and skills you have gained that you can apply to solving the problem. The *levels of performance*—Professional Quality, Approaching Professional Quality, or Needs Quality Improvements—help you and your instructor evaluate your result.

	Your completed project is of Professional Quality if you:	Your completed project is Approaching Professional Quality if you:	Your completed project Needs Quality Improvements if you:
Software Mastery	Choose and apply the most appropriate skills, tools, and features and identify efficient methods to solve the problem.	Choose and apply some appropriate skills, tools, and features, but not in the most efficient manner.	Choose inappropriate skills, tools, or features, or are inefficient in solving the problem.
Content	Construct a solution that is clear and well organized, contains content that is accurate, appropriate to the audience and purpose, and is complete. Provide a solution that contains no errors of spelling, grammar, or style.	Construct a solution in which some components are unclear, poorly organized, inconsistent, or incomplete. Misjudge the needs of the audience. Have some errors in spelling, grammar, or style, but the errors do not detract from comprehension.	Construct a solution that is unclear, incomplete, or poorly organized, containing some inaccurate or inappropriate content; and contains many errors of spelling, grammar, or style. Do not solve the problem.
Format and Layout	Format and arrange all elements to communicate information and ideas, clarify function, illustrate relationships, and indicate relative importance.	Apply appropriate format and layout features to some elements, but not others. Overuse features, causing minor distraction.	Apply format and layout that do not communicate information or ideas clearly. Do not use format and layout features to clarify function, illustrate relationships, or indicate relative importance. Use available features excessively, causing distraction.
Process	Use an organized approach that integrates planning, development, self-assessment, revision, and reflection.	Demonstrate an organized approach in some areas, but not others; or, use an insufficient process of organization throughout.	Do not use an organized approach to solve the problem.

Content-Based Assessments

Project 6K—Inventory

In this project, you will construct a solution by applying any combination of the Objectives found in Projects A and B.

For Project 6K, you will need the following file:

e06K_Inventory

You will save your workbook as
6K_Inventory_Firstname_Lastname

At the end of the winter snow season, in June, Board Anywhere takes an inventory of the winter merchandise in each of the shops. Dana Connolly has had a college student record the number of each item that is currently in stock and the product number. She has placed this information in a workbook and has used a separate sheet for each store. You will use a lookup table to complete the report for each of the three stores. Use the lookup table to enter the product name, description, and unit costs. Then complete the worksheet by determining the value of each item and the total the inventory for each store.

Copy one of the store's worksheets into a summary sheet. Use a 3-D Reference to total the No. in Stock column for all the stores. Insert hyperlinks to move between the worksheets. Use Cell Styles and other formatting skills you have practiced to prepare a professional report. Hide the worksheet that contains the lookup table. Include the File Name and the Sheet Name in the footer on each worksheet. Save the file as **6K_Inventory_Firstname_Lastname** and submit, it as directed.

End **You have completed Project 6K** —————————

Content-Based Assessments

Problem Solving

Project 6L—Expense Budget Template

In this project, you will construct a solution by applying any combination of the Objectives found in Projects A and B.

> **For Project 6L, you will need the following file:**

Expense_Budget (A Microsoft template)

You will save your workbooks as
6L_Expense_Budget_Template Firstname_Lastname (Excel template)
6L_Malibu_Expense_Budget_Firstname_Lastname

Open the Microsoft Budget template named **Expense Budget**. Customize the template by entering the company name—**Board Anywhere**—and the month and year—**For Month of June 2009** Insert the File Name in the Left Footer. Save the file as a template named **6L_Expense_Budget_Template_ Firstname_Lastname** in your **Excel Chapter 6** folder. Then use that template to enter the following budgeted amounts. You will notice that not all items listed in this template will be used for Board Anywhere. Confirm the accuracy of your worksheet. Save the file as **6L_Malibu_Expense_Budget_ Firstname_Lastname** and submit as directed. Submit your work and template as directed.

Personnel	Budget	Actual
Office	1280	1300
Store	3857	3700
Salespeople	4505	4958
Others	259	400
Operating	Budget	Actual
Advertising	380	395
Cash discounts	0	0
Delivery costs	150	135
Depreciation	280	285
Employee benefits	600	623
Insurance	125	95
Interest	100	87
Legal and auditing	25	0
Maintenance and repairs	230	200
Office supplies	200	186
Rent or mortgage	1500	1500
Sales expenses	350	314
Taxes	280	292
Telephone	100	76
Utilities	150	102
Other	75	85

End You have completed Project 6L

Content-Based Assessments

Problem Solving

Project 6M — Tours

In this project, you will construct a solution by applying any combination of the Objectives found in Projects A and B.

> ### For Project 6M, you will need the following file:
>
> e06M_Tours
>
> **You will save your workbook as**
> **6M_Tours_Firstname_Lastname**

Each shop of Board Anywhere sells snow and surf tours. Dana Connolly has requested a report of the tours sold each year. You will complete the report for each shop and prepare one that summarizes the lessons sold for the year.

The sales reports for each store are saved in **e06M_Tours**. Sheet1, Sheet2, and Sheet3 contain the sales data for each store. Sheet4 contains the tour date and tour price for each tour that is offered. Using the skills you have practiced, complete the tour report for the three locations—Big Bear, Malibu, and Redondo Beach. Confirm that the data for the data table on Sheet4 is arranged in the correct order. Name the data table and use the named range in a lookup function to enter the Date and Price of Tours on the three store worksheets. Use a 3-D Reference to prepare a summary report to summarize the tours sold for all the stores for the year. Identify each sheet name and provide hyperlinks between the sheets.

Use Cell Styles and other formatting skills you have practiced to prepare a professional report. Include the File Name and the Sheet Name in the footer on each worksheet. Hide the sheet that displays the lookup table. Save the workbook as **6M_Tours_Firstname_Lastname** and submit it as directed.

> **End** You have completed Project 6M———————

Content-Based Assessments

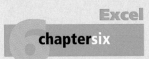

Problem Solving

Project 6N — Withholding

In this project, you will construct a solution by applying any combination of the Objectives found in Projects A and B.

For Project 6N, you will need the following file:

e06N_Withholding

You will save your workbook as
6N_Withholding_Firstname_Lastname

You will assist J. R. Kass by completing the monthly payroll for Board Anywhere. The gross pay for each employee is provided on Sheet1 in the workbook named **e06N_Withholding**. Sheet2 of the workbook displays the insurance and pension information for each employee that will be used to determine the amounts to deduct on the payroll report. The income tax table that is used to determine the amount of income tax to withhold is also displayed in Sheet2.

Complete the payroll. Create a named range for the FICA deduction at 6.2%. Use a lookup function to record the amount of the FICA deduction for each employee. On Sheet2, confirm that the data for the lookup tables are arranged in the correct order. Name the two lookup tables on Sheet2. In the payroll report on Sheet1, use a lookup function to determine the Fed Inc Tax Rate, the No. Insured, the Insurance Deduction, the name of the Pension Plan, and the Pension Withheld. Calculate the Net Pay, and total the columns and rows. J. R. would like to know the number of investors in the AB Growth Fund; use a COUNTIF function to provide that information.

Use Cell Styles and other formatting skills you have practiced to prepare a professional report. Include the File Name and the Sheet Name in the footer and hide the sheet that displays the lookup data. Save the workbook as **6N_Withholding_Firstname_Lastname** and submit it as directed.

End You have completed Project 6N ——————————

Content-Based Assessments

Project 6O — Payroll Summary

In this project, you will construct a solution by applying any combination of the Objectives found in Projects A and B.

For Project 6O, you will need the following file:

e06O_Payroll_Summary

You will save your workbook as
6O_Payroll_Summary_Firstname_Lastname

Board Anywhere has completed the payroll reports for the first three months of the year. You will assist J. R. Kass by creating an annual summary that reports the payroll amounts.

Open the file named **e06O_Payroll_Summary**. Review and complete the monthly payroll reports by calculating the FICA tax and the Net Pay based on the other deductions. Total the columns as appropriate. Insert a new worksheet to summarize the payroll figures by quarters. Copy the column titles of one of the payroll reports and then transpose the data so that the time frame—Quarter 1, Quarter 2, etc.—displays as column titles. Use 3-D References from each of the monthly payroll reports to summarize the data for the first quarter. Use hyperlinks to move quickly between the sheets.

Use Cell Styles and other skills you have practiced to format the worksheet attractively and appropriately. Place the File Name and Sheet Name in the footer. Save the workbook as **6O_Payroll_Summary_Firstname_ Lastname** and submit it as directed.

End You have completed Project 6O _____

Content-Based Assessments

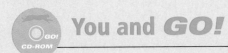
Project 6P — You and *GO!*

In this project, you will construct a solution by applying any combination of the Objectives found in Projects 6A and 6B.

From My Computer, navigate to the student files that accompany this textbook. In the folder **04_you_and_go**, locate and open the folder for this chapter. Open and print the instructions for this project, which are provided to you in Adobe PDF format. Follow the instructions to customize and use a template.

End You have completed Project 6P ————————————

GO! with Help

Project 6Q — *GO!* with Help

In this chapter, you created lookup tables for business applications. In education, a lookup table can be used to determine a student's grades.

In this exercise, you will use Help to create a HLOOKUP for your instructor to use in determining student grades for this class. You will need to have available the grading scale.

1. **Start** Excel to open a new workbook. Display the **Help** window and in the **Search** box, type **HLOOKUP**.

2. Click the HLOOKUP topic and read the contents.

3. In a new workbook, create a worksheet that displays the assignments and points allocated to each assignment. Include all ways that you earn points for the course. Confirm the worksheet is accurate and professionally formatted. In the worksheet, enter the points that you have earned.

4. In another worksheet, create a horizontal lookup table that identifies the letter grade for the course and the points required for each grade. Name the range of the lookup table.

5. In the worksheet that displays the assignments, enter an HLOOKUP formula to determine the final grade. **Save** your workbook and name it **6Q_Grades_Firstname_Lastname**.

6. **Close** the Help window and **Exit** Excel.

End You have completed Project 6Q ————————————

7 chapterseven

Importing Data, Expanding a Table, and Utilizing Database Features

OBJECTIVES

At the end of this chapter you will be able to:

1. Create and Expand a Table and Insert a Calculated Column
2. Create and Sort a Custom List
3. Filter by Using Advanced Criteria
4. Evaluate Data with Database Functions

5. Import Data to Excel
6. Create Lookup Tables in Another Workbook
7. Enter Subtotals and Outline the Worksheet
8. Link and Embed a Worksheet and Chart into Word Documents

OUTCOMES

Mastering these objectives will enable you to:

PROJECT 7A

Sort Data using a Custom List, Filter with Advanced Criteria, Use Database Functions, and Insert a Calculated Column into a Table

PROJECT 7B

Create a Workbook by Importing Data, Use Lookup Tables in Another Workbook, Create Subtotals, and Link and Embed a Worksheet and Chart

DeLong Grant Law Partners

Attorneys at DeLong Grant Law Partners counsel their clients on a wide variety of issues including contracts, licensing, intellectual property, and taxation, with an emphasis on the unique needs of the sports and entertainment industries. Entertainment clients include production companies, publishers, talent agencies, actors, writers, artists—anyone involved in creating or doing business in the entertainment industry. Sports clients include colleges and universities, professional sports teams, athletes, and venue operators. Increasingly, amateur and community sports coaches and organizations with concerns about liability are also seeking the firm's specialized counsel.

Importing Data, Expanding a Table, and Utilizing Database Features

Data that is saved in other Microsoft applications, such as Word and Access, can be imported or copied into an Excel workbook, saving time in re-creating lists from other sources and providing a way to combine several lists into one. Data is usually sorted alphabetically by one column or variable such as customers' last name, but a list in Excel can be customized in any order and by multiple columns or variables. The worksheet can include subtotals and can be linked to other Microsoft applications such as Word and Access.

In this chapter, you will create an Excel workbook by importing data from Access and Word. You will create a table and insert a calculated column that quickly copies a formula in the column. You will create a custom list and sort by that list. You will use functions specific to a database and create a lookup table in another workbook. You will subtotal a worksheet and paste and link worksheet data and a chart into a Word document.

Project 7A **Closed Cases**

In Activities 7.1 through 7.9, you will construct an Excel worksheet for the partners of DeLong Grant Law Partners, Lawrence DeLong and Heather Grant. The worksheet will display the list of cases that were closed during February. You will use database functions to analyze the data. Your completed worksheet will look similar to Figure 7.1.

For Project 7A, you will need the following file:

e07A_Closed_Cases

You will save your workbook as
7A_Closed_Cases_Firstname_Lastname

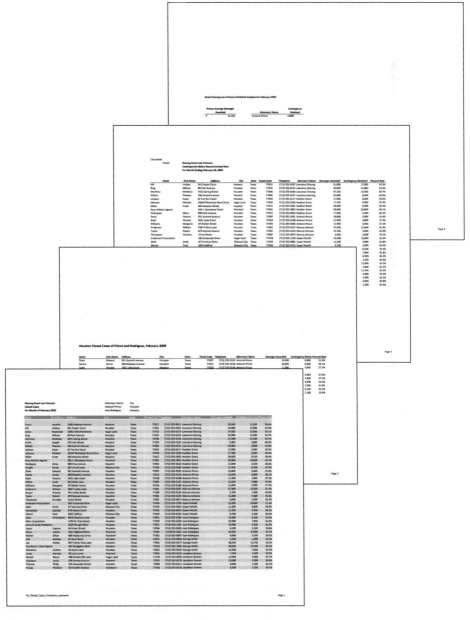

Figure 7.1
Project 7A—Closed Cases

Objective 1
Create and Expand a Table and Insert a Calculated Column

Recall that a **table** is a collected block of data organized so that each row—record—includes all of the data about a single item (a person in an address list or a product in a product catalog, and so on) and each column—field—contains one category of data about that item (for example, the postal code or the catalog number, and so on). Recall that any worksheet can be defined as a table, but a table should include the following characteristics:

- Each column has a unique title that describes the contents of the column.

- Each column contains the same kind of data.

- Each cell contains a single value.

- Each category of data that can be sorted by, searched on, or manipulated individually is in a separate column.

Activity 7.1 Creating and Expanding a Table

Any worksheet can be sorted or filtered, but a Microsoft Excel 2007 table is specifically designed to work with data. In this activity, you will open a worksheet and create a table.

■1 **Start** Excel. From your data files, open the file **e07A_Closed_Cases**. Create a folder named **Excel Chapter 7** and **save** the file in that folder with the name **7A_Closed_Cases_Firstname_Lastname**

■2 Click cell **C9** and on the **Insert tab**, in the **Tables group**, click the **Table** button. In the **Create Table** dialog box, confirm the range of the table—$A$5:$J$44—and then click **OK**. Alternatively, press Ctrl + T or Ctrl + L to access the Create Table dialog box.

Selecting one cell within the worksheet range before accessing the Create Table command enables Excel to determine the dimensions of the table. Your table should not contain blank rows or columns; however, it can contain blank cells. If you select a range of cells within a worksheet, only the selected range will be included in the table. The table is inserted into the worksheet with banded rows. Because there were no column titles in the worksheet, Excel creates **table headers**—Column1, Column2, and so on—to identify each category of data in the table. Table headers are used to sort and filter data and are used in table calculations.

■3 Click cell **A5** and type the following column titles:

Client	First Name	Address	City	State	Postal Code	Telephone	Attorney's Name	Damages Awarded	Contingency Retained

Descriptive headers—column titles—can be entered after the table is created. Column titles, also called headers, must be included in the table and cannot be deleted.

4 Click cell **A46** and add the following client whose case was closed this month:

Shore	Justice	3827 Highland Drive	Pearland	Texas	77581	(713) 555-9203	Jose Rodriguez	36000	12000

When a row is added in a table, it is included in the table range and the row retains the banded color pattern of the table. Likewise, you can add a column to the right of the last column. Using *Auto expansion*—a feature of Excel 2007—the table range adjusts to include the newly added rows and columns.

5 **Save** 💾 your workbook.

Activity 7.2 Naming a Table

Recall that naming ranges and cells assists with proofreading a worksheet. When a table is created, it is given a generic name—Table1, Table2, and so on. A descriptive name that describes the table provides better documentation of that table. In this activity, you will name the table.

1 Click in any cell within the table. On the **Table Tools Design tab**, in the **Properties group**, notice that the Table Name is *Table1*. Click the **Table Name** text box and compare your screen with Figure 7.2.

Table Tools Design tab

Figure 7.2

Table Name text box

Properties group

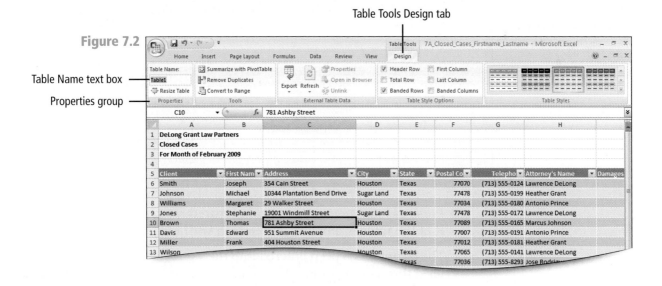

2 In the **Table Name** text box with *Table1* selected, type **February_Closed** and press Enter.

Because the table name cannot contain spaces, place an underscore between words.

3 On the **Formulas tab**, in the **Defined Names group**, click the **Name Manager** button and confirm that the name of the table displays in the **Name Manager** dialog box. Click **Close**.

4 **Save** 💾 your workbook.

Activity 7.3 Inserting a Calculated Column into the Table

When a worksheet is identified as a table, you can quickly create a calculated column. A **calculated column** uses a single formula and adjusts for each row in the table. It automatically expands to the other rows in the table so that you do not have to use the Fill or Copy commands. In this activity, you will create a calculated column that determines the percentage of the contingency retained for the damages awarded.

1 Click cell **K6** and enter a formula that determines the percentage of the damages that are retained. Type **=** click cell **J6**, type **/** click cell **I6** and compare your screen with Figure 7.3.

The formula uses a **structured reference** that displays in the cell and in the Formula Bar. Rather than using cell references, the structured reference uses the table name and column titles in the formula. The name of the table_February_Closed—and the names for the column titles—Contingency Retained and Damages Awarded—are included in the structured reference.

Name of table

Structured reference formula displayed in the Formula Bar

Figure 7.3

Structured reference formula displayed in the cell

Names of column titles

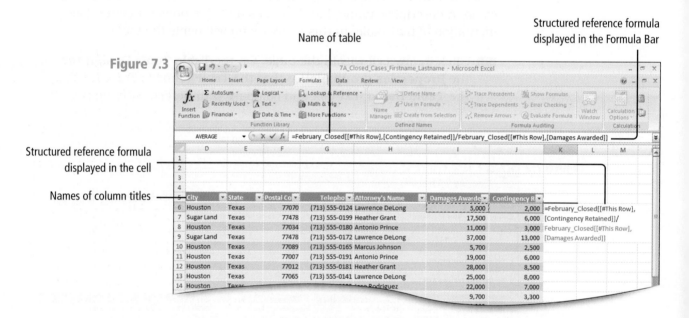

2 Press Enter and notice that the structured reference populates column K of the table. Compare your screen with Figure 7.4.

The formula has been entered into the worksheet and is automatically filled through the range of the table—an Excel feature called **formula replication**. A generic column title is inserted into the column. The

AutoCorrect Options button displays. It may be used to access options for controlling AutoCorrect and to undo the calculated column.

Formula created using structured references

Figure 7.4

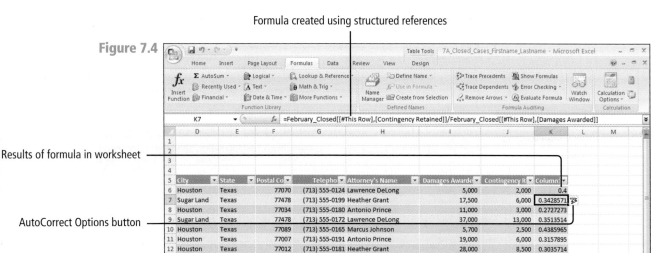

Results of formula in worksheet

AutoCorrect Options button

Alert!

Is your formula not filled in the column?

The AutoCorrect Options button is used to automatically create a calculated column or to turn off the feature. The feature may be turned off or on in the AutoCorrect dialog box. To turn the feature on, from the Office menu, click Excel Options. In the Proofing option, under AutoCorrect options, click AutoCorrect Options. Then click the AutoFormat As You Type tab. The check box under *Automatically as you work* can be checked to *Fill formulas in tables to create calculated columns* and unchecked to turn off the feature.

---

3. Click the **AutoCorrect Options** button 🔻 to display the AutoCorrect Options list and compare your screen with Figure 7.5.

The choices in the AutoCorrect Options button make it available to undo the calculated column or to stop Excel from automatically creating calculated columns. You can turn off AutoCorrect Options when you select Control AutoCorrect Options.

Alert!

Did your AutoCorrect Options button disappear?

The AutoCorrect Options button may disappear while you are reading or if you are interrupted. If that happens, enter the formula again in order to continue.

Figure 7.5

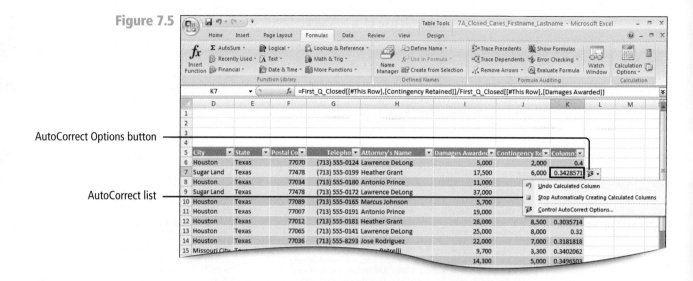

AutoCorrect Options button

AutoCorrect list

4 Click cell **K5**, and type **Percent Rate** Select the range **K6:K46** and format it with **Percent Style** with **one decimal**.

5 Adjust column widths of **columns B to K** to best fit and adjust **column A** to fully display cell **A21**—the longest cell in the column. **Save** 💾 your workbook.

More Knowledge

Control AutoCorrect Options

The AutoCorrect dialog box can be accessed from the AutoCorrect icon or from Excel Options. To access Excel Options, display the Office menu and at the bottom right corner, click Excel Options. On the left side of the Excel Options dialog box, click Proofing and on the right, under AutoCorrect options, click AutoCorrect Options. In the AutoCorrect Options dialog box, click the AutoFormat As You Type tab. To turn off the AutoCorrect feature of using calculated columns, deselect the Fill formula in tables to create a calculated columns check box.

Objective 2
Create and Sort a Custom List

Data is usually sorted in alphabetical or numerical order. Occasionally, there is a need to list items in a different pattern. To sort in another order, create a *custom list*; Excel provides built-in custom lists for the days of the week and months of the year. You can also create your own custom list.

Activity 7.4 Creating a Custom List

When the attorneys of DeLong Grant Law Partners are listed, there is a specific order required, with the named partners at the top of the list and the newest partner at the end of the list. In this activity, you will create a custom list for the attorneys of the firm.

1 Click the **Sheet2 sheet tab**. Click cell **A1** and type the following attorney names in **column A**:

Lawrence DeLong
Heather Grant
Antonio Prince
Marcus Johnson
Susan Petrelli
Jose Rodriguez
Jonathon Somers
George Smith

When creating a custom list, the list can be displayed either in a column or in a row.

2 Select the range of the list—**A1:A8**. Click the **Office** menu , and at the bottom of the menu, click **Excel Options**. On the left side, be sure **Popular** is selected, and then compare your screen with Figure 7.6.

Excel Options
dialog box

Selected option

Figure 7.6

Command selections available

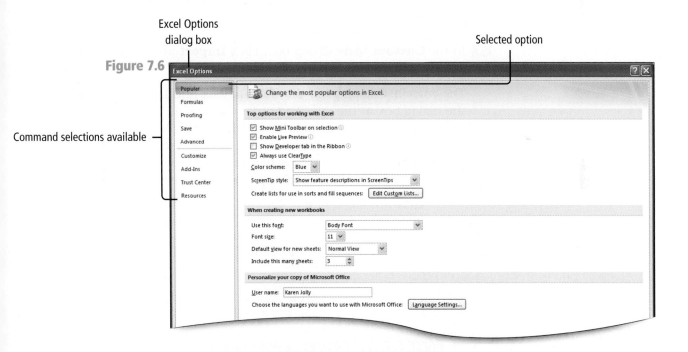

3 On the right side, under **Top options for working with Excel**, click the **Edit Custom Lists** button and compare your screen with Figure 7.7.

The Custom Lists dialog box displays. On the left side are the built-in lists—the days of the week and the months of the year. On the right is the List entries area, which is blank. Below the list boxes, in the *Import list from cells* text area, the range of the selected cells displays using absolute references—$A$1:$A$8.

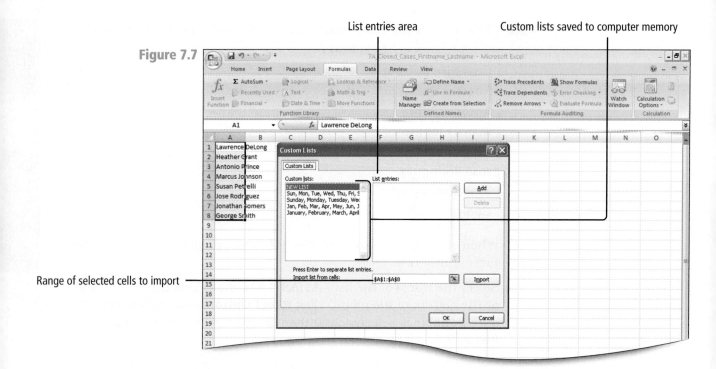

Figure 7.7

List entries area

Custom lists saved to computer memory

Range of selected cells to import

---

4 In the **Custom Lists** dialog box, click **Import** and compare your screen with Figure 7.8.

The entry list displays in the Custom lists and List entries sections of the dialog box in the specified order. Entries in the custom list reside in the memory of the computer on which they were created and are always available. In a classroom or other shared environment, the custom list may be removed when you shut down the computer, depending on the security of your computing environment.

List entries

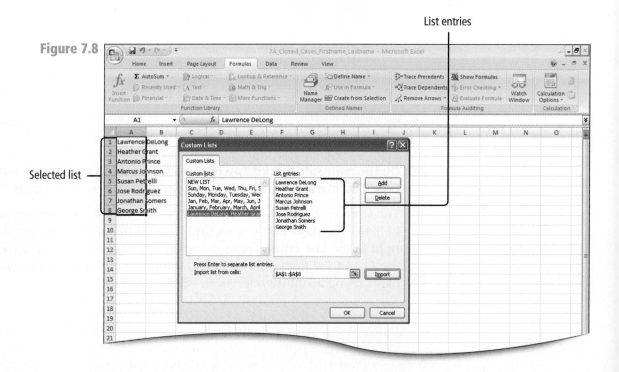

Figure 7.8

Selected list

5 In the **Custom Lists** dialog box, click **OK**. Then in the **Excel Options** dialog box, click **OK**.

Alert!

Did you make an error in the Custom List?

To correct an error in a custom list, first delete the list and then create a corrected list. To delete a list, display the Custom Lists dialog box. Click the Custom list that contains the error, and then click Delete. You will be warned that the list will be permanently deleted; click OK. Then correct and import the corrected list.

6 Delete **Sheet2**. In the **Information** dialog box, click **Delete** to confirm that you will delete a worksheet that contains data. **Sheet3** is now the active sheet.

7 Click the **Closed Cases sheet tab** and click cell **H6**. On the **Data tab**, in the **Sort & Filter group**, click the **Sort** button. Alternatively, on the Home tab, in the Editing group, click the Sort & Filter button arrow and from the list, click Custom Sort.

8 In the **Sort** dialog box, click the **Column Sort by arrow**, and then click **Attorney's Name**. In the **Order** section, click the **Order arrow**, and then click **Custom List**. In the **Custom Lists** dialog box, click the last choice that begins *Lawrence Delong*, and then click **OK**. In the **Sort** dialog box, click **OK**.

The list is now sorted by attorney name in the order determined by the custom list. In column H, the Filtering icon displays by the Attorney's Name column title.

9 On the **Data tab**, in the **Sort & Filter group**, click the **Sort** button. In the **Sort** dialog box, click the **Add Level** button. In the **Then by** box, click the **Then by arrow**, and click **Client**. In the **Order** box, confirm that *A to Z* displays. Using the skills you have practiced, add a third level and sort by **First Name**. Click **OK**.

10 Save your workbook.

More Knowledge

Sort by Month or Day of Week

To sort a list by the days of the week or the months of the year, use one of the built-in custom lists. In the Sort dialog box, under Order, select Custom List, and then select the style of days or months. The days or months will then be listed in calendar order and not in alphabetical order.

Objective 3
Filter by Using Advanced Criteria

Recall that the sorting and filtering arrows are available on a table. Recall also that you can filter on more than one column. Another method to filter on multiple criteria uses the Advanced command for a filter. This command works differently from the Filter command but obtains the same results.

A copy of the filtered data may be extracted and placed in a new location in the worksheet, a feature not available when using the filter arrows. Both the original and filtered lists can be viewed at the same time.

Activity 7.5 Filtering on Two Number Criteria

The **Advanced command** is used to filter a range of cells using complex criteria. The results display in the worksheet. The criteria are typed directly on the worksheet, which keeps them visible.

The partners have decided to review the work of two attorneys, Jose Rodriguez and Antonio Prince. To accomplish this, the partners would like a list of clients in Houston who have had a positive settlement. In this activity, you will use the Advanced command to filter the list of Jose's and Antonio's clients whose cases have been closed.

1 Right-click cell **H5** and click **Copy**. Click cell **D1** and press Ctrl + V to paste the cell. Click the **Paste Options** button 📋 and from the displayed list, click **Match Destination Formatting**.

Although you can type the column title, the data in the cell must identically match the column title. When you copy and paste the column title, you eliminate the possibility of making a typing error.

2 Click cell **E1** and type **City** Alternatively, copy and paste the column title from cell D5 into cell E1.

3 In cell **D2**, type **Antonio Prince** and in cell **D3**, type **Jose Rodriguez** In cell **E2**, type **Houston** and in cell **E3** type **Houston** Adjust column widths to fully display the data. Compare your screen with Figure 7.9.

This range of cells becomes the **filter criteria**—the conditions specified that limit the records displayed. The resulting list will display the clients of Antonio Prince and Jose Rodriguez who live in Houston. On the first row, you placed the column titles, which are the fields included in the filter. On the rows under the column titles, you placed the text or data that identifies the filters needed.

Filter criteria   Column Titles on which to filter

Figure 7.9

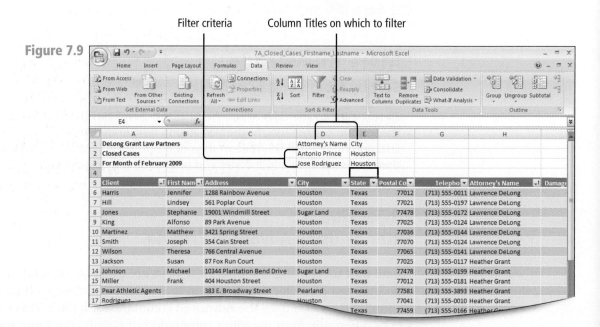

636 **Excel** | Chapter 7: Importing Data, Expanding a Table, and Utilizing Database Features

4 Click in a cell in the **February_Closed** table. On the **Data tab**, in the **Sort & Filter group**, click the **Advanced** button, and then compare your screen with Figure 7.10.

The Advanced Filter dialog box displays. You can choose to filter the list in place, which will replace the existing table, or you can choose to copy the filtered list to another location, which enables both the original table and the filtered list to display in the same worksheet. The *List range* is the range of the table that contains the data, and the *Criteria range* is the location of the criteria that have been entered.

List range selected

Figure 7.10

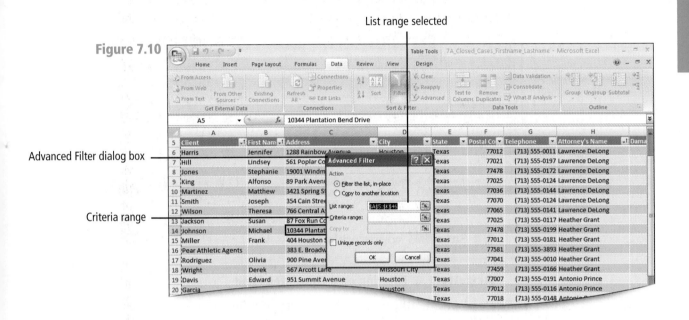

Advanced Filter dialog box

Criteria range

5 In the **Advanced Filter** dialog box, click **Copy to another location**. Confirm that the **List range** includes the range of the worksheet— $A$5:$K$46. In the **Criteria range** text box, click the **Collapse Dialog Box** button and select the criteria range **D1:E3**. Click the **Expand Dialog Box** button . In the **Copy to** box, type **a52** and then click **OK**. Scroll to **row 52** so that the filtered list displays.

The column titles from the table are copied with the filtered list into a new section of the worksheet. The list displays the clients of Antonio Prince and Jose Rodriguez who live in Houston.

6 Select the column titles—**A52:K52**—and format with **Bold** and a **Bottom Border** . Click cell **A50** and type **Houston Closed Cases of Prince and Rodriguez, February 2009** Use the Mini toolbar to format the title with **Bold** and increase the **Font Size** to **14**. Compare your screen with Figure 7.11.

Figure 7.11

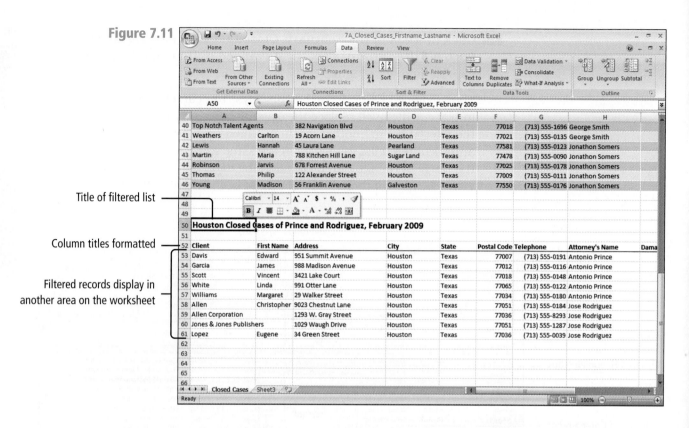

Title of filtered list

Column titles formatted

Filtered records display in
another area on the worksheet

7 Save your workbook.

Activity 7.6 Filtering on a Calculated Field

Data can be filtered on the results of a formula called a *calculated value*. The attorneys at DeLong Grant Law Partners sometimes work on a contingency basis. The client agrees that a percentage of the money from the court-awarded settlement is paid to the attorneys as the fee for their services. The DeLong Grant firm recommends a 35 percent contingency, but not all attorneys at the firm use that same percentage for a contingency fee. In this activity, you will use filters to identify the cases that closed with contingencies less than 35 percent.

1 Click cell **N1** and type **Calculated** Click cell **N2** and type **=j6<35%*i6** and press Enter.

FALSE displays in cell N2. The contingency for the Jennifer Harris case—cell J6—is equal to or greater than 35 percent of the damages awarded. When filtering on a calculated field, enter a title that is not a column title of the worksheet. Because this field requires a formula, the word Calculated was used to identify that. The formula is entered in the cell below the title.

2 On the **Data tab**, in the **Sort & Filter group**, click **Advanced**. In the **Advanced Filter** dialog box, click **Copy to another location**. Confirm the **List range** is the range of the table—**A5:K46**. In the **Criteria range** box, click the **Collapse Dialog Box** button and select the range **N1:N2**. Click the **Expand Dialog Box** button. In the **Copy to** box, click the **Collapse Dialog Box** button, and then click cell **N6**. Click the **Expand Dialog Box** button 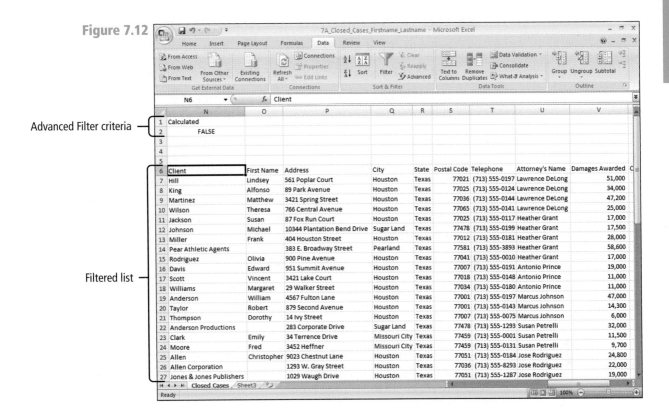, and then click **OK**.

3 Scroll to **column N**, adjust column widths to fully display the data, and, if needed, adjust row heights to remove extra space. Adjust the screen so **column N** is the first column displayed, and then compare your screen with Figure 7.12.

The newly inserted data displays those records where the contingency retained is less than 35 percent of the damages awarded.

Figure 7.12

Advanced Filter criteria —

Filtered list —

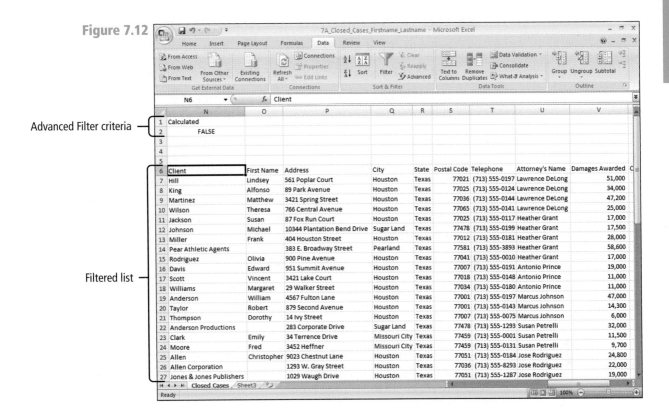

4 Format the column titles in cells **N6:X6** with **Bold** **B**, **Italic** **I**, **Center** alignment, **Wrap Text**, and a **Bottom Border**. In cell **O2**, type **DeLong Grant Law Partners** In cell **O3**, type **Contingencies Below Recommended Rate** and in cell **O4**, type **For Month Ending February 28, 2009** Format this three-line title—**O2:O4**—with **Bold** **B**.

5 **Save** your workbook.

Objective 4
Evaluate Data with Database Functions

Recall that functions are predefined formulas that perform calculations by using specific values, called arguments. Database functions are identified by the letter D—each function starts with a D. The initial D identifies to Excel that a database range will be used in the formula rather than a single column or row of numbers. Excel provides 12 database functions that can be used to evaluate the data in a table. These functions are similar to other Excel functions, such as **_DAVERAGE_** for the average value of a column or field or **_DCOUNT_** for the count of a table column or field.

Activity 7.7 Determining the Average using the DAVERAGE Database Function

The DAVERAGE function determines the average in an Excel table, based on criteria that are set to limit the data to records that match certain conditions. In this activity, you will average the damages awarded for cases handled by Antonio Prince.

1 Click cell **N52** and type **Prince Average Damages Awarded** Format the cell with **Bold** **B**, **Wrap Text** , **Center** alignment , and a **Bottom Border** . Click cell **H52** and copy the cell contents to cell **P52**. Click the **Paste Options** button and click **Match Destination Formatting**. Click cell **N52** and use the **Format Painter** to copy the format to cell **P52**.

Cell P52 will form the first cell in the criteria range for the DAVERAGE function, which must consist of at least two vertical cells. Like the advanced filter, the top cell is the field name that will be searched, and the cell immediately below it is the criteria the function will use in the search.

2 In cell **P53**, type **Antonio Prince** for the search criterion.

3 Click cell **N53**. On the **Formula Bar**, click the **Insert Function** button , and then select the category **Database**. Compare your screen with Figure 7.13.

Notice that all database functions begin with the letter D. DAVERAGE is the function selected. The description of the DAVERAGE function displays in the dialog box.

Figure 7.13

Insert Function dialog box

Select a category section

DAVERAGE function selected

Select a function

Description of the function

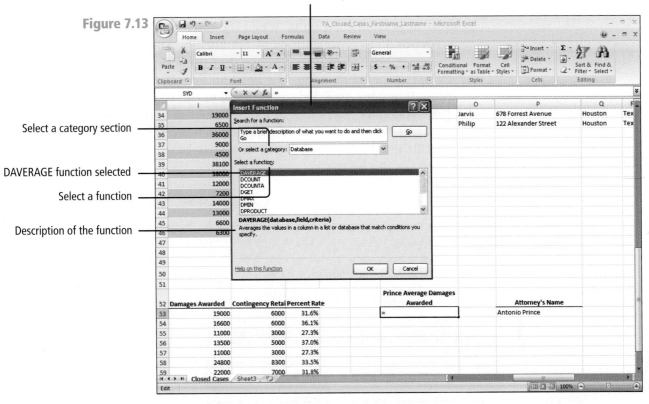

4 Click **OK** to display the **DAVERAGE Function Arguments** dialog box.

In the **Database** text box, click the **Collapse Dialog Box** button 🔳, and then select the range **A5:K46**. Click the **Expand Dialog Box** button 🔳.

The defined name of the table—February_Closed[#All]— displays in the database text box. The selected range of the table—All—is also included in the defined name.

Alert!

Does your database display cell references?

If your dialog box displays cell references rather than the name of the table, click the Collapse Dialog Box button and complete the step again.

5 Press ⟨Tab⟩ so that the insertion point is in the **Field** text box. Scroll in the worksheet and click cell **I5**.

The field or column to be averaged in the database is identified by the column name. The entry includes the name of the table and the column title for the field argument. You will not need to select the range of the data but only the field title.

6 Press ⟨Tab⟩ and in the **Criteria** text box, scroll to and select the range **P52:P53**. Compare your screen with Figure 7.14, and then click **OK**.

The two cells in the criteria range will limit the average calculation to using only those records where *Attorney's Name* is equal to *Antonio Prince*. The function displays in both the Formula Bar and the dialog box.

The arguments of the function are referred to as a **structured reference**—references that use formulas that reference a table and/or portions of a table. When the table range changes, the structured references adjust automatically. The **table specifier** is the outer portion of the reference that is enclosed in square brackets following the table name. The **column specifier** displays the column title—Damages Awarded—and refers to the column data. A **special item specifier** refers to specific parts of the table where the cell is located—#Headers. This information is a header in the table and the specific header is the next text in square brackets.

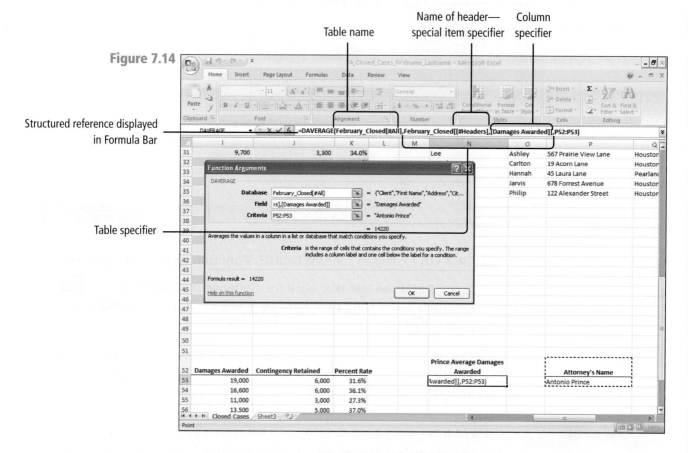

Figure 7.14

7 Format cell **N53** with **Accounting Number Format** $ ▾ with **no decimals**.

The result—$14,220—displays in cell N53. This is the average of the damages awarded to clients represented by Antonio Prince.

8 **Save** 💾 your workbook.

Activity 7.8 Determining the Sum of Certain Contingencies Using the DSUM Function

The **DSUM** function will sum a column of values in a database that is limited by criteria set for one or more cells. In this activity, you will sum the *Contingency Retained* for Antonio Prince.

1 Click cell **N56** and type **Prince Contingency >5000 Retained** and use

Format Painter 🖌 to copy the format from cell **N52** to cell **N56**.

2 Copy the cell contents of cell **J5** to cell **Q52**. Click the **Paste Options** button 🗐 and click **Match Destination Formatting**. Use **Format Painter** 🖋 to copy the format of cell **P52** to cell **Q52**. In cell **Q53**, type **>5000**

3 Click cell **N57**. In the **Formula Bar**, click the **Insert Function** button *fx*, and then, if necessary, select the category **Database**. Scroll to and then double-click **DSUM**.

4 In the **DSUM Function Arguments** dialog box, with the insertion point in the **Database** box, select the range of the database— **A5:K46**—so it displays the table name.

5 Press Tab and in the **Field** text box, click cell **J5.**

6 Press Tab. In the **Criteria** text box, select the range **P52:Q53**, and then click **OK**. Format cell **N57** with **Accounting Number Format** **$ ▾** with **no decimals**. Compare your screen with Figure 7.15.

In this function a compound criteria is used—both the Attorney's Name field and the Contingency field are used to restrict the data that is included in the calculation.

Table name   Column specifier

Figure 7.15

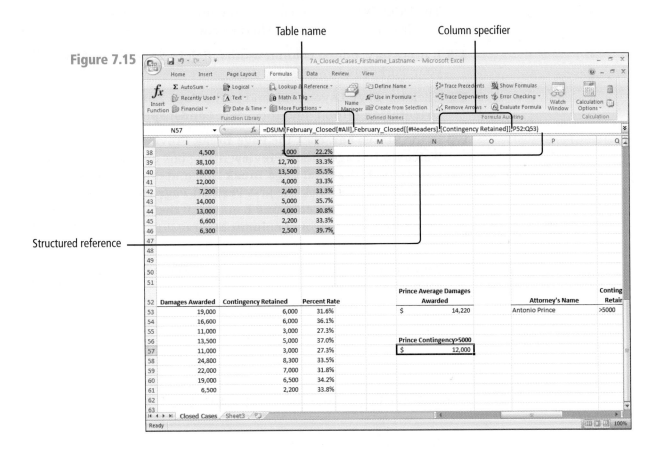

Structured reference

7 Save 🖫 your workbook.

Activity 7.9 Counting Specific Records in a Database

The DCOUNT function is similar to the COUNT function. Within a database table, it counts the number of occurrences of a specified condition. The partners, Lawrence and Heather, would like to know the number of clients who live in Houston who were awarded damages. In this activity, you will use the *DCOUNT* function to determine the number—count—of damages awarded to clients living in Houston.

1 Click cell **N60** and type **Clients in Houston** and copy the format from cell **N56** to cell **N60**. Press Tab two times and in cell **P60**, type **City** and format it the same as cell **N60**. In cell **P61**, type **Houston**

2 Click cell **N61** and on the **Formula Bar**, click the **Insert Function** button *fx* . Double-click the **Database** function **DCOUNT**.

3 In the **DCOUNT Function Arguments** dialog box, position the insertion point in the **Database** text box, select the range of the database—**A5:K46**—so that the table name displays in the box.

4 Press Tab and in the **Field** text box, click cell **I5**.

5 Press Tab. With the insertion point in the **Criteria** text box, select the range **P60:P61**, and then click **OK**.

The DCOUNT function counted the number of clients in the table that live in Houston—the criteria—and located 29.

6 If necessary, adjust column widths, **delete Sheet3** and **Save** your workbook.

7 Click the **Page Layout tab** and in the **Page Setup group**, click the **Orientation** button, and then click **Landscape**.

8 In the **Status bar**, click the **Page Break Preview** button . If the **Welcome to Page Break Preview** dialog box displays, click **OK**. Locate the **Horizontal Page Break line** and drag it so it is between **rows 47** and **48**. Click the first **Vertical Page Break line** and drag it to the right between **columns L** and **M**. If there is a **Vertical Page Break line** to the right of **column M**, drag it to the right edge of the worksheet. Compare your screen with Figure 7.16.

Your worksheet displays on four pages. Manual page break lines—solid lines—identify the four pages.

Figure 7.16

Vertical Page Break line

Page 1

Horizontal Page Break line

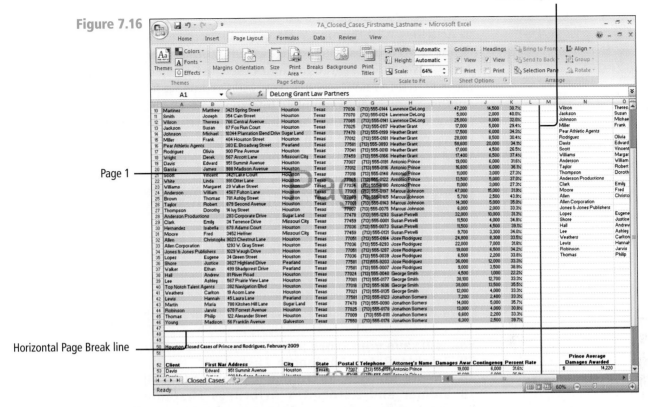

9 Click in the **Normal** button ▦ . Click cell **N49** and type **DeLong Grant Law Partners Statistical Analysis for February 2009** and format it with **Bold** ⊞ .

10 In the **Left Footer** area, enter the **File Name** and in the **Right Footer** area, and type **Page**, press ⎵Space⎵, and then click the **Page Number** button. Then return to **Normal** view and click cell **A1**.

11 Click the **Page Layout tab** and in the **Page Setup group**, click the **Dialog Box Launcher** ⊡ . On the **Margins tab**, center the pages **Horizontally** and **Vertically**, click **Print Preview** to review the worksheet, and then click **Close Print Preview**. Click cell **A1** and **Save** 🖫 your workbook.

12 To submit electronically, follow the instructions provided by your instructor. To print, from the **Office** menu 🔲 , click **Print**. In the **Print** dialog box, under **Print what**, select **Entire workbook**, and then click **OK**. From the **Office** menu 🔲 , click **Close**. **Close** Excel.

End You have completed Project 7A

Project 7B Clients

In Activities 7.10 through 7.18, you will create a list of clients. DeLong Grant Law Partners has merged with two other firms. The firms use Access, Word, or Excel to maintain their list of clients. You will merge these lists into one Excel list. You will then use a lookup table from another worksheet to complete information regarding the billable hours for the attorneys. You will use the outline feature to complete subtotals in the worksheet, and then link and embed worksheet information into a Word memo. Your completed work will look similar to Figure 7.17.

For Project 7B, you will need the following files

New blank Excel workbook
e07B_Clients
e07B_Billable_Rates
e07B_Stevens_Smith_Clients (Access)
e07B_Vidmar_and_Associates_Attorneys (Word)
e07B_Week_Billing_Memo (Word)

You will save your work as
7B_Billable_Rates_Firstname_Lastname
7B_Clients_Merged_Firstname_Lastname (Excel)
7B_Vidmar_and_Associates_Attorneys_Firstname_Lastname (Text)
7B_Week_Billing_Petrelli_Firstname_Lastname (Word)
7B_Week_Billing_Johnson_Firstname_Lastname (Word)

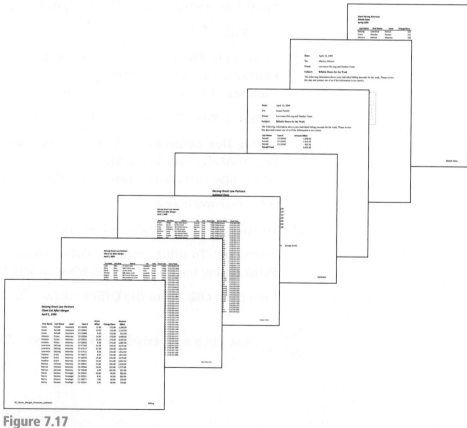

Figure 7.17
Project 7B—Clients

Objective 5
Import Data to Excel

With Microsoft Office software, data may be shared between the applications, and it can be copied and pasted or imported from one application to another.

Data from Access can be inserted into Excel in three ways. You can copy the Access data and paste it into an Excel worksheet. From Access you can export Access data into Excel, or from Excel you can import an Access database into Excel. In order to paste Access data or export from Access, you need to have the Access program available. You may, however, import an Access database without having the Access program on your computer. In Excel, *import* means to make a permanent connection to data that can be refreshed.

Activity 7.10 Importing an Access Database into Excel

DeLong Grant Law Partners has merged with another law firm in the city, Stevens Smith Attorneys. Stevens Smith has maintained their client list in Access. In this activity, you will import an Access database table into a new client list.

1 **Start** Excel. Open a new blank workbook and **Save** it as **7B_Clients_ Merged_Firstname_Lastname** in your Excel Chapter 7 folder. Click cell **A6**. On the **Data tab**, in the **Get External Data group**, click the **From Access** button. In the **Select Data Source** dialog box, navigate to your data files and compare your screen with Figure 7.18.

You have instructed Excel to import an Access database, so only the Access database documents display in this window. Notice the icon used to identify the Access database.

Figure 7.18

Select Data Source dialog box

Access databases available

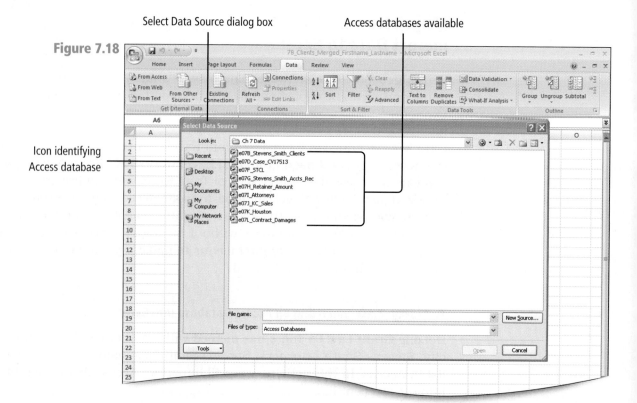

Icon identifying
Access database

2 Click the Access file named **e07B_Stevens_Smith_Clients**, and then click **Open**. In the **Import Data** dialog box, confirm that the **Table** button is selected and that the data will be placed in the **Existing worksheet** in cell **A6**, and then click **OK**.

The Access records are entered into the worksheet as a table. The table begins with record number 8. Access records are numbered as they are entered into the database and when records are deleted, the remaining records are not renumbered.

3 Click cell **A16** and then **Save** your workbook.

More Knowledge

Refresh Access

When Access data is imported into Excel, a connection is made between the Access and the Excel files. When changes are entered in the Access database, they can be reflected in Excel when you refresh the data. To refresh data, in the Data tab, in the Connections group, click Refresh All.

Activity 7.11 Importing a Word Document to Excel

Vidmar & Associates Attorneys is another firm that has merged with DeLong Grant Law Partners. Their client list is in a Word document. Files that are saved as *text*—txt—*files* can be inserted into Excel. A *txt file* contains no formatting and can be read by any text editing or word processing program. A document created in Word can be saved as a txt file. In this activity, you will open a Word document and save it as a txt file so you can import it into the Excel merged client list.

1 From the **Start** menu, open the **Microsoft Office Word 2007** application. Click the **Office** button 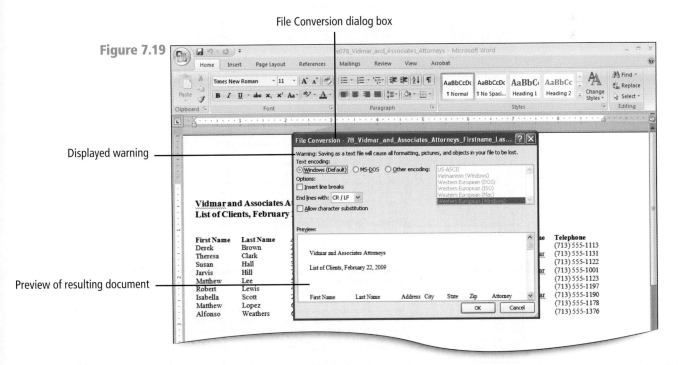, click **Open**, and then navigate to your data files. Locate and **Open** the document named **e07B_Vidmar_and_Associates_Attorneys**.

Alert!

I have paragraph markers in my Word document

Many users prefer to have a paragraph mark ¶ displayed as they work in Word. You may turn the paragraph on or off using the Show/Hide toggle button. In Word, on the Home tab, in the Paragraph group, at the top right, locate the Show/Hide button.

---

2 From the **Office** menu , click **Save As**. Navigate to your **Chapter Excel 7** folder. In the **File name** box, type **7B_Vidmar_And_ Associates_Attorneys_Firstname_Lastname** Click the **Save as type arrow**, scroll down, click **Plain Text**, and then click **Save**. Compare your screen with Figure 7.19.

Excel cannot import a Word document but does import a text file. A *text file* (also a plain text file) contains only ordinary text characters with no formatting and displays the extension *.txt* A Word document must first be saved as a text file.

When a file is saved into another application, a File Conversion dialog box displays. The Warning at the top states that all formatting, pictures, and objects will be lost in this conversion.

File Conversion dialog box

Figure 7.19

Displayed warning

Preview of resulting document

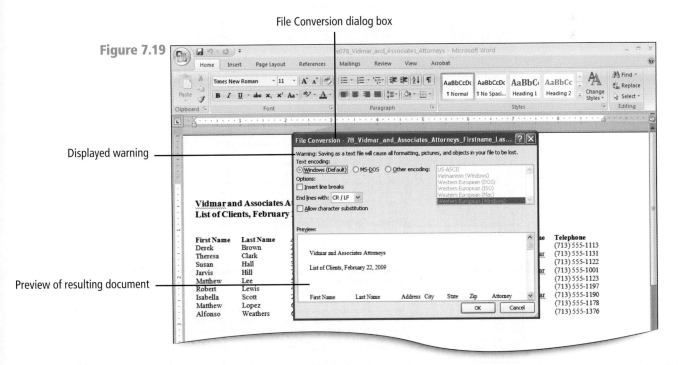

3 In the **File Conversion** dialog box, click **OK**. From the **Office** menu ![office button], at the lower right, click **Exit Word**.

4 In the **Excel** workbook, with cell **A16** active, on the **Data tab**, in the **Get External Data group**, click the **From Text** button. Navigate to your saved files.

The Import Text File dialog box displays the text files available to be imported into Excel. The text icon identifying the document displays and if an extension displays, it is .txt. In the *Files of type* box, *Text Files* displays.

5 Click the txt file **7B_Vidmar_And_Associates_Attorneys_Firstname_Lastname**, and then click **Import**. In the **Text Import Wizard**, click **Next**. In the **Text Import Wizard Step 2 of 3** dialog box, confirm that in the **Delimiters** area **Tab** is selected and the others are not, and then click **Next**.

The title of the worksheet is displayed in column A. It will later be deleted in the worksheet.

6 In the **Text Import Wizard Step 3 of 3** dialog box, click **Finish**. In the **Import Data** dialog box, confirm that the data will be imported into the **Existing worksheet** in cell **A16**, and then click **OK**. Compare your screen with Figure 7.20.

The text file is displayed under the imported table. In the text file, the range for First Name is in column A and in the table, the range for Last Name is in column B.

Figure 7.20

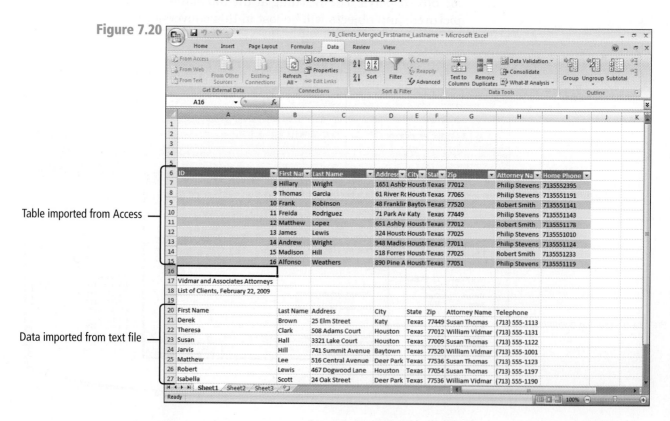

Table imported from Access —

Data imported from text file —

7 In the table, right-click cell **A11**. Point to **Delete** and in the sub-menu, click **Table Columns**.

The numbers in column A are deleted from the table. The table data can be managed independently of data outside of the table. When a group of cells are formatted as a table, you can delete cells from within the table without impacting the rest of the worksheet.

8 **Save** 💾 your workbook.

Activity 7.12 Copying an Excel Worksheet and Editing the Worksheet

Copying Excel data from one workbook to another is the most common method used to insert Excel worksheet data into another worksheet. The format of the original document is retained. When combining data from several sources, it is recommended that you provide a consistent format for the worksheet. In this activity, you will copy Excel data and format the data for consistency.

1 From your data files, open the Excel file **e07B_Clients**. Select the range of the worksheet—**A1:H26**. Right-click, and then click **Copy**. Press [Alt] + [Tab] to display the worksheet named *7B_Clients_Merged_Firstname_Lastname*. Right-click cell **A32**, and then click **Paste**.

2 Press [Alt] + [Tab] to redisplay *e07B_Clients*, and then close the workbook. An Information box displays. Review the Information box, and then click **No**.

Because you just copied a large amount of information to the Office Clipboard, Excel warns that it will be lost when you close this workbook. Because this data has already been used and you will not need it again, you can delete it from the Clipboard and close the box.

3 Click any cell in the banded table—**rows 7:15**. Click the **Table Tools Design tab**. In the **Table Styles group**, click the **More** button 📄, and then at the end of the list, click **Clear**. In the **Tools group**, click the **Convert to Range** button. When warned that this will remove the query definition and convert the table to a normal range, click **OK**.

When you import a database to Excel, a connection is made between the worksheet and the database. The Excel worksheet can be updated—refreshed—so that changes made in the database will be reflected in the Excel worksheet. When you convert the table to a range and remove the query definition, the connection to the Access database is broken and you will no longer be able to update the Excel records. Error indicators appear in several cells because the connection to Access was eliminated.

4 Delete **rows 16:20** and then **rows 25:27**. Adjust the column widths so the data fully displays.

5 Beginning in cell **A1**, enter the worksheet title.

DeLong Grant Law Partners
Client List After Merger
'April 1, 2009

6 Select the range **A1:A3** and format with **Bold** B , **Italic** I , and a **14-point font**. Select the range **A6:H6** and format with **Bold** B , **Center** ≣ , and a **Thick Bottom Border** ⊞ ▾.

7 Select the worksheet data—**A7:H49**. In the **Font group**, click the **Font** button arrow Calibri ▾ , and then click **Calibri**. Click the **Font Size arrow**, and then click **12**. If necessary, adjust the column widths.

The data that was imported from Access is formatted with Calibri 11-point and the other imported or copied text is formatted with Arial 11-point. Text that is imported displays the font used in the original document. When combining data from several locations, using the same font and font size in the worksheet produces a professional appearance.

8 Click cell **F6** and type **Postal Code** Select the range **F7:F49**, which contains the Postal Code data. In the **Number group**, click the **Number Format button arrow** General ▾ , and then click **More Number Formats**. In the **Format Cells** dialog box, in the **Number tab**, click **Special**. On the right, under **Type**, if necessary, click **Zip Code**, and then click **OK.**

9 With the range still selected, in the **Alignment group**, click the **Align Text Right** button ≣ . The error indicator alert displays to the left of some of the cells. Select those cells —**F7:F15**—and click the **Error Checking** button ◈ and from the list, click **Convert to Number**. Adjust the column width to fully display the data in the column.

10 Select the range **H7:H15**, click the **Error Checking** button ◈ , and from the list, click **Convert to Number**.

This section displays the data that was imported from Access. This data was imported as text and is now converted to a number format.

11 Select the data that contains the **Telephone** number—**H7:H49**. In the **Number group**, click the **Number Format button arrow** General ▾ and click **More Number Formats**. In the **Format Cells** dialog box, on the **Number tab**, click **Special**. On the right, under **Type**, click **Phone Number**, and then click **OK**. In the **Alignment group**, click the **Align Text Right** button ≣ .

12 Save 🖫 your workbook.

Activity 7.13 Deleting Matching Names

When data is imported from several sources, it is possible that there may be duplicate records in the list. A ***duplicate record*** occurs when all values of the record match. Use the ***Remove Duplicates*** command to check the list and permanently remove all duplicates. In this activity, you will remove duplicate clients from the list.

1 Press <kbd>Ctrl</kbd> and click the **Sheet1 sheet tab**. Move the mouse to the right and when the down arrow displays between Sheet1 and Sheet2, release the mouse button. Rename **Sheet1 (2)** as **New Client List** and rename **Sheet1** as **Original Clients**

You have copied the worksheet into a new sheet named Sheet1 (2). When manipulating copied data, it is recommended that you make a copy to ensure the original records are retained.

2 In the **New Client List sheet**, delete **column G**, and then click cell **B9**. On the **Data tab**, in the **Sort & Filter group**, click the **Sort** button. In the **Sort** dialog box, under **Column**, click the **Sort by arrow**, and then click **Last Name**. Click the **Add Level** button, display the **Then by** list, and then click **First Name**. Continue in this manner to add sort levels for **City** and **Address**. Confirm that the order for all is **A to Z**, and then click **OK**.

Recall that when you sort items, you can sort on many fields in the records by adding levels.

3 Scroll through the list to determine if there are identical records. Notice there are three records for *Matthew Lee*, all with the same address.

When the list was merged from three firms, it appears that Matthew Lee was a client of all of three firms.

4 Continue checking for identical records and notice the following duplicate names—*Matthew Lopez* and *Alfonso Weathers*.

Although Alfonso Weathers is listed twice, there are different addresses, so this would not be considered a duplicate record.

5 In the **Data Tools group**, click the **Remove Duplicates** button and compare your screen with Figure 7.21.

The Remove Duplicates dialog box displays. Each field of the list is selected. When all checked fields of a record are the same, duplicates will be removed.

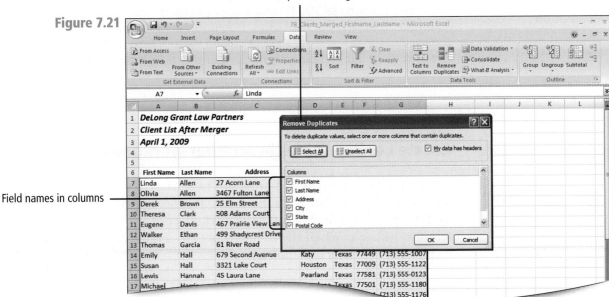

Remove Duplicates dialog box

Figure 7.21

Field names in columns

6 Confirm that all fields are checked, click **OK**, and then compare your screen with Figure 7.22.

An Information box displays and indicates that 4 duplicates have been removed and 39 unique values remain.

Information box displaying number of duplicates removed

Figure 7.22

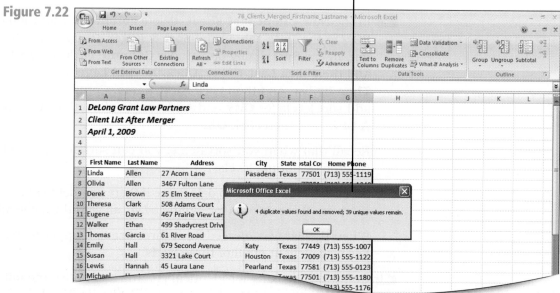

7 Click **OK** and **Save** your workbook. Confirm that there is now one record for Matthew Lee and for Matthew Lopez and that there are two records for Alfonso Weathers.

More Knowledge
Remove Duplicate Dates

If a date is stored as 3/26/09 and another as March 26, 2009, Excel does not consider that they are duplicates. Duplicates are determined by what is displayed in the cell and not the underlying value. When removing data that may contain duplicate dates, first format the dates in the same style.

Objective 6
Create Lookup Tables in Another Workbook

Recall that you use a lookup function to retrieve data from a table array and place it in another worksheet cell. The table array can be displayed in the same worksheet, a different worksheet of the workbook, or in a different workbook. When the table array is in a different workbook, it is considered an *external lookup*.

Activity 7.14 Using an External Lookup

You will create a table array in a new workbook and then create a worksheet that uses an external lookup.

1 From your data files, open the workbook named **e07B_Clients**. Right-click the **Billing sheet tab**, and click **Move or Copy**. Click the **To book box arrow**, and then click **7B_Clients_Merged_Firstname_ Lastname**. In the **Before sheet** box, click the **Original Clients** sheet name, click **Create a copy**, and then click **OK**.

You have copied the Billing worksheet into your 7B_Clients_Merged workbook. Recall that if you move a worksheet, it is deleted from the original workbook, but when you copy it, it is located in both workbooks.

Alert!

A Security Warning appears

Depending on the security settings of your computer, you may have a Security Warning display above the worksheet. If that happens, click Options and from the menu, click Enable this content and then click OK.

2 From your data files, open the workbook named **e07B_Billable_ Rates** and save it in your **Excel Chapter 7** folder as 7B_Billable_ Rates_Firstname_Lastname In the **Left Footer**, insert the **File Name** and in the **Right Footer**, insert the **Sheet Name**.

This workbook contains the table array that will be used to determine the hourly rates for the attorneys.

3 In the **Billable Rates** workbook, click in cell **A5**. On the **Data tab**, in the **Sort & Filter group**, click the **Sort A to Z** button ![A to Z sort icon].

Recall that in a table array, text must be sorted in alphabetical or numerical order.

4 Select the range of the data—**A6:D11**. Click the **Formulas tab**, and in the **Defined Names group**, click the **Define Name** button. In the **New Name** dialog box, replace *DeLong* with **Rate** and then click **OK**. **Save** ![Save icon] your workbook.

5 Click the **View tab**, and in the **Window group**, click the **Switch Windows** button. From the displayed list, click **7B_Clients_ Merged_Firstname_Lastname**. In the **Billing sheet**, click cell **F6**. Click the **Formulas tab**, and in the **Function Library group**, click the **Lookup & Reference** button, and then click **VLOOKUP**.

Recall that a VLOOKUP function is used to retrieve values in a vertically arranged table. The VLOOKUP function looks for a value in the left column of a table, and then returns a value in the same row from another column in the table array that you specify.

6 In the **Lookup_value** box, click cell **B6**, the last name of the attorney. Press Tab. In the **Table_array** box, click the **Collapse Dialog Box** button ![Collapse Dialog icon], and then use Alt + Tab to display the

7B_Billable_Rates_Firstname_Lastname workbook. Select the range **A6:D11**, and then compare your screen with Figure 7.23.

Recall that when you create a lookup table, naming the table array is preferable to using cell references. The collapsed Function Arguments dialog box displays the name of the workbook: 7B_Billable_Rates_Firstname_Lastname; the name of the worksheet: Billable Rates; and the name of the table array: Rate.

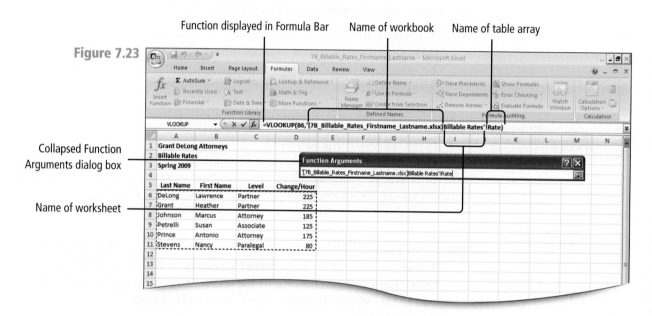

Figure 7.23

Function displayed in Formula Bar · Name of workbook · Name of table array

Collapsed Function Arguments dialog box

Name of worksheet

7 Click the **Expand Dialog Box** button ![button]. Press Tab and in the **Col_index_num** box, type **4** and then compare your screen with Figure 7.24.

The billable rate is in the fourth column of the Rates table array; therefore, 4 is entered as the column index number—the column in the table array where the data will be found. The active worksheet is returned to the *7B_Clients_Merged_Firstname_Lastname* workbook. In the Formula Bar, the arguments are displayed in parentheses, separated by commas. In the Table_array argument, the name of the workbook and the worksheet display surrounded by apostrophes. The exclamation mark (!) separates the worksheet name from the name of the table array—Rate.

Figure 7.24

Function name — Table array—includes name of workbook and worksheet

Name of table array

Column number of table array inserted into worksheet

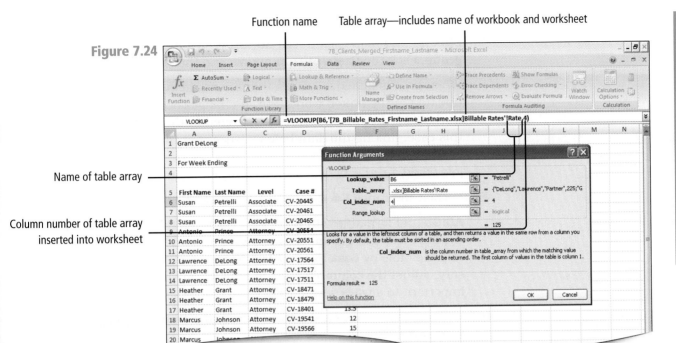

8 Click **OK**. **Copy** the formula down through cell **F24**.

9 In cell **G6**, enter the formula that will determine the amount billed for each case number—Hours Billed times Charge/Hour—and copy the formula through cell **G24**. Format columns **E:G** with **Comma Style** [,].

Even though these are dollar amounts, this worksheet will be sorted and filtered. Recall that when sorting and filtering, the Accounting Number Format should be applied just prior to completion of the report.

10 **Save** [💾] your workbook.

Objective 7
Enter Subtotals and Outline the Worksheet

Subtotals are used to provide a total of a portion of the worksheet data. The Subtotal command provides a quick way to review this data without changing the data or format of the original worksheet. A worksheet that displays several levels of information can have similar data grouped together, and the worksheet can be outlined using the Outline commands.

Activity 7.15 Subtotaling the Worksheet

Lawrence DeLong has asked to review the cases and has asked for totals for each attorney. In this activity, you will use the Subtotal command to provide this information for the current cases.

1 Select and **Copy** the range of the **Billing** worksheet—**A5:G24**. Click **Sheet2**, and then click in cell **A5**. On the **Home tab**, in the **Clipboard group**, click the **Paste button arrow**, and then click **Paste Link**.

When data is linked, changes that are made in one worksheet will be updated in the linked worksheet. If changes occur in the Billing worksheet, they also need to be reflected in the Sheet2 worksheet. In this case, linking the data helps ensure that the data is accurate because the linked data will be updated. Notice that the formatting is lost when a range of cells is copied in this manner.

2 Format the range **E6:G24** with **Comma Style** $\boxed{\text{,}}$. Select the range **A5:G5** and format it with **Bold** $\boxed{B}$. Click cell **B6**. On the **Data tab**, in the **Sort & Filter group**, click the **Sort** button. In the **Sort** dialog box, sort the table by **Last Name**, **First Name**, and then **Case #**. If necessary, adjust the column widths to fully display the data. Note that it is important to always sort a list prior to using the Subtotal command.

3 With cell **B6** active, on the **Data tab**, in the **Outline group**, click the **Subtotal** button.

The Subtotal dialog box displays; here you will specify which subtotals are needed.

4 In the **Subtotal** dialog box, click the **At each change in arrow** to display the list of column titles, and then compare your screen with Figure 7.25.

The column titles display in the order presented on the worksheet.

Subtotal dialog box

Figure 7.25

Fields available for a subtotal

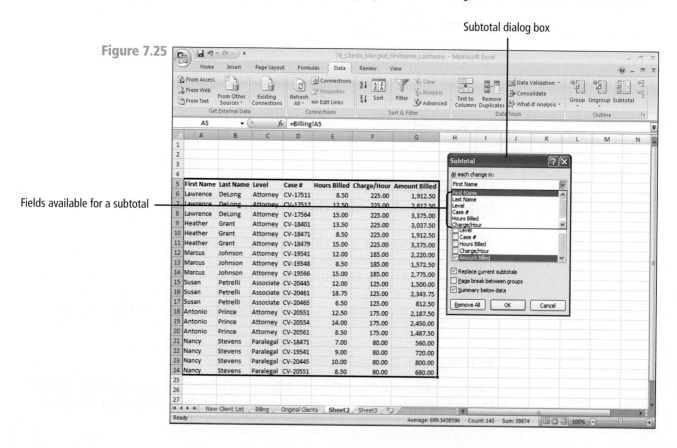

5 Click **Last Name**, and then press Tab. In the **Use function** box, confirm that *Sum* displays. In the **Add subtotal to** list, confirm that **Amount Billed** is selected and clear the other options. Confirm that **Replace current subtotals** and **Summary below data** are both selected. Compare your screen with the dialog box in Figure 7.26.

The subtotal will display for each attorney. When a new last name is encountered in the list, a subtotal will be entered into the worksheet.

There are several functions that can be used in the subtotal command, including Count, Average, Max, Min, and so on. Any of the numeric ranges can include functions that result in formulas, and any of the text ranges can contain functions that can be used with text, such as CountA.

A subtotal may be applied to more than one field of the worksheet. The Add subtotal to section indicates which fields will have a subtotal applied. You can choose to replace current subtotals—if subtotals are already displayed—or display each group on a separate page, or display a summary below the list.

Subtotal dialog box

Figure 7.26

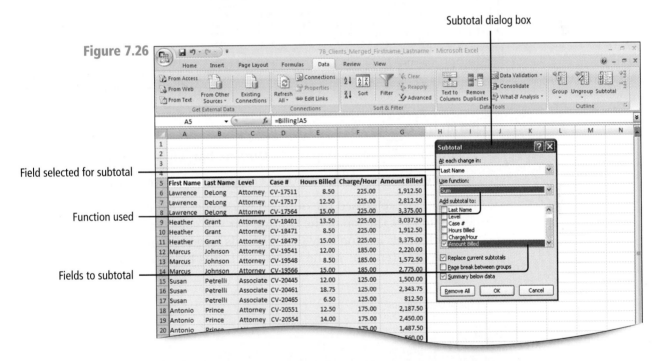

Field selected for subtotal

Function used

Fields to subtotal

6 Click **OK**. Scroll until the last row—**row 31**—displays, and then compare your screen with Figure 7.27.

The totals for the amounts billed for each attorney are displayed in the worksheet. The Subtotal command also outlines the worksheet. At the bottom is the grand total for the entire month. The left side of your screen displays the Outline bar, including Expand Data ⊞ and Collapse Data ⊟ buttons, which are used to display or hide detail in the worksheet rows. At the top of the *Outline bar*—the bar that displays at the left of an outlined worksheet used to expand or collapse the data—are the *Outline Level buttons* 1 2 3 used to expand or collapse the outline.

Figure 7.27

Outline bar | Subtotal Identified | Subtotals

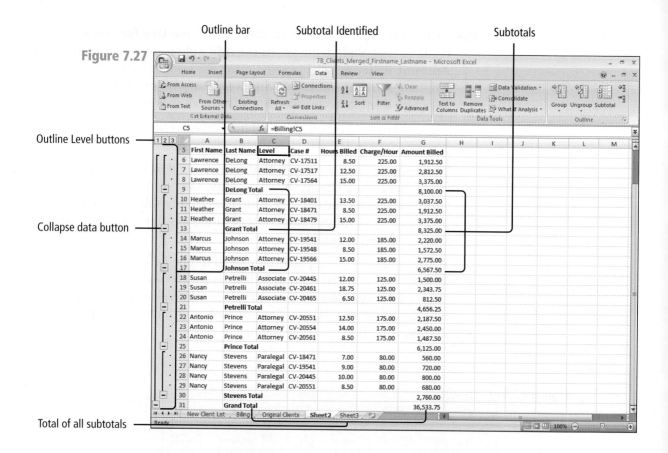

Outline Level buttons

Collapse data button

Total of all subtotals

7 In the **Outline bar**, to the left of **row 9**, click the **Collapse Data** button. At the top of the **Outline bar**, click the **Outline Level 2** button, and then compare your screen with Figure 7.28.

You have collapsed the outlined worksheet. Using the outline level buttons at the top of the Outline bar will collapse or expand the entire worksheet, leaving only the subtotals or grand total for the worksheet. The data remains in the worksheet but is hidden from view.

Expand Data buttons

Figure 7.28

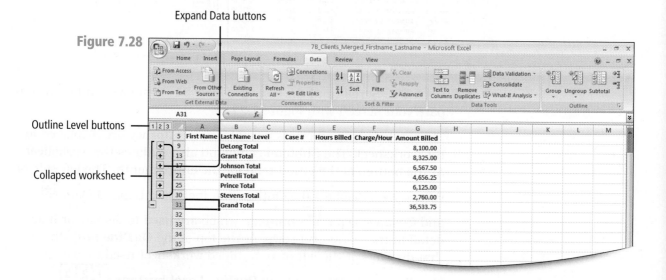

Outline Level buttons

Collapsed worksheet

8 Click in the **New Client List sheet tab**. Select the range **A1:A3**, right-click and click **Copy**, and then click the **Billing sheet tab**. Click cell **A1**, right-click, and click **Paste**. Rename **Sheet2** to **Subtotals** and **Delete Sheet3**. In the **Subtotals** worksheet, click cell **A36**. Type **Attorneys Represented** and in cell **A37**, type **Lawrence DeLong** In the **Formula Bar**, click the **Enter** button ✔ . In cell **A37**, click the fill handle and drag to the right until the ScreenTip displays **George Smith**, and then release the mouse. Increase the width of the columns to display the list.

A custom list can be inserted into a worksheet using the fill handle in the same manner the days of the week or months of the year—built-in lists—can be displayed.

9 **Save** 🖫 your workbook.

More Knowledge

Subtotals Aren't Available in a Table

The Subtotal command is not available when the data is formatted as a table. To use the Subtotal command, first convert the table to a range. When a table is active, the Convert to Range command is available in the Tools group.

Objective 8
Link and Embed a Worksheet and Chart into Word Documents

With the Microsoft Office Suite, text and data from one application can be moved and shared with other applications. Excel data can be pasted or linked into a Word document. When Excel is linked to Word, changes made in the Excel document are automatically reflected in the Word document. *Object Linking and Embedding (OLE)* allows content created and updated in one application to be available in other applications.

Activity 7.16 Embedding a Worksheet into a Word Memo

Lawrence and Heather, the partners, have prepared a memo to the attorneys that discusses their billing amounts for the week. They want to include the worksheet data in the memo. In this activity, you will embed Excel data into the memo that has been started.

1 **Start** Word. Click the **Office** button 🔘, click **Open** and in the **Open** dialog box, navigate to your data files. Locate and **Open** the Word document **e07B_Week_Billing_Memo**. **Save** the file in your **Excel Chapter 7** folder as **7B_Week_Billing_Petrelli_Firstname_Lastname**

2 Scroll to the end of the page until you view the footer. On the footer, right-click, and then click **Edit Footer**. Right-click the footer again, and compare your screen with Figure 7.29. From the displayed list, click **Update Field**. Double-click anyplace above the footer line.

In Word, the footer is not automatically updated when the file name—a *field* in Word—is changed. You will need to do this manually. First select to edit the footer, and then select to update the field.

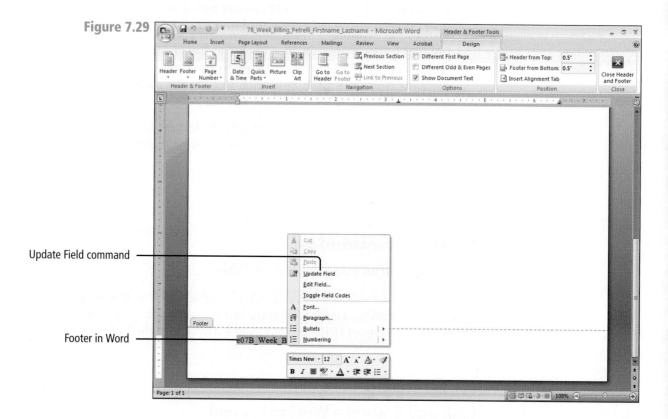

Update Field command

Footer in Word

3 Press [Alt] + [Tab] until the **7B_Clients_Merged_Firstname_Lastname** worksheet icon displays, and then release the keys.

There are several files open. When you hold down the [Tab] key, you will quickly scroll through all of them. In order to locate the one you need, hold down the [Alt] key and press the [Tab] key until the file name you want—**7B_Clients_Merged_Firstname_Lastname**—displays, and then release both keys.

4 In the **Subtotals** worksheet, to the left of **row 21**—the data for Petrelli—click the **Expand Data** button ⊞.

The data for one attorney is displayed while the other data is still collapsed and not visible.

5 Hide **columns C**, **E**, and **F** and **rows 9:17**. Select the range **B5:G21**—the case numbers and the amounts billed for Petrelli. Right-click, and then click **Copy**.

Because you have hidden columns and rows within the range, only the data displayed on the screen is included in the copy area.

6 Press [Alt] + [Tab] to locate the **Word** document and display it on the screen. Click at the end of the memo—just after the word *correct*—and press [Enter]. On the Word **Home tab**, in the **Clipboard group**, click the **Paste** button.

The data is pasted into the Word document. As in Excel, the Paste Options button displays.

7 Click the **Paste Options** button, compare your screen with Figure 7.30, and then click **Paste as Picture**.

There are several options for pasting data. When you select the four options above the line—*Keep Source Formatting*, *Match Destination Table Style*, *Paste as Picture*, or *Keep Text Only*—the worksheet is an **embedded document.** When you insert an embedded worksheet into Word, it becomes part of the Word file. If a change is made in the worksheet, it will not be updated in the Word document.

Paste as Picture command

Figure 7.30

Worksheet data displayed in Word

Choices that will embed the worksheet

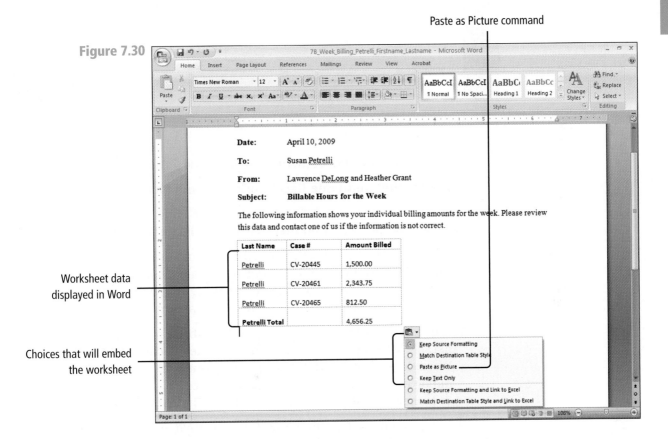

8 Press Enter and compare your screen with Figure 7.31. Then **Save** the **7B_Week_Billing_Petrelli_Firstname_Lastname** memo.

Figure 7.31

Excel data pasted as pictured

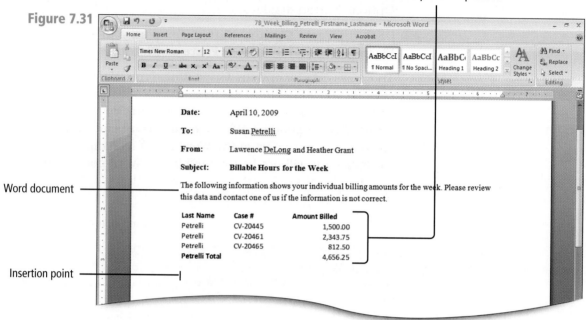

Word document

Insertion point

Date: April 10, 2009

To: Susan Petrelli

From: Lawrence DeLong and Heather Grant

Subject: **Billable Hours for the Week**

The following information shows your individual billing amounts for the week. Please review this data and contact one of us if the information is not correct.

Last Name	Case #	Amount Billed
Petrelli	CV-20445	1,500.00
Petrelli	CV-20461	2,343.75
Petrelli	CV-20465	812.50
Petrelli Total		**4,656.25**

9 **Close** your Word document. Redisplay the **7B_Clients_Merged_ Firstname_Lastname** Excel worksheet and **Save** 💾 it.

Activity 7.17 Linking a Worksheet and a Chart into a Word Memo

Lawrence and Heather have reviewed the memo style and would like to include a chart in the memo in order to visually compare the time spent on each case for the attorney. In this activity, you will link the worksheet and a chart to the memo to one of the firm's attorneys.

1 If necessary, **Start** Word and click the **Office** menu 🔘. From the list, click **Open**. Navigate to your data files, locate and **Open** the Word document **e07B_Week_Billing_Memo**. Display the **Save As** dialog box, navigate to your **Excel Chapter 7** folder and **Save** the document as **7B_Week_Billing_Johnson_Firstname_Lastname**

2 In the memo, select the name *Susan Petrelli* and type **Marcus Johnson** Scroll to the end of the document and right-click the **footer**. Click **Edit Footer**. Right-click the footer again, and from the list, click **Update Field.** Double-click in the Word memo and place the insertion point after the last word in the memo—the word *correct*— and press Enter.

3 Use Alt + Tab to return to the Excel workbook named **7B_Clients_ Merged_Firstname_Lastname** and to the **Subtotals** sheet.

4 Select **rows 5:18**, right-click, and then click **Unhide**. Using the skills you have practiced, hide **rows 6:13**, and then select the range **D5:G16** and select a **Copy** command.

5 Use Alt + Tab to display the Word document named **7B_Week_ Billing_Johnson_Firstname_Lastname**.

6 On the Word **Home tab**, in the **Clipboard group**, click the **Paste** button. Next to the inserted text, click the **Paste Options** button ![paste options icon], and then click **Keep Source Formatting and Link to Excel**. Compare your screen with Figure 7.32.

<table>
<tr><td>**Alert!**</td><td>**Does your Word document look different?**

When you copy and paste data from one application to another, the format of the copied data will use the format specified in the incoming document. Depending on the specific settings of your computer, your Excel data may be formatted slightly differently. For instance, some will display gridlines—in blue—around the data and others will not.</td></tr>
</table>

Figure 7.32

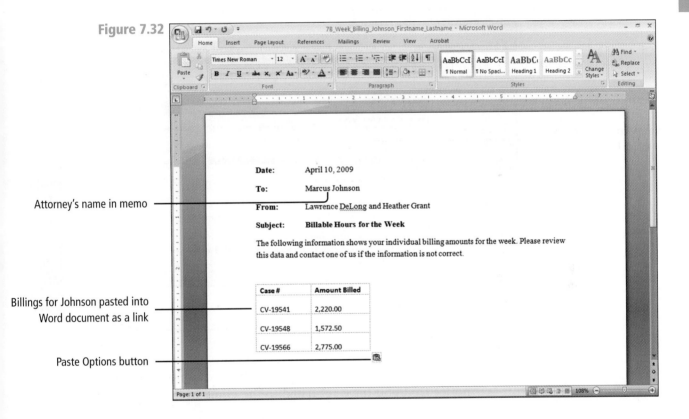

Attorney's name in memo

Billings for Johnson pasted into Word document as a link

Paste Options button

7 Use [Alt] + [Tab] to return to the Excel workbook **7B_Clients_ Merged_Firstname_Lastname**. With the **Subtotals sheet** displayed, press [Esc] to stop the moving border. Confirm that the range **D5:G16** is selected. Click the **Insert tab**, and in the **Charts group**, click the **Column** button. Under **2-D Column**, click the first choice— **Clustered Column**. Point to the top edge of the chart and when the ![pointer icon] pointer displays, drag so that the upper left edge of the chart displays in cell **I5**.

8 With the chart active, right-click and click **Copy**. Display the Word memo **7B_Week_Billing_Johnson_Firstname_Lastname**, confirm the insertion point is below the last line in the worksheet data. On the **Home tab**, in the **Clipboard group**, click the **Paste button arrow**, and then click **Paste Special**.

The Paste Special dialog box displays. At the left are two options buttons—Paste and Paste link. Using this dialog box is another way to paste worksheets or other objects into Word.

9 At the left side, click **Paste link** and in the **As** section, click **Microsoft Office Excel Chart Object**. Compare your screen with Figure 7.33 and read the information about the result under **Result** at the bottom.

Use the Paste Link option when you want to be able to update the content in another application—a Word memo—when changes are made in the source application—Excel. The Paste Special dialog box enables you to control how the image is pasted and what type of object is inserted.

Figure 7.33

Paste button arrow

Paste Special dialog box

To be inserted as a Microsoft Office Excel Chart Object

Paste link button

Description of the result

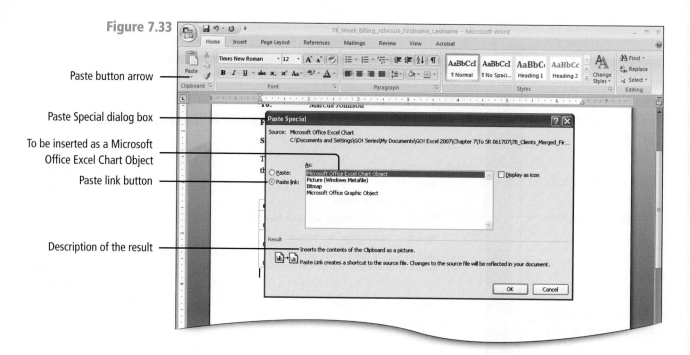

10 Click **OK.** On the right side of the chart, double-click the **legend** and notice that you have returned to the chart in the Excel workbook.

When you are in Word and want to edit the chart, double-click in the chart. Because the chart in Word is linked to the original chart in Excel, the chart in Excel displays as the active worksheet. Notice that the worksheet file name is not displayed in the title bar. Instead, the file name displays just above the column headings.

11 Click the **legend** to select it—recall that sizing handles surround the selected chart part—and press (Delete). Select the text in the chart title—*Amount Billed*—and type **Johnson Billing for Week Ending April 10, 2009** Change the **font size** to **14 point**.

12 **Save** the Excel workbook and use (Alt) + (Tab) to display the Word document named **7B_Week_Billing_Johnson_Firstname_Lastname**.

The title was changed in the Excel worksheet but is not changed in the Word document.

13 Right-click inside the chart, click **Update Link**, and then compare your screen with Figure 7.34.

Figure 7.34

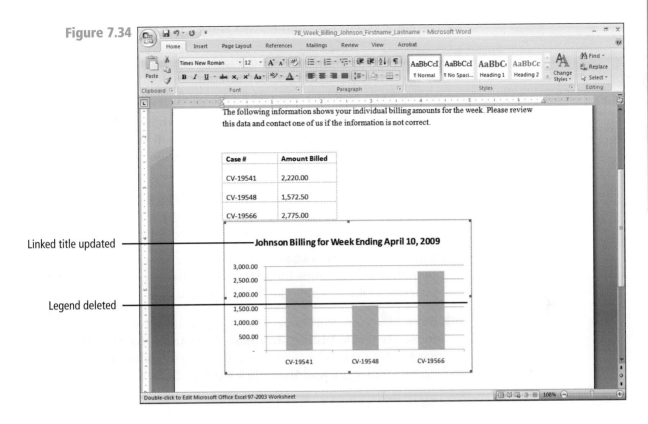

Linked title updated

Legend deleted

14 **Save** the Word document. Press Alt + Tab to display the Excel workbook **7B_Clients_Merged_Firstname_Lastname**. On the worksheet title bar displayed just above the column headings, click the **Maximize** button.

More Knowledge

When to Link and When to Embed Objects

In business, there are times when you want to embed data from an Excel worksheet into Word or other applications, and there are times when you want to link the two files.

When you don't want the data updated, you will embed the document. For instance, if you create a sales report for a specific date and you want that data to always reflect that date, then you will embed the data. This may occur when you have payroll records for a specific period.

When you will use data over and over again in a chart or other report and you want that report to reflect the most current data, choose to link the data. That way the data will always remain current. This may occur when you complete a sales report for a month, but daily or weekly sales information is entered periodically throughout the month.

Activity 7.18 Editing Linked and Embedded Data

Lawrence and Heather have reviewed the work and have noted changes in the billable hours. In this activity, you will correct the billable hours for Petrelli and Johnson and correct the prepared memos.

1 With the **7B_Clients_Merged_Firstname_Lastname** workbook active, click the **Billing sheet tab**, and make these corrections: change cell **E20** to **5** and cell **E7** to **10.50**

For Marcus Johnson, in case CV-19548, there were 8.5 hours billed for a total of $1,572.50, but Marcus actually worked 5 hours on that case. After the hours are changed, note that the amount billed is $925.

For Susan Petrelli, in case CV-20461, there were 18.75 hours billed for a total of $2,343.75, but Susan actually worked 10.5 hours. After the hours are changed, note that the amount billed is $1,312.50.

2 Click the **Subtotals sheet tab** and notice that both Johnson's and Petrelli's total amount billed have been updated. Notice that the chart for Johnson has also been updated.

3 **Save** 🖫 your workbook. Use [Alt] + [Tab] to return to the Word document **7B_Week_Billing_Johnson_Firstname_Lastname**. In the worksheet table, right-click and then click **Update Link**. In the chart, right-click and then click **Update Link** to reflect the change.

Save 🖫 your document.

Because the worksheet and chart were inserted using the Paste Link option, the Word document is a *linked document*, which can be updated when the original worksheet is changed, keeping the linked document current.

4 Open the Word document saved as **7B_Week_Billing_Petrelli_Firstname_Lastname**. In the table, right-click and compare your screen with Figure 7.35.

There is no option for updating the link. This data was pasted into Word as a picture and is an embedded worksheet. Pasting or embedding information provides a picture at a specific date but does not update the worksheet when the data changes.

Recall that when a worksheet or chart is embedded in another document, changes are not reflected. When a worksheet or chart is linked, changes are made and the Word document remains current.

Figure 7.35

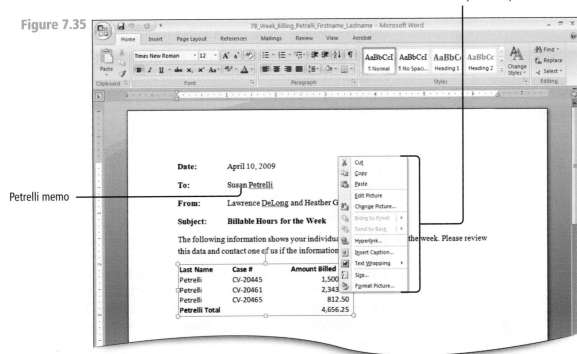

Shortcut menu—no option to update link

Petrelli memo

5 Use Alt + Tab to display the workbook **7B_Clients_Merged_Firstname_ Lastname**. To the left of **row 17**, click the **Collapse Data** button, select row 17, and then click **Hide**.

The data in the chart disappears when the data is no longer displayed on the screen. However, it has not been deleted.

6 Select the range **B5:G21**, right-click, then click **Copy**. Use Alt + Tab to return to the Word memo **7B_Week_Billing_Petrelli_Firstname_ Lastname**. Click at the end of the previous table and press Enter to position the insertion point at the end of the memo. In the **Clipboard group**, click the **Paste** button. Click the **Paste Options** button, and then click **Paste as Picture**. Compare the two tables to notice that the numbers are different. Select the first table picture entered and press Delete. **Save** the memo.

The first table was embedded in the Word document as a picture so it cannot be updated. It provides a picture of the data at a specific time. In order to update an embedded figure, you need to complete the copy and paste function again.

7 Use Alt + Tab to return to the Excel workbook. There is a blank area where the chart was displayed. With that area active, press Delete.

The chart was created for Johnson and then the rows containing the data are hidden from the worksheet. Hidden data cannot be included in a chart. If the rows are unhidden, the range for the chart increases and contains the data from all of the displayed rows. The chart in the Word document will remain visible until you instruct Excel to update that link.

8 Click the **Billing sheet tab** and select the title—**A1:A3**. Right-click and click **Copy**. Click the **Subtotals sheet tab**, right-click cell **A1**, and click **Paste**. Click cell **A2** and type **Subtotal Data**

9 Press ⎡Alt⎤ + ⎡Tab⎤ to return to the **7B_Week_Billing_Johnson_ Firstname_Lastname** Word document and confirm that the chart remains in the document. Then use ⎡Alt⎤ + ⎡Tab⎤ to return to the Excel worksheet.

10 **Select All Sheets** and in the **Left Footer**, insert the **File Name** and in the **Right Footer**, insert the **Sheet Name**. Format the worksheets in **Landscape Orientation**, **Fit to page** and centered **Horizontally** and **Vertically**. **Ungroup** the worksheets and **Save** your workbook.

11 To submit electronically, follow the instructions provided by your instructor. To print, from the **Office** menu, click **Print**. In the **Print** dialog box, under **Print what**, select **Entire workbook**, and then click **OK**. From the **Office** menu, click **Close**. **Close** Excel. Print both the Petrelli and the Johnson **Word** documents. To print in Word, from the **Office** menu, click **Print**. Click **OK**. **Close** both Word and Excel.

More Knowledge

Open a Document That Contains a Link

When you open a file that contains a link, you will be asked if you want to update data. This is an alternate way of making sure linked data remains accurate.

End You have completed Project 7B _____

There's More You Can Do!

From My Computer, navigate to the student files that accompany this textbook. In the folder 02_theres_more_you_can_do, locate and open the folder for this chapter. Open and print the instructions for this project, which are provided to you in Adobe PDF format.

Try It! 1—Filter by Cell Attributes

In this Try It! exercise, you will filter a list depending on the color and attributes of a cell.

Content-Based Assessments

Summary

The Table command is applied to a block of data to facilitate sorting, filtering and other commands that organize and manipulate the data. Inserting a calculated column into a table creates structured formulas that are replicated into the column. Database functions summarize data based on certain conditions.

Data is linked between files using a variety of techniques. A lookup function can be used to link to a table in another workbook. Data can be imported from Access and Word to consolidate data from several sources. Data and charts can be copied to a Word document or linked in a manner that allows you to update the data when changes are made.

Outlining a worksheet and inserting subtotals helps organize data into groups for reporting purposes.

Key Terms

Content-Based Assessments

Match each term in the second column with its correct definition in the first column by writing the letter of the term on the blank line in front of the correct definition.

_____ **1.** A collected block of data organized so that each row—record—refers to an item and each column—field—contains a category of data about that item.

_____ **2.** In a table, used to identify each category of data, such as Column1, Column2.

_____ **3.** When the table range adjusts to include the newly added rows and columns.

_____ **4.** In a table, a single formula that adjusts for each row in the table and fills a column.

_____ **5.** When a formula has been entered into the worksheet and is automatically filled through the range of the table.

_____ **6.** The button that displays when a calculated column is filled, which can be used to undo the calculation.

_____ **7.** A list that is used to sort data in a pattern other than alphabetic or numeric.

_____ **8.** Used to filter a range of cells using complex criteria that display on the worksheet.

_____ **9.** The specified conditions of a filter that limits the records displayed.

_____ **10.** In an advanced filter, the range of the table that contains the data.

_____ **11.** In an advanced filter, the location of the criteria that has been entered.

_____ **12.** The results of a formula.

_____ **13.** The database function that averages the values in a table column.

_____ **14.** The database function that counts a certain item in a table field.

_____ **15.** Used in tables, displays named ranges, column titles, and worksheets names rather than cell references in formulas.

A Advanced command

B Auto expansion

C AutoCorrect Options

D Calculated column

E Calculated value

F Criteria range

G Custom list

H DAVERAGE

I DCOUNT

J Filter criteria

K Formula replication

L List range

M Structured reference

N Table

O Table headers

Content-Based Assessments

Fill in the Blank

Write the correct answer in the space provided.

1. In a structured reference the _____ specifier displays the column title.

2. In a structured reference a specific part of a table is called a _____ _____ specifier.

3. In Excel, making a permanent connection to Access data that can be refreshed is called _____.

4. A file that contains no formatting and can be read by any text editing or word processing program is a/an _____ or _____ file.

5. In a list, when all values of the record match, there is a _____ record.

6. To check the list and permanently remove all duplicates, use the _____ _____ command.

7. When the table array is in a different workbook, it is referred to as a/an _____ _____.

8. In a worksheet containing subtotals, the bar that displays at the left used to expand or collapse the data is the _____ _____.

9. The set of buttons at the top of the Outline bar that are used to expand or collapse the entire outlined worksheet are the _____ _____ buttons.

10. The feature that allows content created in one application to be available in other applications is _____ _____ _____ _____.

11. Pasting a document that cannot be changed into another application is called. _____.

12. A document that can be updated when the original worksheet is changed is called a/an _____ document.

13. To sort data in a specific order that is not alphabetical or numerical, use a _____ _____.

14. To import a Word file, first save it as a _____ _____.

15. The function used in a database to average the values in a column is _____.

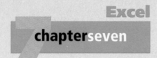

Project 7C — Billable Hours

In this project, you will apply the skills you practiced from the Objectives in Project 7A.

Objectives: 1. *Create and Expand a Table and Insert a Calculated Column;* **2.** *Create and Sort a Custom List;* **3.** *Filter by Using Advanced Criteria;* **4.** *Evaluate Data with Database Functions.*

In the following Skills Review, you will complete an Excel table that displays the billable hours for each attorney and paralegal of DeLong Grant Law Partners. You will filter the data to review partners and senior associates who have smaller billable hours. You will use database functions to evaluate the totals. Your completed workbook will look similar to the one shown in Figure 7.36.

For Project 7C, you will need the following file:

e07C_Billable_Hours

You will save your workbook as
7C_Billable_Hours_Firstname_Lastname

Figure 7.36

First Name	Last Name	Position	Case Number	Hours	Rate	Total
Lawrence	DeLong	Partner	CV-17511	10.00	200.00	2,000.00
Lawrence	DeLong	Partner	CV-17517	30.00	200.00	6,000.00
Lawrence	DeLong	Partner	CV-17564	20.50	200.00	4,100.00
Heather	Grant	Partner	CV-18401	20.00	200.00	4,000.00
Heather	Grant	Partner	CV-18471	10.50	200.00	2,100.00
Heather	Grant	Partner	CV-18479	30.00	200.00	6,000.00
Marcus	Johnson	Senior Associate	CV-19541	20.00	170.00	3,400.00
Marcus	Johnson	Senior Associate	CV-19548	20.00	170.00	3,400.00
Marcus	Johnson	Senior Associate	CV-19566	15.50	170.00	2,635.00
Jose	Rodriguez	Senior Associate	CV-10461	20.00	185.00	3,700.00
Jose	Rodriguez	Senior Associate	CV-23554	15.00	185.00	2,775.00
Jose	Rodriguez	Senior Associate	CV-24465	15.00	185.00	2,775.00
Jonathon	Somers	Senior Associate	CV-13551	20.50	180.00	3,690.00
Jonathon	Somers	Senior Associate	CV-14561	30.00	180.00	5,400.00
Jonathon	Somers	Senior Associate	CV-14662	20.00	180.00	3,600.00
Susan	Petrelli	Associate	CV-20445	20.50	160.00	3,280.00
Susan	Petrelli	Associate	CV-20461	20.00	160.00	3,200.00
Susan	Petrelli	Associate	CV-20465	10.50	160.00	1,680.00
Antonio	Prince	Associate	CV-20551	15.00	150.00	2,250.00
Antonio	Prince	Associate	CV-20554	20.00	150.00	3,000.00
Antonio	Prince	Associate	CV-20561	15.00	150.00	2,250.00
George	Smith	Associate	CV-18730	20.50	160.00	3,280.00
George	Smith	Associate	CV-23554	15.00	160.00	2,400.00
George	Smith	Associate	CV-24465	15.00	160.00	2,400.00
Marty	Hanlon	Paralegal	CV-24483	10.50	95.00	997.50
Marty	Hanlon	Paralegal	CV-24582	15.00	95.00	1,425.00
Marty	Hanlon	Paralegal	CV-24484	9.00	95.00	855.00

Partners and Senior Associates Hours Less Than 20

First Name	Last Name	Position	Case Number	Hours	Rate	Total
Lawrence	DeLong	Partner	CV-17511	10.00	200.00	2,000.00
Heather	Grant	Partner	CV-18471	10.50	200.00	2,100.00
Marcus	Johnson	Senior Associate	CV-19566	15.50	170.00	2,635.00
Jose	Rodriguez	Senior Associate	CV-23554	15.00	185.00	2,775.00
Jose	Rodriguez	Senior Associate	CV-24465	15.00	185.00	2,775.00

Average Associate Hours: 16.83 — Position: Associate

Average Associate Income: $ 2,637.78

7C_Billable_Hours_Firstname_Lastname solutin sent

(Project 7C–Billable Hours continues on the next page)

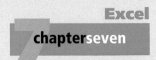

(Project 7C–Billable Hours continued)

1. **Start** Excel and from your data files, open **e07C_Billable_Hours**. **Save** the file in your **Excel Chapter 7** folder as 7C_Billable_Hours_Firstname_Lastname

2. Click any cell in the data and on the **Insert tab**, in the **Tables group**, click the **Table** button. In the **Create Table** dialog box, confirm the range of the table—**A5:F28**. Confirm that **My table has headers** is not selected, and then click **OK**.

3. Click cell **A5** and type the following column titles in **row 5**:

First Name	Last Name	Position	Case Number	Hours	Rate

4. Beginning in cell **A30**, add the following data for a newly hired paralegal:

Marty	Hanlon	Paralegal	CV-24483	10.5	95
Marty	Hanlon	Paralegal	CV-24582	15	95
Marty	Hanlon	Paralegal	CV-24484	9	95

5. Click in any cell within the table. Click the **Table Tools Design tab**, in the **Properties group**, click **Table1** and type **Hours_032009** and then press Enter.

6. Click cell **G5** and type **Total** In cell **G6**, type = click cell **E6** and type * and then click cell **F6** to enter a formula that multiplies the hours times the rate. Press Enter. Select the range **E6:G32** and format the column with **Comma Style**. Adjust the column widths to AutoFit the longest cell in each column.

7. Click the **Sheet2 sheet tab**, and beginning in cell **A1**, enter the following positions in **column A**:

Partner
Senior Associate
Associate
Paralegal

8. Select the range of the list—**A1:A4**. Click the **Office** button, click **Excel Options**. Confirm that **Popular** is selected. Under **Top options for working with Excel**, click **Edit Custom Lists**. In the **Custom Lists** dialog box, near the bottom of the dialog box, confirm the selected range displays—**$A$1:$A$4**—and then click **Import**.

9. With the list displayed in the **List entries** text box, click **OK**. In the **Excel Options** dialog box, click **OK**. Delete **Sheet2** and **Sheet3**. When you delete Sheet2, in the **Information** dialog box, click **Delete** to confirm that you will delete a worksheet that contains data.

10. In the **Billable Hours** sheet, click in the table to make it active. On the **Data tab**, in the **Sort & Filter group**, click the **Sort** button. In the **Sort** dialog box, display the **Sort by** list, and then click **Position**. Click the **Order text box arrow**, and then click **Custom List**. In the **Custom Lists** dialog box, click the choice that begins **Partner, Senior Associate**, and then click **OK**. Click the **Add Level** button. Display the **Then by** list, and then click **Last Name**. Click **Add**

(Project 7C–Billable Hours continues on the next page)

(Project 7C–Billable Hours continued)

Level, click the **Then by text box arrow**, and then click **First Name**. Confirm the sort order for the Last Name and First Name is **A to Z**. Click **OK**.

11. Click cell **D1** and type **Position** Press Tab and in cell **E1** type **Hours** These are the field names that will be used in the filtered list. In cell **D2**, type **Partner** and in cell **D3**, type **Senior Associate**—the data in the Position field to be displayed after the filter is complete. In cell **E2**, type **<20** and in cell **E3**, type **<20**—the value in the Hours column that will be included in the filtered list. Recall that when you use an advanced filter, you first create a criteria range.

12. Click in a cell in the table. On the **Data tab**, in the **Sort & Filter group**, click the **Advanced** button. In the **Advanced Filter** dialog box, click **Copy to another location**. Confirm that the **List range** includes the range of the table—**A5:G32**. In the **Criteria range** text box, select the criteria range in **D1:E3**. In the **Copy to** text box, type **a35**, click **OK**, and scroll down so that row 35 is visible.

13. Select the column titles—**A35:G35**—and format with **Bold** and a **Bottom Border**. Click cell **A34** and type **Partners and Senior Associates Hours Less Than 20 Merge and Center** the title over the range of the worksheet—**A34:G34**—and format with **Bold** with a **Bottom Double Border**. **Save** your workbook.

14. Click cell **A42** and type **Average Associate Hours** Press Tab two times and in cell **C42**, type **Position** Click cell **C43** and type **Associate** and in cell **A45** type **Average Associate Income** Format cell **A42** with **Bold**, **Wrap Text**, and **Bottom Border**. Use the **Format Painter** to copy the format to cell **C42** and cell **A45**. Adjust the column widths so that the titles display on two lines and then adjust the row heights.

15. Click cell **A43**. On the **Formula Bar**, click the **Insert Function** button and then select the **DAVERAGE** function. In the **Database** text box, click the **Collapse Dialog Box** button and then select the range **A5:G32**. Click the **Expand Dialog Box** button. The name of the table displays in the Database argument.

16. Press Tab so the insertion point is in the **Field** text box. Scroll in the worksheet to access and click the **Hours** column title in the table. Press Tab and in the **Criteria** text box, scroll to and select the range **C42:C43**. Then click **OK**. Format cell **A43** with **Comma Style**.

17. Click cell **A46**. On the **Formula Bar**, click the **Insert Function** button and then select the **DAVERAGE** function. In the **Database** text box, click the **Collapse Dialog Box** button, and then select the range **A5:G32**. Click the **Expand Dialog Box** button. The name of the table displays in the Database argument.

18. Press Tab so the insertion point is in the **Field** text box. Scroll in the worksheet to access and click the **Total** column title. Press Tab and in the **Criteria** text box, scroll to and select the range **C42:C43**. Click **OK**. The Average Associate Income—$2,637.78—displays in cell A46. Format the number for **Accounting Number Format**.

(Project 7C–Billable Hours continues on the next page)

Content-Based Assessments

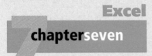
(Project 7C–Billable Hours continued)

19. Insert a row between **rows 4** and **5**. Click cell **C5** and type **Positions Included** Press [Tab] and in cell **D5**, type **Partner** In the **Formula Bar**, click the **Enter** button. Use the fill handle to drag to the right until *Paralegal* is displayed in the ScreenTip, and then release the mouse. This is a reminder of the positions included in this table. Adjust column widths if needed.

20. Display the **Footer** area and in the **Left Footer** area, insert the **File Name**, and in the **Right Footer** area insert the **Sheet Name**. Display the worksheet fit to one page, centered both **Vertically** and **Horizontally**. Confirm in **Print Preview** that the worksheet will display professionally on one page. **Save** your workbook.

21. **Print** the worksheet or submit electronically as directed. If you printed your formulas, be sure to redisplay the worksheet by pressing [Ctrl] + [`]. From the **Office** menu, click **Close**. If you are prompted to save changes, click **No**. **Exit** Excel.

End **You have completed Project 7C** ————————————————

Project 7D — Expert Witnesses

In this project, you will apply the skills you practiced from the Objectives in Project 7B.

Objectives: 5. *Import Data to Excel;* **6.** *Create Lookup Tables in Another Workbook;* **7.** *Enter Subtotals and Outline the Worksheet;* **8.** *Link and Embed a Worksheet and Chart into Word Documents.*

In the following Skills Review, you will prepare a list of the expert witnesses who are often called to testify in specific cases for DeLong Grant Law Partners. Witnesses for each case are kept in separate files. Lawrence DeLong would like a list of all expert witnesses currently working on cases and the rate charged for their services. You will complete a memo that lists the experts in the copyright field. Your completed workbook will look similar to the one shown in Figure 7.37.

For Project 7D, you will need the following files:

New blank Excel workbook
e07D_Witness_Rates
e07D_Case_CV17537

e07D_Case_CV17513 (Access)
e07D_Case_CV17517 (Word)
e07D_Copyright_Memo (Word)

You will save your files as
7D_Expert_Witnesses_Firstname_Lastname
7D_Witness_Rates_Firstname_Lastname
7D_Copyright_Memo_Firstname_Lastname (Word)
7D_Case_CV-17517_Firstname_Lastname (Word)
7D_Case_CV17517_Firstname_Lastname (Text)

Figure 7.37

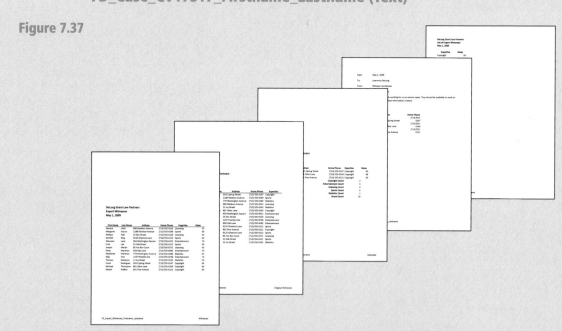

(Project 7D–Expert Witnesses continues on the next page)

(Project 7D–Expert Witnesses continued)

1. **Start** Excel and display a new, blank workbook. **Save** it as **7D_Expert_Witnesses_Firstname_Lastname** Click cell **A6**. On the **Data tab**, in the **Get External Data group**, click the **From Access** button. In the **Select Data Source** dialog box, navigate to your data files, select the Access file named **e07D_Case_CV17513**, and then click **Open**.

2. In the **Import Data** dialog box, confirm that **Table** is selected, that the data will be placed in the **Existing worksheet** in cell **A6**, and then click **OK**.

3. **Start** Word. From the **Office** menu, click **Open** and navigate to your data files. **Open** the file **e07D_Case_CV17517**. From the **Office** menu, click **Save As**, and then navigate to your **Excel Chapter 7** folder. In the **File name** box, type **7D_Case_CV-17517_Firstname_Lastname** and in the **Save as type** box, display the list, scroll, down and click **Plain Text**, and then click **Save**. In the **File Conversion** dialog box that displays, click **OK**. **Exit** Word.

4. In the **7D_Expert_Witnesses_Firstname_Lastname** workbook, click cell **A12**. On the **Data tab**, in the **Get External Data group**, click the **From Text** button. If a security warning displays, click OK and accept the data. Navigate to your **Excel Chapter 7** folder, click the text file **7D_Case_CV17517_Firstname_Lastname**, and then click **Import**. In the **Text Import Wizard**, click **Next**. In the **Text Import Wizard Step 2 of 3** dialog box, confirm in the **Delimiters** text box that only **Tab** is selected, and then click **Next**. In the **Step 3 of 3** dialog box, click **Finish**. In the **Import Data** dialog box, confirm that the data will be imported into the **Existing worksheet** in cell **A12**, and then click **OK**.

5. Right-click cell **A6**. In the shortcut menu, point to **Delete**, and then from the

submenu, click **Table Columns**. **Save** your workbook.

6. Display the **Open** dialog box and navigate to the student data files. Open the file named **e07D_Case_CV17537**. Select the range of the worksheet—**A3:E7**. Right-click and click **Copy**. Press Alt + Tab to display the workbook named **7D_Expert_Witnesses_Firstname_Lastname**. Right-click cell **A20**, and then click **Paste**. Press Alt + Tab to return to the **e07D_Case_CV17537** worksheet and **Close** the workbook.

7. Click any cell in the banded table—**rows 6:11**. Click the **Table Tools Design tab**, and in the **Table Styles group**, click the **More** button, and at the bottom of the gallery, click **Clear**. In the **Tools group**, click the **Convert to Range** button. When warned that you will convert the table to a normal range, click **OK**.

8. Enter the worksheet title beginning in cell **A1**, and format the title lines with **Bold** and **14-point font**.

| DeLong Grant Law Partners |
| Expert Witnesses |
| 'May 1, 2009 |

9. Select the range **A6:E6** and format with **Bold**, **Center**, and a **Bottom Border**. Delete **rows 12:13**. If needed, adjust column widths, allowing the worksheet title to spill over into adjacent columns.

10. Press Ctrl and click the **Sheet1 tab**. Drag the icon to the right of **Sheet1** and release both the Ctrl and mouse to **Copy** the worksheet into a new sheet. Rename **Sheet1** to **Witnesses** and rename **Sheet1 (2)** to **Original Witnesses** in order to preserve the original list.

(Project 7D–Expert Witnesses continues on the next page)

(Project 7D–Expert Witnesses continued)

11. Click the **Witnesses sheet tab**. Click in the data, and then click the **Data tab**. In the **Sort & Filter group**, click the **Sort** button. In the **Sort** dialog box, display the **Sort by** list and then click **Last Name**. Click the **Add Level** button, display the **Then by** list, and click **First Name**. Add another sort level for **Expertise**. Confirm that the order for all is **A to Z**, and then click **OK**.

12. Scroll through the list to determine if there are identical records. In the **Data Tools group**, click the **Remove Duplicates** button. Confirm that all fields are selected, and click **OK**. Two duplicate records are deleted.

13. From your data files, open the workbook named **e07D_Witness_Rates**. **Save** the file in your **Excel Chapter 7** folder as 7D_Witness_Rates_Firstname_Lastname Click cell **A5**. Click the **Data tab**, and in the **Sort & Filter group**, click the **Sort A to Z** button. Select the range of the data— **A6:B10**. In the **Name Box**, type Witness_Rates and press [Enter] to name this range.

14. Click the **View tab**, and in the **Window group**, click the **Switch Windows** button. From the list, click **7D_Expert_Witnesses_Firstname_Lastname**. In the **Witnesses sheet**, click cell **F7**. Click the **Formulas tab**, and in the **Function Library group**, click the **Lookup & Reference** button, and then click **VLOOKUP**.

15. In the Lookup_value text box, click cell **E7**. Press [Tab]. Click the **Collapse Dialog Box** button and then use [Alt] + [Tab] to display the **7D_Witness_Rates_Firstname_Lastname** workbook. Select the range **A6:B10**. Click the **Expand Dialog Box** button. Press [Tab] and in the **Col_index_num** box, type **2** Click **OK**. The number 45 displays in cell F7. **Copy** the formula down through cell F20. In cell **F6**, type **Rates**

and format it the same as cell **E6**. **Save** your workbook.

16. Select the range of the worksheet— **A6:F20**—right-click, and then click **Copy**. Click **Sheet2** and click cell **A5**. On the **Home tab**, in the **Clipboard group**, click the **Paste button arrow**, and then click **Paste Link**. Adjust column widths.

17. Select the data that contains the **Home Phone** number—**D6:D19**. In the **Number group**, click the **Number Format button arrow**, and then click **More Number Formats**. In the **Format Cells** dialog box, in the **Number tab**, click **Special**. From the right under **Type**, click **Phone Number**, and then click **OK**. Click the **Align Text Right** button. Format the range F6:F19 with **Comma Style** with **no decimals**.

18. Select the range **A5:F5** and format with **Bold**. Click cell **E6** and **Sort** the table by **Expertise**. On the **Data tab**, in the **Outline group**, click **Subtotal**. In the **Subtotal** dialog box, under **At each change in**, display the list and click **Expertise**. In the **Use function** section, select **Count**. In the **Add subtotal to** area, click **Expertise** and deselect **Rates**. Confirm that **Replace current subtotals** and **Summary below data** are both checked, and then click **OK**.

19. To the left of the **row headings 13**, **17**, **21**, and **24**, click the **Collapse Data** buttons.

20. Rename **Sheet2** as **Subtotals** and **delete Sheet3**. Click the **Witnesses sheet tab**, **Copy** cells **A1:A3**, display the **Subtotals sheet**, click cell **A1**, and **Paste** the titles. **Save** your workbook.

21. **Start** Microsoft Office Word. From the **Office** menu, display the **Open** dialog box and navigate to your data files. Locate and open the Word document **e07D_Copyright_Memo**. Display the **Save As** dialog box,

(Project 7D–Expert Witnesses continues on the next page)

(Project 7D–Expert Witnesses continued)

navigate to your **Excel Chapter 7** folder, and save the document as **7D_Copyright_Memo_Firstname_Lastname** Scroll to the end of the document, right-click the **Footer** and then click **Edit Footer**. Right-click the **Footer** again, and then click **Update Field**. Double-click in the memo above the Footer line.

22. Use [Alt] + [Tab] until the *7D_Expert_Witnesses_Firstname_Lastname* workbook displays, and then release the buttons. Select and **Copy** the range **A5:D8**.

23. Use [Alt] + [Tab] to display the **Word** document. Click in the memo after the last word—*below*. Then press [Enter]. On the **Home tab**, in the **Clipboard group**, click **Paste**. Next to the inserted text, click the **Paste Options** button, and then click **Keep Source Formatting and Link to**

Excel. **Save** the document. If your instructor asks that you print your work, print the Word memo now and **Exit** Word.

24. In the Excel worksheet, **Select All Sheets**. In the **Left Footer** place the **File Name** and in the **Right Footer** place the **Sheet Name**. Center the worksheet **Horizontally** and **Vertically**. **Save** your workbook.

25. To submit electronically, follow the instructions provided by your instructor. To print, from the **Office** menu, click **Print**. In the **Print** dialog box, under **Print what**, select **Entire workbook**, and then click **OK**. From the **Office** menu, click **Close**. **Close** Excel.

End **You have completed Project 7D**

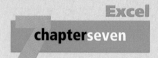

Project 7E — DeLong Hours

In this project, you will apply the skills you practiced from the Objectives in Project 7A.

Objectives: 1. *Create and Expand a Table and Insert a Calculated Column;* **2.** *Create and Sort a Custom List;* **3.** *Filter by Using Advanced Criteria;* **4.** *Evaluate Data with Database Functions.*

Each attorney in the firm keeps track of the hours worked for each of their current cases. You will complete the records for the billable hours for Lawrence DeLong for a week. You will also display a portion of the hours so Lawrence can evaluate the time spent in consultation with clients. Your completed worksheet will look similar to the one shown in Figure 7.38.

For Project 7E, you will need the following file:

e07E_DeLong_Hours

You will save your workbook as
7E_DeLong_Hours_Firstname_Lastname

Figure 7.38

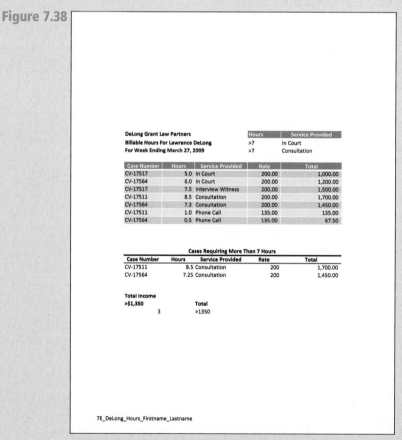

7E_DeLong_Hours_Firstname_Lastname

(Project 7E–DeLong Hours continues on the next page)

Content-Based Assessments

(Project 7E–DeLong Hours continued)

1. **Start** Excel and from your data, open the file **e07E_DeLong_Hours**. **Save** the file in your **Excel Chapter 7** folder as **7E_DeLong_Hours_Firstname_Lastname**

2. Select a cell in the worksheet data and insert a table. Name the table **DeLong**

3. Replace the headers inserted into the table with the following column titles. Center the column titles.

Case Number	Hours	Service Provided	Rate

4. Add the following data about another billable service at the end of the table—row 12:

CV-17564	.5	Phone Call	135

5. In cell **E5** type **Total** Create a formula in cell **E6** that uses the structured reference method to multiply the hours times the rate. Format the **Rate** and **Total** column with **Comma Style**. Format the **Hours** column with **Comma Style** and one decimal, and then adjust column widths if necessary.

6. On **Sheet2**, type a list for the following services provided, and then use **Excel Options** to create a custom list:

In Court
Interview Witness
Consultation
Phone Call

7. After the custom list is created, delete **Sheet2** and **Sheet3**. Display **Sheet1** and **Sort** by **Service Provided** using the order of the custom list you created, and then sort by **Case Number**.

8. Beginning in cell **D1**, create a criteria range and then use an **Advanced** filter to determine which cases required more than 7 hours either in court or for consultation. **Copy** the filtered data to cell **A17**.

9. In the filtered range, format the column titles with **Bold**, **Center**, and a **Bottom Border**. Click cell **A16** and type **Cases Requiring More Than 7 Hours Merge and Center** the title over columns **A:E** and format with **Bold** and a **Thick Bottom Border**.

10. In cell **A22**, type **Total Income >$1,350** and format it with **Bold** and **Wrap Text**, and then adjust the column width so the title displays on two lines; adjust row height if needed.

11. In cell **C22**, type **Total** and copy the format from cell **A22** to cell **C22**. In cell **C23**, type **>1350** In cell **A23**, enter the **DCOUNT** function that will count the number of items in the Total column that exceed 1,350 total billed. The number 3 will display in cell A23.

12. Center the worksheet both **Horizontally** and **Vertically**, and add the **File Name** to the footer.

13. **Print** the worksheet or submit electronically as directed. If you are directed to submit printed formulas, refer to Activity 1.12 to do so. If you printed your formulas, be sure to redisplay the worksheet by pressing [Ctrl] + [`]. From the **Office** menu, click **Close**. If you are prompted to save changes, click **No**. **Close** Excel.

End **You have completed Project 7E**

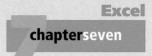

Project 7F — Interns

In this project, you will apply the skills you have practiced from the Objectives in Project 7B.

Objectives: 5. *Import Data to Excel;* **6.** *Create Lookup Tables in Another Workbook;* **7.** *Enter Subtotals and Outline the Worksheet;* **8.** *Link and Embed a Worksheet and Chart into Word Documents.*

Each spring, many students apply to DeLong Grant Law Partners to serve as interns. Part of the screening process is the student's grade point average. The intern director, Tricia Charleston, has asked for the grade point average for students from each law school. Each college or university submits the student data in a different application—some use Access, some use Excel, and some use Word. In this Mastering Excel project, you will place the individual files into one file and then determine the status of each applicant. You will also chart the results and prepare a Word memo that displays the charted results. Your completed files will look similar to those shown in Figure 7.39.

For Project 7F, you will need the following files:

New blank Excel workbook
e07F_UH
e07F_GPA_Table
e07F_RU

e07F__STCL (Access)
e07F_TSU (Word)
e07F_GPA_Memo (Word)

You will save your files as
7F_Interns_Firstname_Lastname
7F_GPA_Table_Firstname_Lastname
7F_GPA_Memo_Firstname_Lastname (Word)
7F_TSU_Firstname_Lastname (Text)

Figure 7.39

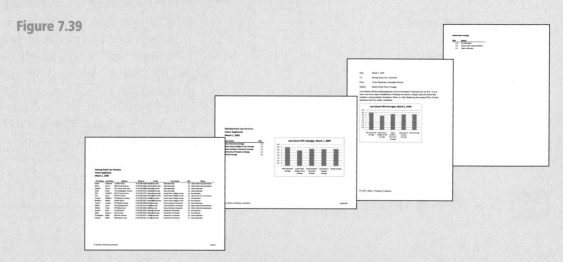

(Project 7F–Interns continues on the next page)

Content-Based Assessments

(Project 7F–Interns continued)

1. **Start** Excel and display a new, blank workbook and **Save** it as **7F_Interns_Firstname_Lastname** Click cell **A5**. On the **Data tab**, in the **Get External Data group**, click the **From Access** button. Navigate to your data files and open the Access file **e07F_STCL** (named for South Texas College of Law) and **Import** the data to Excel.

2. **Start** Microsoft Word. **Open** the Word file **e07F_TSU** (named for Texas Southern University). **Save** the file in your **Excel Chapter 7** folder, as a **Plain Text** file type, with the name **7F_TSU_Firstname_Lastname** and then **Exit** Word.

3. In the **7F_Interns_Firstname_Lastname** workbook, click cell **A10**. On the **Data tab**, in the **Get External Data group**, click the **From Text** button, and import the txt file, **7F_TSU_Firstname_Lastname**. Confirm that **Delimiters** is set to **Tab** and complete the steps. **Delete rows 10:13**. In the table, **Delete column A**.

4. From your data files, open the Excel file **e07F_RU** (named for Rice University). **Copy** the range of the worksheet data excluding column titles—**A6:G9**—into cell **A13** of the **7F_Interns_Firstname_Lastname** worksheet. Open the Excel file **e07F_UH** (named for University of Houston). **Copy** the data—**A6:G10**—and **Paste** it into the **7F_Interns_Firstname_Lastname** workbook in cell **A17**. **Close** workbooks **e07F_RU** and **e07F_UH**.

5. Click any cell in the banded table, and clear the table style, and then convert the table to a range. Format the GPA data in **column G** with **Comma Style** with **one decimal** and adjust the column width. Format the telephone numbers in **column D** for **Phone Numbers** and **Align Text Right**. Format the range **A5:G5** with **Bold**, **Center**, and a **Bottom Border.** Adjust column widths.

In **row 5**, capitalize the **N** in *First Name* and *Last Name* and capitalize the **E** in *E-mail.*

6. Beginning in cell **A1**, enter the worksheet title and format it with **Bold** and a **14-point font**.

| DeLong Grant Law Partners |
| Intern Applicants |
| 'March 1, 2009 |

7. **Copy** the worksheet into a new sheet and rename **Sheet1** to **Interns** and rename **Sheet1 (2)** to **Original Interns**

8. In the **Interns sheet**, sort by **Law School**, and then by **Last Name** and **First Name**. Confirm that the order for all is **A to Z**. Then click **OK**. Remove duplicates, confirm that all fields are checked, and then click **OK**. In cell **H5**, type **Status** and format it the same as cell **F5**.

9. From your data files, open the workbook named **e07F_GPA_Table**. **Save** the file in your **Excel Chapter 7** folder as **7F_GPA_Table_Firstname_Lastname Sort** the grade point averages from smallest to largest. Select the table data and name the range as **GPA**. **Save** the workbook.

10. Display your **7F_Interns_Firstname_Lastname** workbook. On the **Interns sheet**, click cell **H6**, and use the **VLOOKUP** function to determine the status of each applicant based on his or her grade point average. Adjust the column width.

11. **Copy** the intern data beginning with the column titles to **Sheet2**, cell **A5**, and use **Paste Link** to display the data. Name **Sheet2 Subtotals** and adjust the column widths. **Copy** and **Paste** the three-line title from the **Interns sheet** into the range **F1:F3** of the **Subtotals sheet**. Format the column titles with **Bold** and **Thick Bottom Border**.

(Project 7F–Interns continues on the next page)

(Project 7F–Interns continued)

12. Format the phone numbers with the **Number Format** for **Phone Number**, and then click the **Align Text Left** button. Format the grade point averages with **Comma Style** with **one decimal**. Click cell **F18** to deselect the range and retain an active cell in the worksheet.

13. On the **Data tab**, in the **Outline group**, click the **Subtotal** button. At each change in **Law School**, **Average** the **GPA**—make sure that only GPA is selected. In the outline, click on the **Level 2** outline button. **Hide columns A:E** and **column H**. Adjust the column widths.

14. **Start** Word, and from the **Office** menu, display the **Open** dialog box. From the student data files, open the Word file **e07F_GPA_Memo**. Display the **Save As** dialog box, navigate to your **Excel Chapter 7** folder and **Save** the document as **7F_GPA_Memo_Firstname_Lastname** Scroll to the end of the document, right-click the **Footer**, and then click **Edit Footer**. Right-click again, and then click **Update Field**. Double-click in the memo above the Footer line and click after the last word of the memo—*institutions*. Press [Enter].

15. In the Excel file **7F_Interns_Firstname_Lastname**, on the **Subtotals sheet**, select the law school names and the average GPAs, including column titles for the four schools listed and the Grand Average. Click the **Insert tab**, and then create a **2-D Clustered Column** chart. Move the chart so that the left corner of the chart is in cell **J4**. Replace the **title** with **Law School GPA Averages, March 1, 2009** Change the title **Font Size** to **14 point** and then **Delete** the **legend**. With the chart active, use a **Copy** command.

16. Display the **7F_GPA_Memo_Firstname_Lastname** Word document. On the **Home tab**, in the **Clipboard group**, click the **Paste button arrow**, and then click **Paste Special**. Click the **Paste Link** option button, and in the **As** section, click **Microsoft Office Excel Chart Object**. Click **OK**. **Save** the file.

17. There is an error in the GPA for Emily Smith of Rice University. In the **Interns sheet**, correct her GPA to 3.9. In the **Subtotals sheet**, confirm that the average GPA for Rice has changed from 3.2 to 3.5. Display the **7F_GPA_Memo_Firstname_Lastname** Word document and in the chart, right-click and click **Update Link**. **Save** the file.

18. **Print** the Word memo or submit electronically as directed. **Exit** Word.

19. In the **7F_Interns_Firstname_Lastname** Excel file, **Delete** Sheet3. In the **Subtotals sheet**, click cell **F1** to deselect the chart. On all worksheets, place the **File Name** in the left footer and the **Sheet Name** in the right footer. Change the orientation to **Landscape** and **Fit to page**. Center **Horizontally** and **Vertically**. **Save** your workbook. **Ungroup sheets**, right-click the **Original Interns sheet tab**, and click **Hide**. **Save** your workbook.

20. **Print** the worksheets or submit electronically as directed. If you are directed to submit printed formulas refer to Activity 1.12 to do so. If you printed your formulas, be sure to redisplay the worksheet by pressing [Ctrl] + [`]. From the **Office** menu, click **Close**. If you are prompted to save changes, click **No**. **Exit** Excel

End **You have completed Project 7F**

Content-Based Assessments

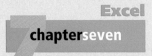
Project 7G—Accounts Receivable

In this project, you will apply the skills you practiced from the Objectives in Projects 7A and 7B.

Objectives: 1. *Create and Expand a Table and Insert a Calculated Column;* **2.** *Create and Sort a Custom List;* **5.** *Import Data to Excel;* **7.** *Enter Subtotals and Outline the Worksheet;* **8.** *Link and Embed a Worksheet and Chart into Word Documents.*

In the following Mastering Excel project, you will complete an accounts receivable report for DeLong Grant Law Partners. The law firm grants credit and payment agreements with its clients and periodically lists the amounts that are owed to the firm. Each of the merged firms has its list of accounts receivable which you will merge into one report. You will then prepare a Word memo summarizing the data. Your completed workbook and memo will look similar to the ones shown in Figure 7.40.

For Project 7G, you will need the following files:

New blank Excel workbook

e07G_AR

e07G_Stevens_Smith_Accts_Rec (Access)

e07G_Vidmar_and_Associates_AR (Word)

e07G_AR_Memo (Word)

You will save your files as
7G_Accounts_Receivable_Firstname_Lastname
7G_AR_Memo_Firstname_Lastname (Word)
7G_Vidmar_and_Associates_AR_Firstname_Lastname (Text)

Figure 7.40

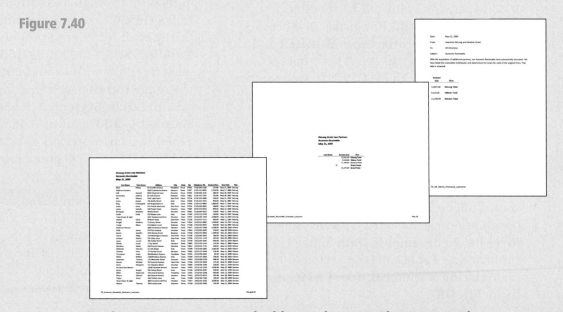

(Project 7G–Accounts Receivable continues on the next page)

Content-Based Assessments

(Project 7G–Accounts Receivable continued)

1. **Start** Excel and display a new, blank Excel workbook. **Save** the workbook as **7G_Accounts_Receivable_Firstname_Lastname**

2. Beginning in cell **A1**, enter the worksheet title:

DeLong Grant Law Partners
Accounts Receivable
'May 31, 2009

3. **Start** Word and from the student files, locate and open the file **e07G_Vidmar_and_Associates_AR**. Save the file to your **Excel Chapter 7** folder as a **Plain Text** file and name it **7G_Vidmar_and_Associates_AR_Firstname_Lastname Close** the Word document.

4. In the Excel **7G_Accounts_Receivable_Firstname_Lastname** workbook, click cell **A5**. Display the **Import Text File** dialog box, select the **7G_Vidmar_and_Associates_AR_Firstname_Lastname** file and import it. In the original Word document there are spaces at the top that are imported as blank rows. Notice that cell **B12** displays an address for Anderson Grocers rather than a first name, and cell **I12** is empty. Select the range **B12:H12** and move them to the right one cell so that the data resides in the range **C12:I12**. **Delete rows 5:8**. Click cell **J5** and type **Firm** In cell **J6**, type **Vidmar** and copy the name down the range through cell **J17**. Then click in the **Paste Options button** and click **Copy Cells**.

5. Click cell **A19**. On the **Data tab**, select to import data **From Access**. Navigate to your student data files and locate and open the Access file **e07G_Stevens_Smith_Accts_Rec** In the **Import Data** dialog box, confirm that **Table** will be inserted into the **Existing worksheet** in cell **A19**, and then click **OK**.

6. From the table, remove the **column A** data. **Clear** the table style and convert the table to a range. Click cell **J20** and type **Stevens** and copy the name down the range through cell **J29**. Confirm that *Stevens* was copied in the range. **Delete rows 18:19**. **Save** your workbook.

7. Click cell **A28**. **Open** the Excel worksheet named **e07G_AR** and **Copy** the range **A6:I20** to the **7G_Accounts_Receivable_Firstname_Lastname** workbook to cell **A28**. Click cell **J28** and type **DeLong** and copy the name down through cell **J42**. **Close** the **e07G_Accounts_Receivable_Firstname_Lastname** workbook.

8. Review the worksheet. Notice that the telephone numbers have imported using the Scientific number format and the due dates have been imported in three different date styles. Also notice that the amount due is not formatted the same. Format the range **A5:J5** with **Bold**, **Center**, and a **Bottom Border**.

9. Select the range **F6:F42** and format with the **Special** number format of **Zip Code** and select to **Align Text Right**. Select the range **G6:G42**. Format the numbers with the **Special** number format of **Phone Number**. Select the range **H6:H42** and format the range with **Comma Style**. Select the range **I6:I42** and format the range with the **Date Style** that displays as **March 14, 2001**. Adjust column widths. Select the **Title—A1:A3**—and format with **Bold**, **Italic**, and **14-point font**. **Save** your workbook.

10. Click the **Sheet2 sheet tab** and in cell **A3** type **DeLong** In cell **A4** type **Vidmar** and in cell **A5** type **Stevens** Select the range—**A3:A5**—and from the **Office** menu, display the **Excel Options** dialog box and create a custom list for these names.

(Project 7G–Accounts Receivable continues on the next page)

Content-Based Assessments

(Project 7G–Accounts Receivable continued)

11. Click the **Sheet1 sheet tab**, and then click cell **B6**. **Sort** the list by **Last Name** and then by **First Name**. Notice that there are two entries for Anderson Grocers and two for Texas Power & Light. **Sort** the list again. For the first field, sort by **Firm** using the **Custom List** you just created—in the order of DeLong, Vidmar, Stevens—then sort by **Last Name** and **First Name**.

12. In the **Data Tools** group, click **Remove Duplicates**. In the **Remove Duplicates** dialog box, click **Select All** and click **OK**. The **Information** box indicates there were no duplicate values found. Although there are duplicate records for two businesses, the fields Amount Due, Due Date, and Firm did not match, so Excel does not consider these duplicate records. Click **OK**.

13. Rename **Sheet1** to **Merged AR Copy** the range of the worksheet—**A5:J42**. In **Sheet3**, click in cell **A7** and **Paste** the data. Click the **Paste Options** button and click **Keep Source Column Widths**. Rename **Sheet3** to **May AR** and delete **Sheet2**.

14. On the **May AR** sheet, click in a cell in the data. In the **Outline group**, click **Subtotal**. In the **Subtotal** dialog box, at each change in **Firm**, use the **Sum** function to create a subtotal for the **Amount Due**.

15. On the Data tab, in the **Outline group**, click **Subtotal** again. At each change in **Firm**, use the **Count** function to count the **Last Name** field. Clear the check box for **Amount Due**, and clear **Replace current subtotals** check box. Click **OK**. Adjust the width of column J.

16. Click the **Level 2** outline button to collapse the detail and display only the total count—37—and total amount due for the

three firms. Adjust the width of **column J** and then **hide columns B:G** and **column I**. **Copy** the range **H7:J50**

17. **Start** Word. From your student data files **Open** the Word file **e07G_AR_Memo** and **Save** it as **7G_AR_Memo_Firstname_Lastname** Scroll to the end of the document, right-click the **Footer**, and then click **Edit Footer**. Right-click again, and then click **Update Field**. Double-click in the document, and click after the last word—*attached*—and then press ⏎. In the **Clipboard group**, click the **Paste** button. By the inserted table, click the **Paste Options** button, and then click **Keep Source Formatting and Link to Excel**. If you are instructed to print your work, from the **Office** menu, click **Print**. **Save** your work, and then **Close** Word.

18. In the Excel workbook, click the **Merged AR sheet tab** and select the worksheet title **A1:A3**. Copy the worksheet title to the **May AR** sheet.

19. Group the worksheet, and in the **Left Footer** place the **File Name** and in the **Right Footer** place the **Sheet Name**. Set the **Orientation** to **Landscape**, **Fit to page**, and centered both **Vertically** and **Horizontally**. **Save** your workbook.

20. **Print** the entire workbook or submit electronically as directed. If you are directed to submit printed formulas refer to Activity 1.12 to do so. If you printed your formulas, be sure to redisplay the worksheet by pressing [Ctrl] + [`]. From the **Office** menu, click **Close**. If you are prompted to save changes, click **No**. **Exit** Excel.

End You have completed Project 7G

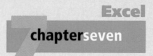
Project 7H — Closed Cases

In this project, you will apply the skills you practiced from the Objectives in Projects 7A and 7B.

Objectives: 1. *Create and Expand a Table and Insert a Calculated Column;* **5.** *Import Data to Excel;* **7.** *Enter Subtotals and Outline the Worksheet;* **8.** *Link and Embed a Worksheet and Chart into Word Documents.*

In the following Mastering Excel project, you will report the closed cases and the amount of each attorney's fees. You will then use subtotals to analyze the data and prepare a memo for Lawrence DeLong. Your completed files will look similar to the ones shown in Figure 7.41.

For Project 7H, you will need the following files:

e07H_Closed_Cases

e07H_Retainer_Amount (Access)

e07H_Cases_Memo (Word)

You will save your files as
7H_Closed_Cases_Firstname_Lastname
7H_Cases_Memo_Firstname_Lastname (Word)

Figure 7.41

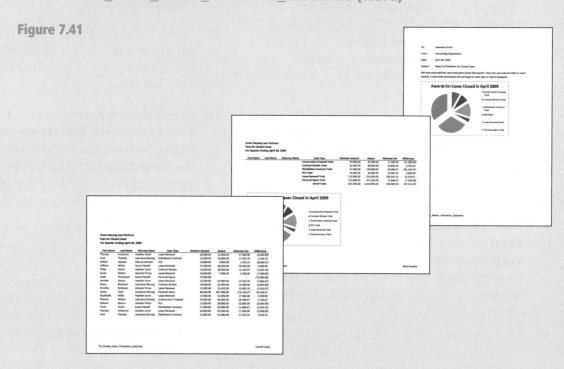

(Project 7H–Closed Cases continues on the next page)

Content-Based Assessments

(Project 7H–Closed Cases continued)

1. **Start** Excel. From the student files locate and open the file named **e07H_Closed_Cases** and **Save** it to your **Excel Chapter 7** folder as **7H_Closed_Cases_Firstname_Lastname**

2. Click cell **A17** and import the Access database **e07H_Retainer_Amount**. **Delete column A** of the table. Clear the table style from the table and convert it to a range. **Delete row 17** to remove the column titles. Adjust column widths and format the cells with a consistent format. Change the format of the range **C17:C22** to match other entries in column C.

3. Select the entire data range and **Insert** a **Table**. In **column G**—*Attorney Fee*—create a structured reference formula to determine the amount of the attorney fee. The attorneys retain one-third of the award—divide the award by 3 to get the amount of the fee. In **column H**—*Difference*—create a structured reference formula to subtract the **Retainer** from the **Attorney Fee** to determine if the retainer is larger or smaller than the actual fee. The difference for Theresa Anderson is −2500, indicating her retainer was larger than the actual fee. Format numbers with **Comma Style** with **no decimals**. The difference should be displayed in cell H6 as a negative number.

4. Clear the table style from the table and convert it to a range. **Copy** the worksheet into a new sheet. Rename **Sheet1** to **Closed Cases** and rename **Sheet1 (2)** to **Data Analysis**

5. In the **Data Analysis** sheet, sort the data by **Case Type**, then by **Last Name** and then **First Name**. Insert **Subtotals** for each **Case Type** that displays the sums for

all of the monetary fields. Collapse the outline to display the totals and grand total. Insert an **Exploded Pie Chart** that displays the **Case Type** and the **Award**. Change the title to display **Awards for Cases Closed in April 2009** Position the chart so it begins in cell **A32**.

6. **Start** Word. From the student data files, open **e07H_Cases_Memo**. **Save** it as **7H_Cases_Memo_Firstname_Lastname** Scroll to the end of the document, right-click the **Footer**, and then click **Edit Footer**, right-click again, and then click **Update Field**. Double-click in the memo above the Footer line and click after the last word of the memo—*displayed*. Press Enter. From the Excel Data Analysis sheet, **Copy** the chart, and then use **Paste Special** to paste link the Excel chart object to the Word memo. **Save** the memo, and then **Print** it if you are required to do so. **Close** Word.

7. In the workbook, click the **Data Analysis sheet tab** and click outside the chart so it is no longer active. **Select All Sheets** and in the **Left Footer** place the **File Name** and in the **Right Footer** place the **Sheet Name**. Format the worksheets to print in **Landscape Orientation**, **Fit to page**, and centered **Horizontally** and **Vertically**. **Save** the workbook.

8. **Print** the entire workbook or submit electronically as directed. If you are directed to submit printed formulas refer to Activity 1.12 to do so. If you printed your formulas, be sure to redisplay the worksheet by pressing Ctrl + `. From the **Office** menu, click **Close**. If you are prompted to save changes, click **No**. **Exit** Excel.

End You have completed Project 7H

Project 7I—April Payroll

In this project, you will apply all the skills you practiced from the Objectives in Projects 7A and 7B.

Objectives: 1. *Create and Expand a Table and Insert a Calculated Column;* **2.** *Create and Sort a Custom List;* **3.** *Filter by Using Advanced Criteria;* **4.** *Evaluate Data with Database Functions;* **5.** *Import Data to Excel;* **6.** *Create Lookup Tables in Another Workbook;* **7.** *Enter Subtotals and Outline the Worksheet;* **8.** *Link and Embed a Worksheet and Chart into Word Documents.*

In the following Mastering Excel project, you will complete a monthly payroll for the Accounting Department. This is the first payroll since the firms have merged and you will import payroll data from Access and Word to combine the data into one payroll report. You will use lookup tables to determine some of the deductions. You will then evaluate the payroll and prepare a Word document for management. Your completed files will look similar to the ones shown in Figure 7.42.

For Project 7I, you will need the following files:

e07I_Admin_Assistants

e07I_Paralegals

e07I_Withholding_Table

e07I_Legal_Assistants (Word)

e07I_Attorneys (Access)

e07I_April_Payroll

e07I_Associates (Word)

You will save your files as
7I_April_Payroll_Firstname_Lastname
7I_Associates_Firstname_Lastname (Word)
7I_Legal_Assistants_Firstname_Lastname (Text)

Figure 7.42

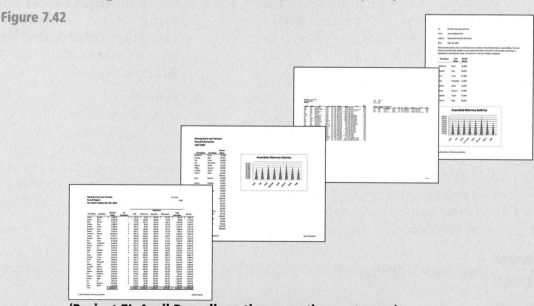

(Project 7I–April Payroll continues on the next page)

(Project 7I–April Payroll continued)

1. **Start** Excel. From your student files, locate and open the file named **e07I_April_Payroll** and **Save** it in your **Excel Chapter 7** folder as **7I_April_Payroll_Firstname_Lastname**

2. On the **Payroll Information sheet tab**, click cell **A5** and import the data **From Access** from the data file named **e07I_Attorneys**. In the table, delete **column A. Clear** the table style and **Convert to Range**. Adjust column widths.

3. **Start** Word. Open the file named **e07I_Legal_Assistants** and **Save** it in your **Excel Chapter 7** folder as a **Plain Text** file named **7I_Legal_Assistants_Firstname_Lastname Close** Word.

4. In your **7I_April_Payroll_Firstname_Lastname** workbook, click cell **A21** and import the **Text File** named **7I_Legal_Assistant_Firstname_Lastname**. **Delete rows 21:23**.

5. Open the workbook **e07I_Admin_Assistants** and **Copy** only the data into the **7I_April_Payroll_Firstname_Lastname** workbook beginning in cell **A28**. Then open the **e07I_Paralegals** workbook and **Copy** its data into your **7I_April_Payroll_Firstname_Lastname** workbook beginning in cell **A31**. **Close** the two workbooks from which you copied the data.

6. Adjust the column widths, **Sort** the data by **Last Name** and then use the **Remove Duplicates** button to remove any duplicate records.

7. In cell **A3**, type **'April 2009** and format it the same as the other title lines. Format the column titles—**A5:J5**—with **Bold**, **Italic**, **Center**, and add a **Bottom Border**. Format the **Zip** column with the **Special** number style of **Zip Code**. Format the **Phone #** column with the **Special** number style of **Phone Number**. Format the **Hire Date**

column with the **Date** style that writes the month in full—the first date displays as *June 1, 1999* Format the **Annual Salary** with **Comma Style** with **no decimals**. Format the column title for **Annual Salary** for **Wrap Text** and adjust column width.

8. **Sort** the list by **Last Name, First Name, Job Title**, and then **City. Copy** the data in the **First Name** and **Last Name** columns—but not the column titles—and **Paste** it into the **April 30 Payroll sheet** beginning in cell **A8**. Click cell **C8** and type = Click the **Payroll Information sheet tab**, and then click cell **J6**. Then type **/12** and press Enter to display the monthly salary. Format the number with **Comma Style** and then copy the data in cell **C8** down through cell **C37**. Adjust columns widths.

9. **Hide column C**. Beginning in cell **D8**, enter the number of exemptions from the list below:

First Name	Last Name	No. Exemptions
Joshua	Barletta	2
Kristen	Berry	0
Rose	Bonner	1
Wesley	Case	3
Wendy	Cohen	2
Matthew	Davis	3
Robert	Davis	1
Lawrence	DeLong	4
Cassidy	Diaz	0
Heather	Grant	3
Hue	Gross	3
Stacey	Henderson	1
Marcus	Johnson	2
Helen	Lee	4
Hugh	McBride	2
Eric	McCoy	3
Susan	Petrelli	0

(Project 7I–April Payroll continues on the next page)

(Project 7I–April Payroll continued)

First Name	Last Name	No. Exemptions
Antonio	Prince	4
Lillian	Rowe	3
Kim	Schneider	4
Robert	Smith	2
Jonathan	Somers	1
Philip	Stevens	3
Edward	Swanson	2
Erin	Swanson	1
Isabelle	Taylor	3
Patrick	Vega	3
Chi	Vu	4
Ima	Watkins	3
Gary	Wolfe	0

10. **Unhide column C**. Click cell **A7**, and display the **Create Table** dialog box. Change the table data to begin with **row 7**. **Sort** by the **No. Exemptions** from smallest to largest. In cell **I1**, type **FICA Rate** and in cell **I2**, type **6.2%**

11. In cell **E8**, create a structured reference formula for the **FICA** deduction—multiply the **Salary** by the **FICA Rate** in cell **J2**—which requires an absolute reference.

Note: If the range is not populated by the formula, click the **AutoCorrect Options** button and select **Overwrite all cells in this column with this formula**.

12. **Open** the workbook named **e07I_Withholding_Table**. Select the range **A5:F10** and define the name as **Withholding**. The withholding table is used to determine the amount of federal income tax to withhold from each employee. The amount depends on the amount of income and the number of exemptions. The amount of income is displayed in column A, and the amount of withholding in the table depends on the number of exemptions.

13. The insurance rates are also included in this worksheet. Select the range **A17:B21** and define the name of that range as **Insurance**

14. Display your **7I_April_Payroll_Firstname_Lastname** workbook, and click cell **F8**. Insert a **VLOOKUP** function that will determine the amount of federal income tax withheld. For the **Lookup_value**, select the Monthly Salary—cell **C8**. For the **Table_array**, display the **e07I_Withholding_Table** workbook and select the range **A5:F10**. For the **Col_index_num**, type **2**—the column that contains the tax withholding amounts for 0 exemptions. Click **OK**. The federal income tax has been inserted into all rows for 0 exemptions.

15. Click the **AutoCorrect Options** and click **Undo Calculated Column**. Copy the formula in cell **F8** to cell **F12**. Click cell **F12** and in the **Formula Bar**, select the last number in the formulas—2—and replace it with **3** In the table array, the amount of withholding for one exemption is in column 3. Use the fill handle to copy the formula through **row 17**. Click cell **F17** and in the **Formula Bar**, select the last number and replace it with **4** Continue in this manner to enter the amount of federal income tax for all employees.

16. Click cell **G8** and insert a **VLOOKUP** function that will determine the amount to withhold for insurance. For the **Lookup_value**, select the No. Exemptions—cell **D8**. For the **Table_array**, display the **e07I_Withholding_Table** workbook and select the range **A17:B21**. For the **Col_index_num**, type **2** and then click **OK**.

Note: If the column does not populate, from the **Office** menu, click **Excel Options**. At the left, click **Proofing**. Click **AutoCorrect**

(Project 7I–April Payroll continues on the next page)

Content-Based Assessments

(Project 7I–April Payroll continued)

Options and in the **AutoFormat As You Type tab**, under **Automatically as you work**, click **Fill formulas in tables to create calculate columns.** Then click **OK.**

17. Click cell **H8** and enter a formula that will display 7% of the salary. The retirement plan for the firm requires that 7% of the salary be withheld from employee pay. The amount of retirement for Kristen Berry is $175.

18. Click cell **I8** and enter a formula that sums the deductions for the employee— the total deductions are the amounts for FICA, Fed Inc Tax, Insurance, and Retirement. Then in cell **J8**, enter the formula to calculate the Net Pay—the **Monthly Salary** minus the **Total Deductions**. Confirm that the formulas are entered throughout the worksheet. The net pay for Kristen Berry is $1,740. **Save** your workbook.

19. **Sort** the list by **Last Name**, and then **First Name. Clear** the table style and convert the table to a range. Format cell **C8** and the range **E8:J8** with **Accounting Number Format**. Format the **No. Exemptions** in **column D** with **Comma Style** with **no decimals**. Format the other numbers in the worksheet with **Comma Style**. Adjust column width and row height, if needed. Monthly Salary, No. Exemptions, and Total Deductions should display on two lines. Review the worksheet and confirm that the body of the worksheet uses Calibri font of 11 points.

20. In cell **A38**, type **Total** and sum **column C** and **columns E:J**. Format the totals with **Bold, Accounting Number Format**, with a **Top and Double Bottom Border.** Adjust column widths.

21. Create a copy of the **Payroll Information sheet** in a new worksheet placed after the **April 30 Payroll sheet. Rename** the sheet **April Evaluation** Beginning in cell **A38**, enter the following list: **Partner, Entertainment Law Specialist, Sports Law Specialist, Attorney, Associate Attorney, Senior Legal Assistant, Legal Assistant, Senior Paralegal, Paralegal, Administrative Assistant Select** the list—**A38:A47**. Create a **Custom List** with these job titles in this order. **Delete** the data created for the custom list.

22. Click cell **I6** and **Sort** by **Job Title** in the order of the custom list just created, and then sort by **Last Name**, and then **First Name.** Create a copy of the worksheet in a new worksheet at the end of the workbook and name it **Salary Data** Adjust column widths.

23. Click the **April Evaluation sheet tab**, and use the **Subtotal command** to determine the sum of the Annual Salary for each job title. Adjust column widths.

24. Click in the **Salary Data sheet tab** and in cell **A38** type **Average Salary – Assistants & Paralegals** and in cell **C38** type **Job Title** Format these cells with **Bold, Wrap Text**, with a **Bottom Border.** Format cell **A38** to **Merge & Center** with cell **B38**. In cell **C39**, type **Legal Assistant** in cell **C40** type **Senior Paralegal** and in cell **C41** type **Paralegal**

25. Click cell **A39** and enter the database function to determine the average salaries for the legal assistants, senior paralegals, and paralegals. For the criteria, use the range **C38:C41**. Format the results with **Accounting Number Format**.

26. Beginning in cell **L1**, create a criteria area for **Job Title** and **Annual Salary**. As the criteria, include **Attorney** and **Associate**

(Project 7I–April Payroll continues on the next page)

(Project 7I–April Payroll continued)

Attorney who have an **Annual Salary greater than $80,000**. Use the **Advanced** filter to display the data that matches this criteria and place the filtered data to begin in cell **L6**. In cell **L5**, type **Attorneys & Associates Earning More Than $80,000** and format with **Align Text Left**. Bold and italic formats are automatically inserted to match the format in cell J5. Adjust column widths.

27. Click the **April Evaluation sheet tab**. **Hide rows 6:16** and **columns C:I** Select the range B5:J24 and insert a **Column Chart** using the **Clustered Cone** chart type to display the Associate Attorney's last name and annual salary. In the chart, display the attorney's **Last Name** and **Annual Salary**. Edit the **Chart Title** to read **Associate Attorney Salaries** and **Delete** the **legend**. Move the chart so the upper left corner begins in cell **L17**. **Copy** the range **A5:J24**.

28. **Start** Word and open the file **e07I_ Associates** and then **Save** it in your **Excel Chapter 7** folder as **7I_Associates_ Firstname_Lastname** In the Word memo, click after the last word of the memo—*assistance*. Press [Enter]. Click the **Paste** button. Click the **Paste Options** button and click **Keep Source Formatting and Link to Excel**. Press [Enter]. Return to the **April Evaluation** sheet in your Excel workbook, **Copy** the chart, return to the Word document—**7I_Associates_Firstname_ Lastname**—and **Paste Link** the chart as a **Microsoft Office Excel Chart Object**. If your document displays on two pages, click between the worksheet and the chart and press **Delete**. If it still displays on two pages, click between the worksheet and the memo and press **Delete** to remove space between the parts.

29. Scroll to the end of the document and **Update** the **Footer**. Double-click in the document to exit the Footer and then **Save** the file.

30. Return to your **7I_April_Payroll_ Firstname_Lastname** workbook. There was an error in the annual salary for Hue Gross. In the **Payroll Information** worksheet, change the **salary** for **Hue Gross** to **81,000** The amount has been updated to display the monthly salary of $6,750.00. in the April 30 Payroll worksheet because they were linked. However, the April Evaluation and the Salary Data worksheets were copies and not links. Change the salary in both of those worksheets. Return to your **7I_Associates_Firstname_ Lastname** Word document and in both the data table and chart, **Update Link**. **Save** the document. **Print** the memo and **Exit Word**.

31. In the workbook, **Group** the worksheets. In the **Left Footer**, place the **File Name** and in the **Right Footer**, place the **Sheet Name**. Format the worksheets to be centered **Horizontally** and **Vertically**, in **Landscape Orientation** and **Fit to page** so that each worksheet prints on one page. **Hide** the **Payroll Information sheet**. **Save** the workbook.

32. **Print** the workbook or submit both the workbook and Word document electronically as directed. Print formulas if you are directed to do so. If you printed your formulas, be sure to redisplay the worksheet by pressing [Ctrl] + [`]. From the **Office** menu, click **Close**. If you are prompted to save changes, click **No**. **Close** Excel.

End You have completed Project 7I

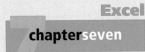 Excel
chapterseven

 CD-ROM

Business Running Case

Project 7J — Business Running Case

In this project, you will apply the skills you have practiced from the Objectives in Projects 7A and 7B.

From the student files that accompany this textbook, open the folder **03_business_running_case**. Locate **07J_Business_Running_Case** and any accompanying files. Follow the instructions and use the knowledge and skills you have gained thus far to assist Emilio Hernandez to meet the challenges of owning and running his multiple-city department store.

End You have completed Project 7J

Rubric

The following outcomes-based assessments are *open-ended assessments*. That is, there is no specific correct result; your result will depend on your approach to the information provided. Make *Professional Quality* your goal. Use the following scoring rubric to guide you in *how* to approach the problem and then to evaluate *how well* your approach solves the problem.

The *criteria*—Software Mastery, Content, Format and Layout, and Process—represent the knowledge and skills you have gained that you can apply to solving the problem. The *levels of performance*—Professional Quality, Approaching Professional Quality, or Needs Quality Improvement—help you and your instructor evaluate your result.

	Your completed project is of Professional Quality if you:	Your completed project is Approaching Professional Quality if you:	Your completed project Needs Quality Improvements if you:
1-Software Mastery	Choose and apply the most appropriate skills, tools, and features and identify efficient methods to solve the problem.	Choose and apply some appropriate skills, tools, and features, but not in the most efficient manner.	Choose inappropriate skills, tools, or features, or are inefficient in solving the problem.
2-Content	Construct a solution that is clear and well organized, contains content that is accurate, appropriate to the audience and purpose, and is complete. Provide a solution that contains no errors of spelling, grammar, or style.	Construct a solution in which some components are unclear, poorly organized, inconsistent, or incomplete. Misjudge the needs of the audience. Have some errors in spelling, grammar, or style, but the errors do not detract from comprehension.	Construct a solution that is unclear, incomplete, or poorly organized, containing some inaccurate or inappropriate content; and contains many errors of spelling, grammar, or style. Do not solve the problem.
3-Format and Layout	Format and arrange all elements to communicate information and ideas, clarify function, illustrate relationships, and indicate relative importance.	Apply appropriate format and layout features to some elements, but not others. Overuse features, causing minor distraction.	Apply format and layout that does not communicate information or ideas clearly. Do not use format and layout features to clarify function, illustrate relationships, or indicate relative importance. Use available features excessively, causing distraction.
4-Process	Use an organized approach that integrates planning, development, self-assessment, revision, and reflection.	Demonstrate an organized approach in some areas, but not others; or, use an insufficient process of organization throughout.	Do not use an organized approach to solve the problem.

Outcomes-Based Assessments

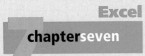
Problem Solving

Project 7K — Referrals

In this project, you will construct a solution by applying any combination of the skills you practiced from the Objectives in Projects 7A and 7B.

For Project 7K, you will need the following files:

e07K_Baytown&Deer_Park
e07K_Katy
e07K_Houston (Access)

**You will save your workbook as
7K_Referrals_Firstname_Lastname**

When DeLong Grant Law Partners prepare for a case, they refer to experts in the field. In the past, the names of these references have been created in Access and Excel. Heather Grant has asked that these lists be combined into one Excel list.

She would like to review the list. Combine the two Excel files—**e07K_Katy** and **e07K_Baytown&Deer_Park**. Import from Access the file named **e07K_Houston**. Prepare a list that displays the entire list of references, sorted first in the order of specialty in this order: transportation, commercial placement, immigration, and recording engineer. Then sort by city, last name, and then first name. She would also like a separate list of all the references that live in Houston who specialize in commercial placement or recording engineer. In another worksheet, use the subtotals to prepare a sheet that provides the total number of each specialty.

Prepare your report in a professional format with each worksheet descriptively named. Use a date of April 30, 2009, for the reports. Confirm that the zip and phone numbers are formatted correctly. Use Comma Style format for the charges per hour. Insert a left footer that includes the file name and a right footer that includes the sheet name. Center the worksheets both vertically and horizontally on the page and name the completed workbook **7K_Referrals_Firstname_Lastname**.

End You have completed Project 7K ——————

Outcomes-Based Assessments

Project 7L — Damages Awarded

In this project, you will construct a solution by applying any combination of the skills you practiced from the Objectives in Projects 7A and 7B.

For Project 7L, you will need the following files:

e07L_Contract_Damages (Access)
e07L_Draft_Agreement_Awards
e07L_Talent_Signing (Text)

You will save your files as
7L_Damages_Awarded_Firstname_Lastname
7L_Talent_Signing_Firstname_Lastname (Text)

In this project, you will create a workbook that displays the damages awarded to DeLong Grant Law Partners. Information about the damages has been saved in Access, Word, and Excel—depending on the type of case. Heather Grant has asked that you combine all of them in one Excel worksheet effective May 31, 2009. Heather has asked that this format be displayed as a table with banded rows.

Combine the following files into an Excel worksheet: **e07L_Contract_Damages** (Access), **e07L_Draft_Agreement** (Excel), and **e07L_Talent_Signing** (Word). (The Word document needs to be saved as a Plain Text document before it is imported.) Create a structured reference calculated column to determine the contingency at 33% of the damages awarded. Copy the data into two new worksheets. In one worksheet, determine the subtotals for the damages and contingencies for each attorney. Recall that a table must be converted to a range in order to use the subtotal feature. In the second worksheet, determine the subtotals for the damages awarded and the contingency awarded for each type of case.

Prepare a professional workbook. Be sure that the consolidated data worksheet is formatted as a table with banded rows and displays in alphabetical order. Add a footer to all the worksheets that includes the file name in the left footer and the sheet name in the right footer. Save the workbook as **7L_Damages_Awarded_Firstname_Lastname** and submit it as directed.

End You have completed Project 7L

Problem Solving

Project 7M—Seminar Requests

In this project, you will construct a solution by applying any combination of the skills you practiced from the Objectives in Projects 7A and 7B.

For Project 7M, you will need the following files:

e07M_Seminar_Requests
e07M_Seminars

You will save your workbook as
7M_Seminar_Requests_Firstname_Lastname
7M_Seminars_Firstname_Lastname

The lawyers and other employees of DeLong Grant Law Partners use seminars as a way to keep current with the law and the findings of recent cases. Each year, a list of seminars is prepared and the employees are then able to quickly determine those that would enhance their work, for which they will register.

The requests that the lawyers and other employees have made for seminars for 2009 are listed in Sheet1 in the **e07M_Seminar_Requests** workbook. The details for each seminar are displayed in the **e07M_Seminars** workbook, which will be used as a lookup table. Lawrence DeLong has asked that you prepare the workbook that contains the seminar requests of the employees. Create a table array from the data in the **e07M_Seminars** that will be used to look up the data.

Save the documents in your folder as **7M_Seminar_Requests_Firstname_Lastname** and **7M_Seminars_Firstname_Lastname**. Create a custom list of the job titles in this order: Partner, Senior Associate, Associate, Entertainment Law Specialist, Senior Law Assistant, Senior Paralegal, Sports Law Specialist. Sort the seminar requests by the custom list first and then by last name and first name. Create lookup functions that will place all the information about each requested seminar in the 7M_Seminar_Requests_Firstname_Lastname workbook. Format the worksheets professionally, include the file name in the left footer, and place the worksheet professionally on the page.

End **You have completed Project 7M**

Outcomes-Based Assessments

Problem Solving

Project 7N—Expenses

In this project, you will construct a solution by applying any combination of the skills you practiced from the Objectives in Projects 7A and 7B.

> **For Project 7N, you will need the following files:**
>
> e07N_Expenses
> e07N_March_Expenses (Word)
>
> **You will save your files as**
> **7N_Expenses_Firstname_Lastname**
> **7N_March_Expenses_Firstname_Lastname (Word)**

The expenses for the attorneys are summarized monthly. DeLong and Grant like to report their travel expenses and the expenses for meals with clients in the same report. A report has been started in Excel but needs to be edited and completed. You will complete and format it in this project.

From the student files, open the file **e07N_Expenses**. The expenses that are reported in the worksheet need to be displayed so that the total of each type of expense—meals, airfare, hotel, and so on—can be easily determined. Create columns for each expense category and transcribe the data so this information can be easily determined.

In a new worksheet, use subtotals to determine the total expenses for each specialty. Prepare a 3-D Column chart that displays the expenses grouped by the type of expense. Use Layout 1 and insert an appropriate title.

Then link the chart as a Microsoft Office Excel Chart Object to the memo to Heather Grant. The memo is started and is located in your data files as e07N_March_Expenses. Save your completed memo as **7N_March_Expenses_Firstname_Lastname** and confirm the footer is correct.

Prepare professional documents. In the worksheet, add a footer that includes the file name in the left footer and the sheet name in the right footer. Position the worksheets professionally on the page and Save the workbook as **7N_Expenses_Firstname_Lastname** and submit it as directed.

End **You have completed Project 7N** _____

Problem Solving

Project 7O—Earnings

In this project, you will construct a solution by applying any combination of the skills you practiced from the Objectives in Projects 7A and 7B.

For Project 7O, you will need the following file:

e07O_Earnings

**You will save your workbook as
7O_Earnings_Firstname_Lastname**

In this project, you will complete a worksheet that reports the annual earnings for 2009 for the attorneys, legal assistants, and paralegals for DeLong Grant Law Partners. The data is on your student data file named **e07O_ Earnings**. Format the worksheet using the table feature, and then complete the Total and Percent of Firm's Total columns, which is the percent each employee contributes to the total income for the firm.

Sort the data first by job title—in the order of Partner, Entertainment Law Specialist, Sports Law Specialist, Senior Associate, Associate, Senior Legal Assistant, and Senior Paralegal—and then by last name and first name.

Copy the report into another worksheet and filter the list to display the Associates who earn more than $80,000. Place this list below the original list. On the same sheet, use the subtotal command to display the total income for each job title. Recall that a table must be converted to range in order to add a subtotal.

Use borders, themes, and font attributes to prepare a professional workbook. Add a footer that includes the file name and sheet name and delete the unused sheets. Adjust column widths so the worksheet prints on one page. Save the workbook as **7O_Earnings_Firstname_Lastname** and submit your work as instructed.

End **You have completed Project 7O** ———————

Outcomes-Based Assessments

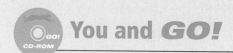
You and GO!

Project 7P—You and GO!

In this project, you will construct a solution by applying any combination of the Objectives found in Projects 7A and 7B.

From My Computer, navigate to the student files that accompany this textbook. In the folder **04_you_and_go**, locate and open the folder for this chapter. Open and print the instructions for this project, which are provided to you in Adobe PDF format. Follow the instructions to create a worksheet that displays something that you collect. You will create a database for your friends and families, sort the list, and use an advanced filter to display only your friends.

 You have completed Project 7P _____

GO! with Help

Project 7Q—GO! with Help

In this chapter, you used advanced filters to place a filtered list in another location of the worksheet. You can filter by innumerable items, including dates and time, even when they change.

1. **Start** Excel and confirm that you are connected to the Internet. At the far right end of the Ribbon, click the **Microsoft Office Excel Help** button.

2. In the search box, type **filter** and then press [Enter]. Locate and click **Filter data in a range or table**. Under **What do you want to do?** locate and click **Filter dates or times**.

3. Read the information that displays, including the sections **Create criteria** and **Dynamic filter**. When you are finished, close the Help window and then close Excel.

 You have completed Project 7Q _____

8 chaptereight

Creating Macros, Using Depreciation and Conditional Functions, and Creating PivotTables and PivotChart Reports

OBJECTIVES

At the end of this chapter you will be able to:

1. Create and Run a Macro
2. Apply Depreciation Functions

3. Evaluate Worksheet Data with Conditional IF Functions
4. Create a PivotTable and PivotChart

OUTCOMES

Mastering these objectives will enable you to:

PROJECT 8A

Create a Comparison of Depreciation Methods and a Depreciation Schedule That Uses Macros

PROJECT 8B

Evaluate Data Using Conditional IF Formulas and Create a PivotTable and PivotChart Report

Penn Liberty Motors

Penn Liberty Motors has one of eastern Pennsylvania's largest inventories of popular new car brands, sport utility vehicles, hybrid cars, and motorcycles. Their sales, service, and finance staff are all highly trained and knowledgeable about their products, and the company takes pride in its consistently high customer satisfaction ratings. Penn Liberty also offers extensive customization options for all types of vehicles through its accessories division. Custom wheels, bike and ski racks, car covers, and chrome accessories are just a few of the ways Penn Liberty customers make their cars personal statements.

Creating Macros, Using Depreciation and Conditional Functions, and Creating PivotTables and PivotChart Reports

When working with Excel, you often complete the same activities repeatedly, such as applying the same formats or inserting the same formulas. You can automate repetitive activities by creating a macro program that can be run as needed to apply the same formats or formulas on worksheets. Depreciation functions are used to determine the amount of depreciation expense that is allowed. This is particularly useful in business when large purchases are made for equipment that will be used over a period of years.

There are several methods of depreciation that are commonly used. In addition to using different methods for determining the depreciation, a Schedule of Depreciation displays the amount of depreciation and the book value throughout the life of the asset. Conditional IF functions are used to evaluate data in a list to determine if the data matches one or more conditions.

PivotTable and PivotChart reports display data in a worksheet in a manner that makes it easy to rearrange so that you can view the results from different perspectives, such as sales by quarter, by product, or by location. This enables you to make comparisons of the data in order to help make business decisions. In this chapter, you will create and run macros, prepare depreciation schedules, use conditional IF functions to analyze data, and complete PivotTable and PivotChart reports.

Project 8A Depreciation

In Activities 8.1 through 8.11, you will create, run, and edit macros that are designed to speed the creation of a worksheet by combining several keystrokes into one shortcut. Marilyn Kellerman, finance manager, is reviewing the depreciation methods used at Penn Liberty Motors. You will create a worksheet that compares the results of three methods used to depreciate an asset for Marilyn and construct a worksheet that displays the depreciation for an asset over its life. You will prepare a macro to format the worksheet title, which can be used with every worksheet you complete. Your completed workbook will look similar to Figure 8.1.

For Project 8A, you will need the following files:

New blank Excel workbook
e08A_Copier_Depreciation

You will save your workbooks as
8A_Depreciation_Firstname_Lastname
8A_Macro_Library_Firstname_Lastname

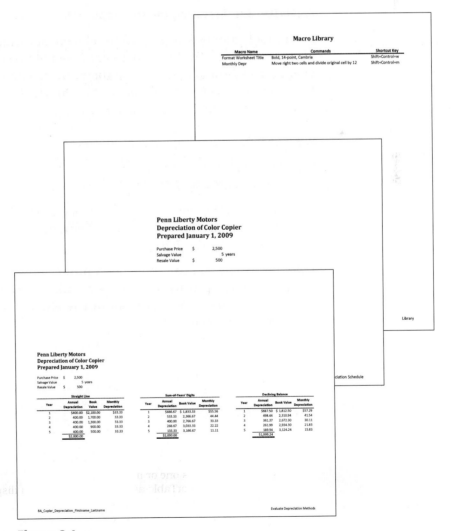

Figure 8.1
Project 8A—Depreciation

Objective 1
Create and Run a Macro

A **macro** is a series of commands—such as selections from menus and dialog boxes, keystrokes, and clicks on toolbar buttons—and functions that are grouped together as a single command.

Create a macro to perform a set of actions quickly with a single mouse click, a keyboard shortcut, or when a workbook opens. When a command requiring several steps is used over and over, a macro can be created to automate those steps and complete them efficiently. For example, you can create a macro that automatically enters employee names in the first column, alphabetizes the names, and then applies a fill color to the cells containing the names.

When you have a sequence of actions that you perform frequently, record them as a macro to automate the actions. Macros can be used to record tasks taking more than an hour manually but take only a minute or two to run, performing complex tasks in a short time.

Activity 8.1 Accessing the Developer Tab

Macro tools are located on the Developer tab, which does not usually display on the Excel Ribbon. There are also macro security settings that disable macros or allow you to use them. In this activity, you will access the Developer tab so it is available on the Ribbon and set the macro settings so you can create and run the macros.

1 **Start** Excel and open to a new, blank workbook.

2 Click the **Office** button [image], and then at the bottom of the displayed menu, click **Excel Options**.

The Excel Options dialog box displays. The list of sections in this dialog box displays at the left—Popular, Formulas, Proofing, Save, Advanced, and others.

3 On the left, confirm that the **Popular** option is selected. At the right, under **Top options for working with Excel**, click the check box next to **Show Developer tab in the Ribbon**, and then compare your screen with Figure 8.2.

Top options for working
with Excel section

Figure 8.2

Excel Options dialog box ———

Popular option ———

Show Developer tab in
the Ribbon check box ———

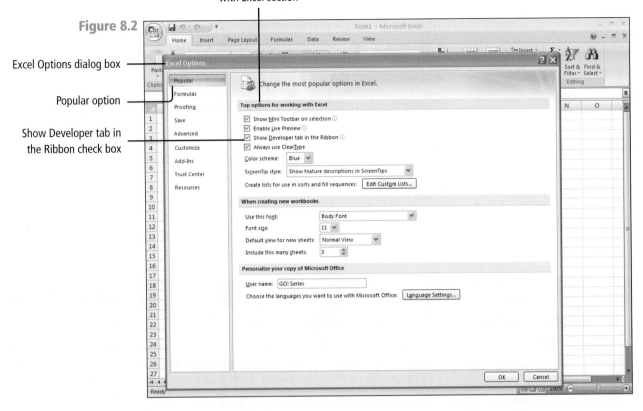

4 Click **OK**. Click the **Developer tab**, and then compare your screen with Figure 8.3.

The ***Developer tab*** has been added to the Ribbon. The Developer tab is used to work with macros, and by developers who customize Excel. The *Code group* on the left displays the buttons used with macros. When macros are available in the worksheet, the Macro button displays on the left side of the status bar.

Figure 8.3

Developer tab ———

Code group ———

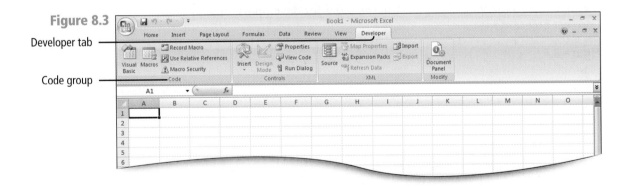

5 In the **Code group**, click the **Macro Security** button.

The Trust Center displays. The Trust Center is where you can find security and privacy settings for the 2007 Microsoft Office system programs.

6 Under **Macro Settings**, click **Disable all macros with notification** and click **OK**. Alternatively, click the Office button ⊞, and then at the bottom of the displayed menu, click Excel Options. Click **Trust Center** and on the right, click **Trust Center Settings**. Under **Macro Settings**, click **Disable all macros with notification**, and then click **OK** two times. Take a moment to study the table in Figure 8.4.

A *macro virus* is unauthorized code that is attached to a macro and may damage or erase files. For this reason, Microsoft has developed security to prevent viruses from being attached to the macro. To protect from this type of virus, you can set the *Macro security* to protect your computer from importing a macro virus.

If your computer has antivirus software installed and the workbook contains macros, the workbook is scanned for known viruses before it is opened. For this reason, in order to work with macros, they need to be disabled and notification will be made to the user.

Macro Settings

Use this macro setting	For the following purpose
Disable all macros without notification	Use when you don't trust macros. All macros in documents and security alerts about macros are disabled. Only documents placed in trusted locations can be run without being checked by the Trust Center security system.
Disable all macros with notification	This is the default macro setting. If you want macros to be disabled but you want to get security alerts if macros are present, use this setting. You can choose when to enable macros on a case-by-case basis.
Disable all macros except digitally signed macros	This is the same as the Disable all macros with notification option, except that if the macro is digitally signed by a trusted publisher, the macro will run if you have already trusted the publisher. If you have not trusted the publisher, you are notified and you can choose to enable them.
Enable all macros (not recommended); potentially dangerous code can run.	Use this setting temporarily to enable all macros to run. Because it makes your computer vulnerable to potentially malicious code, it is not recommended as a permanent setting.
Trust access to the VBA project object model	This setting is for developers only.

Figure 8.4

Activity 8.2 Creating a Macro

Excel uses the *macro recorder* to create a macro. The macro recorder works like an audio recorder—start the recorder, record the steps, and then stop the recorder. With the macro recorder, every keystroke and mouse click is recorded and saved with the macro. When finished, turn off the recorder. A macro can be run (replayed) in any cell or range of cells in any worksheet of the workbook.

When you create a new macro, give it a name so that you can refer to it later. In this activity, you will record a macro that will format the title of a worksheet.

1 Click the **Office** button 🔘, point to **Save As**, and then in the sub-menu, point to **Excel Macro-Enabled Workbook** to review the description, and then compare your screen with Figure 8.5.

Selecting Macro-Enabled Workbook saves the workbook in the XML-based format allowing macros to be saved to the workbook.

Figure 8.5

Save As Excel Macro-Enabled Workbook

Description of Macro-Enabled Workbook file format

Save As command

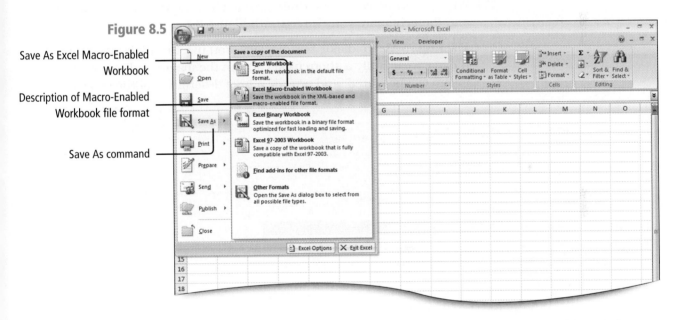

2 Click **Excel Macro-Enabled Workbook**. Navigate to the location where you are saving your files, and create a new folder named **Excel Chapter 8**. In the **File name** box, type **8A_Macro_Library_ Firstname_Lastname** Notice that the **Save as type** box displays **Excel Macro-Enabled Workbook**. Click **Save** Alternatively, you can select to save as an Excel Macro-Enabled Workbook in the Save As type area of the Save As dialog box.

The saved workbook named 8A_Macro_Library_Firstname_Lastname will be used to create and store all of your macros. A macro-enabled workbook stores the macro codes.

3 In the worksheet, in cell **A1**, type your name and then in the **Formula Bar**, click the **Enter** button ✔.

Your macro will use only formatting techniques; none of the text will reside with the macro. However, because it is difficult to visualize formatting in empty cells, the cell content will be used as a sample to display the format.

4 With cell **A1** active, in the **Code group**, click the **Record Macro** button, and then compare your screen with Figure 8.6.

The Record Macro dialog box displays. You use this dialog box to name the macro, identify a shortcut key to run the macro, indicate where the macro will be stored, and provide a brief description of the macro.

Figure 8.6

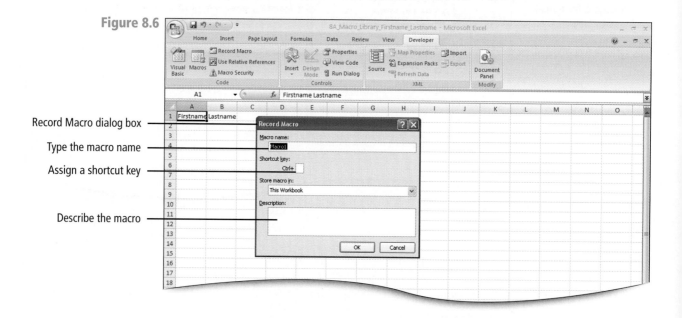

Record Macro dialog box

Type the macro name

Assign a shortcut key

Describe the macro

5 In the **Macro name** box, type **Format_Worksheet_Title** Press [Tab] and in the **Shortcut key** box, press [⇧ Shift] while you type **w** In the **Store macro in** box, confirm that **This Workbook** displays.

The choices are to save the macro in a Personal Macro Workbook, a New Workbook, or This Workbook. Macros that are saved in This Workbook or a New Workbook are available to use whenever that workbook is open on your computer. Similar to range names, macro names cannot include spaces; therefore, an underscore is used between words in the name.

Note — The Personal Macro Workbook

If you want a macro to be available whenever you use Excel at your computer, save the macro in the Personal Macro Workbook. A hidden personal macro workbook is created and the macro is saved in that workbook. This workbook resides on the computer where the macro is created and all macros saved in the workbook are available to use. However, when using the Personal Macro Workbook, the macros cannot be transported to another computer. In a classroom environment, saving to the Personal Macro Workbook allows other students to access your macros but does not make them available to you unless you are sitting at the computer where you created them.

In order to have your macros available at any computer, it is recommended that you save the Macro Library workbook on your USB drive or other portable storage device.

6 In the **Description** box, type **Formats the worksheet title** Then click **OK** and compare your screen with Figure 8.7.

In the Code group, the Record Macro button has changed and now displays Stop Recording. The Macro button displays in the status bar as a shaded blue box to the right of *Ready* with the ScreenTip that displays *A macro is currently recording. Click to stop recording.*

Figure 8.7

Stop Recording button in Code group

Stop Recording button in status bar

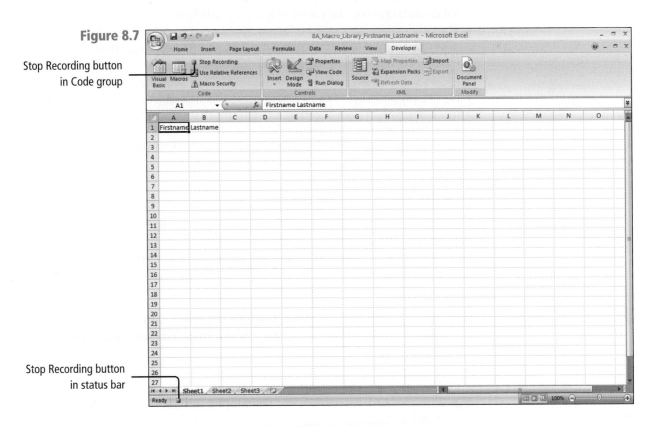

What if I make a mistake while recording?

When the macro recorder is turned on, every keystroke you make will be included in the macro. It is critical that you are cautious when recording a macro. If you make a mistake, delete the macro. To do so, on the Developer tab, in the Code group, click the Macros button. In the Macro dialog box, select the macro to be deleted, click Delete, and then confirm that you do want to delete the macro.

7 Click the **Home tab**; in the **Font group**, click the **Bold** button, and click the **Font Size button arrow** and click on **16**. Click the **Font button arrow**, and in the gallery, click **Cambria**. In the status bar on the left side, click the **Stop Recording** button ▣. Alternatively, on the Developer tab, in the Code group, click Stop Recording.

The macro button displays in the status bar whenever the Developer tab is displayed on the Ribbon. The tab does not need to be active in order to use the Macro button on the status bar to start and stop macro recording. The macro button in the status bar displays a different icon when it is recording and when recording has stopped.

8 Save ▣ your workbook.

More Knowledge
Naming a Macro and Selecting Shortcut Keys

When determining the name of a macro, the first character must be a letter. The other characters may be letters, numbers, or underscores; spaces are not allowed. Using a cell reference will cause an error message that the macro is not valid.

Excel's shortcut keys are a combination of keys, function keys, and some other common keys. As you recall, using the shortcut for functions can be quick and easy. When creating a macro shortcut, you will want to be careful that you don't use a shortcut that Excel has created, as your shortcut will override the Excel one. Use Help to review a list of all shortcut keys available in Excel.

Activity 8.3 Running the Macro

The value of creating a macro is the ability to **run**—play back—**the macro** in order to quickly insert the format, text, or formulas of the macro into the worksheet. Creating a macro that can be used again and again saves time in creating worksheets. In this activity, you will run the macro you created to format the title of a worksheet.

1 Open the file named **e08A_Copier_Depreciation** and **Save** it in your **Excel Chapter 8** folder as **8A_Copier_Depreciation_Firstname_Lastname**

You now have two Excel workbooks open—this one and your Macro Library workbook.

2 With cell **A1** active, click the **Developer tab** and in the **Code group**, click the **Macros** button, and then compare your screen with Figure 8.8.

The Macro dialog box displays the macros that are available to use. Because this macro is saved in another workbook, the workbook name and the macro name both display in the Macro name area. A description of the macro displays at the bottom of the dialog box.

Figure 8.8

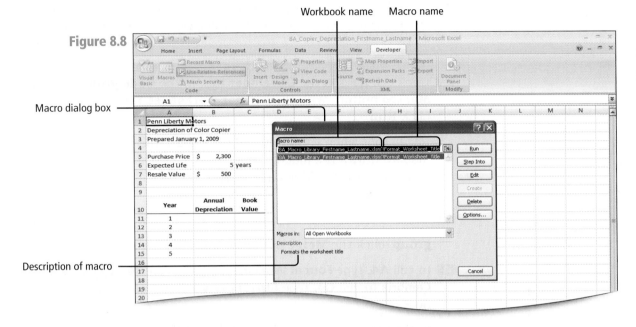

Workbook name   Macro name

Macro dialog box

Description of macro

3 Click **Run**.

Cell A1 is formatted using the same format characteristics that you specified when you created the macro.

4 Select cells **A2:A3** and press Ctrl + ⬆Shift + W.

Cells A2 and A3 are now also formatted. A selected range of cells can be formatted at the same time. The macro runs when you use the shortcut that you established when you created the macro.

5 **Save** your workbook.

More Knowledge
Deleting a Macro

To delete a macro, open the workbook that contains the macro that will be deleted. On the Developer tab, in the Code group, click the Macros button. From the Macros in the list, click This Workbook. In the Macro name box, click the name of the macro that you want to delete, and then click Delete.

Activity 8.4 Preparing a Library Sheet

When a user creates and runs macros, there are usually several macros available. To recall the macros available and what they accomplish, it is good practice to prepare a library sheet that lists the name of the macro, what the macro does, and the shortcut. In this activity, you will begin the library sheet for your macro workbook.

1 Display the **8A_Macro_Library_Firstname_Lastname** worksheet. Delete **Sheet1** and rename **Sheet2** with the name **Library** Click cell **A1** and type **Macro Library** Beginning in cell **A3**, type the following column titles:

Macro Name	Commands	Shortcut Key

2   Click cell **A1**. On the **Developer tab**, in the **Code group**, click the **Macros** button. With the **Format Worksheet Title** macro selected, click **Run**.

Recall that when you first used the macro, the name of the workbook displayed with the macro name. Because the macro resides in this workbook, the workbook name does not display—just the macro name displays.

3   Select the range **A1:C1**, and on the **Home tab**, in the **Alignment group**, click the **Merge & Center** button ⊞ ▾.

4   In cell **A4**, type **Format Worksheet Title** In cell **B4**, type **Bold, 16-point, Cambria** In cell **C4**, type **Ctrl+Shift+w** Adjust column widths as necessary.

In the library sheet, you have identified the name and shortcut for the macro and provided an explanation of what the macro does.

5   **Save** your **8A_Macro_Library_Firstname_Lastname** workbook and **Close** it.

The macros that you create in this assignment may be used in the rest of your Excel course, depending on the preference of your instructor. You may choose to save the 8A_Macro_Library_ Firstname_Lastname workbook in a location that is easy to access.

More Knowledge

Using Digital Signatures to Authenticate a Workbook

Excel provides safeguards that help protect against viruses that can be transmitted by macros. If you share macros with others, you can certify them with a *digital signature* so that other users can verify that they are from a trustworthy source. A digital signature is an electronic, encryption-based secure stamp of authentication on a macro or document. The signature confirms that the macro or document originated from the signer and has not been altered. If a file has been digitally signed, a certificate displays that names the source; then you can decide whether this is a trusted source before you activate the macros. For more information about digital signatures, complete There's More You Can Do! at the end of this chapter.

Activity 8.5   Opening a Document that Contains a Macro

The Excel macro security settings you have used alert you when a document that you will open contains a macro. You may choose to continue to work with the document if it is from a trusted source.

1   Click the **Office** button 🗔, and then click **Open**.

Notice that in the Open dialog box, the icon for the Macro Library workbook displays. Notice how it differs from regular Excel workbooks. The file icon displays only when a macro has been created within that sheet.

2 Open the file named **8A_Macro_Library_Firstname_Lastname** and compare your screen with Figure 8.9.

By default, a **Message Bar** displays security alerts when there is potentially unsafe content in the worksheet that you open.

Figure 8.9

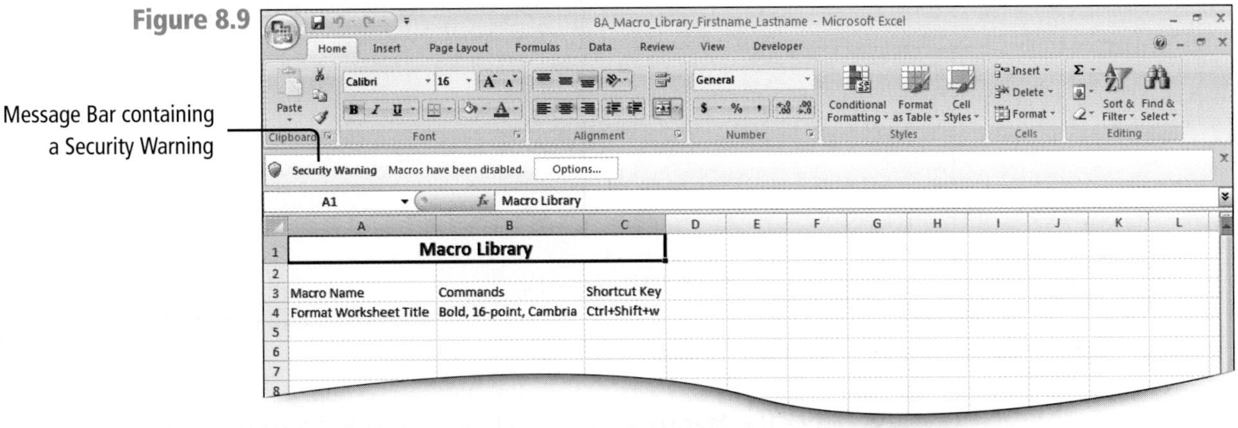

Message Bar containing a Security Warning

Alert!

Where is the Message Bar on my screen?

If you get an information message that indicates you cannot open the file, you will want to confirm that your system will display the Message Bar. To set the Message Bar to display, do the following:

- On the left side of the Excel Options window, click Trust Center. Under Microsoft Office Excel Trust Center at the right, click the Trust Center Settings button.

- On the left side of the Trust Center window, click Message Bar and at the right, confirm that Show the Message Bar in all applications when content has been blocked is checked.

---

3 In the **Message Bar**, click the **Options** button, and then compare your screen with Figure 8.10.

The Microsoft Office Security Options dialog box displays several **security alerts**—messages that Microsoft displays when potentially unsafe tasks are about to be completed. Information about the alert is provided with choices on how to proceed.

Figure 8.10

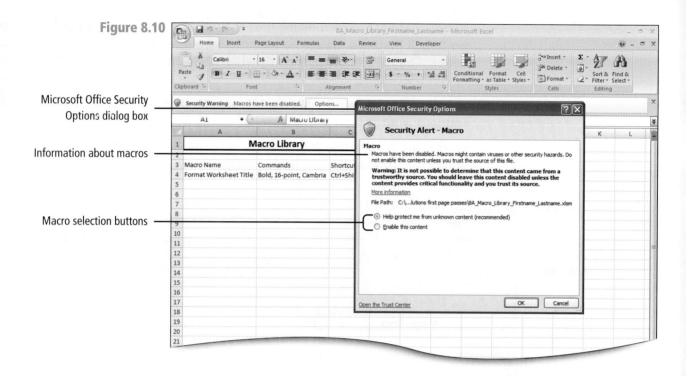

Microsoft Office Security Options dialog box

Information about macros

Macro selection buttons

4 Under the **Macro** section, click **Enable this content**, and then click **OK**.

The Message Bar no longer displays and you are now able to use macros in this workbook.

Activity 8.6 Editing a Macro with VBA Code

When you create a macro, the macro is stored in a module using the *Visual Basic for Applications—VBA*—program. VBA is a programming language used to write computer programs within the Microsoft Windows environment. Each macro is stored in a separate *module*, which is numbered consecutively. As your macro is created, VBA code is created. You can modify the code within VBA. In this activity, you will use VBA to edit the macro you have created.

1 In the **8A_Macro_Library_Firstname_Lastname** workbook, in the **Library** sheet, click the **Developer tab**. In the **Code group**, click the **Macros** button. In the **Macros** dialog box, click **Edit**, and then compare your screen with Figure 8.11.

The Microsoft Visual Basic window displays. Information about VBA projects and properties displays at the left side of the window. The macro code created in your 8A_Macro_Library_Firstname_ Lastname workbook displays on the right side of the window in a module. If the module displays in minimized view, the window at the right may have a separate title bar. Across the top of the window are the Menu bar and the Standard toolbar where command buttons display. The displayed modules also contain a title bar.

The name of the macro displays in the box on the right following the word *Sub*. The name, explanation, and the keyboard shortcut display in green as the first items in the macro.

Figure 8.11

Change font size   Microsoft Visual Basic window

Window title bar

Menu bar
Standard toolbar

Module title bar in
minimized display

VBA code for Macro
Library worksheet

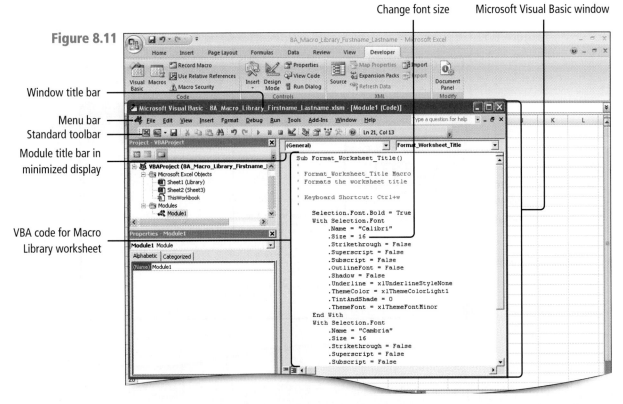

2 In the **Microsoft Visual Basic** window, in the module at the right named **8A_Macro_Library_Firstname_Lastname.xlsm – [Module1 (Code)]**, click the **Maximize** or **Restore Down** buttons in order to display the Visual Basic window in a manner similar to Figure 8.12. Alternatively, use the sizing handles to resize the window.

Every macro begins with the word *Sub* and ends with *End Sub*. Each button click or keystroke is recorded in VBA. The first line is the name of the macro, followed by the description and the keyboard shortcut. The first format choice—Bold—displays on the top line of the code. Each additional format choice begins with *With Selection* and ends with *End With*—which may not be visible on your screen depending on the size of the macro window. In this macro, you made three changes. One is to bold the text and the other two keystrokes changed the font size and the font. In the first set of instructions, the font size is changed to 16. The code in the illustration display these changes. In the second set of instructions, the font is changed to Cambria.

Figure 8.12

First change—size of font

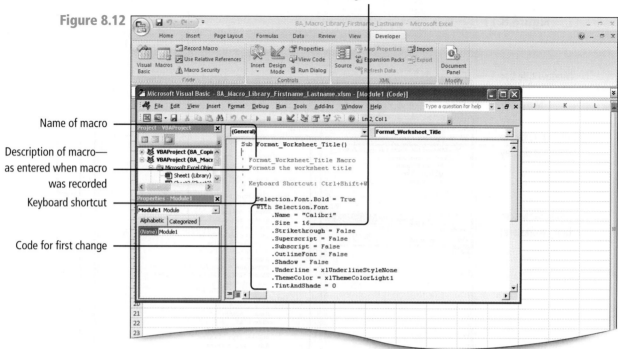

Name of macro

Description of macro—
as entered when macro
was recorded

Keyboard shortcut

Code for first change

3 In the displayed code, use the right scroll arrow to scroll down to
display the second block of code. Just below the first *End With* is
another set of instructions. Compare your screen with Figure 8.13.

The VBA code on the right displays the font name and size and other
attributes of the macro you created.

Changes specified in the macro

Figure 8.13

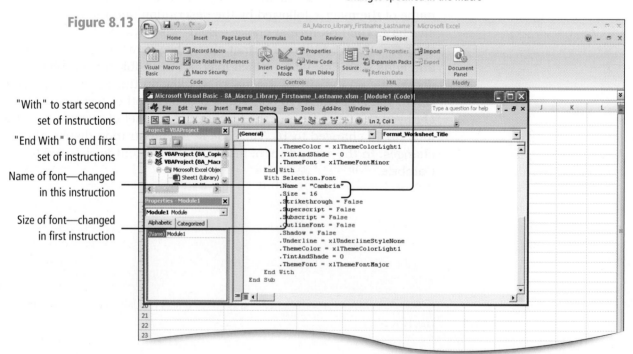

"With" to start second
set of instructions

"End With" to end first
set of instructions

Name of font—changed
in this instruction

Size of font—changed
in first instruction

4 In the second set of instructions, locate the words *Size = 16*. Select **16** and type **14** to change the size of the font of the worksheet title macro. Then compare your screen with Figure 8.14.

With each additional selection, prior format choices display. When you change the format, change it in the last set of instructions—which is the format that Excel will use when the macro is run.

Changed font size

Figure 8.14

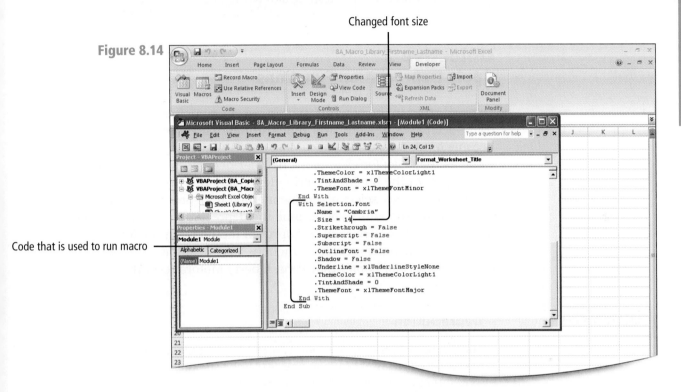

Code that is used to run macro

5 In the Window title bar, click the **Save** button. **Save** *8A_Macro_Library_Firstname_Lastname (Ctrl+S)*. Then on the Microsoft Visual Basic Title bar, click the **Close** button to close the window.

6 In the **8A_Macro_Library_Firstname_Lastname** in the entry for the Format_Worksheet_Title, in cell **B4** change *16* to **14** so the sheet accurately reports the results of the macro.

7 Click the **Sheet3 sheet tab** and in cell **A1**, type your name and press Enter. Click cell **A1** again. On the **Developer tab**, in the **Code group**, click the **Macros** button, click **Format_Worksheet_Title**, and then click **Run**.

The font now displays in 14 point. You have edited the macro by changing the font size. Although the macro is changed, it is not retroactive—formatting completed prior to the change to the font size retains the 16-point size.

8 **Save** and **Close** the **8A_Macro_Library_Firstname_Lastname** workbook.

Planning a Macro

Because every keystroke is recorded with the macro, it is important to plan ahead what you will include in a macro. When preparing a large macro with several steps, it is recommended that you write down the steps needed. In the written instructions, also include a reminder to stop the macro recorder. Macros can be created that save hours of work, but these complex macros require careful planning, testing, and written notes.

Objective 2
Apply Depreciation Functions

Depreciation is the amount that an asset—something of value that you own—decreases in value over time through use, obsolescence—it has become outdated—or damage. Most goods that you purchase lose their value as they age; for example, a new car decreases in value the longer you own it. In the business world, depreciation is an expense to the firm. The business may select a specific method to depreciate the asset. Excel has built-in functions to determine the depreciation using several of these Internal Revenue Service (IRS) approved methods. In the following activities, you will use depreciation functions to consider different depreciation options for a color copier that Penn Liberty Motors recently purchased.

Depreciation

Long-term assets include property and other assets owned by a firm that are expected to last more than one year. The estimated decline in value for a long-term asset is allocated over the expected life of the asset. Each year the asset is used, the value decreases. This decrease in value is *depreciation*. Some of the assets that a company depreciates include computers, automobiles used for business, office furniture, machines used to produce goods for sale, patents, and copyrights. Land cannot be depreciated nor can assets purchased for personal use.

Depreciation is an expense to the firm. Deducting the entire cost of the asset from income in the first year would not reflect the fact that the asset will be used to produce income over a longer period of time. However, calculating the exact portion of an asset used each year would be very difficult. Some assets may wear out evenly over time, some may lose more of their value at the beginning of their use, and some may lose more value toward the end of their life.

To calculate depreciation for an asset, you need to know the terminology that businesses use for the asset, which are shown in the table in Figure 8.15.

The Internal Revenue Service (IRS) determines the rules for the amount that can be depreciated each year. There are several methods for calculating the amount of depreciation, including the straight-line, sum-of-the-years' digits, and declining balance methods. Each of these methods is allowed by law, and different depreciation amounts occur each year over the life of the asset depending on the depreciation method that is used. The IRS also provides rules for the length of time a business can depreciate the asset.

Depreciation Terms

Term	What it means
Cost of the asset	The initial purchase price
Salvage value— Resale value	The sale value at the end of the useful life
Useful life	The number of years of expected use of the asset
Book value	The cost of the asset minus the total amount of depreciation to date

Figure 8.15

Activity 8.7 Depreciating an Asset Using the Straight-Line Method

Straight-line depreciation calculates an equal amount of depreciation for each year of useful life of the asset. The function name for the straight-line depreciation method is **SLN**. In this activity, you will determine the amount of depreciation each year for the life of the color copier.

1 Display the **8A_Copier_Depreciation_Firstname_Lastname** worksheet, and click cell **B11**. On the **Formulas tab**, in the **Function Library group**, click the **Financial** button, scroll through the list, click **SLN**, and then compare your screen with Figure 8.16.

The **SLN Function Arguments** dialog box displays with three required arguments—Cost, Salvage, and Life. The description explains the goal of the function. The Cost argument is described in the dialog box.

Figure 8.16

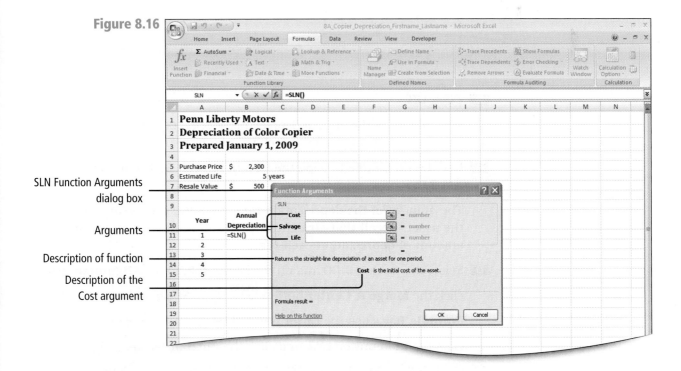

SLN Function Arguments dialog box

Arguments

Description of function

Description of the Cost argument

2 Drag the **Function Arguments** dialog box so that **column B** and **row 10** are visible. In the **Cost** box, type **b5** to enter the purchase price of the copier, and then press F4 so the cell reference is an absolute reference. Press Tab and in the **Salvage** box, type **b7** and then press F4. Press Tab and in the **Life** box, type **b6** press F4, and then compare your screen with Figure 8.17.

The cell references for the function display in the dialog box and the result—*360*—displays in two places in the dialog box. The cells are expressed as absolute references because the formulas will be copied.

Cost argument —

Salvage argument —

Life argument —

Figure 8.17

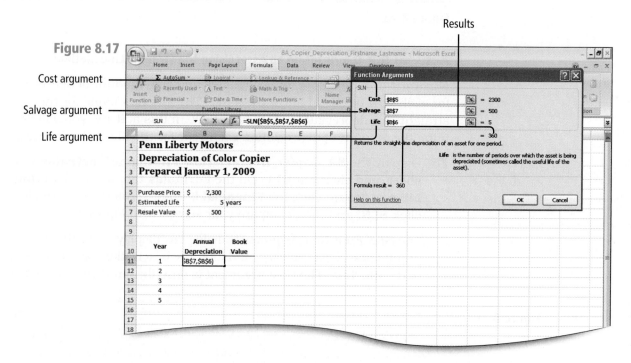

3 Click **OK**.

The amount of the annual depreciation—*$360.00*—displays in the cell. The copier depreciates $360 each year for its expected life of five years.

4 Use the fill handle to copy the formula in cell **B11** down through cell **B15**.

The amount of the depreciation remains $360 each year in the life of the asset. Recall that straight-line depreciation uses an equal amount of depreciation each year.

5 Select the range **A9:C9** and on the **Home tab**, in the **Alignment group**, click the **Merge & Center** button ⊞▾. Type **Straight Line** and in the **Formula Bar**, click the **Enter** button ✔. Then in the **Font group**, click the **Bold** button **B**, and click the **Bottom Border** button ▦▾.

6 Click cell **B16** and press Alt and =, and then on the **Formula Bar**, click the **Enter** button ✔. Format the cell with a **Top and Double Bottom Border**.

Recall that pressing [Alt] and [+] will enter the AutoSum formula. The total amount that the asset depreciates—*$1,800*—displays in the cell. The original cost less the amount depreciated is $500, which is the salvage value of the asset.

7 **Save** 💾 your workbook.

Activity 8.8 Depreciating an Asset Using the Sum-of-Years' Digits Method

The ***sum-of-years' digits depreciation*** method recognizes that an asset will depreciate faster during the early years of its life. The function name for the sum-of-years' digits depreciation method is ***SYD***. In this activity, you will use the SYD method to determine the depreciation amount for each year in the life of the asset.

1 Select the range **A9:C10** and select the **Copy** command. Click cell **E9**, and then click the **Paste** command. Click cell **I9** and click the **Paste** command. Select the range **A11:A15** and **Copy** the range to cells **E11** and **I11**. Click cell **E9** and type **Sum-of-years' Digits**

2 Click cell **F11**. On the **Formulas tab**, in the **Function Library group**, click the **Financial** button and scroll to and click **SYD**.

The SYD Function Arguments dialog box displays with four required arguments—*Cost, Salvage, Life, Per*.

3 In the **Cost** argument box, type **b5** and press [F4]. Press [Tab] and in the **Salvage** argument box, type **b7** and press [F4]. Press [Tab] and in the **Life** argument box, type **b6** and press [F4]. Press [Tab] and in the **Per** argument box, type **e11** and then compare your screen with Figure 8.18.

The Per argument is the period for the amount of depreciation. Recall that the asset will depreciate more in the first years. The argument for the period uses a relative cell reference because the year will change from 1 to 2 to 3, and so on as the formula is copied.

Results

Figure 8.18

Cost argument box —
Salvage argument box —
Life argument box —
Per argument box —

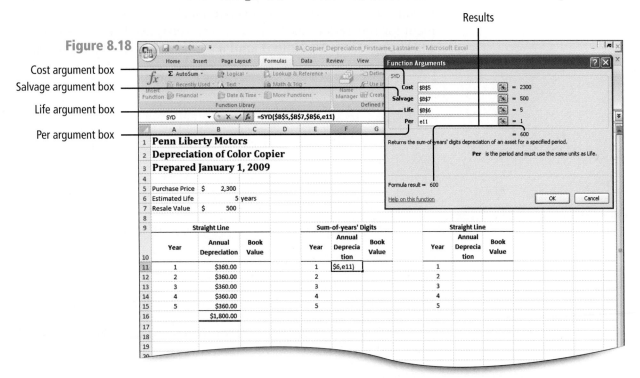

4 Click **OK**, and then copy the formula down through cell **F15**.

5 Click cell **F16** and press [Alt] and [+] to add the range, and then press [Enter]. Format the cell with a **Top and Double Bottom Border**.

The amount that the asset depreciates—*$1,800*—displays in the cell. The original cost less the amount depreciated is $500, which is the salvage value of the asset. The total depreciation is the same for both methods; the amount depreciated each year differs.

6 **Save** 💾 your workbook.

Activity 8.9 Depreciating an Asset Using the Declining Balance Method

The **declining balance depreciation** method also recognizes that an asset will depreciate faster during the early years of its life. The function name for the declining balance depreciation method is **DB**. In this activity, you will determine the depreciation amount for each year in the life of the asset using this method.

1 Click cell **I9** and type **Declining Balance**

2 Click cell **J11**. On the **Formulas tab**, in the **Function Library group**, click the **Financial** button and scroll to and click **DB**.

The DB Function Arguments dialog box displays with four required arguments—*Cost*, *Salvage*, *Life*, *Period*. The Month argument is not a required argument and is used if the asset is purchased during the year and there are fewer than twelve months to depreciate.

3 In the **Cost** argument box, type **b5** and press [F4]. Press [Tab] and in the **Salvage** argument box, type **b7** and press [F4]. Press [Tab] and in the **Life** argument box, type **b6** and press [F4]. Press [Tab] and in the **Period** argument box, type **i11** and then compare your screen with Figure 8.19.

The Period argument is the period for the amount of depreciation. Recall that the asset will depreciate more in the first years. The argument for the period uses a relative cell reference because the year will change from 1 to 2 to 3, and so on as the formula is copied.

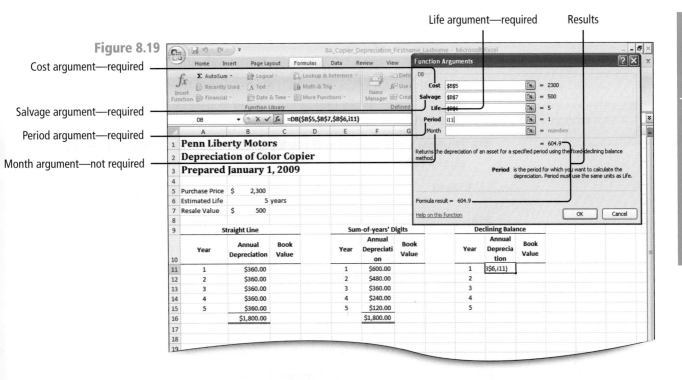

Figure 8.19

Cost argument—required

Salvage argument—required

Period argument—required

Month argument—not required

Life argument—required   Results

4 Click **OK**, and then copy the formula down through cell **J15**.

5 Click cell **J16** and press [Alt] and [+] and in the **Formula Bar**, click the **Enter** button [✓]. Format the cell with a **Top and Double Bottom Border**.

The amount that the asset depreciates—*$1,799.89*—displays in the cell. The original cost less the amount depreciated is $500.11, which is nearly the salvage value of the asset. In this method of depreciation, the complex formula used may not provide the exact resale value, although it is very close. The total depreciation is nearly the same for all methods, but the amount depreciated each year differs.

6 The cost of the copier has increased to $2,500. In cell **B5**, replace the entry with **2500** and as you do, watch the depreciation schedules change to reflect the price. The total Annual Depreciation for the Declining Balance is now $1,999.24.

7 **Save** [💾] your workbook.

Activity 8.10 Preparing a Schedule of Depreciation

When an asset is purchased, Marilyn Kelleman, finance manager, prepares a schedule that displays the amount of depreciation allowed for each year, the total amount of depreciation charged each year, and the resulting book value. Marilyn has determined that she will use the sum-of-years' digits method of depreciation for the copier. In this activity, you will prepare the Schedule of Depreciation for the color copier.

1 Rename **Sheet1** to **Evaluate Depreciation Methods** and rename **Sheet2** to **SYD Depreciation Schedule** Press [⇧ Shift] and click the **Evaluate Depreciation Methods sheet tab** to group the worksheets. Then click

the **Evaluate Depreciation Methods sheet tab** to make it the active worksheet.

2 Select the range **A1:C7**. On the **Home tab**, in the **Editing group**, click the **Fill** button, and then click **Across Worksheets**. In the **Fill Across Worksheets** dialog box, confirm that **All** is selected, and then click **OK**.

3 **Ungroup** the sheets and click the **SYD Depreciation Schedule sheet tab**. Beginning in cell **A9** type the following column titles:

| Year | Annual Depreciation | Total Depreciation | Book Value |

4 Format the column titles with **Bold**, **Center**, **Middle Align**, **Wrap Text**, and **Bottom Double Border**. Adjust the column widths and row heights as necessary. Most of the column titles will display on two lines.

5 Click cell **A10** and type **1** press Enter and in cell **A11**, type **2** Select the range **A10:A11** and use the fill handle to extend the range through the number **5**. Then click the **Center** button.

6 Click cell **B10**. On the **Formulas tab**, in the **Function Library group**, click the **Recently Used** button, and then click **SYD**.

7 In the **SYD Function Arguments** dialog box, in the **Cost** box, type **b5** and press F4. Press Tab and in the **Salvage** box, type **b7** and press F4. Press Tab and in the **Life** box, type **b6** and press F4. Press Tab and in the **Per** box, type **a10** Click **OK**.

The amount of the SYD depreciation for the first year—*$666.67*—displays in the cell.

8 Click cell **C10** and enter a formula that totals the amount of depreciation to date. Type **=b10** Click cell **D10** and type **=b5** press F4 and then type **-c10** and then press Enter.

After the first year of depreciation, the book value of the copier is $1,833.33, which is the purchase price less the amount of depreciation for the first year.

9 Click cell **B10** and drag the fill handle down through cell **B14** to determine the annual depreciation for each year in the life of the asset. Click cell **D10** and drag the fill handle down through cell **D14**.

10 Click cell **C11** and type **=c10+b11** This is the depreciation for the first year plus the depreciation for the second year. In the **Formula Bar**, click the **Enter** button. Use the fill handle to copy the formula down through **row 14**. Format the range **B11:D14** with **Comma Style**. Click outside the worksheet range, and then compare your screen with Figure 8.20.

The depreciation schedule is complete. The total deprecation increases each year until the asset has fully depreciated to $2,000. The book value has decreased each year until the salvage value is $500.

Figure 8.20

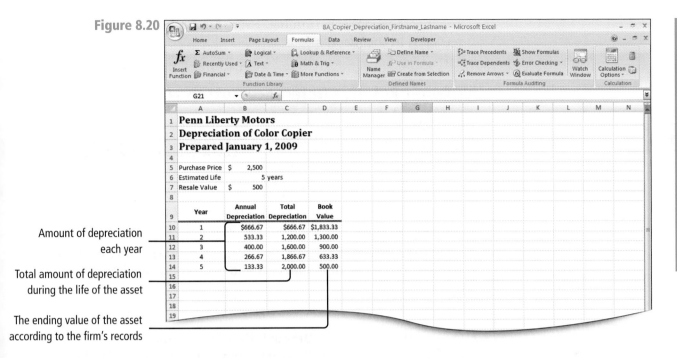

Amount of depreciation each year

Total amount of depreciation during the life of the asset

The ending value of the asset according to the firm's records

11 **Save** your workbook.

Activity 8.11 Create a Macro Using the Relative Reference Feature

The *relative reference* feature for macros is used when the actions in the macro are relative to the selected cell. When the Use Relative References button is selected, it displays in orange. Usually when a macro is recorded and you click in a cell, that exact cell reference is retained in the macro. For instance, if you click in cell B6, that cell becomes active when the macro is run. Using the relative reference feature records the clicks relative to the active cell. Now if cell B5 is active and you click in cell B6, when the macro is run, the active cell will move down to the next row.

In this activity, you will create a macro using the relative reference button that determines the monthly depreciation for the methods.

1 From your files, open the workbook named **8A_Macro_Library_Firstname_Lastname**. If necessary, at the **Security Warning**, click **Options** and click **Enable this content**. Then click **OK**.

Recall that the macro security is enabled and the security warning displays as an alert that macros are contained in this workbook.

2 Click the **Sheet3 sheet tab** and in cell **C3**, type **100** and on the **Formula Bar**, click the **Enter** button. This cell will be a placeholder to use while you are creating the macro.

3 With cell **C3** active, on the **Developer tab**, in the **Code group**, click the **Use Relative References** button. Then click the **Record Macro** button. In the **Record Macro** dialog box, name this macro **Monthly_Depr** For the **Shortcut key**, press ⇧ Shift while you type **m** Confirm that you will store the macro in **This Workbook**. For the **Description**, type **Provide monthly depreciation** and then click **OK**.

The macro recorder is running. Every keystroke and mouse click is recorded in the macro.

> **Note** — **Relative Reference Button**
>
> The Relative Reference button is a toggle switch—it is on or it is off. It is good practice to confirm the need for a relative reference before you create your macro.

4 Press Tab two times and in cell E3 type **=c3/12** and press Enter. Then in the **Code group**, click the **Stop Recording** button.

5 Click the **Library sheet tab**. Click cell **A5** and type **Monthly Depr** In cell **B5**, type **Move right two cells and divide original cell by 12** In cell **C5**, type Ctrl + ⇧ Shift + M Adjust column widths and **Save** 🖫 your workbook.

6 Display the **8A_Copier_Depreciation_Firstname_Lastname** workbook and then click the **Evaluate Depreciation Methods sheet tab**. Right-click the **column D** heading, and then click **Insert** to insert a column to the right of the **Straight Line** information. Insert a column to the right of the **Sum-of-years' Digits** information, leaving two blank columns between these sections of the worksheet.

7 In cell **D10**, type **Monthly Depreciation** and format it like cell **C10**. Copy cell **D10** to cells **I10** and **N10**.

8 Click cell **C11** and type **=b5-b11** and press Enter. In cell **C12**, type **=c11-b12** and in the **Formula Bar**, click the **Enter** button ✔. Use the fill handle to copy the formula down through cell **C15**.

9 Click cell **B11** and on the **Developer tab**, in the **Code group**, click the **Macros** button. In the **Macros** dialog box, click **8A_Macro_Library_Firstname_Lastname.xlsm'!Monthly_Depr**, and then click **Run**. Compare your screen with Figure 8.21.

The monthly amount of depreciation—*33.33333*—displays in cell D11.

Figure 8.21

Use Relative Reference button active

Active cell after macro is run

Monthly depreciation

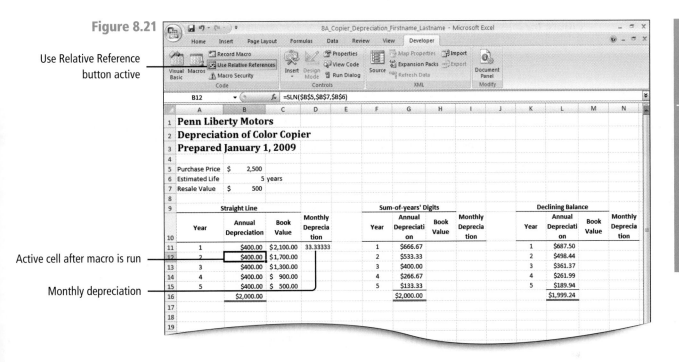

---

10 With cell **B12** active, press Ctrl + ⇧Shift while you type **m** to enter the monthly depreciation for the second year. Using the skills you practiced, insert the macro to complete the monthly depreciation for the straight-line method.

11 Click cell **H11** and enter a formula to determine the book value—the purchase price less the annual depreciation: **=B5-G11**. The book value—$1,833.33—is displayed. Click cell **H12** and enter a formula to determine the book value for the second year: **=H11-G12**. Use the fill handle to copy the formula through **row 15**.

12 Click cell **G11** and press Ctrl + ⇧Shift while you type **m** to use the shortcut keys to run the macro. Using the skills you practiced, run the macro to complete the monthly depreciation for the sum-of-the-years' digits method for all years.

13 Using the skills you practiced, complete the declining balance depreciation information by completing the book value and using the macro to determine the monthly depreciation for all years. Press Ctrl + Home to return to cell **A1. Save** your workbook, and then compare your screen with Figure 8.22.

Figure 8.22

Declining Balance Monthly Depreciation

Declining Balance Book Value

Sum-of-years' Digits Monthly Depreciation

Sum-of-years' Digits Book Value

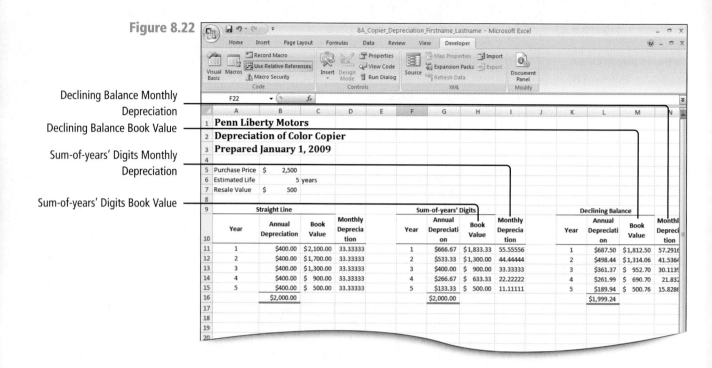

14 Select the range **A9:D9** and on the **Home tab**, click the **Merge & Center** button ⊞ ▾ to unmerge the range, and then click it again to merge and center the title over four columns. Format the range with a **Bottom Border**. Using the skills you practiced, center the Sum-of-years' Digits and Declining Balance titles over the four columns for each depreciation method, and apply a **Bottom Border**.

15 Adjust column widths and row heights as necessary. Use **Format Painter** ◈ to copy the format of cell **B11** to cells **D11**, **I11**, and **N11**. Format the range **B12:D15** with **Comma Style** and use **Format Painter** ◈ to copy the format to cells **G12** and **L12**.

Recall that when a range of cells is formatted with the Format Painter, an identical range will be formatted by clicking the top left cell.

16 **Delete Sheet3**. In both worksheets, in the **Left Footer** area, insert the **File Name** and in the **Right Footer** area, insert the **Sheet Name**. Center the worksheets both **Horizontally** and **Vertically**. Ungroup the worksheets and click the **Evaluate Depreciation Methods sheet tab**. In the **Page Setup group**, click the **Orientation** button and click **Landscape**. In the **Scale to Fit group**, click the **Width button arrow** and then click **1 page**. **Save** 🖫 your workbook.

17 In the **8A_Macro_Library_Firstname_Lastname** worksheet, in the **Library sheet**, select **column B** and on the **Home tab**, in the **Alignment group**, click **Wrap Text**. Adjust **column B** to a width of **45** and adjust **column C** to fully display the contents. Display the worksheet in **Portrait orientation**, centered **Horizontally**. In the **Left Footer** area, insert the **File Name**. **Save** 🖫 your workbook.

18 To submit electronically, follow the instructions provided by your instructor. To print the **8A_Copier_Depreciation_Firstname_Lastname** and the **Library Sheet** in the **8A_Macro_Library_Firstname_Lastname** workbooks, click the **Office** button [icon], and click **Print**. In the **Print** dialog box, under **Print what**, select **Entire workbook**, and then click **OK**. **Close** the workbooks and then **Exit** Excel.

More Knowledge

Working with Macros

If you use macros frequently, it is recommended that you set your computer as follows. These are the settings used in this chapter. If you continue to use the macros you create in this chapter throughout the rest of your Excel course, you will want these settings maintained.

- Display the Developer tab. From the Office menu, click Excel Options. On the left side, click Popular and at the right, under Top options for working with Excel, confirm that Show Developer tab in the Ribbon is checked.

- Display the Message Bar notification. From the Office menu, click Excel Options. On the left side, click Trust Center and at the right, click the Trust Center Settings button. On the left, click Message Bar and confirm that Show the Message Bar in all applications when content has been blocked is checked.

- Set macro security to Disable all macros with notification. On the Developer tab, in the Code group, click Macro Security. Confirm that Disable all macros with notification is checked.

End **You have completed Project 8A** ———————————

Project 8B New Car Sales

In Activities 8.12 through 8.23, you will examine data for the new car sales at Penn Liberty Motors for the first six months of the year. Charlie James, auto sales manager, needs to extract some answers from the data in order to make decisions about training sales representatives, hiring additional sales staff, and evaluating which car models to maintain in stock. In addition to analyzing the data, you will create a PivotTable to evaluate the sales. Your completed workbook will look similar to Figure 8.23.

For Project 8B, you will need the following file:

e08B_New_Car_Sales

You will save your workbook as
8B_New_Car_Sales_Firstname_Lastname

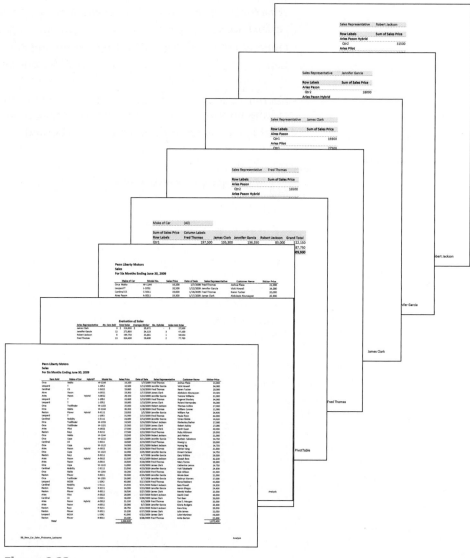

Figure 8.23
Project 8B—New_Car_Sales

Objective 3
Evaluate Worksheet Data with Conditional IF Functions

Business managers analyze worksheet data to gather information that can help them make business decisions. *Conditional functions* test whether a condition is true or false by using logical or comparison expressions. The results of these tests are used by managers to determine if data meets specific conditions. With these functions, the data in the worksheet can be evaluated and included in a formula without rearranging the data.

Activity 8.12 Determining Individual Cars Sold Using the COUNTIF Function

Charlie James, the auto sales manager, wants to know the number of cars that each sales representative sold during this time period. The *COUNTIF function* counts items within a range that match a specific condition. In this activity, you will use the COUNTIF function to count the number of cars each sales representative sold.

1 **Start** Excel. From your student files, locate and open the file named **e08B_New_Car_Sales**. **Save** the file in the **Excel Chapter 8** folder and name it **8B_New_Car_Sales_Firstname_Lastname**

This worksheet reports the car sales for the first six months of the year. You will evaluate this data to answer several questions.

2 Make a copy of the Sales09 worksheet and place it before **Sheet2**. Name the new sheet **Analysis** On the Analysis sheet, select **column B** and insert two columns. Select the range **A6:A47**. On the **Data tab**, in the **Data Tools group**, click the **Text to Columns** button.

Column A contains the car make and model and whether or not it is a hybrid car. Recall that you can separate text into several columns to separate different types of data. The cars listed in column A will be converted to three columns for make, model, and hybrid. Because you will alter this worksheet, it is important to retain a copy of the original.

3 In the displayed **Convert Text to Columns Wizard** dialog box, be sure **Delimited** is selected, and then click **Next**. In **Step 2**, under **Delimiters**, click **Space**, clear all other delimiters, and then click **Finish**.

4 In cell **B5**, type **Model of Car** and in cell **C5**, type **Hybrid?** Then compare your screen with Figure 8.24.

Figure 8.24

Column titles added information about cars—Car Sold, Model, and if it's a hybrid

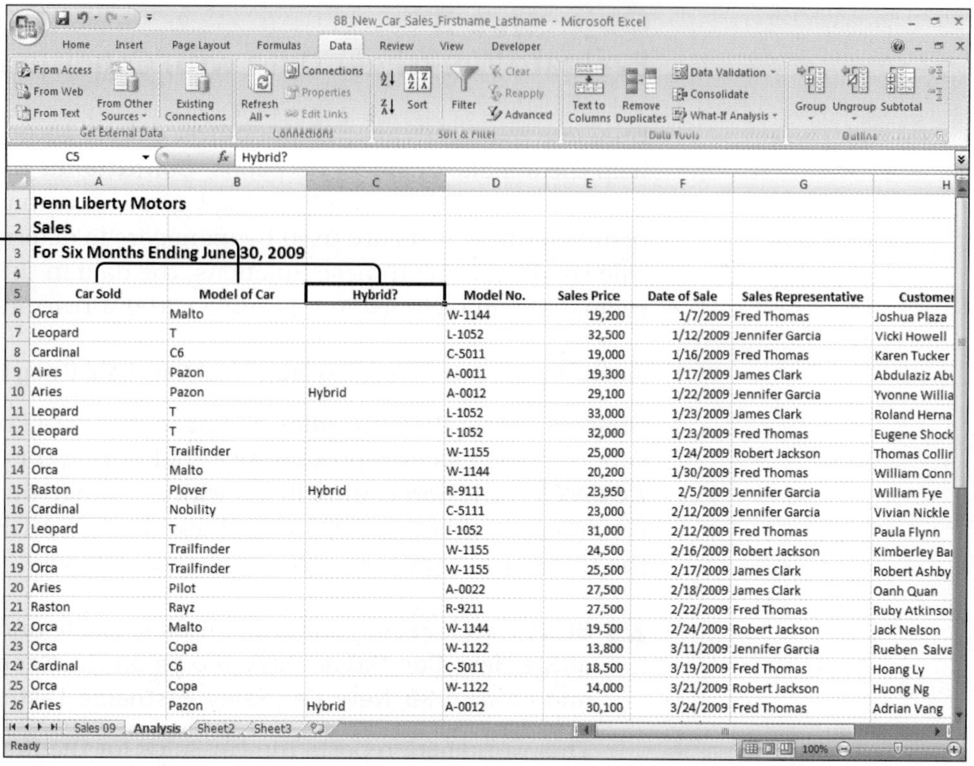

5 In cell **A48**, type **Total** and in cells **E48**—Sales Price—and **I48**—Sticker Price—enter a **Sum** formula. Format these cells with a **Top and Double Bottom Border**. Format cell **A48** with **Bold** **B** , Italic **I** , and **Center** **▤** .

6 Beginning in cell **A52**, enter the following row titles:

James Clark
Jennifer Garcia
Robert Jackson
Fred Thomas

7 Beginning in cell **A51**, enter the following column titles and format with **Bold** **B** , **Italic** **I** , and **Bottom Border** **▦ ▾** . Adjust the column widths to display the column titles in row 51 on one line.

Sales Representative	No. Cars Sold	Total Sales	Average Sticker	No. Hybrids	Sales Amt Aries

8 Click cell **B52**. Click the **Formulas tab** and in the **Function Library group**, click the **More Functions** button. Point to **Statistical**, and then from the submenu, click **COUNTIF**, and then compare your screen with Figure 8.25.

The COUNTIF dialog box displays with two required arguments—Range and Criteria.

Figure 8.25

COUNTIF Function Arguments
dialog box

Range argument

Criteria argument

Description of COUNTIF
function

Description of Range argument

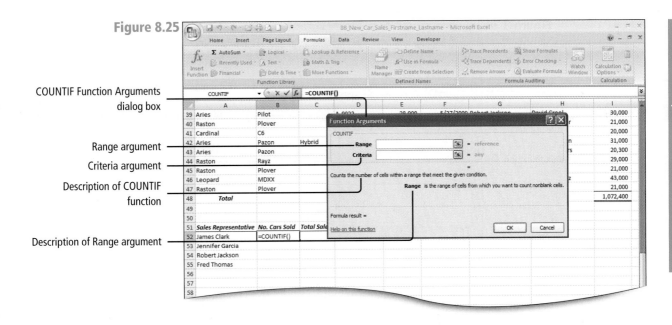

9 With the insertion point in the **Range** box, click the **Collapse Dialog Box** button ![icon], select the range **G6:G47**, and then press F4.

When selecting a range, you can drag from the top to the bottom or from the bottom to the top. The range identified in the dialog box is identical. When a specific sales representative sells a car, his or her name is listed in this column. To determine the number of cars sold, you will count the number of times the name appears in this column.

10 Click the **Expand Dialog Box** button ![icon], press Tab, and in the **Criteria** box, click cell **A52**, and then compare your screen with Figure 8.26.

The name of the sales representative is in this cell. You will copy this formula through the range of the sales representatives, so using the cell reference rather than a specific name allows the formula to be copied. Recall that in a Function Arguments dialog box, the results of each argument display to the right with the result of the function also displayed.

Figure 8.26

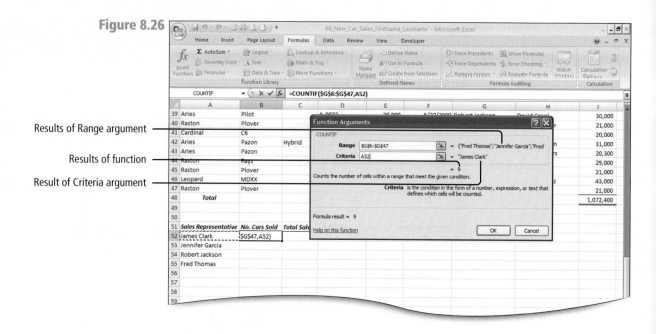

Results of Range argument

Results of function

Result of Criteria argument

11 Click **OK**, and then use the fill handle to copy the function down through cell **B55**.

The number of cars sold by each sales representative during the six-month period is displayed in the cells.

12 **Save** your workbook.

Activity 8.13 Determining Individual Sales Using the SUMIF Function

The **SUMIF function** adds the cells in a range that meet a specific condition. Charlie James wants to know the total sales income for each of the sales representatives. In this activity, you will use the SUMIF function to add the sales for each of the sales representatives.

1 Click cell **C52**, and in the **Function Library group**, click the **Math & Trig** button, and from the list, click **SUMIF**, and then compare your screen with Figure 8.27.

The SUMIF function has two required arguments—Range and Criteria. In this case, the third optional argument—Sum_range—will also be needed.

Figure 8.27

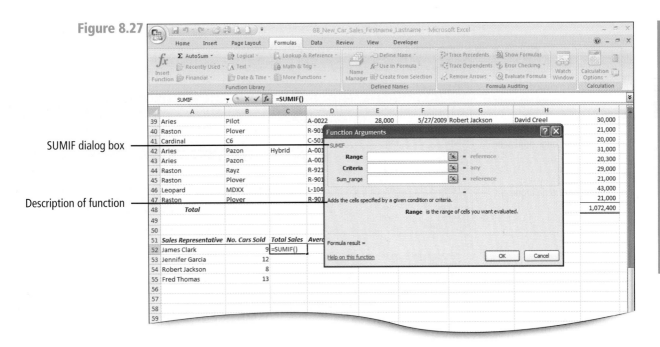

SUMIF dialog box

Description of function

2 With the insertion point in the **Range** box, click the **Collapse Dialog Box** button 🖻, select the range **G6:G47**, and then press [F4].

When a specific sales representative sells a car, his or her name is listed in this column. In order to determine the total amount of sales for each sales representative, we will sum the sales amounts of the cars sold when the sales representative's name appears in the column.

3 Click the **Expand Dialog Box** button 🖼. Press [Tab], and in the **Criteria** box, click cell **A52**.

The name of the sales representative is displayed in this cell. You will copy this formula through the range of the sales representatives, so using the cell reference rather than a specific name allows the formula to be copied. Recall that in a Function Arguments dialog box, the results of each argument displays to the right with the result of the function also displayed.

4 Press [Tab]. In the **Sum_range**, click the **Collapse Dialog Box** button 🖻, select the range **E6:E47**, and then press [F4]. Click the **Expand Dialog Box** button 🖼, and then compare your screen with Figure 8.28.

The range argument is used to identify the range where the criteria is found. When the criteria is matched in that range, the value in the Sum_range argument is summed to determine the total Sales Price of the cars sold by James Clark.

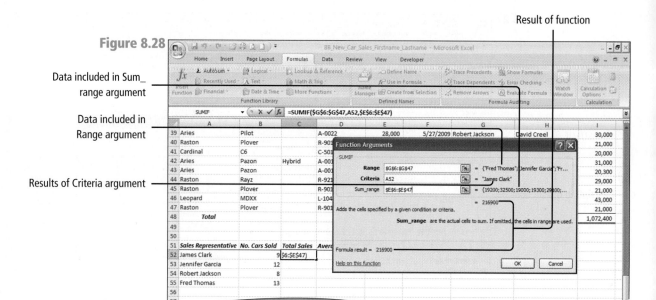

Figure 8.28

Result of function

Data included in Sum_range argument

Data included in Range argument

Results of Criteria argument

5 Click **OK** and confirm the value—*216900*—displays. Use the fill handle to copy the formula down through cell **C55** and display the total sales for each sales representative.

6 **Save** your workbook.

Activity 8.14 Determining Individual Sales Using the AVERAGEIF Function

The *AVERAGEIF function* calculates the average of a range of data that meets a specified condition. It compares data in the worksheet, and if the data matches the criteria, it is included in the average. In evaluating the sales of cars, Charlie uses the average of the sticker price for the sales of each sales representative and compares it with the actual sales price. In this activity, you will determine the average of the sticker price for the cars each sales representative sold using the AVERAGEIF function.

1 Click cell **D52**. In the **Function Library group**, click the **More Functions** button, point to **Statistical**, and then click **AVERAGEIF**. Compare your screen with Figure 8.29.

The AVERAGEIF function has two required arguments: Range and Criteria. It also includes an optional argument—Average_range—which will also be needed.

Figure 8.29

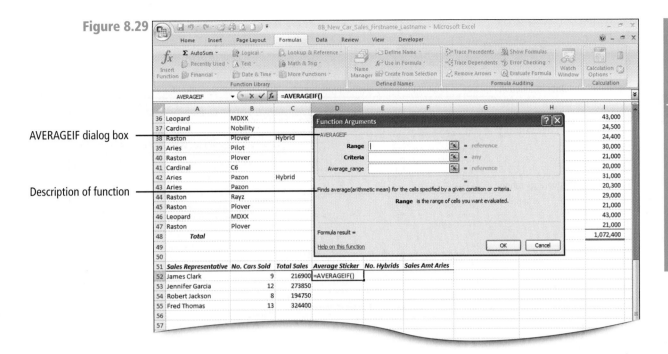

AVERAGEIF dialog box

Description of function

▨ With the insertion point in the **Range** box, click the **Collapse Dialog Box** button ▣, select the range **G6:G47**, and then press F4.

When a specific sales representative sells a car, his or her name is listed in this column. Recall you can select the range by scrolling from the bottom to the top as well as from the top to the bottom.

▨ Click the **Expand Dialog Box** button ▣. Press Tab, and in the **Criteria** box, click cell **A52** to select the cell that displays the sales representative's name.

▨ Press Tab. In the **Average_range** area, click the **Collapse Dialog Box** button ▣, select the range **I6:I47**, and then press F4. Click the **Expand Dialog Box** button ▣, and then compare your screen with Figure 8.30.

To determine the value of the cars sold, include the sticker price of the car sold in the Average_range argument.

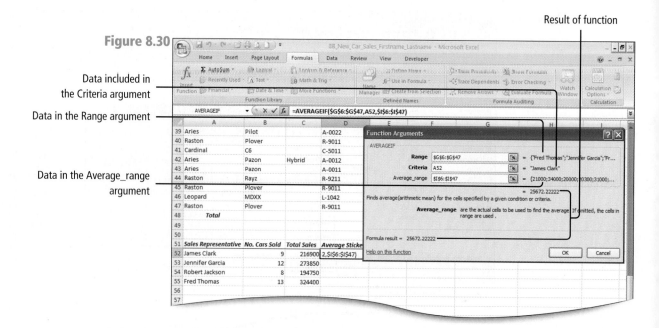

Result of function

Figure 8.30

Data included in the Criteria argument

Data in the Range argument

Data in the Average_range argument

5 Click **OK** and use the fill handle to copy the formula down through cell **D55**. **Save** your workbook.

Activity 8.15 Counting the Number of Hybrids Sold Using the COUNTIFS Function

Kevin Rau, the president of Penn Liberty Motors, has requested information about the sales of the hybrid models and would like to know how many hybrids each sales representative sold. There are two variables for this function—the name of the sales representative and the sale of a hybrid car. To count the number of items in a list when there is more than one condition to be met, use the **COUNTIFS function**. In this activity, you will count the number of hybrid cars each sales representative sold.

1 Click cell **E52**. In the **Function Library group**, click the **More Functions** button, point to **Statistical**, and then from the submenu, click **COUNTIFS**. Compare your screen with Figure 8.31.

There are two required arguments—Criteria_range1 and Criteria1. The numbered criteria indicate that additional arguments may be added.

Figure 8.31

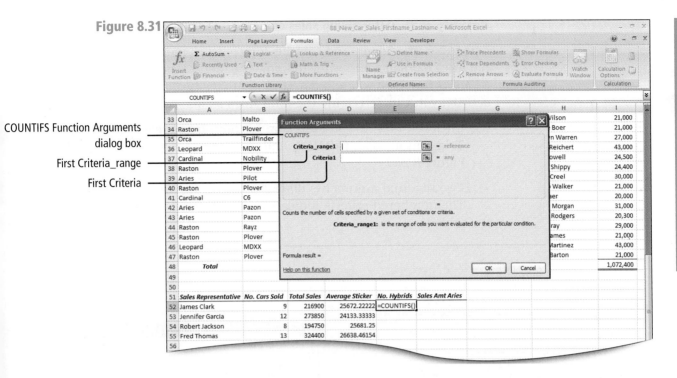

COUNTIFS Function Arguments dialog box

First Criteria_range

First Criteria

2 In the **Criteria_range1** box, click the **Collapse Dialog Box** button , select the range **C6:C47**, and press F4. Then click the **Expand Dialog Box** button .

This range determines if the car is a hybrid. You first determine the condition that the car is a hybrid model.

3 Press Tab and in the **Criteria1** box, type **Hybrid** and then press Tab.

The dialog box expands to include data for a second set of criteria with the arguments Criteria_range2 and Criteria2. The criteria— *Hybrid*—is displayed surrounded by quotation marks, which Excel entered for you. Recall that text entered in a Function Arguments dialog box is surrounded by quotation marks.

4 In the **Criteria_range2** box, click the **Collapse Dialog Box** button , select the range **G6:G47**, and then press F4. Click the **Expand Dialog Box** button .

This range lists the person selling the car.

5 Press Tab, and in the **Criteria2** box, click cell **A52**.

Because you will copy this function for each sales representative, enter the cell reference rather than typing the exact name.

6 Click **OK** and copy the formula down through cell **E55**.

The total number of hybrids sold by each sales representative now displays. Kevin can use this information to assist with education and training of the sales staff.

7 **Save** your workbook.

Activity 8.16 Determining Sales of a Car Make Using the SUMIFS Function

Kevin Rau, president, and Charlie James, sales manager, are reviewing the Aries car sales and want to know the total sales for all Aries cars. The **SUMIFS function** will add data that matches two or more criteria. In this activity, you will determine the total sales for the Aries cars sold.

1 Click cell **F52**. In the **Function Library group**, click the **Math & Trig** button, click **SUMIFS**, and then compare your screen with Figure 8.32.

Two required arguments display—Sum_range and Criteria_range1. The numbered criteria indicate that additional arguments may be added.

Figure 8.32

SUMIFS Function Arguments dialog box

Sum_range

First Criteria_range

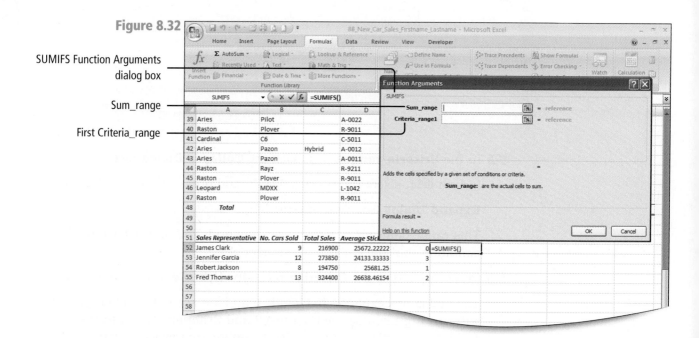

2 In the **Sum_range** text box, click the **Collapse Dialog Box** button, select the range **E6:E47**, and then press F4. Click the **Expand Dialog Box** button.

This range is the sales price for the cars. The numbers in this range will be added when the conditions are met. The Criteria1 box displays after the first argument is entered.

3 Click in the **Criteria_range1** box, click the **Collapse Dialog Box** button, select the range **G6:G47**, and press F4. Then click the **Expand Dialog Box** button.

This range determines the sales representative who made the sale. The criteria ranges must be the same size and shape as the sum range. The dialog box expands to display another required argument—*Criteria1*.

4 Press Tab and in the **Criteria1** box, click cell **A52** to select the sales representative's name. Press Tab.

The dialog box expands to include data for a second set of criteria with the arguments Criteria_range2 and Criteria2.

5 In the **Criteria_range2** box, click the **Collapse Dialog Box** button, select the range **A6:A47**, and press F4. Then click the **Expand Dialog Box** button.

This range lists the make of car sold. Each time the Aries car make is found for the sales representative, the amount of the sale will be included in the sum.

6 Press Tab and in the **Criteria2** text area, type **Aries** and then compare your screen with Figure 8.33.

Criteria1—the first condition,
the sales representative

Figure 8.33

Sum_range—the column
that displays the sales

Criteria_range1—the column
that displays the first condition,
sales representative

Criteria_range2—the column
that displays the second
condition, car make

Criteria2—the second
condition, Aries

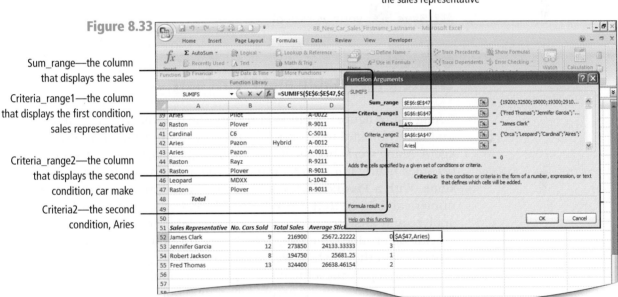

7 Click **OK** and copy the formula down through cell **F55**.

The total sales of Aries cars by each sales representative now displays. Charlie will use this information to assist with education and training of the sales staff.

Alert!

Does the #VALUE! error code display in the cell?

In the SUMIFS function, the argument ranges must be the same size and shape. If the #VALUE! error displays, review the function argument dialog box to be sure each range selected has the same set of beginning and ending row references—row 6 to row 47.

8 Select the range **B52:F55** and format with **Comma Style** with **no decimals**. Format cells **C52**, **D52**, and **F52** with **Accounting Number Format** with **no decimals**. Adjust column widths. In cell **A50**, type Evaluation of Sales and format with **Bold** $\boxed{\textbf{B}}$ and **Italic** $\boxed{\textit{I}}$, increase the font size to **14-point**, and **Merge & Center** $\boxed{\text{⊞}}$ across **columns A:F**.

9 Set this worksheet to print in **Landscape Orientation**. In the **Page Setup group**, click the **Dialog Box Launcher** $\boxed{\text{⌐}}$. In the **Page Setup** dialog box, in the **Page tab**, under **Scaling**, click **Fit to 1 page** wide and **2 pages** tall. In the **Margins tab**, center **Horizontally**. Place the **File Name** in the **Left Footer** and the **Sheet Name** in the **Right Footer**.

10 In the status bar, click the **Page Break Preview** button $\boxed{\text{凹}}$ and in Page Break Preview, move the horizontal page break line between **rows 48** and **49**. Then in the status bar, click the **Normal** button $\boxed{\text{⊞}}$.

11 **Save** $\boxed{\text{💾}}$ your workbook.

Objective 4
Create a PivotTable and PivotChart

A long list of figures is not useful until the data is organized in a manner that is meaningful to the reader and provides information to the managers. Many worksheets contain thousands of rows of data and it becomes nearly impossible to review the data and make business decisions. With a ***PivotTable report*** you can manipulate a large amount of numerical data so that it can be displayed in different ways in order to analyze and answer questions about the data. For instance, you can quickly determine which sales representative had the most sales, what product sold the most, or which month created the largest sales. A PivotTable report uses the data from the original worksheet—the source data—and creates the PivotTable on a new worksheet.

Activity 8.17 Creating a PivotTable

A PivotTable report uses the columns of your worksheet—***fields***—to summarize multiple rows of data. The names of the fields in the PivotTable are the column titles in the worksheet. In this activity, you will assist Charlie James with his sales evaluation by creating a PivotTable so that the data can be manipulated and viewed in different ways.

1 Click the **Sales 09 sheet tab** and click anywhere within the data— **A5:G47**. On the **Insert tab**, in the **Tables group**, click the **PivotTable button arrow**, and then click **PivotTable**.

The PivotTable command is used to create both a PivotTable and a PivotChart. The Create PivotTable dialog box displays with the range of the table—the ***source data***—displayed in the dialog box.

Note — The PivotTable Range

If the PivotTable has not selected the entire range of the data, look for rows or columns that do not contain data. The PivotTable range cannot contain empty rows or columns.

[2] In the **Create PivotTable** dialog box, confirm the range of the data— **A5:G47**—is correct and that **New Worksheet** is selected. Click **OK**. Rename the new sheet **PivotTable** and then compare your screen with Figure 8.34.

A PivotTable can be placed in the current worksheet or in another worksheet of the workbook. This one is placed in a new sheet. At the left side is the ***PivotTable layout area*** where the PivotTable report will be created. On the right side is the ***PivotTable Field List***. The field list displays each of the column titles from the source data in the ***Fields Section***. Below the Fields Section is the ***Areas Section***— which is the area used to place field names into the PivotTable report.

Figure 8.34

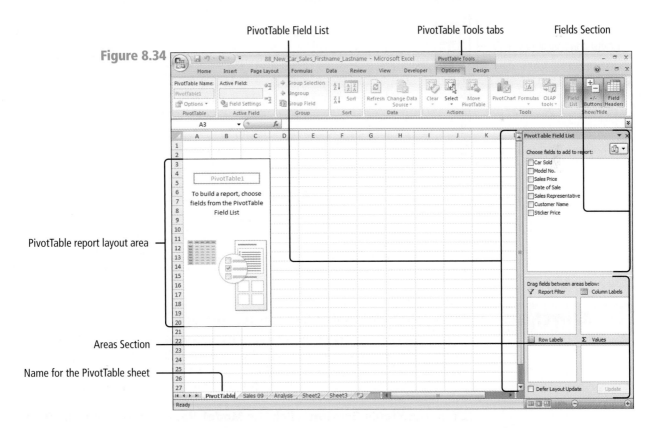

Alert!

Does your PivotTable Field List look different?

The PivotTable Field List can be arranged in several ways. At the upper right corner of the PivotTable Field List, to the right of Choose fields to add to report, is an icon and arrow—the ScreenTip identifies the name of the selected Field List arrangement. When you click the arrow, a gallery displays the choices. Click Fields Section and Areas Section Stacked.

3 In the **PivotTable Field List**, click the **Sales Representative** check box, and then compare your screen with Figure 8.35. Alternatively, right-click the field name and select the field location—Add to Row Labels—from the displayed menu.

As you selected the field name, its field name displays in the Areas Section in the Row Labels area and the names of the representatives display in column A of the layout area. Titles that do not contain numbers are placed as row labels by default. The names of the sales representatives display on the worksheet in the PivotTable layout area as row labels.

Figure 8.35

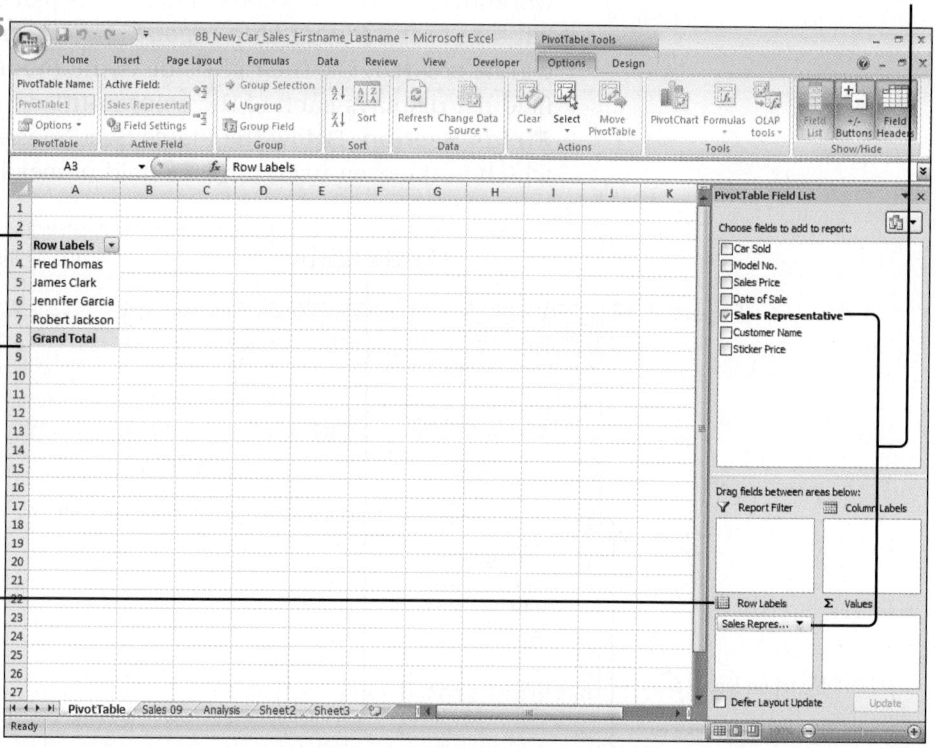

Field(s) displayed as row labels

Row Labels area

Selected field

Alert!   **Did your PivotTable Field List disappear?**

When you click outside the PivotTable and in the worksheet area, the PivotTable Field List is removed from view. To redisplay the Field List, click in the PivotTable displayed at the left of the worksheet.

---

4 In the **Fields Section**, click the **Model No.** check box and the **Sales Price** check box, and then compare your screen with Figure 8.36.

In the Areas Section, fields that do not contain numbers—Sales Representatives and Model No.—display in the *Row Labels area*. The field that contains numbers—Sales Price—displays in the *Values area*, which is used to summarize the data in your PivotTable. In the PivotTable layout area, column A displays the sales representatives, and under each representative, the model number of the cars sold by that representative. The total sales price of each car model and each sales representative's total sales display in column B.

Figure 8.36

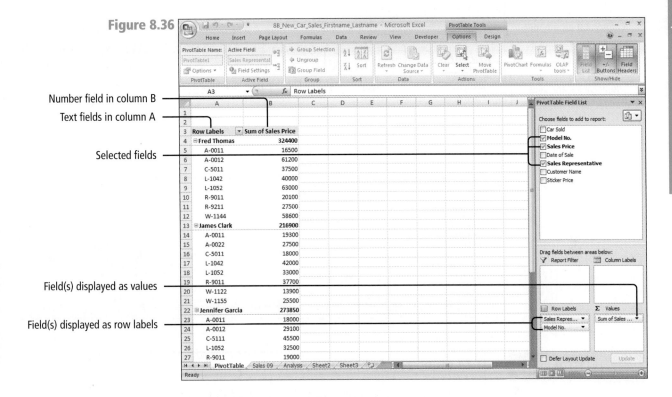

Number field in column B

Text fields in column A

Selected fields

Field(s) displayed as values

Field(s) displayed as row labels

⑤ In cell **A4**—where Fred Thomas is displayed—click the **Collapse Outline** button ▣.

The data about the cars sold is hidden and only the sales representative and his total sales display.

⑥ In the **PivotTable Field List**, in the **Row Labels** area, click on **Model No**. and drag it to the **Column Labels** area. In the **Fields Section**, click the **Car Sold** check box, and then compare your screen with Figure 8.37.

By moving the fields from one area to another, the PivotTable changes to display the data in a different manner. Recall that when you click a field name check box that contains text—Items Sold—it is added to the Row Labels area.

Figure 8.37

Column Labels are the model number

Row Labels are sales representatives and items sold

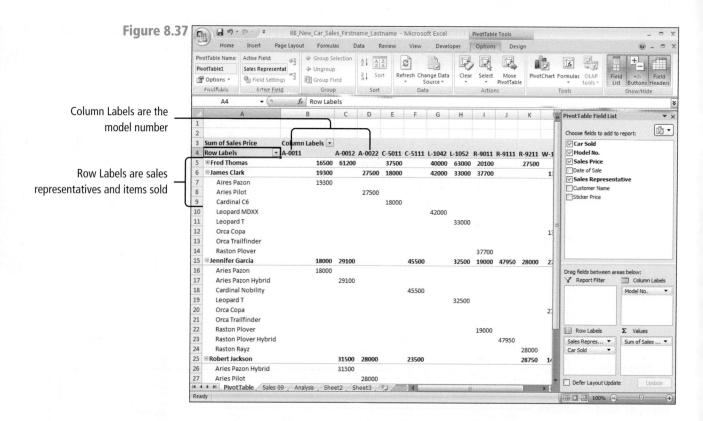

Another Way

To Move Fields in the PivotTable

- In the Fields Section, right-click on the field name and select the area to place the field.
- In the Fields Section, click on the field name and drag to the area in which you will place the field.
- In the Areas Section, click the field name arrow and click the location where you will place the field.

7 Save ⊟ your workbook.

Activity 8.18 Filtering Data

The data in a PivotTable may be filtered to view only specific records. Especially in a large worksheet that contains hundreds of entries, filtering data is useful to review specific details. Charlie James wants to review the performance of the sales representative hired last fall. In this activity, you will of filter the PivotTable report data for Jennifer Garcia to view just her sales.

1 In the **PivotTable Field List**, in the **Fields Section**, clear the **Model No.** check box to remove this field from the PivotTable.

To remove a field, you can deselect the check box, click on the field name and drag it to the Fields Section, or click the arrow by the field name and from the menu, click Remove Field.

2 In the **Row Labels** area, click **Sales Representatives** and drag to the **Report Filter** area.

Sales Representative displays in cell A1, and *(All)* displays in cell B1 of the PivotTable where it can be used as a report filter to display selected sales representatives. The sales representatives' names no longer display as row labels.

3 In cell **B1**, click the **(All) arrow** to display the sales representatives. At the end of the menu, click **Select Multiple Items**. At the top, click the **(All)** check box to clear all check boxes next to the sales representatives' names, and then click the check box for **Jennifer Garcia.** Click **OK**, and then compare your screen with Figure 8.38.

Only the sales for Jennifer display. The Filter button displays in cell B1 beside the name of the filtered field. It is also displayed in the Fields Section of the PivotTable Field List.

Figure 8.38

Filter button

Name of filtered field

Total sales for Jennifer Garcia

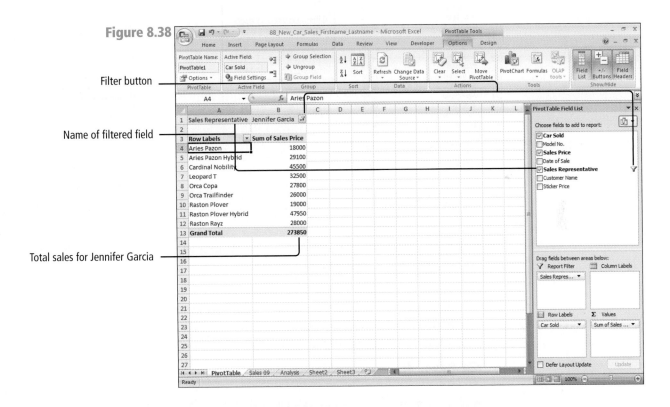

4 In the **PivotTable Field List**, click the **Date of Sale** check box.

Even though a date is a number, it cannot be summarized as a value; therefore, it is entered in the PivotTable as a row label and is listed under each make of car sold.

5 Click cell **A7**. Click the **Options tab** and in the **Group group**, click the **Group Field** button. The **Grouping** dialog box displays as shown in Figure 8.39.

The Grouping dialog box allows specific items to be grouped and displayed together in the PivotTable. The first and last dates displayed in the PivotTable are entered in the Grouping dialog box. Dates or time frames can be specified and you can group the items by several time periods—day, month, quarter, year.

Beginning and End dates from PivotTable

Figure 8.39

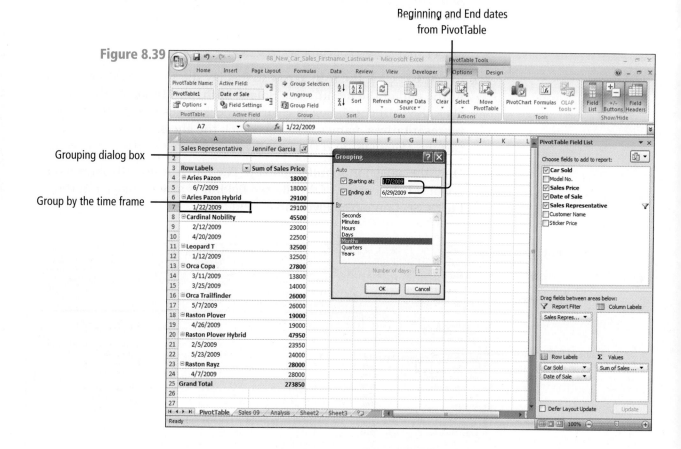

Grouping dialog box

Group by the time frame

6 In the **Grouping** dialog box, click **Quarters** to select it, click **Months** to deselect it, and then click **OK**.

The sale of each car is grouped by quarter nested under the car models that Jennifer sold. Excel has combined the sales for the three months in the first quarter and the next three months in the second quarter and now displays the dates as quarters.

7 **Save** 💾 your workbook.

Activity 8.19 Rearranging the Filtered Data to Display Sales Information

Rearranging the data in a PivotTable allows data to be reviewed in different ways. By moving a field to a new location, a different focus is achieved. When evaluating the sales of Penn Liberty Motors, using a PivotTable quickly provides information about car sales, sales for each sales representative, or the total sales of each model. In this activity, you will rearrange the data to review the sales for each sales representative for each quarter.

1 In the **Pivot Table Field List**, in the **Report Filter** area, drag the **Sales Representatives** field to the **Row Labels** area and place it under the field names that already display in that area. Then drag the **Car Sold** field to the **Report Filter** area.

Notice that the quarter totals are the primary titles and the sales representative is displayed as a secondary title. In the row labels area, the field name that displays first becomes the primary label Field names that display below the primary label are the secondary labels.

2 In the **Row Labels** area, drag the **Sales Representatives** field so that it is listed first—before the **Date of Sale** field.

The sales representative is now the primary title with the quarters being the secondary titles. By moving only two field names, the data on the PivotTable displays with a different focus.

3 In the PivotTable, in the **Row Labels** title—cell **A3**—click the **Filter button** and from the displayed list, click the **(Select All)** check box, and then click **OK**. In cell **A4**, next to **Fred Thomas**, click the **Expand Outline button** to display Fred's sales.

4 Right-click cell **A8** and compare your screen with Figure 8.40.

The shortcut menu displays several commands that relate specifically to the PivotTable.

Figure 8.40

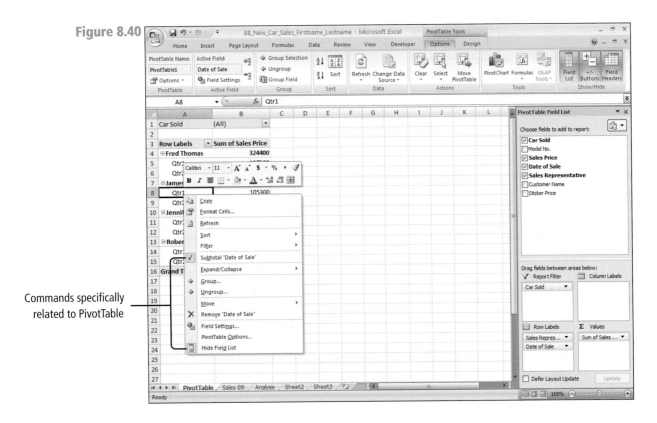

Commands specifically related to PivotTable

5 Point to **Move** and from the submenu that displays, click **Move "Date of Sale" to Columns**, and then compare your screen with Figure 8.41.

The Date of Sale field is now a column title and displays as *Qtr1* and *Qtr2*. The field name has also moved to the Column Labels area in the PivotTable Field List.

The names of the sales representatives now display as row labels and the words *Column Labels* display over the *Qtr1* sales data. The grand totals for each quarter display at the end of each column in row 9.

Note — To Return to the Previous View

To return the data back to the previous view, right-click one of the *Qtr* headings and select *Move "Date of Sale" to Rows*.

Figure 8.41

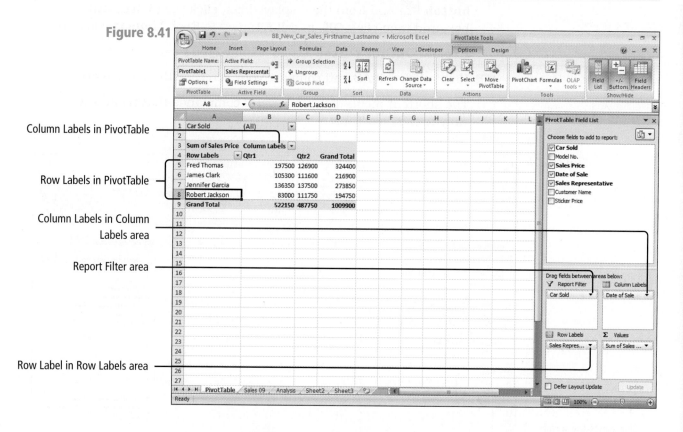

Column Labels in PivotTable

Row Labels in PivotTable

Column Labels in Column Labels area

Report Filter area

Row Label in Row Labels area

6 **Save** your workbook.

Activity 8.20 Removing Filters to Display More Data

In this activity, you will remove the filters to display all the data fields.

1 In cell **B1**, click the **(All) arrow** and at the end of the list, click the **Select Multiple Items** check box to select all items in the list. At the top of the menu, click the **(All)** check box to deselect the check boxes, and then click the check boxes for the three **Orca** models. Click **OK** and compare your screen with Figure 8.42.

The data in the worksheet now displays the sales data for only the Orca cars that were sold. The PivotTable still displays which sales representatives sold the car, in which quarter the car(s) were sold, and their total sales prices. The *(Multiple Items)* arrow in cell B1 now displays the Filter button, which also displays in the Fields Section of the Pivot Table Field List.

Figure 8.42

Multiple Items—Filter button displays

Row Labels

Column Labels

Filter button in Fields Section

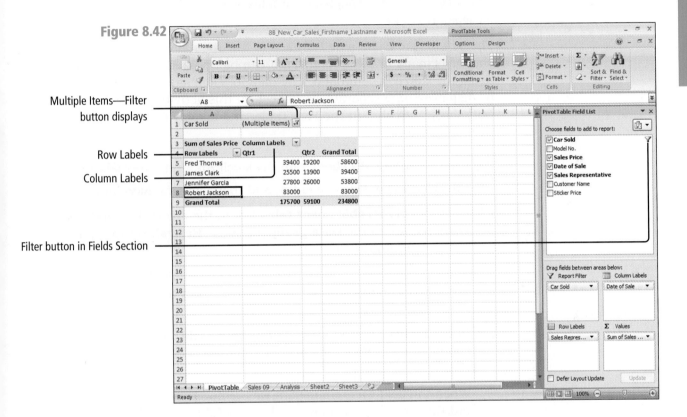

2 Select the range **A6:A7**—James Clark and Jennifer Garcia —right-click and from the displayed menu, point to **Filter**, and from the submenu, click **Keep Only Selected Items**.

Using the shortcut menu is another method used to filter data. Now only the Orca sales by Jennifer Garcia and James Clark are displayed. By reviewing the data, Charlie can identify the Orca sales that were made by these two individuals.

3 In the **Areas Section** of the **PivotTable Field List**, drag the **Sales Representatives** field to the **Report Filter** area, drag the **Car Sold** field to the **Row Labels** area, and then move **Date of Sale** to the **Row Labels** area below the **Car Sold** field.

4 In the **Fields Section** of the **PivotTable Field List**, point to **Sales Representatives**, click the **filter arrow**, and click the **All** check box, and then click **OK**. Using the skills you practiced, display all of the **Car Sold** data.

5 **Save** 🖫 your workbook.

To Remove All Filters

On the Ribbon, click the PivotTable Tools Options tab, and in the Actions group, click the Clear button, and then click Clear Filters.

Activity 8.21 Refreshing the Pivot Table and Displaying the Table on Separate Pages

The data in the PivotTable is linked to the original worksheet. When a change is made in the worksheet, it can be updated in the PivotTable using the *Refresh* command. The data for each sales representative can be displayed on a separate worksheet. In this activity, you will correct the worksheet, refresh it in the PivotTable, and display data on separate worksheet pages.

1 Click the **Sales 09 sheet tab**. Click cell **A5**, and type **Make of Car** Press [Enter] to confirm the entry, and then click the **Save** button 🖫 .

2 Click the **PivotTable sheet tab**, click in the PivotTable, and click the **Options** tab. In the **Data group**, click the **Refresh** button. Click in any cell within the PivotTable.

The Car Sold field name has been updated to *Make of Car*. The PivotTable collapses because the field used in the PivotTable—Car Sold—was changed in the source data.

3 In the **Fields Section** of the **PivotTable Field List**, drag the **Make of Car** field to the **Row Labels** area and place it first, above *Date of Sale*.

When the field was renamed, it was removed from the PivotTable, but the new name displays in the PivotTable Field List. Recall that one way to move fields to the PivotTable is to click on its name in the Fields Section and drag it to the Areas Section.

4 On the **Options tab**, in the **PivotTable group**, click the **Options button arrow**. From the displayed list, click **Show Report Filter Pages** and compare your screen with Figure 8.43.

The Show Report Filter Pages dialog box displays with the field, Sales Representatives, selected.

Figure 8.43

Show Report Filter Pages dialog box

Field for reports

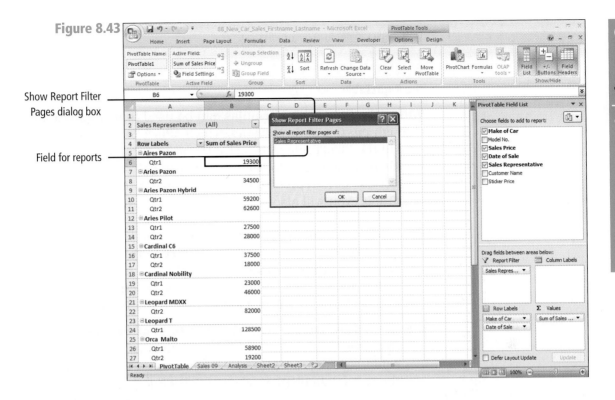

5 Click **OK** and compare your screen with Figure 8.44.

Worksheets have been inserted into the workbook—one for each sales representative. These worksheets display the same information displayed in the PivotTable for each sales representative.

Figure 8.44

Displays an active worksheet—Fred Thomas

Active worksheet

Worksheets inserted for each sales representative

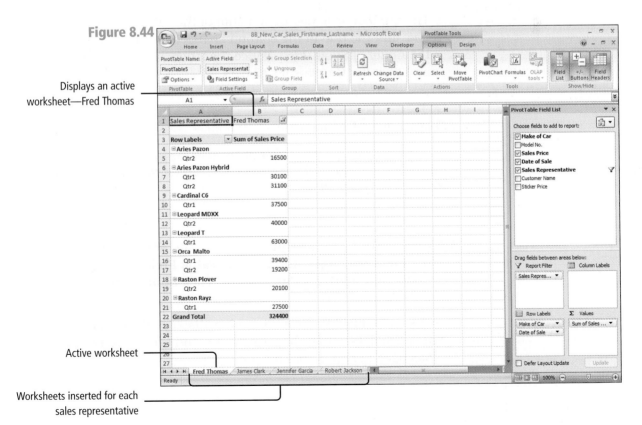

6 Save 🖫 your workbook.

Activity 8.22 Establishing a Custom Calculation and Formatting the PivotTable

Within the PivotTable, formulas can be used to manipulate the data through *custom calculations*, which allows for calculations to be created in the PivotTable. A PivotTable can be formatted using the formatting features of Excel. In this activity, you will determine the bonus for each of the sales representatives and enter that information in the PivotTable. You will also use the formatting features for the PivotTable.

1 Click the **PivotTable Options sheet tab**. In the **Areas Section** of the **PivotTable Field List**, in the **Report Filter** area, click the **Sales Representative arrow**, and from the list, click **Move to Row Labels**. Using one of the techniques you have practiced, move the **Make of Car** field from the **Row Labels** area to the **Report Filter** area.

2 In the **Row Labels** area, click the **Date of Sale arrow**, and then click **Remove Field**. Notice that the heading in cell A4 for the sales representative's data displays *Row Labels*, and the heading in cell B4 for the sales data displays *Sum of Sales Price*.

The PivotTable now displays the sales representatives and their total sales of cars for the six-month period. Excel uses the Sum function to add the fields.

3 Right-click a data cell in **column B**. Point to **Summarize Data By**, and then click **Count**.

The number switches from a sum of the values to a count of the values, and the title in the column changed to reflect this data is now the *Count of Sales Price*. Notice that there were a total of 42 cars sold and Jennifer Garcia sold 12 cars.

Note — Sort Data

You can sort data in a PivotTable. Right-click the subtotal for any of the salespeople, click Sort, and then click Sort Largest to Smallest or Sort Smallest to Largest, depending on your needs.

4 Click cell **B7**. On the **Options tab**, in the **Active Field group**, click the **Field Settings** button. In the **Value Field Settings** dialog box, under **Summarize value field by**, click **Sum**. Compare your screen with Figure 8.45.

The Value Field Settings dialog box displays the fields and specifies how the data will be displayed. Sum and Count are two of the methods used to summarize a field.

Figure 8.45

Custom name used in PivotTable

Value Field Settings dialog box

Name of field

Choice of calculation

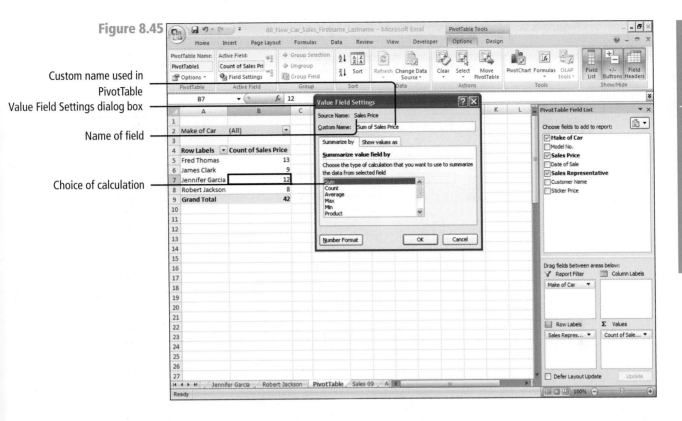

5 In the **Value Field Settings** dialog box, in the lower left corner, click the **Number Format** button. In the **Format Cells** dialog box, click the **Number** category and on the right side, in the **Decimal places** box, click the down **spin box arrow** to select **0** decimal places. Then click **Use 1000 Separator (,)**, and then click **OK**. In the **Value Field Settings** dialog box, click **OK**. Alternatively, right-click the cell and from the shortcut menu, click Number Format.

The heading now displays *Sum of Sales Price* and the numbers have been formatted.

6 On the **Options tab**, in the **Tools group**, click the **Formulas** button. From the displayed list, click **Calculated Field**.

The Insert Calculated Field dialog box that displays is used to create a formula for the calculated field.

7 In the **Name** box, type **Bonus Amount** to name the calculated field you are creating. In the **Formula** box, type **='Sales Price' * 1%** Compare your screen with Figure 8.46, and then click **OK**. Alternatively, press Tab, and in the Fields box, click Sales Price, and then click Insert Field. In the Formula box, type ***1%**

The calculated field is inserted into column C with the column title displayed—*Sum of Bonus Amount*. This column heading displays in the PivotTable Field List as a field name and in the Areas Section in the Values area.

Figure 8.46

Insert Calculated Field dialog box

Name of calculated field

Formula used in field

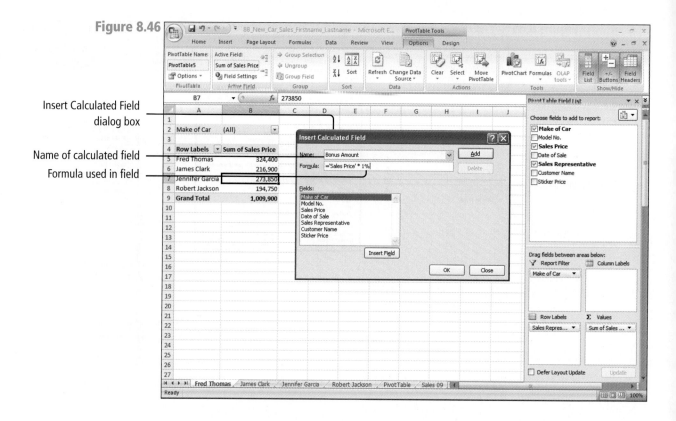

8 Click the **Design tab** and in the **PivotTable Styles group**, click the **More** ⊽ button. Move the mouse over the gallery to display how the format of the PivotTable changes. In the third row, click the sixth column—**Pivot Style Light 19**. In the **PivotTable Style Options group**, click **Banded Rows**.

9 **Save** 🖫 your workbook.

Activity 8.23 Creating a Pivot Chart

In a *PivotChart* you visually display the data and can manipulate it quickly to show different trends. A PivotChart is interactive with the PivotTable upon which it is based, so as you move the data in either the chart or the table, the other object is changed to reflect the change in the organization of the data. In this activity, you will create and manipulate a PivotChart to show the sales of cars by each sales representative.

1 Click in the PivotTable report to make it active. On the **PivotTable Options tab**, in the **Tools group**, click the **PivotChart** button, and then compare your screen with Figure 8.47.

The Insert Chart dialog box displays. Here you select the chart type and subtype.

Figure 8.47

Insert Chart dialog box

Type of charts available

Style of charts

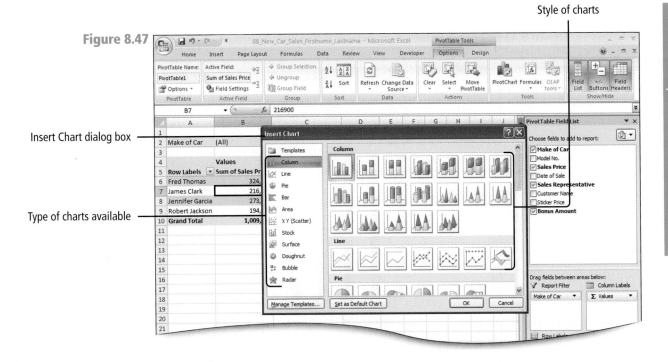

2 On the left, confirm that **Column** is selected and on the right, under **Column**, in the first row, click the fourth chart type—**3-D Clustered Column**—and then click **OK**. Compare your screen with Figure 8.48.

The chart displays on the worksheet, and the PivotChart Filter Pane displays. The PivotChart Tools contextual tab displays four tabs—Design, Layout, Format, and Analyze. The information from the PivotTable displays in the PivotChart Filter Pane—Make of Car is the *Report Filter* and Sales Representative is the *Axis Fields (Categories)*. The Column Labels area is now the *Legend Fields* area and displays the Values, which is the legend in the chart. The chart displays the Sum of Sales Price and the Sum of Bonus Amount.

In the PivotTable Field List, the field names in the Areas Section have changed to reflect the terms in the chart. The Column Labels area is now the Legend Fields area and the Row Labels area is now the Axis Fields area. The data fields that display remain the same. Note that in the figure, some of the parts are moved to better display the items on the screen.

Figure 8.48

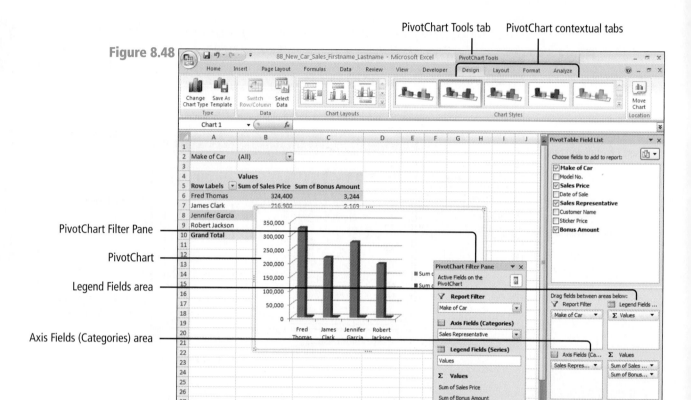

PivotChart Filter Pane

PivotChart

Legend Fields area

Axis Fields (Categories) area

3 In the **PivotChart Filter Pane**, click the **Close** button. Then drag the chart so the upper left corner displays in cell **A19**.

The chart displays the sales representatives and their total sales and bonus.

4 In the **PivotTable Field List Fields Section,** click the **Bonus Amount** check box to deselect it.

This field has been removed from the PivotTable and the PivotChart with the click of the mouse. Both the table and the chart change.

5 In the **Fields Section**, click the **Date of Sale** check box. Now the chart displays the quarterly sales.

Adding, removing, and rearranging the fields instantly changes the PivotChart. Data can quickly be moved so the chart displays different trends.

6 In the **Axis Fields** area, click the **Sales Representative** field and drag it to the **Legend Fields** area. In the **Chart Layouts group**, click **Layout 1**. Select the **Chart Title** and type **Semi-Annual Car Sales, June 2009** Click in the active chart and drag it so the upper left corner displays in cell **A10**. Click in cell **A1** so the chart is no longer active.

7 Arrange the workbook so that the **Analysis** sheet is first, followed by the **Sales 09** sheet, and then the **PivotTable** sheet with the individual sales representatives' sheets in the order inserted. **Delete** the **Sheet2** and **Sheet3** worksheets.

8 Click the **Sales 09 sheet tab**. If necessary, use the **Tab Scrolling** button to view the last worksheet—Robert Jackson. Press ⇧Shift while you click the **Robert Jackson sheet tab** to group all but the Analysis sheet.

9 In the **Left Footer**, place the **File Name** and in the **Right Footer**, place the **Sheet Name.** Format these worksheets with **Portrait Orientation**, **Fit to page**, and centered **Horizontally** on the page.

10 Save your workbook.

11 To submit your work electronically, follow the instructions provided by your instructor. To print, click the **Office** button and click **Print**. In the **Print** dialog box, under **Print what**, click the **Entire workbook** option. Under **Copies**, confirm that **1** is selected. Click **OK**. **Close** the workbook and **Exit** Excel.

More Knowledge

Formatting the PivotChart

When the PivotChart is active, the PivotChart Tools displays. The Design, Layout, and Format tabs match the tabs available with any chart that displays. The Analyze tab displays tools available with the PivotChart.

End **You have completed Project 8B** ⎯⎯⎯⎯⎯⎯⎯⎯

There's More You Can Do!

From My Computer, navigate to the student files that accompany this textbook. In the folder **02_theres_more_you_can_do**, locate and open the folder for this chapter. Open and print the instructions for this project, which are provided to you in Adobe PDF format.

Try It! 1—Digital Signature

In this Try It! exercise, you will create a digital signature for your worksheet.

Summary

In this chapter, you created and ran macros that saved time when formatting and completing your workbook. You used financial functions to determine the depreciation of assets and to produce a schedule of depreciation. Conditional IF functions were used to count, add, and average data that matched criteria. You created PivotTables to review the data from different perspectives. The data can quickly be moved to display the data from a different point of view. In addition, you created a PivotChart to view the data in different ways. The PivotChart can be quickly changed to review the data from a different perspective.

Key Terms

The ⊘ symbol represents Key Terms found on the Student CD in the 02_theres_more_you_can_do folder for this chapter.

Content-Based Assessments

Matching

Match each term in the second column with its correct definition in the first column by writing the letter of the term on the blank line in front of the correct definition.

_____ **1.** A series of commands—such as selections from menus and dialog boxes, keystrokes, and clicks on toolbar buttons—and functions that are grouped together as a single command.

_____ **2.** Added to the Ribbon and used to work with macros and for developers who customize Excel.

_____ **3.** Unauthorized code that is attached to a macro which may damage or erase files.

_____ **4.** Protects your computer from importing a macro virus.

_____ **5.** Works like an audio recorder. Every keystroke and mouse click is recorded and saved with the macro.

_____ **6.** Playing back the macro to quickly insert the format, text, or formulas previously recorded into the worksheet.

_____ **7.** An electronic, encryption-based, secure stamp of authentication on a macro or document.

_____ **8.** An area on your window that displays security alerts when there is potentially unsafe content in the document you open. This is the default.

_____ **9.** Messages that display when potentially unsafe tasks are about to be completed. Information about the alert is provided with choices on how to proceed.

_____ **10.** Programming language used to write computer programs within the Microsoft Windows environment.

_____ **11.** In Visual Basic for Applications, the place where each macro is stored. These are numbered sequentially.

_____ **12.** The amount that an asset decreases in value over time through use, obsolescence, or damage.

_____ **13.** Property owned by a firm that is expected to last more than one year.

_____ **14.** The name of the depreciation method that calculates an equal amount of depreciation for each year of useful life of the asset.

_____ **15.** The function name for the straight-line depreciation method.

A Depreciation

B Developer tab

C Digital signature

D Long-term assets

E Macro

F Macro recorder

G Macro security

H Macro virus

I Message Bar

J Module

K Run macro

L Security Alerts

M SLN

N Straight-line depreciation

O Visual Basic Application (VBA)

Content-Based Assessments

Write the correct answer in the space provided.

1. The methods of depreciation that recognize that an asset will depreciate faster during the early years of its life are _____ and _____.

2. The type of macro used when the actions in the macro are relative to the selected cell is a(n) _____ _____ macro.

3. Tests whether a condition is true or false that uses logical or comparison expressions are _____ _____.

4. The function that counts items within a range that match a specific condition is _____.

5. A function that adds the cells in a range that meet a specific condition is _____.

6. A function that calculates the average of a range of data that meets a specified condition is _____.

7. A function used to count number of items in a range when there is more than one condition to be met is _____.

8. A function that adds data that matches two or more criteria is _____.

9. A report used to manipulate a large amount of numerical data so that it can be displayed in different ways in order to analyze and answer questions about the data is a(n) _____ _____.

10. Columns of a worksheet used in a PivotTable to summarize data are called _____.

11. The range of the table used in a PivotTable is the _____ _____.

12. The _____ _____ _____ appears at the right side of the PivotTable sheet and displays the Fields Section and the Areas Section.

13. In a PivotTable, the area where the field list displays each of the column titles from the source data is the _____ _____.

14. An area used to place field names into the PivotTable report is the _____ _____.

15. When a change is made in the worksheet, use _____ to update the PivotTable.

Project 8C—Office Equip Depreciation

In this project, you will apply the skills you practiced from the Objectives in Project 8A.

Objectives: 1. *Create and Run a Macro;* **2.** *Apply Depreciation Functions.*

In the following Skills Review, you will complete a depreciation report for Penn Liberty Motors. Equipment depreciates yearly, and you will prepare the yearly depreciation figures for 2009. You will also use the declining balance method to create a depreciation schedule for a power generator. To format the report, you will create and run macros. Your completed workbook will look similar to the one shown in Figure 8.49.

For Project 8C, you will need the following files:

e08C_Office_Equip_Depreciation
8A_Macro_Library_Firstname_Lastname

You will save your workbook as
8C_Office_Equip_Depreciation_Firstname_Lastname

Figure 8.49

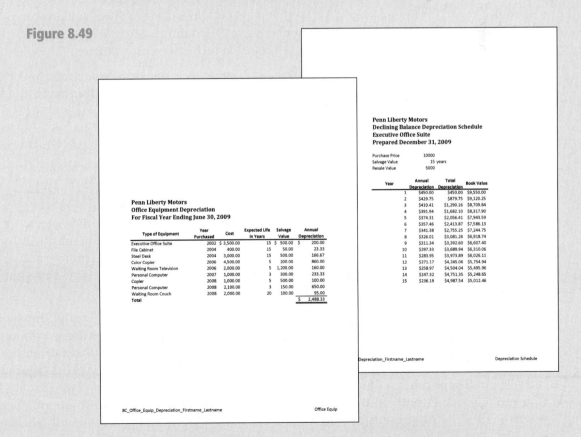

(Project 8C–Office Equip Depreciation continues on the next page)

(Project 8C–Office Equip Depreciation continued)

1. **Start** Excel and open the **8A_Macro_ Library_ Firstname_Lastname** that you created in Project 8A. If the **Message Bar** displays a security warning, in the Message Bar click the **Options** button. In the **Microsoft Office Security Options** dialog box, click **Enable this content**, and then click **OK**. If the Developer tab does not display, click the **Office** button, and then click the **Excel Options** button. Confirm the **Popular** choice is selected. At the right, under **Top options for working with Excel**, select the check box by **Show Developer tab in the Ribbon**, and then click **OK**.

2. **Open e08C_Office_Equip_Depreciation** and **Save** it in your **Excel Chapter 8** folder as 8C_Office_Equip_Depreciation_ Firstname_Lastname

3. Select cells **A1:A3**. Click the **Developer tab** and in the **Code group**, click the **Macros** button, select the macro named **Format_Worksheet_Title**, and then click **Run**.

4. Use Alt+Tab to make the **8A_Macro_ Library** workbook active. Click **Sheet3**. In cell **A5**, type your name—**Firstname_ Lastname**—and in the **Formula Bar**, click the **Enter** button.

5. With cell **A5** active, in the **Code group**, click the **Record Macro** button. In the **Macro name** text area, type **Format_ Column_Titles** In the **Shortcut key** box, press ⇧Shift while you type **c** In the **Store macro in** area, confirm that **This Workbook** displays. In the **Description** text area, type **Formats the column titles** then click **OK**.

6. Click the **Home tab**, and in the **Font group**, click the **Bold** and **Bottom Border** buttons. In the **Alignment group** click the

Center, **Middle Align**, and then **Wrap Text** buttons. Click the **Developer tab**, and in the **Code group**, click the **Stop Recording** button.

7. Click the **Library sheet tab**. In the Macro Library, click the next cell available in **column A**. Type **Format Column Titles** Press Tab and in the cell in **column B**, type **Bold, Bottom Border, Center, Middle Align, Wrap Text** Press Tab and in **column C** type **Ctrl+Shift+c** Adjust column widths. Select the range **A3:C3** and in the **Code group**, click the **Macros** button. Click **Format_Column_Titles**, and then click **Run**. **Save** the workbook.

8. Use Alt + Tab to redisplay the **8C_Office_ Equip_Depreciation_Firstname_Lastname** workbook. Select the range **A5:F5** and press Ctrl + ⇧Shift while you type **c** Adjust column widths and row height to display the titles on two lines.

9. Click the **Developer tab**. In the **Code group**, click the **Macros** button. In the **Macros** dialog box, click **Edit**. Locate the words *Weight = xlThin*. Select **Thin** and type **Medium** to change the bottom border of the column titles macro. In the Window toolbar, click the **Save** button. Then click the **Close** button.

10. With the range **A5:F5** selected, press Ctrl + ⇧Shift + **c** Adjust column widths so no column title displays on more than two lines and adjust row height. **Save** both workbooks.

11. In the 8C_Office_Equip_Depreciation_ Firstname_Lastname workbook, click cell **F6**. On the **Formulas tab**, in the **Function Library group**, click the **Financial** button and from the menu, scroll to and click **SLN**. In the **Cost** argument, click cell **C6**, in the **Salvage** argument, click cell **E6**,

(Project 8C–Office Equip Depreciation continues on the next page)

Content-Based Assessments

(Project 8C–Office Equip Depreciation continued)

and in the **Life** argument, click cell **D6**. Click **OK**, and then copy this formula through cell **F14**.

12. Click cell **A15** and type **Total** Format it with **Bold**. Click cell **F15** and enter a **Sum** formula. Format the cell with **Accounting Number Format** and a **Top and Double Bottom Border**. Format cells **C6**, **E6**, and **F6** with **Accounting Number Format** and other amounts in those columns with **Comma Style** format. **Save** your workbook.

13. Click the **Depreciation Schedule sheet**. Click cell **A2** and edit the title to read **Declining Balance Depreciation Schedule** Select the range **A1:A4** and click the **Developer tab**. In the **Code group**, click the **Macros** button. In the **Macro** dialog box, click the **Format Worksheet Title** macro, and then click **Run**. If you haven't created this macro, format the worksheet title with **Bold**, **Cambria font**, **14-point font**.

14. Select the range **A10:D10** and in the **Code group**, click the **Macros** button. In the **Macro** dialog box, click the macro named **Format Column Titles**, and then click **Run**. Adjust column widths and row heights if needed.

15. Click cell **B11**. On the **Formulas tab**, in the **Function Library group**, click the **Financial** button and click **DB**. In the **DB**

Function Arguments dialog box, in the **Cost** box, type **b6** and press F4. Press Tab and in the **Salvage** box, type **b8** and press F4. Press Tab and in the **Life** box, type **b7** and press F4. Press Tab and in the **Period** box, type **a11** and then click **OK**. Fill the formula down to cell **B25**.

16. Click cell **C11** and enter a formula that totals the amount of depreciation to date—type **=b11** and press Enter. Click cell **D11**, type **=b6** press F4 and type **-c11** and then press Enter.

17. Click cell **C12** and type **=c11+b12** In the **Formula Bar**, click the **Enter** button. Use the fill handle to copy the formula down through **row 25**. Click cell **D11** and fill the formula down through **row 25**. Format the range **B12:D25** with **Comma Style**.

18. **Delete** the **Sheet 3** worksheet. In both worksheets, in the **Left Footer** area, insert the **File Name** and in the **Right Footer** area, insert the **Sheet Name**. Center the worksheets both **Horizontally** and **Vertically**. **Save** your workbook.

19. To submit electronically, follow the instructions provided by your instructor. To print the **8C_Office_Equip_ Depreciation_Firstname_Lastname** worksheet, click the **Office** button, click **Print**. In the **Print** dialog box, under **Print what**, select **Entire workbook**, and then click **OK**. Click the **Office** button and then click **Close**. **Exit** Excel.

End You have completed Project 8C

Project 8D — Customization

In this project, you will apply the skills you practiced from the Objectives in Project 8B.

Objectives: 4. *Evaluate Worksheet Data with Conditional IF Functions;* **5.** *Create a PivotTable and PivotChart.*

In the following Skills Review, you will complete a report for car customizations done by Penn Liberty Motors for the month of August. You will use functions to supply statistical information and complete a PivotTable and PivotChart so the data can be viewed in several different ways. Your completed workbook will look similar to the one shown in Figure 8.50.

For Project 8D, you will need the following file:

e08D_Customization
8A_Macro_Library_Firstname_Lastname

You will save your workbook as
8D_Customization_Firstname_Lastname

Figure 8.50

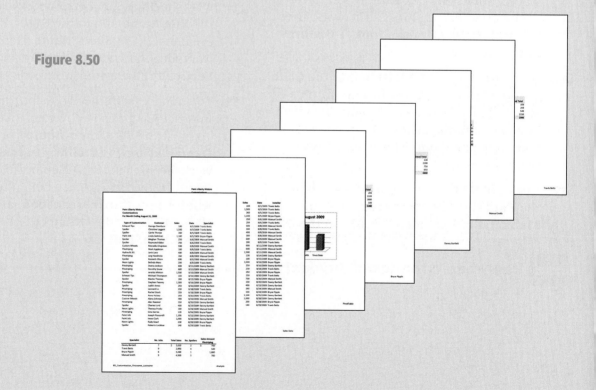

(Project 8D–Customization continues on the next page)

(Project 8D–Customization continued)

1. **Start** Excel. From your student files locate and open the file named **e08D_Customization**. **Save** the file in the **Excel Chapter 8** folder and name it **8D_Customization_Firstname_Lastname** Open the file named **8A_Macro_Library_Firstname_Lastname**.

2. Rename **Sheet1** to **Analysis**. Beginning in cell **A40**, type the following column titles and run the **Format Column Titles** macro. If you haven't created this macro, format the column titles with **Bold**, **Bottom Border**, **Center**, **Middle Align**, and **Wrap Text.** Adjust the column width and row height.

Specialist	No. Jobs	Total Sales	No. Spoilers	Sales Amount Pinstriping

3. Beginning in cell **A41** enter the following row titles:

Danny Bartlett
Travis Betts
Bryce Pippin
Manuel Smith

4. Click cell **B41**. Click the **Formulas tab** and in the **Function Library group**, click the **More Functions** button. Point to **Statistical**, and then from the submenu, click **COUNTIF**.

5. In the **Range** text box, click the **Collapse Dialog Box** button and select the range **E6:E36**, and then press F4. Click the **Expand Dialog Box** button. Press Tab and in the **Criteria** box, click cell **A41**. Click **OK**, and then use the fill handle to copy the function down through cell **B44**. With the range **B41:B44** selected, click the **Center** button.

6. Click cell **C41**, and in the **Function Library group**, click the **Math & Trig** button, and from the list, click **SUMIF**. In the **Range** text box, click the **Collapse Dialog Box** button, select the range **E6:E36**, and then press F4. Click the **Expand Dialog Box** button. Press Tab and in the **Criteria** box, click cell **A41**. Click in the **Sum_range** text box, select the range **C6:C36**, and then press F4. Click **OK** and use the fill handle to copy the formula down through cell **C44**.

7. Click cell **D41**, and in the **Function Library group**, click the **More Functions** button. Point to **Statistical**, and then from the submenu, click **COUNTIFS**. In the **Criteria_range1** box, click the **Collapse Dialog Box** button. Select the range **A6:A36** and press F4. Click the **Expand Dialog Box** button and press Tab. In the **Criteria1** box, type **Spoiler** and press Tab. In the **Criteria_range2** box, click the **Collapse Dialog Box** button and select the range **E6:E36** and press F4. Click the **Expand Dialog Box** button. In the **Criteria2** box, click cell **A41**. Click **OK** and use the fill handle to copy the formula down through cell **D44**. With the range **D41:D44** selected, right-click and then click **Center**.

8. Click cell **E41** and in the **Function Library group**, click the **Math & Trig** button, and then click **SUMIFS**. In the **Sum_range** box, click the **Collapse Dialog Box** button, select the range **C6:C36**, and press F4. Click the **Expand Dialog Box** button. In the **Criteria_range1** box, click the **Collapse Dialog Box** button, select the range **A6:A36**, press F4, and then click the **Expand Dialog Box** button. Press Tab, and in the **Criteria1** box, type **Pin Striping** Using the skills you have practiced, in the **Criteria_range2** box, select the range **E6:E36** and press F4, and in the **Criteria2** box, click **A41**. Click **OK** and copy the formula down through cell **E44**.

(Project 8D–Customization continues on the next page)

(Project 8D–Customization continued)

9. Format the ranges **C42:C44** and **E42:E44** with **Comma Style** with **no decimals**. Format cells **C41** and **E41** with **Accounting Number Format** with **no decimals**.

10. Right-click the **Analysis sheet tab** and click **Move or Copy**. Copy the **Analysis** worksheet and place it before **Sheet2**. Rename the new worksheet as **Sales Data** Delete **rows 40:44**. Click anywhere within the data **A5:E36**. On the **Insert tab**, in the **Tables group**, click the **PivotTable** button. In the **Create PivotTable** dialog box, confirm the range of the data is correct and that the **New Worksheet** is selected. Click **OK**. Name the new worksheet PivotTable

11. In the **PivotTable Field List**, right-click **Type of Customization**, and then click **Add to Report Filter**. Click the **Specialist** and **Sales** check boxes and confirm that **Specialist** is in the **Row Labels** area of the field list and that **Sum of Sales** is in the **Values** area.

12. In cell **B1**, click the **arrow** to display the type of customization. At the end of the menu, click **Select Multiple Items**. At the top, click **(All)** to deselect it, and then click the **Neon Lights**, **Paint Job**, and **Pin Striping** check boxes. Click **OK**.

13. In the **PivotTable Field List**, click the **Date** check box, and then drag it from the **Row Labels** area to the **Column Labels** area. Click cell **B4**. On the **Options tab**, in the **Group group**, click the **Group Field** button. In the **Grouping** dialog box, click **Days** and confirm that **Months** is still selected, and then click **OK**.

14. In the **PivotTable Field List**, in the **Column Labels** area, drag **Date** to the **Row Labels** area and place it below **Specialist**. In cell **B1**, click the **(Multiple Items) Filter** button, click the **All** check box, and then click **OK**.

15. In the **PivotTable Field List**, in the **Row Labels** area, drag **Specialist** to the **Report Filter** area. Move the **Type of Customization** to the **Row Labels** area box and place it below **Date**, and then drag the **Date** to the **Fields Section** to delete it from the PivotTable.

16. Click the **Sales Data sheet tab**. In cell **E5**, replace **Specialist** with **Installer** and press Enter to confirm the entry. Click the **PivotTable sheet tab**, click in the **PivotTable** and click the **Options** tab. In the **Data group**, click the **Refresh** button. In the **Fields Section**, right-click the **Installer** field and select **Add to Report Filter**. On the **Options tab**, in the **PivotTable group**, click the **Options button arrow**. From the displayed list, click **Show Report Filter Pages**. In the **Show Report Filter Pages** dialog box, click **OK**.

17. Click the **PivotTable sheet tab**. Using skills you have practiced, place **Type of Customization** as a **Report Filter** and place **Installer** as a **Row Label** and move **Months** to the field list to deselect it.

18. If necessary, click in the **Pivottable** In the **Tools group**, click the **Formulas** button, and then click **Calculated Field**. In the **Insert Calculated Field** dialog box, in the **Name** box, type **Bonus** and then press Tab. In the **Fields** area, click **Sales**, and then click the **Insert Field** button. In the **Formula** box, type ***4%** and then click **OK**. The field displays the bonus earned, which is 4% of the monthly sales.

19. Click any cell in the **Sum of Sales** column—**B6:B10**. In the **Active Field** group, click the **Field Settings** button. In the **Value Field Settings** dialog box, in the lower left corner, click **Number**

(Project 8D–Customization continues on the next page)

Content-Based Assessments

(Project 8D–Customization continued)

Format. In the **Format Cells** dialog box, click the **Number** category and on the right side, use the **spin box arrow** to select **0** decimal places. Click the **Use 1000 Separator (,)** check box to select it, and then click **OK**. In the **Value Field Settings** dialog box, click **OK**. Using the skills you have practiced, format the numbers in the **Sum of Bonus** column for **Number**, **0** decimal places, and **1000 Separator**.

20. Click the **Design tab** and in the **PivotTable Styles group**, click the **More** button. Under **Medium**, in the first row, click the third column—**Pivot Style Medium 3**.

21. Click the **Options tab**, and in the **Tools group**, click the **PivotChart** button. On the first row, click the fourth choice—**3-D Clustered Column**. Click **OK**. **Close** the **PivotChart Filter Pane**.

22. In the **Fields Section** of the **PivotTable Field List,** click the **Bonus** check box to deselect it. On the **Design tab**, in the **Chart Styles group**, click the fourth option—**Style 4**. In the chart, delete the legend. Select the **Title** and type **Customization Sales for August 2009** Move the chart so the upper left corner is in cell **A11**, and then click cell **A1**.

23. **Delete Sheet2** and **Sheet3**. Arrange the workbook so that the **Analysis** sheet is first, followed by the **Sales Data**, **PivotTable**, then the individual installer sheets in the order inserted. Select all worksheets. In all worksheets, in the **Left Footer** area, insert the **File Name** and in the **Right Footer** area, insert the **Sheet Name**. Center the worksheets both **Horizontally** and **Vertically**. **Save** your workbook.

24. To submit electronically, follow the instructions provided by your instructor. To print the **8D_Customization_Firstname_Lastname** workbook, click the **Office** button, click **Print**. In the **Print** dialog box, under **Print what**, select **Entire workbook**, and then click **OK**. Click the **Office** button, and then click **Close**. **Exit** Excel.

 You have completed Project 8D ——————————————————

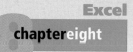

Content-Based Assessments

Excel chapter eight

Mastering Excel

Project 8E — Shop Depreciation

In this project, you will apply the skills you practiced from the Objectives in Project 8A.

Objectives: 1. *Create and Run a Macro;* **2.** *Apply Depreciation Functions.*

In the following Mastering Excel project, you will complete a depreciation report for Penn Liberty Motors. During the year, Penn Liberty Motors has purchased several new pieces of shop equipment. You will prepare a report that compares the annual depreciation for the equipment for the first year using different depreciation methods. To format the report, you will create and run macros. Your completed worksheet will look similar to Figure 8.51.

For Project 8E, you will need the following files:

e08E_Shop_Depreciation
8A_Macro_Library_Firstname_Lastname

You will save your workbook as
8E_Shop_Depreciation_Firstname_Lastname

Figure 8.51

Penn Liberty Motors
New Shop Equipment Depreciation
For Fiscal Year 2009

Type of Equipment	Expected Life in Years	Cost	Salvage Value	Straight Line	Declining Balance	Sum-of-the-Years' Digits
Air Compressor	10	$ 4,000.00	$ 500.00	$ 350.00	$ 752.00	$ 636.36
Air Compressor	10	2,500.00	250.00	225.00	515.00	409.09
Air Lift	20	34,000.00	1,500.00	1,625.00	4,896.00	3,095.24
Air Lift	20	25,000.00	875.00	1,206.25	3,850.00	2,297.62
Arc Welder	15	5,000.00	500.00	300.00	710.00	562.50
Engine Diagnostics Machine	5	30,000.00	4,500.00	5,100.00	9,480.00	8,500.00
Engine Diagnostics Machine	5	35,000.00	4,000.00	6,200.00	12,320.00	10,333.33
Paint Sprayer	15	8,000.00	750.00	483.33	1,168.00	906.25
Pipe Bender	10	12,000.00	2,500.00	950.00	1,740.00	1,727.27
Power Generator	15	10,000.00	2,000.00	533.33	1,020.00	1,000.00
Total				$ 16,972.92	$ 36,451.00	$ 29,467.67

8E_Shop_Depreciation_Firstname_Lastname

(Project 8E–Shop Depreciation continues on the next page)

(Project 8E–Shop Depreciation continued)

1. **Start** Excel and open the **8A_Macro Library_Firstname_Lastname** file you created in Project 8A. If the Message Bar displays a security warning, enable the macros. If the Developer tab does not display, click the **Office** button, and then follow the procedures you have practiced to display the Developer tab.

2. **Open** the file **e08E_Shop_Depreciation** and **Save** it in your **Excel Chapter 8** folder as 8E_Shop_Depreciation_Firstname_ Lastname

3. Select cells **A1:A3** and run the macro named **Format_Worksheet_Title**. Select cells **A5:G5** and run the macro named **Format_Column_Titles**. Alternatively, if you have not created this macro, format the column titles with Bold, Center, Thick Bottom Border, Middle Align, and Wrap Text. Adjust column widths so the titles display on one or two rows and adjust row height.

4. Use Alt + Tab to make the **8A_Macro_ Library** workbook active. Click **Sheet 3**. In an empty cell, type **500.5** and then on the **Formula Bar**, click the **Enter** button. Record a **Macro** named Format_Totals with a shortcut of **Ctrl+Shift+t**. Store the macro in **This Workbook** with a description that reads **Format totals with Top and Double Bottom Borders** and click **OK**.

5. Click **Accounting Number Format** and select a **Top and Double Bottom**. Then click the **Stop Recording** button.

6. Click the **Library sheet tab**. In the first available cell in **column A**, type Format Totals In **column B**, type Accounting Number Format, Top and Double Bottom Border In **column C**, type Ctrl+Shift+t

Adjust column widths if needed. **Save** the Macro Library workbook.

7. Make the **8E_Shop_Depreciation_ Firstname_Lastname** workbook active, and then click cell **E6**. Use the **SLN**— Straight-Line—function to determine the depreciation using the straight-line method. Click in cell **F6** and use the **DB**— Declining Balance—function to determine the depreciation using the declining balance method. In the **Period** text area, type **1** Click in **G6** and use the **SYD**—Sum-of- the-Years' Digits—function to determine the depreciation using the sum-of-the- years' digits method. For the period, type **1** Copy the amount of depreciation for each method down through **row 15**.

8. In cell **A16**, type **Total** and format with **Bold** and **Center**. In the range **E16:G16**, use the SUM function to enter totals. With cells **E16:G16** selected, run the **Format Totals** macro. Format the range **C6:D6** with **Accounting Number Format** and format the range **C7:G15** with **Comma Style**. Adjust column widths if needed.

9. Name **Sheet1** Depreciation Comparison In the **Left Footer**, insert the **File Name**. Place the worksheet in **Landscape orien- tation** and center it both **Horizontally** and **Vertically**. **Delete Sheet2** and **Sheet3** and then **Save** your workbook.

10. To submit electronically, follow the instruc- tions provided by your instructor. To print the **8E_Shop_Depreciation_Firstname_ Lastname** worksheet, click the **Office** but- ton, and click **Print**. In the **Print** dialog box, under **Print what**, select **Entire work- book**, and then click **OK**. Click the **Office** button, and then click **Close**.

End You have completed Project 8E

Project 8F—Accessories Inventory

In this project, you will apply the skills you practiced from the Objectives in Project 8B.

Objectives: 3. *Evaluate Worksheet Data with Conditional IF Functions;* **4.** *Create a PivotTable and PivotChart.*

In the following Mastering Excel project, you will complete a report for a car accessories inventory completed by Penn Liberty Motors in July. You will use functions to supply statistical information and complete a PivotTable and PivotChart so the data can be viewed in several different ways. Your completed worksheets will look similar to Figure 8.52.

For Project 8F, you will need the following file:

e08F_Accessories_Inventory

You will save your workbook as
8F_Accessories_Inventory_Firstname_Lastname

Figure 8.52

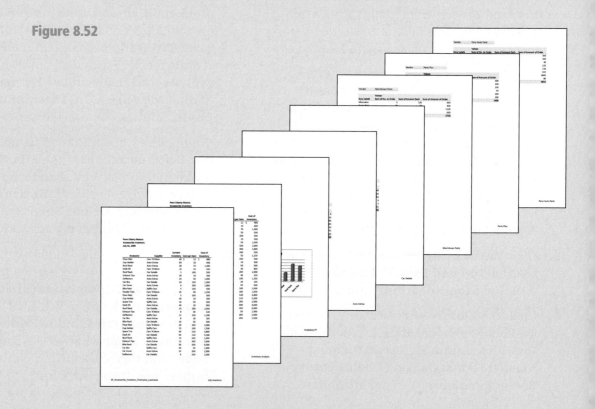

(Project 8F–Accessories Inventory continues on the next page)

Content-Based Assessments

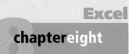

Excel
chaptereight

Mastering Excel

(Project 8F–Accessories Inventory continued)

1. **Start** Excel. From your student files, locate and open the file named **e08F_Accessories_ Inventory**. **Save** the file in the **Excel Chapter 8** folder and name it **8F_Accessories_Inventory_ Firstname_Lastname**

2. Rename **Sheet1** to **July Inventory**. In cell **E5**, type **Cost of Inventory** Format cell **E5** the same as cell **D5**. Adjust column widths and row height.

3. In cell **E6**, enter a formula to multiply the inventory by the cost of each item and then copy the formula down to cell **E35**. Format the amounts in **column E** the same as those in **column D**.

4. Copy the **July Inventory sheet** to a new sheet and name it **Inventory Analysis**. Beginning in cell **A38**, enter the following column titles:

Supplier	Cost of Roof Rack Inventory	Bike Rack Supplier

5. Format the column titles with **Bold**, **Bottom Border**, **Center**, **Middle Align**, and **Wrap Text**.

6. Beginning in cell **A39** enter the following row titles:

Auto Extras
Car Details
Cars 'N More
Spiffy Cars

7. Click cell **B39** and enter a **SUMIFS** function to determine the total cost of the inventory of roof racks sold by each of the suppliers. For the Sum range, use **Cost of Inventory**. For the first criteria range, use the **Accessory** range with **Roof Rack** as the criteria. For the second criteria range, use the **Supplier** range with the criteria as cell **A39**—Auto Extras.

8. In cell **C39**, enter a **COUNTIFS** function to determine the number of bike rack models that Penn Liberty Motors carry and which supplier we order from. For one criteria range, use the **Accessory** that matches **Bike Rack** and for the second criteria range use the **Supplier** to match the ones listed beginning in cell **A39**. The result for Auto Extras is 0.

9. Copy the formulas in the range **B39:C39** down through **row 42**. Format the numbers in the Cost of Roof Rack Inventory and Bike Rack Supplier columns with **Comma Style** and with **no decimals**.

10. With the **July Inventory sheet** active, click anywhere within the data **A5:E35**. Insert a PivotTable into a new worksheet. Name the new sheet **Inventory PT**

11. In the PivotTable, place **Supplier** as the **Report Filter**, **Accessory** as the **Row Label**, and **Cost of Inventory** in the **Values** area. Click in the PivotTable and display a separate PivotTable for each of the suppliers.

12. In the **Inventory PT sheet**, click any cell in the **Sum of Cost of Inventory** column and format the numbers for **Number**, **0** decimal places, and **1000 Separator**. Format the PivotTable using the **Pivot Style Light 15**.

(Project 8F–Accessories Inventory continues on the next page)

(Project 8F–Accessories Inventory continued)

13. Insert a **PivotChart** using the **3-D Clustered Column** style. Move the chart so the upper left corner displays in cell **A17**. Display the chart using **Style 30**. **Delete** the legend and change the title to **Inventory on July 31, 2009**

14. **Delete Sheet2** and **Sheet3**. Arrange the workbook so that the **July Inventory sheet** is first, followed by the **Inventory Analysis sheet**, **Inventory PT sheet**, then the individual supplier sheets in the order inserted.

15. In all worksheets, in the **Left Footer** area, insert the **File Name** and in the **Right Footer** area, insert the **Sheet Name**. Center the worksheets both **Horizontally** and **Vertically**. **Save** your workbook.

16. To submit electronically, follow the instructions provided by your instructor. To print, click the **Office** button, click **Print**. In the **Print** dialog box, under **Print what**, select **Entire workbook**, and then click **OK**. Click the **Office** button, and then click **Close**.

End **You have completed Project 8F**

Content-Based Assessments

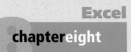
Project 8G — Shop Inventory

In this project, you will apply the skills you practiced from the Objectives in Projects 8A and 8B.

Objectives: 1. *Create and Run a Macro;* **3.** *Evaluate Worksheet Data with Conditional IF Functions;* **4.** *Create a PivotTable and PivotChart.*

In the following Mastering Excel project, you will report the inventory of the items in the shop for Penn Liberty Motors, prepare statistical analysis, and use a PivotTable to prepare the order forms for each vendor to replenish the inventory. Your completed workbook will look similar to Figure 8.53.

For Project 8G, you will need the following files:

e08G_Shop_Inventory
8A_Macro_Library_Firstname_Lastname

You will save your workbook as
8G_Shop_Inventory_Firstname_Lastname

Figure 8.53

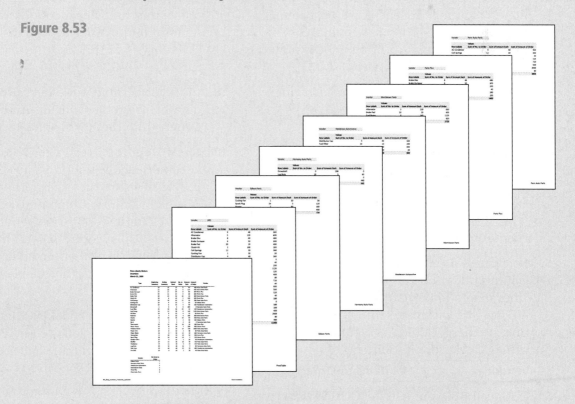

(Project 8G–Shop Inventory continues on the next page)

(Project 8G–Shop Inventory continued)

1. **Start** Excel. From the student files, locate and open the file named **e08G_Shop_Inventory** and **Save** it in your **Excel Chapter 8** folder as 8G_Shop_Inventory_Firstname_Lastname From your saved files, open the **8A_Macro_Library_ Firstname_Lastname** workbook and enable the content.

2. With the **8G_Shop_Inventory_Firstname_Lastname** workbook open, display the **Developer Tab**. Select the range **A1:A3** and run the **Format Worksheet Title** macro or format with **Bold**, **14-point Cambria font**. Select the column titles—**A5:G5**—and run the **Format_Column_Titles** macro or format it with **Bold**, **Thick Bottom Border**, **Center**, **Middle Align**, and **Wrap Text**.

3. Click cell **E6** and enter a formula to determine the number of each inventory item that needs to be ordered—Optimal Stock minus the Ending Inventory=D6-C6 Copy the formula down through cell **E35**.

4. Beginning in cell **A39**, type the following row titles:

Edison Parts
Harmony Auto Parts
Henderson Automotive
Morristown Parts
Parts Plus
Penn Auto Parts

5. Beginning in cell **A38**, type the following column titles and run the **Format Column Titles** macro to format the column titles. Alternatively, format column titles with Bold, Center, Middle Align, and Wrap Text with a Thick Bottom Border.

Vendor	No. Items to Order

6. Click cell **B39** and use the **COUNTIFS** function to count the number of parts that will be ordered from each vendor. For the first criteria range, use the Vendors in **column G** with absolute references, and for the criteria, use the name of the vendor in cell **A39**. For the second criteria, use the No. to Order in **column E** with absolute cell references and with a criteria of **>0** Copy the formula in cell **B39** through cell **B44**. Adjust column widths if needed.

7. Click in the worksheet range and insert a PivotTable in a new worksheet. Select the following fields to appear in the PivotTable—**Type**, **No. to Order**, **Amount Each**, **Vendor**. Rename **Sheet1** to March Inventory and rename **Sheet4** to PivotTable

8. Position the **Vendor** as the **Report Filter**. In the **March Inventory** sheet, insert a column between **columns F** and **G**. In cell **G5**, type **Amount of Order** In cell **G6**, enter a formula that will calculate the total amount of the order to replenish the inventory—=e6*f6 Copy the formula through cell **G35**.

9. In the PivotTable worksheet, **Refresh** the data. Insert the new field—**Amount of Order**—into the PivotTable.

10. **Show Report Filter Pages** so that a worksheet for each vendor displays on its own page. These are the order forms to replenish the inventory. Compare the number of products ordered for each vendor with the number displayed in the March Inventory worksheet. Even when no additional parts need to be ordered, they display in the PivotTable report.

11. Rearrange the workbook so the **March Inventory** is first, followed by **PivotTable**, and then the individual vendor sheets. Delete unused worksheets.

12. Select all worksheets and in the **Left Footer** area, insert the **File Name**. In the **Right Footer** area, insert the **Sheet**

(Project 8G–Shop Inventory continues on the next page)

(Project 8G–Shop Inventory continued)

Name. Format all worksheets so they are centered **Horizontally**. Format the **March Inventory** worksheet to display on **one page** in **Landscape Orientation**.

13. To submit electronically, follow the instructions provided by your instructor.

To print, click the **Office** button, and click **Print**. In the **Print** dialog box, under **Print what**, select **Entire workbook**, and then click **OK**. Click the **Office** button, and then click **Exit Excel**.

 End You have completed Project 8G

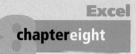

Project 8H — Shop Equipment

In this project, you will apply the skills you practiced from the Objectives in Projects 8A and 8B.

Objectives: 1. *Create and Run a Macro;* **2.** *Apply Depreciation Functions;* **4.** *Create a PivotTable and PivotChart.*

In the following Mastering Excel project, you will complete a depreciation analysis of the shop equipment that Penn Liberty Motors uses. You will create a PivotTable to analyze the data. Two new assets will be purchased and you will complete a depreciation schedule for that purchase. Your completed worksheets will look similar to Figure 8.54.

For Project 8H, you will need the following files:

e08H_Shop_Equipment
8A_Macro_Library_Firstname_Lastname

You will save your workbook as
8H_Shop_Equipment_Firstname_Lastname

Figure 8.54

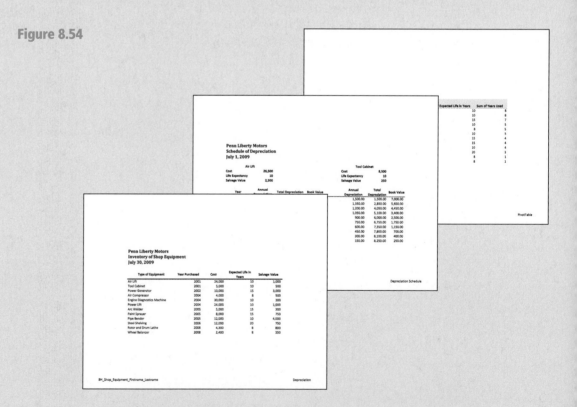

(Project 8H–Shop Equipment continues on the next page)

(Project 8H–Shop Equipment continued)

1. **Start** Excel. From your student files, open the file named **e08H_Shop_Equipment** and **Save** it in your **Excel Chapter 8** folder as **8H_Shop_Equipment_Firstname_Lastname** Open the **8A_Macro_Library_Firstname_Lastname** workbook. In the **Message Bar**, click **Options** and select to **Enable** macros.

2. In the **8H_Shop_Equipment_Firstname_Lastname** workbook, select the range **A1:A3** and run the **Format Worksheet Title** macro. Then select the range **A5:E5** and if it's available, run the **Format Column Titles** macro. If you haven't created this macro, then format the column titles with **Bold**, **Thick Bottom Border**, **Center**, **Middle Align**, and **Wrap Text**.

3. Format the numbers in **columns B** and **D** with **Number style** and **no decimals** and in **columns C** and **E** with **Comma Style** format with **no decimals**.

4. Insert a new worksheet and create a **PivotTable** that displays the **Type of Equipment**, **Year Purchased**, and **Expected Life in Years**. **Rename** the sheet to **PivotTable** Insert a calculated field named **Years Used** that determines the number of years the asset has been used. Recall that dates must be displayed in numbers in order to use mathematical functions and that the PivotTable applies mathematical functions to numbers in a PivotTable. In the **Insert Calculated Field** dialog box, in the **Name** box, type **Years Used** and in the **Formula** box, type **=2009 – 'Year Purchased'** On the **Design tab**, in the **Layout group**, click **Grand Totals** and from the list, click **Off for Rows and Columns**

5. **Sort** the data by **Sum of Years Used** from **Largest to Smallest**. There are two assets that have been used 8 years and both have a life expectancy of 10 years. The firm will consider replacing these two assets and would like to have a schedule of depreciation prepared for replacing both assets with new equipment.

6. Click the **Sheet2 sheet tab**. Beginning in cell **A1**, type the following worksheet title:

Penn Liberty Motors
Schedule of Depreciation
'July 1, 2009

7. Beginning in cell **A5**, enter the following information about the asset:

Air Lift	
Cost	26500
Life Expectancy	10
Salvage Value	2500

8. In cell **F5**, type **Tool Cabinet** and copy the data in the range **A6:A8** to cell **F6**. Beginning in cell **G6**, enter the following data in the column:

8500
10
250

(Project 8H–Shop Equipment continues on the next page)

(Project 8H–Shop Equipment continued)

9. Click cell **A10** and enter the following column titles—leaving cell E10 empty—and then run the **Format Column Titles** macro to format the titles. If you haven't completed this macro, format with **Bold**, **Thick Bottom Border**, **Center**, **Middle Align**, and **Wrap Text**.

Year	Annual Depreciation	Total Depreciation	Book Value	Annual Depreciation	Total Depreciation	Book Value

10. In cell **A11**, type **1** and in cell **A12**, type **2** Select both cells and use the fill handle to fill the series to the life expectancy of the asset—10— in cell **A20**. Format the numbers with **Center** alignment.

11. Click cell **B11**. Penn Liberty uses the sum-of-the-years' digits method of depreciation. Complete the depreciation schedule for both the air lift and the tool cabinet, including the total depreciation and the book value for each asset for each year. Format the numbers in the schedule with **Comma Style**.

12. To format the title in cells **A1:A3**, run the **Format_Worksheet_Title** macro. Adjust column widths and format the information about each asset—ranges **A5:B8** and **F5:G8**—with **Bold**. In the asset information area—the ranges **B6:B8** and **G6:B8**—use **Comma Style** with **no decimals**. Merge and center the asset names over the two columns of their data—Air Lift centered in cells **A5:B5** and Tool Cabinet centered in cells **F5:G5**. Increase the width of the columns, if needed.

13. Create a macro in the Macro Library sheet that will be used for placement of the worksheet on the page. Name the macro **Page_Setup** and use the keyboard shortcut—**Ctrl+Shift+p** In the macro, display the worksheet with **Landscape**, **Fit to page**, and centered both **Horizontally** and **Vertically**. Then stop the macro. Enter the information for the new macro in the **8A_Macro_Library_Firstname_Lastname** workbook. **Save** the workbook.

14. In the **8H_Shop_Equipment_Firstname_Lastname** workbook, **Delete Sheet3**. **Rename Sheet2** to **Depreciation Schedule** In each worksheet, run the **Page Setup** macro. (Note: The macro will not run if you group all worksheets before you create the macro or run it.) On all worksheets, in the **Left Footer** area place the **File Name** and in the **Right Footer** area, place the **Sheet Name**.

15. Arrange the worksheets in the following order: **Depreciation**, **Depreciation Schedule**, **PivotTable**. **Save** the workbook. If asked, save it as a macro-free workbook.

16. **Print** the worksheet or submit electronically as directed. If you are directed to submit printed formulas, refer to Activity 1.12 to do so. If you printed your formulas, be sure to redisplay the worksheet by pressing Ctrl + `. From the **Office** menu, click **Close**. If you are prompted to save changes, click **No. Close** Excel.

End **You have completed Project 8H**

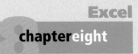

Project 8I — Fleet Purchase

In this project, you will apply all the skills you practiced from the Objectives in Projects 8A and 8B.

Objectives: 1. *Create and Run a Macro;* **2.** *Apply Depreciation Functions;* **3.** *Evaluate Worksheet Data with Conditional IF Functions;* **4.** *Create a PivotTable and PivotChart*

In the following Mastering Excel project, you will report data about a fleet of cars sold to Philadelphia Utilities. You will create PivotTables to display the data of sales for each make of car. As a service to the purchaser, Penn Liberty Motors prepares a depreciation schedule for each automobile purchased using the declining balance method of depreciation. Your completed workbook will look similar to Figure 8.55.

For Project 8I, you will need the following files:

e08I_Fleet_Purchase
8A_Macro_Library_Firstname_Lastname

You will save your workbook as
8I_Fleet_Purchase_Firstname_Lastname

Figure 8.55

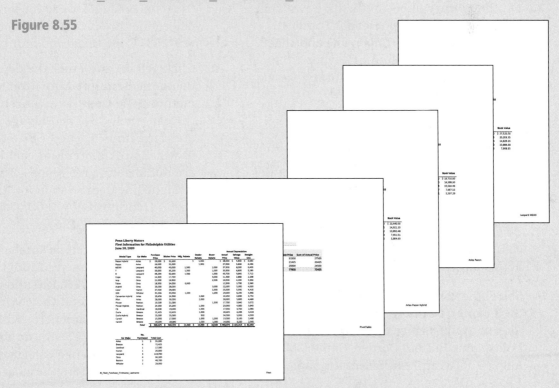

(Project 8I–Fleet Purchase continues on the next page)

Content-Based Assessments

(Project 8I–Fleet Purchase continued)

1. **Start** Excel. From the student files, locate and open the file named **e08I_Fleet_ Purchase** and **Save** it to your **Excel Chapter 8** folder as 8I_Fleet_ Purchase _Firstname_Lastname **Open** the **8A_Macro_ Library_Firstname_Lastname** workbook.

2. With the **8A_Macro_Library_Firstname_ Lastname** worksheet open and macros enabled, display the **Developer tab** if it is not visible. Record a macro in this work- book named **Header_Footer** and use a shortcut key of **Ctrl+Shift+h** In the descrip- tion, type **File Name in Left Footer and Sheet Name in Right Footer** In the **Left Footer**, insert the **File Name** and in the **Right Footer**, insert the **Sheet Name**. Return to **Normal** view and click cell **A1**. On the status bar at the left edge, click the **Stop Recording** button.

3. On the **Library sheet** in the first available cell in **column A**, type **Header/Footer** In **column B**, type **Insert file name and sheet name in footer** In **column C**, type **Ctrl+Shift+h** Then **Save** the Library workbook.

4. Display the **8I_Fleet_Purchase_ Firstname_Lastname** workbook and select the range **A1:A3**. Run the **Worksheet Title** macro or format the title with **Bold** and **14-point Cambria font**.

5. In cell **H4**, type **Annual Depreciation** Beginning in cell **H5**, type the following column titles:

Actual Price	Salvage Value	Straight Line

6. Select the column titles—**A5:J5**—and run the **Format_Column_Titles** macro. Alternatively, format the column titles with Bold, Thick Bottom Border, Center, Middle Align, and Wrap Text. Select the range

H4:J4 and format it with **Bold** and **Merge & Center.**

7. Click cell **H6** and enter the formula to determine the actual purchase price of the car. There are three types of rebates that may be available for each car purchase. These rebates come from the manufac- turer and will be returned to the buyer after the car is purchased. These rebates reduce the actual price of the car and are deducted from the price prior to determin- ing the value of the car and the deprecia- tion. The formula in cell H6 is **=c6-e6-f6-g6** Copy the formula through cell **H25**.

8. Click cell **I6** and determine the salvage value. A car is expected to be maintained by Philadelphia Utilities for five years and they expect the car to have a salvage value of 20% of the purchase price—the price before the rebates are allowed. The formula to determine the salvage value in cell I6 is **=c6*20%** Copy the formula through cell **I25**.

9. Click cell **J6** and enter the depreciation using the **Straight-Line** function **(SLN)** method. The **Cost** is the purchase price of the car —cell **C6**. The **Salvage** is in cell **I6**, and the **Life** is **5** years. Since the details provided are different for each car, these are not absolute references. The annual straight-line depreciation for the first Aries Pazon Hybrid is $4,640.00. Copy the for- mula through cell **J25**.

10. Click cell **B26** and type **Total** and format with **Center** alignment, **Bold**, and **Italic**. Select the range **C26:J26** and enter the **Sum** function to total the columns. Run the **Format_Totals** macro. With the range still selected, format with **no decimals** and with **Bold**. Alternatively, format the totals with Bold, Accounting Number Format

(Project 8I–Fleet Purchase continues on the next page)

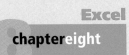
(Project 8I–Fleet Purchase continued)

with no decimals, and a Top and Double Bottom border.

11. Rename **Sheet2** to **Aries Pazon Hybrid** Select the range **A1:A3** and run the **Format Worksheet Title** macro. Select the range **A9:D9** and run the **Format_Column_Titles** macro. Alternatively, format the column titles with Bold, Thick Bottom Border, Center, Middle Align, and Wrap Text. If necessary, adjust the columns and row height so the titles display on one or two lines.

12. Click cell **B6** and type **29000** and in cell **B7**, type **5800** These numbers are the actual price and the salvage value for worksheet Pazon Hybrid listed in the Fleet worksheet.

13. Click cell **B10** and complete the **Declining Balance (DB)** function to determine the depreciation for the life of the asset. Then copy the formula through cell **B14**. Click cell **C10** and enter the total depreciation for the first year. Click cell **C11** and enter the formula to display the total deprecation for the first two years, and copy that formula through cell **C14**. Click cell **D10** and enter the formula to determine the book value for the first year—you will use an absolute reference so you can copy this formula. Copy the formula down through cell **D14**. Format the range **B11:D14** with **Comma Style**. **Save** your workbook.

14. Copy the **Aries Pazon Hybrid sheet** into a new sheet that **28000** just after this one. Click cell **A3** and type **Aries Pazon** For the actual price, type **28000** and for the salvage value, type **5600** and as you do, notice the depreciation schedule changes to reflect the data for this car. Change the sheet name to **Aries Pazon**

15. Create another depreciation schedule on a separate worksheet using the information for the Leopard MDXX that displays in the Fleet sheet in **row 8**. (Depreciation is figured on the actual sales price after all rebates.) Complete the worksheet and rename it **Leopard MDXX** Be sure the name of the car displays in cell **A3**.

16. In the **Fleet sheet,** beginning in cell **A29** type the following row titles:

Car Make
Aries
Breeze
Cardinal
Huron
Leopard
Orca
Raston
Whisler

17. Beginning in cell **B29**, type the following column titles:

No. Purchased	Total Cost

To format the column titles—**A29:C29**— run the **Format_Column_Titles** macro. Alternatively, format the column titles with Bold, Thick Bottom Border, Center, Middle Align, and Wrap Text.

18. In the range **B30:B37**. enter the **COUNTIF** function to determine the number of each make of car purchased. In the range **C30:C37**, enter the **SUMIF** function to determine the actual price received for the purchase of each model of car.

19. Format the numbers in **row 6**, and cell **C30** with **Accounting Number Format** and **no decimals**. Format the money amounts in the worksheet—**C7:J26**—with **Comma Style** and **no decimals**.

(Project 8I–Fleet Purchase continues on the next page)

Content-Based Assessments

(Project 8I–Fleet Purchase continued)

20. Insert a **PivotTable** using the range **A5:J25**. Adjust the PivotTable to display the **Car Make** as the **Report Filter** with the **Model Type**, **Purchase Price**, and **Actual Price** as the fields in the PivotTable. Display the PivotTable so that only the **Breeze** model displays. Rename **Sheet4** to PivotTable

21. Delete Sheet3. Run the **Header/Footer** macro on each worksheet. If you haven't created this macro, group the worksheets and in the Left Footer area, enter the File Name and in the Right Footer area, enter the Sheet Name. Then format with **Landscape Orientation** and **Fit to page** for the Fleet and PivotTable worksheets

and **Portrait Orientation** for the other worksheets. On all worksheets, center both **Horizontally** and **Vertically**. Arrange the worksheets in the following order: **Fleet**, **PivotTable**, **Aries Pazon Hybrid**, **Aries Pazon**, **Leopard MDXX**. **Save** your workbook.

22. Print the worksheet(s), which may include your macro library, or submit it electronically as directed. If you are directed to submit printed formulas, refer to Activity 1.12 to do so. If you printed your formulas, be sure to redisplay the worksheet by pressing ⎡Ctrl⎤ + ⎡`⎤. From the **Office** menu, click **Close**. If you are prompted to save changes, click **No**. **Exit** Excel.

End **You have completed Project 8I**

Content-Based Assessments

Business Running Case

Project 8J — Business Running Case

In this project, you will apply the skills you have practiced from the Objectives in Projects 8A and 8B.

From My Computer, navigate to the student files that accompany this textbook. In the folder **03_business_running_case**, locate and open the folder for this chapter. Open and print the instructions for this project, which are provided to you in Adobe PDF format. Follow the instructions and use the skills you have gained thus far to assist the managers of the Grand Department Store to meet the challenges of keeping records for a large department.

End **You have completed Project 8J** ——————————————

The following outcomes-based assessments are *open-ended assessments*. That is, there is no specific correct result; your result will depend on your approach to the information provided. Make *Professional Quality* your goal. Use the following scoring rubric to guide you in *how* to approach the problem and then to evaluate *how well* your approach solves the problem.

The *criteria*—Software Mastery, Content, Format and Layout, and Process—represent the knowledge and skills you have gained that you can apply to solving the problem. The *levels of performance*—Professional Quality, Approaching Professional Quality, or Needs Quality Improvement—help you and your instructor evaluate your result.

	Your completed project is of Professional Quality if you:	Your completed project is Approaching Professional Quality if you:	Your completed project Needs Quality Improvements if you:
1-Software Mastery	Choose and apply the most appropriate skills, tools, and features and identify efficient methods to solve the problem.	Choose and apply some appropriate skills, tools, and features, but not in the most efficient manner.	Choose inappropriate skills, tools, or features, or are inefficient in solving the problem.
2-Content	Construct a solution that is clear and well organized, contains content that is accurate, appropriate to the audience and purpose, and is complete. Provide a solution that contains no errors of spelling, grammar, or style.	Construct a solution in which some components are unclear, poorly organized, inconsistent, or incomplete. Misjudge the needs of the audience. Have some errors in spelling, grammar, or style, but the errors do not detract from comprehension.	Construct a solution that is unclear, incomplete, or poorly organized, containing some inaccurate or inappropriate content; and contains many errors of spelling, grammar, or style. Do not solve the problem.
3-Format and Layout	Format and arrange all elements to communicate information and ideas, clarify function, illustrate relationships, and indicate relative importance.	Apply appropriate format and layout features to some elements, but not others. Overuse features, causing minor distraction.	Apply format and layout that does not communicate information or ideas clearly. Do not use format and layout features to clarify function, illustrate relationships, or indicate relative importance. Use available features excessively, causing distraction.
4-Process	Use an organized approach that integrates planning, development, self-assessment, revision, and reflection.	Demonstrate an organized approach in some areas, but not others; or, use an insufficient process of organization throughout.	Do not use an organized approach to solve the problem.

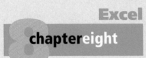

Problem Solving

Project 8K—Accessories Sales

In this project, you will construct a solution by applying any combination of the skills you practiced from the Objectives in Projects 8A and 8B.

For Project 8K, you will need the following file:

e08K_Accessories_Sales
8A_Macro_Library_Firstname_Lastname

You will save your workbook as
8K_Accessories_Sales_Firstname_Lastname

In Project 8K, you will complete a workbook that provides statistical analysis of the monthly sales in the accessories department for Andre Randolph, the sales manager. You will construct a PivotTable to review the sales in different ways in order to restock the items and make recommendations for an increase in sales.

In the worksheet, determine the following statistical analysis:

- The number of items sold from each of the four departments

- The total sales for each of the four departments

Create two PivotTables that display the following:

- The total sales for each department during the first half of the month—before November 16 to include November 15

- The total sales for each department during the last half of the month—after November 15

Format the worksheets, using the available macros that have been created.

Provide appropriate sheet names and delete unused worksheets. Place the worksheets in an appropriate order in the workbook. Run the footer macro or insert a left footer that includes the file name and a right footer that displays the sheet name and a page number. Save the workbook as **8K_Accessories_Sales_Firstname_Lastname** and submit it as directed.

End You have completed Project 8K

Project 8L — Computer Depreciation

In this project, you will construct a solution by applying any combination of the skills you practiced from the Objectives in Projects 8A and 8B.

For Project 8L, you will need the following file:

e08L_Computer_Depreciation
8A_Macro_Library_Firstname_Lastname

You will save your workbook as
8L_Computer_Depreciation_Firstname_Lastname

In Project 8L, you will complete a workbook that displays the depreciation for a computer network using the various depreciation methods in order to determine the method of depreciation most suited to the firm. You will complete and format the worksheet and prepare a PivotTable report to assist in the evaluation.

Complete the depreciation schedule for three depreciation methods—straight-line, declining balance, and sum-of-the-years' digits. Computer equipment has a suggested life of three years. Display only the amount of depreciation for each year. Create and format a PivotTable that displays the Year as the Report Filter and the three depreciation methods as the values. Then insert three PivotTables—one for each year—that display the three depreciation methods for each year.

Format the worksheets, using the available macros that have been created. Use themes and/or font attributes to prepare a professional worksheet. Provide appropriate sheet names and delete unused worksheets. Place the worksheets in an appropriate order in the workbook. Insert a left footer that includes the file name and a right footer that displays the sheet name. Save the workbook as **8L_Computer_Depreciation_Firstname_Lastname** and submit it as directed.

End **You have completed Project 8L** ——————

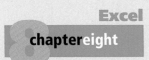

chaptereight

Problem Solving

Project 8M—Hybrid Sales

In this project, you will construct a solution by applying any combination of the skills you practiced from the Objectives in Projects 8A and 8B.

For Project 8M, you will need the following file:

e08M_Hybrid_Sales
8A_Macro_Library_Firstname_Lastname

You will save your workbook as
8M_Hybrid_Sales_Firstname_Lastname

In Project 8M, you will analyze data in a workbook that displays the sales of hybrid cars for the first quarter of the year for Charlie James, the auto sales manager. Prepare the following statistical information in the worksheet:

- The total number of each car make sold

- The total sales for each car make

- The total sales for each sales representative

- The total Aries cars sold by each sales representative

Insert a PivotTable to analyze the total number of each car make sold, grouped by each month, using the Model Type as the Report Filter. Format the PivotTable in a style of your choice. Prepare a PivotTable report for each model type and insert a chart for each type.

Format the worksheets, using the available macros that have been created. Use themes and/or borders and font attributes to prepare a professional workbook. Provide appropriate sheet names and delete unused worksheets. Place the worksheets in an appropriate order in the workbook. Insert a left footer that includes the file name and a right footer that displays the sheet name. Save the workbook as **8M_Hybrid_Sales_Firstname_Lastname** and submit it as directed.

End **You have completed Project 8M**

Project 8N — Power Lift

In this project, you will construct a solution by applying any combination of the skills you practiced from the Objectives in Projects 8A and 8B.

For Project 8N, you will need the following file:

New blank Excel workbook

8A_Macro_Library_Firstname_Lastname

You will save your workbook as
8N_Power_Lift_Firstname_Lastname

In Project 8N, you will complete a comparison of the depreciation methods for a new power lift that Penn Liberty Motors plans to purchase. Kevin Rau, president of Penn Liberty Motors, is working with the accounting department to determine the method of depreciation they should use for this asset.

Prepare the depreciation schedules for the power lift. The lift has a sales price of $38,000. It is expected that the lift will have a usable life of 15 years with a salvage value of $5,000. Complete a schedule of depreciation for each of the three methods that Penn Liberty is considering—straight-line, declining balance, and sum-of-the-years' digits. Be sure to include the depreciation amount for each year in the life of the asset, the total depreciation, and the book value.

Format the worksheets, using the available macros that have been created. You may choose to use borders, themes, and font attributes to prepare a professional workbook. Provide appropriate sheet names and delete unused worksheets. Place the worksheets in an appropriate order in the workbook. Insert a left footer that includes the file name and a right footer that displays the sheet name and the page number. Save the workbook as **8N_Power_Lift_Firstname_Lastname** and submit as directed.

End **You have completed Project 8N** ————————

Outcomes-Based Assessments

Problem Solving

Project 8O — Heating-Cooling

In this project, you will construct a solution by applying any combination of the skills you practiced from the Objectives in Projects 8A and 8B.

For Project 8O, you will need the following file:

e08O_Heating-Cooling
8A_Macro_Library_Firstname_Lastname

**You will save your workbook as
8O_Heating-Cooling_Firstname_Lastname**

In Project 8O, you will analyze data in a workbook that displays the income for the heating and cooling parts and installation for the month of April, for Accessories Sales Manager Andre Randolph. The data is saved in your data files as **e08O_Heating-Cooling**.

For each of the car years, provide statistical data showing the number of parts sold each year and the number of heaters sold each year. Then create a PivotTable that displays the car model, the cost of the parts, and the cost of labor. Chart this data. Prepare individual PivotTable reports for each of the accessories.

Prepare another worksheet to calculate the depreciation on a new vacuum coolant exchange system. The system costs $1,530, has a projected life of 5 years, and a salvage value of $300. Display the first-year depreciation for the three depreciation methods you have practiced.

Format the worksheets, using the available macros that have been created. Use font attributes to prepare a professional workbook. Provide appropriate sheet names and delete unused worksheets. Place the worksheets in an appropriate order in the workbook. Insert a left footer that includes the file name and a right footer that displays the sheet name. Save the workbook as **8O_Heating-Cooling Firstname_Lastname** and submit as directed.

End You have completed Project 8O

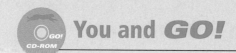

Project 8P—You and *GO!*

In this project, you will construct a solution by applying any combination of the Objectives found in Projects 8A and 8B.

From My Computer, navigate to the student files that accompany this textbook. In the folder **04_you_and_go**, locate and open the folder for this chapter. Open and print the instructions for this project, which are provided to you in Adobe PDF format. Follow the instructions to create a worksheet that lists something you own and then prepare a PivotTable using that data.

End You have completed Project 8P ——————————————

GO! with Help

Project 8Q—*GO!* with Help

In this chapter, you practiced creating PivotTable reports. The Excel Help program includes Web-based tutorials that provide further information and guidance in using this data analysis tool. To complete this exercise, you need to be connected to the Internet.

1. Be sure you are connected to the Internet, and if you have speakers, be sure they are turned on. **Start** Excel and display the Help window. In the **Search** text box, type **PivotTable** and then click **Search**.

2. In the list of topics, locate and click the **PivotTable I: Get started with PivotTable reports in Excel 2007**. This tutorial includes sound on the first page.

3. At the bottom of each screen, click **Next** to move to the next screen. At the end of the session is a practice session for you to complete. Download the practice worksheet to practice creating the PivotTable.

4. Return to the **Search Results** task pane, and then click **PivotTable II: Filter PivotTable reports data in Excel 2007**. Complete the tutorial and then download the practice file and practice in Excel.

5. Return to the **Search Results** task pane, and then click **PivotTable III: Calculate data in PivotTable report in Excel 2007**. Complete the tutorial and then download the practice file and practice in Excel.

6. Explore other topics related to PivotTable reports.

7. After you have completed your practice, close your browser, close Help, and close the worksheet without saving it.

End You have completed Project 8Q ——————————————

9 chapternine

Inserting Graphic Elements into Worksheets and Charts

OBJECTIVES

At the end of this chapter you will be able to:

1. Format with Graphic Images Including WordArt to Enhance Worksheets
2. Insert SmartArt Graphics
3. Create, Edit, and Publish a Web Page

4. Create Specialized Charts
5. Format Column Charts with Pictures and Other Graphic Elements

OUTCOMES

Mastering these objectives will enable you to:

PROJECT 9A
Create Worksheets and Web Pages Using Graphic Elements Including WordArt and SmartArt

PROJECT 9B
Create Line, Area, Scatter, and Other Charts and Use Pictures and Graphic Elements to Format Charts and Workbooks

Cross Oceans Music

Cross Oceans Music produces and distributes recordings of innovative musicians from every continent in genres that include Celtic, jazz, new age, reggae, flamenco, calypso, and unique blends of all genres. Company scouts travel the world attending world music festivals, concerts, and small local venues to find their talented roster of musicians. These artists create new music using traditional and modern instruments and technologies. Cross Oceans customers are knowledgeable about music and demand the highest-quality digital recordings provided in state-of-the-art formats.

Inserting Graphic Elements into Worksheets and Charts

Microsoft graphical elements are available in Excel as well as in other Office programs. Inserting, formatting, sizing, and cropping graphics—including pictures and clip art—is useful in Excel worksheets and charts. Graphic elements can be used to create a company logo, emphasize information, add comments, present tasks, or show relationships, such as an organization chart.

Formatting charts with graphical elements adds interest to the chart. Inserting pictures as background to a chart or using pictures in the data markers of a column or bar chart add to the effectiveness of the chart. In this chapter, you will use graphical elements in worksheets and charts.

Project 9A Quarter1 Sales

In Activities 9.1 through 9.11, you will use graphical elements, including colors, textures, patterns, clip art, and pictures, to enhance the appearance of worksheets. You will also use SmartArt to complete an organization chart and you will create and save a Web page. Your completed workbooks will look similar to Figure 9.1.

For Project 9A, you will need the following files:

e09A_Quarter1_Sales
e09A_Drums

You will save your workbooks as
9A_Quarter1_Sales_Firstname_Lastname
9A_Web_Firstname_Lastname

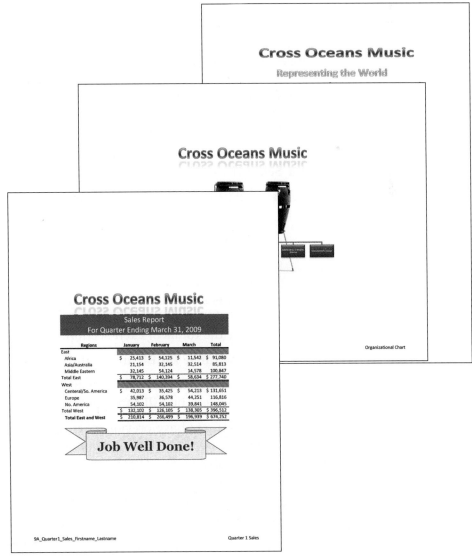

Figure 9.1
Project 9A—Quarter1 Sales

Objective 1
Format with Graphic Images
Including WordArt to Enhance Worksheets

Microsoft Excel provides graphical elements that include shapes, pictures, lines, and clip art in all of the Microsoft Office applications. Text can be formatted as art using WordArt. Each of these elements can be formatted using color, texture, and patterns. Emphasis can be added with gradients of color, where the color transforms from lighter to darker shades within the selected range. In Excel worksheets, graphics are used to help emphasize and highlight specific data.

Activity 9.1 Formatting with Patterns

Cross Oceans Music is growing both in the number of artists and in the sales generated. The first quarter of the year displays considerable growth over previous quarters. Tony Escovedo, president of Cross Oceans Music, is pleased with this growth and has asked for a worksheet that summarizes and displays the income in the East and West regions. He wants the worksheet formatted in a way that displays the excitement over the increase in sales. In this activity, you will complete the worksheet and use patterns in the worksheet.

1 **Start** Excel. From your student files, locate and open the file named **e09A_Quarter1_Sales**. Save the workbook in a folder named **Excel Chapter 9** as **9A_Quarter1_Sales_Firstname_Lastname** Rename **Sheet1** to **Quarter 1 Sales**

2 Select the range **B7:E10** and click the **Sum** button $\boxed{\Sigma \cdot}$. Select the range **B12:E15** and click the **Sum** button $\boxed{\Sigma \cdot}$. Then select the entire range of the worksheet—**B7:E16**—and click the **Sum** button $\boxed{\Sigma \cdot}$. If necessary, adjust column widths to fully display the cell contents.

Recall that a grand total is entered into the worksheet when you select all of the data that will be included in that total. Excel recognizes totals and will add those totals to get the grand total. Recall also that the formula used in the grand total displays the cell references for the totals of each section, starting with the last total.

3 Select the range **B6:E6** and in the **Alignment group**, click the **Dialog Box Launcher** $\boxed{\text{\scriptsize ⌐}}$ to display the **Format Cells** dialog box, and then click the **Fill tab**.

Recall that you have previously entered a fill color from the icon in the Font group. The Fill tab is another way to enter fill color into a cell or range of cells. There are other effects that can also be inserted into the worksheet.

4 On the right side, under **Pattern Style**, click the arrow to display the gallery of patterns, and then compare your screen with Figure 9.2.

Patterns can be inserted into a cell or range of cells, adding texture to the worksheet.

Pattern Style section

Figure 9.2

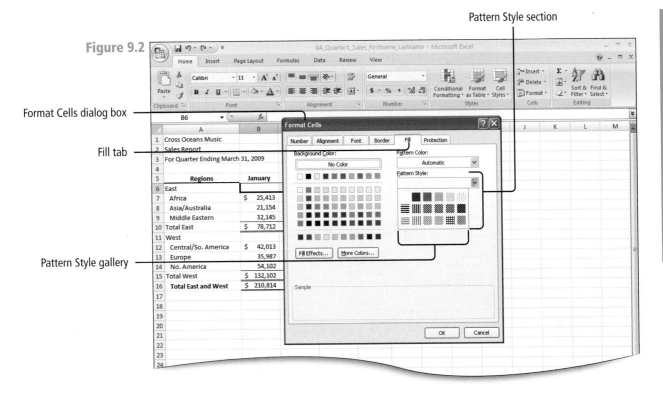

Format Cells dialog box

Fill tab

Pattern Style gallery

5 In the gallery, in the third row, click the third style—**Thin Reverse Diagonal Stripe**. Then click **OK**. In the **Font** group, click the **Fill Color button arrow** and under **Theme Colors**, in the fifth column, click the fourth choice—**Blue, Accent 1, Lighter 40%**. Use the **Format Painter** button to copy the format to the range **B11:E11**.

Rows 6 and 11 do not contain data. Placing a pattern in those cells adds texture to the worksheet. When your manager reviews the worksheet, these intentional entries in these rows indicate nothing is missing.

6 **Save** your workbook.

Activity 9.2 Inserting and Formatting a Shape

A variety of shapes can be inserted into the worksheet. These shapes can be sized and formatted. Text can be inserted into the shape, and the color of the shape can be changed. Texture and colors can be used within a shape. In this activity, you will insert a ribbon shape, change the size of the shape, insert and format text in the shape, and add texture to the shape.

1 Click cell **B19**, and click the **Insert tab**, and then in the **Illustrations group**, click the **Shapes** button. Compare your screen with Figure 9.3.

The Shapes gallery displays a number of shapes that can be used with Excel workbooks. They are grouped according to the type of shape. Shapes can be inserted into a worksheet or chart and can be sized and formatted.

Figure 9.3

Shapes button   Shapes gallery

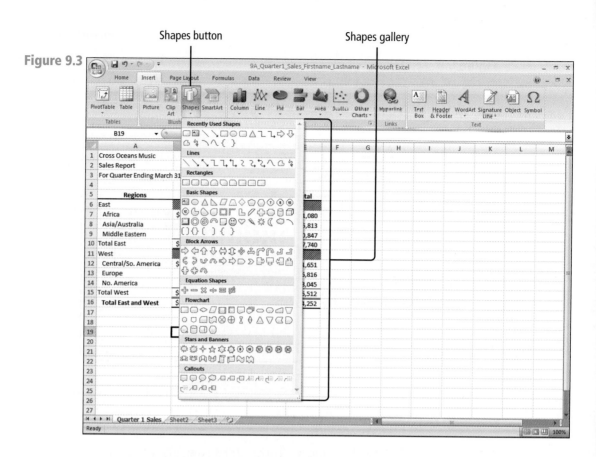

2 Under **Stars and Banners**, in the second row, click the second banner—**Down Ribbon**. With the pointer displaying as [+], click in the upper left corner of cell **B18** and drag to the lower right corner of cell **D20**, and then compare your screen with Figure 9.4.

A blue ribbon is inserted into the worksheet and the Drawing Tools contextual tab displays the Format tab.

The border surrounding the graphic element is active and the sizing handles, adjustment handles, and rotation handle display. **Sizing handles** are the small circles or squares that appear at the corners and sides of the selected—active—object. Dragging on the sizing handles changes the size of the object. **Adjustment handles** are the diamond-shaped handles at the top of the graphic and are used to adjust the appearance but not the size of the shape. The **rotation handle** is the green circle that displays above the selected shape and is used to rotate the shape.

Alert!

Are you dissatisfied with the shape?

To create a shape, click and drag to open the desired shape. When inserting it, you may find it easier to drag in a downward diagonal direction. If you are not satisfied with your first attempt, press [Delete] and try again.

Figure 9.4

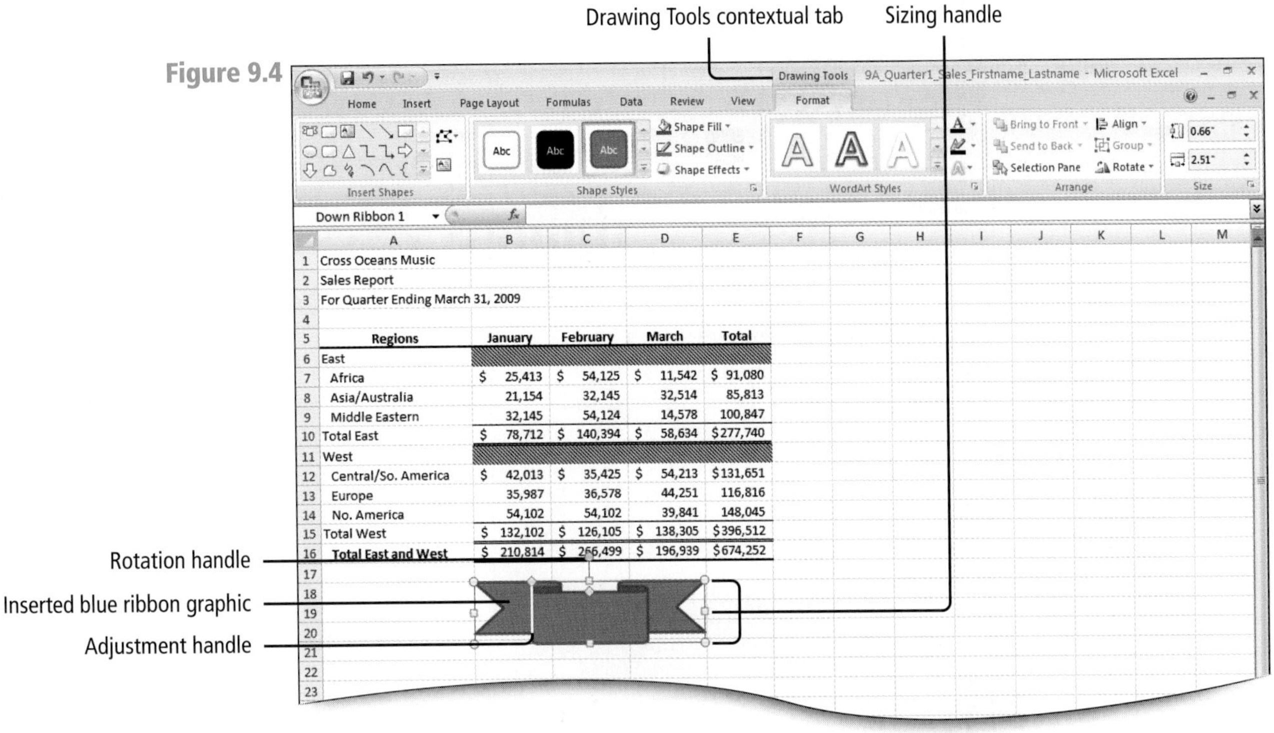

Drawing Tools contextual tab   Sizing handle

Rotation handle

Inserted blue ribbon graphic

Adjustment handle

	A	B	C	D	E	F	G	H	I	J	K	L	M
1	Cross Oceans Music												
2	Sales Report												
3	For Quarter Ending March 31, 2009												
4													
5	Regions	January	February	March	Total								
6	East												
7	Africa	$ 25,413	$ 54,125	$ 11,542	$ 91,080								
8	Asia/Australia	21,154	32,145	32,514	85,813								
9	Middle Eastern	32,145	54,124	14,578	100,847								
10	Total East	$ 78,712	$ 140,394	$ 58,634	$277,740								
11	West												
12	Central/So. America	$ 42,013	$ 35,425	$ 54,213	$131,651								
13	Europe	35,987	36,578	44,251	116,816								
14	No. America	54,102	54,102	39,841	148,045								
15	Total West	$ 132,102	$ 126,105	$ 138,305	$396,512								
16	Total East and West	$ 210,814	$ 266,499	$ 196,939	$674,252								

▣ Point to the **lower-right sizing handle**. When the pointer takes the ⬉ shape, drag at an angle until the ⊞ pointer is at the lower right corner of cell **E22**.

When you use a corner sizing handle, you can increase both the width and the height of the graphic element at the same time.

▣ At the left edge of the graphic, point to the **middle sizing handle**. When the ↔ shape displays, drag to the left until the left edge is at the left edge of **column A**.

▣ Click the left **adjustment handle**—the yellow diamond—and drag to the left until the pointer is in the middle of **column A**.

The adjustment handle now displays in the middle of column A. You have changed the shape of the ribbon by increasing the middle portion of it and decreasing the ends. When changing the width of the graphic, both ends of the ribbon changed at the same time.

▣ Click the **Drawing Tools Format tab**. In the **Shape Styles group**, click the **Shape Fill** button, and then compare your screen with Figure 9.5.

The Format tab displays choices for formatting shapes and other graphic elements. In addition to the Theme and Standard colors, choices of Picture, Gradient, and Texture are available.

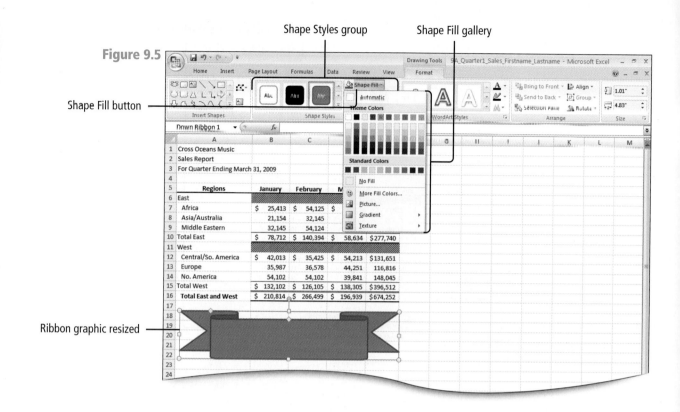

Figure 9.5

Shape Styles group

Shape Fill gallery

Shape Fill button

Ribbon graphic resized

7 In the **Shape Fill gallery**, point to **Texture**. In the gallery that displays, scroll over the selections—Live Preview changes the texture in the ribbon. In the fifth row, click the first choice—**Blue tissue paper**. Click in an empty cell outside the ribbon so the graphic is no longer active. Then compare your screen with Figure 9.6.

Texture may be inserted into a graphic element. In addition to the textures that are included with Excel, other textures can be saved to your computer.

Figure 9.6

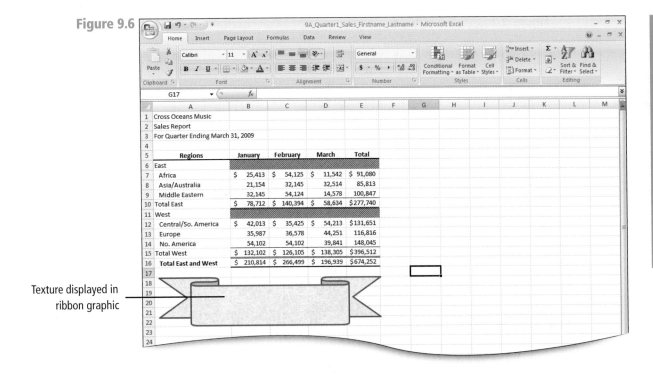

Texture displayed in ribbon graphic

8 **Save** 💾 your workbook.

Activity 9.3 Formatting Text Within a Shape

Within a graphic, the text can be altered by changing the font, font size, and color of font. The lines in a graphic element can also be changed in size, style, and color. In this activity, you will change the font used in the ribbon graphic and change the lines that border the ribbon graphic.

1 Click the ribbon graphic to make it active and then type **Job Well Done!**

As you begin to type, the insertion point becomes active. The default font color is white, no matter the color of the ribbon, so the text is not visible.

2 In the text in the ribbon, triple-click—click the mouse quickly three times—to select the text. Right-click and click the **Font Color button arrow** and click **Automatic**. Then click **Bold** and select a font size of **20 points**. Then confirm the words are correct and are correctly spelled.

The Automatic font color is black, which is the most common color used in fonts.

3 With the text selected, on the **Home tab**, in the **Font group**, click the **Font button arrow** and type **g** to quickly display the fonts that begin with the letter *G*. Notice that Live Preview displays different text styles. Then scroll to and click **Georgia**. Click the **Font Size button arrow** and use Live Preview to display the font sizes, and then click **28** and compare your screen with Figure 9.7.

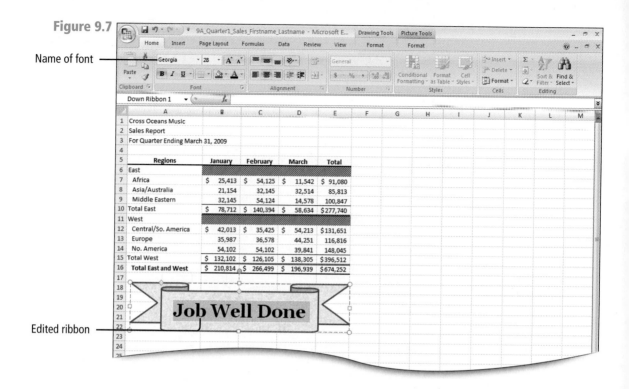

Figure 9.7

Name of font

Edited ribbon

4 With the text selected, click on the **Font Color button arrow** [A] and scroll through the colors to view the Live Preview. In the fifth column, click the last color—**Blue, Accent 1, Darker 50%**.

Selecting commands on the Mini toolbar is convenient because the commands are close to your work. However, Live Preview is available only on the Ribbon, which is helpful when making formatting choices.

5 Click the **Drawing Tools Format tab**. In the **Shape Styles group**, click the **Shape Outline** button and in the displayed gallery, point to **Weight**, and in the submenu, scroll through the menu to review the Live Preview; then click **3/4 pt**.

The line that surrounds the graphic image can be formatted in different ways, including a different point, color, or even a dotted or dashed border.

6 **Save** [💾] your workbook.

Activity 9.4 Inserting and Formatting WordArt

WordArt is a gallery of text styles that transforms text into a stylized image that you can use to create a distinctive logo or heading. WordArt can be formatted with WordArt styles. The fill and outline of the text can be altered. Text effects, such as shadows, glow, and reflections can be used. In this activity, you will use WordArt to insert the company name and then modify the WordArt style.

1 Right-click the **row 1 heading** and from the displayed shortcut menu, click **Row Height**. In the **Row Height** dialog box, type **70** and then click **OK**. Click the **Insert tab**, and in the **Text group**, click **WordArt**, and then compare your screen with Figure 9.8.

The WordArt gallery displays. The letter "A" is formatted in several different styles to provide an example of the style of WordArt that will be displayed.

WordArt button

Figure 9.8

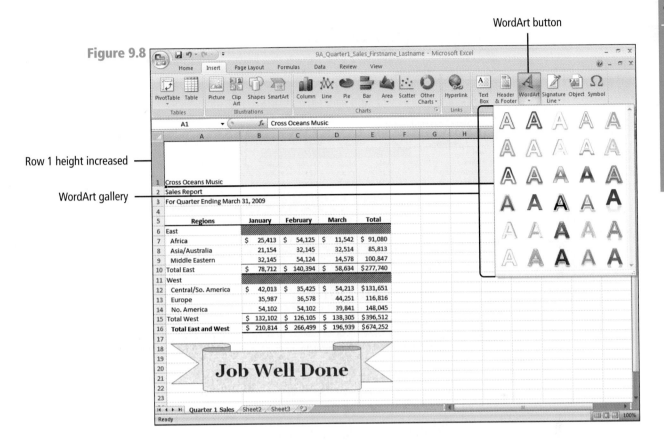

Row 1 height increased

WordArt gallery

2 In the fourth column, click the third choice—**Gradient Fill – Accent 1**—and then compare your screen with Figure 9.9.

WordArt changes text to a graphic element. The text box displays over the worksheet with the words *Your Text Here* inserted as WordArt. The color in the text alternates from light blue to dark blue and back to light blue, which is a gradient style that was selected as part of the format of the WordArt. A *gradient* fill is a gradual progression of colors and shades, usually from one color to another, or from one shade to another shade of the same color.

Figure 9.9

Sizing handles

Rotation handle

Inserted WordArt

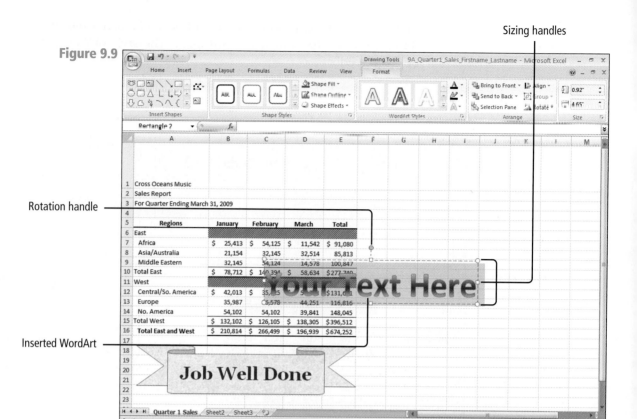

3 Click in cell **A1**, press ⌈Delete⌉, and click in the WordArt. In the **WordArt** text box, point to the top edge of the graphic, and when the pointer displays, drag up to place the upper left corner at the upper left corner of cell **A1**. Triple-click the words *Your Text Here* to select the text, and then type **Cross Oceans Music** On the WordArt, triple-click to select the text again, and then on the **Home tab**, click the **Font Size button arrow** `11 ▾`, scrolldown, and then click **36** to change the size of the font.

Text in WordArt can be edited and formatted in the same manner as other text is formatted.

4 With the text still selected, on the **Drawing Tools Format tab**, in the **WordArt Styles group**, click the **Text Effects** button `A▾` and compare your screen with Figure 9.10.

Text effects change the look of WordArt text by adding other effects such as shadows, reflections, flow, or 3-D rotations or bevels.

Figure 9.10

Drawing Tools Format tab   Text Effects button

Text Effects gallery

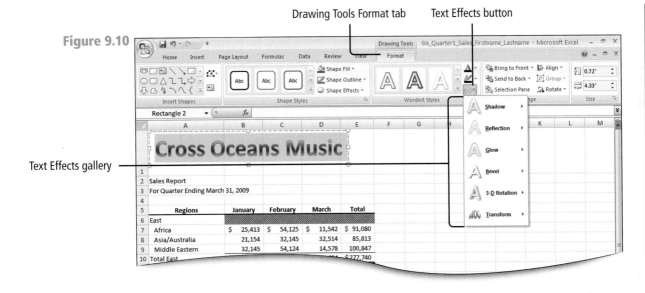

5 Scroll down the list to review the submenus that display. Scroll through a submenu and see how the effect will change the WordArt. Point to **Reflection** and in the gallery, under **Reflection Variations**, in the second row, click the first selection—**Tight Reflection, 4 pt offset**. Then click in the worksheet.

Each of the text attributes provides a different appearance for the WordArt title. When creating a worksheet, use text effects cautiously as it is easy to clutter a worksheet with too many formatting choices.

6 Click in the **WordArt** to select it and point to a border. At the right edge of the WordArt box, point to the **middle sizing handle** and when the ↔ shape displays, drag until the right edge is just to the left of the right cell gridline of cell **E1**.

7 Select the range **A2:E3**. In the **Font group**, click the **Fill Color button arrow** , and under **Theme Colors**, in the fifth column, select the fifth color—**Blue, Accent 1, Darker 25%**. Click the **Font Color button arrow** , and under **Theme Colors**, click the first color— **White, Background 1**. Click the **Font Size button arrow** , scroll to and click **18 point** and then **Merge & Center** cell **A2** over **columns A:E**. Use the **Format Painter** to copy the format from cell **A2** to cell **A3**. Adjust row heights for **rows 2** and **3**.

8 **Save** your workbook.

Objective 2
Insert SmartArt Graphics

A **SmartArt graphic** is a designer-quality visual representation of information that you can create. There are a variety of SmartArt layouts that can be used to quickly, easily, and effectively communicate the information. There are several types of SmartArt graphics available—List, Process, Cycle, Hierarchy, Relationship, Matrix, and Pyramid.

When you create a SmartArt graphic, you should consider the message that you are trying to convey. SmartArt should not be used if there is a large amount of text. The table in Figure 9.11 describes the types of SmartArt layouts and their suggested purposes.

SmartArt Options

Graphic Type	Purpose of Graphic
List	Show nonsequential information
Process	Show steps in a process or timeline
Cycle	Show a continual process
Hierarchy	Show a decision tree or create an organization chart
Relationship	Illustrate connections
Matrix	Show how parts relate to a whole
Pyramid	Show proportional relationships with the largest component on the top or bottom

Figure 9.11

Activity 9.5 Inserting a SmartArt Organization Chart

An organization chart visually displays the relationships of the employees or positions within a firm. Lines are drawn between the employees providing a visual display of the reporting lines. Tony Escovedo, president of Cross Oceans Music, has requested that you prepare an organization chart that displays the relationship of the artistic director and managing director to the president as well as their relationships to the sales representatives from each region. In this activity, you will use SmartArt to prepare the organization chart for the firm.

1 Click the **Sheet2 sheet tab** and rename it **Organization Chart** Click the **Insert tab**, and in the **Illustrations group**, click the **SmartArt** button, and then compare your screen with Figure 9.12.

The Choose a SmartArt Graphic dialog box displays. SmartArt adds color, shapes, and emphasis to your text and data. The categories of SmartArt display at the left of the dialog box. The SmartArt layouts display in the center section with several layout styles available for each type of SmartArt. The area at the right provides a color visual of the completed graphic.

Figure 9.12

Visual display of the selected SmartArt

Displayed List category of SmartArt

Choose a SmartArt Graphic dialog box

Categories of SmartArt available

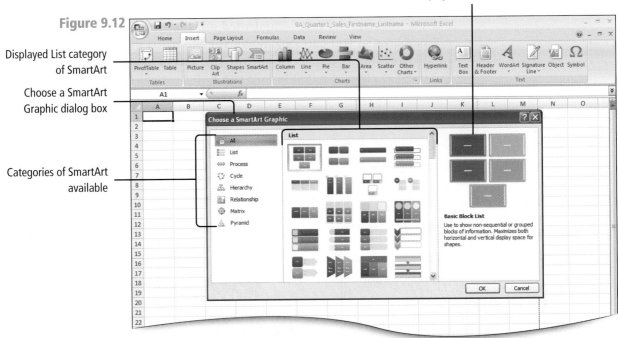

On the left side of the dialog box, click **Hierarchy**. In the center area, click the first chart on the top row—**Organization Chart**—and then compare your screen with Figure 9.13.

The layout section displays the Hierarchy layouts for the Organization Chart category. A graphical example of the Organization Chart and an explanation displays on the right.

Figure 9.13

Visual example of the Organization Chart

Hierarchy layouts

Description of an Organization Chart

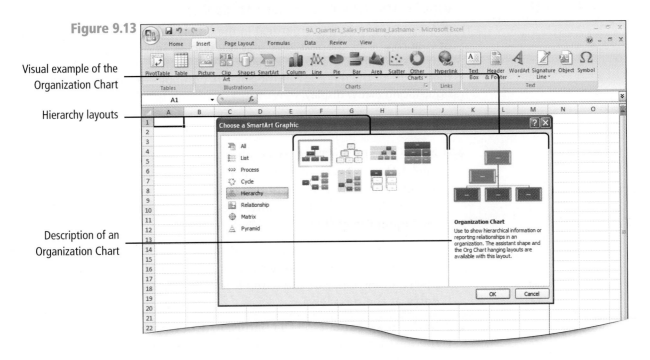

3 Click **OK** and compare your screen with Figure 9.14.

The placeholder text—illustrated as *[Text]* in the SmartArt graphic—displays so you can view how your SmartArt graphic will look. Placeholder text does not print. The **_Text Pane_** at the left may be used to enter the text or you can enter text directly in the graphic.

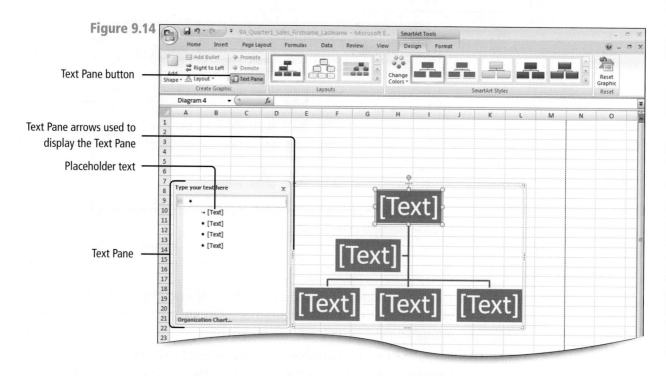

Figure 9.14

Text Pane button

Text Pane arrows used to display the Text Pane

Placeholder text

Text Pane

Alert!

What if the Text Pane does not display?

The Text Pane is used to enter text in the graphic. Depending on prior uses of your computer, the Text Pane may not display. To display the Text Pane, in the Create Graphic group, click the Text Pane button. Alternatively, click in the middle of the left edge of the SmartArt graphic—a left-facing and a right-facing arrow display.

4 At the left, in the **Text Pane**, click by the first bullet. If the placeholder—Text—displays, delete it. Then type **Tony Escovedo, President** and as you do, notice that it is also entered into the first area in the organization chart. Press the ⬇ and type **Amalia Raman, Managing Director** and press Enter.

As you enter data into the organization chart, the sizes of the shapes are altered in order to fully display the entered text. Press Enter to insert a new entry at the same level and press ⬇ to insert a new entry at the next level.

5 In the **Text Pane**, type **Lila Darius, Artistic Director** and press the ⬇. In the next text area, type **Matisse Keita, Africa**, press Enter. Continue typing the regional representatives displayed on the next page and press Enter after each entry.

Morris Connell, Asia/Australia
Raa Ihansa, Middle East
Samuel Beck, North America
Isabella Delia, Central/So. America
Diana Samuels, Europe

6 After the last entry, click the **Text Pane Close** button ✕ . If there are boxes that display the placeholder—Text—click in the box and press Delete. When you are finished, there should be six boxes that display the regional scouts.

7 Position the pointer at the upper, left corner of the organization chart and when the ↖ pointer displays, drag up and to the left until the upper left corner is in cell **A5**. Point to the **bottom center sizing handle**, and when the ↕ pointer displays, drag to **row 24**. Compare your screen with Figure 9.15.

As the size of the organization chart is increased, the text within the chart also increases.

Figure 9.15

Inserted Organization Chart

First-level employee—
President

Second-level employees—
Directors

Third-level employees—
Regional scouts

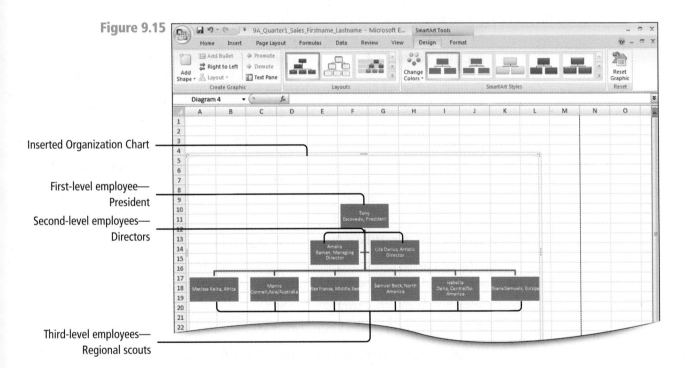

8 Select both worksheets and click the **Page Layout tab**. In the **Page Setup group**, click the **Orientation** button, and then click **Landscape**. Ungroup the sheets, click the **Quarter 1 Sales sheet tab**, and then click the WordArt title at the border two times. When a solid border displays around the WordArt, press Ctrl+C to copy the graphic.

In the WordArt, when a dotted line displays, it cannot be moved or edited. Click twice to get the solid border so the WordArt can be moved or edited.

9 Click the **Organization Chart sheet tab** and in **cell A1**, press Ctrl+V to paste the graphic.

Does your WordArt display as text in the cells?

When the WordArt is displayed with a dashed border, it is copied as text and placed in cells. In order to copy the WordArt as created, the solid border must surround the WordArt before it is copied. WordArt copied in this manner can be edited.

🔟 Position the WordArt and resize it as necessary so that it displays over the range **C1:J4**. **Save** 💾 your workbook.

WordArt Can Be Pasted as a Picture

In order to prevent WordArt from being edited, it can be copied as a picture. A picture can be moved and sized. To copy WordArt as a picture, first select the copy command. Then select Paste Special. In the Paste Special dialog box, select Picture (PNG).

More Knowledge
Picture Formats

Pictures are saved in different formats for different reasons. With some formats, files are compressed to save disk space. Sometimes compressing a file may cause the picture to display in a lower-quality resolution. The common formats are PNG—Portable Network Graphics; GIF—Graphics Interface Format; and JPEG—Joint Photographic Experts Group. If you work with pictures frequently, you will want to understand the differences between the formats used with pictures.

Activity 9.6 Inserting a Picture as Background

Pictures, clip art, texture, or other graphical elements can be inserted as background in a worksheet. In this activity, you will insert a picture that displays behind the organization chart.

1️⃣ Click the organization chart to select it, and then click the **Format tab**. In the **Shape Styles group**, click the **Dialog Box launcher** 🔲. Alternatively, right-click on the border of the organization chart and click Format Object.

The Format Shape dialog box displays. The organization chart can be formatted using this dialog box.

2️⃣ In the **Format Shape** dialog box, confirm that on the left **Fill** is selected. On the right, click **Picture or texture fill**, and then compare your screen with Figure 9.16.

The Format Shape dialog box has expanded the choices for inserting a picture or texture fill. Notice that a texture has been inserted into the organization chart.

Figure 9.16

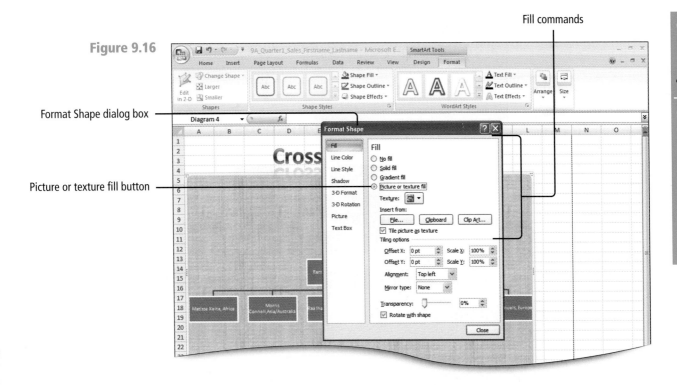

Fill commands

Format Shape dialog box

Picture or texture fill button

Alert!

Is the texture in your chart different?

If this function has previously been used, the texture or picture last selected will display.

> ■ In the **Format Shape** dialog box, under **Insert from**, click **File**. Navigate to your data files for Chapter 9, locate and click the picture named **e09A_Drums**, and then click **Insert**. Click **Close** and compare your screen with Figure 9.17.
>
> The picture that you have inserted is placed behind the organization chart. A picture inserted as background cannot be moved or formatted independently.

Figure 9.17

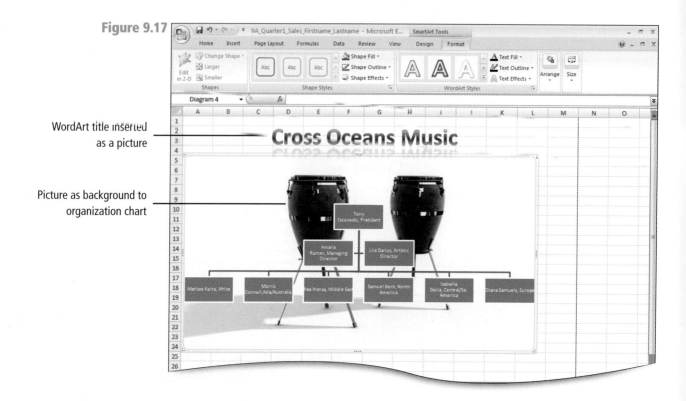

WordArt title inserted
as a picture

Picture as background to
organization chart

4 Save 🖫 your workbook.

Activity 9.7 Formatting SmartArt

The color choices used in the SmartArt boxes, the style of the colors, and the placement of the organization chart can be changed. In this activity, you will change the colors and apply a different style to the SmartArt chart.

1 Click in the **Organization Chart** to select it. Click the **Design tab** and in the **SmartArt Styles group**, click the **Change Colors** button, and then compare your screen with Figure 9.18.

The Change Colors gallery displays the color choices for the layout. The color choice currently displayed is surrounded by a yellow/orange border.

Change Colors button   Change Colors gallery

Figure 9.18

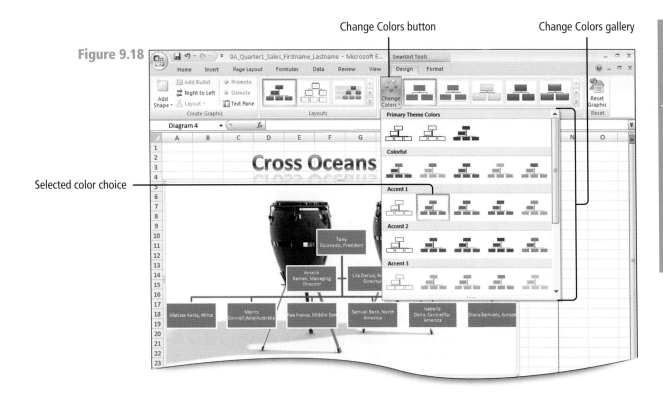

Selected color choice

> **2** Move the pointer over the choices to view the Live Preview. Then under **Colorful**, click the first choice—**Colorful—Accent Colors**.

> **3** In the **SmartArt Styles group**, click the **More** button [▽] to display the styles gallery, and then compare your screen with Figure 9.19.

The styles gallery displays with the Best Match for Document at the top and other 3-D choices display next.

Best Match for Document selections   Styles gallery

Figure 9.19

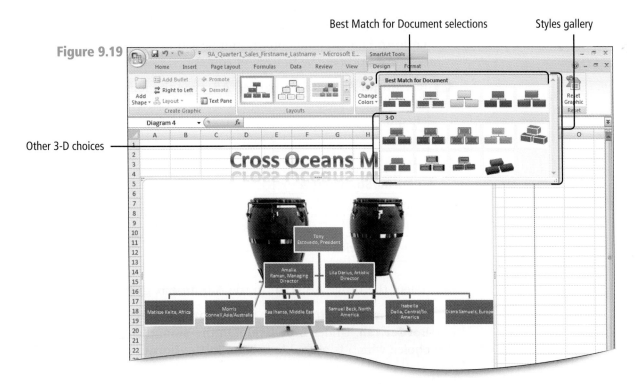

Other 3-D choices

4 Point to different options in the gallery to view the Live Preview. Then under **Best Match for Document**, click in the last choice—**Intense Effect**.

5 Save 💾 your workbook.

Objective 3
Create, Edit, and Publish a Web Page

A **Web page** is a document that displays as a screen that may contain links, frames, pictures, and other features and is uploaded to the World Wide Web—or simply the Web. Documents that are written for the Web are saved in a format used for the Web, called **html—Hypertext Markup Language**. Excel workbooks can be saved in the html format and saved as a Web page.

Activity 9.8 Preparing a Web Page

Cross Oceans Music is creating a Web page to display the regions and the regional directors. Each region will link to information about that region. In this activity, you will create the Web page for Cross Oceans Music.

1 Click the **Sheet3 sheet tab** and rename it **Home Page** Click the **Quarter 1 Sales sheet tab** and select the WordArt title so solid lines display around it. Recall that when solid borders surround the WordArt, it is selected. Then press Ctrl+C to select a Copy command.

2 Click the **Home Page sheet tab**, and click cell **A1**. On the **Home tab**, in the **Clipboard group**, click the **Paste button arrow**, and then click **Paste Special**.

3 In the **Paste Special** dialog box, confirm that **Picture (PNG)** is selected, and then click **OK**. Click the right middle sizing handle and drag to the right so that the WordArt stretches to the right edge of **column H**. Click the bottom middle sizing handle and drag up so the WordArt ends at the bottom of **row 6**.

4 In **column A**, beginning in cell **A8**, type the following data:

Region
Africa
Asia
Central/So. America
Europe
Middle East
North America

5 Select the range **A8:D14**. In the **Alignment group**, click the **Dialog Box Launcher** button 🔲. In the **Format Cells** dialog box, click the **Border tab**. Under **Line Style**, in the second column, click the last choice which is a double border. In the **Border** area, click the vertical border at both the left and right sides. Compare your screen with Figure 9.20, and then click **OK**.

Figure 9.20

Format Cells dialog box

Border tab

Right edge of cells

Double border

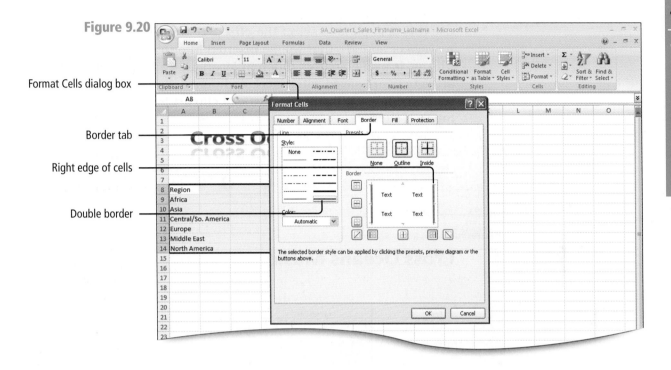

6 Select the range **H8:H14** and using the skills you practiced, place a double-right border at the right side of the range.

7 Beginning in cell **E8**, type the following data

Regional Director
Matisse Keita
Morris Connell
Isabella Delia
Diana Samuels
Raa Ihansa
Samuel Beck

8 Select the range **A8:D8** and in the **Alignment group**, click the **Merge & Center** button and insert a **Thick Bottom border**. Click the **Format Painter** button , and then click cell **E8**.

9 **Save** your workbook.

Activity 9.9 Inserting and Formatting Graphic Elements into a Web Page

Web pages are often advertisements for the firm. Adding graphic elements to provide an attractive Web page enhances the firm's image with customers. Data within the Web page can be formatted and edited, and graphics, pictures, and other shapes can be inserted. In this activity, you will insert and format graphic elements in the Web page.

1 Click in cell **A18**, and on the **Insert tab**, in the **Illustrations group**, click the **Clip Art** button, and then compare your screen with Figure 9.21.

The **Clip Art task pane** displays on the right of the screen. You can use this task pane to select the **clip art**—drawings, photographs, movies, or sound—that will be inserted into the Excel worksheet. Clip art is available from different locations—a limited number of clip art figures are saved with Excel, additional clip art can be saved to your computer, or you can download clip art from Microsoft or other Internet sites.

Figure 9.21

Clip Art button

Clip Art task pane

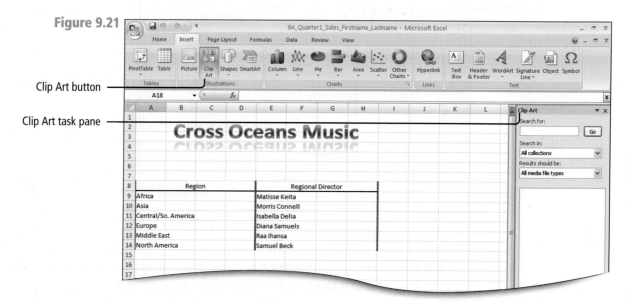

2 In the Clip Art task pane, under **Search for**, type **music** and then click **Go**. Several clip art figures display in the task pane. Locate the clip art image named *Music*—it contains musical notes, as shown in Figure 9.22. Point to the music image to read the ScreenTip—which contains the name of the clip art—and when the arrow displays, click the **Clip Art arrow**, and then compare your screen with Figure 9.22.

Each clip art is named; the name and other technical information about the clip art displays in the ScreenTip. When the pointer rests on the clip art, a border with an arrow displays at the right side of the clip art.

Figure 9.22

Clip Art task pane

Clip Art arrow

Music clip art

Menu displays for clip art icon

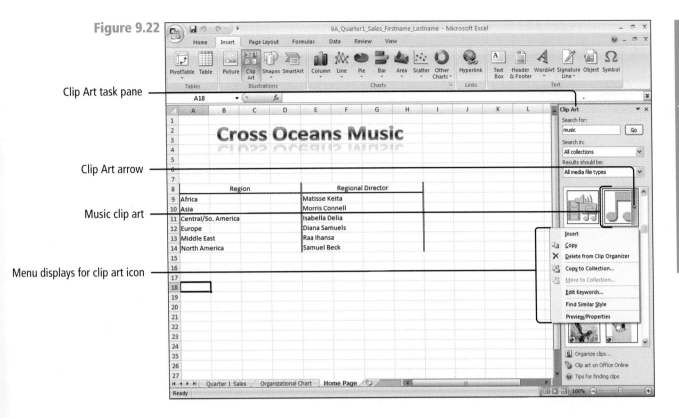

3 In the list, click **Insert**. Alternatively, click in the selected clip art to insert it into the worksheet. Then compare your screen with Figure 9.23.

The graphic image is inserted into the Web page. The sizing handles and the rotation handle display. Recall that the rotation handle is the green circle at the top of the selected image. This handle is used to change the rotation—orientation—of the image. In the task pane, the selected image displays with a border surrounding it.

Figure 9.23

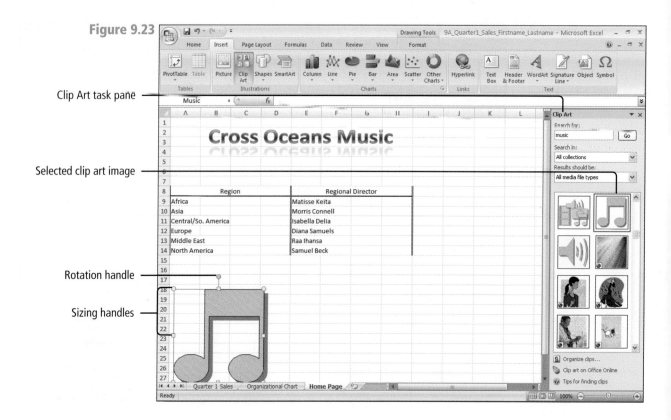

Clip Art task pane

Selected clip art image

Rotation handle

Sizing handles

4 Click in the active clip art image and drag the image until it is centered under the text in the Web page with three blank rows above the image. In the Clip Art window, click the **Close** button ☒.

5 Point to the **rotation handle** and when the ⟳ shape displays, click the mouse. The shape now displays ⟲ as the button becomes active. Click the rotation handle and move the mouse to the left until the image displays at about a **45-degree angle**. Then release the mouse and compare your screen with Figure 9.24.

Figure 9.24

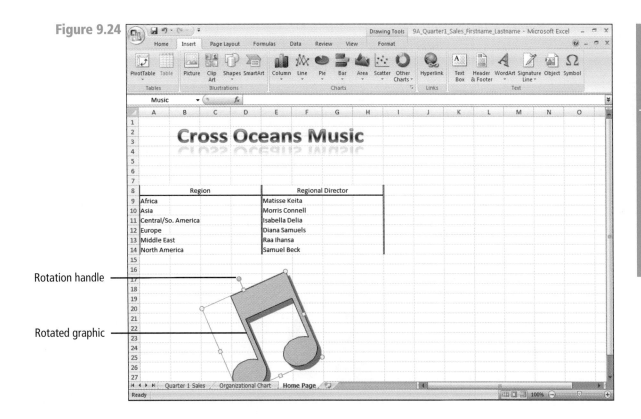

Rotation handle

Rotated graphic

6 Click in the worksheet to deselect the clip art. Click the **Insert tab** and in the **Text group**, click **WordArt**. In the WordArt gallery, in the second column, click the last choice—**Fill - Accent 6, Warm Matte Bevel**.

7 In the selected WordArt, type **Representing the World** Triple-click in the text to select it; then right-click and select a **24 point resize font size**.

8 Move the graphic to the upper left corner of cell **B5**, and so that the right border ends at the gridline line between **columns G and H**. Adjust the size so the graphic is centered in the worksheet covering **rows 5:7**. Decrease the width of **column I** to **0.50 points**. Compare your screen with Figure 9.25.

Figure 9.25

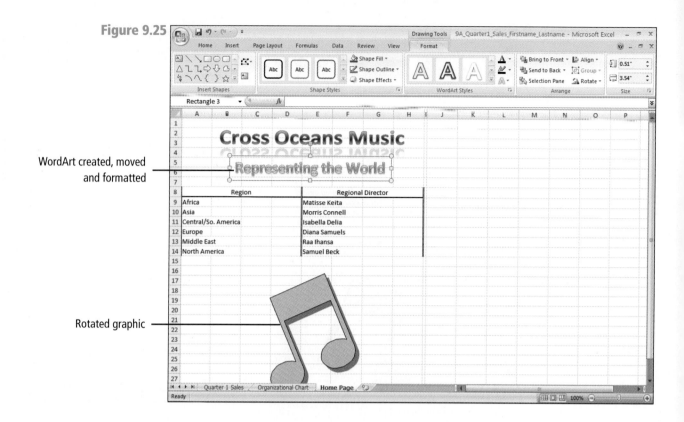

WordArt created, moved and formatted

Rotated graphic

9 On the **Page Layout tab**, in the **Page Setup group**, click the **Dialog Box Launcher** [icon], and in the **Margins tab**, under **Center on page**, click **Horizontally** and **Vertically**. Then click **Print Preview**.

10 Click the **Close Print Preview** button. In cell **A35**, type **Created by Firstname Lastname** replacing *Firstname* and *Lastname* with your own name. **Save** [icon] your workbook.

More Knowledge

Clip Art

Clip art is saved in a separate file on your computer. When clip art is used on your computer, it is placed in the clip art organizer and becomes available each time you insert clip art. The clip art available will vary from one computer to another. In order to ensure that the figures used in this chapter are the correct ones, pictures rather than clip art will be used.

Activity 9.10 Insert Hyperlinks into a Web Page

As you search the Web, you move from page to page with the *hyperlinks* that are inserted in Web pages. Recall that a hyperlink is text or a graphic that you click to go to another location in a worksheet. A hyperlink is also used to take you to another Web page. In this activity, you will insert hyperlinks from the type of music to information about that region.

1 In the **9A_Quarter1_Sales_Firstname_Lastname** worksheet, click the **Home Page sheet tab**.

2 Click cell **A9**. Click the **Insert tab**, in the **Links group**, click the **Hyperlink** button. In the **Insert Hyperlink** dialog box, in the **Link to** area, confirm that *Existing File or Web Page* is selected. In the **Text to display** box, confirm that *Africa* displays. In the Address box, type **http://music.calabashmusic.com/world/africa/** Compare your screen with Figure 9.26, and then click **OK**.

It is possible to link text in a Web page to any address on the Internet. It is important, however, to have the permission of the author of the linked page before linking his or her Web site. It is also important to check the links occasionally to make sure that they are still operative.

The *Text to display* is the text that resides in the cell that contains the link. The text can be changed in the cell or in this text area. In the Insert Hyperlink dialog box, use the ScreenTip button to insert a ScreenTip that further describes the link. Recall that when you inserted a hyperlink to another worksheet, you created a ScreenTip that displayed in the worksheet when the cell is selected.

Figure 9.26

ScreenTip
Link to area
Existing File or Web Page
Address typed

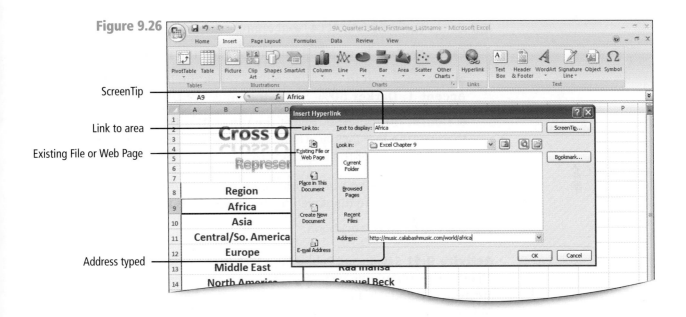

3 Click the link in cell **A9** to confirm that it works.

Your Web browser opens and the Calabash Music Web site displays. When the hyperlink is inserted, the font size reduces to the default size.

Alert!

When you click the hyperlink, do you get an error message?

Web sites change frequently. When you include Web sites in written material, it is important to check frequently that the hyperlinks are still accurate. In a printed textbook such as this, it is not possible to update Web site information. If you do not get an active Web site, hyperlink each of these regions to your school's Web address. Alternatively, search the Web for each of these regions and insert a hyperlink of your choice.

4 Using the skills you have practiced, in cells **A10:A14**, insert hyperlinks to the following web addresses:

Region	URL to Insert
Asia	http://music.calabashmusic.com/world/asia
Central/So. America	http://music.calabashmusic.com/world/south_america
Europe	http://music.calabashmusic.com/world/europe
Middle East	http://music.calabashmusic.com/world/middle_east
North America	http://music.calabashmusic.com/world/north_america

To move between Web pages, each site has a Web address, called the **URL—Uniform Resource Locator**. You can access the Web site either by typing the URL in the text area of your browser or by clicking on a hyperlink to the Web site.

5 Select the range **A8:H14**, and change the **font size** to **18 points**. Click the **Bold** button **B**, and then click the **Font Color button arrow** **A ·** and in the fifth column, click the last item—**Blue, Accent 1, Darker 50%**. Select the range **A9:D9** and click the **Merge & Center** button **⊞ ·**. Select the range **A10:D10** and press [Ctrl]+[Y] to apply the last format. Using the skills you practiced, apply the format to the rest of the regions through row 14.

6 Using the skills you have practiced, merge and center the regional directors that are displayed in the range **E9:H14**.

7 **Save** **🖫** your workbook.

Activity 9.11 Saving and Publishing a Web Page

When saving a multiple-page workbook as a Web page, all of the worksheets are available and can be accessed. You can also save a single worksheet as a Web page. In this activity, you will save a worksheet as a Web page.

1 Right-click the **Home Page sheet tab** and click **Move or Copy**. In the **Move or Copy** dialog box, under **To book**, click the arrow, and then click **(new book)**. Click **OK**.

You have moved the worksheet from the 9A_Quarter1_Sales_Firstname_Lastname workbook into a new workbook.

2 In cell **A32**, type **9A_Web_Firstname_Lastname** and format with **Bold**. Click cell **A1**. From the **Office Menu**, click **Save As**. In the **Save As** dialog box, navigate to the **Excel Chapter 9** folder. Then click the **Save as type arrow** and select **Single File Web Page**. Compare your screen with Figure 9.27.

The file type has changed to **Single File Web Page** and additional options display in the Save As dialog box, such as Page Title, Change Title button, Entire Workbook, Selection: Sheet, and Publish. When Single File Web Page is selected, only the sheet will be saved as a web page.

Figure 9.27

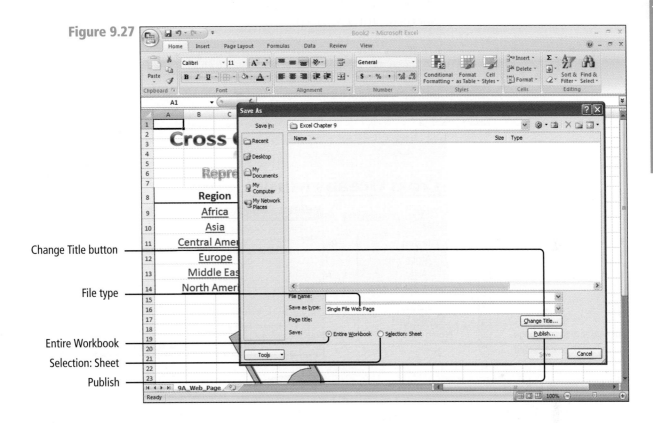

Change Title button

File type

Entire Workbook

Selection: Sheet

Publish

3 At the bottom of the dialog box, in the **Save** section, click the **Selection: Sheet** option button.

When you publish an Excel workbook, you can publish either the entire workbook, which includes the tabbed worksheets, or the selected sheet. You have selected to save only the Home Page worksheet as a Web page.

Alert!

Why isn't *Selection: Sheet* a choice?

The first time you publish the Web page, *Selection: Sheet* displays. If you have already published the worksheet—or made an error and started again—the Save section will read *Republish: Sheet*. Be sure this is the button you select.

4 Click the **Publish** button. The **Publish as Web Page** dialog box displays. In the **File Name** box, delete the text and type **9A_Web_ Firstname_Lastname** Click the **Open published web page in browser** check box to select it, compare your screen with Figure 9.28, and click the **Publish** button.

Under Items to Publish, you can select to publish the entire workbook, entire worksheet, specific items, a range of cells, or only a chart, for a few examples. Use the Title button to insert a title into the Web page if one does not already exist in the Excel worksheet.

The Web page you created opens in the default browser, usually Microsoft Internet Explorer.

Figure 9.28

Publish as Web Page dialog box

Open published web page in browser check box selected

Publish button

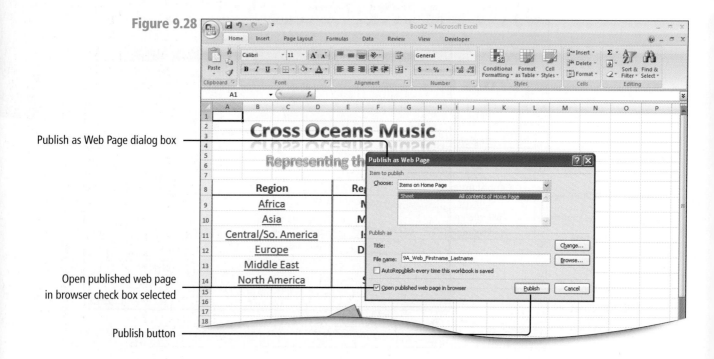

5 **Close** the browser. Display the **9A_Quarter1_Sales_Firstname_ Lastname** workbook, click in the **Quarter 1 Sales sheet tab**, and click **Save** .

6 From the **Start** menu, click **Internet Explorer** or your Internet browser. Near the top, in the **Menu bar**, click **File**, and then click **Open**. In the **Open** dialog box, click the **Browse** button. Navigate to your **Excel Chapter 9** folder, and locate and click the Web page file **9A_Web_Firstname_Lastname**. Click **Open**, and then click **OK** and compare your screen with Figure 9.29.

Figure 9.29

Microsoft Internet Explorer title bar

File command

Menu bar

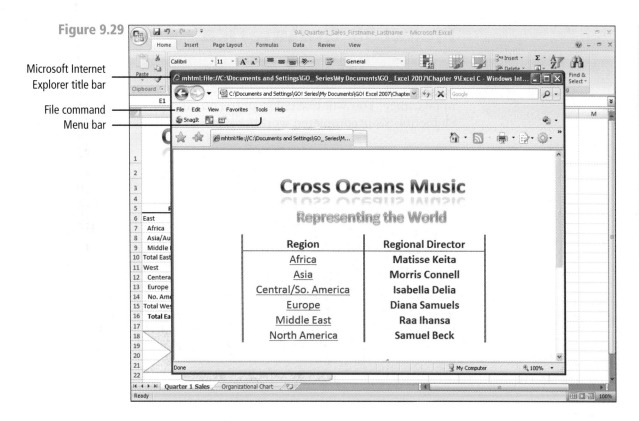

7 In the Web page, click on the hyperlinks to navigate through the World Wide Web. Then close Internet Explorer or your browser.

8 Display the **9A_Quarter1_Sales_Firstname_Lastname** workbook, and then select both worksheets. In the **Left Footer** area, insert the **File Name**, and in the **Right Footer** area, insert the **Sheet Name**

9 Ungroup the worksheets and click the **Organization Chart sheet tab**. In the **Page Setup group**, center the worksheet **Horizontally** and **Vertically**. Then click the **Quarter 1 Sales sheet tab** and center the worksheet both **Horizontally** and **Vertically**. Use **Print Preview** to confirm placement of the worksheet, and then **Save** your workbook.

Alert! **Why isn't my worksheet centered?**

If your graphic image displays into the next column, Excel uses that column width to center the worksheet. Also, if the graphic element displays slightly to the left of the column A gridline, the worksheet also will not center. Be sure that the entire graphic image is within the gridlines of the suggested range. You will want the entire sizing handles to be visible.

10 To submit the workbooks electronically, follow the instructions provided by your instructor. To print, from the **Office** menu, click **Print**. In the **Print** dialog box, under **Print what**, select **Entire workbook**, and then click **OK**. From the **Office** menu, click **Close**. **Exit** Excel.

End You have completed Project 9A

Project 9B SoAmerica

In Activities 9.12 through 9.22, you will create line, area, scatter, and stock charts and use the formatting feature of Excel to enhance their appearance. You will use color, patterns, and pictures to format the chart elements. Your completed workbook will look similar to Figure 9.30.

For Project 9B, you will need the following files:

e09B_SoAmerica
e09B_Bongo Drums
e09B_Maracas
e09B_Blue_Banjo
e09B_Tambourine
e09B_Ocean

You will save your workbook as
9B_SoAmerica_Firstname_Lastname

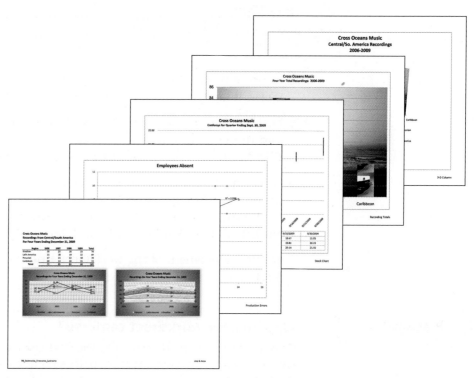

Figure 9.30
Project 9B—SoAmerica

Objective 4
Create Specialized Charts

There are different types of charts available in Excel which are useful when specific types of data need to be displayed in a precise manner. For instance, if you would like to see a pattern in a large amount of data and determine a trend, you would use the scatter chart, which is designed for this type of data. Perhaps you would like to evaluate the stock prices of an investment for a period of time to review the high price, low price, and closing price for the stock. These and other charts, designed for a specific purpose, will be created and formatted with design elements that include texture, pictures, clip art, and gradients.

Each chart is designed to display a specific type of data and you will want to know the purpose of each chart type in order to best display the data. The table in Figure 9.31 displays the primary charts Excel creates and the type of data best displayed in the chart.

Type of chart	Purpose
Column chart	Shows data changes over a period of time or illustrates comparisons among items.
Bar chart	Illustrates comparisons among individual items.
Line chart	Illustrates continuous data over time—ideal for showing trends in data.
Pie chart	Shows the size of items in one data series proportional to the total. It always shows only one data series.
Scatter chart	A scatter chart—also called the XY chart—shows the relationships among numeric values in several data series. It is commonly used for scientific data.
Area chart	Emphasizes the magnitude of change over time and can be used to emphasize the total value across a trend.
Stock chart	Used to display stock price data.

Figure 9.31

Activity 9.12 Inserting a Line Chart

A *line chart* displays data over time and is used to show trends over equal intervals of time. The line chart can be created to display the data in relation to other data or in a manner that also displays the totals. President Tony Escovedo and Artistic Director Lila Darius are reviewing the recordings over the last four years in the Central/South America region. They would like to compare the recordings completed in each region in order to make recommendations about where scouting activity should take place. In this activity, you will create line charts that display the number of recordings made in the regions of Central and South America.

1 **Start** Excel. From your student files, locate and open the file named **e09B_SoAmerica**. **Save** the file in the **Excel Chapter 9** folder as **9B_SoAmerica_Firstname_Lastname**

This worksheet reports the recordings that were made in the Central and South America region for the past four years.

2 Click cell **D7** and on the **Insert tab**, in the **Charts group**, click the **Line** button. Then compare your screen with Figure 9.32.

The Line Chart gallery displays two types of line charts—2-D and 3-D.

Figure 9.32

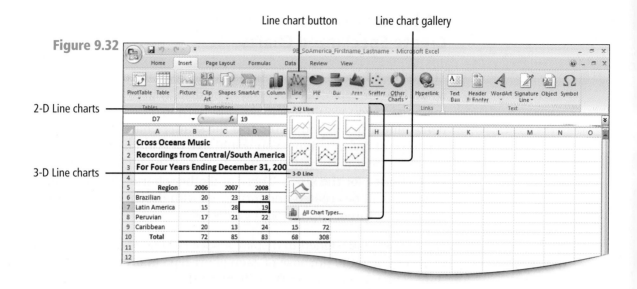

Line chart button   Line chart gallery

2-D Line charts

3-D Line charts

3 Under **2-D**, in the second row, click the first chart—**Line with Markers**. Click in the border of the chart and move it so the upper left corner displays in cell **A12**, and compare your screen with Figure 9.33.

When one cell is selected, Excel automatically plots into a chart all cells containing data that directly surround that selected cell. Because your chart should display the comparison of the sales in each region for each year, totals should not display.

In this chart, charting the totals causes the individual regions to be bunched together so it's difficult to compare the recordings completed for each region. The chart is designed to compare the regions, which is not possible in this chart when the totals are included.

Selected chart range—incorrectly
includes totals

Figure 9.33

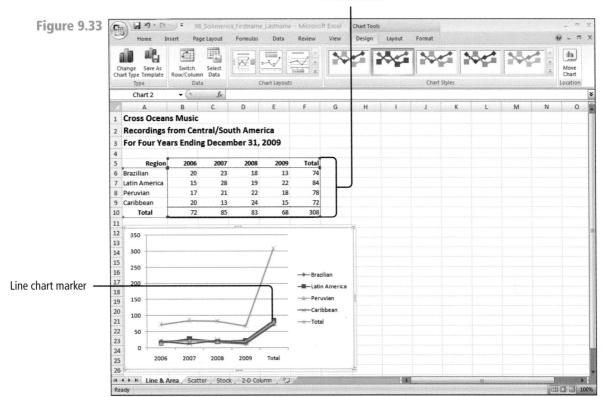

Line chart marker

4 With the chart active, point to the lower right corner of the source data—cell **F10**. When the ↖ pointer displays, drag up to the lower right corner of cell **E9**, and then compare your screen with Figure 9.34. Then point to different areas of the chart and notice that a ScreenTip identifies the parts of the chart.

The totals now do not display in the chart and it is easy to compare the sales between the regions. Recall that when you chart data, you either chart the totals or you chart the details, but you do not compare both in the same chart.

The chart displays in the *plot area* of the chart, which is the area that includes all of the data series. The areas charted are identified in the worksheet by the colored borders. The blue border surrounds the source data—which includes the data without the totals. The green border surrounds the *series names*—the labels for the categories that display in the legend. Recall that the *legend* is a box that identifies the patterns or colors that are assigned to the *data series* in the chart. The value for each data series displays in the *vertical (value) axis*. The purple border surrounds the *horizontal (category) axis*—in this case the years—displayed along the bottom of the chart.

Figure 9.34

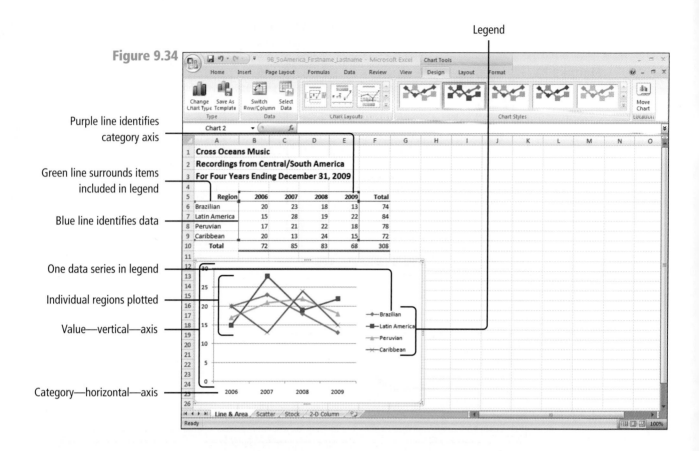

Legend

Purple line identifies category axis

Green line surrounds items included in legend

Blue line identifies data

One data series in legend

Individual regions plotted

Value—vertical—axis

Category—horizontal—axis

Another Way

Selecting Chart Data

Recall that earlier you selected the chart data by dragging through the range of the data that will be included in the chart. As you work with Excel, you will discover that you prefer one method over another when selecting a chart range. Using either of these methods to select the chart range will produce an identical chart.

5 Click the **Chart Tools Design tab** and in the **Chart Layouts group**, click the **More** button. From the displayed gallery, in the third row, click the last choice—**Layout 9**. Then compare your screen with Figure 9.35.

This layout includes a chart title. The series ***data labels***—the numbers displayed by the data markers in the chart—provide information about the data to more easily identify the value of each data marker. Recall that a ***data marker*** is the shape on the chart that represents a value. In the Line Chart, each data marker is a different shape—diamond for Brazilian, square for Latin America, triangle for Peruvian, and X for Caribbean. A value is also called a ***data point***.

Figure 9.35

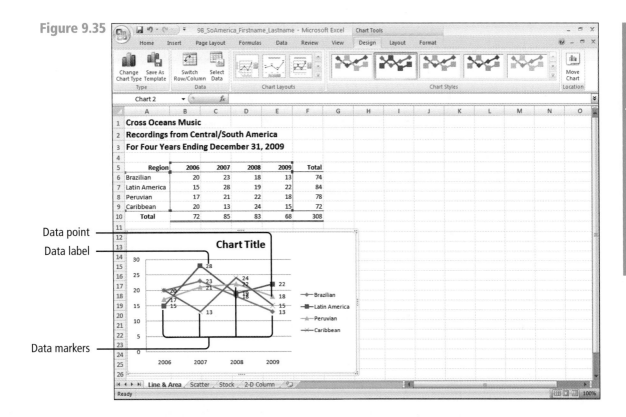

Data point

Data label

Data markers

6 Click the **Layout tab** and in the **Labels group**, click the **Data Labels** button, and then compare your screen with Figure 9.36.

The placement of the data labels within the chart can be prescribed in this gallery. Each placement includes an explanation of the location for the data labels.

Figure 9.36

Data Labels button   Data Labels menu

Placement of Data Label and description

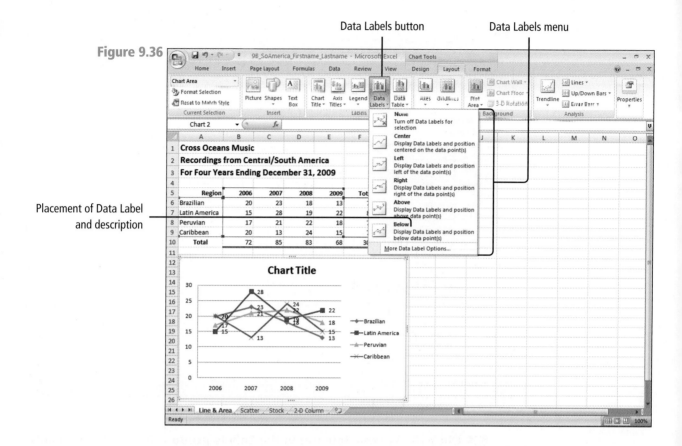

7 Click **Left** and as you do, notice that the data labels now display to the left of the data marker.

8 In the **Axes group**, click the **Gridlines** button. The list displays *Primary Horizontal Gridlines* and *Primary Vertical Gridlines*. Point to **Primary Horizontal Gridlines** to display the submenu, and then compare your screen with Figure 9.37.

Recall that **gridlines** are horizontal or vertical lines that extend across the chart. The **major gridlines** display gridlines for the major units and the **minor gridlines** display the minor units.

Figure 9.37

Gridlines button

Primary Horizontal
Gridlines gallery

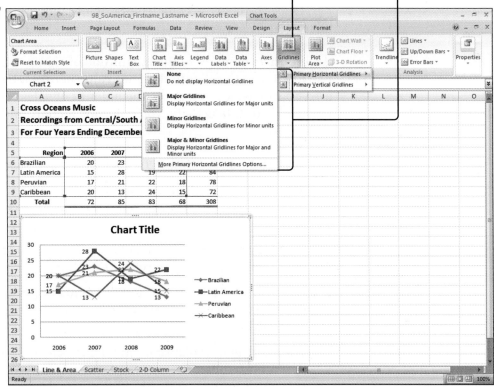

9 Click **Major & Minor Gridlines**.

The major gridlines are displayed in a bold line at the category numbers 5, 10, 15, and so on. The lighter gridlines displayed between the major gridlines are the minor gridlines.

10 Triple-click the **Chart Title** to select the text, and then type **Cross Oceans Music** Press [Enter] and type **Recordings for Four Years Ending December 31, 2009** With the title selected, right-click and in the shortcut menu, select a font size of **12 point**. Click the **Legend** to select it. Click the **Layout tab**, and in the **Labels group**, click the **Legend** button, and then click **Show Legend at Bottom**.

When you select the Legend button, the legend gallery displays an icon with the placement of the legend and a description for each placement of the legend.

11 Save 💾 your workbook.

More Knowledge
Vertical Gridlines

Vertical gridlines display in a chart vertically between the data markers and include both major gridlines and minor gridlines. With a line chart that contains many data markers, using vertical gridlines assists in reading the chart.

Activity 9.13 Copy a Chart and Change Chart Type to Area Chart

Tony and Lila would like to look at the same data but in a different manner. Once the chart is completed, it is not difficult to change the type of chart that displays.

Area charts emphasize the magnitude of change over time and can be used to draw attention to the total value across a trend. Using a stacked area chart visually compares the amount of sales for each of the past four years. In this activity, you will copy a chart and then change it to an area chart.

1 With the chart active, right-click and click **Copy**. To the right of the sheet tabs, click the **New Sheet** button and in the newly inserted sheet, right-click cell **A1** and click **Paste**.

You have copied the chart to a new sheet. The chart is linked to the original worksheet; when a change is made in the worksheet, the chart will be updated to reflect the change.

2 Click the **Design tab** and in the **Location group**, click **Move Chart**. Click **New Sheet** and without changing the name of the sheet, click **OK**.

The chart is now displayed in a chart sheet, named Chart1. Recall that a *chart sheet* is a worksheet that displays a chart on a separate sheet in the workbook. Sheet1 now has nothing displayed in it after you moved the chart to a chart sheet.

3 Click the **Design tab**, and in the **Type group**, click the **Change Chart Type** button. In the **Change Chart Type** dialog box, at the left, click **Area**. On the right, under **Area**, click the second choice—**Stacked Area**. Click **OK**, and then compare your screen with Figure 9.38.

Changing the chart type displays the data in a different manner. In the Stacked Area chart, the color of each data marker displays the sales for one region. A *stacked chart* places the data from each region one on top of the other. In this chart, the data for Latin America is stacked on top of Brazilian, and so on. The chart now displays that the total recordings for 2006 are nearly 70, determined by reviewing the minor gridlines that display.

A stacked chart such as this displays the relationship of the recordings for each region in proportion to the total recordings.

Figure 9.38

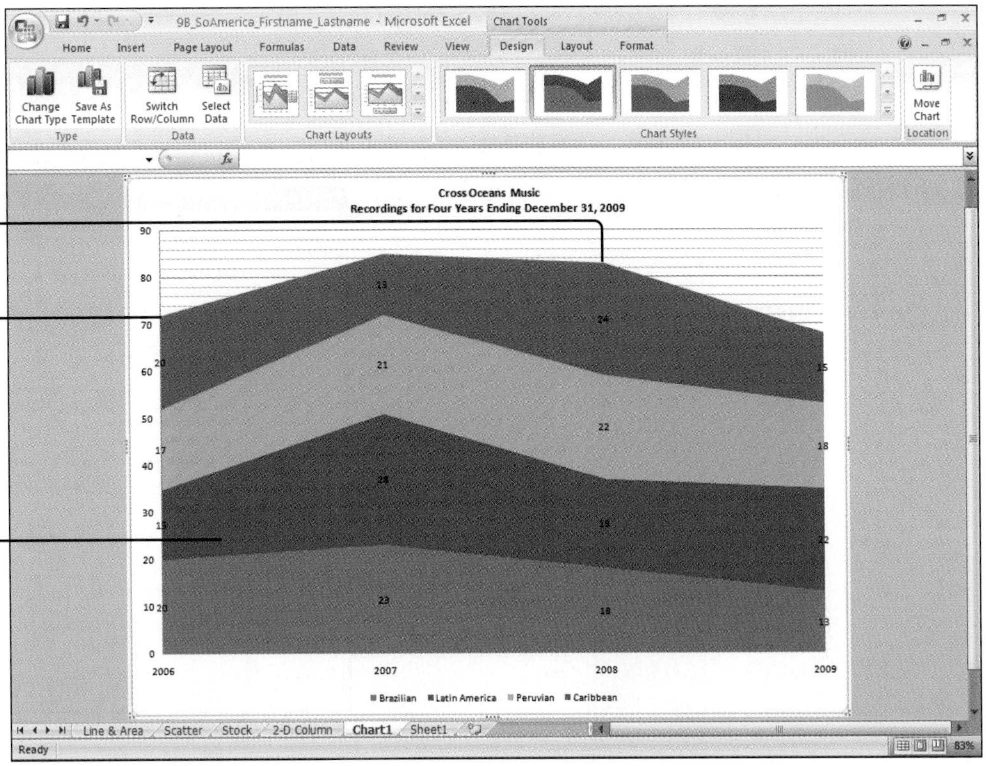

Total recordings for 2008

Total recordings for 2006

Charted data for Latin America

4 **Save** 💾 your workbook.

Activity 9.14 Format Data Series and Chart Area

Each portion of the chart can be independently formatted—the data markers, the chart area, the legend, and so on. The ***chart area*** is the entire chart and all of its elements. In this activity, you will format the data markers and the chart area and add a glowing border to the chart.

1 On the **Design tab**, in the **Chart Styles group**, click the **More**

button 🔽. From the displayed Chart Styles gallery, in the sixth column, click the fourth choice—**Style 30**.

2 Select the first line of the chart title, right-click, and format it with **14-point font**. Format the second line with **12-point font**. Confirm the title is centered over the chart.

3 In the chart, position the pointer in the bottom data series—the ScreenTip displays *Series "Brazilian"* Right-click and in the shortcut menu, click **Format Data Series**. In the **Format Data Series** dialog box, on the left side, click **Fill**. On the right side, click **Picture or texture fill**, and compare your screen with Figure 9.39.

The dark purple data marker in the chart now displays a different picture, color, or texture. When selected to use picture or texture fill, Excel will first insert the last choice made, so your data marker may display a different texture or picture than the one displayed in the figure. Recall there are several formatting choices available in the Format Data Series dialog box. Selecting *Picture or texture fill* is used to insert clip art, a picture, or texture as a data marker.

Figure 9.39

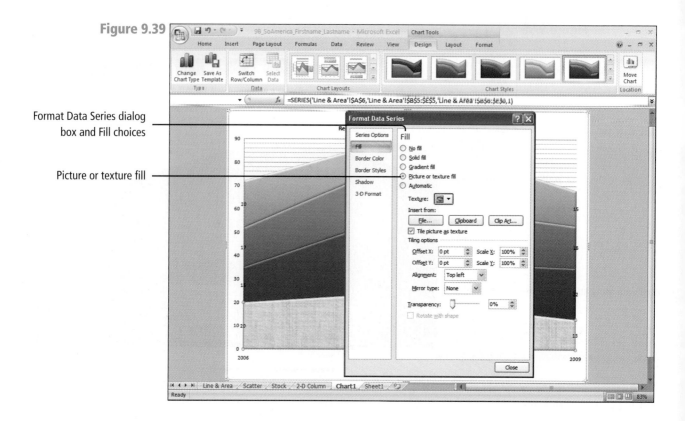

Format Data Series dialog box and Fill choices

Picture or texture fill

4 In the **Format Data Series** dialog box, click the **Texture** button.

The Texture gallery displays textures available. A texture can be inserted in the chart as a data marker or as fill for other chart areas, such as the chart area or the background.

5 In the first row, click the third choice—**Denim**—and then compare your screen with Figure 9.40.

The denim texture replaces the dark purple color in the data series. The color icon in the legend is also changed to match denim. The Format Data Series dialog box remains displayed on the screen so other format choices can be made before closing it.

Figure 9.40

Fill command on Format Data
Series dialog box

Texture button

Denim texture added
to data marker

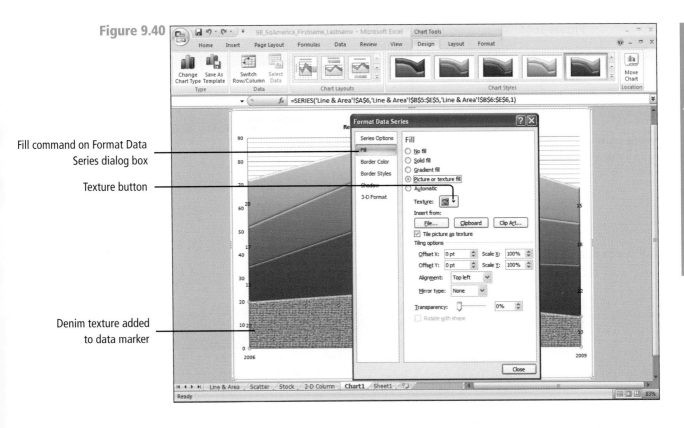

6 With the **Format Data Series** dialog box displayed, in the chart click in the next data series—Latin America. In the **Format Data Series** dialog box, on the left side, click **Fill** and on the right, click **Picture or texture fill**. Click the **Texture** button and from the gallery that displays, in the third column, click the fourth choice—**Pink tissue paper**.

After the Format Data Series dialog box is displayed, several formatting choices can be made before closing the dialog box.

7 Using the skills you have practiced, format the **Peruvian** data series to **Stationery** texture, and the **Caribbean** series with **Water droplets**. **Close** the dialog box, and then compare your screen with Figure 9.41.

Each data marker is formatted with a different texture. The data range displays in the Formula Bar, indicating the source data is in the worksheet named Line & Area.

Figure 9.41

Data source

Selected data range—identified by active handles

Texture used for data markers

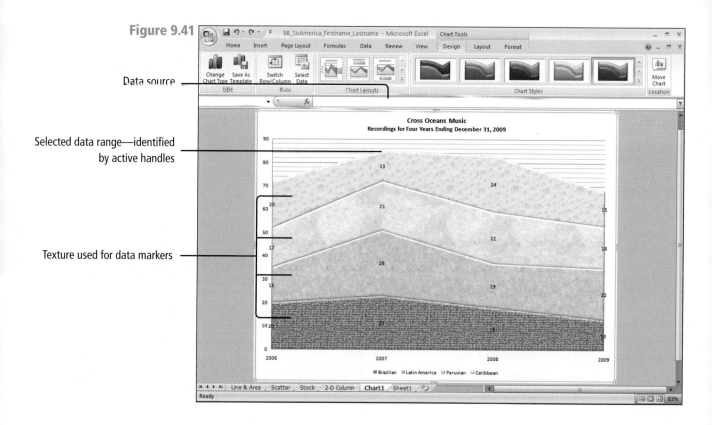

8 In the **Chart**, point to the right of the title until the ScreenTip displays *Chart Area*—it may take a few seconds for the ScreenTip to display. Right-click and click **Format Chart Area**. In the **Format Chart Area** dialog box, on the right side under **Fill**, click **Gradient fill**.

The entire background area of the chart has been filled with the last fill that was selected.

9 Click the **Preset colors** button, and from the gallery, in the second row, click the second choice—**Ocean**. Then click **Close**.

10 In the **Location group**, click the **Move Chart** button. In the **Move Chart** dialog box, click **Object in** and confirm that *Line & Area* displays in the text box. Then click **OK**.

The area chart has been moved from a chart sheet to an embedded chart within the Line & Area sheet. The Chart1 sheet has been deleted from the workbook.

11 Click in the chart border, and when the pointer takes the 🕂 shape, drag the chart so the upper left corner is in cell **I12**.

12 Click in the **Line Chart**, and then point to the right of the title until the ScreenTip displays *Chart Area*, and then right-click and click **Format Chart Area**. In the **Format Chart Area** dialog box, on the right side under **Fill**, click **Gradient fill**. Then click **Close**.

The Ocean gradient fill now displays in the Line Chart and both charts are formatted in a similar manner. Using the same background for both charts provides a consistent style in the charts.

13 With the **Area Chart** active, click the **Format tab**, in the **Shape Styles group**, click the **Shape Fill** button. From the list, point to

Gradient, and then move the pointer the Gradient gallery to view the styles using Live Preview. Under **Variations** in the second row, click the second choice—**From Center**. Click in the **Line & Area sheet tab** and press Ctrl + Y.

The same gradient is applied to the line chart as was applied to the area chart. Recall that Ctrl + Y repeats the last command.

14 With the **Line Chart** active, in the **Shape Styles group**, click the **Shape Effects** button, point to **Glow**, and then in the displayed Glow gallery, move the pointer over the shapes to view the Live Preview effects. In the fifth column, click the last effect—**Accent color 5, 18 pt glow**. The glow effect surrounds the chart. Click the Area Chart to make it active and press Ctrl + Y to repeat the format command, and then compare your screen with Figure 9.42.

Figure 9.42

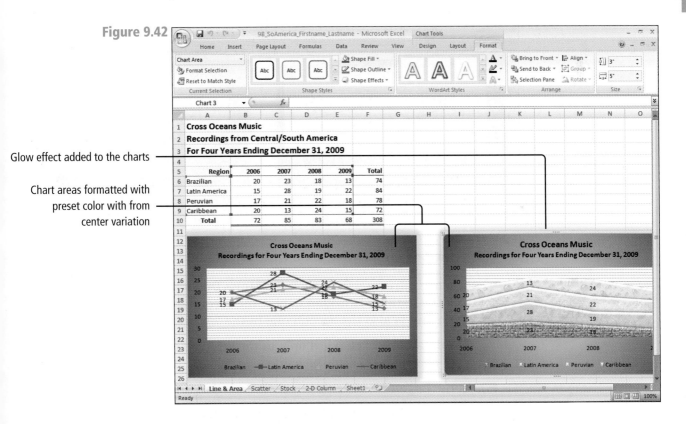

Glow effect added to the charts

Chart areas formatted with preset color with from center variation

15 **Save** your workbook.

Activity 9.15 Rearrange Data Markers

The order that the data markers display in the chart is the same as in the worksheet. In a chart, the order of the data can be rearranged in the Select Data Source dialog box. In this activity, you will rearrange the order of the data markers.

1 With the **Area chart** active, click the **Design tab**, and in the **Data group**, click the **Select Data** button, and then compare your screen with Figure 9.43.

The Select Data Source dialog box displays. In this dialog box you can add, edit, or delete data series and arrange them in different orders. The left side displays the *Legend Entries (Series)* and the right side displays the *Horizontal (Category) Axis Labels*. The entries of the chart display in the window.

Figure 9.43

Select Data Source dialog box

Horizontal Axis Labels area

Legend Entries area

Add button

Edit button

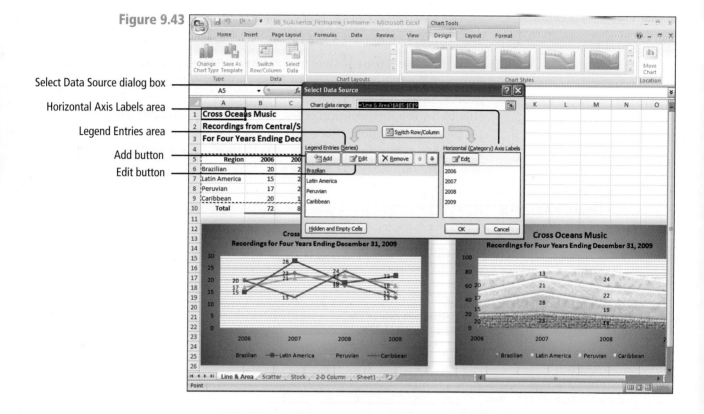

2 In the **Legend Entries** area, click **Brazilian**. At the top right of the Legend Entries section, click the **Move Down** button ⬇ and notice that the data for Brazilian is now the second from the bottom of the chart and is also the second one in the legend.

The data marker changes only in the selected chart, even though both charts have used the same source data.

3 In the **Legend Entries** area, click **Peruvian** and click the **Move Up** button ⬆. Using the skills you practiced, arrange the data markers in the following order from left to right: Peruvian, Latin America, Brazilian, and Caribbean. Then compare your screen with Figure 9.44.

The data markers have been rearranged in the chart using the Select Data Source dialog box.

Figure 9.44

Corrected Legend Entries of Select Data Source dialog box

Chart with data markers rearranged

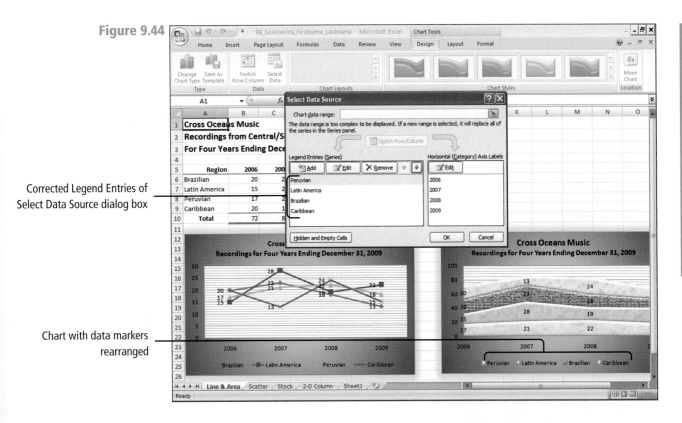

4 In the Select Data Source dialog box, click **OK** and then **Save** 🖫 your workbook.

More Knowledge

Print an Embedded Chart

An embedded chart displays on the same sheet with the worksheet. To print only the chart, select it. Access the Print menu, and in the Print dialog box, under Print what, confirm that Selected Chart is selected. Then click OK and only the chart prints on the page. It enlarges to print on the entire page as if it were a separate chart sheet.

Activity 9.16 Inserting a Scatter Chart

Scatter charts are used for displaying and comparing numeric values, such as statistical data. Scatter charts display the relationship among the numeric values in several data series and plot two sets of numbers at the same time. This type of chart is often used when the data points are at uneven intervals or in clusters.

Music artists regularly record their music for a CD, which is then sold. The production group prepares and produces the CDs. Recently, June Huong, the production manager, noticed an increase in errors in the quality of the completed CD, both in the production and in the packaging. She is concerned that employee absences are contributing to the errors. June has created an Excel spreadsheet that lists the days of production with the number of absences and the number of errors for each day. In this activity, you will chart the errors and determine the relationship between the CD errors and employee absences.

1 Click the **Scatter sheet tab**. This worksheet records the CD errors and the number of employee absences for the past several months

2 Select the ranges that contain the errors and the number of employees absent—**B5:C120**. Click the **Insert tab**, and in the **Charts group**, click the **Scatter** button, and then compare your screen with Figure 9.45.

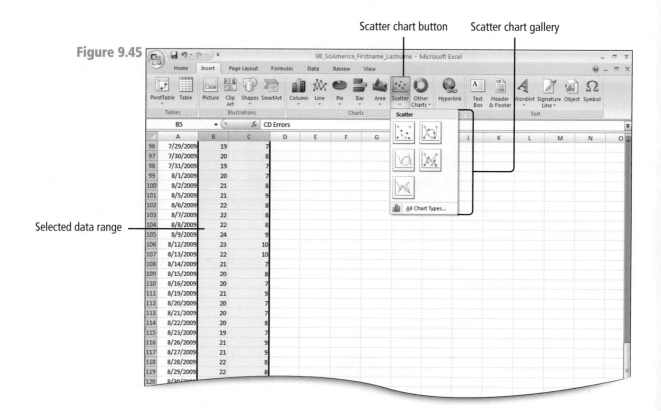

Figure 9.45

Scatter chart button

Scatter chart gallery

Selected data range

3 Click the first choice—**Scatter with only Markers**.

The Scatter chart is inserted into the workbook with *Employees Absent* displayed both as the legend and the title. The data markers indicate the relationship between the number of absences and the errors in CD production.

Each data marker in the chart represents one date in the worksheet. The number of employees absent displays on the vertical axis and the number of errors displays on the horizontal axis. This chart indicates that the more absences that occur, the more errors that are made.

4 In the chart, click in the **Legend**, press Delete, and **Save** your workbook.

Activity 9.17 Inserting a Trendline

A **trendline** is a graphic representation of the trends in a data series. Adding a trendline to a chart will display the trend for the displayed data. In this activity, you will insert a trendline in the scatter chart that will assist the production group in their analysis of the production errors.

1 With the scatter chart active, on the **Layout tab**, in the **Analysis group**, click the **Trendline** button, and then compare your screen with Figure 9.46.

The Trendline list displays with an icon displaying the type of trendlines available and an explanation of each trendline type.

Trendline button

Figure 9.46

Trendline list

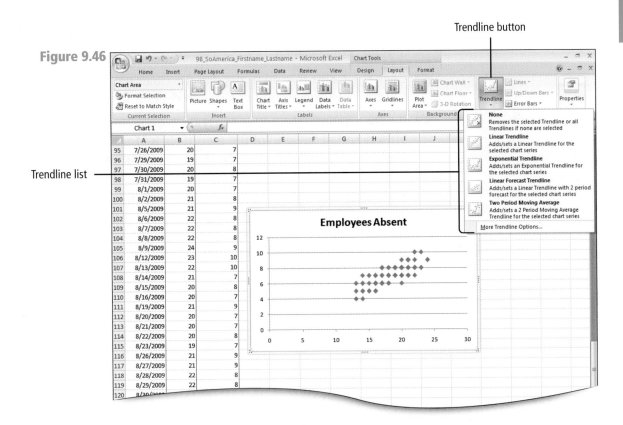

2 Click **Linear Trendline**. Then in the chart, point to the Trendline and when the ScreenTip identifies it as *Series "Employees Absent" Trendline 1*, right-click the Trendline and then in the shortcut menu, click **Format Trendline**.

The trendline has been inserted into the chart and displays an upward slope. This indicates that there is a correlation between the number of absences and the number of errors in CD production.

Is Format Trendline not available in the shortcut menu?

Each time you right-click, a portion of the chart becomes active. Because the trendline is displayed near the data markers and the chart area, a different portion of the chart may be selected. If the area of the chart does not display in the shortcut menu, click in the chart to deselect the area, move closer to the trendline, and click on it again. Alternatively, on the Layout tab, in the Current Selection group, click the Chart Elements button arrow, and from the list click Series "Employees Absent" Trendline1. Then click the Format Selection button.

3 In the **Format Trendline** dialog box, on the left, click **Line Color**, and then on the right, under **Line Color**, click **Solid line**.

The Line Color area expands to include information about the color and its transparency.

4 Click the **Color** button to display the Color gallery. Under **Standard Colors**, click the second choice—**Red**—and then click **Close**.

5 On the **Layout tab**, in the **Analysis group**, click the **Trendline** button and at the end of the menu, click **More Trendline Options**. At the bottom, click in the check box by **Display R-squared value on chart**. Click **Close** and then compare your screen with Figure 9.47.

The R-factor is a formula that is applied to the trendline. The closer the number is to 1 the higher the positive correlation between the numbers. The R-factor in this chart is 0.598, which indicates there is *some* correlation between the numbers but it is not a high correlation. This should indicate to management that the absences do impact the errors, but the correlation between the two is not a strong one.

Figure 9.47

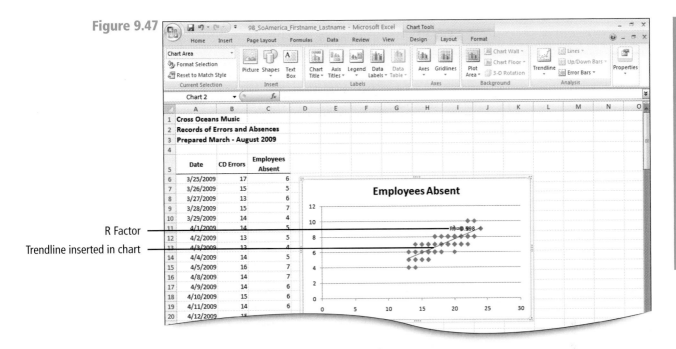

R Factor

Trendline inserted in chart

6 With the chart active, click the **Design tab** and in the **Location group**, click the **Move Chart** button. Move the chart to a new sheet and name the sheet **Production Errors** and click **OK**. Right-click the **Scatter sheet tab** and click **Hide**.

7 Save 💾 your workbook.

Activity 9.18 Inserting Axis Titles

Axis titles are placed next to the vertical axis and the horizontal axis to identify the data displayed on that axis. When the axes contain only numbers, as they do in this scatter chart, it is important to identify the data. Axis titles can be inserted into the chart to explain the data. In this activity, you will insert axis titles into the scatter chart.

1 Click the **Production Errors sheet tab**, and then click the **Layout tab**. In the **Labels group**, click the **Axis Titles** button. From the list, point to **Primary Horizontal Axis Title**, and then compare your screen with Figure 9.48.

The submenu is used to indicate whether or not an axis title will display.

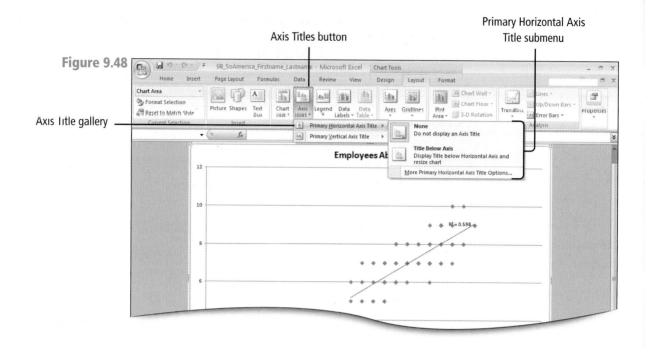

Figure 9.48

Axis Titles button

Primary Horizontal Axis Title submenu

Axis Title gallery

2 In the submenu, click **Title Below Axis**. The **Axis Title** is active—it is surrounded by a solid border. Type **CD Errors** and press Enter. Alternatively, in the axis title, select the text *Axis Title* and type **CD Errors**

A label that describes the horizontal axis is inserted into the worksheet. It is first entered in the Formula Bar but also displays in the axis title when the Enter key is pressed.

3 In the **Labels group**, click the **Axis Titles** button. From the list, point to **Primary Vertical Axis Title**, and then in the submenu, click **Rotated Title**. With the Axis Title active, type **Absences** and press Enter. Alternatively, in the Axis Title area that displays in the chart, triple-click the text *Axis Title* and type **Absences**

The axis labels can be formatted and inserted into any Excel chart. When the data is not clearly identified by the legend or the displayed categories, it is recommended that you provide an axis title to clearly identify the data.

4 Save your workbook.

Activity 9.19 Editing the Axis of a Chart

The data markers in the scatter chart are grouped in a bunch near the middle of the displayed chart area. To more accurately review the relationships of the data, it would help to increase the area that displays the data markers. The charting numbers begin at 0 for both the vertical and horizontal axes. By changing the beginning number in the axis, the data on the chart can display in a larger area, making them easier to view.

In this activity, you will change the axes in order to display the data in a larger space of the chart.

1 In the chart, point to a number on the ***horizontal axis***—the numbers at the bottom of the chart—and when the *Horizontal (Value) Axis* ScreenTip displays, click to select the horizontal axis. Compare your screen with Figure 9.49.

Because the two data fields for this scatter chart are both numbers, the horizontal axis is also a value axis. When the axis is selected, sizing handles display at each corner.

Figure 9.49

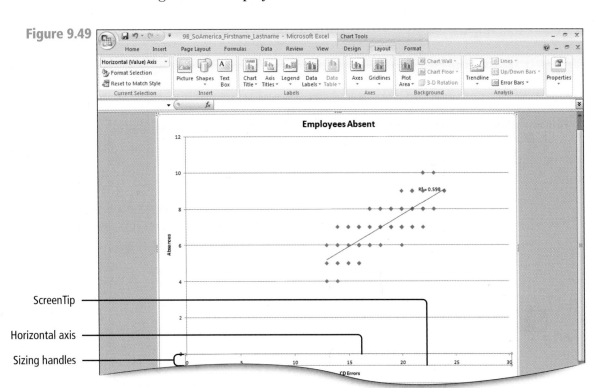

ScreenTip

Horizontal axis

Sizing handles

2 In the horizontal axis, right-click to display the shortcut menu, and then click **Format Axis**. Alternatively, on the Layout Tab, in the Current Selection group, click the Format Selection button.

The Format Axis dialog box displays with the Axis Options displayed on the right.

Alert!

Why don't I have the Format Axis choice?

If the Format Axis command does not display on your shortcut menu, click in the chart to close the shortcut menu and try again with your pointer closer to the bottom left of the axis. Alternatively, access the Format Axis dialog box on the Format tab—in the Shape Styles group, click in the Dialog Box launcher button.

3 On the right side, under **Axis Options**, next to **Minimum** click the **Fixed** option button. The text box becomes active. In the **Minimum** text box, replace the number with **12** and compare your screen with Figure 9.50.

The data for this scatter chart begin with about 12 errors on the horizontal axis. Currently, the data markers are grouped close together. A better sense of the data would occur if it were spread out and covered more of the chart. Beginning the horizontal axis numbering with 12 will remove the empty area on the left side of the chart and will result in the data being spread over a wider area.

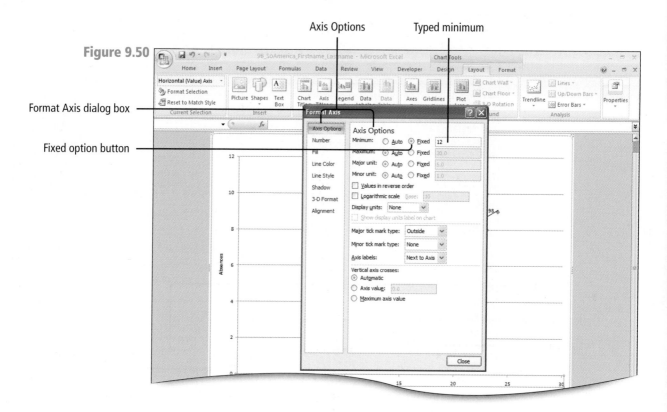

Figure 9.50

Axis Options

Typed minimum

Format Axis dialog box

Fixed option button

4 In the **Format Axis** dialog box, click **Close**, and then compare your screen with Figure 9.51.

Because there is a larger area for the data markers, the relationships are easier to review.

TR Factor

Figure 9.51

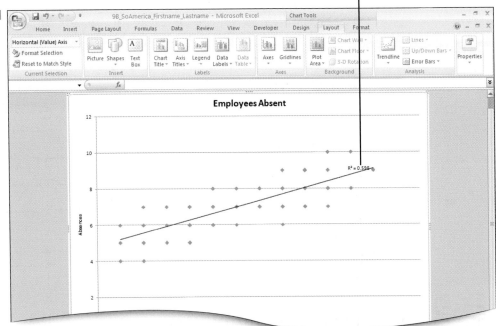

5 In the chart, point to the vertical axis—the numbers at the left side of the chart—and when the *Vertical (Value) Axis* ScreenTip displays, right-click to select the axis. In the shortcut menu, click **Format Axis**. Alternatively, on the Format tab, in the Shape Styles group, click the Dialog Launcher button [icon].

As with the horizontal axis, if the Format Axis command does not display on your shortcut menu, click in the chart to close the shortcut menu and try again closer to the numbers on the left axis.

6 Under **Axis Options**, next to **Minimum**, click the **Fixed** option button. The text box becomes active. In the **Minimum** text box, replace the entry with **3** Click **Close**, and then compare your screen with Figure 9.52.

The data markers now more fully display within the chart and are no longer bunched in a small area.

The data for this scatter chart begin with 4 absences and the data are within a small range of numbers. A better sense of the data occurs if it covers more of the chart. Beginning the numbering with 4 spreads the data over a larger area.

Figure 9.52

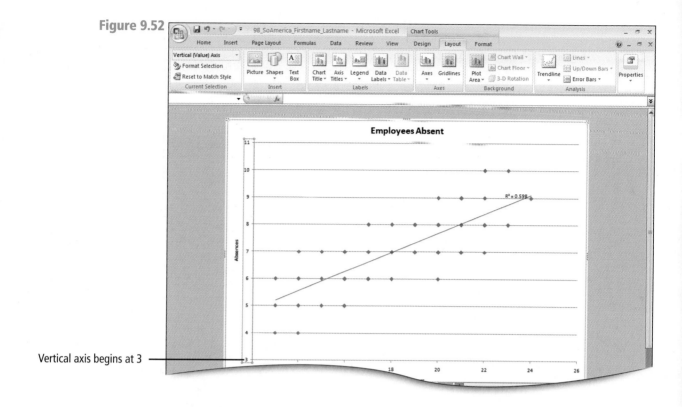

Vertical axis begins at 3

7 Save 💾 your workbook.

Activity 9.20 Creating a Stock Chart

A **stock chart** illustrates the fluctuation of stock prices, providing a history of the stock by displaying the highest price, lowest price, and closing price. The data must be organized in a specific manner with the stock names or stock dates as row headings and the stock prices—high, low, and close—as column headings. Because Cross Oceans Music is an international firm, it holds stock in each of the regions. Tony Escovedo, president, and Amalia Ramon, managing director, are reviewing a stock from Central America. In this activity, you will create a stock chart that tracks the value of a stock over the last quarter.

1 Click the **Stock sheet tab**.

The stock prices for Confersys for the past quarter have been entered into the worksheet. To complete a stock chart, the data must be arranged exactly as displayed—the column headings must be in the order of High, Low, and Close. Dates or stock names can be the row titles.

2 Select the range of the worksheet—**A5:D12**. Click the **Insert tab**, and in the **Charts group**, click the **Other Charts** button, and then compare your screen with Figure 9.53.

Stock, Surface, Doughnut, Bubble, and Radar chart types can be created in Excel. The Stock charts available are the High-Low-Close, Open-High-Low-Close, Volume-High-Low-Close, and Volume-Open-High-Low-Close stock charts. The arrangement of your data needs to match the stock chart type that you plan to use.

Other Charts button

Figure 9.53

Stock chart types

Surface chart types

Doughnut chart types

Bubble chart types

Radar chart types

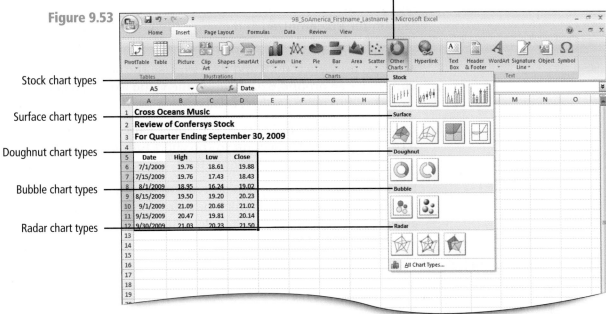

3 Under **Stock**, click the first choice—**High-Low-Close**.

The stock chart is displayed in the worksheet. The vertical lines in the chart area represent the stock prices for one day. The top of the line represents the high value of the stock during the day and the bottom of the line represents the low value of the stock during the day. The small horizontal line along the vertical line represents the ending value for the stock—the value of the stock when the stock market closed.

4 On the **Design tab**, in the **Chart Layouts group**, click the third choice—**Layout 3**.

The legend no longer displays in the chart and the chart displays a title.

5 Triple-click the title and type the following two-line title:

Cross Oceans Music
Confersys for Quarter Ending Sept. 30, 2009

6 In the title, format the company name with **16-point font** and the other line of the title with **12-point font**.

7 On the left side of the chart, display the ScreenTip for *Vertical (Value) Axis*, and then right-click the **Value Axis**. From the shortcut menu, click **Format Axis**. In the **Format Axis** dialog box, confirm that **Axis Options** is selected at the left.

Recall that the *value axis* is the left vertical axis on a chart.

8 On the right side, under **Axis Options**, click the **Minimum Fixed** option button and in the text box, change the number to **16** Click the **Maximum Fixed** button and change the number to **22**

You have instructed Excel to display the stock prices in the value axis that are between 16 and 22. Because the stock prices are close and clustered around $20, limiting the value axes numbers is recommended to more easily compare the stock fluctuations.

9 Click **Close**. Move the chart so the upper left corner begins in cell **A14**, scroll the worksheet up so the chart fully displays, and then compare your screen with Figure 9.54.

Because the vertical axis has decreased the range that is displayed, the data markers for each stock have increased in height, so the actual stock prices are easier to determine.

Figure 9.54

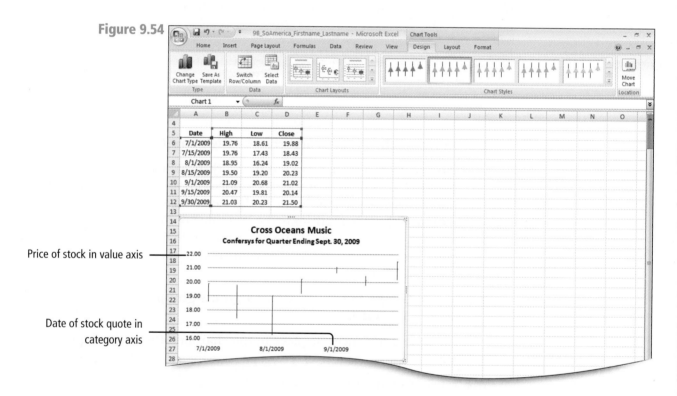

Price of stock in value axis

Date of stock quote in category axis

10 In the chart, position the pointer in the lower right corner and drag until the chart covers **row 29** and **column I**.

By increasing the size of the chart, all of the dates display in the category axis.

11 Click the **Layout tab** and in the **Labels group**, click the **Data Table** button. In the menu, click **Show Data Table**.

A data table is inserted in the chart. A **data table** displays the exact data in the worksheet. In a chart of this type, it is important to know the exact amounts of the stock prices for each day.

12 Click the **Design tab**, and in the **Location group**, click the **Move Chart** button. Place the chart in a new sheet named **Stock Chart** and click **OK**.

Placing the chart in its own chart sheet allows the data markers to display in a size that allows meaningful information to be compared. The data table displays the exact amount of the data displayed in the worksheet.

13 Click a stock data marker to select all of the markers. Click the **Format tab** and in the **Shape Styles group**, click the **More** button ⏷, and in the gallery, in the first column, click the second choice—**Moderate Line – Dark 1**—and then compare your screen with Figure 9.55.

Figure 9.55

High point of stock

Low point of stock

Category labels

Data table

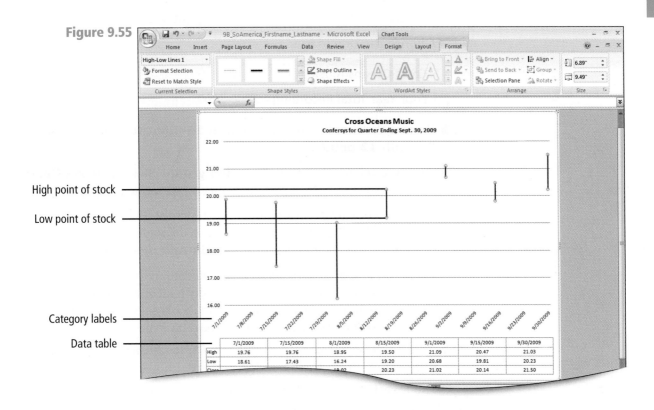

14 Right-click the **Stock sheet tab** and click **Hide**, and then **Save** 💾 your workbook.

Objective 5
Format Column Charts with Pictures and Other Graphic Elements

As you have seen, adding graphic elements to charts adds interest and professionalism. Pictures add a dimension of realism to the chart. Pictures can be used in the background of the chart, in the chart area, or in the data markers. Working with a picture is like working with other graphical elements.

Activity 9.21 Using Pictures to Format a 2-D Column Chart

Adding pictures in the data markers of a column chart adds interest to the chart. Amalia Ramon, the managing director, would like to review the recording totals for the last four years. In this activity, you will create a 2-D column chart and use pictures or clip art for the data markers.

1 Click the **2-D Column sheet tab**. Select the range **A5:A9** and press (Ctrl) while you select the range **F5:F9**.

You have selected nonadjacent ranges to be included in the chart. Because Amalia will review the total recordings for each region, the totals are the data range.

2 On the **Insert tab**, in the **Charts group**, click the **Column** button, and then from the gallery, under **2-D**, click the first choice—**Clustered Column**. In the chart, click in the **Legend** and press (Delete).

3 Change the title to read

Cross Oceans Music
Four Year Total Recordings: 2006-2009

4 Format the first line of the title with **14-point font** and the second line with **12-point font**.

5 On the **Design tab**, in the **Location group**, click the **Move Chart** button. Move the chart to a new sheet and name it **Recording Totals**

6 On the **Recording Totals** sheet, in the chart, click one of the data markers. Recall that each data marker displays the four-year total for that region. Then click in the **Latin America** data marker.

When you first click in a data marker, all data markers are selected. When all are selected, format changes are made in all data markers. When you click a second time, that specific data maker is selected, which enables you to make format changes to that one data maker.

7 Click the **Format tab**. In the **Shape Styles group**, click the **Shape Fill** button. From the list, click **Picture**.

The Insert Picture dialog box displays.

8 In the **Insert Picture** dialog box, navigate to your student files for this chapter and locate and click the **e09B_Bongo_Drums** picture, and then click **Insert**.

The Bongo Drum picture is inserted into the data marker as an elongated figure, called a *stretch data point*. To display the clip art in this style, use the stretch command. When a figure is stretched, it is usually distorted to fit the designated space.

9 Right-click the **Latin America** data marker and from the list, click **Format Data Point**. In the **Format Data Point**, on the left side, click **Fill**. On the right side about halfway through the options, click the **Stack** button, and then compare your screen with Figure 9.56.

Only one of the choices can be selected—Stretch, Stack, or Stack and Scale with. When you selected Stack, the original selection, Stretch, was deleted. To *stack data points* is to place images on top of each other without distorting the image.

Figure 9.56

Excel | chapter 9

Format Data Point dialog box

Stretch choice

Stack choice

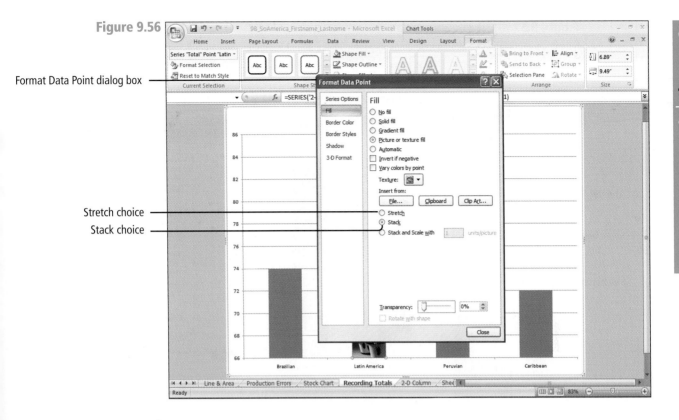

10 Click **Close**. The figure is now stacked in the data point.

11 Right-click the **Brazilian** data point to select it. From the list, click **Format Data Point**. In the **Format Data Point** dialog box, click **Fill** and on the right, click **Picture or texture fill**.

12 Under **Insert from**, click the **File** button. Locate and click the picture named **e09B_Maracas**, and then click **Insert**. Compare your screen with Figure 9.57. Note: In the figure, the dialog box has been moved in order to view the data markers.

The maracas have been inserted as a stretched data marker into the Brazilian data point. It is stretched within the range of the data marker.

Figure 9.57

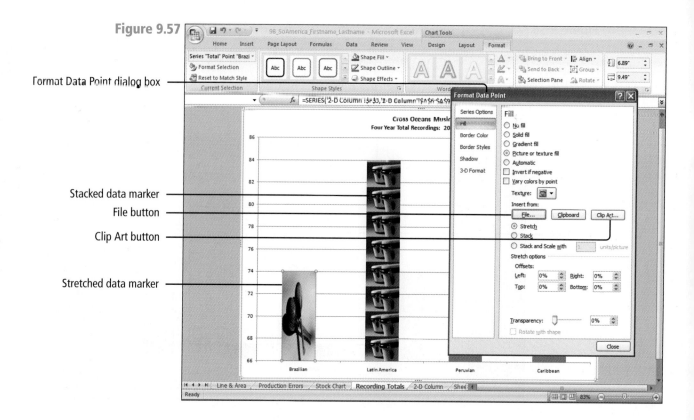

Format Data Point dialog box

Stacked data marker

File button

Clip Art button

Stretched data marker

13 On the right side of the **Format Data Point** dialog box, click the **Stack** button—which deselects stretch.

Now the data marker containing the maracas is also stacked and the figure is not distorted. To change the formatting of other close markers, click in the marker. Complete all of the formatting before you close the Format Data Point dialog box.

14 Using the skills you practiced, click the **Peruvian** data point and insert the **e09B_Blue_Banjo** clip as a stacked figure. In the **Caribbean** data point, insert the **e09B_Tambourine** image as a stacked figure. Then click **Close**.

15 In the space above the Peruvian and Caribbean data markers, notice that the ScreenTip displays *Plot Area*. Right-click and from the list, click **Format Plot Area**. In the **Format Plot Area** dialog box, on the right side, click **Picture or texture fill** and then use the **File** button to locate the **e09B_Ocean** image, and then click **Insert**. Click **Close**.

Recall the plot area is the area bounded by the axes and includes all data series. Placing the ocean picture as a background to the chart identifies the data markers from the Cross Oceans Music store.

16 Right-click the category axis—the data marker labels at the bottom of the chart. In the Mini toolbar, change the **Font Size** to **16**. Using the skills you have practiced, increase the value markers—the numbers at the left side of the chart—to **16** points and then compare your screen with Figure 9.58.

Figure 9.58

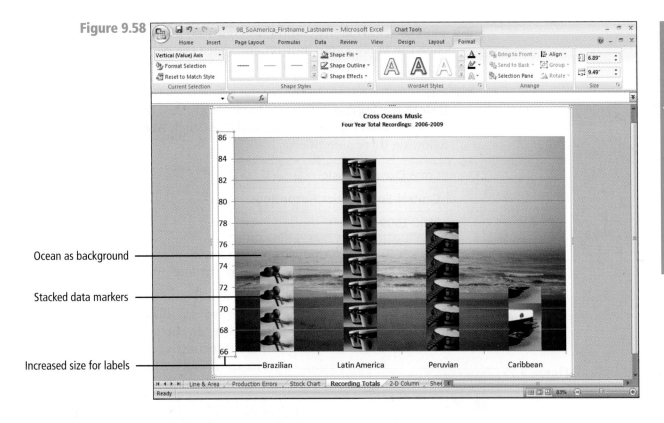

Ocean as background

Stacked data markers

Increased size for labels

17 Save your workbook.

Activity 9.22 Using Pictures to Format a 3-D Column Chart

A 3-D column chart uses three axes to display the data—horizontal, vertical, and depth. It should be used when the categories and values are equally important. In reviewing the progress of recording music in Central and South America, Amalia Raman requests a chart that displays all of the data for the period. In this activity. you will create a 3-D column chart that displays the recordings for the four years for all regions in Central and South America.

1 Click the **2-D Column sheet tab**. Click in a cell in the worksheet and click the **Insert tab**, and in the **Charts group**, click the **Column** button. From the list, under **3-D Column**, click the last choice—**3-D Column**. Move the chart down so you can display all of the data in the worksheet.

Notice in the chart that the data markers are very short except for the ones in the back and the right side—which are the data markers for the totals. Recall that you will chart the data or the totals, but not both on the same chart, as the visual impact is skewed. Recall that when Excel selects the range, it selects all adjoining cells; the totals need to be removed from the chart range.

2 In the worksheet, position the pointer to the lower right of cell **F10**, and when the pointer takes the ⬉ shape, drag up to cell **E9**.

The data markers now fully display, so you can make a visual comparison about the data markers.

3 With the chart active, on the **Design tab**, in the **Location group**, click the **Move Chart** button and move the chart to a new sheet named **3-D Column**

4 The country names in the legend are also displayed in the chart. **Delete** the **legend**. Click the **Layout tab**, and in the **Labels group**, click the **Chart Title** button, and then click **Above Chart**. Insert the following three-line title:

Cross Oceans Music
Central/So. America Recordings
2006-2009

5 Confirm that the formatting for the first row of the title is **20 point** font and the other two rows is **18 point** font. Then compare your screen with Figure 9.59.

The 3-D column chart displays the years and the regions as data markers. Notice that the data markers in the last row are not all visible and some in the third row are difficult to see.

Figure 9.59

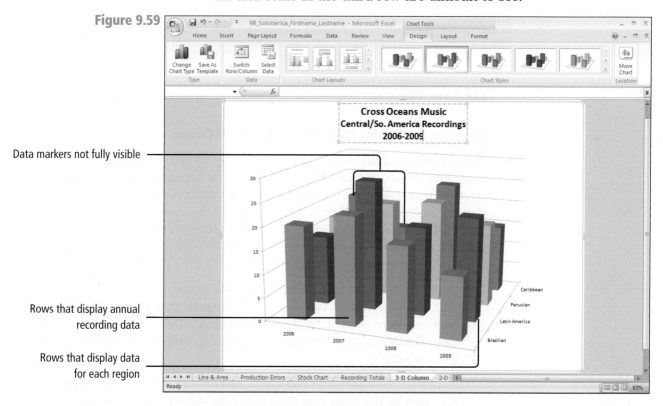

Data markers not fully visible

Rows that display annual recording data

Rows that display data for each region

6 Right-click one data marker to select the data series. On the **Layout tab**, in the **Background group**, click the **3-D Rotation** button. Move the **Format Chart Area** dialog box to one side so you can see most of the data markers on the chart. On the right side of the **Format Chart Area** dialog box, under **Rotation**, in the **X** rotation box, click the **spin box up arrow** to **20**—unless it already displays 20. As the numbers change, notice the Live Preview displays the way the chart will display with these rotation numbers. Click the **Y spin box up arrow** to **30**, and click the **Perspective** box to **15**. Then click **Close** and compare your screen with Figure 9.60.

All of the data markers now fully display and provide a perspective of the recordings for each region for each year.

Figure 9.60

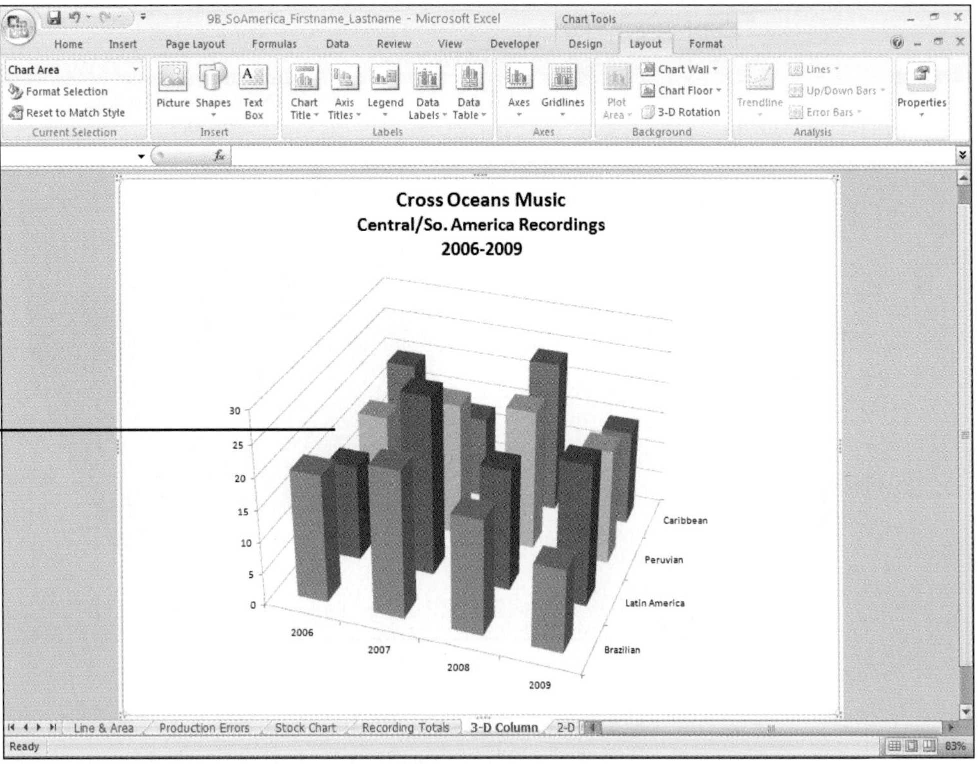

3-D column chart rotated so all
data markers are visible

⬛7 Position the pointer between the 2008 and 2009 columns and when the ScreenTip *Floor* displays, right-click and click **Format Floor**. Under **Fill**, click **Picture or text fill**. Click the **Texture** button and on the first row click the fourth choice—**Woven mat**.

⬛8 In the chart, point to the white area behind the columns and when the ScreenTip displays *Back Wall*, right-click to select the walls, and then click **Format Walls**. The dialog box changes to the **Format Walls** dialog box. Under **Fill**, click **Picture or texture fill**. Either from the **File** or **Clip Art** choices, locate and insert the picture named **e09B_Ocean**. Then click **Close** and compare your screen with Figure 9.61.

Figure 9.61

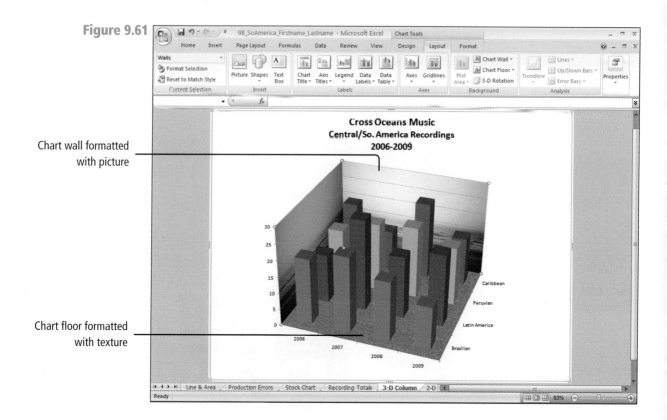

Chart wall formatted with picture

Chart floor formatted with texture

9 Delete **Sheet1**. Right-click the **2-D Column sheet tab** and click **Hide**. Then confirm that the worksheets are arranged in the following order: Line & Area, Production Errors, Stock Chart, Recording Totals, 3-D Column.

10 Click the **Production Errors sheet tab**. Press ⇧Shift and click in the **3-D Column sheet tab**. Click the **Insert tab** and in the **Text group**, click **Header & Footer**. In the **Page Setup** dialog box, in the **Header/Footer tab**, click the **Custom Footer** button. With the insertion point in the **Left section**, click the **Insert File Name** button 🖳. Click the **Right section** and then click the **Insert Sheet Name** button 🖳. Then click **OK** two times.

Recall that you must use the Page Setup dialog box to place a header and footer on a chart sheet.

11 Click the **Line & Area sheet tab**, click cell A1, and then in the **Left Footer** area insert the **File Name** and in the **Right Footer** area, insert the **Sheet Name**. Format it to print in **Landscape Orientation**, **Fit to page**, and centered **Horizontally** and **Vertically**. **Save** your workbook.

12 To submit electronically, follow the instructions provided by your instructor. To print, from the **Office** menu, click **Print**. In the **Print** dialog box, under **Print what**, select **Entire workbook**, and then click **OK**. From the **Office** menu, click **Close**. **Close** Excel.

End **You have completed Project 9B** ——————

There's More You Can Do!

From My Computer, navigate to the student files that accompany this textbook. In the folder **02_theres_more_you_can_do**, locate and open the folder for this chapter. Open and print the instructions for this project, which are provided to you in Adobe PDF format.

Try It! 1—Picture Fun

In this Try It! exercise, you will learn techniques for working with pictures in Excel.

Summary

In this chapter, you used the graphic elements of Excel to format worksheets and charts. Inserting WordArt adds text as a graphic element. WordArt can be moved, edited, resized, and altered with other effects such as glow and reflection. Shapes can be inserted and resized. Text can be entered on shapes. Web pages with hyperlinks have been created.

In a chart, you can add color, texture, or pictures into any chart element, such as the floor, wall, or data marker. These elements can then be formatted with different highlighting effects, adding interest and gloss to provide a professional chart. The chart and other graphic elements can be rotated to display the graphic in several positions on the screen. Other chart types such as a Scatter chart or Stock chart are used for special purposes such as determining if there is a relationship between data or to chart stock performance.

Key Terms

The ⊙ symbol represents Key Terms found on the Student CD in the 02_theres_more_you_can_do folder for this chapter.

Content-Based Assessments

Matching

Match each term in the second column with its correct definition in the first column by writing the letter of the term on the blank line in front of the correct definition.

_____ 1. The small circles or squares at the corners and sides of a graphic element that are used to make the element larger or smaller.

_____ 2. The diamond-shaped handles at the top of a graphic used to adjust the appearance but not the size of a graphic element.

_____ 3. The green circle that appears above the selected shape that is used to change the angle of the shape.

_____ 4. A feature that creates a graphic image of text.

_____ 5. A gradual progression of colors and shades, usually from one color to another or from one shade to another shade of the same color.

_____ 6. The effects that change the look of the text by adding effects such as shadows, reflections, flow, or 3-D rotation.

_____ 7. A designer-quality visual representation of information in a variety of layouts to display a set of information, such as relationships.

_____ 8. The area that displays at the left of a SmartArt diagram and is used to enter text into the diagram.

_____ 9. A document that displays as a screen that may contain links, pictures, and other features and can be uploaded to the World Wide Web.

_____ 10. The format used for documents that are written for the Web.

_____ 11. The area that displays at the right side of the worksheet and is used to insert graphic elements.

_____ 12. Drawings, photographs, movies, or sound clips that can be inserted into an Excel worksheet.

_____ 13. Text or an image that you click to go to another location in a worksheet or another page on the Web.

_____ 14. A specific Web address.

_____ 15. Saving one page of a workbook as a Web page.

A Adjustment handles

B Clip art

C Clip Art task pane

D Gradient

E html

F Hyperlinks

G Rotation handle

H Single File Web page

I Sizing handles

J SmartArt graphic

K Text effects

L Text Pane

M URL

N Web page

O WordArt

Content-Based Assessments

Fill in the Blank

Write the correct answer in the space provided.

1. When displaying data over time, use the _____ chart.

2. The area in a chart that includes all of the data series is the _____ area.

3. The axis on the worksheet that contains categories is the _____ axis.

4. The box in a chart that identifies the patterns or colors that are assigned to the data series is the _____.

5. The area in a chart that displays the values is the _____ axis.

6. In a chart, the numbers displayed by data markers that identify the data are the data _____.

7. Any value in the chart is a data _____.

8. The shape on the chart that represents a value is the data _____.

9. The horizontal and vertical lines that extend across the chart are the _____.

10. A chart that emphasizes the magnitude of change over time is the _____ chart.

11. A chart that places the data from each category one on top of the other is the _____ chart.

12. The entire chart and all of its elements is the _____ area.

13. Charts that plot two sets of numbers at the same time are _____ charts.

14. In a chart, a graphic representation of the trends in the data series is a(n) _____.

15. The chart that displays the highest and lowest point in daily stock prices is the _____ stock chart.

Content-Based Assessments

Project 9C—New Age Sales

In this project, you will apply the skills you practiced from the Objectives in Project 9A.

Objectives: 1. *Format with Graphic Images Including WordArt to Enhance Worksheets;* **2.** *Insert SmartArt Graphics;* **3.** *Create, Edit, and Publish a Web Page.*

In the following Skills Review, you will create a report of New Age music sales for the third quarter, create a Web page that displays the sales, and use a SmartArt illustration to display the top selling types of New Age music. Amalia Raman, the managing director, has reviewed the New Age CD sales for the third quarter and has prepared a report that will be published to the Web. In addition, President Tony Escovedo requests a visual diagram of the best-selling CDs. Your completed worksheets will look similar to those in Figure 9.62.

For Project 9C, you will need the following file:

e09C_New_Age_Sales

You will save your workbook as
9C_New_Age_Sales_Firstname_Lastname (Excel)
9C_New_Age_Web_Firstname_Lastname (Excel)
9C_New_Age_Web_Firstname_Lastname (.mht)

Figure 9.62

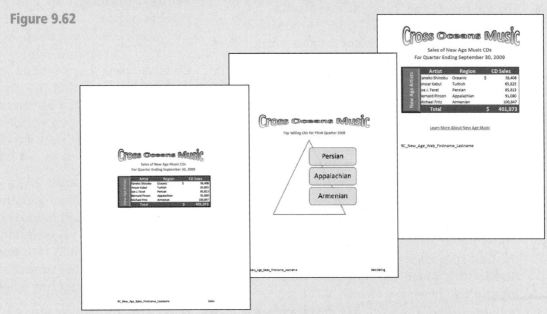

(Project 9C–New Age Sales continues on the next page)

(Project 9C–New Age Sales continued)

1. **Start** Excel. From your student files, locate and open the file named **e09C_New_Age_Sales**. Save the workbook in your **Excel Chapter 9** folder as 9C_New_Age_Sales_Firstname_Lastname

2. Insert a column to the left of **column A**. Select the range **B5:D5** and in the **Alignment group**, click the **Dialog Box Launcher** to display the **Format Cells** dialog box. Click the **Fill tab**. In the **Background Color** section, in the last line of colors, click the second **Blue** color chip. At the right, click the **Pattern Style** arrow. In the first row, select the fifth choice—**12.5% Gray**—and then click **OK**.

3. In the **Font group**, click the **Font Color button arrow** and change the font color to **White, Background 1**. Format the text with **Bold**, **14 point**, and **Center**. Copy the format from the range **B5:D5** to the range **B11:D11**. Format cell **D11** with **Accounting Number Format** with **no decimals**.

4. On the **Insert tab**, in the **Illustrations group**, click the **Shapes** button. From the displayed gallery, under **Rectangles**, click the first shape—**Rectangle**. Click in the upper left corner of cell **F5** and drag to the lower right corner of cell **J7**. With the rectangle active, type **New Age Artists** Triple-click to select the text, and then right-click, and from the Mini Toolbar, change the font size to **14 points**.

5. With the rectangle active, right-click and select **Format Shape**. On the left side of the dialog box, click **3-D Format**, and then under **Bevel**, click **Top**. Under **Bevel**, in the first row, click the fourth option—**Cool Slant**. Click **Close**. Click the **rotation handle** and move the mouse to the left and down until the rectangle is vertical—it is rotated 90 degrees.

6. Drag the rectangle so its top left border is at the top left edge of cell **A5**. Use the bottom center sizing handle to bring the lower edge of the rectangle to the bottom edge of cell **A11**, and use the right sizing handle to move the shape to the right edge of **column A**.

7. Adjust the row height of **row 1** to **54 points**. Click the **Insert tab** and in the **Text group**, click the **WordArt** button. In the third row, click the first choice—**Gradient Outline - Accent 1**. Triple-click to select the words—**Your Text Here**—and then type **Cross Oceans Music** With the text selected, right-click and change the **font size** to **36**.Click in the **WordArt** text box and drag to it **row 1**, between **column A** and **D** of the worksheet. If it does not fully display in row 1, click on the bottom middle sizing handle and drag up to adjust its height to fit.

8. On the **Drawing Tools Format tab**, in the **WordArt Styles group**, click the **Text Effects** button and point to **Transform**. In the submenu, under **Warp**, in the sixth row, click the second choice—**Deflate**. Click the pink diamond adjustment handle and pull down so that the center of the WordArt is as narrow as possible. Click in the right middle sizing handle and drag until the right edge is at, but not touching, the right cell gridline of cell **D1**.

9. Select the range **B2:B3**. Right-click and from the Mini Toolbar, click the **Font Color** button, and in the Standard colors, click **Blue**. With **B2:B3** selected, move the range to cells **A2:A3**. Format with **Bold**, **14 point**, and **Merge & Center rows 2** and **3** over **columns A:D**. Adjust row heights.

10. Select cells **B5:D11**, and in the **Font group**, click the **Borders button arrow**, and then

(Project 9C–New Age Sales continues on the next page)

Content-Based Assessments

(Project 9C–New Age Sales continued)

click **Thick Box Border**. Format cell **D6** with **Accounting Number Format** with **no decimals**, and format the range **D7:D10** with **Comma Style** with **no decimals**.

11. Click the **Sheet2 sheet tab** and rename it Best Selling Increase the height of **row 1** to **48 points**. In cell **A3**, type **Top Selling CDs for Third Quarter 2009** and format it with **14 point**, **Bold**, and font color of **Standard Blue**, and **Merge & Center** it through **columns A:H**.

12. On the **Insert tab**, in the **Illustrations group**, click the **SmartArt** button. On the left side of the dialog box, click **Pyramid**. In the center area, click the third chart— **Pyramid List**.Review the information at the right, and then click **OK**.

13. In the top rectangle, replace *Text* with **Persian** Click in the next rectangle, and type **Appalachian**. In the last rectangle, type **Armenian** On the **Design** tab, click the **Change colors** button, and then under **Accent 1**, click the first choice—**Colored Outline – Accent 1**.

14. Click the border surrounding the SmartArt and drag so the upper left corner of the SmartArt is in the upper left corner of cell **A5**. Click on the lower right corner sizing handle and extend the size to fill the range **A5:H22**.

15. Click the **Sales sheet tab**. Right-click the WordArt title and click **Copy**. Click the **Best Selling sheet tab** and in cell **A1**, right-click and select **Paste Special**. In the **Paste Special** dialog box, confirm that **Picture (PNG)** is selected, and then click **OK**. Click the right middle sizing handle and adjust the size to cover column H. Adjust the height to fit row 1. Recall that when you copy WordArt as a picture, it cannot be edited.

16. Delete **Sheet3**. In both worksheets, in the **Left Footer** area, insert the **File Name**, and in the **Right Footer** area, insert the **Sheet Name**. For the worksheet, in the **Page Setup dialog box**, center the worksheets both **Horizontally** and **Vertically**. Ungroup the sheets, and then **Save** your workbook.

17. Right-click the **Sales sheet tab**, and click **Move or Copy**. In the **Move or Copy** dialog box, under **To book**, click the arrow and click **(new book)**. Click **Create a copy**, and then click **OK**. **Save** the workbook as 9C_New_Age_Web_Firstname_ Lastname

18. In cell **A13**, type **Learn More About New Age Music Merge & center** across **columns A:D**. Click the **Insert tab**, and in the **Links group**, click the **Hyperlink** button. In the **Insert Hyperlink** dialog box, in the **Link to** area, confirm that *Existing File or Web Page* is selected. In the **Address** box, type http://music.calabashmusic.com/ world/New_Age and then click **OK**. In cell **A16**, type 9C_New_Age_Web_Firstname_ Lastname replacing Firstname_Lastname with your name. **Save** your workbook.

19. Click the **Office Menu**, and then click **Save As**. In the **Save As** dialog box, click the **Save as type** arrow and select **Single File Web Page**. At the bottom of the dialog box, by **Save**, click the **Selection: Sheet** option button.

20. Click the **Publish** button. In the **Publish as Web Page** dialog box, click the **Open published web page in browser** check box to select it. In the **File name** box, the entire path of the worksheet displays. Delete the path and type 9C_New_Age_ Web_Firstname_Lastname.mht and then click the **Publish** button.

(Project 9C–New Age Sales continues on the next page)

Content-Based Assessments

(Project 9C–New Age Sales continued)

21. Test the link and if it doesn't work, return to the worksheet and confirm the link is correctly entered. If it still doesn't work, then insert a link to your college. In your browser, click the **Close** button.

22. From the **Start** menu, open the default browser. Near the top, in the **menu bar**, click **File**, and then click **Open**. In the **Open** dialog box, click the **Browse** button. Navigate to your **Chapter 9 Excel** files, and then locate and click the **9C_New_Age_Web_Firstname_Lastname.mht** file

and click **Open**. Then click **OK** to display the Web page. **Close** your Web page, and then **Close** the browser.

23. To submit electronically, follow the instructions provided by your instructor. To print, from the **Office** menu, click **Print**. In the **Print** dialog box, under **Print what**, select **Entire workbook**, and then click **OK**. Print both workbooks and the Web page. From the **Office** menu, click **Close**. **Close** Excel.

End **You have completed Project 9C** ——————————————————

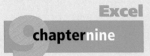

Excel

chapternine   Skills Review

Project 9D — US Festivals

In this project, you will apply the skills you practiced from the Objectives in Project 9B.

Objectives: 4. *Create Specialized Charts;* **5.** *Format Column Charts with Pictures and other Graphic Elements.*

In the following Skills Review, you will create several charts that will display the number of contacts made at music festivals in the United States. The scouts in the United States have attended music festivals over the last three years and have made contacts with artists. Lila Darius, the artistic director, is reviewing the results of the past festivals to identify where the contacts are located and whether any music festival provides more artists than others. Your completed worksheets will look similar to those in Figure 9.63.

For Project 9D, you will need the following files:

e09D_US_Festivals.jpg
e09D_Blue_Banjo.jpg
e09D_Red_Snare_Drum.jpg
e09D_Drummer.jpg
e09D_Ocean.jpg

You will save your workbook as
9D_US_Festivals_Firstname_Lastname

Figure 9.63

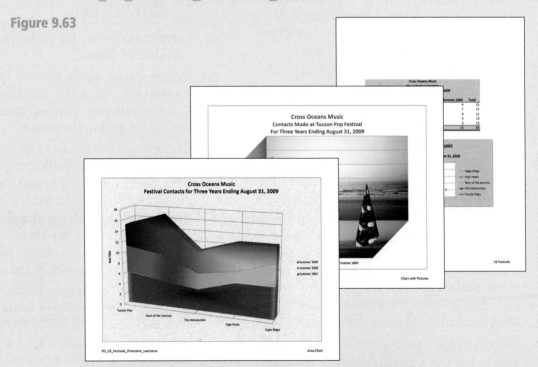

(Project 9D–US Festivals continues on the next page)

(Project 9D–US Festivals continued)

1. **Start** Excel. From your student files locate and open the file named **e09D_US_Festivals**. **Save** the file in the **Excel Chapter 9** folder and name it **9D_US_Festivals_Firstname_Lastname**

2. Click in cell **C7** and on the **Insert tab**, in the **Charts group**, click the **Line** button. Under **2-D**, in the second row, click the first chart—**Line with Markers**. Move the chart so the upper left corner displays in cell **A14**. In the worksheet data, position the mouse on the sizing handle at the lower right corner of the source data—cell **E11**—and drag to the lower right corner of cell **D10**.

3. In the chart, right-click the **Vertical (Value) Axis**, and from the shortcut menu, click **Format Axis**. Under **Axis Options**, next to **Minimum**, click **Fixed**, delete the number entered, and then type **2.0** Next to **Maximum**, click **Fixed**. In the **Maximum** text box, delete the number entered, and then type **7.0** Click **Close**.

4. Click the **Layout tab** and in the **Labels group**, click the **Data Labels** button. Click **Left**. In the **Labels group**, click the **Chart Title** button and click **Above Chart**. Triple-click in the title and type

Cross Oceans Music
Festival Contacts
For Three Years Ending August 31, 2009

5. Format the second and third lines of the title with **12-point font** and the first line with **18-point font**.

6. On the **Chart Tools Format** tab, in the **Current Selection group**, in the **Chart Elements** box, click **Chart Area**. Click the **Format Selection** button. With **Fill** selected, click **Solid fill**. Click the **Color** button. In the sixth column, click the third color—**Red, Accent 2, Lighter 60%**. Click **Close**.

7. With the **Line chart** active, on the **Design tab**, in the **Data group**, click the **Switch**

(Project 9D–US Festivals continues on the next page)

Row/Column button. Click the **Select Data** button, and in the **Select Data Source** dialog box, in the **Legend Entries** area, click **High Peaks**. At the top right of the **Legend Entries** section, click the **Move Up** button **three times**, so that **High Peaks** is the first entry. Continue moving the data labels up or down until the festivals are in alphabetical order (Eagle Ridge is the first festival listed). Click **OK**.

8. Click cell **C8** or another cell within the worksheet data. On the **Insert tab**, in the **Charts group**, click the **Area** button and under **3-D Area**, click the second chart—**Stacked Area in 3-D**. In the worksheet, in the lower right corner of cell **E11**, click the sizing handle and drag up to cell **D10**.

9. Right-click the border of the chart and select **Move Chart**. In the **Move Chart** dialog box, click **New Sheet** and type the sheet name **Area Chart** and then click **OK**. In the **Chart Layouts group**, click **Layout 1**. In the chart title, type the following two-line title:

Cross Oceans Music
Festival Contacts for Three Years Ending August 31, 2009

10. On the **Chart Tools Layout tab**, in the **Axes group**, click the **Gridlines** button. Point to **Primary Vertical Gridlines**, and then click **Major Gridlines**.

11. In the chart, right-click the bottom data series. In the shortcut menu, click **Format Data Series**. In the **Format Data Series** dialog box, on the left side, click **Fill**. On the right side, click the **Gradient fill** button. Click the **Preset colors** button and click the first choice—**Early Sunset**. Click the **Type** arrow and click **Path**.

12. In the chart, click the middle data series, and in the **Format Data Series** dialog box, click **Fill**, and then at the right, click the **Gradient fill** button. Click the **Preset colors** button and from the second column and third row, click **Peacock**. Click the

(Project 9D–US Festivals continued)

Type button, and then click **Radial**. Using the skills you have practiced, change the fill for the top data series to the preset **Gradient** color in the fourth column, second row—**Fire**—and change the **Type** to **Rectangular**. Click **Close**.

13. In the chart, point to the white background and when the Chart Area ScreenTip displays **Chart Area**, right-click, and then click **Format Chart Area**. In the **Format Chart Area** dialog box, on the right side under **Fill**, click **Picture or texture fill**. Click the **Texture** button and in the second column, fourth row, click **Blue tissue paper**. Click **Close** and **Save** your workbook.

14. In the **US Festivals** sheet, select **A5:D6**, click the **Insert tab**, and in the **Charts group**, click the **Column** button. Under **Cone**, click the first chart—**Clustered Cone**. Using the skills you have practiced, move the chart to a new worksheet named **Chart with Pictures**

15. In the title area, type

| Cross Oceans Music |
| Contacts Made at Tucson Pops Festival |
| For Three Years Ending August 31, 2009 |

16. In the title, format the first row with **20-point font** and format the entire title with the **Standard Font Color** of **Dark Red**. Then **Delete** the **Legend**.

17. Click a data point, and then click the data point at the left to select it. Right-click and select **Format Data Point**. In the **Format Data Point** dialog box, click **Fill** and on the right side, click **Picture or texture fill**. Under **Insert from**, click the **File** button. Navigate to your data for Chapter 9 student files and click the **e09D_Blue_Banjo** file. Click **Insert**. In the **Format Data Point** dialog box, click **Stack**.

18. If necessary, move the **Format Data Point** dialog box so you can see the middle data point, then click it to select it. At the left,

click **Fill** and at the right, click **Picture or texture fill**. Under **Insert from**, click **File**, and then insert the picture named **e09D_Red_Snare_Drum** and click **Stack**. Using the skills you practiced, in the third data point, insert the picture named **e09D_Drummer** and **Stack** it. **Close** the dialog box.

19. Right-click between the columns at the base, and then click **Format Floor**. Under **Fill**, click **Picture or texture fill**. Under **Insert from** click **File** and then locate and click the picture **e09D_Ocean** and insert it. Right-click between the gridlines and click **Format Walls**. At the right, under **Fill**, click **Picture or texture fill**. Under **Insert from**, click **File** and locate and click the file named **e09D_Ocean**. **Close** the dialog box.

20. Right-click in the chart and select **3-D Rotation**. In the **Format Chart Area** dialog box, under **Rotation**, in the **X** area, change the rotation to **50** and change the **Y** to **50**. Click **Close**.

21. Delete **Sheet2** and **Sheet3**. Group the **Area Chart** and **Chart with Pictures** sheets. In the **Text group**, click the **Header & Footer** button. In the **Page Setup** dialog box, in the **Header/Footer tab**, click **Custom Footer**. In the **Left Footer** section, insert the **File Name** and in the **Right Footer** section, insert the **Sheet Name**. In the **US Festivals** sheet, in the **Left Footer** area, insert the **File Name** and in the **Right Footer** area, insert the **Sheet Name** and center the worksheet both **Horizontally** and **Vertically**. Arrange the worksheets in this order: **Area Chart**, **Chart with Pictures**, and **US Festivals**. **Save** your workbook.

22. To submit electronically, follow the instructions provided by your instructor. To print, from the **Office** menu, click **Print**. In the **Print** dialog box, under **Print what**, select **Entire workbook**, and then click **OK**. From the **Office** menu, click **Close**. **Close** Excel.

End You have completed Project 9D

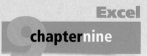

Project 9E—New Artists

In this project, you will apply the skills you practiced from the Objectives in Project 9A.

Objectives: 1. *Format with Graphic Images Including WordArt to Enhance Worksheets;* **2.** *Insert SmartArt Graphics;* **3.** *Create, Edit, and Publish a Web Page.*

In the following Mastering Excel project, you will identify the artists who have recently signed a contract with Cross Oceans Music. You will format the worksheet and then prepare the information using SmartArt. Then you will save a Web page that displays this information. Your completed worksheets will look similar to those in Figure 9.64.

For Project 9E, you will need the following file:

e09E_New_Artists

You will save your workbook as
9E_New_Artists_Firstname_Lastname
9E_New_Artists_Web_Firstname_Lastname.mht

Figure 9.64

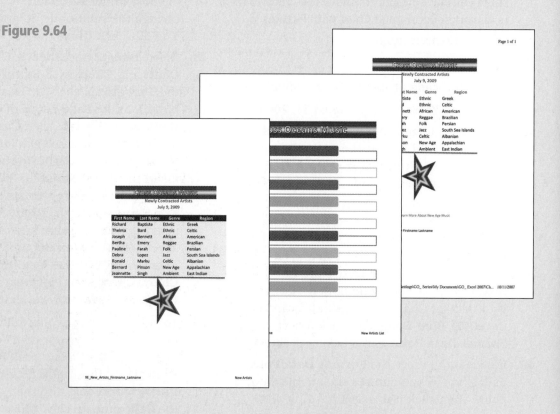

(Project 9E–New Artists continues on the next page)

Content-Based Assessments

(Project 9E–New Artists continued)

1. **Start** Excel. From your student files, locate and open the file named **e09E_New_Artists**. Save the workbook in your **Excel Chapter 9** folder as 9E_New_Artists_Firstname_Lastname

2. Adjust the height of **row 1** to **54 points**. **Insert** the **WordArt** displayed as the first choice in the first row—**Fill - Text 2, Outline - Background 2**. In the WordArt text box, type **Cross Oceans Music** Format the text with **24-point font**. Access the **Format Shape** dialog box and insert a **Gradient fill** with a **Preset color** of **Rainbow**. Position the WordArt rests at the bottom of **row 1**.

3. Format the range **A2:A3** with **Bold**, **14 point**. Change the **Font Color** to **Red**. **Merge & Center** each row across **columns A:D**. Select cells **A5:D5**, right-click, and select **Format Cells**. In the **Fill tab**, select a **Background Color** of **Red**—the last row, the second red color chip. Select the **Pattern Style** of **Thin Diagonal Crosshatch**, and then click **OK**. Change the **Font Color** to **White** and format with **Bold**, **14 point**, and **Center** alignment.

4. Select the range **A6:D14** and format with **14-point font** size and a fill color of **Tan Background 2**. Adjust column widths, if necessary, and adjust the WordArt to cover columns **A:D**.

5. Insert a **Line** shape, and position it at the bottom of **row 14** from the left of cell **A14** continued through the end of cell **D14**. With the shape selected, select a **Shape Style** with **Intense Line – Accent 2**.

6. Insert the **Shape** of a **5-Point Star** and center it under the worksheet data from the left top of cell **B16** to the bottom right of cell **C21**. **Format** the **Shape** with a **Gradient fill** with a **Preset color** of **Rainbow** and a

Type of **Path**. Using the rotate handle, **rotate** the star 90 degrees to the left until the rotatation handle extends from the left side of the selected box. Adjust the star so the top tip just rests at the bottom border of the worksheet.

7. Name **Sheet1 New Artists** Click the **Sheet2 tab** and rename it **New Artists List** Insert a **SmartArt List** named **Vertical Box List**. Display the **Text Pane**. Click the **New Artists sheet tab**, select and **Copy** the last names—**B6:B14**. Click in the **New Artists List sheet tab** and in the **Type your text here** Text Pane, click in the first entry area and select a **Paste** command.

8. **Close** the **Text Pane**. On the **SmartArt Design tab**, change the color of the list to **Colorful - Accent Colors**. Position the SmartArt beginning in cell **A5** and extending through cell **I36**. If there are areas that display *Text* in the SmartArt, delete them. Click in cell **A1**.

9. **Copy** the WordArt title from the **New Artists sheet**, **Paste** it in cell **A1** of the **New Artists List sheet**, and then extend the title through **Column I**. Recall that to copy WordArt, the solid borders must surround the WordArt before selecting a copy command.

10. Delete **Sheet3**. In both sheets, in the **Left Footer** area, insert the **File Name** and in the **Right Footer** area, insert the **Sheet Name**. Center the worksheets **Horizontally** and **Vertically**. Then display the worksheets in **Print Preview**. Caution: Recall that if a graphic element extends into an adjoining cell, it will cause that cell to be included in the data to be centered, resulting in a document that is not centered. The line that you placed at the bottom of the worksheet is a graphic element.

(Project 9E–New Artists continues on the next page)

Content-Based Assessments

(Project 9E–New Artists continued)

11. **Save** your workbook. Copy the **New Artists** worksheet to a new workbook and save the workbook as **9E_New_Artists_Web_ Firstname_Lastname** In cell **A27**, type **Learn More About New Age Music Merge & Center** across **columns A:D**. Insert a **Hyperlink** in the *Existing File or Web Page* that links to the following address: **http://music.calabashmusic.com/world/ New_Age** Note: If this link doesn't work, link to your college's web site.

12. In cell **A30**, type **Web page created by Firstname_Lastname** and replace Firstname Lastname with your name. Save the workbook as a **Single File Web Page**. Confirm that the worksheet will open as a published Web page and the file path is not included in the File name. Name the Web page **9E_New_ Artists_Web_Firstname_Lastname.mht** After

testing the link, in the browser, click the **Close** button.

13. From the **Start** menu, open the default browser, navigate to your **Chapter 9 Excel** files, and then locate and open the **9E_New_Artists_Web_Firstname_Lastname** file. Click **OK**. Test the link. Close the Web page, and then close the browser. **Save** your 9E_New_Artists_Web workbook.

14. To submit electronically, follow the instructions provided by your instructor. To print, from the **Office** menu, click **Print**. In the **Print** dialog box, under **Print what**, select **Entire workbook**, and then click **OK**. Print the Web page, too. From the **Office** menu, click **Close**. **Close** Excel.

End You have completed Project 9E

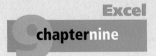

Mastering Excel

Project 9F—Stocks

In this project, you will apply the skills you practiced from the Objectives in Project 9B.

Objectives: 4. *Create Specialized Charts;* **5.** *Format Column Charts with Pictures and other Graphic Elements.*

In the following Mastering Excel project, you will create charts that will display information about the closing prices for European stocks that the company owns. As a company that does business internationally, Cross Oceans Music invests in businesses throughout the world. Amalia Raman, the managing director, periodically reviews the value of the stocks. You will complete and chart the stock data for the European stocks for a day in August and complete a chart that summarizes the closing prices. Your completed workbook will look similar to the one in Figure 9.65.

For Project 9F, you will need the following file:

e09F_Stocks

You will save your workbook as
9F_Stocks_Firstname_Lastname

Figure 9.65

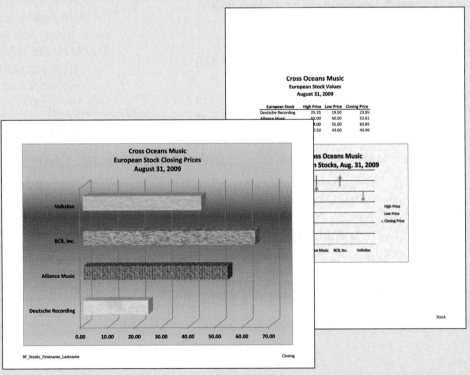

(Project 9F–Stocks continues on the next page)

Content-Based Assessments

(Project 9F–Stocks continued)

1. **Start** Excel. From your student files, open the file named **e09F_Stocks**. **Save** the file in the **Excel Chapter 9** folder and name it 9F_Stocks_Firstname_Lastname

2. Select the ranges **A5:A9** and **D5:D9** and click the **Insert tab**. In the **Charts group**, click the **Bar** button, and under **3-D Bar**, click the first choice—**Clustered Bar in 3-D**. Delete the **Legend**.

3. Replace the title with the following:

Cross Oceans Music
European Stock Closing Prices
August 31, 2009

4. Move the chart to a new sheet named **Closing**. Select the **Deutsche Recording** data marker, and then display the **Format Data Point** dialog box. Click **Fill**, and then add a **Texture** of **Stationery**. Insert the following textures in the data points: **Alliance Music**, **Denim**; **BCB**, **Inc.**, **Granite**; **Volksfon**, **Pink tissue paper**. Close the dialog box.

5. Format both the **Value axis** and the **Category axis** with **14-point font** and **Bold**.

6. Right-click next to the title and select **Format Chart Area**. Click **Fill**, and then add a **Gradient fill** under **Preset colors** of **Calm Water**. Click **Close**.

7. Click the **Stock sheet tab**. Click in cell **C7** and insert a **High-Low-Close stock chart**. Insert the two-line title displayed at the top of the next column at the top of the chart area:

Cross Oceans Music
European Stocks, Aug. 31, 2009

8. Move the chart so the upper left edge is in the upper left edge of cell **A12**. Extend the bottom border of the chart to cell **F31**.

9. Click in the **Chart** and on the **Design tab**, in the **Chart Styles group**, click the **More** button, and from the Chart Styles gallery, in the sixth column, click the third item—**Style 22**.

10. With the chart active, on the **Format tab**, in the **WordArt Styles group**, click the **Text Effects** button and select a **Glow** of **Accent color 1, 5 pt glow**.

11. Right-click the **Chart Area** and click **Format Chart Area**. Format in the **Chart** and **Plot Areas**, with a **Texture** of **Parchment**. Click **Close**.

12. Delete **Sheet2** and **Sheet3**. In all the worksheets, in the **Left Footer** area, insert the **File Name** and in the **Right Footer** area, insert the **Sheet Name**. Click the **Stock sheet tab** and center the worksheet both **Horizontally** and **Vertically**. **Save** your workbook.

13. To submit electronically, follow the instructions provided by your instructor. To print, from the **Office** menu, click **Print**. In the **Print** dialog box, under **Print what**, select **Entire workbook**, and then click **OK**. From the **Office** menu, click **Close**. **Close** Excel.

End You have completed Project 9F

Content-Based Assessments

Mastering Excel

Project 9G—Celtic Festivals

In this project, you will apply the skills you practiced from the Objectives in Projects 9A and 9B.

Objectives: 1. *Format with Graphic Images Including WordArt to Enhance Worksheets;* **4.** *Create Specialized Charts;* **5.** *Format Column Charts with Pictures and other Graphic Elements.*

In the following Mastering Excel project, you will review the attendance at Celtic Music festivals in England over the last three years. You will chart the data using pictures and other formatting techniques. Your completed worksheets will look similar to Figure 9.66.

For Project 9G, you will need the following files:

e09G_Celtic_Festivals.jpg
e09G_Music_Flute.jpg

You will save your workbook as
9G_Celtic_Festivals_Firstname_Lastname

Figure 9.66

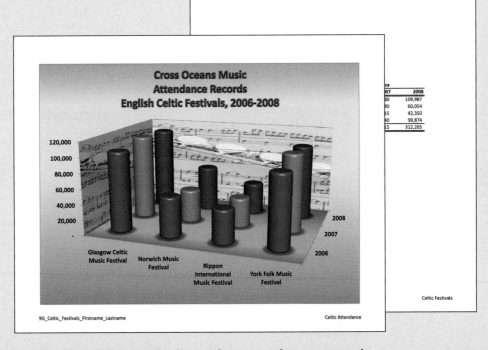

(Project 9G–Celtic Festivals continues on the next page)

(Project 9G–Celtic Festivals continued)

1. **Start** Excel. From the student files, locate and open the file named **e09G_Celtic_ Festivals** and **Save** it in your **Excel Chapter 9** folder as 9G_Celtic_Festivals_ Firstname_Lastname

2. Insert a **WordArt** of **Fill – Accent 2, Warm Matte Bevel** that displays **Celtic Fever** Move the WordArt so it begins in **row 14** and is centered under the worksheet. Then select a **Shape Effects** of **Preset** and select **Preset 9**.

3. Select the worksheet title and format with the **Standard Color** of **Dark Red**. Then **Merge & Center** the title over **columns A:E**.

4. Select the range **A7:E11**, and insert a **3-D Cylinder** chart. Move the chart so you can view both the worksheet and the chart, and then hide **column B**. Delete the **Legend**. Display the chart in a separate chart sheet named **Celtic Attendance**

5. Insert a title above the chart that reads **Cross Oceans Music** on the first line, **Attendance Records** on the second line, and **English Celtic Festivals, 2006-2008** on the third line. Format the title with **24-point font**.

6. Format the three axes text with **Bold** and **14-point font**. Note that in this 3-D chart there are threee axes to format— one identifies the attendance, one the festival names, and one the year of the festival. Format the **Chart Floor** with a **Gradient fill** of **Fog** with a **Linear** direction of **Linear Down**. Format the walls

with the picture named **e09G_Music Flute**.

7. Format the 2008 data series with a **Solid fill** of **Purple, Accent 4, Darker 25%**. Format the 2007 data series with a **Solid fill** of **Aqua, Accent 5, Darker 25%**. Format the 2006 data series with a **Solid fill** of **Blue, Accent 1, Darker 25%**.

8. Format all data series with a **Shadow** of **Outer** style named **Offset Diagonal Bottom Left**. Use **3-D Format** with a **Top Bevel** of **Circle** and a **Bottom Bevel** of **Circle**. Use the **Surface Material** effect under **Standard** of **Plastic**.

9. Format the **Chart Area** with a **Gradient fill** color of **Fog** with the **Direction** of **Linear Up**.

10. Click the chart title and in the **Format tab** in the **WordArt Styles** group, select a **Text Effect** of **Glow Accent color 2, 5 pt glow**.

11. Delete **Sheet2** and **Sheet3**. Do not unhide column B; if you do, the data will display in the chart. Confirm that the order of the worksheets is Celtic Attendance and then Celtic Festivals. In both sheets insert a **Left Footer** that displays the **File Name** and a **Right Footer** that displays the **Sheet Name**. Center the **Celtic Festivals** worksheet **Horizontally** and **Vertically** in **Portrait Orientation**. **Save** your workbook.

12. **Print** the worksheet or submit electroni- cally as directed. From the **Office** menu, click **Close**. **Close** Excel.

End You have completed Project 9G

Content-Based Assessments

Mastering Excel

Project 9H — Tours

In this project, you will apply the skills you practiced from the Objectives in Projects 9A and 9B.

Objectives: 1. *Format with Graphic Images Including WordArt to Enhance Worksheets;* **4.** *Create Specialized Charts;* **5.** *Format Column Charts with Pictures and other Graphic Elements.*

In the following mastering Excel project, you will create a scatter chart with a trendline. After Cross Oceans Music signs a new artist, the artist is taken on a promotional tour to stimulate sales of that artist's CDs. The tours range in length from 12 to 30 days. The artists sometimes have to cancel due to illness or exhaustion. You have been asked to look at the data and create a chart that will see if there is a relationship between the length of the tour and the number of cancellations. Your completed worksheets will look similar to those in Figure 9.67.

For Project 9H, you will need the following file:

e09H_Tours

You will save your workbook as
9H_Tours_Firstname_Lastname

Figure 9.67

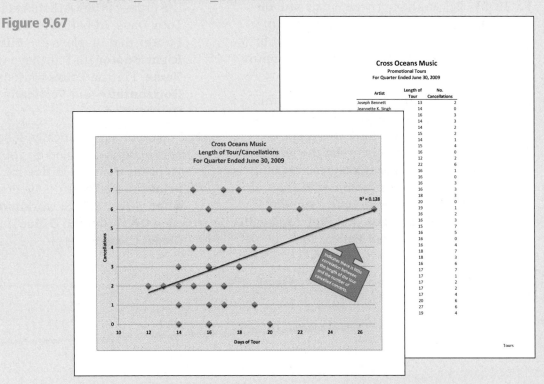

(Project 9H–Tours continues on the next page)

(Project 9H–Tours continued)

1. **Start** Excel. From the student files, locate and open the file named **e09H_Tours** and **Save** it in your **Excel Chapter 9** folder as 9H_Tours_Firstname_Lastname

2. Select the range **B6:C40**, and insert a **Scatter with only Markers** chart. Move the chart to a new worksheet with a name of **Tour Days** and delete the **Legend**.

3. Insert a title above the chart that reads **Cross Oceans Music** on the first line and **Length of Tour/Cancellations** on the second line, and **For Quarter Ended June 30, 2009** on the third line. Format the title with the **Dark Blue, Text 2, Darker 25%** font color and **16 point**.

4. Format the chart with **Chart Style 27**. Insert a vertical axis rotated title that reads **Cancellations** and a horizontal axis title that reads **Days of Tour** Format both axes and their titles with **Bold, 12-point font**.

5. Right-click in the horizontal axis and display the **Format Axis** dialog box. Change the horizontal axis so that the minimum number displayed is **10** and the maximum number displayed is **27**.

6. Add a **Linear Trendline** to the chart and **Display R-squared value on chart**. Notice that the low R-factor indicates there is very little correlation between the length of the tour and the number of concerts cancelled. Format the Trendline with the **Shape Style** of **Intense Line – Accent 2**. Format the **Chart Area** and **Plot Area** with a **Texture** of **Recycled Paper**.

7. Click in the R factor in the chart to select it. Right-click and format with **Bold** and **12-point font size**. With the text selected, drag the R factor up so it is completely visible.

8. Insert the **Block Arrow** shape named **Up Arrow Callout**. Position the callout at the right side of the chart below the trendline so it is located between the horizontal gridlines for 4 and 5 at the top and 1 and 2 at the bottom with it extending between days 22 and 26 on the horizontal axis. It will be a square. In the callout, type **Indicates there is little correlation between the length of the tour and the number of cancelled concerts**. Then use the **Rotation Handle** to point the graphic arrow to the R-factor. Confirm that the color in the shape is **Blue Accent 1** with text color of **White**.

9. Delete **Sheet2** and **Sheet3**. Confirm that the order of the worksheets is Tours and Tour Days. In both sheets, insert a **Left Footer** that displays the **File Name** and a **Right Footer** that displays the **Sheet Name**. For the **Tours** worksheet, center it **Horizontally** and **Vertically** in **Portrait Orientation**.

10. To submit electronically, follow the instructions provided by your instructor. To print, from the **Office** menu, click **Print**. In the **Print** dialog box, under **Print what**, select **Entire workbook**, and then click **OK**. From the **Office** menu, click **Close**. **Close** Excel.

 End **You have completed Project 9H**

Mastering Excel

Project 9I—Recordings

In this project, you will apply all the skills you practiced from the Objectives in Projects 9A and 9B.

Objectives: 1. *Format with Graphic Images Including WordArt to Enhance Worksheets;* **2.** *Insert SmartArt Graphics;* **3.** *Create, Edit, and Publish a Web Page;* **4.** *Create Specialized Charts;* **5.** *Format Column Charts with Pictures and other Graphic Elements.*

In the following Mastering Excel project, you will complete a worksheet and chart the data. During the year, Cross Oceans Music has concentrated on recording its New Age, Folk, and Ambient artists. President Tony Escovedo and Lila Darius, the artistic director, will review the recording totals for these three genres during the year. You will complete the worksheet that reports the number of recordings, and then chart the data in a variety of styles to present to Tony and Lila. Your completed worksheets will look similar to those in Figure 9.68.

For Project 9I, you will need the following files:

e09I_Recordings.jpg
e09I_Flute.jpg
e09I_Drum2.jpg
e09I_Guitar.jpg
e09I_Baton.jpg

You will save your workbooks as
9I_Recordings_Firstname_Lastname
9I_Org_Structure_Firstname_Lastname
9I_Org_Structure_Firstname_Lastname.mht

Figure 9.68

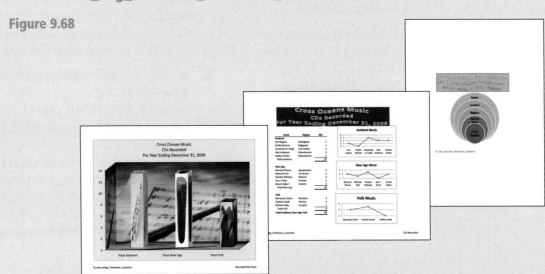

(Project 9I–Recordings continues on the next page)

(Project 9I–Recordings continued)

1. **Start** Excel. From your student files, locate and open the file named **e09I_Recordings** and **Save** it in your **Excel Chapter 9** folder as 9I_Recordings_Firstname_Lastname

2. Insert a **WordArt** style **Gradient Fill – Accent 1, Outline – White, Glow – Accent 2** that displays the following title:

Cross Oceans Music
CDs Recorded
For Year Ending December 31, 2009

3. Select the WordArt title and change the **Font Size** to **20 points**, and then use **Text Effects** to **Transform** the style to **Double Wave 2**. Increase the height of **row 1** to **63 points** and position the WordArt in the range **A1:H2**. Insert a **Shape Fill** of **Dark Blue, Text 2, Darker 25%**.

4. Complete the totals in the worksheet to determine the CDs for each genre of music. In cell **A27**, type **Total Ambient, New Age, Folk** and format with **Bold**. In cell **C27**, use the Grand Total feature to determine the total CDs for these three genres. Format the totals for each genre with **Top and Double Bottom Border** and the Grand Total with a **Thick Bottom Border**.

5. Click the edge of the **WordArt** graphic and copy and paste it to **Sheet2** in the format that can be edited. Position the WordArt to begin in cell **A1**. Insert a **SmartArt** graphic from the **Relationship** list of **Stacked Venn**. In the **Text Pane**, enter the data in the following order, and if necessary, delete any unused circles:

Scout
Location
Region
East or West

6. In the **SmartArt Change Colors**, under **Colorful**, click **Colorful Range – Accent Colors 3 to 4**. Move the graphic so it displays in the range **A7:G21**. In each circle of the SmartArt, change the text to **Bold**, font color—**Automatic**, and **Increase font size** once unless the text breaks into more than one line in the middle of a word. With the East or West circle selected, in the **Create Graphic group**, click the **Add Shape button arrow**, and then click **Add Shape After**. In the shape, type **Cross Oceans** and format it in the same style as the other labels.

7. Decrease the size of the **WordArt** title so it is centered over the SmartArt. Replace *CDs Recorded* with **Organization Structure** and in the date line, delete *For Year Ending*. In the **Shape Styles group**, click the **More** button and select a style of **Colored Fill – Accent 3**. In cell **A24** type 9I_Org_Structure_Firstname_Lastname and change the text color to **Olive Green, Accent 3, Darker 50%**.

8. Rename **Sheet1** to **CDs Recorded** and **Sheet2** to **Organization Structure** Copy the **Organization Structure** sheet to a new workbook and save it as **9I_Org_Structure_Firstname_Lastname** Then publish it as a **Single File Web Page** and name it 9I_Org_Structure_Firstname_Lastname.mht Open it in a Web page to view the results.

9. In your **9I_Recordings** workbook on the **CDs Recorded** sheet, increase the width of **column H** to **16.29 pixels**. Select the ranges **A7:A11** and **C7:C11**. Insert a **Line with Markers** chart. Delete the **Legend**. Insert a title **Above the Chart** that displays **Ambient Music** and format it with **14-point font**. Begin the vertical axis with **1.0**. Move and adjust the size of the chart to cover the range **E3:H11**. In the worksheet,

(Project 9I–Recordings continues on the next page)

(Project 9I–Recordings continued)

select the ranges **A15:A19** and **C15:C19**. Insert a **Line with Markers** chart. Delete the **Legend**. Insert a title **Above the Chart** that displays **New Age Music** and format it with **14-point font**. Begin the vertical axis with **1**. Adjust the size of the chart to cover the range **E13:H20**. Using the skills you have practiced, insert a **Line with Markers** chart to display the Folk CDs. Format the chart as the others are formatted and place it in the range **E22:H30**.

10. Adjust the **WordArt** to cover the range **A1:H2**. Group the worksheets and in the **Left Footer** insert the **File Name** and in the **Right Footer** insert the **Sheet Name**. Center the worksheets **Horizontally** and **Vertically**. Place the **CDs Recorded** worksheet in **Landscape Orientation** and then access **Print Preview**. If the worksheet displays on more than one page, adjust the size and placement of the charts so it displays on one page.

11. Select the following nonadjacent ranges: **A12:C12**, **A20:C20**, and **A26:C26** and insert a **3-D Clustered Column** chart on a separate chart sheet named **Recorded CDs Chart** Delete the **Legend** and insert a three-line title above the chart that displays:

Cross Oceans Music
CDs Recorded
For Year Ending December 31, 2009

12. In the chart, format the vertical and horizontal axes to increase the font size to **14 point bold** with a font color of **Orange, Accent 6, Darker 50%**. Format the **Walls** and **Floor** with the **e09I_Baton** clip art. Format the title with the **WordArt Style** of **Gradient Fill – Accent 6, Inner Shadow**. Format the **Chart Area** with a **Solid fill** color of **Blue, Accent 1, Lighter 80%**.

13. Select the data marker for **Total Ambient** and insert the picture named **e09I_Flute** and confirm that **Stretch** is selected. For the data marker for **Total New Age**, insert the picture named **e09I_Drum2** and stretch the picture. In the **Total Folk** data marker insert the **Stretched** picture named **e09I_Guitar**.

14. In the chart, in the **Left Footer**, insert the **File Name** and in the **Right Footer**, insert the **Sheet Name**. **Hide** the Organization Structure worksheet. Arrange the worksheets in the following order: Recorded CDs Chart and CDs Recorded. Delete **Sheet3**. **Save** your workbook.

15. **Print** the worksheet or submit electronically as directed. From the **Office** menu, click **Close**. If you are prompted to save changes, click **No**. **Close** Excel.

End You have completed Project 9I

Content-Based Assessments

Project 9J—Business Running Case

In this project, you will apply the skills you have practiced from the Objectives in Projects 9A and 9B.

From My Computer, navigate to the student files that accompany this textbook. In the folder **03_business_running_case**, locate and open the folder for this chapter. Open and print the instructions for this project, which are provided to you in Adobe PDF format. Follow the instructions and use the skills you have gained thus far to assist the managers of the Grand Department Store to meet the challenges of keeping records for a large department.

End **You have completed Project 9J** _____

Outcomes-Based Assessments

Rubric

The following outcomes-based assessments are *open-ended assessments*. That is, there is no specific correct result; your result will depend on your approach to the information provided. Make *Professional Quality* your goal. Use the following scoring rubric to guide you in *how* to approach the problem and then to evaluate *how well* your approach solves the problem.

The *criteria*—Software Mastery, Content, Format and Layout, and Process—represent the knowledge and skills you have gained that you can apply to solving the problem. The *levels of performance*—Professional Quality, Approaching Professional Quality, or Needs Quality Improvement—help you and your instructor evaluate your result.

	Your completed project is of Professional Quality if you:	Your completed project is Approaching Professional Quality if you:	Your completed project Needs Quality Improvements if you:
1-Software Mastery	Choose and apply the most appropriate skills, tools, and features and identify efficient methods to solve the problem.	Choose and apply some appropriate skills, tools, and features, but not in the most efficient manner.	Choose inappropriate skills, tools, or features, or are inefficient in solving the problem.
2-Content	Construct a solution that is clear and well organized, contains content that is accurate, appropriate to the audience and purpose, and complete. Provide a solution that contains no errors of spelling, grammar, or style.	Construct a solution in which some components are unclear, poorly organized, inconsistent, or incomplete. Misjudge the needs of the audience. Have some errors in spelling, grammar, or style, but the errors do not detract from comprehension.	Construct a solution that is unclear, incomplete, or poorly organized, containing some inaccurate or inappropriate content; and contains many errors of spelling, grammar, or style. Do not solve the problem.
3-Format and Layout	Format and arrange all elements to communicate information and ideas, clarify function, illustrate relationships, and indicate relative importance.	Apply appropriate format and layout features to some elements, but not others. or, overuse features, causing minor distraction.	Apply format and layout that does not communicate information or ideas clearly. Do not use format and layout features to clarify function, illustrate relationships, or indicate relative importance. Use available features excessively, causing distraction.
4-Process	Use an organized approach that integrates planning, development, self-assessment, revision, and reflection.	Demonstrate an organized approach in some areas, but not others; or, use an insufficient process of organization throughout.	Do not use an organized approach to solve the problem.

Outcomes-Based Assessments

Problem Solving

Project 9K — CD_Sales

In this project, you will construct a solution by applying any combination of the skills you practiced from the Objectives in Projects 9A and 9B.

For Project 9K, you will need the following file:

e09K_CD_Sales

You will save your workbook as
9K_CD_Sales_Firstname_Lastname

In this project, you will create a worksheet for the Tony Escovedo, president of Cross Oceans Music, that highlights the artists with the top-selling CDs for the first quarter of 2009. Use WordArt to create an appropriate title for the data that has been assembled. Tony has asked that you format the data attractively and that you insert the words *Top-Selling Artists for First Quarter* into the shape to highlight the data. He has also asked that you add a filled star in the worksheet.

Create a 3-D column chart that displays the CD sales for each artist—rather than the type of music—for the three months. Use pictures, texture, and other graphic elements in the chart. Place this chart in a separate sheet. Place the data markers in positions that make all of them visible.

In the workbook, insert a footer that includes the file name at the left and sheet name at the right. Delete unused worksheets. Save the workbook as **9K_CD_Sales_Firstname_Lastname** and submit as directed.

End **You have completed Project 9K** ————————————

Project 9L — Promotion

In this project, you will construct a solution by applying any combination of the skills you practiced from the Objectives in Projects 9A and 9B.

For Project 9L, you will need the following files:

e09L_Promotion.wmf
e09L_Quarter_Notes.wmf

You will save your workbook as
9L_Promotion_Firstname_Lastname

In this project, you will complete a 3-D chart for Cross Oceans Music. Recently, Raa Ihansa, the scout for the Middle Eastern region, conducted a promotion to sell the CDs that feature Middle Eastern music. You will complete a chart sheet that displays the type and the total number of CDs sold during the two-week promotion. The data is entered in the file named e09L_Promotion.

On a separate sheet, insert a cylinder, cone, or pyramid column chart to display the totals of the CDs sold. Format the chart area with the quarter notes e09L_Quarter_Notes located with the student files. In the chart, across the cross bar of the quarter notes, use WordArt to display the company name. Complete the entire title of the chart in the same area using the same information that is included in the worksheet. Include a filled star shape in the chart. Format the other chart elements to provide a professional-appearing worksheet and chart.

In both the chart and the worksheet, add a footer that includes the file name at the left and sheet name at the right. Delete unused worksheets. Save the workbook as **9L_Promotion_Firstname_Lastname** and submit it as directed.

End **You have completed Project 9L** ——————————

Problem Solving

Project 9M—Asian Stocks

In this project, you will construct a solution by applying any combination of the skills you practiced from the Objectives in Projects 9A and 9B.

For Project 9M, you will need the following file:

New blank Excel workbook

You will save your workbook as
9M_Asian_Stocks_Firstname_Lastname

In this project, you will complete a stock report for Cross Oceans Music. The president, Tony Escovedo, believes that the company should maintain investments in the regions where they do business. You will complete a worksheet that reports its Asian holdings for one day. You will then complete a stock chart that displays the activity of the stock for October 14, 2009.

Enter the following data in your workbook:

Stock	High	Low	Close
Honshu Bank	15.61	20.50	23.50
Japan Arts	63.85	52.00	61.35
Metals of China	86.44	82.00	84.50
Speedy Train, LTD	23.96	29.75	31.00
TalkEFone	23.95	20.35	22.50

Use borders, themes, WordArt, and other attributes to prepare a professional workbook. Insert a stock chart on a separate sheet that displays the data for the day. In the chart, use the formatting techniques to format the parts of the chart—chart area, chart wall, chart floor, data markers, and so on—to present a professional appearance.

In both the chart and the worksheet, add a footer that includes the file name at the left and sheet name at the right. Save the workbook as **9M_Stocks_Firstname_Lastname** and submit it as directed.

End You have completed Project 9M————————

Outcomes-Based Assessments

Problem Solving

Project 9N — No. Africa

In this project, you will construct a solution by applying any combination of the skills you practiced from the Objectives in Projects 9A and 9B.

For Project 9N, you will need the following file:

e09N_No_Africa
e09N_MusicNotes1
e09N_MusicNotes2 and/or
e09N_MusicNotes3

**You will save your workbook as
9N_No_Africa_Firstname_Lastname**

In this project, you will complete a workbook that displays the North African artists who have signed with Cross Oceans Music during the third quarter of 2009. You will then chart that data.

Lila Darius, the artistic director, tracks the number of artists that each of the scouts signs during the quarter. Matisse Keita, the scout for North Africa, has reported his signings on a worksheet that is saved as **e09N_No_Africa**. Total and format the worksheet using WordArt, color, shapes, and other format techniques.

On a separate sheet, create a column chart that compares the data by month. Use musical notes available in clip art for the data markers. Alternatively, use the music notes in your student files—e09N_MusicNotes1, e09N_MusicNotes2, and/or e09N_MusicNotes3. Format the chart title with WordArt. Review the worksheet to make sure all items included in the chart are easy to read.

Add a footer that includes the file name at the left and page numbers at the right. Delete unused sheets. Save the workbook as **9N_No_Africa_Firstname_Lastname** and submit it as directed.

End You have completed Project 9N ————————

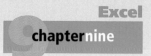

Problem Solving

Project 9O — Recording Costs

In this project, you will construct a solution by applying any combination of the skills you practiced from the Objectives in Projects 9A and 9B.

For Project 9O, you will need the following file:

e09O_Recording_Costs

**You will save your workbook as
9O_Recording_Costs_Firstname_Lastname**

In this project, you will complete a workbook that displays the recording costs for an artist's CD. The data is saved in **e09O_Recording_Costs**.

Use WordArt to create the worksheet title. On the first line you will insert the company name—Cross Oceans Music. You will display the recording costs for Slavia Bachev completed on July 18, 2009. Format the worksheet attractively, but include the following items: a colored font for the data that is coordinated with the other worksheet parts, a texture with a colored fill, and an inserted and rotated shape.

Add a footer that includes the file name and delete the unused sheets. Save the workbook as **9O_Recording_Costs_Firstname_Lastname** and submit it as directed.

End **You have completed Project 9O** ────────────

Outcomes-Based Assessments

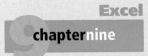

You and GO!

Project 9P — You and GO!

In this project, you will construct a solution by applying any combination of the Objectives found in Projects 9A and 9B.

From My Computer, navigate to the student files that accompany this textbook. In the folder **04_you_and_go**, locate and open the folder for this chapter. Open and print the instructions for this project, which are provided to you in Adobe PDF format. You will record information about stock for one day and then create a worksheet and a stock chart to report the results of those stocks.

 End You have completed Project 9P _____

GO! with Help

Project 9Q — GO! with Help

In this chapter, you created many charts. However, there are still several charts in Excel that you did not use—surface, doughnut, bubble, and radar. You will use Help to select and create a different type of chart.

1 **Start** Excel and confirm that you are connected to the Internet. At the far right end of the Ribbon, click the **Microsoft Office Excel Help** button.

2 In the search box, type the type of chart you will explore—**surface chart**, **doughnut chart**, and so on—and then press Enter. When the search is completed, click on the item that displays *Present your data in a xxx chart*—where the xxx is replaced by the chart you selected.

3 In Help, review the information about the chart. Then using that information, create a worksheet that displays the data appropriate for the chart. Then create the chart and format it professionally.

 End You have completed Project 9Q _____

chapter**ten**

Creating Templates and Creating and Validating Forms

OBJECTIVES

At the end of this chapter, you will be able to:

1. Protect Worksheet Elements
2. Unprotect Elements and Hide Formulas
3. Protect a Workbook
4. Save Worksheet and Chart Templates
5. Complete a Report with Worksheet and Chart Templates

OUTCOMES

Mastering these objectives will enable you to:

PROJECT 10A
Protect and Unprotect Worksheets, Workbooks, and Individual Elements and Hide Formulas

6. Create a Form
7. Validate a Form
8. Insert Macro Command Buttons

PROJECT 10B
Create and Validate a Form and Create and Use a Macro Command Button

Southwest Gardens

The Southwest style of gardening is popular in many areas of the country, not just in the yards and gardens of Arizona and New Mexico. The stylish simplicity and use of indigenous, hardy plants that are traditional in the southwest United States make for beautiful, environmentally friendly gardens in any part of the country. Produced by Media Southwest Productions, the television show *Southwest Gardens* is broadcast nationwide. The show and its Web site provide tips and tricks for beautiful gardens and highlight new tools and techniques, and the show's hosts present tours of public and private gardens that showcase the Southwest style.

Creating Templates and Creating and Validating Forms

Template documents are created for worksheets that are used repeatedly. For example, a sales report is prepared weekly. Completing all of the formatting and formulas in a worksheet and then entering only the variable data saves time. Saving this report as a template that can be used again improves efficiency.

Forms that are used by several different people are created and saved as a template. Certain portions of the form are protected so they cannot be altered. Other areas of the form are available for data entry. To complete the form faster, a macro can be created that is attached to a shape on the form, and when that shape is selected, the macro is run.

Project 10A **Payroll Report**

In Activities 10.1 through 10.11, you will create a worksheet, protect a worksheet, and then save that worksheet as a template. You will also create a chart and then save it as a template. You will assist the Payroll Department of Media Southwest Productions by streamlining the preparation of the weekly report for the hours worked and the corresponding chart. You will create and format the worksheet, protect it so it cannot be altered, and then save it as a template that can be used to report each week's hours worked. In addition, the chart that displays the hours worked will be saved as a template and used each week for the payroll report. Your completed workbook will look similar to Figure 10.1.

For Project 10A, you will need the following files:

New blank Excel workbook
e10A_SW_Garden_Logo

You will save your workbooks as
10A_Payroll_Report_Firstname_Lastname
10A_Payroll_October9_Firstname_Lastname
10A_Payroll_Report_Template_Firstname_Lastname (Template)
10A_Pay_Chart_Temp_Firstname_Lastname (Template)

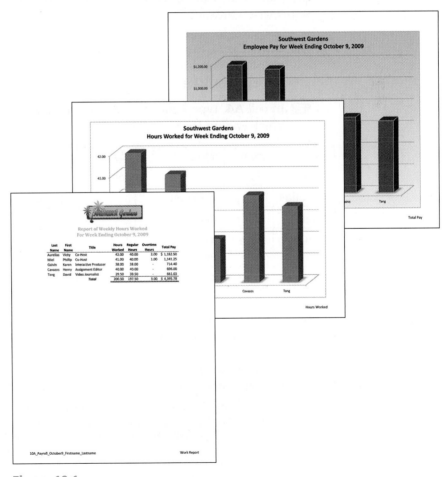

Figure 10.1
Project 10A—Payroll Report

Objective 1
Protect Worksheet Elements

An Excel worksheet is normally saved as ***read-write*** workbook, which means they can be read, edited, and resaved. When a worksheet or workbook is used by several people, it is recommended that the worksheet be protected so changes to the format or formulas cannot be made. There are different levels of protection—from protecting only elements of the worksheet to protecting the entire workbook.

Southwest Gardens prepares a report of the hours worked on the TV show on a weekly basis using an Excel spreadsheet. After several months of completing the same report, the chief accountant of the Payroll Department suggests that a template be created that reports those hours worked to Media Southwest Productions. Then each employee can access the worksheet and enter the hours he or she worked. You will create a new worksheet and set it up with the proper formats, logos, and formulas, and then protect it for future use.

Activity 10.1 Inserting a Picture into a Header

A logo provides a visual identification of the firm that people recognize. Southwest Gardens uses a logo on its worksheets to create a visual identity that is associated with the show. In this activity, you will insert the Southwest Gardens logo into the header of a worksheet.

1 **Start** Excel. Save a blank workbook in a new **Excel Chapter 10** folder with the name **10A_Payroll_Report_Firstname_Lastname** Rename **Sheet1 Work Report**

2 In cell **A4**, type **Report of Weekly Hours Worked** and in cell **A5**, type **For Week Ending** Beginning in cell **A7**, enter the following information:

Last Name	First Name	Title	Hours Worked	Hourly Rate	Regular Hours	Overtime Hours	Total Pay
Aurelias	Vicky	Co-Host		27.50			
Miel	Phillip	Co-Host		27.50			
Galvin	Karen	Interactive Producer		18.80			
Cavazos	Henry	Assignment Editor		17.40			
Tang	Davis	Video Journalist		16.75			

3 Click the **Insert tab**, and in the **Text group**, click the **Header & Footer** button. With the insertion point in the center Header section, in the **Header & Footer Elements group**, click the **Picture** button. In the **Insert Picture** dialog box, navigate to the files for this chapter, click **e10A_SW_Garden_Logo**, and then click **Insert**.

The code &[Picture] is inserted into the header. When the worksheet displays, the picture will display instead of the code.

4 Click in cell **A1**.

The logo in the header is large and displays through several rows of the worksheet. When a picture is inserted into the worksheet, it is inserted in its original size. Often a picture size needs to be modified to fit the designated space.

5 In the **Text group**, click the **Header & Footer** button. In the **Header & Footer Elements group**, click the **Format Picture** button 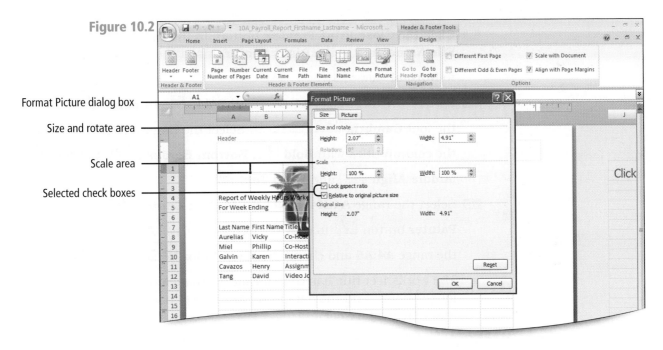, and then compare your screen with Figure 10.2.

The Format Picture dialog box is used to specify the size of the picture. On the Size tab, under the Scale area, the check boxes are selected for *Lock aspect ratio* and *Relative to original picture size*. This confirms that the picture will not be distorted when it is resized.

Figure 10.2

Format Picture dialog box

Size and rotate area

Scale area

Selected check boxes

6 Under **Size and rotate**, in the **Height** box, replace the displayed entry with **1** and then click **OK**. In the **Header & Footer Elements group**, click **Format Picture** and confirm that the Width has been changed to 2.38. Click **OK**, and then click cell **A1**.

When you change either the height or width of a picture, both will be altered in order to retain the original proportions.

7 Press Ctrl + F2 to display Print Preview and the logo in the header, and then compare your screen with Figure 10.3.

The keyboard shortcut quickly displays Print Preview. The logo now displays at the top of the worksheet. The logo also displays while you are in Page Layout view.

Figure 10.3

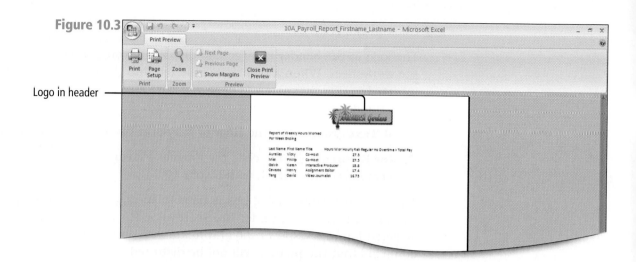

Logo in header

Report of Weekly Hours Worked
For Week Ending

8 Click the **Close Print Preview** button. In the **Left Footer**, insert the **File Name**, and in the **Right Footer**, insert the **Sheet Name**. Return to **Normal** view ⊞ .

9 Format the title—cells **A4:A5**—with **Bold** B , **14 point** 11 ▾ , and the font **Cambria** Calibri ▾ . Select the range **A7:H7** and format the column titles with **Bold** B , **Bottom Border** ▾ , **Center** ▥ , **Middle Align** ▤ , and **Wrap Text** ▤ .

10 Select the range **A4:H4** and click **Merge & Center** ▾ . Use **Format Painter** button ✦ to copy the format from cell **A4** to cell **A5**. Select the range **A4:A5** and change the **Font Color** A ▾ to **Standard Green**.

The worksheet title has been formatted to include the company logo for the name, and the data in the worksheet has been formatted with a complementary color.

11 **Save** ▥ your workbook.

Activity 10.2 Inserting Formulas and Formats into a Report

Before a template is saved, all of the formatting and the formulas should be completed. Then when the hours are reported each week, only the hours need to be entered and the worksheet is completed. In this activity, you will complete the formulas required and format the rest of the worksheet.

1 Adjust column widths as needed to fully display the data. In the range **D8:D12**, enter the following numbers as placeholders:

| 38 |
| 39 |
| 40 |
| 41 |
| 42 |

These numbers are placeholders to use as you develop the worksheet. The number of hours worked is the **input range**—the range that will be filled in each week. Adding data as placeholders helps review the results of the formulas to determine that they are accurate.

2 Click cell **F8** and enter an IF formula to determine the number of regular hours worked. Recall that all hours over 40 each week are overtime hours. Click the **Formulas tab**, and in the **Function Library group**, click the **Logical** button and from the list, click **IF**. In the **IF Function Arguments** dialog box, in the **Logical_test** box, type **d8>=40**

This function tests if the hours worked are equal to or greater than 40, the normal hours in a work week.

3 Press ⇥ and in the **Value_if_true** box, type **40** Press ⇥ and in the **Value_if_false** box, type **d8** and then compare your screen with Figure 10.4.

If the hours worked are equal to or greater than 40, the argument is true and 40 will be entered in the cell. If the results of the logical test is false—the hours worked are less than 40—the actual hours worked will be entered. Recall that the result of the function displays in the Function Arguments dialog box—38 is the result of this function.

Logical test—hours worked are 40 or more

Result of function

Figure 10.4

IF Function Arguments dialog box

Value if true—if hours worked are equal to or greater than 40, enter 40

Value if false—if hours worked are less than 40, enter the hours worked

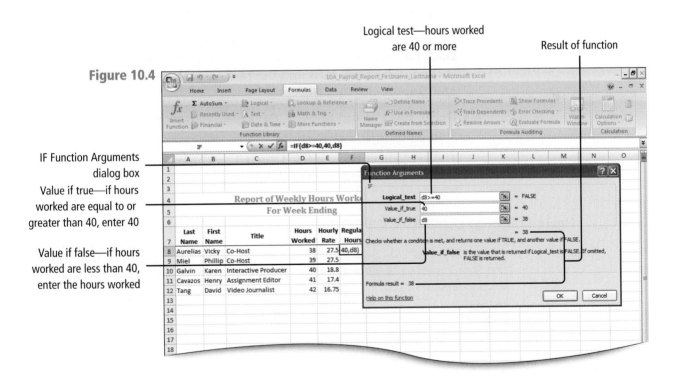

4 Click **OK**. The result of the logical test is false, so the actual hours worked—38—is entered in the cell.

5 Click cell **G8** and type **=d8-f8** This is the formula to determine the overtime hours worked—the difference between the hours worked and the regular hours. Press `Tab` and in cell **H8**, enter the formula for the total pay. It is the regular hours times the hourly rate plus the overtime hours times the hourly rate times 1.5. Type **=f8*e8+g8*e8*1.5** and press `Enter`.

The total pay for Vicky—1045—is entered into the cell.

6 Select the range **F8:H8** and use the fill handle to copy the formulas down through **row 12**. Confirm that the regular hours worked are accurate—no numbers are greater than 40.

Recall when an employee works more than 40 hours a week, all hours over 40 are overtime hours.

7 Click cell **C13** and type **Total** and format cell **C13** with **Bold** $\boxed{B}$, **Italic** $\boxed{I}$, and **Center** $\boxed{≡}$. Click cell **D13**, and then press `Ctrl` and select the range **F13:H13**. Then enter a **Sum** function.

8 Select cells **E8**, **H8**, and **H13** and format them with **Accounting Number Format** $\boxed{\$\,\cdot}$. Select cell **D8** and format it with **Comma Style** $\boxed{,}$. Right-click cell **D8**, and in the Mini toolbar, double-click the **Format Painter** button $\boxed{≼}$, and then click cells **F8:G8**, **D9:H12**, **D13**, **F13**, and **G13**. Press `Esc` to turn off the Format Painter. Select cell **D13** and the range **F13:H13** and insert a **Top and Double Bottom Border**.

9 Delete **Sheet2** and **Sheet3**. **Save** $\boxed{🖫}$ your worksheet and compare your work with Figure 10.5.

The worksheet is completed and when the hours worked are entered, the weekly payroll report will be completed.

Figure 10.5

Completed worksheet —

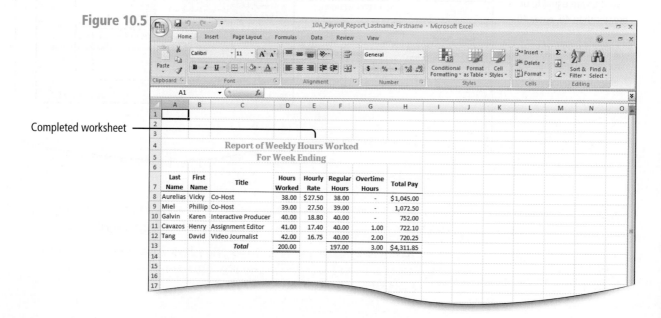

Activity 10.3 Completing a Chart for the Worksheet

When a chart is used to display the worksheet data, it is convenient to place the chart on a separate worksheet within the workbook. In this activity, you will create a chart of the hours worked in the workbook.

1 Select the range **A7:A12** and press Ctrl while you select the range **D7:D12**.

2 On the **Insert tab**, in the **Charts group**, click the **Column** button. In the Chart gallery, under **3-D Column**, click **3-D Clustered Column**. On the **Design tab**, in the **Location group**, click **Move Chart**. In the **Move Chart** dialog box, click **New sheet** and name it **Hours Worked** and then click **OK**.

The chart is now displayed in a separate Chart sheet.

3 Change the title to a two-line title that reads:

> **Southwest Gardens**
> **Hours Worked for Week Ending**

4 In the chart, delete the **Legend**. On the **Design tab**, in the **Chart Styles group**, click the **More** button ⬇, and then in the gallery, click **Style 27**. Compare your screen with Figure 10.6.

Figure 10.6

Title changed ────

Hours Worked chart sheet created ────

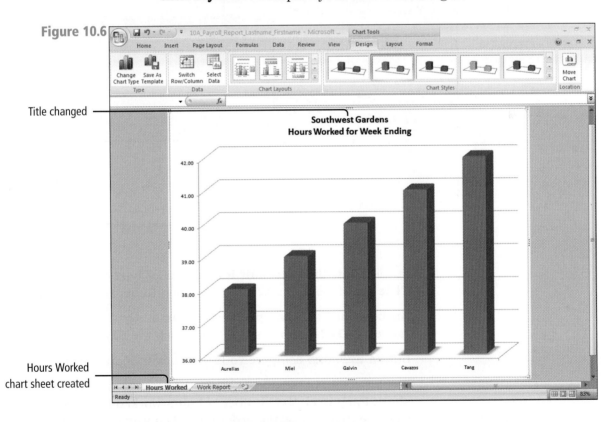

5 Move the **Work Report** sheet to the left of the **Hours Worked** sheet. With the **Work Report** sheet active, click the **Page Layout** tab and in the **Page Setup group**, click the **Dialog Box Launcher** 🔲. In the **Page Setup** dialog box, click the **Margins tab**, and then center **Horizontally**.

6 **Save** your workbook 💾.

Activity 10.4 Protecting Elements of the Worksheet

When a worksheet will be used by several people, it is recommended that the worksheet be **protected**, which means that unauthorized changes cannot be made. Protected worksheets may require a password in order to edit them. Sometimes, however, some cells should be edited or changed. It is possible to leave some cells unprotected while the rest of the worksheet is protected. In this activity, you will protect the worksheet but allow users to enter the hours worked and the date of a pay period.

> **1** Click the **Review tab**, and in the **Changes group**, click the **Allow Users to Edit Ranges** button. Then compare your screen with Figure 10.7.
>
> The Allow Users to Edit Ranges dialog box displays. Here you can enter cells or ranges of cells that will be left unprotected while you protect the rest of the worksheet.

Figure 10.7

Allow Users to Edit Ranges dialog box

New button used to insert new fields

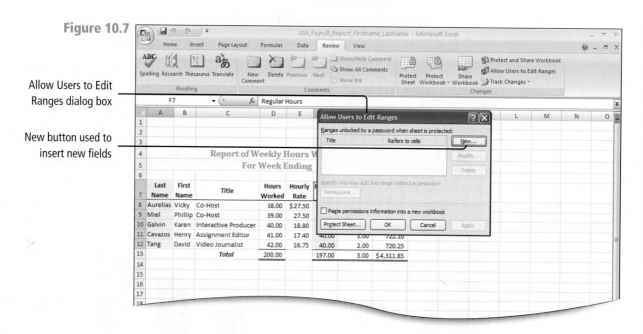

> **2** In the **Allow Users to Edit Ranges** dialog box, click **New**. In the **Title** box, type **Hours_Worked** and then under the **Refers to cells**, in the box, click the **Collapse Dialog Box** button and select the range **D8:D12** and press F4. Then click the **Expand Dialog Box** button , and compare your screen with Figure 10.8.
>
> You have selected to allow changes to a range of cells in the worksheet. Each week the number of hours worked by each employee will be entered. A **password**—which is a way to restrict access to a workbook, worksheet, or part of a worksheet—may be required in order to change an entry in the cell. The password can be entered here. Excel passwords can be up to 255 letters, numbers, spaces,

and symbols; passwords are case sensitive. The password in this dialog box applies to the selected range.

Figure 10.8

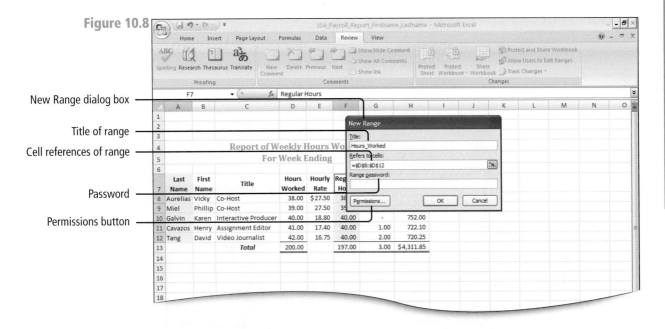

New Range dialog box

Title of range

Cell references of range

Password

Permissions button

3 Click the **Permissions** button, and then compare your screen with Figure 10.9.

You can allow certain areas to be edited in a protected worksheet when **permissions** are granted. When specific people are allowed to edit the worksheet, permissions may be granted in this dialog box. For Southwest Gardens, the small number of employees does not warrant further protection.

Figure 10.9

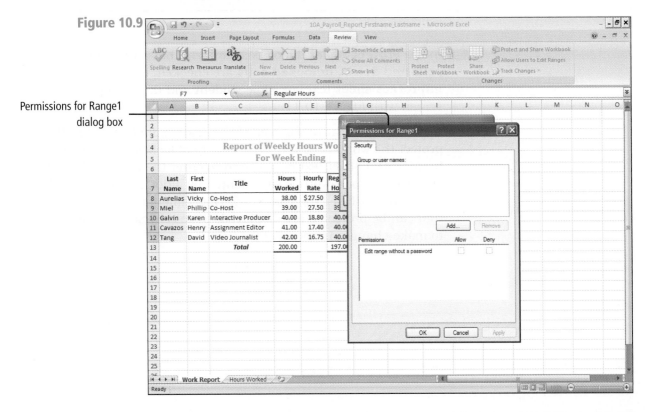

Permissions for Range1 dialog box

4 Click **OK** two times. At the bottom left of the **Allow Users to Edit Ranges** dialog box, click **Protect Sheet**, and then compare your screen with Figure 10.10.

The Protect Sheet dialog box is used to set the protection levels for the worksheet and its elements. A password can be entered and allowance can be given for specific elements of the worksheet to be edited.

Figure 10.10

Protect Sheet dialog box

Area to insert password

Elements that can be edited

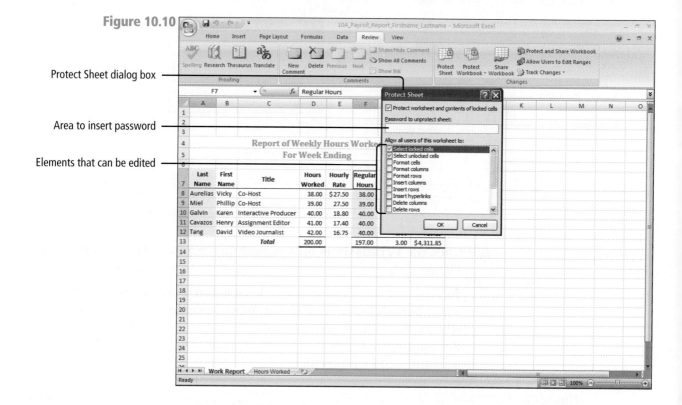

5 In the **Protect Sheet** dialog box, confirm that both **Select locked cells** and **Select unlocked cells** are checked. In the **Password to unprotect sheet** text box, type **student** and then compare your screen with Figure 10.11.

Near the top of the dialog box, the check box indicates that this will protect the worksheet and the contents of locked cells. The Password to unprotect sheet text box is used to enter the password. Each keystroke of the password is represented by a dot. This ensures that no one nearby will see the password. The elements of the worksheet that can be protected are displayed. Boxes checked will allow users to make changes in the selected areas.

Figure 10.11

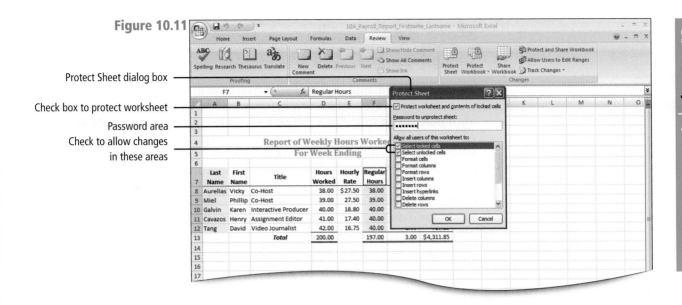

Protect Sheet dialog box

Check box to protect worksheet

Password area

Check to allow changes
in these areas

6️⃣ Click **OK**. In the **Confirm Password** dialog box, again enter the password—**student**—and then click **OK**.

Alert! | **Why does another dialog box display?**

If the confirmation password is incorrectly entered, a dialog box displays warning you that the password was incorrectly entered. Click OK, and then enter the correct password again.

7️⃣ Click cell **A7** and press Delete. Read the displayed warning box, and then click **OK**.

The warning box that displays explains that the cell is locked and you do not have access to change it.

8️⃣ Click in cell **D8** and enter a number. Continue clicking in other cells and attempt to change the cell contents to confirm they are locked. Then select the range **D8:D12** and press Delete to clear the hours worked range.

The cells in this range have not been locked and changes can be made. Other cells have been locked so changes cannot be made. A warning box displays to indicate that the cell or chart is protected and read-only. A **read-only** workbook can be reviewed, but no changes can be made to it. When an employee enters the number of hours worked in a week, only those cells that remain unlocked can be edited.

9️⃣ If necessary, click **OK**, and then **Save** 🔲 your changes.

More Knowledge

Strong Passwords

Microsoft recommends that **strong passwords** be used. A strong password combines uppercase and lowercase letters, numbers that do not make up a word that can be found in a dictionary, numbers, and symbols, such as Y6ieyTy. Note that this sample password appears to randomly alternate between letters and numbers, another feature of a strong password. Weak passwords do not. An example of a weak password is Student1. Passwords should be 8 or more characters in length; however, 14 characters are better. Use passwords that are easy for you to remember but difficult for others to guess. Write down your passwords, and then save them in a secure location.

For more information on password recommendations, access the Microsoft Web site—http://www.microsoft.com—and search for Strong Passwords.

Objective 2
Unprotect Elements and Hide Formulas

Once a worksheet is protected, it can be unprotected and changed. If each element was protected with a password, then that password needs to be entered before the element can be edited. When a worksheet is shared, there are often elements in the worksheet that should not be available for others to view, such as formulas and other sensitive data.

Activity 10.5 Unprotecting Cells in a Protected Worksheet

A protected worksheet sometimes needs to be edited or changed. Cells within a protected worksheet can be unprotected without changing the protection of other elements on the worksheet. In this activity, you will unprotect the cell containing the date so it can be entered for each weekly report.

1 With the **Work Report sheet** active, click the **Review tab**, and in the **Changes group**, click the **Unprotect Sheet** button.

When a worksheet is protected, the command in the Changes group is Unprotect Sheet. The Unprotect Sheet dialog box displays where you will enter the password in order to make changes to the worksheet.

2 In the **Unprotect Sheet** dialog box, type **student** and then click **OK**. Click cell **A5**.

3 On the **Home tab**, in the **Cells group**, click the **Format** button and from the list, under **Protection**, click **Format Cells**. In the **Format Cells** dialog box, click the **Protection tab**, and then compare your screen with Figure 10.12. Alternatively, use the keyboard shortcut of Ctrl + ⇧ Shift + F.

The Protection tab in the Format Cells dialog box is used to lock or hide selected cells in the worksheet. The check box for Locked is selected, which indicates that cell A5 is locked.

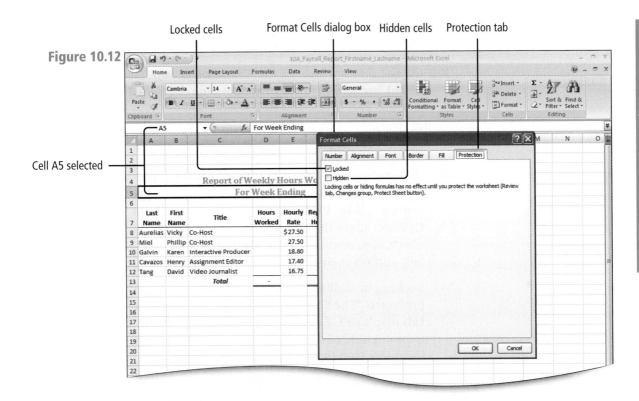

Figure 10.12

Locked cells   Format Cells dialog box   Hidden cells   Protection tab

Cell A5 selected

4 In the **Protection tab**, click **Locked** to deselect it, and then click **OK**. Click the **Review tab**, and in the **Changes group**, click the **Protect Sheet** button. Type the password **student** and click **OK**, and then enter the password again to confirm it. Click OK.

Each week the date of the payroll will be entered in cell A5, so it needs to be unlocked. When additional cells in a protected worksheet need to be locked or unlocked, use the Protection tab in the Format Cells dialog box.

Note

Student Will Be the Password Throughout the Chapter

You should use strong passwords when you complete most work. In this text, the password is *student* because it is easy to remember and your instructor will know the password—just in case you forget your password.

5 Try to change cells in the worksheet to confirm that cells are still locked except cell **A5**—for the date—and the range **D8:D12**—where the hours worked will be entered. **Save** 💾 your workbook.

Activity 10.6 Hiding Formulas and Other Sensitive Information

Because this workbook will be used by all employees, the sensitive information of the hourly rate should be hidden. In addition, the formulas that are used in the worksheet also can be hidden. In this activity, you will hide the hourly rate and the formulas from view.

1 On the **Review tab**, in the **Changes group**, click the **Unprotect Sheet** button. In the **Unprotect Sheet** dialog box, type the password **student** and then click **OK**.

Recall that a protected worksheet cannot be changed, so it must first be unprotected.

2 Hide **column E**. Select the range **F8:H13**, press Ctrl and click cell **D13**. Click the **Home tab**, and in the **Cells group**, click the **Format** button. Under **Protection**, click **Format Cells**, and then in the **Custom Lists** dialog box, on the Protection tab, click the **Hidden** check box, and then click **OK**. Click in the cells that contain formulas, and on the Formula Bar, notice that the formulas are still visible.

Locking or hiding cells does not take effect until the worksheet is protected. The Custom Lists dialog box displays with the **Protection tab** displayed. *Locked cells* cannot be changed after the worksheet is protected. When the worksheet is protected, *hidden cells* hide formulas from other users.

3 On the **Home tab**, in the **Cells group**, click the **Format** button, and then under **Protection**, click **Protect Sheet**. In the **Protect Sheet** dialog box, confirm that the **Protect worksheet and contents of locked cells** check box is selected, and in the **Password to unprotect sheet** box, type **student**

4 Click **OK**, type **student** to confirm the password, and then click **OK**.

Save 🖫 your workbook. Click in the cells that contain formulas and confirm that no formulas display in the Formula Bar.

Note

The Custom Lists Dialog Box Looks Like the Format Cells Dialog Box

When protecting cells, Excel opens the Format Cells dialog box the first time it is used. In each subsequent command, the Custom Lists dialog box is used. The choices in the dialog boxes are the same.

Objective 3
Protect a Workbook

When protecting your work, the entire workbook can also be protected. A password may be required to open the workbook. The structure of the workbook or the way the windows display can be protected. In a business, workbooks are often used by many people and the protection feature prevents workbooks from being altered, either accidentally or maliciously.

Activity 10.7 Protecting a Workbook's Structure and Windows

The **structure** is the basic format of the worksheet that includes the number and order of worksheets. When the structure is protected, hidden worksheets cannot be accessed, you cannot move or copy worksheets or change their names, and you cannot insert or delete worksheets. Protecting the way the windows display includes changing the size and position of the windows when the workbook is opened and moving, resizing, or closing windows. In this activity, you will protect the structure of the workbook so worksheets cannot be inserted or removed.

■1 On the **Review tab**, in the **Changes group**, click the **Protect Workbook** button to display the menu, and then compare your screen with Figure 10.13.

There are two aspects of workbooks that can be protected—the structure and permissions for viewing and/or editing. Recall that you previously deleted extra sheets in the added workbook. Protecting the structure prevents additional sheets from being added.

Protect Workbook button

Figure 10.13

Protect Workbook menu

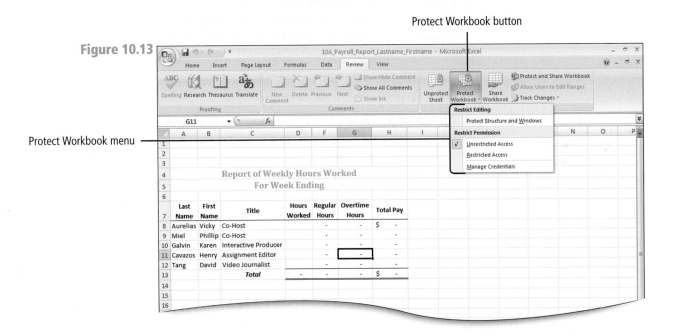

■2 Under **Restrict Editing**, click **Protect Structure and Windows**, and then compare your screen with Figure 10.14.

The Protect Structure and Windows dialog box displays with check boxes to protect either the structure or the windows or both. An optional password may be entered. If a password is not used, then any user can unprotect the workbook and change the protected elements.

Figure 10.14

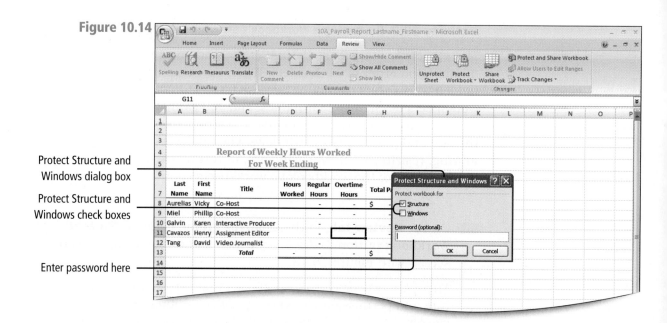

Protect Structure and
Windows dialog box

Protect Structure and
Windows check boxes

Enter password here

3 Confirm that **Structure** is the only item checked. In the **Password** text box, type **student** and then click **OK**. Reenter the password **student** to confirm it, and then click **OK**. In the worksheet, try to insert a column or insert a worksheet.

Because the worksheet structure is protected, changes to the workbook structure cannot be made.

4 Click cell **A1**. Click the **Office** button and point to **Prepare**, and on the right side, point to **Encrypt Document**, and then compare your screen with Figure 10.15.

When you *encrypt* a document, it is encoded—information is scrambled—to increase the security of the document. This also prevents unauthorized access to the document.

Figure 10.15

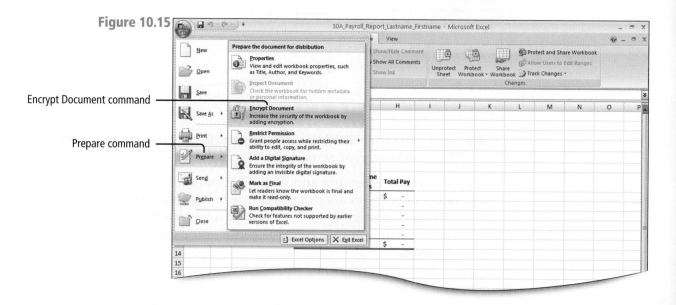

Encrypt Document command

Prepare command

5 Click **Encrypt Document**. In the **Encrypt Document** dialog box, in the **Password** box, type **student** and then click **OK**. In the **Confirm Password** dialog box, type **student** to confirm the password, and then click **OK**.

6 **Save** 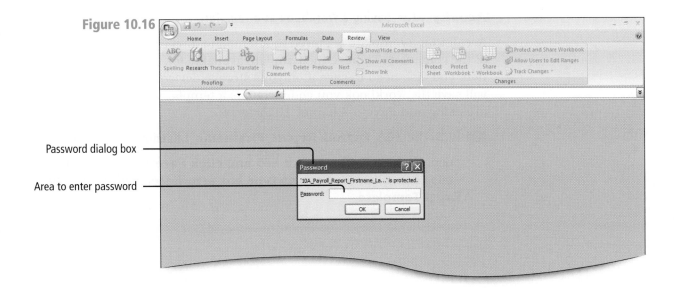 the workbook. The password is saved with the workbook. Then **Close** the workbook.

More Knowledge

Set a Password to Modify a Document

Passwords can be set so that only authorized reviewers can modify the worksheet. To set these passwords, complete the following steps:
- In the Save As dialog box, click Tools, and then click General Options.
- In the Password to modify box, type the password.
- Select the Read-only recommended check box. Opening the worksheet as a read-only document will prevent the user from accidentally modifying the file.
- Click OK. When prompted, retype your password, and then click OK.
- Click Save. If prompted to replace existing document, click Yes.

Activity 10.8 Opening a Protected Workbook

When a workbook is password protected, the password must be entered before you can see the workbook. In this activity, you will open the workbook using the password.

1 **Open** the workbook named **10A_Payroll_Report_Firstname_Lastname**, and then compare your screen with Figure 10.16.

Because this workbook is protected, it can be opened only when you use the password. Saving documents with a password allows only certain users to access the file. When workbooks are placed in a shared space, only those users with the password are allowed to open it.

Figure 10.16

Password dialog box

Area to enter password

2 In the **Password** box, type **Excel** and then click **OK**.

A warning box displays indicating that the workbook is password protected and an incorrect password was used.

3 Click **OK**. Then open the workbook again. In the **Password** box, type **student** and then click **OK**.

The workbook is now open. All of the protection that was set on this worksheet remains in place.

More Knowledge

Unprotect a Workbook

To remove the workbook password protection, from the Office menu, click Save As. In the Save As dialog box, click Tools, and then click General Options. The password is selected; press Delete.

Objective 4
Save Worksheet and Chart Templates

Even though Excel provides numerous preformatted templates, they may not be pertinent for the specific needs of a particular business. Whenever a document is used repeatedly, it is good practice to save it as a template. Then only the variable data needs to be inserted and the worksheet is complete. A chart can also be saved as a template. Once the structure and format of a chart are created, it can be saved so the structure can be used over and over.

Recall that a *template* is a file that is saved in a way that preserves the original file and creates as copy of the file for use each time it is opened. When all formulas and formats are saved with the template, only the variable information needs to be entered.

Activity 10.9 Saving a Workbook as a Template

Recall that a template is stored in a template directory on the hard drive of the computer. To have the template available for use in another location, you also need to save it on your storage device. In this activity, you will save the workbook you completed as a template on the computer you are using and in your Chapter 10 folder.

1 With the **10A_Payroll_Report_Firstname_Lastname** workbook open, click the **Office menu** 🗔 and click **Save As**. In the **Save As** dialog box, click the **Save as type box arrow**, locate and then click **Excel Template**.

2 In the **File name** box, type **10A_Payroll_Report_Template_Firstname_ Lastname** Then click **Save**.

Recall that a template is saved on the computer in a special directory for templates.

3 Click the **Office** button [icon] and click **Save As**. Click the **Save as type box arrow**, and then click **Excel Template**. Navigate to your **Excel Chapter 10** folder and confirm the file name is 10A_Payroll_Report_Template_Firstname_Lastname and that the **Save as type** is **Excel Template**. Then click **Save** [icon]. **Close** the workbook.

Activity 10.10 Creating a Chart to Save as a Template

A chart can be included in the template. A chart can also be saved as a *chart template* and used independently of specific worksheets. Businesses often use a similar chart for their reports. For instance, the monthly sales chart may use the same format when it is prepared each month. In this activity, you will create a chart that displays the total weekly pay for each employee and save it as a template.

1 Open the **10A_Payroll_Report_Firstname_Lastname** workbook; use the password **student** to unprotect it. In **column D**, beginning in cell **D8**, enter the following numbers that are placeholders:

38
39
40
41
42

You will create a chart of the total pay. Having numbers in those cells makes it easier to visualize the completed chart. These placeholder numbers will later be deleted.

2 Select the range **A7:A12**, press ⌃, select the range **H7:H12**, and click the **Insert tab**.

Most of the commands are dimmed and not available. When a worksheet is protected, there are restrictions on the changes that can be made.

3 With the ranges selected, right-click and click **Copy**. Alternatively, on the **Home tab**, in the **Clipboard group**, click the **Copy** button [icon].

Display the **Office** menu [icon], click **New**. Compare your screen with Figure 10.17, and then click **Create**.

Figure 10.17
New Workbook dialog box

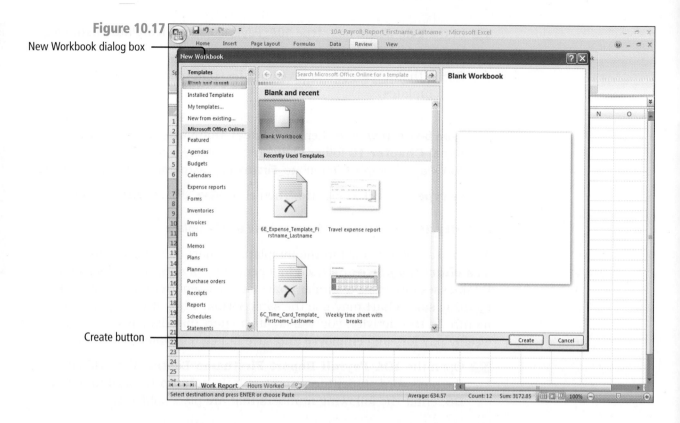

4 In the new workbook, click cell **A7**, and then right-click and click **Paste**. With the range still selected, on the **Insert tab**, in the **Charts group**, click the **Column** button, and then under **3-D Column**, click the first choice—**3-D Clustered Column**.

5 In the chart, click the **Legend** to select it, and then press ⌐Delete⌐.

6 On the **Design tab**, in the **Chart Styles group**, click the **More** button ⌐▼⌐, and in the fourth column, click the second choice—**Style 12**.

Additional formatting may be entered in this worksheet. When a chart is saved as a template, you may want to enhance its visual aspects to give it a professional appearance.

7 On the **Design tab**, in the **Location group**, click the **Move Chart** button. Click **New sheet** and name it **Total Pay** and then click **OK**. **Close** the **10A_Payroll_Report_Firstname_Lastname** workbook and when asked if that you want to save changes, click **No**. The new unnamed workbook remains open.

The changes you entered in the worksheet for the hours worked have not been saved with this workbook.

8 In the open workbook, with the Chart Area active—when you point to the white area surrounding the chart, the ScreenTip displays *Chart Area*—click the **Format tab**, and in the **Shape Styles group**, click the **Shape Fill** button. From the list, point to **Gradient**, and from the submenu, under **Light Variations**, in the first row, point to the second choice—**Linear Down**. Compare your screen with Figure 10.18, and then click **Linear Down**.

Figure 10.18

Shape Fill button

Gradient

Linear Down choice

ScreenTip Identifies
Gradient style

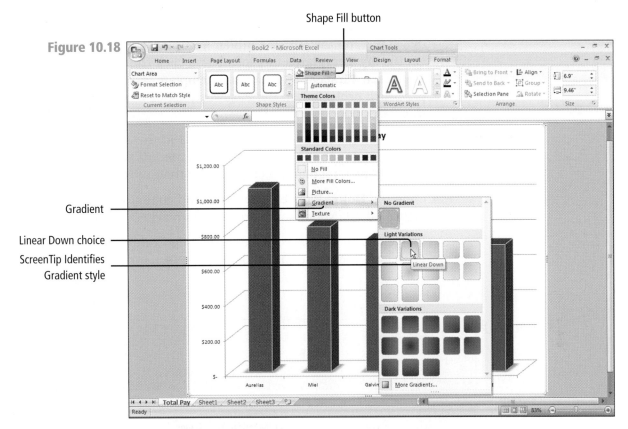

☐ On the **Design tab**, in the **Type group**, click the **Save As Template** button.

The Save Chart Template dialog box displays and the Save as type identifies it as Chart Template Files.

☐ In the **File name** box, type **10A_Pay_Chart_Temp_Firstname_Lastname** and then click **Save**.

This saves the chart template in the template directory on the computer you are using. The title in the title bar does not display the file name. A chart template opens only from the templates folder located on a computer's hard drive. You cannot access it from your student files.

☐ **Save** the **10A_Pay_Chart_Temp_Firstname_Lastname** workbook in the **Excel Chapter 10** folder. Then click the **Close Window** button

☒ to close only the workbook. When asked if you want to save changes, click **No**. Excel remains open but all workbooks are closed and do not display.

Objective 5
Complete a Report with Worksheet and Chart Templates

Southwest Gardens now has the templates needed for the weekly reports. When templates are used, only the variable information is inserted to complete the worksheet and chart.

Activity 10.11 Creating a Worksheet and Charts Using Templates

In this activity, you will use your templates to enter the hours worked for a week and then complete charts that display those hours worked and the total pay for each employee.

1 From the **Office** menu 🗔, click **New**. In the **New Workbook** dialog box, on the left side, under **Templates**, click **My templates**. On the **My Templates** tab, locate and click the **10A_Payroll_Report_ Template_Firstname_Lastname** template, and then click **OK**. It is password protected; in the **Password** dialog box, type **student** and then click **OK**.

The file name in the title bar displays *1* at the end of the file name. This indicates that a copy of the template has been opened and will be saved as a regular Excel file rather than as a template.

2 Click the **Hours Worked sheet tab** and compare your screen with Figure 10.19. Notice there are no data markers in the chart.

The template was saved without the important data—hours worked. Therefore, the chart has no data markers.

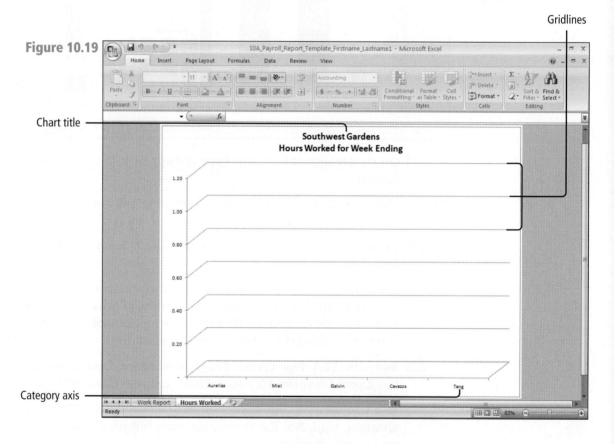

Figure 10.19

Gridlines

Chart title

Category axis

3 Click the **Work Report sheet tab**. Enter the following data for the weekly hours worked in the range **D8:D12**:

Last Name	Hours Worked
Aurelias	42
Miel	41
Galvin	38
Cavazos	40
Tang	39.5

4 Click cell **A5**, and in the **Formula Bar**, place the insertion point after the word *Ending*, press Spacebar, and then type **October 9, 2009** to enter the date.

5 Click the **Hours Worked sheet tab**, and edit the title of the chart to read **Hours Worked For Week Ending October 9, 2009** Compare your screen with Figure 10.20.

The hours worked chart and the work report are now completed using the templates you previously created after entering only the hours each employee worked and the date.

Figure 10.20

Chart title

Data markers

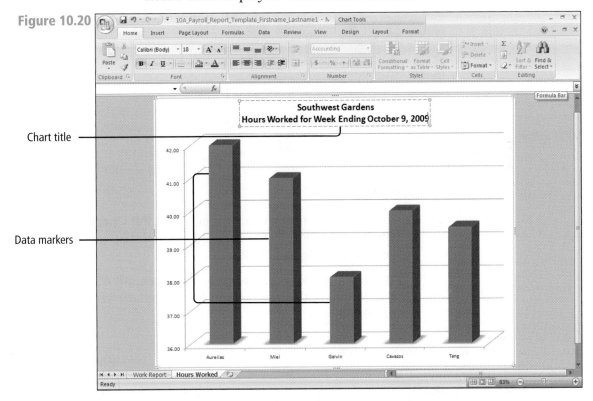

6 Click the **Work Report sheet tab**. Click the **Office** button and click **Save As**. In the **Save As** dialog box, navigate to your **Excel Chapter 10** folder. Then in the dialog box, under **File name**, type **10A_Payroll_October9_Firstname_Lastname** Confirm that **Save as type** is **Excel Workbook**, and then click **Save**.

7 Select the ranges **A7:A12** and **H7:H12**. Click the **Insert** button to insert a chart.

The insert chart buttons are not active. Recall that you are unable to insert a chart because even though the worksheet was saved with a new name, all of the protection still applies to the worksheet and workbook.

8 Click the **Review tab** and in the **Changes group**, click the **Unprotect Sheet** button. In the **Password** dialog box, type **student** and then click **OK**.

9 Confirm that the ranges **A7:A12** and **H7:H12** are still selected, click the **Insert tab**, click the **Column** button, and compare your screen with Figure 10.21.

Because the worksheet is now unprotected, a chart can be inserted.

Column Chart button

Figure 10.21

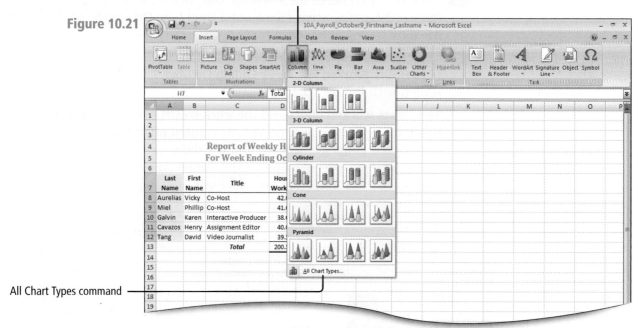

All Chart Types command

10 At the bottom of the chart gallery, click **All Chart Types**. In the **Insert Chart** dialog box, at the left, click **Templates**, and then compare your screen with Figure 10.22.

When you click on any of the chart types, All Chart Types displays at the bottom of the menu. The chart templates that have been created are displayed.

Chart template icon

Figure 10.22

Insert Chart dialog box

Templates command

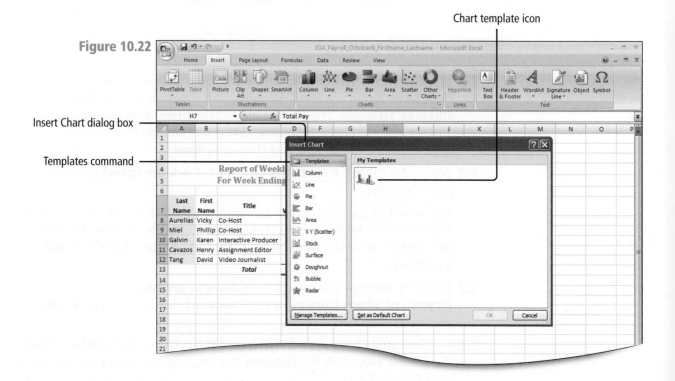

11 In the **My Templates** section, an icon of the 3-D column chart displays. Point at the icon—the ScreenTip displays the saved name of the chart—**10A_Pay_Chart_Temp_Firstname_Lastname** Click on the chart, and then click **OK**.

The formatted chart is inserted into the worksheet.

12 Select the **Title** and enter the following title:

> **Southwest Gardens**
> **Employee Pay for Week Ending October 9, 2009**

13 On the **Design tab**, in the **Location group**, click the **Move Chart** button, and place the chart in a **New sheet** named **Total Pay** Click **OK**, and then compare your screen with Figure 10.23.

You receive an error message stating that the workbook is protected and cannot be changed.

Figure 10.23

Inserted chart template

Protection warning

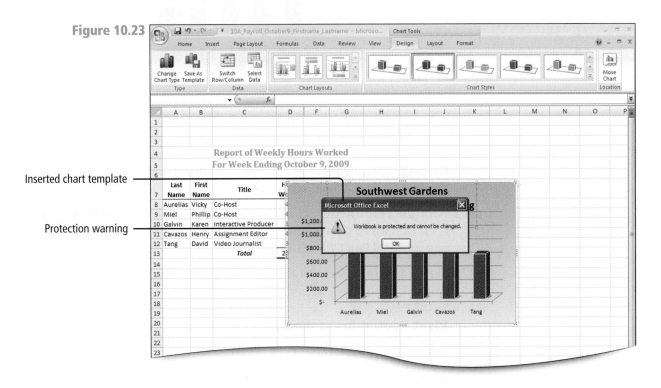

14 Click **OK**, and then in the **Move Chart** dialog box, click **Cancel**. Click the **Review tab** and compare your screen with Figure 10.24.

The structure and windows of the workbook were protected when the template was saved, but the Protect Workbook button still displays *Protect Workbook*.

Figure 10.24

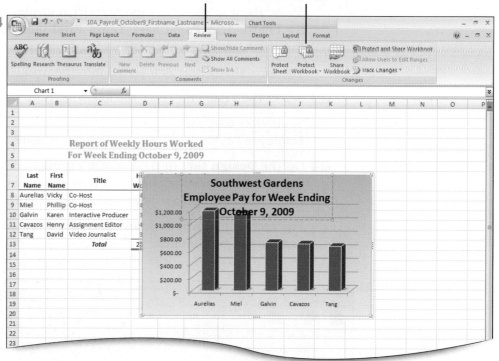

15 In the **Changes group**, click **Protect Workbook**. Under **Restrict Editing**, click **Protect Structure and Windows**. In the **Unprotect Workbook** dialog box, type **student** and then click **OK**.

16 With the chart active, click the **Design tab**. In the **Location group**, click the **Move Chart** button and place the chart in a **New sheet** named **Total Pay** Click **OK**.

17 Place the worksheets in the following order: Work Report, Hours Worked, Total Pay. Select the chart worksheets—**Hours Worked** and **Total Pay**—and in the **Left Footer**, insert the **File Name**, and in the **Right Footer**, insert the **Sheet Name**.

18 **Save** 🖫 your workbook.

19 To submit electronically, follow the instructions provided by your instructor. Print only the **10A_Payroll_October9_Firstname_ Lastname** and the **10A_Payroll_Report_Template_Firstname_ Lastname** workbooks. Click the **Office** button 🔘 and click **Print**. In the **Print** dialog box, under **Print what**, select **Entire workbook**, and then click **OK**. **Close** the workbooks and then **Exit** Excel.

End **You have completed Project 10A**

Project 10B **Time Card**

In Activities 10.12 through 10.24, you will create a form that employees will use to report hours worked. This time card will be saved as a template that can be accessible from the Web. Each employee will be able to enter the hours worked, which will then be used by the accounting department to complete the payroll. Your completed time card form will look similar to Figure 10.25.

For Project 10B, you will need the following files:

e10B_Time_Card
e10B_SW_Garden_Logo

You will save your workbooks as
10B_Time_Card_Firstname_Lastname (Macro-Enabled Worksheet)
10B_Time_Card_Cavazos_Firstname_Lastname (Macro-Enabled Worksheet)
10B_Time_Card_Galvin_Firstname_Lastname (Macro-Enabled Worksheet)
10B_Time_Card_Template_Firstname_Lastname (Macro-Enabled Worksheet)

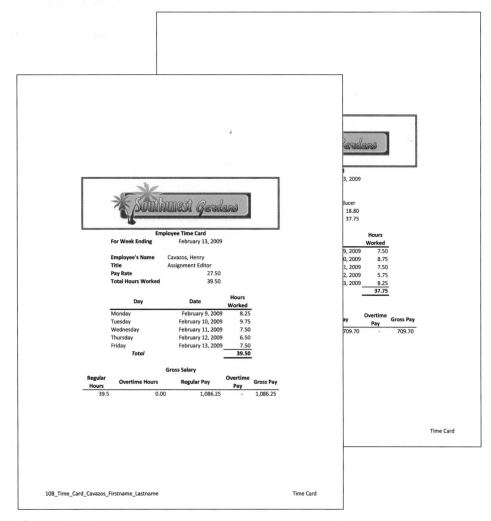

Figure 10.25
Times Cards

Objective 6
Create a Form

When similar information is needed from customers or employees, a form is generally used to record the information. Businesses use forms to report hours worked, travel expenses, orders, and so on. Many of these forms are available on the Internet. Excel can also be used to create these forms. The format and formulas are entered so that only the variable data is entered into the form. Macros can be included in the template and run by clicking a macro command button on a "hot spot" on the form.

Southwest Gardens' employees report their hours worked each week. Posting the time card on the Internet is convenient both to the employee completing the time card and to the accounting department. You will create a form to report the hours worked. The form will include a drop-down list and macro command buttons.

Activity 10.12 Inserting a VLOOKUP to Enter Data

The pay rate for each employee remains the same from week to week and should be entered into the time card for the employee. When an employee enters his or her name, the hourly rate will also be inserted. In this activity, you will insert a lookup function to insert the pay rate for the employee.

1 **Start** Excel. From your student files, locate and open the file named **e10B_Time_Card**. In the **Left Footer**, insert the **File Name** and in the **Right Footer**, insert the **Sheet Name**. From the **Office menu**, point to **Save As** and in the submenu, click **Excel Macro-Enabled Workbook**, and then **Save** the file in the **Excel Chapter 10** folder as 10B_Time_Card_Firstname_Lastname

This worksheet will be used to create a time card form that will be saved as a template.

2 On the **Time Card sheet**, with cell **A1** active, on the **Home tab** in the **Cells group**, click the **Format** button. Under **Cell Size**, click **Row Height**. In the **Row Height** dialog box, type **80** and then click **OK**.

When you want to adjust the row height to a specific height, typing in the measurement is more precise than dragging the row to the required height.

3 With cell **A1** active, on the **Insert tab**, in the **Illustrations group**, click the **Picture** button. Navigate to your student files for Chapter 10 and click **e10B_SW_Garden_Logo**, and then click **Insert**. Use the sizing handles to adjust the size of the logo to cover the range **A1:D2**.

Return to **Normal** ▦ view.

4 Select the range **A3:F3** and click the **Merge & Center** button ▦ ▾.

5 Click the **Pay Rates sheet tab** and click cell **A6**. Click the **Data tab**, and in the **Sort & Filter group**, click the **Sort A to Z** button ↓ to sort the names in alphabetical order.

The employee names will be used in a lookup function. Recall that a lookup range must be arranged in alphabetical order.

6 Select the range **A6:C10**, and on the **Formulas tab**, in the **Defined Names group**, click the **Define Name** button. In the **New Name** dialog box, in the **Name** box, type **Pay_Rates** and then click **OK**.

Recall that when creating a lookup function, it is recommended that you name the range of cells. Recall that you cannot insert a space when defining names.

7 Click the **Time Card sheet tab**, and in cell **B6**, type **Aurelias, Vicky** as a placeholder while you complete the form. Click cell **B7** and confirm the **Formulas tab** is active. In the **Function Library group**, click the **Lookup & Reference** button, and then click **VLOOKUP**.

The VLOOKUP Function Arguments dialog box displays. Recall that the VLOOKUP function has three required fields.

8 In the **VLOOKUP Function Arguments** dialog box, in the **Lookup_value** text box, type **b6** and press F4. Then press Tab. In the **Table_array** text box, type **Pay_Rates**

The lookup value is the data that will be compared in the selected range of cells—the table array—which is the range of cells you named that contains the data. Recall that the lookup value is compared in the lookup range—the table array—in order to find a match.

9 Press Tab and in the **Col_index_num** text box, type **2** because the employee's job title displays in the second column. Press Enter and compare your screen with Figure 10.26.

Vicky's title, *Co-Host*, displays in the cell.

Figure 10.26

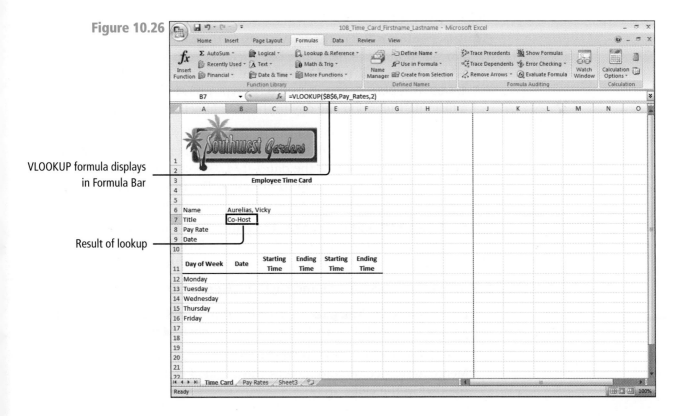

VLOOKUP formula displays in Formula Bar

Result of lookup

10 Click cell **B6** and type **Tang, Davis** and press ⏎ to confirm that the function is accurate and the job title for Tang—*Video Journalist*—now displays.

11 Copy the formula from cell **B7** to cell **B8**. Click cell **B8**, and in the **Formula Bar**, change the **2** to **3** and then press ⏎. Alternatively, enter a VLOOKUP function to determine the pay for the employee.

The amount—*19.75*—displays in the cell, which is the pay rate for Mr. Tang. You have copied the lookup function to the pay rate cell so that Excel will also look up the correct pay rate for the employee. By changing the Col_index_num to 3, it looks up the value in the third column of the Pay Rates table array.

When complex functions are created, it is advisable to copy the function and change the variable information. Not only does this save time in constructing the worksheet, it also ensures accuracy.

12 Click cell **B6** and type **Galvin, Karen** and press ⏎ and confirm that the title—*Interactive Producer*—and the pay rate—*18.8*—display. Format the cell **B8** with **Comma Style** ⟨,⟩.

13 **Save** 💾 your workbook.

Activity 10.13 Inserting Formulas to Display Dates in a Form and Formatting the Input Area

When the time card is completed, the user will enter only one date. You will enter formulas that will calculate all of the other dates displayed in the time card. The area where the user enters data is called the ***input area*** and needs to be easily identified to the user. In this activity, you will enter formulas to display the correct dates of the time card and identify the input area with colored cells.

1 Select **column B**. On the **Home tab**, in the **Cells group**, click the **Format** button. Under **Cell Size**, click **Column Width**. In the **Column Width** dialog box, type **13.5** and then click **OK**. Click cell **B9** and type **1/4/09** as a placeholder. In cell **B12**, type **=b9+1** and press ⏎ to enter a formula that adds one day to the date in cell B9.

The date entered in cell B9 will be the first day of the week—Sunday. Recall Excel identifies dates by a serial number beginning with 1 for January 1, 1900. When the date—1/4/09—is entered into the worksheet, the serial number for that date is the underlying value. Adding 1 to that date will display the next calendar date.

2 Click cell **B13** and type **=b12+1** to enter the formula to get the next date. Then use the fill handle to copy the formula through Friday—cell **B16**. The date for Friday displays as 1/9/2009.

3 Select the range **B6:C6** and click the **Home tab**. In the **Alignment group**, click the **Merge & Center button arrow** ⊞▾ and compare your screen with Figure 10.27, and then click **Merge Across**.

The Merge & Center menu displays different merge commands. The Merge Across command merges the selected cells but does not center the text in the cells.

Merge Across command

Figure 10.27

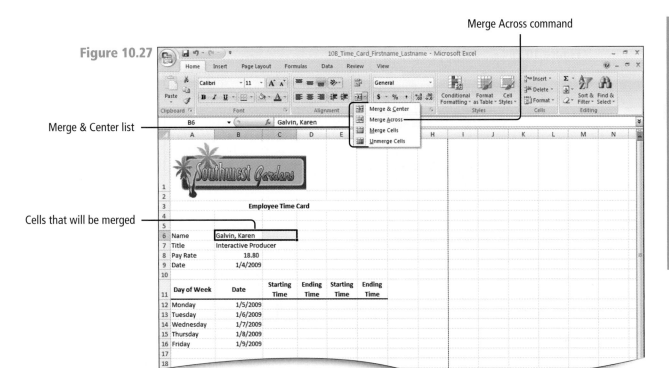

Merge & Center list

Cells that will be merged

4 In the **Font group**, click the **Fill Color button arrow** , and under **Theme Colors**, in the seventh column, click the third choice—**Olive Green, Accent 3, Lighter 60%**. Select the range **B9:C9**, click the **Merge & Center button arrow** , and then click **Merge Across**, and then, in the **Font group**, click the **Fill Color** button .

Because olive green was the last selected color, it remains in the Fill Color button. To format other cells with the same color, simply click on the Fill Color button.

5 In the **Number group**, click the **Number Format button arrow** General and from the list, click **More Number Formats**. In the **Format Cells** dialog box, under **Category**, confirm that **Date** is selected. On the right, under **Type**, click **March 14, 2001**, and then click **OK**. In the **Alignment group**, click the **Align Text Left** button .

6 Select the range **C12:F16** and click the **Fill Color** button .

Save your workbook and compare your screen with Figure 10.28.

The input area is identified by the shaded cells. When each employee completes the time card, he or she will enter data in these shaded cells. Identifying the input area in this manner assists the user in locating the areas he or she needs to complete.

Figure 10.28

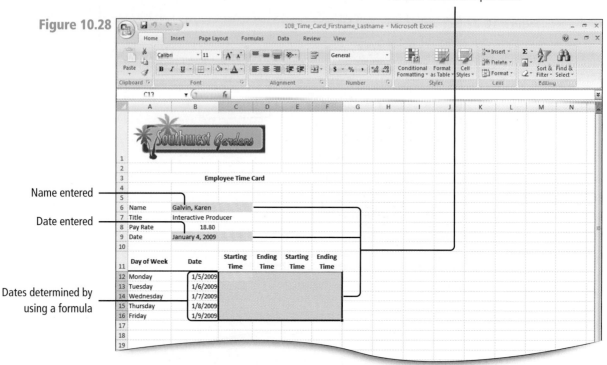

Fill color identifies input areas

Name entered

Date entered

Dates determined by
using a formula

More Knowledge

The Merge Commands

The *Merge Across* command is used to merge cells across the row. When a range of cells is selected that covers two or more columns and two or more rows, this command will merge the columns but not the rows. If you select the *Merge Cells* command, the selected range will be merged into one cell that is the size of the selected range.

Activity 10.14 Creating the Output Area

When a form is completed, it will be submitted to the payroll department and a copy can be printed by the employee for his or her records. Rather than print the original input area, a separate place in the form that summarizes the data will be prepared and printed, called the *Output area*. In this activity, you will begin the output area.

1 Click the **Sheet3 sheet tab**. Select the range **A4:E21**, right-click and click **Copy**. Click the **Time Card sheet tab** and right-click cell **J3**, and then click **Paste**. Select the range **J19:N20**, point to the edge of the selected range, and when the ⬚ pointer displays, drag to the left one column—the data will reside in the range **I19:M20**.

The data that you copied will be the output area of the form.

2 Select the range **I20:M20**, and format with **Bold** **B**, **Bottom Border** ⬚ ▾, **Center** ≡, **Middle Align** ≡, and **Wrap Text** ⬚.

3 Increase the widths of **columns J** and **K** to **18**—131 pixels. Click cell **A1** and **Copy** the logo and **Paste** it in cell **J1**. Adjust it to fit the range **J1:L2**. Click cell **J3** and format with **Bold** **[B]**, and **Merge & Center** **[⊞ ▾]** it in the range **J3:L3**. Select cell **J4** and the range **J6:J9**, and then format with **Bold** **[B]**.

4 Click cell **K6**, type the formula **=b6** and copy the formula down through to cell **K8**. Click cell **K9** and type **=L17**—the cell that will eventually contain the total hours worked. In the **Formula Bar**, click the **Enter** button **[✓]**, and compare your screen with Figure 10.29.

In the output area, you will use the same information that the employee entered in the input area of the form by using formulas to copy those cells. Cell L17 will display the total hours worked.

Cell that will display total hours worked when form is completed

Output area

Figure 10.29

Formula that copies total hours worked

Input area

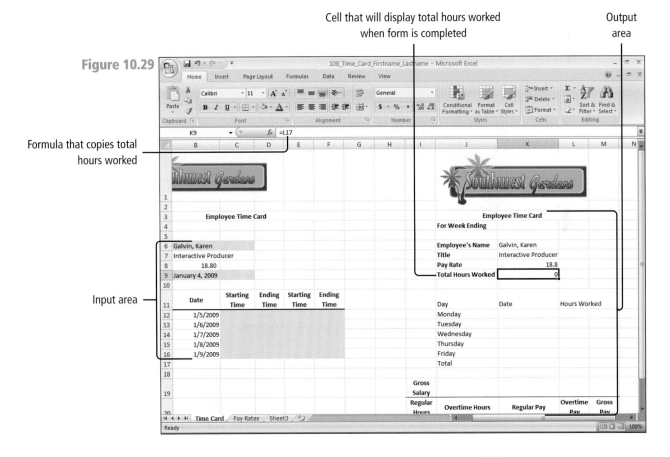

5 Format cells **K8** and **K9** with **Comma Style** **[,]**. Click cell **K12** and type **=b12** and then copy the formula down through cell **K16**. Select the range of the dates—**K12:K16**—and on the **Home tab**, in the **Number group**, click the **Number Format** arrow **[General ▾]**, and then click **More Number Formats**. In the **Format Cells** dialog box, on the **Number tab**, under **Category**, confirm that **Date** is selected, and then at the right under **Type**, click **March 14, 2001**. Click **OK**. Click cell **K12**—confirm that only one cell is selected—and then right-click and click the **Format Painter** button 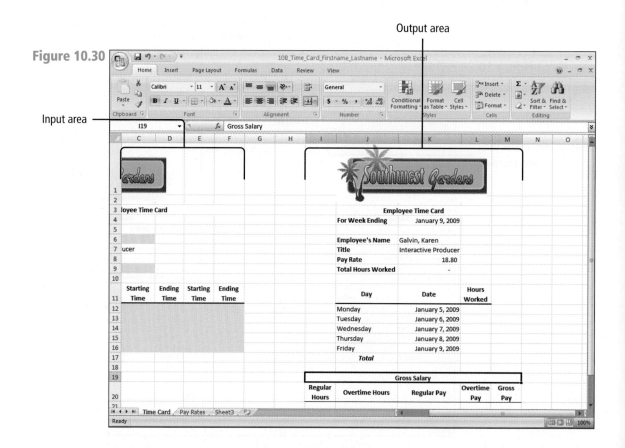, and then click cell **K4**. In cell **K4** type **=k16** and press Enter.

The date of the last day of the work week—Friday—is entered in the output area. The formulas are entered into the worksheet. Recall that the information in the worksheet is used as a placeholder so that you can view the results as you create the output area.

6 Right-click cell **A11** and click the **Format Painter** button. Then select the range **J11:L11**. Click cell **J17** and format with **Bold B**, **Italic I**, and **Center**.

7 Click cell **I19** and format with **Bold B**, and then select the range **I19:M19** and click the **Merge & Center** button. **Save** your workbook and compare your screen with Figure 10.30.

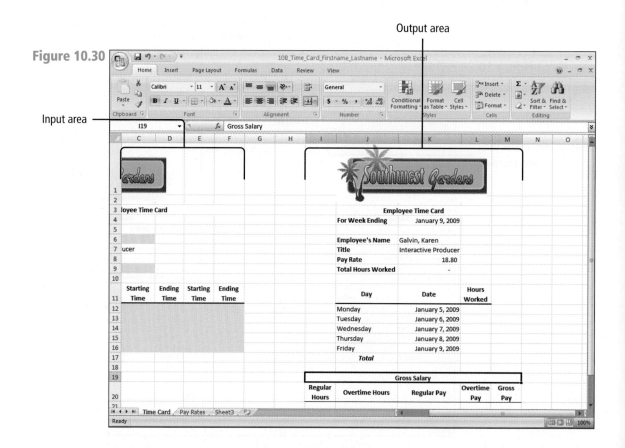

Figure 10.30

Output area

Input area

Activity 10.15 Completing the Formulas in the Output Area

The output area is the area that is printed and is retained by the employee, so the format should have a professional appearance. In the output area for the time card, the employee will print the result of the hours worked and the gross pay. In this activity, you will complete the formulas required for the output area and finish formatting the area.

1 Beginning in cell **C12**, enter the following data, which will be used as placeholders while creating formulas in the starting and ending time section:

Starting Time	Ending Time	Starting Time	Ending Time
7 am	11:30 am	12:30 pm	5 pm
8:15 am	11:45 am	12:30 pm	5 pm
7:45 am	12 pm	1 pm	5 pm
8 am	12 pm	12:45 pm	5 pm
8 am	12 pm	1 pm	5 pm

Type am or pm when you enter the time. Excel recognizes that am and pm identifies the time and will format the numbers accordingly, as long as you enter a space after the time.

2 Click cell **L12** and type **=((d12-c12) + (f12-e12))*24** to create the formula to determine the total hours worked. On the **Formula Bar**, click the **Enter** button ✔. Then compare your screen with Figure 10.31.

The formula calculates the hours worked in the morning—*(d12-c12)*—and adds them to the hours worked in the afternoon—*(f12-e12)*. The outside parentheses are used to ensure that the total is multiplied by 24, the number of hours in a day. The number *9.00* displays in the cell. Because you entered numbers as placeholders, you can view the results of your formulas.

When you multiply by 24, you convert the minutes of time to a decimal fraction—15 minutes to .25 hours. You have entered the formula to determine the hours worked for the day—=((d12-c12)+(f12-e12))*24.

Figure 10.31

Formula used

Placeholders used for afternoon hours

Placeholders used for morning hours

Result

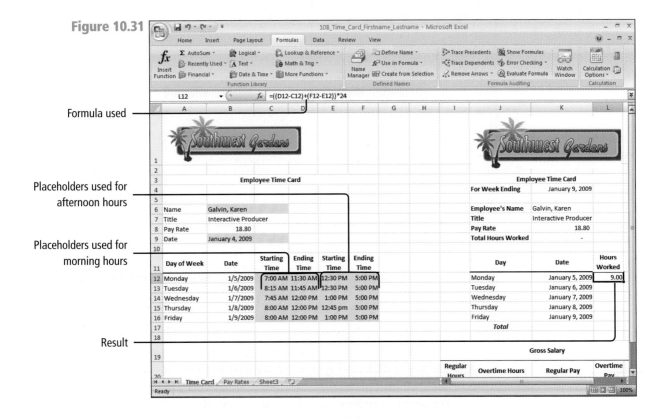

3 Use the fill handle to copy the formula down through cell **L16**. Click cell **L17** and on the **Home tab**, in the **Editing group**, click the **Sum** button $\boxed{\Sigma \, \cdot}$. Format cell **L17** with **Bold** $\boxed{B}$ and insert a **Top and Double Bottom Border**.

Notice that the total hours worked have also been inserted into cell K9.

4 Click cell **I21** and click the **Formulas tab**. In the **Function Library group**, click the **Logical** button, and from the list, click **IF**. Move the **IF Function Arguments** dialog box aside so you can see the data in the worksheet columns.

5 In the **Logical_test** text box, type **L17>=40** Press [Tab] and in the **Value_if_true** text box, type **40** Press [Tab] and in the **Value_if_false** text box, type **L17** and then compare your screen with Figure 10.32. Click **OK**.

The result—40—displays in the Function Arguments dialog box and will be entered in the cell. Recall that the logical test in an IF function compares a cell with a value or formula—in this case the total hours worked will be evaluated and the formula stipulates that the total is greater than or equal to 40. If this is true, 40 is entered in the cell, and if it is not true, the actual hours worked—the value in cell L17— is entered in the cell.

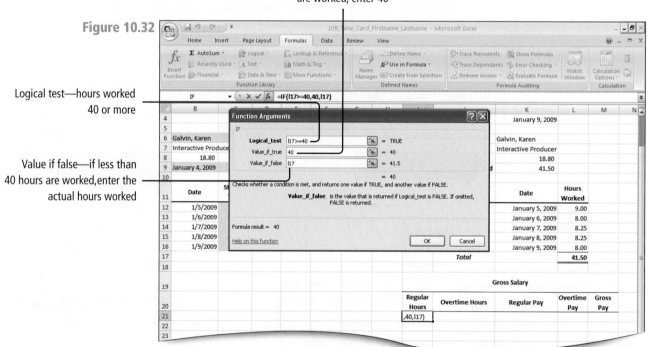

Figure 10.32

Value if true—if 40 or more hours are worked, enter 40

Logical test—hours worked 40 or more

Value if false—if less than 40 hours are worked, enter the actual hours worked

6 Click cell **J21** and type **=L17-I21** and then press [Tab]. In cell **K21**, type **=i21*k8** and press [Tab]. Using the skills you practiced, enter formulas for the **Overtime Pay** and the **Gross Pay**. Recall that overtime pay is the overtime hours times the pay rate times 1.5. Recall also that the gross pay is the regular pay plus the overtime pay. Format cells **I21:J21** with

Comma Style and the range **K21:M21** with **Accounting Number Format**. Then compare your screen with Figure 10.33.

The gross pay—*$794.30*—displays in cell M21.

Results of formulas using
placeholder data

Figure 10.33

Placeholders for hours worked

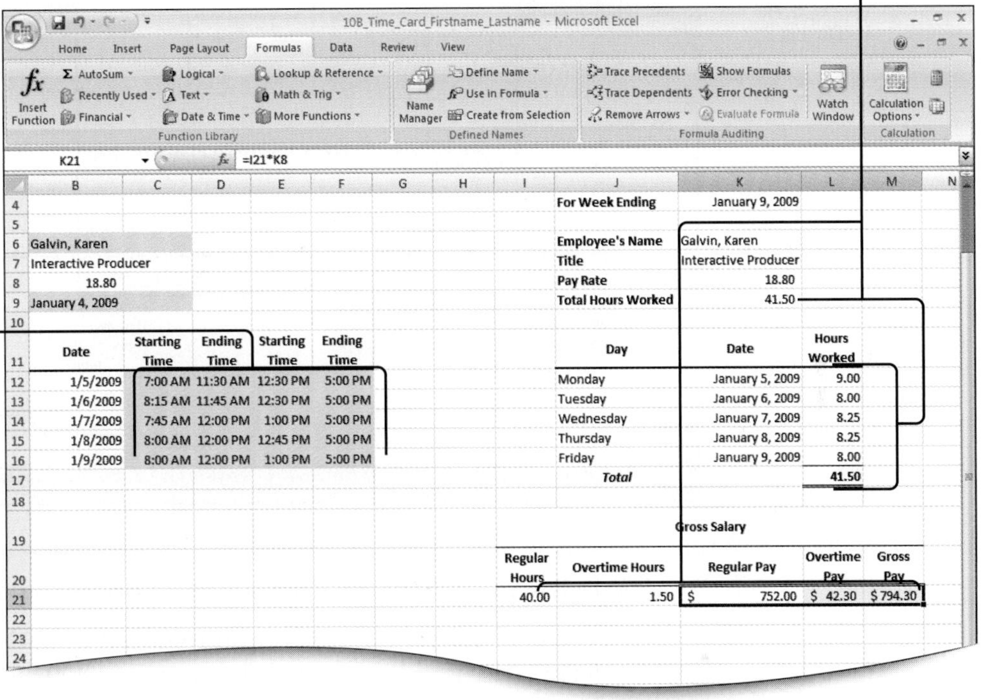

[7] Select the range **I1:M2** and on the **Home tab**, in the **Font group**, click the **Dialog Box Launcher** [icon]. In the **Format Cells** dialog box, click the **Border tab**. Under **Line,** click the last choice in the right column—**double borders**. At the right, under **Presets**, click **Outline**. Compare your screen with Figure 10.34, and then click **OK**.

Figure 10.34

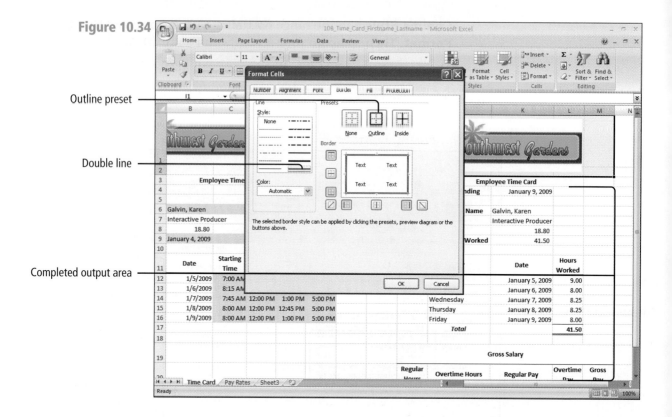

Outline preset

Double line

Completed output area

8 Delete the data in the following cells: **B6**, **B9**, and the range **C12:F16**.

The placeholder data has been removed from the input area of the form. The dates begin with January 1, 1900. The green error indicators at the upper left of the cells display, alerting you that there may be errors in the cells.

9 Click in cell **B7** and click the **Error Checking** button ⬧. From the list, click **Ignore Error**. Using the skills you practiced, removed the error indicators from the worksheet. Recall that you can select a range and remove the error alert in the selected cells at the same time.

The ScreenTip indicates that a value is not available to the formula or function. Because there is a formula in cells K21:M21 with no numbers entered, the #N/A error message displays. This error message will be replaced by valid values when the form is completed.

10 **Save** 🖫 your workbook.

Objective 7
Validate a Form

For a form to be useful, it must be easy to complete so that accurate data is collected. When you create a form, consider questions that may occur and provide directions directly on the form. Use data validation to ensure that accurate data is entered and to provide instructions on how to complete the form, such as information about the required data. Making a form self-explanatory helps ensure that accurate data is entered.

The three types of data validation are settings, input message, and error alert. These settings prevent invalid data from being entered into the cell by blocking entries or by providing additional information about the type of data required. The purpose of each data validation option is displayed in the table in Figure 10.35.

Figure 10.35

Data Validation Options	
Settings	Restricts the criteria entered in the cell
Input Message	Displays a message when the cell is selected
Error Alert	Displays a message that alerts the user when incorrect information is entered into the cell

Activity 10.16 Validating the Form

Data validation is a process of assisting the user to enter correct data in the form. You may place restrictions on the type of data entered, provide instructions on the type of data that you will enter, or block invalid entries. In this activity, you will use data validation to provide instructions about the types of entries allowed and to block invalid data.

1 Click cell **B9**. Click the **Data tab**, in the **Data Tools group**, click the **Data Validation** button, and then compare your screen with Figure 10.36.

The Data Validation dialog box displays with three tabs—Settings, Input Message, and Error Alert.

Settings tab

Figure 10.36

Data Validation dialog box

Input Message tab

Error Alert tab

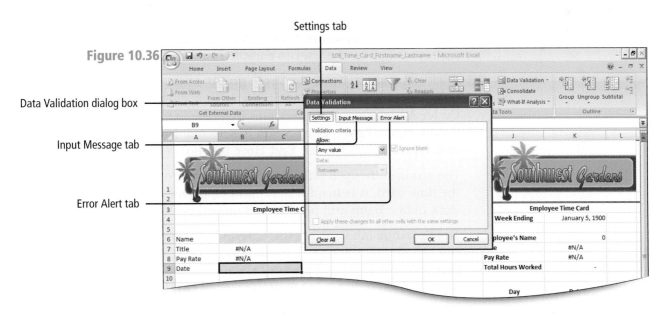

2 Click the **Input Message tab**. Confirm that **Show input message when cell is selected** is checked. In the **Title** text box, type **Date of Payroll** In the **Input message**, type **Insert the Sunday date of the week and the dates of work, Monday through Friday, will be entered for you. If the date you enter is not a Sunday, the dates will not be correct. Use the 1/11/2001 style to enter the date**. Compare your screen with Figure 10.37.

An **input message** displays when the cell is selected. It provides information to the user about the type of information that should be entered into the cell. Because a form is designed to be used without further instruction, it is good practice to place all pertinent information on the form.

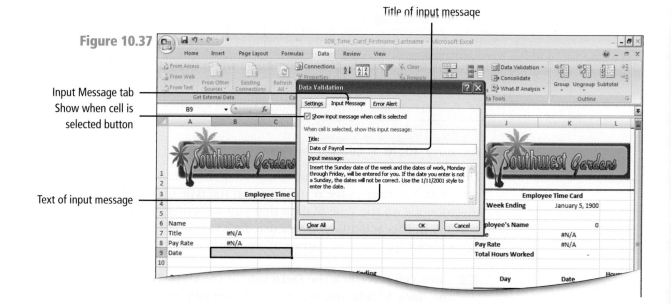

Title of input message

Figure 10.37

Input Message tab
Show when cell is
selected button

Text of input message

3 Click **OK**. Because cell **B9** is selected, the input message displays under the cell. Click in the message and drag it so it displays in **column C** so the dates in **column B** are visible.

The messages that display on the worksheet may be moved to nearby locations. It is important to complete the form in a manner that makes is easy for the user to complete.

4 Click cell **C12**. In the **Data Tools group**, click the **Data Validation** button. In the **Data Validation** dialog box, click the **Settings tab**. Under **Allow**, click the arrow and from the list, click **Time**. In the **Data** box, confirm that **between** is selected. In the **Start time** text box, type **6 am** and in the **End time** text box, type **10 pm**

The studios are open only between the hours of 6 am and 10 pm. In the time card, it is helpful to remind employees they cannot begin work before 6 am and need to be finished by 10 pm.

The **Settings** tab restricts the criteria entered in the cell. In this tab, you will specify the type of validation that you want—from type and length of text to type of numerical data. For the time card, the starting and ending time have limitations that can be controlled in the settings tab.

5 In the **Data Validation** dialog box, click the **Input Message tab**. In the **Title** text box, type **Starting Time** and in the **Input Message**, type **Studios do not open until 6 am. Use am or pm when entering the time.** The input message will display as the starting time is entered into the time card. It is a reminder to the user what data will be accepted.

6 Click the **Error Alert tab**. In the **Title** text box, type **Time Not Valid** and in the **Error message** text box, type **Studio hours are 6 am to 10 pm.**

Enter hours within that range. Confirm that the **Style** is **Stop**. Compare your screen with Figure 10.38, and then click **OK**.

An *error alert* displays a message that alerts the user when incorrect information is entered into the cell. The information you entered displays in the worksheet, which will assist the employee when completing the time card. If an invalid number is entered into cell C12, an error alert box will display with an explanation why the entry was not accepted. A *stop error alert* will prevent invalid data from being entered into the cell.

Figure 10.38

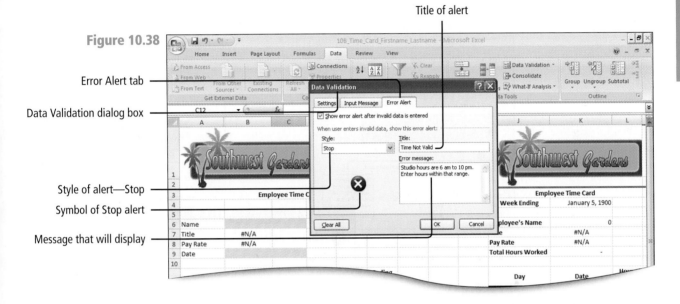

More Knowledge

Error Alerts

There are three types of alert styles—Stop, Warning, and Information. A Stop Alert prevents invalid data from being entered in the cell. A Warning Alert will warn that the information you entered is outside of the accepted range but will allow you to override the alert and enter the data. An Information Alert provides information about the entries but does not prevent an entry from being entered.

7 Save your workbook.

Activity 10.17 Testing the Validation Rule

Testing the validation to confirm that it works as intended is a critical step in creating validation rules. Enter both valid and invalid data to confirm the accuracy of the validation entries. When the validation is accurate, it can be copied to other cells and then edited for those cells. In this activity, you will test the validation you created and copy and edit the validation in the worksheet.

1 Click cell **C12** and notice the message that displays to provide information about the valid data that can be entered. If the message covers the cell, click on it and move it to the side.

The input message will display whenever cell C12 is selected, but it may display from any location on the worksheet.

2 In cell **C12**, type **4 am** and press Enter, and then compare your screen with Figure 10.39.

The Alert dialog box displays. The title of the dialog box is the title you entered—Time Not Valid—and the message is exactly as you typed it. Information about the entry and the reason the starting time was rejected are displayed for the user.

Figure 10.39

Input message

Error message

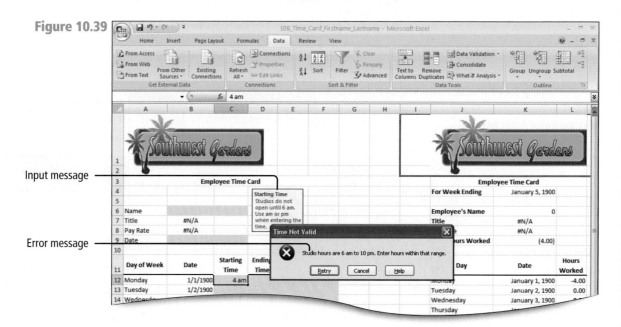

3 In the **Time Not Valid** alert box, click **Cancel**. Then in cell **C12**, type **6:30 am** and press Enter. This time is acceptable. Click cell **C12** and press Delete to remove the number you entered.

4 Copy cell **C12** to cell **D12**, and then click cell **D12** so it is active. In the **Data Tools group**, click the **Data Validation** button. Click the **Input Message tab** and change the title to **Ending Time** Change the **Input message** to **Studios close at 10 pm. Use am or pm when entering the time.** Click **OK**.

5 In cell **D12**, type **11 pm** to confirm the validation is accurate. Click **Cancel**. Then copy cell **C12** to cell **E12** and copy cell **D12** to cell **F12**. Select the range **C12:F12** and use the fill handle to copy the validation down through **row 16**.

Validation can be copied into other cells in the worksheet. When you copy the validation, it is important to review the text and confirm it is accurate for each cell it is copied into.

6 **Save** your workbook.

Activity 10.18 Creating a Drop-Down List

A **drop-down list** displays valid entries that can be entered into the cell, making data entry easier or limiting the items that can be entered. A cell that contains a drop-down list displays an arrow in the cell. In this activity, you will create a drop-down list to insert the employees' names in the worksheet.

1 Click the **Pay Rates sheet tab**. Select the range **A5:A10**, and then click the **Formulas tab**. In the **Defined Names group**, click the **Create from Selection** button. In the **Create Names from Selection** dialog box, confirm that **Top row** is selected, and then click **OK**.

Creating a range name from a selection is another method to name a range of cells. The first cell of the selected range—*Name*— is the name used for the range. When creating a drop-down list, the data must have a defined name.

2 Click the **Time Card sheet tab** and click cell **B6**. Click the **Data tab** and in the **Data Tools group**, click the **Data Validation** button. In the **Data Validation** dialog box, click the **Settings tab**. Under **Allow**, click the arrow and from the list, click **List**. In the **Source** text box, type **=Name** Confirm that **In-cell dropdown** is selected, and then compare your screen with Figure 10.40.

The name of the range of employee names is entered as the source for the list. Be sure that the equal sign (=) is entered before the range name.

Figure 10.40

Allow List

The Source of the list

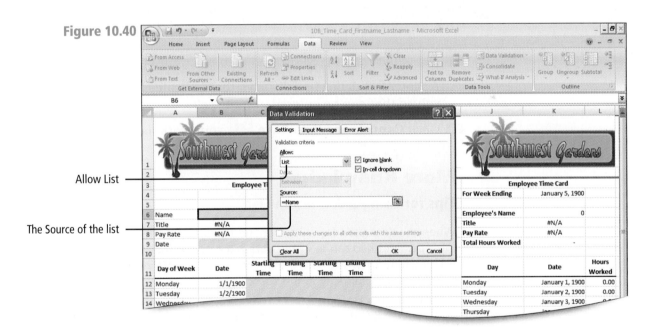

3 Click **OK**. Then click cell **B6** and notice the arrow that displays by the cell. Click the arrow and compare your screen with Figure 10.41. In the list, click **Miel, Phillip**.

As you enter the employee's name, the title and pay rate of the employee is entered into the cells B7 and B8. Recall that you entered lookup functions so these cells would be updated once the name of the employee was entered.

Figure 10.41

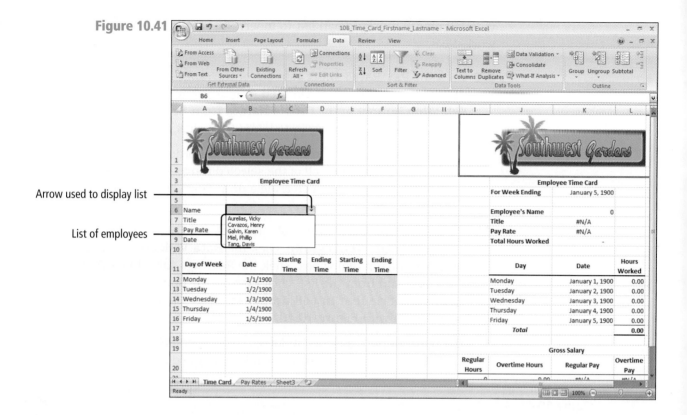

Arrow used to display list

List of employees

4 Delete the entry in cell **B6**, and then type your first name and press Enter.

A Stop Alert dialog box displays that indicates a user has restricted values that can be entered into the cell.

5 Click **Cancel**, and then **Save** your workbook.

More Knowledge

Tips for Using a Validation List

When the data used for a list is on a different worksheet of the workbook, it must be a defined range. If the data is located in the same worksheet as the list, you may enter the cell references in the Data Validation dialog box, on the Settings tab directly in the Source box.

If the validation list is on another worksheet of the workbook, consider hiding and protecting the worksheet to prevent users from making changes.

Activity 10.19 Hiding Formulas

Recall that hiding a formula is a good idea when forms will be shared with others. In this activity, you will hide the formulas used in the form.

1 Select the range **B7:B8** and on the **Home tab**, in the **Cells group**, click the **Format** button. Under **Protection**, click **Format Cells**. In the **Format Cells** dialog box, click the **Protection tab**, click **Hidden**, and then click **OK**. Using the skills you practiced, hide the formulas in the following cells: **K4:K9**, **K12:L17**, and **I21:M21**.

Recall that the formulas will continue to be visible until the worksheet is protected. Recall that the error codes in many of these cells occur because the underlying formulas refer to cells that currently have no content. When the form is completed, the error notations will be replaced by valid data.

2 Click the **Review tab**, and in the **Changes group**, click the **Allow Users to Edit Ranges** button, and then compare your screen with Figure 10.42.

Figure 10.42

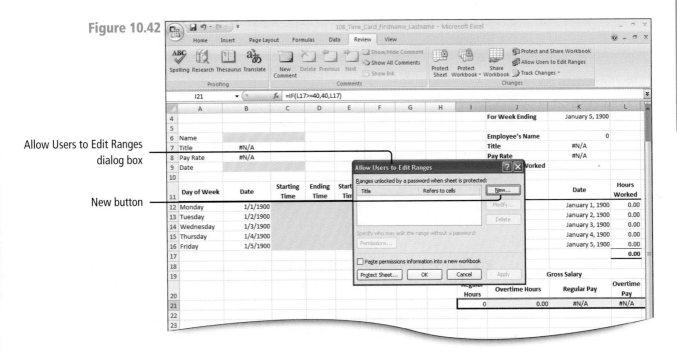

Allow Users to Edit Ranges dialog box

New button

3 In the **Allow Users to Edit Ranges** dialog box, click **New**. In the **Title** area, type **Name** and then press [Tab]. With the reference in the **Refers to cells** text box highlighted, click cell **B6**, compare your screen with Figure 10.43, and then click **OK**.

You have indicated that the user will be allowed to insert his/her name into the form.

Figure 10.43

Title text box

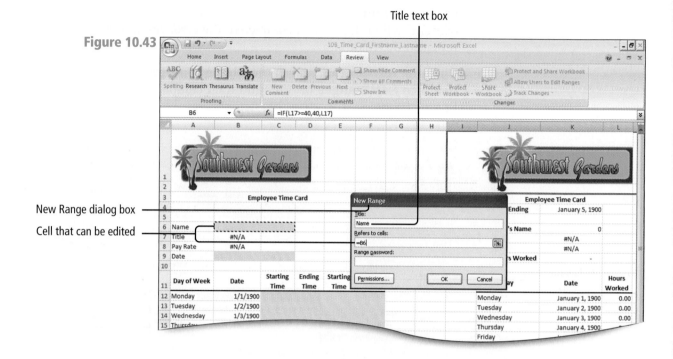

New Range dialog box

Cell that can be edited

4 In the **Allow Users to Edit Ranges** dialog box, click **New**. In the **Title** text box, type **Date** and then press Tab. In the **Refers to cells** box, click cell **B9**, and then click **OK**. Using the skills you practiced, allow users to edit the times area of the worksheet—**C12:F16**—and use the title **Hours Worked** When finished, click **OK**. Then click **OK** again and do not protect the sheet.

5 **Save** your workbook.

Objective 8
Insert Macro Command Buttons

Because the form is designed to be used repeatedly, after it is completed by one employee, it should be cleared for the next employee. Only the output area is to be printed and used as a receipt of the hours worked. Creating macros to automate these activities saves time for the person filling out the form. Creating a button that you click to activate the macros is another way to make the form easy to use.

Activity 10.20 Creating a Print Macro

Printing only the output area is done by selecting a print area and then using the Print command. Because the time card will be used by employees who do not know how to print an area of the worksheet, inserting a macro for that command is helpful. In this activity, you will create a macro to print the output portion of the time card. Recall that a macro needs to be planned before it is executed. In this macro, you select the print area, set the print area, format the area so it is centered horizontally and vertically, and then execute a print command before stopping the macro.

1 Click the **Office** button ⬚, click the **Excel Options** button. In the **Popular section**, under **Top options for working with Excel**, confirm that the **Show Developer tab in the Ribbon** is checked, and then click **OK**.

You have enabled the macro commands to be displayed on the Ribbon.

2 Click the **Developer tab** and in the **Code group**, click the **Record Macro** button. In the **Macro name** text box, type Print_Form and in the **Shortcut key**, type r Confirm that **Store macro in This Workbook** displays, and in the **Description** area, type Print output area of the Time Card and then click **OK**.

Recall that when you click OK, the macro records each keystroke you make and the icon in the status bar indicates a macro is being recorded. Recall also that the Record Macro dialog box is used to assign a macro name and a description of the macro. Placing the macro in the workbook needs to be done in order for the macro to run in the form. Recall also that the workbook containing a macro needs to be opened in order for that macro to run.

3 Select the range **I1:M22** and click the **Page Layout tab**. In the **Page Setup group**, click the **Print Area** button, and then click **Set Print Area**. In the **Page Setup group**, click the **Dialog Box Launcher** ⬚ and in the **Page Setup** dialog box, click the **Margins tab** and center **Horizontally** and **Vertically**, and then click **OK**.

Recall that a **print area** is the portion of the worksheet that is to print and is usually smaller than the entire worksheet. The print area includes one row below the data in the output area.

4 Click the **Office** button ⬚ and then click **Print**. In the **Print** dialog box, click **OK**, and then click the **Developer tab** and in the **Code group**, click **Stop Recording**. Alternatively, on the Status bar, click the Stop Recording button ⬚.

5 Confirm the macro works. Press [Ctrl] + [R], and then **Save** ⬚ your workbook.

Activity 10.21 Creating a Macro to Clear the Input Area

In this activity, you will record a macro that will clear the input areas on the form. In this macro, you will unprotect the worksheet, clear the input area, and then protect the worksheet again. Because the worksheet has not been protected yet, you will first protect the worksheet in order to record a correct macro.

1 Click the **Review tab**, and in the **Changes group**, click the **Protect Sheet** button. Click **OK**.

A worksheet can be protected without using a password. Because the worksheet will be protected and this macro will not run with a protected worksheet, the first step in the macro is to unprotect the worksheet. However, before you can unprotect the worksheet, it needs to first be protected.

2 On the **Status bar**, click the **Record Macro** button. In the **Record Macro** dialog box, enter the **Macro name Clear** and then enter a **Shortcut key** of [⇧ Shift] + [L]. In the **Description** area, type Clear form and start new Compare your screen with Figure 10.44, and then click **OK**.

Figure 10.44

Record Macro dialog box

Record Macro button

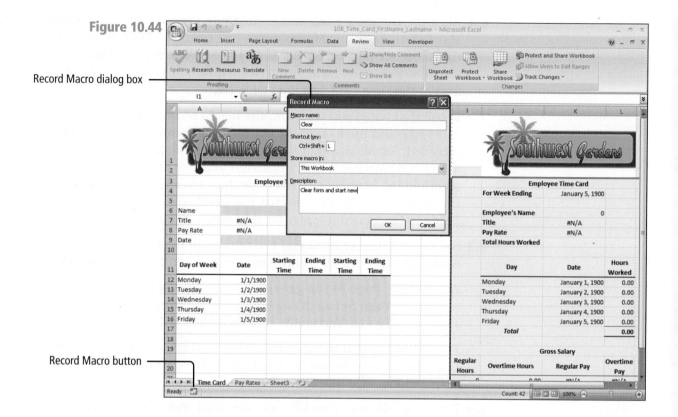

3 On the **Review tab**, in the **Changes group**, click the **Unprotect Sheet** button. Click cell **B6** and press [Delete]. Click cell **B9** and press [Delete], and then select the range **C12:F16** and press [Delete]. In the **Status bar**, click the **Stop macro** button.

Even though there is no data in the cells you deleted, there will be when the form is used.

4 In cell **B6**, click the arrow and select an employee's name. Then press [⇧ Shift] + [Ctrl] + [L] to confirm the macro works by clearing the entry.

Save your workbook.

Activity 10.22 Inserting a Macro Command Button

A *macro command button* is a graphic shape inserted into the worksheet that is assigned to a macro. When you click on the **macro command button**, the macro runs. In this activity, you will insert a macro command button and assign it to a macro.

1 Click the **Insert tab** and in the **Illustrations group**, click the **Shapes** button. Under **Stars and Banners**, click the first starburst— **Explosion 1**. Position the pointer in middle of cell **D3** at the top of the gridline between **rows 2** and **3** and drag down and to the right. End the shape at the bottom right gridline of cell **E5**, as shown in Figure 10.45.

Figure 10.45

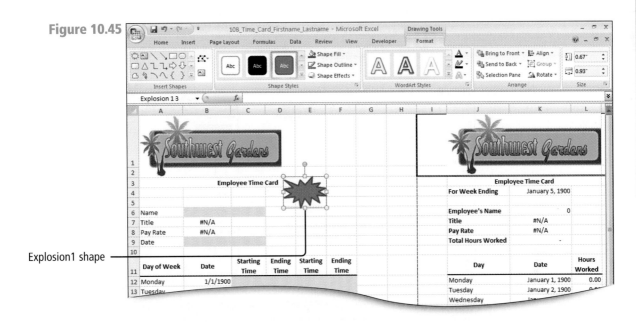

Explosion1 shape

2 Type **Print** in the **Shape Styles group**, click the **Shape Fill** button, and in the seventh column, click the last item—**Olive Green, Accent 3, Darker 50%**.

3 On the **Insert tab**, in the **Illustrations group**, click the **Shapes** button. Under **Stars and Banners**, click the ninth choice—**12-Point Star**. Point at the upper left border of cell **F6** and drag down and to the right to position the star over the range **F6:G9**. Type **Clear**

4 With the **Clear** star selected, right-click and from the shortcut menu, click **Assign Macro**. In the **Assign Macro** dialog box, click **Clear**. Compare your screen with Figure 10.46, and then click **OK**.

The blue starburst has become a *hot spot* on the form—a place that will execute a command when you click on it.

Figure 10.46

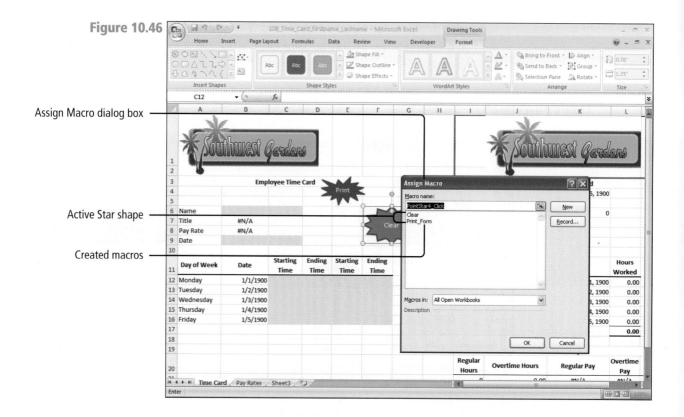

Assign Macro dialog box

Active Star shape

Created macros

Alert!

Why do I show only the name of the macro?

Depending on the way your computer is set, your screen may display only the name of the macro and not the entire file path. It is important that the names of the macros display in the Assign Macro dialog box. You do not need to change the settings on your computer.

5 Right-click the **Print** starburst, and from the shortcut menu, click **Assign Macro**. In the **Assign Macro** dialog box, click **Print_Form**, and then click **OK**.

6 In cell **B9**, type **1/1/2009** and press Enter. Click the **Clear** icon starburst to confirm the macro command button functions.

7 **Save** your workbook.

Activity 10.23 Protecting the Worksheet and Saving It as a Template

This template will be accessible to the employees in the media company so it will be protected without a password. In this activity, you will protect the worksheet and save it as a template.

1 Hide the **Pay Rates** and **Sheet3** worksheets. On the **Review tab**, in the **Changes group**, click the**Protect Workbook** button. In the menu, under **Restrict Editing**, click **Protect Structure and Windows**. Confirm that only **Structure** is protected, and then click **OK**.

There are hidden sheets that you do not want the user to edit. In addition, the Pay Rates worksheet contains the confidential information of each employee's pay rate.

2 In the **Changes group**, click **Protect Sheet**. In the **Protect Sheet** dialog box, confirm that **Select locked cells** and **Select unlocked cells** are checked. Click **OK**.

3 Click cell **B6**. From the **Office** menu ⬛, click **Save As**. Click the **Save as type box arrow**, and then click **Excel Macro-Enabled Template**. Navigate to the **Excel Chapter 10** folder, confirm that the **Save as type** is **Excel Macro-Enabled Template**, type the file name **10B_Time_Card_Template_Firstname_Lastname** and then click **Save**. **Close** the workbook.

Before you save a template, make the first cell that will be used the active cell. For the macros to function appropriately on the template, the template needs to be saved in the Excel Macro-Enabled Template format. This saves a copy of the template file to your folder.

Activity 10.24 Preparing Payroll Reports for a Week

The value in completing a form such as this is the ease in using the form. In this activity, you will use the Time Card form to complete the hours worked for two employees.

1 Click the **Office** button ⬛, and then click **New**. Under **Templates**, click **New from existing**. From your **Excel Chapter 10** folder, select **10B_Time_Card_Template_Firstname_Lastname**, and then click **Create New**.

The template file opens as a new workbook that can be used to enter data.

2 On the **Security Warning** bar, click the **Options** button, and then click **Enable this content** and click **OK**. **Save** the workbook as an **Excel Macro-Enabled Workbook** named **10B_Time_Card_Cavazos_ Firstname_Lastname** Enter the following information: in cell **B6**, click the arrow and select **Henry Cavazos**. In cell **B9**, type **2/8/2009** which is a Sunday. The hours worked are below. If the alert stops you from an entry, then use the earliest or latest time allowed. Use the ⏎ key to move down each column or the ➡ key to move across the rows.

Day of Week	Starting Time	Ending Time	Starting Time	Ending Time
Monday	7:30 am	11:45 am	1 pm	5 pm
Tuesday	10:30 am	2 pm	3:30 pm	9:45 pm
Wednesday	5:30 am	11:30 am	1 pm	3 pm
Thursday	8 am	12 pm	1:30 pm	4 pm
Friday	8:45 am	12:30 pm	1:15 pm	5 pm

3 **Save** 💾 the workbook. Click the **Print** button to print a copy of the time card, and then click the **Clear** button.

4 In the cleared time card, **Save** the worksheet as an **Excel Macro-Enabled Workbook** named **10B_Time_Card_Galvin_Firstname_ Lastname** In the Time Card, enter the following for **Karen Galvin** for the same week—2/8/2009. Use the list to select the employee's name. The hours worked are below. If the alert stops you from an entry, then use the closest acceptable time.

Day of Week	Starting Time	Ending Time	Starting Time	Ending Time
Monday	8:15 am	12 pm	1 pm	4:45 pm
Tuesday	11:45 am	4 pm	5:30 pm	10:15 pm
Wednesday	7 am	11:30 am	1 pm	4 pm
Thursday	10 am	1:30 pm	2:15 pm	4:30 pm
Friday	8 am	12:30 pm	1:15 pm	5 pm

 Click the **Save** button . Click the **Print** button to print a copy of the time card. Then click the **Clear** button.

6 To submit the workbooks electronically, follow the instructions provided by your instructor. If you submit printed copies, you will submit the **10B_Time_Card_Template_Firstname_Lastname** as well as the printed documents you created in Steps 3 and 5 of this activity. **Exit** Excel.

End **You have completed Project 10B**

There's More You Can Do!

From My Computer, navigate to the student files that accompany this textbook. In the folder **02_theres_more_you_can_do**, locate and open the folder for this chapter. Open and print the instructions for this project, which are provided to you in Adobe PDF format.

Try It! 1—Protect Structure

In this Try It! exercise, you will protect the structure of a worksheet.

Content-Based Assessments

Summary

In this chapter, you created a workbook and saved it as a template to be used repeatedly. Prior to saving the workbook as a template, you identified the input and output areas and formatted them so they can be identified by the user. You also created a chart template as a separate template and as part of a workbook. To make a form easier to use, you validated the form by inserting messages that provide instructions for completing the form or preventing inaccurate entries. You inserted a list in the form.

Macros were created to print the form and clear the contents for the next user. These macros were attached to a graphic element—button—in the form. You used the macro to print the form and clear the contents for the next user. You saved the form as a macro-enabled workbook and template, and then used it to enter data. You created a chart template as a separate template and as part of a workbook.

Key Terms

Content-Based Assessments

Matching

Match each term in the second column with its correct definition in the first column by writing the letter of the term on the blank line in front of the correct definition.

_____ **1.** A workbook that can be opened, read, edited, and resaved.

_____ **2.** In a form or template, the range that will be filled in with current data.

_____ **3.** Saving a workbook so that changes cannot be made by others, but it can be viewed without using a password.

_____ **4.** A method used to access a protected workbook, worksheet, or portion of a worksheet.

_____ **5.** The process of allowing only authorized persons to edit portions of the worksheet.

_____ **6.** A worksheet or workbook saved in a manner so that the workbook can be viewed but unauthorized changes cannot be made.

_____ **7.** A combination of uppercase and lowercase letters as well as numbers or symbols used to protect a worksheet or workbook.

_____ **8.** Formatting cells in a worksheet so that the underlying value or formula cannot be viewed.

_____ **9.** Cells in a worksheet that cannot be edited.

_____ **10.** The basic format of the workbook that includes the number and order of worksheets.

_____ **11.** A document technique that encodes and scrambles the data to increase the security of the document.

_____ **12.** The command you will used to merge a range of cells that covers both rows and columns into one cell.

_____ **13.** In a form, the command used to set a separate area of the worksheet to print.

_____ **14.** A message that provides additional information about the entry in the cell and displays when a cell is selected.

_____ **15.** Entering a password a second time to ensure its accuracy.

A Confirm password

B Encryption

C Hiding cells

D Input message

E Input Range

F Locked cells

G Merge cells

H Password

I Permissions

J Protected

K Print area

L Read only

M Read-write workbook

N Strong password

O Structure

Fill in the Blank

Write the correct answer in the space provided.

1. A file that is saved in a way that preserves the original file and creates a copy of the file for use each time it is opened is a(n) _____.

2. A chart that is saved in a way that preserves the original format and style each time it is opened is a(n) _____ _____.

3. In a form, the area where the user will enter data is the _____ _____.

4. In order to combine cells in a row into one cell, use the _____ _____ command.

5. A place in a form that summarizes the data and can be printed is the _____ _____.

6. In a form, use _____ to ensure that accurate data is entered and instruction is provided for completing the form.

7. The data validation that identifies the criteria entered into the cell is the _____.

8. The validation that creates a user-created ScreenTip when a cell is selected is the _____ _____.

9. The validation that creates a ScreenTip message that alerts the user that incorrect information is entered into the cell is the _____ _____.

10. The alert that prevents invalid data from being entered into the cell is a(n) _____ _____ _____.

11. A list that displays the entries that can be made into a cell is the _____ _____ _____.

12. A graphic shape inserted into a worksheet that has a macro assigned to is a(n) _____ _____ _____.

13. On a worksheet or form, the area that will execute the command on the form is a(n) _____ _____.

14. When you use a template to enter data, and then save the completed workbook, save it as a(n) _____ file.

15. When you save a workbook in a format that will allow macros in the worksheet it is a _____ _____ _____.

Content-Based Assessments

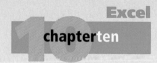
Project 10C—Guest Costs

In this project, you will apply the skills you practiced from the Objectives in Project 10A.

Objectives: 1. *Protect Worksheet Elements;* **2.** *Unprotect Elements and Hide Formulas;* **3.** *Protect a Workbook;* **4.** *Save Worksheet and Chart Templates;* **5.** *Complete a Report with Worksheet and Chart Templates.*

In the following Skills Review, you will create a template to keep track of the guests and the stipends paid to them. Southwest Gardens prides itself on the quality and knowledge of the guests they invite on the show and provides a small stipend for participating. Each show has varying numbers of guests—anywhere from one to four. The guests are paid a standard stipend of $25 per hour. In the following Skills Review, you will create a template to keep track of the guests and the stipends paid to them. Your completed worksheets will look similar to those in Figure 10.47.

For Project 10C, you will need the following files:

New blank workbook
e10C_SW_Garden_Logo

You will save your documents workbooks as
10C_Guest_Costs_Firstname_Lastname
10C_Guest_Costs_Template_Firstname_Lastname (Template)

Figure 10.47

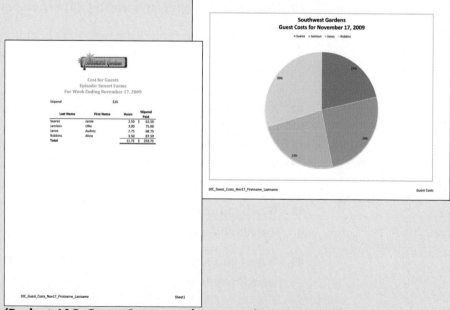

(Project 10C–Guest Costs continues on the next page)

Content-Based Assessments

(Project 10C–Guest Costs continued)

1. **Start** Excel to a new, blank workbook and **Save** it in the **Excel Chapter 10** folder as **10C_Guest_Costs_Firstname_Lastname**

2. Beginning in cell **A1**, type the following worksheet title:

| Cost for Guests |
| For Week Ending |

3. In cell **A5**, type **Stipend** and in cell **B5**, type **$25**. Beginning in cell **A7**, enter the following column titles on one line:

| Last Name | First Name | Hours | Stipend Paid |

4. In the **Left Footer**, insert the **File Name** and in the **Right Footer**, insert the **Sheet Name**. Click in the **Center Header** and in the **Header & Footer Elements group**, click the **Picture** button and navigate to your data files. Locate and insert **e10C_SW_Garden_Logo**. In the **Header & Footer Elements group**, click the **Format Picture** button. In the **Format Picture** dialog box, under **Size and rotate**, in the **Height** box, type **1.5** and then click **OK**. Display the **Page Setup** dialog box and click the **Margins tab**. Set the **Top Margin** to **1.5"**. Return to **Normal** view.

5. Select the range **A7:D7** and format the column titles with **Bold**, **Bottom Border**, **Center**, **Middle Align**, and **Wrap Text**.

6. Select the range **A1:A3** and format the range with **Bold**, **14 point**, change the font to **Cambria** font, and change the **Font Color** to **Standard** color **Green**. Select the range **A1:D1** and in the **Alignment group**, click the **Merge & Center** button. Use the **Format Painter** to copy the format from cell **A1** to cells **A2** and **A3**. Select **columns A** and **B**. In the **Cells group**, click the

Format button, and then click **Column Width**. In the **Column Width** dialog box, type **18.43** pixels.

7. In the range **C8:C11**, enter the following placeholder numbers: **10, 20, 30, 40** In cell **D8**, enter a formula that will multiply the hours by the stipend—**=c8*b5**. Use the fill handle to copy the formula down through cell **D11**. In cell **A12**, type **Total** and format it with **Bold**. Select the range **C12:D12** and enter a **Sum** function. Format the total in the range with a **Top and Double Bottom Border**.

8. Click cell **D12**, press ⟨Ctrl⟩, and select **D8**. Format with **Accounting Number Format**. Select **D9:D11** and format with **Comma Style**. Format **C8:C12** with **Comma Style**. Select the range **C8:C11** and **delete** the placeholder numbers. Delete **Sheet2** and **Sheet3**.

9. Select the range **A8:C11**—the cells that the user can edit. Click the **Review tab** and in the **Changes group**, click the **Allow Users to Edit Ranges** button. In the **Allow Users to Edit Ranges** dialog box, click **New**. In the **Title** box, type **Guest_Data** and then in the **Refers to cells** box, verify that the range **A8:C11** displays as an absolute reference. Click **OK**.

10. In the **Allow Users to Edit Ranges** dialog box, click **New**. In the **New Range** dialog box, in the **Title box**, type **Date** and then in the **Refers to cells** box, click the **Collapse Dialog Box** button, click cell **A3**, and press ⟨F4⟩. Then click the **Expand Dialog Box** button and click **OK**. Using the skills you practiced, allow users to edit cell **A2** and use the title **Episode** Then close the dialog boxes.

11. To hide the formulas, select the range **D8:D12** and press ⟨Ctrl⟩ while you click cell

(Project 10C–Guest Costs continues on the next page)

(Project 10C–Guest Costs continued)

C12. On the **Home tab**, in the **Cells group**, click the **Format** button, and under **Protection**, click **Format Cells**. In the **Format Cells** or **Custom List** dialog box, click the **Protection tab**, click **Hidden**, and then click **OK**.

12. To password protect the worksheet, click the **Review tab**, in the **Changes group**, click the **Protect Sheet** button. In the **Protect Sheet** dialog box, in the **Password to unprotect sheet** text box, type **student** and then click **OK**. Confirm the password by typing **student** again, and then click **OK**.

13. To protect the workbook, on the **Review tab**, in the **Changes group**, click the **Protect Workbook** button, and then under **Restrict Editing**, click **Protect Structure and Windows**. In the displayed dialog box, confirm that **Structure** is the only item checked. In the **Password** box, type **student** and then click **OK**. Reenter the password to confirm it, and then click **OK**.

14. To encrypt the worksheet, click the **Office** menu and point to **Prepare**, and on the right side, click **Encrypt Document**. In the **Encrypt Document** dialog box, in the **Password** box, type **student** and then click **OK**. In the **Confirm Password** dialog box, type **student** again, and then click **OK**. **Save** the workbook.

15. From the **Office** menu, click **Save As**. In the **Save as type** box, click the arrow and click **Excel Template**. In the **File Name**, type **10C_Guest_Costs_Template_Firstname_Lastname** Change the **Save in** location to your **Excel Chapter 10** folder, and then click **Save**. Close the template.

16. Open the **10C_Guest_Costs_Firstname_Lastname** workbook using the password

student Select the range **A8:A11** and type the following placeholders:

Amos
Bond
Clark
Dunn

17. In cells **C8:C11**, type the place holders **10**, **20**, **30**, **40**. Select the range **A7:A11**, press Ctrl, and select the range **D7:D11**. Right-click and click **Copy**. Open a new, blank workbook. Click cell **A7** and select a **Paste** command. With the range still selected, on the **Insert tab**, in the **Charts group**, click **Pie**, and then under **2-D Pie**, click the first choice—**Pie**. On the **Design tab**, in the **Chart Layouts group**, select chart **Layout 2**. In the **Chart Style group**, select **Style 15**.

18. On the **Design tab**, in the **Location group**, click the **Move Chart** button. Click **New sheet** and name it **Guest Costs** and then click **OK**.

19. Display the **10C_Guest_Costs_Firstname_Lastname** workbook, click the **Close Window** button, and when asked if you want to save changes, click **No**. Delete **Sheet2** and **Sheet3** and hide **Sheet1**. With the chart active, on the **Design tab**, in the **Type group**, click the **Save As Template** button. In the **File name** box, type **10C_Guest_Costs_Chart_Temp_Firstname_Lastname** Confirm that the **Save as** type is **Chart Template Files**, then click **Save**. Click the **Close Window** button. When asked if you want to save changes, click **No**.

20. From the **Office** menu, click **New**. In the **New Workbook** dialog box, on the left,

(Project 10C–Guest Costs continues on the next page)

(Project 10C–Guest Costs continued)

under **Templates**, click **New from existing**. In your **Excel Chapter 10** folder, locate and click the **10C_Guest_Costs_Template_Firstname_Lastname** template, and then click **Create New**.

21. To open the template, type the password—**student**—and click **OK**. Beginning in cell **A8**, type the following:

Last Name	First Name	Hours
Suarez	Jamie	2.5
Jamison	Ollie	3
Janos	Audrey	2.75
Robbins	Alicia	3.5

22. In cell **A2**, after *Episode*, type **Sunset Farms** Click cell **A3** and after *For Week Ending*, type **November 17, 2009** From the **Office** menu, click **Save As**. In the **Save As** dialog box, navigate to your **Excel Chapter 10** folder. Then in the **File name** box, type **10C_Guest_Costs_Nov17_Firstname_Lastname** Confirm that **Save as type** is **Excel Workbook**, and then click **Save**.

23. Click the **Review tab** and in the **Changes group**, click **Protect Workbook**. Under **Restrict Editing**, click **Protect Structure and Windows** to deselect it. In the **Unprotect Workbook** dialog box, type the password **student** and then click **OK**. The workbook structure is no longer protected.

24. Select the range **A7:A11** and press Ctrl while you select the range **D7:D11**. Select a **Copy** command. Click the **Insert Worksheet** button, right-click cell **A2**, and click **Paste**. Click the **Insert tab**, click the **Pie** button, and then at the bottom, click **All Chart Types**. On the left, click **Templates**, and in the **My Templates** section, position the pointer over the pie chart and confirm the ScreenTip displays *10C_Guest_Costs_Chart_Temp_Firstname_Last name*. Click the icon, and then click **OK**.

25. Click the **Title** and type the following title:

Southwest Gardens
Guest Costs for November 17, 2009

26. In the **Location group**, click the **Move Chart** button and place the chart in a new sheet named **Guest Costs Hide Sheet 2**. In the chart sheet, in the **Left Footer** area, insert the **File Name**. Center **Sheet1 Horizontally**. **Save** your workbook.

27. To submit electronically, follow the instructions provided by your instructor. **Print** the **10C_Guest_Costs_Nov17_Firstname_Lastname** workbook. To print, from the **Office** menu, click **Print**. In the **Print** dialog box, under **Print what**, select **Entire workbook**, and then click **OK**. From the **Office** menu, click **Close**. **Exit** Excel.

End **You have completed Project 10C**

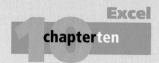
Project 10D — Travel Reimbursement

In this project, you will apply the skills you practiced from the Objectives in Project 10B.

Objectives: 6. *Create a Form;* **7.** *Validate a Form;* **8.** *Insert Macro Command Buttons.*

The hosts of *Southwest Gardens* travel to various locations to present tours of public and private gardens that showcase the southwest style. A form is needed to keep track of travel expenses for reimbursement purposes.

In the following Skills Review, you will create a form to be used to report travel expenses. You will create both an input and output area and create two macro buttons to be used with the form. Your completed worksheet will look like Figure 10.48.

For Project 10D, you will need the following files:

e10D_Travel_Reimbursement
e10D_SW_Garden_Logo

You will save your workbooks as
10D_Travel_Reimbursement_Template_Firstname_Lastname
(Macro-Enabled Template)
10D_Travel_Reimbursement_Tang_Firstname_Lastname
(Macro-Enabled Worksheet)
10D_Travel_Reimbursement_Cavazos_Firstname_Lastname
(Macro-Enabled Worksheet)

Figure 10.48

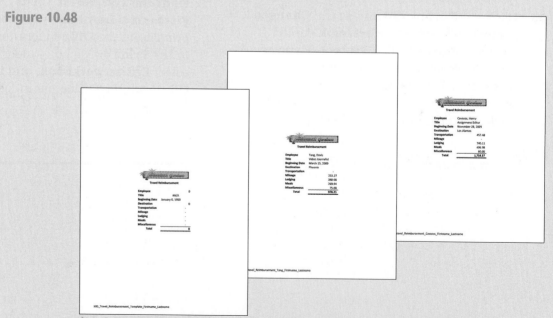

(Project 10D–Travel Reimbursement continues on the next page)

(Project 10D– Travel Reimbursement continued)

1. **Start** Excel. From your student files, locate and open the file named **e10D_Travel_Reimbursement**. From the **Office** menu, point to **Save As** and in the submenu, click **Excel Macro-Enabled Template**, and then save the file in the **Excel Chapter 10** folder and name it **10D_Travel_Reimbursement_Template_Firstname_Lastname**

2. Click the **Employee sheet tab**. Select the range **A3:B7** and on the **Formulas tab**, in the **Defined Names group**, click **Define Name**. In the **New Name** dialog box, in the **Name** box, type **Employees** and then click **OK**. Select **A3:A7** and name the range **Name**

3. Click the **Travel sheet tab** and click cell **B7**. On the **Data tab**, in the **Data Tools group**, click the **Data Validation** button. In the **Data Validation** dialog box, on the **Settings tab**, and under **Allow**, click the **arrow**. From the list, click **List**. In the **Source** box, type **=Name** Confirm that **In-cell dropdown** is selected, and then click **OK**. In cell **B7**, click the **arrow**, and then from the list click **Galvin, Karen**.

4. Click cell **B8** and click the **Formulas tab**. In the **Function Library group**, click the **Lookup & Reference** button, and then click **VLOOKUP**. In the dialog box, in the **Lookup_value** box, type **b7** and then press Tab and in the **Table_array** box, type **Employees** Press Tab and in the **Col_index_num** box, type **2** and then press Enter.

5. Click in cell **B9**, and then click the **Data tab**. In the **Data Tools group**, click the **Data Validation** button, and then click the **Input Message tab**. Confirm that **Show input message when cell is selected** is checked. In the **Title** box, type **Date of Travel** In the **Input message**, type **Enter beginning date in the style of**

1/1/2009 Click **OK**. Copy this cell to **C9**. Edit the **Input message** to read **ending** instead of beginning date.

6. Click cell **B10** and enter a formula that will subtract the beginning date from the ending date and add one day—**=C9-B9+1** In cell **A22**, type **Total Meals** In **B22**, enter a formula that will total the amount spent for meals—**=Sum(a18:e18, a20:e20)**

7. Click cell **B15** and click the **Data tab**. In the **Data Tools group**, click the **Data Validation** button, and then click the **Settings tab**. Under **Allow**, click the **arrow** and from the list, click **Decimal**. In the **Data** box, confirm that **between** is selected. In the **Minimum** box, type **0** and in the **Maximum** box, type **75** Click the **Input Message tab**, and confirm that **Show input message when cell is selected** is checked. In the **Title** box, type **Miscellaneous** In the **Input message** box, type **No more than $75 may be spent for miscellaneous items** Click the **Error Alert tab**. In the **Title** box, type **Amount Not Valid** and in the **Error message** box, type **Cannot enter more than $75** Confirm that the **Style** is **Stop**, and then click **OK**.

8. In cell **B9**, enter the following data as placeholders: For beginning date of travel, type **1/1/2009** In cell **C9**, type **1/5/2009** for the ending date of travel. In cell **B11**, type **Los Angeles** as the destination. In cells **B12:B15**, type **10** for each expense item listed. In the cells in **rows 18** and **20**, type **10** for each meal for the ten days. Format **B12:B15, A18:E18, A20:E20**, and **B22** with **Comma Style**. Format cell **B13** with **no decimals**.

9. Using the Ctrl key, select **B7, B9:C9, B11:B15, A18:E18**, and **A20:E20**. Click

(Project 10D–Travel Reimbursement continues on the next page)

(Project 10D–Travel Reimbursement continued)

the **Fill Color button arrow**. Under **Theme Colors**, in the fifth column, click the third choice—**Blue, Accent 1, Lighter 60%**.

10. Click cell **H1** and on the **Insert tab**, in the **Illustrations group**, click **Picture**. Navigate to your student files for Chapter 10 and click **e10D_SW_Garden_Logo**, and then click **Insert**. Use the sizing handles to fit the picture in **H1:I3**. Click cell **I6**, type the formula **=b7** and copy the formula down through cell **I8**. With cell **I8** selected, in the **Number group**, click the **Number Format button arrow** and from the list, click **More Number Formats**. In the **Format Cells** dialog box, under **Category**, click **Date**. On the right, under **Type**, change the date format to **March 14, 2001**, and then click **OK**. In the **Alignment group**, click **Align Text Left**.

11. In cell **I9**, type the formula **=b11** and copy it through **I10**. Click cell **I11**, type **=b13*.31** to create a formula to multiply the number of miles traveled by 31 cents. In cell **I12**, enter a formula that will multiply the cost of lodging per night by the number of days of the trip minus 1— **=(b10−1)*b14**. In cell **I13**, enter a formula that will result in the total costs of meals, and in cell **I14**, enter a formula that will result in the amount spent on miscellaneous items.

12. In cell **H15**, type **Total** Format with **Bold** and **Center**. In cell **I15**, enter a **Sum** formula and format it with **Bold** and **Top and Double Bottom Border**. Format amounts in **I10:I15** with **Comma Style**.

13. Select the range **I6:I15** and on the **Home tab**, in the **Cells group**, click the **Format** button. Under **Protection**, click **Format Cells**. In the **Format Cells** dialog box, click the **Protection tab**, click **Hidden**, and then click **OK**.

14. Select all cells with a blue background, click the **Review tab**, and in the **Changes group**, click the **Allow Users to Edit Ranges** button. In the **Allow Users to Edit Ranges** dialog box, click **New**. In the **Title** area, type **Input** and then click **OK**. Click the **Protect Sheet** button, and without entering a password, click **OK**.

15. Click the **Developer tab**, in the **Code group**, click the **Record Macro** button. In the **Macro name** box, type **Print_Travel_ Form** and in the **Shortcut key**, type **w** Confirm that **Store macro in This Workbook** displays, and in the **Description** area, type **Print output area of travel reimbursement form** and then click **OK**.

16. Select the range **H1:I16**—because of the logo in row 1, begin the selection in cell **I16**—and then click the **Page Layout tab**. In the **Page Setup group**, click **Print Area**, and click **Set Print Area**. Then in the **Page Setup group**, click the **Dialog Box Launcher** and in the **Page Setup** dialog box, click the **Margins tab** and center **Horizontally** and **Vertically**, and then click **OK**. In the **Office** menu, click **Print**. In the **Print** dialog box, click **OK**. Click the **Developer tab** and in the **Code group**, click **Stop Recording**.

17. On the **Developer tab** and in the **Code group**, click the **Record Macro** button. In the **Macro Name** box, type **Clear_Form** and in the **Shortcut key**, type ⇧ Shift + F Confirm that **Store macro in This Workbook** displays and in the **Description** area, type **Unprotect the sheet and clear input ranges** and then click **OK**. On the **Review tab**, in the **Changes group**, click the **Unprotect sheet** button, and delete all data in cells formatted with a blue background. On the **Developer tab**, in the **Code group**, click the **Stop Recording** button.

(Project 10D–Travel Reimbursement continues on the next page)

Content-Based Assessments

(Project 10D–Travel Reimbursement continued)

18. Click the **Insert tab** and in the **Illustrations group**, click the **Shapes** button. Under **Rectangles**, select the first shape. Position the shape in cells **E7:E8**, and then type **Print** With the **Print** shape selected, right-click, and from the shortcut menu, click **Assign Macro**. In the **Assign Macro** dialog box, click **Print_Travel_ Form**, and then click **OK**. Using the skills just practiced, insert a rectangle shape in cells **E10:E11** that reads **Clear** and assign the **Clear_Form** macro to it.

19. In the **Left Footer**, add the **File Name**. On the **Review tab**, in the **Changes group**, click **Protect Sheet**, and then click **OK** to protect the worksheet without a password. Hide the **Employee sheet** and **Sheet3**.

20. From the **Office** menu, click **Save As**. In the **Save as type** box, click the arrow and click **Excel Macro-Enabled Template**. Navigate to the **Excel Chapter 10** folder. In the **File name** box, type **10D_Travel_ Reimbursement_Template_Firstname_ Lastname** Then click **Save**. **Close** the workbook.

21. From the **Office** menu, click **New**. Under **Templates**, click **New from existing**. From your **Excel Chapter 10** folder, **Open** the **10D_Travel_Reimbursement_ Template_Firstname_Lastname** workbook, and then click **Create New**. **Save** it as an **Excel Macro-Enabled Workbook**— **10D_Travel_Reimbursement_Tang_ Firstname_Lastname** On the **Security Warning** bar, click the **Options** button, and then click **Enable this content** and click **OK**.

22. Enter the following information. Use the drop-down list to select the employee's name. If the alert stops you from an entry, then use the maximum amount allowed.

Employee	Tang, Davis	
Date of travel	3/15/2009	3/19/2009
Destination	Phoenix	
Mileage	817	
Lodging per night	95.00	
Miscellaneous	75	

23. In cells **A18:E18**, enter the costs for meals:

Day 1	Day 2	Day 3	Day 4	Day 5
15.47	45.81	78.00	77.24	53.42

24. Click the **Print** macro button to print a copy of the expense travel reimbursement form. Click **Save**, click the **Clear** macro button, and **Close** the workbook.

25. Using the skills you practiced, open a new from existing template document named **10D_Travel_Reimbursement_Template_ Firstname_Lastname** and create a new workbook. **Save** the file as an **Excel Macro- Enabled Workbook** named **10D_Travel_ Reimbursement_Cavazos_Firstname_Lastname** and enter the following information:

Employee	Cavazos, Henry	
Date of travel	11/28/2009	12/5/2009
Destination	Los Alamos	
Transportation Cost	457.48	
Lodging per night	105.73	
Miscellaneous	60	

(Project 10D–Travel Reimbursement continues on the next page)

(Project 10D–Travel Reimbursement continued)

26. Enter the costs for meals:

Day 1	Day 2	Day 3	Day 4	Day 5
45.37	80.92	53.49	78.03	95.06
Day 6	Day 7	Day 8	Day 9	Day 10
65.98	53.40	24.73		

27. Click the **Print** macro button. Click **Save**, and then click the **Clear** macro button. **Close** the workbook without saving changes.

28. To submit the workbooks electronically, follow the instructions provided by your instructor. Print the following workbooks: **10D_Travel_Reimbursement_Template_Firstname_Lastname, 10D_Travel_Reimbursement_Tang_Firstname_Lastname,** and **10D_Travel_Reimbursement_Cavazos_Firstname_ Lastname**. To print, from the **Office** menu, click **Print**. In the **Print** dialog box, under **Print what**, select **Entire workbook**, and then click **OK**. From the **Office** menu, click **Close**. **Exit Excel**.

End **You have completed Project 10D**

Content-Based Assessments

Project 10E — DVD Sales

In this project, you will apply the skills you practiced from the Objectives in Project 10A.

Objectives: 1. *Protect Worksheet Elements;* **2.** *Unprotect Elements and Hide Formulas;* **3.** *Protect a Workbook;* **4.** *Save Worksheet and Chart Templates;* **5.** *Complete a Report with Worksheet and Chart Templates.*

Media Southwest Productions, tapes the television show, Southwest Gardens, and makes the show DVDs available to the viewing public. In the following Mastering Excel assessment, you will create a workbook that lists the DVD Sales for November and includes a chart and then save it as a template. Your completed work will look like Figure 10.49.

For Project 10E, you will need the following files:

New blank workbook

e10E_SW_Garden_Logo

You will save your files as
10E_DVD_Sales_Firstname_Lastname (Macro-Enabled Worksheet)
10E_DVD_Sales_Nov_Firstname_Lastname (Macro-Enabled Worksheet)
10E_DVD_Sales_Temp_Firstname_Lastname (Macro-Enabled Template)

Figure 10.49

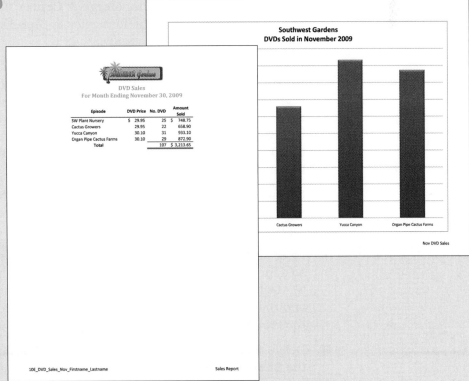

(Project 10E– DVD Sales continues on the next page)

Content-Based Assessments

(Project 10E–DVD Sales continued)

1. **Start** Excel and open to a new, blank workbook. Save it in the **Excel Chapter 10** folder as an **Excel Macro-Enabled Workbook** named **10E_DVD_Sales_Firstname_Lastname** In the **Left Footer**, insert the **File Name** and in the **Right Footer** insert the **Sheet Name**. In the **Center Header**, insert the picture named **e10E_SW_Garden_Logo**. Format the picture with a **Height** of **1.5**. Then insert a top margin of **1.5″**, and center the worksheet **Horizontally**.

2. In cell **A1**, type **DVD Sales** In cell **A2**, type **For Month Ending** Beginning in cell **A4**, type the following data:

Episode	DVD Price	No. DVD	Amount Sold
SW Plant Nursery	29.95		
Cactus Growers	29.95		
Yucca Canyon	30.1		
Organ Pipe Cactus Farms	30.1		
Total			

3. Select the range **A4:D4** and format with **Bold**, **Bottom Border**, **Center**, **Middle Align**, and **Wrap Text**.

4. Format the worksheet title—**A1:A2**—with **Bold**, **14 point**, and change the font to **Cambria**. **Merge & Center** the title lines over the data range, and change the font color to **Standard Green**. Adjust the width of **column A** to **23**.

5. In cells **C5:C8**, enter the following placeholders: **25, 26, 27, 28** In cells **D5:D8**, enter a formula to determine the dollar amount of sales for each episode. Total the number of DVDs sold and the total amount of the sales. Format cell **A9** with **Bold** and **Center**. Format cell **C9** with **Comma Style** with **no decimals** and **D9** with **Accounting Number Format**, and then insert a **Top and Double Bottom Border** in both cells.

6. Format cells **B5** and **D5** with **Accounting Number Format**. Format the range **C5:C8** with **Comma Style** with **no decimals**. Format the ranges **B6:B8** and **D6:D8** with **Comma Style**.

7. Insert a **2-D Clustered Column** chart that shows the total amount sold for each of the episodes. **Select Layout 1** and **Style 28**. **Delete** the **Legend** and move the chart to a new sheet and name it **DVD Sales** and then click **OK**. In the chart worksheet, in the **Left Footer**, insert the **File Name** and in the **Right Footer** insert the **Sheet Name**.

8. Delete **Sheet2** and **Sheet3** and click the **Sheet1 sheet tab**. Position the **Sheet1** worksheet so it is the first worksheet of the workbook

(Project 10E–DVD Sales continues on the next page)

(Project 10E–DVD Sales continued)

Name **Sheet1** Sales Report. Delete the entries in **C5:C8**. Click the **Review tab** and in the **Changes group**, allow users to edit the range of **C5:C8** and cell **A2**. **Hide** the formulas in the range **D5:D9** and cell **C9**. Then **Protect** the worksheet using the password of **student Protect** the workbook to restrict the editing of the workbook **structure** using **student** as the password.

9. From the **Office** menu, click **Prepare** and then **Encrypt Document** using **student** as the password. **Save** this workbook as a **Template** in your **Excel Chapter 10** folder and name it **10E_DVD_Sales_Temp_ Firstname_Lastname Close** the workbook.

10. From the **Office** menu, click **New**. In the **New Workbook** dialog box, under **Templates**, click **New from Existing**. Navigate to your **Excel Chapter 10** folder and open the template **10E_DVD_Sales_ Temp_ Firstname_ Lastname** using the password **student** to open the template. Beginning in cell **C5**, enter the following information for DVD sales: **25, 22, 31, 29** In cell **A2**, edit the date to read **For Month Ending November 30, 2009**

11. Click the **DVD Sales sheet tab**, and then change the title of the chart to read:

> Southwest Gardens
> DVDs Sold in November 2009

12. Click back in the **Sales Report sheet tab** and **save** your workbook as 10E_DVD_Sales_Nov_Firstname_Lastname.

13. **Print** the entire **10E_DVD_Sales_Nov_Firstname_Lastname** work-book or submit electronically. To submit electronically, follow the instructions provided by your instructor. To print, from the **Office** menu, click **Print**. In the **Print** dialog box, under **Print what**, select **Entire workbook**, and then click **OK**. Print the **Template** workbook if you are required to do so. **Close** any open workbooks. **Exit** Excel.

End You have completed Project 10E———————

Content-Based Assessments

Project 10F — Billable Hours

In this project, you will apply the skills you practiced from the Objectives in Project 10B.

Objectives: 6. *Create a Form;* **7.** *Validate a Form;* **8.** *Insert Macro Command Buttons.*

Media Southwest Productions needs a form that can be used to record the time spent by the media technicians and the total cost of filming each episode of the Southwest Gardens television show. In the following Mastering Excel assessment, you will create a form with both an input and output area and create two macro buttons to be used with the form. Your completed work will look similar to Figure 10.50.

For Project 10F, you will need the following files:

e10F_Billable_Hours
e10F_SW_Gardens_Logo

You will save your workbooks as
10F_Billable_Hours_Temp_Firstname_Lastname (Macro-Enabled Template)
10F_Billable_Hours_GSF_Firstname_Lastname (Macro-Enabled Worksheet)
10F_Billable_Hours_DTG_Firstname_Lastname (Macro-Enabled Worksheet)

Figure 10.50

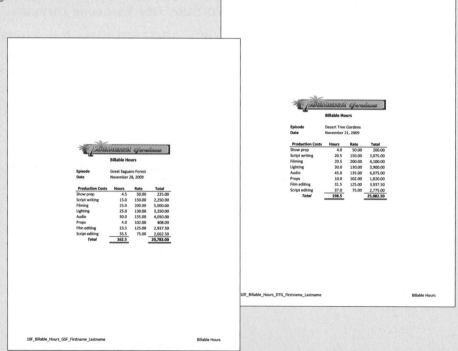

(Project 10F–Billable Hours continues on the next page)

Content-Based Assessments

(Project 10F–Billable Hours continued)

1. **Start** Excel. From your student files locate and open the file named **e10F_Billable_ Hours**. **Save** the file as an **Excel-Macro- Enabled Template** and name it **10F_Billable_Hours_Temp_Firstname_ Lastname** On the **Billable Hours** sheet, in the **Left Footer**, add the **File Name**.

2. On the **Rates sheet**, alphabetize the produc- tion costs, and select the range **A5:B12**. Name the range **Rates** Click the **Episodes sheet tab**, alphabetize the episodes. Select the range **A4:A18** and name it **Episode** Select **B4:B18** and name the range **Show_Dates**

3. Click the **Billable Hours sheet tab**. Select **B6:D6**. Click the **Merge & Center button arrow**, and then click **Merge Across**. Use the **Format Painter** to copy this format to cells **B7**, **G6**, and **G7**.

4. In cell **B6**, use data validation to create a drop-down validation list. For the source, type **=Episode** Select any episode as a placeholder. In cell **B7**, enter a **VLOOKUP function** that will determine the date for the episode. Format **B7** with the date style of **March 14, 2001** and **Align Text Left**. In **C10**, enter a **VLOOKUP** function to determine the hourly rate for each of the production costs. Copy the formula through cell **C17**. Enter numbers in the **Hours column** as placeholders.

5. Enter the necessary formulas in **columns G**, **H**, and **I** in the output area. In **F18**, type **Total** and format it with **Bold**, **Italic**, and **Center**. In **G18** and **I18**, enter a **Sum** formula and format with **Bold** and **Top and Double Bottom Border**. In the input and output areas, format the hours with **Comma Style**, **one decimal**, and all money amounts with **Comma Style**.

6. In **cell G6** create a formula to enter the **Episode Name** and in cell **G7** create the

formula to enter the **date**. Format both cells with **Left Align**.

7. In the **Left Footer**, place the **File Name** and in the **Right Footer**, place the **Sheet Name**.

8. Select **B6** and **B10:B17**. Format with a **Fill Color** of **Aqua, Accent 5, Lighter 60%**, and allow users to edit the selected cells. Title the range **Input** Select the formulas in the output range and format to **Hide** them. **Protect** the worksheet without a password.

9. Record a macro named **Clear Form** that will unprotect the worksheet and clear the input area of the form. Record a macro named **Print Form** that will set the output areas as the **Print Area**—because of the logo, begin the selection of the print area from the bot- tom—center the worksheet **Horizontally** and **Vertically**, and **Print** the form.

10. Insert the basic shape of cloud for each of the macros. Place one shape beginning in the middle of the top border of cell **A19** and ending just over the left border of cell **B20**. Place the other shape beginning in middle of the top border of cell **C19** and ending in the bottom border of cell **D20**, and then assign the recorded macros to the shapes. **Hide** all formulas in the output area and **Hide** the **Rates sheet** and the **Episode sheet**.

11. **Protect** the sheet without a password, and confirm the workbook is saved as an **Excel Macro-Enabled Template** named **10F_Billable_Hours_Temp_Firstname_Lastname**. **Close** the workbook.

12. From the **New from Existing Workbook** dialog box, **Open** the **10F_Billable_Hours_ Temp_Firstname_Lastname** workbook file and enable the macros. Save it as an **Excel Macro-Enabled Workbook** named **10F_Billable_Hours_GSF_Firstname_Lastname** Enter the following hours for the **Great Saguaro Forest** episode.

(Project 10F–Billable Hours continues on the next page)

(Project 10F–Billable Hours continued)

Production Costs	Hours
Show prep	4.5
Script writing	15
Filming	25
Lighting	25
Audio	30
Props	4
Film editing	23.5
Script editing	35.5

Enter the following data for the **Desert Tree Gardens** episode:

Production Costs	Hours
Show prep	4
Script writing	20.5
Filming	20.5
Lighting	30
Audio	45
Props	10
Film editing	31.5
Script editing	37

13. Save. Click the **Print** button to print a copy of the Billable Hours form. Then use the macro button to clear the form. Enter the password, **student** when asked for it. **Save** the workbook again as a **Macro-Enabled Workbook** with the name 10F_Billable_Hours_DTG_Firstname_Lastname

14. Save, **Print**, and **Close** the workbook.

15. To submit the workbooks electronically, follow the instructions provided by your instructor. Print the template and the two completed workbooks. **Close** any open workbooks. **Exit** Excel.

 End **You have completed Project 10F** _____

Content-Based Assessments

Mastering Excel

Project 10G — Show Request

In this project, you will apply the skills you practiced from the Objectives in Projects 10A and 10B.

Objectives: 1. *Protect Worksheet Elements;* **3.** *Protect a Workbook;* **4.** *Save Worksheet and Chart Templates;* **5.** *Complete a Report with Worksheet and Chart Templates;* **6.** *Create a Form;* **7.** *Validate a Form;* **8.** *Insert Macro Command Buttons.*

The popularity of the Southwest Gardens show has increased over the years it has been televised. Each year, hundreds of requests are received from people asking for video taping of their gardens. To more easily manage the requests, a form is needed to gather information about gardens that may be included in the show. In this Mastering Excel assignment, you will create the form that will be used for these requests. Your completed workbook will look similar to Figure 10.51.

For Project 10G, you will need the following files:

e10G_Show_Request
e10G_SW_Garden_Logo

You will save your files as
10G_Show_Request1_Firstname_Lastname (Macro-Enabled Worksheet)
10G_Show_Request2_Firstname_Lastname (Macro-Enabled Worksheet)
10G_Show_Request_Temp_Firstname_Lastname (Macro-Enabled Template)

Figure 10.51

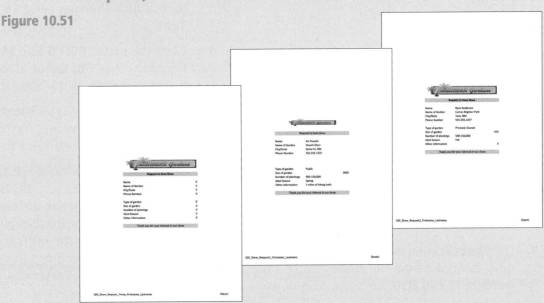

(Project 10G–Show Request continues on the next page)

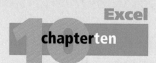
(Project 10G–Show Request continued)

1. **Start** Excel. From the student files, locate and open the file named **e10G_Show_Request** and **Save** it in your **Excel Chapter 10** folder as an **Excel Macro-Enabled Template** named 10G_Show_Request_Temp_Firstname_Lastname

2. In the **Left Footer**, insert the **File Name**, and in the **Right Footer**, insert the **Sheet Name**.

3. Adjust the width of **column A** to display the longest cell. Increase the width of **column B** to **28—201 pixels**. Click the **Sheet2 sheet tab** and in the range **A4:A6**, type the following row titles:

Public
Privately Owned
Park

4. In the range **C4:C7**, type the following:

<500
500–1,500
1,500–3,000
>3,000

5. In cell **E4:E8**, type

Winter
Spring
Summer
Fall

6. Define names for the three ranges you have entered. Name the range in cells **A4:A6 Type_Garden** Name the range in cells **C4:C7 Number_Plantings** Name the range in cells **E4:E7 Season**

7. On **Sheet1**, click cell **B8** and create a drop-down list from the named range Type_Garden. In cell **B10**, create a drop-down

list for the Number_Plantings. In cell **B11**, insert a drop-down list and create a validation list for Season.

8. Select the range **B3:B6** and format with a **Fill Color** of **Orange, Accent 6, Lighter 60%** with a **Bottom Border** in each cell. Copy that format to the range **B8:B12**. Click cell **B12** and click the **Wrap Text** button.

9. Click cell **B3** and enter an **Input Message** with the **Title Name** that reads **Name of person we can contact** In cell **B12**, allow a **Text length** between **0** and **199** characters. Insert an **Input Message** with the **Title** of **Tell Us More** with a message that reads **Provide additional information about the uniqueness, beauty, or other aspects of your garden**

10. Adjust the width of **column E** to **21—152** pixels. Adjust the width of **column F** to **29—208 pixels**. In cell **E1**, insert the picture **e10G_SW_Garden_Logo** and adjust it to fit the range **E1:F4**. Click cell **F7** and type **=b3** Using the skills you practiced, complete the rest of the information in the output area. Format cell **F16** with **Wrap Text**.

11. Click the range **E5:F5** and **Merge & Center**. Use a **Fill Color** of **Red, Accent 2, Lighter 60%** and format it with **Bold**.

12. Click cell **E18** and type **Thank you for your interest in our show** and format the range as you formatted cell **E5: F5**.

13. Allow users to edit ranges **B3:B6**—with the title of **Contact**—and **B8:B12**—with the title of **Garden Protect** the rest of the worksheet without a password. **Set** the **Print Area** as the output area of cells **E1:F19**. Center the print area both **Horizontally** and **Vertically**.

(Project 10G–Show Request continues on the next page)

(Project 10G–Show Request continued)

14. **Unprotect** the worksheet, and then create a macro—**Print_Clear**—that prints and then clears the form. In the range **A14:B18**, insert a **basic shape** of **Hexagon** and assign the **Print_Clear** macro to it. On the shape, type **Print Clear**

15. **Hide Sheet2** and **Sheet3**. **Encrypt** the document with no password and **Save** it as an **Excel Macro-Enabled Template** in your **Excel Chapter 10** folder, and name it **10G_Show_Request_Temp_Firstname_Lastname** Then **Close** the workbook.

16. Open the template as a new from existing file—**10G_Show_Request_Temp_Firstname_ Lastname**—and enter the following information:

Contact name	Ari Passola
Garden name	Desert Glory
City/State	Santa Fe, NM
Phone number	555.555.1232
Type of garden	Public
Size of garden	2,000
Number of plantings	1,093
Season	Spring
Other	5 miles of hiking trails

17. **Save** this form as an **Excel Macro-Enabled Workbook** and name it **10G_Show_Request1_ Firstname_Lastname** and then click the **Print Clear** button.

18. In a new form, enter the following information:

Contact name	Ryan Anderson
Garden name	Cactus Register Park
City/State	Taos, NM
Phone number	555.555.1457
Type of garden	Privately Owned
Size of garden	450
Number of plantings	2,093
Season	Fall
Other	

19. **Save** this form as an **Excel Macro-Enabled Workbook** and name it **10G_Show_Request_2_ Firstname_Lastname** and then click the **Print Clear** button.

20. To submit the workbooks electronically, follow the instructions provided by your instructor. **Close** any open workbooks. **Exit** Excel.

 End **You have completed Project 10G**

Content-Based Assessments

Project 10H—TV Segments

In this project, you will apply the skills you practiced from the Objectives in Project 10A.

Objectives: **1.** *Protect Worksheet Elements;* **3.** *Protect a Workbook;* **4.** *Save Worksheet and Chart Templates;* **5.** *Complete a Report with Worksheet and Chart Templates.*

In the following Mastering Excel project, you will create a template that will be used to report the time and the various program segments that will be a part of the TV show. There may be up to eight segments, but the total time for filming must be exactly 48 minutes for a one-hour show. The remaining time is required by the host stations for previews of other shows, fundraising, and public announcements. Beginning and closing credits begin and end each show, and each takes 3.5 minutes. You will also create a chart template that can be used to compare the amount of time devoted to each segment. Your complete worksheets will look like those in Figure 10.52.

For Project 10H, you will need the following files:

New blank Excel workbook
e10H_SW_Garden_Logo

You will save your files as
10H_TV_Segments_Temp_Firstname_Lastname (Template)
10H_TV_Segments_SG_Firstname_Lastname

Figure 10.52

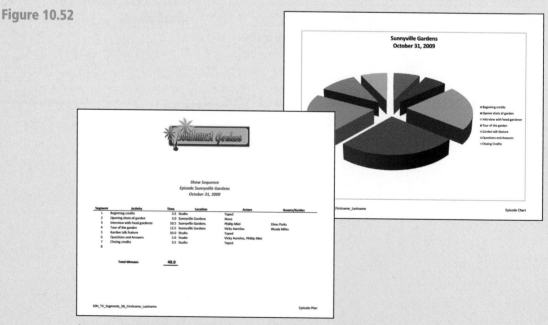

(Project 10H–TV Segments continues on the next page)

Content-Based Assessments

(Project 10H–TV Segments continued)

1. **Start** Excel and open a new blank worksheet. **Save** it as an **Excel Template** in your **Excel Chapter 10** folder as **10H_TV_Segments_Temp_Firstname_Lastname** In the **Left Footer**, insert the **File Name**. In the **Center Header**, insert the picture **e10H_SW_Garden_Logo**. Format the height of the logo to **1.5** and set a **Top Margin** of **1.5"**.

2. Enter the following data beginning in cell **A1**:

Show Sequence
Episode

3. In cell **A3**, type **Date** as a placeholder. Format title cells **A1:A3 Bold**, **Italic**, **14 point** with a **Font Color** of **Aqua, Accent 5, Darker 50%**. **Merge & Center** each line over **columns A:F**. Format cell **A3** using the date style of *March 14, 2001*.

4. Beginning in cell **A6**, enter the following column titles. Place a space between guests and guides so the title will display on two lines.

Segment	Activity	Time	Location	Actors	Guests/ Guide

5. Format column titles with **Bold**, **Bottom Border**, **Center**, **Middle Align**, and **Wrap Text**.

6. Beginning in cell **A7** and in the column, enter the numbers **1–8**. **Center** the numbers. Then enter the following data from a prior show as placeholder information in order to format the template:

Segment	Activity	Time	Location	Actors	Guests/ Guides
3	Interview with Master Gardener	2	Studio	Phillip Miel	
4	Overview of Sunset Gardens	1	Sunset Gardens	Phillip Miel	Miki Alexandros
6	Tour of Sunset Gardens Nursery	8	Sunset Gardens	Vicky Aurelias	
8	Closing Credits	3.5	Studio	On tape	

7. Adjust column widths to fit the longest line and increase **column D** to **180** pixels. Format the times in **column C** with **Comma Style** with **one decimal**. In cell **A17**, type **Total Minutes** Select the range **A17:B17** and format with **Bold** and **Merge & Center**. In cell **C17**, enter a formula to sum the minutes and format it with **Bold**, **14-point**, and a **Thick Box Border**. You have inserted additional rows in the template for flexibility when a show has more than 8 segments.

(Project 10H–TV Segments continues on the next page)

(Project 10H–TV Segments continued)

8. Select cells **C7:C16** and add a data validation input message with the title of **Length of Show** and a message that reads **Entire time can take no more than 48 minutes**

9. Format the worksheet so it is centered **Horizontally** and **Vertically** and change the orientation to **Landscape** and **Fit to page**.

10. Select the **Activity** and the **Time** devoted to each, including column headings, and insert an **Exploded pie chart in 3-D**. Move the chart to a separate worksheet named **Episode Chart** and change the style to **Style 18**. Insert the **File Name** in the **Left Footer** and the **Sheet Name** in the **Right Footer**.

11. Rename **Sheet1** to **Episode Plan** and allow users to edit cells **A2, A3,** and **B7:F16**. **Protect** the worksheet with the password **student** Clear the data from **B7:F14** Move the **Episode Chart** sheet so it is the last sheet and **Delete Sheet2** and **Sheet3**. **Protect** the **structure** of the workbook with the password **student Confirm** the template is named **10H_TV_Segments_Temp_Firstname_Lastname** and **Close** it.

12. Open a **New** workbook and choose a **Template** located at **New from Existing**. In your files, select the template file **10H_TV_Segments_Temp_Firstname_Lastname**, and then click **Create New**. **Save** it as an **Excel workbook** with the name **10H_TV_Segments_SG_Firstname_Lastname** (SG is for Sunnyville Gardens).

13. In cell **A2**, after the word *Episode*, type **Sunnyville Gardens** and replace *Date* with **October 31, 2009** Fill in the activities and time columns as follows:

Segment	Activity	Time	Location	Actors	Guests/Guides
1	Beginning credits	3.5	Studio	Taped	
2	Opening shots of garden	3.0	Sunnyville Gardens	None	
3	Interview with head gardener	10.5	Sunnyville Gardens	Phillip Miel	Elmo Parks
4	Tour of the garden	12.5	Sunnyville Gardens	Vicky Aurelias	Rhoda Miles
5	Garden talk feature	10.0	Studio	Taped	
6	Questions and Answers	5.0	Studio	Vicky Aurelias, Phillip Miel	
7	Closing credits	3.5	Studio	Taped	

14. Click the **Episode Chart sheet tab**. Because the chart template had 8 segments, and this episode had only 7, delete the last color dot from the legend. Change the title to read

Sunnyville Gardens
October 31, 2009

15. **Print** the worksheet and chart or submit electronically as directed. **Close** the worksheet. If you are prompted to save changes, click **No**. **Exit** Excel.

End **You have completed Project 10H**

Mastering Excel

Project 10I — Audiences

In this project, you will apply the skills you practiced from all of the Objectives in Projects 10A and 10B.

Objectives: 1. *Protect Worksheet Elements;* **2.** *Unprotect Elements and Hide Formulas;* **3.** *Protect a Workbook;* **4.** *Save Worksheet and Chart Templates;* **5.** *Complete a Report with Worksheet and Chart Templates;* **6.** *Create a Form;* **7.** *Validate a Form;* **8.** *Insert Macro Command Buttons.*

In the following Mastering Excel project, you will create a worksheet for Karen Galvin, who is in charge of the audience participation for the shows. She determines who will be in the audience, and she likes to have a balance between community members, garden clubs, and tour groups. In this project, you will create a template to identify the audience for each show. You will also create a form that is used as an admittance ticket.

The worksheets of your workbook will look similar to Figure 10.53.

For Project 10I, you will need the following files:

New blank Excel workbook
e10I_Audiences
e10I_SW_Garden_Logo

You will save your files as
10I_Audiences_Temp_Firstname_Lastname (Macro-Enabled Template)
10I_Audiences_May1_Firstname_Lastname (Macro-Enabled Worksheet)
10I_Ticket_Template_Firstname_Lastname (Macro-Enabled Template)
10I_Ticket_May5_Firstname_Lastname (Macro-Enabled Worksheet)

Figure 10.53

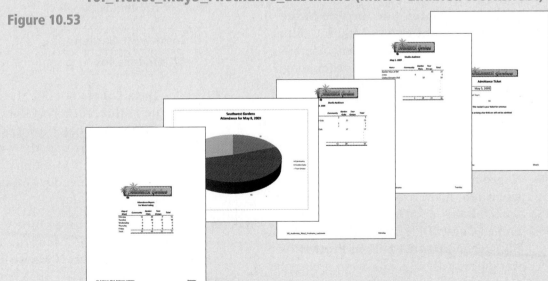

(Project 10I–Audiences continues on the next page)

(Project 10I–Audiences continued)

1. **Start** Excel and open the file **e10I_Audiences**, which is a macro-enabled workbook. If a Security Warning appears, click **Options**, and then in the **Security Link**, click **Enable this content**. This Security Warning displays because there is a hidden worksheet in the workbook, which you will use later.

2. Save the workbook in your **Excel Chapter 10** folder and confirm it is an **Excel Macro-Enabled Template**. Name it **10I_Audiences_Temp_Firstname_Lastname**

3. **Group** the worksheets. **Merge & Center** cell **A1** over the range **A1:E1**. In cell **A2**, type **Date** Format cell **A2** with the date style displayed as *March 14, 2001*. In cell **A14**, type **Total** and format it with **Bold**, **Italic**, and **Center**. In cell **B14**, enter a **Sum** formula that adds the range **B5:B13** and format the cells **B5:B14** with **Comma Style** with **no decimals**. In cell **B14**, add a **Top and Double Bottom Border**. Copy the formula across through **column E**. Click cell **E5** and enter a **Sum** formula that adds columns **B:D** of that row. Copy the formula down through **row 13** and format the range with **Comma Style** with **no Decimals**.

4. In the **Left Footer**, add the **File Name**, and in the **Right Footer**, add the **Sheet Name**. In the **Center Header**, insert the **Picture** named **e10I_SW_Garden_Logo** and change the picture format to a **Height** of **1.25**. Change the **Top margin** to **1.5**. Then center the worksheets **Horizontally**. Click **Print Preview** to review the page layout. Then click **Close Print Preview**.

5. **Ungroup** the worksheets. Click the **Monday sheet tab**. Allow users to edit cell **A2**—named **Date**—and the range **A5:D13**—named **Guests** Hide the formulas in ranges **E5:E13** and **B14:E14**. Then **Protect** the worksheet without a password. Using the

skills you practiced, protect the other sheets of the workbook in this same manner, allowing users access to the input area and hiding formulas. Then **Save** your workbook.

6. Enter placeholder data. In the **Monday** sheet, in cell **B5**, type **4** and in cell **C6**, type **6** and in cell **D7**, type **7 Group** the worksheets, select the range **B5:D7**, and **Fill across worksheets**. Select **All** and click **OK**. **Ungroup** the worksheets.

7. At a worksheet tab, right-click and click **Unhide** and in the **Unhide** dialog box, click **Summary**, and then click **OK**. The summary sheet contains formulas that summarize the worksheets into one sheet. It has been completed for you. Click in the cells of the summary sheet to review the formulas used.

8. In the **Left Footer** insert the **File Name** and in the **Right Footer** insert the **Sheet Name**. Center the worksheet both **Vertically** and **Horizontally**.

9. In the **Summary sheet tab**, select the ranges **B11:D11** and **B17:D17**. Insert a **Pie in 3-D** chart. Move the chart to a Chart Sheet and name the sheet **Attendance Chart** Insert a **Chart Title** above the chart and enter the following title:

| Southwest Gardens |
| Attendance for |

10. Place **Data Labels** outside the data markers. Then **click** in each of the worksheets—Monday through Friday—and delete the data. Arrange the worksheets in the following order: Summary, Attendance Chart, Monday, Tuesday, Wednesday, Thursday, and Friday.

11. **Protect** the **structure** of the workbook without entering a password. **Save** the workbook as an **Excel Macro-Enabled**

(Project 10I–Audiences continues on the next page)

(Project 10I–Audiences continued)

Template—10I_Audiences_Temp_
Firstname_Lastname—in your **Excel
Chapter 10** folder. **Close** the workbook.

12. Open a new, blank workbook. Beginning
in cell **A4**, type the following row titles:

Name
Date
Total Guests

13. Increase the width of **column A** to display
the longest entry. Then increase **column B**
to **25—180 pixels**. Format cell **B5** with the
date style displayed as *March 14, 2001*.
Select the range **B4:B6** and use a **Standard
Fill Color** of **Yellow**. Place a **Bottom Border**
in each of the cells. This is the input area.
Click cell **B4** and insert **Data Validation**
with an **Input Message** of **Enter information
about guests**

14. In cell **E6**, type **Admittance Ticket** In cell
E8, type **Date** and in cell **E10** type **Guest**
and in cell **E12** type **Total** In cell **E14**, type
This receipt is your ticket for entrance and
in cell **E16**, type **Guests arriving after 8:45
am will not be admitted**

15. In cell **E1**, insert the **e10I_SW_Garden_
Logo** and format it to fit the range **E1:I5**.
Format cell **F8** using the **Date** format style
of **March 14, 2001**, with **16-point bold** with
a **red colored font**. Then place an **Outside
Border** around the cell. This cell is formatted so it is easy for the date to be confirmed
as guests enter the studio. In cell **F8**, type
=b5 and in cell **F10**, type **=b4** and in cell
F12, type **=b6** Select the range of the output
area—**E1:I17**— and set it as the **Print Area**.

16. Select the range **E14:I14** and **Merge &
Center** and format with **Bold**. Copy the format to the range **E16:I16**. Format the range

E6:I6 with **Merge & Center**, **Bold**, and
increase the font size to **16-point font**.

17. Record a macro named **Print_Clear** that is
stored in the workbook using the shortcut
key **z** with a description that reads **Print
ticket and clear entries**

18. Insert a **10-point star** that covers the range
B9:B12 and on the shape, type **Print and
Clear** Then assign to it the **Print_Clear**
macro.

19. In the **Left Footer**, add the **File Name**
and center both **Horizontally** and
Vertically. Save the form in your folder as
an **Excel Macro-Enabled Template** and
name it **10I_Ticket_Template_Firstname_
Lastname Close** the workbook.

20. Open the template named **10I_Audiences_
Firstname_Lastname** as a new from
existing file, and **Save** it as an **Excel
Macro-Enabled Workbook** named
**10I_Audiences_May1_Firstname_
Lastname**. In the **Summary sheet tab**, in
row 9, complete the date by typing **May 8,
2009** Enter the following data for two days
of the week—Monday and Tuesday.

21. Click the **Monday sheet tab** and in cell **A2**
replace *Date:* with the date of the show—
May 4, 2009 Enter the following data for
Monday:

Name	Community	Garden Clubs	Tour Groups
Johnsons	2		
Phoenix Garden Club		13	
Calkins	2		
Garcia	7		
Desert Diggers Club		17	

(Project 10I–Audiences continues on the next page)

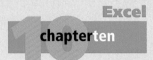
(Project 10I–Audiences continued)

22. Click the **Tuesday sheet tab** and in cell **A2** replace *Date* with the date of the show—**May 5, 2009** Enter the following data for Tuesday:

Name	Community	Garden Clubs	Tour Groups
Garden Tour of SW			22
Jones	4		
Cactus Growers Club		10	

23. Click the **Attendance Chart** and in the title, after *Attendance for*, type **Week Ending May 8, 2009** Then click in the **Summary sheet tab** and **Save** the workbook.

24. Open the **10I_Ticket_Template_ Firstname_Lastname** as a new from existing file. Use the following data for the Input area:

Name	Sunset Tours
Date	May 5, 2009
Total Guests	14

25. **Save** the worksheet workbook as an **Excel Macro-Enabled Workbook** named **10I_ Ticket_May5_Firstname_Lastname**

26. **Print** the worksheets or submit electronically as directed. **Close** all open worksheets. If you are prompted to save changes, click **No**. **Exit** Excel.

End You have completed Project 10I

Content-Based Assessments

Excel

chapterten

Business Running Case

Project 10J—Business Running Case

In this project, you will apply the skills you have practiced from the Objectives in Projects 10A and 10B.

From My Computer, navigate to the student files that accompany this textbook. In the folder **03_business_running_case**, locate and open the folder for this chapter. Open and print the instructions for this project, which are provided to you in Adobe PDF format. Follow the instructions and use the skills you have gained thus far to assist the managers of the Grand Department Store to meet the challenges of keeping records for a large department.

 End **You have completed Project 10J**_____

Rubric

The following outcomes-based assessments are *open-ended assessments*. That is, there is no specific correct result; your result will depend on your approach to the information provided. Make *Professional Quality* your goal. Use the following scoring rubric to guide you in *how* to approach the problem and then to evaluate *how well* your approach solves the problem.

The *criteria*—Software Mastery, Content, Format and Layout, and Process—represent the knowledge and skills you have gained that you can apply to solving the problem. The *levels of performance*—Professional Quality, Approaching Professional Quality, or Needs Quality Improvement—help you and your instructor evaluate your result.

	Your completed project is of Professional Quality if you:	Your completed project is Approaching Professional Quality if you:	Your completed project Needs Quality Improvements if you:
1-Software Mastery	Choose and apply the most appropriate skills, tools, and features and identify efficient methods to solve the problem.	Choose and apply some appropriate skills, tools, and features, but not in the most efficient manner.	Choose inappropriate skills, tools, or features, or are inefficient in solving the problem.
2-Content	Construct a solution that is clear and well organized, contains content that is accurate, appropriate to the audience and purpose, and is complete. Provide a solution that contains no errors of spelling, grammar, or style.	Construct a solution in which some components are unclear, poorly organized, inconsistent, or incomplete. Misjudge the needs of the audience. Have some errors in spelling, grammar, or style, but the errors do not detract from comprehension.	Construct a solution that is unclear, incomplete, or poorly organized, containing some inaccurate or inappropriate content; and contains many errors of spelling, grammar, or style. Do not solve the problem.
3-Format and Layout	Format and arrange all elements to communicate information and ideas, clarify function, illustrate relationships, and indicate relative importance.	Apply appropriate format and layout features to some elements, but not others. Overuse features, causing minor distraction.	Apply format and layout that does not communicate information or ideas clearly. Do not use format and layout features to clarify function, illustrate relationships, or indicate relative importance. Use available features excessively, causing distraction.
4-Process	Use an organized approach that integrates planning, development, self-assessment, revision, and reflection.	Demonstrate an organized approach in some areas, but not others; or, use an insufficient process of organization throughout.	Do not use an organized approach to solve the problem.

Problem Solving

Project 10K — Pledge

In this project, you will construct a solution by applying any combination of the skills you practiced from the Objectives in Projects 10A and 10B.

For Project 10K, you will need the following files:

New blank Excel workbook
e10K_SW_Garden_Logo

You will save your workbook as
10K_Pledge_Firstname_Lastname (Macro-Enabled Template)

The Southwest Gardens show has an annual pledge week where viewers are encouraged to phone in monetary pledges to help keep the program on the air. A pledge form is needed with an input area for name, address, city, state, postal code, telephone, e-mail, and the amount pledged.

Create a pledge form that can be used for the Southwest Gardens show. The output area of the form will be sent as a receipt to those who pledge. It should have the SW Garden logo at the top and a title line of **Pledge Form** It should display the personal information of the person who pledged—name, address, and so on, and also display the amount of the pledged payment in various options—the amount for full payment, for monthly payments, or for quarterly payments. Add an area near the bottom of the form for the person who pledged to sign and date the form. In rows at the bottom of the output area, type the following:

Thank you for your pledge to our program.
Please select your payment option and
return this form to us. We will send you a
receipt as soon as we receive this form.

Allow users to edit the input areas and use a fill color for those areas. Hide the formulas for the payment options, and protect and save the pledge form as a template that may be used for all pledges. Add macros to print and clear the form. Assign them to shapes in the worksheet. Using the skills you have practiced in this chapter, complete and format the workbook attractively and appropriately and confirm its accuracy. Add the file name to the footer and save the workbook as **10K_Pledge_Firstname_Lastname** and submit your file as directed.

End You have completed Project 10K

Problem Solving

Project 10L — Grants

In this project, you will construct a solution by applying any combination of the skills you practiced from the Objectives in Projects 10A and 10B.

For Project 10L, you will need the following files:

e10L_Grants
e10L_SW_Garden_Logo

You will save your files as
10L_Grants_Temp_Firstname_Lastname (Template)
10L_Grants_Q1_Firstname_Lastname
10L_Grants_Q2_Firstname_Lastname
10L_Grants_Q3_Firstname_Lastname

The Southwest Gardens show writes requests for grants from corporate sponsors to fund the program. Quarterly reports are prepared to report this income. You will complete and save the first quarterly report, saved in your data files as **e10L_Grants**. Save the completed document as a template that can be used quarterly. The Southwest Gardens logo should be added at the top of the report, and the logo should also appear in the center footer. Add the file name and the sheet names to the footer area also.

Using the skills you have practiced in this chapter, complete and format the workbook attractively and appropriately, delete unneeded sheets, allow users to edit necessary ranges, and protect the worksheet. Save the file as a template named **10L_Grants_Temp_Firstname_Lastname** and then close the file.

Open the template as a new file and prepare quarterly reports for quarters 2 and 3, naming the files **10L_Grants_Q1_Firstname_Lastname**, changing the name for each quarter report. You will need the following data for the quarterly reports:

Second Quarter:

Hart & Hartley Trust	2000	2000	14000
Bill Chase Corporation	5000		
SW Flower Association	30000		
Grand Insurance Company	10000	10000	10000
HM Menendez Fund	1200	1200	1200
Arizona Nursery Assn			4000
Saguaro Club	5000	5000	5000
Jillson & Martinez Assn.	14500		
Addison Jones Trust	750	750	750

(Project10L–Grants continues on the next page)

Excel

Mastering Excel

(Project 10L–Grants continued)

Third Quarter:

Hart & Hartley Trust	2000	2000	2000
Bill Chase Corporation	1500	1500	1500
SW Flower Association	30000		
Grand Insurance Company	10000	10000	10000
HM Menendez Fund	1000	1000	1200
Arizona Nursery Assn	2500		
Saguaro Club		15000	
Jillson & Martinez Assn.	14500		
Addison Jones Trust	12000	12000	12000

Save the each quarterly workbook separately and submit your files as directed.

 End **You have completed Project 10L** ⎯⎯⎯⎯⎯⎯⎯⎯

Outcomes-Based Assessments

Problem Solving

Project 10M — Weekly Payroll

In this project, you will construct a solution by applying any combination of the skills you practiced from the Objectives in Projects 10A and 10B.

For Project 10M, you will need the following files:

e10M_Weekly_Payroll
e10M_Cooking_With_Doug_Logo

You will save your files as
10M_Weekly_Payroll_Temp_Firstname_Lastname (Template)
10M_Weekly_Payroll_Nov5_Firstname_Lastname

Media Specialists, the producers of the Southwest Garden show, were impressed with the payroll template produced for the garden show. The payroll specialist has asked that you produce the same type of template for the show *Cooking With Doug* to use each week.

The payroll report has been started in Sheet1 of the e10M_Weekly_Payroll workbook. Insert the e10M_Cooking_With_Doug_Logo and center it at the top of the worksheet. After creating the necessary formulas and formatting the worksheet, hide the column that displays the pay rate and hide all formulas and unneeded worksheets. Insert a column chart that displays the number of hours each show employee works per week. Place it in a new sheet and save it as a chart template. Protect the Payroll sheet. Add the file name to the footer and save it as a template file named **10M_Weekly_Payroll_Temp_Firstname_Lastname** and then close the file.

Open a new copy of the template and prepare a weekly payroll for the week ending November 5 with the following information: Douglas Gritz worked 43 hours, Emilio Bondurant worked 38.5 hours, Ramona Othus worked 40 hours, Lenita Hornsby worked 39 hours, and Paco Esposito worked 42.5. The pay rates are as follows Gritz–$16.25, Bondurant– 15.83, Othus–12.55, Hornsby–14.15, and Esposito–13.50.

Save the worksheet workbook as **10M_Weekly_Payroll_Nov5_Firstname_Lastname** and submit your files as directed.

End **You have completed Project 10M** _____

Outcomes-Based Assessments

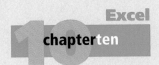
Problem Solving

Project 10N — Contributions

In this project, you will construct a solution by applying any combination of the skills you practiced from the Objectives in Projects 10A and 10B.

For Project 10N, you will need the following file:

e10N_Contributions

You will save your files as
10N_Contributions_Temp_Firstname_Lastname (Macro-Enabled Template)
10N_Contributions_Randell_Firstname_Lastname (Macro-Enabled Worksheet)
10N_Contributions_Geist_Firstname_Lastname (Macro-Enabled Worksheet)

The Southwest Gardens show solicits contributions from viewers. When contributions are made, David Tang would like to have a form that can be used as a receipt for the contributor. At various levels, contributors become members of a "circle." For example, a donor who gives $5,000 or more is part of the Saguaro Cactus Circle. A donor who gives $25 is part of the Desert Marigold Circle. The circle categories for the levels of giving are found in the Levels sheet of the data e10N_Contributions file.

On the Contributions sheet, finish creating the output portion of the form. In cell D19, use a lookup function to retrieve the type of circle for which the contribution qualifies. After you have created the form, hide formulas, allow users to edit data in input ranges, hide unneeded sheets, and protect the worksheet. Create a macro that will print the output area and then clear the form. Add the file name to the footer and save the file as a macro-enabled template named **10N_Contributions_Temp_Firstname_Lastname** and then close it.

Open the template and complete the form for the following contributions: Nedda & James Randell have contributed $5,500. Their address is 4044 Alameda SW, Phoenix, AZ 85003, telephone (480) 555-1212, e-mail njrandell@ccc.com. Their gift is in memory of Virgil Randell. Save the file as **10N_Contributions_Randell_Firstname_Lastname**

Alonzo Geist, $75, 1525 NW Main Street, Dallas, TX 75226, telephone (214) 555-5151, e-mail **ageist@mno.com.** Save the file as **10N_Contributions_Geist_Firstname_Lastname** and submit your files as directed.

End You have completed Project 10N

Outcomes-Based Assessments

Problem Solving

Project 10O — Camera Crew

In this project, you will construct a solution by applying any combination of the skills you practiced from the Objectives in Projects 10A and 10B.

> ### For Project 10O, you will need the following file:
>
> e10O_Camera_Crew
>
> **You will save your files as**
> **10O_Camera_Crew_Temp_Firstname_Lastname (Macro-Enabled Template)**
> **10O_Camera_Crew_Hoag_Firstname_Lastname (Macro-Enabled Worksheet)**

The Southwest Gardens show would like you to create a time card for the camera crew that will total the number of hours worked per week and multiply total hours by pay rate to determine gross salary. Dates should be enter automatically in the time card when Sunday's date is typed in the input area. Add data validation so employees cannot start before 7 am or end after 9 pm.

After you have created the form, hide formulas, allow users to edit data in input ranges, hide unneeded sheets, and protect the worksheet. Create a macro that will print and then clear the form. Add the file name to the footer and save the file as a template named **10O_Camera_Crew_Temp_Firstname_Lastname** and then close a macro-enabled template. Open the template as a new file and save the workbook as **10O_Camera_Crew_Hoag_Firstname_Lastname** Use the following information to determine the gross salary for Arvin Hoag for the week beginning on Sunday, November 1, 2009. Add data validation so employees cannot start before 7 am and end after 9 pm.

Day of Week	Starting Time	Ending Time	Starting Time	Ending Time
Monday	7:30 am	11:30 am	1 pm	8 pm
Tuesday	9:30 am	12 pm	2:30 pm	9:15 pm
Wednesday	6:30 am	11:30 am	1 pm	3 pm
Thursday	8 am	11:45 am	1:30 pm	4:30 pm
Friday	8:45 am	12:30 pm	1:15 pm	9:30 pm

Save the file and submit your workbooks as directed.

End You have completed Project 10O

Outcomes-Based Assessments

 You and *GO!*

Project 10P — You and *GO!*

In this project, you will construct a solution by applying any combination of the skills you practiced from the Objectives found in Projects 10A and 10B.

From My Computer, navigate to the student files that accompany this textbook. In the folder **04_you_and_go**, locate and open the folder for this chapter. Open and print the instructions for this project, which are provided to you in Adobe PDF format. You will create a template to track your income for the last two months.

End **You have completed Project 10P** _____

GO! with Help

Project 10Q — *GO!* with Help

In this chapter, you protected worksheets and workbooks. Elements of the worksheet can also be protected. You will use Help to read about protecting worksheet elements.

1 **Start** Excel and confirm that you are connected to the Internet. At the far right end of the Ribbon, click the **Microsoft Office Excel Help** button.

2 In the **Search** box, type **protect structure** and click **Search**. Read the information about **Protect** worksheet or workbook **elements**.

3 In Help, review the information about locking and unlocking graphic objects, cells, or ranges you want others to change. Then using that information, create a worksheet that has a graphic element, a formatted title, and a SUM function. Then using Help, protect the sheet so that all of the data may be changed, except for the title, graphic element, formats, and formulas.

End **You have completed Project 10Q** _____

11 chaptereleven

Nesting Functions and Consolidating Worksheets

OBJECTIVES

At the end of this chapter you will be able to:

OUTCOMES

Mastering these objectives will enable you to:

---

1. Nest One Function within Another
2. Use 3-D References and Nested Lookups
3. Check Accuracy with Excel's Auditing Tools

PROJECT 11A
Create Complex Formulas by Nesting Functions and Using Auditing Tools

---

4. Consolidate Workbooks
5. Share and Merge Workbooks

PROJECT 11B
Consolidate and Merge Workbooks

Wild Islands Breeze

Wild Islands Breeze is a "quick casual" franchise restaurant chain with headquarters in Jacksonville, Florida. The founders wanted to create a restaurant where the flavors of the Caribbean islands would be available at reasonable prices in a bright, comfortable atmosphere. The menu features fresh food and quality ingredients with offerings like grilled chicken skewers, wrap sandwiches, fruit salads, mango ice cream, smoothies, and coffee drinks. All 150 outlets offer WiFi Internet connections, making Wild Islands Breeze the perfect place for groups and people who want some quiet time.

Nesting Functions and Consolidating Worksheets

Complex formulas can be created by nesting functions one within another. You can nest any of the functions using the function arguments dialog boxes. A lookup table can be nested within a function, using the lookup only when other values match.

Workbooks can be shared and merged together. They can also be consolidated so that the data from several workbooks is automatically combined into one workbook. The structure of the workbooks that are consolidated needs to be the same. In this chapter, you will nest functions to create complex formulas, merge and consolidate workbooks, and use auditing tools to confirm the accuracy of your work.

Project 11A **Server Bonus**

In Activities 11.1 through 11.10, you will nest functions within each other and nest a lookup table within another function. You will use auditing tools and the Watch Window to evaluate your work. Your completed workbooks will look similar to Figure 11.1.

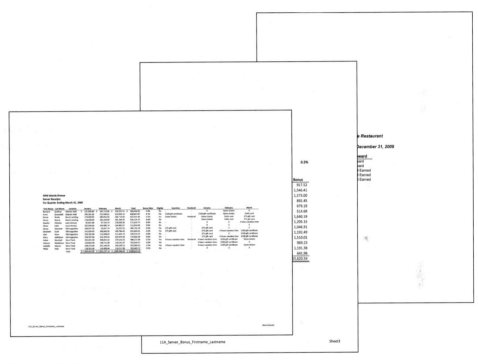

Figure 11.1
Project 11A—Server Bonus

Objective 1
Nest One Function within Another

Recall that functions are used for complex business solutions. In Excel, you can **nest functions**—place one function within another function—to create an even more complex formula. For instance, you may want to provide a reward for outstanding sales. By inserting a lookup table within an IF function, when a condition is met, the lookup table contained in the formula is used to determine the reward. This reduces the number of steps that it takes to determine the reward that is earned. You can nest up to 64 levels of functions.

Activity 11.1 Creating a Nested Function

Martin Famosa, vice president of marketing, wants to review the revenues the servers have generated in the first quarter. All who generate more than $750,000 in revenues during the quarter will earn a 0.2% bonus of their revenues. In this activity, you will assist Mr. Famosa by writing a formula that will nest a SUM function within an IF function to determine the rate of the bonus.

1 **Start** Excel. From your student files, locate and open the file named **e11A_Server_Bonus**. **Save** it in a new **Excel Chapter 11** folder and name it **11A_Server_Bonus_Firstname_Lastname**

Sheet1 reports the receipts each server has generated during the first quarter of the year.

2 Click cell **G6** and click the **Formulas tab**. In the **Function Library group**, click the **Logical** button, and from the list, click **IF**. Move the **Function Arguments** dialog box to the side so the worksheet is visible.

3 With the insertion point in the **Logical_test** text box, at the left end of the **Formula Bar**, click the **Name Box arrow**, and locate the **SUM function**. If it is not listed, at the bottom of the list, click More Functions, and then compare your screen with Figure 11.2.

The Insert Function dialog box displays.

IF Function Arguments dialog box

Figure 11.2

Insert Function dialog box

Select a category

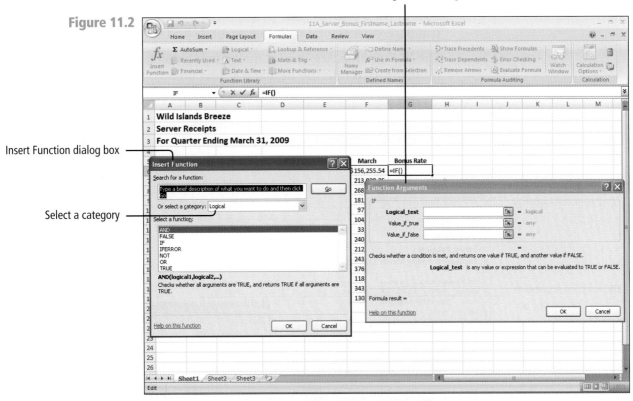

Click the **Or select a category list arrow** and click **Math & Trig**. In the **Select a function** area, type **s** and then scroll to and click **SUM**. Click **OK**, and then compare your screen with Figure 11.3.

The SUM Function Arguments dialog box displays with the range D6:F6 inserted. This range includes the sales for the employee and is correct.

SUM formula entered in Formula Bar

Figure 11.3

IF function started

Selected range to SUM

SUM Function Arguments dialog box

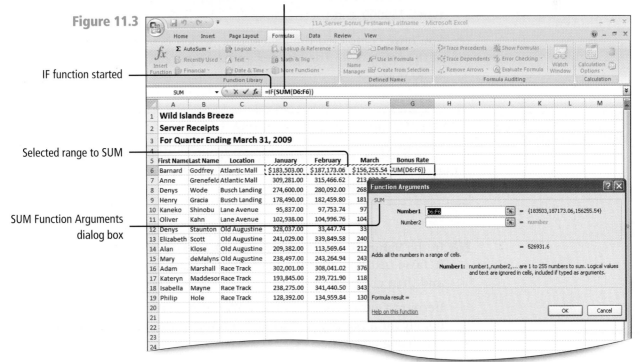

5 Confirm that the range *D6:F6* displays in the **Number1** argument box. In the **Formula Bar**, position the insertion point in the **IF** name, compare your screen with Figure 11.4, and then click in the **IF**.

The IF Function Arguments dialog box redisplays with the SUM formula inserted into the logical test text box.

Formula displayed

Figure 11.4

Insertion pointer located in IF in the Formula Bar

SUM Function Arguments dialog box

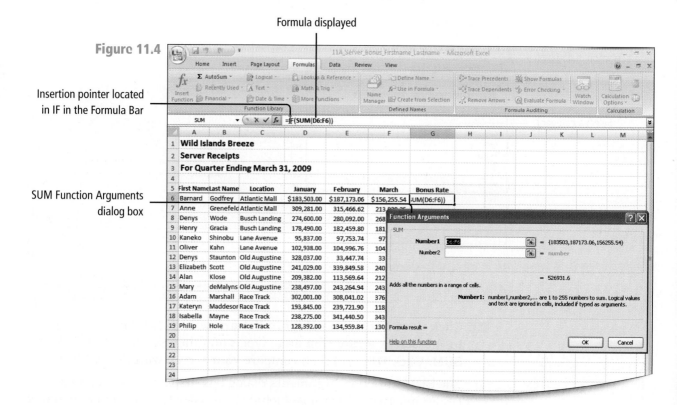

6 In the **Logical_test** box, after the arguments for the SUM formula, type **>750000** and press [Tab].

You have completed the logical test, which is to compare the sum of the receipts for the quarter and determine if they are greater than $750,000.

Another Way ┤ **To create the logical test formula**

You can also type the logical test directly in the Logical_test box, rather than using the SUM function dialog box. Recall that the range to be summed must be within parentheses.

---

7 In the **Value_if_true** text box, type **0.2%** and press [Tab]. In the **Value_ if_false** text box, type **0** and compare your screen with Figure 11.5, and then click **OK**.

Bernard Godfrey has less than $750,000 in receipts and does not qualify for a bonus, so 0 will be entered in the cell, as identified in the dialog box.

Figure 11.5

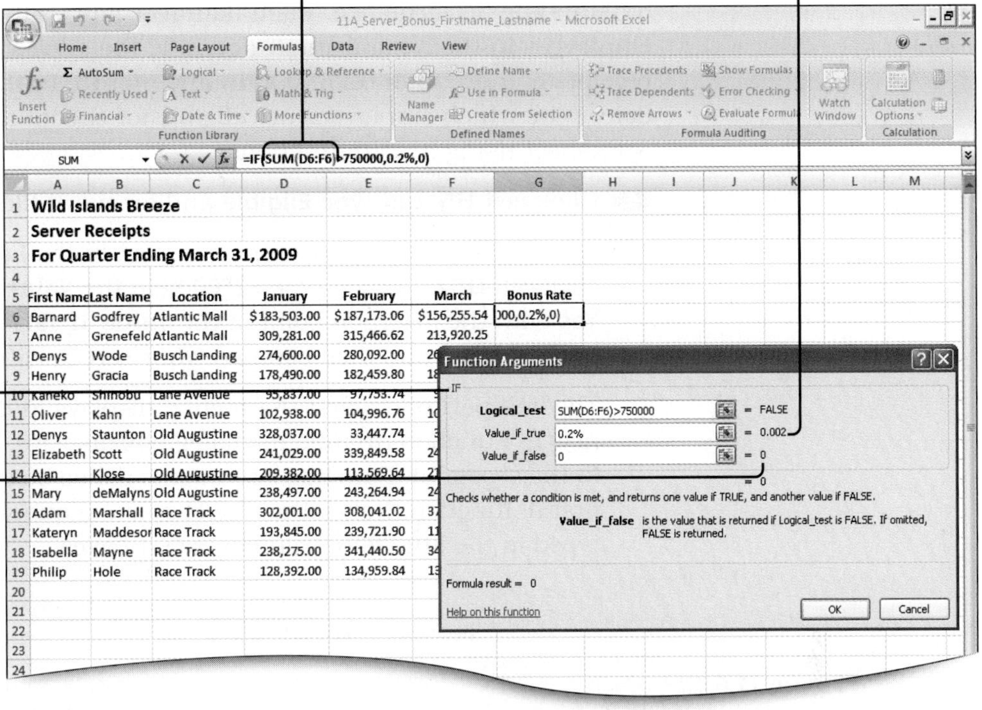

SUM function nested into IF function

Result that will be
entered if test is true

Completed IF Function
Arguments dialog box

Result that will be entered
if test is false

	First Name	Last Name	Location	January	February	March	Bonus Rate
1	Wild Islands Breeze						
2	Server Receipts						
3	For Quarter Ending March 31, 2009						
4							
5	First Name	Last Name	Location	January	February	March	Bonus Rate
6	Barnard	Godfrey	Atlantic Mall	$183,503.00	$187,173.06	$156,255.54	00,0.2%,0)
7	Anne	Grenefeld	Atlantic Mall	309,281.00	315,466.62	213,920.25	
8	Denys	Wode	Busch Landing	274,600.00	280,092.00	26	
9	Henry	Gracia	Busch Landing	178,490.00	182,459.80	18	
10	Kaneko	Shinobu	Lane Avenue	95,837.00	97,753.74		
11	Oliver	Kahn	Lane Avenue	102,938.00	104,996.76	10	
12	Denys	Staunton	Old Augustine	328,037.00	33,447.74	3	
13	Elizabeth	Scott	Old Augustine	241,029.00	339,849.58	24	
14	Alan	Klose	Old Augustine	209,382.00	113,569.64	27	
15	Mary	deMalyns	Old Augustine	238,497.00	243,264.94	24	
16	Adam	Marshall	Race Track	302,001.00	308,041.02	37	
17	Kateryn	Maddeson	Race Track	193,845.00	239,721.90	11	
18	Isabella	Mayne	Race Track	238,275.00	341,440.50	34	
19	Philip	Hole	Race Track	128,392.00	134,959.84	13	

8 Use the fill handle to copy the function through cell **G19** and format
the results with **Percent Style** with **one decimal**, and **Center**
the results. **Save** your workbook.

Workshop

Evaluate Nested Functions

The syntax of a nested function takes some study to fully understand. Recall
that the syntax for an IF function is =IF(logical test, value if true, value if false).
The name of the function is displayed first, followed by the arguments of the
function.

When an argument includes a formula, that formula will be inserted in the
function and enclosed in parentheses.

The function created in Activity 11.1 is =IF(SUM(D6:F6)>750000,0.2%,0)

Using the syntax of the IF function, the logical test is SUM(D6:F6)>750000

Within the logical test is another function—SUM(D6:F6).

The value if true is 0.2% and the value if false is 0.

Activity 11.2 Nesting IF Functions

Wild Islands Breeze has developed an incentive for each of the servers for outstanding performance. Each manager has a different incentive for the employees in the restaurant. To qualify, the server must generate receipts of more than $250,000 in any month. In this activity, you will determine which employees are eligible for the incentive by creating a worksheet using nested functions.

1 Click cell **H5** and type **Eligible** and format it like cell **G5**.

2 Click cell **H6** and insert an **IF** function. In the **Logical_test** text box, click cell **D6** and then type **>250000** In the **Value_if_true** text box, type **Yes** With the insertion point in the **Value_if_false** text box, in the **Name** Box, click **IF**, and then compare your screen with Figure 11.6.

The first part of the first IF function displays in the Formula Bar and a new IF Function Arguments dialog box displays. The arguments placed in the second IF Function Arguments dialog box will be nested in the first IF function. Notice that Excel places a quotation mark around text typed in the Function Arguments text boxes.

Beginning of second IF function

Figure 11.6

First IF function logical test (in Formula Bar)

IF Function Arguments dialog box for second IF function

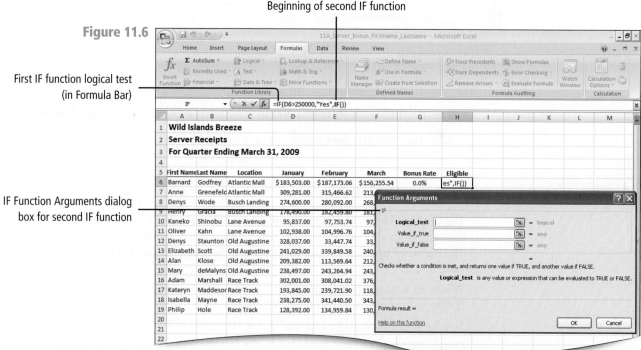

3 In the **Logical_test** text box, click cell **E6**, and then type **>250000** In the **Value_if_true** text box, type **Yes** and press `Tab`. With the insertion point in the **Value_if_false** text box, in the **Name** Box, click **IF**.

A third IF Function Arguments dialog box displays where you will enter the third IF function.

4 In the **Logical_test** text box, click cell **F6**, and then type **>250000** In the **Value_if_true** text box, type **Yes** and press `Tab`. In the **Value_if_false** text box, type **No** and then click **OK**. Take a few minutes to review the formula in the **Formula Bar** and compare your screen with Figure 11.7.

There are three IF statements in this function. Each of them compares the receipts for a month with $250,000. If either is true, an incentive will be awarded. If none of the receipts are large enough, the answer is false and "No" is entered into the cell.

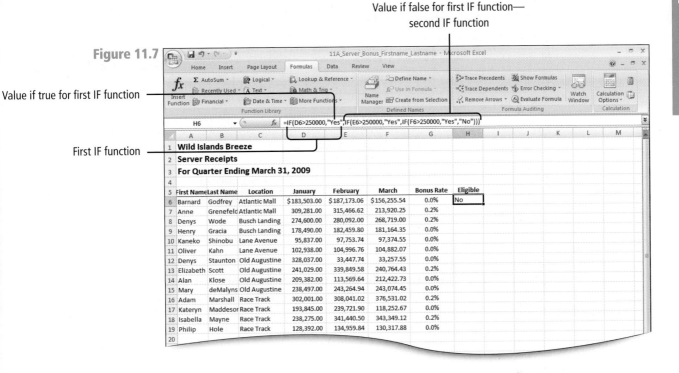

Value if false for first IF function—
second IF function

Figure 11.7

Value if true for first IF function

First IF function

5 ▸ Copy the formula in cell **H6** through cell **H19**, **Center** the column, and then **Save** your workbook.

Activity 11.3 Nesting IF Functions to Determine the Incentive for Sales for One Month

The incentive for each restaurant varies, depending on the manager. In this activity, you will use nested functions to determine the incentive for each employee.

1 ▸ Click cell **I5** and type **Incentive** and format it like cell **H5.**

2 ▸ Click cell **I6** and insert an **IF function**. Click cell **C6** and type **="Atlantic Mall"** Press ⎋Tab and with the insertion point in the **Value_if_true** text box, in the **Name** Box, click **IF**. In the **Logical_test** text box, click cell **H6** and type **="Yes"** Press ⎋Tab and in the **Value_if_true** text box, type **$100 gift certificate** Press ⎋Tab and in the **Value_if_false** text box, type **"-"** Then compare your screen with Figure 11.8.

You have completed the nested IF function. Review the formula in the Formula Bar and notice that the IF formula displayed is completed, but the first IF formula is not completed. The value if false area is not completed, which is why there are two right parentheses next to each other.

First IF function that is not completed

Figure 11.8

Second IF function

Formula for IF function
in Formula Bar

Completed IF Function
Arguments dialog box

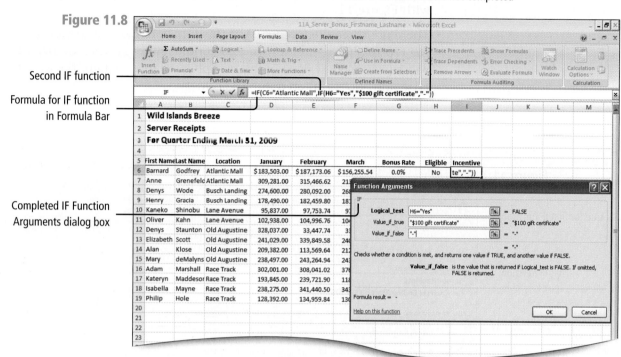

3 In the **Formula Bar**, position the insertion point in the first **IF**, click it, and then compare your screen with Figure 11.9.

The first IF Function Arguments dialog box redisplays with the Value_ if_false text box empty.

Figure 11.9

First IF in Formula Bar

First IF Function Arguments
dialog box

Value_if_false
not completed

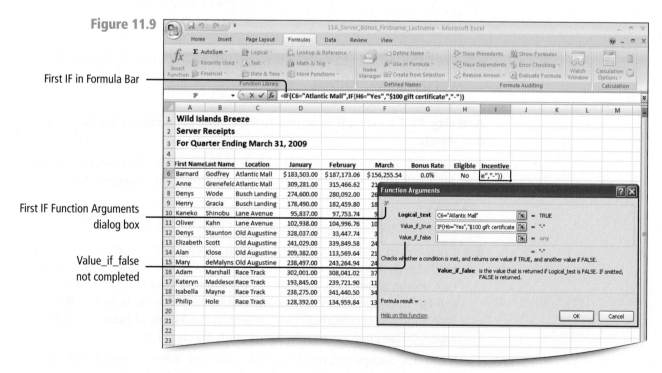

4 Click the **Value_if_false** text box and type **"-"** and then click **OK**.

While this server is at the Atlantic Mall, he is not eligible for the incentive, so a hyphen is entered into the cell. Notice in the Formula Bar that the Value_if_false value of "-" is entered before the final right parenthesis, which completes this IF formula.

5 Copy the formula through cell **I8**. The incentive for the Busch Landing location is different and needs to be corrected. Click cell **I8** and in the **Formula Bar**, select the text *Atlantic Mall*, and then type **Busch Landing** In the Formula Bar, select the text *$100 gift certificate* and replace it with **Game tickets** Compare your screen with Figure 11.10, press Enter, and then copy the formula through cell **I10**.

Figure 11.10

Location changed ——

Award changed ——

Cells used in formula ——

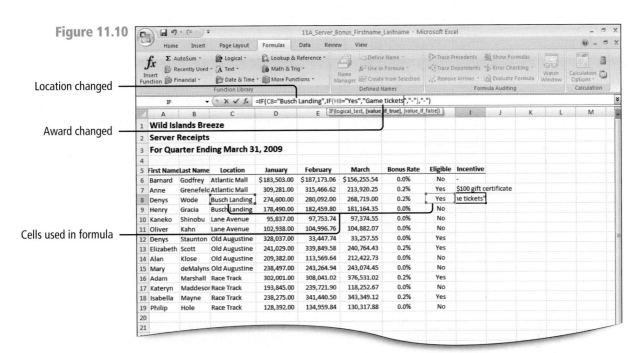

6 Using the skills you practiced, edit the formula for the other three locations by changing the locations and incentives. The incentive for **Lane Avenue** is a **Debit Card** and for **Old Augustine** the incentive is **$75 gift card** and for **Race Track** the incentive is **4 hours vacation time** Adjust column widths, and then compare your screen with Figure 11.11.

Editing a complex formula is another way to complete complex formulas. The worksheet now displays the incentive for the servers who will earn a bonus.

Figure 11.11

Results when match
is Lane Avenue

Formula displayed
in Formula Bar

Results when match
is Busch Landing

Results when match
is Atlantic Mall

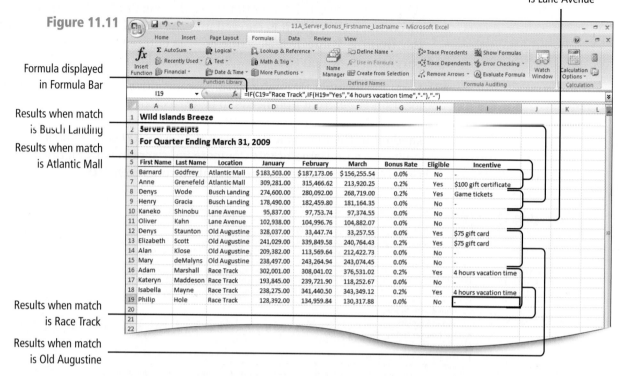

Results when match
is Race Track

Results when match
is Old Augustine

7 **Save** your workbook.

Activity 11.4 Nesting IF and AND Functions to Determine the Weekend Recipients

Martin Famosa, vice president of marketing, has offered a weekend in St. Augustine for all employees who have generated more than $250,000 in receipts for each of the three months of the quarter. In this worksheet, you will nest IF and AND functions to determine which employees qualify.

1 Click cell **J5** and type **Weekend** and format it like cell **I5**.

2 Click cell **J6** and on the **Formulas Tab**, in the **Function Library group**, click the **Recently Used** button and click **IF**. With the insertion point in the **Logical_test** text box, click the **Name Box arrow**, and then click **AND**.

The AND Function Arguments dialog box displays. The Formula Bar displays the function with the AND function displayed in parenthesis just after the IF function.

Alert!

What if AND does not display in the list?

The functions that display in the Name Box are the most recently used functions. If the AND function does not display, at the bottom, click More Functions to access the Insert Function dialog box where you can locate the function needed. AND is a logical function.

3 In the **AND Function Arguments** dialog box, in the **Logical1** text box, type **d6>250000** and press Tab. In the **Logical2** text box, type **e6>250000** and press Tab. In the **Logical3** text box, type **f6>250000** and then compare your screen with Figure 11.12.

In the AND Function Arguments dialog box, you have entered the comparisons for the function—the sales for each of the three months are greater than $250,000. All of these comparisons need to be true in order for the function to be true.

Figure 11.12

Partial IF function in Formula Bar

AND function in Formula Bar

AND Function Arguments dialog box

Arguments

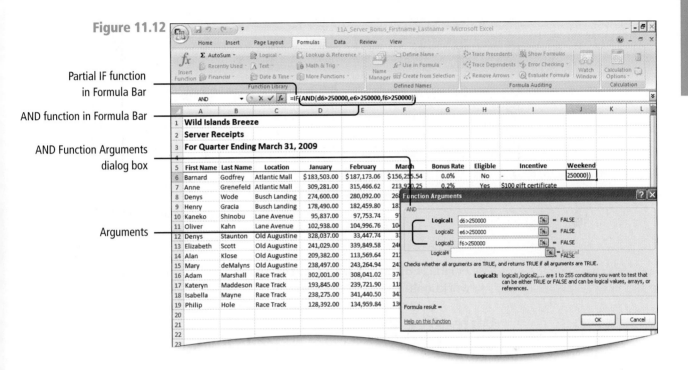

4 In the **Formula Bar**, point to **IF** and click it to redisplay the **IF Function Arguments** dialog box. In the **Value_if_true** text box, type **Weekend** and in the **Value_if_false** text box, type **"-"** Click **OK** and copy the formula through cell **J19**, and then compare your screen with Figure 11.13.

Two employees qualify for the weekend trip. Recall that Excel will place double quotation marks around text that is entered in a Function Arguments text box.

Figure 11.13

AND function in Formula Bar

Formula in Formula Bar

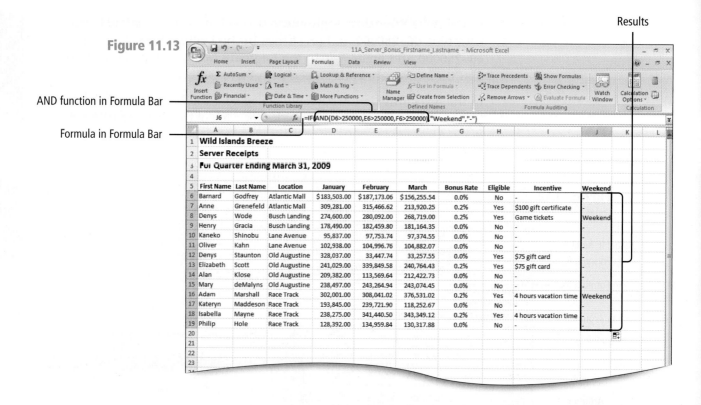

The formula bar shows: `=IF(AND(D6>250000,E6>250000,F6>250000),"Weekend","-")`

	A	B	C	D	E	F	G	H	I	J
1	Wild Islands Breeze									
2	Server Receipts									
3	For Quarter Ending March 31, 2009									
4										
5	First Name	Last Name	Location	January	February	March	Bonus Rate	Eligible	Incentive	Weekend
6	Barnard	Godfrey	Atlantic Mall	$183,503.00	$187,173.06	$156,255.54	0.0%	No	-	
7	Anne	Grenefeld	Atlantic Mall	309,281.00	315,466.62	213,920.25	0.2%	Yes	$100 gift certificate	-
8	Denys	Wode	Busch Landing	274,600.00	280,092.00	268,719.00	0.2%	Yes	Game tickets	Weekend
9	Henry	Gracia	Busch Landing	178,490.00	182,459.80	181,164.35	0.0%	No	-	
10	Kaneko	Shinobu	Lane Avenue	95,837.00	97,753.74	97,374.55	0.0%	No	-	
11	Oliver	Kahn	Lane Avenue	102,938.00	104,996.76	104,882.07	0.0%	No	-	
12	Denys	Staunton	Old Augustine	328,037.00	33,447.74	33,257.55	0.0%	Yes	$75 gift card	-
13	Elizabeth	Scott	Old Augustine	241,029.00	339,849.58	240,764.43	0.2%	Yes	$75 gift card	-
14	Alan	Klose	Old Augustine	209,382.00	113,569.64	212,422.73	0.0%	No	-	
15	Mary	deMalyns	Old Augustine	238,497.00	243,264.94	243,074.45	0.0%	No	-	
16	Adam	Marshall	Race Track	302,001.00	308,041.02	376,531.02	0.2%	Yes	4 hours vacation time	Weekend
17	Kateryn	Maddeson	Race Track	193,845.00	239,721.90	118,252.67	0.0%	No	-	
18	Isabella	Mayne	Race Track	238,275.00	341,440.50	343,349.12	0.2%	Yes	4 hours vacation time	-
19	Philip	Hole	Race Track	128,392.00	134,959.84	130,317.88	0.0%	No	-	
20										
21										
22										
23										

5 Format **column J** with **Center** alignment and **Save** your workbook.

Objective 2
Use 3-D References and Nested Lookups

When using nested functions, you can use 3-D references within a function. Recall that a **3-D reference** is a reference to the same cell or range of cells on multiple worksheets. Lookup functions can be nested within other functions, creating a complex lookup function.

Activity 11.5 Using Nested 3-D References

Restaurant managers are also rewarded based on their receipts for the year. When a store sells more than $1.5 million in a year, the manager earns a reward. In this activity, you will complete a report that uses nested 3-D references to determine which managers will receive a reward this quarter.

1 Open the **e11A_Receipts** workbook, and save it in your **Excel Chapter 11** folder as **11A_Receipts_Firstname_Lastname**

This workbook displays the 2009 Sales Report for the locations. The Annual Award sheet that will be used to determine which of the store managers will earn a reward for the store's annual receipts.

2 In the **Annual Award sheet**, click cell **B6** and insert an **IF function**. With the insertion point in the **Logical_test** text box, click the **Busch Landing sheet tab**.

The name of the worksheet displays in the Logical_test text box. Single quotation marks surround the name and it is followed by an exclamation mark (!).

3 In the **Busch Landing sheet**, click cell **F11**, press F4 to convert the cell reference to an absolute reference, and then type **>1500000** Press Tab and in the **Value_if_true** text box, type **Award Earned** and in the **Value_if_false** text box, type **No Award** Compare your screen with Figure 11.14, and then click **OK**.

The total sales for the Busch Landing restaurant did not meet the minimum so the manager will receive no award.

Figure 11.14

Logical test refers to a cell in the Busch Landing worksheet

Value if true

Value if false

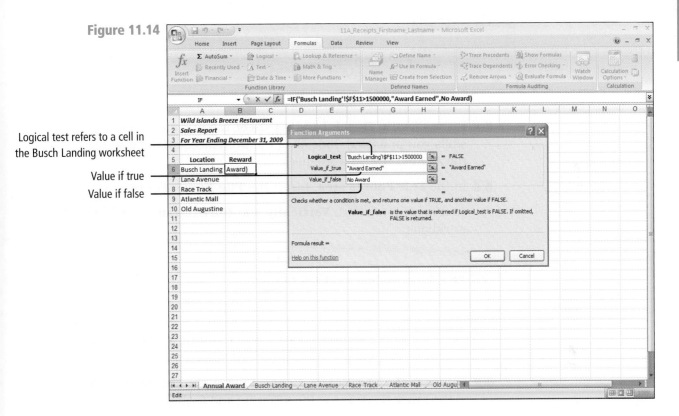

4 Click cell **B7** and insert an **IF function**. With the insertion point in the **Logical_test** text box, click in the **Lane Avenue sheet tab**, and then click cell **F11**. Press F4, and then type **>1500000** In the **Value_if_true** text box, type **Award Earned** and in the **Value_if_false** text box, type **No Award** Then click **OK**.

The receipts of the Lane Avenue restaurant also did not meet the goal so the manager does not receive an award.

5 Click cell **B7** and copy the formula to cell **B8**. With **B8** active, in the **Formula Bar**, select *Lane Avenue*, and type **Race Track** and then press Enter. Using the skills you practiced, complete the formulas for the Atlantic Mall and the Old Augustine locations. Adjust the width of **column B** to fit the longest cell entry in the column, and then compare your screen with Figure 11.15.

You have determined which managers are eligible for a reward for annual sales.

Figure 11.15

Results of function

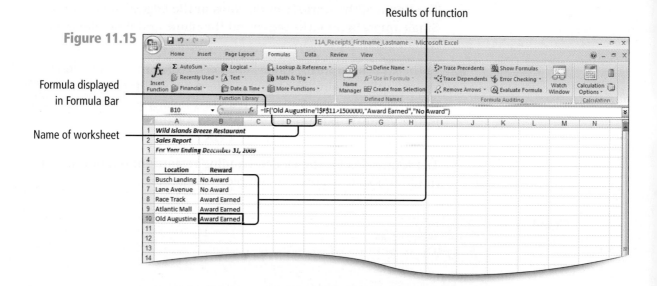

Formula displayed in Formula Bar

Name of worksheet

6   Right-click the **Busch Landing sheet tab** and click **Hide**. Using the skills you practiced, hide all of the worksheets of the workbook except the **Annual Award** worksheet.

7   In the **Left Footer area**, insert the **File Name**. Format the worksheet so it is centered both **Vertically** and **Horizontally**. **Save** 💾 your workbook.

Activity 11.6 Nesting a Lookup Function

Awards are provided for quality receipts for each month for all employees who have generated receipts of more than $175,000 in a month. The rewards differ for each store and month as a way of ensuring a variety of incentives. In this activity, you will determine which rewards the servers have earned.

1   Return to the **11A_Server_Bonus_Firstname_Lastname** workbook and in the range **K5:M5** type the following and format the cells like cell **J5:**

January	February	March

2   Rename **Sheet1** to **Bonus Results** and rename **Sheet2** to **Incentive**

The Incentive sheet displays the incentives for each restaurant for the first three months of the year. Each month, different incentives are offered, and they vary depending on the restaurant.

3   In the **Incentive sheet**, in cell **A4**, type **Restaurant** and format it in the same style as cell **B4** is formatted. Select the range of the worksheet—**A5:D9**—and on the **Formulas tab**, in the **Defined Names group**, click **Define Name**. Name the range **Award** and then click **OK**.

4   Click the **Bonus Results sheet tab**, click cell **K6**, and enter an **IF function**. In the **Logical_test** text box, type **d6>175000** and press Tab.

5   With the insertion point in the **Value_if_true** text box, click the **Name Box arrow** and from the list, click **VLOOKUP**. In the **Lookup_value** box, type **c6** and press F4 three times to make this a mixed reference—**$C6**.

A *mixed reference* is the cell reference in which either the column or the row reference is absolute (does not change no matter where it is copied) and the other reference remains relative (changes according to where it is copied—$C2 or C$2 are examples of mixed cell references. In this mixed reference, the reference to column C will remain no matter which row the formula is copied to. This formula will be copied to the February and March columns, and when it is, the reference will remain at the Location—column C in this formula. If you did not use a mixed reference, then the reference to column C will change as the formula is copied to other columns.

6 In the **Table_array** text box, type **Award** and in the **Col_index_num** text box, type **2** and then compare your screen with Figure 11.16.

In the Formula Bar, the IF function is started but not completed. If an award is earned, Excel uses the lookup table to determine the award. Because this is January and January is displayed in the second column, the column index number is 2.

Figure 11.16

IF function logical test

IF function value is true—result retrieved from lookup table

VLOOKUP Function Arguments dialog box

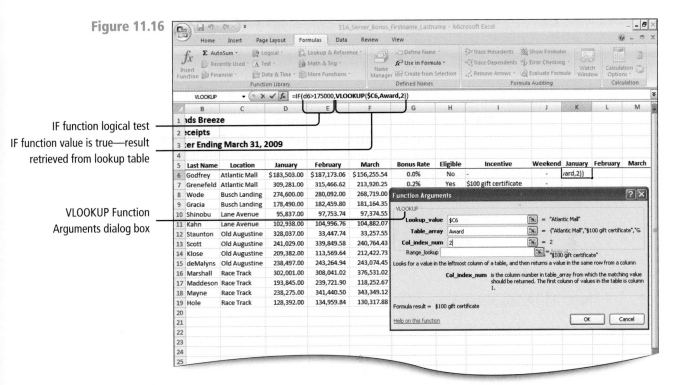

7 In the **Formula Bar**, click **IF** to redisplay the **IF Function Arguments** dialog box. In the **Value_if_false** box, type **0** and then in the **Formula Bar**, click the **Enter** button ✔. Compare your screen with Figure 11.17.

The IF function is completed with a lookup table nested within it.

Figure 11.17

Result of nested functions

IF function value if true

IF function logical test

Nested VLOOKUP function

IF function value if false

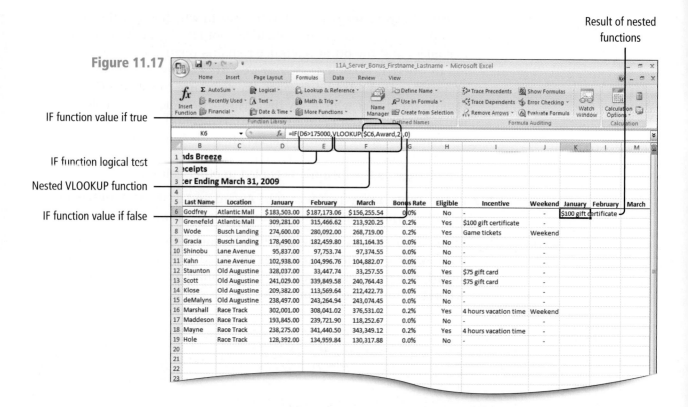

8 With cell **K6** selected, copy the formula through cell **K19**. Then copy **K6** to cell **L6**. With cell **L6** active, in the **Formula Bar**, in the VLOOKUP section of the formula, change from column *2* to **3** and compare your screen with Figure 11.18. Then on the **Formula Bar**, click the **Enter** button ✓.

The column index number argument is changed to 3 because the February rewards are listed in column 3. The reward, Game tickets, displays in cell L6.

Figure 11.18

Column number changed to 3

Lookup arguments in Formula Bar

Formula in cell L6

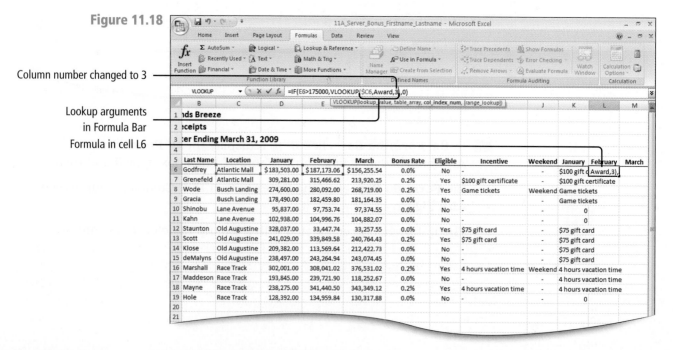

9 Copy cell **L6** to cell **M6**. With cell **M6** as the active cell, in the **Formula Bar**, in the VLOOKUP section, change from column 3 to **4** and press Enter.

10 Select the range **L6:M6** and copy the range down through **row 19**. Adjust all column widths. Select the range **K6:M19**, **Center** the data, and then compare your screen with Figure 11.19. **Save** your workbook.

Results of March receipts

Figure 11.19

Formula for active cell— VLOOKUP nested within IF function

Results of February receipts

Results of January receipts

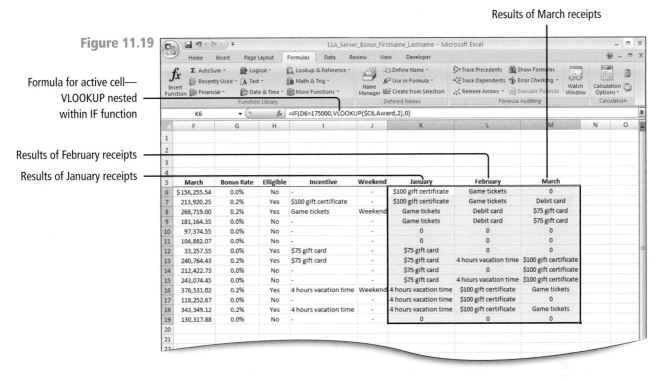

Objective 3
Check Accuracy with Excel's Auditing Tools

The accuracy of a worksheet is critical. Errors can lead to analysis that is incorrect or business statements that are inaccurate, resulting in faulty business decisions. As Excel has become more sophisticated, error detection methods have been added to the program, including the error message feature. Viewing formulas for proofreading is one method that helps in the accuracy of the worksheet. Using Excel's *auditing tools* provides additional assistance to help locate possible errors.

Activity 11.7 Evaluating Formulas

Sometimes understanding how a nested formula calculates the final result is difficult because there are several calculations and logical tests. By using the *Evaluate Formula* dialog box, you can see the different parts of a nested formula evaluated in the order that the formula is calculated. In this activity, you will use the Evaluate Formula dialog box to review a nested formula.

1 In the **Bonus Results sheet**, click cell **H6**. On the **Formulas tab**, in the **Formula Auditing group**, click the **Evaluate Formula** button and compare your screen with Figure 11.20.

As you evaluate the formula, each portion of the formula is underlined in the Evaluation box—currently D6 is underlined. Underlining a portion of the formula isolates it in order to more carefully evaluate each portion of the complex formula.

Figure 11.20

Evaluate Formula dialog box

Reference

Evaluation area

Explanation of use

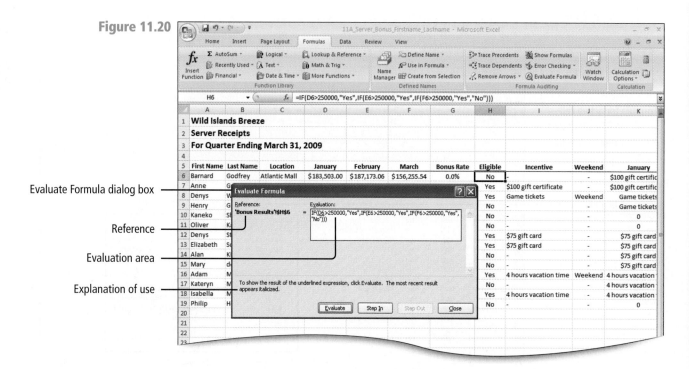

2 Click **Evaluate** to examine the value of the underlined reference. Then compare your screen with Figure 11.21.

In the Evaluation area, the value of the cell—183503—is displayed in italics. In order to assist with evaluating the formula, the value of the selected cell is displayed.

Figure 11.21

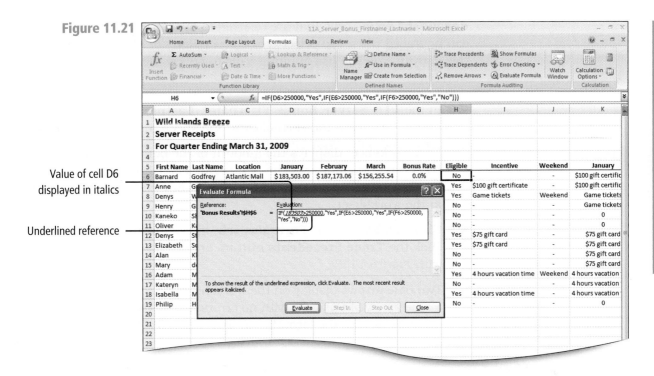

Value of cell D6 displayed in italics

Underlined reference

---

3 Click **Evaluate** again.

The result of the first logical test displays as *FALSE*. The cell in the Logical test for the second IF function—E6—is underlined. At the bottom of the dialog box, the Step In button becomes available.

4 Click **Step In** and notice that the value of cell E6 is displayed.

The second formula displays in the dialog box with the value of E6 displayed. When you *Step In* to the formula, the nested formula is evaluated.

5 Click **Step Out** and notice that the nested function is underlined. Click **Evaluate**.

Step In is again available because the next cell reference is part of another nested function. Some parts of formulas that use the IF function are not evaluated, and #N/A is displayed in the Evaluation box.

6 Click **Evaluate** until the **Restart** button becomes available. Notice that the final evaluation of this formula is *No*, and then click **Close**.

You have completed the evaluation and have stepped in to evaluate the nested functions. Before closing the dialog box, you could click Restart to evaluate the formula again.

7 **Save** your workbook.

Activity 11.8 Using Auditing Tools to Trace Precedents and Dependents

The formulas in a worksheet may be *audited*—examined to check their accuracy—to show relationships between data and formulas. When auditing the Excel worksheet, tracer arrows show the flow of formulas and the results. The *precedent cells*—cells that are referred to in a formula—or *dependent cells*—cells that are referred to by a formula in another cell—can be traced when you select *trace precedents* or *trace dependents*. In this activity, you will use auditing tools to review the formulas used in the worksheet.

1 In the **11A_Server_Bonus_Firstname_Lastname** workbook, rename it **Bonus Amount** and then click in the sheet and review the data.

This worksheet displays the amount of the bonus that each server has earned in January. The bonus rate is 0.5% and is located in cell E2. As you review the worksheet, it appears there are several errors in the worksheet.

2 Click cell **E6**. On the **Formulas tab**, in the **Formula Auditing group**, click the **Trace Precedents** button, and then compare your screen with Figure 11.22.

Two blue arrows display on the worksheet and identify the precedents; a blue arrow shows cells with no errors. Recall that a precedent identifies cells used in the formula—in this case cells D6 and E2.

Figure 11.22

Line indicates the cell—E2—is used in the formula in cell E6

Line indicates the cell—D6—is used in the formula in cell E6

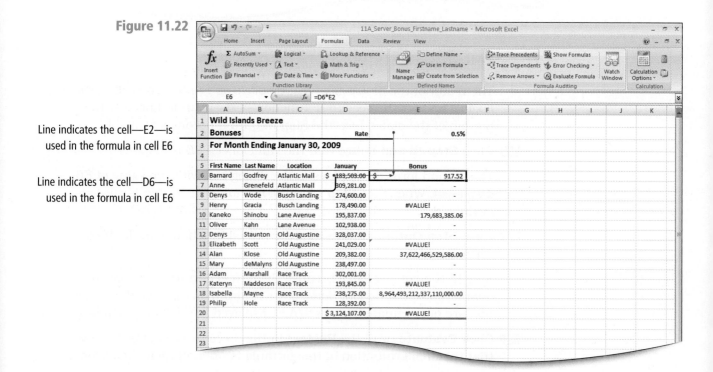

3 Click cell **E13** and in the **Formula Auditing group**, click the **Trace Precedents** button, review the cells involved in the formulas, and compare your screen with Figure 11.23.

The arrows display and identify the precedents for the formula in cell E13. The red arrow indicates a cell that can cause an error. The formula refers to cell E9, which contains a #VALUE! error, which would cause this error.

Figure 11.23

Excel | chapter 11

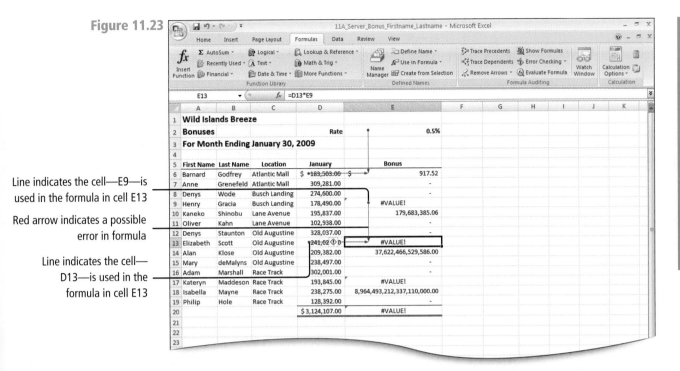

Line indicates the cell—E9—is used in the formula in cell E13

Red arrow indicates a possible error in formula

Line indicates the cell—D13—is used in the formula in cell E13

4 Click cell **E7** and in the **Formula Auditing group**, click the **Trace Precedents** button and review the formula.

This formula includes cell E3, which contains no data. The formula in cell E6 that was originally copied, contains an error. Since the bonus rate should be multiplied in all of the cells, the original formula required an absolute reference for cell E3 so that it could be accurately copied.

5 Click cell **E13**, which is the cell containing precedents arrows the furthest from the first cell—cell E2. In the **Formula Auditing group**, click the **Remove Arrows button arrow** to access the menu, and then compare your screen with Figure 11.24.

The three choices on the displayed list are to Remove Arrows, Remove Precedent Arrows, or Remove Dependent Arrows. When you use Remove Precedent Arrows in a cell that contains an arrow, the arrows are removed one at a time. If the selected cell does not contain a Precedent Arrow and you click the Remove Precedent Arrows, all arrows are removed. It is recommended that you begin reviewing the precedents with the cell the furthest from the formula.

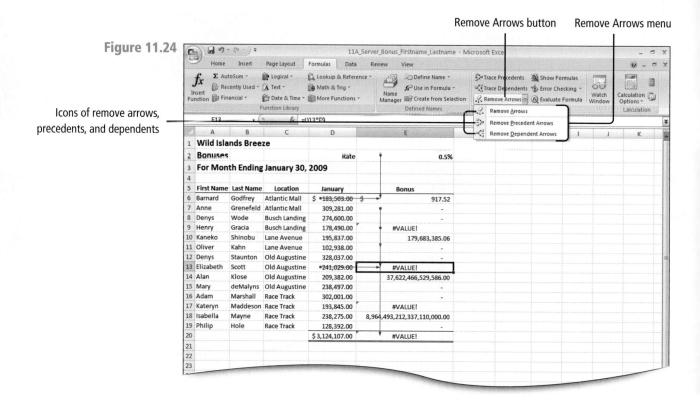

Figure 11.24

Remove Arrows button   Remove Arrows menu

Icons of remove arrows, precedents, and dependents

6 In the **Remove Arrows** list, click **Remove Precedent Arrows** to remove one precedent arrow. Then display the list again and click **Remove Arrows** to remove all arrows from the worksheet.

7 Click cell **E9** and in the **Formula Auditing group**, click **Trace Dependents**. Then click cell **E13** and click **Trace Dependents**, and then click **E17** and click **Trace Dependents**. Then **Save** your workbook.

Recall that a dependent is a cell that is used in a formula. Again, the red arrow displays to indicate a cell that causes an error. When the workbook is saved, the Trace Error command is no longer in effect and all tracer arrows are removed from the worksheet.

Activity 11.9 Using Error Checking

When a worksheet is completed, Excel uses certain rules to check for errors in formulas, called *error checking*. These rules do not guarantee that the worksheet is error-free but they help in finding common mistakes (and sometimes the built-in rules point to potential problems even if they do not contain errors). You can also use the Evaluate Formula dialog box to review the parts of a complex formula. In this activity, you will evaluate the structure of a formula.

1 Click cell **E9**. In the **Formula Auditing group**, click the **Error Checking button arrow**, and then compare your screen with Figure 11.25.

Figure 11.25

Error Checking button

Error Checking menu

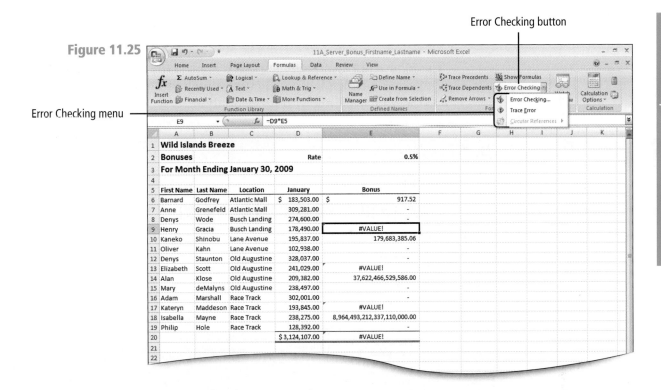

2 Click **Trace Error**. The arrows that identify the precedents display.

3 Click the **Error Checking button arrow**, click **Error Checking**, and compare your screen with Figure 11.26. If you need help with Error Checking, you would click *Help on this error*.

The Error Checking dialog box displays. The formula in the cell is entered in the dialog box. Several choices are located at the right side of the dialog box. The Options button displays options in Excel for changes related to formula calculation performance and error handling.

Figure 11.26

Formula in the worksheet

Error Checking dialog box

Choices for assistance in checking errors

Options button

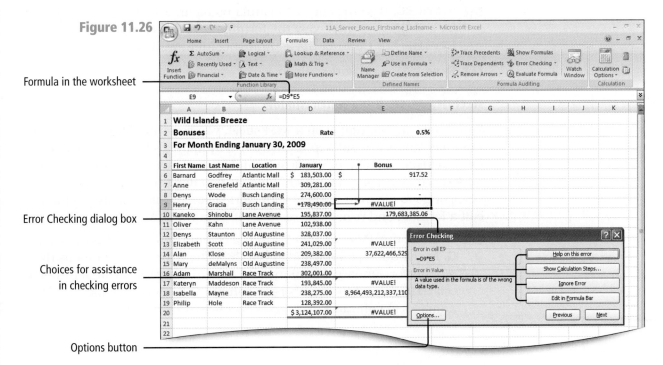

4 Click **Show Calculation Steps** and move the dialog boxes so both are visible. Then compare your screen with Figure 11.27.

The Evaluate Formula dialog box displays. In the Evaluation section, the formula is displayed as actual values rather than cell references as a way of assisting with its evaluation.

Figure 11.27

Evaluate Formula dialog box

Evaluation of formula

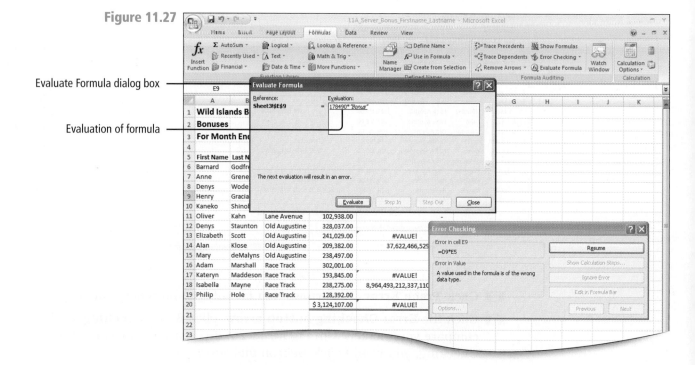

5 In the **Evaluate Formula** dialog box, click **Close**. In the **Error Checking** dialog box, click **Next** to move to the next error. Continue clicking **Next** until all errors have been checked, and then click **OK**.

6 In cell **E6**, type the correct formula using an absolute cell reference for cell E2, and then copy the formula through **row 19**. Format **E7:E19** with **Comma Style**. Adjust column widths.

7 Save your workbook.

Activity 11.10 Using Watch Window

When cells are not visible on a worksheet, you can watch those cells, their formulas, and the results in the **Watch Window**—a small window that is used to inspect, audit, or confirm formula calculations and results in large worksheets. By using the Watch Window, you don't need to repeatedly scroll or go to different parts of your worksheet. In this activity, you will edit a formula and review the results with the Watch Window.

1 In the **Bonus Results sheet**, insert a column between **columns F** and **G**. In cell **G5**, type **Total** and in cell **G6**, enter a formula that totals the receipts for January, February, and March. **Copy** the formula through cell **G19**. Format the numbers in **column G** to match the format of the numbers in **column F**.

2 Click cell **C20** and type **Total** and then enter totals in the range **D20:G20** and format with **Accounting Number Style** $ ▾ and add a **Top and Double Bottom Border**. Adjust column widths if necessary.

3 Click the **Formulas tab**, and in the **Formula Auditing group**, click the **Watch Window** button, and then compare your screen with Figure 11.28.

The Watch Window task pane displays above the Excel worksheet with its name in the title bar. The **Add Watch** button displays and the blank area is available to insert specific information about the formulas to watch.

Figure 11.28

Watch Window title bar

Add Watch button

Watch Window menu bar

Area to display Watch Window information

Watch Window button

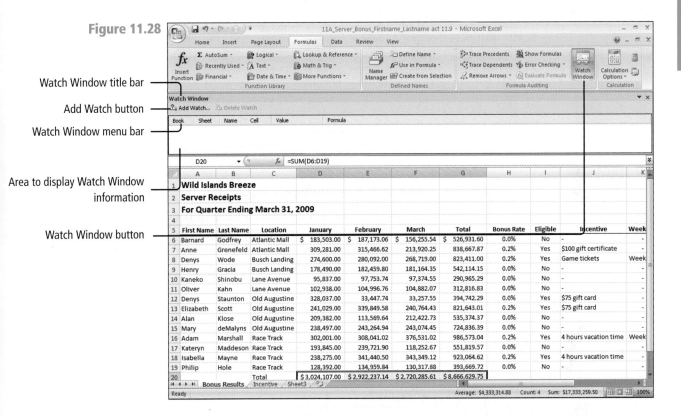

Alert!

What if my Watch Window doesn't match the picture in the text?

If the Watch Window is floating on your screen, double-click the title bar so it displays above the worksheet. The Watch Window task pane can be also be resized. Position the pointer at the edge of the Watch Window and drag it to the size displayed in Figure 11.29.

4 Click cell **G20** and in the **Watch Window**, click the **Add Watch** button. Then compare your screen with Figure 11.29.

The Add Watch dialog box displays the address of the cells you would like to watch, including the sheet name.

Figure 11.29

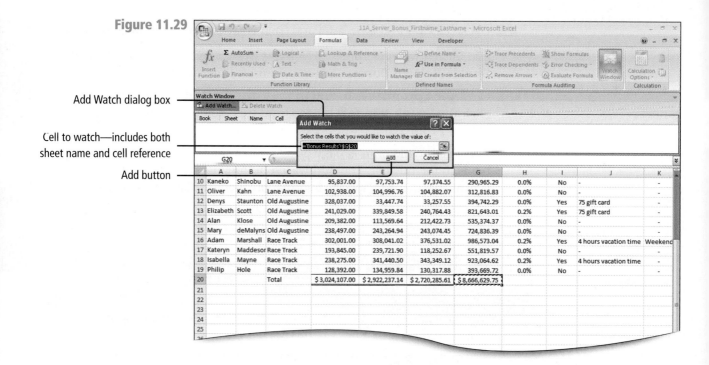

Add Watch dialog box

Cell to watch—includes both sheet name and cell reference

Add button

▐5▌ In the **Add Watch** dialog box, click **Add**.

The data about this cell has been added to the Watch Window task pane. The information includes the name of the workbook, the worksheet, the specific cell, and the results and formula of that cell.

▐6▌ Select the range **L6:N6** and in the **Watch Window**, click the **Add Watch** button and confirm the cell location in the **Add Watch** dialog box by clicking **Add**. Then compare your screen with Figure 11.30.

A range of cells can be identified as a group, but each cell displays individually in the Watch Window task pane.

Sheet name Cell reference   Formula in each cell

Figure 11.30

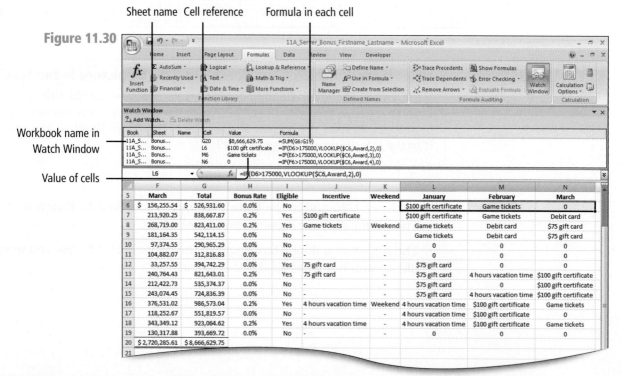

Workbook name in Watch Window

Value of cells

7 Scroll the worksheet so **column A** displays and the last columns are not displayed. Then click cell **D6** and type **125,038** and as you press ⌷Enter⌷, review the results of the Value column in the Watch Window.

All of the cells being reviewed are not visible on the screen, but you can see the results in the Watch Window.

8 Click cell **F10** and type **178,029** and review the results in the Watch Window toolbar as you press ⌷Enter⌷. On the **Watch Window** at the right side, click the **Close** button ⌷X⌷ to close the Watch Window.

9 Select all sheets and in the **Left Footer** insert the **File Name** and in the **Right Footer**, insert the **Sheet Name**. **Hide** the **Incentive sheet**. Format the **Bonus Results sheet** in **Landscape Orientation**, **Fit to page**, and center it both **Vertically** and **Horizontally**. In the **Page Setup** dialog box, click the **Sheet tab**, click in the text box for **Columns to repeat at left**, and click **columns A** and **B** so $A:$B displays.

Recall that on a large worksheet, column and row titles display on all pages of the worksheet. The first name and last name will display on all printed pages of this worksheet.

10 Click the **Bonus Amount sheet tab**, and format the worksheet for **Portrait Orientation** and center it both **Vertically** and **Horizontally**. Click in the **Bonus Results sheet tab**, and **Save** your workbook.

11 **Print** the visible sheets in both files—**11A_Server_Bonus_Firstname_ Lastname** and **11A_Receipts_Firstname_Lastname**—or submit electronically as instructed. **Close** the workbook and **Exit** Excel.

End You have completed Project 11A ————————————

Project 11B Sales Report

In Activities 11.11 through 11.17, you will combine worksheets from the different restaurants and combine them—consolidate—the data into one workbook. You will also share workbooks and merge workbooks into one workbook. Your completed workbooks will look like Figure 11.31.

For Project 11B, you will need the following files:

e11B_Sales_Report
e11B_Coffee
e11B_Quarter
e11B_Wkly_Sales_Rept

You will save your workbooks as
11B_Sales_Report_Firstname_Lastname
11B_Quarter_Firstname_Lastname
11B_Coffee_Firstname_Lastname
11B_Completed_Wkly_Sales_Rept_Firstname_Lastname

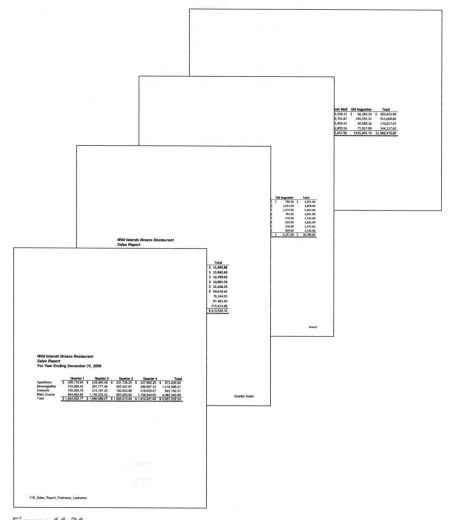

Figure 11.31
Project 11B—Sales Report

Objective 4
Consolidate Workbooks

To summarize and report results from separate worksheets, you can **consolidate**—combine—data from each separate worksheet into a master worksheet. The worksheets can be in the same workbook or in separate workbooks.

There are three methods to consolidate data—consolidate by position, category, or formula.

Activity 11.11 Consolidating by Position

Ron Mueller, of the accounting department, has received the sales report from each of the restaurants for the fourth quarter of the year. He would like to prepare one report for the Jacksonville restaurants, which you will consolidate.

When you **consolidate by position**, you arrange the data in all worksheets in an identical order and location. To consolidate by position,

- Be sure each range of data is in list format, each column has a label in the first row, each row and column contains similar facts, and there are no blank rows or columns in the list.

- Put each range of data on a separate worksheet.

- Use a new, blank worksheet for the consolidation.

- Confirm that each range has the same layout—column and row titles in the same location.

- Name each range.

In this activity, you will consolidate the sales reports from each restaurant into one report by using Consolidate by Position.

1 **Start** Excel. Locate and open the file named **e11B_Quarter**. Save it in your **Excel Chapter 11** folder and name it **11B_Quarter_Firstname_ Lastname**

This workbook displays the sales report for each of the Jacksonville restaurants for the fourth quarter. Each worksheet uses the same structure for the report, including the four cost centers—Appetizers, Beverage/Bar, Desserts, and Main Course—and the monthly earnings.

2 Click the **Insert Worksheet** button and move the inserted worksheet so it is the first sheet of the workbook. Rename **Sheet1** to **Quarter Sales** Group the **Quarter Sales** and **Busch Landing** worksheets and display the **Busch Landing sheet**. Select the range of the worksheet—**A1:E11**—and on the **Home tab**, in the **Editing group**,

click the **Fill** button and click **Across Worksheets**. In the **Fill Across Worksheets** dialog box, confirm **All** is selected, and then click **OK**.

3 Select all worksheets and in the **Left Footer** area insert the **File Name** and in the **Right Footer** area insert the **Sheet Name**. Center the worksheets both **Vertically** and **Horizontally**. Return to **Normal** view with cell **A1** active.

4 **Ungroup sheets** and in the **Quarter Sales sheet**, delete the data in the range **B7:D10**. Click cell **A2** and press Delete, and then move the data from the range **A3:A4** to **A2:A3**. Adjust the width of **column A** to fully display the row titles. Then click in all worksheets to confirm that the structure is identical in all sheets—all columns have the same column and row titles, the data covers the same range, **A6:E11**— and there are no blank rows or columns within the data range.

The structure of the Quarter Sales worksheet exactly matches the structure of the worksheet for each restaurant. The **worksheet structure** refers to the data range in all worksheets, which must be identical—the same range of cells is used. The column and row titles must be the same. There can be no empty rows or columns within the data range. The empty rows between the worksheet title and the data do not affect the consolidation process. The extra blank row in the Quarter Sales report is necessary in order to have the column titles begin in cell A6 on all worksheets.

5 Click the **Busch Landing sheet tab** and select the range of the data—**B7:E11**. Click the **Formulas tab**, and in the **Defined Names group**, click the **Define Name** button. In the **New Name** dialog box, in the **Name** box, type **Busch_Landing** and then click **OK**. Alternatively, select the range of data, click the Name Box, type **Busch_Landing** and then press Enter.

6 Click the **Lane Avenue sheet tab** and select the range of the data— **B7:E11**. Using the skills you practiced, define the name of this range as **Lane_Avenue** Using the skills you practiced, define the name of the ranges for the Race Track, Atlantic Mall, and Old Augustine restaurants.

When you consolidate data, the ranges must be named. Recall when you name cells or ranges, spaces are not allowed, so replace the space with an underscore.

7 Click the **Quarter Sales sheet tab** and click cell **B7**.

To start the consolidation, click the upper left cell in the area where you want the consolidated data to appear.

8 On the **Data tab**, in the **Data Tools group**, click **Consolidate** and compare your screen with Figure 11.32.

The Consolidate dialog box displays. There are four areas in the dialog box—*Function, Reference, All references,* and *Use labels in.*

Figure 11.32

Consolidate dialog box ———

Function area ———

Reference area ———

All references area ———

Use labels in area ———

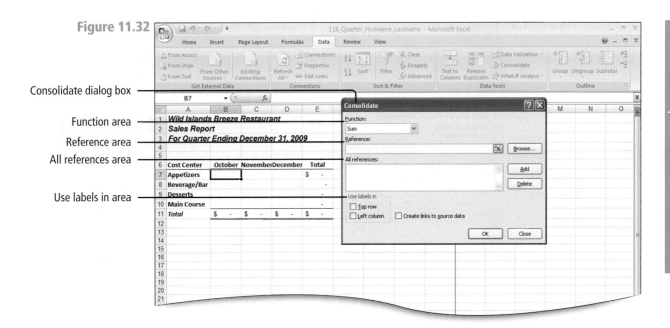

9 ▸ In the **Consolidate** dialog box, in the **Function** text box, click the arrow to review the available functions and click **Sum**.

To consolidate these worksheets, you will add the sales for each of the worksheets to get the total sales for the year.

10 ▸ At the end of the **Reference** box, click the **Collapse Dialog Box** button 📧, then click the **Busch Landing sheet tab**. Select the range of the data—**B7:E11**—then click the **Expand Dialog Box** button 📧. In the **Consolidate** dialog box, click **Add** and compare your screen with Figure 11.33.

You have selected the range of the data that will be used to determine the total sales for the year. The name of the worksheet—followed by an exclamation mark—and the selected range displays in the Reference area.

Figure 11.33

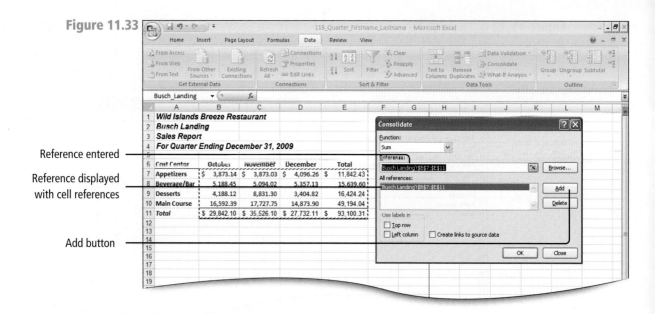

Reference entered

Reference displayed with cell references

Add button

11 Click the **Lane Avenue sheet tab**.

The reference now displays Lane Avenue and the correct range.

12 In the **Consolidate** dialog box, click **Add** to add the Lane Avenue reference to the All references box. Then click in the **Race Track sheet tab**, note that the correct range is already selected, and click **Add**. Using the skills practiced, add the data from the **Atlantic Mall** and **Old Augustine** sheets.

13 Click the **Create links to source data** check box, and then click **OK**. Adjust column widths, click in cell **A1**, and compare your screen with Figure 11.34.

The data is entered in the worksheet using subtotals. Expand buttons display at the left. The data is linked because you checked *Create links to source data*. When a change is made in one of the worksheets, it will be updated in this worksheet.

Completed consolidated worksheet

Figure 11.34

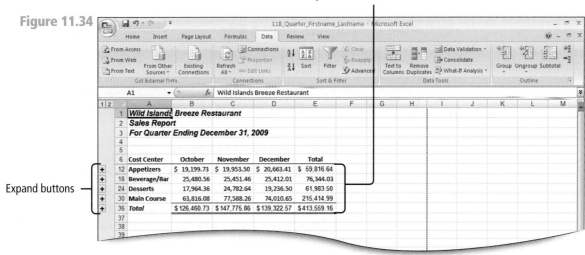

14 In the subtotal area at the left, click the first **Expand** button 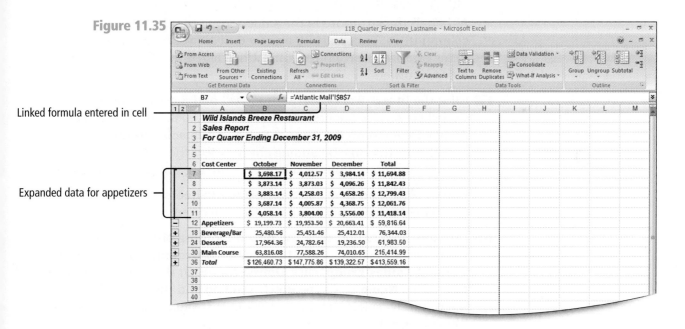 to display the numbers used for appetizers from the five restaurants. Click cell **B7** and in the **Formula Bar**, review the formula that is linked to the original data and compare your screen with Figure 11.35.

Figure 11.35

Linked formula entered in cell

Expanded data for appetizers

15 **Hide** all worksheets except the **Quarter Sales sheet**, and if necessary, adjust column widths in the sheet. **Save** your workbook.

More Knowledge

The Consolidate Dialog Box

When using Consolidate by Position, the Use labels in Rows and Columns check boxes should be left unchecked. Excel does not copy the row or column labels in the source ranges to the consolidated data.

Activity 11.12 Consolidating by Category

When you ***consolidate by category***, the data in each row in the worksheets does not have to be arranged in the same order. The same column and row titles must be used so that the master worksheet can match the data, but the categories in each row and column do not have to be in the same order. Each of the restaurants has reported the same data, but they have not been consistent with the way they reported the data. In this activity, you will consolidate the worksheets by category.

1 From your student files, open the file named **e11B_Sales_Report**. Save it in your **Excel Chapter 11** folder and name it **11B_Sales_Report_Firstname_Lastname** Then click in the worksheets and review the data. Notice that each worksheet lists the food categories in a different order.

Although the structure is the same—same number of rows, same column titles, data starting on row 6 in all worksheets, and the totals on row 11—each restaurant has listed the cost centers in a different order.

2 Click the **Insert Worksheet** button 🗐 and move the inserted worksheet so it is the first sheet of the workbook. Rename **Sheet1** to **Annual Sales** Group the **Annual Sales** and **Busch Landing** worksheets and display the Busch Landing sheet. Select the worksheet title—**A1:A4**—and on the **Home tab**, in the **Editing group**, click the **Fill** button 🔽, and then click **Across Worksheets**. In the **Fill Across Worksheets** dialog box, confirm **All** is selected, and then click **OK**.

3 **Ungroup sheets** and click the **Busch Landing sheet tab** and select the range of the data—**A6:F11**. Click the **Formulas tab**, and in the **Defined Names group**, click **Define Name**. In the **New Name** dialog box, in the **Name** box, type **Busch_Landing** and then click **OK**. Alternatively, select the range, click in the Name Box, type **Busch_Landing** and then press Enter.

Recall that when naming cells, there can be no spaces. Instead, place an underscore between words.

4 Click the **Lane Avenue sheet tab** and select the range of the data—**A6:F11**. Using the skills you practiced, define the name of this range as **Lane_Avenue** Using the skills you practiced, define the name of the ranges for the Race Track, Atlantic Mall, and Old Augustine restaurants.

Recall that when consolidating data, the ranges must be named.

5 Click the **Annual Sales sheet tab**. Click cell **A6**, the upper left cell of the area in which you want the consolidated data to appear. Then on the **Data tab**, in the **Data Tools group**, click the **Consolidate** button.

6 Confirm that the **Function** is **Sum**. In the **Reference text** box, type **Busch_Landing** click the **Add** button, and then compare your screen with Figure 11.36.

Because you named the range the same as the worksheet name, typing the range name enters the data range in the All Reference box.

When you Consolidate by Category, you can enter the defined name of the reference area, which you could not do when you Consolidate by Position.

Figure 11.36

Named range entered

Range selected on the Busch Landing sheet

Named range added to the All references list

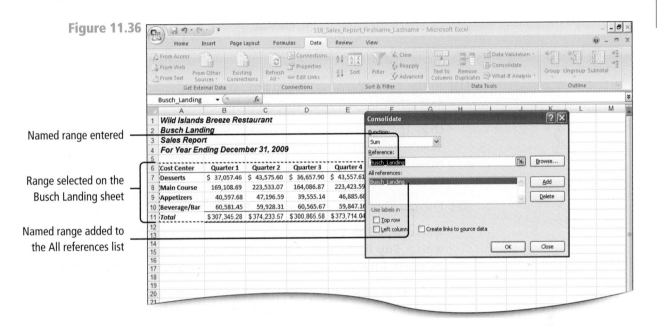

7 Click in the **Lane Avenue sheet tab** and note that the range displays in the Reference area. Click **Add**. Using the skills you practiced, add the ranges from the Race Track, Atlantic Mall, and Old Augustine sheets.

8 In the **Use labels in** section, click the **Top row** and **Left column** check boxes, and then click **OK**. Adjust the column widths and review the results in the worksheet.

The labels from the row titles and column titles are entered into the worksheets, as instructed. Excel matched the data for each of the menu items and quarter sales and entered the sum in the summary worksheet.

9 Delete the contents of cell **A2** and move cells **A3:A4** to **A2:A3**. Select the range **A7:A10** and on the **Data tab**, in the **Sort & Filter group**, click the **Sort A to Z button** and compare your screen with Figure 11.37.

The Sort Warning dialog box displays. Because there are entries in the cells adjacent to the selected range, Excel asks you to confirm that you want to alphabetize only the selected cells.

Figure 11.37

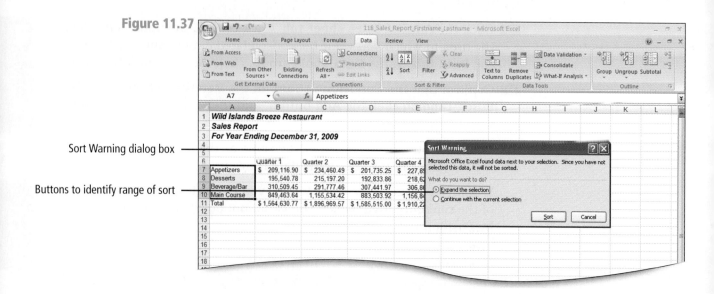

Sort Warning dialog box

Buttons to identify range of sort

10 In the **Sort Warning** dialog box, confirm the button by **Expand the selection** is checked, and then click **Sort**.

Only the row titles were selected. If you had sorted by the current selection, the numbers in the rows would not be sorted to match their row title. When you expand the selection, the entire range of cells is sorted.

11 Format the column titles with **Bold** **B** , **Align Text Right** ≣ ,
with a **Bottom Border** . Select the range **B11:F11** and format with a **Top and Double Bottom Border**. Confirm that **Accounting Number format** is applied to the ranges **B7:F7** and **B11:F11**.

12 **Hide** all worksheets except the **Annual Sales sheet** and adjust column widths, if needed. In the **Left Footer** area, insert the **File Name**.

Center the worksheet both **Horizontally** and **Vertically**. **Save**
your workbook.

More Knowledge
Consolidate by Formula

There are three methods to consolidate workbooks. In addition to Consolidate by Position and Consolidate by Category, you can Consolidate by Formula, which has been covered previously.

To consolidate by formula, use a 3-D reference—a reference to a range that spans two or more worksheets in a workbook. To use a 3-D reference, the structure of the worksheets needs to be the same. Click in the cell that contains the data, type = then the name of the function, and then click in the tab of the first worksheet and press ⇧ Shift while you click in the last worksheet. The data in the intervening worksheets will be included in the formula. The Consolidate dialog box is not used when you Consolidate by Formula.

Objective 5
Share and Merge Workbooks

Workbooks can be shared, allowing more than one user to enter data into the workbook. In a **shared workbook** you can track changes to determine who used the workbook, when it was used, and what changes were made. Shared workbooks can also be merged into one workbook.

Activity 11.13 Using a Shared Workbook

The five Jacksonville restaurants enter sales data in the same shared workbook, which is available to them on the company Web site. The workbook tracks changes that were made, so the history of the changes—who made the change, what it was, and when it was made—can be determined. In this activity, you will access the shared workbook, enter the changes for the Atlantic Mall restaurant, and then review the changes that were made in the workbook.

1 From your student files, open the file named **e11B_Coffee**. **Save** it in your **Excel Chapter 11** folder as **11B_Coffee_Firstname_Lastname**

This workbook is a shared workbook. Notice in the Title bar that *[Shared]* displays after the file name.

2 Beginning in cell **E6**, enter the data below for the Atlantic Mall coffee sales. These sales would be completed on this worksheet by the employees at the Atlantic Mall and then forwarded to the accountant.

Vanilla Almond Coffee	1011
Cappuccino	1143
Cafe Mocha	1199
Espresso	769
Island Coffee	629
Iced Mochaccino	854
Iced Mint Frappachino	487
Iced Island Coffee	729

3 Click **Save** 🖫 .

4 On the **Review tab**, in the **Changes group**, click the **Track Changes** button and compare your screen with Figure 11.38.

When others use one workbook, use *Track Changes* to see who made changes, when they were made, and what the changes are. You can also accept or reject any changes that were made.

Figure 11.38

Track Changes menu

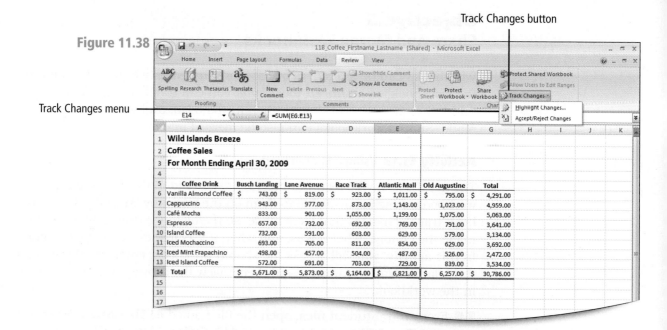

5 Click **Highlight Changes**. In the **Highlight Changes** dialog box, under **Highlight which changes**, click **When** and **Who**. After **When**, click the arrow and select **All**. **Deselect** the check box by **Highlight changes on screen** and **Select** the check box by **List changes on a new sheet**. Then compare your screen with Figure 11.39.

Excel can be set so that you can track all changes made to the workbook since it was developed. You can view all of the changes, the ones that were created since you last saved, or changes from a specific date. You can also select to save changes made by any person or by all users. You can also isolate a portion of the worksheet and review only the changes made to those cells.

You can choose to highlight the changes on the original worksheet or display them on a worksheet named the History sheet.

Figure 11.39

Highlight Changes dialog box

Display—list—changes on a new sheet

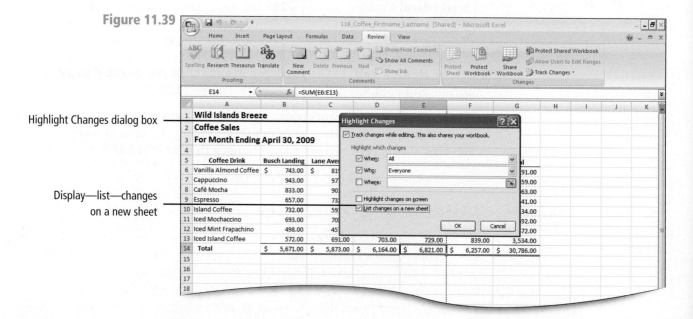

6 Click **OK** and compare your screen with Figure 11.40. Then review the History sheet and note that the changes that have been made to the title and to correct the entry in cell A6.

The new worksheet named **History** displays the recent history of the workbook. You can see who created the change, which cells were changed, and when the changes were made. In the Who column, you can see who made the changes. Note that the name of your computer is displayed for the changes you just made.

Figure 11.40

What was changed—old value and new value
Location of change
Who made the change
Date of change

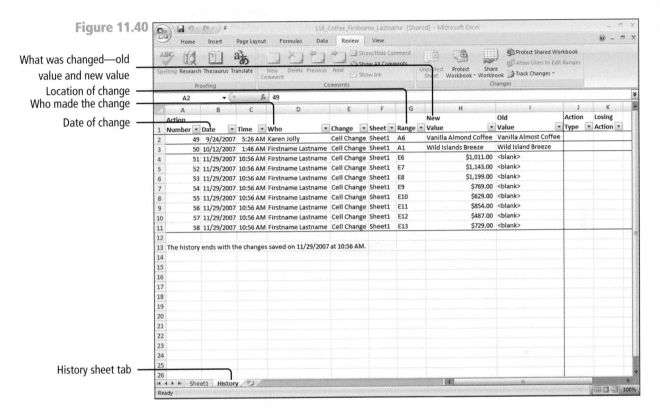

History sheet tab

7 Select both worksheets and in the **Left Footer**, insert the **File Name** and in the **Right Footer**, insert the **Sheet Name**. If a warning box displays indicating that Page Layout view is incompatible with Freeze Panes, click **OK** to continue. Format the workbook to display in **Portrait Orientation**, **Fit to page**, and center both **Horizontally** and **Vertically**. If your instructor requires you to submit printed copies, **Print** the **History** page now.

8 Click **Save** and **Close** the workbook.

Notice that when you save your work, the History page disappears. The history log remains with the document, but it does not remain as a permanent worksheet in the workbook.

Activity 11.14 Creating a Shared Workbook

When you **merge workbooks**, individual workbooks containing similar data are combined into one workbook. For instance, the sales records of an individual restaurant may be merged with data from the other restaurants. The accounting department places the monthly data in one workbook. The data is received from each restaurant on a separate

sheet, and you will merge them into one workbook. In order to merge a
workbook, it must be saved as a shared document. In this activity, you
will create the shared document that will later be used to merge data
from all restaurants.

1 From your student files, open the file named **e11B_Wkly_Sales_Rept**
and **Save** it as **11B_Wkly_Sales_Rept_Firstname_Lastname** In the worksheet title, correct the name of the firm to **Wild Islands Breeze**

2 Click the **Review tab** and in the **Changes group**, click the **Share
Workbook** button. In the **Share Workbook** dialog box, on the
Editing tab, click **Allow changes by more than one user at the
same time**. This also allows workbook merging. Compare your
screen with Figure 11.41.

To share a workbook so that others can also edit or change the
workbook, it needs to be saved as a shared workbook.

Figure 11.41

Share Workbook dialog box

Editing tab

Allow changes by others

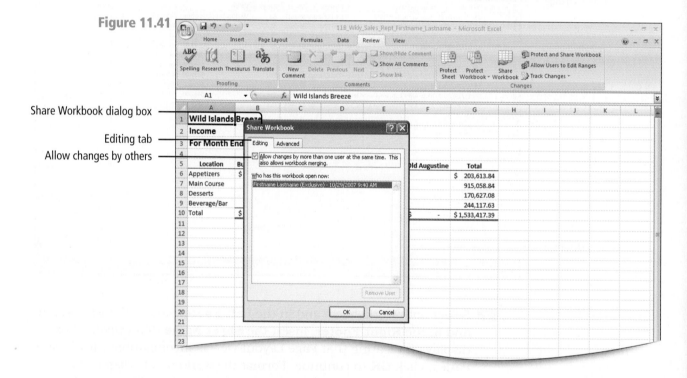

3 Click **OK**. At the dialog box that indicates the action will now save
the shared workbook, click **OK**.

The word *Shared* displays in the title bar, indicating this workbook is
a shared workbook. You will enter the Atlantic Mall data, and the
changes made to this workbook will be recorded—tracked as changes.

4 **Save** the workbook, and then **Close** it.

Activity 11.15 Entering Data into a Shared Workbook

When merging workbooks, the data is entered on a copy of the original
workbook and saved as a copy. In this activity, you will open the original
workbook, save it as a copy, and enter the data for the Old Augustine
restaurant. The data from the other restaurants has already been merged
into the workbook.

1 Click the **Office button** 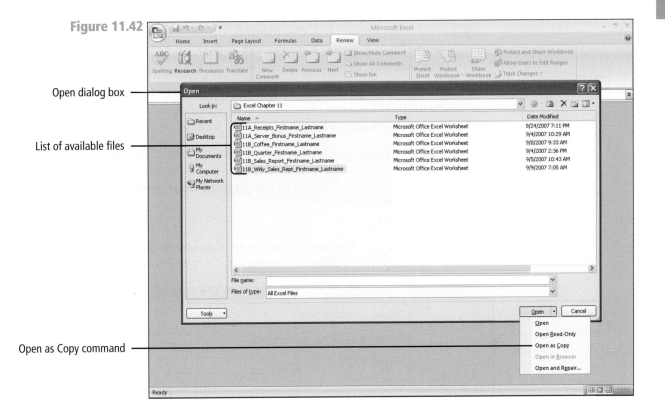, and click **Open**. In the **Open** dialog box, click the **11B_Wkly_Sales_Rept_Firstname_Lastname** file, and then at the lower right of the dialog box, click the **Open button arrow** to display a list of options for opening this file and compare your screen with Figure 11.42.

The list displays the ways a workbook can be accessed. When you click Open, you have full access to the worksheet and you can edit, format, and save it. When you open a **read-only** workbook, you are looking at the original file. If changes are made, the file needs a new name. When you **Open as Copy**, a duplicate file is opened. The file is given a new name—the default is to add *Copy (1)* to the beginning of the file name.

Figure 11.42

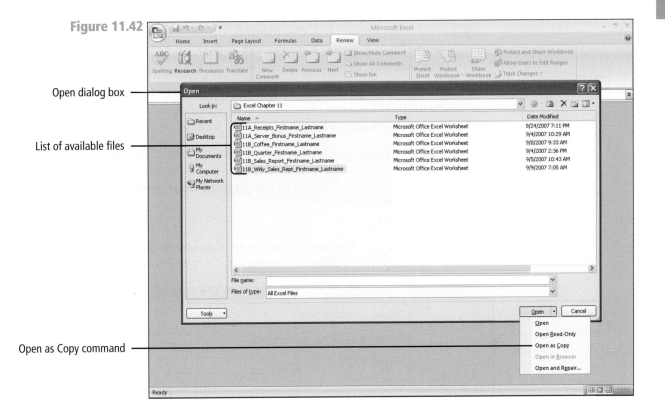

Open dialog box

List of available files

Open as Copy command

2 From the displayed list, click **Open as Copy**.

The shared document opens as a copy of the original document. Note in the Title bar this is *Copy (1) 11B_Wkly_Sales_Rept_Firstname_Lastname* and is a shared workbook, which is used when merging workbooks.

3 Beginning in cell **F6**, type the monthly sales displayed below for the Old Augustine restaurant.

Appetizers	66,383.23
Main Course	246,595.31
Desserts	50,098.16
Beverage/Bar	71,927.00

4 **Save** 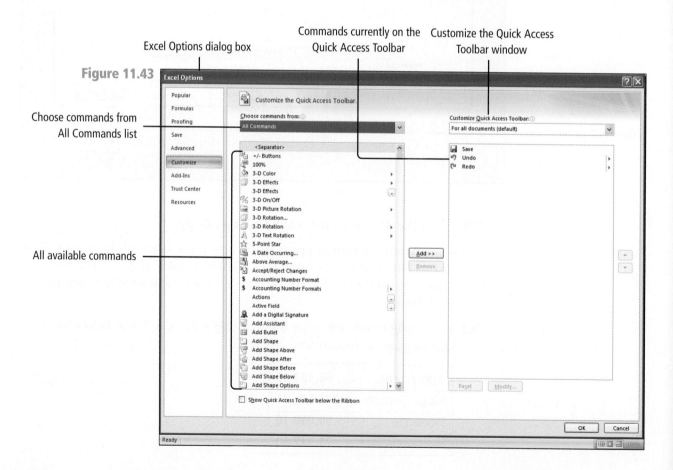 your workbook with the name **Copy (1)11B_Wkly_Sales_ Rept_Augustine_Firstname_Lastname Close** the workbook.

Activity 11.16 Display the Compare and Merge Button

The *Compare and Merge Workbooks* command is used when you compare similar workbooks and merge the data into one workbook. The Compare and Merge command does not display on a Ribbon, but you can add it to the Quick Access Toolbar. In this activity, you will access the Compare and Merge Workbooks command by placing the command on the Quick Access Toolbar.

1 Click the **Office** button and at the bottom right corner, click the **Excel Options** button.

2 In the left pane, click **Customize**. Under the **Choose commands from**, click **Popular Commands arrow**, and then click **All Commands**. Compare your screen with Figure 11.43.

This list is used to add button commands to the Quick Access Toolbar. When you customize your computer, you can place the most frequently used commands on this toolbar.

The Compare and Merge Workbooks command is only available as a button, so in order to utilize the feature, the button must be added to the toolbar. It is used to merge data from several workbooks into one workbook.

Figure 11.43

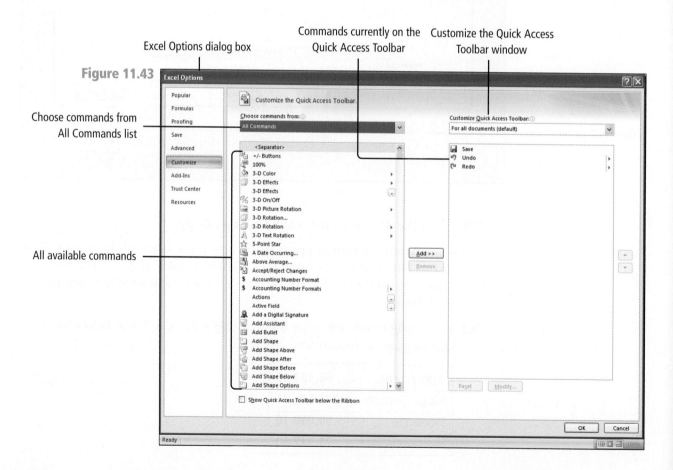

3 Scroll down the list, click **Compare and Merge Workbooks**, click the
Add button, and compare your screen with Figure 11.44.

At the right side of the window, the Compare and Merge Workbooks
button displays. It is added to the Quick Access Toolbar.

Customize the Quick Access Toolbar

Figure 11.44

Compare and Merge
Workbooks command button

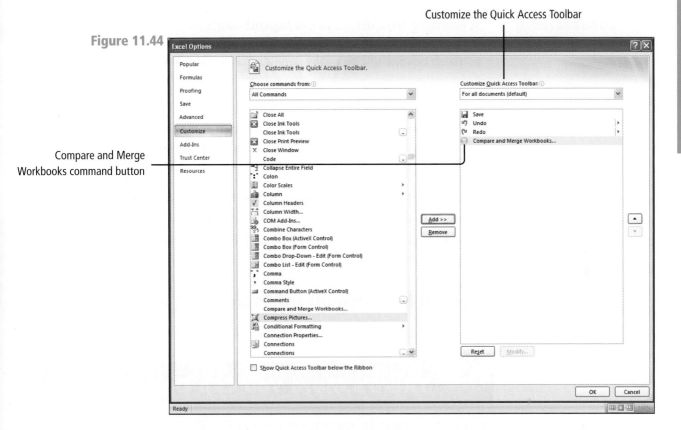

4 At the bottom right, click **OK**.

The icon for Compare and Merge Workbooks ☐ displays on the
Quick Access Toolbar.

Activity 11.17 Merge Workbooks

Now that you have received the data from all restaurants, you will merge
it into one workbook. In this activity, you will open the workbooks that
will be merged together and save the work as a final monthly sales report.

1 **Open** the workbook named **11B_Wkly_Sales_Rept_Firstname_
Lastname**.

2 On the **Quick Access Toolbar**, click the **Compare and Merge
Workbooks** button ☐. In the **Select Files to Merge Into Current
Workbook** dialog box, from your **Excel Chapter 11** folder, click
Copy (1)11B_Wkly_Sales_Rept_Augustine_Firstname_Lastname,
and then click **OK**.

The data from the Old Augustine restaurant has been entered into
the workbook.

3 In the **Left Footer** area, enter the **File Name**. Place the workbook in **Landscape Orientation** and center both **Vertically** and **Horizontally**.

4 **Save** the completed workbook as **11B_Completed_Wkly_Sales_Rept_Firstname_Lastname**

5 Click the **Office** button , click **Open**, and open the **Excel Chapter 11** folder. Click the worksheet named **Copy (1)11B_Wkly_Sales_Rept_Firstname_Lastname** and press Delete. In the **Confirm File Delete** warning box, click **Yes**. In the same manner, delete the worksheet named **11B_Wkly_Sales_Rept_Firstname_Lastname**. Then in the **Open** dialog box, click **Cancel**.

6 Print your files or submit electronically as instructed. **Close** all workbooks and **Exit** Excel.

End **You have completed Project 11B** ——————————

There's More You Can Do!

From My Computer, navigate to the student files that accompany this textbook. In the folder **02_theres_more_you_can_do**, locate and open the folder for this chapter. Open and print the instructions for this project, which are provided to you in Adobe PDF format.

Try It! 1—Consolidated Workbooks

In this Try It! exercise, you will consolidate workbooks to complete a combined sales report.

Content-Based Assessments

Excel
chaptereleven

Summary

In this chapter, you nested functions in order to create complex formulas. You have nested SUM, IF, VLOOKUP, and other functions. You used Excel's auditing tools to check for errors and examine formulas and the Watch Window to see changes made in other parts of the worksheet. You consolidated the data from several separate worksheets into one worksheet that reports the sum of each sheet. In addition, you created shared workbooks and merged workbooks from shared sources.

Key Terms

Content-Based Assessments

Matching

Match each term in the second column with its correct definition in the first column by writing the letter of the term on the blank line in front of the correct definition.

_____ **1.** Placing one function within another to create complex formulas.

_____ **2.** A reference to the same cell or range of cells on multiple worksheets.

_____ **3.** A cell reference where either the column or the row will remain the same as the formula is copied.

_____ **4.** The tools that provide additional assistance to help locate possible errors.

_____ **5.** Used to evaluate the nested formula within another formula.

_____ **6.** Examine a worksheet to check its accuracy.

_____ **7.** Cells that are referred to in a formula.

_____ **8.** Cells that are referred to by a formula in another cell.

_____ **9.** Rules that Excel uses to review formulas for accuracy.

_____ **10.** A small window used to inspect, audit, or confirm formula calculations and results in a large worksheet.

_____ **11.** Combine data from separate worksheets into a master worksheet.

_____ **12.** Using the position of data from separate worksheets to combine into a master worksheet.

_____ **13.** The data range in all worksheets that includes empty rows or columns, the rows that are used, and the row and column titles.

_____ **14.** Using the same categories in individual worksheets to create a combined workbook.

_____ **15.** Workbooks that allow more than one user to enter data in the same workbook.

A 3-D reference

B Audit

C Auditing tools

D Consolidate

E Consolidate by category

F Consolidate by position

G Dependent cells

H Error checking

I Mixed reference

J Nest functions

K Precedent cells

L Shared workbook

M Step In

N Watch Window

O Worksheet structure

Content-Based Assessments

Fill in the Blank

Write the correct answer in the space provided.

1. Review a nested formula in the order the formula is calculated in the _____ _____ dialog box.

2. To identify the cells with an arrow that are referred to in a formula is to _____ _____.

3. The cell reference B$5 is an example of a/an _____ _____.

4. To identify the cells with an arrow that are referred to by a formula is to _____ _____.

5. Combining worksheets with similar data into one workbook is _____ _____.

6. A file which can be viewed but not changed is a(n) _____ _____ file.

7. When you open a duplicate copy of a read-only file, select the _____ _____ _____ command.

8. The feature that is used to merge data from several workbooks into one workbook is _____ and _____.

9. Place a frequently used command on the _____ _____ _____ by accessing Excel Options.

10. Placing an AND function within an IF function is an example of _____ _____.

11. The area where you can review the results of a formula from another part of the worksheet is the _____ _____.

12. In the Open dialog box, to open a workbook as a copy or as a read-only document, click the _____ button arrow.

13. The ability to see who made changes, when they were made, and what the changes are when using a shared workbook is available when you select to _____ _____.

14. The worksheet that displays who created the change, which cells were changed, and when the changes were made is named the _____ sheet.

15. When a workbook has the same number of rows and columns with the same row and column titles, but the rows and columns are not arranged in the same order, use _____ by _____ to merge the workbooks.

Content-Based Assessments

Skills Review

Project 11C — Chocolate Sales

In this project, you will apply the skills you practiced from the Objectives in Project 11A.

Objectives: 1. *Nest One Function within Another;* **2.** *Use 3-D References and Nested Lookups;* **3.** *Check Accuracy with Excel's Auditing Tools.*

In the following Skills Review, you will complete a worksheet that evaluates the sales of specialty chocolate menu items at the Wild Islands Breeze restaurants. Special chocolate items were added to the restaurants' menus as a trial and Chef Jimmy wants to evaluate their success and report to Executive Chef Maxine Hylton-Pert. In this worksheet, you will evaluate the success of the chocolate items and determine whether or not each item should be added to the regular menu. In addition, the employees of the stores who have sold larger amounts of the chocolate items will be awarded with a small gift. Your completed worksheets will look like Figure 11.45.

For Project 11C, you will need the following file:

e11C_Chocolate_Sales

You will save your workbook as
11C_Chocolate_Sales_Firstname_Lastname

Figure 11.45

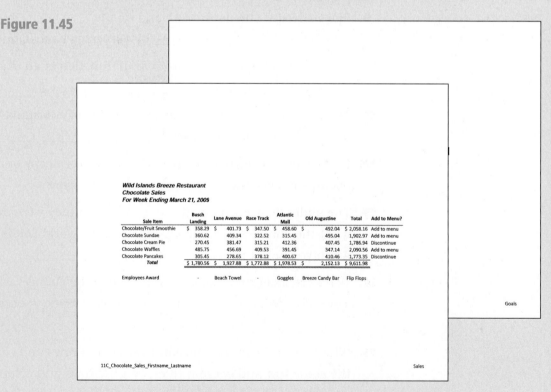

(Project 11C–Chocolate Sales continues on the next page)

Excel

chapter eleven   Skills Review

(Project 11C–Chocolate Sales continued)

1. **Start** Excel and from the student files, open **e11C_Chocolate_Sales** and **Save** it in your Excel Chapter 11 folder as **11C_Chocolate_Sales_Firstname_Lastname**

2. If the average sales of a chocolate item are more than $375, the item will be added to the menu permanently. On the **Sales sheet**, in cell **H5**, type **Add to Menu?** and format it the same as cell **G5**. Click cell **H6** and click the **Formulas tab**. In the **Function Library group**, click the **Logical** button, and from the list click **IF**.

3. With the insertion point in the **Logical_test** text box, click the arrow by the **Name Box** and select the **AVERAGE** function. If it is not listed, at the bottom of the list click **More Functions** and locate it in the Insert Function dialog box. Recall that AVERAGE is a Statistical function.

4. With the insertion point in the **Number1** text box, type the range **B6:F6** In the **Formula Bar**, click the **IF** function name to redisplay the IF Function Arguments dialog box.

5. In the **Logical_test** box, after the AVER-AGE function, type **>375** In the **Value_if_true** text box, type **"Add to menu"** In the **Value_if_false** text box, type **"Discontinue"** and then click **OK**. **Copy** the formula through cell **H10**.

6. If a store sells over $1,900 worth of the chocolate menu items, all employees of that store will receive an award. Each store manager has decided on a different award, which is found on the Awards sheet. **Click** the **Awards sheet tab** and **sort** so that the first column is in alphabetical order. Select the range of the table, click in the **Name** box, type **Award** and then press Enter.

7. In the **Sales sheet**, click cell **A13** and type **Employees Award** Click cell **B13**, and insert an **IF** function. In the **Logical_test** box, type **b11>1900** In the **Value_if_true** text box, click in the **Name** Box and select the **VLOOKUP** function. In the **Lookup_value** text box, click cell **B5**; in the **Table_array** text box, type **Award**, and in the **Col_index_num** box, type **2**

8. In the **Formula Bar**, click in the **IF** function name to redisplay the IF Function Arguments dialog box. In the **Value_if_false** text box, type **"-"** and then click **OK**. Copy the formula to the right through cell **F13**. **Center** the range **B13:F13** and adjust the column width as necessary. The employees of the Busch Landing and Race Track restaurants will not receive an award.

9. Click cell **H6**, and on the **Formulas tab**, in the **Formula Auditing group**, click **Trace Precedents**. The arrow begins in cell B6, and a blue box surrounds B6:F6, the cells used in the Average function. Click cell **C11**, and in the **Formula Auditing group**, click **Trace Precedents**. The blue arrow begins in cell C6.

10. Click cell **E13** and click **Trace Precedents**. A dotted line displays to and from a worksheet icon, indicating that some of the formula depends on data in another worksheet. Click the **Remove Arrows button arrow** to display the list, and then click **Remove Precedent Arrows**.

11. Click the **Goals sheet tab** and click cell **D6** and in the **Formula Auditing group**, click the **Watch Window** button. Then click **Add Watch**. Confirm that cell D6 in the Goals worksheet displays in the **Add Watch** dialog box, and then click **Add**. Confirm that cell D6 is selected in the Watch Window.

(Project 11C–Chocolate Sales continues on the next page)

Content-Based Assessments

(Project 11C–Chocolate Sales continued)

12. Click the **Sales sheet tab**, and in cell **D6** type **347.50** and review the result in the **Watch Window** as you press Enter. **Close** the **Watch Window**.

13. Hide the Awards sheet. In the remaining sheets, in the **Left Footer** area, insert the **File Name**, and in the **Right Footer** area, insert the **Sheet Name**. **Center** the worksheets both **Horizontally** and **Vertically** and change to **Landscape Orientation**. **Save** your workbook.

14. Print the worksheets or submit electronically as instructed. **Close** the workbook and **Exit** Excel.

End You have completed Project 11C

Project 11D — Drink Sales

In this project, you will apply the skills you practiced from the Objectives in Project 11B.

Objectives: 4. *Consolidate Workbooks;* **5.** *Share and Merge Workbooks.*

In the following Skills Review, you will create a summary of drink sales by Wild Islands Breezes restaurants during the months of March and April. Maxine Hylton-Pert, the executive chef, has been collecting data for the drink sales for each store for these two months. You will create a summary sheet for all the Jacksonville restaurants that summarizes the drinks sold.

You will also create a shared workbook to be used to collect sales data for April. Your completed worksheets will look similar to those in Figure 11.46.

For Project 11D, you will need the following files:

e11D_Drink_Sales
e11D_Drink_Sales_April

You will save your workbooks as
11D_Drink_Sales_Firstname_Lastname
11D_Drink_Sales_Merged_Firstname_Lastname
Copy (1)11D_Italian_Soda_Drink_Sales_April_Firstname_Lastname

Figure 11.46

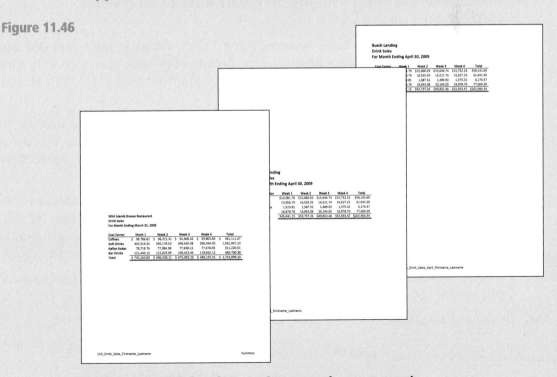

(Project 11D–Drink Sales continues on the next page)

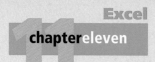
(Project 11D–Drink Sales continued)

1. **Start** Excel and open the **e11D_Drink_Sales** file and **Save** it in your **Excel Chapter 11** folder with the name 11D_Drink_Sales_Firstname_Lastname

2. Click the **Insert Worksheet button** and move the new worksheet so it is the first sheet of the workbook. Rename **Sheet1** to Summary Group the **Summary** and **Busch Landing** worksheets and display the **Busch Landing sheet**. Select the range of the worksheet—**A1:F10**. On the **Home tab**, in the **Editing group**, click the **Fill** button, and then click **Across Worksheets**. In the **Fill Across Worksheets** dialog box, confirm **All** is selected, and then click **OK**.

3. **Ungroup** sheets and in the **Summary sheet**, delete the data in the range **B6:E9**. In cell **A1**, type Wild Islands Breeze Restaurant Adjust the width of **column A** to fully display the row titles.

4. Click the **Busch Landing sheet tab** and select the range of the data—**B6:F10**. Click the **Formulas tab**, and in the **Defined Names group**, click **Define Name**. In the **New Name** dialog box, in the **Name** box, type Busch_Landing and click **OK**.

5. Using the skills you practiced, define the name of the data ranges for the Lane Avenue, Race Track, Atlantic Mall, and Old Augustine worksheets.

6. Click the **Summary sheet tab** and click cell **B6**. On the **Data tab**, in the **Data Tools group**, click the **Consolidate** button and confirm that the displayed function is **SUM**. At the end of the **Reference section**, click the **Collapse Dialog Box** button, and then click the **Busch Landing sheet tab**. Select the range of the data—**B6:F10**—then click the **Expand Dialog Box** button. In the **Consolidate** dialog box, click **Add**. Using the skills just practiced, add the data from the **Lane Avenue**, **Race Track**, **Atlantic Mall**, and **Old Augustine** sheets.

7. In the **Consolidate** dialog box, click the **Create links to source data** check box, and then click **OK**. Adjust column widths.

8. **Hide** the **Busch Landing**, **Lane Avenue**, **Race Track**, **Atlantic Mall**, and **Old Augustine** worksheets. In the **Summary Sheet**, in the **Left Footer** area, insert the **File Name**, and in the **Right Footer** area, insert the **Sheet Name**. Center the worksheet both **Horizontally** and **Vertically**. **Save** and **Close** your workbook.

9. The drink sales report for the Busch Landing restaurant is missing the data for the Italian Sodas. You will save this workbook as a shared file so it can be merged with the Italian soda data. From your student files, open the file named **e11D_Drink_Sales_April**. **Save** it in your folder as 11D_Drink_Sales_April_Firstname_Lastname

10. Click the **Review tab** and in the **Changes group**, click the **Share Workbook** button. In the **Share Workbook** dialog box, click **Allow changes by more than one user at the same time**, and then click **OK**. At the **message** dialog box that indicates the action will now save the workbook, click **OK**. Confirm that *Shared* displays in the title bar. **Close** the workbook.

11. From the **Open** dialog box, click **11D_Drink_Sales_April_Firstname_Lastname**. Click the **Open arrow** and click **Open as Copy**.

12. Beginning in cell **B8**, enter the data below for Italian soda sales:

Italian Sodas	1523.81	1587.32	1489.93	1575.31

(Project 11D–Drink Sales continues on the next page)

Content-Based Assessments

(Project 11D–Drink Sales continued)

13. From the **Office** menu, click **Save As** and name the workbook **Copy (1)11D_Italian_Soda_Drink_Sales_April_Firstname_Lastname** and click **Save**. Then **Close** the workbook.

14. **Open** the **11D_Drink_Sales_April_Firstname_Lastname** file.

15. If the **Compare and Merge Worksheets** button is not on the **Quick Access Toolbar**, do the following: Click the **Office** button, and at the bottom click **Excel Options**. In the **Customize** category, in the **Choose commands from list**, click **All Commands**. In the list, click **Compare and Merge Workbooks**, click the **Add** button, and then click **OK**.

16. In the **Quick Access Toolbar**, click the **Compare and Merge Workbooks** button. In the **Select Files to Merge Into Current Workbook** dialog box, from your **Excel Chapter 11** folder, click the **Copy (1)11D_Italian_Soda_Drink_Sales_April_Firstname_Lastname** file, and then click **OK**.

17. In the **Left Footer** area, insert the **File Name**. Center the worksheet both **Horizontally** and **Vertically** and change to **Landscape** orientation.

18. **Save** the workbook and name it **11D_Drink_Sales_Merged_Firstname_Lastname** Recall that a warning box may display indicating you have corrupted content. Click **OK** and save your file.

19. **Delete** the workbooks saved as **11D_Italian_Soda_Sales_Firstname_Lastname**, **11D_Drink_Sales_April_Firstname_Lastname**, and **Copy (1)11D_Drink_Sales_April_Firstname_Lastname**.

20. **Print** the **11D_Drink_Sales_Firstname_Lastname**, **11D_Drink_Sales_Merged_Firstname_Lastname**, and **Copy (1)11D_Italian_Soda_Drink_Sales_Firstname_Lastname** workbooks. If you submit your work electronically, follow the directions of your instructor. **Close** the workbooks and **Exit** Excel.

 You have completed Project 11D _____

Content-Based Assessments

Project 11E — Tropical Promotion

In this project, you will apply the skills you practiced from the Objectives in Project 11A.

Objectives: 1. *Nest One Function within Another;* **2.** *Use 3-D References and Nested Lookups;* **3.** *Check Accuracy with Excel's Auditing Tools.*

In the following Mastering Excel project, you will nest functions and use auditing tools. Wild Islands Breeze restaurants feature tropical items during the month. Chef Maxine Hylton-Pert has developed special recipes and has promoted these items. After sales for each week are received, Maxine will send a certificate to the restaurants that have met the sales goal, decide which restaurants will get special advertising on the Web, and set goals for the next week. You will prepare this information for Maxine.

Your completed worksheets will look similar to those in Figure 11.47.

For Project 11E, you will need the following file:

e11E_Tropical_Promo

You will save your workbook as
11E_Tropical_Promo_Firstname_Lastname

Figure 11.47

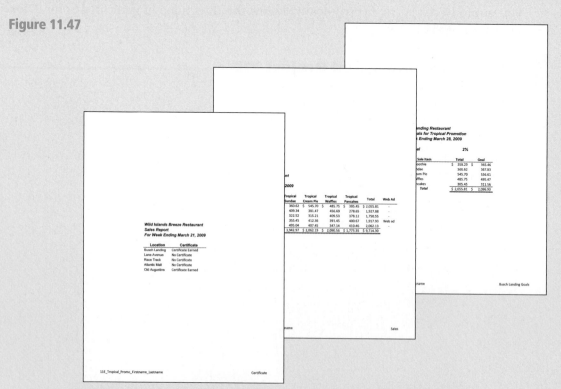

(Project 11E–Tropical Promotion continues on the next page)

Content-Based Assessments

(Project 11E–Tropical Promotion continued)

1. **Start** Excel and from the student files open **e11E_Tropical_Promo** and **Save** it in the **Excel Chapter 11** folder with the name **11E_Tropical_Promo_Firstname_Lastname** This worksheet displays the combined sales of tropical menu items for a week.

2. If a branch sells a total of $2,000 of the featured tropical menu items in a week, the branch will be awarded a framed certificate to display in the restaurant. To the left of the **Sales sheet**, click in the **Certificate sheet**, click in cell **B6** and insert an **IF** function. With the insertion point in the **Logical_test** text box, click in the **Busch Landing sheet tab** and click cell **B12**. Press F4 and type **>2000** and press Tab.

3. In the **Value_if_true** text box, type **"Certificate Earned"** and in the **Value_if_false** text box, type **"No Certificate"** and then click **OK**.

4. **Copy** the formula through cell **B10**, and then edit each formula so that it refers to the correct worksheet name. Only the Old Augustine restaurant earned the certificate.

5. Click the **Sales sheet tab**. Click cell **H5** and type **Web Ad** and format it like cell **G5**. If the sales total for each tropical menu item at a location are over $350, an advertisement for that store will be added to the Web site for the next week.

6. Click cell **H6** and insert an **IF** function. With the insertion point in the **Logical_test** text box, in the **Name** box, access the **AND** function.

7. In the **AND Function Arguments** dialog box, in the **Logical1** text box, type **b6>350** and press Tab. In the **Logical2** text box, type **c6>350** Continue adding the logical argument for cells **D6:F6** to be greater than 350.

8. On the **Formula Bar,** click the **IF** to access the IF function dialog box. In the **Value_if_true** text box, type "**Web ad**" and in the **Value_if_false** text box, type **"-"** Click **OK** and copy the formula through cell **H10**. **Center** the range **H6:H10**. Only the Atlantic Mall sales were high enough for the Web ad.

9. The Busch Landing manager has set a sales goal of a 2% increase for the next week of the tropical sale. Click the **Busch Landing Goals sheet**—the last worksheet. Notice the amounts in **column B** are linked to the Sales sheet. Change cell **A2** to read **Busch Landing Sales Goals** There are errors in some of the formulas. Click cell **C8** and **Trace Precedents**. Click cell **C9** and **Trace Precedents**. Continue tracing precedents for the formulas in **column C** until you see the error in the formula. Correct the formula in cell **C8** and copy it down the column. Complete the worksheet and format the numbers in column C as they are formatted in column B. Remove all arrows.

10. Click cell **B10** and add this cell to a Watch Window. Click the **Sales sheet tab**, and change the amount for **Tropical Cream Pie** sold at **Busch Landing** to 545.70. Notice the change in the Watch Window as you press Enter. **Close** the Watch Window.

11. **Hide** the individual location sheets. You will have three sheets remaining and arranged in this order—**Certificate, Sales,** and **Busch Landing Goals**. In all worksheets, in the **Left Footer** area, insert the **File Name**, and in the **Right Footer** area, insert the **Sheet Name**, center the worksheets both **Horizontally** and **Vertically** and **Fit to page**. **Save** your workbook.

12. **Print** the worksheets or submit electronically as instructed. **Close** the workbook and then **Exit** Excel.

End You have completed Project 11E

Project 11F—Hours

In this project, you will apply the skills you practiced from the Objectives in Project 11B.

Objectives: 4. *Consolidate Workbooks;* **5.** *Share and Merge Workbooks.*

In the following Mastering Excel project, you will report the hours worked for the month for the employees of the Lane Avenue Wild Islands Breeze Restaurant. The hours are reported on weekly worksheets and will be shared and consolidated into the monthly report. Your completed worksheets will look similar to those in Figure 11.48.

For Project 11F, you will need the following files:

e11F_Hours
e11F_May2_Hours

You will save your workbooks as
11F_Hours_Firstname_Lastname
11F_May2_Hours_Firstname_Lastname

Figure 11.48

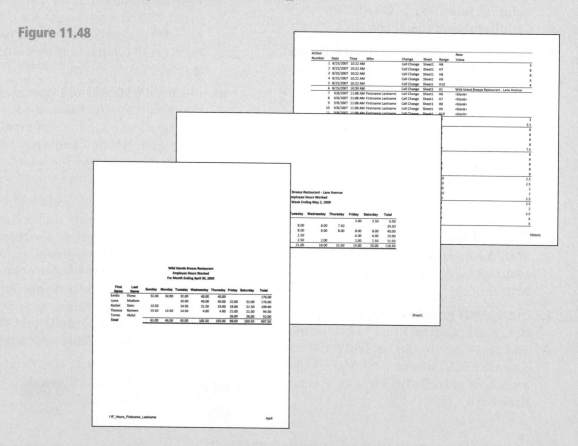

(Project 11F–Hours continues on the next page)

Excel

chaptereleven | Mastering Excel

(Project 11F–Hours continued)

1. **Start** Excel. Locate and open **e11F_Hours** and save it in your **Excel Chapter 11** folder as 11F_Hours_Firstname_Lastname

2. Click the **Insert Worksheet** button and move the worksheet so it is the first sheet of the workbook. Rename the sheet **April** Use **Fill Across Worksheets** to copy the data from a weekly sheet to the **April sheet**. In the **April sheet**, delete only the hourly data and not the formulas for the totals. Edit cell **A3** to read **For Month Ending April 30, 2009**

3. The employee names in the rows in the weekly report sheets are not in the same order. In the **April sheet**, **alphabetize** the names by **last name**. From the weekly sheets, name the data range—**B5:I10**—to match the sheet name, omitting the space—**Week1**, **Week2**, etc.

4. In the **April sheet**, click cell **B5**. Display the **Consolidate** dialog box to sum data by category. In the **Reference** box, type **Week1** and then click **Add**. Using the skills you have practiced, add the other named ranges.

5. Click the **Top row** and **Left column** check boxes, and then click **OK**. Adjust column widths. **Hide** all worksheets except the **April sheet**. In the **Left Footer**, insert the **File Name**, and in the **Right Footer**, insert the **Sheet Name**. Center the worksheet both **Horizontally** and **Vertically**. Confirm that the employee first and last names are correct—Emilio Florez, Lyssa Madison, Rachel Stein, Therese Romero, and Tomas Abdul. Recall that the labels used for consolidating the data are the last names and that the first names were not part of the consolidation range. **Save** your workbook.

6. From your student files, open the file named **e11F_May2_Hours**. Save it in your **Excel Chapter 11** folder as 11F_May2_Hours_Firstname_Lastname Notice it is a shared workbook.

7. Beginning in cell **C9**, enter the data below for Theresa Romero. When you have completed the hours, **Save** the workbook.

Last Name	Sunday	Monday	Tuesday	Wednesday	Thursday	Friday	Saturday
Romero	2.5	2	2.5			6	6

8. Track the changes and create a History sheet. **Hide** all worksheets except the **April sheet**.

9. In the **Left Footer** area, insert the **File Name**. Center the worksheets both **Horizontally** and **Vertically**, change to **Landscape Orientation**, and **Fit to page**. **Print** the **History sheet**.

10. Print your workbooks or submit electronically as instructed. **Save** and **Close** the workbooks and **Exit** Excel.

 End You have completed Project 11F ————————————————

Content-Based Assessments

Project 11G—Beverage Contest

In this project, you will apply the skills you practiced from the Objectives in Projects 11A and 11B.

Objectives: 1. *Nest One Function within Another;* **2.** *Use 3-D References and Nested Lookups.*

In the following Mastering Excel project, you will complete the results of a contest for introducing new beverages. Wild Islands Breeze is promoting beverages of all types—coffee, alcoholic, and fruit beverages. They have established a contest in their restaurants in two states—Georgia and Florida. Each entrant is awarded a cash bonus for developing the recipe, but the amounts of the rewards differ in each state. In this project, you will nest functions to determine the cash bonus for each participant. Your completed worksheets will look similar to those in Figure 11.49.

For Project 11G, you will need the following file:

e11G_Beverage_Contest

You will save your workbook as
11G_Beverage_Contest_Firstname_Lastname

Figure 11.49

Wild Islands Breeze
Beverage Contest Results
July 15, 2009

First Name	Last Name	Location Name	Street Address	City	State	Postal Code	Beverage Name	Type	Reward
Dorothy	Cullens	Newton Court	1074 Newton Court	Atlanta	GA	30331	Caribbean Coffee	Coffee	$ 100
Rebecca	Foster	Pelican Pointe	21 Pelican Pointe	Atlanta	GA	30303	Mango Margarita	Alcohol	95
Benjamin	Medina	Brooksville	8000 West Orange	Brooksville	FL	34601	A Day At The Beach	Alcohol	90
Forest	Jones	Conquest	463 Conquest Boulevard	Crystal River	FL	34429	Banana Colada	Alcohol	90
Vincent	Hays	University	3562 University Avenue	Cutler Bay	FL	33189	Green Iguana Margarita	Alcohol	90
Bill	Estes	Evans	94 West 102nd Street	Evans	GA	30809	Three Alarm Coffee	Coffee	100
Seth	Santiago	Old Augustine	11345 Old Saint Augustine	Jacksonville	FL	32258	Cool Breeze Tea	Alcohol	90
Peggy	Hardin	Lane Avenue	475 Lane Avenue South	Jacksonville	FL	32205	Pineapple Mojito	Alcohol	90
Kelly	Cook	Race Track	1499 Race Track Road	Jacksonville	FL	32259	Three Fruit Smoothie	Fruit	75
Nathan	Garcia	Shining Moss	34 Shining Moss Road	Lake Mary	FL	32746	South Beach Ice Tea	Alcohol	90
Shirley	Forward	Elm	1001 Elm Street	Melbourne	FL	32934	Beachcomber Smoothie	Fruit	75
Susann	Mitche	Moultrie	500 Shining Court	Moultrie	GA	31768	Pineapple Guava Smoothie	Fruit	75
Amanda	Hicklin	Bash Road	70712 Bash Road	Oldsmar	FL	34677	Caribbean Romance	Alcohol	90
Frank	Cho	Visionary Way	1744 Visionary Way	Oldsmar	FL	34677	Florida Tropical Storm	Alcohol	90
Celestine	Jones	Donec Palm Beach	5676 Donec Road	Palm Beach Gardens	FL	33403	Pink Flamingo	Alcohol	90
Alina	Shelton	Spring Hill	1485 Sagittis Street	Spring Hill	FL	34606	Blueberry Blitz Smoothie	Fruit	75
Justin	Bott	West Fifth	24 West Fifth	St. Petersburg	FL	33710	Acapulco Zombie	Coffee	50

11G_Beverage_Contest_Firstname_Lastname

Beverage

(Project 11G—Beverage Contest continues on the next page)

(Project 11G–Beverage Contest continued)

1. **Start** Excel. From the student files, locate and open the file named **e11G_Beverage_Contest** and **Save** it in your **Excel Chapter 11** folder as **11G_Beverage_Contest_Firstname_Lastname** Right-click cell **D10** and click the **Format Painter** button. **Select** the range **D11:D22** to copy the format. On both sheets, in the **Left Footer**, insert the **File Name** and in the **Right Footer**, insert the **Sheet Name**.

2. Click the **Contest sheet tab** and beginning in cell **A4**, enter the following data. Recall that when using a lookup function you must arrange text in alphabetical order.

	FL	GA
Alcohol	90	95
Coffee	50	100
Fruit	75	75

3. On the **Formulas tab**, in the **Define Names group**, click the **Name Manager** and confirm the range **A5:C7** has been named **results** Then close the **Name Manager** dialog box.

4. On the **Beverage sheet** in column J, enter a formula that will result in listing the award in the column. The award will depend on the type of beverage and the store location. You will nest two lookup functions into an IF function. In cell **J5**, type **Reward** and format it like cell **I5**.

5. Click cell **J6** and insert an **IF** function. In the **Logical_test**, type **f6="GA"** In the **Value_if_true** text box, insert a **VLOOKUP**

function. In the **VLOOKUP Function Arguments** dialog box, for the **Lookup_value** click cell **I6**. Click in the **Table_array** text box and type **results** In the **Col_index_num** box, type **3** because the Georgia rewards are displayed in the third column of the lookup range.

6. In the **Formula Bar**, click in the **IF** to redisplay the **IF Function Arguments** dialog box. In the **Value_if_false** text box, insert another **IF function**. For the **Logical_test**, use **f6="FL"** In the **Value_if_true** text box, insert a **VLOOKUP** function. Using the skills practiced, use the VLOOKUP function to look up the value in cell **I6**. For the **Table_array**, use the lookup range named **results** If the match is made, return the value found in column **2** for those entrants from Florida. In the **Formula Bar**, click in the second **IF** to redisplay the second **IF Function Arguments** dialog box, and in the **Value_if_false** text box, type **0** The result—*100*—is entered in cell J6.

7. **Copy** the formula through **row 22**. Format cell **J12** with **Accounting Number style** and **no decimals**. Format the rest of the column with **Comma Style** and **no decimals**. Hide the **Contest sheet**.

8. Format the worksheet with **Landscape Orientation**, centered **Vertically** and **Horizontally**, and **Fit to page**. **Save** your workbook.

9. **Print** the worksheet or submit electronically as directed. **Close** the workbooks and **Exit** Excel.

End You have completed Project 11G

Project 11H—Third Quarter Coffee

In this project, you will apply the skills you practiced from the Objectives in Projects 11A and 11B.

Objectives: **4.** *Consolidate Workbooks.*

In the following Mastering Excel project, you will complete the report for the income from coffee beverages during the third quarter of the year. Each restaurant has completed its individual income report which have been combined into one workbook. In this project, you will review the individual income reports and consolidate them into one report. Your completed worksheet will look like Figure 11.50.

For Project 11H, you will need the following file:

e11H_ThirdQ_Coffee

You will save your workbook as
11H_ThirdQ_Coffee_Firstname_Lastname

Figure 11.50

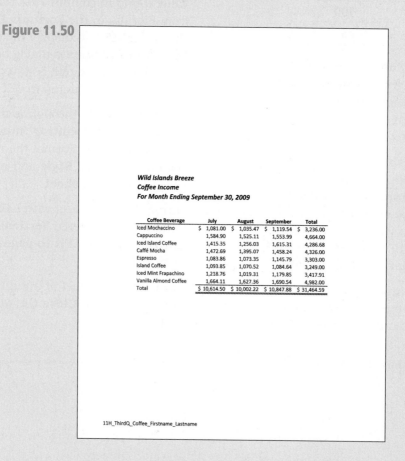

Wild Islands Breeze
Coffee Income
For Month Ending September 30, 2009

Coffee Beverage	July	August	September	Total
Iced Mochaccino	$ 1,081.00	$ 1,035.47	$ 1,119.54	$ 3,236.00
Cappuccino	1,584.90	1,525.11	1,553.99	4,664.00
Iced Island Coffee	1,415.35	1,256.03	1,615.31	4,286.68
Caffé Mocha	1,472.69	1,395.07	1,458.24	4,326.00
Espresso	1,083.86	1,073.35	1,145.79	3,303.00
Island Coffee	1,093.85	1,070.52	1,084.64	3,249.00
Iced Mint Frapachino	1,218.76	1,019.31	1,179.85	3,417.91
Vanilla Almond Coffee	1,664.11	1,627.36	1,690.54	4,982.00
Total	$ 10,614.50	$ 10,002.22	$ 10,847.88	$ 31,464.59

11H_ThirdQ_Coffee_Firstname_Lastname

(Project 11H–Third Quarter Coffee continues on the next page)

Content-Based Assessments

(Project 11H–Third Quarter Coffee continued)

1. **Start** Excel. From the student files, locate and open the file named **e11H_ ThirdQ_Coffee** and **Save** it to your **Excel Chapter 11** folder as **11H_ThirdQ_Coffee_ Firstname_Lastname**

2. Click in each worksheet to review the order of the data and notice that the order is different in each worksheet. You will use the Consolidate by Category method.

3. Insert a new worksheet and name it **Q3 Summary** Click in the **Atlantic Mall sheet tab**, and select the range **A1:A4**. Copy that title to the **Q3 Summary sheet tab**, beginning in cell **A1**. Delete **row 2**.

4. In each of the restaurant worksheets, define the name of the worksheet range, which includes the row and column titles and the totals. Name each range using the same name as the sheet name.

5. Click in the **Q3 Summary sheet tab** and click cell **A6**. Click the **Data tab** and display the **Consolidate** dialog box. Insert the

references required to consolidate all restaurant worksheets into the Q3 Summary sheet. Recall the row titles are not in the same order in all worksheets, so use the labels needed. Be sure to create links and complete the consolidation.

6. Adjust the column widths and **Delete column B**. Confirm that all columns and rows have titles. Format the column titles with **Bold**, **Center**, and a **Bottom Border**. Confirm there is a **Top and Double Bottom Border** at the total row.

7. **Hide** all worksheets except the **Q3 Summary sheet**. In the sheet, in the **Left Footer** area, insert the **File Name**. Center the worksheet both **Horizontally** and **Vertically**.

8. **Print** the Q3 Summary worksheet or submit electronically as directed. **Close** the workbook and **Exit** Excel.

End You have completed Project 11H

Content-Based Assessments

chaptereleven *Excel*

Mastering Excel

Project 11I—Tropical Days

In this project, you will apply all the skills you practiced from the Objectives in Projects 11A and 11B.

Objectives: **1.** *Nest One Function within Another;* **2.** *Use 3-D References and Nested Lookups;* **3.** *Check Accuracy with Excel's Auditing Tools;* **4.** *Consolidate Workbooks;* **5.** *Share and Merge Workbooks.*

In the following Mastering Excel project, you will complete the report of the sales of the Tropical Days specials for a month. Wild Islands Breeze restaurants have been running a summer special of tropical beverages and desserts. They are tracking the sales of these items in order to consider offering them again as a seasonal item or placing them on the permanent menu. You will merge workbooks, consolidate workbooks, and use nested functions to evaluate the sales of the tropical menu items. You will use error-checking features to help evaluate the work. Your completed workbook will look similar to Figure 11.51.

For Project 11I, you will need the following files:

e11I_Tropical_Busch
e11I_Tropical_Sales_Summary

You will save your workbook as
11I_Tropical_Sales_Summary_Firstname_Lastname
Copy (1)11I_Tropical_Busch_Wk4_Firstname_Lastname

Figure 11.51

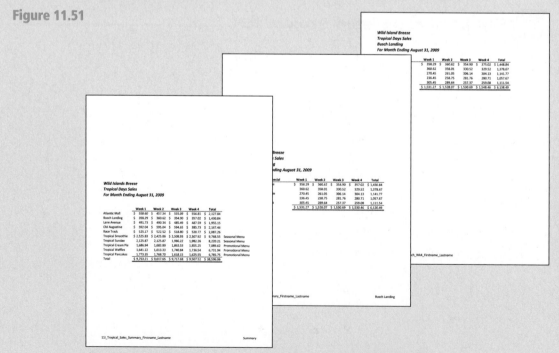

(Project 11I—Tropical Days continues on the next page)

(Project 11I–Tropical Days continued)

1. **Start** Excel. From your student files, open the file named **e11I_Tropical_Busch** and **Save** the workbook in your **Excel Chapter 11** folder with the name **11I_Tropical_Busch_Firstname_Lastname**

2. The Busch Landing restaurant has had a change in personnel and found that their data was entered in different workbooks. You will use the Compare and Merge Workbooks command to place the data on one workbook. On the **Review tab**, click the **Share Workbook** button. In the **Share Workbook** dialog box, click **Allow changes by more than one user**, and then click **OK**. In the **message** box, click **OK**. Notice that *Shared* is indicated in the title bar. **Close** the workbook.

3. Open a copy of **11I_Tropical_Busch_Firstname_Lastname** and beginning in cell **E7**, enter the following data for Week 4:

Tropical Smoothie	357.02
Tropical Sundae	329.52
Tropical Cream Pie	304.13
Tropical Waffles	280.71
Tropical Pancakes	259.08

4. Save the workbook as **Copy (1)11I_Tropical_Busch_Wk4_Firstname_Lastname** and **Close** your workbook.

5. Confirm that you have the **Compare and Merge Workbooks** button available in the Quick Access Toolbar. From the **Open** dialog box, click **Copy (1)11I_Tropical_Busch_Firstname_Lastname**

6. In the **Quick Access Toolbar**, click the **Compare and Merge Workbooks** button. Click the **Copy (1)11I_Tropical_Busch_Wk4_Firstname_Lastname** file and click

OK. The merged workbook displays. Recall that the week 4 data entry was completed at another location. **Save** the workbook as **11I_Tropical_Busch_Firstname_Lastname**

7. Open the workbook named **e11I_Tropical_Sales_Summary** and **Save** it in your **Excel Chapter 11** folder with the name **11I_Tropical_Sales_Summary_Firstname_Lastname** Insert a new sheet at the beginning of the workbook. Name the sheet **Summary**

8. On the **Atlantic Mall sheet**, select the range of the title—**A1:A4**—right-click, and click **Copy**. In the **Summary sheet**, click cell **A1** and **Paste** the title. Delete **row 3**.

9. Display the **11I_Tropical_Busch_Firstname_Lastname** workbook. Right-click the **Sheet1 tab** and click **Move or Copy**. **Copy** the worksheet to the **11I_Tropical_Sales_Summary_Firstname_Lastname** workbook and place it before the **Lane Avenue sheet**. Rename the sheet **Busch Landing**. **Close** the **11I_Tropical_Busch_Firstname_Lastname** workbook.

10. In each of the restaurant worksheets, select the range **A6:F12** and define the name of the range to match the sheet name.

11. Click the **Summary sheet tab** and click in cell **A6**. Display the **Consolidate** dialog box and add the named ranges from the worksheets into the **All references** box. Select the check boxes for **Top row**, **Left column** and **Create links to source data**. Then click **OK**. In the **Summary sheet**, adjust the column widths and **Delete column B**. Format the column titles with **Bold**, **Center**, and **Bottom Border**. In the totals on **row 42**, place a **Top and Double Bottom Border**.

(Project 11I–Tropical Days continues on the next page)

(Project 11I–Tropical Days continued)

12. Click the **Expand Buttons** and in the range **A7:A11**, type the following row titles:

| Atlantic Mall |
| Busch Landing |
| Lane Avenue |
| Old Augustine |
| Race Track |

13. Copy the restaurant names to the rest of the expanded worksheet so there are row titles in all rows. Display the worksheet so only the Tropical Smoothie section is expanded and **Save** the workbook.

14. Add a new worksheet and name it **Menu** In cell **A3**, type **Tropical Items Merge and Center** cells **A3:B3** and format with **Bold**. Beginning in cell **A4**, enter the following data:

0	Drop Item
300	Promotional Menu
400	Seasonal Menu
500	Permanent Menu

15. Adjust column widths. Select the range **A4:B7** and name it **Tropical_Item** Then **Save** your workbook.

16. On the **Summary sheet**, click cell **G12** and display the **VLOOKUP Function Arguments** dialog box. With the insertion point in the **Lookup_value** box, click the **Name box arrow** and insert the **AVERAGE** function. In the **Number1** box, select the range **B7:E11**. In the **Formula Bar**, click **VLOOKUP** and click in the **Table_array** text box. Type **Tropical_Items** For the **Col_index_num**, type **2** and then click **OK**. *Permanent Menu* is entered in cell G12.

17. Copy the formula from cell **G12** through cell **G36**, adjust column widths, and **Save** your workbook.

18. In the **Summary sheet**, click cell **F12**. In the **Formula Auditing group**, click the **Watch Window** button. In the **Watch Window**, click **Add Watch**, and in the **Add Watch** dialog box, click **Add**. Click cell **G12** and add it to the Watch Window.

19. In reviewing the data, it was discovered that there were errors in entering data for the Tropical Smoothie. Make the following corrections and as you do, watch the results in the Watch Window.

Sheet Tab	Week	Change to
Atlantic Mall	2	457.34
Old Augustine	4	385.73

20. The total for Tropical Smoothies is now *$9,768.55* and the menu type is now a *Seasonal Menu*. **Close** the **Watch Window**.

21. Select all worksheets and in the **Left Footer**, enter the **File Name** and in the **Right Footer**, enter the **Sheet Name**. Format the worksheets in **Portrait Orientation**, **Fit to page**, and centered both **Horizontally** and **Vertically**. **Hide** all of the worksheets except the **Summary** and **Busch Landing** worksheets. **Save** your workbook.

22. Delete all workbooks except **11I_Tropical_Sales_Summary_Firstname_Lastname** and **Copy (1)11I_Tropical_Busch_Wk4_Firstname_Lastname**. **Print** the remaining worksheets or submit electronically as directed. **Close** the workbooks and **Exit** Excel.

End **You have completed Project 11I**

Content-Based Assessments

Project 11J — Business Running Case

In this project, you will apply the skills you have practiced from the Objectives in Projects 11A and 11B.

From My Computer, navigate to the student files that accompany this textbook. In the folder **03_business_running_case**, locate and open the folder for this chapter. Open and print the instructions for this project, which are provided to you in Adobe PDF format. Follow the instructions and use the skills you have gained thus far to assist the managers of the Grand Department Store to meet the challenges of keeping records for a large department store.

End You have completed Project 11J _____

Outcomes-Based Assessments

Rubric

The following outcomes-based assessments are *open-ended assessments*. That is, there is no specific correct result; your result will depend on your approach to the information provided. Make *Professional Quality* your goal. Use the following scoring rubric to guide you in *how* to approach the problem and then to evaluate *how well* your approach solves the problem.

The *criteria*—Software Mastery, Content, Format and Layout, and Process—represent the knowledge and skills you have gained that you can apply to solving the problem. The *levels of performance*—Professional Quality, Approaching Professional Quality, or Needs Quality Improvement—help you and your instructor evaluate your result.

	Your completed project is of Professional Quality if you:	Your completed project is Approaching Professional Quality if you:	Your completed project Needs Quality Improvements if you:
1-Software Mastery	Choose and apply the most appropriate skills, tools, and features and identify efficient methods to solve the problem.	Choose and apply some appropriate skills, tools, and features, but not in the most efficient manner.	Choose inappropriate skills, tools, or features, or are inefficient in solving the problem.
2-Content	Construct a solution that is clear and well organized, contains content that is accurate, appropriate to the audience and purpose, and is complete. Provide a solution that contains no errors of spelling, grammar, or style.	Construct a solution in which some components are unclear, poorly organized, inconsistent, or incomplete. Misjudge the needs of the audience. Have some errors in spelling, grammar, or style, but the errors do not detract from comprehension.	Construct a solution that is unclear, incomplete, or poorly organized, containing some inaccurate or inappropriate content; and contains many errors of spelling, grammar, or style. Do not solve the problem.
3-Format and Layout	Format and arrange all elements to communicate information and ideas, clarify function, illustrate relationships, and indicate relative importance.	Apply appropriate format and layout features to some elements, but not others. Overuse features, causing minor distraction.	Apply format and layout that does not communicate information or ideas clearly. Do not use format and layout features to clarify function, illustrate relationships, or indicate relative importance. Use available features excessively, causing distraction.
4-Process	Use an organized approach that integrates planning, development, self-assessment, revision, and reflection.	Demonstrate an organized approach in some areas, but not others; or, use an insufficient process of organization throughout.	Do not use an organized approach to solve the problem.

Project 11K — Jacksonville Employees

In this project, you will construct a solution by applying any combination of the skills you practiced from the Objectives in Projects 11A and 11B.

Shannon Reina, the manager of the Human Resources Department, is evaluating the employee earnings in the Jacksonville restaurants. She has asked that you provide analysis of their hourly wage and their years of service in order to make recommendations about the salary structure.

You will use nested functions to assist Shannon with the evaluation. The data is in the workbook named **e11K_Jacksonville_Employees**. In the Employees worksheet, determine the actual number of years each employee has worked for the restaurant; notice that the date of the worksheet is March 1, 2009. Then use nested functions to determine the following:

- Shannon would like to raise the salaries by 3% for all employees who have worked with the company more than 3 years and are currently earning less than $10.50 an hour. Determine the ending hourly wage for the employees who will get the raise. (*Hint*: You will nest IF and AND functions.)

- Shannon recognizes that the hosts, those who bus tables, and the cooks deserve recognition. She will provide them with an extra $50 in their next paycheck. Use nested functions to determine which employees will receive this bonus.

Use borders, font attributes, and appropriate page orientation to prepare a professional worksheet. If the worksheet prints on more than one page, repeat appropriate row or column titles on each page. Insert a left footer that includes the file name and a right footer that displays the page number. Save the workbook as **11K_Jacksonville_Employees_Firstname_ Lastname** and submit as directed.

End You have completed Project 11K ──────────

Outcomes-Based Assessments

Problem Solving

Project 11L — June Receipts

In this project, you will construct a solution by applying any combination of the skills you practiced from the Objectives in Projects 11A and 11B.

For Project 11L, you will need the following file:

e11L_June_Receipts

You will save your workbooks as
11L_Final_June_Receipts_Firstname_Lastname

In this project, you will use a shared workbook and merge data that reports the receipts for the Jacksonville restaurants for the month of June.

Using the data in the e11L_June_Receipts shared workbook, merge the Busch Landing data into the workbook. The data for Busch Landing follows:

Location	Appetizers	Main Course	Desserts	Beverage/Bar
Busch Landing	40,772.27	169,994.72	37,105.31	60,723.18

Use shared workbooks to prepare the final report for the monthly receipt. Review that the formulas in the final report are correct. Use borders and font attributes to prepare a professional worksheet. Add a footer that includes the file name in the left footer. Save the workbook as **11L_Final_June_Receipts_Firstname_Lastname** and the copy of the file that you used when you merged the workbooks. Submit your work as directed.

End **You have completed Project 11L** ————————

Problem Solving

Project 11M—Dessert Contest

In this project, you will construct a solution by applying any combination of the skills you practiced from the Objectives in Projects 11A and 11B.

For Project 11M, you will need the following file:

e11M_Dessert_Contest

You will save your workbook as
11M_Dessert_Contest_Firstname_Lastname

In this project, you will complete a workbook that displays the rewards that will be distributed as a result of the request for new desserts. Marlin Taylor, the quality assurance manager, has provided an incentive for the chefs to develop new desserts. They will receive cash awards for their efforts.

You will use nested functions to determine the awards that the dessert chefs will receive. There are four dessert categories—cake, frozen desserts, pie, and other desserts. The amount of the reward varies according to the location of the restaurant. You will nest a lookup table within an IF function in order to determine the amount of each reward.

Use borders, font attributes, and appropriate page orientation to prepare a professional workbook. Add a footer that includes the file name at the left and sheet name at the right. Save the workbook as **11M_Dessert_Contest_Firstname_Lastname** and submit it as directed.

 End **You have completed Project 11M** ————————

Outcomes-Based Assessments

Problem Solving

Project 11N — Annual Sales

In this project, you will construct a solution by applying any combination of the skills you practiced from the Objectives in Projects 11A and 11B.

For Project 11N, you will need the following file:

e11N_Annual_Sales

**You will save your workbook as
11N_Annual_Sales_Firstname_Lastname**

In this project, you will complete a workbook that displays the annual sales for Wild Islands Breeze. The quarterly reports have been completed and you will consolidate the data into an annual sales worksheet. Use borders, font attributes, and appropriate page orientation to prepare a professional workbook. Add a footer that includes the file name at the left and the sheet name at the right. Save the workbook as **11N_Annual_Sales_Firstname_Lastname** and submit it as directed.

End **You have completed Project 11N** ————————

Problem Solving

Project 11O—Days Worked

In this project, you will construct a solution by applying any combination of the skills you practiced from the Objectives in Projects 11A and 11B.

For Project 11O, you will need the following file:

e11O_Days_Worked

You will save your workbook as
11O_Days_Worked_Firstname_Lastname

In this project, you will complete a workbook that identifies the awards earned for days worked. The Jacksonville restaurants have had unusual absences during the previous quarter. The managers of the Atlantic Mall and Busch Landing restaurants would like to reward the servers who work steadily during this quarter. The worksheet is prepared that reports the days worked in each of the three months. You will use nested IF functions to determine the awards earned.

The goal for January is to work 18 days or more during the month; the goal for February is 20 days or more during the month; and the goal for March is 22 days or more during the month. If the server works the suggested number of days and is employed at the Atlantic Mall or Busch Landing restaurant, indicate YES in the rewards area for each month.

For the Total, all employees will earn a bonus depending on the average number of days they worked. If the average days worked is at least 18 days a month, they will earn $25; if the average is at least 21 days, they will earn $50; if the average is at least 23 days, they will earn $75; and if the average is at least 25 days, they will earn $100.

Use borders, and font attributes to prepare a professional workbook. Add a footer that includes the file name, delete the unused sheets, and hide any sheets that have lookup information. Adjust column widths so the worksheet prints on one page. Save the workbook as **11O_Days_Worked_Firstname_Lastname** and submit it as directed.

End You have completed Project 11O ——————————

Outcomes-Based Assessments

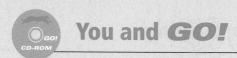
Project 11P—You and *GO!*

In this project, you will construct a solution by applying any combination of the Objectives found in Projects 11A and 11B.

From My Computer, navigate to the student files that accompany this textbook. In the folder **04_you_and_go**, locate and open the folder for this chapter. Open and print the instructions for this project, which are provided to you in Adobe PDF format. Follow the instructions to create a worksheet that merges workbooks with a classmate's.

End You have completed Project 11P ————————————

GO! with Help

Project 11Q—*GO!* with Help

Businesses are sharing workbooks and workspace to complete many of their day-to-day projects, which enables collaboration on many work projects. In this *GO!* with Help, you will review sharing and collaboration techniques available with Excel.

1 **Start** Excel and confirm that you are connected to the Internet. Click the **Microsoft Office Excel Help** button.

2 In the search box, type **shared workbooks** and then press [Enter]. Locate and click **Overview of sharing and collaborating on Excel data**.

3 Review the articles available on **Using Excel Services to share data while maintaining one version of the workbook**, **Collaborating on workbooks on a document management server**, and **Distributing data through e-mail, by fax, or by printing**.

4 When you are finished, **Close** the Help window and then **Exit** Excel.

End You have completed Project 11Q ————————————

chaptertwelve

Working with Data Tables, Scenarios, Solver, XML, and the Document Inspector

OBJECTIVES

At the end of this chapter you will be able to:

OUTCOMES

Mastering these objectives will enable you to:

1. Create a Data Table
2. Create a Scenario
3. Use Solver

PROJECT 12A

Complete What-If Analysis to Evaluate Worksheet Data Using Data Tables, Scenarios, and Solver

4. Prepare a Document for Distribution
5. Use XML to Enhance Security

PROJECT 12B

Prepare Documents for Distribution and Use XML to Improve Document Security

Image Medtech

Located in the northern part of the greater New York metropolitan area, Image Medtech develops, manufactures, and distributes medical imaging equipment for the diagnosis and research of conditions and diseases. The equipment records images and also processes and stores them and provides a means for printing and distributing them electronically. The company is a leader in state-of-the-art, noninvasive diagnostic methods such as measurement of body temperature and blood flow. The company's products are used in a variety of health-care environments, including hospitals, doctors' and dentists' offices, imaging centers, and pharmaceutical companies.

Working with Data Tables, Scenario, Solver, XML, and the Document Inspector

In addition to maintaining financial records, businesses use Excel for "what-if" analysis of business situations. What-if analysis is a process of changing the values in cells to see how those changes affect the outcome of formulas on a worksheet. A data table can evaluate the results of changing one or two variables in a financial formula. A scenario is a set of values that can be substituted into the original formula to help forecast results. Solver, an Excel add-in, works with a group of related cells and adjusts the values in the changing cells to produce a specific result. When information is shared with people outside of a company, it is important to remove proprietary information and data, which can be done using the Document Inspector and XML.

Project 12A **Analysis Tools**

In Activities 12.1 through 12.7, you will use what-if analysis tools to review the interest rates for a loan and the requirements for a loan for starting up manufacturing a piece of equipment and to determine the manufacturing goals for the year. Your completed worksheet will look similar to Figure 12.1.

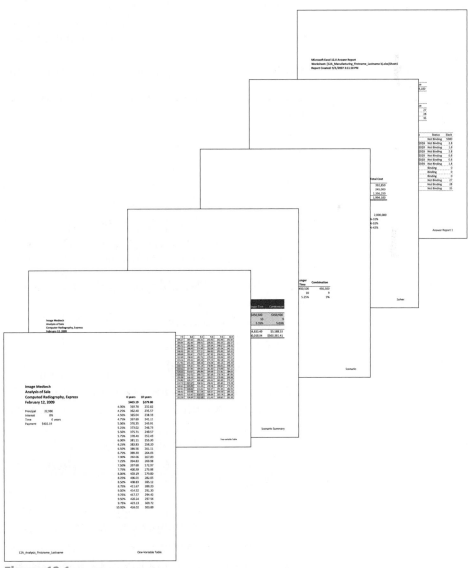

Figure 12.1
Project 12A—Analysis Tools

Objective 1
Create a Data Table

What-if analysis is a process of changing the values in cells to see how those changes affect the outcome of formulas on the worksheet. Data tables are part of a suite of commands that are called what-if analysis tools. A **data table** is a range of cells that shows how changing certain values in your formulas affects the results of the formulas. Data tables provide a shortcut for calculating multiple versions in one operation and a way to view and compare the results of all the different variations together on your worksheet.

Depending on the number of variables you want to test, you can create one-variable or two-variable data tables. A **one-variable data table** uses one variable with one or more formulas. For example, to show how a change in interest rates would affect a loan, you could use a one-variable data table to show the interest paid over the term of the loan. A **two-variable data table** uses two variables and one formula. You would use a two-variable data table to display the effect of different interest rates and different loan terms on the payment required to purchase medical equipment.

Activity 12.1 Creating a One-Variable Data Table

The vice president of marketing, Joel Lieber, is reviewing the sale of computed radiography machines to a local hospital. The hospital is negotiating the terms of the loan for the machine. In a one-variable data table, the formula must refer to the same cell—called the **input cell**. This is the cell in which each input value from a data table is substituted. In this activity, you will use a one-variable data table to review the results in the sale of the equipment depending on the interest rate.

1 **Start** Excel. From the student files open **e12A_Analysis** and save it in a new **Excel Chapter 12** folder. **Save** the worksheet as **12A_Analysis_Firstname_Lastname**

2 In the **One-Variable Table sheet**, beginning in cell **A2**, enter the following title:

Analysis of Sale
Computed Radiography, Express
'February 12, 2009

3 Beginning in cell **A6**, enter the following data and format the cells in **column A** with **11-point Calibri** font, that is not bold.

Principal	22,996	
Interest	8%	
Time	6	years
Payment		

You have inserted the information known about the radiography machine—the amount of the sale, the expected interest rate, and the length of the loan.

4 Format the four-line title—**A1:A4**—with **Bold** **B** and **14-point font** **11** ▾.

⑤ Click cell **B9**. Click the **Formulas tab** and in the **Function Library group**, click the **Financial button**. In the list, scroll to and click **PMT** to access the **PMT Function Arguments** dialog box. For the **Rate**, click cell **B7** and type **/12**

Recall that the interest rate is expressed as an annual rate and in order to determine a monthly payment, the interest rate needs to be converted to the monthly interest rate by dividing the annual rate by 12.

⑥ Press [Tab] and in the **Nper** text box, click cell **B8** and type ***12**

Recall that the length of the loan—time—will also be expressed by number of months, so multiply the number of years for the loan by 12 months in a year.

⑦ Press [Tab] and in the **Pv** text box, click cell **B6** to insert the purchase price of the equipment into the function. Then click **OK** and in the **Formula Bar**, between the equal sign and PMT, type – and then press [Enter]. The result—*$403.19*—displays in cell **B9**.

Recall that the PMT function reduces the amount of a loan so the result displays as a negative number. Recall also that the the Fv and Type arguments are optional.

⑧ Click cell **G5** and type **4%** and in cell **G6**, type **4.25%** Select the range **G5:G6** and use the fill handle to copy the interest rates down until *10%* displays in cell **G29**. If necessary, format the range with 2 decimals.

These interest rates are the ***input values*** and are the values that will be tested. These values may be either down a column or across a row. You have inserted interest rates in quarter-percent increments from 4 to 10 percent in a column.

⑨ Click cell **H4**. In the **Formulas tab**, in the **Function Library group**, click the **Recently Used button** and from the list that displays, click **PMT**. Enter the same PMT formula that you entered in cell **B9**. Be sure to add a minus sign in the formula so the result is a positive number. Alternatively, type **=B9** to link this formula with the one in cell B9. Click cell **H4** and compare your screen with Figure 12.2.

The formula for the data table is entered in the row above and one cell to the right of the column values.

Figure 12.2

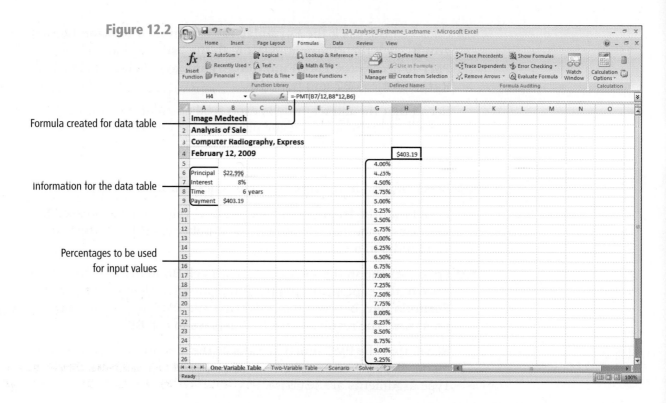

Formula created for data table

Information for the data table

Percentages to be used for input values

10 Select the range **G4:H29**. Then click the **Data tab** and in the **Data Tools group**, click the **What-If Analysis button**. In the list, click **Data Table**, and then compare your screen with Figure 12.3.

The Data Table dialog box displays with areas for the row input cell and the column input cell.

Figure 12.3

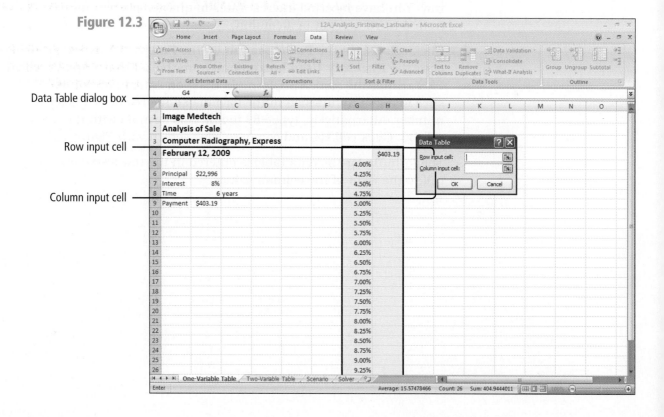

Data Table dialog box

Row input cell

Column input cell

11 Click in the **Column input cell** text box, and then click cell **B7**.

Cell B7 is the input cell—the cell that contains the changing values, which in this case is the interest rate. Because the range of rates that is being considered is in a column, you entered the interest rate from the related formula in the Column input cell box. If the variable—input cell—had been displayed in a row, then the changing value would have been entered in the Row input cell box.

12 Click **OK**. Format the range **H5:H29** with **Comma Style**. Then compare your screen with Figure 12.4.

The values in column H display the amount of the payment at the varying interest rates. To read the table, the monthly payments at 4 percent will be $359.78 and the monthly payments at 7 percent will be $392.06.

Amount of payment at corresponding interest rate

Figure 12.4

Column used for input

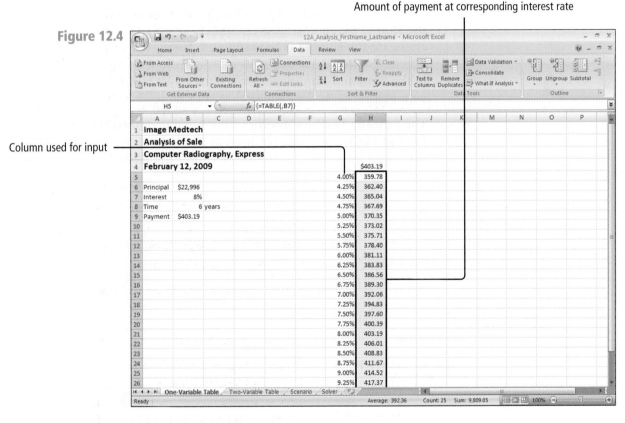

13 **Save** your workbook.

Activity 12.2 Adding a Formula to the One-Variable Data Table

Other formulas can be added to the one-variable data table, but they must refer to the same input cell. Joel would like to consider the payments if the loan were ten years instead of six years. In this activity, you will add a formula to the data table to determine the payments when the loan is for ten years.

1 Click cell **I4**. Using the skills you practiced, enter the PMT function for the loan of the radiography machine. Use the data in the worksheet, changing the length of the loan to ten years. When completing the function, enter the actual time in total number of months—**10*12**—in the Function Arguments dialog box. Then compare your screen with Figure 12.5.

The formula used for another data table is entered into the cell to the right of the existing formula in the top row of the table. The input cell must refer to the same cell in the formula—the interest rate in this case.

Figure 12.5

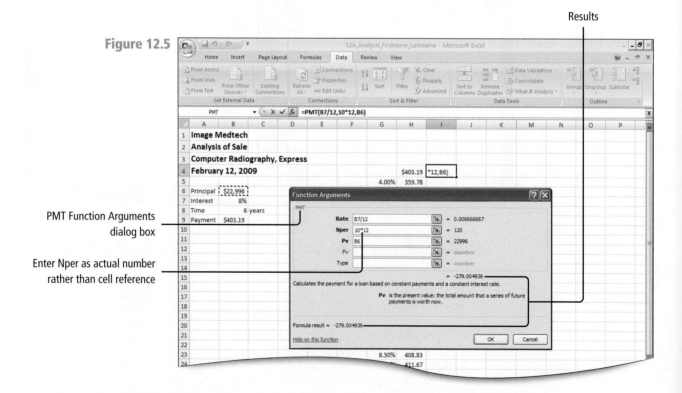

Results

PMT Function Arguments dialog box

Enter Nper as actual number rather than cell reference

2 Click **OK** to calculate a new payment amount for a ten-year loan. Position the insertion point between the equal sign and PMT and type − (a minus sign). Select the range of the data table—**G4:I29**. In the **Data Tools group**, click the **What-If Analysis button**, and then click **Data Table**. In the **Data Table** dialog box, click the **Column input cell**, click cell **B7**, and then click **OK**. Format the numbers in the range **I5:I29** with **Comma Style**.

The payments for the loan are lower because the length of the loan is for a longer period of time.

3 In cell **H3**, type **6 years** and in cell **I3**, type **10 years** Select the range **H3:I4** and format it with **Bold** **B**. Then compare your screen with Figure 12.6.

The first column displays the payments at various interest rates for a six-year loan. The second column displays the payments at various interest rates for a ten-year loan. As management reviews the results of the loan, it is easy to determine the payments at various interest rates for two different lengths of the loan.

Payments if loan is ten years

Figure 12.6

Payments if loan is six years

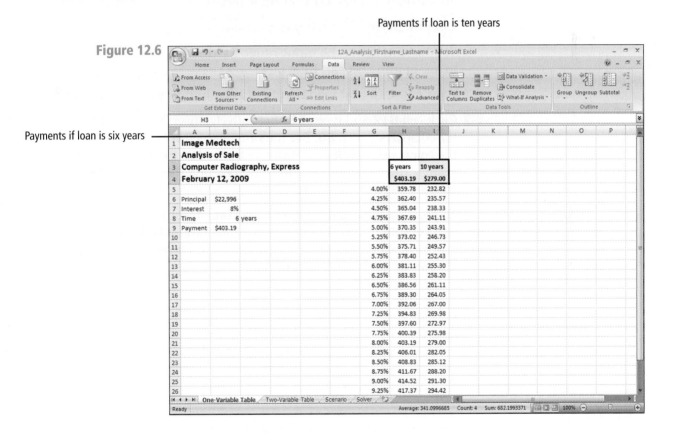

4 **Save** your workbook.

Activity 12.3 Creating a Two-Variable Data Table

As Joel Lieber is negotiating the rates for the radiography machine, he realizes that there are other factors in addition to the interest rates. He would like to evaluate the payments for the machine when both the interest rates and the length of the loan vary. You will create a two-variable data table that will display these results.

1 Group the **One-Variable Table** and **Two-Variable Table sheets**. With the **One-Variable Table** on top, select the range **A1:C9** and on the **Home tab**, in the **Editing group**, click the **Fill button** ⬇▾ and click **Across Worksheets**. In the **Fill Across Worksheets** dialog box, confirm that **All** is selected, and then click **OK**.

2 **Ungroup worksheets** and click the **Two-Variable Table sheet tab**. Click cell **B13** and type **4%** In cell **B14**, type **4.25%** Select cells **B13:B14** and copy down the column until **9%** displays in cell **B33**. Format the numbers for **Percent Style** % with **two decimals**. In cell **A13**, type **Interest** and in cell **A14**, type **Rates** and format the cells with **Bold** B .

You have inserted the input range for the interest rates in quarter-percent increments.

3 Click cell **C12** and type **4** press ⇥Tab and in cell **D12**, type **4.5** Select the range **C12:D12** and use the fill handle to extend the row until *10* and displays in cell **O12**. Format this range with **Bold** B and **Comma Style** , with **one decimal**.

You have inserted the input range for the length of time of the loan in six-month (.5 year) intervals.

4 Click cell **C11** and type **Length of Loan** and format with **Bold** B .

5 Click cell **B12** and type **=B9** Alternatively, insert the same PMT function that displays in cell **B9**. For the rate, use cell **B7** and divide by 12. For the **Nper**, use cell **B8** and multiply by 12. For the **Pv**, use cell **B6**. Display the result as a positive number, and then click **OK**. Compare your screen with Figure 12.7.

To create a two-variable data table, one input range must be located in a column and the second input range must be located in a row. The formula that is used for the tables must reside in the cell that intersects the two input ranges.

Figure 12.7

Row input range

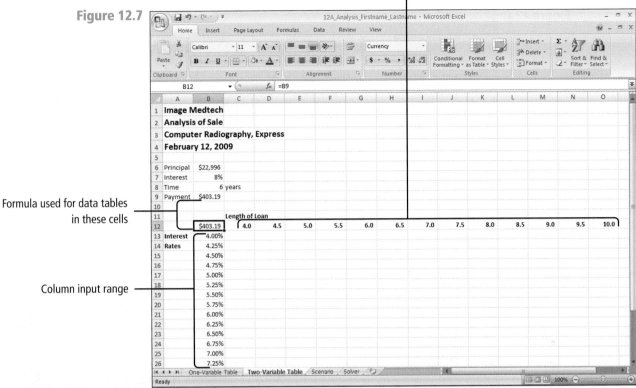

Formula used for data tables in these cells

Column input range

More Knowledge

Inserting the Formula in a Data Table

When the formula used in a data table is displayed in another part of the worksheet, you can link the formulas by using the formula in a cell that equals another cell, such as =b9. When one formula changes, they both change. You need to be cautious when doing this, however, in case you want one of the formulas to change but not both.

6 Select the range of cells that contains the formula and both the row and column of values—the range **B12:O33**. Click the **Data tab** and in the **Data Tools group**, click the **What-If Analysis button**. From the list, click **Data Table**.

7 In the **Data Table** dialog box, in the **Row input cell** text box, click cell **B8**—the cell that displays the number of years of the loan. In the **Column input cell** text box, click cell **B7**—the cell that displays the interest rates for the loan. Then compare your screen with Figure 12.8.

The row input cell—B8—is the cell in the formula that corresponds to the years displayed in row 12. The column input cell—B7— is the cell in the formula that corresponds to the interest rate displayed in column B.

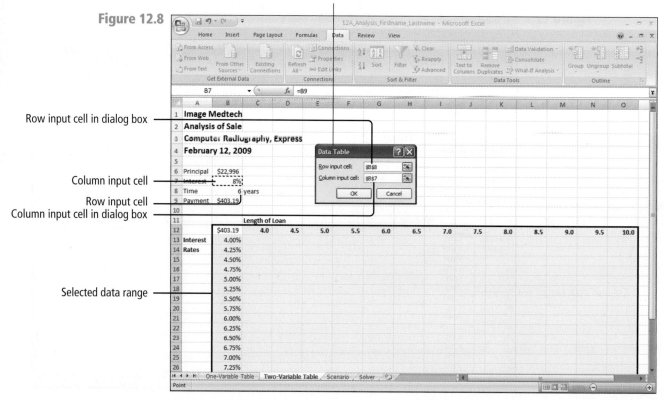

Figure 12.8

Data Table dialog box

Row input cell in dialog box

Column input cell

Row input cell
Column input cell in dialog box

Selected data range

8. In the **Data Table** dialog box, click **OK**. Select the range of the data—**C13:O33**—and format it with **Comma Style** `,`. On the **Home tab**, in the **Font group**, click the **Borders button arrow**, and then click **All Borders**.

9. To read the table, determine the length of the loan and the interest rate. Follow both numbers to the intersection of the row and column. The number is the amount of the payment for that number of years and interest rate. Compare your screen with Figure 12.9.

   The payment for a 7-year loan—column I—at 5.75%—row 20—is $333.19.

Figure 12.9

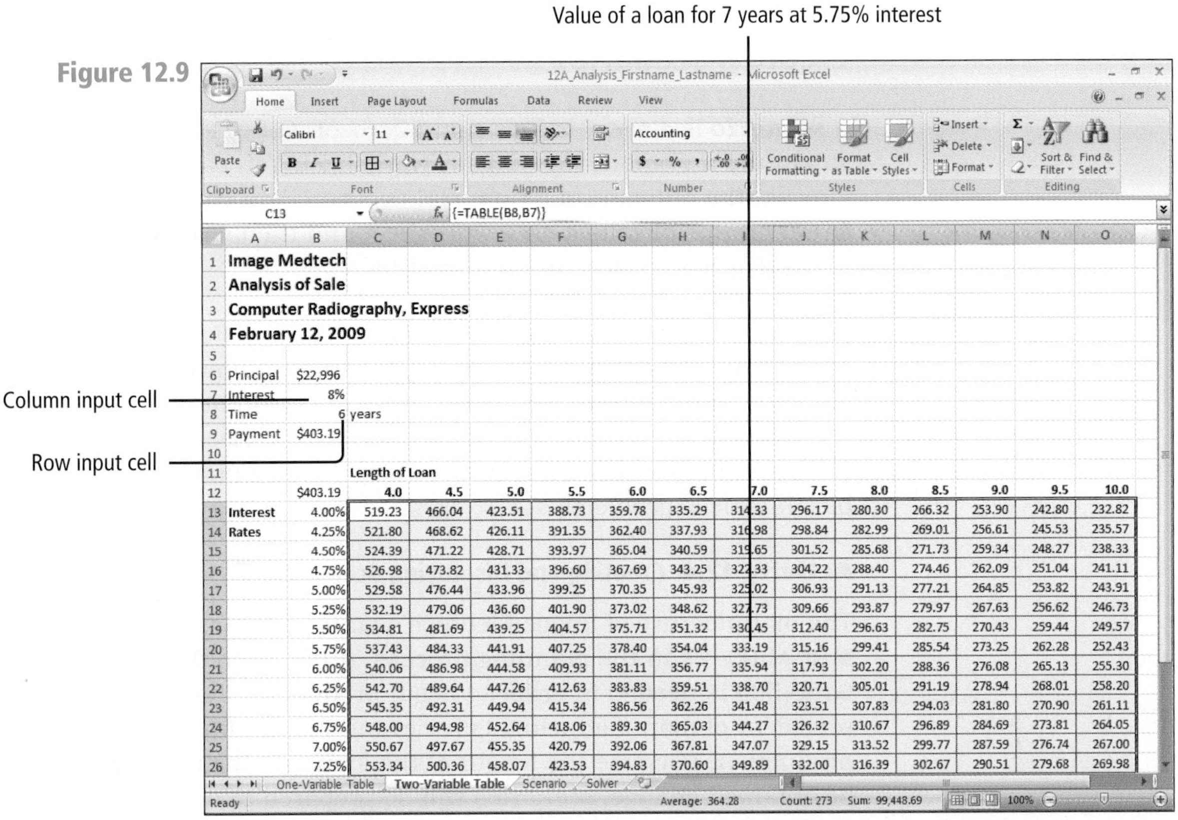

Value of a loan for 7 years at 5.75% interest

Column input cell

Row input cell

10 Joel would like to make payments between $320 and $330 each month. Select cells **I16:I18**—the cells that meet these payment requirements—and in the **Font group**, click the **Fill Color button** and select a **Standard Color** of **Yellow**. Review the data of the data table and highlight all cells that contain the desired amount of payment.

11 **Save** your changes.

More Knowledge

Data Table Calculations

To Speed Up Calculation on a Worksheet with Data Tables

Calculation is the process of computing formulas and then displaying the results as values in the cells that contain the formulas. To avoid unnecessary calculations, Microsoft Office Excel automatically recalculates formulas only when the cells that the formula depends on have changed.

When a worksheet contains data tables, each cell contains a formula that needs to be recalculated. You can speed up the calculation option by skipping the data tables when the rest of the workbook is recalculated.

On the Formulas tab, in the Calculation group, click Calculation Options and from the list, click Automatic Except for Data Tables.

Objective 2
Create a Scenario

A *scenario* is a set of values that Microsoft Office Excel saves and can substitute automatically on your worksheet. You can use scenarios to forecast the outcome of a financial decision. You can create and save different groups of values on a worksheet and then switch to any of these new scenarios to view different results.

Scenarios are useful when the data is uncertain. For instance, in preparing a budget, the firm is forecasting future, unknown data. By using several different amounts for the variables and switching between several scenarios, what-if analysis is easily performed. Because a scenario may contain up to 32 variables, the Scenario feature finds solutions to complex business problems.

Activity 12.4 Creating and Displaying Scenarios

The manufacture of Image Medtech's state-of-the-art MRI machine—the MRI–4500—is in the planning process. It has been determined that $450,500 is needed in order to begin production. Karine Soika, the vice president of manufacturing, is reviewing the funding sources to begin production. Because the length of the loan and the interest rate that can be obtained change, scenarios will be prepared to determine the results with these varying factors. In this activity, you will create scenarios to evaluate the factors for borrowing funds to start production.

1. Click the **Scenario sheet tab**.

   This worksheet displays four possible lending options for Image Medtech. The start-up costs are the same in all four options, but the interest rate and the length of the loan differ. Image Medtech is reviewing the lending options in order to obtain the most beneficial financial position before it begins production.

   When several factors may change—interest rate and length of loan, in this case—it is more difficult to evaluate the data by changing only a cell or two on the worksheet. Therefore, create and use the Scenario feature for evaluating complex business data such as this.

2. Click cell **B10**, and click the **Formulas tab**. In the **Function Library group**, click the **Financial button**, and then from the list, locate and click **PMT**. Complete the function, using the numbers in the range **B6:B8**. For the **Rate**, enter **B8/12** For the **Nper**, enter **B7*12** For the **Pv**, enter **B6** Express the result as a positive number.

3. Click cell **B11** and enter a formula to determine the total amount paid for this loan. Multiply the amount of the payments times the length of the loan times 12—there are 12 payments in a year. Adjust column width if necessary. Format this cell with **Bold** $\boxed{B}$. **Save** $\boxed{}$ your workbook.

   Data for the four other options—scenarios—has been entered on the worksheet. The approved loan is for an 8-year loan at 5.25% interest.

4 Click the **Data tab**, and in the **Data Tools group**, click the **What-If Analysis button**, and then click **Scenario Manager**. Then compare your screen with Figure 12.10.

The Scenario Manager displays and is blank. No scenarios are added.

Figure 12.10

Scenario Manager dialog box

No Scenarios defined

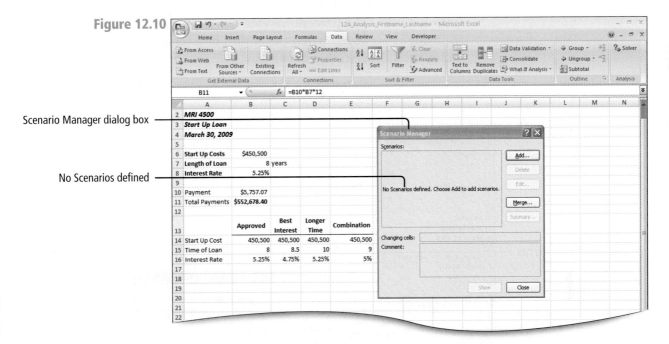

5 In the **Scenario Manager**, click **Add**. Then compare your screen with Figure 12.11.

The Add Scenario dialog box displays the areas needed to complete the scenario. Each scenario will display a name to help identify it. The **Changing cells** are the cells on the original worksheet that contain the estimates; these are the cells that will change when the scenario is completed.

Figure 12.11

Add Scenario dialog box

Scenario name area

Changing cells area

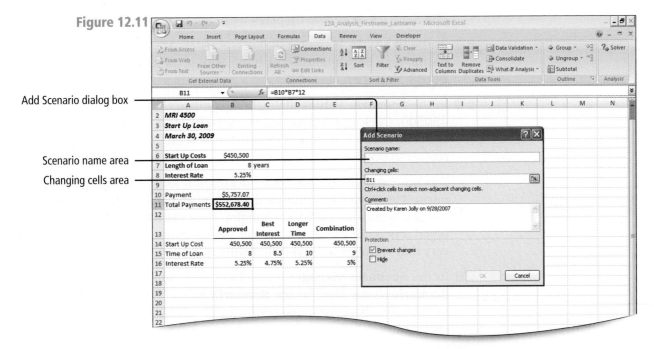

6 In the **Scenario name** text box, type **Approved** In the **Changing cells** text box, select the range **B6:B8**. Under **Protection**, confirm that **Prevent changes** is checked. Click **OK**, and then compare your screen with Figure 12.12.

The Scenario Values dialog box displays with the values of the selected cells. The percentage rate has been changed to a decimal equivalent—0.0525. When the values of a scenario change, you will enter the values in this dialog box.

Values for the scenario

Figure 12.12

Scenario Values dialog box

Cells identified in the scenario

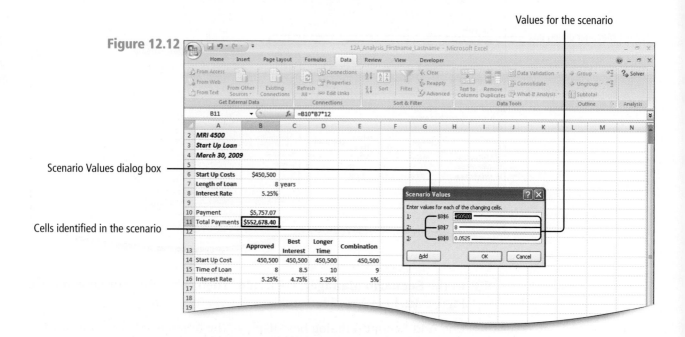

7 Because the numbers for the approved loan are those entered in the worksheet, the values in the Scenario Values dialog box are correct. Click **OK**.

The Scenario Manager displays with one scenario—*Approved*—listed.

8 In the **Scenario Manager** dialog box, click **Add**. For the **Scenario name**, type **Best Interest** and confirm that the **Changing cells** are **B6:B8**, and then click **OK**.

9 In the **Scenario Values** dialog box, confirm that the first number is 450500. Click in the text box to the right of **2:**—$B$7—and type **8.5** the time of the loan in the Best Interest scenario. In the **3:** text box, replace *0.0525* with **4.75%**, and then click **OK**.

You have entered the variable information for the Best Interest scenario. The Scenario Manager dialog box displays with the names of the two scenarios with the changing cells identified. Although you typed a percent into the Scenario Values dialog box, Excel will convert that number to its decimal equivalent.

10 In the **Scenario Manager** dialog box, click **Add**. In the **Add Scenario** dialog box, for the **Scenario name**, type **Longer Time** and for the changing cells, confirm that *B6:B8* displays, and then click **OK**.

11 In the **Scenario Values** dialog box, enter the values of the changing cells for the Longer Time scenario which are listed in cells **D14:D16**. Then compare your screen with Figure 12.13.

Variables entered for the
Longer Time scenario

Figure 12.13

Scenario Values dialog box

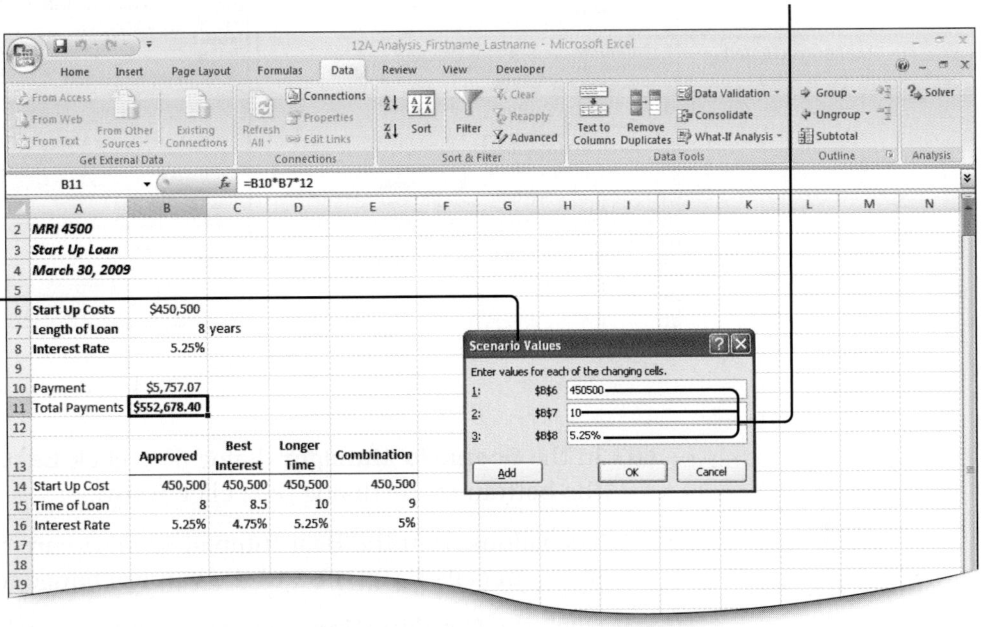

12 Click **OK** to accept that scenario, and then click **Add** to add another. The **Add Scenario** dialog box displays. Using the skills you practiced, enter the data required for the **Combination** scenario, displayed in cells **E14:E16**. Then click **OK** and compare your screen with Figure 12.14.

Four scenarios are entered in the Scenario Manager dialog box, displayed by their names.

Figure 12.14

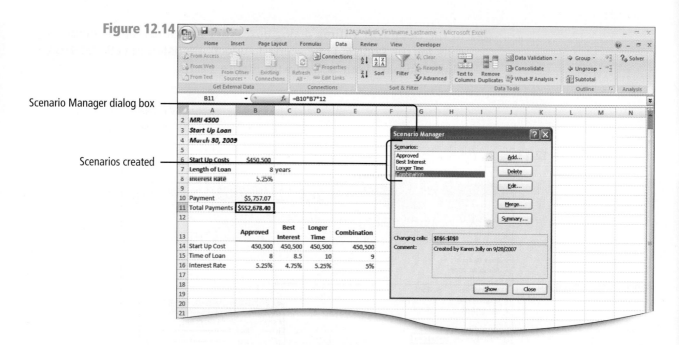

Scenario Manager dialog box

Scenarios created

13 In the **Scenario Manager** dialog box, click **Best Interest** and then at the bottom of the dialog box, click **Show**.

The values from the Best Interest scenario are entered into the worksheet in cells B10:B11 and the values change to reflect this scenario.

14 Click the **Combination** scenario, and then click **Show** to review the results of this scenario. In the **Scenario Manager**, click **Close**, and then **Save** 🖫 your workbook.

Activity 12.5 Creating a Scenario Summary Report

To compare the results of the scenarios in one place, you can create a *Scenario Summary report*—a report that displays the variable information along with the results of several scenarios on the same page. In this activity, you will create the Scenario Summary report for the loan options.

1 On the **Data tab**, in the **Data Tools group**, click the **What-If Analysis** button, and then click **Scenario Manager**.

The Scenario Manager dialog box displays. The scenarios that were created remain with the worksheet.

2 In the **Scenario Manager** dialog box, click **Summary.**

The Scenario Summary dialog box provides two types of summaries— Scenario summary or Scenario PivotTable report.

3 In the dialog box, under **Report type**, confirm that **Scenario summary** is selected. For the result cells, select cells **B10:B11**, and then click **OK**. Compare your screen with Figure 12.15.

The Scenario Summary displays in a new worksheet named *Scenario Summary*. The *result cells*—cells whose values are changed by the scenarios—are also displayed in the Scenario Summary in order to view the results of all the options in one worksheet.

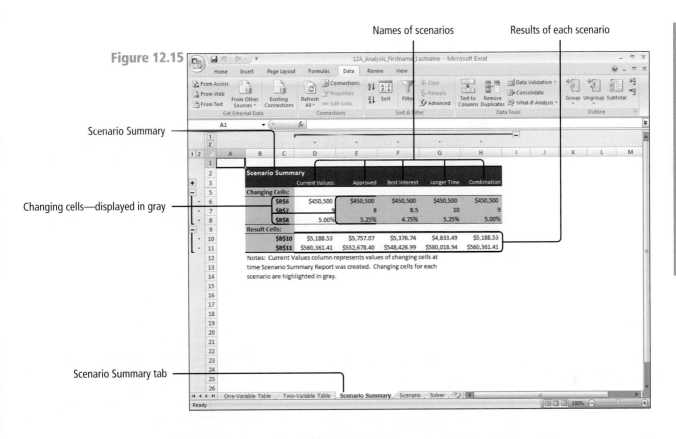

Figure 12.15

Names of scenarios

Results of each scenario

Scenario Summary

Changing cells—displayed in gray

Scenario Summary tab

4 **Select all worksheets** and in the **Left Footer area**, insert the **File Name** and in the **Right Footer area**, insert the **Sheet Name**. Format the worksheets in **Portrait orientation**, **Fit to page**, and centered both **Horizontally** and **Vertically**. **Ungroup** the worksheets. Click the **Two-Variable Table sheet tab** and change the **orientation** to **Landscape**. Confirm that the worksheets are in this order: **One-Variable Table, Two-Variable Table, Scenario Summary**, and **Scenario**.

5 **Save** your workbook. Print the worksheets or submit electronically as instructed and then **Close** the workbook.

Objective 3
Use Solver

Solver is part of the What-If analysis tools of Excel. With **Solver**, you can find an optimal value for a cell on a worksheet. Solver works with a group of cells that are related to the formula and adjusts the values in a group of cells to determine the optimal value. This type of analysis tool is useful for finding minimums or maximums when several variables are involved.

Activity 12.6 Loading Solver

Solver is an **add-in**—a supplemental program that adds custom commands or features—that is available when you install Excel. To use the Solver Add-in, however, you must first load it, which you will do in this activity.

1 From the data files, open **e12A_Solver** and **Save** it to the **Excel Chapter 12** folder named **12A_Solver_Firstname_Lastname**. Click the **Office Button** 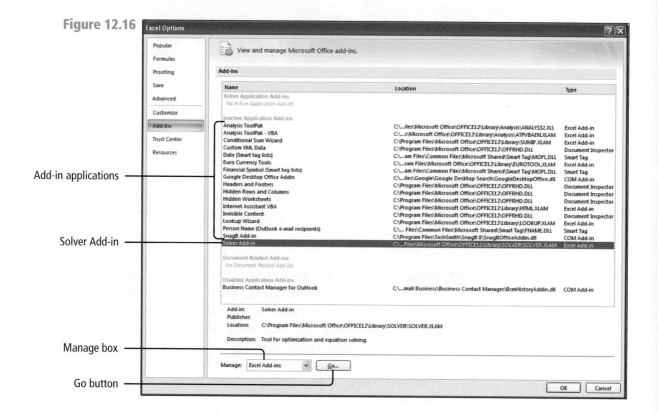 and at the end of the list, click **Excel Options**.

2 From the list on the left, click **Add-Ins**. The **View and manage Microsoft Office add-ins** list displays on the right. Scroll down if necessary to locate and then Click **Solver Add-in**. Compare your screen with Figure 12.16.

Figure 12.16

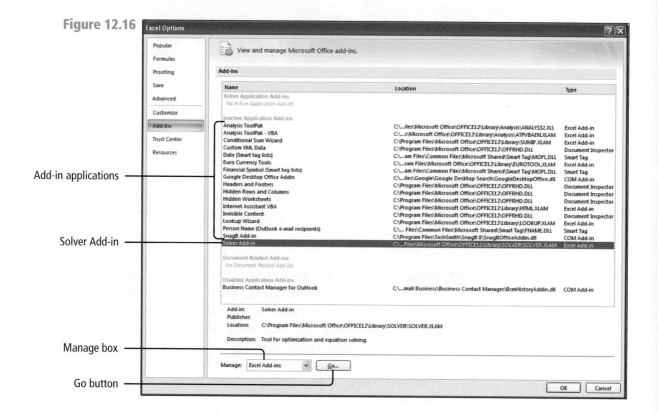

Add-in applications

Solver Add-in

Manage box

Go button

3 Confirm that the **Manage box** displays **Excel Add-ins**, and then click **Go**.

4 In the displayed **Add-Ins** dialog box, in the **Add-Ins available** section, click **Solver Add-in**, and then click **OK**.

The Solver button now displays on the Data tab in the Analysis group.

Alert! **Why doesn't my dialog box display Solver Add-in?**

If the Solver Add-in is not listed in the Add-Ins available list, click browse to locate the add-in. If a message box displays to inform you that the Solver Add-in is not currently installed on your computer, click *Yes* to install it.

---

5 Click the **Data tab**, in the **Analysis group**, click the **Solver button**, and then compare your screen with Figure 12.17.

Figure 12.17

Solver button

Solver Parameters dialog box ————

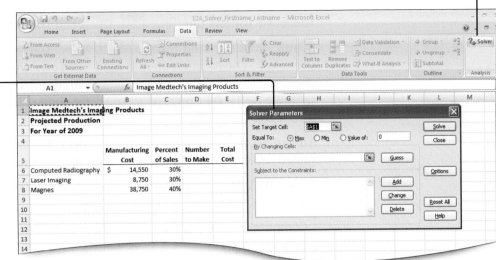

▣ **6** In the **Solver Parameters** dialog box, click **Close** to close Solver. You have successfully installed the add-in.

More Knowledge

To Remove Solver and Other Add-ins

Click the Office button, and then click Excel Options. Click the Add-Ins category. In the Manage box, click Excel Add-Ins, and then click Go. In the Add-Ins dialog box, under the list of available add-ins, clear the check box next to the add-in that you want to remove, and then click OK.

Activity 12.7 Using Solver

Hospitals are increasing their use of high-tech equipment such as the equipment manufactured by Image Medtech manufactures. As this diagnostic equipment is used more frequently, the manufacturing department will increase the number of units made. To meet the demand of the industry and maintain a stock of needed equipment, Karine Soika needs to determine the number of each type of equipment to manufacture during the next year.

Medtech has budgeted $2 million for production costs. In the past, the sales of Magnes, an advanced imaging machine, has been 40 percent of the total number of machines sold, and the computed radiography and laser imaging machines have accounted for 30 percent each of the total number sold.

You will assist Karine by using Solver to determine how many of each machine to manufacture this year to meet the increased demands and stay within the $2 million production budget.

1 In cell **A9**, type **Total Available** Format the cell with **Bold** [B] and **Increase Indent** one time [≔]. Click cell **D9** and in the **Editing group**, click the **SUM button** [Σ ▾]. Select the range **D6:D8**, and then press [Enter]. The formula should read *=SUM(D6:D8)*. In cell **E6**, calculate the Total Cost by multiplying the manufacturing cost by the number to make—**=B6*D6** Copy the formula through cell **E8** and insert a total in cell **E9**.

To use Solver, the formulas in the worksheet first need to be completed, even though there is no data in the worksheet.

2 In cell **B13**, type **Constraints:** Beginning in cell **D13**, type the following:

Total cash available	2,000,000
Computed Radiography	28%-32%
Laser Imaging	28%-32%
Magnes	38%-42%

3 Select the range **D13:D16** and in the **Alignment group**, click the **Align Text Right button** [≡].Widen **column E** to **11.00**.

The ***constraints*** are the restrictions that limit the values that Solver will review. It is good practice to display the constraints on the worksheet as a reminder of the assumptions made when using this model. The constraints should be maintained as a range rather than as an exact number. For instance, the goal is to have 40% of the equipment be the Magnes machine. However, using the exact constraint of 40% limits the results, which may mean a result is unavailable.

4 Click cell **D9**, click the **Data tab** and in the **Analysis group**, click the **Solver button**. Position the **Solver Parameters** dialog box on your screen so that the data on the worksheet is visible, and then compare your screen with Figure 12.18.

In the Solver Parameters dialog box, the active cell is identified in the **Set Target Cell** box. The ***target cell*** is the cell that contains the goal to be achieved. Your goal for Solver is to determine the total number of pieces of equipment to produce within a cost of $2 million.

Figure 12.18

Solver Parameters dialog box ———

Target Cell ———

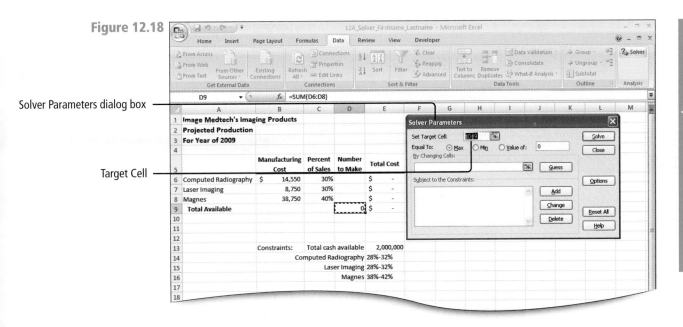

5 In the area next to **Equal To:** confirm that the **Max** option button is selected.

The three option buttons determine if Solver will find the maximum or minimum value or solve for a specific value.

6 Under **By Changing Cells**, click the text box and select the range **D6:D8**. Alternatively, click the Collapse Dialog Box button and select the range **D6:D8**, and then click the **Expand Dialog Box button**. Then compare your screen with Figure 12.19.

The number of each piece of equipment to manufacture will change depending on the results of Solver. Similar to scenarios, the changing cells are the cells that contain the variables that will be changed to achieve the results within the constraints that have been identified. When you can view the range of changing cells, it is not necessary to use the Collapse Dialog Box button to enter the selected range of cells.

Figure 12.19

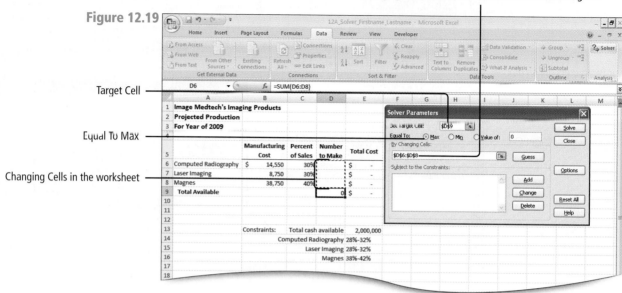

Changing Cells identified in Solver Parameters dialog box

Target Cell

Equal To Max

Changing Cells in the worksheet

7 At the right of the **Subject to the Constraints** text box, click **Add**. In the **Add Constraint** dialog box, in the **Cell Reference** area, select the range **D6:D8**. In the center area—that displays the mathematical operators—click the arrow and select **int**. Confirm that in the **Constraint** box, *integer* displays, and then click **OK**.

8 In the **Solver Parameters** dialog box, click **Add** to display the **Add Constraint** dialog box. In the **Cell Reference**, select the range **D6:D8**, for the mathematical operator, select **>=**, and in the **Constraint** box, type **0**

You have instructed Excel to enter only whole numbers—integers—that are positive—greater than or equal to zero.

9 Click **Add** to add another constraint. For the **Cell Reference**, click cell **E9**. At the right, under **Constraint**, click cell **E13**. Confirm that the mathematical symbols between the two text boxes displays **<=** and compare your screen with Figure 12.20. This constraint limits the total cost to $2 million or less.

When you have a series of constraints to add, you can move directly to the next constraint without redisplaying the Solver Parameters dialog box. Each time you click Add, the boxes are cleared so another constraint can be added.

Figure 12.20

Constraint to limit total cost to $2 million

Add Constraint dialog box

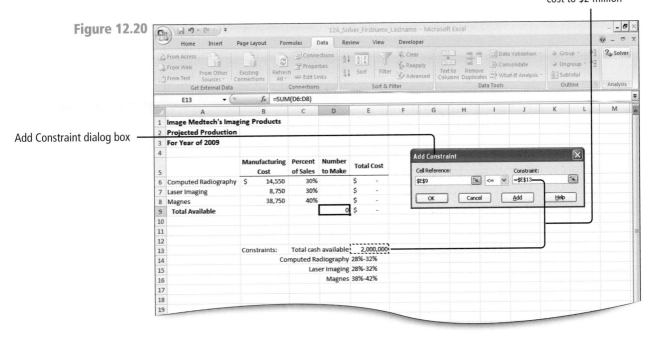

10 In the **Add Constraint** dialog box, click **Add** to add another constraint. For the **Cell Reference**, click cell **D6**, change the mathematical operator to **>=**, and then in the **Constraint** box, type **28%*d9**

This constraint indicates that the number of the Computed Radiography machines should be greater than or equal to 28% of the total machines produced. Excel automatically changes the reference to an absolute cell reference.

11 In the **Add Constraints** dialog box, click **Add**. In the **Cell Reference**, click cell **D6**, confirm the mathematical operators is <=, and for the constraint, type **32%*d9**

By entering two constraints for the same cell, you have indicated that the number of Computed Radiography machines should be between 28% and 32% of the total machines produced. When the constraints are limited with a range, you will need two constraints—the lower number and the upper number. It is good practice to enter a range for the constraints rather than an exact number, which would limit the results and may not allow Solver to find a solution.

12 In the **Add Constraint** dialog box, click **Add** to enter a new set of constraints. For the **Cell Reference**, click cell **D7**, change the mathematical operator **>=** and in the **Constraint** box, type **28%*d9** Click **Add** and complete this constraint with the cell reference D7>= 32%*d9.

13 Using the skills you practiced, click **Add** and enter the constraints for the number of Magnes machines. The number of machines to produce in cell D8 is greater than or equal to 38% of the total in cell D9 and less than or equal to 42% of D9. Click **OK**, and then compare your screen with Figure 12.21.

The constraints that you entered display in the Solver Parameters dialog box.

Figure 12.21

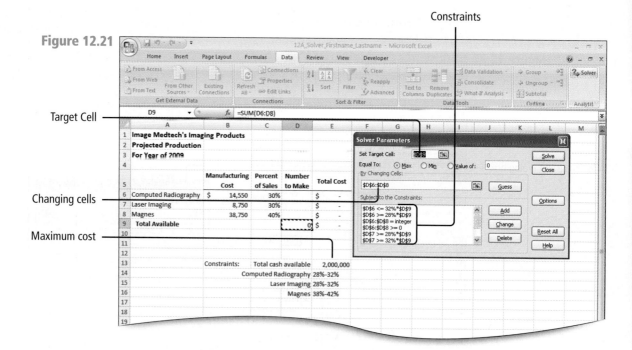

Target Cell

Changing cells

Maximum cost

Constraints

14 As you review the constraints, you notice an error. In the **Subject to the Constraints** box, click *$D$7>= 32%*$D$9* and click **Change**. In the **Change Constraint** dialog box, click the mathematical operator to **<=** and then click **OK**.

15 In the **Solver Parameters** dialog box, click **Solve**. The **Solver Results** dialog box displays indicating a solution has been found. Confirm that **Keep Solver Solution** is selected and compare your screen with Figure 12.22.

The worksheet has been completed with the results of the Solver. The results recommend manufacturing 90 machines for a total cost of $1,994,100.

Figure 12.22

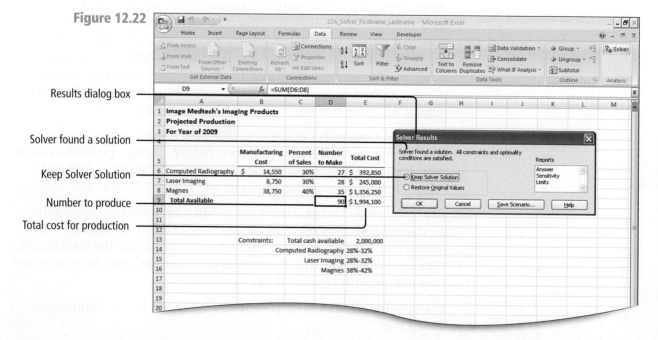

Results dialog box

Solver found a solution

Keep Solver Solution

Number to produce

Total cost for production

Alert!

Is your answer different?

Solver computes complex mathematical operations quickly. If your answer is different, you will want to close Excel and then complete the activity again. It is recommended that you close Excel and then open it again before using Solver.

16 In the **Solver Results** dialog box, under **Reports**, click **Answer**, and then click **OK**.

An additional worksheet, named *Answer Report 1*, is inserted in the workbook to the left of the Solver worksheet.

17 Select the range **D9:E9** and add a **Top and Double Bottom Border**.

Format the range **E7:E8** with **Comma Style** `,` with **no decimals**.

18 Click the **Answer Report 1 sheet tab** and compare your screen with Figure 12.23.

The Answer Report lists the Target Cell and the adjustable cells with their original value and the value of the results. Information is provided about the constraints. This report can be used by management to study the results and assist in making decisions.

Constraints identified

Figure 12.23

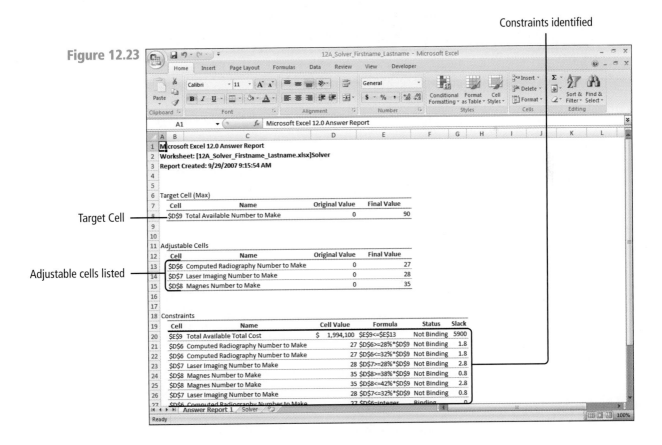

Target Cell

Adjustable cells listed

19 **Select both worksheets** and in the **Left Footer**, insert the **File Name**, and in the **Right Footer**, insert the **Sheet Name**. Format the worksheets in **Portrait orientation**, **Fit to page**, and centered both **Horizontally** and **Vertically**. Move the **Solver sheet** so it is the first worksheet in the workbook.

20 **Save** 🖫 your workbook. Print the worksheets or submit electronically as instructed.

End **You have completed Project 12A** ————————————

Project 12B Price List

In Activities 12.8 through 12.23, you will prepare for a meeting with Vinit Singh, president of Image Medtech. Vinit has been informed by his information technology (IT) staff that the new Excel 2007, PowerPoint 2007, and Word 2007 programs provide opportunities to improve security and document management. Because you are more familiar with the procedures and people in the company and the types of information contained in the documents they create, he wants you to familiarize yourself with the new security features and the new file format used in Excel 2007 so that you can work as a liaison between his office and the IT staff on document security and management issues. You will use a workbook that Vinit intends to send to a customer as an example to demonstrate what can be done. The worksheet of your workbook will look similar to Figure 12.24.

For Project 12B, you will need the following files:

e12B_Price_List
e12B_Logo.jpg

You will save your files as
12B_Price_List_Firstname_Lastname
12B_Price_List_Inspected_Firstname_Lastname
12B_core_Firstname_Lastname.xml
12B_sheet1_Firstname_Lastname.xml

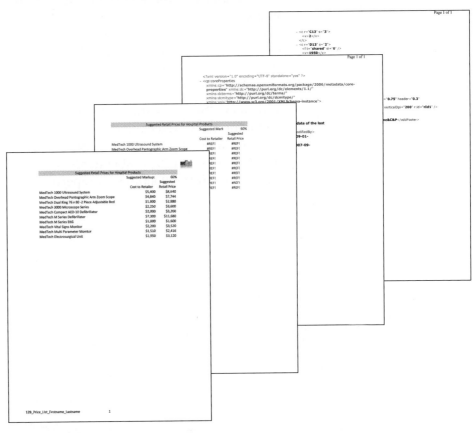

Figure 12.24
Project 12B Price List

Objective 4
Prepare a Document for Distribution

Documents include information about the user, the time and date of creation, and other information that is used by company employees to identify the document and the people who were involved in its creation. Some of this information could be confidential and the document should be checked before it is distributed outside the company.

An example of this type of information would be the user name. Someone outside the company might try to contact the person whose name appears as the user and bypass the company's designated representative.

Activity 12.8 Changing the User Information

You can designate the name of the person who is associated with Microsoft Office 2007. If several different people use the same computer, they can each be designated as a user of the computer as long as they are assigned separate user accounts. The user name is used to identify who was the last person to save a file or the author of new files. In this activity, you will change the user information on the machine you are using.

1 **Start** Excel. In the **Office** menu 🗔 at the bottom of the menu, click **Excel Options**.

2 In the panel at the left, confirm that **Popular** is selected. On the right, under **Personalize your copy of Microsoft Office**, in the **User name** box, make note of the name displayed in this box if it is not your name. If you are not using your own computer, you will restore the user name to its original value at the end of this project. Select the name and type your name: **Firstname Lastname** Compare your screen with Figure 12.25.

Your name becomes the user name for the Office 2007 programs including Word, Excel, and PowerPoint. By changing the user name to your name, it will appear in several places in the document information and you will be able to identify where the program has placed your name in the document properties.

Figure 12.25

Excel Options dialog box ————

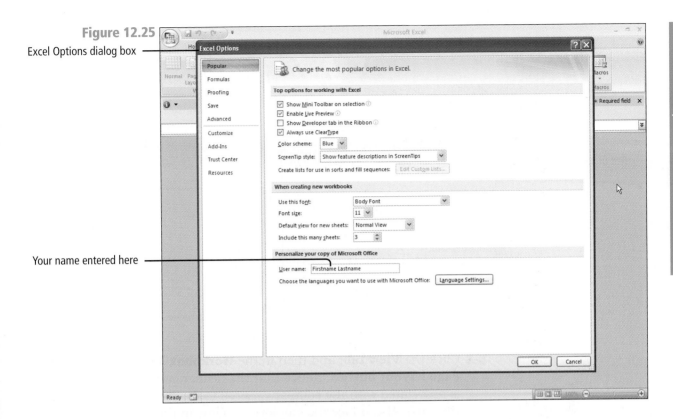

Your name entered here ————

3 At the bottom of the **Excel Options** dialog box, click **OK**.

Activity 12.9 Examining a File for Sensitive Information

You begin by examining the file that Vinit Singh, president of Image Medtech, provided as an example to see what types of information should be removed before a workbook is sent outside the company.

1 Locate and open **e12B_Price_List**. Save the file in your **Excel Chapter 12** folder, as **12B_Price_List_Firstname_Lastname**

2 Notice that the headings for column B and column C are not displayed, which indicates that they are hidden. Select column headings **A** and **D**. Click the **Home tab** and in the **Cells group**, click the **Format button**. Under **Visibility**, point to **Hide & Unhide**, and then on the submenu, click **Unhide Columns**. Alternatively, right-click the selected columns and click Unhide.

These columns contain costs and profit markup values that should not be shared with anyone outside the company. The calculations of cost and suggested retail price in columns D and E use the values in columns B and C.

3 Click the **Undo button** to hide **columns B** and **C**.

4 Point to cell **A4** to display the comment. Compare your screen with Figure 12.26.

Comments like this one are intended for other company team members and should not be shared with outsiders.

Figure 12.26

Comment about product quality

Red triangle indicates
a comment

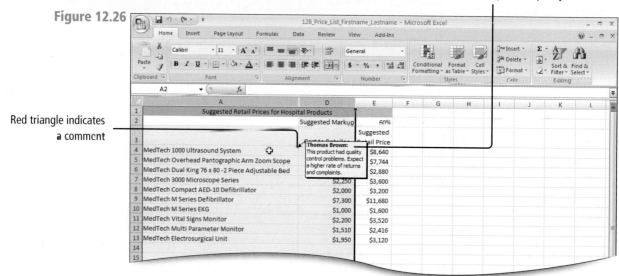

5 Click the **View tab**, and then in the **Workbook Views group**, click the **Page Layout button**. Notice that the header contains an image that is associated with the company. Scroll to the footer at the bottom of the page. Also notice the employee's name in the footer. Scroll back to the top of the document. Compare your screen with Figure 12.27.

The company has designed a new logo and the image in the header might be replaced in the near future. It would be useful if there were a way to replace this image in all of the existing documents without doing it one at a time. The employee's name in the footer should be kept if the document is stored for internal use but removed if shared with outsiders.

Logo image may need to be replaced

Figure 12.27

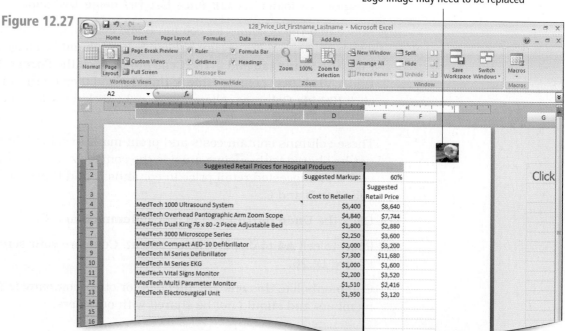

6 From the **Office** menu 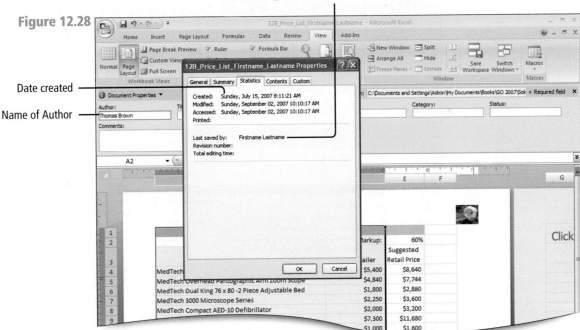, point to **Prepare**, and then click **Properties**.

The Document Properties panel displays a name in the Author box. The name that appears in this box is the name of the primary user of the copy of Excel 2007 that was used to create the file. This might be the name of a worker. This information should not be shared with outsiders, but it is useful to know who to contact if a document needs updating.

7 On the **Document Properties** panel, click the **Document Properties arrow**, and then click **Advanced Properties**. Click the **Statistics tab**. Notice the program records the date when the document was created, modified, and accessed. It displays your name as the person who last saved this file. Compare your screen with Figure 12.28.

The dates are valuable if the document is kept within the company, but they do not need to be shared with outsiders. If the company is charging a client for the time spent on a project or gave it a starting date that is different from the date shown, the client could use these dates to dispute the charges. Managing this information could be important to Vinit and the IT department.

Name of registered user of Excel on this computer

Figure 12.28

Date created

Name of Author

8 In the displayed dialog box, click **Cancel**.

Activity 12.10 Using Document Properties

The Document Properties panel has boxes for attaching information to the document that could be useful within the company for storing and retrieving files.

1 In the **Document Properties panel**, click the **Title** box and type **Hospital Products**

2 Click the **Subject** box. Alternatively, press the Tab key to move to the next box in the Document Properties panel. Type **Suggested Retail Prices**

3 Click the **Keywords** box and type **Hospital, Prices**

Keywords are used by programs that search through documents. Adding keywords to documents make them easier to find if they are stored on a company computer but would be less useful on a document shared with outsiders.

4 Click the **Category** box and type **Hospital**

The category designation would be useful if the categories were well defined within the company. There is no list from which to choose, so it would be hard to standardize employee use of this field. It would not be very useful to outsiders.

5 Click the **Comments** box and type **Prices valid for 30 days from the date of the last modification** Compare your screen with Figure 12.29.

This type of comment is for internal use only and should not be shared with others.

Figure 12.29

Entries made to the document properties

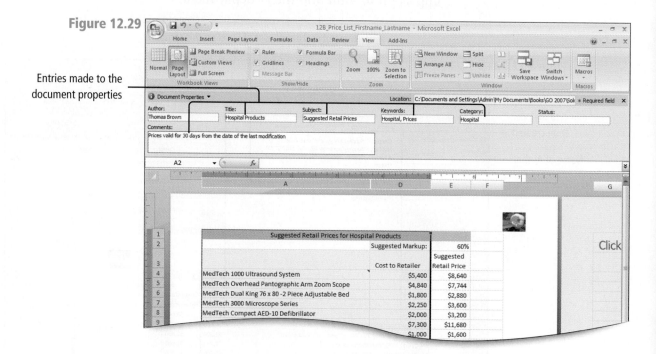

6 Save the changes you have made to your workbook.

Activity 12.11 Restricting Permissions Using Encryption and Information Rights Management

Recall that access to files can be restricted with an *encryption* technique—scrambling the contents—using a program that requires a password to display the contents of the file in usable form. This feature has been available in earlier versions of Excel. The problem with using passwords is that they can be forgotten or the person who applied the password might leave the company. Excel 2007 provides a means to transfer the management of file access to the IT department. This is a topic that Vinit wants you to know about if you are to be the liaison with the IT department on security issues.

1 From the **Office** menu , point to **Prepare**, point to **Restrict Permission**, and then click **Restricted Access**. The **Microsoft Office** dialog box displays. Compare your screen with Figure 12.30.

To use this feature, you have to have the Vista operating system or you have to download and install the ***Windows Rights Management client*** in Windows XP. This program allows you to enable ***Information Rights Management (IRM)***, which is a formal system that designates who can read or edit the file. The IT department is accustomed to working with this type of system when they assign rights to users of the company's network. To learn more about this topic, see the Workshop at the end of this activity.

Figure 12.30

Information about IRM displays —

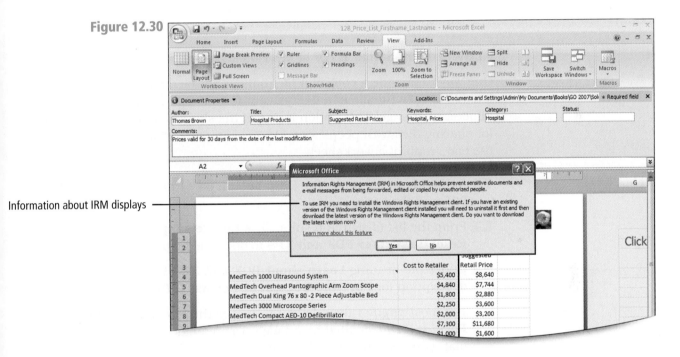

2 In the **Microsoft Office** dialog box, click **No**.

You will need to know more about this topic before you meet with the IT staff.

Using Information Rights Management (IRM)

To implement an IRM system, you need to create a system to reliably identify each employee by assigning *digital credentials* that are used to identify a person electronically. Your IT department can create groups of users that have certain rights, and you would assign employees to one or more of those groups. You can use IRM to prevent unauthorized users from forwarding, copying, modifying, printing, faxing, or pasting content. You can set expiration dates on a file so that the person cannot open the file after a certain date. This system requires time and expertise to administer and the value of securing the documents needs to be weighed against the time and effort required to protect them. Typically, the staff in an IT department would be familiar with this type of security system because it is similar to what they do to manage access to different resources on a company's computer network.

Activity 12.12 Saving as PDF or XPS Formats

One way to provide a copy of a file that cannot be changed or manipulated is to save the file in a fixed-layout format that is easy to share but difficult to change. This option is one of the simplest and best solutions for sharing files with people outside of a company who just want to see the end result of a worksheet.

1 In the **Menu** bar, click the **Help button** ⓘ. In the **Search** box, type **PDF** and then press Enter.

2 From the list of search results, click **Enable support for other file formats, such as PDF and XPS** to open the help topic on this subject.

3 Under the heading **Learn about PDF and XPS file formats**, read the description for **Portable Document Format (PDF)**.

The most popular fixed-layout format is the **Portable Document Format (PDF)**, created by Adobe®. To create documents in PDF format, you needed to purchase and install Adobe Acrobat®. To read files that were already saved in the PDF format, you could download and install the Adobe Reader®, which is free. The PDF format is widely used and because the reader is free, anyone can open and view files saved in PDF. If you install a special add-in program from Microsoft, you can create and read PDF files without purchasing Adobe Acrobat®.

4 Under the heading **Learn about PDF and XPS file formats**, read the description for **XML Paper Specification (XPS)**.

Microsoft introduced its version of a fixed-layout format in Office 2007 and it is named **XML Paper Specification (XPS)**. There is an add-in to the Save As menu that must be downloaded and installed to create and read XPS files. To read XPS files, a free viewer is available for download. No download is necessary if you have the Microsoft Vista operating system.

5 **Close** the **Excel Help** window.

The ability to create fixed-layout versions of your files is very important if you want someone outside the company to view the final results of your worksheets. Your company should have the ability to create PDF or XPS files and you will need to learn more about them. You need to have permission to download and install programs on the computer you are using before installing this add-in to Office 2007.

Activity 12.13 Checking for Features Not Supported in Earlier Versions of Excel

The new file format used for Excel 2007 files will not open in earlier versions of Excel unless a compatibility pack has been downloaded and installed. Instead of placing this burden on your customers, you can save your file in the older file format. If you plan to share an Excel 2007 workbook with someone who is using an older version of Excel, it is a good idea to check for compatibility problems first.

1 From the **Office** menu 🔘 , click **Prepare**, and then click **Run Compatibility Checker**. The **Compatibility Checker** dialog box displays. Compare your screen with Figure 12.31. Notice that it found three occurrences of features in this workbook that are not supported in earlier versions, but you do not have the option of examining each one to see what effect it would have.

The shading—fill color—used in the first row is not available in earlier versions of Excel. A different color will be substituted if you save this file in an earlier version.

Compatibility Checker displays results

Figure 12.31

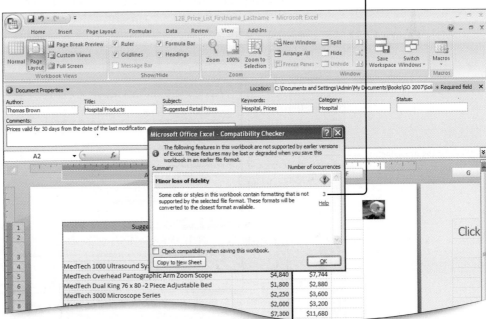

2 Click **OK**.

More Knowledge

Features That Are Not Supported

One example of a feature that is not backwardly compatible is the use of advanced conditional formatting. There are more graphical display options in Excel 2007, such as new background colors, that are not available in previous versions.

Activity 12.14 Using the Document Inspector

The Document Inspector can be used to clear the contents from several areas where personal or private information is likely to be found, such as footers and document properties. The Document Inspector is provided to make it easy to clean out this information.

1 **Save** 🖫 the **12B_Price_List_Firstname_Lastname** workbook.

The Document Inspector can make permanent changes to a workbook before you see what it did. Therefore, it is recommended that you save the workbook before you use the Document Inspector, and then save it by a different name to create a backup file.

2 From the **Office** menu 🖫 , click **Save As** and save this file as **12B_Price_List_Inspected_Firstname_Lastname** to create a backup copy of your file.

3 From the **Office** menu 🖫 , click **Prepare**, and then click **Inspect Document** to open the **Document Inspector** dialog box. Compare your screen with Figure 12.32. Notice that all of the check boxes are selected.

The program will look for the types of information that you select.

Figure 12.32

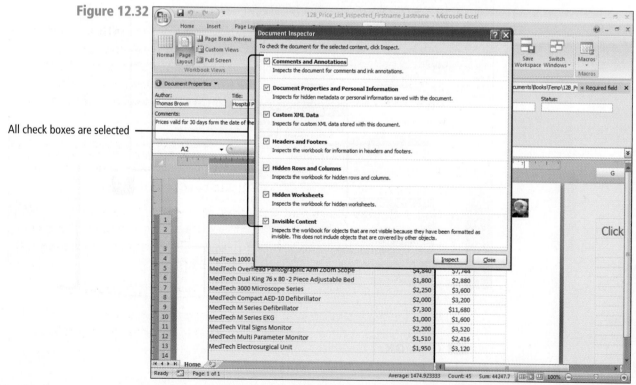

All check boxes are selected

4 In the **Document Inspector** dialog box, click **Inspect**. Notice that the program found that this file has comments, personal information, headers and footers, and hidden columns, as indicated by the red exclamation point. Compare your screen with Figure 12.33.

Figure 12.33

Removable content found

Scroll to view more options

Found 2 hidden columns

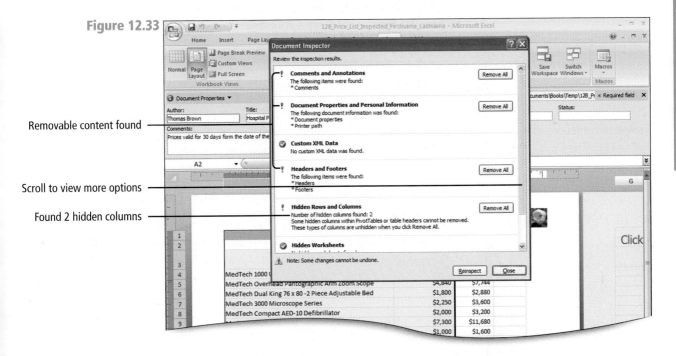

5 Under **Comments and Annotations**, notice that the program does not show you the content of the comment. It does not give you the opportunity to select some comments for removal and leave others.

6 To the right of **Comments and Annotations**, click the **Remove All button** to remove all comments.

7 Under **Document Properties and Personal information**, notice that it does not distinguish between the properties you can see in the Document Properties panel and the advanced properties, which include the printer path. To the right of **Document Properties and Personal information**, click the **Remove All button** to remove the properties and printer path.

The printer path identifies where the printer is located on the network.

8 To the right of **Headers and Footers**, click the **Remove All button** to remove the text and images in the header and footer.

9 Under **Hidden Rows and Columns**, notice that it does not indicate where these columns are or what is in them. To the right of **Hidden Rows and Columns**, click the **Remove All** button to remove the hidden columns, and then click the **Close button**.

10 Click cell **A4**. Notice that the comment is no longer present.

If you plan to use this option, workers would have to be trained not to use comments to convey information to customers or outsiders.

11 Notice that the image in the header has been removed. Scroll to the bottom of the first page and notice that the name in the footer is gone and so is the page number.

12 In the **Document Properties** panel, notice that the information from all of these boxes has been removed. Compare your screen with Figure 12.34.

Figure 12.34

Document properties cleared ──

Footer removed including
the page number ──

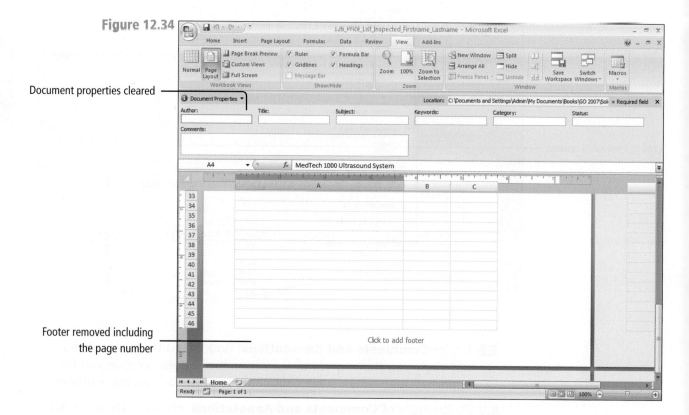

13 On the **Document Properties** panel, click the **Document Properties arrow**, and then click **Advanced Properties**. In the displayed dialog box, click the **Summary tab**. Notice all of this information has been cleared. Click the **Statistics tab**. Notice the information about who saved the file last is deleted. Notice the date the file was created is changed to the current date.

It is important to know that removing the document properties did not remove these dates, which are *automatically updated properties*—properties that are set by the operating system or by the Microsoft Office program. The name of the user who last saved the file is deleted but this will be replaced the next time the file is saved. The date of creation was reset and might be misleading.

14 In the displayed dialog box, click **Cancel**. Click cell **B4**. Notice that this formula now displays a reference error—*#REF!*— because the values it formerly used were in hidden columns that were deleted. The formula in *C4* uses the value in *B4*, so it also displays a reference error.

It is common practice to hide columns or rows that contain intermediate steps or data to make the worksheet appear less cluttered. Deleting hidden columns or rows is risky and should not be done unless you first find any hidden columns, rows, or worksheets and decide what would happen if they were deleted.

Activity 12.15 Marking the Workbook as Final

Another option for sharing a workbook is to save it in a form where the user can only view its contents but cannot make changes.

1 From the **Office** menu 🗒, point to **Prepare**, and then click **Mark as Final**.

The Microsoft Office Excel dialog displays and asks you to confirm that you want to mark this file as final and save it.

2 In the **Microsoft Office Excel** dialog box, click **OK**.

The Microsoft Office Excel dialog box displays a message that explains that the status will be changed to *final*, and then saved. A final file is a *read-only file*—one that can be viewed but not changed.

3 Click **OK**. In the **Document Properties** panel, notice the status is *Final*. In the **Title bar** at the top of the window, notice that *[Read-Only]* has been inserted after the file name, and in the status bar, the Marked as Final icon displays. Compare your screen with Figure 12.35.

Title bar displays [Read-Only]   Marked as Final

Figure 12.35

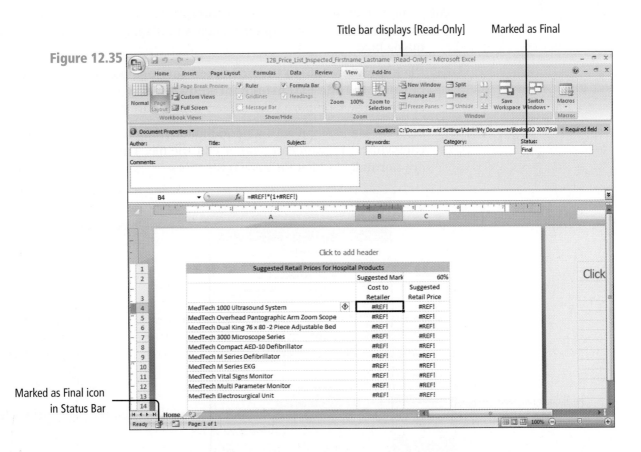

Marked as Final icon in Status Bar

4 Click any cell in the worksheet and attempt to type a number or text. Notice that nothing happens.

5 From the **Office** menu 🗒, click **Close**.

Objective 5
Use XML to Enhance Security

The Document Inspector does not give you the opportunity to preview the content of the elements that it deletes and it is designed to work with files one at a time. Excel 2007, Word 2007, and PowerPoint 2007 use a new file format that enables you to edit files in more detail, and someone who knows how to write programs can create a program that will make changes to groups of files that use this format. This feature gives you more options for securing your documents and to prevent unwanted information from leaving the company. Excel 2007 files use a new file extension and a new method of storing a file as groups of smaller files. To see these files, you display file extensions and rename the file so that it can be uncompressed to reveal its structure.

Activity 12.16 Renaming an Excel 2007 File and Displaying Its Structure

Under the new file structure, files are stored as a group of files where each type of file performs a specific function. These files always have the same names, and simple programs can be used to make changes to them. In this activity, you see the internal structure of an Excel 2007 file.

1 From the **Start** menu, click **My Computer**. On the menu bar, select **Tools**, and then click **Folder Options** to display the **Folder Options** dialog box.

2 Click the **View tab**. In the **Advanced settings** box, click the check box next to **Hide extensions for known file types** to remove the check mark. Compare your screen with Figure 12.36.

Most file names end with a period followed by a few letters that indicate which program can read or edit the file. These *file extensions* are normally hidden for known file types.

Figure 12.36

Check mark removed

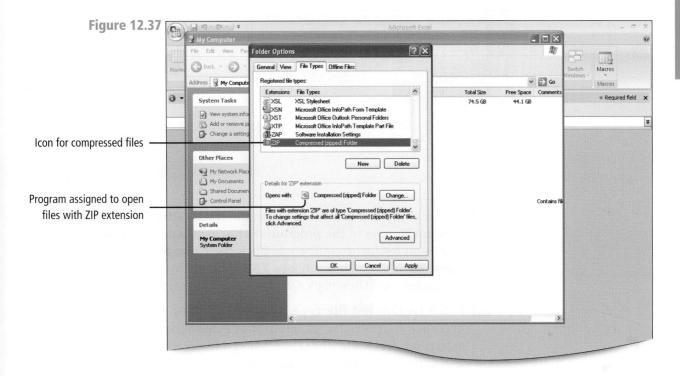

3 Click the **File Types tab**. In the **Registered file types** box, scroll to the bottom of the list of file extensions. (It may take a few minutes for the Registered file types to populate the box.) Under **Extensions**, click **ZIP**. Compare your screen with Figure 12.37.

Files can be combined, compressed, or uncompressed using a procedure named ZIP. This function can be performed by a program provided with Windows XP or by third-party software such as WinZip. The default is the program provided with Windows XP that is named *Compressed (zipped) Folder*.

Figure 12.37

Icon for compressed files

Program assigned to open files with ZIP extension

4 If your computer displays **Compressed (zipped) Folder** as the registered file type for ZIP, go to the next step. If your computer is not set to use the **Compressed (zipped) Folder** program with ZIP files, make note of the program that is associated with this extension for future reference—you will return to this dialog box at the end of the project to restore the default values. Click the **Change button** and from the list of available programs, be sure **Compressed (zipped) Folder** is selected, and then click **OK**.

5 In the **Registered file types** window, scroll up to the **XML** extension and click it. Compare your screen with Figure 12.38.

The default program for files with the XML extension is probably XML Editor.

Figure 12.38

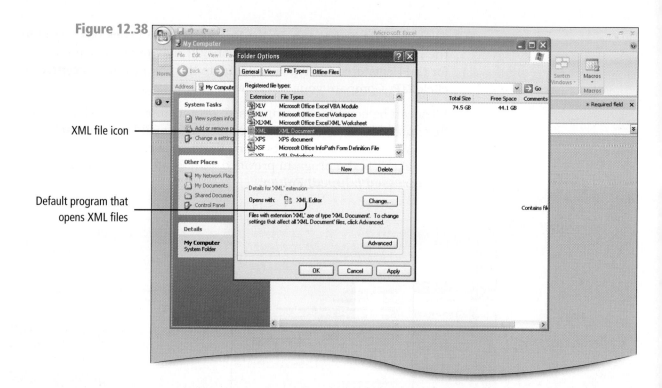

XML file icon ——

Default program that
opens XML files ——

6 If your computer is not set to use the **XML Editor** program with XML files, make note of the program that is associated with the XML extension for future reference. Click the **Change button** and in the **Open With** dialog box, choose **XML Editor** from the list of available programs, and then click **OK**. Otherwise, continue to the next step.

7 In the **Registered file types** window, scroll up to the **JPG** extension and click it. Notice the program that is associated with this file extension. Click the **JPEG** extension and notice the program that is associated with this extension. They are probably the same because they both refer to the same file type.

The **JPG** or **JPEG** file extension identifies image files that are stored using the JPEG compression procedure that was developed by the Joint Photographic Experts Group. There are several programs that could be used as the default for viewing this type of file. The Windows Picture and Fax Viewer program will be used later in this project to display an image, but you do not have to change the default for this file type if another program is specified.

8 At the bottom of the **Folder Options** dialog box, click **OK** if you have not made any changes; otherwise, click **Close**.

You will return to this dialog box at the end of the project to restore the default values.

9 On the **Standard Buttons** toolbar, click the **Folders button**, if necessary, to display the Folders pane on the left. In the **My Computer** window, navigate to your **Excel Chapter 12** folder, and click the file **12B_Price_List_Firstname_Lastname.xlsx**. On the **Standard Buttons** toolbar, click the **Views button** 🔳▾, and then click **Details**. Maximize the window. On the right side of the window, drag the vertical line on the right of the **Name** column heading to the right to widen the **Name** column until the full file name displays, including its extension. Compare your screen with Figure 12.39.

File name extension for Excel 2007 files

Figure 12.39

Icon for Excel 2007 files

10 Right-click the file name **12B_Price_List_Firstname_Lastname.xlsx**, and from the shortcut menu, click **Rename**. Edit the name to replace the file extension *xlsx* with **zip** Do not delete the period between the file name and the extension. Press Enter.

The Rename dialog box displays warning you that by changing the extension, the file might become unusable.

11 Click **Yes** to make the change. Compare your screen with Figure 12.40.

The new file format used by Excel 2007 is a ***container*** of files called ***parts*** that are compressed using the ZIP procedure. The zip file is called the container, and the files and folders within it are called the parts. Reducing the file size—***zipping***—is accomplished by identifying repetitive words or phrases and storing them in a table along with a list of locations where they were in the original document. The new files are up to 75 percent smaller than files stored in previous versions of Microsoft Office. The document can be regenerated—***unzipped***—from this table of information. By changing the file extension, you will be able to view these files using the Compressed (zipped) Folder program.

Zip file extension—.zip—replaces xlsx

Figure 12.40

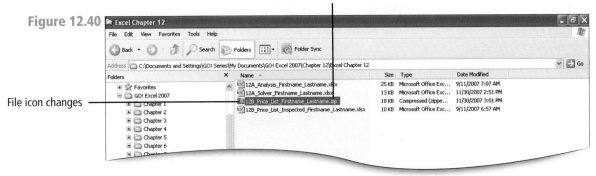

File icon changes

More Knowledge

Working with ZIP files

When you double-click a file with the zip extension, the My Computer window displays the folders and files within the zipped file. The *Compressed (zipped) Folder* program allows you to open the files individually without uncompressing (extracting) all of the files. If you drag a file into the pane that displays the contents of the zipped file, the *Compressed (zipped) Folder* program will compress the new file and add it to the container file.

Activity 12.17 Identifying the Functions of Folders and Files

The files that make up an Excel 2007 file are grouped into folders by their functions. After you know where to look for a certain type of information, you can find it in any Excel 2007 file. In this activity, you will open a container and examine its parts to identify their functions.

1 Double-click the **12B_Price_List_Firstname_Lastname.zip** file name.

Another window opens to display the contents of this zip file. The Compress (zipped) Folders program displays the internal structure of the file because it is the program that is now associated with the ZIP file extension.

Alert!

What if a warning displays a potential security risk?

If you are accessing your files over a network, or from a file server, you may see warning box suggesting that there may be a potential security risk. If this displays, click Yes to continue.

2 On the **Standard Buttons** toolbar, click the **Folders button**.

The Folders pane displays on the left side of the window.

3 In the **Folders** pane, click the plus sign next to the **xl** folder to display its subfolders. Compare your screen with Figure 12.41.

A single Excel 2007 file is made up of a group of approximately 20 individual files in almost a dozen different folders. One advantage of this system is that the same type of information is always found in the same folder for all Excel 2007 workbooks.

Folders in the xl folder

Figure 12.41

Container

Parts

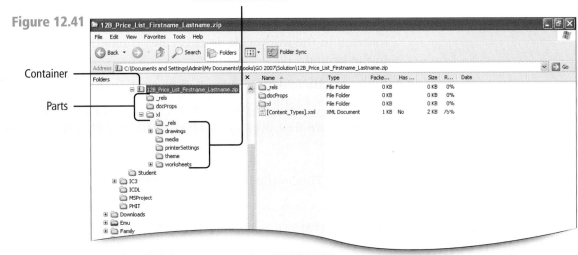

4 In the **Folders** pane, just under the **12B_Price_List_Firstname_ Lastname.zip** file, notice the folder named _rels.

This folder contains a file that describes the relationships between the files and folders in the first level of files and folders.

5 In the **xl** folder, notice the folder named _rels.

This _rels folder contains a file that describes the relationships between files and folders in the xl folder.

6 Next to the **worksheets** folder, click the plus sign. In the **worksheets** folder, notice the folder named _rels. Next to the **drawings** folder, click the plus sign. In the **drawings** folder, notice the folder named _rels.

The _rels folders contain files that describe the relationships between the files in the folder and the other files and folders in the workbook and in drawings, respectively.

7 In the **Folders** pane, click the **docProps** folder. On the right side of the window, notice this folder contains two files, *app.xml* and *core.xml*.

The ***docProps folder*** contains files that define the document properties. The ***core.xml file*** contains text that identifies the author, key search words, descriptions, and the dates the file was created and modified.

8 In the **Folders** pane, click the **worksheets** folder. On the right side of the window, notice this folder contains *sheet1.xml*.

This workbook only contains one worksheet. If it had more worksheets, there would be a separate file for each of them. These files contain the data in each worksheet, the column formatting, and the header and footer information.

9 In the **Folders** pane, notice the *xl* folder.

The xl folder contains the files and folders that describe the workbook. It also contains folders for elements that are inserted into the workbook such as pictures.

10 In the **xl** folder, click the **media** folder.

The media folder contains pictures and other media files that are inserted in the workbook. In this case, it has the picture that is used in the header.

11 In the **media** folder, double-click **image1.jpeg**. Compare your screen with Figure 12.42.

The program that is associated with the jpeg file extension starts and displays the image. If your computer uses a different program to display jpeg files, your screen may look different but the image will be the same. This is the image in the header of the worksheet.

Program associated with jpeg files   Image used in the header

Figure 12.42

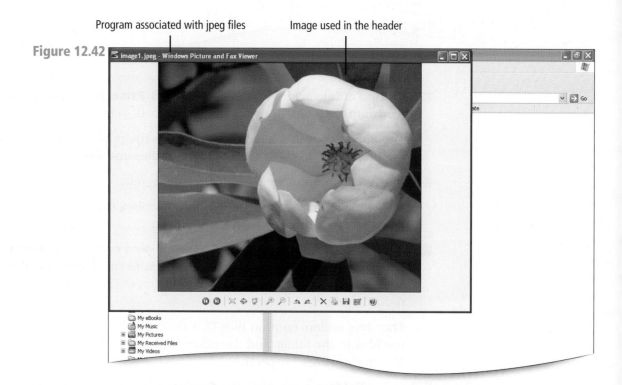

12 **Close** the program that is displaying the image1.jpeg file but leave the **My Computer** window open.

Activity 12.18 Replacing a Picture in the Media Folder

Picture files are stored in the media folder. In this case, the picture that is used in the header is named image1.jpeg. If the company logo changes, all the logos could be changed by writing a program to replace this image with a new one in all of the Excel 2007 or Word 2007 files. In this activity, you will locate the logo image and replace the current picture with the new logo:

1 On the taskbar, click the **Excel Chapter 12 button** to display the My Computer window that displays this folder. Alternatively, if this button does not display, click Start and click My Computer to open another window of My Computer. On the Standard Buttons toolbar, click the Folders button. Navigate to the student data files for this chapter, locate **e12B_Logo.jpg**, right-click the image, and then click **Copy**.

2 Navigate to your **Excel Chapter 12** folder, right-click the folder, and then from the shortcut menu, click **Paste**. Right-click **e12B_Logo.jpg** and click **Rename** from the shortcut menu. With the file name selected, type **image1.jpeg** and press Enter. Click **Yes** to confirm the change.

3 Right-click **image1.jpeg**. From the shortcut menu, click **Cut**. Leave the **My Computer** window that displays the content of the **Excel Chapter 12** folder open.

The image1.jpeg file is deleted from the Excel Chapter 12 folder and placed on the Clipboard.

Note

You should have two windows of My Computer open. One window displays the parts of the container—zip file—12B_Price_List_Firstname_Lastname.zip that is in use by the *Compressed (zipped) Folder* program. The other window is used to locate the file you want to paste into the container.

---

4 On the **taskbar**, click the **My Computer button** that displays the content of the **xl/media** folder. If necessary, on the **Standard Buttons** toolbar, click the **Views button**, and then click **Details** to display the type and size information. In the **Size** column, notice the size of the file.

5 Right-click the right side of the window and click **Paste** to place a new version of **image1.jpeg** into the **media** folder. The **Confirm File Replace** dialog box appears. Compare your screen with Figure 12.43.

Because you are pasting a file that has the same name into the media folder, a dialog box displays that asks if you would like to replace the existing file.

Current image1.jpeg file   File size

Figure 12.43

Media folder selected

Confirm File Replace dialog box

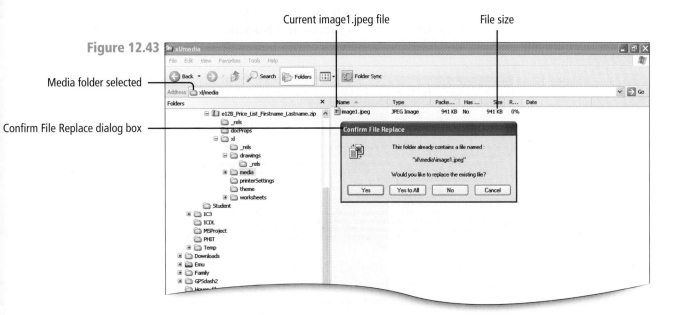

6 Click **Yes**. Notice the new file has a much smaller size and a different date in the details view.

This new image will appear in the header in place of the old logo when you are finished editing the file.

Note — Tracking Relationships Between the Parts in the Container

The files in the _rels folders keep track of the relationships between the parts in the container. If you replace a file, it is easiest if you use the same file name so that you do not have to find and modify the files in the _rels folders that refer to this file by name.

Activity 12.19 Identifying the Characteristics of an XML File

Most of the files in the container that comprise an Excel 2007 file use the xml file extension. This type of file uses *Extensible Markup Language (XML)*—a set of rules used to create a language. Unlike the previous Excel file formats that used proprietary numeric codes to manage the files, Excel 2007 files are written in plain text using XML rules that can be read using a text editor once they are unzipped. To understand how this new file format can be used to improve flexibility and security, you will examine the characteristics of several of the files that make up a single Excel workbook. In this activity, you will look at the xml file that contains the Document Properties information.

1 Display the Folders pane, if necessary. In the **Folders** pane, click the **docProps** folder; in the **Detail** pane on the right, double-click the **core.xml** file. An Internet Explorer window will open and display the content of the file using the XML Editor program. The Information Bar notice box might display. If it does, click the **Close button** ☒. Compare your screen with Figure 12.44.

Because the XML Editor program is associated with files that end with xml, it will start automatically when you double-click a file that has this extension. Because we are only examining the file, you do not have to click the security bar to activate the ActiveX controls.

Figure 12.44

Defines this as an XML file

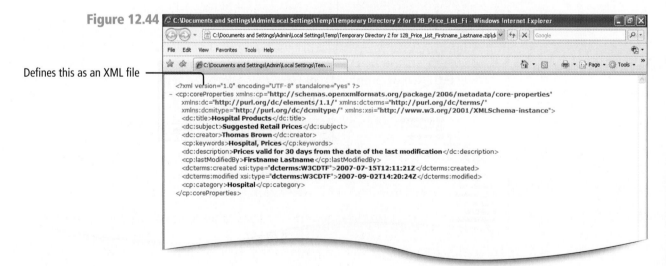

2 Notice that the first line begins with *<?xml version="1.0"*

This code tells any program that opens this file that it is an XML file.

Note — How XML Uses Namespaces

Unlike other computer languages that have a set of predefined terms, in XML you get to make up your own labels for data. You or your organization creates a dictionary of these data labels and stores them in a ***namespace***. If an organization wants to allow all of its members to use the same set of data labels, it makes its namespace available on the Internet. If you want to be able to read a file that uses an organization's data, your computer program can find this namespace on the Internet and read the data.

3 In the first few lines, locate *xmlns:dc="http://purl.org/dc/elements/1.1/"*.

In this statement, xmlns stands for XML namespace, and http://purl.org/dc/elements/1.1 is the namespace created by the Purl organization. Because namespace references are typically long Internet addresses, a short nickname or ***alias*** is assigned. In this example, the namespace is given the alias *dc*. In the lines following this statement, any data label that is preceded by dc is a data label that is defined in the Purl organization's namespace.

4 Near the middle, notice *<dc:creator>Thomas Brown</dc:creator>*.

The alias dc tells you that the following data label—creator—comes from the Purl namespace described in the previous step. The code *<dc:creator>* is the ***start tag*** that marks the beginning of the data. The ***end tag***, *</dc:creator>* marks the end of that type of data.

5 Notice that the start tag, *<dc:creator>*, and the end tag, *</dc:creator>*, are the same except that the end tag has a forward slash in it.

The start and end tags are used to enclose data.

6 In the second line locate the start tag, *<cp:coreProperties*. The end tag, *</cp:coreProperties>*, is at the end of the file. Notice that other pairs of tags, such as *<cp:/creator>* and *</cp:creator>*, are located between the start and end tags of coreProperties. Notice that the XML Editor emphasized this situation by indenting the lines between the start and end tags for coreProperties.

Some tags are used to define data that describes other data. If a pair of tags is enclosed within another pair of tags, the relationship is called a ***parent-child relationship***, where the parent tags enclose the child tags to indicate that the data enclosed by the child tags is a component of the data enclosed by the parent tags.

7 Notice that all the document properties are listed, including the date created and date modified and your name as the person who last modified the file. Compare your screen with Figure 12.45.

Figure 12.45

Alias   Namespace

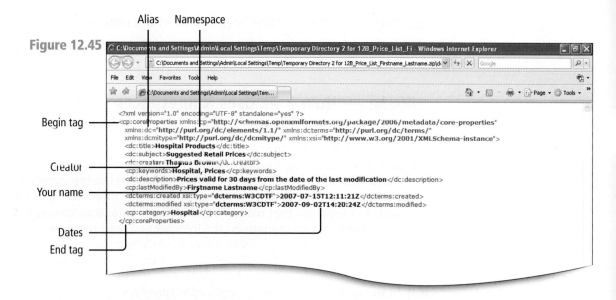

Begin tag

Creator

Your name

Dates

End tag

More Knowledge

XML Schemas

XML allows developers to specify rules that the data in the XML files must obey. For example, the rule could require that all of the child tags contain data for a given parent tag, thus preventing partially completed worksheets. The rules are stored in a file called a *schema*. An organization can give a schema an Internet address and make it available to everyone. If you receive an XML file from an organization and the file contains Internet references to the namespace and schema, your computer can open the file and use the data. Microsoft adopted this approach for Excel 2007, Word 2007, and PowerPoint 2007, which makes it possible for programmers in a company's IT department to write simple programs that can remove sensitive data because it is always in the same file in each Word 2007, Excel 2007, or PowerPoint 2007 file.

Activity 12.20 Editing an XML File

The XML Editor displays the structure of an XML file using color and indented lines, but it does not allow you to change the text it displays. To change the text in one file, you use a simple text editor program named Notepad that is included with Windows XP, which allows you to edit the unformatted text. In this activity, you will edit the XML file using Notepad.

1 With the code of the **core.xml** file displayed in the Internet Explorer window by the XML Editor, click the **View** menu, and then click **Source** to open **Notepad** and display the unformatted text.

2 In the **Notepad** window, click the **Format** menu and then click **Word Wrap**, if necessary, to activate this feature. Maximize the window. Compare your screen with Figure 12.46.

The XML codes are harder to read in Notepad than they are in XML Editor but you can make changes in this program.

Text wrapped to next line

Figure 12.46

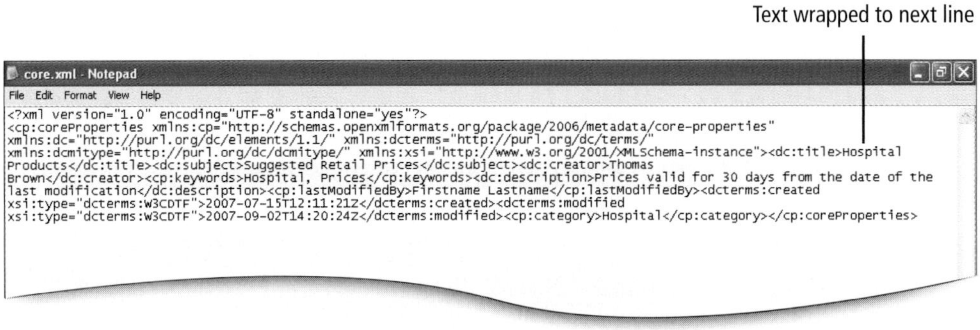

3 In the **Notepad** window, click the **Edit** menu, and then click **Find**.

The Find dialog box displays. Because the text is not indented and there are many confusing codes, it is often faster to use the Find feature than it is to scroll down the screen looking for what you want.

4 In the **Find what** box, type **creator** and then click **Find Next** to locate the start tag of the creator field. Notice that the creator is **Thomas Brown**. Compare your screen with Figure 12.47.

Start tag for the creator field

Figure 12.47

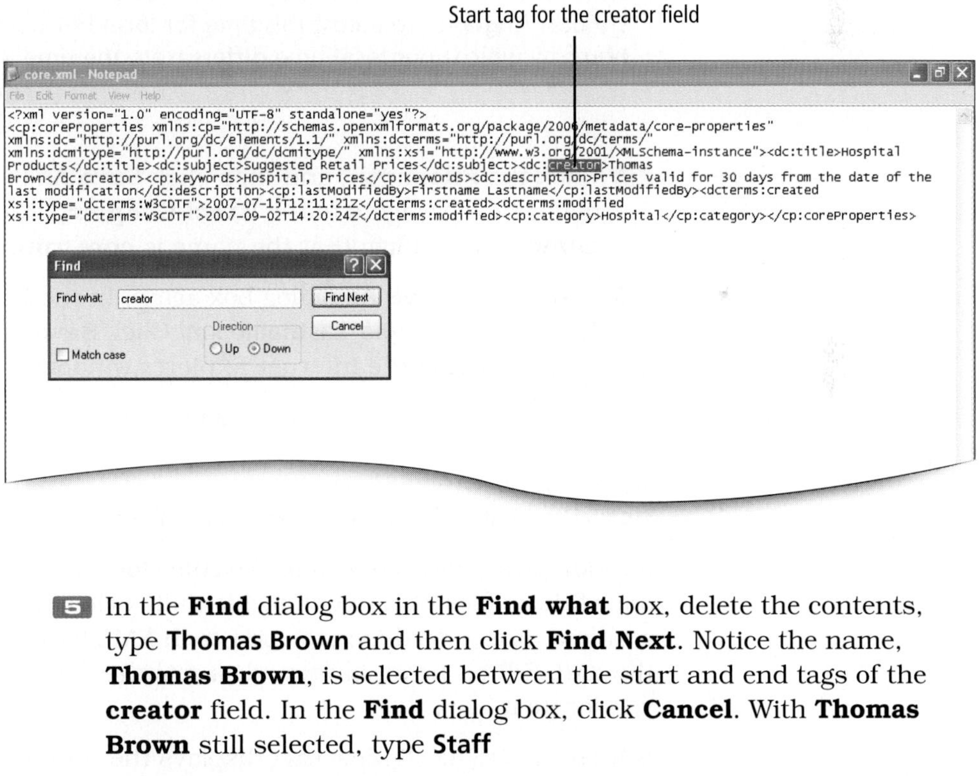

5 In the **Find** dialog box in the **Find what** box, delete the contents, type **Thomas Brown** and then click **Find Next**. Notice the name, **Thomas Brown**, is selected between the start and end tags of the **creator** field. In the **Find** dialog box, click **Cancel**. With **Thomas Brown** still selected, type **Staff**

6 Click **Edit**, and then click **Find**. In the **Find what** box, type **created** and then click **Find Next** to locate one of the tags that identifies the date the file was created. This is a long tag. Look for a date that starts with 2007.

7 In the **Find** dialog box, click **Cancel**. In the **Notepad** window, select the date, **2007-07-15T12:11:21Z**, between the start and end tags and type **2009-01-01T14:00:00Z** Compare your screen with Figure 12.48, and be sure that you made the changes correctly. If you do not have exactly the right date and time format, it will confuse the Excel program later when you try to open this file.

New name

Figure 12.48

New time

Note — Times in the Document Properties

Even though the time of day when the file was created was not displayed in the Advanced Properties box in Excel, it was actually recorded. In this example—T14:00:00Z—the T stands for Time; 14:00:00 stands for the time in hours, minutes, and seconds; and the Z stands for Zulu or zero longitude, which is a line that runs through the Royal Greenwich Observatory in London, England. To adjust this time for local time, you add or subtract the hours by which your local time differs from the time at the zero longitude.

8 Click the **File** menu, and then click **Save As** to display the **Save As** dialog box. Navigate to the **Excel Chapter 12** folder. In the **File name** box, confirm that the name is **core.xml**. Click **Save**.

9 Display the **Save As** dialog box again. In the **File name** box, type **12B_core_Firstname_Lastname.xml** Click **Save**. Close the **Notepad** window. **Close** the Internet Explorer window.

The file is saved a second time using your name for grading purposes only.

Activity 12.21 Checking XML Files for Valid Structure

All XML files must conform to the rules for an XML file. When you edit one of these files, you might accidentally delete a character that is required. It is a good idea to open each XML file that you have edited in the XML Editor. If you have made a mistake, the XML Editor will help you locate it.

1 Switch to the window that displays the content of the **Excel Chapter 12** folder. Double-click the **core.xml** file. If it is a valid XML document, it will open in the XML Editor window. Check the changes you made. If you made a mistake, read any messages provided by the XML Editor, then close the XML Editor and repeat activities 12.19 and 12.20. **Close** the XML Editor in the Internet Explorer window.

Alert! What if my core.xml file does not open?

The XML rules that govern the structure of an XML file have to be met for any program to open an XML file. If you accidentally deleted part of a start or end tag, it would not match its corresponding tag and the file would not open. If you paste an invalid XML file into the container of an Excel file, the Excel file will not open and it will be hard to fix. It is important to check the validity of any XML file before you paste it into the container for an Excel file. Fortunately, this is easy to do. You double-click the file and open it in the XML Editor before you paste it into the Excel file container. If you accidentally corrupted the file by deleting a necessary part, the XML Editor will provide an error message that gives you a clue regarding the problem. It will probably be easier to start the editing procedure over again and save a new version of the edited file. Be careful when you select text to replace in Notepad. Selecting codes that are adjacent to the text you want to change is the most common error.

2 Display the **My Computer** window that displays the parts of the XML container, and then in the **Folders** pane click the **12B_Price_List_Firstname_Lastname.zip** folder. Compare your screen with Figure 12.49.

Parts

Figure 12.49

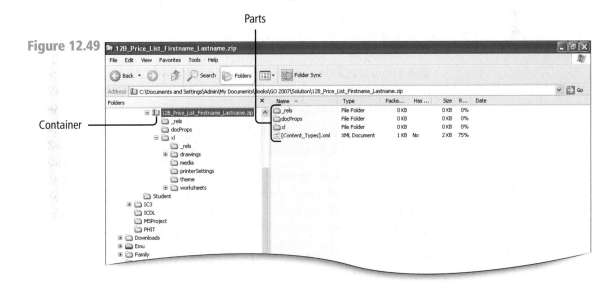

Container

3 In the **Folders** pane, click the **worksheets** folder, and in the Detail pane on the right, double-click the **sheet1.xml** file. An Internet Explorer window opens and displays the content of the file using the XML Editor program. Scroll to the bottom of the window and notice that **Thomas Brown** is part of the footer. Thomas was the creator of the document and he placed his name in the footer.

4 With the code of the **sheet1.xml** file displayed in the browser window by the XML Editor, click the **View** menu, and then click **Source** to open **Notepad** and display the unformatted text. **Maximize** the Notepad window.

5 In the **Notepad** window, click the **Edit** menu, and then click **Find**. In the **Find what** box, type **Thomas Brown** and then click **Find Next** to locate this name in the footer.

6 In the **Find** dialog box, click **Cancel**. In the **Notepad** window be sure that **Thomas Brown** is selected, and then type **12B_Price_List_ Firstname_Lastname** Compare your screen with Figure 12.50.

Figure 12.50

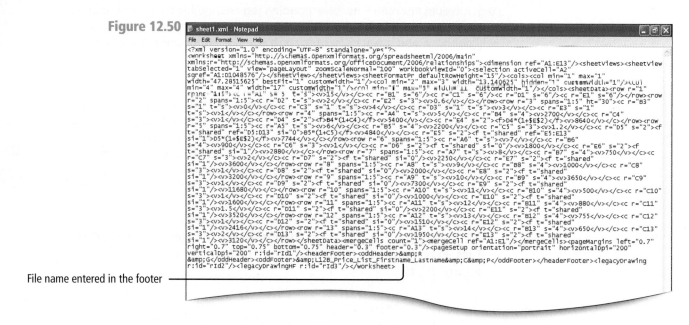

File name entered in the footer

7 Click the **File** menu, and then click **Save As** to copying the **Save As** dialog box. Navigate to your **Excel Chapter 12** folder. In the **File name** box, confirm that the name is **sheet1.xml**, and then click **Save**.

8 Display the **Save As** dialog box again. In the **File name** box, type **12B_Sheet1_Firstname_Lastname.xml** and then click **Save**.

9 Switch to the window that displays the content of the **Excel Chapter 12** folder. Double-click the **sheet1.xml** file. If it is a valid XML document, it will open in the XML Editor window. Check the changes you made. If you made a mistake, start this part of the activity again. **Close** the XML Editor in the Internet Explorer window. **Close** the Notepad window.

Activity 12.22 Replacing Parts and Zipping the Container File

You can replace parts of the Excel file by copying the replacement files into the Compressed (zipped) Folder window and replacing the existing file. The files must be the same name. When you close the window, the program compresses all of the files into the single container file.

1 Switch to the window that displays the content of the **Excel Chapter 12** folder. Locate **core.xml**, right-click the file, and then click **Cut**.

2 Switch to the window that displays the unzipped container of files. Click the **docProps** folder. Point to the pane on the right side that contains the **app.xml** and **core.xml** files. Right-click, and then click **Paste**. Click **Yes** to confirm that you want to replace the file that has the same name.

3 Switch to the window that displays the **Excel Chapter 12** folder. Locate **sheet1.xml**, right-click the file, and then click **Cut**. Close the window that shows the content of the **Excel Chapter 12** folder.

4 Switch to the window that displays the unzipped container of files. Click the **worksheets** folder. Point to the pane on the right side that contains the **sheet1.xml** file. Right-click, and then click **Paste**. Click **Yes** to confirm that you want to replace the file that has the same name.

5 Close the **worksheets** window that displays the unzipped container of files.

Closing the window will cause the Compressed (zipped) Folder program to compress the new files back into the single file that is a container for all of the related files and folders that comprise an Excel 2007 file.

6 Display the **Excel** window, navigate to your **Excel Chapter 12** folder and locate **12B_Price_List_Firstname_Lastname.zip**. Right-click on the file name and click **Rename**. Replace the **zip** extension with **xlsx** and press [Enter] and click **Yes** to confirm that you want to change the extension.

The xlsx file extension identifies this file as one that can be opened by Excel 2007.

7 Double-click **12B_Price_List_Firstname_Lastname.xlsx**.

Because Excel 2007 is associated with the xlsx file extension, Excel 2007 starts and opens this file. If an older version of Excel is associated with this file extension, close the file. Start Excel 2007 and open the file using the Excel 2007 menu options.

8 Notice the new picture in the header.

The new picture is the new company logo that you placed in the media folder.

9 Scroll to the bottom of the page and notice the file name in the footer and the page number in the center of the page.

10 From the **Office** menu, point to **Prepare**, and then click **Properties**. In the **Document Properties** panel, notice that the **Author** box now contains **Staff** instead of the actual author. Compare your screen with Figure 12.51.

Figure 12.51

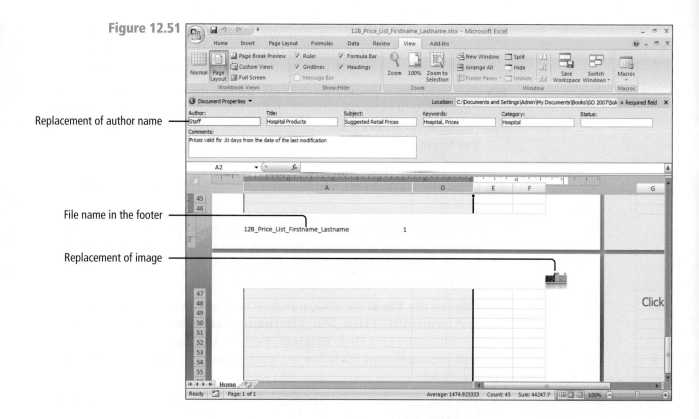

Replacement of author name

File name in the footer

Replacement of image

11 On the **Document Properties panel** click the **Document Properties arrow**, and then click **Advanced Properties**. Click the **Statistics tab**. Notice the date and time to the right of **Created** is the date you entered and the time is the time you entered, which has been adjusted for your local time zone. Notice the times next to **Modified** and **Accessed** are the dates and times that you worked on the file.

Note

Because the document properties are stored in a separate XML file that always uses the same tags for information such as the creator of the document, a simple program can be written by the IT staff to make this change to each Excel, Word, or PowerPoint 2007 file before it is electronically transferred out of the company.

12 In the displayed dialog box, click **Cancel**. Review the summary information for managing document security in the table in Figure 12.52.

Summary of Security Issues and Options

Issue	Staff Training	Manage from Excel	Edit individual XML Files	Programs written by IT Dept.
Employee name in Property Documents		Remove author name using Document Properties	View the source code of core.xml in Notepad and change the name	Program to remove the creator's name from the core.xml file in all the documents that leave the company
Employee name in header or footer	Do not put name in header or footer	Use Document Inspector to clear headers and footers		
Date of creation and modification in the Document Properties			View the source code of core.xml in Notepad and change the date	Program to replace the creation, modified, and saved dates in all the documents that leave the company
Images in the document		Edit images in individual files	Paste a replacement into the images folder	Program to replace the image in all the documents in a given folder
Hidden rows, columns, worksheets	Do not place comments or text that shouldn't be shared in hidden elements	Use Document Inspector to discover hidden elements. Do not delete hidden elements		
Comments	Do not use comments to communicate with outsiders	Use Document Inspector to remove comments		Write a program to remove comments
View the final results		Use Mark as Final to make it read-only or save as PDF or XPS		
Intended user does not have Excel 2007		Check for compatibility, then save as xls file		

Figure 12.52

13 Center the **Home** sheet **horizontally** and **Save**  your file. Print all of the files created, or submit electronically as instructed. **Close** all files. Leave Excel open for use in the next activity.

Activity 12.23 Renaming the File and Restoring Default Values

If you changed the default views of file extensions, the default associations between file extensions and programs, or the user name, you should put them back the way you found them, especially if you are using a computer that is not yours.

1 From the **Office** menu , click **Excel Options**. In the pane at the left, confirm that **Popular** is selected. Under **Personalize your copy of Microsoft Office**, in the **User name** box, select the name and type the name that was there originally and click **OK**. **Close** Excel Options and **Exit** Excel.

2 From the **Start** menu, click **My Computer**. Click the **Tools** menu, and then click **Folder Options**, to display the **Folder Options** dialog box.

3 Click the **View tab**. In the **Advanced settings** box, click the check box next to **Hide extensions for known file types** to replace the check mark if it was there when you started.

The file extensions are hidden for extensions that are associated with programs. An icon usually provides a visual tip on what program is associated with a file name.

4 Click the **File Types tab**. If you changed any of the programs that were associated with the **ZIP**, **XML**, or **JPEG** extensions, restore the original associations.

5 Click **OK** to close the **Folder Options** dialog box and **Close** the My Computer window.

End You have completed Project 12B ————————————

There's More You Can Do!

From My Computer, navigate to the student files that accompany this textbook. In the folder **02_theres_more_you_can_do**, locate and open the folder for this chapter. Open and print the instructions for this project, which are provided to you in Adobe PDF format.

Try It! 1—Save a File in PDF and XPS Format

In this Try It! exercise, you download and install the Save As add-in and save a file in PDF and XPS format. Then you view the XPS version of the file using the add-in and view the PDF file using Adobe Reader.

Content-Based Assessments

Summary

What-If Analysis tools are used to help businesses make financial and other decisions. These tools provide additional information to the user by evaluating data for the firm. Using Data tables, scenarios, and Solver helps provide a clearer picture of the financial data on which to base decisions. Preparing workbooks to be shared with others outside of the organization removes confidential or sensitive information. Learning basic XML language is helpful in order to make global changes.

Key Terms

Content-Based Assessments

Matching

Match each term in the second column with its correct definition in the first column by writing the letter of the term on the blank line in front of the correct definition.

_____ **1.** A process of changing the values in cells to see how those changes affect the outcome of formulas on the worksheet.

_____ **2.** A range of cells that shows how changing certain values in formulas affects the results of those formulas.

_____ **3.** A data table that may use more than one formula.

_____ **4.** A data table that uses more than one variable.

_____ **5.** In a data table, the cell in which each input value from the table is substituted.

_____ **6.** The values that will be tested in a data table.

_____ **7.** A set of values that is saved in Excel and can be substituted automatically on a worksheet when completing What-If analysis.

_____ **8.** The cells that change when the Scenario or Solver is completed.

_____ **9.** A report that displays the variable information along with the results of several scenarios on one page.

_____ **10.** The cells whose values are changed by the scenarios.

_____ **11.** A What-If analysis tool used to find an optimal value for a cell on a worksheet by working with a group of related cells.

_____ **12.** A supplemental program that adds custom commands or features to Excel.

_____ **13.** With Solver, the restrictions that limit the values that will change.

_____ **14.** With Solver, the cell that contains the goal to be achieved.

_____ **15.** Scrambling the contents of a document to restrict their availability.

A Add-In

B Changing cells

C Constraints

D Data table

E Encryption

F Input cell

G Input values

H One-variable data table

I Result cells

J Scenario

K Scenario Summary report

L Solver

M Target cell

N Two-variable data table

O What-If analysis

Content-Based Assessments

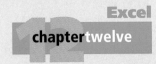
Fill in the Blank

Write the correct answer in the space provided.

1. A Windows XP program that allows you to enable IRM is a Windows Rights Management _____.

2. A format system that designates who can read or edit a file is _____ _____ _____.

3. In order to reliably identify each employee to implement an IRM system, use _____ _____.

4. A format widely used so the reader can open and view files without making changes is the _____ _____ _____.

5. Microsoft's version of a fixed-layout format is _____ _____ _____.

6. Properties that are set by the system or by the Office program are _____ _____ properties.

7. When the Document Inspector is set to _____, it makes the file read-only.

8. A few letters at the end of a file name that indicate which program should be used to open the file is a/an _____ _____.

9. The ZIP program that is provided with Windows XP is the _____ _____ _____.

10. The zip file that is created with the ZIP feature of Windows XP is the _____.

11. The files and folders within a Compressed (zipped) Folder are the _____.

12. A program used to reduce the file size is a/an _____ program.

13. A regenerated zipped file is _____.

14. The folder that contains files that define the document properties is the _____ folder.

15. A short nickname assigned to a namespace reference is a/an _____.

Excel

chaptertwelve

Skills Review

Project 12C — Building

In this project, you will apply the skills you practiced from the Objectives in Project 12A.

Objectives: 1. *Create a Data Table;* **2.** *Create a Scenario;* **3.** *Use Solver.*

In the following Skills Review, you will use Excel Data Tables, Scenarios, and Solver to assist with Image Medtech's ambitious building project. A new wing will be added to the plant. It will be necessary to make some comparisons for financing, to negotiate with contractors to obtain the best possible bids, and to determine how many square feet can be added for a cost of $2.5 million. The added space will be used for manufacturing, warehousing, and office activities. The completed files will look similar to those in Figure 12.53.

For Project 12C, you will need the following files:

e12C_Building
e12C_Building_Solver

You will save your workbook as:
12C_Building_Firstname_Lastname
12C_Building_Solver_Firstname_Lastname

Figure 12.53

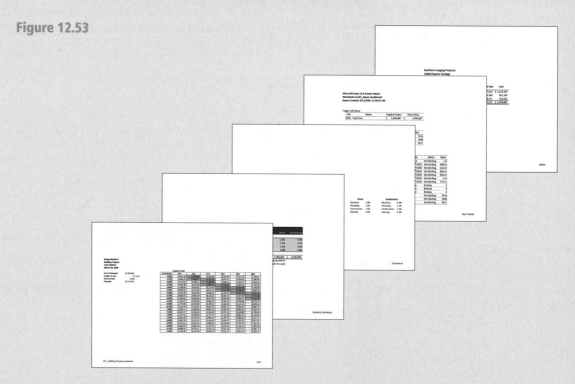

(Project 12C–Building continues on the next page)

Content-Based Assessments

(Project 12C–Building continued)

1. **Start** Excel. From your student files, locate and open the file named **e12C_ Building**. Save it in the **Excel Chapter 12** folder with the name **12C_Building_ Firstname_Lastname**

2. Rename **Sheet1** to **Loan** Click cell **G6** and type **15** Press ⇥ and in cell **H6** type **16** Select the range **G6:H6** and use the fill handle to extend the column until *20* displays. Format this range with **Comma Style, one decimal, Center**, and **Bold**. Click cell **G5** and type **Length of Loan** and format with **Bold**.

3. Click cell **F7** and type **4.00%** Press Enter and type **4.25%** Select the range **F7:F8** and use the fill handle to extend the series until *9.00%* displays.

4. Click cell **B9** and enter a **PMT** function. For the **Rate**, use cell **B8** and divide by 12. For the **Nper**, use cell **B7** and multiply by 12. For the **Pv**, use cell **B6** and display the solution as a positive number. In cell **F6**, insert a **PMT** function like the one in cell **B9** and express it as a positive number.

5. Select the range of cells that contains the formula and both the row and column of values— **F6:L27**. From the **Data tab**, in the **Data Tools group**, click the **What-If Analysis button**. From the list, click **Data Table**.

6. In the **Data Table** dialog box, for the **Row input cell**, click cell **B7**—the cell that displays the number of years of the loan. For the **Column input cell**, click cell **B8**—the cell that displays the interest rate for the loan. Click **OK**. Select the range of the data and format with **Comma Style**.

7. Select the range of the data table— **F6:L27**—and on the **Home tab**, in the **Font group**, click the **Border Button arrow**, and then from the list, click **All**

Borders. Format the range **F6:F27** with **Bold**. If necessary, adjust column widths.

8. The goal of the financial manager is to have payments in the $17,000 to $18,000 range. Select the range **H7:H8** and on the **Home tab**, in the **Font group**, click **Fill Color arrow** and select a **Standard Color** of **Light Blue**. In the data table, highlight the other cells that also display payments between $17,000 and $18,000. **Save** your workbook.

9. The building contractors have agreed to discount some of their work, but Paul Peterson, project manager for Medtech, feels that he may be able to negotiate further discounts and would like several scenarios to see what the savings might be. Click **Sheet2** and rename it **Contractors** In cell **D7**, enter a formula to display the negotiated costs by the percentage listed in column **C**—**=B7-(C7*B7)** Copy the formula through cell **D10** and enter a total in cell **D11**. Format the numbers in **column D** the same as those in **column C**.

10. Confirm that the format for cells **D7** and **D11** is **Accounting Number Format**. Format the range **D8:D10** with **Comma Style**. Data for the scenarios has been entered on the worksheet for you. On the **Data tab**, in the **Data Tools Group**, click **What-If Analysis**, and then click **Scenario Manager**.

11. In the **Scenario Manager**, click **Add**. In the **Scenario name** text box, type **Best** In the **Changing cells** text box, select the range **C7:C10**. Under **Protection**, confirm that **Prevent changes** is selected, and then click **OK**.

12. For the **Scenario Values**, enter the percents that match the Best scenario information on the worksheet—found in **column G**. Click in the first box, and type

(Project 12C–Building continues on the next page)

Content-Based Assessments

(Project 12C–Building continued)

5% the amount of the discount in the best scenario. In the second box, type **3.5%** In the third box, type **5%** and in the fourth box, type **4.5%** Click **OK**.

13. In the **Scenario Manager**, click **Add**. In the **Add Scenario** dialog box, for the **Scenario name**, type **Worst** and for the changing cells, confirm that the range **C7:C10** is entered. Then click **OK**. In the **Scenario Values** dialog box, enter the values of the changing cells for the **Worst** scenario found in **column J**, and then click **OK**.

14. Click **Add**. In the **Add Scenario** dialog box that displays, use the skills you practiced to enter the data required for the **Combination** scenario. Then click **OK**. In the **Scenario Manager** dialog box, click **Summary**. Confirm that **Scenario summary** is selected. For the **result cells**, click **D11**, and then click **OK** to create a Scenario Summary on a new worksheet.

15. In all worksheets, in the **Left Footer** area, insert the **File Name** and in the **Right Footer** area, insert the **Sheet Name**. Center **Horizontally** and **Vertically**. Change to **Landscape orientation** and **Fit to page**. **Save** your changes.

16. From your student files, open **e12C_Building_Solver** save it in your **Chapter 12** folder as **12C_Building_Solver_Firstname_Lastname**. Rename the **Solver sheet tab** as **Sq Footage** Image Medtech has projected a cost of $2.5 million for the additional space and plans to devote about half of the space to manufacturing, 30% to office space, and 20% to warehouse space. You will use Solver to determine the total square footage for the addition and the amount devoted to each of the areas.

17. In cell **A9**, type **Total** and format the cell with **Bold**. Click cell **D9** and insert a **SUM**

formula that adds the range **D6:D8** so the formula reads =*SUM(D6:D8)*. In cell **E6**, multiply the cost per square foot by the square feet—=**B6*D6 Copy** the formula through cell **E8** and insert a total in cell **E9**. Format **D9:E9** with a **Top and Double Bottom Border**. Format cell **E6** and **E9** with **Accounting Number Format** with **no decimals**, and the ranges **D6:D9** and **E7:E8** with **Comma Style** with **no decimals**.

18. Click cell **E9**, and then click the **Data tab** and in the **Analysis group**, click the **Solver button**. Recall that to access Solver, from the Office menu, click Excel Options. At the left, click **Add-Ins**. From the Add-ins list, click **Solver** and at the bottom by Manage, click **Go**. In the **Add-Ins** dialog box, click **Solver Add-in** and click **OK**.

19. For the **Set Target Cell**, click cell **E9**. In the **Equal To:** area, confirm that the **Max** option button is selected. Under **By Changing Cells**, select the range **D6:D8**.

20. At the right of the **Subject to the Constraints** text box, click **Add**. In the **Add Constraint** dialog box, in the **Cell Reference** area, select the range **D6:D8** and for the mathematical operator, click the arrow and click **int**. Click **Add**. For the second constraint, for the **Cell Reference**, select the range **D6:D8**, and for the mathematical operator select **>=** and for the **Constraint** type **0**

21. For the next constraint, click **Add**. For the **Cell Reference**, click cell **E9**. At the right, under **Constraint**, click cell **C13**. Confirm that the mathematical operator between the two text boxes displays **<=**. Then click **Add**.

22. In the **Add Constraints** dialog box, for the **Cell Reference**, click cell **D6**, confirm the mathematical operators is **<=** and for the constraint, type **53%*d9** then click **Add**.

(Project 12C–Building continues on the next page)

(Project 12C–Building continued)

In the **Add Constraints** dialog box, for the **Cell Reference**, click cell **D6**, change the mathematical operator to **>=** and for the constraint, type **47%*d9** then click **Add**.

23. Using the skills you practiced, enter the upper and lower constraints for the Office and Warehouse space using the values found in cells **C15** and **C16**, respectively. After entering all of the constraints, click **OK**.

24. Carefully review your constraints. When you are satisfied they are correct, click **Solve**. The Solver Results dialog box displays indicating a solution has been found. (The results are an additional 15,517 square feet at a cost of $2,499,877.) Confirm that **Keep Solver Solution** is selected. In the **Solver Results** dialog box, under **Reports**, click **Answer**, and then click **OK**. Adjust column widths if needed.

25. Click **Answer Report 1 sheet tab** and rename it **Sq Ft Solver**

26. In all worksheets, in the **Left Footer** area, insert the **File Name**, and in the **Right Footer** area, insert the **Sheet Name**. Center **Horizontally** and **Vertically**. Change to **Landscape orientation** and **Fit to page**. **Save** your changes.

27. To submit electronically, follow the instructions provided by your instructor. Be sure to submit worksheets from both workbooks: 12C_Building_Firstname_Lastname and 12C_Building_Solver_Firstname_Lastname. To print, from the **Office** menu, click **Print**. In the **Print** dialog box, under **Print what**, select **Entire workbook**. Under **Copies**, confirm that 1 is selected. From the **Office** menu, click **Close**. If you are prompted to save changes, click **No**. **Exit** Excel.

End You have completed Project 12C

Content-Based Assessments

Skills Review

Project 12D — Consultant

In this project, you will apply the skills you practiced from the Objectives in Project 12B.

Objectives: 4. *Prepare a Document for Distribution;* **5.** *Use XML to Enhance Security.*

In the following Skills Review, you will review a worksheet for Joel Lieber, Vice President of Marketing, that shows a list of prices for imaging center equipment. He wants to enlist the aid of an outside consultant to compare Image Medtech's prices with the competition, but he does not want the consultant to know too much about Image Medtech's internal operations. Joel would like to learn about the options available for concealing certain types of information. You will assist Joel by demonstrating the options for removing sensitive information so that the consultant does not know what employees worked on the document, when it was first created, or any of the company's internal costs to make the products. The completed files will look similar to those in Figure 12.54.

For Project 12D, you will need the following files:

e12D_Consultant

e12D_Logo.jpg

You will save your work as
12D_Consultant_Firstname_Lastname
12D_Consultant_Inspected_Firstname_Lastname
12D_core_Firstname_Lastname.xml
12D_sheet1_Firstname_Lastname.xml

Figure 12.54

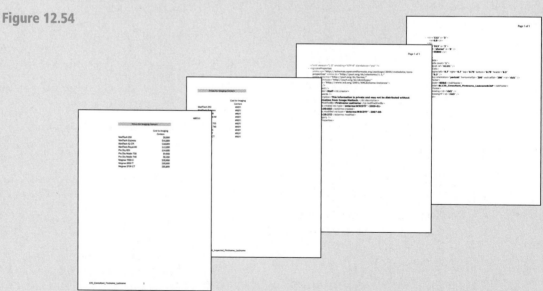

(Project 12D–Consultant continues on the next page)

Content-Based Assessments

(Project 12D–Consultant continued)

1. **Start** Excel. Locate and open **e12D_Consultant**. Save the file in your **Excel Chapter 12** folder, as **12D_Consultant_Firstname_Lastname**

2. Notice that the headings for **column B** and **column C** are not displayed, which indicates that they are hidden. Select column headings **A** and **D**. Click the **Home tab** and in the **Cells group**, click **Format**. Under **Visibility**, point to **Hide & Unhide**, and then in the submenu, click **Unhide Columns**. Notice the hidden columns contain company costs and markup data. Click the **Undo button** to hide **columns B** and **C** again.

3. Click the **View tab**, and then in the **Workbook Views group**, click the **Page Layout button**. Scroll down to the footer. Notice that the footer contains the name of a company employee who worked on the workbook.

4. From the **Office** menu, point to **Prepare**, and then click **Properties**. In the **Author** box, the **Document Properties** panel displays the registered name associated with the copy of Excel that was used to create this document. In the **Comments** box, type **This information is private and may not be distributed without authorization from Image Medtech**

5. From the **Office** menu, point to **Prepare**, and then click **Run Compatibility Checker**. The **Compatibility Checker** dialog box displays. Notice that no major problems exist. Click **OK**.

6. From the **Office** menu, at the bottom of the menu, click **Excel Options**. In the pane at the left, confirm that **Popular** is selected. On the right, under **Personalize your copy of Microsoft Office**, in the **User name** box, make note of the name in this box. If necessary, select the name and

type your name: **Firstname Lastname** and then click **OK**.

7. **Save** the workbook. From the **Office** menu, click **Save As** and save this file again as **12D_Consultant_Inspected_Firstname_Lastname**

8. From the **Office** menu, click **Prepare**, and then click **Inspect Document** to open the **Document Inspector** dialog box. In the **Document Inspector** dialog box, click **Inspect**. Notice that the program found that this file has comments, personal information, headers and footers, and hidden columns.

9. In the **Document Inspector** dialog box, click the four **Remove All buttons** to remove the comments, personal information, headers and footers, and hidden columns. Click the **Close button**. Removing the hidden columns renders the worksheet useless because they contain necessary data. You can use a copy of this worksheet to demonstrate the problem to Joel. Observe that the comments, header, and footer have been erased.

10. Insert the **File Name** in the **Left Footer**. From the **Office** menu, point to **Prepare**, and then click **Mark as Final** to make the file read-only. Close the message windows. **Close** the file and **Close** Excel.

11. From the **Start** menu, click **My Computer**. Click the **Tools** menu, and then click **Folder Options** to display the **Folder Options** dialog box. Click the **View tab**. In the **Advanced settings** box, next to **Hide extensions for known file types**, click the check box to remove the check mark.

12. Click the **File Types tab**. In the **Registered file types** box, scroll to the bottom of the list of file extensions. Under Extension, click **ZIP**. Confirm that this program is

(Project 12D–Consultant continues on the next page)

(Project 12D–Consultant continued)

associated with **Compressed (zipped) Folder**. If not, click the **Change button** and select this file from the list. Scroll to **XML** and confirm that these types of files are associated with the **XML Editor**. At the bottom of the **Folder Options** dialog box, click **OK** if you have not made any changes; otherwise click **Close**.

13. On the **Standard Buttons** toolbar click the **Folders button**. In the My Computer window, navigate to your **Excel Chapter 12** folder, and click the file **12D_Consultant_Firstname_Lastname**. If necessary, on the **Standard Buttons** toolbar, click the **View button**, and then click **Details**. If necessary, drag the vertical line between column headings to widen the **Name** column to display the full file name, including its extension.

14. Right-click the file name **12D_Consultant_Firstname_Lastname.xlsx** and from the shortcut menu, click **Rename**. Edit the name to replace the file extension **xlsx** with **zip** Do not delete the period between the file name and the extension. Press [Enter]. Click **Yes** to make the change.

15. Double-click the file name **12D_Consultant_Firstname_Lastname.zip** to display the structure of the file. On the **Standard Buttons** toolbar, click the **Folders button** to display the **Folders** pane. In the **Folders** pane, click the plus sign next to the **xl** folder.

16. In the **Folders** pane, click the **media** folder. On the right side of the window, notice this folder contains a jpeg file, **image1.jpeg**. Click **Start** and click **My Computer** to open another window of My Computer. Alternatively, if a second window of My Computer is still open on your screen—one that does not display the parts of the zip container—you can switch

to the other My Computer window. Be sure the Folders pane displays on the left.

17. From the student files, locate **e12D_Logo.jpg**, right-click the image, and then click **Copy**. Navigate to the **Excel Chapter 12** folder, right-click and from the shortcut menu, click **Paste**. Right-click **e12D_Logo.jpg** and click **Rename**. With the name selected, type **image1.jpeg** and press [Enter]. Click **Yes** to confirm the change.

18. Right-click **image1.jpeg**. From the shortcut menu, click **Cut**. Close the **My Computer** window. Switch back to the **My Computer** window that displays the content of the **xl/media** folder. On the right side of the window, in an open area, right-click and click **Paste** to place a new version of image1.jpeg into the media folder. In the **Confirm File Replace** dialog box, click **Yes**.

19. In the **Folders** pane, click the **docProps** folder; in the detail pane on the right, double-click the **core.xml** file to display the contents of the file using the XML Editor program. With the code of the **core.xml** file displayed, click the **View** menu, and then click **Source** to open Notepad and display the unformatted text.

20. In the **Notepad** window, from the menu bar, choose **Format**, **Word Wrap**, if necessary to turn on this feature. **Maximize** the window. In the **Notepad** window, from the menu, choose **Edit**, **Find**. In the **Find what** box, type **creator** and then click **Find Next** to locate the start tag of the creator field.

21. In the **Notepad** window, select the name, **Joseph Smith**, between the start and end tags, and type **Staff** Display the **Find** dialog box. In the **Find what** box, type **created** and then click **Find Next** to locate the start tag of the **created** field. In the **Find** dialog box, click **Cancel**. In the **Notepad**

(Project 12D–Consultant continues on the next page)

(Project 12D—Consultant continued)

window, select the date, **2007-07-15T12:11:21Z**, between the start and end tags, and type **2009-01-01T14:00:00Z**

22. Click the **File** menu and click **Save As**. In the **Save As** dialog box, navigate to your **Excel Chapter 12** folder. In the **File name** box, confirm that the name is **core.xml**, and then click **Save**. Display the **Save As** dialog box again. In the **File name** box, select the name and type **12D_core_Firstname_Lastname.xml** and then click **Save**. **Close** the Notepad window. **Close** the Internet Explorer window.

23. In the **Folders** pane, in the **xl folder**, click the **worksheets** folder; in the detail pane on the right, double-click the **sheet1.xml** file to display the content in the XML Editor program. Scroll to the bottom of the window and notice that *Prepared by Joseph Smith* is part of the footer. Joseph was the creator of the document and he placed his name in the footer.

24. Click the **View** menu, and then click **Source** to open Notepad and display the unformatted text. **Maximize** the Notepad window. In the **Notepad** window, using the skills you have practiced, display the **Find** dialog box. In the **Find what** box, type **Joseph** and then click **Find Next** to locate his name in the footer field.

25. Close the **Find** dialog box. In the **Notepad** window, select **Prepared by Joseph Smith**. Do not select the codes on either side. Type **12D_Consultant_Firstname_Lastname**

26. Display the **Save As** dialog box. Navigate to the **Excel Chapter 12** folder. In the **File name** box, confirm that the name is **sheet1.xml**, and then click **Save**. Display the **Save As** dialog box again. Edit the **File name** to **12D_sheet1_Firstname_Lastname.xml** and then click **Save**. **Close**

the Notepad window. **Close** the Internet Explorer window.

27. Click **Start** and click **My Computer** to open another window of My Computer. Display the **Folders** pane. Navigate to your **Excel Chapter 12** folder. Locate **core.xml** and double-click the file. Confirm that it is a valid XML file and that the edits you made were correct; then close the XML Editor window. In the **Excel Chapter 12** folder, locate **sheet1.xml** and double-click the file to confirm that it is a valid XML file and that the edits you made were correct.

28. In the **Excel Chapter 12** folder, right-click the **core.xml** file, and then click **Cut**. Switch to the window that displays the unzipped container of files. Click the **docProps** folder, point to the pane on the right side that contains the **app.xml** and **core.xml** files. Right-click, and then click **Paste** to place the revised core.xml file in this folder. Confirm that you want to replace the file that has the same name.

29. Using the skills you have practiced, switch to the window that displays the **Excel Chapter 12** folder, locate and **Cut** the **sheet1.xml** file. Switch to the window that displays the unzipped container of files. Click the **worksheets** folder, and then **Paste** the sheet1.xml file to this folder and confirm that you want to replace the file that has the same name. Close the window that displays the unzipped container of files to recompress them into a single container file.

30. In the My Computer window that displays the **Excel Chapter 12** folder, locate **12D_Consultant_Firstname_Lastname.zip**. Right-click on the file name and click **Rename**. Replace the **zip** extension with **xlsx** and press [Enter]. Click **Yes** to confirm that you want to change the extension.

(Project 12D—Consultant continues on the next page)

(Project 12D–Consultant continued)

Double-click **12D_Consultant_ Firstname_Lastname.xlsx** to open the file.

31. On the **View tab**, click the **Page Layout button** and notice the new picture in the header. From the **Office** menu, click **Prepare**, and then click **Properties**. In the **Document Properties** panel, click the **Document Properties arrow**, and then click **Advanced Properties**. Click the **Statistics tab**. Notice that the **Last saved by:** name is *Staff* and the **Created** date is *January 1, 2009*. **Close** the dialog box. Center the worksheet **horizontally**, and **Save** your file. Print all of the files created or submit electronically as instructed. **Close** the file.

32. Return the settings to their previous information. From the **Start** menu, click **My Computer**. Display the **Folder Options** dialog box. On the **View tab**, in the **Advanced settings** box, click the check box next to **Hide extensions for known file types** to replace the check mark if it was there when you started. Click the **File Types tab**. If you changed the programs that were associated with the **ZIP or XML**, restore the original associations. Click **OK** to close the **Folder Options** dialog box, and then close the My Computer window. From the **Office** menu, click **Excel Options**. Replace the user name if you changed it for this exercise. **Close** Excel.

End You have completed Project 12D

Mastering Excel

Project 12E — Production

In this project, you will apply the skills you practiced from the Objectives in Project 12A.

Objectives: 1. *Create a Data Table;* **2.** *Create a Scenario;* **3.** *Use Solver.*

Image Medtech has received additional orders and is considering adding an evening shift to the production staff. To add another shift, Image Medtech will need funding for this increase in production. You will complete a worksheet that includes the variables for a loan. You will then review the orders that have been received to determine those that will take the fewest number of hours to fill in order to decide which orders to complete first. Then use Solver to assist with scheduling the evening shift. Your completed workbooks will look similar to those in Figure 12.55.

For Project 12E, you will need the following files:

e12E_Production
e12E_Evening_Shift_Solver

You will save your workbook as
12E_Production_Firstname_Lastname
12E_Evening_Shift_Solver_Firstname_Lastname

Figure 12.55

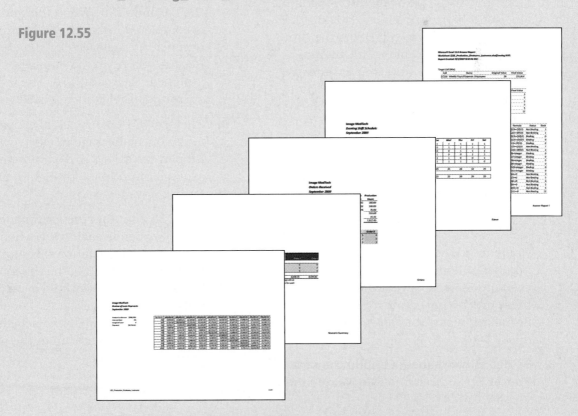

(Project 12E–Production continues on the next page)

(Project 12E–Production continued)

1. **Start** Excel. From the student files, locate and open **e12E_Production**. In your **Excel Chapter 12** folder, Save the file as **12E_Production_Firstname_Lastname**

2. Click the **Loan sheet tab**. Complete the worksheet to determine the amount of the payment, displayed as a positive number. The amount of the loan is $500,000 with an interest rate of 8% for 6 years. In **row 6**, beginning in cell **F6**, enter the possible amounts for the loan in 50,000 increments, from 450,000 to 900,000.

3. In **column E**, beginning in cell **E7**, enter the possible length of the loan, in 6-month increments, from 4.5 years to 10 years. Format the range with **one decimal**.

4. In cell **E6**, enter the payment formula and express it as a positive number. Create a data table with these amounts, using the amount to borrow from cell B6 and the length of the loan in cell B8 as the input cells. Format the table with **Comma Style**. Format the values in **column E** and **row 6** with **Bold**. Format the Data Table with **All Borders**. In the table, use a **Yellow Fill Color** to highlight the cells where the payments will be between $10,000 and $10,500 a month—the amount of monthly payments management is targeting.

5. Click the **Orders sheet tab**. Image Medtech has three orders for goods and wants to use scenarios to determine the number of hours required to produce each order. Create scenarios for each of these orders and create a Scenario Summary report that shows the total cost in cell **D10**.

6. **Select all worksheets** and in the **Left Footer** area, insert the **File Name**, and in the **Right Footer** area, insert the **Sheet Name**. Center the worksheets both **Horizontally** and **Vertically**. Position the worksheets in **Landscape orientation** and **Fit to page**.

7. Open the worksheet named **e12E_Evening_Shift_Solver** and save it in your **Excel Chapter 12** folder as **12E_Evening_Shift_Solver_Firstname_Lastname**. Select the range **A6:A11**. These are the possible schedule shifts. The plant will be in production seven days a week and each employee needs two consecutive days off. Those working Schedule A will have Sunday and Monday off—in the row, there is a 0 inserted for those days, indicating that an employee for Schedule A will NOT be assigned those days. This pattern is used for each shift schedule.

8. Click cell **C13** and review the formula in the Formula Bar. When the work schedule is completed, this cell will contain the total number of employees for the evening shift. Because there are no employees yet assigned, the result is 0. The red border surrounds the changing cells.

9. Click cell **C17**. This cell displays the formula for the average weekly wage. Employees earn $15.15 an hour—on the average—multiplied by eight hours a day for five days a week.

10. Cell **C18** contains the formula for the total payroll expense each week when the schedule is determined. The numbers in the range E15:K15 is the minimum number of employees required each day. The cells in this row will be the constraints. The number of employees scheduled must be equal to or greater than the number required each day.

(Project 12E–Production continues on the next page)

(Project 12E–Production continued)

11. Display the **Solver Parameters** dialog box. The target is the weekly payroll expense—**C18**—to **Min**, and the changing cells are surrounded with a red border. Enter the following constraints:

C6:C11=integer

C6:C11>=0

E13:K13>=E15:K15

12. Solve the problem. Then create the **Answer Report**, You will need 36 employees total with 12 employees working Schedule F with Saturday and Sunday off. The total payroll for the week will be $21,816.

13. Select both worksheets and in the **Left Footer** area, insert the **File Name**, and in the **Right Footer** area, insert the **Sheet Name**. Center the worksheets both **Horizontally** and **Vertically**. Position the **Answer Report** in **Portrait orientation** and the **Solver** sheet in **Landscape orientation** and **Fit to page**. Move the **Answer Report 1 sheet** so it is the last sheet in the workbook.

14. **Save** your workbook. **Print** the workbooks, or submit electronically as directed. **Close** your workbook and **Exit** Excel.

End You have completed Project 12E —————————————

Project 12F — Sales Force

In this project, you will apply the skills you practiced from the Objectives in Project 12B.

Objectives: 4. *Prepare a Document for Distribution;* **5.** *Use XML to Enhance Security.*

In the following Mastering Excel project, you will edit a worksheet for Joel Lieber, Vice President of Marketing, who intends to send out a worksheet to the sales force that shows the items available for use in doctor's offices. One worksheet is intended for the salespeople. The second sheet is for the area manager's eyes only. The second sheet contains a list of products and the cost to produce them. The area manager can approve discounts for special clients that cannot go below the cost. The first sheet shows the base price, the sales commission, and the suggested retail price. Salespeople can discount the suggested retail price up to the value of their own commission. To discount the price further, they must get approval of the area manager, who knows the company's cost.

Joel has heard that the new file format for Excel allows users to see the content of the files. He wants you to check the file and remove any references to the person who wrote it—Margaret Williams—and he wants you to make sure that the salespeople cannot see the hidden costs in the second sheet without the password. Joel wants you to list the elements of the worksheet that contain Margaret's name which can be removed using the normal Excel editing options, and he wants you to list the occurrences of Margaret's name that had to be removed by editing the source code of the XML file parts. Finally, he wants you to document what you found out about the security of the password-protected sheet. You will use another workbook to record your findings, and then you will copy that worksheet into the original workbook. Your completed workbook will look similar to the one in Figure 12.56.

For Project 12F, you will need the following files:

e12F_Sales
e12F_Sales_Documentation

You will save your workbook as
12F_Sales_Firstname_Lastname
12F_Sales_Documentation_Firstname_Lastname
12F_Sales_Secure_Firstname_Lastname

Figure 12.56

(Project 12F–Sales Force continues on the next page)

(Project 12F–Sales Force continued)

1. **Start** Excel and open the **e12F_Sales** workbook. **Save** the workbook in your **Excel Chapter 12** folder as 12F_Sales_Firstname_ Lastname Open **e12F_Sales_ Documentation** and save it in the **Excel Chapter 12** folder as 12F_Sales_ Documentation_Firstname_Lastname

2. In the **12F_Sales_Firstname_Lastname** file, click the **Area Managers sheet tab**. Use the password **Medtech** to unprotect this sheet.

3. Unhide **column B**. Notice the values in this column. These values should not be visible to the salespeople when the column is hidden and the sheet is protected. Choose values to look for in future files such as $120.00 for the *Fly Weight Wheelchair* and $47.00 for the *Dermascope*.

4. Save the **12F_Sales_Firstname_Lastname** workbook as a precaution before you run the **Document Inspector**. Run the **Document Inspector** but do not remove any of the elements using it. Notice the types of elements that exist in this document so that you know what to check. **Close** the Document Inspector without removing any elements.

5. Click the **SalesForce sheet tab**. Display the footer area and notice that it has Margaret's name in it. Delete her name and insert the **File Name**.

6. Display the **12F_Sales_Documentation_ Firstname_Lastname** workbook. This workbook will be used to document the actions taken. In cell **B6**, type **Replaced with file name** to record the action you just took to replace Margaret Williams's name in the footer. In the **12F_Sales** workbook, check the headers and footers on both worksheets for Margaret's name and remove it if necessary. Switch to the **12F_Sales_**

Documentation workbook and describe the action taken or not taken for each header or footer in the Sales workbook.

7. Switch to **12F_Sales_Firstname_ Lastname**. Display the comments on the **SalesForce** sheet. Determine if the comment is intended for the salespeople or for internal use. Delete the comments that are not intended for the salespeople to see. Edit the remaining comments (if any) and change the name in the comment from **Margaret Williams** to **Staff** Document what you did with each comment in the **12F_Sales_Documentation** workbook. Examine the **Area Managers** sheet for comments and document any action taken.

8. In the **12F_Sales workbook**, display the **Document Properties** panel. For both worksheets, replace any occurrence of Margaret's name with **Staff**

9. Display the **Advanced Properties** box. Examine each tab and document if Margaret's name appears and what action is taken, if any. If you find an instance Margaret's name—or another one other than Staff—that you cannot edit, make note of it.

10. Click the **Area Managers sheet tab**. Hide **column B**. Protect the **Area Managers** sheet. Use **Medtech** as the password. In the **12F_Sales_Documentation** workbook, record the effect of this action.

11. Save **12F_Sales_Firstname_Lastname**. Then save **12F_Sales_Firstname_ Lastname** as 12F_Sales_Secure_Firstname_ Lastname and then close it. Leave **12F_Sales_Documentation_Firstname_ Lastname** open.

12. Start **My Computer** and in the **Folder Options** dialog box, display hidden file

(Project 12F–Sales Force continues on the next page)

(Project 12F–Sales Force continued)

name extensions and set the program associated with XML files to **XML Editor**. In your **Excel Chapter 12** folder, rename **12F_Sales_Secure_Firstname_Lastname.xlsx** as **12F_Sales_Secure_Firstname_Lastname.zip** and then double-click it to display its contents.

13. Use the XML Editor to look at each file in the container file that has an **.xml** file extension. Look for any instance of Margaret's name and look for any instance of the hidden data in **column B**, such as *$120* and *$47*.

14. If you find Margaret's name in a file—or any name other than *Staff*—replace it with **Staff**. If your name or the registered user name appears you may leave it in place without comment. If you find the hidden data, report it. Document your actions and findings in the **Documentation** sheet of the **12F_Sales_Documentation_Firstname_Lastname** workbook.

15. Complete your edit of the parts of the XML container. Be sure to move any changed files into the appropriate container (folder) in the My Computer window that displays the extracted xml files. Close the **My Computer** window that displays the container parts to reassemble the file. Rename the **12F_Sales_Secure_Firstname_Lastname.zip** file as **12F_Sales_Secure_Firstname_Lastname.xlsx**

16. Open **12F_Sales_Secure_Firstname_Lastname.xlsx**. Switch to **12F_Sales_Documentation_Firstname_Lastname**. Copy the **Documentation** sheet into **12F_Sales_Secure_Firstname_Lastname**. Close 12F_Sales_Documentation.

17. Be sure the **File name** displays in the **Left footer** of all three sheets. Center each of the three worksheets **horizontally** and **Save** the file. Print the worksheets or submit the file electronically as directed. **Close** the workbook and **Exit** Excel.

End **You have completed Project 12F**

Content-Based Assessments

Project 12G—Budget

In this project, you will apply the skills you practiced from the Objectives in Projects 12A and 12B.

Objectives: 1. *Create a Data Table;* **2.** *Create a Scenario;* **5.** *Use XML to Enhance Security.*

In the following Mastering Excel project, you will use Excel scenarios to assist with Image Medtech's budget for next year and then create a data table to forecast the possible results of a proposed investment. Managers have been asked to cut their expenses for next year, but they are hopeful that profits might allow for a budget increase. You have been asked to prepare a scenario for either possibility regarding a long-term investment the company is considering. Because this workbook will be shared, you will edit the document properties. Your completed workbook will look similar to the one in Figure 12.57.

For Project 12G, you will need the following file:

e12G_Budget

You will save your files as
12G_Budget_Firstname_Lastname
12G_core_Firstname_Lastname.xml

Figure 12.57

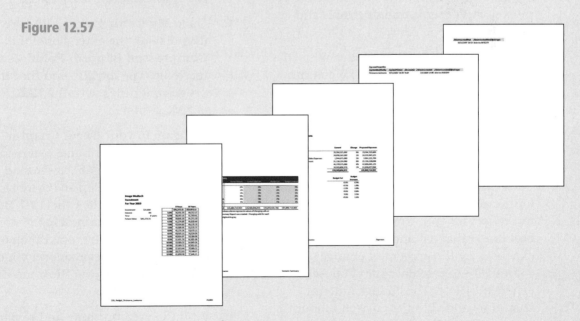

(Project 12G–Budget continues on the next page)

(Project 12G–Budget continued)

1. **Start** Excel. From your student files, locate and open the file named **e12G Budget**. Save the workbook in the **Excel Chapter 12** folder with the name **12G_ Budget_Firstname_Lastname** Name **Sheet1** 25,000 In cell **B8**, enter the Financial function for **FV**—Future Value. For **Rate** use cell **B6**. For **Nper** use cell **B7**. Leave Pmt empty, and then for **Pv** use **B5**. Express the results as a positive number. In cell **E5**, enter the same FV function.

2. In cell **F5**, enter a **FV** function for 10 years. The formula will be the same as the one in cell B8 except the **Nper** will be **10** instead of the contents of cell B7. Express the results as a positive number. In cell **E4**, type **8 Years** and in cell **F4**, type **10 Years** Format the range **E4:F5** with **Bold** and **Center** alignment.

3. Beginning with cell **D6**, enter **5%** Continue with interest rates in increments of .5 until cell **D20** reads *12.00%*. Format the interest rates with **Percent**, **one decimal**, and **Bold**.

4. Select the range **D5:F20**. Under What-If Analysis, click **Data Table**. The column input cell will be the cell in **column B** that contains the interest rate. Format the data table with **Comma Style** and **two decimals**. Select the range **D5:F20** and format with **All Borders**.

5. Click **Sheet2** and rename it **Expenses** Data for the scenarios has been entered on the worksheet for you. Create formulas for **column D** that will increase the current expenses by the percent of change— column C—to calculate the proposed expenses. (Note: The change amount should be added to the current amount.) The formula will read *=B6+(B6*C6)*. The result will be identical to the number in the *Current* column. Copy the formula

through cell **D11**, and then format the numbers the same as those in column B. Enter a **SUM** formula in cell **D12** and format with a **Top and Double Bottom Border** and **Bold**. If necessary, increase column widths.

6. Use **Scenario Manager** to display scenarios for Current Expenses, Budget Cut, and Budget Increase, using the **Change** column values as the changing cells. The Scenario Values dialog box displays only five cells on each screen; use the scroll bar to access all of the data information. **Show** the **Budget Increase** scenario and then create a summary sheet that displays the **Result cell** of D12.

7. In all worksheets, in the **Left Footer** area, insert the **File Name**, and in the **Right Footer** area, insert the **Sheet Name**. Center the worksheets both **Horizontally** and **Vertically**. **Save** your changes. **Close** the workbook and **Exit** Excel.

8. Open **My Computer**. Make sure that your files display the extensions, that **Compressed {zipped} Folder** is the registered file type for ZIP, and that the default program for files with the **XML** extension is XML Editor.

9. Navigate to your **Excel Chapter 12** folder and locate the file name extension on the file **12G_Budget_Firstname_ Lastname.xlsx**. Replace extension **xlsx** with **zip** Double-click the **12G_Budget_ Firstname_Lastname.zip** file name. From the **docProps** folder, open the **core.xml** file. In the Internet Explorer window by the XML Editor, click the **View** menu, and then click **Source**.

10. Find the creator name and replace it with **Staff** In the **Notepad** window, select the first date and type **2009-01-01T14:00:00Z**

(Project 12G–Budget continues on the next page)

Content-Based Assessments

(Project 12G–Budget continued)

11. Click the **File** menu, and then click **Save As**. Navigate to the **Excel Chapter 12** folder. In the **File name** box, confirm that the name is *core.xml*. Click **Save**. Display the **Save As** dialog box again. In the **File name** box, type **12G_core_Firstname_ Lastname.xml** Click **Save**. Close the **Notepad** window. **Close** the Internet Explorer window.

12. Locate **core.xml** in your **Excel Chapter 12** folder, and double-click the file to be sure that it opens in the XML Editor program. Close the XML Editor program. Right-click the **core.xml** file name, and then click **Cut**. Switch to the window that displays the unzipped container of files. In the **docProps** folder, replace the **core.xml** file with your newly saved one.

13. In the **Excel Chapter 12** folder, replace the extension of **12G_Budget_Firstname_ Lastname.zip** with **xlsx** Open the revised file. Display the document properties to see that the creator name has been changed to Staff and the creation date has been changed to January 1, 2009. Close the document properties panel.

14. Print your worksheets or submit electronically as instructed.

End **You have completed Project 12G**

Content-Based Assessments

chaptertwelve | Mastering Excel

Project 12H — Production Mix

In this project, you will apply the skills you practiced from the Objectives in Project 12A and 12B.

Objectives: 2. *Create a Scenario;* **3.** *Use Solver;* **4.** *Prepare a Document for Distribution.*

Image Medtech is in the process of evaluating the past sales and production results and forecasting information for the future. They want to estimate how many pieces of equipment they can produce with a $3 million budget. Because their newer equipment is out-selling the older equipment, they have changed their production mix. In addition, they are projecting a net profit for next year based on sales of the last two years. You will use Document Inspector to prepare the document for distribution. Your workbook will look similar to Figure 12.58.

For Project 12H, you will need the following files:

e12H_Production_Mix
e12H_Projection

You will save your workbook as
12H_Production_Mix_Firstname_Lastname
12H_Projection_Firstname_Lastname

Figure 12.58

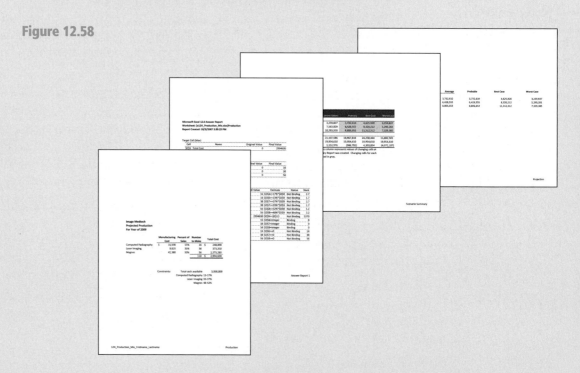

(Project 12H–Production Mix continues on the next page)

(Project 12H–Production Mix continued)

1. **Start** Excel, locate and open the file **e12H_Production_Mix**, and then save the file in your **Excel Chapter 12** folder as 12H_Production_Mix_Firstname_Lastname

2. Enter the formulas required for this worksheet in **column E**—multiply Manufacturing Cost by Number to Make—and enter totals in cells **D9:E9**. Format the totals with **Top and Double Bottom Border**.

3. Display the **Solver Parameters** dialog box. For the **Set Target Cell**, use the total cost of all equipment as Max. The changing cells are the Number to Make in column D. Use the following constraints:

   D6:D8=integer

   D6:D8>=0

   D6<=17%*D9

   D6>=13%*D9

   D7<=37%*D9

   D7>=33%*D9

   D8<=52%*D9

   D8>=48%*D9

   E9<=E13

4. Carefully review the constraints for accuracy and then **solve** the problem and create an **Answer Report**. Format the ranges **D6:D9** and **E7:E8** with **Comma Style** with **no decimals**, and cells **E6** and **E9** with **Accounting Number Format** with **no decimals**. Place the Production sheet in front of the Answer Report 1 sheet.

5. Locate and open **e12H_Projection**, and then save it in your **Excel Chapter 12** folder as **12H_Projection_Firstname_Lastname**

6. Image Medtech is forecasting their sales for the next year using three different scenarios—one that is the most likely, one that is optimistic, and one that is pessimistic.

7. Complete the worksheet by determining the average sales for the three pieces of equipment for the last two years using the AVERAGE function. Then determine the sales possibilities by entering numbers for three possibilities. For the **Probable** scenario, use the average for the last two years. For the **Best Case** scenario, take the highest sales of the two years and add 10% For the **Worst Case** take the smallest sales of the two years. Format amounts with **Comma Style** with **no decimals**.

8. Use the Scenario Manager to create four scenarios: the three you have determined the numbers for—Probable, Best Case, and Worst Case—as well as a **Current** scenario using the 2009 numbers. Use cells **C8:C10** as the changing cells, and for each scenario replace the numbers with the values you calculated in step 6. Display the Scenario Summary, using cells **C11**, **C18**, and **C20**. To enter more than one result cell, place a comma after each cell reference.

9. In all sheets of both workbooks, in the **Left Footer** area, insert the **File Name** and in the **Right Footer** area, insert the **Sheet Name**. Format all worksheet centered **Horizontally** and **Vertically** and in **Portrait orientation**, **Fit to page**.

10. For both worksheets, access **Document Inspector** to inspect the document. Remove all document properties and personal information, except for headers and footers, and remove hidden rows and columns. Mark the document as final.

11. Submit your work as instructed.

End You have completed Project 12H

Mastering Excel

Project 12I — New Facility

In this project, you will apply the skills you practiced from all of the Objectives in Projects 12A and 12B.

Objectives: 1. *Create a Data Table;* **2.** *Create a Scenario;* **3.** *Use Solver;* **4.** *Prepare a Document for Distribution;* **5.** *Use XML to Enhance Security.*

In the following Mastering Excel assessment, you will create worksheets that will assist in the installation of Image Medtech's equipment in a new facility. As Image Medtech sells digital imaging equipment, they also work with the purchasing hospital for installation and other requirements. Image Medtech is working with Providence and Warwick hospital as it designs its new facility. The hospital has requested assistance with the space needs for the equipment as well as assistance with the financial impact of the equipment. In this activity, you will use the What-If Analysis tools to assist management in making these decisions. Your completed workbook will look similar to Figure 12.59.

For Project 12I, you will need the following files:

e12I_New_Facility
e12I_Data_For_P&W_Hospital

You will save your files as
12I_New_Facility_Firstname_Lastname
12I_New_Facility_Inspected_Firstname_Lastname
12I_Data_For_P&W_Hospital_Firstname_Lastname
12I_core_Firstname_Lastname.xml

Figure 12.59

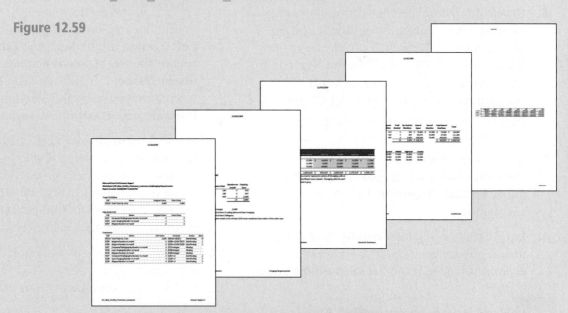

(Project 12I–New Facility continues on the next page)

(Project 12I–New Facility continued)

1. **Start** Excel. If you are continuing from another project, be sure that you close Excel and then open it again; Solver is used in this project. From the student files, open **e12I_New_Facility** and save it in your **Excel Chapter 12** folder as 12I_New_Facility_Firstname_Lastname

2. Providence and Warwick Hospital has maintained records for the use of the imaging equipment. Based on past history, management knows that the radiography and laser imaging machines are equally used. However, the demand for the Magnes equipment is approximately 25 percent more than that for either of the other two machines. As a result, the number of machines ordered must meet this demand. The hospital also know it needs a minimum of two radiography and laser imaging machines and a minimum of three Magnes machines. Currently, the hospital has planned 3,500 square feet for this new facility. These constraints are displayed in this worksheet. In the **Imaging Requirements sheet**, click cell **C10** and enter a **SUM** formula for the range **C7:C9**—even though the range is now blank, these are the changing cells for Solver.

3. Complete the formulas required in the worksheet to determine the total square feet required for each machine and the total for the hospital. Format the range **C10:D10** with a **Top and Double Bottom Border**. Format the numbers in the **Number to Install** and **Total Sq. Feet** columns with **Comma Style** with **no decimals.**

4. If Solver is not available, add it to your computer. Display the **Solver Parameters** dialog box. Set the **Target Cell** as **D10** equal to **Max**. For the **Changing Cells**, use **C7:C9**.

5. Click the **Add button**. Add the following constraints:

    C7:C9=int

    C7>=2

    This constraint is to confirm that at least two Computed Radiography machines will be installed.

6. Add constraints so that cell **C8** is at least 2 and cell **C9** is at least 3. Add the constraint **D10<=C13** to keep the space limited to 3,500 square feet.

7. Add the following constraints to cell C9— >=125%*C7 and >=125%*C8. These constraints are required so that there are 25% more Magnes machines than the others.

8. Use **Solver** to find a solution. When a result has been found, insert the **Answer Report**. In the **Imaging Requirements sheet**, adjust column widths to fully display cell contents. You will install 13 machines in the hospital—4 Computed Radiography, 3 Laser Imaging, and 6 Magnes.

9. Click in the **Install Costs sheet tab** and edit the column title in cell **G5** to read *Total Cost of Machines*. Image Medtech manufactures machines of different quality. Warwick and Providence Hospital has asked for a comparison of the total costs depending on the machine quality purchased and the cost per square foot.

10. Click cell **C6** and type = Click the **Imaging Requirements sheet tab**, and click cell **C7** and press Enter. Complete the total needed using the results of Solver and include a total in cell **D9**. If your Solver did not bring the results identified in step 8, then use the results listed there.

11. Complete the formula in **column D**, which is the total square feet needed for all of the machines. In **column E**, enter a formula to

(Project 12I–New Facility continues on the next page)

Content-Based Assessments

(Project 12I–New Facility continued)

calculate the cost of the space, which is $125 per square foot. In **column G**, enter the total cost for all machines ordered, and in **column H**, complete the worksheet by creating a formula to calculate the total cost—the cost of space plus the cost of machines.

12. Place totals in cells **C9**, **D9**, **E9**, **G9**, and **H9**. Format with a **Top and Double Bottom Border** and in **E9**, **G9**, and **H9**, format with **Accounting Number Format** with **no decimals**. Format the range **E6:H6** with **Accounting Number Format** with **no decimals**. Delete the data in **row 17**.

13. Display the Scenario Manager. Create four scenarios using the data entered in the range **A13:E17**. The changing cells are **F6:F8**. As you evaluate the results, leave the scenario to show the **Combo** scenario. Create a Scenario Summary sheet to display cell **H9** in the results. In the **Install Costs sheet**, adjust column widths if necessary. Using Find and Replace or by proofreading the document, make the two corrections from **Computer Radiography** to **Computed Radiography**.

14. Rename **Sheet2** to **Table of Costs** You will use this worksheet to create a two-variable data table that evaluates the costs of the facilities, including the cost per square foot and the cost of the equipment.

15. Using the results of the Combo Scenario in the **Install Costs sheet** place the amount of of Sq Feet for machines and the Total cost of machines (equipment) into the **Table of Costs** works cells **B6** and **B9**. In **cell B7**, enter $125, **the cost per square foot**. In cell **B8**, enter a formula to determine the cost of space. **In cell B10** enter a formula to determine the total cost of the building and the equipment.

16. Edit cell **A6** to read **Sq Feet for Machines**, **A8** to read **Cost of Space** and cell **A9** to read **Total Cost of Machines** and adjust column widths if needed.

17. Format the numbers in **column B** with **Comma Style** and **no decimals**. Place a **Bottom Border** under cell **B7** and a **Top and Double Bottom Border** in cell **B10**.

18. You will create a data table that examines the total cost depending on the cost per square foot for construction and the type of equipment ordered. Beginning in cell **G7**, enter the following cost per square foot options across the row:

100	110	120	125	130	140	150

19. Beginning in cell **E8**, type the equipment costs shown below. These numbers are the results of the scenario; you will obtain these results when you **Show** the scenario in the **Install Costs sheet**. Recall that the prices vary depending on the model of the equipment that will be installed.

Low End	389,935
Middle	590,935
High End	739,935
Combo	599,935

20. Click cell **F7** and enter the formula that determines the total cost.

21. Select the range of the data table and insert the table. Format the data with **Comma Style** and **no decimals**, and the entire table with **All Borders**. Apply **Bold** to both the **row titles—F7:M7**— and the **column titles—E8:F11**. In the data table, highlight the cells that are between $1,000,000 and $1,100,000 with **Yellow Fill**.

22. Delete **Sheet3**. **Select all worksheets** and in the **Left Footer** area, enter the **File Name** and in the **Right Footer** area, enter

(Project 12I–New Facility continues on the next page)

(Project 12I–New Facility continued)

the **Sheet Name**. In the **Center Header**, insert the **Date**. Center the worksheets both **Vertically** and **Horizontally**. Place all worksheets in **Landscape orientation** and **Fit to page**. **Save** the workbook.

23. Resave the workbook and name it **12I_ New_Facility_Inspected_Firstname_Lastname** From the **Office** menu, display the Document Inspector and remove the hidden rows and columns from the workbook. **Save** and **Close** the workbook.

24. From the student files, open the file **e12I_Data_For_P&W_Hospital**, and then save it in your **Excel Chapter 12** folder as **12I_Data_For_P&W_Hospital_Firstname_Last name** and then **Close** the file.

25. Open **My Computer** and confirm that your computer is set to display file extensions. Navigate to your **Excel Chapter 12** folder. Right-click the file name **12I_Data_For_ P&W_Hospital_Firstname_Lastname.xlsx** , and from the shortcut menu, click **Rename**. Edit the name to replace the file extension **xlsx** with **zip** Do not delete the period between the file name and the extension. Press Enter, and click **Yes** to confirm the change.

26. Double-click the **12I_Data_For_P&W_ Hospital_Firstname_Lastname.zip** file name. On the **Standard Buttons** toolbar, click the **Folders button**. In the **Folders** pane, click the **docProps** folder. In the detail pane on the right, double-click the **core.xml** file. If an **Information Bar** notice box appears, click the **Close button**. With the code of the **core.xml** file displayed in the Internet Explorer window by the XML Editor, click the **View** menu, and then click **Source**.

27. In the **Notepad** window, if necessary, click the **Format** menu, and then click **Word**

Wrap. **Maximize** the window. In the **Notepad** window, click the **Edit** menu, and then click **Find**.

28. In the **Find what** box, type **creator** and then click **Find Next** to locate the start and end tags of the creator field. In the **Find** dialog box, click **Cancel**. In the **Notepad** window, select the name that is displayed between the start and end tags and type **Staff**

29. Click the **Edit** menu, and then click **Find**. In the **Find what** box, type **created** and then click **Find Next**. In the **Find** dialog box, click **Cancel**. In the **Notepad** window, select the date between the start and end tags and type **2009-01-01T14:00:00Z**

30. Click the **File** menu, and then click **Save As** to display the **Save As** dialog box. Navigate to your **Excel Chapter 12** folder. In the **File name** box, confirm that the name is **core.xml**. Click **Save**.

31. Display the **Save As** dialog box again. In the **File name** box, type **12I_core_ Firstname_Lastname.xml** Click **Save**. Close the **Notepad** window. **Close** the Internet Explorer window.

32. Switch to the window that displays the content of the **Excel Chapter 12** folder. Double-click the **core.xml** file. If it is a valid XML document, it will open in the XML Editor window. Check the changes you made. If you made a mistake, start over at step 23. **Close** the XML Editor.

33. Navigate to the **Excel Chapter 12** folder, right-click the **core.xml** file, and then click **Cut**. Switch to the window that displays the unzipped container of files. Click the **docProps** folder. Point to the pane on the right side that contains the *app.xml* and

(Project 12I–New Facility continued)

core.xml files. Right-click, and then click **Paste**. Click **Yes** to confirm that you want to replace the file that has the same name.

34. Navigate to the **Excel Chapter 12** folder, right-click on **12I_Data_For_P&W_Hospital_Firstname_Lastname.zip**, and click **Rename**. Replace the **zip** extension with **xlsx** and press Enter and click **Yes**. Double-click **12I_Data_For_P&W_Hospital_Firstname_Lastname.xlsx**. If you receive an error message, click **OK** or

Yes to continue. Display the Properties Pane to make sure the author and date corrected were changed. **Close** the Properties Pane.

35. From the **Office** menu, click **Prepare**, and then click **Mark as Final**. In the **Microsoft Office Excel** dialog box, click **OK** twice.

36. **Print** all the worksheets or submit electronically as directed. **Close** your workbooks and **Exit** Excel.

End **You have completed Project 12I** ⎯⎯⎯⎯⎯⎯⎯⎯⎯⎯⎯⎯⎯⎯⎯⎯⎯⎯⎯⎯⎯

Content-Based Assessments

Project 12J — Business Running Case

In this project, you will apply the skills you have practiced from the Objectives in Projects 12A and 12B.

From My Computer, navigate to the student files that accompany this textbook. In the folder **03_business_running_case**, locate and open the folder for this chapter. Open and print the instructions for this project, which are provided to you in Adobe PDF format. Follow the instructions and use the skills you have gained thus far to assist the managers of the Grand Department Store to meet the challenges of keeping records for a large department.

End You have completed Project 12J ——————

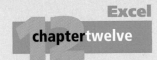

Rubric

The following outcomes-based assessments are *open-ended assessments*. That is, there is no specific correct result; your result will depend on your approach to the information provided. Make *Professional Quality* your goal. Use the following scoring rubric to guide you in *how* to approach the problem, and then to evaluate *how well* your approach solves the problem.

The *criteria*—Software Mastery, Content, Format and Layout, and Process—represent the knowledge and skills you have gained that you can apply to solving the problem. The *levels of performance*—Professional Quality, Approaching Professional Quality, or Needs Quality Improvements—help you and your instructor evaluate your result.

	Your completed project is of Professional Quality if you:	Your completed project is Approaching Professional Quality if you:	Your completed project Needs Quality Improvements if you:
1-Software Mastery	Choose and apply the most appropriate skills, tools, and features and identify efficient methods to solve the problem.	Choose and apply some appropriate skills, tools, and features, but not in the most efficient manner.	Choose inappropriate skills, tools, or features, or are inefficient in solving the problem.
2-Content	Construct a solution that is clear and well organized, contains content that is accurate, appropriate to the audience and purpose, and is complete. Provide a solution that contains no errors of spelling, grammar, or style.	Construct a solution in which some components are unclear, poorly organized, inconsistent, or incomplete. Misjudge the needs of the audience. Have some errors in spelling, grammar, or style, but the errors do not detract from comprehension.	Construct a solution that is unclear, incomplete, or poorly organized, containing some inaccurate or inappropriate content; and contains many errors of spelling, grammar, or style. Do not solve the problem.
3-Format and Layout	Format and arrange all elements to communicate information and ideas, clarify function, illustrate relationships, and indicate relative importance.	Apply appropriate format and layout features to some elements, but not others. Overuse features, causing minor distraction.	Apply format and layout that does not communicate information or ideas clearly. Do not use format and layout features to clarify function, illustrate relationships, or indicate relative importance. Use available features excessively, causing distraction.
4-Process	Use an organized approach that integrates planning, development, self-assessment, revision, and reflection.	Demonstrate an organized approach in some areas, but not others; or, use an insufficient process of organization throughout.	Do not use an organized approach to solve the problem.

Outcomes-Based Assessments

Problem Solving

Project 12K — Markup

> **For Project 12K, you will need the following file:**
>
> e12K_Markup
>
> You will save your workbooks as
> 12K_Markup_Firstname_Lastname
> 12K_Price_List_Firstname_Lastname

Image Medtech is interested in knowing how a change in the markup rate will affect the final price of their products. The equipment is expensive to manufacture, and the prices must reflect the research and development, labor, and other factors that go into manufacturing. You have been asked to create scenarios for several markup possibilities. After you complete the scenarios, show the Combination scenario in the worksheet and create a Summary sheet.

Because this workbook may be distributed to hospitals, you will hide the column that shows the cost and the markup percentage as well as the scenario data. You will also hide the total row and the Summary sheet.

On each worksheet, apply appropriate number formatting; use borders and fill colors and choose font styles and font sizes to create professional-looking worksheets. Add a footer to each worksheet that includes the file names, center the worksheets on the page, and delete unused sheets. Save your workbook as **12K_Markup_Firstname_Lastname** Save the workbook a second time with the name **12K_Price_List_Firstname_Lastname** Use Document Inspector to remove all items from the 12K_Price_List_Firstname_Lastname workbook except for hidden rows and columns. When you have completed an accurate workbook, mark the workbook as final. Submit your workbooks as directed.

End You have completed Project 12K ———————————

Outcomes-Based Assessments

Problem Solving

Project 12L — Machinery

In this project, you will construct a solution by applying any combination of the skills you practiced from the Objectives in Projects 12A and 12B.

> **For Project 12L, you will need the following file:**
>
> e12L_Machinery
>
> **You will save your workbook as**
> **12L_Machinery_Firstname_Lastname**

Image Medtech must replace some of its production equipment and would like financial information to assist in determining the finance method for this upgrade. A worksheet has been started for you. You will need to determine the amount to borrow and the payment. To determine the total cost of the loan, multiply the payment by the time by 12 months. The interest expense is the total cost less the amount borrowed. The annual cost is the payment for 12 months.

Create a data table that has two formulas in it—use IPMT and PPMT functions. At the left column of the data table, enter varying percentages in increments of 0.5% beginning with 4.5% and ending with 11.5%.

Apply appropriate number formatting; use borders, fill colors, and font styles and sizes to create a professional worksheet. Add a footer to the worksheet that includes the file name, center the worksheet on the page, and delete unused sheets. Save the workbook as **12L_Machinery_ Firstname_Lastname** and submit it as directed.

End **You have completed Project 12L** ⸺⸺⸺⸺

Problem Solving

Project 12M — Income

In this project, you will construct a solution by applying any combination of the skills you practiced from the Objectives in Projects 12A and 12B.

For Project 12M, you will need the following file:

e12M_Income

You will save your workbook as
12M_Income_Firstname_Lastname

Complete the income statement for Medical Technology, Inc. IQ CR. You will total the revenue and expenses. In the Net Income section, deduct the expenses from the revenue. Then prepare scenarios based on the current values. Create three scenarios—decrease costs, increase price, and a combination of the two. The data for the scenarios is included in the data worksheet. Include a Scenario Summary in your results.

On each worksheet, apply appropriate number formatting; use borders, fill colors, and font styles and sizes to create a professional-looking worksheet. Add a footer to each worksheet that includes the file name, center the worksheets on the page, and delete unused sheets. Save the workbook as **12M_Income_Firstname_Lastname** and submit it as directed.

End **You have completed Project 12M**

Outcomes-Based Assessments

Problem Solving

Excel

chapter twelve

Project 12N—Weekly Shift

In this project, you will construct a solution by applying any combination of the skills you practiced from the Objectives in Projects 12A and 12B.

For Project 12N, you will need the following file:

e12N_Weekly_Shift

You will save your workbooks as
12N_Weekly_Shift_Firstname_Lastname
12N_Work_Schedule_Firstname_Lastname

Production of machinery at Image Medtech occurs seven days a week. Medtech needs to review the shift requirements for the week for the three shifts the plant runs—day, evening, and night. They will also need to determine the total number of hours required. The constraints—the issues you need to take into consideration—and the minimum number of employees needed for each shift are displayed on the worksheet. You will use Excel Solver to determine the number of employees needed for the day, evening, and night shifts by changing the number of employees for each of the shifts. Prepare an Answer Report. Add the file name to the footer of both worksheets and delete unused sheets. Save your file as **12N_Weekly_Shift_Firstname_Lastname**

Resave the file as **12N_Work_Schedule_Firstname_Lastname** Hide the Answer Report sheet and the constraints. Change it to a Zip file and edit the code file to change the name of the creator to Staff and to change the date to 2009-01-01T14:00:00Z. Test your results and replace the file in the zip container folder. Rename the file to an .xlsx file and open it.

Use the Document Inspector to fully protect all properties of the workbook, except for the header and footer, and to mark it as a final copy. Submit your workbooks as directed.

End **You have completed Project 12N** ——————

Problem Solving

Project 12O — Magnes

In this project, you will construct a solution by applying any combination of the skills you practiced from the Objectives in Projects 12A and 12B.

For Project 12O, you will need the following file:

e12O_Magnes

You will save your workbook as
12O_Magnes_Firstname_Lastname

Image Medtech has scheduled the production of 60 Magnes machines. Of that total, the number of each model produced will be a certain percentage, which is listed on the worksheet located in your student files. After you solve the problem of the number of each model to produce, create an Answer Report.

Add a footer to each worksheet that includes the file name, center the worksheets on the page, and delete unused sheets. Save the workbook as **12O_Magnes_Firstname_Lastname** and submit it as directed.

End You have completed Project 12O ——————————

Outcomes-Based Assessments

You and *GO!*

Project 12P—You and *GO!*

In this project, you will construct a solution by applying any combination of the Objectives found in Projects 12A and 12B.

From the student files that accompany this textbook, open the folder **04_you_and_go**. Locate the **You_and_GO** project for this chapter and follow the instructions to create a data table to compare vehicle loan terms.

 End You have completed Project 12P ───────────

GO! with Help

Project 12Q—*GO!* with Help

In this chapter, you used data tables, scenarios, and Solver. Solver is a flexible tool that can help you consider alternatives in a wide variety of situations. Excel offers additional information about Solver from outside sources. In this exercise, you will use Help to learn more about Solver.

1 **Start** Excel and click the **Help button** . In the **Type words to search for** box, type **Solver** and click **Search**. From the list, click **Perform What-If Analysis with the Excel 2007 Solver Tool**. Read the information contained there to give you additional tips about using Solver.

2 In the menu bar, click the **Back** arrow 🄴 and in the menu, click **Analyze business results with Excel 2007**. Read the information about data tables.

3 When you are finished, **Close** the **Help** window, and then **Exit** Excel.

End You have completed Project 12Q ───────────

Glossary

3-D reference A reference to the same cell or range of cells on multiple worksheets.

Absolute cell references Refer to cells by their *fixed* position in the worksheet and do not change when the formula is copied.

Accounting Number Format Numbers displayed with two decimal places, fixed U.S. dollar sign at the left gridline, and thousand comma separators.

Active area The rectangle formed by all rows and columns that contain entries in a worksheet.

Active chart A chart that is identified by the double border surrounding it and may be edited, formatted, and moved.

Active workbook The workbook that is visible on the screen where changes can be made.

Active worksheet The worksheet where text and data will be entered. The sheet tab of the active sheet is highlighted, while the sheet tabs of the inactive sheets are dimmed.

Add-in A supplemental program that adds custom commands or features that is available when you install Excel.

Adjacent cells Cells that are next to each other that form a range of cells.

Adjustment handles The diamond-shaped handles at the top of the graphic that are used to adjust the appearance but not the size of the shape.

Advanced command A command used to filter a range of cells using complex criteria that display in the worksheet.

Alias A short nickname assigned to a namespace reference.

Amortization table A report that shows each monthly payment, the amount paid for interest, and the remaining amount due until the loan is fully paid. Also called a loan payment schedule.

AND function A logical function that tests two or more arguments to see if they are true or false, and returns TRUE if all arguments are true and FALSE if any argument is not true.

Area charts A chart that emphasizes the magnitude of change over time and can be used to draw attention to the total value across a trend.

Areas Section In the PivotTable, the section used to place field names into the PivotTable report.

Arguments The values that an Excel function uses to perform calculations or operations.

Arithmetic operators Provide basic mathematical operations such as addition, subtraction, multiplication, and division. Also used to combine numbers and produce numeric results.

Ascending order The order from the smallest number to the largest number or from A to Z.

Audit Examine a worksheet to check for accuracy.

Auditing tools The tools that provide additional assistance to help locate possible errors.

Authenticity The digital signature helps assure that the signer is who he or she claims to be.

Auto expansion Inserted rows or columns are automatically included in the table format and are formatted as the table.

Auto Fill Generates a series of values into adjacent cells, based on the value of other cells.

Auto Fill Options button A button that displays just to the right of copied formula, providing options for filling the text as a copy or series and the format choices.

AutoComplete The feature that uses previous text entries to complete the remaining characters for you.

AutoCorrect Assists in your typing by automatically correcting and formatting text as you type.

AutoCorrect Options button The button is used to undo the calculated column and to access options for controlling AutoCorrect.

AutoFit Column Width Adjusts the column width to fully display the contents of the *selected* cell or cells.

Automatically updated properties Properties that are set by the operating system or by the Office program.

AVERAGE function A formula that adds a group of values and divides the result by the number of values in the group.

AVERAGEIF function Calculates the average of a range of data that meets a specified condition.

Axis titles Titles that display at the far left and bottom of the chart that identify the type of data in that area.

Banded columns In a worksheet, columns that alternate colors or shades of color.

Border line The line that surrounds the title or other chart element.

Border style The style of the border line.

Brightness Used with graphics to indicate the relative lightness of the graphic element.

By Changing cell In Goal Seek, the cell that will change.

Calculated column In a table, after a single formula is entered the column automatically expands to include additional rows so the formula is immediately extended to those rows.

Calculated value The results of a calculated formula.

Calculation operators Specifies the type of calculation that will be performed on the elements of a formula.

Calculations The process of computing formulas and then displaying the results as values in the cells that contain the formulas.

Category axis Labels that display along the bottom of the chart to identify the category of data; also called the horizontal axis.

Category labels The labels that display along the bottom of the chart to identify the category of data.

Cell The intersection of a column and a row.

Cell address Another term for cell reference.

Cell content Anything typed into a cell.

Cell reference Cell identification that is the intersection of the column letter and row number; sometimes called cell address.

Cell Styles A defined set of formatting characteristics, such as fonts and font sizes, number formats, borders, and shading.

Cell Styles gallery Displays a palette of styles than can be applied to selected cells or ranges.

Certificate Authority (CA) The certificate associated with a digital signature that is issued to the reputable signer.

Changing cells The cells that will change when the Scenario or Solver is completed.

Chart A graphic representation of data in a worksheet.

Chart area The entire chart and all of its elements.

Chart layout Combination of chart elements including title, legend, labels for the columns, and the table of charted cells.

Chart Layouts gallery Predesigned chart layouts.

Chart range The range of cells that are included in the chart.

Chart sheet A chart displayed on a separate sheet in a workbook.

Chart styles Used to determine the colors used in the chart.

Chart Styles gallery The gallery that displays styles available for the chart and includes charts formatted in shades of an individual color, shades of black and white, or multiple-colors.

Chart template A template of a chart that can be used independently of a specific worksheet.

Chart titles Descriptive text that is aligned to an axis or centered at the top of a chart.

Chart type The way chart data is presented—as a column, line, bar, pie, or other graphical element that displays the relationship among the data.

Circular reference Occurs when the cell in which the formula is created is included in the range of cells or arguments used in the formula.

Clear command Clears the format and contents of the cell.

Clip art Drawings, photographs, movies, or sound clips that can be inserted into the Excel document.

Clip Art task pane When accessing clip art, the area that displays at the right side of the worksheet used to display clip art choices.

Clipboard task pane An area to the left of the screen used to collect copied data.

Clipboard The storage area that contains data that has been copied.

Collapse Dialog Box button Collapses the Function Arguments dialog box and displays only the entry area for the selected argument.

Color scales A conditional format that uses gradients of the color to visually compare values.

Column A vertical group of cells in a worksheet.

Column chart A chart used to display changes over a period of time or for illustrating comparisons among categories of related numbers.

Column headings The letters at the top of each column that identify the column.

Column Index Number In a lookup, the column number in a table from which the matching value will be returned. In the table the first column is column 1, the second column 2, etc.

Column specifier In a structured reference, the column title.

Column title Text that identifies the data in the column.

Comma Style Numbers displayed with two decimal places and thousand comma separators.

Comment A remark that is attached to a cell.

Comment indicator A red triangle in the upper right corner of a cell that indicates a comment is attached to the cell.

Compare and merge workbooks Merging data from several workbooks into one workbook.

Comparison operator A mathematical operator that compares two values.

Compatibility Mode Indicating a workbook that was created in an earlier version of Excel that can be converted to open in Excel 2007.

Compound interest The interest paid on the principal plus the previously accumulated interest.

Compressed (zipped) Folder The program provided with Windows XP that is used to ZIP— combine, compress, or uncompress files.

Conditional format Any format, such as cell shading or font color, that is applied to cells that meet certain conditions and emphasizes that data.

Conditional Formatting Rules Manager A dialog box that uses predetermined rules for applying a conditional format. New rules can be added, or rules can be edited or removed.

Conditional functions Tests whether a condition is true or false by using logical or comparison expressions.

Consolidate Combine data from each separate worksheet into a master worksheet in the same workbook or a different workbook.

Consolidate by category Using the same categories in individual worksheets to create a consolidated workbook.

Consolidate by position Using the position of data in individual worksheets to create a consolidated workbook.

Constant value Any data in a cell.

Constraints The restrictions that limit the values that will change with Solver.

Container The zip file that is created with the ZIP feature.

Context-sensitive Commands that are associated with a particular selection.

Contextual tabs Contain related groups of commands that you will need when working with the selected area or object.

Contextual tools Enable specific commands related to the selected area or object.

Contrast The difference between the lightest and darkest areas of a graphic.

Copy Contents of the cell can be placed in additional locations within the worksheet, workbook, or in a different workbook.

Copy and paste The action of copying cell contents into another location.

core.xml file Contains text that identifies the author, key search words, descriptions, and the dates the file was created and modified.

COUNT function A statistical function that counts the number of cells in the selected range that contain numeric values.

COUNTA function A statistical function that counts the number of cells in the range that are not empty.

COUNTIF function A function that counts the number of cells within a range that meet the given condition.

COUNTIFS function Used to count the number of items when there is more than one condition to be met.

Create from Selection Used to create cell and range names from existing row and column titles by using a selection of cells in the worksheet.

Criteria Conditions you specify in filtering data.

Criteria range In an advanced filter, the location of the criteria that have been entered.

Crop Reducing the size of a graphic element by removing the horizontal and vertical edges.

Cryptography The process of converting ordinary text into unintelligible gibberish in order to maintain security of the original data.

Currency number format Used for general monetary values—the U.S. dollar sign is the default symbol.

Custom calculations Formulas that allow for calculations to be created in the PivotTable.

Custom list A list that is used to sort by an order other than alphabetic or numeric.

Custom number format Used to create your own number format.

Data Numbers, text, dates, or times of the day that are used in Excel.

Data bar With a Conditional Format, a colored bar that displays in a worksheet cell where the length of the data bar represents the value in the cell.

Data labels The numbers displayed by the data markers in the chart.

Data marker In a chart, a column or portion of the chart that represents the value in a cell in the worksheet.

Data point A value in the chart.

Data series Related data points that are plotted in a chart.

Data table In a worksheet, a range of cells that is used to determine how changing certain values in formulas affects the results of the formulas.

Data table In a chart, a table that is inserted to display the exact data in the worksheet.

Data validation A method that ensures accurate data is entered. Instructions are provided that assist with the completion of the form and alerts the user if an error is made.

Database A collection of data. Also called a table or list.

Date number format Provides many common ways to display dates.

DAVERAGE function A function that determines an average in a database.

DB The function name for the declining balance depreciation method.

DCOUNT function A function that counts specific items in a database.

Declining balance depreciation Recognizes that an asset will depreciate faster during the early years of its life.

Deduction An amount that is withheld from your paycheck.

Default font The font Excel uses in its workbooks and worksheets.

Defined name A name that represents a cell, range of cells, formula, or constant value.

Deleting cells Cutting cells from the worksheet.

Delimited Determining column fields from a list by a symbol, such as a space, comma, tab, or semicolon.

Delimiters In converting text to columns, the symbols used to separate fields, such as a space, comma, tab, or semicolon.

Dependent cells Cells that are referred to by a formula in another cell.

Depreciation The amount that an asset decreases in value over time through use, obsolescence, or damage.

Descending order The order from the largest number to the smallest number or from Z to A.

Destination The cell or range of cells into which data will be copied.

Destination cell The cell into which data will be copied. In a range, the destination cell is the upper left cell.

Destination range The range of cells into which data will be copied.

Developer tab Used to work with macros and for developers who customize Excel.

Dialog box A box that displays and requests additional information about the command or requires a decision.

Dialog Box Launcher Displays in some groups on the Ribbon and opens a related dialog box that provides additional options and commands related to the group.

Digital credentials Data used to implement an IRM system to reliably identify each employee .

Digital signature An electronic, encryption-based secure stamp of authentication on a macro or document.

Displayed value Data displayed in a cell.

docProps folder Contains files that define the document properties.

Document theme Used to format workbooks and individual worksheets. Themes are available in all Microsoft Office applications to provide a consistent format throughout a group of documents.

Double-click Quickly clicking the left mouse button two times.

Drag Move cell contents from one location in the worksheet to another; the action of dragging includes releasing the mouse button at the desired time or location.

Drag-and-drop A technique that uses the mouse to move or copy selected text from one location to another. Press Ctrl as you move the cells to copy the cell contents.

Drop-down list Displays valid entries that can be entered into a cell in the form. A cell that contains a drop-down list displays an arrow in the cell.

DSUM function In a database, the function that will sum a column of values in a database that is limited by criteria set for one or more cells.

Duplicate record An identical record. A record is considered a duplicate record when all values of the records match.

Edit Change values of a worksheet.

Ellipses String of three periods following a command that indicate a dialog box will open when that command is selected.

Embedded chart A chart that displays as an object within the worksheet.

Embedded document Pasting a document into another application that cannot be changed. Selecting Keep Source Formatting, Match Destination Table Style, Paste as Picture, or Keep Text Only creates an embedded document.

Encrypt A method for scrambling information to increase security during data transmissions.

Encryption The process of restricting access to files by scrambling the contents with a program.

End tag Code that marks the end of that type of data in a namespace.

Enter data by range Selected range where the data will be entered so the active cell will move to the next cell where data will be entered.

Error alert Creates a dialog box that alerts the user that incorrect information is entered into the cell.

Error checking Rules Excel uses to check for errors in formulas.

Error Checking button Reviews the formulas that are entered in the worksheet and alerts you to potential errors in creating a formula.

Error indicator A green triangle that displays in the upper left corner of the cell and indicates a potential formula error.

Error value Indication that a type of error has been detected.

Evaluate formula When reviewing a formula, this enables you to see the different parts of a nested formula in order to evaluate the formula in the order it is calculated.

Expand Dialog Box button Fully displays the Function Arguments dialog box.

Expand Formula Bar button Increases the height of the Formula Bar to display lengthy cell content.

Exploded pie chart A style of pie chart that displays one or more data markers "outside" or unattached to the chart.

Extensible Markup Language (XML) A set of rules used to create a language.

External lookup The term used in a lookup when the table array is in a different workbook.

Field An individual category of data.

Fields Columns of a worksheet used in a PivotTable.

Fields Section In the PivotTable Field List, the section that displays each column title from the source data.

File extension A few letters following the file name that indicate which program should be used with the file. These file extensions are normally hidden for known file types.

Fill The color or pattern in the interior of a shape, line, or character.

Fill Across Worksheets The feature that allows you to copy data from one worksheet to the exact cells in other worksheets of the workbook.

Fill handle The small black square in the lower right corner of a selected cell used to copy text or a formula to adjacent cells.

Filter Displays only the rows that meet specific criteria.

Filter button The button that displays as a visual reminder when a column is filtered.

Filter criteria The specified conditions of a filter that limits the records displayed.

Final Used with Document Inspector to make the file read-only.

Financial functions Functions used to assist businesses in making financial decisions, such as calculating a loan payment or reviewing the depreciation allowed on an asset.

Find and Replace Searches the cells in a worksheet—or in a selected range—for matches and then replaces each match with a replacement.

Fixed width Determining fields that are a specific width when converting text to columns.

Font A set of characters with the same design and shape.

Font size The size of characters.

Font style Characteristics of a font such as bold and italic.

Footer Text, page numbers, and graphics that display and print at the bottom of every page.

Format Painter Copies a format from one cell and pastes it into another cell or cells.

Formatting The process of determining the appearance of cells and the overall layout of a worksheet.

Formula An equation that directs Excel to perform mathematical calculations.

Formula AutoComplete After you type = (equal sign) and the beginning letters of the function, Excel displays a dynamic list of valid functions, arguments, and names that match the letters.

Formula Bar Displays the value or formula contained in the active cell; also permits entry or editing of values or formulas.

Formula replication The term used when the formula has been entered into the worksheet and is automatically filled through the range of the table.

Fraction number format Displays fractional amounts as actual fractions rather than as decimal values.

Freeze Panes A command that is used to display specific rows or columns when scrolling through the worksheet.

Full Screen The entire screen displays the worksheet without the ribbon, scroll bars, or other aids.

Function A prewritten formula that takes one or more values, performs an operation, and then returns a value or values.

Function Arguments dialog box The location where you enter the arguments—values—used for the function.

Function keys Keys across the top of the keyboard labeled F1, F2, F3, and so on that are used for special tasks.

Future value The amount that an investment made today will be worth in the future.

Gallery A display of potential results to the format of the worksheet.

General number format The default format used when numbers are typed in the cell, excluding the trailing zeros to the right of a decimal point.

Goal Seek An Excel "what-if" analysis tool that is used to find a specific value for a cell by adjusting the value in another cell.

Gradient A gradual progression of colors and shades, usually from one color to another or from one shade to another shade of the same color.

Gradient fill A gradual progression of colors and shades, usually from one color to another color, or from one shade to another shade of the same color.

Grand total The total of the individual sums in the selected range.

Gridlines Horizontal and vertical chart lines that extend from any horizontal and vertical axes across the plot area of the chart.

Gross pay The amount of earnings before any deduction.

Grouped Data and formatting can be entered in all worksheets at the same time.

Header Displays at the top of every page and may be used to print text, page numbers, and graphics.

Help button Displays the Excel Help.

Hidden cells Cells that have hidden formulas that other users cannot see when the worksheet is protected.

Hide columns Removing columns of data from the worksheet view without losing the data.

Hide rows Removing rows of data from the worksheet view without losing the data.

Hide Sheet The command that hides the worksheet so it does not display in Print Preview and does not print with the workbook group. The worksheet remains in the workbook.

History sheet The worksheet that displays the history of the workbook and displays who created each change, which cells were changed, and when the changes were made.

HLOOKUP function The function that compares the values in a cell with a defined horizontal list and when a match is found, places a corresponding value in the original worksheet.

Horizontal axis The axis along the bottom of a chart that usually contains categories; also called the category axis.

Horizontal lookup The full name of the HLOOKUP function.

Horizontal page break line The line placed between rows to indicate the placement of the page break.

Hot spot A place on a form that will execute a command when you click on it.

html—Hypertext Markup Lanugage The format of documents that are written for the Web.

Hyperlinks Text that you click to move to another location in a worksheet or another page on the Web.

Icon set A group of similar icons that are used to add emphasis to the conditional format of a list.

IF function A logical function that performs a test to determine whether a condition is true or false.

Import Inserting data from one application to another application.

Inactive chart A chart that cannot be edited; it is identified by the single line border.

Increase Font Size button Increases the font size with each click.

Information Rights Management (IRM) A formal system that designates who can read or edit a file.

Input area Areas in a worksheet where the user enters information.

Input cell The cell in a data table in which each input value from a data table is substituted.

Input message Displays when the cell is selected. It provides information to the user about the type of information that should be entered into the cell.

Input range The range in a template that will be filled in with data needed to complete the form.

Input values The values that will be tested in a data table—may be either down a column or across a row.

Insert Options button Provides suggestions for formatting a newly inserted column.

Insertion point The point in the cell, Formula Bar, or text box that indicates where additional text will be entered and is identified by a vertical line.

Inside preset Used to place borders that surround each cell within the selected range of cells.

Integrity The digital signature helps to assure that the content has not been changed or tampered with.

Interest In a loan, the amount of money charged for the use of the money. In a savings or investment, interest is the amount paid for the amount saved or invested.

Interest rate The percentage rate that is charged for a loan.

IPMT—Interest Payment—function A financial function that calculates the amount of interest that will be charged for a given period.

JPG A file extension that identifies image files that are stored using the JPEG compression procedure.

Keyboard shortcut An individual keystroke or a combination of keys pressed simultaneously that can either access an Excel command or navigate to another location on your screen.

Landscape orientation Printing and displaying a worksheet when the paper is wider than it is tall.

Legend The box in a chart that identifies the patterns or colors assigned to the data series or categories in the chart.

Line chart A chart designed to display data over time using lines that join data markers. A line chart is used to show trends over equal intervals of time.

Linked The term used when a worksheet and a chart are connected.

Linked document A document that can be updated when the original worksheet is changed, keeping the linked document current.

List A collection of data. Also called a table or database.

List range In an advanced filter, the range of the table that contains the data.

Live Preview Live Preview is a technology that displays the results of applying an editing or formatting change as you move the pointer over the items presented in the gallery or list.

Loan payment schedule A report that displays each monthly payment, the amount paid for interest, and the amount the loan is decreased with each payment. Also called an amortization table.

Locked cells Worksheet cells that cannot be changed after the worksheet is protected.

Logical functions A group of functions that compares data to a set of conditions and returns results based on the comparison.

Logical test Any value or expression that is evaluated as being true or false.

Long Date A date format that displays the day of the week and the date written in full.

Long-term assets Property owned by a firm that is expected to last more than one year.

Lookup list Another term for table array. A table of text, numbers, or logical values in which data is looked up.

Lookup value The entry in the worksheet that will be compared in the lookup list.

Macro A series of commands—such as selections from menus and dialog boxes, keystrokes, and clicks on toolbar buttons—and functions that are grouped together as a single command.

Macro command button A graphic shape inserted into the worksheet that is assigned to a macro.

Macro recorder Works like an audio recorder. Every keystroke and mouse click is recorded and saved with the macro.

Macro security Protects your computer from importing a macro virus.

Macro virus Unauthorized code that is attached to a macro which may damage or erase files.

Major gridlines The gridlines in a chart that identify the major units.

Manual page break line The solid blue page break line that displays when the page break position is set by the Excel user.

Maximum Function (MAX) Displays the largest number in the selected cells.

Median A statistical function that finds the value at the midpoint of a series of numbers.

Merge Across command A command used to merge cells across a row.

Merge Cells command When used, the selected range is merged into one cell that is the size of the selected range.

Merge workbooks command Combining individual workbooks containing similar data into one workbook.

Merged cell A single cell created by combining two or more selected cells.

Message Bar An area on your window that displays security alerts when there is potentially unsafe content in the document you open and displays by default.

Microsoft Excel Help Used to answer specific questions and, in some cases, provides step-by-step instruction.

Microsoft Office Clipboard Allows you to copy multiple text and graphical items from Office documents and paste them into another Office document.

Mini toolbar Brings common commands closer to selected text so that your mouse does not have to travel so far to select a commonly used formatting command.

MINIMUM function A statistical function that displays the smallest number in the selected range of cells.

Minor gridlines The gridlines in a chart that identify the minor units.

Mixed reference A cell reference where either the column or the row will remain the same as the formula is copied. $A1 and A$1 are mixed references.

MODE function A statistical function that finds the value that occurs the most often in a list of numbers.

Module The place where each macro is stored in Visual Basic Application (VBA) code. These are numbered sequentially.

Name Box Displays the name of the selected cell, table, chart, or object.

Name Manager The command that accesses the dialog box where you can create, edit, or delete names used in the workbook.

Named cell A cell that is identified by a name, which is used in a formula rather than the cell reference.

Named range A range that is identified by a name, which is used in a formula rather than the cell references.

Namespace The place where labels for data is stored.

Navigate Move within a worksheet, between workbooks, or to the drive on which you will be storing your folders and workbooks.

Nest functions Functions that are placed within one another to create complex formulas.

Net pay The amount of pay after deductions are withheld. Also called take-home pay.

Non-repudiation The digital signature helps to prove to all parties the origin of the signed content. Repudiation refers to the act of a signer's denying any association with the signed content.

Nonadjacent cells Cells that are not next to each other.

Nonadjacent ranges Ranges of cells that are not next to each other.

Normal View The default view.

NOW function A Date & Time function that returns the current date and time in the cell.

Nper argument The total number of payments needed to pay off the loan.

Number format The ways numbers are displayed, such as General, Accounting Number, Comma Style, and Custom.

Object Linking and Embedding (OLE) The feature that allows content created and updated in one application to be available in other applications.

Office button Displays a menu of commands related to things you can do *with* a workbook, such as opening, saving, printing, or sharing.

One-variable data table A data table that uses one variable with one or more formulas used for "what-if" analysis.

Open as Copy The command used to open a duplicate file, which is given a new name—usually by adding *Copy (1) of* to the front of the file name.

OR function The logical function that tests two or more arguments to see if they are true or false, and returns TRUE when any one of the arguments is true.

Orientation Within a cell, refers to a diagonal angle or vertical position of data.

Outline bar The bar that displays at the left of an outlined worksheet and is used to expand or collapse the data.

Outline Level buttons The buttons in the Outline bar that expand or collapse the outline.

Outline preset Used to insert a border that outlines a selected range of cells.

Output area An area in the form that summarizes the data that will be prepared and printed.

Overtime All hours worked in excess of 40 hours per week and paid at a higher rate of pay, usually 1H times the regular pay rate.

Overwrites Replaces any existing cell content.

Page break lines Dark blue dotted lines that display where the pages will break.

Page break preview The screen that displays the suggested page breaks.

Page breaks The location in a worksheet where the worksheet will split—break—between pages when it is printed.

Page Layout View Displays the horizontal and vertical rulers, margins, headers and footers, and the edges of the page.

Parent-child relationship A pair of tags enclosed within another pair of tags. The parent tags enclose the child tags.

Parts The files and folders within a Compressed (zipped) Folder.

Password A word that is unknown to others used to restrict access to a workbook, worksheet, or part of a worksheet.

Paste Used to insert copied data into a new cell or range of cells.

Paste Options button Displays just under and to the right of the destination and is used to confirm what will be pasted.

Paste Values A command used to paste only the results of the cell and that clears any underlying formula.

PDF format The abbreviation for Portable Document Format. A format that cannot be changed and enables file sharing. It ensures that when the file is viewed or printed, the exact format is retained and data cannot be easily changed.

Per argument The argument that identifies the period for which you want to find the interest.

Percentage number format Multiplies the cell value by 100 and displays the result with a percent sign and two decimal places.

Permissions May be granted to enable certain areas to be edited in a protected worksheet.

Pie chart A round chart that shows the relationship of parts to the whole.

PivotChart Visually displays the data and can be manipulated quickly to show different trends. It is interactive with the PivotTable upon which it is based.

PivotTable Field List At the right side of the PivotTable sheet, a pane that displays the fields section and the layout—areas—section. The field list displays each of the column titles from the source data in the Fields Section. Below the Fields Section is the Areas Section—which is the area used to place field names into the PivotTable report.

PivotTable Layout Area The area of the PivotTable where the PivotTable is created by inserting fields and data.

PivotTable report Used to manipulate a large amount of numerical data so that it can be displayed in different ways in order to analyze and answer questions about the data.

Plot area In a chart, the area bordered by the axes, including all data series, category names, tick-mark labels, and gridlines.

PMT—Payment—function Calculates the payments for a loan based on constant payments and a constant interest rate.

Point-and-click method Clicking in the cell to enter its cell reference in a formula.

Points How the font size is measured. There are 72 points in an inch and most fonts contain 10 or 11 points.

Portable Document Format (PDF) A software program created by Adobe™. A format widely used because the reader is free and anyone can open and view files saved in PDF. With a special add-in program from Microsoft, users can create and read PDF files without purchasing Adobe Acrobat™.

Portrait orientation Printing and displaying a worksheet when the paper is taller than it is wide.

PPMT—Principal Payment—function A financial function that calculates the amount of the payment that will be applied to the principal.

Precedent cells Cells that are referred to in a formula.

Present value The amount of money that must be invested today in order to have a specific amount of money at a future time. Alternatively, the total amount that a future amount is worth now.

Primary sort The first level of a sort.

Principal The original amount of a loan or the amount still owed.

Print area A defined area of the worksheet that is to print—usually smaller than the entire worksheet.

Print Preview The feature that displays the worksheet and its placement on the screen.

Proper case When the first letter of each word is capitalized.

PROPER function A text function that capitalizes the first letter of each word in a cell entry that contains text.

Protected A worksheet or workbook in which unauthorized changes cannot be made.

Pt. The abbreviation for point.

Pv In the IPMT function, the present value—the amount that it would take today to completely pay the loan or the amount still owed.

Pv argument—Present Value Depending on the function, the lump-sum amount that a series of future payments is worth now or the total amount that a series of future payments is worth now.

Quick Access Toolbar Displays buttons to perform frequently used commands with a single click. Frequently used commands in Excel include Save, Undo, and Redo. Butttons for the commands that *you* use frequently can be added to the Quick Access Toolbar.

Range A group of cells.

Range lookup The argument in a lookup function that is used when an exact match must be made.

Rate The interest percentage rate charged for a loan.

Read-only A worksheet that can be reviewed, but no changes can be made to it unless it is saved with a new name.

Read-only file A file that can be read, but not changed.

Read-write Workbooks that can be read, edited, and resaved.

Recently Used menu In the Function Library group, a menu that displays a list of recently used functions.

Record The related data for that person, place, or thing.

Redo Reverses a previous Undo command.

Refresh Used to update the PivotTable when a change is made in the worksheet.

Relative cell reference When a cell reference is copied, it changes to reflect the new location.

Relative reference (macro) Used when the actions in the macro are relative to the selected cell.

Remove Duplicates The command used to check the list in the worksheet and permanently remove all duplicates.

Result cells Cells whose values are changed by the scenarios.

Ribbon Groups the commands used for performing related workbook tasks.

Right-click Click the right mouse button.

Rotation The command that changes the orientation and perspective of the selected chart element.

Rotation handle The green circle that appears above the selected shape that is used to rotate the shape.

Row A horiztontal group of cells in a worksheet.

Row heading The numbers along the left side of the worksheet that indicate the row number.

Row Labels area The section of the PivotTable Field List that identifies row titles of the PivotTable. These fields do not contain numbers.

Run macro Playing back the macro to quickly insert the format, text, or formulas previously recorded into the worksheet.

Sans serif A font that does not have small line extensions on the ends of the letters.

Scaling Adjusts the size of the printed worksheet to fit on one page and is convenient for printing formulas.

Scatter charts Charts that plot two sets of numbers at the same time and are used for displaying and comparing numeric values.

Scenario A set of values that Microsoft Office Excel saves and can substitute automatically on a worksheet.

Scenario Summary Report A report that displays the variable information along with the results of several scenarios on the same page.

Schema The XML standard that allows developers to specify rules that data in the XML files must obey.

Scientific number format Displays numbers in scientific (exponential) notation and is useful with large numbers.

ScreenTip Additional information about the button or command that appears when the mouse is pointed at the button or command.

Scroll arrows Used to scroll one column or row at a time.

Scroll bars The bars located at the right side and bottom of a worksheet used to scroll the Excel window up and down or left and right.

Scroll boxes The boxes within the scroll bars used to move the position of a window up and down or left and right.

Secondary sort The levels of the sort after the first level.

Security Alerts Messages that display in the Message Bar when potentially unsafe tasks are about to be completed. Information about the alert is provided with choices on how to proceed.

Select Highlighting cells by clicking or dragging with your mouse.

Select All box Used to select all the cells in a worksheet.

Series A group of similar or related items that come one after another in succession.

Series names The labels for the categories in a chart that display in the legend and in a ScreenTip when you point to a data marker.

Serif font A font that includes small line extensions on the ends of the letters to guide the eye in reading from left to right.

Set cell In Goal Seek, the cell that contains the formula that will be set to a specific value by changing the value in another cell used in the formula.

Settings Used to specify the type of validation you want to set—from type and length of text to type of numerical data.

Shared workbook Workbooks that enable more than one user to be able to enter data in the same workbook.

Sheet tabs Tabs that are used to identify and change the active worksheet in a workbook.

Shortcut menu A list of context-related commands that displays when you right-click selected cells.

Single File Web Page Single File Web Page is selected when only the sheet will be saved to the Web.

Sizing handles In a selected object, the small circles or squares that appear at the corners and sides of the object and are used to change the size of an embedded chart or other object.

SLN function The function name for the straight-line depreciation method.

SmartArt graphic A designer-quality visual representation of information that provides a variety of layouts that can be used to quickly, easily, and effectively communicate the information.

Solver Part of the What-If analysis tools and used to find an optimal value for a cell on a worksheet. It works with a group of cells that are related to the formula and adjusts the values in a group of cells to determine the optimal value.

Sorting Arranging data according to its value or alphabetically.

Sorting and Filtering arrow An arrow that display in a column title indicating that the column can be sorted or filtered.

Source cell The cell that will be copied into another location.

Source data Data that is copied. Alternatively, the range of data included in a PivotTable.

Source range The range of cells that will be copied into another location.

Special item specifier In a structured reference, specific parts of the table.

Special number format Used primarily with database functions such as postal codes, telephone numbers, and taxpayer ID numbers.

Spelling Checker Compares the text in the worksheet with a built-in dictionary and identifies words that are possibly misspelled.

Spreadsheet Another term for worksheet.

Stack data points Pictures inserted as data points stacked on top of the others without distorting the image.

Stacked chart A chart that places the data from each category one on top of the other.

Start tag Code that marks the beginning of the data in a namespace.

Static A date or time that remains the same and does not change.

Static date A date that will not update; it always remains the same date.

Static time A time that will not update.

Statistical functions A group of functions that provide statistical analysis of the worksheet for the purpose of evaluating data.

Status bar Displays at the bottom of the screen, On the left side the current cell mode, page number, and other information display. On the right side, buttons to control how the window looks is displayed. When numerical data is selected, common calculations such as Sum, Average, and Count display.

Step-In A feature used when evaluating a nested formula.

Stock chart A chart that illustrates the fluctuation of stock prices, providing the history of the stock by displaying the highest price, lowest price, and closing price.

Stop error alert Alerts the user and prevents invalid data from being entered into the cell.

Straight-line depreciation Calculates an equal amount of depreciation for each year of useful life of the asset.

Stretch data point A picture inserted as a data point that is stretched to fit the designated space, often causing a distortion of the image.

Strong password A combination of uppercase and lowercase letters, numbers, and symbols that is used to restrict access to a workbook, worksheet, or part of a worksheet.

Structure The basic format of the workbook that includes the number and order of worksheets.

Structured reference Used in database functions; displays named ranges, worksheet names, and so on, rather than cell references. When a structured reference is used, the cell references included in the table automatically use the names in the worksheet in the formulas.

Sum-of-years' digits depreciation The method of depreciating an asset that recognizes that an asset will depreciate faster during the early years of its life.

SUMIF function Adds the cells in a range that meet a specific condition.

SUMIFS function Adds data that matches two or more criteria.

SYD function The function name for the sum-of-years' digits depreciation method.

Syntax The language rules used by Excel to complete an instruction or command.

System Clipboard A temporary storage area maintained by the Windows operating system that contains the latest data in a copy command.

Tab scrolling buttons Used to move sheet tabs into and out of view so the worksheets can be selected.

Table A collected block of data organized so that each row—record—includes all of the data about a single item and each column—field—contains one category of data about that item. Also called a list or database.

Table array A table of text, numbers, or logical values in which data is looked up.

Table headers Column titles that identify each category of data in the table, which are used to sort and filter data and are used in calculations.

Table specifier In a structured reference, the outer portion of the reference that is enclosed in brackets following the table name.

Table Styles gallery Displays the styles that can be applied to a table.

Take-home pay The amount of pay after deductions are withheld. Also called net pay.

Target cell The cell in Solver that contains the goal to be achieved.

Template A workbook that has the structure—the format and formulas are completed—already determined. A template can be used over and over.

Text Words used in a worksheet that provide information about the text or numbers in other worksheet cells.

Text box A box that is used to add additional information to a chart or worksheet.

Text effects Effects that change the look of the text by adding other effects, such as shadows, reflections, flow, or 3-D rotations or bevels.

Text file The file type that contains no formatting and can be read by any text editing or word processing program; it uses the extension .txt..

Text format Formats number as if it were text.

Text functions A group of functions that are used to format text.

Text Pane The area that displays at the left of a SmartArt diagram that is used to enter text.

Text to Columns The feature that converts data in one cell into several fields and places the data in the number of cells required to display the fields separately.

Theme A format applied to a worksheet that is a combination of complementary colors, fonts, and effects.

Time The length of time it takes to pay off a loan.

Time number format Provides many common ways to display time.

Title bar Indicates the name of the current workbook and the program name and displays the program-level buttons.

To value box In Goal Seek, the amount that you want the Set Cell to display.

TODAY function A Date & Time function used to return the current date.

Toggle button A button that you click once to turn on and click again to turn off.

Trace dependent Identifying the cells that are referred to by a formula.

Trace precedent Identifying the cells that are referred to in a formula.

Track changes In a shared workbook, displaying who made changes, when they were made, and what the changes are.

Transpose Shifts the vertical and horizontal orientation of the data in the worksheet.

Trendline A graphic representation of the trends in a data series.

TRIM function The function that removes all spaces from text except for spaces between words.

Truncated Cell contents that do not fully display in the cell.

Two-variable data table A data table that uses two variables and one formula.

txt file The extension used for a text file.

Underline button Places a line under only the text or numbers within a cell or range of cells.

Underlying formula The formula displayed in the Formula Bar.

Underlying value Data displayed in the Formula Bar.

Undo command Used to reverse up to 16 past keyboard actions.

Unzip To regenerate a zipped file.

URL—Uniform Resource Locator The Web address. It is used to access specific Web addresses.

Use in Formula list A list that displays all names of defined cells and ranges available to use in the active workbook.

Value Data entered into a cell. It may be numbers, text, dates, or times of day.

Value axis In a chart, a numerical scale upon which the charted data is based; also called the vertical axis.

Values area The section of the PivotTable Field List used to summarize data in the PivotTable.

VBA Programming language used to write computer programs within the Microsoft Windows environment. Also referred to as Visual Basic Application.

Vertical (Value) axis The axis on the left edge of the chart that usually contains numeric values. A second vertical axis may also display on the right edge of the chart. Also called the value axis.

Vertical lookup The full name of the VLOOKUP function.

Vertical page break line The page break line that is placed between columns.

View options Contains buttons for viewing the workbook in Normal, Page Layout View, or Page Break Preview; also Zoom Out and Zoom In.

Visual Basic Application Programming language used to write computer programs within the Microsoft Windows environment. Also referred to as VBA.

VLOOKUP function A function that looks for a value in the left column of a table, and then returns a value in the same row from another column in the table array that you specify.

Volatile A Date & Time function that is updated each time the worksheet is used.

Watch Window A small window that is used to inspect, audit, or confirm formula calculations and results in large worksheets.

Web page A document that displays as a screen that may contain links, frames, pictures, and other features and is uploaded to the World Wide Web.

What-If analysis A process of changing the values in cells to see how those changes affect the outcome of formulas on the worksheet.

Windows Rights Management client A Windows XP program that allows you to enable Information Rights Management (IRM).

WordArt A style of text that can be added to Excel—and other Microsoft documents—that creates decorative effects.

Workbook A collection of worksheets.

Workbook-level buttons Minimizes or restores the displayed workbook.

Worksheet The primary document used in Excel to store and work with data; organized in a pattern of uniformly spaced horizontal and vertical lines.

Worksheet grid Displays the columns and rows that intersect to form the workbook's cells.

Worksheet structure The data range in all worksheets that includes the same range of cells, the same column and row titles, with no empty rows or columns.

Worksheet title The area of the worksheet that identifies the organization, purpose, and date of the worksheet.

Workspace A group of worksheets that are saved together in one file name that can be opened simultaneously. When you save a workspace, information about the workbook is saved, including window sizes, screen positions, and links to the actual workbooks.

Wrap text Allows text entries to display on multiple lines within the cell.

x-axis Another name for the category axis.

XML Paper Specification (XPS) Microsoft's version of a fixed-layout format in Office 2007. There is an add-in to the Save As menu that must be downloaded and installed to create and read XPS files. To read XPS files, a free viewer is available for download. No download is necessary with the Microsoft Vista operating system.

y-axis Another term for the value axis.

Zip Used to reduce the file size.

Zoom control Provides a method to quickly decrease or increase the worksheet and is one method used to view and work in more areas of the worksheet.

Zoom to Selection Changes the size of the worksheet so the currently selected range of cells fills the entire window.

Index

 The CD symbol represents Index entries found on the CD (see CD file name for page numbers).

module, 718
money, borrowing, 484–485
More arrow, 67, 427
mouse
  double-click, 23
  moving worksheets with, 233
  right-click, 27
Move Chart button, 69
Move Chart dialog box, 349
Move or Copy, 160, 169, 182, 200, 233, 382,
  386, 418, 431, 577, 603, 655, 772, 826, 871,
  1053
moving
  active cell location, 13
  data, 254
  worksheets with mouse, 233
multiple-sheet workbooks, 114–158
  exercises, 194, 204, 211, 220
  footers in, 188–189
  formatting data in, 115–118
  formatting page placement in, 188–189
  insert columns into, 150–153, 194, 204, 216, 220
  insert rows into, 153–158
    exercises, 194, 204, 216, 220
    relative cell references in, 153–158
Multiplication operator symbol, 54
music clip art, 821

N

name box, 5, 8, 14
Name Manager, 549, 552
named cells, 542–545
  quarterly totals with, 555–557
  from row/column titles, 545–548
named ranges, 542
  changing data in, 554
  formula creation with, 548–593, 601,
    607, 613
  pasting lists of, 557–558
  rules for, 544
#NAME?, 186
namespaces, 1113
naming
  Excel files, 1104–1108
  macros, 714
  rules for ranges, 544
  sheet tabs/worksheets, 118, 120–121
  tables, 629
#N/A, 186
navigating, 7, 114
  worksheets, 9–13, 114
    exercises, 80, 87, 93, 96
negative numbers, 279, 283
nested 3-D references, 1003–1005
nested functions, 992–1003
  auditing tools, 1008–1017
  creating, 992–995
  evaluating, 995
  IF and AND functions, 1001–1002
  IF functions, 996–1000

VLOOKUP, 1005–1008
net pay, 243
New Age Sales-9C, 869–872
New Artists-9E, 876–878
New Car Sales, 734–763
New Folder dialog box, 7
New Range dialog box, 907, 944
New Workbook dialog box, 72, 918
nonadjacent cells, 55
nonadjacent ranges, 16
nonadjacent worksheets, selecting, 150
non-repudiation ⊙, 764
Normal view, 6, 31
North Africa-9N, 893
Not equal to symbol, 242
Not in Dictionary, 49–50
NotePad, 1114–1116. *See also* XML
Notes
  Border button, 30
  clear print area, 294
  Decrease Indent button, 271
  deleting comments, 478
  deleting items from Office Clipboard, 137
  Formula AutoComplete, 467
  formula display keyboard shortcut, 41
  grand total does not display, 147
  namespaces, 1113
  negative numbers, 283
  Not in Dictionary, 50
  Office Clipboard size difference, 136
  page break, 286
  password is *student*, 911
  paste action/pressing enter, 130
  Personal Macro Workbook, 713
  PivotTable range, 747
  PMT function/optional arguments, 487
  Relative Reference button, 730
  screen resolution, 4, 114
  sort data in PivotTable, 758
  text box size/shape, 369
  times in Document Properties, 1116
  unhiding worksheets, 566
NOW function, 469–470
Nper argument, 486
#NULL!, 186
number(s)
  entered in worksheets, 21–22
  formatting, 280–284
  negative, 279, 283
  sorting, 382–385
Number Filters, 416–418
number formats, 22, 279–284
  Accounting, 26–27, 63, 82, 279, 281
  Comma Style, 26, 63, 279
  Currency, 281
  Custom, 282
  Date, 281
  exercises, 303, 313, 316, 320, 324
  Fraction, 282
  General, 22, 281
  Percentage, 281
  Scientific, 282

SINGLE PC LICENSE AGREEMENT AND LIMITED WARRANTY

READ THIS LICENSE CAREFULLY BEFORE OPENING THIS PACKAGE. BY OPENING THIS PACKAGE, YOU ARE AGREEING TO THE TERMS AND CONDITIONS OF THIS LICENSE. IF YOU DO NOT AGREE, DO NOT OPEN THE PACKAGE. PROMPTLY RETURN THE UNOPENED PACKAGE AND ALL ACCOMPANYING ITEMS TO THE PLACE YOU OBTAINED THEM. *THESE TERMS APPLY TO ALL LICENSED SOFTWARE ON THE DISK EXCEPT THAT THE TERMS FOR USE OF ANY SHAREWARE OR FREEWARE ON TH E DISKETTES ARE AS SET FORTH IN THE ELECTRONIC LICENSE LOCATED ON THE DISK:*

1. GRANT OF LICENSE and OWNERSHIP: The enclosed computer programs ("Software") are licensed, not sold, to you by Prentice-Hall, Inc. ("We" or the "Company") and in consideration of your purchase or adoption of the accompanying Company textbooks and/or other materials, and your agreement to these terms. We reserve any rights not granted to you. You own only the disk(s) but we and/or our licensors own the Software itself. This license allows you to use and display your copy of the Software on a single computer (i.e., with a single CPU) at a single location for academic use only, so long as you comply with the terms of this Agreement. You may make one copy for back up, or transfer your copy to another CPU, provided that the Software is usable on only one computer.

2. RESTRICTIONS: You may not transfer or distribute the Software or documentation to anyone else. Except for backup, you may not copy the documentation or the Software. You may not network the Software or otherwise use it on more than one computer or computer terminal at the same time. You may not reverse engineer, disassemble, decompile, modify, adapt, translate, or create derivative works based on the Software or the Documentation. You may be held legally responsible for any copying or copyright infringement which is caused by your failure to abide by the terms of these restrictions.

3. TERMINATION: This license is effective until terminated. This license will terminate automatically without notice from the Company if you fail to comply with any provisions or limitations of this license. Upon termination, you shall destroy the Documentation and all copies of the Software. All provisions of this Agreement as to limitation and disclaimer of warranties, limitation of liability, remedies or damages, and our ownership rights shall survive termination.

4. DISCLAIMER OF WARRANTY: THE COMPANY AND ITS LICENSORS MAKE NO WARRANTIES ABOUT THE SOFTWARE, WHICH IS PROVIDED "AS-IS." IF THE DISK IS DEFECTIVE IN MATERIALS OR WORKMANSHIP, YOUR ONLY REMEDY IS TO RETURN IT TO THE COMPANY WITHIN 30 DAYS FOR REPLACEMENT UNLESS THE COMPANY DETERMINES IN GOOD FAITH THAT THE DISK HAS BEEN MISUSED OR IMPROPERLY INSTALLED, REPAIRED, ALTERED OR DAMAGED. THE COMPANY DISCLAIMS ALL WARRANTIES, EXPRESS OR IMPLIED, INCLUDING WITHOUT LIMITATION, THE IMPLIED WARRANTIES OF MERCHANTABILITY AND FITNESS FOR A PARTICULAR PURPOSE. THE COMPANY DOES NOT WARRANT, GUARANTEE OR MAKE ANY REPRESENTATION REGARDING THE ACCURACY, RELIABILITY, CURRENTNESS, USE, OR RESULTS OF USE, OF THE SOFTWARE.

5. LIMITATION OF REMEDIES AND DAMAGES: IN NO EVENT, SHALL THE COMPANY OR ITS EMPLOYEES, AGENTS, LICENSORS OR CONTRACTORS BE LIABLE FOR ANY INCIDENTAL, INDIRECT, SPECIAL OR CONSEQUENTIAL DAMAGES ARISING OUT OF OR IN CONNECTION WITH THIS LICENSE OR THE SOFTWARE, INCLUDING, WITHOUT LIMITATION, LOSS OF USE, LOSS OF DATA, LOSS OF INCOME OR PROFIT, OR OTHER LOSSES SUSTAINED AS A RESULT OF INJURY TO ANY PERSON, OR LOSS OF OR DAMAGE TO PROPERTY, OR CLAIMS OF THIRD PARTIES, EVEN IF THE COMPANY OR AN AUTHORIZED REPRESENTATIVE OF THE COMPANY HAS BEEN ADVISED OF THE POSSIBILITY OF SUCH DAMAGES. SOME JURISDICTIONS DO NOT ALLOW THE LIMITATION OF DAMAGES IN CERTAIN CIRCUMSTANCES, SO THE ABOVE LIMITATIONS MAY NOT ALWAYS APPLY.

6. GENERAL: THIS AGREEMENT SHALL BE CONSTRUED IN ACCORDANCE WITH THE LAWS OF THE UNITED STATES OF AMERICA AND THE STATE OF NEW YORK, APPLICABLE TO CONTRACTS MADE IN NEW YORK, AND SHALL BENEFIT THE COMPANY, ITS AFFILIATES AND ASSIGNEES. This Agreement is the complete and exclusive statement of the agreement between you and the Company and supersedes all proposals, prior agreements, oral or written, and any other communications between you and the company or any of its representatives relating to the subject matter. If you are a U.S. Government user, this Software is licensed with "restricted rights" as set forth in subparagraphs (a)-(d) of the Commercial Computer-Restricted Rights clause at FAR 52.227-19 or in subparagraphs (c)(1)(ii) of the Rights in Technical Data and Computer Software clause at DFARS 252.227-7013, and similar clauses, as applicable.

Should you have any questions concerning this agreement or if you wish to contact the Company for any reason, please contact in writing:

Multimedia Production
Higher Education Division
Prentice-Hall, Inc.
1 Lake Street
Upper Saddle River NJ 07458